The Kinks

ALL DAY AND ALL OF THE NIGHT

by **Doug Hinman**

Day-by-day concerts, recordings and broadcasts, 1961–1996

Backbeat
Books

THE KINKS
all day and all of the night

Doug Hinman

A BACKBEAT BOOK
First edition 2004
Published by Backbeat Books
600 Harrison Street,
San Francisco, CA94107, US
www.backbeatbooks.com

An imprint of The Music Player Network United
Entertainment Media Inc.

Published for Backbeat Books by Outline Press Ltd,
Unit 2a Union Court, 20-22 Union Road, London,
SW4 6JP, England.
www.backbeatuk.com

ISBN 0-87930-765-X

Dedicated to the memory of Jane Guild Hinman

ART DIRECTOR: Nigel Osborne
EDITOR: Tony Bacon
DESIGN: Paul Cooper Design
PICTURE RESEARCH: Andy Neill

Origination and Print by Colorprint (Hong Kong)

04 05 06 07 08 5 4 3 2 1

contents

Introduction

In 1996 Ray Davies was asked what prompted him to write *X-Ray*, his "unauthorised biography". He replied, "The publishers came to me, I think in 1988, and asked me to write an autobiography. I refused initially because I don't like those sort of books, just recounting the dates, facts and figures. Let somebody else document that."

Well, I guess I'm that guy. And here is that sort of book.

So what exactly are you holding? It's primarily a piece of research that attempts to document all the professional activities of The Kinks during their career from 1961-1996. That includes their personal appearances in concert, on TV and on radio, and their work in recording studios. The band's activities are documented in diary style so that it's possible to learn more or less everything they did professionally, as they did it.

This book isn't a conventional biography of the band or its members. It is not a look at their private lives, beyond the basic public details of marriage, family and area of residence where relevant to the story. The focus here is on what the band did in order to create music.

Both of the principal Kinks – Ray Davies and Dave Davies – have written and published their own books: Ray's *X-Ray* in 1994 and Dave's *Kink* in 1996. These are first-hand accounts of the band's history from their unique perspectives. Nothing could begin to act as a substitute for either book – each as different in style and content as the disparate personalities from which they spring. Reading both is essential to begin to understand the personalities that drove this band.

But a hole remains. There is no reliable historical account of their career. A number of conventional stories of The Kinks have been written over the years, offering a range of insights into the creative process and personal dynamics of the band. Each has a basic retelling of the facts of their long career, generally presented in broad brushstrokes and with highlights of the band's operation. These books have their own strengths and each is worth seeking out. However, none of them is built upon a foundation of in-depth research – and I think that this is the only way to establish a reliable history and to separate fact from fiction, especially in an area where myth-making is so much a part of the game.

The principal aim of this book is to create as thorough and as accurate as possible a historical record of this often tumultuous musical career. It must be admitted that lurking beneath the surface of The Kinks' history is a darker underbelly at times rife with bitterness and acrimony, an undeniable undercurrent of dysfunctional emotional turmoil and violence. Perhaps this results from a combination of the classic artistic temperament of highly creative personalities and the much heralded sibling rivalry between the brothers Davies. There's also the almost intentionally imposed air of tension that fuels the creative process, ever in search of freshness, spontaneity and what Ray describes as "an edge". While these are often the aspects of The Kinks' story that find the most favour in the press, I will leave them to others to explore. The focus here remains on just the facts, ma'am.

Researching the history of The Kinks is particularly difficult, for a number of reasons. There are problems associated with trying to track an occupation that for a good while was viewed as essentially ephemeral in nature and perhaps unworthy of preservation. But the main difficulty stems from the fact that the nature of the operation over the years was largely a reflection of the personal style of leader Ray Davies. He tended to operate in an atmosphere of spontaneity, chaos, conflict, and even secrecy. A state of confusion, indeed. These methods probably help to create a creative atmosphere – and in large part contribute to the air of intrigue and mystery that has always surrounded the band. From a researcher's point of view, it creates a very real challenge.

Concerts and broadcasts

One of the main parts of my job has been to track the paper trail usually left by public performance in concert and appearances on broadcast media. These are events designed to promote public exposure and derive income, and so normally they are planned in advance and advertised to attract attention and awareness. Radio and television research has been relatively straightforward. Tracking concert appearances, particularly in the 1960s, proved to be full of problems. Memories of the people involved are of only marginal help because recollections can be remarkably inaccurate for all kinds of reasons.

There are almost no surviving private sources that cover the coveted 1960s era. No booking-agency records or management-agency records from this era are known to survive. The legendary Ray Davies diaries of that era are still the Holy Grail, and they would answer many questions. But as a source they remain out of reach, barring the few tempting titbits revealed in Ray's book, *X-Ray*. For large periods of time there were no published reports of concert activities in the music press. There's often a complete lack of print advertising locally, with the band instead relying on radio or leaflets and posters to announce a concert appearance. And the conventional press often failed to even mention rock'n'roll events taking place in their area because back then they took a particularly conservative and dim view of this music.

As well as these hurdles, one must add the tendency for The Kinks to book shows without allowing enough time to advertise, and to shuffle tour schedules at the last minute. They took an often cavalier attitude to the last-minute cancelling of shows – or would just simply not turn up. I felt at times that The Kinks probably cancelled as many shows as they actually played. All these factors make it difficult years later to try to piece together what they did and when they did it. The concert histories reconstructed in this book were largely created by painstakingly trawling through hundreds of local newspapers and music papers around the globe, verifying eyewitness reports, and using every last ounce of research skill in order to track down information.

Uncovering touring timelines from 1971 onwards was a slightly less daunting task. The process has been aided by the existence of band itineraries, and some band members' diaries have been accessible. Even then, unravelling the real facts can still be complex. Tours are scheduled, cancelled, shuffled and rebooked to an amazing degree. From the early 1970s onwards, shows are generally listed, advertised and reviewed in print, and while this presents a large and complicated task, it is a surmountable one. The results here represent 17 years of ongoing research. While not perfect – and it never can be – the concert history in this book is thorough and certainly indicative of the pace and breadth of the band's public life.

The Kinks in the studio

Documenting the band's recording sessions presented its own set of complications. Unlike a relatively straightforward subject such as The Beatles – who primarily recorded at one studio, where administration personnel kept virtually every tape and maintained detailed documentation of recording activity – no evidence of The Kinks' recording activities in the 1960s survives.

Unlike EMI, for whom The Beatles recorded, Pye Records and Pye Studios where the Kinks did most of their studio work in the 1960s kept very few session tapes (they generally recorded over them). No records of the work done at Pye studios survived into the mid 1980s when research was properly begun on this project. Again, the only likely source for details of these '60s sessions would be Ray Davies's diaries, which might at least identify the precise days a certain song was worked on or when recording was started.

The studio information included here is the best the author has been able to reconstruct from a wide range of sources. I've put the picture together from the recollections of people involved, evidence from surviving master-tape lists, acetate labels, song publishing data, record company tape logs, published secondary sources from the time, and circumstantial evidence. But there is no unimpeachable source for this information and the reader should be aware of this from the outset.

Many people seem to believe that simply because something appears in print on, say, the CD booklet of an official record company reissue, it must be accurate. Yet no one has very good information on The Kinks' recording history – and certainly not the record companies who now own that material. Everyone faces the same problem: a dire lack of reliable original sources. Virtually every bit of recording data included on any reissued Kinks CDs from the 1990s onwards originates from research done for this book and for my Kinks discography, *You Really Got Me* (privately published in 1994). Thus any such information included on any officially-issued record by The Kinks carries no added authority by virtue of its proximity to the record label or the band. This is true not just of the reissues of the Pye recordings (1964-71) but also the Velvel reissues of the records made for RCA (1971-76) and Arista (1976-85). In every instance, in the absence of their own information (which is almost none), the record companies have turned to the author for what can only be described as "best available information" – and often such a description was not included on the CDs, even though I requested it.

The reader must understand that little included in this book regarding the time, location and circumstances of recording sessions is faultless. The author in many cases is able to make extremely informed guesses only, knitted together from clues of varying reliability. In an effort not to attach too much weight to any given piece of questionable information, I have tried to characterise anything less than a reasonable conclusion or an almost certain guess as "probably" or "possibly", or to suggest several possibilities in the case where multiple pieces of information seem equally likely. I hope, by being honest about less-than-certain conclusions, that those pieces of information presented without qualification can take on an air of reasonable certainty. Throughout the book I've attempted to present what I know and when possible or within reason how I know it, and if something is purely my opinion that it is presented as such and as nothing more.

Determining who played on certain recordings is sometimes a matter of conjecture rather than proven fact. Again, I am forced to rely largely on a combination of less than perfect sources, including the recollection of participants (often in conflict), musical evidence (largely subjective but necessary), and reasonable assumption (for example, if a track was recorded in 1972, it would be presumed to be John Dalton on bass as he was in the band at the time, and with no evidence to the contrary, it is a logical conclusion).

Little attempt has been made to attempt to distinguish in the later multitrack years whether Ray or Dave might be the guitar player on a minor part of a recording. In virtually every instance Dave would be the soloist when one is present, but whether it is Ray or Dave playing an additional rhythm part – often multitracked and layered – is probably not of much interest beyond knowing that it is one or the other. Through the band's recording career, Ray often adds keyboard parts on his own, and when known this fact is stated. But when the parts are minor embellishments rather than featured performances, little effort has been exerted to make an absolute distinction. This goes back to the earliest stages of their career, when keyboard player Nicky Hopkins – normally easily identifiable – might not be so obvious when asked to play a simple part that could easily have been played by Ray – and on audio evidence alone could be either of them. Further complicating the picture is the fact that from the outset it has been Ray's tendency in the studio to record backing tracks without the luxury of a guide vocal, such that the other players are often not even aware of the title of the piece at the time.

Especially in the multitrack era, individual performances can be added, erased and replaced with such ease, and in some cases over extended periods of time, that it becomes difficult to know just whose part remains in the final recording. In fact, recording in the digital age has rendered as largely irrelevant the traditional discographic itemisation of a particular personnel performing in a certain location on such-and-such a date. Added to that is the tendency of The Kinks from the start of their career to record multiple versions of songs over time. Separating out the details years after the fact is also prone to the natural human tendency to blur and compress events of the past.

Then we come to the matter of unreleased recordings. Very few of these are known to survive from the 1960s, and it can be reasonably assumed that what is known to survive is documented in this book. But when we come to the recordings made from the RCA period onwards, and especially since 1973 when The Kinks opened their own recording studio, it should be realised that all recording was done under their own control, and so our knowledge of the detail of endless hours of unfinished and unreleased material is limited. Until and unless there is some access to the vaults and files of Konk Studios, this aspect of The Kinks' recorded legacy will remain far short of definitive.

The reader is asked to view the recording information contained in this book with all these considerations in mind, and to consider it as the best available information gathered into a single place – but by no means the last word on the subject.

Presenting the facts

It is with all these caveats in place that *The Kinks: All Day And All Of The Night* is presented. One of the great tasks has been to whittle down the mountain of information I have collected for this project. It has been my rather odd lifelong passion – perhaps it is a curse – to obsessively and methodically collect any and all material about the band, since I first saw them on American TV on January 20th 1965. But the real challenge has always been to distil and present the facts of such a long, productive and complex career into a manageable and usable form. In the end it came down to some rather tough decisions, and the intentional decision to let the research and the words of the band speak for themselves.

Almost by their own design, The Kinks have always been an elusive and mysterious entity. Unravelling and making some sense of the mystery by the power of research has for some reason always been with me. With the band inactive since 1996 – although hopefully they will return to life, perhaps in 2004 – enough time has passed for the dust to settle and for me to muster the energy to complete this project. The story of The Kinks can never be perfectly told. But I hope that those interested in learning more about their music and career will find that this book serves the purpose and offers some entertainment value of its own.

To Ray and Dave, and every member of The Kinks over the years, my thanks for the perpetually fascinating mosaic of a career and the rich musical legacy you have left behind, and most of all ... thank you for the days.

DOUG HINMAN Rumford, RI, October 2003

Early years

In London, as war broke out in 1939, the working-class Davies family moved from densely-packed King's Cross to the city's northern reaches and the suburban calm of Muswell Hill. It was here that the band that became known as The Kinks had its origins.

The immediate family of Fred and Annie Davies consisted of six girls born between 1924 and 1938 in King's Cross. As war broke out in 1939 the family moved out of central London to East Finchley, and then in January 1940 to neighbouring Muswell Hill, to Denmark Terrace just off Fortis Green. (Fortis Green is the name of a road.) A seventh child and the first boy, Raymond Douglas Davies, was born on June 21st 1944, and finally David Russell Gordon Davies was born on February 3rd 1947. Besides the immediate family, there were many aunts, uncles, cousins and, later, nieces and nephews.

Money was tight as the large family grew up, but they were resourceful and would help each other out. In the lean years following the war, times were hard. But the two brothers found music an ever-present relief. Their older sisters had an enthusiasm for pop music, and they would all take turns playing the family's old upright piano, a cornerstone of the front room.

At parties on Saturday nights the entire extended family would assemble at the home on Denmark Terrace and the older generation would sing popular music-hall standards. Fred Davies never needed much prompting to dance, sing or play banjo. It was in this lively family atmosphere that the two boys began to soak up all kinds of musical influences.

Dave was a free-spirited, mischievous kid, where Ray was quiet and emotionally troubled as he grew up. But music continued to interest them and provided an outlet for the introspective Ray, who soon started to play. His sister Rene in particular helped nurture his talents, teaching him some piano as well as encouraging an interest in guitar.

But tragedy struck in an especially cruel manner, and for Ray would profoundly tie the joy of music to an eternally painful memory. On his 13th birthday, in June 1957, he was given a new Spanish guitar, funded by sister Rene. But that same night Rene died while out ballroom dancing, the victim of a childhood heart defect. The event drove the young Ray further inside himself, and deeper still into his music. He continued to practice and play his guitar diligently and became accomplished fairly quickly. He was further assisted by lessons from Mike Picker, husband of sister Peg and a musician who studied classical guitar and would in turn pass on his knowledge to Ray.

Dave too showed a similar interest in the instrument and at age 12, on December 4th 1959, received his first guitar, a Harmony Meteor electric model bought by his mother on hire purchase (an instalment plan). Dave applied himself with determination, and was similarly fuelled by a love of folk, country and especially rock'n'roll.

By this time Ray was mainly living with his sister Rose, her husband Arthur and their son Terry, but before long the brothers – both enrolled at the William Grimshaw Secondary Modern School in Muswell Hill – would regularly pair up to play guitars together.

Ray Davies: solo guitarist

During 1959 Ray played a few solo shows on guitar. He received a 30-watt Watkins Dominator amplifier for his 15th birthday in June that year and this probably made him think about performing publicly. His electric guitar was probably a Maton model. He later recalled that his earliest performances were at local pubs, including The Clissold Arms on Fortis Green, The Stag in neighbouring East Finchley, and The Victoria in Highgate to the south, and even a folk club in Potters Bar to the north.

Ray's earliest guitar inspirations were from the worlds of jazz (Tal Farlow and Charlie Christian), country (Chet Atkins), and the slightly earthier sounds of Arthur "Guitar Boogie" Smith. He worked up a few of his own instrumentals, and would recall that one of his earliest compositions was "a cowboy thing called 'Rocky Mountain'".

At 15, Ray was about to leave school, and began to wonder what to do. He later remembered being sent for an interview at the Youth Employment Office during this period. "You'd go to this guy who'd talk to you for about five minutes and decide whether you were going to work at the factory down the road or were going to be a baker. I decided I was going to have to fight my way out."

During the winter of 1960, uneasy at school and seeing no point in staying there, Ray answered an ad in the London Evening Standard newspaper and left school for a job with a central-London publisher. "But there was no future in it," he said, "so after six months I went back to school. It was my renaissance as a student – I became sports captain and house captain and we actually won things. I studied art and painting."

Ray's return to Grimshaw and concentration on art would lead him two years later to the affiliated Hornsey College of Art & Crafts. "I was a very quiet kid," said Ray, "but I knew what I wanted to do. I knew the limitations of myself and what I was good at. If I wasn't good at something I wouldn't put energy into it. I was good at making up stories, drawing pictures, and running. I could invent situations. I lived in an absolute dream world."

Earlier in 1960, probably on April 15th, 13-year-old Dave attended a concert performance by American guitar wizard Duane Eddy at the Finsbury Park Empire in north London. This was a defining moment in the young guitarist's education. As recalled in Kink, it was Dave's brother-in-law Mike Picker who provided the matinee tickets for Dave to see his guitar hero in person, complete with genuine American band. The concert made a great impression on Dave, now more determined than ever to play rock'n'roll guitar.

The Kelly Brothers

It was obvious that the next musical step should be for Ray to team up with younger brother Dave. Around December 1960 the duo played some performances, billing themselves on at least one occasion as The Kelly Brothers ("Kelly" was borrowed from their grandmother's maiden name).

Dave would recall that he was the rhythm guitar player and Ray the instrumentalist in the duo, and they'd play instrumental tunes written by Ray. "We did our first gig … in the pub across the road [The Clissold Arms], only because my dad used to frequent the place. We'd do this sort of Chet Atkins thing. Ray had classical training … I would just pick [like bluegrass banjo player] Earl Scruggs or something, but I didn't know what I was doing."

Dave's recollections identified standards like 'Sweet Sue' and 'Sweet Georgia Brown' as typical of the songs the two would perform. In his book, *Kink*, Dave remembered an early composition by Ray called 'South' that he said would become the basis for 'Tired Of Waiting For You'. Dave maintained that he and Ray recorded a proper version of 'South' as a demo at Regent Sound Studio in central London at the time, though there is no other evidence for this early example of the Davies' burgeoning musical talents. So it is that our story begins.

day by day

1961–1996

kinks'61

1961

This year marked the first appearance of a band that, over the course of the following two years, became The Kinks. Three-quarters of the first classic line-up – Ray Davies, Dave Davies and Pete Quaife – came together under typical circumstances of the time: as teenagers at school with some raw talent, rudimentary ability, and no experience. What they also had was boundless energy and a determination to create something greater than the sum of their parts, and along the way hoped to impress their friends and peers.

September

Ray and Dave are still students at the William Grimshaw Secondary Modern School in Muswell Hill, north London, with 17-year-old Ray in his final year as part of Grimshaw's experimental extended-year courses. The most popular of these is the art and crafts course that Ray is taking, with many students moving on to the closely affiliated Hornsey College of Art.

Also attending Grimshaw at this time is another artistically-inclined student, Pete Quaife (born December 31st 1943). Quaife is in the same year as Ray and, like Ray, is enrolled for an extended period so that he can gather arts coursework that will qualify him for entry to art college.

Ray is known to Pete but they have not yet become friends. They end up in the same music class this autumn, taught by a Mr Wainwright. According to Quaife's later recollection, Wainwright polls the class to see who can play an instrument, and both he and Ray confess to playing guitar. Next lesson they each bring in their guitar and play something for the class. Pete recalls being duly impressed and somewhat intimidated by Ray's obvious mastery of the instrument, which he rates as beyond his own limited ability.

With Wainwright's prompting, the two students decide that they should work together and even form a band. Quaife suggests his best friend, John Start, as drummer. Start is a year down from Ray and Quaife, but like many young British lads has played around in a skiffle band on washboard, inspired by Lonnie Donegan's 1956 hit 'Rock Island Line'. Quaife, whose parents have been friendly with the Starts since the war, has been known to join in on guitar with Start's makeshift skiffle combo. Start has long had a passion for playing drums, and has been taking lessons since he was about eight.

Ray's recommendation is that his younger brother Dave should join him, Quaife and Start as an obvious fourth member, also on guitar. Quaife will recall that at this time he doesn't know Dave is Ray's brother, or a guitar player, only that Dave has a reputation in school as a hellion.

The band's early task is to quickly put together a repertoire as they have the opportunity to provide musical entertainment for the school's upcoming autumn dance. Quaife is also playing guitar, so in effect The Kelly Brothers – Ray and Dave – are augmented by Quaife and Start as rhythm section for this new schoolboy danceband. They begin rehearsing at Start's house on Ringwood Avenue in Muswell Hill, the drummer's parents happy to encourage the ambitious venture.

Ray is clearly the most accomplished musician of the band, which now calls itself The Ray Davies Quartet. Dave says later: "I was 14 when I joined my first group, The Ray Davies Quartet. We played school dances and things. The group played a lot of instrumentals, material by people like Chet Atkins and Arthur Smith. We were a skiffle group really, I suppose."

October

It is most likely during this month that the debut performance of The Ray Davies Quartet occurs at the *Autumn Dance* at the William Grimshaw School's Assembly Hall in Muswell Hill, north London, featuring Ray, Dave and Quaife on guitars, powered by one amplifier, and Start on drums. The band performs on stage for a crowd of dancers on the main floor. It's apparently a big success and encourages the four students to continue as a performing ensemble.

The band's repertoire consists of a mix of guitar instrumentals and rock'n'roll vocal numbers. Among the instrumentals are some by Ray's favourites, The Ventures, including 'Walk Don't Run' and 'Perfidia'. Also included are popular instrumental hits of the day, including The Shadows' 'Apache', apparently with Quaife on lead guitar prior to his switch to bass, The Ramrods' 'Riders In The Sky', and The String-A-Longs' 'Wheels'. The band plays tunes by Dave's favourite, Duane Eddy, including 'Ramrod' and probably 'Peter Gunn', country-flavoured instrumentals by Chet Atkins, the R&B leanings of Arthur Smith's 'Guitar Boogie', and even a few big-band standards, including a Gene Krupa favourite 'Big Noise From Winetka', and 'St. Louis Blues'. A feature piece for Ray is the standard 'Malequena', which over time will become a showpiece for Ray playing guitar behind his back, T-Bone Walker-style.

From the start both Ray and Dave tackle some vocal numbers, although both prefer instrumentals. Start recalls that Ray does some Buddy Holly material, probably including 'Oh Boy', 'Rave On' and 'Everyday', as well as Cliff Richard's 'Move It' and 'Living Doll'. They try at least one Everly Brothers song, 'All I Have To Do Is Dream', plus Bobby Freeman's 'Do You Want To Dance' and Barrett Strong's 'Money (That's What I Want)'. Dave is noted for nailing Little Richard's 'Good Golly Miss Molly' which he later recalls as one of their first numbers performed on stage. Also thrown into the mix is a song that will carry on into The Kinks, Elvis Presley's 'One Night With You', as well as some Chuck Berry ('Johnny B. Goode' and 'Memphis') and a few skiffle numbers, including 'Greenback Dollar' (a hit for Chas McDevitt in Britain in 1957). Following this successful debut the band readies itself for the next engagement. Quaife moves from guitar to bass, acquiring a Framus bass guitar that he recalls buying without a case in which to carry it home.

November

It's probably this month that The Ray Davies Quartet makes its second appearance, at The Athenaeum ballroom in Muswell Hill. Following the success of the Grimshaw school dance, the Davies' brother-in-law Brian Longstaff books the band for one of a regular series of Saturday night dances at this local gathering place for teens, described by Quaife as a hangout for rockers. The dances at The Athenaeum are very popular, but are generally viewed by local residents as a magnet for "teenage hooliganism", especially in the Fortis Green area where the Davies live.

However, outside their safe school environment, the band is unceremoniously booed off stage by the large, vocal and opinionated crowd, which Start estimates later at well over 1,000. All they have is Ray's little Watkins Dominator amp to power the show. Start's only other recollection is of his drums sliding helplessly forward as he tries to play with no anchor to hold them in place.

1962

For the first part of the year, the schoolboy outfit slowly spread into territory beyond their immediate neighbourhood, and scrambled for any gig, anywhere – simply for the thrill of playing out and gaining experience. Mid-year marked a crisis point of a kind as all but drummer John Start left school. While the commitment among the band remained firm, the ever-ambitious Ray, ensconced in art college and influenced and encouraged by its Bohemian culture, began to pursue musical side-projects, and by the end of the year these temptations led him to stray from but not abandon his Quartet.

→ Through the winter and spring into 1962 The Ray Davies Quartet continues to pick up gigs at any local spots that will have them. They play occasional church dances, teen centres, coffee bars, and amateur talent nights in the Muswell Hill area. There's a handful of gigs at the lounge in the back of The Clissold Arms, the pub across the street from the Davies home on Denmark Terrace. The band will play as a quartet, or as a trio without Start – because sometimes the drums simply will not fit into the smaller coffee bars and pubs.
"It was all social clubs, youth clubs, scout huts, pubs," says Dave later. "It was really good, that time, starting out doing sort of folk and skiffly things." Around this time, Dave acquires his first two amps: a Linear amplifier and speaker bought through Exchange & Mart magazine, and a small Elpico combination amp-and-speaker from a local radio shop. These will serve him into 1963 when he will get a more professional Vox amplifier.

→ ● RECORDING Attempts are made around now to do some home recording, probably with guitars only (no drums). Using a tape recorder belonging to the Davies' brother-in-law Mike Picker a few songs are recorded, including an echo-laden attempt at the standard 'Malequenia' and the more ambitious Jimmy Guiffre jazz number 'The Train And The River'.
→ Ray is uncomfortable with the vocal chores even when divided among him and Dave, and feels they should be looking for a singer to front the band. The first candidate for this position is fellow Grimshaw student and football enthusiast Rod Stewart (born in nearby Highgate on January 10th 1945). During spring 1962 the band holds a series of rehearsals with Stewart at Start's home on Ringwood Avenue. Stewart is a big fan of American rocker Eddie Cochran, also one of Dave's early inspirations.
Start recalls later that his mother cannot bear the sound of Stewart's vocal style – even then a raspy-toned instrument – and insists they not practice in the house as usual but clear the garage and practice out

there. She is presumably not aware that Stewart is known locally as the Elvis of Muswell Hill.
They rehearse for a new booking at the Coldfall Youth Club, in a hall on the council estate at the edge of Muswell Hill. The band plays at least this one date with Stewart, but it is immediately evident that there are musical and personality clashes and that the association will not work out. Stewart will go on to form his own band, Rod Stewart & The Moonrakers, who for a short while are in competition with the Quartet.
☆ Also in the spring of 1962 Start's father, keen to support his son's efforts, buys the band uniforms from an outfitters in nearby Wood Green. These apparently consist of black satin trousers, shirt and tie, and blue cardigan.

April

Wednesday 4th

At a church hall in nearby Finchley a legendary fight takes place, later recounted by Quaife in the liner notes for the *Kinda Kinks* LP. A Muswell Hill street gang, the Mussies, battle with rival faction the Finchley Boys, resulting in a number of serious stabbings. Mussie member Quaife, realising the seriousness of the situation, escapes detection and arrest by clinging to the bottom of a nearby parked car. The experience will cure him of his involvement in the delinquent gang.

→ After failing to acquire Rod Stewart as a permanent vocalist, The Ray Davies Quartet tries out a second singer, a Greek youth by the name of Pete Georgious. Start remembers rehearsing with Georgious in preparation for a booking at the Muswell Hill Youth Club at Carisbrooke House in Colney Hatch Lane, Muswell Hill, where the band play regularly on Friday nights for a six to eight-week stretch around this time. Start recalls that Georgious's feature number is Cliff

kinks'62

Richard's 'Living Doll', but other than possibly one show at Carisbrooke he too does not work out. Ray's recollection is that by this time Rod Stewart has formed The Moonrakers who are the regular Saturday night band at the same Carisbrooke youth club.

☆ Other performances the band is known to have made during this time include dances at Hendon Police College, where they play probably three or four bookings through a connection with the Davies' brother-in-law, policeman Mike Palmer. Other dances at schools include one in Crouch End and another in Edmonton (all north London).

June

Dave is expelled from William Grimshaw School for general truancy and for being caught in compromising circumstances with his girlfriend Sue on Hampstead Heath. He has only completed three and a half years of his secondary schooling. His best friend George Harris has already been thrown out, earlier in the spring. Harris is also a guitar player and has quite a large collection of records. Dave says later: "I left school and as I didn't want to work I didn't do anything for three or four months. The group were working on occasional dates then and I realised that all I really wanted to do was make a career in music."

July

Ray and Quaife finish their final year at William Grimshaw school. The last assembly is held – doubtless the inspiration for the song of the same name from the 1975 Kinks album *Schoolboys In Disgrace*.

→ Unknown to the Muswell Hill band, at this time Kink-to-be Mick Avory attends two rehearsals at a pub, The Bricklayers Arms, in central London for a nascent version of The Rolling Stones. Mick Jagger, Keith Richards, Brian Jones, Ian Stewart, and Dick Taylor are present. Avory is brought in to rehearse when the band's semi-regular drumming candidate Tony Chapman proves unavailable. Avory is possibly at the Stones' regular Wednesday and Friday rehearsals, perhaps on July 6th and 11th. The band has been given a trial spot opening for Long John Baldry at London's Marquee Club on Thursday July 12th. Although Avory is listed ("Mike Avery") as a band member in an announcement for this show, Chapman instead plays the Stones debut performance after he is tracked down and promises to show up.

→ Around now The Ray Davies Quartet auditions a third potential singer in the Davies' front room, remembered by Quaife only as a South African keen on Elvis Presley and Rick Nelson-type numbers and whose featured song is Elvis Presley's 'Suspicion'. The vocalist's pop leanings fail to impress and no more is heard of him.

September

Monday 24th

Ray and Quaife begin their first classes at the Hornsey College of Art & Crafts on Crouch End Hill. Ray is enrolled in a four-tier diploma course, studying fine art, painting, sculpture, and art history.

October

Quaife either leaves or is expelled from Hornsey College, three weeks into the autumn session (so probably in the middle of this month). He subsequently finds employment as assistant to the art editor of menswear magazine *The Outfitter*. He will work in this position until quitting a little over a year later, at the point when The Kinks turn fully professional.

→ Aware that Quaife is now working and that Start, though still at Grimshaw, works occasionally at his father's jewellery store, Dave decides around now that with the summer long gone he too should get a job. Following a number of failed interviews elsewhere, he becomes a stock-room assistant at the warehouse of Selmer's music shop on Charing Cross Road in central London, where he helps to repair wind instruments. He lasts about six months there before being fired.

→ At this time it seems that whoever books a gig can name the band, so there are appearances by The Pete Quaife Quartet and The Dave Davies Quartet.

Again, Start does not always play, depending on the size of the venue and the space required for drums, and so the billing is sometimes reduced from Quartet to Trio.

→ **Railway Tavern** *Crouch End, north London* The Ray Davies Trio/Quartet

A steady twice-a-week gig around this time at this pub in Park Road, just down the street from Hornsey Art College. The band is able to pull its repertoire together during this stretch and map out some musical identity.

→ **El Toro Coffee Bar** *Muswell Hill, north London* The Ray Davies Trio

A regular hangout at the time where the Davies brothers and Quaife often perform as a trio.

→ Around now Granada Television broadcasts a programme on Big Bill Broonzy as part of its series *This Wonderful World*. It marks a turning point for Ray and Dave, introducing them to the blues and laying bare Broonzy's raw, honest, authentic music. Around the same time Ray sees the movie *The Seven Samurai* which triggers his interest in the art of film-making.

→ Keen for wider musical experiences, Ray plays some duo and trio gigs at Hornsey College of Art with his pianist friend Geoff Prowse and an unidentified bass player.

December

Saturday 15th

→ Alexis Korner's Blues Incorporated perform at Hornsey College's Christmas dance, the band including a pre-Stones Charlie Watts on drums. The ambitious Ray approaches Korner for advice on how to get a job in an R&B band.

Korner gives Ray his phone number, and when he calls the following day he's referred to the Piccadilly club in Soho, central London, where he should ask for Giorgio Gomelsky – blues impresario, club manager, and documentary film-director.

Gomelsky's Piccadilly club has been running regular Friday R&B nights with Dave Hunt's band since November 23rd, and opens its Chinese Twist Club on Saturdays starting December 15th, also with Hunt. (The Piccadilly will shortly be renamed The Scene, by which it is better known.)

At least since December 8th Hunt also has a regular Sunday night residency at the Station Hotel in Richmond, west London, another venue run by Gomelsky.

Friday 21st

Following Korner's advice, Ray visits the Piccadilly Jazz Club on Great Windmill Street in central London Ray, attending an 8:00pm show with Dave Hunt's Rhythm & Blues Band supported by The Rollin' Stones (as they are billed).

Ray sits in with the Hunt band (something he will do so a second time, probably next Friday). Gomelsky is looking for younger players for Hunt, particularly on guitar, as the older traditional jazz ("trad") players with whom Hunt is familiar are either banjo players or guitarists with no ability to play the newer R&B styles. With his schooling in trad jazz and modern styles, Ray is an ideal candidate.

The audition goes well, but it is the interval band that catches Ray's attention. The Rollin' Stones are more like the sort of band he hopes to join. Ray later recalls this occasion, his first sighting of the Stones. "The band leader [Dave Hunt] said, 'Come on, let's go over the pub.' … I said, 'No, I wanna stay and see the other band,' because they all looked about the same age as me – I was the baby of the [Hunt] group. He said, 'Don't watch 'em. They're a skiffle group.' I sat down and I saw them play, and I saw energy. I saw Brian Jones – a total star. I saw Keith … I saw Jagger, not so prominent then. They stood in a line, the three of 'em, all in their round button collars and their little shirts. The sound was exciting. Couldn't hear the vocal, but that was great – he was just there, a really trebly, bad PA … I think that was the best I've ever seen 'em play. Really!"

☆ The Wednesday-night spot at the Piccadilly is held down by Cyril Davies & His All-Stars, easily the best British R&B band of the time, including future Kinks session pianist Nicky Hopkins.

Friday 28th

➜ Probably tonight Ray attends another Dave Hunt performance at the Piccadilly and sits in again. He is asked to join, starting the following week, and ponders his decision.

Monday 31st

Lyceum Ballroom *central London* The Ray Davies Quartet
New Year's Eve, and the band plays its most prestigious show, as a cabaret opening act to Cyril Stapleton & His All-Star Orchestra, a popular big-band. This is the same ballroom where Ray's sister Rene collapsed and died in June 1957. The symbolism for him working as a musician here must be profound.

It may be that the image of an orchestra in a ballroom sticks with Ray and in part inspires the setting of the videos for 'Come Dancing' (1982) and 'Don't Forget To Dance' (1983), both of which rely heavily on imagery from his youth and the formative days of The Kinks.

Ray will refer to tonight in later interviews as the point when he decides to pursue music as a possible career, moving on from local gigs and joining Dave Hunt's outfit – a real "London band" with older, experienced players.

1963

This was a year filled with major upheavals and transitions that saw Ray, Dave and Pete Quaife – the core of what became The Kinks – transform themselves from a fledgling schoolboy band into determined contenders with their sights set firmly on becoming a successful, professional outfit. They were mightily inspired by the almost unimaginable runaway success of a provincial working-class outfit, The Beatles. They also found themselves amid a rapidly emerging London R&B scene, right in their own back yard, and by the autumn Muswell Hill's Three Musketeers of rock'n'roll were committed to doing whatever it took to reach their goal.

January

Friday 4th

Piccadilly Jazz Club *central London* 8:00-11:00pm, The Dave Hunt R&B Band
Almost certainly the day that Ray joins the Dave Hunt band as an official member. The full billing is Dave Hunt's Rhythm & Blues Band featuring Hamilton King. Beside Hunt on trombone and King on vocals there is Lol Coxhill on saxophone, an older trad pianist, a bassist, and a drummer, the latter three players' names lost to time. Ray later describes the drummer as having a rock background, which probably indicates a younger player.

Hunt's band, managed by Giorgio Gomelsky, is an interesting attempt at combining older trad players with younger art-student types learning to play from scratch. Prior to Ray joining, Charlie Watts has on occasion played drums for Hunt. Watts will join the rival Rollin' Stones on January 17th after filling in with them at the Marquee club. Hunt later claims that his band has never had a permanent line-up and players are always coming and going, despite Gomelsky providing steady residencies.

When Ray joins, the band usually plays three nights per week. They don't seem to have a Saturday night residency now, which probably allows him to pursue Ray Davies Quartet dates. The Hunt band's repertoire varies, and is later described by Ray as "a lot of mainstream jazz numbers and a lot of traditional jazz, and a few blues numbers".

kinks'63

Sunday 6th

Station Hotel *Richmond, west London* The Dave Hunt R&B Band

As a member now, Ray performs at this residency that began for Hunt back in November, providing the club's first house band.

Wednesday 9th, 16th & 23rd

Six Bells Jazz Club, The Six Bells *Chelsea, central London*
The Dave Hunt R&B Band

This residency is at a pub on the King's Road.

Thursday 10th

Elm Park Hotel *Hornchurch, east London* The Dave Hunt R&B Band

Friday 11th, 18th, 25th

Piccadilly Jazz Club *central London* 8:00-11:00pm, The Dave Hunt R&B Band

Sunday 13th, 20th, 27th

Station Hotel *Richmond, west London* The Dave Hunt R&B Band

February

Sunday 3rd & 10th

Station Hotel *Richmond, west London* The Dave Hunt R&B Band

The show on the 10th is possibly Ray's last performance with the Hunt band (a date advertised for the following Sunday is apparently cancelled due to bad weather). Ray's decision to leave may be because he wants to play with younger musicians. It prompts Hunt to split the band and give up this key residency. Ray will say later that he leaves the band because of the demands of his upcoming exams.

In his book *X-Ray* Ray implies it is tonight that renowned British guitarist Davy Graham wanders into the club and sits in during the break, playing an impromptu performance after borrowing Ray's guitar – and in Ray's mind miraculously transforming the sound of his Gretsch copy into a fine instrument.

Hunt's residency at Gomelsky's club is taken over on February 24th by The Rolling Stones, which turns out to be their big break as the R&B trend explodes. From April 14th the Station Hotel club becomes known as the Crawdaddy, clearly defined as an R&B club.

☆ Ray is keeping a busy schedule. He is taking weekend classes at a local drama school in addition to his college course. Shortly he will join forces with Hunt's singer Hamilton King, leaving the trad material behind to play a repertoire of American blues and R&B along with other younger players. He also still plays with Dave, Quaife and Start when gigs are available.

Saturday 16th

Town Hall *Hornsey, north London* St. Valentine's Carnival Ball
The Ray Davies Quartet, with Harry Pitch & His Band

A beauty contest to choose Miss Valentine, with The Ray Davies Quartet providing instrumental backing. This booking underlines Ray's continuing commitment to play with Dave, Quaife and Start on home turf, even though he's off at art college and has been playing in a pro London-based outfit.

The Hornsey Journal writes: "More than 600 young people attended [the ball] organised by the management committee of Thanet Boys Club, Kentish Town … Saturday's dance raised £50. Music was provided by Harry Pitch and his band, and the Roy Davis Quartet [sic],

the members [of which] are pupils of William Grimshaw School." This is probably one of the last dates booked as the Quartet; the band will rename itself The Ramrods during this spring.

→ ● **RECORDING** (probably) IBC Studios *central London*. Although it's impossible to date, the Quartet makes its first proper recording session around this time. The location is known to be Great Portland Street in central London, which almost certainly identifies it as IBC Studios. Start clearly recalls playing two separate demo sessions (the second one documented as April 16th 1963). These earliest demos are probably instrumentals, titles unknown.

March

→ Hamilton King's band, variously known as the Blues Messengers and the R&B Group, consists of King on vocals and harmonica, Ray on electric guitar, Peter Bardens on piano, and Dave Ambrose on bass guitar, with an unnamed drummer. This version of the King band will break up in June, but King continues with new musicians at least into 1965. In his book *Kink* Dave tells of seeing this band at the Kaleidoscope club on Gerrard Street in central London, and describes them as "the genuine article, raw, authentic". Dave also alludes to an influential song that they play, 'Oh! Yeah', a "heavy blues riff-based piece which was very hypnotic and repetitive". Ray has said little about his brief time with the band, although King does acquaint Ray with West Indian music, a new influence that will come through in later Kinks recordings such as 'I'm On An Island' and 'Apeman'.

Peter Bardens, later of 1970s band Camel, recalls that the King outfit is his first band, which he joins while still at art school. "I'd just met Mick Fleetwood [who] didn't start off playing with the band – he used to come along to rehearsals and watch. The band had Ray Davies on lead guitar. Hamilton King was this West Indian, a big bear of a fellow. He used to play harmonica and sing in a very high-pitched voice. [As a lead guitarist, Ray] was very good. He used to do all the things like playing it behind his head, rolling on the ground and kicking his legs in the air. He only sang on one or two numbers."

April

→ Following Ray's brief six-week interlude with Hunt's band, and his stint now with the King band, the Quartet begins the process that will see it renamed The Ramrods. It's taken from a Duane Eddy single, 'Ramrod', a favourite of Dave's. Dave says that he and Quaife conceive the change while Ray is "off playing in some blues band", likely referring to King's outfit.

While Ray is always part of the venture – though sometimes characterised as a floating member – his energies are clearly focused elsewhere, and by his own later admission for a while he looks down on the Quartet. During these periods of Ray's diminished commitment it seems likely that Dave is exerting more influence over the direction and identity of the band.

Quaife and Start do not recall any point where Ray ceases to be involved, and say the core band is always tangible but that Ray simply shifts his level of commitment. Quaife recalls that Dave is easily the most consistent driving force in keeping the band going, especially during the periods of Ray's preoccupations elsewhere. Looking back, Start doesn't even recall Ray being in other bands at the time, so seamless is his multi-band involvement.

Dave says later: "Until Ray decided to [commit to] our band, the people he played with were coming out of the jazz-influenced side of music, and I think what we were doing was more unique, purely rock and blues influenced, and something the musicians he had been working with looked down on."

Probably not a coincidence is that around the same time this spring, Dave is fired from his job at Selmer's central-London music shop, and begins to devote more time to the band as a full-time career.

Saturday 13th
Town Hall *Hornsey, north London* Easter Saturday Holiday Dance
The follow-up to the February 16th beauty contest, the quartet again providing instrumental backing. The name used by the band for this booking is unknown.

Tuesday 16th
● **RECORDING** R.G. Jones Recording Studios *Morden, south-west London*. Probably today, the band – Ray, Dave, Quaife and Start – has its second demo session. (This is also the date of an early Rolling Stones demo session at which Gomelsky recalls bumping into Ray, finishing his own session prior to the Stones.)

Start recalls that one of the probable two recordings was an original song by Dave called **'(something) Sunshine'**. (The full titles seems to be lost to time, as in 2003 neither Dave nor Quaife can remember it.) Start says that at the time Ray is not writing any original material other than instrumentals. Ray is apparently continuing his involvement with the Quartet, despite his other musical projects, and Dave is clearly active, writing and singing on at least one of these early demos.

➜ Ray is working with the King band as they get their repertoire together at rehearsals in the Kaleidoscope club in Soho. Among the many King originals are Ray Charles covers and R&B standards including 'Night Train' and 'Night Time Is The Right Time'. Barry Fantoni, an art-college colleague of Ray's (and later TV personality and author), sits in on saxophone at one rehearsal. Likely places that the King band plays in its short existence in this line-up include London clubs such as The Kaleidoscope, possibly The Top Ten Club and/or Roaring Twenties in Carnaby Street, Count Suckle's Cue Club, and a Jamaican club probably near Edgware Road tube station.

May

6th, 13th or 20th
All Nighter, The Flamingo *central London*
Hamilton King's band, with Ray, reportedly plays an R&B audition/gig here, opening for residents Georgie Fame & The Blue Flames.
☆ Around this time, future Kinks session pianist Nicky Hopkins leaves Cyril Davies's All Stars due to ill-health. Ray, Quaife and Start have seen Cyril's band at the Marquee and certainly will have caught Hopkins in action prior to his departure.

June

Ray leaves Hamilton King's Blues Messengers some time this month as the band in its current guise apparently falls apart. Peter Bardens forms his own R&B band, The Cheynes, in July with his good friend, drummer Mick Fleetwood, signing with the Rik Gunnell Agency and quickly become a staple on the London R&B circuit.

➜ Although specific gigs are unknown, The Ramrods continue to play

regularly, with Ray's departure from the King band likely signalling a renewed interest on his part. Start recalls a few out-of-town performances, including shows in Peterborough and Southampton. The band is keen to get work at the various US Air Force bases littered around the country, and will succeed in securing such gigs in July and August. Other regular gigs possibly played around now are at a West End nightclub in Oxford Street, and the TOC-H on Pages Lane in Muswell Hill, where Quaife recalls playing driving sets of blues-based and rock'n'roll songs. Start recalls that, despite everyone's interest in R&B in recent months, his time in the band is dominated mostly by traditional rock'n'roll, and that the band's shift to R&B is more likely to have occurred after he leaves the band (probably next month).

July

Ray completes one year of studies at Hornsey College of Art, but leaves because the school has no course in film studies, a subject now of great interest to him and one which he wants to pursue rather than his current fine arts course. Ray wants to go to the Central School of Art & Design in central London but is too late to apply, so instead he settles for a spot at Croydon School of Art in south London, biding his time until he can get a grant to attend film school.

John Start finishes at William Grimshaw school and, almost certainly this month, announces that he will no longer be a member of The Ramrods. Start recalls that it has very little to do with any dissatisfaction with the group, but that he simply prefers to pursue his love of boat racing on the weekends rather than rehearsing with the band. He is also about to begin studies to become a surveyor, and the timing just seems natural. Once he leaves the band, Start will never again see or speak to Ray or Dave, despite their rise to fame, but remains a casual friend of Quaife's. He never returns to music. It falls to Quaife to find a permanent replacement on drums, but until they find someone the band seems to rely on fill-in players on a gig-by-gig basis.

At about the same time as Start's departure, the band signs with or at least begins getting work from booking agent Danny Haggerty. Dave later says that Haggerty secures them work at US bases and at private parties. Haggerty has apparently already found Ray occasional work as a guitarist, and now books him as part of a pick-up band to back black bodybuilder and singer Rick Wayne ("Mr. Southern England") on a series of gigs at clubs on American Air Force bases. Apparently Quaife and Dave too are used as the basis of the band, with various pick-up drummers, billed as Rick Wayne & The Muscle Men. Ray misses some dates due to illness. A series of appearances in Germany is booked by Haggerty but falls through. The home bookings continue into August.

Another regular gig, possibly at this time, involves providing instrumental music at the Dance Institute of London in Oxford Street, central London, where Ray with Dave and Quaife plus different drummers play for the dancers. Haggerty may well have secured this gig, too.

August

Sometime this month Quaife finds a replacement drummer in Mickey Willett from Palmers Green, north London. Willett is slightly older than the others, and Quaife recalls he looks much like pop crooner Matt Monro. Willett is proud of having been a former member of Tommy Bruce & The Bruisers, a band that had a series of singles on Columbia in 1960-61 (a number 3 with 'Ain't Misbehavin'' in summer 1960 and a number 36 with 'Broken Doll' that autumn – plus a number 50 for Bruce with 'Babette' in late winter 1962, though Willett may not

kinks'63

have been a member then). Willett has something of a seasoned pro's outlook, in contrast to the scruffy and naive college-kid style of Ray, Dave and Quaife.

September

➔ Moving ever closer to what becomes The Kinks, the band – Ray, Dave, Quaife and Willett – are now performing more R&B-flavoured material, but have an eye out for a proper vocalist as Ray continues to be uncomfortable in the role. This seems to have increased after his time with relatively authentic R&B singer Hamilton King, and Dave is apparently handling a large portion of the vocal chores.

Jonah Jones, a good friend of the band, has long wanted to be their vocalist, but besides an occasional chance to sit in, he instead becomes the band's right-hand man – an early roadie of sorts, a role in which he will continue during the band's early years.

Willett recalls intensive rehearsals at pubs in the local area and occasionally in the front room at the Davies' home on Denmark Terrace. With Willett committed to the group and the musical direction shifting to R&B, the band takes advantage of the changes to transform itself from The Ramrods to The Boll-Weevils. The name is Dave's suggestion and is taken from another of Dave's big influences, Eddie Cochran, whose 1959 single 'Somethin' Else' had as its B-side 'Boll Weevil Song'. Although derived from this rock'n'roll track, the name conjures an American blues vibe, as in the traditional 'Boll-Weevil Blues' which may be known to the band in its Leadbelly recording.

Dave pictures the newly-named Boll-Weevils dressed entirely in black, as a distinct break from the clean-cut look of the John Start era. This also seems to be the point where Ray abandons his musical side-trips and commits himself solely to The Boll-Weevils. He will say later that as he starts at Croydon art college he becomes consumed with the idea of not just playing music but succeeding with it, and his competitive ambition kicks in.

✪ At summer's end, aspiring singer Robert Wace together with his manager and close friend Grenville Collins are looking for a "beat group" to back Wace at various society parties. Wace encounters music-business figure Terry Kennedy, manager of The Ivy League among others, who suggests that he phone a drummer friend, one Mickey Willett. Willett suggests that Wace and Collins come and see the band he's playing with, and arranges a visit to one of the The Boll-Weevils' informal rehearsals.

Sunday 8th

➔ Probably today, Robert Wace and Grenville Collins see Ray, Dave and Quaife at a Sunday rehearsal at The Athenaeum ballroom in Muswell Hill, where in effect both parties audition each other. Willett doesn't seem to be present, though later everyone meets up at The Clissold Arms pub across from the Davies home to discuss the possibility of working together.

While Wace is by no means what the band have in mind as an R&B vocalist, a mutually beneficial relationship is established. The Boll-Weevils can pick up some better-paid "society" gigs by backing Wace, who will do a relatively short feature spot, typically a four-song segment at the end of a set by The Boll-Weevils.

Regular rehearsals follow. Collins advances the band money to buy new outfits from the John Stephen boutique on Carnaby Street, central London, including pink tab-collar shirts and dark blue corduroy trousers. These are urgently needed to replace the abandoned, worn-thin matching cardigans and shirts bought by Start's father. Now that Wace and Collins are in the picture, agent Haggerty is phased out.

➔ Ray enters Croydon College of Art in south London as a theatre-design major on a scholarship (grant) from Middlesex County Council.

Sunday 15th

The Boll-Weevils audition for booking agent Rik Gunnell at the Flamingo club in central London, but don't impress him.

Monday 16th

Wace and Collins visit the Davies' home on Denmark Terrace to hold a meeting with Ray, Dave and Quaife.

Tuesday 17th

The Boll-Weevils rehearse at The Duke Of Edinburgh pub in neighbouring Wood Green. Wace and Collins bring along some of their friends, hoping to interest them in hiring the band for assorted social events. From this point the band is billed as Robert Wace & The Boll-Weevils.

Wednesday 18th

Ray, Dave and Quaife rehearse at the Davies home.

Thursday 19th

A proposed rehearsal at the Davies home is cancelled as drummer Willet announces he will be unavailable due to a proposed holiday in Manchester. Wace and Collins come by to talk things over.

Saturday 21st

A low-key rehearsal is held at the Davies home with Wace and Collins. Dave notes in his diary that he's building a new amplifier and speaker cabinet.

Thursday 26th

Wace has contacted Beatles manager Brian Epstein, who agrees to come and see The Boll-Weevils at an upstairs rehearsal area of The Camden Head pub in Islington, north London. This is evidently a combination rehearsal and audition with just Ray, Dave and Quaife present (no Willett). According to Wace, Epstein is possibly interested in Ray as a solo, and not the band itself, but nothing comes of this.

Friday 27th

Everybody is scrambling around today to find a fill-in drummer for tomorrow night's gig.

Saturday 28th

Robert Wace & The Boll-Weevils play a wedding date with fill-in drummer Johnny Bremner. The venue may be the prestigious Dorchester Hotel in central London. According to Ray's recollection the first booking the band performs as backing group to Wace is at a private party at the Guildhall in central London, the first of many such social affairs the band will play at private central-London residences around well-heeled Belgravia and Sloane Square. Wace usually sings around four songs, drawn from material like Buddy Holly's 'It's So Easy', 'Rave On', 'Peggy Sue' and 'Think It Over' and recent hits such as Trini Lopez's 'If I Had A Hammer', Freddie & The Dreamers' 'I'm Telling You Now', Billy J. Kramer's 'Bad To Me', Gerry & The Pacemakers' 'I Like It', and The Isley Brothers' 'Twist And Shout' (popularised this summer in the UK by The Beatles).

October

Wednesday 2nd

A full band rehearsal for tomorrow's show is held at a local school on Summers Lane in Finchley, possibly the Compton School. Also today,

Wace buys a new Vox AC-30 amplifier for the band, which definitely brings their sound up a notch. Later this winter, Dave will combine his Elpico amp (the fabled "little green amp") with the Vox.

Thursday 3rd
Grocer's Hall *central London* Robert Wace & The Boll-Weevils
According to Dave in his later book, *Kink*, tonight's performance is well received, with promises of more bookings. "We played this place called the Grocer's Hall, some rich do where the guy would throw a massive party for his daughter. So we would get to drink champagne all night – and shag posh women, which is why I was put on earth, I'm sure! So we had a lot of that around us, and Ray was absorbing all of these influences. I was always the demonstrative one; if there was a party happening I was always the one in the middle of it. But I think this was how Ray's writing developed, just from being in the band and picking up these things – seeing a different side of society and how society was changing."

→ **Brady's Club** *east London* Robert Wace & The Boll-Weevils
This is likely the scene of one of the band's last performances backing Wace (though Ray will claim in *X-Ray* that they play one more date in Mayfair after this). Wace is unceremoniously booed by the crowd at this club, which is outside his usual circuit. From now, The Boll-Weevils will continue without their add-on vocalist. Among their repertoire at this time are 'Got Love If You Want It', 'Johnny B. Goode', 'Route 66', 'Little Queenie', 'Bo Diddley', 'Poison Ivy' and similar R&B material. The band's feature numbers are 'Smokestack Lightning' and 'Money (That's What I Want)', both of which they regularly extend into long rave-ups.

Sunday 13th
A landmark night in British pop music as The Beatles appear on the ITV show *Val Parnell's Sunday Night At The London Palladium*, an influential showbiz programme. The Boll-Weevils are also probably aware that The Rolling Stones have now left the London club scene and are currently on a national package tour with Bo Diddley and The Everly Brothers.

Monday 14th
At the Davies home, Dave notes in his diary that he, Ray and Quaife collaborate on a new song, 'One Fine Day'.

→ Wace and Collins form an informal partnership to finance and co-manage The Boll-Weevils. Collins has convinced Wace to give up his ambitions as a singer and instead to move into management, spurred their fascination with Brian Epstein's success with The Beatles. Nonetheless, it is evidently Ray's suggestion that Wace and Collins manage the band. Collins continues to work as a stockbroker in London, but Wace quits his job as a sales representative at his father's manufacturing company to devote time to managing the band, relying on his 50 percent interest in management income.

Saturday 19th
● **RECORDING** Regent Sound Studios *central London*. The Boll-Weevils' first proper demo session takes place at this Regent Street studio. Recorded today are at least two songs – **'I Believed You'**, written by Dave and Ray, and Leiber & Stoller's **'I'm A Hog For You'** – of which there is at least one surviving acetate disc. The choice of one original and one cover may be intended to showcase both aspects of the group's abilities. Dave's diary entry notes that they "must record new songs we wrote", but it seems that while 'One Fine Day' is finished in time it is not yet recorded. Wace and Collins then shop around acetates

of the two songs to the various record companies and publishing houses on Denmark Street in central London. ('I Believed You' will be first issued in 1999 on the two-CD Dave Davies set *Unfinished Business: A Dave Davies Kronikle, 1963-1998*. 'I'm A Hog For You' will be relegated to bootleg-only status when a copy comes to light in 1997.)

Sunday 20th
Ray attends a concert at the Fairfield Halls, Croydon, south London where blues harmonica great Sonny Boy Williamson performs.

Tuesday 22nd
A management contract is drawn up with today's date by the four Boll-Weevils and Wace and Collins. The contract will be superseded by another signed on February 12th 1964 with Boscobel Productions Ltd, the company later formed by Wace and Collins.

Thursday 24th
Denmark Productions Ltd, which will soon become involved with the band, is registered as a company. It is started by Austrian-born music publisher Edward Kassner as an artist-management arm of his own much larger Edward Kassner Music Co in a 50-50 partnership with Larry Page. Page acts as general manager and principal representative, while Kassner remains a behind-the-scenes partner. Kassner and Page form the partnership so that they can benefit from each other's talents and resources. As the streetwise and entrepreneurial Page signs up new talent, Kassner will potentially have a piece of these new recording acts, as Page passes on publishing rights to Kassner's publishing company in exchange for a placement fee. In addition to these lucrative fees, Page will have the resources and influence of a powerful publisher behind him, and thus be able more easily to attract young talent. The company will last 30 years, being dissolved on October 19th 1993. It will be another five or six weeks before the Davies brothers cross paths with Page.

Friday 25th
Another business meeting is held at the Davies' home as Wace and Collins explain the new contract arrangements.

Thursday 30th
Brady's Club *east London* The Boll-Weevils
The band plays at this club tonight for expenses for their session-drummer friend, Bobby Graham – who will go on to do early session work with The Kinks.

November

→ Following the universal dismissal of their acetate demo by record companies, the band and their managers shift tactics and will now approach music publishers, for which they decide they will need a new demo of 100 percent original material. They are probably becoming aware that in the case of unproved bands, publishers and record companies are more interested in hearing the original songs an artist is capable of creating.

Saturday 16th
● **RECORDING** R.G. Jones Recording Studios *Morden, south-west London*. Wace books more studio time, not this time in the relatively expensive studios of central London but at this cheaper place in south London that the Start-era band used back in April. The R.G. Jones studio is gaining a reputation for reasonable prices and good results. Acts such as The Rolling Stones have worked here, and next month The Yardbirds will use the studio.

For their second set of demos, The Boll-Weevils work at a session from 10:00am to 12midday, presumably overseen by house engineer Ronald G. Jones junior. Dave's diary notes that two band originals are recorded: Ray and Dave's **'One Fine Day'** is tackled, with Dave singing lead, plus one of Ray's first solo compositions, **'I Took My Baby Home'**, on which he sings. The surviving studio log lists Wace's name only, along with his address (45 Boscobel Place) and phone number, and notes that the band consists of three guitars, vocals and drums.

➔ The Boll-Weevils play some more private parties this month. In London the band plays at the 21st birthday party of Jackie Rufus Isaacs, grandchild of Rufus Isaacs, the 1st Marquess of Reading. He is a highly distinguished Jewish barrister who served as Attorney General, Lord Chief Justice of England, Viceroy of India, British Ambassador, and Secretary of State for Foreign Affairs. In Belgravia, central London, the band appears at a private birthday party for Greek shipping magnate and financier George P. Livanos. They play overtime, and a dispute over money occurs with Willett. A further event this month sees the band in a tent in Lewisham, south-east London.
☆ Late this month drummer Mickey Willett's girlfriend Maria comes across a receipt for a gig fee that amounts to far more than the £5 apiece the band receives, and she prompts Willett to challenge Wace about it.
☆ With another demo in hand, Wace continues to shop for interest in his charges at various music publishers, and gets some response from one Tony Hiller at Mills Music. Wace possibly leaves copies of one or both of their demos at the Mills office.
☆ Inspired by director Roger Corman's new horror movie *The Raven*, which is based on the famous Edgar Allan Poe poem of the same name, the band changes its name again, possibly prompted by criticism of the rather uncommercial Boll-Weevils. The band will be The Ravens for less than two months, yet it is this name most associated with their pre-fame, pre-Kinks period, even though they were The Boll-Weevils for longer.

Saturday 23rd
Methodist Youth Hostel *Muswell Hill, north London* The Ravens
Almost certainly the band's first booking with the new name.

➔ **Daily Mail newspaper offices** *central London*
Around this time Mickey Willett is fired as the band's drummer, after a performance at a private press reception here, where The Ravens provide entertainment. Willett is apparently not happy with the style and direction that the new management team is taking, and also challenges them on money matters.
Wace will recall: "We got rid of [Willett] very quickly [and] found someone else who was really quite a good drummer, but older than [the rest of the band]." This new, older drummer recruited to replace Willett remains anonymous, though it may be Johnny Bremner, who filled in for Willett back in September. Ray will refer later in *X-Ray* to "Johnny Green" but like many of the less-prominent figures in his book, the surname is probably a fabrication, though the forename is generally agreed upon.
➔ Despite the interest in the demo disc from Mills Music, Wace also approaches Kassner Music and is directed to one Larry Page. Wace is able to convince Page to come and see his band in person. Page manages a number of other artists including The Orchids, Shel Naylor, and Johnny B Great, and the first two will soon record compositions by the Davies brothers.
☆ Larry Page goes to see The Ravens play, apparently in the East End of London, which may imply Brady's Club where the band has played

before. Some later accounts place Page at a pub rehearsal, probably The Camden Head in Islington. Whatever the location, Page likes what he sees and hears, and becomes more interested in the band. He offers to help manage them, initially to get a recording contract but also to provide traditional management activities such as advising them on business and stage matters and helping to shape their musical direction.
It is agreed verbally in principle to give Page's management company Denmark Productions, 10 percent of the band's earnings, and Page sends an informal letter of agreement to Wace and Collins to this effect, until a formal contract can be drawn up between their respective companies – though in fact this will not be signed until February 26th 1964. Nonetheless, Page goes to work almost immediately, eager to prove his worth.

December

➔ The Ravens continue to play dates around London, and it is likely now that they do a good number of the lucrative private parties drawn from Collins and Wace's social circles, particularly as the Christmas season draws near.
☆ Keen to show his abilities, Larry Page takes the band's existing acetates to Dick Rowe at Decca Records, with whom he has a good working relationship. But Rowe rejects The Ravens, possibly because the company has The Rolling Stones and does not feel the need for what they perceive as a similar band.
☆ Now that it seems likely a business agreement will be made with Page's Denmark Productions, Wace and Collins form their own limited company to handle all future management business. Wace sells a prized set of golf clubs to raise the £100 necessary to register the company, which they call Boscobel Productions after Wace's address on Boscobel Place, off Eton Square, a prestigious address in Belgravia, central London.

Thursday 5th
● **RECORDING AUDITION** Philips Recording Studios *central London*. This session is arranged by Page (or possibly Wace) with Philips head of A&R, Jack Baverstock. The Ravens record two originals (which they've already recorded themselves): Ray and Dave's **'I Believed You'** and Ray's **'I Took My Baby Home'**. Baverstock rejects the band.

➔ The band's small cache of original material is clearly not impressing record companies, and they are offered some Kassner-published material for recording. After hearing what is proposed, they are unimpressed, offering instead to work on more original material. It is at this point that Ray, encouraged by Page, begins to consider songwriting seriously. "They'd given us songs of theirs, the publishing guys," he says later, "but we didn't want to do them, so I started writing." The band is still keen to hire a lead singer at this point, but Page discourages them. He wants to develop Ray's songwriting and singing, saying that Ray should write material to suit his vocal limitations.
☆ With events beginning to snowball, on successive Saturdays (possibly the 7th, 14th and 21st) the three principal Ravens assemble for on-location filming by friend and fashion photographer John Cowan in and around Hyde Park, central London. The project is never finished. One scene has the band driving through a car-wash in a convertible with the top down. Even before signing a record deal, it seems that Ray is thinking of the band in terms of film as well as music.
➔ The entry of American record producer Shel Talmy into the story now is complex, with at least three widely differing versions of the sequence of events.

Talmy maintains that he hears an acetate of the band at Mills Music and feels they have the kind of potential he's interested in working with. He considers them candidates for a new independent production deal he is negotiating with Pye Records. Wace confirms this version of the story and says the band's eventual signing to Pye is solely Talmy's accomplishment. There is the indisputable fact that it is Talmy's name that appears on the Pye contract. In his later book *Kink*, Dave too leans towards this version.

Larry Page is equally sure that it is he who makes the deal with Pye, but concedes that Pye is forced to take the band through Talmy and his new independent recording deal with them. Page probably does approach Pye on his own when soliciting all the major record companies in search of a deal.

Ray will present a third version of the story in *X-Ray*, recalling that Page suggests meeting Talmy, a business associate with whom Page has worked already, and that Page, Ray and Talmy meet and agree to work together.

One can only imagine that the truth lies somewhere between these versions. Bearing in mind the various enmities that will develop later, what emerges as the most likely scenario is that both Page and Talmy have an interest in the band, and both approach Louis Benjamin at Pye Records, probably independently of one another. Our conclusion is that it seems likely that Talmy's influence at Pye secures the deal, especially as he has a signed production deal with them, regardless of who saw or dealt with whom immediately beforehand.

Monday 16th

● **RECORDING** Regent Sound Recording Studios (No.2) *central London*. Page takes The Ravens into one of his favourite studios, literally across the road from his office on Denmark Street. Presumably with house engineer Bill Farley, the band records two songs, **'Ooladiooba'**, probably a Kassner-published composition, and an instrumental, **'Revenge'**, an early embodiment of what becomes The Kinks' sound.

The songwriting for the latter track is attributed to Ray Davies and Larry Page, but Ray later claims this is simply the age-old publisher's ploy to derive further income from a client's songwriting, and that the piece is entirely Ray's. It's also notable as the last distant echo of the primarily instrumental Ray Davies Quartet.

A two-sided Regent Sound acetate disc survives. Ray sings lead vocal on the top side, 'Ooladiooba', and plays harmonica on both. The drummer for the session is anonymous, though the amateurish, rudimentary style makes it clear it is not someone of the calibre of Bobby Graham, who had already played with the band. It may even be Larry Page deputising for the lack of a regular drummer.

The acetate lists no artist, perhaps implying that the name of the band is already under reconsideration as part of Page's new advice. Page presumably shops the demo around to various record companies but he is still turned down by everyone. (The acetate will be sold at auction in 1993 and acquired by an employee of Sequel Records, a subsidiary of Castle Music, who purchases it for potential issue as part of an *Early Kinks* release, which ultimately does not happen.)

'Revenge' is received for US copyright filing on December 18th, making it the earliest copyrighted Ray Davies composition. Ray says later: "We were being given bad Beatles copies to record and I thought I can do better than that. So I was an accidental singer and reluctant songwriter."

Tuesday 17th

Town Hall *Hornsey, north London* 8:00pm-12midnight, *The Ravens Christmas Party*
A privately promoted concert arranged by the band's management. Crates of Coca-Cola are purchased by Wace and Collins who sell it as refreshment for the evening.

Wednesday 18th

Archway Tavern *Holloway, north London* The Ravens
A listing in Dave's diary marks this evening as "Xmas party" and is likely a booking for the band at a private celebration.

➜ Ray is at a Christmas dance at the Croydon College of Art around this time, sitting in on harmonica with the band. One of its members, guitarist Ralph McTell, later recalls the event.

Twycross Country Club *Twycross, Leics* The Ravens
The band reportedly performs at a Christmas dance here at this time.
➜ Quaife will say in an interview next year that the change of name from The Ravens to The Kinks is made some time around this Christmas. But it seems more likely that the band fulfil any remaining gigs into January 1964 as The Ravens and save the new name for their official launch on February 1st. As with most things at this stage, at least four people are credited with the idea for the new name: booking agent Arthur Howes (see 31st); an anonymous friend of Robert Wace; first Kinks photographer Bruce Fleming; and Larry Page (the most adamant and indeed likely candidate).

Ray recalls later that Page witnesses an event in a pub: "[Dave and Quaife were] dressed in black leather, and some old boozer at the bar said, 'Hey, look, there's a couple of Kinks.'" Other influences on the name-change may include Honor Blackman's famous leather "kinky boots" that she wears as the Cathy Gale character in the British TV series *The Avengers*, as well as an August 1963 single by The John Barry Seven, 'Kinky'.

Future Kink drummer Mick Avory says later: "Dave and Pete used to go round wearing cloaks and things, which was pretty way out for the times. People used to say they were 'kinky', so Larry [Page] picked up on that and [said,] 'That's what you should be called, The Kinks.' And that was that."

Tuesday 31st

Town Hall *Hornsey, north London* 8:00pm, *The Ravens Grand New Year's Eve Carnival Ball*
Lotus House Restaurant *central London* late show, The Ravens
Quaife's 20th birthday. The appearance at the Lotus House on Edgware Road is booked by Wace, a private New Year's Eve party at a show-business hangout and attended by influential Beatles promoter Arthur Howes. He is impressed by The Ravens' performance and tells Wace and Collins that they should phone him in two days to discuss him becoming their booking agent. Howes apparently thinks The Ravens have similar potential to The Beatles. Wace and Collins are concerned that Howes might not remember or value his impressions in the clear light of day, but when Collins phones him Howes is still very impressed and maintains his offer to become their agent. This key event tips the scale in The Ravens' favour, and everything else will quickly go their way in the coming weeks and months.

1964

This was the year that The Kinks appeared as a band and went to almost instant success, with all the personal and professional upheavals that accompany such a speedy rise to fame. From amateurs with no experience of touring or residencies and only hit-and-miss club and private-party experience, they were thrust into a whirl of sessions and concerts and personal appearances, and had to deal with complex business arrangements that would have tested even a more mature outfit's endurance. They would spend a good deal of the next ten years reacting against all of this.

As with many new bands in the first flurry of professional activity, contracts were signed that would have unforeseen consequences and that followed them for the rest of their lives. And yet at that time the band was still looking for a drummer and was still hoping to find a lead singer. Ray Davies had only written a couple of songs, with little sign that he would soon develop into a world-class composer.

Finally they did find drummer Mick Avory and a little over a week after his audition he was on national TV and then straight out on tour. He and the band would spend much of the following 20 years on the road.

The changes in their lives were immediate and profound. Dave Davies was already a conventional workforce dropout; Pete Quaife and Mick Avory held down proper jobs; Ray was a full-time student until the early days of January. It was a dream come true to be able to walk away from a dreary future and step onto a stage night after night to play music, but as with all young hopefuls the distance between the dreams and the reality quickly became apparent once money and heavy workloads were introduced.

Early attempts to mould the band into a conventional showbiz package misfired miserably, whether an enforced recording of a cover song in an alien style, or fitting Ray with caps to hide the gap in his front teeth. Every step of the way the band rebelled against anything that didn't feel right, relying on their inherent instinct of self-identity and survival. From the first recording session – where they went along with the conventional wisdom, and produced a dud – the battle-lines were drawn.

For 'You Really Got Me', the third and potentially last single, a fiercely determined Ray fought to get his song done his own way, proving everyone else wrong, and in the process giving the world a timeless slice of rock'n'roll magic. It was a fantastic achievement … but it also unleashed a monster of sorts.

From this point on, the pressure was always on Ray to create commercial magic at the last second to keep the band afloat. And because he had been so spectacularly right about 'You Really Got Me' where everyone else was wrong, later he would often recreate similar circumstances so that he could again save the band and prove that he needed to fight against all the odds. Add to this the insecurities of a creative personality plus some self-destructive tendencies that somehow aided self-preservation, and a long battle was underway pitching artistic values against commercial realities. The result was a major fight within The Kinks upon almost every single release until 1973.

But for now The Kinks arrived as the original, authentic punks, and true rebels, not simply part of a manufactured image like The Rolling Stones. As we shall see later, the brisk ride to fame continued into 1965, but the brakes would be quickly applied.

➡ INDICATES EVENT AROUND THIS TIME BUT WITH NO FIRM DATE

January

➜ After a discussion with the band's managers (Robert Wace and Grenville Collins) Arthur Howes agrees to become their booking agent. With the band now poised for a professional career, Ray Davies consults his Croydon Art College counsellor Freddie Crooks on New Year's Day: should he stay at college, or pursue music? Crooks agrees that Ray should give music a chance for six months – and if that doesn't work he can simply resume his studies in the autumn, with no effect on his future. Once Ray decides to drop out of college and devote himself to the band, things happen very quickly, especially once the influential agent Howes is involved. Ray completes two more weeks of school to qualify for his grant money, and probably finishes on the 17th.

Shel Talmy persuades Pye Records to sign the band, although the contract is not signed until just after the first Pye recording, which will make their first studio visit in effect a test session. Pressure is now on Ray to produce a suitable song for the band to record at their first proper recording session. No separate song-publishing contract is arranged or signed, but Larry Page will soon become contractually empowered to assign to Kassner Music any songs written by either of the Davies brothers, as soon as they are composed. This arrangement will be formalised in February. (The publishing of songs and printing of them for sale is standard record industry practice, even though the sale of compositions in recorded form long ago eclipsed that of printed music, and publishers still wield considerable power in the industry. A writer's compositions are "published" by a publishing company, and a portion of the ownership is given, or "assigned", to that publisher.)

Once the decision is made for the band to go professional, the current (temporary) drummer gives in his notice, presumably because he doesn't want to endanger his day job. Probably at this point Viv Prince, the flamboyant and legendary drummer, is set up for an audition, but he either fails to turn up at all or simply comes along for a rehearsal. Whatever the circumstances, he does not join – and in the next few months will become a member of The Pretty Things.

Monday 6th

According to Kassner Music files, Ray's very first written-for-hire composition, 'That's All I Want', is assigned to them as publisher today. It follows the arrangement worked out with Larry Page that he will formally pass the rights along to Kassner Music, and this is soon confirmed by contract. The song is almost certainly very similar to or even the same as 'A Little Bit Of Sunlight', which will be included in a group of songs assigned to Kassner in May 1965.

➜ Around this time Arthur Howes signs the band to his agency and agrees to put them on a major package tour with The Dave Clark Five starting late in March. Howes will get a 10 percent cut from the band's earnings, part of the 40 percent that Boscobel deducts as a total from The Kinks' gross earnings. Terry McGrath is assigned as the agent handling the account, while one G.T. Sumner, a booking agent based in Runcorn, Liverpool, briefly becomes their northern representative. The band is initially sent north to gather some experience out of town before the Clark package tour begins.

Wace will later claim that Howes is not happy with the presence of Larry Page within the band's management and from the start is keen to remove him. Wace and Collins defend Page's role and stand by their decision to include him, a fact that is especially significant now because the two parties are still only bound by a letter of agreement and not by a formal contract. Apparently encouraged by the signing to the Howes Agency, Pye warms to Talmy's band and an initial recording date is set. Arrangements to draw up a formal recording contract are started and the first recording session is slated a few weeks hence.

Tuesday 7th – Sunday 12th

With a record deal agreed, Larry Page is now pushing Ray to write original material for the upcoming Pye recording session. Ray is hoping, of course, that one of his own compositions will merit A-side status. Page will later claim that he specifically encourages Ray to write songs that emphasise "you" and "me" in a bid to give the songs a more direct appeal for the listener.

➜ Around this time Ray produces at least two completely new songs, 'You Still Want Me' and 'You Do Something To Me'. The former is apparently the main contender for the first A-side as it is immediately filed for US copyright registration (and received by the US Copyright Office on January 16th). This implies that at least in Larry Page's eyes the song is probably the one intended for release as the first single, before Howes persuades otherwise. Also up for consideration is 'I Don't Need You Anymore', another song probably written at this point. Ray says later that this batch of songs is his second shot at writing a single for the band, particularly 'You Still Want Me' – implying that he considers 'That's All I Want' as his first attempt.

Monday 13th

● **RECORDING** Regent Sound Studios *central London*. This is probably the day a demo session is booked to record three of Ray's new songs for consideration for recording at Pye in the coming week. Although completely undocumented, the studio is probably Regent where likely **'You Still Want Me'**, **'You Do Something To Me'** and **'I Don't Need You Anymore'** are recorded. Demos of the first two have never surfaced, adding to speculation, though a long-standing rumour suggests a two-sided Emidisc acetate of them does exist. A one-sided Emidisc of 'I Don't Need You Anymore' will turn up at a Christie's auction in 1990. The acetate is marked "The Kinks" indicating that the new bandname has almost certainly been decided upon by now.

Tuesday 14th

Publishing is assigned to Edward Kassner Music Ltd for five original Ray Davies songs: 'You Still Want Me', 'You Do Something To Me', and 'I Don't Need You Anymore', plus two titles composed earlier, 'I Took My Baby Home' and 'I Believed You'. Beside 'You Still Want Me', none of the other songs assigned with Kassner today is ever filed for US copyright – implying less than complete faith in their commercial prospects.

Friday 17th

Arthur Howes phones the morning after The Beatles' opening night concert at the Olympia in Paris and advises management of his opinion that The Kinks should record Little Richard's classic 'Long Tall Sally', a consistent highlight of The Beatles' set but as yet unrecorded by them. The Ravens – now The Kinks – have included a number of Little Richard songs in their repertoire, but this is not one of them. On short notice, presumably over the weekend, the band works up a Merseybeat-style arrangement of the song. Shel Talmy probably works with the band to finalise arrangements before the session takes place.

Monday 20th

● **RECORDING** Pye Studios (No.1) *central London*. Although undocumented, this is the most likely day when for the first time The Kinks visit Pye Studios in ATV house near Marble Arch in central London. The session is in the original full-size studio 1, which at 35 by 40 feet is large enough to record a full orchestra. The smaller 20x22 studio 2 is where most of their subsequent recordings at Pye will be done, but this is only opened this month and not quite ready yet. The session's producer is Shel Talmy, the engineer Ray Prickett, and the band records tonight on the studio's 3-track machine.

Ray Davies is armed with his Maton electric guitar and harmonica,

Dave Davies his Harmony Meteor guitar, and Pete Quaife his Framus bass guitar. On drums is their friend, session drummer Bobby Graham. Also present are Arthur Howes, Terry McGrath and Larry Page.

Put on tape during this reportedly six-hour session are **'Long Tall Sally'**, **'I Took My Baby Home'**, **'You Still Want Me'**, **'You Do Something To Me'** and **'I Don't Need You Anymore'**. Dave Davies recalls later: "We signed with Pye and were given a three-hour recording session to do about six tracks – quarter-inch tape, that sort of thing. Pye weren't willing to spend much money on this bunch of long-haired unknowns, so we had to work very fast." Despite Dave's 'six', accounts in Ray's later book, *X-Ray*, and *The Official Biography* suggest four songs were done. There is no surviving evidence of a sixth song or what it would be, though the likely candidate is 'I Believed You' – or an unknown non-original. Quaife recalls that 'One Fine Day' is recorded as a Kinks master at some point for possible inclusion on their first LP, but this is also unlikely as it has not yet been assigned to Kassner, and no further details are known. ('I Don't Need You Anymore' is later issued as a bonus track on the 1998 CD reissue of *The Kinks* album.)

Tuesday 21st

A press release announces that The Kinks are signing to Pye Records. Scheduled for release on February 4th is 'Long Tall Sally' as their first single, and their debut TV appearance will be on Associated-Rediffusion's *Ready Steady Go!* on February 7th.

Thursday 23rd

Boscobel Productions formally signs a recording contract with Pye Records on behalf of Ray, Dave and Quaife, who are all too young to sign on their own account. The original contract is for three singles (six sides) with five one-year options for renewal. (The first one-year option will be picked up in August 1964, only after the third single, 'You Really Got Me', proves successful. The contract is then entirely renegotiated in the summer/autumn of 1966 and continued for a further five years until 1971, when The Kinks deem the contract fulfilled and sign a new deal with RCA.)

Back in 1964, this first deal is for the band to be paid two percent of retail price (domestic) and one percent of retail (foreign) on 85 percent of record sales, the 15 percent being a standard allowance for returns and defective product. Recording costs are charged directly to Shel Talmy Productions, contrary to the industry standard established shortly afterwards where recording costs will be deducted directly from artist royalties. The deal is an even split of four percent between Talmy and The Kinks, meaning that each party gets two percent of retail (domestic). Although Shel Talmy Productions is written into the deal and The Kinks will submit their recordings through that company, Talmy points out later that The Kinks are not signed directly to his production company, even though that would have been to his advantage later, but directly to Pye Records. This will be at odds with standard independent production deals that evolve in the industry in the coming years, where the artist signs directly to the independent producer who then secures the record deal as their representative (and thereby gives the producer control).

☆ In the band's continuing quest for a drummer, Mick Avory is contacted by The Kinks' management in response to an ad he placed in today's *Melody Maker* (dated January 25th): "Drummer. Young, good kit, read, seeks pro-R&B groups. MOL 4615."

With a single recorded and poised for release, and a debut concert and major TV appearance set for a week's time, The Kinks are desperate to hire a drummer. In a later interview, Dave implies that the auditioning process has been ongoing: "He was the best drummer we'd seen, but I didn't really have a gut feeling that he was the right guy. But the pressure was mounting to do stuff and he looked good, he was a nice guy, played well and stuff, but I wasn't happy with it at the start," says Dave.

Auditions are held as soon as the next day, in Islington, north London. Avory gets his hair cut for the event, apparently asking for a Beatle-style cut, but the barber ends up cutting it too short and Avory is unsure about fitting in with the band's image.

Friday 24th

Almost certainly today at The Camden Head pub in Islington, at their regular spot in an upstairs room, the band auditions Avory with managers Robert Wace and Grenville Collins present. Avory recalls a second appearance two nights later, which may mean the band has a gig booked for the Saturday.

Sunday 26th

Probably back at The Camden Head in Islington for a second audition with Mick Avory, with Arthur Howes and Larry Page present.

Monday 27th

Avory is officially hired as the band's new drummer today, according to his own recollection. He says it's a date he'll always remember because it changes his life forever.

Thursday 30th

'Louie Louie' by The Kingsmen, on the Pye label, enters *Record Retailer*'s British charts for a seven-week run, peaking at number 26. Larry Page becomes familiar with the song and apparently encourages the band to emulate the same type of sound.

Tuesday 28th – Friday 31st

Further rehearsals are held at The Camden Head to familiarise Avory with The Kinks' repertoire – his first performance is only days away. This includes among others six Chuck Berry songs ('Too Much Monkey Business', 'Bye Bye Johnny', 'Little Queenie', 'Talkin' 'Bout You', 'Sweet Little Sixteen', 'Beautiful Delilah'), three by Bo Diddley ('Cadillac', 'Who Do You Love', 'Bo Diddley'), and other staple pieces of the period such as 'Poison Ivy', '(Get Your Kicks On) Route 66', 'Smokestack Lightning', 'I'm Your Hoochie Coochie Man', 'Money (That's What I Want)', 'Tutti Frutti', 'Long Tall Sally', 'Good Golly Miss Molly', 'Got Love If You Want It', 'I'm A Lover Not A Fighter', 'I'm A Hog For You', and 'Louie Louie'. They also play 'Revenge' by Ray Davies and Larry Page.

Dave says later: "When we first started we would do the odd Sonny Boy Williamson song and Bo Diddley, like 'Who Do You Love', and then we might throw in a couple of Buddy Holly songs. It was just a very experimental mix. And we used to do 'Smokestack Lightning'. It just had more soul, more grit, more expression." No doubt Avory's lessons are made easier because so many of these songs are standards that will be familiar to him. Maybe it is short notice to add a drummer, but the band is quickly becoming used to this kind of rushed and hurried method of doing things.

☆ The first photo session of The Kinks is held at photographer Bruce Fleming's studio in Great Newport Street, near Leicester Square, central London. The band dresses in various outfits of their own design. All wear leather jackets except Ray who has a suit jacket; all four have cloth caps (Quaife's was leather); Dave wears tweed pants; Ray has a huge white turtleneck sweater. Some photos are taken casually as they gather around a couch or a piano, others have the band brandishing whips. The shots seem to be done hastily in order to get a photo to accompany the management-financed *NME* ad (February 7th) for the release of the first single, 'Long Tall Sally'. Pye rejects use of the shots with whips, though some appear later in various pop magazines.

Friday 31st

A possible warm-up gig for Avory, likely at The Camden Head, but billed as The Ravens (according to Dave in *Kink*).

➜ INDICATES EVENT AROUND THIS TIME BUT WITH NO FIRM DATE

February

Saturday 1st

Town Hall *Oxford* 8:00-11:45pm, opening for Downliners Sect
The first concert with the band billed as The Kinks; Avory has been a member only a matter of days. No ads are published in local newspapers and the exact date is only confirmed from a ticket stub published in 1996 in Dave's book *Kink*. Oxford Town Hall periodically holds beat concerts at this time: The Rolling Stones appeared on January 4th, and The Tornados on February 22nd. Ray later recalls this first professional show as so poorly attended that the other musicians on the bill serve as the audience for each other's set. Only after tonight's low turn-out are further shows heavily advertised in the press. Avory says later that there are two sets tonight. Sect member Don Craine's recollection of the night is that The Kinks bus in a load of fans to ensure at least some enthusiasm in front of the stage.
☆ Underlining the wisdom of the band's name change, Oriole Records group The Ravens appear tonight at Cellar 64 in Manchester.
☆ This is also probably the first date on which the new name, The Kinks, is heard on TV as Brian Matthew is said to mention them on ABC TV's *Thank Your Lucky Stars* programme. Matthew apparently says: "There are so many groups coming up these days, I even heard of one the other day called The Kinks!" Maybe he read last week's brief mention of them signing to Pye Records?

Monday 3rd – Thursday 6th

More rehearsals probably held today at The Camden Head. The Kinks are photographed by Bruce Fleming on location and at his studio. This is the first proper image-shaping photo session. The band now has a matching set of three-piece brown suits with black leather trim and unique two-button fronts to the jackets, purchased from fashion designer John Stephen's boutique in Carnaby Street, central London. They all wear Cuban-heel boots, too. Some captions to the black-and-white press shots refer to the suits as bottle (very dark) green, so it's possible there is a second set. Also this week, Ray is fitted with temporary caps for his front teeth so that he is in perfect shape for the "proper" photo session.

Friday 7th

Goldhawk Beat Club, Goldhawk Social Club *Shepherds Bush, west London* with The Detours
❏ **TV** Television House (Studio 9) *central London*. ATV **Ready Steady Go!** lip-synch 'Long Tall Sally'.
The Kinks make their TV debut as they appear on *Ready Steady Go!* hosted by Cathy McGowan, and Dave is briefly interviewed by Michael Aldred. Other scheduled guests are American singer Ben E. King, Manfred Mann, Kiki Dee, and Danny Seyton & The Sabres. After the performance a photo is taken of a crowd of fans outside the studio – composed of friends and family members. Later, there's a gig to the west of town, where The Detours have a Friday residency at the Goldhawk. Drummer Doug Sandom clearly recalls opening for The Kinks at the Goldhawk just at the time of the release of 'Long Tall Sally'. His group's name changes from The Detours to The Who by February 20th, and Sandom will leave The Who in April.
'Long Tall Sally' single released in the UK. Although slated for Tuesday 4th, the slight delay may be because of a production error that causes an almost indetectable skip (just before the first chorus), long thought to have been a bad edit. Ray must be pleased by the *NME*'s review and its compliment for his song: "Another R&B speciality brought up to date and injected with the resonant group sound of the moment. ... It lacks the basic down-to-earth feel so essential to this type of music but the thunderous beat will provide plenty of pleasure to dancers. My preference is for 'I Took My Baby Home' with its hypnotic

twist beat and pleasing melody." The monthly *Big Beat* says "many critics have said that ['I Took My Baby Home'] should have been the A-side. However, the final choice was with the record company". The reviewer in *Record Mirror* reckons the group "give 'Long Tall Sally' a Chuck Berry treatment and commercially it comes off. Pounding stuff!" But Liverpool's *Mersey Beat* is far less kind: "How can anyone make such an exciting song so boring?" The record does not even merit a review in the *Melody Maker*.
☆ Probably today, The Kinks give their first published interview, with Chris Roberts of *Melody Maker*, published in the February 22nd issue. Besides discussing the band's unusual name, the musicians are bluntly honest when speaking of the planted crowd outside the TV studio. "They're not really followers – we've got large families." When asked if the Davies brothers are related, Ray chimes in: "Yeah, we're sisters."
☆ Half-page ad on *NME* cover launches band's first 45, 'Long Tall Sally'.
☆ It has long been said that the debut broadcast of The Kinks' first single was on the BBC Light Programme's *Housewives' Choice* show, but research shows that the record is not included any time between January 24th and February 14th. The story may well be an early example of Kinks humour.
☆ The Beatles leave Britain for New York today for their American debut on *The Ed Sullivan Show* on the 9th. Accompanying the group is Brian Sommerville in his capacity as their press officer. Somerville will later be hired by The Kinks' management – when 'You Really Got Me' takes off in the charts – underlining their philosophy to hire the best professionals money can buy to help launch The Kinks. (Unconfirmed gig likely the day following.)

Long Tall Sally single

A **'Long Tall Sally'** (E. JOHNSON, R. PENNIMAN, R. BLACKWELL).
B **'I Took My Baby Home'** (R. DAVIES).

UK release February 7th 1964 (Pye 7N 15611).
US release March ?27th 1964 (Cameo 308).
Musicians Ray Davies lead vocal, harmonica, rhythm guitar. Dave Davies lead guitar, backing vocal. Pete Quaife bass guitar, backing vocal. Bobby Graham drums.
Recorded Pye Studios (No.1); *central London*; January ?20th 1964; 3-track mixed to mono.
Producer Shel Talmy (for Shel Talmy Productions).
Engineer Ray Prickett.
Chart high UK 42; US none.

Tuesday 11th

The song **'I've Got That Feeling'** is assigned to publisher Kassner Music, implying that today or the day before a demo of the song may be recorded, possibly at Regent Sound. US copyright filing is received February 17th.

Wednesday 12th

The band signs a formal agreement with Boscobel Productions Ltd, the company formed by Robert Wace and Grenville Collins for the purposes of managing The Kinks. It is agreed that Boscobel Productions receives a 40 percent commission on all earnings by the band (later slightly rearranged to exclude income from songwriting). Of the 40 percent of earnings, half stays with Boscobel, a quarter is subcontracted out to the Larry Page-run Denmark Productions, and the final quarter to the Arthur Howes agency. This contract replaces the one signed October 22nd 1963 by The Ravens prior to the establishment of Boscobel Productions. Because of their ages, group members must have their parents countersign on their behalf.

Thursday 13th

'Long Tall Sally' enters the *Melody Maker* chart (the February 15th edition is on sale today) where it resides for just this week at number 42. Dave will say later in *Kink* that there is a rumour now that the chart placing was "bought". Of course this can never be proved , but certainly at the time it is not impossible to be able to influence the lower reaches of certain charts.

Friday 14th

A club date almost certainly happens tonight, but its location is unconfirmed. A date at Klooks Kleek at the Railway Hotel in West Hampstead, north-west London, has been mentioned as an early Kinks date but no evidence has been found. Another rumoured early club date is at the Ram Jam Club in Brixton, south London, but this too is unconfirmed. Quaife at least doesn't recall ever playing there.

→ Probably at the start of this week, Larry Page employs Shel Talmy's services to oversee the recording of a Dave song, **'One Fine Day'**, by one of his stable of artists, Shel Naylor (born Robert Woodward), at Decca Studios, north-west London. Publishing of the song is assigned to Kassner Music today. The song has languished unfiled since October 1963. (A US copyright filing is received on March 12th, implying an [unfulfilled] intention to release it there.)

The Naylor recording bears a Talmy/Stone production credit (Shel Talmy and his early partner Charles Stone), with musical direction attributed to Charles Blackwell. Musicians are the usual array of Talmy's preferred session players, in this case guitarist Jimmy Page, bassist John Paul Jones, and probably drummer Bobby Graham. This recording captures more of the future Kinks sound than anything recorded during their debut Pye session, and is an example of how Ray envisioned the early Kinks sound: "The Ventures with lyrics on top." Take away the vocal here, and it's easy to hear the backing track as a thrilling Ventures-style instrumental.

Saturday 15th

Moravian Church Hall *Hornsey, north London* 7:30-10:30pm, *Dance'n'Listen*, with The Argonauts; sponsored by Hornsey & Wood Green British Red Cross

This is probably The Kinks' third or fourth performance. It's the second in a series of local Dance'n'Listen concerts, and it is a sell-out. The performance, says the *Hornsey Journal*, is a success because of the band's ability to ad lib a song almost indefinitely when it is apparent that it is being well received. Leader Ray Davies is said to be playing some piano in addition to guitar and harmonica, and the band described as wearing "David Copperfield-style suits".

Tuesday 18th

The instrumental 'Revenge' is assigned to Kassner Music today, though the song and a demo of it were completed back in mid December. US copyright filing was received, 'incomplete', on December 18th 1963.

As an instrumental it may not have been assigned earlier because it is not felt worthy for consideration for The Kinks' initial recording session. Larry Page may be trying to peddle it to another artist and so feels the need now to properly assign it for publishing, especially since he is listed as a co-writer with Ray.

☆ Ray attends a session at Decca Studio 2 in West Hampstead, north-west London for the recording of his composition 'I've Got That Feeling' by the Page-managed band of schoolgirls, The Orchids, at which Page again employs Shel Talmy as producer.

Friday 21st

The Cavern Club *Liverpool* 12noon-2:15pm, lunchtime session
The band begins a series of occasional trips north to play in the Liverpool/Manchester area, booked by northern agent G.T. Sumner of Runcorn in co-operation with the Arthur Howes Agency. For touring purposes the band has just acquired an old ambulance, driven by the Davies' brother-in-law, Brian Longstaff. Not being able to afford proper accommodation, the band sleeps in the vehicle en route overnight and clean themselves up in the morning inside the washroom at Liverpool train station. Also accompanying the band is friend Jonah Jones as roadie and the Davies' nephew, Phil Palmer. This is another of The Kinks' very early performances, here at an already legendary club made famous by The Beatles. But the local music paper *Mersey Beat* has already slammed The Kinks' first record (see February 7th).
☆ While at the Cavern the band stages a separate performance filmed by Granada Television. This apparently goes unaired at the time but is found over 30 years later on a wrongly marked reel of film, and a portion of 'Long Tall Sally' is shown as part of a documentary in 1995.
Mersey View Ballroom *Frodsham, Ches* two shows, with The Liverbirds
Ray later maintains that the band drives back to London tonight. There is a possible second appearance at this venue, the following Wednesday, February 26th, reported in *Mersey Beat* on the day of the show as a showcase for interested agents to check them out. This seems unlikely.
☆ The popularity of the term "kinky" is reinforced with the release today of the single 'Kinky Boots' on Decca in the UK by Patrick MacNee and Honor Blackman, stars of British ABC TV series *The Avengers*.
☆ Following the photo session and the TV appearance, with temporary teeth-caps in place, Ray is scheduled to be fitted with permanent caps for his front teeth. But he leaves the dentist's office at the last minute and never returns. He later sees this as one of his first acts of rebellion against the star-making machinery that will attempt to strip him of his individual identity.

→ According to Ray's later book, *X-Ray*, The Kinks audition for the BBC at this time but fail to pass the corporation's criteria for performance standards. No evidence of this survives in the otherwise well-maintained BBC archives.

Wednesday 26th

Boscobel Productions (Robert Wace and Grenville Collins) signs a formal agreement with Denmark Productions (Edward Kassner and Larry Page). The agreement provides for the management services of Denmark Productions, for which a quarter of Boscobel's 40 percent commission is allotted. Significantly, it also provides Denmark Productions with the right to place the publishing of original songs by Ray Davies and Dave Davies – which of course they will place with Edward Kassner Music Co Ltd – and for which it has been arranged between Page and Kassner that Page will receive a placement fee as a financial incentive.

Friday 28th

Friday Beat Club, Glenlyn Ballroom *Forest Hill, south London* 7:30-11:00pm
Kinks paid £65. (Unconfirmed gig likely the day following.)

March

Friday 6th

ABC Cinema *Wigan, Lancs* 6:20 & 8:35pm, The Billy J. Kramer Show, featuring Billy J. Kramer & The Dakotas, Gene Pitney, Cilla

The Kinks perform 'Long Tall Sally' on their first TV appearance, for the influential British pop show Ready Steady Go! on February 7th 1964.

Black, The Remo Four, The Escorts; compèred by Billy Burden
The Kinks appear as a substitute for The Swinging Blue Jeans who were part of the formal billing but unavailable tonight due to a prior commitment. This date no doubt tests The Kinks' ability to cope with the package-show experience, and will be alluded to in the 1987 song 'The Road'. The concert is described as Merseybeat-heavy by the *Wigan Observer*, which says the only value to the audience of The Kinks, The Escorts and The Remo Four is their long haircuts. This is the first date when the band meets their road manager, Malcolm Cooke, who will join for the upcoming Dave Clark Five tour. (Unconfirmed gig the day following.)
'One Fine Day' single by Shel Naylor released in the UK, a song by Dave Davies.

Sunday 8th
Popular Music Club, Clayton Lodge *Newcastle-Under-Lyme, Staffs*
A local advertisement boasts: "First appearance outside London of the Pye hit recorders of 'Long Tall Sally' … These boys make the Beatles look like 4 Yul Brynners. Seeing them will be the big talking point in town next week." Admission is 5/- (25p) for members, 6/- (30p) guests.
☆ This date is later alluded to in *X-Ray* as the venue where Ray meets one of his first serious female fans, dubbed "Cindy" for anonymity in the book. It is very likely that she is the inspiration for 'You Really Got Me', written just days later back in Muswell Hill.

Monday 9th – Thursday 12th
Ray composes a new song, 'You Really Got Me', on the piano in the front room of the Davies family home some time this week. The band works up an arrangement and reportedly tries it out at a club in Manchester later in the week. In an interview in *Record Mirror* later in the year Ray says that the song as originally written was a light, jazzy tune that bore little resemblance to its final form on disc. "But when the rest of The Kinks heard it and played around with the tune for several hours," the *Mirror* writer continued, "they realised the immense potential that it had. That night Dave Davies ace guitarist had a dream it would be a hit. So the boys rushed down to Regent Sound [the next week] where they cut a demo of it and took it along to Pye."

Ray recalls later: "When I came up with ['You Really Got Me'] I hadn't been writing songs very long at all. It was one of the first five I ever came up with. I wanted it to be a jazz-type tune, because that's what I liked at the time. It's written originally around a sax line. I remember we had that song about four or five months before the record company would even listen to it. They had heard us play live and thought there was no way we could ever make a record out of it. Dave ended up playing the sax line in fuzz guitar and it took the song a step further." Dave, too, has a later recollection about the birth of the song: "Ray was a great fan of Gerry Mulligan, who was in [the *Jazz On A Summer's Day* movie], and as he sat at the piano at home he sort of messed around in a vein similar to Mulligan and came up with this figure based on a 12-bar blues."

Friday 13th
Bodega Club *Manchester* with Mr Smith, Some People
This is probably the performance debut of 'You Really Got Me', given that Ray claims it was first played at a club in Manchester and that the song's publishing is assigned six days later. (Unconfirmed gig the day following.)
'I've Got That Feeling' single by The Orchids released in the UK, a song by Ray Davies. "I like [this disc] much better than their last one because they are no longer borrowing from Phil Spector," writes Derek Johnson in *NME*. "The melodic content is not strong but there's a foot-tapping beat and the arrangement is catchy."

Sunday 15th
Popular Music Club, Clayton Lodge *Newcastle-Under-Lyme, Staffs* "until 11:00pm", with The Liverbirds
Co-op Hall *Droylsden, Manchester*
A double booking for the night. The Clayton Lodge date is hastily added following the positive reception the week before, and The Kinks are once again paired with the all-female Liverbirds.

Monday 16th – Tuesday 17th
Likely rehearsals in London for upcoming demo session. "When I wrote 'You Really Got Me'," Ray says later, "almost every day when we were rehearsing [in the front room] neighbours would knock on the door and the walls of my parents' Muswell Hill house and threaten to call the police. This kind of thing urged me on."

Wednesday 18th
● **RECORDING** Regent Sound Studios *central London*. Probably on this day or the next The Kinks are back here to demo some more new songs: **'It's You'**, **'It's Alright'** and **'You Really Got Me'**. Ray remembers later: "They wanted us to write some Beatle-type material. I remember doing four or five demos in Regent Sound in Denmark Street, and they said, 'Yeah, the first three, they're what's happening. We don't want to hear the last one ['You Really Got Me'].'" Despite Ray's recollection of "four or five", these three titles seem to be the extent of what is assigned to Kassner at this time, so he may be merging the January 14th submission of Beatlesque originals. Of this demo version of 'You Really Got Me' Ray says: "It had very way-out words and a funny sort of ending that didn't. We did it differently on the record because [this] was really rather uncommercial."

Thursday 19th
Ray submits for assignment to Kassner Music at least three new songs including 'It's You', 'You Really Got Me' and 'It's Alright'. (Unconfirmed gig likely the day following.)

Saturday 21st
Plaza Ballroom *Handsworth, Birmingham*
This is another early performance that will be alluded to in the 1987 career-reviewing song 'The Road' when in the lyrics Ray refers to Birmingham.

Sunday 22nd
Palace Theatre *Manchester* 6:15 & 8:30pm, with Gene Vincent (headliner), The Undertakers, Shane Fenton & The Fentones, Tommy Bruce & The Bruisers, The Harbour Lights, The Four Pennies
Not only do The Kinks get to play alongside US rock'n'roll legend Gene Vincent in this 2,185-seat venue, they are also billed at this Manchester date with former drummer Mickey Willet's old band, Tommy Bruce & the Bruisers. (Likely time off back in London follows during the coming week.)

Friday 27th
Club Noreik *Tottenham, north London* with The Falcons
The Falcons are another local north-London band that at the time includes guitarist Mick Grace, who will later fill in for Ray in The Kinks for a week during March 1966.

→ **'Long Tall Sally'** single released in the US around this time. The Kinks' debut 45 is out in America on the Philadelphia-based Cameo label. Only a brief listing is warranted in the music trade magazine *Cash Box* (April 11th) with no review, but rated B+ for the flip-side (actually listed as the A-side) and a B rating for 'Long Tall Sally'. The leading trade magazine *Billboard* takes no notice at all.

→ INDICATES EVENT AROUND THIS TIME BUT WITH NO FIRM DATE

Saturday 28th
West Cliff Cavern *Ramsgate, Kent* with Vince Eager & His Puppets

Ray cites an early performance in the coastal town of Margate as the first place where an audience is clearly receptive to 'You Really Got Me'. This appearance in neighbouring Ramsgate is most likely what he meant as no gig at Margate is recorded at the time. Ads for this show claim: "Direct from Beatleland!" (The venue is alternatively known as Westcliffe Dance Hall.)

☆ The following day in nearby Clacton sees one of the first "mods and rockers" clashes between rival youth factions.

➪ **TOUR STARTS** *Dave Clark Five Show: UK Tour* (Mar 29th – May 14th). Line-up: Ray Davies (lead vocal, guitar), Dave Davies (guitar, vocal), Pete Quaife (bass), Mick Avory (drums). An Arthur Howes, Harold Davidson & Leslie Grade Presentation. Compère: Frank Berry.

Sunday 29th
Coventry Theatre *Coventry* 6:00 & 8:30pm, with The Dave Clark Five (headliners), The Hollies, Mark Wynter, The Trebletones, The Mojos

First night on the Dave Clark Five tour. Journalist Richard Green reviews this performance for the *NME* in an audience of 2,100 and bluntly feels that The Kinks "relied too much on almost entirely copying The Rolling Stones with long hair, tie-less shirts and even Jagger-type dances. Their drummer impressed, doubling drums and maracas on 'Bo Diddley', but the rest of their act was below average." He rates The Mojos as a first-class outfit who shouldn't be stuck in the opening spot, which he suggests should belong to The Kinks – advice that is acted upon two nights later. This is the first national review for the band – and a very poor one at that.

Set-list: typical set by The Kinks is of just four songs, drawn from at least: 'Bo Diddley', 'You Really Got Me', 'Long Tall Sally', 'Smokestack Lightning', 'Tutti-Frutti', 'Too Much Monkey Business', 'Got Love If You Want It', and 'Beautiful Delilah'. The set for one night is 'Talkin' Bout You', 'Bye Bye Johnny', 'Louie Louie' and 'You Still Want Me'.

☆ Radio Caroline begins broadcasting, the first all-day all-pop pirate radio station that, despite limited reach, becomes a huge influence on the listening public.

Monday 30th
Futurist Theatre *Scarborough, Yorks* 6:25 & 8:45pm, with The Dave Clark Five (headliners), The Hollies, Mark Wynter, The Trebletones, The Mojos

Tuesday 31st
DeMontfort Hall *Leicester* two shows, with The Dave Clark Five (headliners), The Hollies, Mark Wynter, The Trebletones, The Mojos

Promoter Arthur Howes telegrams the theatre telling the tour manager to drop The Kinks back to first act of the night. This is a very serious demotion so soon into the tour and no doubt sends the band and management into a frenzy of self-examination.

April

Wednesday 1st
ABC Cinema *Cleethorpes, Lincs* 6:15 & 8:30pm, with The Dave Clark Five (headliners), The Hollies, Mark Wynter, The Trebletones, The Mojos

Thursday 2nd
ABC Cinema *Carlisle* 6:15 & 8:30pm, with The Dave Clark Five (headliners), The Hollies, Mark Wynter, The Trebletones, The Mojos

Friday 3rd
City Hall *Newcastle Upon Tyne* 6:00 & 8:30pm, with The Dave Clark Five (headliners), The Hollies, Mark Wynter, The Trebletones, The Mojos

Saturday 4th
City Hall *Sheffield* 6:10 & 8:40pm, with The Dave Clark Five (headliners), The Hollies, Mark Wynter, The Trebletones, The Mojos

Sunday 5th
Gaumont Cinema *Bradford, Yorks* 6:00 & 8:30pm, with The Dave Clark Five (headliners), The Hollies, Mark Wynter, The Trebletones, The Mojos

Monday 6th
Granada Cinema *Woolwich, south-east London* 7:00 & 9:10pm, with The Dave Clark Five (headliners), The Hollies, Mark Wynter, The Trebletones, The Mojos

Tuesday 7th
ABC Cinema *Gloucester* 6:15 & 8:30pm, with The Dave Clark Five (headliners), The Hollies, Mark Wynter, The Trebletones, The Mojos

Wednesday 8th
Granada Cinema *Tooting, south London* 6:00 & 8:30pm, with The Dave Clark Five (headliners), The Hollies, Mark Wynter, The Trebletones, The Mojos

Thursday 9th
ABC Cinema *Cambridge* 6:15 & 8:30pm, with The Dave Clark Five (headliners), The Hollies, Mark Wynter, The Trebletones, The Mojos

Friday 10th
Granada Cinema *Bedford* 7:00 & 9:10pm, with The Dave Clark Five (headliners), The Hollies, Mark Wynter, The Trebletones, The Mojos

As a somewhat desperate measure, management brings in an outside consultant, Hal Carter, formerly Billy Fury's road manager, to help advise the rough-and-tumble Kinks about improving their stage act. Carter comes from traditional entertainment and his ideas are often at odds with those of The Kinks. Among his suggestions is to cut many of the blues songs that the band are so fond of. Carter and Ray even collaborate on a few unpublished original compositions: one song intended for Billy Fury is 'I'll Tell Her Tomorrow' and another for The Mojos is '(Come On Baby) Got My Rabbit's Foot Working'. The location of this collaboration is said to be Bridlington, Yorks but there is no indication that this tour visited the town.

Saturday 11th
Theatre Royal *Norwich* 6:20 & 8:30pm, with The Dave Clark Five (headliners), The Hollies, Mark Wynter, The Trebletones, The Mojos

Sunday 12th
Embassy Theatre *Peterborough* 5:30 & 8:00pm, with The Dave Clark Five (headliners), The Hollies, Mark Wynter, The Trebletones, The Mojos

Monday 13th
A day off in London, and it's probably now that the band is outfitted with new custom-made hunting jackets. They are ordered from Berman's, the pre-eminent theatrical costumiers in central London, and probably first worn on April 25th.

Tuesday 14th

ABC Cinema *Dover, Kent* 6:15 & 8:30pm, with The Dave Clark Five (headliners), The Hollies, Mark Wynter, The Trebletones, The Mojos

Wednesday 15th

ABC Cinema *Romford* 6:45 & 9:00pm, with The Dave Clark Five (headliners), The Hollies, Mark Wynter, The Trebletones, The Mojos

Thursday 16th

Odeon Cinema *Chelmsford* 6:15 & 8:30pm, with The Dave Clark Five (headliners), The Hollies, Mark Wynter, The Trebletones, The Mojos

Friday 17th

ABC Cinema *Lincoln* 6:15 & 8:30pm, with The Dave Clark Five (headliners), The Hollies, Mark Wynter, The Trebletones, The Mojos
'You Still Want Me' single released in the UK. The legendary second Kinks single is issued and sinks without a trace – though not for lack of trying by management who likely pay themselves for a prominent front-page ad on today's edition of the *NME* that announces the record's arrival. The conventional wisdom is that The Kinks are not aware of its release, but this is not surprising as at the time record companies routinely issue singles if nothing is happening in the charts for a band. And 'You Still Want Me' was the main A-side contender for the first release, before 'Long Tall Sally' was forced upon them.

'You Still Want Me' reflects Ray's attempt to write Merseybeat-style pop to order. The *NME* recognises that "although they are not a Northern group ... The Kinks have learned much from Mersey trends" and optimistically notes the A-side's "forceful driving beat combined with a plaintive vocal. The melody is quite ear-catching and an improvement on their first disc". The best that music paper *Disc Weekly* can offer is that "the foursome chant and twang with steady style on this their second disc".

You Still Want Me single

A 'You Still Want Me' (R. DAVIES).
B 'You Do Something To Me' (R. DAVIES).

UK release April 17th 1964 (Pye 7N 15636).
Musicians Ray Davies lead vocal, rhythm guitar. Dave Davies lead guitar, backing vocal. Pete Quaife bass guitar, backing vocal (A). Bobby Graham drums.
Recorded Pye Studios (No.1), *central London*; January ?20th 1964; 3-track mixed to mono.
Producer Shel Talmy (for Shel Talmy Productions).
Engineer Ray Prickett.
Chart high UK none.

Saturday 18th

Apollo Theatre *Ardwick Green, Manchester* 6:15 & 8:30pm, with The Dave Clark Five (headliners), The Hollies, Mark Wynter, The Trebletones, The Mojos

Sunday 19th

Odeon Cinema *Guildford, Surrey* 6:00 & 8:15pm, with The Dave Clark Five (headliners), The Hollies, Mark Wynter, The Trebletones, The Mojos

Following (20th) is a day off in London, possibly rehearsing new material for the upcoming recording session.

Tuesday 21st

Gaumont Cinema *Doncaster, Yorks* 6:15 & 8:30pm, with The Dave Clark Five (headliners), The Hollies, Mark Wynter, The Trebletones, The Mojos

Wednesday 22nd

Granada Cinema *Mansfield, Notts* 6:20 & 8:30pm, with The Dave Clark Five (headliners), The Hollies, Mark Wynter, The Trebletones, The Mojos

Thursday 23rd

Granada Cinema *Shrewsbury* 6:15 & 8:30pm, with The Dave Clark Five (headliners), The Hollies, Mark Wynter, The Trebletones, The Mojos

Friday 24th

Capitol Theatre *Cardiff, Wales* 6:30 & 8:50pm, with The Dave Clark Five (headliners), The Hollies, Mark Wynter, The Trebletones, The Mojos

Saturday 25th

Winter Gardens *Bournemouth* two shows, with The Dave Clark Five (headliners), The Hollies, Mark Wynter, The Trebletones, The Mojos
This is said to be the first show where the band wear their new red hunting jackets, trying out their new image. While strangely at odds with their rough-and-tumble rebellious nature, the outfits nonetheless give the band a unique and identifiable look and style.

Sunday 26th

The Hippodrome *Brighton* 6:00 & 8:30pm, with The Dave Clark Five (headliners), The Hollies, Mark Wynter, The Trebletones, The Mojos

Monday 27th

● **RECORDING** Pye Studios *central London*. Today is a day off from the tour but a busy one nevertheless. Early on the band is interviewed and photographed on location at the Battersea Park Fun Fair in south London for a July feature in *Fabulous* magazine. In the afternoon they head back to central London for a recording session at Pye Studios for The Kinks' third and contract-fulfilling single. Ray wants to record 'You Really Got Me' but this is not allowed by Pye who are still pressuring them to record another Merseybeat-style number and have no desire that they even attempt the R&B-flavoured original. While there is no hard evidence, it is possible that the song **'It's You'** is recorded at this time. The song was part of the March 13th demo-reel of new songs prepared by the band in anticipation of this session. It's possible that the other new song written for the March 13th demo, **'It's Alright'**, is recorded at this time (though possibly at the next session, in mid June); it will end up as the B-side of the third single. The battle over which recording will be on the contentious A-side occupies the coming three months. Bobby Graham is still on drums for recordings at this point.

Tuesday 28th

ABC Cinema *Northampton* 6:30 & 8:45pm, with The Dave Clark Five (headliners), The Hollies, Mark Wynter, The Trebletones, The Mojos

Wednesday 29th

Gaumont Cinema *Wolverhampton* 6:30 & 8:40pm, with The Dave Clark Five (headliners), The Hollies, Mark Wynter, The Trebletones, The Mojos

---

→ INDICATES EVENT AROUND THIS TIME BUT WITH NO FIRM DATE

Thursday 30th

Gaumont Cinema *Taunton, Somerset* 6:25 & 8:40pm, with The Dave Clark Five (headliners), The Hollies, Mark Wynter, The Trebletones, The Mojos

May

Friday 1st

Gaumont Cinema *Southampton* 6:15 & 8:40pm, with The Dave Clark Five (headliners), The Hollies, Mark Wynter, The Trebletones, The Mojos

Saturday 2nd

Astoria Theatre *Finsbury Park, north London* 6:45 & 9:10pm, with The Dave Clark Five (headliners), The Hollies, Mark Wynter, The Trebletones, The Mojos

This venue is later re-named the Rainbow Theatre, and The Kinks will play prominent shows there in the 1970s and record two well-known concert programmes for the BBC.

Sunday 3rd

Odeon Cinema *Lewisham, south-east London* 6:30 & 8:45pm, with The Dave Clark Five (headliners), The Hollies, Mark Wynter, The Trebletones, The Mojos

Day off in London follows.

Tuesday 5th

ABC Cinema *Hull* 6:15 & 8:30pm, with The Dave Clark Five (headliners), The Hollies, Mark Wynter, The Trebletones, The Mojos

Wednesday 6th

ABC Cinema *Huddersfield* 6:15 & 8:30pm, with The Dave Clark Five (headliners), The Hollies, Mark Wynter, The Trebletones, The Mojos

Thursday 7th

Globe Cinema *Stockton-on-Tees, Co Durham* 6:15 & 8:30pm, with The Dave Clark Five (headliners), The Hollies, Mark Wynter, The Trebletones, The Mojos

Friday 8th

Gaumont Cinema *Hanley, Stoke-On-Trent, Staffs* 6:30 & 8:45pm, with The Dave Clark Five (headliners), The Hollies, Mark Wynter, The Trebletones, The Mojos

☆ The Pretty Things issue their first single 'Rosalyn' today (also employing session drummer Bobby Graham). They are noted as an even rawer version of the Stones, and help further to pave the way on the British airwaves for the R&B sound.

Saturday 9th

Gaumont Cinema *Derby* 6:00 & 8:30pm, with The Dave Clark Five (headliners), The Hollies, Mark Wynter, The Trebletones, The Mojos

Sunday 10th

Granada Cinema *Walthamstow, north-east London* 6:00 & 8:30pm, with The Dave Clark Five (headliners), The Hollies, Mark Wynter, The Trebletones, The Mojos

Monday 11th

Odeon Cinema *Southend-on-Sea* 6:35 & 8:50pm, with The Dave Clark Five (headliners), The Hollies, Mark Wynter, The Trebletones, The Mojos

Tuesday 12th

Colston Hall *Bristol* two shows, with The Dave Clark Five (headliners), The Hollies, Mark Wynter, The Trebletones, The Mojos

Wednesday 13th

Granada Cinema *Harrow, north-west London* 6:45 & 9:00pm, with The Dave Clark Five (headliners), The Hollies, Mark Wynter, The Trebletones, The Mojos

Thursday 14th

Granada Cinema *Kingston-on-Thames, south-west London* 7:00 & 9:10pm, with The Dave Clark Five (headliners), The Hollies, Mark Wynter, The Trebletones, The Mojos

This is the final night of the Dave Clark Five package tour, and this further London-area date gives The Kinks a chance to feel at home for a few moments before heading back on the road in their own right with a series of steady dates. These will include many bookings in the north where so far they have connected most effectively with the audience. Meanwhile both The Dave Clark Five and The Hollies top off their tour with an appearance on *Ready Steady Go!* the following night, but The Kinks at this stage are not yet worthy of a return appearance.

Friday 15th

Goldhawk Beat Club, Goldhawk Social Club *Shepherds Bush, west London*

Tonight is the first of a fully-booked schedule of club and ballroom dates, many of which will find the band back in areas of Lancashire and Yorkshire that might almost be called strongholds. In fact on at least one occasion they are billed as being "direct from Liverpool". For tonight's show the band is paid £90.

Saturday 16th

Savoy Ballroom *Southsea, Hants* 7:30-11:45pm, with The Residents

Ray refers to this performance in *X-Ray* as the first time he feels the band connects with the audience, and that the band has finally found an identity and a sound uniquely theirs. The confidence gained from this realisation will help in Ray's fight to get onto record the one song that embodies that sound.

Sunday 17th

The Scene *Redcar, Yorks*

In *X-Ray*, this is given as the date that the Davies' sister Rose, her husband Arthur and their son Terry depart for Australia, although Dave and Quaife recall it as November 1963. Whenever it is, it seems to trigger a crisis for Ray. He is accompanied to this show by his girlfriend (called "Anita" in *X-Ray*) and recalls an emotional scene on the beach in frustration over his sister's departure and the failure of the band's records so far. In *X-Ray* it is characterised as a pivotal moment when he decides to continue to fight the might of the music industry and somehow prevail with a successful record.

Monday 18th

Possible concert in Wakefield, Yorks. Ray's future wife Rasa recalls later that it is here that she first sees The Kinks at this time, but the gig remains unconfirmed.

Tuesday 19th

Esquire Club *Sheffield*

Dave meets two Bradford girls, Eileen Fernley and her friend Rasa Didzpetris. Rasa is introduced to Ray backstage afterwards, and the two will subsequently meet again in London in August. Ray will eventually marry her in December 1964. Eileen will be Dave's date at that wedding, but subsequently sues him in a paternity suit after she becomes pregnant shortly after the December wedding. Dave is cleared of charges at a court hearing in Bradford on May 5th 1966. (Unconfirmed gig the day following.)

Thursday 21st

City Hall *Salisbury* with Dick Delmont & The Strangers
"Howard-Lock Entertainment present Decca Recording Artists: The Kinks." No doubt Pye is not amused. (Unconfirmed gig next day.)

Saturday 23rd

Pier Ballroom *Hastings, Sussex* with Earl Sheridan & The Houseshakers
Unconfirmed gigs in the days following include a possible date with Millie & The 5 Embers, with whom the band certainly plays around now.

Wednesday 27th

Corn Exchange *Bristol* 7:30-10:45pm, with Dene King, Danny Alpine & The Cardinals

Thursday 28th

Astoria Ballroom *Oldham* 7:30-10:30pm
Unconfirmed gig the day following.

Saturday 30th

Stamford Hall *Altrincham, Ches* 8:00-11:00pm, with The Mustangs
Gigs likely at unconfirmed venues the two days following.

June

Tuesday 2nd

Paar Hall *Warrington* with The Saxons
There are also unconfirmed shows during the days following.

Friday 5th

Public Hall *Wallington, Surrey* 7:30 pm, with Glen Athens & The Trojans
Advertising touts the show as "Mod dancing" and, probably to the band's chagrin, notes: "If you like The Rolling Stones, you will love The Kinks."

Saturday 6th

Memorial Hall *Northwich, Ches* 7:45-11:45pm, with Tommy Quickly & The Remo 4 (headliners), The Secrets

Sunday 7th

Forum Cinema *Bath* 7:00pm, with Gene Vincent (headliner), The Dennisons, The Fenmen
The Kinks again open for Gene Vincent, the legendary 1950s rockabilly singer. Years later, Ray recalls how he realises he never wants to end up like Vincent, who by now is an alcoholic and addicted to pain-killers. Vincent will die at age 36 in 1971 from a bleeding ulcer.

Tuesday 9th

Easy Beat Club, Gray's *Tottenham, north London*
A late-night booking at this club. It's possible that earlier in the day The Kinks play at a private costume party at a mansion in Sussex. It is not beyond the band's scope even in this early hunting-jacket period to be booked for private parties. The only clue is a recollection that the band played in Tottenham afterwards, but the costume party is significant because it is probably a partial inspiration for the hunting-jacket dream sequences in the much later video made for the song 'Don't Forget To Dance' (1983). (There are also likely but unconfirmed shows in the days following.)

Friday 12th

Jung Frau *Manchester*
Unconfirmed show the day following.

Sunday 14th

King George's Hall *Blackburn* 6:00 & 8:15 pm, with The Four Pennies (headliners), Shane Fenton & The Fentones

→ The band likely returns to London for the week for a break from their tour schedule. It is also about this time that Hal Carter leaves as The Kinks' temporary road manager and performance advisor. The Davies' brother-in-law Brian Longstaff returns as a replacement.
● **RECORDING** Pye Studios (No.1) *central London*. It is at this time that the band is given another chance to record at Pye. As Ray later recalls: "We went on one-nighters all over the country, topping the bill in clubs. We worked a lot round Manchester – and then we did some sessions and decided to record **'You Really Got Me'**. We had to get permission from the record company to record it! They said, 'You're going to go in the studio and they're going to let you do 'You Really Got Me'. You're happy now, are you?'"
It's generally acknowledged that Shel Talmy is much more in control of this unreleased-master version of 'You Really Got Me'. He uses his usual crew of musicians, possibly with Ken Lewis, John Carter and Perry Ford (The Ivy League) on backing vocals. The recording, later described by Ray as echo-laden, is probably similar to the Spector-like sound Talmy used on The Orchids' cut of Ray's song 'I've Got That Feeling' a few months earlier.
Talmy's later recollection is different: "[This] version of 'You Really Got Me' was a much bluesier version than the one you know, and much slower. We did it, oh, about 25 percent slower – and if you picture the riff, you'll see that it really goes well with blues. It certainly wasn't a Phil Spector version. I don't know what that is. It was extremely good and a totally different concept from the one that eventually came out. We all liked it at the time, decided to try it the other way, and then decided the later version should be the one that came out." Ray remembers: "I think Shel overproduced [this unreleased master] to a certain extent, with every good intention. He gave it this big sound, and it lost the character of the group." (It's also possible that the flip-side, **'It's Alright'** is recorded at this time.)

Friday 19th

Today probably sees a show at an unconfirmed northern location.
☆ In today's *NME* an ad appears on the front page featuring various Pye artists, including a photo of The Kinks that is captioned as "recorders of the ravin' R&B disc 'Long Tall Sally'" on the same day that The Beatles' version comes out on EP. Promotion of The Kinks is still based around the paltry chart showing of their first disc, with no mention of the failed second single.

Saturday 20th

Astoria Ballroom *Rawtenstall, Lancs* 7:30pm, with The Warriors, The Electones

Sunday 21st

According to the sequence of events he recalls later in *X-Ray*, Ray travels to London by coach today. Otherwise today likely sees an unconfirmed gig.

Monday 22nd

Majestic Ballroom *Reading, Berks*
Likely unconfirmed shows in the days following.
The exact timing is unconfirmed, but around now (and prior to The Kinks' own first hit) they play some dates with The Nashville Teens,

→ INDICATES EVENT AROUND THIS TIME BUT WITH NO FIRM DATE

who will enjoy some success in the charts with 'Tobacco Road' in July.

☆ In the days following the recording session around the 15th, Ray's dissatisfaction with the results grows. He objects to issuing the finished recording of 'You Really Got Me' and protests to all three managers – Wace, Collins and Page – as well as producer Shel Talmy, none of whom want to bother to change it. Slightly later, after further prompting, Page decides to break the stalemate and threatens Pye director Louis Benjamin that his partner Edward Kassner, as the song's publisher (Kassner Music), will withhold the mechanical licence necessary for the record's release, as a means of forcing Pye to delay issuing the record. Pye, after initially threatening legal action itself, is forced to agree to the delay and the re-recording of the song – on the condition that the band pays for the additional session time itself. Collins and Wace subsequently agree to this and raise the money to finance a further session a few weeks later, in mid July.

Friday 26th

Lido Ballroom *Winchester, Hants* 8:00-11:30pm, with Roy Starr & The Cherokees

☆ The Rolling Stones' fourth British single, 'It's All Over Now', is issued today and rapidly goes to number 1 in some British charts.

Saturday 27th

Stamford Hall *Altrincham, Ches* with Ivan's Meads
"Another star R&B night!" (Unconfirmed show the day following.)

Monday 29th

Oasis Club *Manchester* with The Meads
Unconfirmed shows in the days following.

July

Thursday 2nd

Broadway Cinema *Filwood Park, Bristol* 6:15 & 8:30pm, with Bob Grant & The Democrats, Paul Vernon & The Raiders, The Chequers, The Buccaneers

Friday 3rd

Pier Ballroom *Hastings, Sussex* 11:00pm-3:00am, with The Classmates; sponsored by Hastings College of Further Education Students' Union

☆ 'House Of The Rising Sun' by The Animals, issued only two weeks ago, is number 1 in this week's *NME* charts, bumping from the top Roy Orbison and 'It's Over', which itself had followed a run by Cilla Black's 'You're My World'. The fact that The Animals have managed to get a traditional R&B song to the top of one of the British singles charts is not lost on Ray, though his particular goal is to do the same with an original composition.

Saturday 4th

Club Noreik *Tottenham, north London* 12:00midnight-6:00am, *All Nite Rave*, with Jimmy Crawford & The Shantells

Sunday 5th

Mister Smith's *Manchester* with The Stirlings
The Kinks are originally booked to appear at another Manchester club, the Jung Frau, but this was evidently cancelled.

Monday 6th

Whiskey A-Go-Go *Salford*
The band is originally booked to appear in Broughton, Cheshire, but this was evidently cancelled. (Unconfirmed shows in days following.)

Thursday 9th

Majestic Ballroom *Luton* with The Prowlers

Friday 10th

Tonight's show is at an unconfirmed venue and location.

☆ The R&B boom storms the pop charts: in this week's *NME* The Animals and 'House Of The Rising Sun' are still number 1, while The Rolling Stones are at number 2 with 'It's All Over Now'.

Saturday 11th

Town Hall *Clacton-On-Sea, Essex* with The Trends, Tony Rivers & The Castaways

Sunday 12th

ABC Cinema *Great Yarmouth, Norfolk* with PJ Proby and others
Provocative American-born singer PJ Proby is high in the charts with his first UK hit 'Hold Me'.

➔ ● **RECORDING** IBC Studios *central London*. Following the band's dissatisfaction with the unreleased master recording of '**You Really Got Me**', a further attempt is made around this time. Ray is no doubt aware of the currency of the R&B sound in the charts with The Animals and The Rolling Stones in top positions. Hearing these records on the radio, he is even more determined not only to achieve that sound but to be the first with an original song that embodies the R&B feel.

The new recording of 'You Really Got Me' is made at IBC and not Pye Studios, as The Kinks – or at least their management – are paying for the session themselves. IBC (Independent Broadcasting Company) is a major studio in Portland Place, central London where producer Shel Talmy often records his independent acts and is comfortable and familiar with the studio and its engineer, the young Glyn Johns.

Although IBC is one of the most modern and well-equipped studios in town, it offers a full range of recording options from basic single-track to 4-track recording. Ray wants a rawer sound than was achieved on the 4-track attempt at Pye and, perhaps also prompted by considerations of cost, opts for the cheaper basic machine. He recalls later: "When we recorded 'You Really Got Me' at Pye we did it on 4-track ... After it was done I said it was over-produced and I didn't want to put it out, [and that] we should do it on 1-track and get the raw sound we wanted. To double-track we just copied it on to another machine and did the vocals whilst they were copying it."

The line-up is the four Kinks, with Avory on tambourine and Bobby Graham on drums, augmented by session pianist Arthur Greenslade playing the simple keyboard part, and another guitarist from Kassner's office – likely Harry, possibly Bob or Vic, surname unknown – playing rhythm on a Fender Telecaster. (It's not clear if Ray plays on this version, but if he does he doubles the rhythm on his Maton guitar.) Dave plays his Harmony Meteor through his Elpico amp with a punctured speaker to get the distinctive guitar sound, which is in turn fed through a Vox AC-30 amplifier. Quaife plays his Fender bass.

The instrumental track is recorded live with these supplemental musicians to give the fullest sound possible on tape. The backing is recorded to a single track, and the vocals are overdubbed as the instrumental track is bounced to a second single-track tape. According to *X-Ray*, two takes are attempted, the second being the "keeper". The main vocal is done three or four times, Ray says later, "and it came out American, so I just sang the way I felt it and it sounded like me". The session was of the standard three-hour length, but probably only this song is recorded.

Dave later remembers the session well. "When we started recording we couldn't argue with the [record] company. But this time we insisted on doing what we wanted. Well, what could we lose? ... The song came out of a working-class environment, people fighting for something." Ray also remembers a feeling of spontaneity. "When I left that studio I felt great. It may sound conceited, but I knew it was a great record … I said I'd never write another song like it, and I haven't."

The aim to make an original R&B record is now fulfilled. Ray says that up to this point, many consider The Kinks a joke. "Everybody thought we would last five minutes. We weren't cool enough to be treated with respect by the Marquee musos – yer Erics [Clapton] and Jimmy Pages. A lot of our contemporaries who'd had hits before us – Manfred Mann, The Rolling Stones, The Yardbirds [in fact their hit was afterwards] – were much more accomplished than we were as far as blues went. But when it came to making pop records, they went for the common denominator: they made 'Do Wah Diddy Diddy', 'For Your Love' … It was almost a sin that we were the first to have a hit with what was vaguely a blues thing."

It may be this condescending attitude to the 'Marquee musos' that has helped feed stories about Jimmy Page playing the solo on 'You Really Got Me'. He did not. The Kinks have been plagued by rumours that sessionmen – and in particular Jimmy Page – were present on their recordings, along with the assumption that it must be the manic guitar solos that were done for them. Maybe it started because more accomplished bands resented the sometimes musically inept Kinks soaring to the top of the charts with the original and powerful 'You Really Got Me'. Publicity for Jimmy Page's first solo recording, 'She Just Satisfies', released in February 1965 and recorded four months earlier, listed The Kinks among his session credits, presumably to underline The Kinks-like sound of his single.

Ray says in *Melody Maker* in December 1965: "To clear up anything that's ever been said … Dave Davies plays every solo on every record we've ever made and does it better than anyone else." Page put his side in 1972: "The Kinks didn't really want me around when they were recording … I didn't really do that much on The Kinks' records … I know I managed to get a couple of riffs in on their album, but I can't really remember – I know that [Ray] didn't really approve of my presence." Five years later in *Trouser Press*, Page sounded angrier: "I never played tambourine on the damned records. I played guitar. But I didn't play on 'You Really Got Me' … I played on the subsequent records … On the [first LP] it's more apparent. There are a few little bits and pieces that come in where I'm just there."

Although Quaife recalls Page's presence in place of Ray primarily on acoustic guitar on a few sessions subsequent to the first LP, Talmy is certain that he only hired Page to substitute for an initially insecure Ray on the debut album. "After Ray got his sea legs," says Talmy, "he didn't want anybody else to play guitar, and his acoustic playing was always good – and under-rated."

So it's summer 1964 … and it's likely that Pye would have dropped The Kinks had 'You Really Got Me' flopped. Ray suggests as much later: "The record company were going to put out a slower version I didn't like, and if it wasn't a hit they were going to drop us. At that time it had never been heard of for a group to say they didn't like a record. We fought and fought and eventually got the version we wanted out."

Knowledge of these realities no doubt drives Ray and the band – and certainly adds to the pressure for the third Pye single to be the record that will make The Kinks. The strength of the remade 'You Really Got Me' is immediately evident to many, and a return booking to *Ready Steady Go!* is arranged as quickly as possible to tie in with the record's release date, which is set for August 4th.

Thursday 16th
Fab R&B Ball, Assembly Hall *Worthing, Sussex* 7:30-10:45pm, with The Paramounts, The Preachers and others; admission 5/- (25p) Unconfirmed show the day following.

Saturday 18th
The Dungeon *Nottingham*
It's probably this club date (not Southend) that Larry Page refers to in

the later *Official Biography*, comparing the audience reaction on this gig just before 'You Really Got Me' came out and another (August 9th) just after its release. At today's booking it's hard for the band to get a response; three weeks and one record later the audience will go wild.

Sunday 19th
Princess Theatre *Torquay The Billy J. Kramer Show*, with Billy J. Kramer & The Dakotas (headliners), Billy Maxwell & His Orchestra, The Barracudas, Chris Carlsen, The Other Two
The Kinks also back up The Other Two from behind the stage curtain for this show. (Following day off or unconfirmed show.)

Tuesday 21st
Fabulous Queens Ballroom *Cleveleys, Blackpool* with Barry Langtree & The Lancastrians; compère DJ Dave Lee Travis

Friday 24th
Friday Beat Club, Glenlyn Ballroom *Forest Hill, south London* 7:30-11:00pm
The band is paid £95 for tonight's show. (Unconfirmed show day following.)
☆ The Beatles are number 1 with 'A Hard Day's Night' in *NME's* chart.

Sunday 26th
Domino Club *Manchester* early show
Princess Club *Manchester* late show

Monday 27th – Thursday 30th
Unconfirmed shows and likely days off in London. With advance word on the street that The Kinks will have a chart smash on their hands, Ray tracks down old girlfriends, including "Margie" and "Anita", and an argument with "Anita" inspires him to write 'Stop Your Sobbing'.

➔ The Kinks do a major photo session in Hyde Park, central London around this time, wearing their hunting jackets. The shots will be used constantly during the coming demand for press photos.

Friday 31st
❏ **TV** Television House (Studio 9) *central London*. ATV **Ready Steady Go!** live performance 'Got Love If You Want It', lip-synch 'You Really Got Me'. Also, likely gig tonight at unconfirmed venue and location.
☆ Manfred Mann are at number 1 with 'Do Wah Diddy Diddy'.
☆ Ray recalls in *X-Ray* that following tonight's show he has a confrontation with his old Croydon Art School friend "Margie" at a celebration in Mayfair, central London where he says she physically assaults him in a fit of rage because Ray has "sold out".

August

Saturday 1st
Tonight's show is at an unconfirmed venue and location.
☆ 'You Really Got Me' is reviewed on two influential TV shows broadcast today: on BBC-1's *Juke Box Jury* by panellists Sue Stranks, Pete Murray and Alma Cogan; and on *Thank Your Lucky Stars* in its record-rating segment, where the new single wins out over the very popular Dave Clark Five's latest, 'Thinking Of You Baby'.

Sunday 2nd
Gaumont Cinema *Bournemouth* with The Beatles (headliners), Mike Berry, Adrienne Posta
This is the scene of the now infamous encounter between The Beatles

and The Kinks, as told in *X-Ray* and embellished further in Ray's later solo show *Storyteller/20th Century Man*. According to manager Collins, The Kinks definitely win the crowd, which irritates The Beatles who follow directly afterwards. Reportedly, when The Kinks are next included on a show with The Beatles they are given the closing spot of the first half of the show rather then directly preceding The Beatles. When the two bands meet one final time at the *NME* Pollwinner's Show in London in April 1965, The Kinks are forced to follow The Beatles' stunning performance – and turn in one of their most disappointing performances ever. It is reported that backstage in London Lennon snaps at Collins: "There's yer payback for Bournemouth." Dave recalls: "The Beatles were very wary of us when we did shows together. I don't know why. ... We always had this ability to ruffle people's feathers for some reason, in all shapes and forms."

→ Press agent and former *Daily Express* journalist Brian Sommerville, whose most famous clients have been The Beatles since the start of this year, is hired by The Kinks' management to help to create a public image for the band and an angle for selling that image. The first piece to appear in the national music press is based on a band interview with Peter Jones for the *Record Mirror* of August 15th.

☆ It is likely that classic red-hunting-jacket shots with The Kinks in various poses around the Tower Of London and sitting on a cannon are taken at this time. They are used extensively in early promotional material. The session may well have been at the urging of new press officer Brian Sommerville upon the launch of his campaign to smarten up the band's image. Also, Summerville seeks to represent them as symbols of Englishness, a notion that will in time sell well to the American market.

Tuesday 4th

'**You Really Got Me**' single released in the UK. Although it is customary to issue records on Fridays in Britain at this time, Pye Records experiments with Tuesday releases during this period. The single will already score in some local charts by Friday 7th. Ray later claims that demand for the record is so great upon release that pressing of all other Pye records is put on hold to produce only copies of 'You Really Got Me'. Some of the pop papers and even some chart entries attempt to correct the song title's grammar and list the record as 'You've Really Got Me'.

Small ads run in some papers during the first week, but no review of the disc is published in the *NME*, possibly because of the Tuesday release date – and by the following week the record is very well known. *Disc Weekly* says: "Middle rock from The Kinks as they present a choppy repeater... . Some gimmicky tribal noise may get sales too. [B-side] 'It's Alright' is a little wilder in the R&B mould." The reviewer in *Record Mirror* writes, "Highly promising group with strong guitar sound and a compact sort of vocal performance. Mid-tempo but bustling song should sell well."

Singer Dave Berry is played 'You Really Got Me' in a blindfold test for *Melody Maker*. "Great! The Kingsmen?" he wonders. "It sounds like that from the intro. It's fabulous, this one. I like these records that sound as if they've gone into a recording studio and done what they wanted to on the spot. It's got a good chance of being a big hit. On second thoughts, I'd say it was British." The comment has a profound effect on Ray; in the 1970s he remembers: "When it came out it was reviewed in the *Melody Maker* by a guy called Dave Berry, who'd had a few hits – so he mattered. He said, 'This group sounds like they actually recorded what they wanted.' That said it all for me."

Thursday 6th

Debut radio airing of 'You Really Got Me' on the BBC Light Programme's new pop show, *Top Gear*.

You Really Got Me single

A '**You Really Got Me**' (R. DAVIES).
B '**It's Alright**' (R. DAVIES).

UK release August 4th 1964 (Pye 7N 15673).
US release September ?2nd 1964 (Reprise 0306).
Musicians Ray Davies lead vocal, harmonica (B), rhythm guitar. Dave Davies lead guitar, backing vocal. Pete Quaife bass guitar, backing vocal. Bobby Graham drums. Unknown rhythm guitar (A). Arthur Greenslade piano. Mick Avory tambourine.
Recorded IBC Studios, *central London*; A: mid-July 1964, 1-track to 1-track mono; B: April 27th or mid June 1964, 3-track mixed to mono.
Producer Shel Talmy (for Shel Talmy Productions).
Engineers Glyn Johns (A), probably Bob Auger (B).
Chart high UK number 1; US number 7.

Friday 7th
The Cavern *Manchester*

The success of 'You Really Got Me' is virtually instantaneous. The band is committed to bookings made long before their instant fame, and so find themselves back up north, still playing their usual small club dates.

Saturday 8th
Imperial Ballroom *Nelson, Lancs* 7:30-11:30pm, with The Mustangs, The Saracens

Sunday 9th
The Dungeon *Nottingham*

Monday 10th
The band assembles back in London and is given the news that Pye Records has now authorised the recording of an LP, to be finished by the end of August for a late-September release. At this time Pye also picks up its option for the next of five one-year options. Manager Wace reportedly asks for an increase in the royalty rate but is flatly refused by indignant Pye director Louis Benjamin. Pye meanwhile wastes no time with a proven seller and involves their biggest US associate, Reprise Records. For the initial period of the band's Pye contract, Reprise picks up US release rights, for which it has first refusal. This is a benefit at first because The Kinks are represented in the largest world market by a young but well-connected and well-distributed label. Reprise is a subsidiary of Warner Brothers, and was started as something of a vanity label for legendary American crooner Frank Sinatra.

☆ A press release – probably the first in a long time not trashed – announces a basic biography. It also notes the recording of an LP next week and that 'You Really Got Me' is rush-released in the US this week.
☆ Brief interview by Peter Jones in *Record Mirror* reveals a plan (unfulfilled) to record 'You Really Got Me' in various languages.

Tuesday 11th
London newspaper *The Daily Sketch* previews this week's *NME* charts and shows 'You Really Got Me' entering at number 22. Topping the chart is Manfred Mann, with The Beatles at number 2, The Rolling Stones at 3, and The Nashville Teens at 5. In *Disc* The Kinks win the Ace Award for distinctive new talent – and alongside is one of the earliest appearances of the now famous hunting-jacket shots, pushing an image of the band as country gentlemen with hunting dogs in tow.

kinks'64

Wednesday 12th

❏ **TV** Television Centre *Bristol*. TWW ***Discs A Go Go*** lip-synch 'You Really Got Me' broadcast August 17th (7:00-7.30pm). Videotaping of an appearance on the west-country pop show, lip-synching one of many performances of the new single. The programme's other guests are Kenny Lynch and Kiki Dee. It is at this taping that Bradford singer Dee tells Ray that Rasa, the girl he met in Sheffield in May, is in London. She gives him a phone number where Rasa can be reached at Rasa's sister's flat.

Thursday 13th

Probably a rehearsal day with Shel Talmy for the first round of recording of the band's LP next week. During the week, The Kinks are interviewed by Penny Valentine for an article in *Disc* that will be headlined "People Don't Laugh At The Kinks Now". It reveals that the stage version of 'You Really Got Me', written almost exactly five months ago, ended dead on the vocal refrain and did not include the staccato-chords ending of the released single. Another mention is made of producer Talmy's intention to get Ray to overdub the vocal in French, German, Spanish and Japanese, though this never happens.

☆ It is likely that Ray phones Rasa tonight and meets her at Tottenham Court Road tube station in central London.

Friday 14th

Wallington Public Hall *Wallington, Surrey*

According to *X-Ray* the band is quickly rebooked for *Ready Steady Go!* on short notice due to the sudden and immense response to 'You Really Got Me'. The show is broadcast from Studio 8 at Television House in central London, not too far from Wallington, but The Kinks are not noted as guests in any TV listings.

Saturday 15th

St. George's Ballroom *Hinckley, Leics*

Sunday 16th

Opera House *Blackpool* with The Beatles (headliners), The High Numbers

Tonight's concert presents one of the more memorable triple billings of the 1960s. The Kinks are added to this bill at the last minute, and do not appear in most ads for the show. The High Numbers will revert back to their original name, The Who, early in November when they record their heavily Kinks-influenced song 'I Can't Explain'. Avory first witnesses Who drummer Keith Moon now. (The band drives back to London afterwards to be available for press duties and their upcoming recording session.)

Monday 17th

Today is likely devoted to the press. The Kinks are interviewed by Cordell Marks for the *NME*, and they tell him the usual stories of their pre-success experiences. Ray says: "I never thought we'd get this far. Course, our parents are pleased at what's happened. They can't quite believe it. They keep going around mumbling, 'Strewth, that mob have actually got a job.' They can't quite believe it."

The Kinks are interviewed again by Chris Roberts for *Melody Maker*, the piece tellingly headlined "Kinks Ready For New Wave". Ray explains how he is already planning for future changes in the music scene beyond the current beat craze. "We are still trying hard to develop. In about four years time, or before then – you can never follow public taste – we might be augmenting the group to form a [big] band. This was our original plan, if we hadn't any luck with the records – that would probably have been at the end of the year." Dave pipes in: "We're already looking for new sounds. Ray likes Indian music." Ray: "Yeah, I like going to Indian restaurants and listening to the records there. I like that drone they got on them." This predates their landmark

recording of 'See My Friends' by about six months. "We've got a bit of a drone on ['You Really Got Me'] about halfway through."

Roberts explains that on stage and in the recording studio The Kinks are perfecting their own ideas for sounds. "One of which is using 'feedback' from a guitar amplifier," he writes, "a constant or increasing hum obtained by holding the guitar in front of the amplifier's loudspeaker." This in turn predicts the sound used on 'I Need You' by another half-year. Already conscious of the need for a follow-up single to 'You Really Got Me', Ray says: "Well, we've got about half way through it. We haven't quite decided what it's going to be, yet." Dave: "It's either going to be completely different, or very similar to this one. We haven't made up our minds completely."

Tuesday 18th

● **RECORDING** Pye Studios (No.2) *central London*. The Kinks begin the first sessions for their debut LP at Pye. Short on original material, Ray suggests his own choice of covers – to avoid doing further covers favoured by Talmy. Although no studio records survive, this initial session is most likely when the Chuck Berry, Bo Diddley and Slim Harpo numbers are done: **'Beautiful Delilah'**, **'Too Much Monkey Business'**, **'Cadillac'** and **'Got Love If You Want It'**. 'Smokestack Lightning' is reportedly considered for recording but rejected as it has already been recorded by many other bands. (Alternate takes of 'Too Much Monkey Business' and 'Got Love If You Want It' survive, with the former issued as a bonus track on the 1998 CD reissue of *The Kinks* album, the latter on bootleg.)

Wednesday 19th

❏ **TV** Playhouse Theatre *Manchester*. BBC-1 ***Top Of The Pops*** lip-synch 'You Really Got Me' broadcast this evening.

☆ The Kinks are interviewed for Liverpool-based *Mersey Beat* magazine where they extol the virtues of playing to northern audiences, their favourite area of the country to play outside London clubs. Ray says they will probably do some Odetta numbers on the new LP which they've just started recording. Today is also notable because the band flies to Manchester from London, their first plane ride, and the fact is used as a publicity angle at the time.

Thursday 20th

❏ **TV** ATV Studios *Borehamwood, Herts*. ATV ***For Teenagers Only*** lip-synch 'You Really Got Me' 6.40-7.00pm. Also on today's show are Chad & Jeremy, The Wolves, and Marianne Faithful.

Friday 21st

Jung Frau *Manchester*

Today sees the first ad appear for the newly formed fan club, Kinkdom Kome, run from the offices of Boscobel Productions.

Saturday 22nd

Market Hall *Redhill, Surrey*

Sunday 23rd

A date at the Princess Theatre in Torquay originally set for this date is rescheduled to allow more time for recording and/or preparation for recording. This is very likely the timing of a day off where Ray and Rasa stay at the house of her sister's friend in Isleworth, west London. Ray says in *X-Ray* this is the night their daughter Louisa is conceived.

Monday 24th

● **RECORDING** Pye Studios (No.2) *central London*. The Kinks resume their sessions at Pye. In *X-Ray* this is recalled as a morning session that includes recording of the backing track for the as yet unnamed **'Tired Of Waiting For You'**, referred to at the time simply as 'So Tired'. Dave says later: "That song had been around quite some

Backstage around August 1964 – standing (L-R) are Mick Avory, Ray Davies and Pete Quaife, with Dave Davies sitting.

years. It was an instrumental that Ray and I used to play together – and then wrote a lyric to it and we recorded it, but it didn't sound right. The guitar parts weren't strong enough. So I went in [in December 1964] and put the heavier rhythm guitar part on last, after it was finished."

☆ A press release announces that The Kinks have been added to a Gerry & The Pacemakers tour for November.

Tuesday 25th

● **RECORDING** Pye Studios (No.2) *central London*. This is probably the day that Talmy has set aside for recording his traditional arrangements, and the Odetta songs are recorded, and most likely the day that Jimmy Page and Jon Lord are hired to come in and augment the sound for these folk covers. In what is probably a standard three-hour session, maybe four songs are put down on tape, possibly: **'I'm A Lover Not A Fighter'**, **'Bald Headed Woman'**, **'I've Been Driving On Bald Mountain'** and **'Long Tall Shorty'**.

Jimmy Page has been credited for guitar work on the first three, and according to Ray plays tambourine on 'Long Tall Shorty'. On 'I'm A Lover Not A Fighter' Ray plays lead with Jimmy Page backing on 12-string, and Page also plays 12-string on 'I've Been Driving On Bald Mountain' and possibly on 'Bald Headed Woman'. Jon Lord is clearly heard on organ on 'Bald Headed Woman' and possibly plays percussion parts on 'Long Tall Shorty'. Bobby Graham is probably on drums for the entire session. Ray later admits: "On 'Lover Not A Fighter' there's a guitar solo … and I'm doing it, and I'm the worst guitar player in the world. Jimmy Page was playing rhythm guitar. I remember Jimmy saying, 'Go on mate, knock yourself out' – [he was] sending me up!"

Wednesday 26th

The Cavern *Manchester*

❑ **TV** Playhouse Theatre *Manchester*. BBC-1 ***Top Of The Pops*** lip-synch 'You Really Got Me'.

The band is interviewed by Jay Martin for *Combo Musical Weekly* where it is mentioned they are now working hard on the LP that will be out "in one or two months".

Thursday 27th

Today's activities are unaccounted for, but in addition to a scheduled concert they possibly include the taping of a further TV appearance.

Friday 28th

Goldhawk Beat Club *Shepherds Bush, west London* 7:30pm, with The Clique

☆ Probably today The Kinks are interviewed for *Record Mirror* by Norman Jopling where 'So Tired' ('Tired Of Waiting For You') is first mentioned as one of the ballads recorded for their new LP in progress.

Saturday 29th

Merseyview Ballroom *Frodsham, Ches*

Sunday 30th

Queen's Theatre *Blackpool* 6:00pm & 8:10pm, with The Searchers, The High Numbers, Jon Best & The Challengers, Val McCallum

The second appearance inside a month with The High Numbers (soon renamed The Who). Other than a very large festival date in Lincoln in May 1966, The Kinks will only ever appear with The Who once more, with The Kinks as the opening act, in Chicago in October 1969.

Monday 31st

● **RECORDING** Pye Studios (No.2) *central London*. Likely late today or early the next, one last session is completed at Pye for remaining work on the LP, including mixing and/or overdubs. Possibly recorded at this time is **'I Gotta Move'**, a track that will end up as the B-side of the

next single. "I remember on the last sessions for that album," says Dave, "there were actually people hammering on the door to get in because we were running a bit over time."

☆ A press release announces that The Kinks' first LP – some tracks of which are completed this week – is due for release next month, and that the band has been added to a Billy J. Kramer tour.

September

Tuesday 1st

Town Hall *High Wycombe, Bucks* 7:30-10:30pm

Wednesday 2nd

❑ **TV** Playhouse Theatre *Manchester*. BBC-1 ***Top Of The Pops*** lip-synch 'You Really Got Me'. This will become almost a routine, and the band probably flies up to Manchester and back this day. In addition to appearing on this evening's broadcast, earlier in the afternoon they tape another appearance that will be aired the following Wednesday (when they will be in London).

'You Really Got Me' single released in the US. This was scheduled for August 26th but delayed until this week. While Reprise pays for an impressive full-page ad in *Billboard* dated September 5th, the record itself warrants no review the following week, only a listing in "special programming". Nevertheless, while slow to enter the charts (not until September 26th) the record steadily builds steam once it is heard and will rise to number 7 a full two months later.

☆ Ray is interviewed by Les Hall in *Mersey Beat* and when asked about their next single he says, "I think we've got it now, and it's a ballady beat type of number. We've already recorded the single after our next one." The "ballady beat" song to which Ray refers is probably the newly-written 'I Just Wanna Walk With You', which would go unrecorded and was never heard of again. Apparently a demo is committed to tape during the next few days. And what Ray calls "the single after" is 'Tired Of Waiting For You'.

Thursday 3rd

Neald Hall *Chippenham, Wilts*

In London, publishing assignments are entered for Ray's original songs from the just-completed debut LP: 'Stop Your Sobbing', 'So Mystifying' and 'Just Can't Go To Sleep', plus two songs to be held for subsequent singles, 'Tired Of Waiting For You' and 'I Gotta Move'. This implies the recordings aren't fully completed until this week.

Friday 4th

Mecca Ballroom *Basildon, Essex* two shows, with The Swinging Blue Jeans

"Kink-crazy fans run amok at the Mecca," runs the headline in the *Basildon Reporter*. The reviewer writes: "Hordes of screaming and hysterical teenage girls mobbed the stage … at midnight on Friday in a bid to reach long-haired parade idols, The Kinks. There was pandemonium as the girls – some of them sobbing – swept towards the rostrum on which The Kinks were playing and dragged off [Dave] after a cordon of shirt-sleeved Mecca men gave way under the pressure."

☆ Today there is a meeting at Edward Kassner's office in central London about the next single. Ray submits for consideration two new songs, 'Don't Ever Let Me Go' and 'I Just Wanna Walk With You', and these are likely demoed today. This would also seem to be the time of Kassner's offer to sign Ray directly to a publishing deal that would provide £40 a week for life for his compositions, and of an offer by Larry Page that would completely take away management control from Wace and Collins. There is also possibly a meeting now with Arthur Howes to discuss plans for upcoming bookings.

Saturday 5th
Locarno Ballroom *Brighton*

Sunday 6th
Princess Theatre *Torquay* 6:00pm & 8:30pm, with Tommy Quickly & Company
The Kinks were originally scheduled to appear at the ABC Cinema, Great Yarmouth, but this was cancelled in August. After tonight's performance the band travels to London by train where they hear the news that 'You Really Got Me' has reached number 1 in the upcoming issue of *NME*.

Monday 7th
Silverblades Ice Rink *Streatham, south London* 7:30-10:00pm
))) RADIO Playhouse Theatre *central London*. BBC Light Programme *Saturday Club* live performance 'Got Love If You Want It', 'Little Queenie', 'Cadillac', 'You Really Got Me' broadcast September 19th. This is *the* moment where, as Ray later describes it, everything is perfect and everyone on The Kinks team is in harmony and working to the same end. The day starts as Ray awakes to receive a telegram formally confirming the number 1 position of 'You Really Got Me', and publicist Brian Sommerville makes The Kinks available for press functions upon this announcement. The band is taken to central London for interviews and photographs. The day is a busy one, with a radio recording session and a prominent show the same night. At the Playhouse Theatre with producer Bernie Andrews and engineer Alistair Taylor the band records four titles for its BBC radio debut. ('Cadillac' will be released in 2001 on *The Kinks BBC Sessions 1964-77*.) The band later performs a 30-minute set in Streatham during which Ray is pulled from the stage during 'Got Love If You Want It'. After the show the band celebrates achieving number 1 with a champagne toast, with the Davies family there to congratulate everyone.
☆ A press release announces that the band's debut LP, *The Kinks*, is due for release on September 25th and that it will consist of 14 songs, including six originals.

Tuesday 8th
● RECORDING Pye Studios (No.2) *central London*. A session probably today is intended to produce a follow-up single, the likely candidates being two songs recently submitted to Kassner, **'I Just Want To Walk With You'** and **'Don't Ever Let Me Go'**, although these will be completely rejected and never heard from again (the latter eventually appearing as a bootleg in the 1990s). Pressure was on Ray at this time to write a suitable follow-up to 'You Really Got Me' in a similar vein, and this is one of the first candidates. It's possible that some minor changes are made now to some of the tracks already recorded for the debut LP, resulting in a week's delay in the release date from September 25th to October 2nd.

→ Band meeting around this time at Arthur Howes's office on Greek Street in central London to read press accounts and discuss tours.

Wednesday 9th
100 Club *central London* 7:30-11:00pm, with Danny & The Torinos

Thursday 10th
'You Really Got Me' peaks at number 1 in the *NME* and *Record Mirror* charts dated September 11th/12th.

→ Probably today the *Pye Press Party Celebrating The Kinks At Number One* is held at Pye Records, ATV House, central London.
☆ Ray is interviewed by a couple of journalists around this time. When

Ray Coleman of *Melody Maker* asks if The Kinks are trying to push ahead on the strength of a rebellious image, Ray replies: "You mean are we trying to do a Stones? No, of course not ... There's a bit of rebel in us but we are not doing a Stones. And we don't play R&B. That's best left to people like Muddy Waters who know what it's all about. I call our stuff more expression. It's an outlet to us." The resulting article that appears in the *Melody Maker* is inevitably headlined "Kinks Deny Stones Copy" ... but the band is at least afforded a cover story and a feature interview with Ray.
Ray mentions to Peter McGill of *Pop Weekly* that The Kinks have already recorded four or five songs for consideration for the next single, but that no decision has been made about which will be issued as the A-side. Asked about the forthcoming LP and if he thinks it might be a bit premature, Ray responds in a manner predicting his future actions. "You're right. I don't like putting out an LP so early. I'd like to spend about three months on an album. But the record company have got to make their money, I suppose."

Friday 11th
Princess Ballroom *Halifax, Yorks* 7:30-11:00pm

Saturday 12th
Memorial Hall *Northwich, Ches* 7:45-11:45pm, with Johnny Ringo & The Colts

Sunday 13th
Queen's Theatre *Blackpool* 6:00pm & 8:10pm, with The Nashville Teens

Monday 14th
Majestic Ballroom *Newcastle-upon-Tyne* 7:30-11:00pm, with The Teenbeats
A near-riot erupts at the start of the show and the performance is stopped after only three songs. A hundred girls faint as the crowd surges forward and presses against the stage barrier. The crowd then breaks through and rushes the stage, and The Kinks' performance is stopped. Ray Davies is injured in the process. Local papers also report that the band does not appear in their trademark hunting jackets tonight but rather in grey sweaters and brown trousers.
☆ A press release says *The Kinks* LP release is now moved from September 26th to October 2nd.

Tuesday 15th
Fabulous Queens Ballroom *Cleveleys, Lancs* 7:45-11:45pm, with "three local bands"
❐ TV Playhouse Theatre *Manchester*. BBC-1 *Top Of The Pops* lip-synch 'You Really Got Me' broadcast following day.

Wednesday 16th
A show at an unknown venue and location.

Thursday 17th
Booking agent Jack Green of the powerful Associated Booking Corporation flies in to London to discuss the possibility of US visits for The Kinks, The Honeycombs, and The Barron Knights.

Friday 18th
R&B Scene, Cubiklub *Rochdale, Lancs* 7:00-11:00pm
At 2:00am, following the band's performance, the car in which they and Rasa are travelling is involved in a crash with a truck. The band has just been given the new car this week. No one is seriously injured and the performance the following night continues as scheduled. However, the crash is probably used as an excuse to cancel three concerts later in the

week: it will be said that Ray and Dave collapse on stage in Sheffield on Sunday because of a delayed reaction to the accident.

Saturday 19th
Palais de Danse *Bury, Lancs* 7:30-11:00pm, with The Trendsetters
Formby Hall *Atherton, Lancs* doors open 7:30 pm
☆ Ray Davies writes 'All Day And All Of The Night' today.

Sunday 20th
Mojo Club *Sheffield*
☆ The band works out the arrangement for 'All Day And All Of The Night' while still in the north of England.

Monday 21st
The Kinks are scheduled to appear at the Golden Diamond Social Club, Sutton-In-Ashfield, Notts with The Teenseens but cancel hours before showtime. The fictitious reason given is that a delayed shock from the car crash (now portrayed as Saturday night) caused two members of the band to collapse on stage in Sheffield the previous evening. The Teenseens play instead to a very disappointed crowd. The club is assured that doctor's certificates of certified injury will be forwarded by management. Although The Kinks are solidly booked for months, management offers as a gesture of consolation to the club to rebook The Kinks on October 5th, the first open date available – but the club already has plans and passes on the offer.
☆ Perhaps not uncoincidentally, Rasa returns to St. Joseph's Roman Catholic girl's school in Bradford today, which may help explain the cancellations. Ray's meeting with Rasa in a local park causes a scene that will result in her being expelled from school a short time later, because of the disruptive attention that is caused by her relationship with Ray.

Tuesday 22nd
The band is scheduled to appear at the Lotus Ballroom, Forest Gate, north-east London but cancel on the day of the show. It is rescheduled for October 27th. The band possibly remain up north today.

Wednesday 23rd
The Kinks are scheduled to appear at the Gaumont Cinema, Ipswich, Suffolk as part of the Billy J. Kramer Show but again cancel on the day of the show. They will join this package tour on a regular basis on October 7th.

Thursday 24th
Carlton Club *Erdington, Birmingham*

→ ● **RECORDING** Pye Studios (No.2) *central London*. In a fit of inspiration Ray composed a new song, **'All Day And All Of The Night'**, only a few days earlier while on tour in northern England. It was quickly rehearsed then, and around now, squeezed between live shows, is recorded in a 10:00am to 1:00pm session at Pye. **'I Gotta Go Now'** is also recorded at the session, another song apparently written in recent days and inspired by Rasa's return to school.
☆ Around this time Ray writes an interesting piece for *Melody Maker* entitled "What A Kink Thinks" (published October 3rd issue). He reveals a good deal about his outlook that will shape his career. "When I was at art school as a student what I got out of it was colour, expression," he writes. "Now I find you turn out a bad song for the same reason you turn out a bad painting – insincerity. If you are sincere – if you do what you want – you can't turn out a bad thing. It's time the groups got wise and did what they want to do. This is where [The Kinks are] one up because even if we don't have another hit for a year, we will have another hit. We can't lose, because we entertain, and we're always trying to get something different."

Friday 25th
Casino Club *Burnley, Lancs* 8:00pm, with The Avalons, The Mustangs

Saturday 26th
Vaughn Hall *Shotton, Flints, Wales*
The one-hour show includes 'I'm A Lover Not A Fighter', 'Cadillac', 'So Mystifying', 'Bald Headed Woman', 'Revenge', 'You Really Got Me' and 'All Day And All Of The Night', plus one or two Muddy Waters songs, probably at least 'I'm Your Hoochie Coochie Man'. 'All Day And All Of The Night' is introduced as the band's new single which has been recorded just a few days ago. The Kinks were scheduled to appear at the Royal Lido Ballroom at Prestatyn in Flintshire but again cancel only hours before the show, citing a car crash as the reason for their inability to appear.
A local band, The Raynes, fills in and plays to a crowd of 1,100, with The Kinks rescheduled to appear on October 31st. Based on a local fan's recollection only, apparently the band instead play this impromptu booking in Shotton – perhaps it's where they happen to be stranded. With a record topping the charts, it surely is not too difficult to gather an audience at short notice.

Sunday 27th
Queen's Theatre *Blackpool* 6:00pm & 8:10pm, with Marianne Faithful, The Paramounts, Jerry Stevens, The Quotations, The Puppets, The Rustiks
Oasis Club *Manchester* with Herman's Hermits
There is also possibly an appearance at the Cavern in Manchester.

Monday 28th
Jubilee Hall *Burton-on-Trent, Staffs* 7:45-10:45pm, with The Vibrons
☆ A press release announces that the new single 'All Day And All Of The Night' is ready for release.

Tuesday 29th
Theatre Royal *Kings Lynn, Norfolk* 6:30 & 8:45pm, *Top-In-Pops No.2*, opening for The Merseybeats, with Russ Sainty & The Nu-Notes, The Other Two, The Herd, The Missing Links
➪ **TOUR STARTS** *Billy J. Kramer Show: UK Tour* (Sep 30th, then Oct 7th – 18th). **Line-up**: Ray Davies (lead vocal, guitar), Dave Davies (guitar, vocal), Pete Quaife (bass), Mick Avory (drums). An Arthur Howes & Brian Epstein Presentation. Compèred by Tim Connor.

Wednesday 30th
Odeon Cinema *Glasgow, Scotland* 6:40 & 9:00pm, with Billy J. Kramer & The Dakotas (headliners), The Ronettes, Cliff Bennett & The Rebel Rousers, The Bill Black Combo, The Yardbirds, The Nashville Teens
First night of the Billy J. Kramer tour. Dave is dragged into the audience by fans and sustains a cut hand. The Kinks fly to Glasgow from London Airport, and then return to London the same night.

October

Thursday 1st
❏ **TV** BBC Television Centre (Studio 4) *west London*. BBC-2 **Beat Room** live performance 'You Really Got Me', 'Got Love If You Want It' broadcast October 5th. The band rehearses and then videotapes these songs. Among other acts appearing are John Lee Hooker (with future Groundhogs guitarist Tony McPhee) and The Syndicats (with future

Tomorrow and Yes guitarist Steve Howe). A video clip from this performance of 'You Really Got Me' will also be broadcast on BBC-1's *Time Out!* on November 12th. The tapes from this show fortunately survive and will be used repeatedly in various documentaries.

Friday 2nd

Floral Hall Ballroom *Morecambe, Lancs* 8:00pm-2:00am
The Kinks album released in the UK. "Some wild R&B tracks," says Allen Evans in *NME*, "including a raucous 'Long Tall Shorty' [and] a jerky, dramatic piece in 'Stop Your Sobbing'. The backing they supply for themselves moves along with a rock steady beat, and is punctuated with good guitar work and exciting harmonica-drums rhythm." Meanwhile Nigel Hunter in *Disc* writes: "Impressive first set by Those Kinks ... It follows the now dominant commercial rhythm and blues pattern à la Britain ... crammed full of guitaristics and solid-drum-foundationed beat," and concludes: "The Kinks have mixed up a nice concoction of contrasting songs which keep the interest going."

Saturday 3rd

Astoria Ballroom *Rawtenstall, Lancs* 7:30pm, with Ian Dean & The Brystals, Curt's Creatures

---

The Kinks album

A1 **'Beautiful Delilah'** (C. BERRY).
A2 **'So Mystifying'** (R. DAVIES).
A3 **'Just Can't Go To Sleep'** (R. DAVIES).
A4 **'Long Tall Shorty'** (D. COVAY, H. ABRAMSON).
A5 **'I Took My Baby Home'** (R. DAVIES).
A6 **'I'm A Lover Not A Fighter'** (J. MILLER).
A7 **'You Really Got Me'** (R. DAVIES).
B1 **'Cadillac'** (E. MCDANIEL).
B2 **'Bald Headed Woman'** (TRADITIONAL/ARR. S. TALMY).
B3 **'Revenge'** (R. DAVIES, L. PAGE).
B4 **'Too Much Monkey Business'** (C. BERRY).
B5 **'I've Been Driving On Bald Mountain'** (TRAD'L/ARR. S. TALMY).
B6 **'Stop Your Sobbing'** (R. DAVIES).
B7 **'Got Love If You Want It'** (J. MOORE).

UK release October 2nd 1964 (Pye NPL 18096 mono; NSPL 83021 stereo).
US release See *You Really Got Me* November 25th 1964.
Musicians Ray Davies lead vocal except as noted (no vocal on Revenge), rhythm guitar, lead guitar (A6), harmonica, backing vocal. Dave Davies lead vocal (A1, A4, A6, B5), electric guitar, backing vocal. Pete Quaife bass guitar, backing vocal. Mick Avory drums (B1, B2, B4- B6, B7), tambourine, maracas. Bobby Graham drums (all except Avory as noted). Jimmy Page 12-string acoustic (A6, B5, possibly B2). Perry Ford piano (B2, B6). Jon Lord organ (B2). Rasa Didzpetris backing vocals (B6).
Recorded Pye Studios (No.2), *central London*; A1-A4, A6, B1-B7: probably August 18th, 24-25th, 31st, September 1st 1964, A5: see single released February 7th 1964 (mixed to stereo September 1964), A7: see single released August 4th 1964; all 3-track mixed to mono and stereo (except A7 mono only).
Producer Shel Talmy (for Shel Talmy Productions).
Engineer Bob Auger.
Chart high UK number 4.

Sunday 4th

New Pyramid Beat Club *Rochdale, Lancs* 8:40pm & 9:50pm

Monday 5th

A TV recording is scheduled for today, probably a regional TV spot. The band offers to cancel the TV commitment for an appearance today as a make-up for the September 21st cancellation in Sutton-In-Ashfield, but this is not required as the club has a prior commitment.

Tuesday 6th

Probable press functions for the band occur during the day in London. Not until today does the BBC review board consider The Kinks' debut BBC session that was recorded on September 7th, and gives a thumbs-up for further work.

Wednesday 7th

ABC Cinema *Carlisle* 6:15 & 8:30 pm, with Billy J. Kramer & The Dakotas (headliners), Cliff Bennett & The Rebel Rousers, The Bill Black Combo, The Yardbirds, The Nashville Teens
The Kinks join the remainder of the dates on the *Billy J. Kramer Show* tour, replacing The Ronettes who have done the dates up to this point – although The Ronettes are included in a review of the show from October 11th, indicating they stayed on for at least one more date than advertised.
Set-list: typically of package shows, The Kinks' set consists of just four songs and normally includes both 'You Really Got Me' and 'All Day And All Of The Night'.

Thursday 8th

Odeon Cinema *Bolton* 6:15 & 8:30pm, with Billy J. Kramer & The Dakotas (headliners), Cliff Bennett & The Rebel Rousers, The Bill Black Combo, The Yardbirds, The Nashville Teens
Fans rush the stage, climb over the orchestra pit, and grab hold of Ray, who is uninjured.
☆ Today's edition of *Mersey Beat* includes a short piece headed "Kinks Write Song For Former Fan Club Secretaries". It says that Jeanette Ross and Gita Mivrenieks revealed at a recent Liverpool show by The Escorts that they formed a vocal duo, The Pixies. The two originally started The Kinks' fan club which they had run until earlier this year. "Ray wrote us a number and told us to record it," says one of the girls, "and The Kinks' manager Larry Page thought it was a good idea. Then Ray wrote another number for us and something that started off as a giggle ended up seriously.
"Larry became our manager and Arthur Howes, The Kinks' agent, became our agent. Our first engagement as The Pixies was at a club in Boscombe and we have appeared in several London clubs and on *Ready Steady Go!* and *Top Of The Pops*, as dancers. We'd really like to go on tour, and our first record should be released shortly." No such record is ever issued and nor is any more heard from this obscure and probably unsanctioned project.

Friday 9th

Granada Cinema *Grantham, Lincs* 6:20 & 8:30pm, with Billy J. Kramer & The Dakotas (headliners), Cliff Bennett & The Rebel Rousers, The Bill Black Combo, The Yardbirds, The Nashville Teens

Saturday 10th

ABC Cinema *Hull* 6:15 & 8:30pm, with Billy J. Kramer & The Dakotas (headliners), Cliff Bennett & The Rebel Rousers, The Bill Black Combo, The Yardbirds, The Nashville Teens

Sunday 11th

Granada Cinema *East Ham, east London* 6:00 & 8:30pm, with Billy J. Kramer & The Dakotas (headliners), The Ronettes, Cliff

Bennett & The Rebel Rousers, The Bill Black Combo, The Yardbirds, The Nashville Teens

The Kinks are getting reactions equal to those of the headlining Billy J. Kramer. Cordell Marks in *NME* notes how Ray and Dave encourage the crowd's excitement by moving to the very edge of the stage and then jumping back at the last minute. He says the perpetual screaming of the crowd is heightened by flashing lights and Dave's weird "crippled jockey" dance. Inclusion in the set of The Drifters' classic 'Save The Last Dance For Me' (as well as 'It's Alright', 'You Really Got Me' and 'All Day And All Of The Night') provides an early taster of some of the material on the second Kinks album. On that record, a shortlived fascination will be evident with the classic early-1960s soul-ballads coming from Atlantic Records in New York, including 'Don't Ever Change' and 'Something Better Beginning'.

Monday 12th

The band is in London for a day off from the tour.

Tuesday 13th

Granada Cinema *Bedford* 7:00 & 9:10pm, with Billy J. Kramer & The Dakotas (headliners), Cliff Bennett & The Rebel Rousers, The Bill Black Combo, The Yardbirds, The Nashville Teens

Wednesday 14th

Granada Cinema *Brixton, south London* 7:00 & 9:10pm, with Billy J. Kramer & The Dakotas (headliners), Cliff Bennett & The Rebel Rousers, The Bill Black Combo, The Yardbirds, The Nashville Teens

Thursday 15th

Odeon Cinema *Guildford, Surrey* 6:00 & 8:15pm, with Billy J. Kramer & The Dakotas (headliners), Cliff Bennett & The Rebel Rousers, The Bill Black Combo, The Yardbirds, The Nashville Teens

Friday 16th

ABC Cinema *Southampton* 6:15 & 8:30pm, with Billy J. Kramer & The Dakotas (headliners), Cliff Bennett & The Rebel Rousers, The Bill Black Combo, The Yardbirds, The Nashville Teens

Saturday 17th

ABC Cinema *Gloucester* 6:15 & 8:30pm, with Billy J. Kramer & The Dakotas (headliners), Cliff Bennett & The Rebel Rousers, The Bill Black Combo, The Yardbirds, The Nashville Teens

Sunday 18th

Granada Cinema *Tooting, south London* 6:00 & 8:30pm, with Billy J. Kramer & The Dakotas (headliners), Cliff Bennett & The Rebel Rousers, The Bill Black Combo, The Yardbirds, The Nashville Teens
The last date of the *Billy J. Kramer Show* tour, after which the band heads north to Scotland for a series of concert dates and a regional television appearance.

→ ● **RECORDING** Pye Studios (No.2) *central London.* During a single daytime session probably at least two tracks are put down for the upcoming *Kinksize Session* EP: **'I've Got That Feeling'** and **'Louie Louie'**. The latter is an obvious cover as the band has included it in shows since the beginning of the year. Originals are not in abundance at this point; **'I've Got That Feeling'** is an early composition of Ray's from the start of 1964. A third song, **'Things Are Getting Better'**, is possibly done at this session, but more likely on November 16th.

Monday 19th

Barrowland Ballroom *Glasgow, Scotland* 8:00-11:00pm, *Top Of The Charts*, admission 5/- (25p)

Tuesday 20th

Town Hall *Elgin, Morays, Scotland* 9:00pm-1:00am, with The Copycats; sponsored by the Two Red Shows Ballroom

Wednesday 21st

Beach Ballroom *Aberdeen, Scotland* 8:30pm-1:00am

Thursday 22nd

❏ **TV** Scottish Television Studios *Cowacaddens, Glasgow, Scotland.* STV *Dig This!* live, probably 'All Day And All Of The Night'.

Friday 23rd

City Hall *Perth, Scotland* 8:00pm-1:00am, with The Embers, The Vikings
'All Day And All Of The Night' single released in the UK. *NME's* reviewer writes: "The same [overall feel and effect of their previous hit] applies to their new one and again I'm impressed by the muffled, authentic-sounding atmosphere created on this disc. Another Ray Davies composition, it features him soloing with chanting support – plus insidious strumming, drums thumps and cymbal bashing, and twangs galore. They could get very close to No. 1 again with this one."

All Day And All Of The Night single

A 'All Day And All Of The Night' (R. DAVIES).
B 'I Gotta Move' (R. DAVIES).

UK release October 23rd 1964 (Pye 7N 15714).
US release December 9th 1964 (Reprise 0334).
Musicians Ray Davies lead vocal, rhythm guitar. Dave Davies lead guitar, backing vocal. Pete Quaife bass guitar, backing vocal. Bobby Graham drums (A). Mick Avory drums (B), tambourine (A). 'Johnny B. Great' backing vocal (A). Perry Ford piano (A). Jimmy Page (possibly) 12-string acoustic (B). Recorded Pye Studios (No.2), central London; A: September 23rd or 24th 1964, B: probably August 31st, September 1st 1964; 1-track to 1-track to mono.
Producer Shel Talmy (for Shel Talmy Productions).
Engineer Bob Auger.
Chart high UK number 2; US number 7.

Saturday 24th

Eldorado Ballroom *Leith, Edinburgh, Scotland* 7:30-11:00pm, with Bobby King & The Jesters, The Embers

Sunday 25th

The Human Jungle *Oldham*

Monday 26th

The band are probably busy with a variety of media functions in London during the day today, including a photo-studio session with Derek Berwin that produces the well-known shot of the band among powder kegs.

Tuesday 27th

Lotus Club *Forest Gate, north-east London*
This is the make-up date for the September 22nd cancellation.
☆ At Philips Studios, which is situated in central London, the session

→ INDICATES EVENT AROUND THIS TIME BUT WITH NO FIRM DATE

guitarist Jimmy Page records his debut one-off solo single, titled 'She Just Satisfies' and which is based very closely on The Kinks' album track, 'Revenge'. This marks the beginning of the rush to sound like the chart-topping Kinks.

Wednesday 28th
Twisted Wheel *Manchester*

Friday 30th
))) **RADIO** Playhouse Theatre *central London*. BBC Light Programme *Top Gear* studio recordings 'I'm A Lover Not A Fighter', 'Long Tall Shorty', 'You Really Got Me', 'Too Much Monkey Business', 'All Day And All Of The Night', 'Bye Bye Johnny' broadcast November 19th. (Two of the tracks from this session, 'You Really Got Me' and 'All Day And All Of The Night', will be released in 2001 on *The Kinks BBC Sessions 1964-1977*.)

❐ **TV** Television House *central London*. Rediffusion **Ready Steady Go!** lip-synch 'All Day And All Of The Night'. Double media duty today. First they are at the Playhouse with producer Bernie Andrews to tape five numbers for BBC radio's *Top Gear*. Aural evidence suggests that Ray's girlfriend Rasa is present, adding backing vocal to 'All Day And All Of The Night'. Later, the band appears on this evening's broadcast of *Ready Steady Go!*.

Saturday 31st
Royal Lido Ballroom *Prestatyn, Flints, Wales* 8:00-11:45pm, with Jack Ellis & The Autocrats
The following day is probably a day off.

November

Monday 2nd – Tuesday 3rd
On the eve of a long string of tour dates, the early part of the week includes a clutch of press commitments and photo sessions.

Among the interviews, Ray talks to Alan Freeman for *Rave* and the whole band joins David Griffiths for *Record Mirror*. Besides the usual discussions about having to keep up the image expected of The Kinks, part of the band's secret weapon is revealed. "Fortunately for the group," writes Griffiths, "Pete [Quaife] has a rampant imagination and is always ready to make up the most outrageously improbable stories to delight (and confuse) journalists."

Meanwhile Ray talks seriously to *Rave* about the band's music and the new sounds they are experimenting with. "The public might get tired if we stuck with the same formula all the time so we've been trying out different types of guitars and amplifiers, looking for something new. I've found that by using a lot of distortion on my amplifier and then using even more distortion in the recording booth we can make my guitar sound like a whole group of violins!"

Among photo sessions is a visit to Dezo Hoffman's studio in central London, resulting in such demeaning poses as the band clutching playing cards in their mouths and – for an unlikely-seeming tie-in campaign – the band holding apples to promote healthy eating habits among teenagers.

→ Around now Ray misses a scheduled radio interview with Chris Hutchins, to have been taped at BBC Broadcasting House in central London for broadcast on the Light Programme's *Teen Scene*. Ray writes a letter slightly later to the show's producer Wilfred D'Ath to apologise, saying that their road manager failed to turn up. The producer replies in a letter dated November 19th: "I realise it was not your fault and I will certainly not take any steps to blacklist your group in the eyes of the BBC as a result of this one incident."

Wednesday 4th
❐ **TV** Playhouse Theatre *Manchester*. BBC-1 *Top Of The Pops* lip-synch 'All Day And All Of The Night' (three versions) broadcast November 5th, 12th, 26th. The Kinks spend a doubtless long day at BBC Manchester videotaping three different inserts, presumably with different outfits and/or stage settings, for upcoming editions of *Top Of The Pops*, in anticipation of the new record's virtually assured success and The Kinks' busy touring schedule. A separate taping on the 18th (broadcast 19th) will provide a solid month of weekly appearances on this cornerstone music show.

→ At this time, and without obvious reason unless related to the missed interview appointment (see 2nd/3rd), the BBC evidently cancels the band's upcoming scheduled TV spot on *Beat Room* for taping November 26th and broadcast on the 30th. The Kinks would have co-starred with The Isley Brothers.

Thursday 5th
While it is possible a local TV show is done today, there is certainly media-related activity going on, with Dave for example interviewed by Geoff Leack for *Mersey Beat*.

Friday 6th
))) **RADIO** Playhouse Theatre *central London*. BBC Light Programme *Joe Loss Pop Show* live performance 'All Day And All Of The Night', 'It's Alright', 'I'm A Lover Not A Fighter', 'You Really Got Me' broadcast November 13th. With TV spots covered, The Kinks focus today on the radio waves and tape this appearance before an invited audience at one of the theatres regularly used by the broadcasting company. BBC files erroneously list the final song as 'You Really Got A Hold On Me', but this is almost certainly a clerical error – although no tape survives to confirm this. Exactly the same error occurs later, and that one certainly is the band's first hit and not the Smokey Robinson & The Miracles song.

↪ **TOUR STARTS** *Gerry & The Pacemakers Show: UK Tour* (Nov 7th – Dec 6th). **Line-up**: Ray Davies (lead vocal, guitar), Dave Davies (guitar, vocal), Pete Quaife (bass), Mick Avory (drums). Another arthur howes/Brian Epstein Presentation. Compèred by Bryan Burdon.

Saturday 7th
Granada Cinema *Walthamstow, north-east London* 6:30 & 9:00pm, with Gerry & The Pacemakers, Gene Pitney, Marianne Faithful, The Mike Cotton Sound, Bobby Shafto & The Roof Raisers, Kim Weston & The Earl Van Dyke Band

Opening date of the *Gerry & The Pacemakers Show* tour, with a collection of talent that includes a number of people who will have future influence or associations with The Kinks, as well as at least one future superstar. The Mike Cotton Sound's leader, trumpeter and trombonist John Beecham, will eventually become part of The Kinks in the early 1970s. Mid-tour, Cotton's Sound hire a new bass player, a young Jim Rodford – who will join The Kinks in that capacity in 1978. The line-up also includes keyboardist and future Animal and Kink-buddy Dave Rowberry.

As the tour progresses, The Kinks become enamoured of Motown vocalist Kim Weston's backing band, a solid R&B outfit with a jazz background that features drummer Uriel Jones, whose distinctive playing provides the inspiration for The Kinks' experimental single 'Ev'rybody's Gonna Be Happy' recorded following this tour. Among the members of The Manish Boys who play the final dates of the tour (see December 1st) is a young David Jones, later David Bowie, on vocals and tenor saxophone.

During the tour The Kinks close the first half of the show, and for tonight's debut they are, according to Ian Dove in *NME*, "ecstatically received" by the audience. Titles and lyrics are unintelligible among the shouting and screaming, he reports, but some good harmonica work on a routine blues does cut through the atmosphere.

Mike Ledgerwood reviews the gig too, for *Disc Weekly*, and he also raves about The Kinks. "For sheer excitement and an excellent stage act, I give full marks to those clever Kinks ... Their kacophony of brash beat kaptivated the audience so much that they were klamouring for more, and sorties of girls were kontinually trying to slip past the attendants and on to the stage. The klimax kame when two teenagers klambered up and threw themselves on Kink Ray Davies midway through a song."

Marianne Faithfull will write about the tour later in her autobiography. "The Kinks were very gothic. Creepy and silent. They never spoke," she says. "They were uptight and fearful of everyone. Terrified. Underneath which there was all this weird dysfunctional family stuff going on. They hated each other. ... It was all very odd."

Monday 9th

Royal Albert Hall *Kensington, central London* Top Beat Show, with Gerry & The Pacemakers, Gene Pitney, The Hollies, The Honeycombs, Lulu, Cliff Bennett, The Pretty Things, Martha & The Vandellas, The Mike Cotton Sound

Tonight's show is not part of the *Pacemakers* tour but rather a separate TV-based special, broadcast on BBC-2 on November 11th at 7:45 pm. The Kinks probably perform 'All Day And All Of The Night'; BBC files show The Kinks' fee is £100. This appearance alongside Martha & The Vandellas playing their hit 'Dancing In The Streets' probably adds to the general inspiration that led to The Kinks' covering the song at the end of the sessions for what became their second LP, *Kinda Kinks*, in February 1965.

☆ *The Daily Express* exclusively reveals the news of Ray's marriage to Rasa Didzpetris in Bradford in December. Journalist Judith Simons has evidently uncovered the fact buried among the church's published listing of upcoming marriage announcements in the previous day's *Bradford Argus*. The *Express* quotes Rasa's father: "Ray has been hoping to keep the event quiet as he thinks it might harm the group."

Tuesday 10th

ABC Cinema *Romford* 6:45 & 9:00pm, with Gerry & The Pacemakers, Gene Pitney, Marianne Faithful, The Mike Cotton Sound, Bobby Shafto & The Roof Raisers, Kim Weston & The Earl Van Dyke Band

Back to the *Gerry & The Pacemakers Show* tour.

Wednesday 11th

ABC Cinema *Harrow, north-west London* 6:30 & 8:45pm, with Gerry & The Pacemakers, Gene Pitney, Marianne Faithful, The Mike Cotton Sound, Bobby Shafto & The Roof Raisers, Kim Weston & The Earl Van Dyke Band

Thursday 12th

ABC Cinema *Northampton* 6:30 & 8:45 pm, with Gerry & The Pacemakers, Gene Pitney, Marianne Faithful, The Mike Cotton Sound, Bobby Shafto & The Roof Raisers, Kim Weston & The Earl Van Dyke Band

Friday 13th

ABC Cinema *Lincoln* 6:15 & 8:45pm, with Gerry & The Pacemakers, Gene Pitney, Marianne Faithful, The Mike Cotton Sound, Bobby Shafto & The Roof Raisers, Kim Weston & The Earl Van Dyke Band

☆ Today's *NME* reveals in *Tailpieces*, the paper's back-page gossip column, that "on December 12th Ray Davies (leader of The Kinks) marries art student Rasa [Didzpetris]".

Saturday 14th

City Hall *Sheffield* 6:10 & 8:40pm, with Gerry & The Pacemakers, Gene Pitney, Marianne Faithful, The Mike Cotton Sound, Bobby Shafto & The Roof Raisers, Kim Weston & The Earl Van Dyke Band

Sunday 15th

Hippodrome Theatre *Birmingham* 5:30 & 8:10pm, with Gerry & The Pacemakers, Gene Pitney, Marianne Faithful, The Mike Cotton Sound, Bobby Shafto & The Roof Raisers, Kim Weston & The Earl Van Dyke Band

According to the *Birmingham Evening Mail* the audience at this show is relatively quiet except for their enthusiasm for The Kinks, which takes the form of accurate aiming of various missiles.

Monday 16th

● **RECORDING** Pye Studios (No.2) *central London*. The song **'Things Are Getting Better'** is assigned to Kassner Music today. Owing to the presence of pianist Nicky Hopkins on this one cut, it is very possible that this additional recording for the soon-to-be-released *Kinksize Session* EP is done today at Pye rather than at the October 18th session. Hopkins is just entering the session scene following an 18-month layoff from playing after retiring from Cyril Davies & His All-Stars in May 1963. He will not record again with the band until a session for *The Kinks Kontroversy* LP late in 1965.

Tuesday 17th

Granada Cinema *Bedford* 7:00 & 9:10pm, with Gerry & The Pacemakers, Gene Pitney, Marianne Faithful, The Mike Cotton Sound, Bobby Shafto & The Roof Raisers, Kim Weston & The Earl Van Dyke Band

Wednesday 18th

ABC Cinema *Chester* 6:15 & 8:30pm, with Gerry & The Pacemakers, Gene Pitney, Marianne Faithful, The Mike Cotton Sound, Bobby Shafto & The Roof Raisers, Kim Weston & The Earl Van Dyke Band

❒ **TV** Playhouse Theatre *Manchester*. BBC-1 *Top Of The Pops* lip-synch 'All Day And All Of The Night'.

The close geographic proximity of tonight's show to Manchester gives the band time earlier in the day to do a fresh mimed performance that will be included in the following evening's edition of *Top Of The Pops*.

Thursday 19th

Broadway Theatre *Eccles, Manchester* 6:15 & 8:30pm, with Gerry & The Pacemakers, Gene Pitney, Marianne Faithful, The Mike Cotton Sound, Bobby Shafto & The Roof Raisers, Kim Weston & The Earl Van Dyke Band

☆ The Kinks are featured guests on the BBC Light Programme's *Top Gear* (see October 30th).

Friday 20th

Granada Cinema *Shrewsbury* 6:15 & 8:30pm, with Gerry & The Pacemakers, Gene Pitney, Marianne Faithful, The Mike Cotton Sound, Bobby Shafto & The Roof Raisers, Kim Weston & The Earl Van Dyke Band

Typical of the era, the music press latches on to Quaife's recent acquisition of a pet toy poodle, one Earl Ruthara Dino Kinkly II. As for more down-to-earth matters, according to Ray's account in *X-Ray* it is after this show that he receives a telegram from Rasa who has been hospitalised for internal bleeding. Ray visits her in Bradford. Later, Rasa has to admit to her parents that she is three-months pregnant.

☆ In today's *NME* Shel Talmy speaks with Cordell Marks and mentions The Kinks. "There's never enough time," says the producer. "They're always rushing around all over the place and I can never keep them in the studio for as long as I'd like. I'd like to spend more time finding out what they can do." He says that The Kinks, like many other groups, prefer recording at night when they are more relaxed, but that unlike other producers he doesn't like rehearsing numbers before recording them. "It kills any feel a person might have for a composition. [And] I'm not that concerned with the technical quality of a record. The sound is the important thing."

Saturday 21st

Gaumont Cinema *Derby* 6:00 & 8:30pm, with Gerry & The Pacemakers, Gene Pitney, Marianne Faithful, The Mike Cotton Sound, Bobby Shafto & The Roof Raisers, Kim Weston & The Earl Van Dyke Band

Sunday 22nd

Coventry Theatre *Coventry* 6:00 & 8:30pm, with Gerry & The Pacemakers, Gene Pitney, Marianne Faithful, The Mike Cotton Sound, Bobby Shafto & The Roof Raisers, Kim Weston & The Earl Van Dyke Band

Monday 23rd

The Kinks are photographed by Dezo Hoffman at his London studio.

Tuesday 24th

ABC Cinema *Dover, Kent* 6:15 & 8:30pm, with Gerry & The Pacemakers, Gene Pitney, Jackie DeShannon, The Mike Cotton Sound, Bobby Shafto & The Roof Raisers, Kim Weston & The Earl Van Dyke Band

❏ **TV** Unknown location *London*. CBS **The Red Skelton Show** filming 'Got Love If You Want It' and others, broadcast March 30th 1965. Earlier today the band is at a London-area soundstage (probably Twickenham or Shepperton) where an insert for this American TV show is filmed.

While it is not known how many songs are filmed, only one is ultimately shown, and strangely this is not one of their hits but rather 'Got Love If You Want It'. It is aired on the March 30th 1965 edition of this primetime CBS network show. (The programme will also be broadcast in the UK by Rediffusion on August 4th 1967.)

Red Skelton is a weekly comedy and variety show hosted by the American comedian. British acts are hot property on American TV at this time and Skelton has booked appearances by a number of British acts, filmed in London and later inserted into the show. This is especially useful to CBS as the Skelton show would be running opposite NBC's popular *Hullaballoo* during the next season.

Wednesday 25th

ABC Cinema *Cambridge* 6:15 & 8:30pm, with Gerry & The Pacemakers, Gene Pitney, Jackie DeShannon, The Mike Cotton Sound, Bobby Shafto & The Roof Raisers, Kim Weston & The Earl Van Dyke Band

You Really Got Me album released in the US this week . The LP shares a full-page ad with Sandie Shaw in the secondary trade magazine *Cash Box*. It reads: "The Kinks – for whom The Beatles may have been a curtain raiser." Market-leader *Billboard* runs a typical review of the time: "Herein the boys dredge up their gutsy musical ribaldry in potent commercial style," and adds an ironic note: "Stereophiles will get added enjoyment from the special audio treatment." At this time it is enough simply to title the album after the huge hit it contains in order to ensure good sales, and indeed the record achieves a respectable showing, peaking at number 29 during a 26-week run in the charts.

Thursday 26th

Ritz Cinema *Luton* 6:30 & 8:45pm, with Gerry & The Pacemakers, Gene Pitney, Marianne Faithful, The Mike Cotton

---

You Really Got Me album

A1 'Beautiful Delilah' (C. BERRY).
A2 'So Mystifying' (R. DAVIES).
A3 'Just Can't Go To Sleep' (R. DAVIES).
A4 'Long Tall Shorty' (D. COVAY, H. ABRAMSON).
A5 'You Really Got Me' (R. DAVIES).
B1 'Cadillac' (E. MCDANIEL).
B2 'Bald Headed Woman' (TRADITIONAL/ARR. S. TALMY).
B3 'Too Much Monkey Business' (C. BERRY).
B4 'I've Been Driving On Bald Mountain' (TRAD'L/ARR. S. TALMY).
B5 'Stop Your Sobbing' (R. DAVIES).
B6 'Got Love If You Want It' (J. MOORE).

US release November 25th 1964 (Reprise R 6143 mono; RS 6143 stereo). Identical credits to UK The Kinks LP except three tracks omitted, different cover, and A5 in reprocessed stereo for stereo version.
Chart high US number 29.

Sound, Bobby Shafto & The Roof Raisers, Kim Weston & The Earl Van Dyke Band

Tonight is future Kink Jim Rodford's first gig as the new bass player for fellow tour-band The Mike Cotton Sound.

☆ 'All Day And All Of The Night' peaks at number 2 in the *Melody Maker* chart.

☆ A scheduled taping of *Beat Room* at BBC Television Centre, west London, due for broadcast November 30th, was cancelled on the 6th, perhaps due to the *Teen Scene* problem (see November 2nd/3rd).

Friday 27th

ABC Cinema *Kingston-upon-Thames, south-west London* 6:45 & 9:00pm, with Gerry & The Pacemakers, Gene Pitney, Marianne Faithful, The Mike Cotton Sound, Bobby Shafto & The Roof Raisers, Kim Weston & The Earl Van Dyke Band
Kinksize Session EP released in the UK.

Kinksize Session EP

A1 'Louie Louie' (R. BERRY).
A2 'I Gotta Go Now' (R. DAVIES).
B1 'Things Are Getting Better' (R. DAVIES).
B2 'I've Got That Feeling' (R. DAVIES).

UK release November 27th 1964 (Pye NEP 24200).
Musicians Ray Davies lead vocal, piano (A1, B2, or Perry Ford), harmonica (B1). Dave Davies electric guitar, backing vocal. Pete Quaife electric bass, backing vocal. Mick Avory drums. Nicky Hopkins piano (B1).
Recorded Pye Studios (No.2), central London; A1, B2: October 18th 1964, A2: September 23rd 1964, B1 possibly November 16th (or October 18th) 1964; 1-track to 1-track mono.
Producer Shel Talmy (for Shel Talmy Productions).
Engineer Bob Auger.
Chart high UK number 1 (EP chart).

Saturday 28th

Winter Gardens *Bournemouth* two shows, with Gerry & The Pacemakers, Gene Pitney, Marianne Faithful, The Mike Cotton Sound, Bobby Shafto & The Roof Raisers, Kim Weston & The Earl Van Dyke Band

Sunday 29th

Colston Hall *Bristol* two shows, with Gerry & The Pacemakers, Gene Pitney, Marianne Faithful, The Mike Cotton Sound, Bobby Shafto & The Roof Raisers, Kim Weston & The Earl Van Dyke Band (Day off in London following.)

December

Tuesday 1st

ABC Cinema *Wigan, Lancs* 6:20 & 8:45pm, with Gerry & The Pacemakers, Gene Pitney, Marianne Faithful, The Mike Cotton Sound, Bobby Shafto & The Roof Raisers, Kim Weston & The Earl Van Dyke Band, The Manish Boys

Wednesday 2nd

ABC Cinema *Hull* 6:15 & 8:30pm, with Gerry & The Pacemakers, Gene Pitney, Marianne Faithful, The Mike Cotton Sound, Bobby Shafto & The Roof Raisers, Kim Weston & The Earl Van Dyke Band, The Manish Boys

Thursday 3rd

ABC Cinema *Edinburgh, Scotland* 6:30 & 8:50pm, with Gerry & The Pacemakers, Gene Pitney, Marianne Faithful, The Mike Cotton Sound, Bobby Shafto & The Roof Raisers, Kim Weston & The Earl Van Dyke Band, The Manish Boys

Friday 4th

ABC Cinema *Stockton-on-Tees, Co Durham* 6:15 & 8:30pm, with Gerry & The Pacemakers, Gene Pitney, Marianne Faithful, The Mike Cotton Sound, Bobby Shafto & The Roof Raisers, Kim Weston & The Earl Van Dyke Band, The Manish Boys
Venue possibly moved to the Globe Theatre.

Saturday 5th

City Hall *Newcastle Upon Tyne* 6:30 & 8:40pm, with Gerry & The Pacemakers, Gene Pitney, Marianne Faithful, The Mike Cotton Sound, Bobby Shafto & The Roof Raisers, Kim Weston & The Earl Van Dyke Band, The Manish Boys

Sunday 6th

Futurist Theatre *Scarborough, Yorks* 6:00 & 8:30pm, with Gerry & The Pacemakers, Gene Pitney, Marianne Faithful, The Mike Cotton Sound, Bobby Shafto & The Roof Raisers, Kim Weston & The Earl Van Dyke Band, The Manish Boys
The end of the long *Gerry & The Pacemakers Show* tour, as The Kinks move straight into another (non-touring) package with Gene Pitney.

Monday 7th

New Theatre *Oxford*

Tonight is the opening night of a week-long residency of *The Gene Pitney Show*. Pitney is backed by The Mike Cotton Sound, and the opening acts besides The Kinks include The Falling Leaves, Val McAllum, and Bobby Shafto & The Roofraisers. The *Oxford Times* reviewer dislikes The Kinks and says that their records leave him cold, as does their stage act. He feels they rely too much on the "grotesque appearance of so many of the beat groups of the day".

Tuesday 8th

New Theatre *Oxford*

The *Gene Pitney Show* continues.

Wednesday 9th

New Theatre *Oxford*

>>> **RADIO** Piccadilly Theatre Studios *central London*. BBC Light Programme **Saturday Club** studio recordings produced by Bernie Andrews 'I'm A Lover Not A Fighter', 'I've Got That Feeling', 'Stop Your Sobbing', 'All Day And All Of The Night', 'Louie Louie' broadcast December 12th.

'All Day And All Of The Night' single released in the US. "Another potent entry by the Englishmen," says *Billboard*. "Raw gutsy delivery is maintained along with raunchy guitar sound. Hot follow-up to 'You Really Got Me'." *Cash Box* tags it as Pick Of The Week, describing "a similarly styled raunchy-rocker that should flip the teeners. Shel Talmy produced the lid [A-side]". *Variety* calls it "a hard rhythm number which the British combo belts out in characteristic dissonant style". No doubt designed as a spoiler, just a week ago Cameo Records reissued The Kinks' weak-by-comparison debut single 'Long Tall Sally' in the US. Released at the same time in the US is The Who's heavily Kinks-influenced debut 'I Can't Explain'.

➜ ● **RECORDING** Regent Sound Studios *central London*. Two more demos are made around this time, of **'Everybody's Gonna Be Happy'** and **'Something Better Beginning'**. The songs are assigned to publisher Kassner on December 10th, implying the demos are made on the 9th. Probably no Pye session is held until December 22nd and 23rd, which is when proper recordings of these songs are probably made. Larry Page often works up demos of new songs with the band in order to refine arrangements. Unsurprisingly, Page has since said he often preferred his demos to Talmy's finished masters.

Thursday 10th

New Theatre *Oxford*

Ray's marriage to Rasa Didzpetris is announced on the front page of her hometown newspaper, the *Bradford Argus*. It reports she has just left St. Joseph's College and resides at 31 Howard Street in Bradford.

Friday 11th

New Theatre *Oxford*

Final date of *The Gene Pitney Show*. Larry Page drives Ray to Bradford after the show.
☆ In today's issue of *NME* the full results are published of its readers poll of the year's top artists, discs and music programmes. For the coveted Best New Group, The Kinks' 685 votes place them a distant number 2 behind The Rolling Stones (2,094 votes), followed by Manfred Mann (675 votes) and The Animals (668 votes).
For the title of British R&B Group, the Stones again take number 1 (8,682 votes) but The Kinks manage the number 4 position (2,998 votes), behind The Animals (3,297) and Manfred Mann (3,186). In the British Vocal Group category The Kinks are number 6 behind The Beatles, The Rolling Stones, The Bachelors, The Searchers, and Manfred Mann.
In Best New Disc Of The Year 'You Really Got Me' is at number 7 after The Animals' number 1 'House Of The Rising Sun', The Beatles and 'A Hard Day's Night', The Rolling Stones with 'It's All Over Now' and 'Little Red Rooster', Manfred Mann's 'Do Wah Diddy Diddy' and Dusty Springfield's 'I Just Don't Know'. The Kinks do not receive a top award, but it's important to remember that they had only two charting discs out at the time of the voting. The *NME*-sponsored concert – in effect the awards presentation for the winners of the pop paper's poll – will be held on April 11th 1965.

➜ INDICATES EVENT AROUND THIS TIME BUT WITH NO FIRM DATE

Saturday 12th

Ray Davies marries Rasa Didzpetris at St. Joseph's Church, Packington, Bradford in a traditional Lithuanian ceremony.

Dave is the best man, and while Kinks managers Robert Wace, Grenville Collins and Larry Page along with publicist Brian Sommerville attend, neither Quaife nor Avory are present – or evidently invited. The couple is given three days off from Kink duties following the wedding, which they spend in Exeter. Upon their return Ray and Rasa rent an attic flat in Muswell Hill, north London, as their first residence.

Wednesday 16th – Thursday 17th

❏ **TV** Haliford Studio, Shepperton Film Studios, *Shepperton, Middx.* ABC **Shindig!** live performance 'You Really Got Me', 'All Day And All Of The Night', 'Beautiful Delilah', 'I'm A Lover Not A Fighter' broadcast January 20th 1965 and September 1st 1965. The Kinks reconvene at this studio complex not too far from London in order to film various appearances for the top American TV music show of the day, *Shindig!*.

The filming is produced by Leon Mirrell who is in London to shoot a series of black-and-white inserts for future episodes of this popular new weekly rock'n'roll show hosted by Los Angeles DJ Jimmy O'Neil. Sparked by the success of The Beatles and the British Invasion, the American networks for a short while give rock'n'roll primetime slots. The *Shindig!* show, which is based in Los Angeles, will often undertake filming in London, shooting popular British acts who would otherwise be unable to appear.

On a simple soundstage The Kinks are filmed performing four numbers, and it is notable that they are actually performing rather than the customary lip-synching. The two hits are aired a month later, on January 20th 1965, marking The Kinks' debut on US television and the first opportunity for US fans of their two records to match a visual image to the sounds. While neither performance can quite match the power of the studio recordings, they are real, exciting, and very close.

The two further numbers, 'Beautiful Delilah' and 'I'm A Lover Not A Fighter', are both sung by Dave, revealing the band's rock'n'roll roots as well as Dave's own appeal to the teenage audience. These final two clips are not shown until September 1st 1965.

The inserts are introduced by host Jimmy O'Neil with mock amazement: "They have shoulder length hair … no wonder they're called The Kinks!" Films of this entire series of programmes survive and this appearance will be widely re-broadcast, including video releases in the 1980s.

✫ On the 16th a show is scheduled but likely cancelled at the Corn Exchange, Bristol, as is a show on the 17th at the Pavilion Theatre, Llandudno, Wales.

Friday 18th

Poplar Baths *Poplar, east London* with Manfred Mann, The Falcons, The Prospectors
A scheduled date at the Crystal Ballroom, Shotton, Flints, Wales, is cancelled.

Saturday 19th

❏ **TV** BBC Television Centre (Studio 4) *west London.* BBC-1 **Top Of The Pops '64** lip-synch 'You Really Got Me' broadcast December 24th.

Sunday 20th

The Celebrity Club *central London* 8:00pm, with Cops'n'Robbers

Monday 21st

Probably a rehearsal takes place today for the upcoming recording session. The band evidently receives the required inoculation shots for their world tour, causing some illness the following day.

Tuesday 22nd – Wednesday 23rd

● **RECORDING** Pye Studios (No.2) *central London.* These two days see work begin on the band's next LP, with masters completed of '**Ev'rybody's Gonna Be Happy**', '**Something Better Beginning**', '**Who'll Be The Next In Line**' and '**Come On Now**'. Ray is at the piano rather than on guitar for the first three and completes doubled-tracked lead vocals. On 'Ev'rybody's Gonna Be Happy', done in three takes, assorted girlfriends (probably Nicola and Eileen) and a wife (Rasa) contribute handclaps. Shel Talmy is producing.

A surviving partial session tape reveals that eight takes are attempted to get the final backing track for 'Who'll Be The Next In Line'. A lead vocal overdub is done in a single take and a doubled lead vocal in two, resulting in the finished recording. 'Come On Now' has Ray moving over to second guitar, and the backing track is done in five takes. Dave's lead vocal and the backing vocals, including Ray, Pete and Rasa, are completed together in four takes.

Demos were done earlier in the month for 'Ev'rybody's Gonna Be Happy' and 'Something Better Beginning', but only two other songs, 'Come On Now' and 'Who'll Be The Next In Line', were assigned with Kassner at this time (on the 23rd) implying that no other original material is ready now. It is likely that all these titles except 'Come On Now' were contenders for possible A-sides. (When 'Something Better Beginning' is rejected in February 1965 it is handed to The Honeycombs.) With the band about to leave for an extended period of time it is no doubt considered prudent at least to try to have the next single – the one after 'Tired Of Waiting For You'– in the can and ready. The implication may even be that the second LP was expected to be essentially complete at this time but, because there is not enough new material ready, the full LP sessions are stalled until immediately following the upcoming Australian tour.

Thursday 24th

New Century Hall *Manchester* 7:30-11:45pm, with Just Four Men, The Factotums, DJ Peter Doyle
The band has Christmas Day and Boxing Day off.

✫ US dates negotiated in October for The Kinks to appear as part of Murray The K's Xmas Show were tentatively announced but the appearances eventually cancelled. The show runs from December 25th to January 3rd at the Fox Theater, Brooklyn, New York City with Chuck Jackson, Ben E. King, The Drifters, The Shirelles, The Shangri-Las, Dionne Warwick, The Zombies, Patti LaBelle & The Bluebelles, and others. Ultimately, The Nashville Teens and The Hullabaloos are added to the final Kink-less line-up.

Sunday 27th

The Whitehall *East Grinstead, Sussex*

Monday 28th

Eltham Baths *Eltham, south-east London*

Tuesday 29th

● **RECORDING** IBC Studios *central London.* The Kinks shift again to IBC where '**Don't Ever Change**' is put down on tape and may be considered as another potential single. But the song that was set aside from the album sessions (see August 24th) and earmarked as the next single, '**Tired Of Waiting For You**', is given some fattening-up today as Dave overdubs its distinctive sliding chord figure. Two further backing tracks are supposedly done at this time but no other original titles are assigned to Kassner Music, so titles are unknown (though '**Don't Ever Change**' is assigned to Kassner on December 30th). Too late to issue a press release, management phones around with news for this week's pop papers that 'Tired Of Waiting For You' will be the new Kinks single.

✫ A scheduled concert in Nottingham tonight is cancelled.

kinks'65

Wednesday 30th
Town Hall *Stourbridge, Worcs*

Thursday 31st
❏ **TV** BBC Television Centre (Studio 3) *west London*. BBC-2 **Beat In The New...** live performance 'You Really Got Me', 'It's Alright'.
❏ **TV** Television House *central London*. ATV **The New Year Starts Here** lip-synch 'All Day And All Of The Night'.
The Kinks do double TV detail on this important viewing night. They

report to BBC producer Barry Langford for a rehearsal at 9:30am and by early afternoon videotape live performances for a special 90-minute year-end edition of *Beat Room* aired this same night. Later they head over to the ATV studios in Kingsway, central London where they lip-synch to 'All Day And All Of The Night' on a special New Year's edition of *Ready Steady Go!* that airs from 11:05pm to midnight. To top off the day, it is Quaife's 21st birthday. The pop press captures him backstage at the BBC pouring champagne and posing with the Beat Beat Room girls, revelling in his new found glory and smoking a cigar.

1965

Arguably this was the defining year of The Kinks' entire career. All the elements for success had been set in place in 1964, and now the band's commercial fortunes quickly reached a peak – and then a long battle began to regain control of their own destiny. The initial crisis came as the band arrived home from a world tour that put them in a similar league to The Rolling Stones, a band second only to The Beatles in world pop domination. The band's management teams and record producers were also in conflict among themselves, heightening the confusion. Mid-year, following a legendarily disastrous tour of the United States, The Kinks began the long process of purging the "winning team" of 1964 that had helped put them in the spotlight. First they broke one of their management contracts, then they signed a publishing deal that brought them into further conflict with the existing publishing arrangement.

At the centre of all the uproar was Ray, clearly at odds with the traditional rules of showbiz success. Despite any image created to the contrary, acts like The Beatles and Rolling Stones were generally considered reliable outfits to do business with. But The Kinks proceeded to self-destruct their way around the world, largely fuelled by complete irreverence if not outright contempt for the entertainment business. In the process they alienated promoters, union officials, hotel keepers, and sometimes even their own fans. Perhaps they were breaking down at least some of the less desirable aspects of the game, to the benefit of the rock'n'rollers who followed. Even more so than today, young artists were exploited and worked liked dogs, and at the end of the day had little to show for it.

Ray in particular proved to be a curious combination of tremendous creativity and fierce competitiveness, allowing The Kinks' career to last almost four decades. They were a talented lot, and willing to fight to do things their own way, even if that was sometimes at the expense of their own advancement. In his later book, X-Ray, Ray characterised this pivotal year as "an age of blind reckless innocence", one that would be followed by "an era fraught with litigation, emotional turmoil and paranoia".

January

Friday 1st
California Ballroom *Dunstable* with Linda Laine & The Sinners

Saturday 2nd
Doubled-booked for Adelphi Ballroom, West Bromwich, Staffs and

Smethwick Baths, Smethwick, Staffs – but both shows are rescheduled at short notice to February 27th. Today was probably kept as time off or cleared to make room for another (unknown) booking.

Sunday 3rd
❏ **TV** Alpha Television Studios *Aston, Birmingham*. ABC **Thank Your Lucky Stars** lip-synch 'Tired Of Waiting For You' broadcast January 9th. There is almost certainly a concert date today, details unknown.

Monday 4th

Bath Pavillion *Bath* Teenbeat Dance

Wednesday 6th

❏ **TV** Playhouse Theatre (Studio A) *Manchester*. BBC-1 *Top Of The Pops* lip-synch 'Tired Of Waiting For You' broadcast January 21st/28th and February 4th/11th. Flying north to the BBC, today is spent videotaping two inserts of next week's new single (presumably with different backdrops and attire) for use by the BBC on *Top Of The Pops* while the band is abroad on the upcoming world tour. The BBC pays the band's airfare of £4/17/- each (£4.85, about $13.50 then, around £55 or $80 in today's money). The evening is probably occupied with a performance in the Manchester area, details unconfirmed.

Thursday 7th

Royal Hall *Harrogate, Yorks* 6:30 & 8:30pm, with Rocking Al Oliver, Small Paul & The Young Ones, The Rocking Barrons, Melanie Waters, compère: Barry Dean
❏ **TV** Playhouse Theatre *Manchester*. BBC-1 *Top Of The Pops* lip-synch 'Tired Of Waiting For You'.

Friday 8th

Spa Royal Hall *Bridlington, Yorks* 8:00pm-6:30am *All Night Ball*, with ten local bands
The *Bridlington Free Press* reports that 2,000 attend this show. Tonight is likely one of the inspirations for Ray Davies's 1970 song 'Lola'. He later referred to an "early gig in Bridlington" where he may have been a victim of mistaken sexual identity. Something similar will happen to manager Robert Wace in a nightclub in Paris in April this year.

Saturday 9th

Tower Ballroom *New Brighton, Wallesey, Ches* with Small Paul & The Young Ones, Vince Earl & The Talismen, The Adds
The Kinks are interviewed by *Mersey Beat* reporter Jeff Rigby, who asks about the pop scene. Quaife has some insight, saying: "It's such a rat race, you've got to be a rat!"

Sunday 10th

A booking at the Palais in Peterborough, Northants is rescheduled for March 13th. No doubt this is to give the band some time off with their families before the world tour begins in a few days.

Monday 11th

Today seems to be set aside for a day-long series of interviews at publicist Brian Sommerville's office on Charing Cross Road in central London. Among others, Quaife is interviewed by *Record Mirror* and says that "we've got a new LP coming out in a couple of months. We've already cut a few tracks for it. It'll be better than our last LP, although we didn't think that was too bad, considering how rushed it was ... We hope to make [the new one] varied". The whole band is interviewed by Keith Altham for the *NME* and they talk, not surprisingly, about the new single and the upcoming trip to Australia. Speaking to Laurie Henshaw in *Disc Weekly* they enthuse about the American leg, where Dave Davies wants to see the Empire State Building, and Quaife hopes to fly over the Grand Canyon. Ray is silent on this subject, only showing excitement at the prospect of visiting his sister Rose in Adelaide, Australia, where he's been told that it's "sunshine all the time".

Tuesday 12th

The band travels from London to Paris today where they are interviewed at Europa Studios for the French radio programme *Musicorama*. A brief first tour of Sweden had originally been set for January 12th-14th but is pushed back until the beginning of March in favour of a French TV offer (see following).

Wednesday 13th – Thursday 14th

❏ **TV** on location *Marseille, France* and on-board USS Saratoga. ORTF *Dim-Dam-Dom* lip-synch 'You Really Got Me', 'All Day And All Of The Night' broadcast probably March 7th. This French television programme will also be submitted as France's entry for the Montreux TV Festival, to be held this coming May. Filming is done both on the streets of Marseille and off-shore in the Mediterranean aboard an American battleship, the USS Saratoga. The band and film crew are shuttled by helicopter to the ship, where they are staged to play along to their two hit records. At the insistence of the ship's captain, The Kinks perform an impromptu mini-concert on the top deck for the ship's crew of approximately 4,000 seamen, playing two or three songs with makeshift equipment on hand. The band is shuttled back to land by ferry only after they are almost forced to remain due to rough weather conditions – which would have meant a side trip to Egypt.

Friday 15th

❏ **TV** Television House (Studio 9) *central London*. ATV *Ready Steady Go!* lip-synch 'Tired Of Waiting For You'. A busy day even by Kinks standards. The band travels in the morning from Marseilles to London where they are interviewed by the pop press, including Keith Altham (*NME*) and Laurie Henshaw (*Disc Weekly*). During the mid-afternoon rehearsal for the evening's broadcast they are further interviewed and photographed for Liverpool's *Combo Musical Weekly* and no doubt a growing line of reporters. For the *Ready Steady Go!* appearance the band has acquired a new set of stage jackets, bottle green rather than the red ones they've been using since last spring.
'Tired Of Waiting For You' / 'Come On Now' single released in the UK. It is met with almost unanimous praise in the pop press.
　　Also out is the first serious challenge to The Kinks' sound, by the former High Numbers, now billed as The Who. Their debut single is 'I Can't Explain', produced by Shel Talmy, and it borrows heavily from the sound achieved on The Kinks' first two hits. The Who's single will do well (it reaches number 8 in the UK) and launches a spectacular career that eventually outshines the commercial success of The Kinks and produces another acclaimed British songwriter in Pete Townshend. This is the first time The Kinks' sound has been copied outright – and by their own producer, no less. While The Who would quickly move to define their own sound in their own way, their record's success will certainly add to The Kinks' desire to shift from their formula sound. 'Tired Of Waiting For You', out today, already marks a departure from the chunky rock sound with which they launched their career, a fact not lost on the *NME*'s reviewer: "Change of character for The Kinks sees a departure from their raucous broken-beat approach ... more subdued – really it's a rock ballad with a slow shake-shuffle beat. Very nice it is too!"

Saturday 16th

Day off in London. Ray implies later in *X-Ray* that work is done on the new LP at this time. A quick session is possible, details unknown.
➪ **TOUR STARTS** Australasia/Singapore/Hong Kong Tour (Jan 20th – Feb 8th). Line-up: Ray Davies (lead vocal, guitar), Dave Davies (guitar, vocal), Pete Quaife (bass), Mick Avory (drums). The Australian segment is promoted by Aztec Services Pty and Stadiums Pty, through London agent Cyril Berlin, and in New Zealand by Kerridge Odeon in association with Aztec Services.
　　As the band departs from London Airport for their trip around the world they have two top-ten hits under their belts, and what will be their third chart-topper, 'Tired Of Waiting For You', was issued only days before in the UK. To maintain their media presence in England during their absence a number of prime radio and TV appearances plugging the song have already been taped and, as a safety measure, two further separate inserts have been filmed for the BBC's weekly TV chart programme, *Top Of The Pops*. All this is aimed to preserve their

Tired Of Waiting For You single

A 'Tired of Waiting For You' (R. DAVIES).
B 'Come On Now' (R. DAVIES).

UK release January 15th 1965 (Pye 7N 15759).
US release around February 24th 1965 (Reprise 0347).
Musicians Ray Davies lead vocal (A), electric guitar. Dave Davies electric guitar, backing vocal, lead vocal (B). Pete Quaife bass guitar. Bobby Graham drums (A). Mick Avory drums (B).
Recorded Pye Studios (No.2) central London. A: probably August 25th 1964, with guitar overdubbed at IBC Studios, central London December 29th 1964; 3-track mixed to mono. B: December 22nd & 23rd 1964; 1-track to 1-track mono.
Producer Shel Talmy (for Shel Talmy Productions).
Engineer Bob Auger.
Chart high UK number 1; US number 6.

presence for the competitive, fickle pop audience while the tour continues.

A promotional visit to the US is included as part of the tour – pending approval of work visas – and will also allow the band their first taste of the American experience.

Furthermore, the Australian trip is symbolic for the brothers Davies who, while in Adelaide, will be able to visit their recently-emigrated sister Rose and her family. When the family left last year, The Kinks were barely getting by after two failed singles had left them waiting to make it or quit. But the August 1964 release of 'You Really Got Me' had completely changed their fortunes.

Now the brothers are able to make a triumphant visit halfway around the world as international stars, an almost unimaginable dream for them just eight months earlier. The trip is as much a victory and a cause of celebration for the Davies family, and The Kinks are seen off at the airport by many of their relatives. Significantly, none of the band's business handlers (Robert Wace, Grenville Collins, Larry Page) accompany the band. Instead, booking agent Arthur Howes sent his own drill sergeant-like Johnny Clapson as the man in charge of the tour.

The first leg of the trip on Air India takes the band to Moscow for refuelling, and the passengers are allowed off the plane for a stretch – but only after armed guards collect all passports. The band are used to being magnets for controversy, so it's no surprise that Quaife is forced back on to the plane at gunpoint after making a wisecrack about Premier Kruschev. The flight continues to New Delhi and then Bombay for an evening stopover.

Monday 18th

The entourage is put up at the Sun 'n' Sands Hotel in Bombay, and Ray has since cited the six-hour overnight stopover as the source of his inspiration for 'See My Friends', which is at least conceived and partially written during this tour. Ray has often recalled since the sight of local fishermen reeling in their nets in the early morning hours as the visual catalyst for the song. Following the brief rest stop, the journey continues with refuelling stops in Madras, then Singapore, and finally on to Perth on the west coast of Australia.

Tuesday 19th

In typically sarcastic language of the day, Perth's *Herald* is scarcely able to conceal adult contempt for the adolescent pop stars. "Fifteen of Britain's noisiest entertainers arrived in Perth early today... in silence,"

ran the report. "After 34 hours in the air, The Honeycombs, The Kinks and the Manfred Mann group were all pale and tired. They were too exhausted even to get out among their fans." Everyone has a full night's sleep to prepare for the start of a string of shows across the imposing continent.

For the Australian dates The Kinks appear just before Manfred Mann, in effect second on the bill. Manfred Mann are about level with The Kinks' chart success, having hit big with 'Do Wah Diddy Diddy' and 'Sha La La', but tip the scale as tour headliners because of their ascension to the charts just before The Kinks hit with 'You Really Got Me'. By the time the tour ends, The Kinks will have raced ahead of Manfred Mann in the charts, returning to England at the peak of their initial commercial success. They will have claimed three smashes in a row, putting them in line to challenge the mighty Rolling Stones. The Stones are also on tour in Australia at this time on a competing package show that features US singer Roy Orbison, and The Newbeats.

Wednesday 20th

Capitol Theatre *Perth, Western Australia, Australia* 6:00 & 8:45pm, *The Big Show*, with Manfred Mann (headliners), The Honeycombs, Tony Sheveton, Tony Worsley & The Blue Jays
The Kinks' filmed appearance on *Shindig!* is aired tonight in the US (see December 16th-17th 1964) where they are introduced by host Jimmy O'Neil in mock shock: "They have shoulder length hair ... no wonder they're called The Kinks!" Also on: The Rolling Stones, The Dave Clark Five, Petula Clark, Gerry & The Pacemakers. This is the televisual event that in effect started this book.

Thursday 21st

Centennial Hall *Wayville, Adelaide, South Australia, Australia* 6:00 & 8:45pm, *The Big Show*, with Manfred Mann (headliners), The Honeycombs, Tony Sheveton, Tony Worsley & The Blue Jays
Both shows in this 2,500-capacity venue are sell-outs. The reviewer for Adelaide's *Advertiser* thinks The Kinks rely on their clothes, hairstyles and some remarkable acrobatic feats to win the audience's approval. Their stage outfits are described as green jackets, grey tapered trousers, yellow ruffled shirts, and red socks. It is also noted that "the acoustics were as poor as usual in the Centennial Hall, and with the amplifiers turned to full volume, and the singers and bands performing as loudly as possible, a high-pitched microphone whistling persisted for the full two hours".

Upon arrival in Adelaide earlier in the day, the Davies brothers are reunited at the Grand Hotel with their sister Rose, her husband Arthur and son Terry. After the day's show the brothers visited Rose's semi-detached home in a "designed community", a village called Little Elizabeth, just outside Adelaide. This was Ray's inspiration for the song 'Shangri-la' and the album *Arthur*.

Friday 22nd

Festival Hall *Melbourne, Victoria, Australia* 8:30pm, *The Big Show*, with Manfred Mann (headliners), The Honeycombs, Tony Sheveton, Tony Worsley & The Blue Jays
The bands are greeted at Essendon Airport by about 1,000 screaming teens. After a brief press conference at the airport's VIP room they are shuttled off in an airport bus to the Southern Cross Hotel.

Saturday 23rd

Festival Hall *Melbourne, Victoria, Australia* 8:30pm, *The Big Show*, with Manfred Mann (headliners), The Honeycombs, Tony Sheveton, Tony Worsley & The Blue Jays

Sunday 24th

A day off for the band, and sister Rose visits again, flying in from

Adelaide for the day. Ray is writing 'This Strange Effect' around now, as well as 'See My Friends' and some songs that would end up on *Kinda Kinks*. He is probably feeling pressure to have new material ready for the recording sessions booked to start the day of their return to London. Fly to Brisbane following day, with brief press conference at the airport before heading to Lennon's Hotel, where the Stones are also holed up.

Tuesday 26th

Festival Hall *Brisbane, Queensland, Australia* 8:30pm, *The Big Show*, with Manfred Mann (headliners), The Honeycombs, Tony Sheveton, Tony Worsley & The Blue Jays

While The Rolling Stones perform two shows again tonight at the smaller Brisbane City Hall, The Big Show features a single two-hour performance in this almost-sold-out 5,400-capacity hall. Brisbane's *Courier* reports that more than 30 teenagers had to be physically removed from the stage in attempts to attack and hug their favourite artists.

Wednesday 27th

Century Theatre *Broadmeadow, Newcastle, New South Wales, Australia* 8:30pm, *The Big Show*, with Manfred Mann (headliners), The Honeycombs, Tony Sheveton, Tony Worsley & The Blue Jays

The entourage flies from Brisbane to Newcastle and is scheduled for a 2:30pm press conference in the lounge of the Great Northern Hotel. In downtown Brisbane however the groups are besieged by up to 2,000 fans requiring 15 extra policemen to control the mob and escort the bus to the hotel. Some 300 teenagers have gathered there and caused a disturbance, delaying the band's entry to the hotel for over an hour, after which the scheduled press conference eventually gets underway. A typical highlight of the event is quoted in the *Newcastle Morning Herald*: "When one shaggy youth was asked if he was one of The Kinks, he replied, 'Find out and ask again.' He was." (Fly from Newcastle to Sydney day following.)

Friday 29th – Saturday 30th

Sydney Stadium *Sydney, New South Wales, Australia* 8:30pm, *The Big Show*, with Manfred Mann (headliners), The Honeycombs, Tony Sheveton, Tony Worsley & The Blue Jays

Sunday 31st

Although a day off, a photo session at Sydney's famed Bondi Beach is staged where The Kinks are perversely photographed in their winter-travel clothing in the scorching Australian summer heat. No would-be surfing poses here. The photo will run in the February 5th *NME* back home as a reminder to the British pop audience of The Kinks' whereabouts as they race up the charts once again. A party is held tonight for the Australian band Tony Worsley & The Blue Jays who end the tour here. In a contemporary press report in *Disc Weekly*, Dave reveals that tonight he is taught hypnotism by Paul Shannon of The Blue Jays. Dave later reveals in his book *Kink* that tonight he successfully hypnotises a girl but never bothers to bring her out again. The band flies out of Sydney the following morning for the first of their New Zealand dates.

February

Monday 1st

Town Hall *Auckland, North Island, New Zealand* 6:00 & 8:30pm, *The Big Show*, with Manfred Mann (headliners), The Honeycombs (headliners), Tony Sheveton, Tommy Adderley & The Merseymen

Tuesday 2nd

Founder's Theatre *Hamilton, North Island, New Zealand* 6:00 & 8:30pm, *Swingin' 65*, with Manfred Mann (headliners), The Honeycombs (headliners), Tony Sheveton, Tommy Adderley & The Merseymen

Wednesday 3rd

Town Hall *Wellington, North Island, New Zealand* 6:00 & 8:30pm, *Swingin' 65*, with Manfred Mann (headliners), The Honeycombs (headliners), Tony Sheveton, Tommy Adderley & The Merseymen

The band flies in to Wellington Airport this afternoon where a straight-faced local reporter asks Dave if he ever wears his hair in a bow like the fashionable London mods. Dave dryly replies, "You're joking." After the evening's performances to capacity crowds, it is time for Dave's 18th birthday celebration back at the Royal Oak Hotel, no doubt a night to remember. Manfreds singer Paul Jones later recalls this evening as among the wildest on the tour, with the power cut by the theatre management during his band's performance in an effort to subdue the crowd's apparently boundless enthusiasm.

Thursday 4th

Majestic Theatre *Christchurch, South Island, New Zealand* 6:00 & 8:30pm, *Swingin' 65*, with Manfred Mann (headliners), The Honeycombs (headliners), Tony Sheveton, Tommy Adderley & The Merseymen

The earlier show begins as scheduled but within minutes the house PA system fails and after an hour's attempt to repair it the entire first show is cancelled. An angry and disappointed crowd is turned away and promised either a refund or a ticket for another upcoming pop show. The second show continues as planned after the PA system is replaced with another. The Kinks at the second show earn a shower of screams, streamers and sweets. Songs include 'All Day And All of the Night', 'You Really Got Me', and 'Long Tall Shorty'. The Honeycombs finish the tour now, moving on to Japan where they are hugely popular.

Friday 5th

The Kinks and the Manfreds fly back to Sydney and then on to Hong Kong the following morning. On the way they learn that *Melody Maker* lists 'Tired Of Waiting For You' at number 2 in the charts, beating the competing 'Come Tomorrow' by Manfred Mann. It's also around now that Quaife is informed by phone that they have in fact reached number 1 in the upcoming but still unavailable issue, though without evidence the others consider his claim to be premature. Quaife's inside scoop will be confirmed in a few days.

Saturday 6th

Hong Kong Football Club Stadium *Hong Kong* 7:00pm, *Big Beat 1965*, with Manfred Mann (headliners), D'Swooners, Tony Myatt, The Kontinentals

According to the *Tiger Standard*, pandemonium breaks loose as a crowd of 2,000 teens throw seating mats, orange peel and paper cups at Manfred Mann during their first show. The Kinks and the rest of the performers apparently go on without incident. Around this time, The Kinks receive notice of the arrival of their visas for the proposed end-of-tour US visit. While the Manfreds will return to London directly after the Singapore shows of the next few days, The Kinks head on eastward, completing what will be a round-the-world trip.

Sunday 7th – Monday 8th

Singapore Badminton Stadium *Singapore* 6:15 & 9:15pm, *Goodwood's Kong Hee Fatt Choy Show*, with Manfred Mann (headliners), The Crescendos, Frantic Fran, The Dutch Swing College Band

The bands stay at the luxurious Goodwood Hotel, sponsors of the concert. Later in *X-Ray* Ray describes the hotel as "one of the great symbols of the old empire". It is evidently on Monday that Ray receives a telegram from London informing him that 'Tired Of Waiting For You' has indeed reached the number 1 spot in the upcoming issue of *Melody Maker* (out on Thursday, but chart positions are calculated and known to the industry as early as the Sunday before). While other band members are busy partying, Ray orders a bottle of champagne and, half way around the world, enjoys a moment to savour his accomplishments.

Tuesday 9th

The Kinks leave Singapore and head for Honolulu via Saigon (Vietnam), Manila (Philippines) and the Island of Guam, crossing the international dateline and in effect travelling 24 hours but arriving the same day they leave. After the one-hour stopover in Vietnam their plane is escorted back into the air by American fighter planes as a precaution against local hostilities in the escalating conflict. The band perhaps plays an impromptu show at a small location at Honolulu International Airport. There is also a brief stopover in San Francisco, providing the band's first taste of California, and perhaps a radio interview. They then head on to New York via Chicago.

Wednesday 10th

The Kinks arrive in New York City and are met by Marvin Deane, head of artist relations at Reprise Records, and George Lee, the company's Eastern Operations director. They are ushered around the city where they visit writers at trade paper offices and DJs at various radio stations. Tonight and the following nights the band visits various nightspots, including the legendary Peppermint Lounge and the Copa Club. They also see avant-garde jazz legend Ornette Coleman perform. The band is ultimately discouraged from travelling up to Harlem where they wanted to catch some of their favourite "coloured acts".

Thursday 11th

Rehearsals are held at NBC Studios (Studio 8H) in Rockefeller Plaza, New York City, for the following day's taping of the network music variety programme *Hullabaloo*.

Friday 12th

❒ **TV** NBC Television Studios (Studio 8H) *New York, NY*. NBC *Hullabaloo* lip-synch 'You Really Got Me', 'All Day And All Of The Night', broadcast February 16th, June 22nd. *Hullabaloo* is a weekly network all-music programme that debuted on January 12th, created to rival ABC's popular rock'n'roll offering *Shindig!*. The New York-based show is notable for broadcasting in colour, still unusual at the time; few other youth-oriented shows are afforded such luxury. The Kinks segment cleverly features the band in a city back-alley, with Ray planted on a garbage can to hide his foot which is swollen from an insect bite inflicted while in Singapore earlier in the week. The show's producers are apparently angered by the fact that during a cameo spot in the taping Ray and Avory do a cheek-to-cheek dance instead of the rehearsed routine. In the final airing they refrain, suggesting a retake was done. Ever embroiled in controversy, the band at least initially refuses to join the American Federation of Television & Recording Artists (AFTRA) for this appearance, which will cause problems with the union later in the year during their first proper US tour.

Saturday 13th

The band needs to get back to London to record. The original plan, perhaps before the recording session was booked, was to return to London on the 16th. Indeed, filming in Los Angeles for the network TV program *Shindig!* was pencilled in for today and tomorrow, but this fails to materialise. These final two days are also mentioned as possible concert dates, but these too do not happen.

Sunday 14th

The Kinks arrive at London Airport today, with 'Tired Of Waiting For You' topping the charts, their third major hit in a row. They are now characterised in the music press as neck-to-neck with The Rolling Stones in the battle for the coveted spot behind the invincible Beatles as the leading British band. Having been away for an entire month, they face a tough schedule of work, including the immediate completion of an album (*Kinda Kinks*) in addition to the non-stop round of radio, TV, press, and concert appearances. Rather than continue into the regular whirlwind of a chart-topping pop act, the band begins a long, slow and somewhat haphazard process of rebellion against the star-making machinery, challenging every business arrangement put in place for them, and in the process staking out their idiosyncratic musical destiny.

Monday 15th – Wednesday 17th

● **RECORDING** Pye Studios (No.2) *central London*. While Ray sees a specialist for treatment of his foot bite on Monday morning, the others continue press duties, including interviews with Keith Altham for *NME*, mostly recounting stories of their world tour. Dave says: "You could say we complained our way around the world." Rod Harrod concludes in *Disc Weekly* that complaining is all part of the latest Kinks scheme to "drive people out of their minds".

Recording sessions continue over three days. Road manager Brian Longstaff is sent around London music shops to buy a 12-string electric guitar for the sessions for Dave, but comes back empty-handed. The sessions are devoted to completing work on all tracks for the new LP, scheduled for release in just two weeks time, on March 5th. Tracks recorded are: **'So Long'**, **'Look For Me Baby'**, **'Nothin' In This World (Can Stop Me Worryin' 'Bout That Girl)'**, **'Got My Feet On The Ground'**, **'Wonder Where My Baby Is Tonight'**, **'Naggin'**, and **'You Shouldn't Be Sad'**. Recorded apparently in desperation on the final day is a cover of the Martha & The Vandellas hit **'Dancin' In The Street'**. Two backing tracks reportedly made at IBC Studios on December 29th 1964 may be used among the tracks completed now.

Thursday 18th

❒ **TV** Playhouse Theatre *Manchester*. BBC-1 **Top Of The Pops** lip-synch 'Tired Of Waiting For You'. The Kinks are present on the set this time after four consecutive recorded inserts (two inserts, both repeated) were shown in their absence.
Plaza Ballroom *Manchester* 7:00-11:00pm, with Fitz & Startz
The Kinks resume their concert schedule. Upon leaving the building they are mobbed so fiercely by the crowd that all are bruised and shaken. Quaife describes the scene as being like World War II. It is later suggested that the mobbing was partially "allowed" to happen for publicity purposes, and it does provide the band with national press coverage. But it also makes the band aware of their physical vulnerability now they have reached a Beatles-like level of popularity.

Friday 19th

❒ **TV** ABC Television Centre *Birmingham*. ABC **Thank Your Lucky Stars** lip-synch 'Tired Of Waiting For You', broadcast February 20th.
Hillside Ballroom *Hereford* 8:00pm-12:00midnight, with The Roadhogs
After a routine television taping the band presses on to tonight's show, where a crowd of 900 appreciative teens is considered tame by the *Hereford Evening News* reporter in contrast to previous crowds.
☆ With The Kinks at the peak of their commercial appeal, two related singles are released in the UK today. 'Revenge' / 'Raunchy' is the debut single by Scottish big-band The Ray McVay Sound, a Larry Page production with the A-side a Ray Davies composition that becomes the latest new theme song for *Ready Steady Go!*. 'She Just Satisfies' / 'Keep Moving' is Jimmy Page's first 45, released with ads in the music

weeklies that mention his work on Kinks sessions. Neither single makes the charts.

Saturday 20th

Main Hall, Subscription Rooms *Stroud, Gloucs* 8:00-11:30pm, with The Roadhogs
Promoter Bill Reid doubles the normal entrance fee from 5/- to 10/- in an effort to keep the crowd size to a controllable level. The band performs two 30-minute shows with 650 attendance. Extra police are brought in for crowd control – which mostly consists of preventing screaming girls from getting onto the stage. Fainting girls are routinely carried away. The band's fee is reported as £300. (Day off in London following.)

Monday 22nd

Eltham Baths *Eltham, south-east London*

Tuesday 23rd

Olympia Theatre *Paris, France* with Johnny Rivers, and unidentified French singer
Among the entourage of 12 making this quick visit are manager Larry Page and Rasa, arriving at Le Bourget Airport at 1:00pm. During the afternoon the band is interviewed for the French radio programme *Salut les Copains* at Europe Studio No.1 in Paris. *NME* reporter (and future Kinks publicist) Keith Altham is one of those along for the trip, interviewing them individually for four separate forthcoming articles. The concert is initially marred by the promoter's poor excuse for amplification equipment which the band deems useless during rehearsal. Replacement amps are found but The Kinks' appearance is in jeopardy until the last minute. Everyone is disappointed by the disorganisation and the poor accommodation provided. But the concert, attended by 2,400, goes well. "The Kinks chalked up yet another success for Britain at Paris Olympia where they topped the bill," says *Melody Maker*. "Despite the handicap of inadequate amplifiers they stormed through a programme of six numbers and left a packed house clamouring for more." The set-list is reported as 'Bye Bye Johnny', 'You Really Got Me', 'Long Tall Shorty', 'All Day And All Of The Night' and 'Tired Of Waiting For You', plus one other song, all of which are taped and broadcast on Europe 1 Radio's weekly Sunday programme *Musicorama* on the 28th.

Wednesday 24th

❒ **TV** ORTF Studios *Paris, France*. ORTF channel 1 *Discorama* lip-synch (probably) 'Tired Of Waiting For You' broadcast 26th 12:30-1:15pm. This popular weekly French TV programme is hosted by Denise Glaser.
'Tired Of Waiting For You' / 'Come On Now' single released in the US this week.

Thursday 25th

Olympia Theatre *Reading* with The Dawn Breakers
The band travels from Paris to London early this morning and almost immediately on to this evening's concert appearance.

Friday 26th

))) **RADIO** Playhouse Theatre *central London*. BBC Light Programme *Joe Loss Pop Show* live performance 'Come On Now', 'Tired Of Waiting For You', 'All Day And All Of The Night', 'Naggin'', rehearsals from 9.30am, broadcast 1:00-3:00pm.
Town Hall *Lydney, Gloucs* 9:00pm-12:30am, with The Roadhogs
'Just Can't Go To Sleep' single by Formula One (from Birmingham) produced by Larry Page released in the UK on Warner Brothers. This is a song by Ray Davies, part of a bid by The Kinks' manager to maintain a steady stream of recorded Davies compositions.

Saturday 27th

Adelphi Ballroom *West Bromwich, Staffs* 8:45pm
Smethwick Baths *Smethwick, Staffs* 10:15pm
This pair of ballrooms in the Birmingham area is routinely double-booked for many bands at the time.

Sunday 28th

Possibly a concert this evening at an unconfirmed university, perhaps with Downliners Sect and Manfred Mann.

March

Monday 1st

Student Union, University of Manchester *Manchester* with The Honeycombs
Part of the university's Rag Ball celebration, a notoriously rowdy event. Both bands are forced off stage because the audience are throwing beer bottles and pint glasses. The Kinks are never able to complete a song and finally just leave. However, sugar has been poured into the petrol tank of their car, causing further inconvenience. A press release issued today says that a Kinks/Manfred Mann tour of the UK proposed for April is abandoned after neither would accept second billing.

Tuesday 2nd – Thursday 4th

Meanwhile, a tour of Denmark, Sweden and Finland to include concerts, TV and radio, announced in mid-February and planned for March 2nd-10th, is postponed; quickly-arranged bookings fill the gaps. The Scandinavian dates eventually take place in September.

Friday 5th

Leyton Baths **Leyton, north-east London**
Crowd mania continues as Dave is mauled by over-eager fans.
Kinda Kinks album released in the UK. The band's quickly recorded second LP is rushed to the shops today. "These Londoners produce an appropriate Negroid sound in their singing, yet still have a bit of the Cockney too," writes Allen Evans in *NME*. "They take their bluesy songs with an ease that is relaxing even for beat music. They instil some charm into their work which is probably why they are so successful." In *Disc Weekly* Nigel Hunter raves most about the two folk songs, 'Nothin' In This World' and 'So Long', noting them as among Ray's best. "The rest of the tracks are goodish exercises in beatdom," he says, "with some hints of Tamla-Motown in 'Wonder'." *Melody Maker* thinks it's their best, "sometimes a little scrappy instrumentally but at all times it has driven the characteristically attractive arrogance in The Kinks' voices – and life".
Palais *Wimbledon, south-west London* 7:30pm
Dave is again mauled by the crowd and this time suffers delayed concussion. He is subsequently advised by doctors to take a week off from concert appearances in order to recover.

Sunday 7th – Wednesday 10th

While Dave is recuperating, a string of previously booked dates are cancelled outright or rebooked for later. The affected shows are: March 8th Top Rank Suite, Doncaster, Yorks (originally set for City Hall in Sheffield for the first of four shows with The Animals, but later Manfred Mann appear in place of The Kinks); March 9th Regent Ballroom, Brighton, Sussex; March 10th Top Rank Ballroom, Hanley, Stoke-on-Trent, Staffs; March 11th Majestic Ballroom, Luton, Beds. Unexpectedly freed-up from concert commitments, the band and management take care of some business affairs, including the incorporation of The Kinks as a limited company, intended to better handle their new-found monetary success.

Thursday 11th

The band's accountant files for the establishment of Kinks Productions Ltd, and the incorporation is routinely certified two weeks later, on March 25th. The business is apportioned with the following personnel and percentage of interest. The named directors are accountant Robert Ransom and principal managers Robert Wace (1 percent) and Grenville Collins (1 percent), with the group members' interests split between Ray Davies (24 percent), Dave Davies (24 percent), Mick Avory (25 percent) and Pete Quaife (25 percent). Despite the token interests of management, it is worth pointing out that at this point Larry Page has no representation in this venture at all, reflecting his role in the operation and foreshadowing his imminent ousting.

Meanwhile Dave, afforded some unexpected free time this week, goes hunting with Avory for that they describe as a "ravers flat" in Muswell Hill, north London. They put down money on a place in Connaught Gardens at the start of the next week. Dave is still living at home and looking to have more freedom and independence. Avory too is in theory still living at his parent's home in south London, and practically needs to be located in Muswell Hill near to the rest of the members for ease and convenience when returning home from out-of-town commitments, which by now is quite a regular occurrence. He has

been periodically staying when convenient in Muswell Hill with the Davies' sister and brother-in-law, Gwen and Brian Longstaff.

Friday 12th

Co-op Ballroom *Nuneaton, Warwicks* 5:00 & 8:30pm

Saturday 13th

Palais *Peterborough* 8:00-11:45pm

A local paper reports that the screams of the teenage girls nearly raised the roof of the Palais.

Set-list: 'Louie Louie', 'Long Tall Shorty', 'You Really Got Me', 'Tired Of Waiting For You', 'All Day And All Of The Night'.

Sunday 14th

City Hall *Newcastle Upon Tyne* 6:15 & 8:30pm, *Big Beat Night Out*, with The Animals, The Pretty Things, Screaming Lord Sutch, Dodie West, Sean Buckley & The Breadcrumbs

Melody Maker reports that Ray has his pants torn by overly excited fans during this show.

Monday 15th

Ray phones the music papers to deny a rumour about The Kinks breaking up that has apparently spread over the weekend and is reported to be a story planted by a competing band.

With the recent formation of a proper limited company for The Kinks, it seems surely to be unfounded. Quaife is asked by Mike Ledgerwood for *Disc Weekly* how they get along as a group. "Very well. We have our arguments. We even have fights! When we were in America we had a good old punch-up once. As far as we were concerned it was a damn good laugh, but everybody there thought it was for real. It just didn't mean anything. It was a blow-up for five minutes and then it was all over."

He denies the stories of a break-up. "No, definitely not! It's just one of those rumours floating around the business. When we came back from the Australian tour, word was put round by one of the big groups that Ray Davies was quitting. They said he was going to start up on his own, set up a new group. I can tell you there's absolutely no truth in it at all. We'd be mugs to split now, anyway. We want to stay at the top as long as we can, obviously."

☆ The Kinks fail to appear for a scheduled appearance on the Southern TV programme *Three Go Round* at Southern Television Studios in Southampton, Hants, due for broadcast on Thursday 18th. Although the exact taping date is unconfirmed, it's cancelled at the last minute due to Ray's refusal. "I said I won't stand for this shit any more," Ray explains much later. The show, presumably minus The Kinks, airs on ITV on Thursday this week, 5.25-5.55 pm. Ray also refuses to honour a number of interviews at the time. Later he offers this observation: "We'd had two number ones and one number two in our first four months and I wanted it to stop. I'm an introverted person and this was becoming an invasion of my privacy. I found it very difficult and dealt with it very badly. I didn't turn up for interviews, which was unheard of in those days. I ran away, basically, and it caused the band to have a dip."

Tuesday 16th

The band, likely minus Ray, is interviewed probably today at the Ideal Home Exhibition at Olympia Exposition Centre, west London for the BBC Light Programme's *Pop Inn*. Other publicity stunts around this time include a photo session around some big computers at *The Daily Mirror* newspaper offices. The Kinks pull out at the last minute from a concert tonight at Assembly Hall, Tunbridge Wells, Kent with The Dynes and Sons Of Mad. The official reason is that Ray is ill. The other three Kinks appear at the hall to apologise to an angry, disappointed crowd of 1,200.

Kinda Kinks album

A1 'Look For Me Baby' (R. DAVIES).
A2 'Got My Feet On The Ground' (D. DAVIES, R. DAVIES).
A3 'Nothin' In This World (Can Stop Me Worryin' 'Bout That Girl)' (R. DAVIES).
A4 'Naggin'' (J. WEST, J. ANDERSON).
A5 'Wonder Where My Baby Is Tonight' (R. DAVIES).
A6 'Tired Of Waiting For You' (R. DAVIES).
B1 'Dancin' In The Street' (W. STEVENSON, M. GAYE).
B2 'Don't Ever Change' (R. DAVIES).
B3 'Come On Now' (R. DAVIES).
B4 'So Long' (R. DAVIES).
B5 'You Shouldn't Be Sad' (R. DAVIES).
B6 'Something Better Beginning' (R. DAVIES).

UK release March 5th 1965 (Pye NPL 18112).
US release August 11th 1965 (Reprise R 6173 mono / RS 6158 [simulated] stereo) The US release omits 'Naggin'' and 'Come On Now', substitutes the recent A-side 'Set Me Free' in place of 'Tired of Waiting For You' (as the final song on side A) and adds 'Ev'rybody's Gonna Be Happy' as the lead-off song on side B.
Musicians Ray Davies lead vocal except as noted (see entry for Dave Davies), electric rhythm guitar, acoustic guitar (A3, B2, B4), piano (A5, B5, B6). Dave Davies lead vocal (A2, A4, A5), electric guitar, backing vocal. Pete Quaife bass guitar, backing vocal. Mick Avory drums. Rasa Davies backing vocal (A1, B1, B5, B6).
Recorded Pye Studios (No.2) central London; B6: December 22nd-23rd 1964; A1-A5; B1, B4-B5: February 15th-17th 1965. IBC Studios central London; B2: December 29th 1964; A6 & B3: see single released January 15th 1965; 1-track mono to 1-track mono.
Producer Shel Talmy (for Shel Talmy Productions).
Engineers Bob Auger; probably Glyn Johns (B2).
Chart high UK number 3.

➜ INDICATES EVENT AROUND THIS TIME BUT WITH NO FIRM DATE

Wednesday 17th

Day off in London. A concert originally scheduled for City Hall, Salisbury, Wilts with The Troggs is rescheduled for April 21st.

Thursday 18th

Locarno Ballroom *Swindon* 7:45pm, with Les Fleur De Lys
A capacity crowd composed largely of screaming and fainting girls witnesses the band's single 30-minute set.

Friday 19th

Fairfield Halls *Croydon, south London* 6:45 & 9:00pm, *Big Beat Nite Out*, with The Animals, The Pretty Things, Dodie West, Sean Buckley & The Breadcrumbs, The Caravelles
'Ev'rybody's Gonna Be Happy' / 'Who'll Be The Next In Line' single released in the UK. Although the 45 stalls in the charts, reviews are mildly positive. "Hardly their best single but of course it's a hit. Quite catchy after a couple of plays," says *Disc Weekly*, "but slightly messy and repetitive." Tony Ward of *Pop Weekly*, otherwise a passionate supporter of The Kinks, thinks it has little melody line, no feeling, and "even less of a commercial prospect than a recording of banks and braes by the Argyll and Sutherland Highlanders". Never breaking out of the top 20 in Britain, 'Ev'rybody' was at the eleventh hour rejected by Reprise Records for release now in the US. Dave says later: "We thought we'd broken new ground with 'Ev'rybody's Gonna Be Happy' which we had for a funky R&B vibe, but it wasn't a commercial success."

Saturday 20th

Starlite Green *Boston, Lincs* two shows 7:00-11:40pm, with Brian Diamond & The Cutters, The Shake
Quaife has said in the press that the band will attend tonight's debut of the Tamla-Motown Revue tour at Finsbury Park Astoria, north London, but it's more likely they go the following night.

Sunday 21st

A concert at Colston Hall, Bristol, Gloucs with The Fenmen is cancelled due to a booking dispute on the day of the show. The promoters claim an airtight contract with deposit paid in advance. The Kinks say today was long scheduled as a day off. It is more likely that the band played hooky as they evidently attend the Tamla-Motown Revue at the Hammersmith Odeon, west London, tonight, to see The Supremes, Martha & The Vandellas, Stevie Wonder, Smokey Robinson & The Miracles, and The Earl Van Dyke Six, plus for good measure Georgie Fame & The Blue Flames. The band are big fans of these artists and in particular the Earl Van Dyke backing band. Quaife later reveals to the press that they are snubbed backstage after the show.

Monday 22nd

Town Hall *Birmingham* 6:30 pm & 8:45pm, *Big Beat Nite Out*, with The Animals, The Pretty Things, Screamin' Lord Sutch, Dodie West, Sean Buckley & The Breadcrumbs

Tuesday 23rd

Ray files for the establishment of a limited company, Ray Davies (Entertainments) Ltd, in order to handle more wisely the income generated from his songwriting. The incorporation is routinely certified on April 1st. The directors named are Ray and Kinks accountant Robert Ransom. Meanwhile, tonight is likely when Dave and his date Lesley Duncan attend a promotional party for The Honeycombs held at the Country Club in Hampstead, north-west London to launch their new single, the Ray Davies composition 'Something Better Beginning', set for release this coming Friday. Tomorrow marks the start of a string of Scottish dates.

Ev'rybody's Gonna Be Happy single

A **'Ev'rybody's Gonna Be Happy'** (R. DAVIES).
B **'Who'll Be The Next In Line'** (R. DAVIES).

UK release March 19th 1965 (Pye 7N 15813).
US release (A/B sides reversed) July 21st 1965 (Reprise 0366).
Musicians Ray Davies piano, lead vocal. Dave Davies electric guitar, backing vocal (A). Pete Quaife bass guitar, backing vocal (A). Mick Avory drums. Rasa Davies and assorted girlfriends, backing vocal (A).
Recorded Pye Studios (No.2) central London: December 22nd-23rd 1964; 1-track to 1-track mono.
Producer Shel Talmy (for Shel Talmy Productions).
Engineer Bob Auger.
Chart high UK number 20; US number 34 (B-side as A).

Wednesday 24th

Kinema Ballroom *Dunfermline, Fife, Scotland* 8:00pm-12:00midnight, with The Red Hawks
Kinks-Size album released in the US today or the 31st.

Thursday 25th

Albert Hall *Stirling, Scotland* 6:30 & 8:45pm, with Marianne Faithful, Johnny Mike & The Shades, Julie Grant, Eric Burns, The Jacobeats, The Montrose Showband
Ray collapses during the performance, suffering from physical exhaustion and showing signs of pneumonia.

Friday 26th

The remainder of the UK tour is cancelled today, further compounded by Dave also becoming ill, with bronchitis. All members are still in Stirling, Scotland today. Cancelled today is a concert at City Hall, Perth, Scotland with The Black Diamonds and The Hoods.

Saturday 27th

Quaife returns to London in the band van while Ray returns by train. Cancelled today is a concert at the New Palladium Ballroom, Greenock, Scotland with The Beat Brothers, The Black Orchids, and The Echo Sounds, rescheduled for the end of May.

Sunday 28th

Dave and Avory return to London by air. Cancelled today is the band's appearance at Caird Hall, Dundee, Scotland with The Hollies, Marianne Faithful, Julie Grant With The Shades, and The Jacobeats, and the concert proceeds without The Kinks.

Monday 29th

Ray and Dave are both back home recuperating when Quaife suffers concussion in a fall after fainting while at a showing of *The Ipcress File* at the Odeon Cinema in Muswell Hill. Three-quarters of the band are now out of commission due to illness. Cancelled today is a concert at the Barrowland Ballroom, Glasgow, Scotland, rescheduled for the end of May.

Tuesday 30th

Band members continue recuperating from their various maladies. Quaife is hospitalised and has stitches but is well enough to be interviewed by journalist Mike Ledgerwood for *Disc Weekly*. With the

---

Kinks-Size album

A1 'Tired Of Waiting For You' (R. DAVIES).
A2 'Louie Louie' (R. BERRY).
A3 'I've Got That Feeling' (R. DAVIES).
A4 'Revenge' (R. DAVIES, L. PAGE).
A5 'I Gotta Move' (R. DAVIES).
B1 'Things Are Getting Better' (R. DAVIES).
B2 'I Gotta Go Now' (R. DAVIES).
B3 'I'm A Lover Not A Fighter' (J. MILLER).
B4 'Come On Now' (R. DAVIES).
B5 'All Day And All Of The Night' (R. DAVIES).

US release probably March 24th 1965 (Reprise R 6158 mono / RS 6158 stereo/[simulated] stereo). A US-only compilation of assorted tracks. Identical credits to previously issued UK releases: Kinksize Session EP, 'All Day And All Of The Night' single, 'Tired Of Waiting For You' single, Kinks LP ('Revenge', 'I'm A Lover Not A Fighter'). **Chart high** US number 13.

---

new single 'Ev'rybody's Gonna Be Happy' performing poorly, the pressure is applied to Ray to produce a new song quickly to bounce The Kinks back into the charts. Cancelled today is the band's appearance at the Capitol Theatre, Aberdeen, Scotland; the show proceeds with The Yardbirds replacing The Kinks.

Wednesday 31st

Band members are still recuperating, though at least Ray and Dave get together to record demos for a new batch of Ray's compositions, in preparation for proper recording of their next single. Evidently only rough home recordings are made of five new songs, all of which are deposited for assignment with Kassner Music on April 1st. The new titles are 'Set Me Free', 'I Need You', 'See My Friends', 'Never Met A Girl Like You Before', and 'Such A Shame'.

Cancelled is the band's scheduled taping today for French TV on location at the Cavern Club, Liverpool. The programme is filmed by the BBC and broadcast on ORTF-TV Paris, and does feature Sandie Shaw, Manfred Mann, Gerry & The Pacemakers, Gene Vincent, and Petula Clark.

April

Thursday 1st

Band members recuperating. Cancelled today is a spot on BBC TV's *Top Of The Pops* at the Playhouse Theatre, Manchester, and the band's appearance at the Pier Pavilion, Worthing, Sussex, where they are replaced by The Four Pennies.

Friday 2nd

Band members recuperating. Cancelled today is a concert at the Maple Ballroom, Northampton. The show is said to be rescheduled for "late April" but is ultimately set for May 28th – which will also be cancelled.

Saturday 3rd

Band members recuperating. Cancelled today is a concert at Marcam Hall in March, Cambs, postponed initially to May 29th and then again until August 7th.

Sunday 4th

❏ **TV** Alpha Television Studios *Aston, Birmingham*. ABC **Thank Your Lucky Stars** lip-synch 'Ev'rybody's Gonna Be Happy' broadcast April 10th. The first in a new-look version of the programme has an emphasis on a magazine style, featuring more filmed inserts and with the audience size greatly increased to 700. The Kinks are also slated to appear on a Radio Luxemburg special, *The Kinks Versus The Pretties*, for broadcast today, details unknown, possibly cancelled. Certainly cancelled today is a concert at the Marcam Ballroom in Cambridge.

Monday 5th

❏ **TV** Granada Television Centre *Manchester*. Granada **Scene At 6:30** lip-synch 'Ev'rybody's Gonna Be Happy'.
Paar Hall *Warrington* with The Rondeks
The Kinks resume their normal schedule of ballroom dates. A press release confirms this and says that dates cancelled due to illness will be rescheduled.

Tuesday 6th – Wednesday 7th

Two days spent almost entirely on publicity matters with interviews and photo shoots at various locations around London, including Brian Somerville's office on Charing Cross Road, and at the Denmark Productions offices on Denmark Street (for the cover of Larry Page's *Kinky Music* LP). Photographers Chris Walters and Stu Richman corner the band at the Museum of British Transport in Clapham, south London for *Music Echo*, while *Fabulous* magazine's Bent Rej gets formal individual shots in the red hunting jackets and yellow frilly shirts, suitable for pin-up duty.

Thursday 8th

Industrihotellet *Nykøbing, Falster, Denmark* 9:30pm, with Danny & The Royal Strings, The Namelosers, The Bellies, Marty Daily, Scots Dale Trio, The Shouts
The Kinks travel today to Copenhagen accompanied by manager Grenville Collins plus road managers Jay Vickers and Brian Longstaff. The first call is a rather casual press conference at the Galleri Birch, an art gallery in the Admiralgade district. Ray says his music is influenced by Bob Dylan, Joan Baez and oriental music, that their next record – 'See My Friends' – is inspired by their recent trip to India, and he has arranged it for bongo drums and guitar. This refers to the home demo made a week earlier rather than the finished master recording, which will not be attempted for another week. At some point during the stay the band is the subject of a photo shoot at the docks in Copenhagen by photographer "Bent Rej" for British pop magazine *Fabulous*. He then accompanies the band as they take a bus for the hour's ride to the west-coast town of Nykøbing for this evening's show, where he also takes concert photos, all of which will be used in the programme for the upcoming *Kinks Show* tour. Back home, 'Ev'rybody's Gonna Be Happy' peaks in the *Melody Maker* chart at number 20 and the *Kinda Kinks* LP at number 3.

Friday 9th

Tivoli Koncertsal *Tivoli Gardens, Copenhagen, Denmark* 9:00pm, with The Honeycombs, Danny & The Royal Strings, The Joe E. Carter Group, The Telstars, The X-Group, Jette Ziegler & The Sharks, Sir Henry & His Butlers, compère: Jorgen Mylius
The concert turns ugly when about 40 policemen with truncheons storm in from the back of the hall early in The Kinks' set after some girls had rushed the stage to embrace their idols. A brutal confrontation between police and approximately 2,000 wild fans erupts after the police demand that the band stop playing and attempt to clear the hall. The Kinks are pulled off stage by the promoter and locked into a small room backstage as the confrontation escalates into an all-out battle between police and fans. Windows, mirrors and furniture are smashed

by the irate crowd, and ten people are arrested.

As a result, the following night's performance is cancelled and the band adjourns to the Hotel Europa in disbelief at the turn of events. A promptly inebriated Dave smashes a mirror with a brandy bottle in the hotel bar and assaults a hotel porter. He and road manager Jay Vickers are arrested by Danish police and put in jail. Manager Grenville Collins goes to bail him out and is informed that Dave will have to spend the night there, though the police assure Collins that he has not been harmed.

Despite all this, one reviewer is generally positive about the music he manages to hear from The Kinks during their soundcheck, which he describes as oriental – implying he witnesses the band run through the new and demoed-only 'See My Friends'.

☆ The Rolling Stones played at Tivoli on March 28th and 30th without incident.

Saturday 10th

The Kinks hold a press conference at La Carrousel, a restaurant in Copenhagen owned by Danish businessman Kaj Paustian. (Paustian's daughter Annette and niece Lisbet Thorkil-Petersen were introduced to Quaife and Dave the previous day. No one knew it at the time, but both Kinks have just met their future first wives.) To business, however, and the press conference discusses the previous night's riot. Remarkably, the media almost unanimously blames it on over-zealous police rather than the audience or The Kinks. Dave's drunken episode is also discussed with the press, with the suggestion that the inebriated musician started smashing up his room after his new female acquaintance was not allowed in.

☆ The line-up for the two houses at the Tivoli Koncertsal in Copenhagen tonight would have been The Kinks, The Honeycombs, The Lollipops, Sir Henry & His Butlers, The Bristols, The Moonlighters. A possible TV appearance is cancelled as well. The Kinks remain in town tonight as arrangements are already in place for their flight to London tomorrow.

Sunday 11th

Empire Pool *Wembley, north-west London* NME Poll Winners' *Concert* with (in order of appearance) The Moody Blues, Freddie & The Dreamers, Georgie Fame & The Blue Flames, Twinkle, The Seekers, Herman's Hermits, The Ivy League, Sounds Incorporated, The Bachelors, Wayne Fontana, The Rolling Stones, *intermission*, The Rockin' Berries, Cilla Black, Donovan, Them, Tom Jones, The Searchers, Dusty Springfield, The Animals, The Beatles, awards presentations by Tony Bennett, The Kinks. Presenters are Jimmy Saville, Keith Fordyce, Cathy McGowan. Broadcast on ITV television as *Poll Winners Concert (The Big Beat Show Of The Year) Part 1* on April 18th 1965 (and *Part 2* the following week, without The Kinks). Ten-thousand fans attend this long-sold-out pop extravaganza, with The Kinks performing 'You Really Got Me' and 'Tired Of Waiting For You'. The *NME* has previewed the band's arrival in the April 9th issue: "Kinks fans will be wishing any fog away from London Airport on Sunday afternoon. The group is flying in from Copenhagen, arriving at 12.19pm, and a fast car will be rushing them to the Empire Pool."

It's notable that The Kinks go on stage after The Beatles. In one respect this is a high compliment, but it backfires somewhat for The Kinks who turn in a particularly disappointing performance. The order of appearance is perhaps best explained by two simple facts. First, The Beatles have another commitment after the show. Second, The Kinks simply arrive too late from Denmark for their scheduled spot. They are allowed to play following the show's scheduled climax, the awards presentation. In any event, manager Grenville Collins maintains that John Lennon remarks afterwards that this was payback for the way The Kinks had upstaged The Beatles at Bournemouth the previous summer (see August 2nd 1964). One TV viewer, writing to *Music Echo*, says that

The Kinks' broadcast performance was so bad vocally and musically that Ray apologised after each number, and ends his letter by questioning the band's professionalism. In fact Ray's only apology is for being late – but their performance is undeniably diabolical.

Between The Beatles and The Kinks came the presentations of the *NME* awards by American crooner Tony Bennett. The awards culminate a fan-voted popularity contest conducted by *NME* at the end of the previous year (see December 11th 1964). The Kinks receive Runner Up: Best New Group.

Monday 12th

According to Ray's later recollection in *X-Ray* it is at this time that he refuses to appear for a TV booking in Southampton and decides he wants to quit the business, prompting an angry reaction from his father, but this may be a blurring of two separate incidents. Ray's temporary quitting is equally likely to have occurred in the first days of March, when the "Davies is quitting" rumours were publicly leaking and the planned March 18th broadcast could be the Southampton no-show.

☆ A press release announces that a three-week US tour is being arranged to start June 11th.

Tuesday 13th – Wednesday 14th

● **RECORDING** Pye Studios *central London.* Reportedly booked into the larger studio No.1, presumably as No.2 is booked but the band must squeeze in studio time to get another single ready. Ray is under considerable pressure by management to produce a guaranteed chart success that harks back to the identifiable sound of The Kinks' first three hits. '**Set Me Free**' was written and recorded as just such a single. A contemporary report in *Beat Instrumental* reveals that it is done in four takes, with the band playing live. Only the doubled vocal and probably the backing vocals and tambourine are dubbed. Ray, Dave and Quaife will all say that they dislike this safe return to the Kinks formula, and it is perhaps no surprise that they immediately turn their attentions to recording something truly original for a follow-up.

Once 'Set Me Free' is completed, the band has a day and a half to build up a store of recordings, including another strong return to the Kinks early hit sound with '**I Need You**'. Tracks from these sessions are earmarked for the upcoming single and EP. Also probably done at this time is a first attempt at the experimental '**See My Friends**' although evidence points to the released version being re-recorded on May 3rd. Further recordings done now are '**Never Met A Girl Like You Before**' and '**Such A Shame**' (both previously demoed, and assigned to publishing on April 1st), although the released version of the latter will likely be redone in August as part of the sessions for 'A Well Respected Man'.

Session guitarist Jimmy Page will claim in 1977 that he thinks he plays "the opening bit" on 'I Need You', but Ray, Dave, Quaife and producer Shel Talmy all confirm later that it is certainly done by Dave alone. Ray in particular will paint a vivid picture in *X-Ray* of engineer Bob Auger grabbing at the faders on the mixing desk (board) to perfectly capture Dave's spontaneous opening guitar phrase to tape. Quaife recalls that Dave's perfectly matched slashing barre-chorded rhythm is likely Dave doubled (overdubbed) playing rhythm in place of Ray, and that as always it is Dave playing the manic solo.

Thursday 15th

❑ **TV** Playhouse Theatre *Manchester.* BBC-1 *Top Of The Pops* lip-synch 'Ev'rybody's Gonna Be Happy'.

Friday 16th

❑ **TV** Rediffusion Television Studio (No.1) *Wembley, north-west London.* ITV *Ready Steady Goes Live!* live performance 'Ev'rybody's Gonna Be Happy', 'Hide And Seek'. The debut for this show of regular "live" performances instead of lip-synching to records. Also on: Adam

Faith & The Roulettes, Herman's Hermits, Doris Troy. Future Kinks drummer Bob Henrit is the drummer for The Roulettes. The show's finale is a sort of jam session including members of The Kinks joining in with Faith and The Roulettes on a version of the Dee Dee Ford hit 'I Need Your Loving', including supporting vocals from John Lennon and George Harrison.

☆ A concert at the Theatre Royal in Boston, Lincs is cancelled.

☆ Announced and scheduled today is a visit to the US from April 16th to the 25th as part of Soupy Sales' Easter Show at the newly reopened landmark Paramount Theater on Broadway in New York City, alongside Little Richard, The Hullabaloos and others. However, this is never finalised for The Kinks and a US visit is delayed again until June.

Saturday 17th
Pavilion Gardens Ballroom *Buxton, Derbys*
Originally scheduled for the Gaumont Cinema, Bradford, Yorks.

Sunday 18th
DeMontfort Hall *Leicester* two shows, with The Pretty Things, Tommy Quickly, The Walker Brothers, Micky Finn, The Remo Four, Sounds Incorporated, compère: Tony Marsh

Monday 19th
Futurist Theatre *Scarborough, Yorks* 6:20 & 8:45pm, with Goldie & The Gingerbreads, Tommy Quickly, The Walker Brothers, Micky Finn, The Remo Four, Sounds Incorporated, compère: Tony Marsh
Set-list: 'Louie Louie', 'Tired Of Waiting For You', 'Ev'rybody's Gonna Be Happy', 'All Day And All Of The Night', 'You Really Got Me'.
☆ A press release announces a three-week US tour to start June 9th.

Tuesday 20th
))) **RADIO** BBC Maida Vale Studios *central London*. BBC Light Programme *Saturday Club* studio recordings 'Dancing In The Street', 'Naggin", 'Ev'rybody's Gonna Be Happy', 'Nothin' In This World (Can Stop Me Worryin' 'Bout That Girl)', 'You Shouldn't Be Sad' broadcast April 24th.
☆ An advertised appearance at the Boneyard club, Bolton, Lancs with The Warriors (featuring a pre-Yes Jon Anderson) fell through a week or so ahead of the date.

Wednesday 21st
City Hall *Salisbury* 8:00pm, with That Group

→ ❒ **TV** unconfirmed location *London*. KHJ-TV *Cherio A Go Go* (later *Hollywood A Go Go*) broadcast May 1965. This rather obscure Los Angeles show started as a competitor to the prime US TV music shows *Shindig!* and *Hullaballoo*, syndicated nationally by Four Stars Television. It debuted late in May and while The Kinks are scheduled to film an insert, it is unknown if this is done or shown or indeed which songs are performed.

Friday 23rd
The band is in Paris, France for some TV and live work over the coming days. Quaife is interviewed on the phone by Penny Valentine for *Disc Weekly* and relates the band's hopes to present something new in future for their audiences. The ambitious plans include sketches between numbers and a grand finale with all the acts together, though he admits it isn't feasible to have this ready for their first headlining package show, due to start on the 30th. But it shows that The Kinks regularly want to take things a step further … somehow.

With time off in Paris, the band visits clubs around town. In a contemporary interview Quaife says that during a previous visit there was no time for such fun, so two days (23rd and 25th) are specifically scheduled for this trip. They are ushered about by Xavier, their French record-company promotion man, who takes them to the Castiles Club, a notoriously wild, exotic, no-holds-barred venue. Ray will later claim it is here that the encounter occurs between manager Wace and a mademoiselle who is in fact a man, providing in part the inspiration for the 1970 hit 'Lola'.

Saturday 24th
Palais de la Mutualité *Paris, France*
Concert before a live audience filmed tonight and broadcast July 26th on ORTF Channel 1 programme *Discorama* (10:00-10:20pm). The programme was originally set to air on July 7th but The Kinks' segment was hastily removed two days prior. The show's directors were horrified upon previewing the band's live act, which was deemed too wild for primetime TV. However, public outcry from the programme's young viewers resulted in The Kinks' segment being reinstated on a later show. A brief clip of the band performing 'Louie Louie' will later be exhumed and used in a 1993 French TV special about the band, indicating that the broadcast still exists. (More nightclubbing and sightseeing in Paris following day.)

Monday 26th
Grand Bretagne Hotel *Paris, France*
After this final French show the band returns to London the following day.

Wednesday 28th – Thursday 29th
Scheduled rehearsal days for the upcoming tour probably turns into days off or rehearsal for Monday's recording session. A concert on the 28th at the Maple Ballroom, Northampton, rescheduled from April 2nd, is cancelled.

➪ **TOUR STARTS** *The Kinks Show: UK Tour* (Apr 30th – May 19th). **Line-up**: Ray Davies (lead vocal, guitar), Dave Davies (guitar, vocal), Mick Avory (drums), Pete Quaife (bass). The first package tour with The Kinks featured as headliners. The band's road manager is Sam Curtis, a newly hired hand from outside the family circle.

Friday 30th
Adelphi Cinema *Slough* 6:30 & 8:30pm, with Mickey Finn, Jeff & Jon, The Yardbirds, The Riot Squad, Val McKenna, Goldie & The Gingerbreads; compère: Bob Bain
Norman Jopling in *Melody Maker* describes The Kinks as having powerful music and an energetic stage act, and that as a result they give an all-round entertaining show. Norrie Drummond in the *NME* notes early theatrical leanings as the show begins with a darkened stage and then a pinpoint spot that spreads as the band launches into 'You Really Got Me'.
Set-list (2nd show): 'You Really Got Me', 'Beautiful Delilah', 'It's Alright', 'Tired Of Waiting For You', 'Ev'rybody's Gonna Be Happy', 'It's All Over', 'All Day And All Of The Night', 'Hide And Seek'.

May

Saturday 1st
Granada Cinema *Walthamstow, north-east London* 6:30 & 8:30pm, with Mickey Finn, Jeff & Jon, The Yardbirds, The Riot Squad, Val McKenna, Goldie & The Gingerbreads; compère: Bob Bain
Among the well-wishers tonight is Beatles manager Brian Epstein who telegrams The Kinks at the theatre: "All the best for what I am sure will prove a very successful tour for you all."

Sunday 2nd
Odeon Cinema *Lewisham, south-east London* 6:30 & 8:30pm, with Mickey Finn, Jeff & Jon, The Yardbirds, The Riot Squad, Val McKenna, Goldie & The Gingerbreads; compère: Bob Bain

Monday 3rd
● **RECORDING** Pye Studios (No.2) *central London*. With a day off from the tour the band returns to Pye to re-record **'See My Friends'**, first tried at the April 13th-14th sessions. The issued 'See My Friends' exhibits a good deal of tape hiss, due to multiple overdubs and running the recording through a compressor for effect. The song features Ray or Dave on a 12-string guitar, played close to the amp to achieve the droning feedback effect. Probably also done today is a new composition by Dave, **'Wait Till The Summer Comes Along'**.

Tuesday 4th
Guildhall *Portsmouth* 6:30 & 8:30pm, with Mickey Finn, Jeff & Jon, The Yardbirds, The Riot Squad, Val McKenna, Goldie & The Gingerbreads; compère: Bob Bain

Wednesday 5th
ABC Cinema *Aldershot, Hants* 6:30 & 8:30pm, with Mickey Finn, Jeff & Jon, The Rockin' Berries, The Riot Squad, Val McKenna, Goldie & The Gingerbreads; compère: Bob Bain

Thursday 6th
Granada Cinema *Kingston-Upon-Thames, south-west London* 6:30 & 8:30pm, with Mickey Finn, Jeff & Jon, The Yardbirds, The Riot Squad, Val McKenna, Goldie & The Gingerbreads; compère: Bob Bain

Friday 7th
Granada Cinema *East Ham, east London* 6:30 & 8:30pm, with Mickey Finn, Jeff & Jon, The Yardbirds, The Riot Squad, Val McKenna, Goldie & The Gingerbreads, Unit Four Plus Two; compère: Bob Bain

Saturday 8th
Gaumont Cinema *Hanley, Stoke-On-Trent* 6:30 & 8:30pm, with Mickey Finn, Jeff & Jon, The Yardbirds, The Riot Squad, Val McKenna, Goldie & The Gingerbreads; compère: Bob Bain

Sunday 9th
Coventry Theatre *Coventry* 6:30 & 8:30pm, with Mickey Finn, Jeff & Jon, The Yardbirds, The Riot Squad, Val McKenna, Goldie & The Gingerbreads; compère: Bob Bain

Monday 10th
● **RECORDING** RGM Sound Studios *north London*. A day off from the tour, and Ray records a piano-and-vocal demo of a new composition, **'Emptiness'**, at Joe Meek's studio on Holloway Road. The song is meant specifically for The Honeycombs as a follow-up to their last single 'Something Better Beginning', another Ray composition. It is ultimately rejected, presumably by Pye, and relegated to the band's second LP *All Systems Go!* issued at the end of 1965.

Tuesday 11th
Odeon Cinema *Swindon* 6:30 & 8:30pm, with Mickey Finn, Jeff & Jon, The Yardbirds, The Riot Squad, Val McKenna, Goldie & The Gingerbreads; compère: Bob Bain

Wednesday 12th
Odeon Cinema *Southend-on-Sea* 6:30 & 8:30pm, with Mickey Finn, Jeff & Jon, The Yardbirds, The Riot Squad, Val McKenna, Goldie & The Gingerbreads; compère: Bob Bain

Thursday 13th
Granada Cinema *Bedford* 6:30 & 8:30pm, with Mickey Finn, Jeff & Jon, The Yardbirds, The Riot Squad, Val McKenna, Goldie & The Gingerbreads; compère: Bob Bain

Friday 14th
❏ **TV** Rediffusion Television Studios *Wembley, north-west London*. ITV **Ready Steady Goes Live!** live performance 'Set Me Free', 'Wonder Where My Baby Is Tonight'. An exclusive preview performance of the band's next single, due for release the following Friday.
Granada Cinema *Tooting, south London* 6:30 & 8:30pm, with Mickey Finn, Jeff & Jon, The Yardbirds, The Riot Squad, Val McKenna, Goldie & The Gingerbreads; compère: Bob Bain

Saturday 15th
Winter Gardens *Bournemouth* 6:30 & 8:30pm, with Mickey Finn, Jeff & Jon, The Yardbirds, The Riot Squad, Val McKenna, Goldie & The Gingerbreads; compère: Bob Bain

Sunday 16th
Gaumont Cinema *Ipswich* 6:30 & 8:30pm, with Mickey Finn, Jeff & Jon, The Yardbirds, The Riot Squad, Val McKenna, Goldie & The Gingerbreads; compère: Bob Bain
Day off following.

Tuesday 18th
Gaumont Cinema *Taunton, Somerset* 6:30 & 8:30pm, with Mickey Finn, Jeff & Jon, The Yardbirds, The Riot Squad, Val McKenna, Goldie & The Gingerbreads; compère: Bob Bain
Avory and Dave are involved in a serious punch-up after Dave returns from a post-show party and attacks the drummer. Dave is forced to go on stage in Cardiff the following day with sunglasses to cover his two black eyes.

Wednesday 19th
Capitol Theatre *Cardiff, Wales* 6:30 & 8:30pm, with Mickey Finn, Jeff & Jon, The Yardbirds, The Riot Squad, Val McKenna, Goldie & The Gingerbreads; compère: Bob Bain
A fight breaks out on-stage during the start of the second song of the band's first show. Avory knocks down Dave with his hi-hat stand after Dave verbally insults him, then kicks over his drums after finishing the opening song 'You Really Got Me' and starting (probably) 'Beautiful Delilah'.
    Dave is hospitalised at Cardiff Royal Infirmary and receives 16 stitches to his head. Avory flees the theatre in terror, fearing he has killed his bandmate and attempting to avoid the police. The second show proceeds as scheduled but without The Kinks. Police are called in to investigate the incident but are convinced by Kinks management that the whole affair is just the stage show gone awry.
    The band returns to London and Dave recuperates at sister Joyce Palmer's home for most of the next ten days. Avory meanwhile hides out at journalist Keith Altham's house in New Malden, Surrey. The Kinks cancel their remaining four appearances on the tour – May 20th Gaumont Cinema, Wolverhampton; 21st Odeon Cinema, Bolton; 22nd Odeon Cinema, Leeds; 23rd Gaumont Cinema, Derby – and The Walker Brothers are poised to fill the spot.

Thursday 20th
Avory hides out with Altham who fronts the story that the Kink is at his parents' house in Molesey as the national press seizes this latest incident in what some of them now call "the Kinks Kontroversy".

Friday 21st

'**Set Me Free'** / '**I Need You'** single released in the UK. Reviews are generally positive, though many acknowledge the return to a more calculated "Kinks sound". *NME* headlines their review: "Not So Kinky As Usual, But It's Still A Hit," going on to note that "a characteristic raucous guitar introduction leads into 'Set Me Free' which is considerably slower than The Kinks' previous offering – only just above a rock ballad." Dave recalls later: "The only single I was never totally happy with in the early days was 'Set Me Free'. As it happened, it worked. When we recorded it … we were trying to parody ourselves. And it worried me. We'd just come off a difficult record … I think we had to backtrack a bit and try and get on course again. 'Set Me Free' … kind of turned out like a perfect pop record."

Sunday 23rd

A daughter, Louisa, is born to Rasa and Ray Davies at Alexandra Maternity Hospital, Muswell Hill. Reportedly, Ray writes the song 'I Go To Sleep' while waiting for the news. He is particularly unhappy about leaving home to tour the vastness of America for a month within weeks of his first-born's arrival.

Set Me Free single

A '**Set Me Free'** (R. DAVIES).
B '**I Need You'** (R. DAVIES).

UK release May 21st 1965 (Pye 7N 15854).
US release May 26th 1965 (Reprise 0379).
Musicians Ray Davies lead vocal, rhythm guitar. Dave Davies lead guitar (possibly doubled rhythm on B), backing vocal. Pete Quaife bass guitar. Mick Avory drums. Rasa Davies backing vocal.
Recorded Pye Studios (likely No.1) central London; April 13th-14th 1965; 1-track to 1-track mono.
Producer Shel Talmy (for Shel Talmy Productions).
Engineer Bob Auger.
Chart high UK number 8; US number 23.

Monday 24th

● **RECORDING** Regent Sound *central London*. A demo session for seven of Ray's compositions: '**Tell Me Now, So I'll Know'**, '**A Little Bit Of Sunlight'**, '**When I See That Girl Of Mine'**, '**There's A New World (That's Opening For Me)'**, '**I Go To Sleep'**, '**Bet You Won't Stay'**, and '**This Strange Effect'**. All seven are assigned with Kassner Music today. Most will eventually be recorded by other artists, so it's likely the demos were intended for offering around rather than for Kinks purposes. It may not be a coincidence that the Music Publishers Association's First British Song Festival is running from today to Wednesday, and the songs may have been rushed to tape in order to hawk to potential clients at the event. (Back in mid February The Kinks were slated as one of many bands appearing as part of the festival on May 24th and 25th at the Dome in Brighton, but have already dropped out by the time the acts are finalised.)

Dave Davies and Avory are not present at the recording, in the wake of the recent stage battle, but Quaife is probably the bass player. The hastily arranged drummer is future Hendrix Experience man Mitch Mitchell, who as a member of The Riot Squad had just the day before finished the Kinks package tour. Ray later recalls that Mitchell is willing

to fill Avory's spot if it becomes necessary for him to be replaced – and it seems that for a brief moment this week Avory's departure is seriously considered. It is even suggested that a proper Kinks rehearsal with Mitchell occurs at this time, based on the assumption that Avory will not be able to continue. However, Avory returns to the fold in a matter of days, and the issue is quickly forgotten. ('I Go To Sleep' will be issued as a bonus track on the 1998 CD reissue of the *Kinks Kontroversy* album.)

At management's insistence, Avory is hauled before the press in an effort to further downplay the Cardiff incident and to stifle rumours that he is leaving the band. Management and publicist alike are forced to pursue this angle – if for no other reason than to appease the police who want to charge Avory with Grievous Bodily Harm. The solution is to prop up the story that it was a stage act gone awry. Avory tells *Disc Weekly*: "[We] had worked out a routine for 'You Really Got Me' [and] as the song reaches its height, Dave is leaping around and ends by whirling his guitar round his head and pretending to throw it to the audience. It was then that my 18-inch crash cymbal was knocked over and fell on him. It's untrue that we had rowed and are going to break up. It was just an unfortunate incident. The whole thing worked out fine the night before in Taunton."

Wednesday 26th

The band's appearance on the prestigious June 7th holiday weekend radio special *The Beatles Invite You To Take A Ticket To Ride*, due for taping today at BBC Piccadilly Studios, is cancelled. The BBC is provided with a letter from Dave's physician explaining the seriousness of his injuries. The Hollies replace The Kinks at short notice. Furthermore, four make-up dates in Scotland that had to be cancelled in March were all cancelled after the Cardiff incident. The four-date tour would have begun tonight and continued through May 29th with dates at City Hall, Perth; Caird Hall, Dundee; New Palladium Ballroom, Greenock; and Barrowland Ballroom, Glasgow.

'**Set Me Free'** / '**I Need You'** single released in the US. "Hot item on the heels of their 'Tired Of Waiting For You' smash comes this downhome blues rhythm material with a good teen lyric," says *Billboard*. Competing in the American charts with The Kinks this week are The Rolling Stones with '(I Can't Get No) Satisfaction'.

Friday 28th

A crucial business meeting is held with Larry Page at the Denmark Productions offices in central London. Page convinces the band to reassemble in order to fulfil upcoming commitments, including the US tour. A minor concession seems to be to push the start of the tour back from June 9th to the 17th, though this may legitimately be due to some of the proposed earlier dates simply failing to materialise. Cancelled today is a concert at the Maple Ballroom, Northampton, the second rescheduled date after the original April 2nd cancellation.

Saturday 29th

In an effort to reduce public perception of the extent of his injuries, Dave makes a personal appearance signing autographs for charity for the *NME* at the Variety Club Star Gala at Battersea Park Festival Gardens, south London. The event is sponsored by *The News Of The World* newspaper to benefit the Variety Club's Children's Charities. The event runs from 2:00-6:00pm with a long list of other celebrities in attendance.

☆ Meanwhile, Kinks publicist Brian Somerville heads to the US for some advance work on the upcoming US tour. Booking agent Arthur Howes also visits the US to help make arrangements in advance for what is perceived as a crucial step in the band's career, one that that will define them as major players in the pop sweepstakes. Howes will rendezvous with the band during parts of the tour.

☆ Cancelled today is a concert at Marcam Hall, March, originally slated for April 3rd and now pushed to August 7th.

Sunday 30th

While Dave is recuperating, tonight's date at the Locomotive Club in Paris, France is cancelled.

Monday 31st

Cancelled at short notice is a scheduled appearance on a French TV programme in Paris for transmission to the US and other parts of the world via the Early Bird satellite. It was hoped that Dave would be better in time, but this is not the case.

☆ A press release announces that the US tour will continue as planned but with a new later start date of June 17th, and is said to include a Canadian date. The delay is attributed to the early dates falling through, but it's possible the band needs another week to recover and Ray probably wants to spend time with his family.

➜ ● **RECORDING** Regent Sound *central London*. Probably today a demo session is held for two more new compositions by Ray, '**This I Know**' and '**When I'm Walking**', both of which are assigned to Kassner Music today. 'This I Know' is filed for US copyright slightly later on July 15th, but the other song is never filed in the US and is never mentioned again.

June

Tuesday 1st

Proposed TV dates in Belgium and The Netherlands for June 1st to 3rd are cancelled.

Wednesday 2nd

❑ **TV** TWW Television Centre *Bristol, Gloucs*. ITV **Discs A Go Go** lip-synch 'Set Me Free' broadcast June 8th. Also on: The Hollies, The Riot Squad, Donnie Elbert.

Thursday 3rd

❑ **TV** Playhouse Theatre *Manchester*. BBC-1 **Top Of The Pops** lip-synch 'Set Me Free' broadcast June 10th.

Friday 4th

❑ **TV** Rediffusion Television Studios (No.1) *Wembley, north-west London*. ITV **Ready Steady Go!** live performance 'Set Me Free'. Also on: Les Surfs, The Rolling Stones, The Yardbirds.

Saturday 5th

Astoria Ballroom *Rawtenstall, Lancs* 7:30pm, with The Deltas, The Scorchers
The Kinks' first concert appearance since the on-stage incident of May 19th.

Sunday 6th

❑ **TV** Alpha Studios *Aston, Birmingham*. ABC **Thank Your Lucky Stars** lip-synch 'Set Me Free', 'I Need You' broadcast June 12th. Also on: the ever-present Rolling Stones, Lulu, Little Frankie, Ian Whitcomb, Boys Blue, The Fortunes.

Monday 7th – Sunday 13th

The original start date for the US tour was June 9th, planned as a four-week package with The Kinks and The Moody Blues. The cancelled plans are: June 9th travel to New York City; 10th WPIX Studios, New York City, appearance on *Clay Cole Show*; 11th start Kinks/Moody Blues tour JFK Coliseum, Manchester, NH; 12th Ketchum High School, Wappingers Falls, NY (or Academy Of Music, New York, NY); 13th tentative date Boston, MA; 14th tentative date Rhode Island Auditorium, Providence, RI; 15th tentative date New Haven, Bridgeport or Hartford, CT; 16th Stambaugh Auditorium, Youngstown, OH.

☆ This week Ray sees a house for sale just down the street from his childhood Denmark Terrace home on Fortis Green in East Finchley and arranges to buy it. He asks manager Collins to arrange an advance on royalties of £9,000 through Kassner so that he, Rasa and the baby will have a place once he returns from the US tour. He moves in at the end of July, the deal likely secured while the US tour is underway. Meanwhile, Quaife's white Vespa GS motor scooter is stolen from Hornsey High Street this week.

Monday 14th

Ray says in an interview the following day that he spends today writing and arranging guitar duets. These may have been for the ultimately abandoned *Kinky Folky* EP that will be announced in the press the following week. Following the forced return to a safe, identifiable sound with 'Set Me Free' it's quite possible that Ray wants to make another departure. The release of an EP of folk material would certainly be different.

☆ Dave is at the Marquee club in central London tonight for a show by American soul singer Solomon Burke. On with Burke is The Mike Cotton Sound, which in addition to the future Kinks horn section of the the early 1970s features future Kinks bassist Jim Rodford.

Tuesday 15th

The Kinks are at the Denmark Productions offices in central London undertake a battery of press interviews, further attempting to shore up the negative publicity they have been getting and in an effort to help keep their name in the press while they are in the US for the next four weeks. Larry Page plays the soon-to-be-released *Kinky Music* LP for the *Melody Maker*'s Chris Welch, inspiring some dry, sarcastic comments from Ray: "We are very proud of the album. It's got Keith Richard on lead guitar … feeling he had to be jesting. It's all my own arranging, I picked the musicians and A&R'd the session. This album is part of my ambition, yes. It's very well recorded and has people like Bobby Orr on drums. Anybody who criticises this is an idiot. The only thing it can fall down on is melodic content, which is my fault. Playing-wise, it can't be bettered because they are such good musicians."

↪ **TOUR STARTS** US Tour (Jun 18th – Jul 10th). **Line-up**: Ray Davies (lead vocal, guitar), Dave Davies (guitar, vocal), Mick Avory (drums), Pete Quaife (bass). A bit of last-minute business at Denmark Productions on Wednesday 16th requires the four Kinks to formally sign an application to join the American Federation of Musicians, the US musicians' union, a necessity for working in America. The band is accompanied on tour by personal manager Larry Page and road manager Sam Curtis, and they regularly see publisher Edward Kassner as well. The tour is booked by Ken Kendall Associates in New York City. Five of 16 finalised shows (in Indianapolis, Louisville, Rockford, San Jose, and San Diego) are cancelled just prior to leaving, resulting in the addition of hastily arranged dates in Peoria, Springfield and Denver, and a double booking in Honolulu.

Thursday 17th

The entourage departs at midday London time and arrives in New York City early in the afternoon Eastern Daylight Time. After checking in to their hotel The Kinks are promptly whisked off to WPIX Television Studios in downtown Manhattan to tape a guest spot on the *Clay Cole Show*, broadcast on local New York channel 11, WPIX TV. They perform a spontaneous routine, dancing along to the record of 'Set Me Free', and are subsequently interviewed by the show's host.
Later attempts are made to syndicate the series, but this appearance by the band is limited to the New York area.

kinks '65

Friday 18th

The Academy Of Music *New York, NY* 7:00pm, with The Dave Clark Five (headliners), The American Dreams, Fish & Chips; tickets $3.50, $4.50, $5.50; promoted by Sid Bernstein's Associated Booking Group

Right at the start there's an indication of how this tour will go: on the theatre's marquee, the band is mistakenly billed as The Kings. A newspaper ad promises "one parent admitted free with all ticket holders". At the Grantham Hotel The Kinks are subjected to the usual teen press interviews and snapping cameras. They have been added to this evening's bill after having to cancel the June 12th and then 19th matinee dates.

Kinky Music album by The Larry Page Orchestra released in the UK. Ray says later: "When the Kinks were first successful a tribute album came out – an orchestral tribute to our music. That was appalling! Horrible! I reviewed it for Melody Maker at the time and slammed it. It's wonderful to have your work appreciated, but that was just jumping on the back of a craze … total and utter exploitation."

Saturday 19th

Convention Hall *Philadelphia, PA* 8:00pm, with The Dave Clark Five (headliners), The Supremes, with various local bands, compère: WIBG disc jockey Hy Lit; tickets $2.75, $3.75, $4.75; promoted by Don Battles

Tonight's bill at this 13,000-capacity venue was originally scheduled with The Moody Blues, who are unable to enter the US for any of this tour. They are replaced here by The Supremes. Also scheduled today was a 1:00pm matinee with the Moodies at New York's Academy Of Music, but that was replaced with the booking on the 18th.

☆ Co-manager Larry Page is arrested and briefly jailed the following day for failure to pay a local tax demanded by a visiting local union official. The problem is resolved but it sets the tone as the first of many events that will tarnish the tour.

Sunday 20th

Exposition Gardens *Peoria, IL* 5:00 & 9:00pm, with Paul Peterson, The Hollywood Argyles (billed as Bobby & The Argyles), The Rivieras, local acts, compère: DJ Tommy Kirk; promoted by WSIV radio

The band takes an early flight to St. Louis and then heads north into Illinois by bus. After two relatively prestigious shows in sophisticated major east-coast cities, they now find themselves deep in the heart of America's Midwest where attitudes toward long-haired British invaders are far less tolerant. No one is happy with this 700-capacity booking. It is not considered a suitable concert venue and the stage is makeshift at best. The originally scheduled date with The Moody Blues set for the Fairgrounds Coliseum in Indianapolis, IN, was replaced at very short notice by this Peoria booking. What appears to be the only ad runs in the local newspaper on the day of the show. On the phone two days later to the *NME*, Quaife refers to this as their only "ropey" deal so far on the tour. It is almost certainly the location of an encounter with a redneck punk who drives the band around for the promoter, brandishing a gun in the process. The incident leaves a deep impression on an unhappy and frightened Ray, who will immortalise the incident years later in his book *X-Ray* and stage show *Storyteller*.

Monday 21st

Arie Crown Theater, McCormick Place *Chicago, IL* 7:30pm, *Summer Of Stars '65*, with The Thunderbirds, The Blue Knights, The Ventrills; promoted by Frank Field/Triangle Productions

The Moody Blues are billed to appear right up to the day of the show but are unable to perform due as they still lack the proper working papers, and finally cancel tonight. At the show the power goes out and The Kinks have to leave the stage and return about five minutes later

to continue their performance.

☆ Ray Davies, 21 today, is presented with birthday cakes by the crowd before the show.

Tuesday 22nd

A day off in Chicago, the first break on the tour. Quaife is interviewed by phone late tonight and gives a blow-by-blow account of the tour so far to the *NME*. Tonight was originally scheduled with The Moody Blues for the Convention Center, Louisville, KY, but that show is replaced instead by a Dave Clark Five concert on June 21st at the Kentucky Fair & Expo Center.

Wednesday 23rd

Illinois State Armory *Springfield, IL* 8:00pm, with Dick & Dee Dee, Paul Peterson, The Hollywood Argyles, The Rivieras; promoted by Springfield Jaycees (proceeds to Scholarship Fund)

Another late booking, and at showtime the venue still has abundant school desks in evidence. Only years later does it become apparent that the vice president of the Jaycees who organises the event and is responsible for bringing The Kinks to Springfield is Chicago serial killer John Wayne Gacy, convicted and executed in 1994 for his gruesome murder of 33 boys and young men. Gacy was largely known as an upstanding, civic-minded citizen at the time, and The Kinks probably had no direct encounter with him.

The originally scheduled booking with The Moody Blues was at the National Guard Armory, Rockford, IL; this replacement in Springfield was again at short notice and apparently with only a local-newspaper ad on the day of the show. Like Peoria, tonight's show is likely not a very well-run affair and contributes to the band's growing feeling that the tour is not shaping up as promised. They make the almost 700-mile trip to Denver by bus, probably requiring an overnight drive.

Thursday 24th

City Auditorium Arena *Denver, CO* 8:00pm, with The Police, and three other unconfirmed local acts; promoted by Patnik Productions

Another fill-in booking that did not appear on the originally planned Moody Blues date sheet. One of the local bands includes future Poco drummer George Grantham. During The Kinks' trip to Reno the following day their plane hits severe turbulence, scaring everyone on board.

Friday 25th

Centennial Coliseum *Reno, NV* with Dobie Gray, other acts unconfirmed; promoted by Betty Kaye Productions

For this next set of dates and with The Moody Blues definitely absent, newcomers Sonny & Cher are added to bolster the billing. In fact, they fail to appear tonight as Cher refuses to board their flight to Reno from Los Angeles after she hears the news of a horrific crash earlier today in which a US Air Force plane taking off from El Toro, CA, went down killing all 84 aboard.

The concert suffers from extremely poor attendance, due in part to a lack of advertising. Also, the very popular 32nd Annual Reno Rodeo opens a three-day run tonight at the Washoe County Fairgrounds – and Mitch Miller with the entire Sing-along Gang are at the Circus Room Theater Restaurant.

The Kinks allegedly perform only 20 minutes of a contracted 40-minute set because the promoter only offers half the agreed payment upfront, promising the balance after the following night's show. Ray says later in *X-Ray* that the band also irked the promoters by allowing the audience to move down to the front to diminish the gap between the fans and the isolated Coliseum stage. The promoters objected to almost every aspect of The Kinks' performance. Dave writes a postcard where he notes: "Armed police escorts are with us everywhere we go, and even at the hotel the police are on guard outside our bedrooms." Publisher Edward Kassner is in town and joins what is becoming something of a travelling circus.

Ray is picking up on the strong resentment of British bands, not only by the conservative Midwesterners, but also by the US music business who can scarcely disguise their disgust for these young long-haired upstarts who have put their industry in a tailspin. This is compounded by business being too slow to make much money for the promoters and those affiliated with the dates – which would normally be enough to conveniently temper their feelings.

Saturday 26th

Sacramento Memorial Auditorium *Sacramento, CA* 8:00pm, with Sonny & Cher, Dobie Gray, Linda Dawn, The Coachmen, The Fugitives; promoted by Betty Kaye Productions

Further problems over payment result in a dispute with Kaye. She is offended by the band's "unprofessional conduct" after they allegedly play a full 45-minute set but fill much of it with a prolonged version of 'You Really Got Me', and by Larry Page's threat of a law suit to collect the unpaid portion of the Reno money. Kaye apparently later wins this point because the band had only played half the set in Reno. She subsequently files a complaint with the American Federation Of Musicians and in part successfully initiates a blacklisting of the band from playing in the US for the next four years.

The ban was instigated after other complaints were filed by union employees in Los Angeles and, probably, San Francisco. The ban was apparently only lifted four years later in spring 1969 after she receives a written apology from The Kinks and their management. After tonight's show, the band travels to Los Angeles by air where they spend the evening looking around the city on this unexpected night off, with Avory going to see the great jazz drummer Shelly Manne at his Shelly's Manne-Hole club.

Sunday 27th

An unexpected day off as a scheduled appearance at Stockton Civic Memorial Auditorium, Stockton, CA, also promoted by Berry Kaye productions, was cancelled on June 22nd, probably due to poor advance ticket sales for a Sunday-night show. The cancellation partly reflects the booking agent's feeling that The Kinks are seen merely as a set of cheap Beatle substitutes; the show is originally billed as "Direct from Liverpool – The Kinks!"

Monday 28th

❏ **TV** KABC Studios, ABC Television Center *Hollywood, CA*. KABC Channel 7 *Shivaree* lip-synch 'Set Me Free', 'All Day And All Of The Night' broadcast July 3rd 7:00-7:30pm EDT. Virtually the entire week is set aside for TV and promotional work while in Hollywood. This afternoon is devoted to press functions, and during one interview with Rod Alan Barker for *KEWB Magazine* Dave learns that his beloved black Guild guitar has been lost by an airline. Ray gets a sample of West Coast hospitality when he's treated to a late-night hamburger and a malt by Barker at a drive-in on Sunset Boulevard.

➜ While in Los Angeles, Kinks publisher Edward Kassner promotes Ray's song catalogue and in the course of the week secures four agreements to record Davies material. Two are with Capitol Records artists, resulting in the prestigious recording by Peggy Lee of 'I Go To Sleep', while fading teen-idol Bobby Rydell will cut 'When I See That Girl Of Mine'. With Liberty Records, Kassner places 'I Bet You Won't Stay' with the San Diego-based Cascades. The same group also take 'There's A New World Opening For Me' as a second single, but while this will be recorded it is never issued.

Meanwhile, Larry Page meets Cher, takes a great interest in her blossoming career as part of Sonny & Cher, and at LA's fabled Gold Star Studios this week he successfully convinces her to record the same song that Peggy Lee picked up, 'I Go To Sleep'.

None of these songs has yet been recorded by The Kinks, and only one (shortly thereafter) is ever recorded and released by them. A Ray demo, 'This I Know', is shopped around too but is never placed. (Years later the original Kinks demo of this will appear on bootlegs.) Kassner and Page even get Reprise's own Dean Martin to consider recording one of Davies's songs (title unknown) but the singer rejects it shortly afterwards.

Tuesday 29th

➜ ❏ **TV** KCOP Television Studios *Hollywood, CA*. KCOP Channel 13 Los Angeles *The Lloyd Thaxton Show* lip-synch 'Set Me Free', 'I Need You'. Probably this evening the band appears on this daily local music variety programme, which is also syndicated around the US on videotape.

☆ The band is given a tour of Warner Brothers Studios today where they meet Dean Martin and Buddy Greco among others. Avory: "Our record company showed us around recording sessions … and we were able to pick up quite a few ideas. For example, the Americans use more echo on percussion."

Wednesday 30th

➜ ● **RECORDING** Gold Star Studios *Hollywood, CA*. Singer Cher was finishing sessions for her debut solo LP on Imperial earlier this week at Gold Star and had been talked into recording Ray's 'I Go To Sleep' by Larry Page. This inspires Page to book time at the studio, almost certainly today, for the band to record a potential new single, **'Ring The Bells'**. The Kinks were certainly keen to record in a US studio; a plan to work at Warner Brothers studios had gone nowhere. Producer Shel Talmy will later object as the band has readied 'See My Friends' for their next UK single release upon their return to Britain. Once Talmy discovers Page's recording plans in the States he will serve legal papers on the band to prevent them recording anything without his direct supervision. This recording of 'Ring The Bells', possibly engineered by Stan "Choo Choo" Ross, is never issued, and the song will subsequently be re-recorded back in England. It is very possible that UK Musicians Union officials are upset by the band's recording in the US without prior agreement, further fuelling union displeasure with The Kinks.

At a separate evening session booked by the producers of *Shindig!*, a backing track for **'Long Tall Shorty'** for use on the band's appearance on the programme tomorrow. American Federation Of Musicians rules insist on a new, separate recording session for the closing number of the TV show, and The Kinks as this week's featured artists have chosen 'Long Tall Shorty' for the slot.

At the recording, lone Kink Dave is on rhythm guitar, backed by The Shindogs: James Burton on lead guitar, and probably Joey Cooper (bass guitar), Chuck Blackwell (drums), and Glen D. Hardin (musical director and piano), plus possibly Delaney Bramlett on rhythm guitar. This house band is composed of some of the cream of LA musicians. Guitarist Burton played the guitar solos on most of Ricky Nelson's hits, and is one of The Kinks' main guitar heroes. To have Burton playing on their session is a remarkable honour for the band, the enormity of which was not lost on them. Ray recalls later, "The biggest thrill, the only good thing about that first American tour, was when James Burton played with us … and he played my Fender Telecaster."

It is perhaps not coincidental that The Kinks would soon begin featuring in their set a cover of the old blues standard 'Milk Cow Blues', taken partly from Ricky Nelson's arrangement featuring Burton. Furthermore, Burton's sound will be credited as the inspiration behind Dave's solo on the band's soon-to-be-recorded single 'Till The End Of The Day'.

July

Thursday 1st

❏ **TV** ABC Television Center *Hollywood, CA*. ABC network **Shindig!** lip-synch 'It's Alright', 'Set Me Free', 'Tired Of Waiting For You', 'I'm A Lover Not A Fighter', 'Who'll Be The Next In Line' , 'Long Tall Shorty' broadcast (except 'Who'll Be…') July 7th. Also on: Paul Revere & The Raiders, Sonny & Cher, Marianne Faithful, Aretha Franklin. Following a likely day-long rehearsal, this evening before a live audience The Kinks are taped miming to four records and, for the show closer, the previous evening's sound recording of 'Long Tall Shorty'. These classic TV performances mark the debut of Dave's newly-acquired Gibson Flying V guitar, a hasty replacement for the black Guild that disappeared at the airport upon arrival in Los Angeles. The lip-synch performance of 'Who'll Be The Next In Line' is scheduled for September 16th, but evidently is not used until included on a commercial video release in 1992.

Friday 2nd

❏ **TV** The Cinnamon Cinder *North Hollywood, CA*. ABC network **Where The Action Is** lip-synch 'You Really Got Me', 'Set Me Free', 'Ev'rybody's Gonna Be Happy' broadcast July 23rd, 'Who'll Be The Next In Line', 'Tired Of Waiting For You', 'All Day And All Of The Night' broadcast August 18th. The Kinks appear at this local teen club for a daytime location shoot for Dick Clark's new weekday afternoon music series and are taped miming to songs both inside and outside the club. (Originally scheduled for today but cancelled is an appearance at San Jose Fairgrounds, San Jose, CA.)

This is almost certainly the site of the legendary incident where Ray is involved in a fight with an official from the American Federation Of Television & Radio Artists union. Dave pointedly refuses to sign a union contract, at which point the union man allegedly threatens to have The Kinks banned from playing in the US. Ray will recall later, in The Official Biography, "I remember a guy came down – they kept on harassing us for various reasons … and this guy kept going on at me about, 'When the Commies overrun Britain you're really going to want to come here, aren't you?' I just turned round and hit him, about three times. I later found out that he was a union official. Page and Kassner were there and, I discovered later, they fell out with a promoter on the West Coast called Betty Kaye." The tale will be incorporated into Ray's song 'Americana' performed on the Storyteller one-man show in the late 1990s. This incident marks the point where the tour sours completely, and Ray retreats to his hotel room.

'This Strange Effect' single by Dave Berry released in the UK, a song by Ray Davies.

Saturday 3rd

The Hollywood Bowl *Los Angeles, CA* 8:15pm, *The Beach Boys Summer Spectacular*, with The Beach Boys, The Righteous Brothers, The Byrds, Sonny & Cher; Sam The Sham & The Pharaohs, The Sir Douglas Quintet, Donna Loren, Dino Desi & Billy, Ian Whitcomb; tickets $2.75, $3.75, $4.75, $5.75; promoted by Irving Granz & American Productions in association with radio station KFWB

Following the afternoon soundcheck Ray tells Larry Page that he refuses to perform, but is ultimately persuaded to do so. An exasperated Page departs for London first thing the following morning, announcing his intentions to the other Kinks but without informing Ray. Page arranges to leave the band with temporary tour manager Don Zacharlini, described later by Quaife as the owner of a chain of laundromats and "a huge, rough loudmouth", but despite all that "the only guy who knew where we were going".

The Kinks' performance is captured on silent eight-millimetre film, a short excerpt of which is later sold commercially through ads in the back of teen magazines. The show at the world-famous 18,000-plus-capacity venue is a sell-out, and merits coverage by Charles Champlin, entertainment editor of *The Los Angeles Times*. Champlin's teenage daughters rate their top three acts: The Beach Boys first, followed by The Kinks, and then The Byrds.

✪ Tonight at Los Angeles International Airport, Ray and Quaife pick up Rasa and Quaife's girlfriend Nicola after the show.

Sunday 4th

The Cow Palace *San Francisco, CA* 4:00pm, *The Beach Boys' Firecracker*, The Beach Boys (headliners), Sonny & Cher, The Ronettes, Donna Loren, Sam The Sham & The Pharaohs, Ian Whitcomb, Drusalee & The Dead, The Emeralds with Linda Dawn, The Westwinds, The Decibels, The Coachmen, four unidentified local acts; promoted by Betty Kaye

As the band is about to fly from Los Angeles to San Francisco this morning Ray learns that Larry Page has left earlier in the morning to return to London. An impromptu meeting at the airport is held by the band and they decide on the spot to somehow remove Page from their operation upon their own return. Apparently Ray is furious about what he considers to be an abandonment.

The Kinks are present at The Cow Palace but don't perform due to a disagreement about cash payment in advance. The show, on the national 4th-of-July holiday, is a fiasco. It is very poorly attended, with 3,500 present out of 14,000 tickets offered for sale (technically the venue has a capacity of over 17,000). The promoter loses a great deal of money and is only able to offer the band a cheque. Later, Ray will maintain in *X-Ray* that the promoter does not explain the reason for preventing the band's performance. But in *Kink*, Dave will recall a more likely scenario, confirmed by a member of supporting act The Coachmen, that The Kinks refuse to perform because a lack of cash receipts means the promoter cannot pay up-front. Musician Cyril Jordan, later of The Flamin' Groovies, offers an even more direct version of events: "I was backstage since 10 in the morning watching Ray Davies scream about cash – no checks, man. So they went on-stage, [made a dismissive gesture] to everybody, and split." However, an audience eyewitness remembers that the band simply waved quickly to the crowd, which drew a combination of screaming and some booing.

Despite the differing accounts, in Ray's view the scene was a culmination of many occasions when the band was taken advantage of by promoters – and in this case the same promoter over a series of dates. Ray later admits: "We got banned … for asking for our pay: people didn't want to pay us and we started lawsuits."

Promoter Kaye complains to the AFM (American Federation of Musicians) musicians' union about the band's unprofessional behaviour. This in part will cause the informal blacklisting that prevents The Kinks from returning to the US in a professional capacity. Following the debacle, The Kinks travel back to Los Angeles by air where they stay the night before heading on to Hawaii.

Monday 5th

The Kinks depart from Los Angeles via Pan American Airways and at 11:47am arrive in Honolulu where they are given a traditional Hawaiian greeting by local fans. The band has the night off to rest before the back-to-back shows the following day. A concert with The Moody Blues was originally scheduled for the Community Concourse, San Diego, CA, today but is one of the many cancellations from the original itinerary.

Tuesday 6th

Conroy Bowl, Schofield Barracks *Island of Oahu, HI*
A special late-afternoon performance for theUS Army personnel.
Honolulu International Center Arena *Honolulu, Island of Oahu, HI* 7:00-11:30pm, K-POI's Royal Ball, with The Spirits, The Casuals, The Mop Tops; tickets $2

➜ INDICATES EVENT AROUND THIS TIME BUT WITH NO FIRM DATE

Local radio station KPOI regularly brings top names to Hawaii including many other British acts of the day such as The Yardbirds and The Who.

Wednesday 7th

Today is off in Waikiki with the band departing this evening for the long flight to Seattle. This is clearly Ray's inspiration for his later song 'Holiday In Waikiki' that will admit is "like Chuck Berry". When asked another time about his best holiday ever, he names Hawaii. "I thought it would be spoilt and commercialised, but I was wrong," he tells *Rolling Stone*. "There were still many beautiful, peaceful beaches where we could relax. Still, as soon as you got inland there were troops and bases. The atmosphere was tense – as if the H-bomb was going to fall any moment. It was an interesting place, and with lots of sunshine too."

✰ Back in London Larry Page in an *NME* phone interview states his intention to issue the recording made at Gold Star of 'Ring The Bells' as the next Kinks single. Shel Talmy, also on the phone for *NME*, counters that the next single is to be his recording of 'See My Friends' and that as their producer and recording manager he has the final say. Talmy has perhaps foreseen the battle and as a precautionary measure served legal notice on the group prior to their US tour to prevent them from recording in the US without him. His statement in the press was that he does not "intend to allow any record by them being released unless I supervise it". Page counters that "as their publisher, I have the final say on any recordings by them". Enormous battles of egos are waging within The Kinks' management camp, with Wace against Page, and Page against Talmy.

Thursday 8th

The Coliseum *Spokane, WA*

Other acts unconfirmed; likely not the same package as the following two nights, or a much scaled-down version with The Kinks headlining with perhaps some local acts. While family favourites The King Family Singers receive profuse coverage in the local press for a show at the same venue two weeks earlier, there is no mention whatsoever of the Kinks booking, scarcely concealing the establishment's comtempt for such teenage "entertainment". This attitude accords with Ray's later recollection in *X-Ray* that he was confronted by police at a coffee shop at Spokane airport for kissing his wife in public.

Friday 9th

University of Puget Sound Field House *Tacoma, WA* 8:00pm, *1965 Summer Spectacular*, with Jan & Dean, The Righteous Brothers, Ian Whitcomb, The Liverpool Five, Jay & The Americans, The Wailers, The Sonics, Sam The Sham & The Pharaohs, plus orchestra; promoted by KJR's Pat O'Day and Dick Curtis

According to the *Tacoma News Tribune* the three headliners – The Righteous Brothers, The Kinks, Jan & Dean – drew "one continuous roar from the crowd through the second half".

Saturday 10th

Seattle Center Coliseum *Seattle, WA* 8:00pm, *1965 Summer Spectacular*, with The Righteous Brothers, Jan & Dean, Ian Whitcomb, The Liverpool Five, Jay & The Americans, Ray Stevens, The Sonics, Sam The Sham & The Pharaohs, plus orchestra; tickets $3, $4, $5; promoted by KJR's Pat O'Day and Dick Curtis

Reviewer Marshall Wilson reports: "This music must be good or the 10,000 young voices would have tired of cheering during the long, long hours of yesterday evening … But sometimes it was difficult for anyone a generation or even a half generation removed to understand just why they cheered. Whatever the teenagers might say, it was difficult to tell the difference between most of the many groups that rocked and rolled." It is evident the reviewer left before The Kinks and the other headliners even came on-stage as there is no mention in his condescending review of the final portion of the show. Ian Whitcomb

will recall in his book *Rock Odyssey* another typically antagonistic encounter with local police who are present at the Edgewater Hotel where the bands stay. Whitcomb is punched by officers for allegedly being in a girl's room to sign a plaster cast on her broken thigh – even though she is accompanied by her mother.

✰ Ray later recalls that at some point during the stay in Seattle he writes the song 'I'll Remember' on a harmonica.

Sunday 11th

With the tour over, Quaife and Avory stay behind in the US for ten days, taking time off in Los Angeles. Ray and Dave arrive back in London today, furious with Larry Page for what they perceive as his abandonment of the band in LA. Robert Wace picks them up at the airport, and they emphatically convey their feelings to him. (A Canadian date, almost certainly in Vancouver, BC, was originally mentioned for today in early tour plans but never finalised.)

Monday 12th

Back in London, the dispute over the next single is resolved as Larry Page agrees to release 'See My Friends'. *Billboard* explains: "Page backed down from insisting Pye should issue one of the tracks he waxed with the group in Hollywood recently. It was concluded that The Kinks are not on a lease tape deal but signed to Pye, with indie producer Talmy contracted to supervise sessions."

✰ A press release from Ken Kendall Associates, The Kinks' US booking agency, optimistically announces that with "such a successful US tour" behind them the band is now planning a second tour.

➔ Shortly following his return from the US tour, Ray goes on holiday to the traditional English resort town of Torquay, Devon and stays with Rasa at the exclusive Imperial Hotel. However, they leave prematurely after a week, feeling that Ray is looked down upon by the hotel and its clientele, especially once he is recognised and suddenly asked to play golf by a hotel guest. The incident inspires a new song, 'A Well Respected Man', which will be written at the new house on Fortis Green. "The 1960s was a lie, a total lie," Ray explains later. "I said, 'I'm not gonna play fucking golf with you. I'm not gonna be your caddy so you can say you played with a pop singer.' So I decided I was going to use words more, and say things. I wrote 'Well Respected Man'. That was the first real word-oriented song I wrote."

Ray theorises later that the tumultuous US visit has cured him of his envy of American music and underlines his own British identity. "I had abandoned any attempt to Americanise my accent," he will write in X-Ray, where he also suggests that the ban on working in America gives The Kinks an increased "air of mystique". No formal notice of a ban is actually given, but Dave recalls later: "We couldn't get visas for three years. I think it was because of the inexperience of our management. I think they rubbed up the unions the wrong way. I don't think they realised how powerful the unions were. In England, the union was always a bit of a joke, but in America they were actually powerful. I think they rubbed a few people the wrong way and it ended up putting us in shit."

Wednesday 21st

'Who'll Be The Next In Line' / 'Ev'rybody's Gonna Be Happy' single released in the US. A planned American release with the original British a/B-side had been halted, and the single is now issued with the sides reversed after a Los Angeles DJ broke 'Who'll Be The Next In Line', effectively forcing Reprise to issue the 45 with that as the A-side.

✰ Ray and Rasa move into their new house on Fortis Green, East Finchley, north London. Meanwhile Avory along with Quaife and his girlfriend Nicola return to London from Los Angeles. Quaife makes the news as he has a gun confiscated by US customs upon leaving America.

Monday 26th

A session at BBC Television Centre in London taping for *Gadzooks!* is cancelled at the last minute. Press duties resume this week in London with interviews and photo sessions to promote the new single, 'See My Friends', of which the band is universally proud. They view it as different and experimental, and a departure from the calculated sound of the last one, 'Set Me Free'.

Wednesday 28th

❑ **TV** TWW Television Centre *Bristol, Gloucs*. TWW ***Discs A-Go-Go*** lip-synch 'See My Friends' broadcast August 3rd. Also on: Eleanor Toner, Geno Washington & The Ram Jam Band, Sue Thompson.

Thursday 29th

Assembly Hall *Worthing, Sussex*

Friday 30th

❑ **TV** Rediffusion Television Studios (Studio 1) *Wembley, north-west London*. Rediffusion ***Ready Steady Go!*** live performance 'See My Friends'.

'See My Friends' / 'Never Met A Girl Like You Before' single released in the UK. "So nagging in its insistence and repetition that it almost hypnotizes you into playing it over and over again," writes Derek Johnson in *NME*. "It has a distinct R&B flavour and a plaintive quality. A twangy strident riff opens the track, and underlines the vocal throughout." P.J. Proby says in *Melody Maker*: "I like it. It's the best they've done since 'Tired Of Waiting For You' and that was the only one of theirs I liked … [but] I thought they were breaking up."

Saturday 31st

Quaife picks up Sonny & Cher at the airport as the American duo arrive in Britain to start a two-week promotional tour. They will primarily make TV and radio appearances, but also a one-off show at the 100 Club in central London on August 5th.

Kinks manager Larry Page has signed on as their European business manager and personally escorts the duo for the duration of their stay. Meanwhile, Kinks publicity man Brian Sommerville has been signed as Sonny & Cher's British publicist.

August

Sunday 1st

Futurist Theatre *Scarborough, Yorks* 6:20 & 8:40pm, with Peter Jay & The Jaywalkers, The Mike Cotton Sound (with future Kinks-men Jim Rodford, bass, and Mike Cotton and John Beecham, horns).

Monday 2nd

Ray and Robert Wace meet with lawyer Michael Simkins to discuss terminating Boscobel's contract with Denmark Productions. Simkins advises them that according to his interpretation of their contract Ray is free to sign whatever publishing deal he wishes. Simkins says Ray is not personally bound to Kassner beyond the songs that have been assigned so far, because there was never a signed contract directly between Davies and Kassner.

Tuesday 3rd

Ray visits a Sonny & Cher recording session at Pye Studios in central London. Larry Page, now the American duo's European business representative, is also there. Ray objects to Page recording Sonny & Cher and one of his compositions ('Set Me Free'). He also voices the desire that Page terminate his involvement with The Kinks.

See My Friends single

A **'See My Friends'** (R. DAVIES).
B **'Never Met A Girl Like You Before'** (R. DAVIES).

UK release July 30th 1965 (Pye 7N 15919).
US release September 29th 1965 (Reprise 0409).
Musicians Ray Davies lead vocal, acoustic 12-string guitar (A), rhythm guitar (B). Dave Davies electric guitar, backing vocal. Pete Quaife bass guitar. Mick Avory drums.
Recorded A: Pye Studios (No.1 or 2) central London; A: May 3rd 1965, B: April 13th-14th 1965; 1-track to 1-track mono.
Producer Shel Talmy (for Shel Talmy Productions).
Engineers Alan MacKenzie (A); probably Bob Auger (B).
Chart high UK number 11; US number 111.

Wednesday 4th

❑ **TV** Twickenham Film Studios *St. Margaret's, Twickenham, south-west London*. ABC ***Shindig!*** 'See My Friends' (live vocal over record backing) broadcast October 7th 1965, 'Milk Cow Blues' (live performance) broadcast December 30th 1965, 'I Gotta Move' (live vocal over record backing) broadcast January 6th 1966. Three separate inserts for future *Shindig!* programmes.

Thursday 5th

❑ **TV** BBC Television Centre (studio 2) *west London*. BBC-1 ***Top Of The Pops*** lip-synch 'See My Friends'.

→ ● **RECORDING** Pye Studios (No.2) *central London*. A return to Pye this week to record at least three new songs. **'A Well Respected Man'** is another stylistic departure for The Kinks and is reportedly done live in the studio with live vocals. Ray says later that it is his first attempt at trying not to sound American, in reaction to his recent experience in America. It could also be viewed as an act of rebellion against Larry Page's more formulaic attitude toward the established Kinks sound. Also recorded at this time is the folk-ish **'Don't You Fret'**, which dramatically climaxes in a decidedly non-folk ending, adding organ to the band's sound. Third song is **'Having A Good Time'**, but nothing more is known of this, and it has never surfaced since. They almost certainly re-record **'Such A Shame'**, attempted at the April 13th/14th sessions. **'Ring The Bells'**, the song tried out in a US studio in late June, is registered on August 6th and is also likely re-recorded at this session, though this is unconfirmed. While ultimately rejected as an A-side, it is later used to flesh out the *Kink Kontroversy* LP.

Friday 6th

))) **RADIO** BBC Aeolian Hall (Studio 1) *central London*. BBC Light Programme ***You Really Got...*** studio recordings 'You Really Got Me', 'Hide And Seek', 'Never Met A Girl Like You Before', 'This Strange Effect', 'Milk Cow Blues', 'See My Friends' broadcast August 30th 1965. ('This Strange Effect' and 'See My Friends' will be released in 2001 on *The Kinks BBC Sessions 1964-1977*.)

☆ Despite the tensions among the parties involved, publishing is assigned today to Kassner Music for 'Having A Good Time', 'A Well Respected Man', 'Don't You Fret' and 'Ring The Bells'.

Saturday 7th

Marcam Hall *March, Cambs* 8:00-11:45pm, with The Elite

Ray at a soundcheck in the summer of 1965 playing his acoustic 12-string guitar.

Sunday 8th

❏ **TV** Alpha Television Studios *Aston, Birmingham*. ABC ***Thank Your Lucky Stars*** lip-synch 'See My Friends' broadcast August 14th. A concert at the Princess Theatre, Torquay, Devon with The Ivy League is cancelled at the last minute to do this TV show. A clearly annoyed Ray is interviewed during the show. He makes a number of controversial remarks, notably, "I think I could outsing Tony Bennett and Andy Williams put together, I'm sure I could for feeling for a song, and everything." This will later draw pointed criticism in the press. Later still, in *X-Ray*, Ray will carefully point to this as a prime example of how his words are skewed by the media, maintaining that what he said was that he could sing his own song, 'You Really Got Me', better than these two singers. Also during the *Lucky Stars* interview Ray clarifies his relationship to Larry Page's *Kinky Music* LP, which he had jokingly taken arranging credit for back in June – comments that also drew criticism in the press. He backpedals now, admitting he wasn't actively involved in any aspect of the record's creation, but asking for understanding that the arrangements on *Kinky Music* were essentially reproductions of his original recordings with The Kinks, and so effectively were his arrangements. A particularly caustic Ray also complains of the boredom of performing the hits, citing a particular dislike of and embarrassment with their last single, 'Set Me Free'. Finally, he lashes out at Rolling Stones manager Andrew Loog Oldham who in a *Melody Maker* Blind Date record-review session called Dave Berry's record of Ray's composition 'This Strange Effect' "boring".

Tuesday 10th

⟩⟩⟩ **RADIO** Playhouse Theatre *central London*. BBC Light Programme ***Saturday Club*** studio recordings 'Never Met A Girl Like You Before', 'Milk Cow Blues', 'Got My Feet On The Ground', 'See My Friends', 'Wonder Where My Baby Is Tonight', plus Ray Davies interview with Don Moss, broadcast September 4th. ('Milk Cow Blues' and 'Wonder Where My Baby Is Tonight' will be released in 2001 on *The Kinks BBC Sessions 1964-1977.*)

❏ **TV** BBC Television Centre (Studio 2) *west London*. BBC-1 ***Top Of The Pops*** lip-synch 'See My Friends' broadcast August 12th.

Wednesday 11th

Kinda Kinks album released in the US.

➜ ❏ **TV** unknown studio, *probably London*. Around this time The Kinks appear in a pilot for TV series ***Discotech***, ultimately not aired. Hosted by DJ Simon Dee, the pilot also includes P.J. Proby, The Walker Brothers, Sandie Shaw.

Thursday 12th

Palace Theatre *Douglas, Isle Of Man*

Friday 13th

Travel from Isle of Man to London and from there to Berlin.

Saturday 14th

Die Waldbuhne *Berlin, West Germany* 4:00 & 8:00pm, Die Show des Jahres, with The Fortunes, Screaming Lord Sutch & The Savages

A riot erupts among the 20,000 fans at the show. Lord Sutch causes a furore by accidentally stabbing his saxophone player during the act. The Kinks complain after they are chased through a tunnel from the dressing room to the stage by about 50 fans that police are standing idly by. The band is refused service in four different restaurants afterwards as word seems to travel quickly that these British rock'n'rollers are the cause of the trouble. They finally eat at a pavement café after the owner takes pity on the otherwise well-dressed and smartly-groomed young men.

Sunday 15th

Stadthalle *Bremen, West Germany*

Travel day home to London follows.

Tuesday 17th

'I Bet You Won't Stay' single by The Cascades released in the US, a song by Ray Davies.

Wednesday 18th

Corn Exchange *Bristol* with The Pentagons

Fan Julian Bailey remembers the band wearing their new matching grey suits and pink shirts.

The band plays an exciting set consisting of their first three hits as well as 'Louie Louie' and others.

Thursday 19th

❏ **TV** BBC Television Centre (Studio 2) *west London*. BBC-1 ***Top Of The Pops*** lip-synch 'See My Friends'.

Friday 20th

➜ Ray Davies and Pete Quaife are interviewed by Norman Jopling in a third-floor Soho office on a sweltering hot August day. Ray remarks on the mild reception that 'See My Friends' is receiving in the charts. "It's the record," he says. "[It's] the only one I've really liked, and they're not buying it. You know, I put everything I've got into it … I can't even remember what the last one ['Set Me Free'] was called – nothing. It makes me think they must be morons or something. Look, I'm not a great singer, nor a great writer, nor a great musician. But I *do* give everything I have ... and I did for this disc."

Saturday 21st

Matrix Hall *Coventry*

Following day travel to Scotland to fulfil previously cancelled dates.

Monday 23rd

Barrowland Ballroom *Glasgow, Scotland* 8:00-11:00pm, with Studio Six, Hi-Fi Showband

Tuesday 24th

Town Hall *Elgin, Morays, Scotland*

Possibly switched to the Princess Ballroom, Nairn. Originally scheduled was Caird Hall, Dundee, Angus but this is cancelled.

Wednesday 25th

Palais *Fountainbridge, Edinburgh, Scotland* 8:00pm-1:00am, with unnamed local acts

Palladium, Greenock, Renfrews originally scheduled but cancelled.

Thursday 26th

Beach Ballroom *Aberdeen, Scotland* 8:30pm-12:30am, with Johnny Scott & His Big Band, Maureen & Tucker

Friday 27th

City Hall *Perth, Scotland* 8:30pm-1:00am, with first and second place winners of the *East of Scotland Beat Championships* (held 25th and 26th): The Phoenix, The Syndicates, The Merjers, The Fontanas

'I Go To Sleep' single by The Applejacks released in the UK, a song by Ray Davies.

Saturday 28th

Ayr Ice Rink *Ayr, Scotland* 7:30-10:30pm, with The Ravens, The Cravats

The following day the band travels back to London.

➜ INDICATES EVENT AROUND THIS TIME BUT WITH NO FIRM DATE

September

➪ **TOUR STARTS** *Sweden/Finland/Denmark/Iceland Tour* (Sep 1st – 18th). **Line-up**: Ray Davies (lead vocal, guitar), Dave Davies (guitar, vocal), Mick Avory (drums), Pete Quaife (bass).

Wednesday 1st

❏ **TV** Cirkus Television studios *Stockholm, Sweden*. Swedish TV *Drop-In* lip-synch 'Set Me Free', 'Wonder Where My Baby Is Tonight', 'See My Friends' broadcast December 31st 1965.

After two cancelled tours, The Kinks finally make it to Sweden. Accompanied by road manager Sam Curtis, the band arrives this morning at Arlanda Airport but no one is there to meet them. Eventually their Swedish driver appears but he suffers a heart attack during the journey and the car is involved in a near collision. Once at the TV studio it becomes clear that management has neglected to bring along instrumental backing tracks for the band to sing live to, and a lip-synched performance is done instead, using issued records as backing.

Ray is interviewed by *Expressen* and takes the opportunity for another dig at 'Set Me Free'. "I'm ashamed of that song. I can stand to hear and even sing most of the songs I've written night after night, but not that one. It's built around pure idiot harmonies that have been used in thousands of songs." He tells *Aftonbladet*: "Back home in England we're tired of pure beat music. Now it's got to be soft songs with lyrics that tell a story. We don't know much about your pop groups – only that they like heavy pop. Therefore The Kinks will come out with a record made especially for Sweden, Denmark and Germany on which we are going to play raw numbers." This never happens.

☆ Meanwhile on the American airwaves, The Kinks are seen on ABC network's *Shindig!*, broadcast 8:30-9:30 pm EDT. Dave sings 'Beautiful Delilah' and 'I'm A Lover Not A Fighter' as filmed at Twickenham Studios on December 16th-17th 1964.

Folkets Park *Knivsta, Sweden* with The Shanes
Thanks to the cold and equipment difficulties, The Kinks play only a 20-minute set to a small crowd of 350 on the park's open-air stage.

Thursday 2nd

Day off in Stockholm, Sweden, though a photo session is held at Hagaparken around this time, and later used for the cover of the Swedish EP *The Kinks In Sweden*. Later the band travels the approximately 400 miles to Göteborg on the west coast of Sweden.

☆ Back in London, papers are served on Denmark Productions by The Kinks' management, Boscobel Productions, stating the intention to terminate the existing contract between the two parties.

Friday 3rd

Liseberg *Gothenburg, Sweden*
Today's show is on the open-air stage at the city's amusement park where ten minutes into the first of two shows a riot occurs among a crowd of 15,000. About 150 police are present as hysterical and fainting girls are carted off and 13 fans are injured, requiring ambulance care. The second show proceeds as scheduled and a light rain helps cool down the crowd. As a result of the rioting at the first show all future scheduled pop shows at the Liseberg are cancelled. The threat did not prevent the often provocative Who from coming into town a little over a month later and playing at Cirkus Lorensberg.

Saturday 4th

Kommunalhusets *Vara, Sweden* with Larry Finnegan
The third and final Swedish show on this tour is at this small, rural village 70 miles northeast of Gothenburg. The originally scheduled location is the Friluftsscenen, but this is deemed unsafe, and is shifted to the town hall where the band plays on the balcony to the fans below.

Sunday 5th

Travel day back eastward to Stockholm and then by boat on to Finland. Upon their arrival at the coastal city of Turku the band's rented car is twice overturned by fans anxious to show their appreciation.

Monday 6th

Turun Konserttisal *Turku, Finland* 7:00pm, with The Cherry Stones, Sami & The Barricades, The Firestones. The Shoutin' Saints
Despite the wild reception yesterday in Turku, this and all the Finnish concerts pass without incident.

Tuesday 7th

Peacock Theatre *Linnanmäki, Helsinki, Finland* 7:00 & 9:00pm, with The Cherry Stones, Needles, Rondo Four, Leaners
The band moves on to Finland's capital city where their evening show – in an open-air theatre within the city's amusement park – is preceded by a press conference at which it is noted they behave "like gentlemen".

Wednesday 8th

Field House *Lahti, Finland* 8:00pm, with The Cherry Stones, The Creatures
A scheduled appearance on the Finnish TV2 teen programme *Nuorten Tanssihetkessa* is evidently cancelled at the last moment, with Swedish band Lenne & The Lee Kings appearing instead.
☆ In London, Denmark Productions formally responds to Boscobel Productions, stating their intention to maintain the existing contract between the two, forcing Boscobel to up the ante and further challenge the existing contract.

Thursday 9th

A press conference is held at the Arena House in Copenhagen, Denmark.

Friday 10th

Fyens Forum *Odense, Denmark* with The Defenders, Arons, Rocco, Nalle, Les Amis
Aside from the slow night at Knivsta, it is reported that tonight's show is the first concert in Scandinavia at which The Kinks are able to play all the way through without the show being stopped by police. The band personally thank the promoter who naturally can't stop the 2,300 crowd from screaming through the entire show but at least keeps them calm enough for the band to complete its 25-minute show.

A review in *Wez Fyens Stiftstidende* notes The Kinks as fine musicians but says they will probably be best remembered for their provocative movements on stage. "With their long hair swinging from side to side," the imaginative reviewer writes, "they look like cavemen unable to find their way home in the dark."

The *Ekstrabladet* man goes deeper: "They know that the main ingredient in pop is sex. They look at their audience, play with them, tease them and cool them down – a sort of continuous wireless communication. Dave is an untamed person both on and off stage, while it's hard to believe that it's the tall, stylish and thoughtful Ray, who otherwise only talks about how much he misses his wife and daughter, who almost becomes one with the microphone. His harmonica playing and his 'striptease' dance astonished even the most hardened journalists and photographers."

In a brief interview with *BT* newspaper, Ray reveals: "I must have written about 100 songs. I'm writing a musical at the moment. It's about people. Everything I write is about people."

Saturday 11th

KB-Hallen *Copenhagen, Denmark* 8:30 & 11:00pm, with Peter Belli & Les Rivals, Cheetas, The Kids, Defenders, Blackpools, Konrads

The much anticipated return to Copenhagen, scene of rioting last April, and all eyes are on The Kinks to see what will happen at this sell-out show in very hot weather. At the first house, concert manager Niels Wenkens orders them to stop playing so that the guards can regain control of the audience, much to the band's displeasure. However, the second show goes off without problems, and there's a celebration at a private party after the show. Dave meets up again with Lisbet and the romance blossoms.

Sunday 12th

With the tension lifted after a largely incident-free appearance in the Danish capital, the band heads back to London with a night off at home before heading on to the largely uncharted pop-music territory of Iceland, far into the North Atlantic.

Monday 13th

The band arrives at Keflavík International Airport in Iceland's capital city, Reykjavik, where a press conference is held. News footage of the band's arrival is filmed and broadcast, and will be exhumed later in the 1980s for a number of documentaries on the band's career.

Tuesday 14th – Saturday 18th

Austurbæjarbioi *Reykjavik, Iceland* 7:15pm (plus late second show Sat/Sun), with Tempo, Bravo

A residency at this local cinema where the band plays nightly through Saturday. TV cameras are again present and the opening number, 'You Really Got Me', leading into 'I'm A Lover Not A Fighter', is caught on film and shown along with yesterday's airport arrival on the Danish programme *Hvad Morer-Iisland* broadcast February 14th 1966.

☆ In London, Boscobel Productions formally responds to Denmark Productions' lawyer, stating that it is their intention to renegotiate a new contract with The Kinks that prevents Boscobel from signing away any management responsibilities. The implication is that Boscobel considers the original contract null and void and that their new contract with the band will preclude any such original arrangement. It effectively signals to Denmark Productions that they are being excluded from Kinks business.

Friday 17th

Kwyet Kinks EP released in the UK. As note the inclusion of 'A Well Respected Man'. The *NME* succinctly states: "Kinks give you four Kwyet numbers and they're just as attractive as softies! You can listen to the words on this one and the singing is good." As the EP format is alien to the US market, these songs will later form the basis of a US-only LP, *Kinkdom* (see November 24th 1965).

'I Bet You Won't Stay' single by The Cascades released in the UK, a song by Ray Davies from his demo session of May 25th and here receiving its only British outing. It fails to chart.

Sunday 19th – Monday 20th

While the band evidently enjoys a few days off in Iceland, back in Britain a press release announces that they are currently considering an offer for a three-week Christmas show at the Brooklyn Fox Theater in New York City. The offer is never fulfilled, most obviously because of problems obtaining working visas, in addition to the band's growing aversion to such package deals.

Tuesday 20th

Travelling from Iceland back to London, followed by three days off.

Thursday 23rd

Cancelled today is a concert at the Town Hall, Kidderminster, Worcs.

Friday 24th

❐ **TV** Rediffusion Television Studios *Wembley, north-west London*. ITV *Ready Steady Go!* live performance 'A Well Respected Man', 'Don't You Fret'. Also on: Zoot Money, Wayne Fontana, Lou Johnson.
☆ Cancelled today is a concert at the Starlite Ballroom, Greenford, Middx, rescheduled to October 31st. An Irish tour scheduled for September is put back to November 5th-7th.

Monday 27th

Concert today at the Pavilion, Bath, is possibly cancelled.

Wednesday 29th

→ 'See My Friends' single released in the US. *Billboard* says: "Guys lean toward a folk-rock sound that ought to get them listens." Unfortunately it didn't.
→ 'When I See That Girl Of Mine' single by Bobby Rydell released in the US, a song by Ray Davies. This is released months ahead of The Kinks' own version.

October

➾ **TOUR STARTS** *Beat '65: Gemrany/Switzerland/France Tour* (Oct 1st – 17th). **Line-up**: Ray Davies (lead vocal, guitar), Dave Davies (guitar, vocal), Mick Avory (drums), Pete Quaife (bass). Sponsored by German pop magazine *Musik Parade*. Most of the tour is done by bus, though the Hamburg and Swiss dates require air travel. The Kinks' tour manager is Alex King, and road manager Sam Curtis.

Friday 1st – Sunday 3rd

PN Hit House *Munich, West Germany* with The Lords (from Berlin), Tony Sheridan & His All Stars, The Black Stars (from Bremen), The Renegades

The band travels to Munich in plenty of time for tonight's show, but their equipment is held up at London Airport and arrives virtually at showtime, causing some delays. The concert is partially taped by an audience member and reveals an interesting slice of The Kinks live in concert at this crucially under-represented period. The Lords are from Berlin; The Black Stars from Bremen. Tony Sheridan made early recordings in Germany with The Beatles in 1961-62, and is still well

Kwyet Kinks EP

A1 'Wait Till The Summer Comes Along' (D. DAVIES).
A2 'Such A Shame' (R. DAVIES).
B1 'A Well Respected Man' (R. DAVIES).
B2 'Don't You Fret' (R. DAVIES).

UK release September 17th 1965 (Pye NEP 24221).
Musicians Ray Davies lead vocals except as noted, acoustic guitar, 12-string guitar (A1). Dave Davies lead vocal (A1), electric guitar, backing vocal. Pete Quaife bass guitar. Mick Avory drums.
Recorded Pye Studios (No.2) central London. A1: May 3rd 1965; A2, B1, B2: around August 3rd 1965; 1-track to 1-track mono.
Producer Shel Talmy (for Shel Talmy Productions).
Engineer probably Alan MacKenzie.
Chart high UK number 1 (EP chart).

known to German audiences.

Set-list: 'You Really Got Me', 'Beautiful Delilah', 'Tired Of Waiting For You', 'Got Love If You Want It', 'Come On Now', 'All Day And All of the Night'.

Monday 4th

Appearance likely on West German TV, probably for the news and variety show *Drehscheibe* broadcast from Mainz, details unconfirmed.

Tuesday 5th

Hans-Sachs Haus *Gelsenkirchen, West Germany* 4:00 & 8:00pm, with The Lords, Tony Sheridan & His All Stars, The Black Stars
In a phone interview with *Record Mirror*, Quaife says that because of recent trouble at a Rolling Stones concert in Munich the police presence tonight is doubled to avoid trouble, though there are still bloody disturbances between police and audience members. He also mentions that the band will be making an LP upon their return. "It should be ready for Christmas. Ray has written most of the stuff and I've done a few. If we don't think they're suitable for us, we'll give them to other people. There's a lot of stuff we write that we never record." There's no evidence that any of Quaife's songs were recorded.
Set-list: 'Tired Of Waiting For You', 'It's Alright', 'Come On Now', 'All Day And All Of The Night', 'See My Friends', 'Set Me Free', 'You Really Got Me'.

Wednesday 6th

Parkhalle *Iserlohn, West Germany* 5:30pm, with The Lords, Tony Sheridan & His All Stars, The Black Stars
Neue Schützenhalle *Lüdenscheid, West Germany* 8:30pm, with The Lords, Tony Sheridan & His All Stars, The Black Stars

Thursday 7th

Stadhalle *Koblenz, West Germany* 4:30 & 8:15pm, with The Lords, Tony Sheridan & His All Stars, The Black Stars
Venue possibly changed to Rhein-Mosel-Halle.

Friday 8th

Fridayedrich-Ebert-Halle *Ludwigshafen, West Germany* 8:00pm, with The Lords, Tony Sheridan & His All Stars, The Black Stars

Saturday 9th

Olten-Hammer Restaurant *Olten, Switzerland* 3:00pm, with The Lords, The Counts, The Black Stars
Allmend Brunau *Zürich, Switzerland* 4:00 & 8:00pm, with The Lords, The Counts, The Black Stars
The Zürich date features The Kinks in an outdoor tent.

Sunday 10th

Palais Des Fêtes *Mulhouse, France* 5:30pm, with The Lords, Tony Sheridan & His All Stars, The Black Stars
Gundeldinger-Casino *Basel, Switzerland* 8:15pm, with The Lords, The Counts, The Black Stars
Tonight's concert was suitable "only for people with strong eardrums", writes the reviewer in *Volksblatt*, noting The Kinks as the highlight and reporting that "after the concert things got a bit out of hand and several windows were smashed". Cancelled today are originally scheduled concerts at the Casinos in Bern and Biel, Switzerland. The Basel date had originally been booked for October 9th.

Monday 11th

TuS-Sporthalle *Neunkirchen, West Germany* 4:30 pm, with The Lords, Tony Sheridan & His All Stars, The Black Stars
Fruchthalle *Kaiserslautern, West Germany* 8:30 pm, with The

Lords, Tony Sheridan & His All Stars, The Black Stars
☆ Back home, a press release announces cancellation of scheduled late-October dates in order to record the new LP, though some of the shows will go ahead anyway.

Tuesday 12th

Union Theatre *Bochum, West Germany* 5:30 pm, with The Lords, Tony Sheridan & His All Stars, The Black Stars
Vestlandhalle *Recklinghausen, West Germany* 8:15pm, with The Lords, Tony Sheridan & His All Stars, The Black Stars
Cancelled today is a concert in Berlin, West Germany.

Wednesday 13th

Stadthalle *Darmstadt, West Germany* 4:30pm, with The Lords, Tony Sheridan & His All Stars, The Black Stars
Kurfürstliches Schloss *Mainz, West Germany* 8:30pm, with The Lords, Tony Sheridan & His All Stars, The Black Stars

Thursday 14th

Niedersachsenhalle *Hanover, West Germany* 5:30 & 8:15pm, with The Lords, Tony Sheridan & His All Stars, The Black Stars
Cancelled today is a concert in Celle, West Germany.

Friday 15th

Munsterlandhalle *Munster, West Germany* 8:00 pm, with The Lords, Tony Sheridan & His All Stars, The Black Stars

Saturday 16th

Nordmarkhalle *Rendsburg, West Germany* 4:00pm, with The Lords, Tony Sheridan & His All Stars, The Black Stars
Ostseehalle *Kiel, West Germany* 8:00pm, with The Lords, Tony Sheridan & His All Stars, The Black Stars
Tour roadie Sam Curtis is hospitalised after being hit by a bench-seat thrown by angry audience members reacting to his removal of fans from the front of the stage.

Sunday 17th

Delmenhalle *Delmenhorst, West Germany* 4:00 pm, with The Lords, Tony Sheridan & His All Stars, The Black Stars
Weser-Ems-Halle *Oldenburg, West Germany* 8:00pm, with The Lords, Tony Sheridan & His All Stars, The Black Stars
The end of this tour marks the end of the hunting jackets as the regular stage uniform. From now the band often wears white turtlenecks (as they had in Zurich) and other more casual attire.

Monday 18th

The exhausted Kinks travel back to London where they are expected to record an entire LP's worth of material in the coming week following a few British dates.

Tuesday 19th – Wednesday 20th

→ Ray is under pressure to write material for the new LP and the band begins rehearsals.

Thursday 21st

Town Hall *Kidderminster, Worcs*

Friday 22nd

32 Club *Harleston, Norfolk*

Saturday 23rd

Cancelled today is a concert at the Imperial Ballroom, Nelson, Lancs. Two dates for four shows in The Netherlands have been announced in the Dutch music press, for October 23rd at Hontrusthal, The Hague (early show) and Veilinghal, Tiel (8:00pm show) and the 24th at Veilinghal, Beverwijk (two shows). But these are pushed back until November 20th and 21st respectively. Further dates are promised for October 25th-30th but never booked.

Sunday 24th

Day off for writing time and preparation for LP recording.

Monday 25th – Tuesday 26th

➜ ● RECORDING Pye Studios (No.2) *central London*. It has been planned that the band will record their entire next album during this week at Pye, but probably only two days are done now and another two in early November (see 3rd/4th). In addition to the 12 songs of the original release (see November 26th), songs recorded but unused may include the rejected potential single **'Listen To Me'** and the track **'I'll Remember'** which will be included on the Face To Face album in 1966. A further recording, **'Time Will Tell'**, may be from these sessions, but there is no known publishing assignment. The surviving recording, which will be only briefly released in 1983 on a withdrawn bonus disc accompanying a greatest hits collection, contains what must be merely a guide vocal, with Ray's voice breaking at times. The impression is of a failed and unfinished experiment never meant for commercial release.

This is the first session where pianist Nicky Hopkins is brought in, and he will be used regularly for the next two and a half years as the band's studio piano player. Drummer Clem Cattini, newly departed from his most recent band The Ivy League and starting out as a full-time session drummer, is brought in by producer Shel Talmy for this set of sessions, probably to ensure a strong performance for the next single, a strategy Talmy had employed before. But Cattini seems to be used for much of the album too, probably because he can adapt quickly to new material, though doubtless this agitates Avory. Hereafter, Avory will perform on all sessions, without question.

Wednesday 27th

Locarno Ballroom *Stevenage, Herts*
An unperturbed band plays an hour-long set to a hysterical crowd. Fainting girls are revived with smelling salts and promptly returned to the screaming fray. "We get this sort of reception most places we play," Dave assures the *Stevenage News*.

Thursday 28th

Glen Ballroom *Llanelli, Carmarths, Wales* with The Eyes of Blue, The Wheels Of Fortune

Friday 29th

Co-op Hall *Gravesend, Kent*
'A Little Bit Of Sunlight' single by The Majority released in the UK, a song by Ray Davies.

Saturday 30th

Gliderdrome *Boston, Lincs* 7:15-11:40pm (2 shows) with Little Frankie & The Country Gents, Just Four Men

Sunday 31st

Starlite Ballroom *Greenford, Middx*

November

➜ Famed US songwriter Mort Schuman visits Ray at home around this time and provides some encouragement to the young songsmith evidently in the midst of writer's block. The same night of the visit Ray comes up with 'Till The End of the Day', and sessions for the new LP are seemingly concluded quickly this week. "We had to write the songs in a very short space of time," Ray will recall a few years later. "They were all written together ... so they were together in a way. They were connected ... it's unified. It wasn't gold tracks, old tracks and new tracks, just for an LP. We were very pleased with it altogether."

Tuesday 2nd

Winter Gardens *Great Malvern, Worcs* Big Beat Session, with The Huskies
"If the screaming girls had bothered to listen to the music," says the *Malvern Gazette*, "they would have joined some of the older and less vocal members of the audience who decided that a soft drink offered more entertainment than what was going on in the hall. Off-stage The Kinks cut little more ice, and after walking about answering three questions out of the side of their mouth with the assumed authority of Royal Command performers, lead vocalist Ray Davies, when asked where he would most like to play, replied Kidderminster. Perhaps he thought he was being funny."

Wednesday 3rd – Thursday 4th

➜ ● RECORDING Pye Studios (No.2) *central London*. Probably the balance of work on the new single and LP is completed now (see also October 25th/26th). Ray, Dave and Pete are briefly interviewed by Richard Green for *Record Mirror* at the studio at the time **'Till The End Of The Day'** is cut.

Ray says: "We record our own numbers for singles because we know best what material suits us. On LPs we do other stuff, but for singles, we like to stick to stuff I've written. We usually record three or four songs and pick the best for the single. This afternoon we're cutting our next single as well as some LP tracks."

'A Well Respected Man' / 'Such A Shame' single released in the US. Such is the quick descent into near oblivion for the band in the US – following the poor showing of 'Who'll Be The Next In Line' and in quick succession the non-charting of 'See My Friends' – that *Billboard* doesn't tip the new single, even as Top 60 material, and there is no review.

➪ **TOUR STARTS** *Northern Ireland/Ireland Tour* (Nov 5th – 7th).
Line-up: Ray Davies (lead vocal, guitar), Dave Davies (guitar, vocal), Mick Avory (drums), Pete Quaife (bass). The band's first tour of Ireland and Northern Ireland. Shows are presented by promoter Trevor Kane.

Friday 5th

Romano's Ballroom *Belfast, Northern Ireland* 9:00pm-1:00am, with The Silhouettes
Castle Ballroom *Banbridge, Co Down, Northern Ireland* 10:00pm-2:00am, with The Grenadiers
Cancelled today is a concert at the Top Hat, Lisburn, Co Antrim.

Saturday 6th

Queen's Ballroom *Newtownards, Co Down, Northern Ireland* 9:00-12:00midnight, with Broadway
Milano's Ballroom *Bangor, Co Down, Northern Ireland* 8:00pm, with The Red Admirals

Sunday 7th
Adelphi Theatre *Dundalk, Co Louth, Ireland*
Return to London following day.

Monday 8th
Eltham Baths *Eltham, south-east London*

➔ Around this time Ray is introduced to music publisher Freddy Beinstock. Beinstock is a mutual client of Kinks lawyer Michael Simkins, runs Belinda Music Ltd, and is notable for his administering of the Elvis Presley publishing catalogue in Europe. Belinda's offices are at 17 Savile Row, a prestigious central-London address, and the company is affiliated with an even larger publishing conglomerate, the influential Aberbach Group.

Ray soon signs a five-year exclusive publishing contract with Belinda, with the plan that Ray will form his own publishing firms within the company. Davray in the UK will be formed in July 1966 and Mondavies in the US in November '66, at which time the affiliation will shift to Carlin Ltd, another of Beinstock's companies.

Edward Kassner makes a personal appeal to Ray not to sign with Belinda. But Kassner, once his advances are rebuffed, goes ahead and registers 'Till The End Of The Day' with the Performing Right Society as Kassner Music's. Larry Page of Denmark Productions writes letters to the various TV companies and the BBC claiming that any broadcast of 'Till The End Of The Day' will be an infringement of copyright on the broadcaster's part.

Writs are served jointly by Kassner Music and Denmark Productions against Ray Davies, Boscobel Productions, Belinda Music, and Pye Records. Kassner and Denmark Productions also claim damages, breach of contract, and conspiracy. This is all in addition to the suit brought by Denmark Productions against Boscobel Productions for breach of contract.

Wednesday 10th
A press release announces that writs are served by Kassner Music on Belinda Music, Pye Records, and Boscobel Productions over the release of the next Kinks single, 'Till The End Of The Day', which is announced as scheduled for release on November 27th. Kassner claims publishing rights on the single's two new songs and will be applying for an injunction to prevent its release. It is further stated that Denmark Productions has now served a writ on Boscobel Productions for breach of contract and intend to enforce their claim for part-management of The Kinks.

☆ Plans from September to appear on the Murray The K Christmas show in the US are now dropped, and the new album, appropriately titled Kinks Kontroversy, is set for November 26th release.

Friday 12th
Cancelled today is a concert at the California Pool Ballroom, in Dunstable, Bedfordshire. Quaife instead attends a performance by visiting US soul singer Wilson Pickett, probably at central London's Flamingo club.

Saturday 13th
Top Twenty Club *Droylsden, Lancs*

Sunday 14th
Manor Lounge *Stockport, Ches*

Monday 15th
Silverblades Ice Rink *Birmingham*
The Kinks fill-in for The Hollies at short notice due to illness of Hollies singer Alan Clarke.

Tuesday 16th
With a new single rush-released this week, the band would normally be doing the rounds of press, TV and radio. However, their opportunities to do so are limited until a court clears the threat of an injunction and imminent legal challenges.

Wednesday 17th
A press release says Pye is issuing 'Till The End Of The Day' as the new Kinks single ahead of schedule, despite competing publishing claims – and in effect to prevent its release being stopped by injunction. TV and radio appearances are however still in jeopardy.

Thursday 18th
Empire Entertainments & Social Club *Neath, Glamorgan, Wales* early show
A local reviewer begrudgingly admits admiration of the band's musical abilities, but complains that they showed up late, took almost an hour to tune up, and their attitude towards the fans and management was "disgusting". One unnamed member of the group is reported as particularly offensive both on and off stage, and is described as "sullen, conceited and ignorant".
Grand Pavilion *Porthcawl, Glamorgan, Wales* late show

Friday 19th
))) **RADIO** Camden Town Theatre *Camden Town, north London*. BBC Light Programme *Joe Loss Pop Show* live performance 'A Well Respected Man', 'Milk Cow Blues', 'Never Met A Girl Like You Before', 'You Really Got Me'. 'Till The End Of The Day' is barred from inclusion for broadcast in this live performance before an invited audience, because of threats of legal reprisal from Kassner Music. Also as a result of the continuing publishing dispute, The Kinks scheduled appearance on tonight's edition of *Ready Steady Go!* is cancelled. And the band doesn't show either for their spot at the Empire Pool, Wembley, north-west London at the *Glad Rag Ball* with The Hollies, Donovan, The Who, The Merseybeats, Wilson Pickett, Georgie Fame & The Blue Flames, The Barron Knights, John Lee Hooker, The Birds, Ted Heath & His Music, Geno Washington & The Ramjam Band, and The Masterminds.

'Till The End Of The Day' / 'Where Have All The Good Times Gone' single is released in the UK. The release date of the legally embroiled disc is brought forward a week to avoid any injunction that might prevent its availability. Ads run in much of the music press this weekend, and reviews are generally positive. *Record Mirror* declares it a certain hit though perhaps not distinctive enough to be a "really big biggie". *NME* thinks it has all the ingredients of classic Kinks but that, while "exhilarating rhythmically", the "material's disappointing". Indeed the *NME* reviewer favours the B-side, which he finds "fractionally slower with a plaintive quality and a stronger R&B influence". The record is a relatively slow starter and doesn't reach the top 30 for three weeks.

'A Well Respected Man' single is released in The Netherlands, in anticipation of The Kinks' visit there.

➔ **TOUR STARTS** *Netherlands/West Germany Tour* (Nov 21st). **Line-up:** Ray Davies (lead vocal, guitar), Dave Davies (guitar, vocal), Mick Avory (drums), Pete Quaife (bass). After the false start of a delayed October booking, The Kinks finally make their first visit to The Netherlands, through promoter Paul Acket and sponsored in conjunction with leading teen-music magazine *Muziek Express*. Acket is under pressure from the venue managements to run incident-free shows after rioting at a show with The Rolling Stones in Scheveningen the previous year caused serious damage to a hall and badly stained the promoter's reputation for beat shows in Holland. But other factors conspire to affect the shows as fierce weather forces the cancellation of the first two. The Kinks themselves are seen as a risky booking because of their reputation for troublesome shows, so a great deal is resting on these events taking place without incident.

Saturday 20th

With their plane fogged in at London's Gatwick Airport the band is forced to travel by ferry because the Dutch destination, Schipol Airport in Amsterdam, is also closed, due to frost, for only the second time in its history.

As a result their appearance at a 3:00pm concert at Houtrusthal, The Hague, Netherlands with The Golden Earrings is cancelled, disappointing the 3,500 fans present. They also cancel their 8:00pm show at Veiling Septer, Tiel, Netherlands, with Ed Curston & The Black Devils, Terry Gordon & His Virtuals, Jumping Whirlwinds, Don Devil & The Drifters, and F.J. King.

Sunday 21st

VEB-garage *Beverwijk, Netherlands* 2:30pm, with The Bintangs, The Sindychoos, The Golden Earrings, The Gamblers
The Kinks travel from Harwich by ferry to Hoek van Holland after airport closures. The ferry is delayed due to a very bad storm while crossing the English channel and everyone is made ill by the rough ride. Arriving a full day late, they make this Sunday afternoon show, playing to 2,500 eager Dutch fans.
Feestgebouw *Winterswijck, Netherlands* 8:00-12:00pm, with The Blue Comets, The Black Rockets, The Lightnings, The Scamps, Les Baroques; sponsored by The Rootie Tootie Club
The Kinks' 25-minute set begins with 'Louie Louie' and includes the usual early hits plus 'A Well Respected Man' and, reportedly, an extended instrumental. About 600 attend. Pete recalls that a heater in the dressing room catches fire and the band narrowly escapes catastrophe.

An evening concert was originally booked and advertised for Philips Schouwburg, Eindhoven for 8:00pm but was cancelled only a week or so earlier and replaced with this booking.

Monday 22nd

Travel to Offenbach in West Germany; possible rehearsal day. Cancelled today is a TV taping at Dutch AVRO/Ch 2 in Den Haag for *Rooster* and *Tiener* shows.

Till the End Of The Day single

A **'Till The End Of The Day'** (R. DAVIES).
B **'Where Have All The Good Times Gone'** (R. DAVIES).

UK release November 19th 1965 (Pye 7N 15981).
US release March 2nd 1966 (Reprise 0454).
Musicians Ray Davies lead vocal except as noted, electric guitar (A), acoustic guitar (B). Dave Davies electric guitar, co-lead vocal (B), backing vocal (A). Pete Quaife bass guitar, backing vocal (A). Mick Avory drums (B), tambourine (A). Clem Cattini drums (A). Nicky Hopkins piano. Rasa Davies backing vocal (A).
Recorded Pye Studios (No.2) central London; probably November 3rd-4th 1965; 1-track to 1-track mono.
Producer Shel Talmy (for Shel Talmy Productions).
Engineers Alan MacKenzie, assistant Alan "Irish" O'Duffy.
Chart high UK number 6; US number 50.

Tuesday 23rd

❏ **TV** Stadthalle *Offenbach, West Germany*. Hessischer Rundfunk ***Beat Beat Beat*** lip-synch 'A Well Respected Man', 'I'm A Lover Not A Fighter', 'Milk Cow Blues', 'You Really Got Me', 'Till The End Of The Day', 'Cadillac' broadcast January 7th 1966 (except 'Cadillac'). The first of a new *Ready Steady Go!*-styled show. Also on: Kenny Lynch, The Coogers. (After the performance and an overnight stay, the band travels back to London the following day.)

Wednesday 24th

Back home, a press release announces that the threat of injunction against Belinda Music by Kassner Music has been dropped pending a future court decision. A judge has ruled that all monies earned by Ray from publishing are to be put into a secure escrow account that for now will be held by law firm Rubenstein & Nash pending the resolution of the suit.

In the meantime, Ray will only receive songwriting income for radio and TV performances, via PRS (Performing Right Society). The suit will not be decided until October 1970, when an out-of-court settlement determines that all monies accrued are finally released. Thus Ray will receive no income from actual record sales from now until 1970.

✰ Cancelled today is an appearance at TWW TV Studios, Bristol, Gloucs and rescheduled for December 22nd.

➔ *Kinkdom* album released in the US.

Friday 26th

Locarno Ballroom *Swindon* with The Essex
The Kinks Kontroversy album released in the UK. "There's a relaxing sound about the Kinks' best music, a lazy blues sound," says *NME*. "One of the best tracks is 'It's Too Late' ... [However,] some of the instrumental backing is a bit unimaginative." *Melody Maker* deemed it "an excellent album ... Ray's talents as a songwriter come through strongly."

Saturday 27th

Sophia Gardens *Cardiff, Wales* with Peter Budd & The Rebels, The Concords, The Sect Maniacs
A brave return to Cardiff, scene of the legendary onstage brawl. Controversy haunts the band still. "As they began their third number 'You Really Got Me' leader Ray Davies stormed off the stage after one of the microphones went dead," reported the *South Wales Argus*. "He wound down the curtain on the rest of the group who were still playing. He flung down his guitar and paced up and down in the wings as many of the dancers began booing and jeering.

"Then," the *Argus* reporter continued, "the group's road manager, Sam Curtis, wound back the curtain and pleaded with Davies to go on with the act as the other Kinks stood there bewildered. 'Not until whoever pulled out that mike lead [cord] puts it back,' yelled Davies. And once again the curtain fell as hasty talks were held with dance officials and The Kinks. Meanwhile records were played for the dancers until The Kinks finally reappeared to a mixture of jeers and cheers to continue their act. 'Every time we come to South Wales there is a fiasco,' said 20 year-old Ray."

Sunday 28th

❏ **TV** ABC Television Centre *Birmingham*. ABC ***Thank Your Lucky Stars*** lip-synch 'Till The End Of The Day' broadcast December 4th. This appearance was initially in jeopardy back in mid November when the threat existed of an injunction over the publishing rights of 'Till The End Of The Day', preventing performance of the song on TV. With the withdrawal of that threat, television bookings now resume.

➔ INDICATES EVENT AROUND THIS TIME BUT WITH NO FIRM DATE

Brothers on stage: Ray (left) and Dave among the lights and microphones, late in 1965.

Kinkdom album

A1 'A Well Respected Man' (R. DAVIES).
A2 'Such A Shame' (R. DAVIES).
A3 'Wait Till The Summer Comes Along' (D. DAVIES).
A4 'Naggin'' (J. WEST, J. ANDERSON).
A5 'Never Met A Girl Like You Before' (R. DAVIES).
A6 'See My Friends' (R. DAVIES).
B1 'Who'll Be The Next In Line' (R. DAVIES).
B2 'Don't You Fret' (R. DAVIES).
B3 'I Need You' (R. DAVIES).
B4 'It's Alright' (R. DAVIES).
B5 'Louie Louie' (R. BERRY).

US release around November 24th 1965 (Reprise R 6184 mono / RS 6184 [simulated] stereo). A US-only compilation of assorted tracks. Identical credits to previously issued releases: UK Kwyet Kinks EP, 'See My Friends' single, 'Set Me Free' single (B-side), 'Ev'rybody's Gonna Be Happy' (B-side); Kinda Kinks LP ('Naggin'); Kinksize Session EP (Louie Louie); 'You Really Got Me' single (B-side).
Chart high US number 47.

December

→ ● **RECORDING** Central Sound central London. At this small Denmark Street studio Ray, alone on acoustic guitar and vocal, demos **'All Night Stand'**. It was written especially for a Shel Talmy band on Talmy's new Planet Records label and designed to coincide with the release of a controversial novel, Thom Keyes' *All Night Stand*, published by another new Talmy venture, book publishing company Talmy Franklin.

It's possibile but unconfirmed that Ray records a second demo, **'Never Say Yes'**. Elvis Presley's UK publisher (also Belinda Music) have asked him to submit one or two songs for consideration for the next Presley film, *Spinout*, which at first is intended to be titled *Never Say Yes*. Ray submits 'Never Say Yes' and possibly one other. Although the song(s) are never used, film producer Joe Pasternak apparently does express interest in them. Backing tracks for the film are done in Hollywood on February 15th 1966, by which time Ray's songs have been rejected.

While Ray is pursuing his writing projects, Dave does some work at an unconfirmed "small demo studio in Soho" (it's possible that this studio is also Central Sound). He records blues material, including Spider John Koerner songs, with long-time schoolfriend and now aspiring singer and guitarist George Harris. As Dave relates later in *Kink*, nothing came of the recordings. (Harris dies of a drug overdose in the late 1960s.)

Friday 3rd
Palais *Wimbledon, south-west London*

Saturday 4th
Adelphi Ballroom *West Bromwich, Staffs* 8:45pm
Smethwick Baths *Smethwick, Staffs* 10:15pm
Another Birmingham-area two-header for the band.

Sunday 5th
Oasis *Manchester*

Monday 6th
❏ **TV** *London locations*. BBC-1 **A Whole Scene Going** broadcast Jan 19th 1966. The BBC films a short segment for this TV show with Ray, in interview and strolling along Muswell Hill Broadway. The segment will later be included in the 1986 video *The Story Of The Kinks*.
● **RECORDING** Unconfirmed studio (possibly Central Sound) *central London*. It's possible some demos are recorded today in preparation for upcoming Kinks sessions.
☆ A press release says that Ray has submitted two tunes to Elvis Presley, and announces new concert dates.

Thursday 9th
❏ **TV** Playhouse Theatre *Manchester*. BBC-1 **Top Of The Pops** lip-synch 'Till The End Of The Day'.
☆ Ray is interviewed by *Melody Maker* on a variety of subjects. On money: "Unfortunately it ruins a lot of friendships." On war: "There's a world war on at the moment, only no one can see it. Travelling round so much makes me see it." Music publishers: "Very nice people, but unfortunately they have to be very businesslike. They frighten me." On sessionmen: "I always dreamed I'd like to be a sessionman. They can be of great help to a group who don't know much about recording studios. They should be given more publicity. I'd like to see a section for them in the popularity polls." On Jimmy Page: "Nearest thing to James Burton we've got [in Britain]. To clear up anything that's ever been said, Dave Davies plays every solo on every record we've ever made and does

The Kinks Kontroversy album

A1 'Milk Cow Blues' (J. ESTES).
A2 'Ring The Bells' (R. DAVIES).
A3 'Gotta Get The First Plane Home' (R. DAVIES).
A4 'When I See That Girl of Mine' (R. DAVIES).
A5 'I Am Free' (D. DAVIES).
A6 'Till The End Of The Day' (R. DAVIES).
B1 'The World Keeps Going Round' (R. DAVIES).
B2 'I'm On An Island' (R. DAVIES).
B3 'Where Have All The Good Times Gone' (R. DAVIES).
B4 'It's Too Late' (R. DAVIES).
B5 'What's In Store For Me' (R. DAVIES).
B6 'You Can't Win' (R. DAVIES).

UK release November 26th 1965 (Pye NPL 18131 mono).
US release March 30th 1966 (Reprise R 6197 mono / RS 6197 [simulated] stereo).
Musicians Ray Davies lead vocal except as noted, electric guitar (A1, A3, A6), acoustic guitar (A2, A5, B2, B3), harmonica (A3), piano (A2). Dave Davies electric guitar (A1, A3-A6, B1-B6), acoustic guitar (A2), lead vocal (A5, B5), co-lead vocal (A1, B3, B6), backing vocal. Pete Quaife bass guitar, backing vocal (A5, A6). Mick Avory drums (A1, A2, possibly B1, B4), tambourine (A6), maracas (A3), bell (B2). Clem Cattini drums (A3-A6, B1-B6, possibly B1, B4). Nicky Hopkins piano all tracks except (A2). Shel Talmy electric guitar (B4). Rasa Davies backing vocal (A6).
Recorded Pye Studios (No.2) central London; early August 1965 (A2), rest probably October 25th, 26th 1965 and/or November 3rd, 4th 1965; 1-track to 1-track mono.
Producer Shel Talmy (for Shel Talmy Productions).
Engineers Alan MacKenzie, assistant Alan "Irish" O'Duffy.
Chart high UK number 4; US number 95.

it better than anyone else. I think [British session guitarist] Jim Sullivan is just ahead of Jimmy Page."

Friday 10th

Town Hall Greenwich, south-east London

❏ **TV** Rediffusion Television Studios *Wembley, north-west London.* ITV *Five O'Clock Club* lip-synch 'Till The End Of The Day', 'Milk Cow Blues'. This makes up for the November 19th booking when The Kinks were barred from *Ready Steady Go!*. Ray is interviewed on the show. On showbiz: "I get very sick of it sometimes. Like last week, I wanted to give it up completely. If it hadn't been for the other three I'd have packed it in and gone off and done what I wanted. I dislike the pop business, but I enjoy playing. It annoys me intensely sometimes not to be able to do what I want to do." He goes on: "I'd like to stop playing for three months and just write songs," which is essentially what will happen. And perhaps for the first time Ray utters what will become an oft-repeated sentiment: "[Our on-stage image is] very unprofessional – but we're not professionals anyway. One of our aims is to stay amateurs. As soon as we become professionals, we'll be ruined."

☆ Today's *NME* announces the full results of its 1965 readers' poll. The Kinks make a very poor showing this year, not even making the top 20 position in the World Group category. This is topped by The Beatles (9,320 votes) and The Rolling Stones (6,002 votes). The band doesn't even rival Sonny & Cher (at number 12 with 434 votes) or the rapidly fading Dave Clark Five (at 20 with a mere 230 votes). The Kinks fare slightly better at 14 in British vocal group (320 votes), a category again topped by The Beatles (10,002) and the Stones (6,295 votes), appearing below the upstart Yardbirds (at 11 with 558 votes) and The Who (12; 547 votes). In "British R&B Group" the Stones top with 5,984 votes followed closely by the Animals (5,800) and a surprisingly strong Manfred Mann (3,624). The Kinks limp in for 10th place (262 votes) behind The Yardbirds, The Who and The Pretty Things. Ray Davies is nowhere in the top 25 British male singers, nor is a Kinks record present in Best New Discs Of The Year. Accordingly, The Kinks are not booked for the *NME* Pollwinners Concert held on May 1st next year.

☆ Also announced in today's *NME* is the launching of Planet Records, a joint business venture by Kinks producer Shel Talmy and booking agent Arthur Howes. Today the first three singles are issued, none of which lights up the charts. (The band probably has a gig tomorrow, details unconfirmed.)

Saturday 11th

Princess Ballroom Manchester with Mr Kelly's Citizens

The following week the club's regular ad says, "Thank you, thank you, thank you for a fantastic appearance from The Kinks."

Monday 13th

⟩⟩⟩ **RADIO** Playhouse Theatre *central London.* BBC Light Programme *Saturday Club* studio recordings 'A Well Respected Man', 'Where Have All The Good Times Gone', 'Milk Cow Blues', 'Till The End Of The Day', 'I Am Free' broadcast December 18th 10:00am-12midday. Quaife is interviewed at least for the syndicated airing of these recordings on the BBC Transcription Services radio programme *Top Of The Pops*. He alludes to Ray having just written "the title song for a film", *All Night Stand*, and says the band is currently not playing many concert dates but instead concentrating on TV and radio. ('Where Have All The Good Times Gone' and 'Till The End Of The Day' will be released in 2001 on *The Kinks BBC Sessions 1964-1977*.)

Tuesday 14th

➜ Interviewed by Keith Altham at the Boscobel Productions offices in London, Ray reveals he is working on an LP with an unnamed jazz pianist friend. He says it will include portions of spoken narration and use a full orchestra for a new song he's written about the death of an

actor (he may mean 'Fallen Idol'). He names 'You've Lost That Loving Feeling' by The Righteous Brothers as the perfect pop record – and years later he will pay homage to the record with a musical quote in his own 'Now And Then' on 1989's *UK Jive* album. Ray also mentions that Dave is considering managing his friend George Harris.

Wednesday 15th

Majestic Ballroom Newcastle Upon Tyne 8:00pm-1:00am, Kinksize Rave, with The Ken Colyer Jazzmen, Tony Blake Combo, The Outlines; sponsored by College Of Further Education, Charles Trevelyan Technical College

Thursday 16th

❏ **TV** Playhouse Theatre *Manchester.* BBC-1 *Top Of The Pops* lip-synch 'Till The End Of The Day'.

Friday 17th

Unconfirmed concert.

All Systems Go! album by The Honeycombs released in the UK, with 'Emptiness' by Ray Davies.

Saturday 18th

Palais Peterborough

Sunday 19th

The Kinks minus Quaife but with Rasa make an unusual in-person appearance at a charity event, The Third Annual Oxfam Christmas Concert, co-sponsored by the charity and *The Daily Mail*, in Trafalgar Square, central London. Dave is virtually mauled by the crowd as he approaches the stage. While the three Kinks do not perform, they lend their now very public faces to the event in a good cause and join in the singing of Christmas carols.

➜ Ray writes 'Dedicated Follower Of Fashion' after hosting a Christmas party and ending up in a brawl with a fashion-designer guest who makes remarks about the old pullover Ray is wearing. 'Mr Reporter' is also written around this time.

Tuesday 21st

➜ ❏ **TV** BBC Television Centre *west London.* BBC-1 *Top Of The Pops Special Christmas Day Edition* lip-synch 'Tired Of Waiting For You' broadcast December 25th.

➜ ❏ **TV** Rediffusion Television Studios *Wembley, north-west London.* ITV *Ready Steady Go!* live performance 'Till The End Of The Day', 'All I Want For Christmas Is My Two Front Teeth' broadcast December 24th 8:00-9:00pm. Also on: The Who, The Hollies, The Animals, Herman's Hermits, Cilla Black, Chris Farlowe; hosted by Cathy McGowan. In the first portion of the show The Kinks perform 'Till The End Of The Day' and make other guest performances, while in the second they join all the guests in a pantomime of *Cinderella*. In the third and last portion of the show the guests sing assorted Christmas songs, with a finale of everyone singing 'White Christmas'. Ray was asked to write an original song for the Christmas portion but did not complete one. The Kinks do an off-the-cuff rendition of 'All I Want For Christmas Is My Two Front Teeth', The Who contribute 'Jingle Bells', The Animals 'Santa Claus Is Back In Town', The Hollies 'Winter Wonderland', and Herman's Hermits 'Rudolph The Red Nosed Reindeer'.

Wednesday 22nd

➜ ❏ **TV** TWW Television Centre *Bristol, Gloucs.* TWW *Now!* live performance 'Till The End Of The Day' broadcast December 29th. Hosted by Wendy Varnals and Michael Palin (Palin will later come to fame in *Monty Python*).

kinks'65

Thursday 23rd

A later news report in *Melody Maker* suggests that a "new single" is recorded "before Christmas". This may be a reference to the first attempt to record 'Dedicated Follower Of Fashion', though it seems too close to its inspiration (just days ago) so may refer to the making of a demo of the song.

→ Ray does a number of interviews around this time. He tells *Record Mirror* that he wants to advance his songwriting skills and write more descriptive and introverted songs. "We've got an amateur approach and it shows, and we don't care. Start tarting us up into a showbiz sort of thing and you can wave good-bye to The Kinks," he says to *Beat Instrumental*. "We like wild rock but we know we've got to change. I'm worrying all the time about the songs I write. I want to get more complicated lyrics going. Not just lovey-dovey stuff. I want to change our basic tempo, too … even to having several switches of pace inside the same record. I'll do narrative bits in the middle of songs, too, if it fits."

→ ● **RECORDING** Unconfirmed studio (possibly KPS) *central London*. Demos for upcoming recording session.

Tuesday 28th

⟩⟩⟩ **RADIO** Lyceum Theatre (likely) *central London*. Radio Luxembourg ***Ready Steady Radio!*** broadcast January 2nd 1966. The bands appearing are interviewed and mime to their latest record in front of an invited audience.

Wednesday 29th or Thursday 30th

● **RECORDING** Pye Studios (No.2) *central London*. Producer Shel Talmy and engineer Alan MacKenzie oversee a 3-track session where **'You're Looking Fine'**, **'Sittin' On My Sofa'** and an unnamed song thought to be **'And I Will Love You'** are recorded. Two further backing tracks are recorded and presumably later dropped or re-recorded. One is described as having a "Chinese-ish feel" and another in 3/4 time. This may also be the time of the first version of **'Dedicated Follower Of Fashion'** (see also December 23rd) that Ray describes as far too elaborate and which will later be re-recorded twice (see February 2nd and 7th 1966).

☆ *Music Echo* reports on a "secret" Kinks session. The reporter is told that release dates are not fixed because the band does not work best when dates are hanging over their heads. They don't like to rush things, preferring to work steadily, as they are now. "We're in the studio again next week," says Ray, "and in between we're doing demo sessions for the LP. The EP is more or less done. We've got ten tracks to choose from [and] it will probably come out early [in 1966]."

Friday 31st

❏ **TV** Rediffusion Television Studios *Wembley, north-west London*. ITV ***Ready Steady Go! The Year Starts Here*** lip-synch 'A Well Respected Man' broadcast 10.52pm-12midnight; possibly videotaped earlier. Quaife features in a pantomime skit with Pete Townshend of The Who and Hilton Valentine of The Animals, the latter replacing Ray's originally planned appearance.

→ INDICATES EVENT AROUND THIS TIME BUT WITH NO FIRM DATE

1966

The almost relentless pressure of the recording, promoting and touring cycle continued, and again some band members were hit by maladies and injuries. Ray was the first and most serious casualty, victim of a nervous and physical breakdown in March that brought his life to a grinding halt. It forced a considerable shift in priorities within the band as touring commitments were scaled back and studio time became more plentiful, with Ray taking increasing control.

Quaife was the next casualty as an accident took him out of commission for much of the second half of the year – and brought with it some doubts about whether he would remain a member. Dave was ill too, and this cut into some recording time and caused a few shows to be cancelled.

But the biggest changes were on the business front. From a position of strength at the top of the charts, Ray forced the hand of the record company and renegotiated the deal. While this caused a delay in the release of a new album and single, it did bring about a better contract. The year was still overshadowed by the looming court battles intended to solve management and publishing disputes.

Amidst all the calamity in the lives of the band members and those immediately surrounding them, Ray emerged as a prolific and inspired writer. The Kinks were producing wonderful results in the studio, a place to which the band regularly retreated and that increasingly became the focus of their energies.

January

Saturday 1st
Memorial Hall *Northwich, Ches* with The Notions, The Pack of Cards

Monday 3rd
Ray Davies is at the Boscobel offices on Kingly Street, central London and sings a new song, 'I'm Not Like Everybody Else', for a fan who has stopped by to chat.

➔ It is reported that the band is working on tracks for a forthcoming EP, possibly as demos only and without Shel Talmy who is in the United States on business.

Thursday 6th
❏ **TV** Playhouse Theatre *Manchester*. BBC-1 *Top Of The Pops* lip-synch 'Till The End of the Day'. Promotion of the new single, which is about to peak in the charts.

Friday 7th
Raith Ballroom *Kirkcaldy, Fife, Scotland* 7:30pm-1:00am, with The Andy Ross Orchestra; admission 7/6 (38p)
The band heads north for a trio of Scottish dates, a risky business in the heart of winter, but all goes relatively smoothly. Tomorrow's venue and location unconfirmed.

Sunday 9th
Unknown venue *Glasgow, Scotland*
Possibly at the Barrowland Ballroom. The band returns to London the following day.

➔ Dave Davies is interviewed again by *NME* journalist Keith Altham and discusses the influence of an Elektra LP he recently acquired. *Spider Blues* is by American folk-blues singer-guitarist Spider John Koerner, who uses a seven-string guitar to achieve some unusual sounds. Later Dave will record 'Good Luck Child' from the album. Dave also says that a song he wrote ('Sittin' On My Sofa') will appear as the B-side of the new as-yet unnamed single.
☆ Demos are probably made around this time of two songs, titles unknown, that Ray submits to Dave Berry and The Moody Blues for consideration, but which ultimately are not used. Ray is collaborating regularly with Barry Fantoni on material for a jazz-pop LP.

Wednesday 12th
Top Rank Suite *Bristol*

Thursday 13th
Victoria Ballroom *Chesterfield, Derbys*
❏ **TV** Playhouse Theatre *Manchester*. BBC-1 *Top Of The Pops* lip-synch 'Till The End of the Day'. The band tapes an insert for inclusion in tonight's programme so that they can make the Chesterfield show this evening. The single hits its peak position this week in the British charts, as does the accompanying album, *Kink Kontroversy*.

Friday 14th

❏ **TV** Rediffusion Television Studios *Wembley north-west London*. ATV **Ready Steady Go!** lip-synch 'Till The End of the Day', 'Where Have All The Good Times Gone'. During the show's recent "all live" policy the sound quality achieved has been poor and so is no longer wholly live now, reverting in some cases to lip-synching to the record or playing to pre-recorded backing tracks.

Saturday 15th

Floral Hall *Southport, Lancs*

Monday 17th

Silver Blades Ice Rink *Streatham, south London* with The Blades; tickets 5/6

A press release announces that the band plans to issue a series of satirical EPs, the first one on the "boutique business" and said to be due in mid-February.

Tuesday 18th

→ Dave reviews records for *Melody Maker*, giving a thumbs-up to The Lovin' Spoonful's 'You Didn't Have To Be So Nice' and Frank Sinatra's 'It Was A Very Good Year', but a surprising thumbs-down for Bob Dylan's 'Can You Please Crawl Out Your Window' which he describes as "meaningless".

Wednesday 19th

❏ **TV** BBC Television Centre (Studio 2) *west London*. BBC-1 **A Whole Scene Going** lip-synch 'A Well Respected Man', 'All Day And All Of The Night' 6:30-7:30pm. Hosted by Barry Fantoni and Wendy Varnels, the programme also includes a film shot on December 6th 1965 featuring a short interview with Ray. *Melody Maker* later reports that Quaife horrifies BBC staff with a gruesome fake-thumb gag. Fantoni is hanging out with Ray, who is writing him a song to record soon. Ray is also writing for Leapy Lee.

Friday 21st

Majestic Ballroom *Accrington, Lancs*

Monday 24th

Top Rank Suite *Doncaster, Yorks* 7:00-11:00pm

Tuesday 25th

Majestic Ballroom *Newcastle Upon Tyne* with The Sect 7:30-11:00pm; admission 6/- (30p)

Thursday 27th

Pier Pavilion *Worthing, Sussex*

→ ● **RECORDING** Pye Studios (No.2) *central London*. Sessions for the next single that started at the end of December continue now, with Shel Talmy returning from the US later this month to supervise the finished product.

The sessions are at first intended to produce an entire four-song EP to spoof the boutique business. Given the great success of *Kwyet Kinks*, the EP format is seen by Ray as an ideal medium to expand his writing; Pye, meanwhile, prefers the single. Subsequently the lead EP track will be relegated to an A-side. **'Sittin' On My Sofa'**, announced as by Dave and destined for the B-side, will emerge with a label credit for Ray Davies, though it's recorded as a co-composition and all copyright records show a co-writing credit.

A report in the *NME* suggests that drummer Avory is absent from these sessions, while *Melody Maker* notes that Ray has bought himself a grand piano.

February

Wednesday 2nd

● **RECORDING** IBC Studios *central London*. Still unhappy with the Talmy-produced recording of **'Dedicated Follower Of Fashion'** made probably late last year (see December 23rd and 29th/30th 1965), Ray insists on trying it again with a more straightforward approach. "The way we recorded it at first was too elaborate," he tells *NME*. "I got Shel Talmy to come back from America, where he is busy suing The Who, and we did it again, simplifying the arrangement." Rather than try it again at Pye Studios, the band moves to IBC and remakes 'Dedicated Follower Of Fashion' and a new song, **'Mr Reporter'**. The four Kinks are joined by Nicky Hopkins on piano, almost certainly with Glyn Johns engineering. Both recordings are ultimately rejected, and will only emerge unofficially on a bootleg CD in 2000 after the long-lost tape reel somehow turns up in private hands.

Friday 4th

Notre Dame Hall *central London*
Not a religious centre but a popular London club.
'The World Keeps Going Round' single by The Lancastrians released in the UK, a cover version of the Kinks song.

Saturday 5th

Pavilion Gardens Ballroom *Buxton, Derbys* with The Yaks

Sunday 6th

❏ **TV** ABC Television Centre *Birmingham*. ABC **Thank Your Lucky Stars** lip-synch possibly 'A Well Respected Man' broadcast February 12th.

Monday 7th

● **RECORDING** Pye Studios (No.2) *central London*. A further attempt at **'Dedicated Follower Of Fashion'**. The basic arrangement developed on the 2nd seems to be considered an improvement, but Ray is still dissatisfied with the sound of the recording. So The Kinks return to Pye for this session starting at 10:00am with Shel Talmy producing and Alan MacKenzie engineering, again with Nicky Hopkins on piano. The now familiar brash opening and ending chords are introduced at this point in an attempt to catch the listener's attention and give the song a trademark Kinks sound. It is one of the few session tapes to survive in the Pye archive, and records show the song was done in ten takes, with number ten being the master. Also at this session, a backing track for **'She's Got Everything'** is completed in three takes, with vocal and overdubs added shortly afterwards, but the completed song will not be issued until June 1968, as the B-side of 'Days'. (A rough stereo mix of an alternate take of 'Dedicated Follower Of Fashion' will be issued as a bonus track on the 1998 CD reissue of the *Kinks Kontroversy* album.)

In some ways the problems associated with the recording of 'Dedicated Follower' echo the trouble encountered two years ago with 'You Really Got Me'. A pattern of recording and re-recording will soon develop into something of a routine for The Kinks. At the end of today's session still no one is too happy with the results. Ray will tell John Savage, "I wasn't pleased with it. Got to the point, though, where [we recorded 'Dedicated Follower Of Fashion'] three times, [and] what more can we do?" Later Ray says it "wasn't a particularly good recording" and that it was "just a statement I wanted to make". The single will go on to do its job well in the charts, but apparently at a high cost in terms of pressure and bad feeling within the band.

Wednesday 9th

Wolsey Hall *Cheshunt, Herts*

→ INDICATES EVENT AROUND THIS TIME BUT WITH NO FIRM DATE

Thursday 10th

City Hall *Salisbury* 7:45-11:45pm, with That Group; tickets 10/- (50p)

Erroneously advertised as their final appearance before leaving for America (they were off to Denmark). US music trade magazine *Cash Box* gets in a muddle too, placing the band in Belgium at present, but at least having them on their way to Denmark. It all points to the chaotic nature of The Kinks' ever-mutating schedule.

● **RECORDING** Pye Studios (No.2) *central London*. In a rush to complete and issue **'Dedicated Follower Of Fashion'** as the new single, a late-night vocal session following the concert is booked at Pye, either to get an acceptable vocal track or add the band's backing vocals.

Friday 11th

Arriving in Copenhagen, Denmark the band stage a press conference at the Whiskyklubben. Dave and Quaife have good reasons to return to the city as both have serious female acquaintances in waiting.

Saturday 12th

Fyens Forum *Odense, Denmark* 7:00pm, with The Hitmakers and 24 other bands

K.B. Hallen *Copenhagen, Denmark* 11:30pm, with The Beefeaters, The Stoke Sect, Joe E Carter Group, The Dandy Swingers, Annisette, Sir Henry & His Butlers, Master Joseph & His Disciples

At Odense, the first of two shows today, they perform for 3,000 extremely vocal fans. Copenhagen seems set for a repeat of the riot that occurred during the band's last visit in April 1965 as a crowd of 3,000 surges to the stage when The Kinks start their performance, and part of the stage and a number of seats are damaged. The show is momentarily stopped by promoter Niels Wenkens after the second song, but once the audience have calmed down and returned to their seats the show proceeds without incident. The performance is highly rated musically. Ray says afterwards, "I'm beginning to get tired of writing good tunes and lyrics and perform them to the best of my ability to an audience, who are only interested in creating trouble." At least a portion of the concert is filmed by Danish TV crews, broadcast on February 14th on *Hvadmorer-I Island* along with footage shot the previous September in Iceland. Some of this material will be included in Kinks documentaries made in the 1980s.

Monday 14th

A press release announces 'Dedicated Follower Of Fashion' for rush release on February 25th, saying that the song was intended as the title track for a new EP but that it will now be the next single. A tour of Holland originally scheduled for February is rescheduled for May 7th-9th.

Tuesday 15th

Today is Avory's 22nd birthday, and tonight he celebrates at London's prestigious Talk Of The Town with Quaife and members of The Shadows.

Wednesday 16th

Hippodrome *Dudley, Worcs* with The Walker Brothers, Twinkle, The Sorrows, Finders Keepers; two shows

Thursday 17th

Town Hall *Kidderminster, Worcs*

Friday 18th

The pressure surrounding the recording of the new single behind him, Ray moves on to some outside projects, including a session for his art-school tutor and friend Barry Fantoni at Philips Recording Studios, central London with producers Peter Eden and Geoff Stephens. The musicians are all sessionmen with no Kinks members involved, though Ray is present. At least two songs are recorded, including the eventual A-side 'Little Man In A Little Box', written by Ray for Eden and Stephens's Peter Piped Piper Productions. The B-side, 'Fat Man', is written by Fantoni in an extremely Ray-like style.

Saturday 19th

Drill Hall *Grantham, Lincs* 7:45-11:45pm, with Beats Ltd, The Rising Sons; admission 10/- (50p)

Sunday 20th

Top Rank Ballroom *Southampton*

→ ● **RECORDING** IBC Studios *central London*. During this week Ray produces a session for singer Leapy Lee, who is managed by Kinks' managers Wace and Collins. Ray's song **'King Of The Whole Wide World'** is recorded. It's a rare instance of a recording where key members of The Kinks back another singer. The band has Dave on guitar and Quaife on bass, with the drum spot probably filled by a session player. The organist is also unidentified. Backing vocals are handled by Margo Crocitto and Carole MacDonald of the American girl-group Goldie & The Gingerbreads.

→ ● **RECORDING** KPS Studios *central London*. Around this time the band is at KPS, a 2-track facility built in 1965 by native South African Eddie Kramer. Later famed for his work with Jimi Hendrix and others, Kramer had briefly been at Pye Studios in 1964 as an assistant to engineer Bob Auger, reportedly including some Kinks sessions (though Shel Talmy does not recall any). In May this year KPS will be bought by Regent Sound and becomes Regent Sound A. Ray's **'I'm Not Like Everybody Else'** is recorded as a demo, but is initially deemed unsuitable for The Kinks. Subsequently it's offered to The Animals who consider it around March/April but also ultimately pass. The Kinks will return to the song and evidently record their master on May 12th.

Thursday 24th

❏ **TV** BBC Television Centre *west London*. BBC-1 *Top Of The Pops* lip-synch 'Dedicated Follower Of Fashion' broadcast March 10th. A full day of promotional activities, including a *Top Of The Pops* insert and a new photo shoot at Dezo Hoffman's studio that will adorn the

---

Dedicated Follower Of Fashion single

A **'Dedicated Follower Of Fashion'** (R. DAVIES).
B **'Sittin' On My Sofa'** (R. DAVIES, D. DAVIES).

UK release February 25th 1966 (Pye 7N 17064).
US release April 27th 1966 (Reprise 0471).
Musicians Ray Davies lead vocal, acoustic guitar. Dave Davies electric guitar, backing vocal. Pete Quaife bass guitar. Mick Avory drums. Nicky Hopkins piano.
Recorded Pye Studios (No.2) *central London*. A: February 7th, 10th-11th 1966. B: December 29th-30th 1965; 3-track mixed to mono.
Producer Shel Talmy (for Shel Talmy Productions).
Engineer Alan MacKenzie.
Chart high UK number 2; US number 36.

cover of *Record Mirror*. Hoffman also does some location shots at the TV studio. There are assorted interviews, including Ray telling *Disc* that he prefers clothes from the Victorian era rather than the currently trendy op art fashions.

'Dedicated Follower Of Fashion' / 'Sittin' On My Sofa' single released in the UK. *NME*: "Never thought I'd compare The Kinks with Herman's Hermits, but this is certainly Herman-type material, with bouncy beat and cute novelty lyric. Of course, the sound is quite different, with the London lads grinding out their familiar strident raucous twang, exaggerated by an excess of 'top'." *Melody Maker*: "This doesn't sound like the same group who recorded 'Till The End of The Day' because they've issued a humorous jogging Joe Brown-type semi-comedy number. This mild send-up of the fashion conscious mods might not be an ardent R&B fan's idea of a good Kinks release. But it's original and catchy enough to be a hit."

Saturday 26th

Imperial Ballroom *Nelson, Lancs*
Earlier in the day is a scheduled appearance at the opening ceremony of a new boutique, The Inn Place in Blackburn. It represents what Ray considers to be crass exploitation of the very image of trendiness that he caustically criticises in the new single. It may be among the factors that will contribute in a few weeks to Ray's dramatic firing of the band's publicist, Brian Sommerville, who arranges such things.

Sunday 27th

❏ **TV** ABC Television Centre *Birmingham*. ABC ***Thank Your Lucky Stars*** lip-synch 'Dedicated Follower Of Fashion' broadcast March 5th.

March

➪ **TOUR STARTS** *Switzerland/Austria Tour* (Mar 1st – 6th). **Line-up**: Ray Davies (lead vocal, guitar), Dave Davies (guitar, vocal), Mick Avory (drums), Pete Quaife (bass). The band flies into Switzerland on Monday February 28th to begin a week of dates, though the scheduled performance on that day at the Tonhalle in St. Gallen, Switzerland at 8:15pm is cancelled due to local rioting.

Tuesday 1st

Hotel Union *Luzern, Switzerland* 8:15pm, with Les Sauterelles, The Times

Wednesday 2nd

Hotel Schaffhauserhof *Schaffhausen, Switzerland* 8:15pm, with Les Sauterelles, The Times

'Till The End Of The Day' / 'Where Have All The Good Times Gone' single released in the US. *Billboard* says: "Hot follow-up to their smash 'A Well Respected Man' is this rockin' dance beat wailer with up-beat lyric."

Thursday 3rd

Hotel Spirgarten *Zürich, Switzerland* 8:15pm, with Les Sauterelles, The Times

Friday 4th

Kursaal *Bern, Switzerland* 3:00pm, Les Sauterelles, The Times
Maison de Syndicats *Neuchâtel, Switzerland* 8:15pm, with Les Sauterelles, The Times

Saturday 5th

Kino Union *Basel, Switzerland* 8:15pm, with Les Sauterelles, The Times

Originally scheduled was a concert in Chur, Switzerland at 2:00pm but this is cancelled due to the riots at St. Gallen earlier in the week.

Sunday 6th

Messehalle *Dornbirn, Austria* 8:30pm, *Beat Monstershow 66*, with Les Sauterelles, The Times, The Slaves, The Sheapes

Monday 7th

The band returns to London, with Ray's physical health in rapid decline.

Tuesday 8th

Ray sees a doctor today who diagnoses influenza and nervous exhaustion. He is ordered to stay in bed and rest, and to refrain from all concert appearances. Nevertheless, he does at least fulfil a scheduled interview with *NME*'s Keith Altham at home at Fortis Green. He says that 'Dedicated Follower Of Fashion' has "proved that we can do something completely different from our previous singles" though adds dismissively that "it means nothing to me now". He also plays an acetate of Fantoni's recording of 'Little Man In A Little Box'. "My greatest trouble," Ray declares, "is that I'm a composer with no time. All my work is done while we are travelling. It's tough. I've no time to do all the things I want to get over."

Wednesday 9th

A press release announces The Kinks are cancelling all scheduled appearances this week and that, with Ray's physical and mental condition worsening, a replacement for him is being considered for the upcoming Belgian-French tour. With Ray refusing and unable to do press interviews, the responsibility falls largely to Dave because it is important to be in the press as their record continues to move up the charts. Among others Dave speaks to *Melody Maker* today about influences on the band, citing an LP by Albert Schweitzer playing Bach and Miles Davis's *Quiet Nights* album. He reveals that the very first two recordings by the nascent Kinks were his own compositions (likely referring back to the Ray Davies Quartet demos from 1962-early '63). He also says that 'Dedicated Follower Of Fashion' was influenced by World War II ukulele star George Formby.

Ray's illness severely limits the band's ability to do conventional TV spots and as an alternative a film without the band is considered. Just such a film, filled with scenes of Carnaby Street accompanying the audio track of 'Dedicated Follower Of Fashion', will surface later. It's also notable that no BBC radio sessions are done from now until August 1967, creating an unfortunate gap in the band's radio-performance history at this creatively important time.

☆ Bookings tonight for the Leveshume and Devonshire sporting clubs, both in Manchester, are cancelled due to Ray's illness.

Thursday 10th

The Kinks audition and hire a local friend, guitarist Mick Grace of The Cockneys, to replace Ray on guitar for the upcoming tour. In *Record Mirror* Dave, who will now be singing lead vocals, says Ray has approved the idea. Dave will write later in *Kink*: "The managers were standing there, they were like six foot five, and I said, 'Don't look at me, what do you want me to do?' So they said, 'What about getting a hall together and just rehearse some of the songs?' So we did that with me singing, and then they suggested we do the tour. We did ten days and I was totally stoned the whole time. We played Brussels and some outlying areas of France. I didn't know very much about those two weeks. But we got [Grace], a rhythm guitarist, to just sort of fill in … We'd known this guy for ages and he knew the material and looked not dissimilar to Ray, [though his] left-handed guitar was a bit too [different]. We were in Belgium and this wise spark of a kid yells out to his friend, 'Hey, he's not Ray Davies.' But another drink and a few more

pills and we'd go out and do the next show. It was a disaster. It was awful."
☆ Scheduled but cancelled is a TV taping for *Scene At 6:30* at Granada Television Centre in Manchester. The February 24th taped performance of 'Dedicated Follower of Fashion' probably goes out on *Top Of The Pops* tonight, and later in *X-Ray* Ray says that the sight of seeing himself performing the song on TV prompts him to try to throw his set out the kitchen window. He settles for sticking it inside his gas oven, still plugged in and with the image of Ray and the band never disappearing. Maybe this is literary license at work, but the imagery surely conveys his state of mind at the time and the effect of the starmaking machinery surrounding him.

Friday 11th

The Ray-less Kinks plus manager Grenville Collins travel to Paris where the band is interviewed and possibly perform on a TV show, details unknown.

❑ **TOUR STARTS** *France/Belgium Tour* (Mar 12th – 20th). **Line-up**: Ray Davies (lead vocal, guitar), Dave Davies (guitar, vocal), Mick Avory (drums), Pete Quaife (bass). Other acts appearing at various dates include Oliver Despax, Carol Friday, Chris Sanford, Les Sunlights, John's Four.

Saturday 12th

Eden Ranch *Loison-Sous-Lens, France* Bal du Boxing-Ring Lensois
An early evening annual ball, and not part of the package tour. One account suggests attendance is poor because people are unsure if this is the real Kinks or a hoax.
Place Gerard Kasier *Mouscron, Belgium* 4:00pm, with (in addition to tour regulars) Little Jimmy & The Shamrocks, Liberty 6, Les Challengers, The Kings Five, Les Relatifs, R & Rs, The Black Shieks
The official opening of the package tour.

Sunday 13th

Unknown venue *Amiens, France*
Unknown venue *St. Quentin, France*

Monday 14th

Salle Roger Salengro *Lille, France* 9:00pm
Meanwhile in London, a press release says Ray is still ill and that Mick Grace is doing Belgian dates and may continue to perform with the band when they return to Britain. Ray does some limited press from his home, speaking for example with reporter Judith Simons of *The Daily Express*. "[At art school] I tried to find a medium to describe the monotony of modern life," he tells her. "I could not manage to achieve this in painting or poetry. But with songs I found a way. I studied French, jazz, Indian and Chinese music, which, used the right way, I find very moving." At present in bed with flu, Ray is trying another medium to describe monotony: he is writing a play about some characters who attempt to escape from the tedium of their lives.

Tuesday 15th

Koningen Elisabethzaal *Antwerpen, Belgium*
Back in the house on Fortis Green in London, Ray's condition worsens.

Wednesday 16th

Kursaal *Boulogne, France*

Thursday 17th

Coliséum *Verviers, Belgium* 8:00pm, with (in addtion to tour regulars) The Gamblers
In London the chaos continues. A delirious Ray tries to punch Kinks publicist Brian Sommerville after apparently running the six miles or so

from his home to Sommerville's central-London office. Ray is subsequently pursued by the police for assault, and of all places seeks refuge in former publisher Edward Kassner's office until manager Robert Wace, accompanied by a doctor, is able to rescue him. The doctor assures the police that his patient has had a relapse and will again be confined to bed. Sommerville resigns his position as publicist for The Kinks the following day.

Ultimately, Ray makes it clear that he doesn't want to do any more long tours. In essence it is agreed to fulfil existing commitments through October but that for now nothing major will be booked after that. This is an important moment for Ray in particular, because he is in effect rejecting the lifestyle that puts him and the band on a seemingly never-ending treadmill of touring. Management view touring as a means of generating income, and the higher the record is in the charts, the higher the fee. As a contrast, income from the paltry record deal is minimal at best.

Once Ray recovers, he is persuaded to fulfil all the tour plans in place until later in the year, but from that point concert appearances will be drastically reduced in number. Battle lines have already been drawn by Boscobel Productions between Denmark Productions and Kassner Music, and Sommerville's firing represents the removal of another key part of the original business team. Now, Arthur Howes and the remaining management team are forced to accept a new understanding of how touring will proceed in future. The next battlefront for Ray will be the recording contract with Pye Records.

Friday 18th

Liège Palace *Liège, Belgium* 11:00pm
While the Ray-less package tour continues in Europe, back in London Ray goes for a drive with Robert Wace as a bit of therapy. Wace is shopping for a new home out of town, likely the inspiration for Ray's song 'A House In The Country'.
'King Of The Whole Wide World' single by Leapy Lee released in the UK, song and production by Ray Davies, some Kinks members playing (see February 20th). It does not chart, and the planned recording of a full album with Lee is abandoned.

Saturday 19th

Salle de l'Été *Brussels, Belgium* 3:00 & 8:00pm, without Oliver Despax, but plus The Shamrocks, The Kings Five, The King Bees, Deny Vinson; sponsored by Le Club de Rock and Roll

Sunday 20th

Unknown venue *Bruay, France*
Unknown venue *Dunkirk, France*

Monday 21st – Wednesday 23rd

As a tired and exasperated band travels back to London on Monday, a press release reveals that Ray suffered a relapse last Thursday, but nevertheless the release optimistically announces upcoming Kinks concert dates. Ray continues to recuperate at home, reportedly writing new material.

Thursday 24th

Cancelled today is an appearance on tonight's edition of *Top Of The Pops* from BBC Television Centre in west London.

Friday 25th

Cancelled today is a concert at the Ross Group Sports Club Dance in the Mecca Gaiety Ballroom, Grimsby, Lincs. At one point it is intended to do this show and other British dates with Mick Grace continuing to stand in for Ray, but ultimately this scheme is rejected. At Grimsby, The Fourmost, The Nashville Teens, and The She Trinity appear instead, with The Kinks rebooked for August 19th. Meanwhile as the band unexpectedly has time off Dave attends the opening show of The Walker Brothers/Roy Orbison tour at the Finsbury Park Astoria in north London.

Saturday 26th

Surprisingly, Ray is able to honour a long-standing booking and makes an appearance at BBC Television Centre where he is a panellist on this evening's edition of *Juke Box Jury* on BBC-1. However, tonight's gig at the Bromel Club at the Bromley Court Hotel in Bromley, Kent is not fulfilled. The Kinks minus Ray make the effort to appear at the club but don't perform, at least allowing them to mingle with fans as a gesture of good faith and to help reduce any public backlash for the string of cancelled concerts. The Bromel show is rescheduled for May 1st.

Sunday 27th

Ray is still recuperating. Had plans been finalised, today (Easter Sunday) would have marked the start of a ten-day stay for The Kinks in New York City as part of the Murray The K Show at the Paramount Theater with Gene Pitney and The Shangri-Las. Optimistic tour plans for America are nonetheless still being made, in the absence of any firm statement by the US Labor Department or union officials about the band's apparently unwelcome status there.

Monday 28th

A press release confirms that Ray is still ill and that all concert dates are cancelled. Today's booking was for the Carousel Club, Farnborough, Hants, cancelled the day before and rescheduled for May 16th. Nonetheless, some time this week Ray reviews new record releases for *Disc Weekly*.

Wednesday 30th

The Kinks hire Allan MacDougall's Project Publicity company as their new publicists, with partner Frank Smyth also handling the Kink account.
The Kinks Kontroversy album released in the US. *Billboard* says it is a "hot package of rockin' blues sounds, sure to delight the dance-beat set".

Thursday 31st

❏ **TV** BBC Television Centre *west London*. BBC-1 **Top Of The Pops** lip-synch 'Dedicated Follower Of Fashion'. Dave and Ray, interviewed by Norrie Drummond, mention that The Animals are currently considering Ray's 'I'm Not Like Everybody Else' for possible recording, and that Ray is collaborating with satirical cartoonist Gerald Scarfe. Backstage at the show Ray offers a new composition, 'This Is Where I Belong', to The Seekers, who ultimately do not respond. The Kinks will record the song in May.

April

➡ Cancelled concerts originally planned for this period include: April 1st Top Spot Ballroom, Ross-On-Wye, Herefords rescheduled June 10th; April 3rd Guildhall, Portsmouth with The Small Faces and Lou Christie; April 6th Locarno Ballroom, Stevenage, Herts rescheduled August 31st; April 7th Locarno Ballroom, Streatham, south London rescheduled May 12th; April 9th Palais de Danse, Bury, Lancs and Oasis Club, Manchester with The Rockin' Vicars.

Monday 4th

While Ray is home writing new material, manager Robert Wace phones in this week's news to the music papers from his Mayfair office. He says The Kinks hope to resume their bookings this weekend, and that a US tour this summer with Roy Orbison, June 22nd-July 31st, is under consideration.
☆ 'Dedicated Follower Of Fashion' peaked the previous week at number 2 in *Melody Maker* and is now dropping. It is time to think about the next single that might take its place. Ray will report later in *X-Ray* that management turns up on his doorstep with just such a question, and that he replies that his only desire is to leave the business and become a painter.

➡ *Jackie* magazine reveals around this time that "Ray has started writing a stage musical. Says it's going to be about the Prime Minister, Bobby Charlton, himself, and practically anyone else he can think of".

Sunday 10th

In a burst of creativity, Ray reportedly writes six new songs today. One of his recent new songs is described as a patriotic song about England, 'You Ain't What You Used To Be', though nothing more is heard of it.
☆ Today's scheduled concert is way up north at the Cosmopolitan Club in Carlisle where it is announced: "Owing to the sudden illness of Ray Davies, The Kinks will not be appearing." Chris Farlowe & The Thunderbirds play instead.

Monday 11th

Ray is interviewed by Bob Dawbarn for *Melody Maker* at the Capricorn club in Soho, central London, where Ray talks of his anti-social nature, his political views of England, his recent illness, and the new songwriting binge that the illness has allowed. Tonight's scheduled concert at the Casino Ballroom in Blackpool is another late cancellation.

Monday 11th or Tuesday 12th

● **RECORDING** Pye Studios (No.2) *central London*. The Kinks finally reassemble at Pye early this week with producer Shel Talmy where an initial session is held with a new EP in mind. *Disc Weekly* reports on the results and says the planned EP is about various occupations. The paper describes some songs only by subject, but they are probably '**Mr. Reporter'** (about a pop writer) and '**Everybody Wants To Be A Personality'** (about showbiz people), and possibly '**Sir Jasper'** (about a school teacher). There are also specifically named songs: '**Party Line'**, '**Fallen Idol'** and '**A Girl Who Goes To Discotheques'**, the latter probably an early incarnation of 'Big Black Smoke' or 'Little Miss Queen Of Darkness'. Work on the EP continues the following week at Pye. Besides 'Party Line', nothing from this session is ultimately used.
☆ A press release says Ray's illness has caused cancellation of the weekend's gigs and mentions that the band has been in the studio this week and recorded a new EP. A new single is said to be already written but not recorded.

Saturday 16th

Locomotive Club *Paris, France*
Ray's first concert appearance following his six-week absence while recovering from physical and nervous exhaustion is at this famous Parisian discotheque. Ray is now publicly sporting his recently grown moustache. The Kinks are scheduled for an afternoon and evening show, but the afternoon appearance is considerably delayed due to problems getting the band's equipment through customs, and the band doesn't play to the afternoon crowd until after 7:00pm. The appearance is evidently filmed and a portion later broadcast during the summer on a French television programme, probably *Discorama*, but the performance is described as very uninspired. Ray makes a few comments to Karel J. Beer, who reviews the show for *NME*. Asked if he has tired of being a Kink, he says: "No, I like playing with the boys. The money is in staying home writing songs, but I don't do that because I

Spring 1966 and the band poses for the camera: Dave at the front, Ray behind, Pete Quaife left, Mick Avory right.

get a kick out of playing. We are going for a wider audience now with numbers like 'Dedicated Follower Of Fashion'." (Day following spent travelling back to London.)

Monday 18th
Silver Blades Ice Rink *Streatham, south London*
☆ US band The Lovin' Spoonful make their British debut tonight at the Marquee club in Wardour Street, Soho, central London. The band's easygoing folk-blues style is a probable influence on the emerging Kinks sound.

→ ● RECORDING Pye Studios (No.2) *central London.* Back again at Pye this week the band according to *NME* and *Rave* works on two songs already begun, **'The Reporter'** (aka 'Mr. Reporter') and a song about Charlton Heston (possibly **'Fallen Idol'**), plus a new one, **'End Of The Season'**, about football.

Ray will recall much later in *X-Ray* that three further titles have their origin at this time, **'Holiday In Waikiki'**, **'Most Exclusive Residence For Sale'**, and **'A House In The Country'** (though the latter is more likely done on May 12th/13th). The session may have forced the cancellation of some planned dates in Scotland set to commence on April 20th at the Kinema Ballroom in Dunfermline, Fife, but only the weekend gigs are fulfilled.

Friday 22nd
'I Go To Sleep' single by The Truth released in the UK, a song by Ray Davies. It fails to chart.

Saturday 23rd
City Hall *Perth, Scotland* 8:30-11:55pm, with The Barons, The New Fontanas

Sunday 24th
McGoo's Club *Edinburgh, Scotland*

Monday 25th-Wednesday 27th
On Monday The Kinks travel back to London. Avory is now ill with tonsillitis, the latest Kink to be physically incapable of performing in concert. A tentative appearance on Wednesday at the Winter Gardens, Eastbourne, Sussex is rescheduled for May 11th, though possibly for unrelated reasons. The press is notified this week of Avory's illness and that a substitute is being sought. It is also revealed that The Kinks have been recording and plan to issue an EP on May 13th.
'Dedicated Follower Of Fashion' / **'Sittin' On My Sofa'** single released in the US. *Billboard* says: "Clever, music-hall melody and lyric in the bag of their smash 'A Well Respected Man' should prove just as successful."

Thursday 28th
Sherwood Rooms *Nottingham* 9:00pm-3:00am, with The Bonzo Dog Doo Dah Band, Blues & Roots
Part of the University of Nottingham's Arts Ball, the theme of which is the James Bond movie *Thunderball*. According to the recollection of one of the student sponsors, The Kinks are paid £700 for their appearance, the Bonzo Dog Band £70. As a prank, Bonzo members Vivian Stanshall and Legs Larry Smith throw smoke bombs on stage during The Kinks' performance. Session drummer Clem Cattini replaces Avory, who is too ill to perform.

Friday 29th
City Hall *Newcastle Upon Tyne* 6:15 & 8:15pm, with Dave Dee Dozy Beaky Mick & Tich, Wayne Fontana & The Opposition
Possibly also with Clem Cattini in place of Avory, though unconfirmed.

Saturday 30th
Ray is interviewed by Richard Green in *Record Mirror* and mentions working on a new satirical EP where each of the tracks is about a person in a different job. Ray says that this new EP will include a song called 'A Reporter' (aka 'Mr. Reporter'). He also tells Green that three of his songs are under consideration by The Seekers, The Animals, and The Walker Brothers.

May

Sunday 1st
Bromel Club, Bromley Court Hotel *Bromley, Kent*
Meanwhile across town tonight the prestigious 1966 NME Poll Winners Concert is happening at the Empire Pool in Wembley, featuring The Beatles, The Rolling Stones, The Who, and The Yardbirds … but alas no Kinks this year.

Tuesday 3rd
Cancelled today is a concert that had been planned for the Town Hall, High Wycombe, Bucks.

Thursday 5th
Dave appears in court in Bradford, Yorks regarding a paternity suit in which he has been named by former girlfriend Eileen Fernley. She claims Dave is the father of her 13 month-old son. A suit like this could seriously damage a pop career, and Kink managers make every effort to ensure success in court. After a seven-hour hearing before three magistrates, Dave is cleared of all charges.

Friday 6th
DeMontfort Hall *Leicester* with Dave Dee Dozy Beaky Mick & Tich

Saturday 7th
Irenehal, Jaarbeursgebouw *Utrecht, Netherlands* 3:00pm, *PvdA's Meifestival*, with Boudewijn de Groot, The Motions, Golden Earring, Low Down Blues Group '65, The Clungells
Hotel De Kruisweg *Marum, Netherlands* 8:00pm
The PvdA festival is sponsored by the Dutch Labour Party and attracts an estimated 12,000 teenagers. The festival began in Margriethal but the stage there is crushed in a riot during The Motions' set, so The Kinks' appearance is moved to the adjacent Irenehal. The evening appearance in a nearby hotel is attended by 2,000 fans, possibly with The Motions also playing.

Sunday 8th
Garage Wijkermeerweg *Beverwijk, Netherlands* 3:00pm, with The Bintangs, The Black Ventures, The Hamlets, René & His Alligators, The Rowdys
Scheveningen Casino *Scheveningen, Netherlands* 11:00pm
At Beverwijk The Kinks play for just 20 minutes, the set consisting of 'Louie Louie', 'A Well Respected Man', 'You Really Got Me', 'Dedicated Follower Of Fashion', 'Till The End Of The Day'. The Scheveningen show, possibly broadcast on local radio, is a make-up date for a Den Haag gig cancelled last November.

Monday 9th
Sporthal *Den Helder, Netherlands* Beatfestival, with The Kingbeats, The Motions; sponsored by The Derby Club

Tuesday 10th
Travel to London by air. Quaife flies to Copenhagen for a day and then on to London.

→ INDICATES EVENT AROUND THIS TIME BUT WITH NO FIRM DATE

Wednesday 11th

Winter Gardens *Eastbourne, Sussex* 7:30pm, with The Shades

Thursday 12th – Friday 13th

● **RECORDING** Pye Studios (No.2) *central London*. Shel Talmy is producing and Alan MacKenzie engineering, using the studio's 3-track machine. Songs recorded on the first evening include **'Sir Jasper'**, later attempted in June when it will be referred to as 'Lilacs And Daffodils'. Another abandoned song is **'Yes Man'** that will reappear almost three years later in completely rewritten form as 'Plastic Man'. These two songs are still intended for the planned EP, along with 'Mr. Reporter' and one other. Also recorded are **'I'm Not Like Everybody Else'**, written back in January, and **'This Is Where I Belong'**. **'A House In The Country'** is probably done at this time too.

An early take of 'Sunny Afternoon' is done toward the end of the session on Thursday but is saved for a fresh try on Friday morning, when sessions continue from 10:00am to 3:00pm. Besides completing a fully finished master of **'Sunny Afternoon'**, The Kinks also put **'Fancy'** on tape that day. Nicky Hopkins overdubs a Hohner Melodica, a sort of harmonica with a keyboard, on to the backing track of 'Sunny Afternoon', and Ray, Dave and Rasa add backing vocals.

"'Sunny Afternoon' was made very quickly, in the morning," Ray will recall later in *Rolling Stone*. "It was one of our most atmospheric sessions. I still like to keep tapes of the few minutes before the final takes, things that happen before the session. Maybe it's superstitious … [Quaife] went off and started playing funny little classical things on the bass, more like a lead guitar, and Nicky Hopkins was playing 'Liza' – we always used to play that song. Little things like that helped us get in the feeling of the song.

"At the time I wrote 'Sunny Afternoon' I couldn't listen to anything. I was only playing the *Greatest Hits* of Frank Sinatra and Dylan's 'Maggie's Farm', I just liked its whole presence. I was playing the *Bringing It All Back Home* LP along with my Frank Sinatra and Glen Miller and Bach. It was a strange time."

University Of Kent *Canterbury, Kent*

This evening show on the Friday night – after the second day of recording – is presumably honoured. A scheduled appearance on Thursday at the Locarno Ballroom in Streatham, south London was cancelled at short notice.

Saturday 14th

King's Hall *Stoke-On-Trent* with The Eyes
Golden Torch Ballroom *Tunstall, Stoke-On-Trent*

The King's Hall concert may occur as scheduled today or perhaps is delayed into the summer.

Sunday 15th

Birmingham Theatre *Birmingham* with The Yardbirds, Lewis Ruch, The Bo Street Runners

Monday 16th

Carousel Club *Farnborough, Hants* 7:30pm, with unnamed support

A press release announces 'Sunny Afternoon' as the new Kinks single and says producer Shel Talmy has already completed the new LP due in July.

Tuesday 17th – Thursday 19th

➔ ● **RECORDING** Pye Studios (No.2) *central London*. Probable recording dates for more album tracks.

Friday 20th

University of London, Goldsmiths College *New Cross, south-east London*

'Little Man In A Little Box' single by Barry Fantoni released in the UK, a song by Ray Davies. The *NME* today pans 'Little Man' as "plodding". *Disc & Music Echo* says: "This is so obviously a Ray Davies number with [its] lovely insinuating line and sound creeping in and around you [but chartwise I] don't know about it at all." It does indeed fail to chart.

Saturday 21st

Pavilion Gardens Ballroom *Buxton, Derbys*

An originally announced appearance at the Floral Ballroom, Southport, Lancs is cancelled.

Sunday 22nd

Town Football Club *Edgware, north-west London* with The Small Faces

The Kinks are present at this gig but refuse to appear due to a dispute with the promoters over billing. The Kinks were billed in ads as headliners but are told at showtime that The Small Faces will go on last. Manager Robert Wace tells *Disc & Music Echo*: "It placed The Kinks in an impossible situation – either they topped the bill or they didn't appear."

Monday 23rd

A press release says 'Sunny Afternoon' will be released as the new single on June 3rd and describes the song as the third in a trilogy of Ray Davies compositions about society.

Monday 23rd – Wednesday 25th

New material is worked on at a rehearsal room in the London offices of Belinda Music, the band's music publisher. Ray is interviewed by Bob Dawbarn for *Melody Maker*. He discusses the band's bad reputation and their permit problems with the US unions, and plays a preview acetate of 'Sunny Afternoon' for Dawbarn to review. Ray says he wants to use brass and go for "a rotten trad sound" on the next single – almost certainly a reference to 'Dead End Street', a song already half written at this time.

Ray writes a piece for the British music paper *Disc & Music Echo* that will be headlined "Wake Up Kinks Fans: Stop Looking For The Fights – Listen To The Music". During the article he says he has a preference for Continental audiences and fans, who tend to appreciate the band more for their records. The home fans seem more interested in catching a Kinks brawl onstage. Asked about his new moustache in a separate piece in the same issue, Ray replies: "[It] detracts from the gap in my teeth, which detracts from my long nose, which detracts from my big ears, which detract from my shaggy hair, which detracts from my crooked spine."

It's possible that the song **'Big Black Smoke'** is recorded at this time either as a demo or as an early master (later re-recorded), but details are unclear.

Thursday 26th

Palais *Ashton-Under-Lyne, Lancs*

A previously announced booking for the band slated to take place at the Town Hall in Cranford, Northamptonshire, appears to have ended up as a cancellation.

Friday 27th

Fairfield Halls *Croydon, south London* 6:45 & 9:00pm, with Dave Dee Dozy Beaky Mick & Tich, Sean Buckley & The Breadcrumbs

Saturday 28th

Supreme ballroom *Ramsgate, Kent* 8:00pm-12:00midnight, with The Fingers

kinks'66

Lincoln City Football Club *Lincoln* 12noon-10:30pm, *Top Pop Festival*, with The Who (headliners), The Yardbirds, The Small Faces, The Alan Price Set, Georgie Fame, The Creation, The Barron Knights, The Ivy League, Dave Dee Dozy Beaky Mick & Tich, The Children, Crispian St. Peters, Screaming Lord Sutch, The Koobas, The She Trinity, The Dimples

Major pop festival held on the Whit Monday holiday. In retrospect the line-up would seem to guarantee a big crowd, but attendance is far less than hoped for, and the sponsoring football club loses a considerable amount of money. This is a very early appearance by The Creation, which sprang from the ashes of The Mark Four whose bass player, John Dalton, will soon join The Kinks.

June

Wednesday 1st

Top Rank Suite, Mecca Ballroom *Brighton*

Thursday 2nd

Locarno Ballroom *Sunderland* 7:00-11:30pm

Friday 3rd

Central Pier Marine Ballroom *Morecambe, Lancs* 7:30pm, with The Directors, Harold Graham

Quaife and roadie Jonah Jones are involved in a serious crash after this gig on the M6 in Lymm, Cheshire, as the equipment van hits a truck. Both men are hospitalised at Warrington Hospital. Quaife suffers a broken foot and requires stitches to his scalp. Jones suffers more serious injuries as he was thrown through the windscreen (windshield), fracturing his pelvis and sustaining head injuries.

'Sunny Afternoon' / 'I'm Not Like Everybody Else' single released in the UK.

Saturday 4th

The band travels to London minus the injured Quaife in order to recoup and consider their various upcoming commitments. A concert originally scheduled today at the Imperial Ballroom, Nelson, Lancs is cancelled.

Sunday 5th

Cancelled today is the band's appearance at two shows at the Odeon Cinema, Glasgow, Scotland with Dave Dee Dozy Beaky Mick & Tich, Dean Ford & The Gaylords, The Pathfinders, The Meridians, and The Vipers, again due to Quaife's injuries.

❏ **TV** ABC Television Centre *Birmingham*. ABC *Thank Your Lucky Stars* lip-synch 'Sunny Afternoon' broadcast June 11th (June 12th London). The Kinks decide to honour this scheduled TV taping and appear as a trio, minus Quaife. *Thank Your Lucky Stars* will be cancelled as of June 26th due in part to a Musicians Union ban on miming performances.

Monday 6th

● **RECORDING** Pye Studios (No.2) *central London*. The three-piece Kinks head to Pye to work on tracks for the upcoming LP from 6:00pm to 12midnight. Ray says later in *X-Ray* that backing tracks to six songs are recorded with a session bass player: **'Rosie Won't You Please Come Home'**, **'Session Man'**, **'Too Much On My Mind'**, **'You're Looking Fine'**, **'Fallen Idol'**, and **'Rainy Day In June'**. The last three have certainly been worked on previously, underlining a developing trend at this time for the band to re-work recordings if they feel dissatisfied after initial attempts. But it is not clear if Ray's

Sunny Afternoon single

A **'Sunny Afternoon'** (R. DAVIES).
B **'I'm Not Like Everybody Else'** (R. DAVIES).

UK release June 3rd 1965 (Pye 7N 17125).
US release July 20th 1965 (Reprise 0497).
Musicians Ray Davies lead vocal (A), acoustic guitar (A), electric guitar (B), backing vocal. Dave Davies lead vocal (B), electric guitar, backing vocal (A). Pete Quaife bass guitar. Mick Avory drums. Nicky Hopkins piano, melodica (A). Rasa Davies backing vocal (A).
Recorded Pye Studios (No.2) central London; May 12th-13th 1966; 3-track mixed to mono.
Producer Shel Talmy (for Shel Talmy Productions).
Engineer Alan MacKenzie, "Irish" aka Alan O'Duffy (assistant).
Chart high UK number 2 (1 in some charts); US number 14.

recollection is completely accurate. Producer Shel Talmy says later: "I don't remember hiring a bassist to do [any such] marathon session. I was using [session bassist] Herbie Flowers at the time, and none of that stuff sounds like Herbie, who had a distinctive style." Quaife also says later that the bass playing on these six songs sounds like his style – but that if anyone else wants to take credit for them he doesn't object.

☆ A press release announces news of Quaife's injury and the resulting cancelled appearances.

Tuesday 7th

Cancelled today is a concert at Winter Gardens, Great Malvern, Worcs due to Quaife's injuries. The date is rescheduled for July 12th.

Wednesday 8th

❏ **TV** BBC Television Centre *west London*. BBC-1 **A Whole Scene Going** lip-synch 'Sunny Afternoon' broadcast June 8th 6:30-7:30 pm. The band appears again as a trio. Also on: The Yardbirds, Indian sitar player Ravi Shankar.

Thursday 9th

Early in the afternoon at a rehearsal room in the central-London Savile Row offices of Belinda Music, John Dalton is hired as a temporary bass player for The Kinks so that the band can continue its bookings until Quaife is well enough to return. Dalton is brought in by Bill Fowler, who works for Carlin Music and is The Kinks' record plugger. The band quickly run through 'Sunny Afternoon' and another song and announce to the startled Dalton that he has the job and will be appearing on television with them a short while later.

❏ **TV** BBC Television Centre *west London*. BBC-1 **Top Of The Pops** lip-synch 'Sunny Afternoon' broadcast June 16th. The band are at the TV Centre from the afternoon until 7:00pm, as a quartet again, now with Dalton.

● **RECORDING** Pye Studios *central London*. *NME* reports on this session, from 9:00pm until beyond one in the morning, at which four songs are done: two that have already been put on tape – **End Of The Season** and **Fallen Idol** – and two that are mentioned in the press for the first time – **Most Exclusive Residence For Sale** and **Dandy**. The *NME* piece notes that Dalton is not recording with the band; if that's so, it implies that maybe only overdubs are being added to existing tracks. Ray later tells *Disc & Music Echo* that he wrote 'Dandy' after seeing the movie *Alfie*, which opened in London on March 24th. "It's about a bachelor," says Ray, "who's a mixture of Alfie

and the *Saturday Night, Sunday Morning* bloke."
☆ Cancelled today is a gig at the Ram Jam club in Brixton, south London.

Friday 10th
Ray shaves off his moustache, first grown back in March. Cancelled today is a concert at the Top Spot Ballroom, Ross-On-Wye, Herefords.

Saturday 11th
Plaza Ballroom *Handsworth, Birmingham*
Plaza Ballroom *King's Heath, Birmingham*
John Dalton's live debut with The Kinks is marked by this double booking. With Dalton aboard the band can resume its schedule of concerts and maintain the momentum that is shooting the new 'Sunny Afternoon' single up the charts. Dalton and Ray will both recall that musically this first performance left much to be desired due to Dalton's unfamiliarity with Quaife's equipment and the band's repertoire. (Day off following.)

Monday 13th
Sala de Fiestas Yulia *Madrid, Spain* 8:30pm & 1:00am, with numerous local acts
The band arrives at 12:40pm at Aeropuerto Barajas in Madrid and stays at the El Washington Hotel. Travelling with them is newly-hired road manager Stan Whitley, a friend of Quaife's who will replace the ailing Jonah Jones, and publicist Allan MacDougall. The set tonight is 'Louie Louie', 'You Really Got Me', Little Richard's 'She's Got It', 'All Day And All Of The Night', and 'Milk Cow Blues'.

After this first of a booked three-night engagement the Spanish promoters say that because all four original members are not present they refuse to pay the full amount for the performance so far. New bassist Dalton is jailed for the evening and some of the band's equipment is confiscated. Veteran roadie Sam Curtis flies in to help resolve some of the problems.

The remaining dates are cancelled and eventually the band is able to leave with their equipment intact. *NME* reports that The Kinks file a suit against the club for £10,000 damages.

Tuesday 14th – Wednesday 15th
While in Madrid the band visits the Prado Museum and Ray is reportedly impressed by close views of masterworks by Goya and others. The band is photographed both here and at the Plaza de Municipal, where they are harassed by Spanish police. On Wednesday they return to London via Paris.

Thursday 16th
Nordstrandshallen *Oslo, Norway* 8:00pm, with The Beatnicks, Mojo Blues, The Missing Links, Little Earl & The Sapphires, Jan & Freddy, Four Chiefs, 2nd Evolution Corps
The Kinks arrive very late, having travelled from London to Copenhagen by commercial airline and then Copenhagen to Oslo by private plane, and do not play until 1:00am.

Friday 17th
Landåshallen *Bergen, Norway* 7:00pm, with Rhythmic Six
Two 30-minute shows here, as well as a press conference at Bergen Airport.

Saturday 18th
Earlham Park *Norwich* Ad Hocs Jazz & Blues Festival, with New Jazz Orchestra, Terry Lightfoot Jazzmen, Geno Washington & The Ram Jam Band, Collegians Jazz Band, Anna & Albert with JB Quartet, Broad City Blue Blowers
The band flies back to England and then travels up to an unusual booking where they play to a crowd of almost 7,000 at a predominantly non-pop event, but still seem to attract a screaming and fainting crowd. The festival aims to raise money for the local football (soccer) team, so having The Kinks as headliners is probably intended to attract a larger paying audience.

Sunday 19th
Top Ten Club, New Elizabethan Ballroom *Manchester*
Controversy as Ray obstinately refuses to perform the two recent Kinks hits, 'Sunny Afternoon' and 'Dedicated Follower Of Fashion'.

Monday 20th
❐ **TV** Granada Television Centre *Manchester*. Granada *Scene At 6:30* lip-synch 'Sunny Afternoon' broadcast June 22nd.

Tuesday 21st
University Of Oxford: Balliol College *Oxford*
The band also attends a birthday party for Ray, 22 today, in Muswell Hill.
● **RECORDING** Pye Studios *central London*. '**Little Miss Queen Of Darkness**' is recorded at some point during this busy day in a one-off session for the new LP and will constitute Dalton's one confirmed contribution to the *Face To Face* album.

Wednesday 22nd
Today was planned as the start of a proposed US tour with Roy Orbison that would have continued through July 31st. But late in May, after delaying the start to June 28th, all plans were dropped once it became obvious that the required visas for The Kinks to work in the US would not be forthcoming.

Thursday 23rd
Casino Ballroom *Rochester, Kent*
❐ **TV** BBC Lime Grove Studios *west London*. BBC-1 *Top Of The Pops* lip-synch 'Sunny Afternoon'.

Friday 24th
❐ **TV** Rediffusion Television Studios *Wembley, north-west London*. ATV *Ready Steady Go!* live performance 'Sunny Afternoon', 'Dandy'. As well as the expected hit single, the band previews 'Dandy', a track from their forthcoming album.
☆ Dave tells *Melody Maker* he's disappointed that 'See My Friends' was not recognised as the record that virtually introduced the Indian music influence to pop music. He also mentions his love of guitarists Django Reinhardt and Joe Venuti, and reveals that he has been jailed briefly in both Denmark and Australia … but not so far in Spain.

Ray chats with *Disc & Music Echo* and discusses the sudden flurry of requests for his songs by other artists, and the benefit to his writing when he has time off from touring. "Much of the stuff that's done so well lately was written while I was recuperating from my recent nervous breakdown. In fact I penned some 40 songs for our next LP. The stuff we used to do and our new records ... belong to two different worlds. We've got to work on our stage act to suit this new style. The better your stage act the longer you last."
☆ Meanwhile, at the Rehearsal Club in central London, Welsh band The Iveys – later to become Badfinger – audition for Kinks manager Robert Wace.
☆ Ray reveals later that he decides now to renegotiate the Pye Records contract, and moves to this end are made in the coming weeks.

Saturday 25th
Corn Exchange *Hertford*
Cancelled today is a concert at California Pool Ballroom, Dunstable, Beds due to double booking, and The Honeycombs appear instead.

Monday 27th – Tuesday 28th

● **RECORDING** Pye Studios *central London*. Ray is at Pye assisting in the mixing and/or sequencing of the new LP. Apparently he decides to add two more tracks to the 14 planned so far. A corrected press release announces that the new LP *Face To Face* will have 16 tracks and is due out at the end of July, with two new tracks to be recorded this week, including **'Lilacs And Daffodils'** (aka 'Sir Jasper') with a vocal contribution by Avory. Although not tied to these sessions, a song written by Dave, **'She's My Girl'**, is believed to be recorded among the sessions for the next album this spring, although ultimately rejected for inclusion. It is said to be recorded for release by The Attraction later this year, though this never materialises.

✰ A booking set for Monday at the Bath Pavilion set for tonight is pushed back a week to July 4th.

Wednesday 29th

Cancelled today is a scheduled recording session at Pye Studios as Dave is ill, apparently halting the chance of adding two tracks to the album. Ray will later say that Dave was suffering his own physical breakdown at this time, another indication that the lifestyle and demands of The Kinks' busy schedule is taking its toll on the band members.

Thursday 30th

Pier Ballroom *Worthing, Sussex*

In an attempt to placate fans and perhaps to help repair the band's reputation for cancelling shows, Ray and the others travel to this gig and assure the audience that Dave is seriously ill with tonsillitis and that the performance just cannot be done. They play 'Sunny Afternoon' as a trio and leave.

Earlier in the day Ray is interviewed by Keith Altham for *NME* at the Boscobel offices in central London. He refers to 'Sunny Afternoon' making number 1 in the paper's chart, of Talmy's great job in mixing the track, and of Pye's lousy job designing their previous LP covers. He says he is assisting with the design of the next LP (though in fact it will be executed by Pye's Art Department). Discussing the controversy of the band not playing their last two hits in concert, he says they would like to overhaul their stage act and do fewer ballrooms and clubs, instead focussing on cabaret and summer season venues, including pantomime. Ray tells *NME* he has little interest in touring the US following last year's fiasco there, and especially states his dislike for the Dick Clark package tours – the only outlet for a lot of British bands at the time. He says he feels the only way to do a proper US tour would be to cover the whole country in a massive operation, or preferably to do two or three key national TV appearances.

✰ 'Sunny Afternoon' single peaks at number 2 in *Melody Maker* but in *Record Retailer*, *NME*, and *Disc & Music Echo* it makes number 1, displacing The Beatles and 'Paperback Writer'.

✰ A repeat airing of the previous week's taping of 'Sunny Afternoon' is included in this evening's *Top Of The Pops* on BBC-1.

July

Friday 1st – Sunday 3rd

➔ ● **RECORDING** Pye Studios (No.2) *central London*. Ray is reportedly at Pye again, restoring traditional breaks between tracks after Pye objects to the continuous linking of them with sound effects, and making a final track selection. Dave is still recuperating, and more concerts are cancelled as a result, including: July 1st Municipal Hall, Pontypridd, Glamorgan, Wales; 2nd Civic Hall, Barnsley, Gloucs; 3rd Opera House, Blackpool with Tom Jones.

'A House In The Country' single by The Pretty Things released in the UK, a song by Ray Davies. It reaches only number 50 in the charts.

Monday 4th

Pavilion *Bath* 7.30-10.30pm; tickets 5/- (25p)

Earlier in the day at Pye Studios, Ray talks to the press about the new Kinks LP, and 'Sunny Afternoon' being at number 1. Significantly, he comments to one local paper: "This is the turning point for The Kinks' career. Having made number 1 with a non-rock'n'roll-type song we have the chance to change completely and contemplate things like Christmas pantomime." A little later he will recall, "When 'Sunny Afternoon' was number one I did want to quit … I couldn't see the point of carrying on. I wanted to branch out. Be the manager of a football team. Anything. Then I realised if I stayed with the group I could do more within that framework."

Tuesday 5th

● **RECORDING** Pye Studios (No.2) *central London*. Back at Pye, Ray is doing final mixing and sequencing on the now finalised and completed 14-title album.

Wednesday 6th

Master tapes of the *Face To Face* album are submitted to Pye Records ready for production. A new press release announces this final version of the album with 14 songs and now due for August 12th.

Thursday 7th

❏ **TV** BBC Lime Grove Studios *west London*. BBC-1 ***Top Of The Pops*** lip-synch 'Sunny Afternoon'. On top of the charts, if not the world, The Kinks are back at Lime Grove, with Quaife present but Dalton performing on screen. It is announced that Quaife is expected to resume concerts on July 14th.

✰ Illustrating the high media demand, Ray also tapes an interview for the radio programme *Roundabout* for the BBC African Service. Some time this week he answers readers' questions for *Disc & Music Echo* and when asked how he writes his fabulous songs, says: "I try to get beneath the surface, especially of people. It's like being the man with the X-ray eyes."

Asked what he would do if The Kinks broke up, Ray says it's probably inevitable that he'd go solo. "But I can't ever imagine working without the group. They're such a part of my singing style. I think I'd be a Mr. Micawber – [I'd] wait and see what comes along."

Friday 8th

Romano's Ballroom *Belfast, Northern Ireland* 10:30pm, with The Silhouettes
Strand Ballroom *Portstewart, Co Londonderry, Northern Ireland* 12:45am (Saturday morning), with Walter Lewis

With Dave back in sufficient health the band resumes dates with a second tour of Ireland. Dalton vividly recalls doing these dates, bombing around the Irish countryside in Dave's newly acquired sports car, no doubt Dave's present to himself for The Kinks' return to the top of the charts.

Saturday 9th

Milano's Ballroom *Bangor, Co Down, Northern Ireland* 10:30pm, with The Federals

A previously announced date at Manor Lounge, Stockport, Ches is cancelled.

Sunday 10th

Abbey Ballroom *Drogheda, Co Louth, Ireland* 9:00pm-2:00am, with The Kings

Monday 11th

Astoria Ballroom *Bundoran, Co Donegal, Ireland* 9:00pm, with The Black Aces

Tuesday 12th

While The Kinks return to London, pressing business takes precedence over bookings and a rescheduled appearance at the Winter Gardens, Great Malvern, Worcs is again cancelled.

Wednesday 13th – Thursday 14th

Ray and Kinks managers Robert Wace and Grenville Collins, and their accountant Robert Ransom, abruptly depart for the US to meet with up-and-coming manager Allen Klein at his offices in New York City. Klein has already demonstrated his hard-nosed approach by renegotiating contracts for The Rolling Stones to impressive effect. He is recommended to Kinks management by an industry associate of theirs, Peter Grant, currently road manager for The Animals (and later of great renown as manager of Led Zeppelin). The aim is to sign a business management deal giving Klein the authority to negotiate on behalf of The Kinks, and to discuss terms for his renegotiation of their recording contract with Pye Records. Ray will return on Friday or Saturday, but Wace and Collins stay behind, possibly continuing to Los Angeles to deliver master tapes for the *Face To Face* LP (they will be logged into the Reprise tape vaults on July 18th). Also signed at this time is an independent production agreement with Klein, to allow for possible recording by The Kinks in the US. A potential settlement with producer Shel Talmy is also discussed to free The Kinks from his production ties.

Thursday 14th

Dreamland Amusement Park Ballroom *Margate, Kent* 8:00pm, with Davey Sands & The Essex
The Kinks without Ray show up and apologise to the audience that their performance must be cancelled. David Garrick backed by The Iveys (later Badfinger) substitutes for The Kinks at short notice, arranged by Robert Wace who as manager of Garrick takes the opportunity to steer the young singer and his newly-hired backing band into the spotlight.
☆ A repeat airing of the previous week's taping of 'Sunny Afternoon' is included in this evening's *Top Of The Pops* on BBC-1.

Sunday 17th

Plaza De Toros *Palma, Mallorca, Spain* 7:30pm, *Beat 66*, with The Exotics, The Trixons, Los Beta Quartet, Four Winds, Los 5 del Este, Grupo 15
The band was also scheduled to appear in Barcelona yesterday but that was probably cancelled. They definitely make this Spanish appearance, playing at a huge beat music festival in a bullring. Ray later recalls his lasting memory of the stench of bull shit in their dressing room.

Monday 18th

The band travels back from Spain to London. A press release announces that The Kinks are signing with Allen Klein as their US business manager and that an independent production deal is being set up. It is further revealed that Pye Records director Louis Benjamin has now flown to New York City to meet with Allen Klein to discuss renegotiation of the contract with The Kinks (and with Pye artist Donovan who is also represented by Klein).

Tuesday 19th

The Kinks TV appearance on an episode of *The David Frost Show* due for taping today at Twickenham Studios in west London is cancelled at the last minute over a disagreement about song selection. Presumably the TV people want the band to play their new hit, but details of the dispute are unknown.

Wednesday 20th

Ayr Ice Rink *Ayr, Scotland* 7:30-10:30 pm, with The Redhawks,

The Vikings, The Hi-Fi Combo, The Meridiens
With the band topping the charts they are expected to fill this 4,000 capacity venue.
'Sunny Afternoon' / 'I'm Not Like Everybody Else' single released in the US.

Thursday 21st

Lamlash Hall *Lamlash, Isle Of Arran, Scotland*

Friday 22nd

Raith Ballroom *Kirkcaldy, Fife, Scotland* 7:30pm-1:00am, with The Andy Ross Orchestra; tickets 7/6

Saturday 23rd

Drill Hall *Dumfries, Scotland*
Market Assembly Hall *Carlisle* with The London M.I.5., The Jaguars
The second show of the evening finds the band temporarily back on English soil in the north of Cumberland.

Sunday 24th

Mr McGoo's *Edinburgh, Scotland* 9:30pm
The Scottish visit ends with a club date.

Monday 25th

Presumably at the suggestion of new business manager Allen Klein, papers are filed in London today by The Kinks' accountants for the formation of Ray's own publishing company, Davray Music Ltd. Registration will be accepted on August 23rd.

➜ Ray reviews the new Beatles LP *Revolver* for *Disc & Music Echo*. He's generally in favour, but says he thinks *Rubber Soul* is a stronger LP overall. In a typically sensationalist move, the paper subtitles the piece: "Really it's a load of rubbish". This is taken from a critical remark Ray directs towards a single song, 'Yellow Submarine', and certainly does not characterise his feeling about the album as a whole. Perhaps Ray feels now that he should have released his scathing indictment of the pop press, 'Mr Reporter'?
Dave is also pressed into publicity duties for the week, including a chat with Norrie Drummond for *NME* in which he says that in this future The Kinks will have to broaden their appeal and will probably begin to limit and become more selective about their personal appearances. Asked if he's ever considered making his own record, Dave replies: "I wanted to make a solo disc, and I asked Ray if he would write a song for me. But he wouldn't and so I never made the record."

Thursday 28th

Public Hall *Barrow-In-Furness, Lancs* 7:30pm, with Chapter Five, Five Of A Kind; tickets 5/- (25p) & 3/6 (33p)
Tonight's "concert" is followed by a dance from 10:00pm-1:30am with a separate admission and licensed bar.
☆ In London publishing is assigned today for the new songs on the *Face To Face* LP. The slight delay on this is probably due to the wait to register them with Ray's own just-formed company, Davray.

Friday 29th

Top Spot Ballroom *Ross-on-Wye, Herefords*

Saturday 30th

Outdoor event *Pinhoe, Devon* 6:00pm-12midnight, *Bumper Beat Bar-B-Q*, with Trendsetters Limited, The Variations, The Condiaks, The Cordettes
This is the now-legendary night where The Kinks arrive two hours late

for their performance after waiting in London until the World Cup Final is finished on TV, with England famously beating West Germany. After arriving at 11:45pm they play for just 10 minutes as the show must stop at midnight. The crowd of 6,000 are openly angry and boo the band. The Kinks seem to have an increasingly jaded attitude towards their genuinely enthusiastic fans.

Sunday 31st
It is not clear if The Kinks appear for their scheduled performance at the Princess Theatre, Torquay tonight, but on balance it seems unlikely. Among the others acts booked are The Troggs, managed by Larry Page, who are heading to the top of the charts with 'A Girl Like You', their follow-up to 'Wild Thing' that made number 2. The Troggs clearly base their sound on a revival of the early Kinks sound. Ray will refer later in *X-Ray* to his hopes that Page will drop his claims on The Kinks now that he has regained success with his new discovery – but this will not be the case.

August

Monday 1st-Sunday 14th
The official start of the band's annual holiday during the traditional British holiday period. Ray and family spend time in Norfolk while Dave heads off to Copenhagen to visit Lisbet as well as Quaife, who has stationed himself there temporarily with girlfriend Annette. The holiday was originally planned through the 10th but stretched to the 14th because of business considerations.

Wednesday 10th
The Kinks Greatest Hits album released in the US. *Billboard* says: "Here's a blockbuster sales item based upon all of the group's hits ... should hit fast and hard with the teen market." It will do just that, staying in the *Billboard* charts for an amazing 64-week run and earning a Gold Record Award for retail sales of $1million.

Thursday 11th
Newly appointed US business manager Allen Klein arrives in London for three days to continue contract negotiations with Pye Records. During the quick visit Klein will evidently pass an acetate of 'Dandy' to British producer Mickie Most (yet another who employs Klein as his business manager). Most promptly decides it would be a perfect vehicle for Herman's Hermits who have this week arrived back from a US tour. The Hermits record their own version, virtually identical to that of The Kinks, probably the following week at De Lane Lea Studios in central London, and MGM receives the master tape on August 24th.
☆ Various weekend concerts are cancelled at this time, and it's likely that tonight's scheduled gig at the Palace Ballroom on the Isle of Man is also scratched.

Friday 12th
The *Face To Face* album was originally scheduled for release today in the UK, but is delayed because of the contract renegotiations. Its release is first pushed to late August, then September, and finally October.

Saturday 13th
Gaumont Cinema Bournemouth 6:30 & 9:00pm, with The Walker Brothers, Dave Dee Dozy Beaky Mick & Tich (headliners), The Creation, The Wishful Thinking, Hamilton & The Hamilton Movement, The Quotations
According to Dalton (who remembers the show well as his buddies from his former band The Creation are on the bill) Dave does not show up and the three Kinks present simply do half of 'Sunny Afternoon'

> ## The Kinks Greatest Hits album
> **A1** 'You Really Got Me' (R. DAVIES).
> **A2** 'Tired Of Waiting For You' (R. DAVIES).
> **A3** 'Set Me Free' (R. DAVIES).
> **A4** 'Something Better Beginning' (R. DAVIES).
> **A5** 'Who'll Be The Next In Line' (R. DAVIES).
> **B1** 'Till The End Of The Day' (R. DAVIES).
> **B2** 'Dedicated Follower Of Fashion' (R. DAVIES).
> **B3** 'A Well Respected Man' (R. DAVIES).
> **B4** 'Ev'rybody's Gonna Be Happy' (R. DAVIES).
> **B5** 'All Day And All Of The Night' (R. DAVIES).
>
> **US release** August 10th 1966 (Reprise R 6217 mono/RS 6217 [simulated] stereo). Comprised entirely of previously-issued singles and one album track (A4).
> **Chart high** US number 9.

before apologising and walking off, forced to cancel for the evening. (Cancelled anyway today is the band's announced appearance at the Gliderdrome, Boston, Lincs.)

Sunday 14th
The Kinks cancel a prestigious summer Sunday headlining spot set for today at the Opera House in Blackpool.

Monday 15th
The Birdcage Club, Kimbells Ballroom Southsea, Portsmouth
With Allen Klein's departure from London, The Kinks resume their normal schedule with this club date.

Tuesday 16th
Town Hall Torquay 8:00pm-1:00am, with The Travellers, Reaction, Last-Tik Band, Package Deal
This visit down to Devon probably provides inspiration for the song 'Village Green' which Ray recalls later he conceives while in a pub in Devon where he is disappointed to discover that the beer comes from a pressurised metal keg instead of a traditional wooden barrel. He also observes a trend in Devon for the ruination of country life by modern building.

Wednesday 17th
Flamingo Ballroom Redruth, Cornwall 7:45pm, with The Undecided, Johnny & The Giants
A concert originally announced for tonight at Queen's Hall, Barnstaple, Devon is rescheduled for September 1st.

Friday 19th
Mecca Gaiety Ballroom Grimsby, Lincs 8:00pm-1:00am

Saturday 20th
Rutland County Agricultural Showground Oakham, Rutland 7:30-10:30pm, *Big Beat Festival*, with The Applejacks, Brian Poole & The Tremeloes, The Essex
Tonight's appearance is part of a charity show for the local village, Langham, promoted by one David Watts, a retired major. He will inspire a song in his name as a result of events after the show. The Festival itself is something of an anti-climax for the promoters with a relatively disappointing turnout of about 2,000. Blamed are wild local

rumours of 15,000 mods and rockers pouring into the site, which scares off much of the potential audience. The over-cautious organisers hire some 60 police officers armed with walkie-talkies and four teams of Alsatian patrol dogs.

Following the three opening acts, The Kinks are received with a screaming welcome as they begin their 30-minute show (for which they are paid £450). The crowd enjoy the performance and leave peacefully, with no reported incidents of bad behaviour or vandalism. The promoters just about break even and consider the event a failure.

Afterwards drink flows late into the evening and Ray rescues his brother Dave from the advances of David Watts, whom the band subsequently befriend. Ray will soon immortalise Watts in song. Perhaps the nature of the event, a benefit for a local village, was a further inspiration for Ray's song 'Village Green', which will be first recorded in November.

Sunday 21st
ABC Cinema Great Yarmouth, Norfolk with Paul & Barry Ryan, Tony Rivers & The Castaways, Billy Davis

Tuesday 23rd
Cancelled today is a concert at the Winter Gardens, Great Malvern, Worcs.

Thursday 25th
Locarno Ballroom Burnley, Lancs 7:00pm
Ray will recall this concert specifically in X-Ray as one where the band's current roadie, Stan Whitley, manages to arrive without a single wrong turn. He also notes that Edward Kassner and Larry Page are not relenting in their pursuit of damages over publishing and management rights begun last year.

Friday 26th
Belle Vue Ballroom Manchester

Saturday 27th
Spa Royal Hall Bridlington, Yorks with The C Beats, The Small Four
☆ A three-night return to Mr McGoo's, Edinburgh, Scotland slated for the 28th-30th during the Edinburgh Festival is cancelled.

Monday 29th
Dreamland Amusement Park Ballroom Margate, Kent 8:00pm, with The Writ

Wednesday 31st
Cancelled today is a gig that was due to take place at the Locarno Ballroom, Stevenage, Herts.

September

Thursday 1st
The Kinks cancel a rescheduled date at Queen's Hall in Barnstaple, Devon.

Friday 2nd
New Cornish Riviera Lido Carlyon Bay, Cornwall
Well Respected Kinks album released in the UK. With the proper "new" Kinks album, *Face To Face*, held up by contract negotiations, Pye throws together this budget-priced hits collection so that some kind of new product is on sale while the band's popularity in the singles charts with 'Sunny Afternoon' is still fresh in fans' minds.

Saturday 3rd
Houtrusthallen Den Haag, Netherlands 8:00pm, with Ferre Grignard, Rob Hoeke R&B Group, Hu & The Hilltoppers, The Clungels, The Zipps, The Key
A one-off show in Holland, though the band will return in a few weeks. (Travel back to London tomorrow.)

Monday 5th
According to this week's NME Ray is writing a song for Australian star Normie Rowe.

Monday 5th – Saturday 10th
Time off in London.

Sunday 11th
Quaife gives notice that he is leaving The Kinks. He has decided to stay in Copenhagen, Denmark with his girlfriend and announces his decision to quit the pop business.

Monday 12th
John Dalton, who has continued as the band's temporary bass player, is hired as The Kinks' new full-time bassman.
☆ In the US Herman's Hermits, another of Allen Klein's clients, debut their version of Ray's song 'Dandy' on two US network TV shows – *Hollywood Palace* on ABC (17th) and *The Ed Sullivan Show* on CBS (18th) – and the single is rush-released in America this week. Ray says later in his book X-Ray that he was unaware that Klein offered the song to Mickie Most, the producer of Herman's Hermits, and that he felt undermined by Klein giving it to them. He says it had been intended as the next Kinks A-side.

Tuesday 13th
A press release announces Quaife's departure from The Kinks. Two concerts on the 13th and 14th at the Austurbaejarbioi Cinema in Reykjavik, Iceland are cancelled at the last minute, much to the local promoter's displeasure.
☆ The imminent European tour will mark Dalton's first appearances as an official member of The Kinks, now no longer Quaife's temporary stand-in. A general ban on photo sessions is lifted and pictures with Dalton begin to appear in the European pop press. But in fact this will be Dalton's only tour as an official Kink until his return in April 1969,

Well Respected Kinks album

A1 'A Well Respected Man' (R. DAVIES).
A2 'Where Have All The Good Times Gone' (R. DAVIES).
A3 'Till The End Of The Day' (R. DAVIES).
A4 'Set Me Free' (R. DAVIES).
A5 'Tired of Waiting For You' (R. DAVIES).
B1 'All Day And All Of The Night' (R. DAVIES).
B2 'I Gotta Move' (R. DAVIES).
B3 'Don't You Fret' (R. DAVIES).
B4 'Wait Till The Summer Comes Along' (D. DAVIES).
B5 'You Really Got Me' (R. DAVIES).

UK release September 2nd 1966 (Marble Arch MAL 612 mono/MALS 612 [simulated] stereo). Comprised entirely of previously-issued single and EP tracks.
Chart high UK number 5.

because Quaife will soon rejoin the band after reconsidering his hasty decision to quit.

☆ The Kinks leave for Utrecht, Netherlands on a chartered Trident jet which is used for most of the tour. They are accompanied by two roadies, Jay Vickers and Dave Duffield.

➪ **TOUR STARTS** *European Tour* (Sep 17th – 29th). **Line-up**: Ray Davies (lead vocal, guitar), Dave Davies (guitar, vocal), Mick Avory (drums), John Dalton (bass).

Saturday 17th

Circusresidente Toni Boltini *Soesterberg, Netherlands* 2:00pm, with Peter & The Blizzards, The Bintangs, The Key
Hotel De Kruisweg *Marum, Groningen, Netherlands* 8:00pm with Peter & The Blizzards, The Bintangs; The Key
The band's set at the Soesterberg appearance consists of 'You Really Got Me', 'Till The End Of The Day', 'A Well Respected Man', 'Sunny Afternoon', 'Milk Cow Blues'. At Groningen they perform a 25-minute set to 1,800 teenagers.

Sunday 18th

Session Club '66, Gemeentelijke Autobusbedrijven *Dordrecht, Netherlands* 2:00pm, with The Bintangs, The Key, Optical Illusion
Feesttent *Hoorn, Netherlands* 7:30pm, Bierfeesten Hoorn '66, with The Motions
The evening gig finds 5,000 people under a tent. The Motions are the number one Dutch band at the time. The date was originally set for Roermond, Netherlands but changed to Hoorn.

Monday 19th

❏ **TV** Hessischer Rundfunk Studios *Frankfurt, West Germany.* ARD/ZDF *Zwischen Beat Und Bach* lip-synch 'Sunny Afternoon', 'Party Line' broadcast September 23rd 1967 9.25-10.10pm.

Tuesday 20th

Stadthalle *Vienna, Austria* 9:00pm, with The Rangers, The Bonds, The Rainbows
The Kinks miss a direct commercial flight to Vienna and arrive at the last minute via Graz. *Kronen Zeitung* reports that 107 fans from a crowd of "10,000 beat-brawlers" are charged for vandalism. "The Kinks should not have come to Vienna," insists the reporter. "Not because of their loud music – we can endure that – but because of all the riots the band is provoking." The show is reportedly recorded by local radio but apparently never broadcast.

Wednesday 21st

Sportpalast *Berlin, West Germany* 8:00pm, *Stars Hit Popmusik*, with Chris Andrews (headliner), Graham Bonney, Elisa Gabbal, Marion, The Maglos, The Rainbows

Thursday 22nd

A press conference for the band is held at Torslanda Airport, Gothenburg, Sweden.

Friday 23rd

Liseberg Konserthallen *Gothenburg, Sweden* with The Red Squares, The Gonks

Saturday 24th

Sporthallen *Eskilstuna, Sweden* 8:00pm, with The Goofers, The DeeJays, The Outsiders
Club 700 *Örebro, Sweden* 12midnight, with The Moderations, The Gents, The DeeJays

At Eskilstuna, where there is a record crowd for the venue of 2,500, the set is 'You Really Got Me', 'Till The End Of The Day', 'A Well Respected Man', 'Sunny Afternoon', 'Milk Cow Blues'. 'All Day And All Of The Night'.

Sunday 25th

Mariekällsskolan *Södertälje, Sweden* probably early show
Nalen *Stockholm, Sweden* probably early evening show, *Popgala*, with The Maniacs and seven other bands, sponsored by Swedish music magazine *Bildjournal*
The Stockholm show is scheduled for TV broadcast, but The Kinks' appearance is not filmed due to a dispute.

Monday 26th

Press conference in Copenhagen, Denmark. The band also visits Quaife, who's living here with his Danish girlfriend.

Tuesday 27th

Fyens Forum *Odense, Denmark* 7:00pm, with The Baronets, The Rockfighters, The Red Squares, The Bluebirds
Hit Club *Ålborg, Denmark* 12:30am (Wednesday morning)
Eskilstunakuriren newspaper reports that police dogs are set on a wild crowd at Odense. "During the concert the audience threw chunks of metal on to the stage they had loosened from the floor. The band could have been badly injured had they been hit. The youths stormed the police station once the concert was over because some of their mates had been thrown out for not paying. Broken windows and destroyed mailboxes were proof that there is still life in pop music." The performance at Ålborg is delayed because the band has to return to Odense to pick up the rest of their equipment after failing to get it all on to the first plane, and it becomes apparent that one of Ray's favourite guitars is lost or stolen. At both shows filming is done backstage by Danish TV for broadcast in October, though it's probably never shown.

Wednesday 28th

The band is booked to play The Hit House in Copenhagen but refuse to perform, claiming the venue is "unsuitable". Equipment is subsequently confiscated by the promoters, almost preventing them from going to Sweden the following day. The Scandinavian Musicians' Union imposes a ban on further Kinks concerts after this incident.

Thursday 29th

MFF Stadion *Malmö, Sweden* early show, with The Nursery Rhymes, The Caretakers, The Namelosers
Beat House Club *Ängelholm, Sweden* 11:00pm, *Popbal*, with The Stoke Sect, The Moderations, The Nursery Rhymes, The Caretakers
At Malmö The Kinks play only 15 minutes due to a delay in their trip from Copenhagen. At Ängelholm the set is 'Till The End Of The Day', 'A Well Respected Man', 'Sunny Afternoon', 'Milk Cow Blues', 'You Really Got Me', 'All Day And All Of The Night'.

Friday 30th

Ray recalls in *X-Ray* that today in Copenhagen Quaife formally signs his resignation from The Kinks and their company, Kinks Productions Ltd. The band has evidently returned to the city to face a preliminary hearing about their non-appearance at The Hit House two days earlier. A concert tentatively scheduled for today in Helsinki, Finland is cancelled.

'**All Night Stand**' single by The Thoughts, '**Oh What A Day It's Gonna Be**' single by Mo & Steve, '**End Of The Season**' single by The Uglys all released in the UK. With new recordings from The Kinks deadlocked by contract negotiations this flood of recordings of new Ray songs by other artists hits the market, but none makes the charts.

October

Saturday 1st

The band arrives back in London. Cancelled today is a concert at the Imperial Ballroom, Nelson, Lancs, due to "illness"; The Who replace The Kinks at short notice.

Monday 3rd

A press release announces the cancellation of an upcoming Swiss/Austrian tour because the band is busy renegotiating their US deal. A second release later this week states that The Kinks will effectively terminate all concert appearances for the remainder of 1966.

Tuesday 11th – Tuesday 18th

Ray and Colin Wadie, a new litigation lawyer from the Simkins firm assigned to the case, head off to New York City on a business trip to meet with Allen Klein to finalise a new, direct deal with Reprise for the US. Pye Records director Louis Benjamin is also in New York City meeting with Allen Klein to settle the arrangements with Pye over the renegotiated British deal. Holed up at the Warwick Hotel, Ray and Wadie also give depositions for two days regarding the Kassner case and receive advice on the management dispute awaiting settlement in court.

A US holding company, Bethevin Productions Ltd, is created on behalf of The Kinks and is the party with which the new separate contract with Reprise Records is made and signed at this time.

The Kinks' contract with Reprise Records via Bethevin is for a five-year period and gives Reprise perpetual rights to all submitted masters. The back catalogue is licensed by Reprise from Pye for a nine-year period with all rights reverting to Pye after that. The Kinks sign a new contract with Pye in Britain, also for a five-year period, with perpetual rights to all submitted masters for the remainder of the world excluding the US.

The negotiation is accelerated by the Kinks giving up their demand for "coupling rights" to Pye, which will allow Pye (and the subsequent companies that purchase its catalogue) the right to repackage and reassemble Kinks tracks in any order or combination they see fit. It accounts in part for the seemingly random shuffling of Kinks tracks over a long stream of compilation LPs for years to come.

Ray, Wadie and Wace arrive back in London Monday 17th or Tuesday 18th.

Saturday 15th

Publishing is assigned today for 'Big Black Smoke', a fact that further implies that at least a demo recording of this song has already been completed.

Tuesday 18th

A press release says that recording deals have been finalised and that the new LP is now scheduled for October 28th release. No new single is planned as no suitable material is in the can, it suggests, but new recordings will take place shortly.

☆ Now that a new deal has been settled with Pye Records, recording can begin at Pye Studios under the new arrangement. Rehearsals for new material are held this week at the Savile Row, central-London offices of the band's music publisher, now Carlin Music.

'All Night Stand' single by The Thoughts released in the US, a song by Ray Davies. It does not chart.

Friday 21st

Sunny Afternoon album, otherwise the same as the imminent UK *Face To Face* album, released in The Netherlands.

Friday 21st – Saturday 22nd

● **RECORDING** Pye Studios *central London*. The Kinks are finally back at Pye in Marble Arch where the first new sessions are held since June, and the first with John Dalton as an official Kink. Shel Talmy is back in the producer's seat, with Alan MacKenzie engineering, and they now regularly use Pye's more versatile (and expensive) 4-track tape machine, allowing further room for experimentation in the studio.

'Dead End Street' is recorded. At first the band is augmented by tour manager Bill Collins on organ, an unidentified jazz pianist, and French-horn player Albert Hall (remarkably a real name). Ray will recall that this first session is done with Talmy. Then, he says, at a session later the same evening and without Talmy, just the four Kinks with Ray on piano re-record the song, and then bring in a trombonist to play an overdub. Ray says that the first attempt is "very cold" but that the trombone "added a lot of warmth to it".

'Dead End Street' was evidently half written as early as May and demoed in some form, possibly then, but the final lyrics are only completed now. Ray says later that his recent visit to New York was a partial inspiration for the song, as was the recent Aberfan disaster, where a school full of children in Wales is buried by a mountain of coal waste. He also says the lyrics reflect the plight of coal miners generally and the overall feeling of depression in a Britain in the midst of government cutbacks.

It's reported later that five other songs are ready and recorded over these two days, though precise details are not available. Both Dalton and Quaife have recollections of recording '**Big Black Smoke**', and as the issued version is a 4-track recording and this is believed to be the first session using that format, it seems the issued version is done at this time, despite conflicting evidence. Anything else recorded at these sessions is likely unused or at best re-recorded once Quaife is back in the band.

Friday 28th

Face To Face album is released in the UK. The *NME* summarises "a very varied assortment, all from the versatile pen of Ray Davies – a remarkable achievement".

Monday 31st

A press release announces a new single set for November 18th release and notes plans to produce an accompanying film. The 'Dandy' single by Herman's Hermits peaks at number 5 in the US *Billboard* chart.

November

➜ In one of the stranger twists of the band's history, The Kinks now find themselves negotiating for Quaife's return as their bass player, within a matter of weeks of his withdrawal on September 11th and formal resignation on the 30th. Quaife has returned to London with his girlfriend and is temporarily living at his mother's house until moving into a new place. (Dave will recall later in *Kink* that he persuades Quaife to come to Pye Studios for a session, as recording of the new single hadn't gone well without him. But this probably refers to a slightly later event than the recording of 'Dead End Street', the re-recording of which seems to just pre-date Quaife's return.)

Monday 14th

A press release announces Quaife officially returns as a member of The Kinks. His replacement John Dalton has been informed of the decision and returns to his former job as a coalman.

☆ Today The Kinks shoot an accompanying film for the new single, 'Dead End Street', intended for TV music programmes such as *Top Of*

kinks'66

The Pops. Filmed on location in Camden Town, north London it hints at the style of 1920s silent movies and, especially towards the end, The Keystone Cops. All four Kinks, including the reinstated Quaife, appear as characters: Avory as a boy scout, the other three as undertakers. The slightly macabre film has the undertakers collecting a corpse – played by Kinks roadie Stan Whitley – who at the climax leaps from the coffin and runs away down the street. While the BBC eventually rejects the film, it will be shown on the Continent without problems, including the French TV programme *Le Moulin Rouge* in February 1967 and Belgian show *Vibrato* on March 8th. The film is probably offered for broadcast in the US but is almost certainly not aired there now.

☆ *The Kinks Greatest Hits* album peaks in the US *Billboard* chart at number 9.

Tuesday 15th

Probably today the newly reunited original band lines up at Dezo Hoffman's London studio for a new set of press photos. Fresh interviews are also done with the press. Ray tells *Melody Maker*, presumably deadpan, that he has bought a trombone so that he might be able to play the part on 'Dead End Street' himself in concert, and that Dave has bought and is learning to play a tenor saxophone. He also says he has been asked to write some material for a new band called The Iveys (later Badfinger) whom he met through their association with temporary Kinks road manager Bill Collins. He goes to see them play a showcase one afternoon at the Cavalier Club in Golders Green, north-west London, as he is thinking of producing some acts.

☆ The band rehearses new material at publisher Carlin's offices on Savile Row, central London. The new routine is to work material up, record demos … and then go to Pye to do the masters. This is designed to save time and money, particularly as the band are moving from 3-track to 4-track recording, which commands a higher charge at Pye.

Friday 18th

'Dead End Street' / 'Big Black Smoke' single released in the UK. Bob Dawbarn in *Melody Maker* raves: "If it didn't sell a single copy The Kinks would deserve some sort of an award for this. Once again Ray Davies has come up with some fabulous lyrics and a marvellous melody, and combined with a great production, it should be a great hit."

Monday 21st

A press release says that the 'Dead End Street' promotional film has been submitted to the BBC.

Wednesday 23rd

Rehearsals held for the upcoming recording session. Quaife has two songs written and ready for consideration.

Thursday 24th – Friday 25th

● **RECORDING** Pye Studios (No.2) *central London*. Back in the studio to begin the next round of serious recording for the next LP, with Quaife back on board. Again journalist Keith Altham provides a glimpse into the sessions with a report in *NME*. A composition by Ray and Dave, title unknown, is considered for a possible new single, and material is said to be recorded for a US single.

'Village Green' and 'Priscilla & Sybilla' (aka 'Two Sisters') are committed to tape. It's likely they will be re-recorded in February 1967 and that these earlier versions will remain unreleased. Reports suggest two further songs are worked on around this time, probably including an early version of 'Afternoon Tea'. Another early song possibly recorded around now that will be re-recorded is 'Sand In My Shoes' (later with new lyrics becoming 'Tin Soldier Man'.) It will only surface many years later on an outtake reel that somehow finds its way out of Pye Studios.

It's also around this time that a plan begins to make an ambitious new

---

Face To Face album

A1 'Party Line' (D. DAVIES, R. DAVIES).
A2 'Rosy Won't You Please Come Home' (R. DAVIES).
A3 'Dandy' (R. DAVIES).
A4 'Too Much On My Mind' (R. DAVIES).
A5 'Session Man' (R. DAVIES).
A6 'Rainy Day In June' (R. DAVIES).
A7 'A House In The Country' (R. DAVIES).
B1 'Holiday In Waikiki' (D. DAVIES).
B2 'Most Exclusive Residence For Sale' (R. DAVIES).
B3 'Fancy' (R. DAVIES).
B4 'Little Miss Queen Of Darkness' (R. DAVIES)..
B5 'You're Looking Fine' (R. DAVIES).
B6 'Sunny Afternoon' (R. DAVIES).
B7 'I'll Remember' (R. DAVIES).

UK release October 28th 1966 (Pye NPL 18149 mono/NSLP 18149 stereo).
US release December 7th 1966 (Reprise R 6228 mono/RS 6228 stereo).
Musicians Ray Davies lead vocal except as noted, guitar. Dave Davies lead vocal (A1), guitar, backing vocal. Pete Quaife bass guitar except as noted. John Dalton bass guitar (B4). Mick Avory drums. Nicky Hopkins piano, harpsichord, melodica (B6). Rasa Davies backing vocal (B6). (Ray says in X-Ray that a session bassist plays on A2, A4-A6, B5 from a single June 6th session, but Quaife feels they are his playing style and thus were recorded prior to his June 3rd accident. No definitive resolution to the confusion is available.)
Recorded Pye Studios (No.2) central London; mid April-mid June 1966 except following specific dates as noted. B3, B6: May 13th 1966; B4 June 21st 1966; B7: October/November 1965; B5: initially recorded December 29th-30th 1965, possibly re-recorded; 3-track mixed to mono and stereo (except B6 mono only, B7 probably 1 or 2-track mixed to mono only).
Producer Shel Talmy (for Shel Talmy Productions). Original sleevenotes credit Shel Talmy as "Recorder", Raymond Davies as "Musical Director", with "arrangements" by Raymond Davies and Dave Davies.
Engineer Alan MacKenzie, "Irish" aka Alan O'Duffy (assistant).
Chart high UK number 8; US number 135.

LP for which the song 'Village Green' will be a catalyst. Ray will later tell *Rolling Stone* that he originally wanted it to be "*Under Milk Wood*, something like that".

Under Milk Wood, A Play For Voices was poet Dylan Thomas's final masterwork, completed just prior to his death in 1953. The play's storyline revolves around a spring day in a small Welsh coastal town. It opens just before dawn with a brilliant sunrise as a typically noisy day in the life of the townspeople unfolds, and closes as "the rain of dusk brings on the bawdy night".

Ray's concept evolves over time. It is initially sidelined as not appropriate for a band project – perhaps lending new meaning to the eventual title of the next Kinks album, *Something Else By The Kinks* – and more appropriate as a Ray Davies solo album.

Eventually it leads to the 1968 album *The Kinks Are The Village Green Preservation Society*, which in turn inspires the more ambitious *Preservation Acts 1 & 2* from 1973-74. The concept will take on many twists and turns over the next two years, and will play a central role in

---

→ INDICATES EVENT AROUND THIS TIME BUT WITH NO FIRM DATE

Dead End Street single

A 'Dead End Street' (R. DAVIES).
B 'Big Black Smoke' (R. DAVIES).

UK release November 18th 1966 (Pye 7N 17222).
US release November 30th 1966 (Reprise 0540).
Musicians Ray Davies lead vocal, piano (A), acoustic guitar (B). Dave Davies bass guitar (A), acoustic guitar (A), electric guitar (B), backing vocal. John Dalton bass guitar, backing vocal. Mick Avory drums. Stan Whitley backing vocal (A). John Matthews (or John Marshall) trombone (A).
Recorded Pye Studios (No.2) central London; October 21st 1966; 4-track mixed to mono.
Producer Ray Davies (A), Shel Talmy (for Shel Talmy Productions) (B).
Engineer Alan MacKenzie.
Chart high UK number 6; US number 73.

the story of The Kinks during this time.

☆ Quaife tells *Record Mirror* that much of pop music is getting more tuneful, saying that for example The Kinks just recorded a song that went from having three or four chords to seven.

And Ray talks to another publication, *Music Maker* magazine, saying: "I now look upon making a song as a production – rather like making a film. I know it's the wrong way to do it, but it makes it more exciting for me. You know how actors live their parts? Well, I try to do that. I try to get into the character I am writing about. Producing a successful song is just a question of getting the most important ideas – the basic story of the song."

Saturday 26th

Palais *Wimbledon, south-west London* with Long John Baldry, Twice As Much
The stage debut of the reinstated Kinks. Despite the mid-October statement that the band would not perform for the rest of this year, a couple of shows are booked on the quiet, probably designed to keep the band's playing well-oiled. This one may have been booked originally as a warm-up date for a set of German dates to have begun the next day.

Sunday 27th

Again, despite the announcement not to tour this year, a string of dates had been arranged in West Germany to begin today, with a scheduled return to London on December 5th. The dates will eventually be honoured, rescheduled for January of the new year – at first set to begin on January 5th and then the 15th.

Tuesday 29th

Press screening of 'Dead End Street' promotional film in London.

Wednesday 30th

The BBC announces it will not use the film for 'Dead End Street' submitted for the December 1st broadcast of *Top Of The Pops*, saying they feel the film is in poor taste, and the disc only is played during the show.

'Dead End Street' / 'Big Black Smoke' single released in the US. "Composer Davies comes up with another exceptional off-beat item and the result is a surefire smash," writes *Billboard*. "Driving dance beat in strong support."

December

Wednesday 7th

Face To Face album released in the US. *Billboard* again: "Chalk up another album chart winner for the hot British group as they add their own special treatments to new pop material and spotlight their own singles hit 'Sunny Afternoon'. Their version of 'Dandy' is extremely well done. Compositions and arrangements are by Raymond Davies with the off-beat 'Fancy' and 'I'll Remember' among the standouts."

Thursday 8th

❒ **TV** BBC Lime Grove Studios *west London*. BBC-1 **Top Of The Pops** lip-synch 'Dead End Street', repeated December 22nd.
☆ *Face To Face* album peaks at number 8 in UK *Melody Maker* chart.
☆ Quaife is interviewed by *Beat Instrumental* around this time, revealing that the band is hoping to have an EP out for the new year. He says they have uncovered the tape that the Ray Davies Quartette made on a home tape recorder back when Ray, Dave and Quaife first got together and that they may try to re-record some of the songs, including a solo performance of the standard 'Maleguena' with just Ray on echo-laden guitar. Quaife also suggests that a film offer for the band is in hand.

Friday 9th

The *NME* on sale today announces this year's poll results. The Kinks do better than last year's miserable placing in World Vocal Group, scoring 16th place, with 426 votes, slightly ahead of The Who at number 18. Surprisingly, The Beach Boys win the top spot from The Beatles, with The Walker Brothers at 3 and the Stones at 4.

The Kinks also place in British Vocal Group, at 12, and in British R&B Group at 9, a category topped this year by The Spencer Davis Group who beat the ever-present Rolling Stones. Ray even places in British Male Singer, at 21, where Cliff Richard is number 1, and at 15 in British Vocal Personality. Finally, 'Sunny Afternoon' gets to 10th place in the Best British Disc This Year.

Despite these modest successes, the group chooses not to participate in the NME Poll Winners Show that will be held on May 7th 1967, instead accepting an invitation to appear at a competing show, the Daily Star Record Show, in April.

➔ Around this time Avory has fun with a reporter and insists that the band are holding rehearsals at a scout hut near the Avory family house at West Molesey, Surrey in an attempt to put together an entirely new stage show. He tells the hapless journalist, who apparently swallows the lot without question, that during these rehearsals two Bob Dylan songs are tried out – 'Most Likely You'll Go Your Way And I'll Go Mine' and 'Absolutely Sweet Marie'. There is no likelihood that any of this really happens.
☆ A three-week US tour taking in a TV appearance on the important *Ed Sullivan Show* is negotiated and delayed until early 1967, but in fact never happens.

Saturday 17th

Spa Royal Hall *Bridlington, Yorks* with Three Plus One, The Zeros
Another one-off show, only their second since the end of September. An audience estimated at around 1,000 attends this pre-Christmas pop bash.

Friday 23rd

The band is due to appear at Rediffusion Television Studios in Wembley, north-west London for what will be the final transmission of

kinks'67

Ready Steady Go! alongside an all-star line-up of guests from the show's three-and-a-half-year run in what becomes a farewell party. But The Kinks cancel after being told they would only be miming a short excerpt of 'Sunny Afternoon'. The Small Faces, also present, leave as well. The Who stay on, as do Eric Burdon, Donovan, Paul Jones, The Spencer Davis Group, Keith Relf and Paul Samwell-Smith of The Yardbirds, plus a host of others.

Tuesday 27th

A press release says a new EP (with 'Sunny Afternoon', 'Dandy', 'Dedicated Follower Of Fashion', 'Sybilla & Priscilla') is planned for the end of January, that a new single for the US has been recorded, and that a West German tour, planned to have started on January 5th, is delayed until the 15th.

Thursday 29th

'Dead End Street' single peaks at the number 6 position in the UK *Melody Maker* chart.

Saturday 31st

The Davies family hold their annual celebration at the Queen Alexandra pub in Muswell Hill, north London.

1967

The Kinks struck a balance between extended time in the studio and a comfortable level of live work, allowing members to devote some energy to their personal lives. Two members secretly married and started families, and Ray was already in that position, so this year the pace slowed considerably, reflected in the increasing suburban themes of Ray's writing. The youth-culture revolution and the accompanying drug culture that blossomed this year largely passed The Kinks by. Dave emerged as a songwriter and performer in his own right, adding another element to the complex questions surrounding the band's direction.

Behind the scenes, turmoil still lurked as the first round of the court battle between management factions took place, and appeals would carry on into the following year. Internally, crises revolved around Ray's reluctance to continue to be what he saw as a one-man hit-single machine. Instead, he pushed his attention to album-length works and projects in other mediums, including stage, film and TV, causing some blurring of the band's identity that would persist throughout their career.

January

→ ● **RECORDING** Pye Studios (No.2) *central London*. This month sees intensive recording work on material for both a new LP and a new single. Likely tracks recorded during January (if not late last month) are early takes of **'David Watts'** and **'Harry Rag'**, briefly considered for coupling as a single. Both songs will be re-recorded after the band returns from Germany in February. Reports imply **'No Return'** is recorded now, a track that winds up on the next LP, though there are suggestions it is written as a possible number for samba star Astrud Gilberto.

Thursday 5th

❏ **TV** BBC Lime Grove Studios *west London*. BBC-1 **Top Of The Pops** lip-synch 'Dead End Street'.

↪ **TOUR STARTS** *Beat In Carneval: German Tour* (Jan 16th – 22nd). Line-up: Ray Davies (lead vocal, guitar), Dave Davies (guitar, vocal), Mick Avory (drums), Pete Quaife (bass). Booked by one Herr Lange, Musikproduktion West, Dusseldorf. The package show is already under way, with dates without The Kinks January 13th-15th. The band travels from London to Frankfurt via Cologne.

Sunday 15th

● **RECORDING** Maximum Sound Studio *south-east London*. Evidently squeezed in just prior to heading off on tour, at a small studio in the Old Kent Road Ray produces three demos for The Iveys, the band that has taken his interest. Recorded but only released in the 1990s on bootleg CD are 'I Believe In You Girl' (Ron Griffiths), 'Taxi' (Pete Ham) and 'Sausages And Eggs' (Pete Ham).

Monday 16th

Stadthalle *Offenbach am Main, West Germany* 5:00pm, *Beat In Carneval*, with David Garrick, The Creation, The Impact
Kongresshalle *Frankfurt am Main, West Germany* 8:00pm, *Beat In Carneval*, with David Garrick, The Creation, The Impact, The Mods and others

Tuesday 17th

Niederrheinhalle *Krefeld, West Germany* 5:30pm, *Beat In Carneval*, with David Garrick, The Creation, The Impact, The Monks, The Phantoms, The Generals
Reinhalle *Düsseldorf, West Germany* 8:15pm, *Beat In Carneval*, with David Garrick, The Creation, The Impact, The Monks, The Icens, The Dressman-Guys

→ INDICATES EVENT AROUND THIS TIME BUT WITH NO FIRM DATE

kinks'67

Wednesday 18th

ESV-Halle *Ingolstadt, West Germany* 5:30pm, *Beat In Carneval*, with David Garrick, The Creation, The Impact, The Red Rooster Group, The Mods, The Strolling Rags, The Players Group

Sporthalle *Augsburg, West Germany* 8:30pm, *Beat In Carneval*, with David Garrick, The Creation, The Impact, The Beat-Garde

Following day off in Munich.

Friday 20th

Unknown venue (probably Liederhalle) *Stuttgart, West Germany* 7:30 pm, *Beat In Carneval*, with David Garrick, The Creation, The Impact

Universum Kino *Pforzheim, West Germany* 10:30pm, *Beat In Carneval*, with David Garrick, The Creation, The Impact

Saturday 21st

Bürgerverein *Bonn, West Germany* 5:00pm, *Beat In Carneval*, with David Garrick, The Creation, The Impact

Sporthalle *Cologne, West Germany* 8:00pm, *Beat In Carneval*, with David Garrick, The Creation, The Impact

Sunday 22nd

Circus Krone Bau *Munich, West Germany* 11:00am, *Beat In Carneval*, with David Garrick, The Creation, The Impact, The Beatstones, The Others

Messehalle *Nürnberg, West Germany* 5:00pm, *Beat In Carneval*, with David Garrick, The Creation, The Impact, The Knights, The Souls United, The New Alliance

Monday 23rd

Travel Frankfurt to London. Ray says of the tour: "Yes, it was great [in Germany]. I don't usually enjoy touring too much – the travelling. I like playing, though, and in Germany the audiences were fine. Perhaps a bit older than [in England]." One report says that in Germany The Kinks performed an off-the-cuff version of the Teresa Brewer standard 'Music Music Music' (aka 'Put Another Nickel In the Nickelodeon'). Quaife later recalls playing 'David Watts' to German audiences, so it's possible it was played on this tour to test audience reaction to a potential A-side.

☆ A press release announces a likely Arthur Howes package tour with The Kinks and Dave Dee Dozy Beaky Mick & Tich for the spring.

→ ● **RECORDING** Pye Studios (No.2) *central London.* Sessions for the next single continue. Possibly **'Mister Pleasant'** is recorded around now in an early, ultimately unused version. Ray is interviewed by *Record Mirror* and, asked what the other Kinks think of the type of songs they're now recording, says: "I think that Pete and Dave are happier playing rock'n'roll. Mick and I seem to prefer the kind of thing we're doing now, but I'd like to make a rock'n'roll record – as a single. Yes! I think that we're capable of it, but I am afraid everyone would think we were copying The Troggs."

Ray also speaks to Penny Valentine of *Disc & Music Echo* and makes some prophetic statements. "I don't think people understood those last Kinks singles. 'Dead End Street' shouldn't have been a record. It should have been a film." And he says, "I'd like to own the group. I want to run them by myself. There's too many people at the moment. You work six hours on a new record, then your manager walks through the door and says, 'That's *never* your new single,' and you're shattered and furious."

Saturday 28th

Imperial Ballroom *Nelson, Lancs* with The Bystanders, Ways & Means

February

Saturday 4th

King's Hall *Stoke-on-Trent* 7:30-11:45pm, with The Pacifics, The Heatwaves

The Kinks are originally announced on the bill of a charity concert for the blind today with Herman's Hermits, Paul Jones, and Normie Rowe at the Royal Albert Hall, central London, but the appearance is never finalised.

Sunday 5th

Granada Cinema *Bedford* with Dave Dee Dozy Beaky Mick & Tich

Pilot concert for a potential Arthur Howes package tour that never materialises, due mainly to The Kinks' disapproval of the billing and package shows in general.

Monday 6th

→ ● **RECORDING** Pye Studios *central London.* Ray tells *Melody Maker* that he'd like to tour soon with The Mike Cotton Sound. This is almost certainly because The Kinks use the MCS horn section – Mike Cotton trumpet, John Beechan trombone, and Johnny Crocker saxophone – in the studio on at least one new track, in its early incarnation known as **'Sand In My Shoes'** (re-recorded later as **'Tin Soldier Man'**) and featuring saxophone, trombone and flute. Although the idea has been floated to the press that Ray and Dave have taken up brass instruments, Quaife later confirms that neither was ever capable of playing these in the studio, and that any horn parts at this time were done by MCS members, or session players. The Kinks and MCS have been good friends since at least early 1964, running into each other at early rehearsals at the Athenaeum in Muswell Hill and touring together in '64.

Over the coming weeks the band cancels a tour of Europe with dates in Italy, Austria and Switzerland to make way for further recording time. Believed done at this time are re-recordings of **'David Watts'** and **'Harry Rag'**, first recorded in January (or late December) as a possible new single.

According to Ray's later account in *X-Ray* the issued versions of both **'Village Green'** and **'Two Sisters'** are also re-recorded this month, replacing the initial recordings on November 24th-25th 1966. And probably from this time is the re-recorded master of **'Mister Pleasant'**, with Nicky Hopkins prominently on piano and possibly John Beecham on trombone, and which will be released in April.

It is during this stretch of recording that Monkee Mike Nesmith visits The Kinks at Pye while he is in London on a short visit, most likely stopping by on Thursday 9th.

With less pressure to constantly tour, the band is developing their routine of re-recording songs, and now has the luxury of time to let the recordings sit a while rather than rushing them out for release. Combined with their general practice over the next few years of simply stockpiling material and not targeting a next LP or a next single, this makes precise dating of recordings during this period particularly difficult, especially as no studio logs survive.

Monday 20th

→ ☐ **TV** Astridplein *Antwerpen, Belgium.* Belgian TV *Vibrato* lip-synch 'Sunny Afternoon' broadcast February 21st. In one of their more bizarre TV appearances, The Kinks mime to 'Sunny Afternoon' amid the obvious cold and fresh snow at this outdoor park. The film survives and is used in a 1980s documentary on the band.

Friday 23rd – Saturday 24th

Alhambra Théâtre *Paris, France* with Nursery Rhymes, Vigon

kinks'64

Sunday 25th

Casino de Royat *Clermont Ferrand, France* 5:00pm, with nine other unspecified bands

The day before the show Quaife fractures his leg in a fall while sightseeing on a local mountain in the Puy-de-Dôme. For publicity purposes, however, it is reported that the accident occurred during the concert in Paris the night before. The band travels back to London the following day.

March

● **RECORDING** Pye Studios (No.2) *central London.* Sessions continue at the expense of a planned tour of Belgium and Switzerland pencilled in for March 1st-8th, followed by further cancelled dates mid-month in Poland and Czechoslovakia. Among the tracks possibly recorded during an intense period of studio activity in February and March are the re-recordings and master recordings of **'Afternoon Tea'** and probably **'Situation Vacant'** and **'Love Me Till The Sun Shines'**, though it's possible the masters of these are recorded as late as May, June or July.

The Kinks are also known to have demoed songs during February and March at Central Sound, a London studio they routinely use for such purposes.

Monday 6th

A press release announces a new Kinks EP set for release on April 14th. The proposed track listing is 'Two Sisters', 'Mr Reporter', 'Village Green', 'And I Will Love You', 'This Is Where I Belong'. Although the EP is ultimately never issued, it does make it to test-pressing stage, where 'Mr Reporter' is replaced with 'Mister Pleasant'. The inclusion of the song 'Village Green' among the EP's track list is noteworthy as it perhaps underlines Ray's uncertainty at this time about what to do with the piece.

Sunday 12th

Ray and Dave play in the *Melody Maker* Ravers football match. Weekly Sunday games become a regular activity for the brothers.

→ ● **RECORDING** Pye Studios (No.2) *central London.* With Shel Talmy producing, Alan MacKenzie engineering and Nicky Hopkins on piano, The Kinks around this time probably record **'Act Nice And Gentle'**, eventually used as the UK B-side of 'Waterloo Sunset'. It is certainly now that the band first tackles a backing track for **'Waterloo Sunset'**, but Ray is unhappy with (reportedly) two separate recordings, and arranges to re-record it secretly to his own satisfaction. *Disc & Music Echo* describes Kinks recording activities now as "marathon all-night sessions".

Monday 20th

A press release announces that The Kinks have been approached to appear at the Monterey International Pop Festival in Monterey, CA, June 16th-18th. They will decline, probably because they still can't obtain the necessary working visas for the US.

Monday 27th

A press release says that a new Kinks single will be issued in one month, although the title is not yet available. This refers to 'Waterloo Sunset', not yet recorded in a satisfactory version.

Tuesday 28th

❑ **TV** ATV Television Studios *Elstree, Herts.* US ABC *Piccadilly*

Palace lip-synch 'Dandy', 'A Well Respected Man' broadcast July 29th. Dave also makes a cameo appearance in a comedy skit.

Wednesday 29th – Friday 31st

Scheduled dates in Scotland cancelled (Glasgow April 1st goes ahead).

April

Saturday 1st

Kelvin Hall *Glasgow, Scotland* 6:30 & 9:30pm, *Scene '67 Theatre*, with Sounds Incorporated, The Fortunes

Recorded on the 4-track Pye Mobile Recording Unit. The Kinks' appearance is the finale of ten star-studded days of music in a teen festival sponsored by the local Scene discotheque club and the Glasgow newspaper *The Daily Record*.

Monday 3rd

→ ● **RECORDING** Pye Studios (No.2) *central London.* Dissatisfied with the recently recorded Talmy-produced versions, Ray secretly books into Pye around this time (evidence points to the 3rd) to recut **'Waterloo Sunset'**, producing it himself and not using pianist Nicky Hopkins.

This version is recorded in stages. First is the basic rhythm track: just Ray on acoustic guitar with Quaife and Avory on bass and drums. At separate sessions a week later, Dave's guitar is added, and then vocals. Probably about ten hours in total spent on the remake.

Also during the early to middle part of April, post-production work is completed at Pye on the live recordings taped in Glasgow on April 1st. Besides choosing and assembling the tracks, it appears that some overdubs are made (noticeable for example on the released album's guitar solo on 'Till The End Of The Day', and the differing guitar solos between the mono and stereo mixes of 'You Really Got Me'). The high level of crowd noise in the mix may be intentional on Ray's part; clearly the album is seen as a document of the full in-concert experience with The Kinks as scream-inducing pop icons.

☆ A press release announces that recordings for a live album have been made in Scotland, with further plans to record at the Paris Olympia on April 23rd. The live record is set for late spring release. It also says a single of 'Mister Pleasant' is set for European release, with no new UK single due for at least a month (and which only the band knows will be 'Waterloo Sunset').

Thursday 6th

Belle Vue Hall Ballroom *Manchester* Big Sound '67, with Sounds Incorporated, Cliff Bennett & The Rebel Rousers, The Tremeloes, The Move

Charity show for cancer research. Following is a day off, with Ray and Dave playing in a Showbiz XI football match.

Monday 10th

→ ● **RECORDING** Pye Studios (No.2) *central London.* Probable date of the session to record Dave's electric guitar track for **'Waterloo Sunset'**.

Thursday 13th

● **RECORDING** Pye Studios (No.2) *central London.* According to Ray's later account in *X-Ray* this is the date of the session where the backing-vocal tracks for **'Waterloo Sunset'** are recorded with Ray, Dave, Pete and Rasa, and then later the same evening Ray puts on the lead vocal.

After that, Ray personally makes the mono mix with engineer Alan MacKenzie, cutting an acetate for his personal use so that he can

It's April 16th 1967: Ray (left) and Dave heat up the stage at The Daily Express Record Star Show, Wembley.

kinks'67

Mister Pleasant single

A 'Mister Pleasant' (R. DAVIES).
B-NL 'This Is Where I Belong' (R. DAVIES).
B-US 'Harry Rag' (R. DAVIES).

Netherlands release (A/B-NL) April 21st 1967 (Pye 7N 17314).
US release (A/B-US) May 24th 1967 (Reprise 0587).
Musicians Ray Davies lead vocal, acoustic guitar (A), electric guitar (B-NL). Dave Davies electric guitar, backing vocal. Pete Quaife bass guitar, backing vocal (A). Mick Avory drums. Nicky Hopkins piano (A). John Beecham (or unconfirmed session player) trombone (A). Rasa Davies backing vocal (A).
Recorded Pye Studios (No.2) central London; A/B-US: February 1967, 4-track mixed to mono; B-NL: May 13th 1966, 3-track mixed to mono.
Producer Shel Talmy (for Shel Talmy Productions).
Engineer Alan MacKenzie, "Irish" aka Alan O'Duffy (assistant).
Chart high Netherlands number 2; US number 80.

decide if it should be issued as the next Kinks single. Ray says in *X-Ray* that the recording was of such a personal nature that he briefly hesitated in releasing it at all.

This further session arranged in the absence of regular Kinks producer Shel Talmy underlines the role Ray has now effectively assumed as the band's studio producer. Precise details of the change in the business arrangement are unknown, though Talmy will say later that it was by mutual agreement between the two parties and that his contract with the band simply lapsed.

It is possible that in the course of renegotiating their record contract with Pye the previous autumn The Kinks had also renegotiated their arrangement with Talmy, which would allow for such a relatively painless separation now. In any event, it's significant that no production credit for Shel Talmy Productions will appear on the label of the 'Waterloo Sunset' single, and in fact no production credit appears at all. Similarly, no production credit of any kind will appear on British pressings of the forthcoming live album, or the *Something Else* LP, or Dave's first solo record.

Only upon release of the 'Autumn Almanac' single in October will a "produced by Ray Davies" label-credit suggest a transition before the new arrangement is formally worked out. A press release in July announcing the *Something Else* LP will however state that it is the first to be produced by Ray Davies.

As a large portion of the recording for The Kinks' next studio album is essentially already done, it seems that after this point Talmy's presence in the studio ceases or very rapidly comes to an end.

It is not clear to what degree re-recording of any Talmy-produced recordings occur, but it is certainly the case that the resulting LP will be a mixture of Ray Davies-produced and Shel Talmy-produced recordings.

Sunday 16th

Empire Pool *Wembley, north-west London* 1967 *Daily Express Record Star Show*, with The Alan Price Set, The Troggs, The New Vaudeville Band, Julie Felix, Paul Jones, Dave Dee Dozy Beaky Mick & Tich, The Tremeloes, The Move, Cream, Chris Farlowe, Dave Berry, Cliff Bennett, Geno Washington, Lulu, David & Jonathan, Freddie & The Dreamers; hosted by DJs David Jacobs, Simon Dee, Alan Freeman, Don Moss, Pete Murray; presented by Stars

Organisation For Spastics
While the Kinks never appeared at another of the *NME*-sponsored all-star shows after the 1965 debacle, they do turn up at this similar event held at the same venue, sponsored by one of Britain's most popular daily newspapers. The Kinks' spot only features two songs, 'Till The End Of The Day' and 'Dandy'. Highlights only of the show are broadcast April 26th 6.17-6.47 pm on BBC-1 TV, without The Kinks.

→ Some time this spring Quaife secretly marries his now pregnant girlfriend Annette Pautison, familiarly known as Bitten, at the Finsbury Park Registry Office, north London. Meanwhile in April, Dave secretly marries Annette's cousin Lisbet Thorkil-Peterson, at the Town Hall, Frederiksberg, Copenhagen, Denmark. Lisbet will give birth to their first son, Martin, in September. The marriage and the birth are successfully hidden from the press, to maintain Dave's public image. Shortly hereafter Dave purchases a house in Cockfosters, north London, just a few miles north of his parents' Muswell Hill home. This will mean that three-quarters of the Kinks are now young suburban family men (Avory is the sole bachelor for now), a fact certainly not publicised, but one that explains in part the relatively quiet period for the band during 1967-68.

☆ A surviving advance "acetate" disc shows that it is briefly considered to couple 'Waterloo Sunset' with 'Village Green' as the new British single. While such a pairing would have made an amazing single, Ray keeps pulling back 'Village Green', saving it for a bigger but as yet unformulated concept.

Friday 21st

'Mister Pleasant' / 'This Is Where I Belong' single briefly planned for UK release is instead released in The Netherlands. Plans for the British release are apparently advanced enough that copies have been pressed ready for sale, but once 'Waterloo Sunset' appears as a contender it is decided to hold back UK release and export copies instead to sell on the Continent – where it becomes hugely popular. For France and Spain, where the EP is the major format, two as-yet-unreleased tracks, 'Two Sisters' and 'Village Green', are added to the Dutch single cuts. This marks a release for 'Village Green' nearly two years ahead of its inclusion on *The Village Green Preservation Society* album that it inspires.

Sunday 23rd

A concert was planned for tonight at the Olympia, Paris, France where more tracks were to be recorded for the upcoming live LP, but the appearance is scrapped. In London, Ray and Dave play another Showbiz XI football match.

Monday 24th

Top Rank Suite *Cardiff, Wales* with Johnny Howard Band, Simon Dupree & The Big Sound, The Creation
It's reported that The Kinks also play some shows in Welsh border towns in the days following this Cardiff appearance, but details are unknown. The unusual, low-key bookings are almost certainly intentional on Ray's part, so that he has an excuse to visit a few coastal villages similar to those that inspired Dylan Thomas's play *Under Milk Wood*, based on daily life in such towns, and also set in springtime. It could help provide inspiration for Ray's developing ideas for his *Village Green* concept.

☆ A press release says the band will be off to The Netherlands for a TV appearance and to Scandinavia, May 8th-15th, then to Scotland May 3rd-5th, and to Greece in September. The Greek dates will not happen.

→ Ray attends legal strategy meetings around this time with the counsel for Boscobel Productions for the upcoming trial where

Denmark Productions is suing Boscobel for damages for breach of contract.

☆ Ray visits Graham Nash of The Hollies at his home to try the Mellotron, a new tape-loop-based keyboard instrument. The instrument proves attractive to Ray as it offers a wide array of sounds that can be used in recording in place of hiring wind, string and other assorted session players.

☆ The Kinks assemble at Leale-Clareville Photography Studios in London for a major photo session with Mike Leale on behalf of Pye Records for two upcoming LP releases, *Live At Kelvin Hall* and *Something Else By The Kinks*. The so-called concert shots used on the live LP sleeve will in fact be these posed photo-studio pictures. In a rare tip of the hat to the current flower-power rage, the band is also staged among a setting of artificial flowers in their finest fashions of the day. At the same time the band poses for a location shot using a rented psychedelic car, prominently featured on the cover of the Marble Arch album *Sunny Afternoon* later in the year.

Friday 28th

❏ **TV** Nederland 1 TV Studio *Zaandam, Netherlands*. VARA TV **Fan Club** lip-synch 'Mister Pleasant', 'This Is Where I Belong' broadcast May 5th. The band arrives at Schipol Airport in Amsterdam, Netherlands at 10:30am for two days of press and TV appearances to promote their Continent-only new single 'Mister Pleasant'. Another British band, Pink Floyd, tape their segment the following day for the same show. The Kinks are captured in a photo session outside the TV studio; the results surface on the Dutch-only 1967 LP *Greatest Hits*.

Saturday 29th

❏ **TV** VPRO Television Studios (A) *Hilversum, Netherlands*. VPRO TV **Adele Bloementhal Show** lip-synch 'Dead End Street', 'Sunny Afternoon', 'Mister Pleasant' broadcast June 5th. The band returns to London the following day.

Waterloo Sunset single

A 'Waterloo Sunset' (R. DAVIES).
B-UK 'Act Nice And Gentle' (R. DAVIES).
B-US 'Two Sisters' (R. DAVIES).

UK release (A/B-UK) May 5th 1967 (Pye 7N 17321).
US release (A/B-US) July 26th 1967 (Reprise 0612).
Musicians Ray Davies lead vocal, acoustic guitar (A, B-UK), backing vocal, piano chord at end (A). Dave Davies electric guitar, backing vocal. Pete Quaife bass guitar, backing vocal. Mick Avory drums. Rasa Davies backing vocal (A). Nicky Hopkins piano (B-UK), harpsichord (B-US). David Whitaker string arrangement (B-US).
Recorded Pye Studios (No.2) central London; A: early April 1967, final session April 13th; B-UK: probably March 1967; B-US: November 24th/25th 1966 and February 1967; 4-track mixed to mono.
Producer Ray Davies (A); Shel Talmy (B-UK, B-US). (No production credit on UK label; US label credits Shel Talmy Productions.)
Engineer Alan MacKenzie.
Chart high UK number 2; US none.

May

→ During the first week of May Kinks managers Robert Wace and Grenville Collins make an arrangement with Andrew Loog Oldham and Tony Calder of Immediate Records to take over management responsibilities of The Small Faces for one year. This is part of a move by Calder and Oldham to avoid a conflict of interest with their Immediate label.

Wednesday 3rd

Edinburgh University *Edinburgh, Scotland* *Jazz'n'Beat Ball*
The Kinks replace originally-booked Dave Dee Dozy Beaky Mick & Tich at a few weeks' notice.

Thursday 4th

❏ **TV** BBC Lime Grove Studios *west London*. BBC-1 **Top Of The Pops** lip-synch 'Waterloo Sunset'. The band's long-awaited new single is a featured new release on the all-important BBC record show, the day before it reaches the shops. The Jimi Hendrix Experience also appear, plugging their third British single 'The Wind Cries Mary', which is also out tomorrow. Ray will later recall that Hendrix is very complimentary to him.

☆ Indicating that The Kinks are behind schedule in the US, Reprise receives master tapes of 'Waterloo Sunset', 'Mister Pleasant', 'Harry Rag' and 'Two Sisters' for release over two singles. Initially, Reprise couples the two potential A-sides from among the tracks – 'Mister Pleasant' backed with 'Waterloo Sunset' – but will realise their error prior to production.

Friday 5th

University of Glasgow *Glasgow, Scotland* *Summer Ball*, with Zoot Money & His Big Roll Band, Bonzo Dog Doo Dah Band
'Waterloo Sunset' / 'Act Nice And Gentle' single released in the UK. *NME* says: "A thoroughly interesting and very clever disc by The Kinks bristling with contrasts in influences. ... A very catchy tune and an absorbing lyric make this an extremely good pop record. Ray Davies emerges with credit as composer and producer for his intelligent technical approach."

Melody Maker's reviewer writes: "The Kinks have taken a well-deserved and obviously reflective breather from the recording scene, but here they blossom again with that evergreen Kinks sound, noticeably matured, becoming more subtle and less aggressive."

☆ Ray recalls later in *X-Ray* that *Disc & Music Echo* journalist Penny Valentine phones at the time to tell him that 'Waterloo Sunset' is the best record he will ever make.

☆ Ray says later in *The Official Biography* that some inspiration for 'Waterloo Sunset' came from the time when as a child he was in St. Thomas's Hospital in Waterloo, by the Thames in central London.

"I nearly died," Ray recalled for Jon Savage. "I had a tracheotomy and the balloon burst. I was attached to a machine and I had a nightmare and pulled all the things out of my arms. Then two or three or four days later I couldn't speak because of the operation. Two nurses wheeled me out on to the balcony, where I could see the River Thames. It was just a very poetic moment for me. So [when I wrote 'Waterloo Sunset'] I thought about that time – I wanted to write a really great London song."

Saturday 6th

Earlham Park *Norwich* *Rag Barbeque*, with Chris Farlowe & The Thunderbirds

Monday 8th

Scheduled start of Swedish tour delayed to May 11th.

Tuesday 9th

Ray, interviewed by the *NME*, says he has considered using a stand-in during the band's concert appearances so that he can devote more time to recording, in the same way as Brian Wilson of The Beach Boys has done. In typical fashion the piece carries the inflammatory headline "Ray Davies Quitting Kinks?" and management does some quick damage control.

Wednesday 10th

❑ **TV** Playhouse Theatre *Manchester*. BBC-1 *It's Dee Time* lip-synch 'Waterloo Sunset' broadcast May 18th. A scheduled departure afterwards to Sweden is delayed another day and the band returns to London.

Thursday 11th

Yet again the start of the Swedish tour is rescheduled as Quaife's wife suffers complications during childbirth. At first only today's show is cancelled, but soon the rest of the dates go too. Shows are tentatively rescheduled for September, but are never done. Due to the secret nature of Quiafe's marriage, details of the cancellation are not given to the press. Cancelled dates: May 11th Liseberg Konserthallen, Gothenburg; 12th Rígeletto, Jönköping (cancelled three and a half hours before show; Red Squares perform instead); 13th Högbo Bruk, Sandviken; 14th Norrmalmia, Piteå and Ishallen, Boden; 15th Gröna Lund, Stockholm and recording for Swedish radio at Radiohuset, Stockholm.

☆ With some unexpected free time, Ray does some press work. While pub hopping at Jack Straw's Castle and the Bull And Bush in Hampstead, north-west London with *NME* journalist Keith Altham he elaborates further on his ideas for the future, including the first mention publicly that he is working on a solo LP "with a London theme" on which he "sings a few songs and has composed all the music".

He says he would "like to do something on the stage in a controlling capacity and eventually make films, but again in more of a behind-the-camera position". Altham further reveals that Ray would like Dave to write the next single – which is essentially what will happen – and feels his brother's work is now much improved. "I feel I should exploit him more," says Ray.

Talking to *Melody Maker*, he says that EMI has expressed interest in signing him as a producer, and while nothing will come of the EMI connection, it is an area that Ray will investigate.

Monday 15th

● **RECORDING** Pye Studios *central London*. A press release reveals The Kinks are currently recording. No details are known but it is possible that Dave's **'Funny Face'** is recorded.

Tuesday 16th

Ray and Robert Wace phone the music press to deny reports that Ray is leaving The Kinks.

Wednesday 17th

❑ **TV** BBC Lime Grove Studios *west London*. BBC-1 **Top Of The Pops** lip-synch 'Waterloo Sunset' broadcast May 18th.

☆ The Kinks are photographed in separate sessions by Harry Hammond and US freelance photographer Linda Eastman (who later marries Paul McCartney). Eastman's shots are the first new pictures of the band to be published in America since those taken during the summer 1965 visit, and are featured in *Hit Parader* and *Crawdaddy* later in the year.

☆ The scheduled release of the 'Mister Pleasant' / 'Waterloo Sunset' single in the US is delayed until May 24th. The B-side will be dropped (to be replaced by 'Harry Rag') as 'Waterloo Sunset' charts in the UK,

and will later be issued in the US in its own right as an A-side.

→ ❑ **TV** Radio Bremen Studios *Bremen, West Germany*. ARD-TV **Beat-Club** lip-synch 'Mister Pleasant' broadcast May 20th, 'Waterloo Sunset' broadcast June 24th. The taping of 'Mister Pleasant' features an impromptu on-camera appearance of Kinks manager Grenville Collins as the group's pianist (not Nicky Hopkins) and the show's co-host, British DJ Dave Lee Travis, on trombone.

This session also includes a performance by manager Robert Wace in his alter ego, The Marquis Of Kensington, promoting his debut single on the Immediate label, 'The Changing Of The Guard', for broadcast on June 24th.

A photo session follows including shots with the colourfully-garbed Kinks holding clocks, a private joke with the German photographer who knows well the band's propensity for being late.

→ ❑ **TV** Southern Television Studios *Southampton*. ITV **As You Like It** lip-synch 'Waterloo Sunset' broadcast May 23rd.

Saturday 20th

The Upper Cut *Forest Gate, north-east London* 7:00pm
A now rare London club booking for the band, included in ads only days before the event, though it's unclear if they actually appeared. The venue was formerly the Lotus Club, where The Kinks played in 1964.

→ Around this time Dave is interviewed by Bob Farmer for *Disc & Music Echo* and discusses the rumours of Ray's departure from the band, mentions a new song called 'Funny Face' he's just written, and says the new LP will feature 20 percent of his material.

The ever-opinionated Quaife speaks to *Melody Maker* and explains how he's known Ray for years. "Like I can't remember not knowing him. All the punch-ups we had together at school ... him going on to oil-painting before I did. How can you sum him up? I just reckon he's a bloody good songwriter. If it wasn't for Ray and his songs, we wouldn't be where we are now. He's very unpredictable, but I understand the way he thinks."

As for the band, Quaife tells his interviewer: "We don't want to push ourselves as a popular group any more. To push yourself is death. This group has terrible contrasts in personalities and it's part of our success. It's probably one of the most physically violent groups. It doesn't take much to get us going. One wrong word and you walk away with a black eye. We haven't got many friends in showbiz. Showbusiness, ha ha!"

☆ A press release announces an upcoming series of UK ballroom dates, plus TV in Germany on June 5th-6th followed by concerts there on the 20th-21st, as well as a possible booking at the 7th Annual Jazz & Blues Festival at Windsor, England in August.

Tuesday 23rd

At the High Court trial in central London of Denmark Productions (Larry Page and Edward Kassner) versus Boscobel Productions (Robert Wace and Grenville Collins) about the Denmark contract begins, presided by Judge Widgery. Page and Kassner, and former road manager Sam Curtis, testify on behalf of Denmark Productions.

Wednesday 24th

The Denmark v. Boscobel trial continues, with Kinks' accountant Robert Ransom, Kassner's accountant David Dane, manager Robert Wace, and Dave Davies all testifying.
'Mister Pleasant' / **'Harry Rag'** single released in the US. *Billboard* says: "Clever novelty material penned by Ray Davies with an easy dance beat in strong support should skyrocket the group back to the top of the Hot 100."

Thursday 25th
The Denmark/Boscobel trial continues and Ray begins his testimony today.
☆ 'Waterloo Sunset' peaks at number 2 in UK *Melody Maker* chart.

Friday 26th
Grand Ballroom Coalville, Leics
Earlier in the day Ray continues his testimony at London's High Court.

Saturday 27th
Derbyshire Miners' Holiday Centre Skegness, Lincs Trend
'67 Festival – National Young Communist Rally Dance

Monday 29th
Probable concert booking on this Bank Holiday, details unknown.

Tuesday 30th
A press release says Ray will finance a TV pilot to be filmed early in July, the first of a number of planned Ray Davies solo projects. It's an ambitious combination of live bands, filmed inserts, and a 20-piece orchestra … which never happens. Tour dates are also announced.

June

Thursday 1st
❏ **TV** BBC Lime Grove Studios *west London*. BBC-1 **Top Of The Pops** lip-synch 'Waterloo Sunset'.

Friday 2nd
Starlite Ballroom Belfast, Northern Ireland
Top Hat Lisburn, Co. Antrim, Northern Ireland

Saturday 3rd
Corn Exchange Bristol

Monday 5th
At the High Court in London Judge Widgery's decision is handed down. The contract between Denmark Productions and Boscobel Productions is deemed "frustrated" and the relationship between the two parties is considered legally terminated, only requiring payment of commissions due for the period June 30th-September 14th 1965. A stay of execution is granted, and Denmark files for appeal to the House Of Lords, which will extend the dispute into the following spring. The nine-day trial is reported to have cost £10,000 and becomes a textbook case in British contract law.

→ ● **RECORDING** Pye Studios (No.2) *central London*. The emphasis is on getting a few of Dave's numbers on tape. **'Death Of A Clown'**, a new just-completed composition of Dave's with Ray assisting, is recorded, with the band augmented by Rasa Davies and Nicky Hopkins. Perhaps started in mid-May, three more songs are completed by June 12th, including another of Dave's new compositions, **'Funny Face'** and two new Ray songs **'Lazy Old Sun'**, and **'Little Women'**. 'Lazy Old Sun' is an experimental track, more like a poem read over an impressionistic backing, and probably their first recording to feature Mellotron, the versatile tape-loop-based keyboard recently acquired by Ray (it's also heard on the other songs here). 'Little Women' is a backing track that will never have a vocal added and will remain unreleased until included as a bonus on the 1998 CD reissue of Face To Face. In an interview with *Beat Instrumental* at the time Quaife says he might sing on a Kinks recording of Tim Hardin's 'How Can We Hang On To A Dream', but this never happens.

Saturday 10th
Floral Hall Southport, Lancs
Touring has been very light lately, but with the court case out of the way the band commits to a series of dates around England as summer gets underway.

Sunday 11th
A scheduled appearance at the *Golden Trophy Party* at Le Plessis-Robinson in Paris, France is evidently cancelled.

Wednesday 14th
Top Rank Suite Swansea, Wales 7:00-11:00pm; tickets 7/6 (38p)
Billed as "for the very first time in Swansea, the phenomenal Kinks".

Thursday 15th
Locarno Ballroom Hull

Friday 16th
Ben Memorial Ballroom Rugby, Warwicks

Saturday 17th
Plaza Ballroom Oldhill, Birmingham
Plaza Ballroom Handsworth, Birmingham 7:45pm-2:00am

Sunday 18th
Plaza Teen Club Huddersfield with Hepworth's Good Impressions

Monday 19th
A press release announces solo discs are due from Dave Davies and Ray Davies, and that The Kinks are to develop a new stage act and eventually a TV special.

Tuesday 20th – Wednesday 21st
Scheduled concert dates in Germany, possibly not fulfilled.

Friday 23rd
University of Exeter Exeter *Summer Ball*, with The Bonzo Dog Doo Dah Band, Zoot Money & His Big Roll Orchestra

Death Of A Clown single by Dave Davies
A 'Death Of A Clown' (D. DAVIES, R. DAVIES).
B 'Love Me Till The Sun Shines' (D. DAVIES).

UK release July 5th 1967 (Pye 7N 17356).
US release August 2nd 1967 (Reprise 0614).
Musicians Ray Davies acoustic guitar, backing vocal (A). Dave Davies lead vocal, electric guitar. Pete Quaife bass guitar. Mick Avory drums. Nicky Hopkins piano (A), organ (B). Rasa Davies backing vocal (A).
Recorded Pye Studios (No.2) central London; A: early June 1967; B: spring 1967; 4-track mixed to mono (stereo for album).
Producer Ray Davies (no label credit in UK; credited to Shel Talmy Productions on US label).
Engineer Alan MacKenzie, "Irish" aka Alan O'Duffy (assistant).
Chart high UK number 3; US none.

Saturday 24th

New Cornish Riviera Lido *Carlyon Bay, Cornwall* 8:00-11:45 pm, with The Cousin Jacks

Following day off; Ray and Dave play another football match in London.

Monday 26th

A press release announces Dave Davies's 'Death Of A Clown' single for July 7th, a new Kinks album for the end of July, and a Ray Davies solo LP for September. (The "solo LP" probably refers either to Ray's plan for a collection of songs with a London theme, à la 'Waterloo Sunset', an idea that seems to appear and disappear quickly, or his *Village Green* concept, the one that seems to take hold.)

→ ● **RECORDING** Pye Studios *central London*. Ray is reported to be at Pye this week, presumably doing overdubs, mixing and track selection for the new Kinks LP, a chore he must accomplish on his own as producer Shel Talmy is now out of the picture. He says later that this is something he isn't yet ready to do. As the final track listing will not be published until late in July it is likely the process takes until then.

☆ Dave kicks into high gear doing advance publicity for his first solo single, 'Death Of A Clown', including a chat with *Melody Maker* where he wisely tries to explain from the outset that issuing the record in no way means the end of The Kinks. But he still needs to develop something of a solo image, and does a photo shoot with Mike Leale after a visit to the local theatrical hire company, outfitted in finest Edwardian foppery and resulting in a classic 1960s image.

July

Saturday 1st

Rectory Field *Blackheath, Colchester* 3:00pm-12midnight, *South East R&B Festival*, with The Small Faces, Georgie Fame, John Mayall

Ray is ill but performs nevertheless. The show is sponsored by *Melody Maker* and is evidently the inspiration for the later song 'All Of My Friends Were There'. The following day is off and Ray recuperates.

Monday 3rd

Publishing is assigned today for 'Tin Soldier Man' and 'Love Me Till The Sun Shines' as this coupling is issued as a Kinks single in France. Around the same time two songs are logged into Reprise Records' tape vaults, 'Love Me Till The Sun Shines' and 'No Return', possibly intended as an alternative coupling for a Kinks single in the US and, it is rumoured, in Scandinavia.

☆ A press release announces that an August tour of Australia is postponed to January 1968.

Wednesday 5th – Thursday 6th

● **RECORDING** Pye Studios *central London*. The Kinks are reported to be back at Pye to record three or four new tracks for the next single or album, details unknown.

Friday 7th

'**Death Of A Clown**' / '**Love Me Till The Sun Shines**' single by Dave Davies released in the UK. *Record Mirror* is cautious: "The younger Davies Kink on a solo item, with the usual guitar trimmings behind. Slightly wailing in concept, but a good song with a haunting quality, this ... should make the charts easily enough though I wouldn't bank on it being a giant." *Disc & Music Echo* misses the mark entirely: "Here we have Dave, younger fun-crazed brother of sad Ray Kink, on a delightful song which isn't going to be a hit."

→ Work is scheduled to start on Ray's 55-minute TV show featuring live bands and filmed inserts at Granville Theatre Studios in Fulham, west London, early to mid month. The project is never started, but it's possible a short promotional clip shown prior to Dave's appearance on *Top Of The Pops* on July 27th is made at this time instead.

Thursday 13th

❏ **TV** BBC Lime Grove Studios *west London*. BBC-1 *Top Of The Pops* lip-synch Dave Davies 'Death Of A Clown'.

Saturday 15th

Hinckley Football Ground *Hinckley, Leics* Beat Festival, with The Troggs, Whistling Jack Smith, The Mindbenders, The Koobas, Humphrey Lyttelton's Band, The Bats; compères Simon Dee, Jimmy Savile; Bob West Promotions

→ ● **RECORDING** Pye Studios (No.2) *central London*. Ray finally completes all work on the new Kinks album around now. Some Dave Davies recording is reported but unconfirmed.

→ ❏ **TV** Radio Bremen Studios *Bremen, West Germany*. ARD-TV *Beat-Club* lip-synch Dave Davies 'Death Of A Clown' broadcast July 22nd.

Tuesday 18th

Winter Gardens *Malvern, Worcs*

Thursday 20th

Assembly Hall *Worthing, Sussex*

Saturday 22nd

The Kinks begin their annual holiday for two weeks until August 3rd. Ray and family head down to Cornwall. Dave is ill over the weekend and into Monday but will spend time promoting his single during the coming week.

Monday 24th

A press release announces a new album, *Something Else*, for September 2nd and that Ray has been approached to write the music for an unnamed independent film-maker's project.

Tuesday 25th

With 'Death Of A Clown' jumping into the Top 10 at number nine this week, Dave spends most of a *Record Mirror* interview squashing rumours that he's going solo permanently, and speaks of a lack of material for any solo LP he might do.

Wednesday 26th

'**Waterloo Sunset**' / '**Two Sisters**' single released in the US. Following the poor showing of 'Mister Pleasant' in America, little support is evident from Reprise for this new single. No trade ads appear and it is only cursorily reviewed in the trades.

Billboard says under its Top 60 Pop Spotlight: "Currently riding high on the British charts, this infectious soft rock ballad has all the earmarks of a hot sales item here," while New York's *Go* magazine says: "The boys have tried something entirely different on this one." Amazingly, the record creeps into the bottom end of the *Cash Box* charts at a dismal number 141.

Thursday 27th

❏ **TV** BBC Lime Grove Studios *west London*. BBC-1 *Top Of The Pops* lip-synch Dave Davies 'Death Of A Clown'. Dave is mistakenly introduced as Ray Davies by *TOTP* host Alan Freeman. A short film clip by Ray (content unknown) is shown directly before Dave's appearance.

→ INDICATES EVENT AROUND THIS TIME BUT WITH NO FIRM DATE

Still unwell, Dave collapses from exhaustion shortly afterwards, and he takes a few days holiday in Cornwall through August 2nd.

Monday 31st
A press releases announces that Dave is to record a solo LP next week to be released in September when he will be in the US for promotion, that representatives from Warner Brothers Films will arrive next week to discuss The Kinks writing and performing the title song for a Warners movie for the coming autumn, and that a new LP and single are due in September.

August

Wednesday 2nd
'Death Of A Clown' / 'Love Me Till The Sun Shines' single by Dave Davies released in the US. Apparently no promotional copies are sent out to the trade magazines as not a single review seems to be published. Commercial copies of this release are extremely scarce, implying that only a very small amount are ever pressed and distributed. It's almost as if the record's release is cancelled following its pressing, or possibly delayed and then cancelled – and the scrapping of Dave's week-long promotional trip to the US arranged for September by US business manager Allan Klein at this time lends weight to the theory.

Thursday 3rd
❏ **TV** BBC Lime Grove Studios *west London*. BBC-1 *Top Of The Pops* lip-synch Dave Davies 'Death Of A Clown'. Dave is decked out in an elaborate cavalier uniform, again a one-day rental from the theatrical costume shop.

Friday 4th
))) **RADIO** Playhouse Theatre *central London*. BBC Light Programme *Saturday Club* studio recordings 'Death Of A Clown' broadcast August 5th and 26th, BBC Transcription Service 'Love Me Till The Sun Shines', 'Good Luck Charm' broadcast around September 15th. After an absence of more than a year and a half, The Kinks are finally back at the BBC to record unique versions for broadcast.

Today's visit is technically a Dave Davies session, but the four Kinks plus session pianist Nicky Hopkins and Rasa Davies recreate performances very close to the studio recordings of both sides of Dave's solo single, plus a cover version of a song by American blues singer/guitarist Spider John Koerner, 'Good Luck Child', slightly retitled by the BBC as 'Good Luck Charm'.

Oddly, only 'Death Of A Clown' is aired on *Saturday Club* on the BBC's Light Programme station. The remaining tracks and a brief interview with Dave by host Brian Matthew will be syndicated overseas on the BBC Transcription Service programme *Top Of The Pops* the week of September 15th. ('Death Of A Clown' and 'Good Luck Charm' will be released in 2001 on *The Kinks BBC Sessions 1964-1977*.)

Saturday 5th
Nautilus Club, South Pier Pavilion *Lowestoft, Suffolk* 7:30pm

Sunday 6th
Pier Ballroom *Hastings, Sussex* 7:30-11:00pm

Tuesday 8th
Town Hall *Torquay* 8:00pm-1:00am, *Summer Spectacular*, with The Phaze, The Last-Tik Band, A Collexion, The Q-Set; plus go go girls, mod fashion parade

The Live Kinks or Live At Kelvin Hall album

A1 'Till The End Of The Day' (R. DAVIES).
A2 'A Well Respected Man' (R. DAVIES).
A3 'You're Looking Fine' (R. DAVIES).
A4 'Sunny Afternoon' (R. DAVIES).
A5 'Dandy' (R. DAVIES).
B1 'I'm On An Island' (R. DAVIES).
B2 'Come On Now' (R. DAVIES).
B3 'You Really Got Me' (R. DAVIES).
B4 medley 'Milk Cow Blues' (J. ESTES) / 'Batman Theme' (N. HEFTI) / 'Tired Of Waiting For You' (R. DAVIES).

UK release January 12th 1968 (Pye NPL 18191 mono/NSPL 18191 stereo).
US release August (probably 16th) 1967 (Reprise R 6260 mono/RS 6260 stereo).
Musicians Ray Davies lead vocal except as noted, acoustic guitar (A2, A4, A5, B1) otherwise electric guitar. Dave Davies lead vocal (A2, B7, B4 co-lead with Ray), electric guitar, backing vocal. Pete Quaife bass guitar, backing vocal. Mick Avory drums.
Recorded Kelvin Hall Glasgow, Scotland; April 1st 1967. Overdubs and mixing April 1967 at Pye Studios (No.2) central London; 4-track mixed to mono and stereo.
Producer Ray Davies listed as "Musical Director".
Engineers Alan MacKenzie; assistants: Alan O'Duffy, Vic Maile.
Chart high UK none; US number 162.

Wednesday 9th
Flamingo Ballroom *Redruth, Cornwall* 7:45pm

Thursday 10th
'Death Of A Clown' hits its peak at number 3 in the UK *Melody Maker* charts, and the strain of the attention is maybe revealed as Dave cancels at the last minute a scheduled TV taping at the BBC's Lime Grove Studios, west London for *It's Dee Time*, due for broadcast on the 17th.

Friday 11th
The Kinks cancel an appearance at the Windsor Jazz & Blues Festival in Berkshire, and tentatively scheduled concerts are cancelled for August 11th-13th at Casino Tharon in Normandy, France.

Saturday 12th – Sunday 13th
Caught off guard by the success of 'Death Of A Clown' Dave is under increasing pressure to make a follow-up single and an LP's worth of material. To flesh out an LP, Dave considers recording some favourite old blues songs, primarily by Big Bill Broonzy and Leadbelly. Work on an EP is planned to start this weekend at Pye Studios. Dave says later that the eventual follow-up single, 'Susannah's Still Alive', is loosely based on a Leadbelly song and so may have developed out of these initial sessions, although the song is probably recorded later.

Monday 14th
A press release says Ray and Dave are to appear in a British-made film early in 1968, and that the band is in the studio working on a new Kinks single and a Dave Davies LP.

→ ● **RECORDING** Pye Studios (No.2) *central London*. The Kinks are holed up at Pye during the latter half of the month in concentrated sessions to produce the next Kinks 45 and for continued work on a Dave Davies EP. However, no useable Kinks track is produced and, likely under pressure from Pye, it is briefly announced that 'Mister Pleasant' will be issued as the next Kinks A-side. Further sessions are scheduled for September and 'Mister Pleasant' will ultimately be relegated to a B-side. A surviving acetate coupling the Spider John Koerner song **'Good Luck Child'** and Ray's **'Lavender Hill'** suggests these two are from the same session. It further suggests that 'Lavender Hill' is possibly in the running as a potential A-side for the all-important follow-up to 'Waterloo Sunset' (but will be rejected as such). Also under pressure to come up with another song is Dave who lacks anything new. It's said that three different songs by Ray are at least considered for recording by Dave. Reportedly attempted by Dave at this time is another cover song, **'Et Moi Et Moi Et Moi'** by French rocker Jacques DuTronc, but it's probably never finished.

☆ More concert casualties: a tentative planned tour of Australia and the Far East is delayed until January 1968, and an August 15th concert set to take place at Bournemouth Pavilion is cancelled to make way for more recording time.

Wednesday 16th

→ *The Live Kinks* album released in the US. The equivalent LP *Live At Kelvin Hall* is released in mainland Europe around this time, but the record's British release will be delayed until January 12th 1968. Criticism will rage for years about the style of recording of this show, with one channel of the 4-track entirely devoted to the audience's roars of approval and mixed high. In retrospect it will be seen to capture the atmosphere of a typical Kinks concert at the height of their chart-topping 1960s incarnation, and it's quite possible Ray may have mixed it like this deliberately.

Tuesday 22nd

Dave reviews records for this week's *Melody Maker* with a thumbs up to 'We Love You' by the Stones and 'The Burning Of The Midnight Lamp' by Jimi Hendrix.

Saturday 26th

Cancelled today is the band's appearance at the *Festival Of The Flower Children* at Woburn Abbey, Beds.

Monday 28th

Hastings Stadium *Hastings, Sussex* 2:00pm-12midnight, *Hastings United's Festival Of Music*, with Dave Dee Dozy Beaky Mick & Tich, Arthur Brown, Geno Washington, Robb Storme, Winston Fumbs, Hip Hooray Band

A bank holiday pop package show attended by 6,000 fans.

☆ A press release announces 'Mister Pleasant' as a single for UK release on September 22nd. Around this time a tentatively booked Dave Davies solo appearance on September 3rd at the *National Youth Festival* in Bergen, Norway with David Garrick is cancelled.

September

Friday 2nd

Imperial Ballroom *Nelson, Lancs* with Michael's Angels, The Beatovens

Saturday 9th

Concertgebouw *Amsterdam, Netherlands* Mode Happening, with Donovan, Outsiders, Armand, Q65, Shoes, Full House, Daddy's

Something Else By The Kinks album

A1 **'David Watts'** (R. DAVIES).
A2 **'Death Of A Clown'** (D. DAVIES, R. DAVIES).
A3 **'Two Sisters'** (R. DAVIES).
A4 **'No Return'** (R. DAVIES).
A5 **'Harry Rag'** (R. DAVIES).
A6 **'Tin Soldier Man'** (R. DAVIES).
A7 **'Situation Vacant'** (R. DAVIES).
B1 **'Love Me Till The Sun Shines'** (R. DAVIES).
B2 **'Lazy Old Sun'** (R. DAVIES).
B3 **'Afternoon Tea'** (R. DAVIES).
B4 **'Funny Face'** (R. DAVIES).
B5 **'End Of The Season'** (R. DAVIES).
B6 **'Waterloo Sunset'** (R. DAVIES).

UK release September 15th 1967 (Pye NPL 18193 mono/NSPL 18193 stereo).
US release January (around 24th) 1968 (Reprise RS 6279 stereo/R 6279 mono promotional only).
Musicians Ray Davies lead vocal except as noted, electric guitar, acoustic guitar, keyboards. Dave Davies lead vocal (A2, B1, B4), electric guitar, backing vocal. Pete Quaife bass guitar, backing vocal. Mick Avory drums. Nicky Hopkins piano. Rasa Davies backing vocal (A2, A6, B2-B4, B6).
Recorded Pye Studios (No.2) central London; A1, A3, A5: February 1967; A4: January 1967; A6, A7, B3: February-July 1967; B1: spring 1967; A2, B2: June 1967; B4: May-June 1967; B6: April 1967; B5: April-June 1966; 4-track mixed to mono and stereo (except probably B5 3-track mixed to mono and stereo).
Producer Ray Davies and Shel Talmy (no label credit in UK; credited to Shel Talmy Productions on US label).
Engineer Alan MacKenzie, assistant "Irish" aka Alan O'Duffy.
Chart high UK none; US number 153.

Act, Elly Nieman, Theo Van Es, Wally Tax, Shirley, The Dutch Swing College Band, Davy Jones, Jacco Van Rennesse; fashion ball sponsored by Bal Boutique

→ ● **RECORDING** Pye Studios (No.2) *central London*. Pressure from management and record company for a new Kinks single sees them again back at Pye around this time.

Now it seems like Ray has the goods with **'Autumn Almanac'**, inspired by his gardener Charlie, a hunchbacked, elderly man who has long been a well-known figure in the Muswell Hill area. Ray later reveals in *X-Ray* that while he once feared the man's disability, he would go on to recognise him as an inspiration, identifying with his ability to endure happily through quiet accomplishment and fortitude of character.

Although partially written during the spring, the song in its final version reportedly grows out of an unfinished recording called **'My Street'** that, when played-back in reverse, helped Ray develop the final concept and melody. Ray's Mellotron is again used, this time in place of what would normally be horn parts.

Mention is also made at this time of another recording and a candidate for an A-side, **'The Interview'**, which Ray will mention a little later as a potential LP track, but after that nothing more is heard of the song.

Friday 15th

Something Else By The Kinks album released in the UK. *Melody Maker* raves: "Comic lunacy ... mixed with pathos and gentle understanding into a gallery of brilliant musical portraits. The Kinks are not terribly fashionable at this given moment in time, but the material Ray Davies feeds them reveals a depth of thought that commands respect. .... One of the best albums of the year."

→ ● **RECORDING** Pye Studios (No.2) *central London*. Ray completes a mixing session to finish '**Autumn Almanac**'.
☆ Cancelled around now are a tour of Scandinavia from the 20th to the 22nd and a tour of Greece, including 23rd Salonika and 24th Athens. The Greek dates are cancelled due to a military coup which has just occurred in the country.

Monday 25th

A press release says Scandinavian dates are now set for November, an Australian/Far East tour for January, and a new single for release October 13th.

Saturday 29th

Starlite Ballroom *Belfast, Northern Ireland* with The Fugitives
The billing – "Britain's top group: Kinks with Dave Davies – Death of a Clown" – reflects the promoter's desire to emphasise Dave's new status as a hit-maker.

Sunday 30th

New Arcadia Ballroom *Bray, Co. Wicklow, Ireland* 9:00pm, with The Greenbeats
A 5,000-capacity room, sponsored by local promoter Tom Costello.

October

Monday 1st

Autumn Almanac single

A '**Autumn Almanac**' (R. DAVIES).
B-UK '**Mister Pleasant**' (R. DAVIES).
B-US '**David Watts**' (R. DAVIES).

UK release (A/B-UK) October 13th 1967 (Pye 7N 17400).
US release (A/B-US) November 29th 1967 (Reprise 0647).
Musicians Ray Davies lead vocal, acoustic guitar, piano and Mellotron (A, or Nicky Hopkins). Dave Davies electric guitar, backing vocal. Pete Quaife bass guitar, backing vocal. Mick Avory drums. Nicky Hopkins piano and Mellotron (A, or Ray Davies), piano (B-UK, B-US). John Beecham (possibly) trombone (B-UK). Rasa Davies backing vocal (A).
Recorded Pye Studios (No.2) central London; A: September 1967; B-UK, B-US: February 1967; 4-track mixed to mono.
Producer Ray Davies (A); Ray Davies & Shel Talmy (B-UK); US label credits Shel Talmy Productions (B-US).
Engineer Alan MacKenzie.
Chart high UK number 5, US none.

Arcadia Ballroom *Cork, Ireland* 8:00pm with The Kerry Blues
Further Irish dates were set for the next two days with a scheduled (but unconfirmed) return to London on the 4th.

→ ● **RECORDING** Pye Studios (No.2) *central London*. It's likely that Dave's next A-side, '**Susannah's Still Alive**', is recorded or begun around this time.

Friday 5th
Working Men's Club *Langley Mill, Derbys*

Saturday 6th
Kyrle *Birmingham* 8:00pm, with Agency, Jigsaw
Grand opening night of a new club.

Sunday 7th
Savoy Ballrooms *Southsea, Hants*

Thursday 12th
❏ **TV** BBC Lime Grove Studios *west London*. BBC-1 *Top Of The Pops* lip-synch 'Autumn Almanac'. The long-awaited follow-up to 'Waterloo Sunset' is previewed. Promotion for the single begins in earnest too, with Ray doing assorted interviews, including *Melody Maker* and *Record Mirror*.
☆ Reprise Records receives master tapes of 'David Watts' / 'Afternoon Tea' for scheduled release as the next US single. This coupling is eventually scrapped in favour of the current UK release, 'Autumn Almanac'.

Friday 13th
'**Autumn Almanac**' / '**Mister Pleasant**' single released in the UK. *NME* enthuses under the headline Lyrical Kinks – A Big Hit: "There are few groups more capable of painting vivid and descriptive verbal pictures than The Kinks. This follows the tradition of 'Waterloo Sunset' by latching on to everyday happenings and giving them an absorbing lyrical quality … I wouldn't class it as one of their very best discs, if only because the melody has a certain similarity with past releases. But a big one for sure."

Monday 16th – Tuesday 17th
Belgian concert dates originally pencilled in for this time are likely shifted to November. Dave now heads back to the Continent for another quick round of solo TV appearances and, presumably, more press duties.
At home in London, Avory is offered up to the press to help promotion for the new *Something Else* Kinks LP.

→ ❏ **TV** Stadthalle *Offenbach, West Germany*. HR TV *Beat Beat Beat* lip-synch 'Death Of A Clown' broadcast October 16th.
→ ❏ **TV** *Antwerp, Belgium*. Belgian TV *Vibrato* lip-synch 'Death Of A Clown' broadcast October 24th.

Wednesday 18th
Skyline Ballroom *Hull, Yorks* 8:00pm, with The Travellers Express, The Mandrakes, Herbie's iiis

Saturday 21st
❏ **TV** Playhouse Theatre *Manchester*. BBC-1 *It's Dee Time* lip-synch 'Autumn Almanac' 6:45 pm.
Student Union, University of Liverpool *Liverpool* 9:45pm
The TV appearance is possibly cancelled because of a scheduling dispute with the University.

Monday 23rd

A press release says a US trip is planned for November/December and Belgian dates for November 17th/18th, that the band is now recording a new single for January, and that the new US single 'David Watts' / 'Afternoon Tea' is issued this week.

Monday 23rd – Tuesday 24th

→ ● **RECORDING** Pye Studios (No.2) *central London*. The Kinks are scheduled at Pye around this time, details unconfirmed. Work on Dave's new single is at least completed by this time. Otherwise likely is work on material for the proposed Ray Davies solo album, or just new Kinks tracks.

Wednesday 25th

))) **RADIO** BBC Maida Vale Studios (Studio 4) *central London*. BBC Radio 1 *Top Gear* studio recordings produced by Bernie Andrews and Bev Phillips 'David Watts', 'Harry Rag', 'Sunny Afternoon', 'Susannah's Still Alive', 'Autumn Almanac', 'Mister Pleasant' broadcast October 29th. The band re-records a handful of recent songs in a BBC studio for broadcast, thanks as ever to the Beeb's "needle time" agreement with the UK Musicians Union designed to maintain work for musicians. However for 'Autumn Almanac' here, they simply add extra vocals to the existing single. Like many bands at the time they cannot hope to reproduce the sound of their increasingly elaborate recordings in a typical three-hour BBC session, and some choose to add material to existing records or session tapes to create a unique BBC version. ('Harry Rag' will be released in 2001 on *The Kinks BBC Sessions 1964-1977*.)

❏ **TV** BBC Lime Grove Studios *west London*. BBC-1 *Top Of The Pops* lip-synch 'Autumn Almanac' broadcast October 26th.

Thursday 26th

Refectory, University Of Leeds *Leeds* 8:00pm, *Rag Ball*, with Brian Auger & The Trinity With Julie Driscoll, Monty Sunshine Jazz Band, Clockwork Oranges

Monday 30th

A press release says a new Dave Davies single is out November 24th and that The Kinks will record in the US on an upcoming promotional trip.

→ Ray undertakes the usual press chores, including interviews with Nick Cohn and then Keith Altham for *NME*. A more unusual venue for one interview is London Zoo, with Penny Valentine of *Disc & Music Echo*. Ray the ever-frustrated film director reveals: "I write a song and think how much nicer it would be to make a three-minute film of it instead, to show people what I really mean. I want to make a proper film, anyway. They keep offering me the chance to write film music, but I'm not Benjamin Britten or anything. And although it would be nice to do, I really want to do *everything* myself. To have my own idea, film it, write the score, produce, direct, star ..." Valentine notes that Ray fades away here "as the full extent of the idea took over".

November

→ Quaife is interviewed by Chris Welch for *Melody Maker* and, speaking of the band's lack of personal appearances, explains: "Oh, we'll get around to everybody. We are working consistently and do two jobs a week. We need the other five to recover. There isn't much left to do in this country, anyway."

● **RECORDING** Pye Studios (No.2) *central London*. Around now the emphasis shifts to a planned Ray Davies solo album. It's likely that at

Sunny Afternoon album

A1 'Sunny Afternoon' (R. DAVIES).
A2 'I Need You' (R. DAVIES).
A3 'See My Friends' (R. DAVIES).
A4 'Big Black Smoke' (R. DAVIES).
A5 'Louie Louie' (R. BERRY).
B1 'Dedicated Follower Of Fashion' (R. DAVIES).
B2 'Sittin' On My Sofa' (R. DAVIES).
B3 'Such A Shame' (R. DAVIES).
B4 'I'm Not Like Everybody Else' (R. DAVIES).
B5 'Dead End Street' (R. DAVIES).

UK release November 17th 1967 (Marble Arch MAL 716mono/MALS 716 [simulated] stereo). Comprised entirely of previously issued single and EP tracks.
Chart high UK number 9.

least one if not more of the "older" tracks on what will finally appear as 1968's *Village Green Preservation Society* album may come from this original project. **'Mr. Songbird'** in particular, Ray will tell *Crawdaddy!*, was done "a long time before" the rest of *Village Green*, possibly now.

☆ Rescheduled Scandinavian dates pencilled in for this time are cancelled, presumably in order to focus on recording.

Saturday 4th

St. George's Ballroom *Hinckley, Leics* with The Carlings

Monday 6th

A press release says the live album will be out in the UK in January, and that a US trip is being negotiated. A separate release announces that Dave Dee Dozy Beaky Mick & Tich will be undertaking a headlining tour of Australia – which is probably in place of The Kinks who now seem to have been dropped by the Arthur Howes booking agency.

Thursday 9th

❏ **TV** BBC Lime Grove Studios *west London*. BBC-1 *Top Of The Pops* lip-synch 'Autumn Almanac'.
☆ 'Autumn Almanac' peaks in the UK charts at number 5.

Tuesday 14th

Reprise Records in the US receives master tapes of the *Something Else* LP plus the 'Autumn Almanac' and 'Susannah's Still Alive' singles, and release is set for early next year, after the Christmas season.

Friday 17th

Zaal Roma *Antwerpern, Belgium*
The Kinks begin a quick weekend swing into the Continent where they are still in great demand in concert. In an interview with local journalist Guy Mortier for *Humo* magazine Ray says he has "almost completed" a solo album, though this is most likely an optimistic overstatement, as there is no evidence of any undiscovered cache of truly solo recordings. *Sunny Afternoon* album released in the UK. In a similar fashion to last year's *Well Respected Kinks*, this is another budget-priced Pye collection of single and EP sides, this time with a psychedelicised Kinks cover to generate some Christmas income. As before, it has the effect of cheapening The Kinks' classic back catalogue and emphasising their

Susannah's Still Alive single by Dave Davies

A 'Susannah's Still Alive' (D. DAVIES).
B 'Funny Face' (D. DAVIES).

UK release November 24th 1967 (Pye 7N 17429).
US release January 31st 1968 (Reprise 0660).
Musicians Ray Davies acoustic guitar, piano (A), harmonica (A), piano/organ (B, or Nicky Hopkins). Dave Davies lead vocal, electric guitar. Pete Quaife bass guitar. Mick Avory drums. Nicky Hopkins piano/organ (B, or Ray Davies). Rasa Davies backing vocal (B).
Recorded Pye Studios (No.2) central London; A: October 1967; B: May-June 1967; 4-track mixed to mono.
Producer Ray Davies.
Engineer Alan MacKenzie.
Chart high UK none; US none.

image as a singles band at a time when they want attention paid to their full-price long-players.

Saturday 18th

Margriet Youth Club *Mechelen, Belgium* 8:30pm, with Adam's Recital, The Liberty Six
Corso Club, Zaal Casino *Lebbeke, Belgium*

Sunday 19th

Club '67 *Ertvelde, Belgium*
Open air festival *Kieldrecht, Belgium*

A riot reportedly erupts at Kieldrecht. The band travels back to London the following day.

Monday 20th

A press release says the band will visit the US in December for promotional purposes.

Friday 24th

'Susannah's Still Alive' / 'Funny Face' single by Dave Davies released in the UK. The *NME* review, headlined Dave Deserves Kinky Hit, is in favour: "This strikes me as a much more likely hit than did 'Death Of A Clown' when I first played it. It's an excellent pop record – well produced and very commercial."

Saturday 25th

Ready Steady Club, Pearce Hall *Maidenhead, Berks* 7:00pm
➜ Ray signs a contract to write a song a week for ten weeks for the BBC series *At The Eleventh Hour*, a variety show combining music and satire, starting on December 30th. It realises his ambitions to work in other media, outside the strict confines of The Kinks and not as a conventional pop/rock act. The songs are based on current news items from his local paper, *The Hornsey Journal*. Scripts for the show will be submitted on Wednesdays, the song written on Thursday, recorded Friday, and aired Saturday. Ray's songs are to be performed by singer Jeannie Lamb backed by an orchestra with The Mitchell Singers, and the show will feature actress Miriam Margoyles, poet Roger McGough and The Scaffold, Richard Neville of *Oz* magazine, and producer Alan Shallcross . Ray will later remark that he enjoys the challenge of writing for hire.

Wednesday 29th

'**Autumn Almanac' / 'David Watts'** single released in the US. *Billboard* includes the single in their Special Merit Spotlight for records not tipped for the Top 60: "A happy beat entry with intriguing lyrical content and good teen dance appeal." The consummately British single is lost in a rapidly changing American marketplace. While 'Mister Pleasant' trailed along on the tail of chart successes from 1966, 'Waterloo Sunset' was a complete no-show, and the momentum in the US singles market has been lost, with record stores not even bothering to stock Kinks singles now.

December

➜ At the start of the month Dave dutifully undertakes a barrage of interviews – for *Melody Maker*, *Disc & Music Echo*, *Record Mirror*, *Jackie* and others – inundating the press with his words and image to try to propel the second single up the charts with the same success as 'Death Of A Clown'.

☆ On sale the first week of the month in the US is issue 12 of *Crawdaddy!* magazine with a feature-length article, *The Kinks vs. The Doors*, by Sandy Pearlman.

The piece not only features the first contemporary photos of The Kinks published in America in two years, but also helps give the band US underground credibility following what amounted to an exile from the American singles chart this year.

While distribution of the magazine is expanding, it is essentially aimed at the college crowd in the liberal East and West Coast cities and the key areas between. The article is essentially a career-wide review of their albums, culminating with *The Live Kinks*.

Despite that album's curious position following such an artistically successful LP as *Face To Face*, the *Crawdaddy!* article does help to start the so-called "underground cult" of The Kinks in the US. Ray will presumably be given a copy while visiting New York later this month, thus beginning his awareness of the new rock underground and the partial acceptance of The Kinks within it – at least by the critics.

Thursday 7th

❏ **TV** BBC Lime Grove Studios *west London*. BBC-1 **Top Of The Pops** lip-synch Dave Davies 'Susannah's Still Alive'. Ray is at the studio for moral support and says later how impressed he is with Dave's image as a standalone artist. Dave has abandoned the theatrical rental-shop chic and now sports a stylish black leather jacket, more suitable for the retro feel of his new single.

He later argues that the record heralds a return to rock'n'roll basics that bands like The Beatles and Stones were months away from, still wallowing in their most pretentious and relatively unsuccessful psychedelic phases this Christmas with *Magical Mystery Tour* and *Their Satanic Majesties Request*.

➜ Around this time the scheduled two-week trip to the US falls through, including the planned recording session at the Reprise-linked Warner Brothers studios in Burbank, CA, as do TV-show bookings to promote the new US single. It seems the plan comes close to fruition, but is ultimately sunk because proper visas could not be obtained by their US manager Allen Klein, due to of the problems associated with their 1965 US tour.

One rumour has some dates booked but cancelled, including an aborted show at Quinnipiac College, Wallingford, CT. The non-appearance of The Kinks in the US even prompts one unscrupulous promoter to create a bogus version of the band consisting of American musicians posing as Londoners, and the outfit does apparently play some dates in Texas.

kinks'67

Wednesday 13th

With plans for the US abandoned, Dave is scheduled for further press interviews to keep the momentum for his single. He tells an *NME* interviewer that 'Susannah' is "much more my disc than 'Death Of A Clown'. Ray wrote the lyrics for that and the music, but this one is all my own work .... I never even knew that ['Clown'] was coming out, they just phoned me up and said it's been released".

Monday 18th – Wednesday 20th

Ray travels to New York City without The Kinks following the cancellation of the US plans and while there he holds business meetings with Allen Klein to discuss the possibility of writing music for a Hollywood movie. While in town he also attends a birthday party for Klein, which is held at the manager's home in Queens and is reported in New York's *Go* magazine. Back home, a concert booked for the 19th at the Marine & Technical College, South Shields, Co. Durham is evidently cancelled.

☆ A press release announces Dave Davies solo dates and a *Kinks Greatest Hits* double LP, both set for January 1968.

Thursday 21st

Ray travels back to London. Scheduled TV bookings for The Kinks in the US, 21st to 23rd, are cancelled.

Friday 22nd

Majestic Ballroom *Retford, Notts*

It's unclear if this scheduled concert was fulfilled.

Saturday 30th

Broadcast on BBC-1's *At The Eleventh Hour* and sung by Jeannie Lamb is the first of Ray's weekly TV-show songs, 'You Can't Give More Than What You Have' (often referred to as 'He Spent More Than He Had'). It's likely Ray had settled down at home at Fortis Green in the preceding days to write the song.

➔ INDICATES EVENT AROUND THIS TIME BUT WITH NO FIRM DATE

1968

The tremendous political and social turmoil in the world and its reflection in pop culture and music was not lost on Ray, who saw the staunchly conservative land of a few years earlier turned upside down and inside out by the same kids he'd performed for – only now their innocence was ripped bare and they were fighting for an identity of their own in a disturbingly turbulent time.

And while the unrest spread to Europe, The Kinks were holed up in suburban Muswell Hill, north London, exiled from the US, the band members largely balancing new-found family lives and trying to figure how or even if The Kinks had a place or a future.

Last year had allowed some relative peace as they continued to recover from the mayhem of 1964-66, but still enjoying chart success and some artistic satisfaction. This year, however, lawsuits were still pending, the future was uncertain, and it was unclear where Ray's muse was leading him. The band retreated almost exclusively to the studio, losing touch with their audience and often at odds with Ray's creative visions.

The release of the artistically adventurous but commercially unwise single 'Wonderboy' in the spring was followed by a perhaps ill-advised old fashioned package tour of Britain. The Kinks were on a downward spiral as their commercial credibility plummeted at home.

With no hope of salvaging their lost career in the US, the remainder of the year was largely spent completing a new album. It was finally decided to build it around the pivotal recording 'Village Green', first put on tape in November 1966 and only now embraced by the band and developed into the cornerstone album that it would become for The Kinks. In the middle of the process, however, Ray further aggravated the growing disunity in the band by moving out of Muswell Hill into the affluent countryside and, coupled with the almost complete lack of live work and commercial failure of the resulting album at year's end, the band was left sliding into virtual obscurity.

January

Monday 1st – Wednesday 3rd

At home in East Finchley, Ray Davies writes his weekly song for the BBC's *At The Eleventh Hour* TV show. This week's offering, sung by Jeannie Lamb, is 'If Christmas Day Could Last Forever', broadcast on BBC-1 on January 6th.

Tuesday 2nd – Saturday 6th

In the US, Warners-Seven Arts (Reprise's parent company) sends four teams of executives to a total of 22 cities to launch 14 new LPs for release on their labels later this month, including The Kinks' *Something Else* LP. It is announced at these meetings that the releases are now exclusively in stereo and that monaural production has been halted except in the case of radio promotion copies.
➜ ☆ Ken Jones is hired as the band's new road manager at this time. He will stay with The Kinks in this capacity for 24 years, until the end of 1991.

Saturday 6th

The Kinks are scheduled for a concert tonight up at the Imperial Ballroom in Nelson, Lancs, but cancel at the last second.

Monday 8th – Wednesday 10th

Ray writes his weekly song for the BBC's *At The Eleventh Hour* TV show at home in East Finchley. This week's offering, sung by Jeannie Lamb, is 'We're Backing Britain', broadcast on BBC-1 on January 13th.

Wednesday 10th

A scheduled concert at the Pavilion Ballroom, Hemel Hempstead, Herts is cancelled.

➜ *NME* reports that Kinks manager Robert Wace has signed another new artist, Oscar Bicycle, a Bristol-based band with a debut disc, 'On A Quiet Night', out January 26th on CBS.

Friday 12th

❏ **TV** Radio Bremen Studios *Bremen, West Germany*. ARD television **Beat-Club** lip-synch Dave Davies 'Susannah's Still Alive' broadcast January 13th.
Live At Kelvin Hall album released in the UK. Despite a typical amount of advertising in the pop papers and magazines, this belated release (the US version came out last August) gets no press support from The Kinks. They are busy in the studio developing what they likely perceive as the mature music that will lead on from 'Waterloo Sunset',

and they probably view the *Kelvin Hall* album as irrelevant to a post-*Sgt Pepper* world. Although a perfect embodiment of the screamfest mid-1960s British pop concert, the live album was recorded at the very end of that phenomenon, and the delay of its release until now marks it out as clearly dated. Says the *NME*: "Those Scottish girls cheer and scream with the best of them. In this vast arena in Glasgow The Kinks had every encouragement to give a good show and what you can hear above the audience noise is good. I don't know if I like a backing of whistles and screams."

Sunday 14th

❏ TV BBC Television Centre *west London*. BBC-1 *Meeting Point: My Song Is Me*. Ray and Dave Davies appear as panellists on this talk show discussing songwriting along with other guests Alan Price, Spencer Davis, and Cat Stevens.

Monday 15th

Pavilion *Bath* 7:30 & 10:30pm

Monday 15th – Wednesday 17th

At home in East Finchley Ray writes his weekly song for the BBC's *At The Eleventh Hour* TV show. This week's offering, sung as ever by Jeannie Lamb, is 'Poor Old Intellectual Sadie', broadcast on BBC-1 on January 20th.

✫ A scheduled tour of Australia and the Far East with Dave Dee Dozy Beaky Mick & Tich due to start at this time has been scrapped since the autumn. This marks the formal parting from the Arthur Howes Agency that intended the band to work this tour.

Monday 22nd

A press release announces that this week Dave is holding auditions for a backing band (which never materialises) for upcoming European dates: Germany in the last week of February, Sweden in late March, and Belgium and France at the end of April. Dave's announcement of solo plans precludes too much Kinks activity at this time, and they temporarily drift further into an identity crisis of solo projects. The press release also notes a Kinks/Tremeloes/Herd package tour for April. It's also around now that The Kinks briefly use Danny Betesch as their booking agent by agreeing to this tour. It seems to be a stopgap arrangement before Harold Davison fills the role, as manager Collins says he has to almost beg Davison to take them on. The first mention of bookings by Davison will come in an April 1st press release.

✫ This week Ray writes his weekly song for the BBC's *At The Eleventh Hour* TV show at home in East Finchley. Performed again by Jeannie Lamb, it's 'Could Be You're Getting Old', broadcast on BBC-1 on January 27th. Ray later reveals this song was inspired by the recent resignation amid a scandal of Malcolm Muggeridge, rector at the University of Edinburgh.

● **RECORDING** Pye Studios *central London*. There are no firm details of the studio work by The Kinks during this period, except that from autumn last year to March this year a number of recordings are quietly stockpiled for future use. In that time it is generally the policy for the whole band simply to put songs down on tape, with their fate for ultimate release as Kinks records or as Ray or Dave solo releases unknown. Based on their grouping on a tape list of extracted masters, two such titles – '**Monica**' and '**Phenomenal Cat**' – are probably recorded closely together, but could have been done at any time from autumn 1967 to March or even May 1968.

Wednesday 24th

Something Else By The Kinks album released in the US. Says *Billboard*: "Still specialising in inventive lyrics and melodic take-offs, The Kinks have another in their series of bright albums. Suggestions of vaudeville are evident in 'End Of The Season', while Romberg's 'The

Desert Song' is recalled in ['Tin Soldier Man']." Reviewer Ty Davis in the *Providence Evening Bulletin* asks, "So what makes The Kinks one of the top groups in the world, although nobody knows it? The answer is in the songs – mostly in the lyrics. Ray Davies's painted-pathos characterizations qualify him as one of the top ten rock songwriters."

The underground press begins to broaden and get behind The Kinks, with James Pomeroy writing in *Rolling Stone*: "This is the best album The Kinks have made yet, but paradoxically may be the last they will release in this country. This is unfortunate, for it shows great improvement in The Kinks' music since *Face To Face* and wide possibilities for the future …. When they are doing their things, The Kinks are marvelous to listen to. The listener is amused and confused, enchanted and entertained, and always questioning. And *Something Else* is The Kinks at their questionable best, their thing."

Robert Somma in the alternative rock magazine *Crawdaddy!* says: "No album that you can get your hands on this year will open up on a higher level of performance or sheer harmonic achievement than *Something Else*. There are simply no other groups operating on the Kink wavelength of a consistent and unchanging self-conception and musical assurance."

The promotional campaign for the LP is marginal. Beyond a multi-artist Warner/Reprise "new this month" ad in *Billboard*, a full page ad for the LP does appear in *Crawdaddy!*, which has carried regular items on The Kinks during its short lifespan. The ad is further evidence of an attempt to direct interest in The Kinks away from the Top 40 singles market and towards the hip, underground followers.

✫ At the urging of his song publisher, Ray today travels to Cannes, France to attend the *2nd Annual MIDEM Music Publishers Festival* held at the Festival des Palais. MIDEM is an international music industry convention and Ray attends to try to boost his recognition among record-industry people. He stays at the Carlton Hotel, where he gets inspiration for the song 'Big Sky'.

Saturday 27th

Student Union, Lanchester College Of Technology *Coventry* Ray returns to London today, the last day of the MIDEM festival, in time for this performance. Quaife plays the date with his wrist in a plaster cast. The Kinks are interviewed and photographed for the college newspaper. When questioned about the cast on his wrist, Quaife implies it is the result of a personal scuffle with an unnamed colleague, ignoring the innocuous excuse reported in the music press that it results from a fall at home, and avoiding the real reason: a band argument.

Monday 29th

A press release says that the Herd/Tremeloes/Kinks package tour starts April 6th, produced by Peter Walsh/Danny Betesch Productions.

✫ Probably because he was out of town, Ray does not produce a song for BBC TV's *At The Eleventh Hour* this week. Instead the show's musical director John Cameron provides one.

Wednesday 31st

'**Susannah's Still Alive**' / '**Funny Face**' single by Dave Davies released in the US. The single rates not one mention or review in the music trade papers, with the only apparent coverage in the New York-based radio station music weekly, *Go!*.

February

Saturday 3rd

On his 21st birthday Dave discusses with *Disc & Music Echo* the relative inactivity of The Kinks while Ray is busy writing songs. He says he might as well keep busy himself with solo projects, and reckons the band still averages a couple of concerts a week, though journalist Bob Farmer implies this is a generous estimate. Dave says he will start touring this month in Germany and Scandinavia, and in March in Belgium and France, followed by a British ballroom tour, all with his own backing band. All these plans will be in fact be scrapped.

Sunday 4th

Ray and Dave take part in a charity football match at Stags Meadow, Windsor, Berks as part of a *Top Of The Pops* team that plays an Entertainment XI.

Monday 5th

A press release belatedly revives the story that Quaife has suffered a broken wrist, saying he is still scheduled to play the band's upcoming Belgian dates.

Monday 5th - Wednesday 7th

Ray writes his weekly song for the BBC at home in East Finchley. This week's is 'Just A Poor Country Girl', sung by Jeannie Lamb on BBC-1's *At The Eleventh Hour* broadcast on February 10th.

Friday 9th

A tentative Dave Davies solo appearance at the Fanny Boutique, Croydon, south London never happens.

Monday 12th - Wednesday 14th

At home in East Finchley, Ray writes his weekly song for the BBC's *At The Eleventh Hour* TV show. This week's offering, sung by the tireless Jeannie Lamb, is 'The Man Who Conned Dinner From The Ritz', broadcast on BBC-1 on February 17th.

Friday 16th- Sunday 18th

Théâtre 140 Brussels, Belgium 3.30pm (Sat, Sun) & 6:00pm (Fri-Sun)
Quaife plays with a cast on his wrist. It's possible the February 16th show is cancelled. Travel day to London on the Monday following.

Monday 19th - Wednesday 21st

Ray writes his weekly song for the BBC at home in East Finchley. This week's song, as usual sung by Jeannie Lamb, is 'Did You See His Name?', broadcast on BBC-1's *At The Eleventh Hour* on the 24th.

Friday 23rd

Granby Halls Leicester *Rag Rave*, with Traffic, The Move, The Bonzo Dog Doo-Dah Band; sponsored by Leicester University

→ Two weeks of Dave Davies solo concerts in West Germany and Scandinavia are cancelled, seemingly due to Dave's reluctance to actively undertake a solo career now and, Dave claims later, because of a disagreement with management over percentages.

Monday 26th - Wednesday 28th

At home in East Finchley, Ray writes his last weekly song for the BBC's *At The Eleventh Hour* TV show. Sung by Jeannie Lamb, his final offering is 'That Is What The World Is All About', broadcast on BBC-1 on March 2nd.

→ Some time this spring, as part of a general effort to keep band members occupied while various solo obligations are fulfilled, Avory is given the chance to do some fashion modelling. With model Debbie Delacey he is photographed by Mike McGrath, modelling clothes for designer John Stephen. The pictures are published in British magazines *Vanity Fair* and *Men Only*, and also in *Disc & Music Echo*. Avory also does a modelling gig along with singer Kiki Dee around this time.

☆ Also this spring, Ray is approached by Granada Television who want to work with his still evolving *Village Green* idea, but there are problems and that plan is scrapped. Then it's suggested that he write a musical about the decline and fall of the British Empire, and a later report says Ray wants to write the script with British poet John Betjeman. The latter plan does not reach fruition.

March

→ With Ray's obligation to write songs for BBC TV's *At The Eleventh Hour* now completed, all attention evidently returns to The Kinks and to resuming an intensive period of recording, concentrating on a new single in time for next month's package tour. The only known scheduled concert appearance for March, on Friday 8th at the University of Birmingham, is cancelled at the last minute and the band is replaced by The Foundations.

→ ● **RECORDING** Pye Studios (No.2) *central London*. The entire month is likely a productive one at Pye. '**Wonderboy**' is written and recorded as Rasa and Ray try for a second child which at this time they hope will be a boy. (A daughter will be born to them on Christmas Day this year.) Ray later describes this as a particularly happy time, and that he is inspired by the intentional creation of a new life. Also possibly recorded at this time are '**Polly**', '**Lincoln County**' and '**There Is No Life Without Love**'. 'Polly' is interesting in its direct reference to Polly Garter, a character in Dylan Thomas's *Under Milk Wood*, pointing to Ray's continued interest in the work as an inspiration for his own similarly framed *Village Green* concept. An acetate coupling of '**Animal Farm**' with '**Did You See His Name**' probably places these titles too during this period, if not the same session. Avory recalls doing the former in Pye No.1, which means it's possible the latter was also done there.

Another surviving acetate coupling of '**Rosemary Rose**' and '**Berkeley Mews**' suggests more songs from this time being considered as potential Kinks singles (though these two could also come from a slightly earlier time).

There are changes at the Pye studio some time this spring as long-serving engineer Alan MacKenzie moves on, with new arrival Brian Humphries taking his place. Humphries is definitely in position by May, but it is not clear exactly when the change took place.

→ Late in the month Dave and Avory are interviewed by Bob Farmer for *Disc & Music Echo* at a local pub in London and discuss the upcoming tour, The Kinks' lack of exposure in the UK lately, and the band's reputation for missing gigs.

The piece is headlined "Kinks: Breaking The Lazy Image – But Only Just!" Farmer puts it to them that the band has a complete lack of interest in British tours or even ballroom dates, though Dave explains in their defence that the band don't play ballrooms any more as that scene has ground to a halt.

Dave assures Farmer that The Kinks have every intention to show up at concerts, and the bad reputation is one they've not yet recovered from. He suggests there are sometimes conflicting obligations to "football matches and trips abroad or film offers".

Monday 25th

A press release says a new Kinks single will be out April 5th, title still undecided, and a Dave Davies single on April 12th.

☆ Now that Dave is 21 he is able to form his own companies, and Kinks accountant Robert Ransom today files papers for the creation of

Dave's own publishing company, Dabe Music, formally incorporated as of April 23rd. Dabe Music will exist into the 1990s, though it will almost always be affiliated with a larger publishing company. Initially, Dabe goes through Carlin Music, the same publisher that handles Ray's Davray business.

☆ *NME* has an intriguing report that Dave is to start a restaurant in North London, an idea that never happens.

Monday 25th – Friday 29th

All this week at the Court Of Appeal in Westminster, central London, Justices Winn, Harman and Salmon hear the appeal case in the contract dispute of Denmark Productions Ltd vs. Boscobel Productions Ltd.

➔ At the end of this week, 'Wonderboy' is chosen as the new A-side from a backlog of available recordings, none of which have been especially earmarked as single material. The decision is made so late that evidently no promotional copies are manufactured and only simple white-label test pressings with handwritten titles are used for promotional purposes.

Friday 29th

● **RECORDING** Pye Studios (No.2) *central London*. '**Johnny Thunder**' and two instrumentals, '**Easy Come There You Went**' and the bizarrely titled '**Mick Avory's Underpants**', are recorded in what is probably the last session before the next Kinks single is chosen.

April

Monday 1st

A press release announces that the new single is 'Wonderboy', rush-released on April 5th, that Dave's next single is 'Lincoln County' / 'There Is No Life Without Your Love', due at the end of April, and notes tour plans through June including Italian dates and a Swedish tour. The announcement effectively heralds a significant return to the public eye for the hibernating Kinks.

Tuesday 2nd

➔ A lip-synched black-and-white promotional film of 'Wonderboy' is shot this week at a London film studio, likely intended for use as an insert for foreign TV companies in lieu of Kinks travelling to various cities to appear locally. It's an effort to minimise the promotional obligations associated with a new record, without committing commercial suicide. The clip will show up years later on the 1987 video compilation *The Kinks Music Biography*.

Wednesday 3rd

❏ **TV** BBC Lime Grove Studios *west London*. BBC-1 **Top Of The Pops** lip-synch 'Wonderboy' broadcast April 18th.

Thursday 4th

➔ ❏ **TV** Southern Television Studios *Southampton*. ITV **Time For Blackburn** lip-synch 'Wonderboy' broadcast April 13th. The show's producer is Mike Mansfield who works with The Kinks a number of times in the 1960s and '70s.

Friday 5th

'Wonderboy' / 'Polly' single released in the UK. Prominent ads appear in all the music weeklies. *Record Mirror* enthuses: "Still they come up with something which is so darned catchy that one cannot help humming along with it. No specific changes in the overall sound: just Ray doing his charmingly sophisticated attack on the lyrics. Not

necessarily their best but then they set exceptionally high standards. Philosophy-pop is the phrase I've just created for them. Flip: Rather more rhythmic, maybe with moments of crashingness. Again, it's distinctive and makes up a value-for-money coupling. Chart certainty."

NME headlines "Philosophic Kinks Deserve Hit" and continues: "Ray Davies has an incredible flair for writing lyrics of a beautifully descriptive nature – he always gets straight to the point, combining simplicity of thought with a penchant for the more colourful and pleasurable things in life. And his dislike of complex, enigmatic words is again evident in this charming philosophic song ... This is a very good pop record indeed ... Deserves to be big – and it will be!" In fact, the single is a flop. To put it in perspective, 'Waterloo Sunset' sold 220,000 copies, 'Autumn Almanac' 226,000, and even Dave's 'Susannah's Still Alive' managed a respectable 59,000. 'Wonderboy' will go on to sell just 26,000 copies.

Wonderboy single

A '**Wonderboy**' (R. DAVIES).
B '**Pretty Polly**' (R. DAVIES).

UK release April 5th 1968 (Pye 7N 17468).
US release May 15th or 22nd 1968 (Reprise 0691).
Musicians Ray Davies lead vocal, guitar. Dave Davies electric guitar, backing vocal. Pete Quaife bass guitar, backing vocal. Mick Avory drums. Nicky Hopkins piano. Rasa Davies backing vocal. Ken Jones bongos (A). David Whitaker (possibly) string arranger (B).
Recorded Pye Studios (No.2) central London; A: March 1968; B: probably March 1968; 4-track mixed to mono.
Producer Ray Davies.
Engineer probably Brian Humphries.
Chart high UK & US none.

⇨ **TOUR STARTS** *The Kinks/Herd Show: UK Tour* (Apr 6th – 28th). **Line-up**: Ray Davies (lead vocal, guitar), Dave Davies (guitar, vocal), Mick Avory (drums), Pete Quaife (bass). A Kennedy Street Enterprises Ltd (Danny Betesch) and Peter Walsh presentation. Compèred by Ray Cameron.

Saturday 6th

Granada Cinema *Mansfield, Notts* 6:00 & 8:30pm, with The Herd, The Tremeloes, Rain, Ola & The Janglers, Life'n'Soul
The Kinks must surely swallow their professional pride to accept a dreaded package tour, this of two shows nightly around the country's movie houses where they will bang out a string of hit-song performances. Although this method of promoting pop acts is fading quickly in the burgeoning era of expanded single-artist concerts, The Kinks at this point cannot command headliner bookings on their own and have to be presented in a safer setting.

The Herd are flavour of the year, with two big chart successes already – 'I Can Fly' and 'From The Underworld' – and a new single to promote, 'I Don't Want Our Lovin' To Die'. Their singer is a young Peter Frampton, who will go on to be a 1970s solo superstar. Also on the bill are The Tremeloes, who had a string of big hits in 1967: 'Here Comes My Baby', 'Silence Is Golden', and 'Even The Bad Times Are Good', currently riding with 'Suddenly You Love Me'. Rain is former Walker Brother Gary Walker's band, with future Badfinger member Joey Molland. Ola & The Janglers are from Sweden. Ray will recall later that the tour marks a crisis point in the band's career, describing it as uncomfortable and unhappy. He senses that management and booking agent alike feel the writing is on the wall for The Kinks. When 'Wonderboy' fails to chart it seems that their winning streak has come to a halt and that the band cannot last much longer.

Sunday 7th

Granada Cinema *Walthamstow, north-east London* 6:00 & 8:30pm, with The Herd, The Tremeloes, Rain, Ola & The Janglers, Life'n'Soul

David Hughes reports for *Disc & Music Echo* that the venue is only a quarter full, though they are an enthusiastic crowd of screamers. He notes that if the houses don't improve, Britain will shortly be conducting an inquest on the death of the package show. "The Kinks seemed sadly out of place," writes Hughes. "They're not a teenage group by any standards, and Ray's beautiful songs do not suit a cinema stage. 'Waterloo Sunset' and 'Sunny Afternoon' are fantastic to sit back in the sun by a record player and listen to, but for crowds of fans who really want to scream loudly at lots of noise, they fall a bit flat. Still, Dave was very chuffed to be working again, and Pete Quaife was zany as ever, but Ray seemed a bit bored by the whole business – his 'sad clown' face forcing the occasional toothy grin to convince us he was really having a ball! The group also played it safe, sticking exclusively to a selection of its many hits, which were vocally good and instrumentally rather dire! And it was all over – ending as something of an anti-climax to the audience and I would imagine considerable relief to the artists."

Monday 8th

Granada Cinema *Bedford* 7:00 & 9:10pm, with The Herd, The Tremeloes, Rain, Ola & The Janglers, Life'n'Soul

Tuesday 9th

ABC Cinema *Exeter* 6:15 & 8:30pm, with The Herd, The Tremeloes, Rain, Ola & The Janglers, Life'n'Soul

Wednesday 10th

ABC Cinema *Gloucester* 6:15 & 8:30pm, with The Herd, The Tremeloes, Rain, Ola & The Janglers, Life'n'Soul

Thursday 11th

Capitol Theatre *Cardiff, Wales* 6:15 & 8:45pm, with The Herd, The Tremeloes, Rain, Ola & The Janglers, Life'n'Soul
Day off follows.

Saturday 13th

City Hall *Newcastle Upon Tyne* 6:00 & 8:30pm, with The Herd, The Tremeloes, Rain, Ola & The Janglers, Life'n'Soul

Sunday 14th

DeMontfort Hall *Leicester* 5:45 & 8:00pm, with The Herd, The Tremeloes, Rain, Ola & The Janglers, Life'n'Soul

Monday 15th

Town Hall *Birmingham* 6:30 & 8:45pm, with The Herd, The Tremeloes, Rain, Ola & The Janglers, Life'n'Soul
In London, a press release is issued announcing that a writ has been served by Davray and Carlin Music on Philips Records, Northern Songs, and Arcusa Records claiming copyright infringement against Dave Davies's 'Death Of A Clown' by Spain's Eurovision Song Contest winner, Massiel. Her entry 'La La La', written by Ramon Arcusa and Manuel de la Calva, was performed at the Royal Albert Hall in London on April 6th. The charge will later be dropped by Davray and Carlin, but for now it adds to the mounting pile of litigation with which The Kinks are embroiled.

Tuesday 16th

ABC Cinema *Northampton* 6:30 & 8:45pm, with The Herd, The Tremeloes, Rain, Ola & The Janglers, Life'n'Soul

Wednesday 17th

ABC Cinema *Peterborough* 6:15 & 8:30pm, with The Herd, The Tremeloes, Rain, Ola & The Janglers, Life'n'Soul

Thursday 18th

ABC Cinema *Chesterfield, Derbys* 6:10 & 8:25pm, with The Herd, The Tremeloes, Rain, Ola & The Janglers, Life'n'Soul

Friday 19th

ABC Cinema *Chester* 5:40 & 8:30pm, with The Herd, The Tremeloes, Rain, Ola & The Janglers, Life'n'Soul
Set-list: 'Waterloo Sunset', 'You Really Got Me', 'All Day And All Of The Night', 'Death Of A Clown', medley 'Milkcow Blues' / 'Batman Theme', 'A Well Respected Man', 'Wonderboy', 'You Are My Sunshine'.
Dave Davies Hits and *The Kinks* EPs released in the UK. Dave's EP contains both sides of his first two singles, while the band disc has four tracks from the *Something Else …* album. They seem to be attempts by Pye to shore up sales after the relative failure of the new single.

Saturday 20th

An odd night to have off from the tour, given that Saturday is normally the big night out of the week.

Sunday 21st

Empire Theatre *Liverpool* 6:15 & 8:00pm, with The Herd, The Tremeloes, Rain, Ola & The Janglers, Life'n'Soul

Monday 22nd

Odeon Cinema *Manchester* 6:15 & 8:45pm, with The Herd, The Tremeloes, Rain, Ola & The Janglers, Life'n'Soul
Reprise Records logs in master tapes for the new Kinks single 'Wonderboy' / 'Polly'. The band has the following day off.

Wednesday 24th

ABC Cinema *Cambridge* 6:15 & 8:30pm, with The Herd, The Tremeloes, Rain, Ola & The Janglers, Life'n'Soul

Thursday 25th

Adelphi Theatre *Slough* 6:40 & 8:50pm, with The Herd, The Tremeloes, Rain, Ola & The Janglers, Life'n'Soul

Friday 26th

Central Hall *Chatham, Kent* 6:15 & 8:30pm, with The Herd, The Tremeloes, Rain, Ola & The Janglers, Life'n'Soul

Saturday 27th

Winter Gardens *Bournemouth* 6:15 & 8:15pm, with The Herd, The Tremeloes, Rain, Ola & The Janglers, Life'n'Soul

Sunday 28th

Coventry Theatre *Coventry* 6:00 & 8:30pm
This closing night of the tour is attended by 1,800. Over 30 years later Ray will succinctly sum up this time: "People thought it was over for The Kinks, but they always thought it was over for The Kinks. They're even saying it now."
Set-list (1st show): 'Sunny Afternoon', 'A Well Respected Man', 'Dedicated Follower Of Fashion', 'Dandy', 'Wonderboy', 'Love Me Till The Sun Shines', 'Death Of A Clown', 'Milk Cow Blues', 'You Really Got Me'.

May

Wednesday 1st – Friday 3rd

Hearings resume at the Court Of Appeal in Westminster, central London as Justices Winn, Harman and Salmon review the case of Denmark Productions Ltd vs. Boscobel Productions Ltd.

Sunday 5th

Ray & Dave join the *Melody Maker* football team, which also includes folk singer Jon Betmead, for a match at Hounslow Football Club in aid of mentally handicapped children.

→ ● **RECORDING** Pye Studios (No.2) *central London*. The Kinks return to Pye after the tour and reportedly record some upbeat numbers inspired by playing live – after becoming essentially a studio band during the last year. It also reflects what Ray will admit later is a desire to connect to his audience again. Typically of The Kinks at this time, they tend to work on a handful of songs at a time and then choose the best for the next single. At this post-tour session **'Days'**. and **'Misty Water'** are recorded, although **'Days'**.will be revisited later in the month (see 27th) due to dissatisfaction with today's efforts. Evidence from tape files and existing acetates suggests that **'Picture Book'** is also done some time this month. 'Misty Water' has an unabashed classic-early-Kinks break in the middle, partly inspired by the band's return to the stage. Production in all cases is by Ray Davies, with Nicky Hopkins on piano when Ray is not at the keyboard. Brian Humphries is now engineer at Pye No.2, still using the 4-track machine.

→ Dave is interviewed for *Disc & Music Echo*, the resulting article provocatively headlined "Ray Davies: No Longer a Wonder Boy?" Ray isn't doing interviews now, but Dave defends the relative chart failure of 'Wonderboy' and what the press perceives as the band's first serious blip since 'You Really Got Me'. He defends charges of poor attendance on the recent package tour and criticism that they appeared bored and unenthusiastic. He says the band no longer want to rely on stage antics to get their music across, and that they were generally well received. Dave tells *Disc* that the band is busy working out tracks for their upcoming LP between occasional bookings abroad.

☆ In the rush to get a new Kinks single out to follow 'Wonderboy' it is evidently decided to push the proposed May release of Dave's 'Lincoln County' back to July 19th to avoid interfering with Kinks sales. Ray seems to have taken the relative failure of 'Wonderboy' to heart and wants to get another Kinks single on to the market as soon as possible to reinstate the band's chart reputation.

Wednesday 15th

→ **'Wonderboy' / 'Polly'** is released in the US (or possibly 22nd). The single warrants part of a full-page ad in *Billboard* and the record-trade magazine reviews it in their Special Merit category (the fate of singles not tipped for the Top 60). The reviewer uses the parlance of the day, but it seems doubtful he/she bothered to listen to the record because it's described as an "infectious rocker loaded with teen appeal and currently rising up the British sales charts". New York's *Go* magazine also gives it a tip – but that will be the extent of the record's industry exposure, and it vanishes without a trace of radio airplay and minimal availability in record stores.

Saturday 18th

Stadsschouwburg *Sittard, Netherlands* 8:00pm, with Full House, Fagham, Blues Dimension

This show starts a string of weekend dates that interrupt the band's focus on recording. Originally booked are The Small Faces, who cancel at short notice due to "illness", though they too are evidently busy in the

studio for much of this month recording their *Ogden's Nutgone Flake* LP. The two bands share management, though The Small Faces part company with Wace and Collins around this time. The substitution is at such short notice that no mention of The Kinks appears in the national press, only locally in newspapers.

Sunday 19th

De Eurobeurs *Apeldoorn, Netherlands* 2:00pm, with The Mozarts, Full House, Experience, Fagham, Blues Dimension
Zaal Beyering *Vlagtwedde, Netherlands* 8:00pm, with Full House, Fagham, Blues Dimension

Ray tells a local journalist that the band's fortunes have declined so fast in Britain that some singles don't even chart. He says he realises that something has to be done and so has signed several contracts to tour Britain, Scandinavia and some other European countries. He wants to get back in touch with his audience and experience their reaction to his new songs.

Monday 20th

The Kinks travel back to London and presumably straight back into Pye Studios. A press blurb this week notes however that progress on the new Kinks single is "unusually slow".

→ It is announced that the scheduled Italian visit – May 29th Piper's Club, Milan; May 30th-31st TV in Rome; June 1st Piper's Club, Rome – is cancelled in order to make more studio time. However, The Kinks do meanwhile accept a one-off short-notice booking near Dublin, Ireland.

☆ Around this time Ray is purchasing a Tudor-style "estate" out into the country north of London at Borehamwood, Herts. He is convinced by his sister that this is the proper thing for a successful person to do.

Monday 27th

● **RECORDING** Pye Studios (No.2) *central London*. Two songs are recorded: a new composition, **'Pictures In The Sand'**, and a new or revised version of **'Days'** (first attempted May 5th). 'Days' is worked on extensively to achieve the required result.

This session sees the incident reported later in *X-Ray* and *Kink* where Quaife doodles on the song's tape box, by legend writing 'Daze' in place of 'Days'. Both Ray and Dave will point to this as symbolic of the reappearance of Quaife's dissatisfaction with the band. Ray will say in *X-Ray* that he sees the writing of 'Days' and its subject matter ("days I'll remember all my life") as a prediction of the end of the group, and recognises that his angry outburst over Quaife's subconscious doodling shows how far apart the two have grown by this time.

Quaife says later that the "days to daze" part of the tale is "a convenient and fabricated literary image and not a factual part of the otherwise truthful and symbolically correct story. [We] had a big fight over ['Days']," he says. "Ray kept us in the studio so damned long I was beginning to lose my mind. ... After a while it became colossally boring to sit there listening to this thing over and over and over again. So what I was doing was doodling; I was drawing this little man ... and Ray saw it and got really upset [that] I was doodling [rather] than listening to the damn music."

June

Saturday 1st

New Arcadia Ballroom *Bray, Co. Wicklow, Ireland* 9:00pm-2:00am, with The Greenbeats

Quaife intentionally misses the flight to Dublin from London for tonight's show, boarding the plane with The Kinks and manager Collins but slipping off just prior to takeoff. The band doesn't realise he's not there until road manager Ken Jones meets them at the airport in Dublin. Collins arranges to have Rasa pick up Quaife back in London to catch a later flight, still in time to do the show. However, even though they have time to make it to the airport, they arrive too late and The Kinks are forced to cancel the evening's performance. In retrospect the incident will be seen as a major signal that Quaife's days in the band are numbered and that he is unhappy with his role. At the time it may well seem like just another crisis among many in a band used to personal and artistic clashes. Accordingly, there seems to be a resolve to pull together following the Swedish tour and record an album that everyone really wants to make.

→ ● **RECORDING** Pye Studios (No.2) *central London*. Back in London the recording of **'Days'** is certainly finished by this week, before heading off to Sweden, and the band now have an LP's worth of material to submit to Reprise Records. Ray will later express dissatisfaction with the final recording of 'Days', implying that he wants to re-record the track but that there is no time left to do so. Like many of Ray's best 1960s singles 'Days' is finished at the last possible moment and under pressure.

✮ Ray is still holding on to the 'Village Green' song for his "solo LP", but slowly this and the next Kinks album have mutated into one. As far as the band is concerned now, the next British album will be the *Village Green* record. But in the US, The Kinks are contractually bound to submit a completed LP right away to Reprise. (The band is on different contractually-determined schedules in terms of submitting their UK and US albums.)

Fifteen completed recordings (in both mono and stereo mixes) are selected by the end of this week from the band's available backlog. The American album is to be titled *Four More Respected Men*, probably Reprise's idea to associate it with the band's 1965 US hit 'A Well Respected Man'.

It takes at least two more weeks until the tapes are logged in at Reprise, on June 20th, implying more mixing is done (probably stereo mixes, still considered secondary to mono, done by engineer Brian Humphries in Ray's absence). They do not include the 'Village Green' song, but do include a number of songs in common with the later *Village Green Preservation Society* album.

Reprise makes no move whatsoever upon receipt of the tapes, and will not begin to prepare the *Four More Respected Men* LP for a scheduled November release until October, trimmed to 11 of the submitted 15 tracks.

Pye in the UK meanwhile seems to have afforded the band an extra few months to record a new clutch of songs following the Swedish tour, though the resulting *Village Green Preservation Society* album will not be released until the Christmas season.

✮ The choice of 'Days' as the next UK single is only now confirmed as the band leaves for the Swedish tour. Ray chooses for its B-side 'She's Got Everything', a recording that has been languishing in the vaults for well over two years. Perhaps this is an intentional juxtaposition of a classic early-Kinks sound with the A-side's farewell to that era.

↪ **TOUR STARTS** *Sweden public parks* (June 8th – 23rd). **Line-up**: Ray Davies (lead vocal, guitar), Dave Davies (guitar, vocal), Mick Avory (drums), Pete Quaife (bass). The band's third tour of Sweden begins after two riotous visits in 1965 and 1966. It's arranged through FPC Productions, a Stockholm-based booking agency, who liaise with The Kinks' new agent, Barry Dickens (representing the Harold Davison agency). The band is evidently unaware of the nature of the bookings in advance, and are somewhat disappointed when they discover they are playing a series of outdoor public parks. From the booking agent's point of view, the band's reputation is at such an all-

time low that this tour is the only way to generate some reasonable, steady income for them. The tour reinforces the point that their career is seriously waning and that it is time to push hard to resolve the problems in the US and start touring there again (but not before another symbolic low-point later this year: the dreaded cabaret dates). The Swedish shows are normally 30-40 minutes long and consist of the usual string of hits, with no songs after 'Waterloo Sunset' included – 'Wonderboy' is already considered irrelevant, and 'Autumn Almanac' too complex to perform well in concert.

Saturday 8th
Brunnsparken Örebro, Sweden 6:00pm, with String Tones
Folkets Park Tallunden Kristinehamn, Sweden 9:00pm, with Wärmländers
Opening with 'Till The End of the Day', the band plays at such a volume they rattle the stage and seats, much to one reviewer's dismay. He also feels that the audience's response is weak considering the enthusiasm of the band.

Sunday 9th
Mariebergsskogen Karlstad, Sweden 3:00pm
The Kinks play to an afternoon crowd of 2,000 for almost an hour, launching into the opening number while the curtain is still closed. Day off following, when a press release back home announces the new single as 'Days' to be issued in the UK on June 28th.
Set-list: 'Till The End Of The Day', 'Set Me Free', 'See My Friends', 'Sunny Afternoon', 'Waterloo Sunset', 'A Well Respected Man', 'Milk Cow Blues', 'You Are My Sunshine'.

Tuesday 11th
Liseberg Konserthallen Gothenburg, Sweden 8:00pm, with Blue & Yellow, Voces, Rainy Day Women
A reviewer rates the performance highly, though finding it "jumbled and messy" at times, and says that Swedish act Rainy Day Women draws more applause. The Kinks' set includes a medley of 'A Well Respected Man' / 'Dedicated Follower of Fashion' / 'Sunny Afternoon', plus 'Waterloo Sunset', 'See My Friends', 'Death of A Clown' and 'Rip It Up'.

Wednesday 12th
Alingsåsparken Alingsås, Sweden 9:30pm, with Schytts

Thursday 13th
Folkets Park Hunnebostrand, Sweden 10:00pm, with Johnny Öhrbergs Orkester

Friday 14th
Folkets Park Malmö, Sweden 8:00pm
There are sound problems this evening, and the performance is harshly criticised as uninspired and full of mistakes.

Saturday 15th
Folkets Park Åhus, Sweden afternoon
Bellevueparken Karlshamn, Sweden 11:00pm, with The West Coasters, Leif Jörgens

Sunday 16th
Parken Oskarshamn, Sweden 8:00pm, with Tobbes Sextett med Per-Olof
Sound problems plague The Kinks' performance resulting in inaudible lyrics. The band is criticised in the local press for a monotonous and lacklustre performance that never grabs the crowd.
Folkets Park Kalmar, Sweden 10:00pm, with Leif Hobrings Sextett
Day off following.

Tuesday 18th

Folkpark *Gamleby, Sweden* 9:00pm, with Magnus Kvintett
Folkets Park *Hultsfred, Sweden* 11:00pm, with Ingmar Nordströms, No Nox

Wednesday 19th

Folkets Park *Finspång, Sweden* 9:00pm, with Sol Crept, Maarz
The band plays to a somewhat reserved crowd of 600, though a reviewer finds the music "excellent and energetic".

Thursday 20th

Stora Scenen, Gröna Lund *Stockholm, Sweden* 8:00pm
Jump-In, Gröna Lund *Stockholm, Sweden* 11:00pm, with The Peeps, The Greyhounds
The Jump-In is a club within the amusement park.
☆ Reprise Records in the US logs into its tape vault 17 new tracks, including Dave's single ('Lincoln County' / 'There Is No Life Without Love') plus the 15-title mono and stereo master tapes for the proposed Kinks LP *Four More Respected Gentlemen*. Songs received are: 'She's Got Everything', 'Monica', 'Mr Songbird', 'Johnny Thunder', 'Polly', 'Days', 'Susannah's Still Alive', 'Berkeley Mews', 'There Is No Life Without Love', 'Autumn Almanac', 'Phenomenal Cat', 'Misty Water', 'Did You See His Name?', 'Animal Farm', 'Picture Book'. Initially only a 12-title version of the LP (with the first 12 of these 15 songs) is proposed. However, Reprise refrains from scheduling an imminent release, because it seems that word comes from The Kinks' management that an alternative album is to be submitted for September release in place of this collection of songs. For the moment these tapes lie dormant in the Reprise vaults, with only the mono mixes of 'Days' and 'She's Got Everything' used, for a single release in July.

Friday 21st

Park *Eskiltuna, Sweden* early show
Shake-In *Heby, Sweden* late show

Saturday 22nd

Folkets Park *Fagersta, Sweden* 8:00pm, with Curt Görans, Helge Werners
A 30-minute set mostly of the old hits, termed "very professional" but lacking that extra spark.
Folkets Park *Borlänge, Sweden* 11:00pm, with Lill-Babs
The Kinks play to an enthusiastic crowd of 3,000, charming the audience with great success according to one reviewer. His only disappointment is the lack of newer songs, with the band relying almost exclusively on hits and older material.

Sunday 23rd

Folkets Park *Bollnäs, Sweden* 7:00pm, with The Fockins Souls, Janssons Frestelse
Folkparken *Gävle, Sweden* 9:00pm, with Arne Bills, Eddie Üsts

Monday 24th

The band travels back to London where they almost immediately dig into the necessary promotional duties to push the new single, 'Days', due out at the end of the week. The Swedish tour has further brought home the poor state of the band's touring career. Dave will recall later that from this point on The Kinks are determined to return to the States in order to regain their former stature as an exciting live act.

Wednesday 26th

❏ **TV** Hippodrome *Golders Green, north-west London*. BBC-1 **The Basil Brush Show** lip-synch 'Days' broadcast June 28th.
❏ **TV** BBC Lime Grove Studios *west London*. BBC-1 **Top Of The Pops** lip-synch 'Days' broadcast August 1st. The band tapes two TV inserts for *Top Of The Pops*, following a BBC policy that allows for a single that does well in the chart to be featured even if the artist is unavailable.
☆ Almost certainly today The Kinks are photographed by official BBC photographer Harry Goodwin, used for a full front-page ad in the July 6th *NME*. The same shot is earmarked for the cover of the eventually scrapped *Four More Respected Gentlemen* LP.

Thursday 27th

❏ **TV** Southern Television Studios *Southampton*. ITV **Time For Blackburn (Pop People & Places)** lip-synch 'Days' broadcast July 6th.

Friday 28th

At the Court Of Appeal in Westminster, central London the final rulings by Justices Winn, Harman and Salmon are handed down in the contract dispute between Denmark Productions Ltd and Boscobel Productions Ltd. The basis of the findings of the lower court of simple "frustration" of the contract are not supported, but the appeals court instead concludes the contract was nevertheless breached by virtue of Page's abandonment of the band in Los Angeles on July 4th 1965. While the legal analysis differs, the same effect results, and the court maintains that Denmark Productions is not entitled to its ongoing claim of ten percent of The Kinks' income. The court orders only the repayment of unpaid commissions for the period June 30th to September 14th 1965, at which point the contract between the two parties was terminated by virtue of Boscobel's repudiation of it on that date. This ends the management dispute, pending an appeal which is filed at the House Of Lords but ultimately rejected on October 9th this year. At least one daily newspaper picks up on the story and quotes Judge Salmon: "I think that almost anything a manager might do, however harmless or trivial, could induce hatred and distrust in a group of highly temperamental, jealous and spoilt adolescents." The separate matter of Kassner Music's continued claim to Ray's publishing, which has caused all of Ray's publishing income to be held in escrow, will not be settled until October 1970, and that will be out of court.
'Days' / 'She's Got Everything' single released in the UK. Ray will recall later: "['Days'] had an air of finality about it. Which I really liked. Pop musicians aren't meant to go on forever. And around this time, whenever I finished a session, I thought maybe this is the last record I'd ever make. That's why is has that strange emotion to it. The band knew it too. Fortunately though The Kinks went on to make other records." Ray also appears to be saying goodbye to Fortis Green and in effect leaves behind his whole childhood. "It was obvious I was saying goodbye not only to a house, but to a way of life, a time, an inspiration."
There is prominent advertising for and reviews of the new single in all the music weeklies. The *NME* headlines their lead review "Kinks Head For Charts" and *Melody Maker* says that, following the last disappointing outing, "this is great – better than they've done for ages ... a really pleasant record that should do very, very well". Keith Moon of The Who, reviewing records in *Melody Maker*, is less sure. "Memoirs of Ray Davies," is Moon's description of 'Days'. "This sounds very much like a demo with Ray on acoustic guitar. I just heard a bass drum so Mick Avory must be on it as well. So it's The Kinks. Sounds pretty dated, like one of these songs Pete [Townshend] keeps under his sink. I dig what The Kinks do, but I've never thought of them as a group." *Record Mirror*'s reviewer says it's the sort of song that once or twice heard is never forgotten.

Saturday 29th-Sunday 30th

Quaife is spotted filling cars with petrol (gas) at the Lynton Garage in Muswell Hill, north London which somehow triggers rumours that he may have left the band. In fact he was filling a car for his brother. The incident doubtless indicates to the pop readership Quaife's nonchalance about his pop-star status.

➜ INDICATES EVENT AROUND THIS TIME BUT WITH NO FIRM DATE

Days single

A **'Days'** (R. DAVIES).
B **'She's Got Everything'** (R. DAVIES).

UK release June 28th 1968 (Pye 7N 17573).
US release July 24th 1968 (Reprise 0762).
Musicians Ray Davies lead vocal, acoustic guitar (A), electric guitar (B). Dave Davies electric guitar, backing vocal. Pete Quaife bass guitar. Mick Avory drums. Nicky Hopkins piano, Mellotron (A). Rasa Davies backing vocal (A).
Recorded Pye Studios (No.2) central London; A: May-early June 1968, 4-track mixed to mono; B: February 7th & 10th 1966, 3-track mixed to mono.
Producer Ray Davies (A); Shel Talmy (B).
Engineer Brian Humphries (A); Alan MacKenzie (B).
Chart high UK number 10; US none.

July

Monday 1st

))) **RADIO** BBC Piccadilly Studios (No.1) *central London*. BBC Radio 1 *Top Gear* studio recordings produced by Bernie Andrews 'Days', 'Monica', 'Love Me Till The Sun Shines', 'Waterloo Sunset' broadcast July 7th 2:00-4:00pm, repeated August 4th. Energised by their recent touring and recording activity, the band is in fine form for this session of fresh recordings. ('Days', 'Love Me Till The Sun Shines' and 'Waterloo Sunset' will be released in 2001 on *The Kinks BBC Sessions 1964-1977*.)

☆ Rehearsals for the new album begin. Ray will say later in *Crawdaddy!* that much time is spent in the front room of his house on Fortis Green, East Finchley rehearsing for what became the *Village Green Preservation Society* album. It seems that July is a good time for the band as they put the material together for the record in rehearsal and in the studio.

☆ Despite the recent studio confrontation between Quaife and Ray, and Quaife's no-show in Ireland, the recent tour seems to have helped the band at least temporarily work out some of the disagreements and move forward to complete the new LP. More important, perhaps, 'Days' is making a healthy dent in the UK charts, relieving some of the pressure for the band to prove their commercial worth. In retrospect, both Ray and Quaife will describe this as an enjoyable period.

Monday 8th

A press release reveals that Ray and Dave are to form a record production company that will focus on developing new acts, though no record company outlet is yet established for it.

Tuesday 9th

))) **RADIO** BBC Playhouse Theatre *central London*. Radio-1 *Saturday Club* studio recordings 'Susannah's Still Alive', 'Monica', 'Love Me Till The Sun Shines', 'Days' broadcast July 13th, repeated one-song-a-day on *Afternoon Pop Show* during the week July 22nd-26th. The highlight of this broadcast is a frenzied version of 'Love Me Till The Sun Shines', later released on *The Kinks BBC Sessions* CD in 2001 (as is 'Monica').

Thursday 11th

❏ **TV** BBC Lime Grove Studios (Studio G) *west London*. BBC-1 *Top*

Of The Pops live vocal over record backing 'Days' 7.29-8.00pm. Despite a back-up performance that already exists on videotape, the band is back at the Beeb for an appearance on this evening's transmission of *TOTP*.

Monday 15th

A press release announces The Kinks' debut as a pantomime act for an eight-week run at Christmas in the Midlands, probably Birmingham, and as a cabaret act in the autumn. The pantomime is almost certainly intended as a staged version of the *Village Green* LP currently being worked on, but it never happens. The release also says a new LP is due for September, at this point planned to include some of Dave's compositions, that Irish ballroom dates are set for August, West German dates for September, and that Dave's 'Lincoln County' single is delayed yet again, until August 16th.

➜ ● **RECORDING** Pye Studios (No.2) *central London*. While much of the beginning of July is evidently spent rehearsing in Ray's front room at the Fortis Green house in East Finchley, the middle to end of the month seems to be an intense period of recording at Pye.

There is apparently no live work at all this month, with just a couple of Scottish dates slated but written off. Recordings known to be already finalised on tape are 'Phenomenal Cat', 'Picture Book', 'Monica', 'Johnny Thunder', 'Mr Songbird', 'Days' and 'Village Green', so five new songs will be needed to flesh out the planned 12-title version of the new album.

Probably recorded now are **'Do You Remember Walter'**, **'Wicked Annabella'**, **'Starstruck'** and **'People Take Pictures of Each Other'**. As all the songs will be remixed when prepared for the final 15-title version, they are probably only mixed very quickly in August. Also recorded by now but not included on the 12-title LP is 'Sitting By The Riverside', which will be included on an upcoming TV session (for which see July 22nd).

Nicky Hopkins's appearance on 'People Take Pictures of Each Other' marks probably the last use of the session pianist who a few months later would forsake his busy studio schedule and begin a US tour with The Jeff Beck Group. This is yet another nail in the coffin of the classic 1960s Kinks sound.

Tuesday 16th

Publishing for 'Monica' is assigned with Carlin Music, probably necessary due to its inclusion in recent BBC radio programmes.

Friday 19th

Cancelled is a scheduled show at the Kinema Dance Hall, Stranraer, Scotland. The Kinks are replaced at the event by The Boutique from Northern Ireland.

☆ Today's scheduled release of Dave's 'Lincoln County' single is again put back, to August 23rd, because it seems unwise to release any new Kinks-related product while 'Days' is still rising in the chart.

But a few promotional copies are in fact sent out, and some music weeklies publish reviews. In typical Kinks fashion, the decision about 'Lincoln County' seems to have been made just late enough to cause confusion in the marketplace.

Saturday 20th

The Kinks are billed as the headline act at the *Scottish Week Opening Dance* at Agnew Park Marquee, Stranraer, Scotland with The Corsairs, but do not appear.

The band had turned down the booking once it was made clear to them that it was to be staged inside what amounted to a large tent. Honeybus appear in place of The Kinks, and the promoter has to apologise to a disappointed crowd.

kinks'68

Monday 22nd

❑ **TV** BBC Television Centre (Studio 8) *west London*. BBC-2 **Late Night Line-Up – Colour Me Pop** probably lip-synch, medley 'Dedicated Follower Of Fashion' / 'A Well Respected Man' / 'Death Of A Clown', 'Sunny Afternoon', 'Two Sisters', 'Sitting By The Riverside', 'Lincoln County', 'Picture Book', 'Days' broadcast July 26th.

The band videotapes a featured appearance on this early colour show by the BBC, the first colour broadcast in Britain by The Kinks. Rehearsals take place in the late morning, while the taping is done in the late afternoon.

Also shown as an insert is a separate BBC-shot film of unknown content for which 'She's Got Everything' is used as a soundtrack. Sadly the videotape of this classic TV appearance seems to have been erased some time after its only broadcast.

Wednesday 24th

'Days' / 'She's Got Everything' single released in the US. No trade ads appear although the record does rate a *Billboard* review in the Top 60 Spotlight: "This infectious rhythm number will fast prove their first big hit of 1968." Despite this encouraging prediction, 'Days' fails to get airplay besides a few limited spins by Anglo-supportive DJs in the bigger cities like LA and New York, though it reportedly gets some decent regular action in San Francisco.

☆ In a publicity blitz between recording sessions Pye arranges a press free-for-all with The Kinks at the company's central London offices, designed to propel 'Days' further up the UK charts. Dave is interviewed by Richard Green for *NME* and reveals to the music paper that the LP they are working will be called *Village Green* and is about a town and its people.

"It's the best thing we've ever done," says Dave. "Ray wrote most of it and I added a few songs. All Ray's songs came at the right time for us, just when we were wondering what to do next." Dave also plugs his still unreleased solo single: "I want people to know what's in me, I want to be taken seriously, but people never will. This record is all I've got in me."

Ray tells Tony Norman for *Melody Maker*: "I'm happy the way the recordings are coming out. I'm getting over to the group more. We're doing what I think the group wants, although it's hard, sometimes, to feel the same way." Although at times Ray feels that his music is ahead of what's going on, he is happy about The Kinks' forthcoming album, which he originally intended to be a solo album. "It's something I wanted to do two years ago, and I've got the feeling that it is going to work the way I want it to. It will be what I've always wanted."

Ray pronounces to *Record Mirror*: "I Feel The Kinks don't have a position in the pop world today. Our status as musicians is really important to us alone. If we stand the commercial aspects aside, we have only our artistic integrity at stake and I put a high value on that. ... I don't want to push myself into writing faster and churning out single after single so we can remain in the public eye, via TV, radio and the charts."

Disc & Music Echo is not ignored. Dave reveals that the new album was originally Ray's idea "as a stage musical" but that never came off. "So we did it on an LP. It's about a town and the people that have lived there, and the village green is the focal point of the whole thing. Ray wrote most of the songs months ago, and now we've recorded most of it – in fact there's only two tracks to do. I think it's probably the best thing we've ever done."

Saturday 27th +

The start of The Kinks' annual two-week holiday. It's at this time that Ray and family leave his East Finchley semi-detached house on Fortis Green and move to a larger, Tudor house in the deep suburbs of Borehamwood, Herts. One report suggests that Ray wanted to move to nearby Highgate but could not find a suitable place. Ray's decision to

leave Fortis Green will have a huge effect on both his songwriting and the future of The Kinks.

Before, everything centred on that stretch of road, including the inspiration for many of his songs. Symbolically, Ray's move out of the general Muswell Hill area into the outer suburbs signals another step towards the end of the original Kinks team. With Ray's north London base gone, it will force members of the band to travel out to Borehamwood to prepare and rehearse new material.

Perhaps as the result of a publicity ploy to boost the appearance of their success, the press reports that Avory is buying a house in West Molesey, Surrey near where he grew up, but this is not true.

No mention is made of Dave's or Quaife's activities at this time, but it is likely that one or both of them head off to Copenhagen with their wives and families.

August

Monday 12th

→ ● **RECORDING** Pye Studios (No.2) *central London*. Their holiday finished on Sunday 11th, The Kinks reassemble this week at Pye to work on a new piece, **'The Village Green Preservation Society'**, which becomes the title track of the new album – and is the last song recorded before its last-minute withdrawal and consequent expansion to 15 titles. Prior to this recording the working title was likely to have been based on the track simply called 'Village Green'. With a deadline looming for submission of the new record, Ray does final mixing of the first version of the newly-titled *Village Green Preservation Society* LP this week.

Wednesday 14th

→ Ray reviews new and recent singles in *Disc & Music Echo* where he pans Simon & Garfunkel but gives high marks to Arthur Brown's 'Fire' and the new Bee Gees single.

Thursday 15th

❑ **TV** BBC Lime Grove Studios *west London*. BBC-1 **Top Of The Pops** lip-synch 'Days' broadcast August 15th.
☆ 'Days' single peaks at number 10 in the UK *Melody Maker* chart.

Friday 16th

Publishing is assigned for the *Village Green Preservation Society* tracks, indicating that all work on the first version is complete and the tapes sent to Pye to be prepared for release. With the recording finished, The Kinks are photographed around this time by Barry Wentzel on Hampstead Heath, north-west London for the sleeve of the new album.

Monday 19th

→ Ray begins press interviews leading up to the new LP's release. He tells *Record Mirror* of his recent move out of East Finchley into the suburbs of Borehamwood, hoping that a change of scenery will be good for him and for his songwriting. He says he will produce an album for Dave at the end of the year. Speaking to Keith Altham for *NME* with perhaps a hint of early work on the next project (*Arthur*), Ray says he is "currently concerned with writing about birth and 'war mothers'," possibly a reference to the song 'Some Mother's Son'. Altham says that the chart success of 'Days' pleases Ray greatly because it proves The Kinks can come back after a dud single like 'Wonderboy'. Ray says of that record: "It should have never have been released. I didn't want it released. We did it as a favour to someone!"

Ray speaks further of his interest in becoming a film producer, and reveals that he was once asked to produce a record for footballer George Best. Alluding to the new album, Altham writes in the *NME*

→ INDICATES EVENT AROUND THIS TIME BUT WITH NO FIRM DATE

piece of plans for Ray to produce and sing on a solo album of his own, but that these seem to have been shelved. "I've asked the group to sing and play on it with me," says Ray, "and they have kindly consented. I would like to make it clear that I've always wanted to do an LP with The Kinks anyway!"

☆ Most likely around this time, Dave produces some tracks for his friend Ewin Stephens, using session guitarist Albert Lee, at Marquee Studios, central London. Among the songs recorded is an early version of Dave's own 'Mindless Child Of Motherhood' which is completed but never issued.

Saturday 24th

❑ **TV** BBC Lime Grove Studios *west London*. BBC-1 *It's Dee Time* lip-synch Dave Davies 'Lincoln County'. A preview performance, as Dave's new single is not due in the shops until the following Friday.

→ ❑ **TV** Southern Television Studios *Southampton*. Southern Independent Television Network *Time For Blackburn (Pop, People and Places)* lip-synch Dave Davies 'Lincoln County' broadcast August 31st.

Friday 30th

'Lincoln County' / 'There Is No Life Without Love' single by Dave Davies released in the UK. With 'Days' now safely falling from the charts, Dave's long-delayed and rescheduled third solo single is finally issued. It gets generous advertising in the music papers and positive reviews everywhere, but frustratingly fails to even dent the charts. *NME*: "I think the hurdy-gurdy bits at the beginning definitely grow on one and his voice has that desperate sort of earthiness that is very appealing. Perhaps a bit complicated but, nevertheless, a nice one." *Record Mirror*: "Dave, straining at the vocal leash, hammers home a song that seems sometimes messy but overall adds up to a likely biggie." *Disc & Music Echo*: "A very pretty, unusual sound that only Dave Davies can get, and a hit." *Melody Maker*: "That slightly out-of-tune voice gives [Dave] a very personal style. I think this will make it if it gets enough plays. I like it."

☆ Also in today's *Disc & Music Echo* it is reported that Kinks publisher Kassner Music will take legal action against the publishers of Los Angeles band The Doors, claiming copyright infringement over the American band's new single 'Hello I Love You', which is clearly Kinks-influenced.

Lincoln County single by Dave Davies

A **'Lincoln County'** (D. DAVIES).
B **'There Is No Life Without Love'** (D. DAVIES, R. DAVIES).

UK release August 30th 1968 (Pye 7N 17514).
Musicians Dave Davies lead vocal. Ray Davies organ (A), guitar (B). Pete Quaife bass guitar. Mick Avory drums. Nicky Hopkins (probably) harpsichord (B).
Recorded Pye Studios (No.2) central London; A: March 1968; B: probably March 1968; 4-track mixed to mono.
Producer Ray Davies.
Engineer probably Brian Humphries.
Chart high UK none.

September

→ ❑ **TV** South Bank Television Centre *central London*. ITV *Ticker Tape* broadcast September 8th. Ray tapes this unusual TV appearance around now where he recites a poem, details unknown. The show is hosted by Bernard Braden.

→ ● **RECORDING** Pye Studios (No.2) *central London*. With the band's new album probably finished, The Kinks are probably back in the studio around this time to record a one-off song that Ray has written as the title track for the forthcoming movie version of the TV hit *Till Death Us Do Part*. It will be included in the film (see December 20th) but relegated to the closing credits only. Its appearance on the film's soundtrack LP will not be credited to The Kinks, but instead to Chas Mills whose new vocal appears in place of Ray's, along with the original backing track remixed to stereo. The proper Kinks' recording of **'Till Death Us Do Part'** will not appear on record until 1973's *Great Lost Kinks Album* (see January 25th 1973).

Wednesday 4th – Friday 6th

A concert tour of Germany around this time announced back in mid July is not finalised, and TV dates are planned instead, with a return to *Beat-Club* in Bremen scheduled but never done. Quaife later recalls trying out on German audiences some *Village Green*-era material, including 'Days' and 'Phenomenal Cat', so it is possible that there are at least a few unconfirmed dates around now in Germany before heading on to Belgium.

Thursday 5th

In London The Doors appear on BBC-1 TV's *Top Of The Pops* performing live their Kinks-inspired hit 'Hello I Love You'. On the following two days they appear at shows at London's Roundhouse, filmed footage of which forms the basis for a Granada TV documentary *The Doors Are Open*, broadcast October 4th. It is directed by Jo Durden Smith, who has already approached Ray to work on a programme for Granada.

Saturday 7th

Unknown venue *Emerchten, Belgium*

Sunday 8th

Gemeentepark *Châtelet, Belgium* *Teenagers Festival*, with Opus, Marian Maxel, Mistircis Renovation, The Sharons, Jean-Marie Merny, Sweet Feeling, Patricia & Serge Lama, Eric Charden, Gibert Bécaud, The Pebbles, Micky Day, Nicoleta, Systeme Tony, Jacques DuTronc, Pink Floyd
The Kinks are scheduled to play at 2:00pm at this all-day festival.
De Toekomst *Putte, Belgium* 6:30pm, with The Jumpers
Travel day following.

Wednesday 11th

→ Dave comments on new and recent charting records for *Disc & Music Echo* including 'Hey Jude' from The Beatles ("not the best they've done, but very effective") and rates The Bee Gees, Johnny Nash, and Aretha Franklin highly.

→ Probably about a week ahead of the *NME* dated September 21st, Keith Altham reviews an advance tape copy of *The Kinks Are The Village Green Preservation Society* album. But Ray has the record's release stopped at the last moment and UK production is halted. Production masters have already been made and in some cases sent to foreign affiliates, and the release goes ahead in Scandinavia, France,

Italy, and New Zealand. A very small number of UK test-pressings are made, but only for technical purposes, and none are sent out for review. The last-minute decision to halt release points to a major conflict that is brewing, one that will unfold over the coming weeks and months. Ray says later he feels Pye treat him like a hit machine, interested only in his singles and showing no support for the full-length LP works. He seems to draw a line in the sand now, deciding not to hand Pye any recordings earmarked as singles.

☆ Also for the September 21st music papers, Ray counters an earlier report that he intends to sue The Doors over their recording of 'Hello I Love You', telling *Disc & Music Echo* that he has no intention of doing so – and hasn't even heard the record.

Monday 23rd

NME this week has an ad for upcoming releases that includes the *Village Green Preservation Society* album. This same week The Beatles' new album is announced as an ambitious double-LP set due for November. Meanwhile around this time Ray and Dave are busy playing charity football matches.

Friday 27th

Today is the scheduled release date of the original 12-title version of *The Village Green Preservation Society* LP, but it does not reach the shops after production is halted earlier in the week.

Monday 30th

A press release says The Kinks intend to book a US tour for the end of the year, and that a new album is due in a month to include at least 18 songs on two LPs packaged together.

October

→ Avory is interviewed by Peter Jones for *Beat Instrumental*. Discussing the temporarily sidetracked *Village Green Preservation Society* LP, he says that they are trying to get 20 songs spread over two LPs to sell for the price of one. (Pye will refuse this evidently for financial reasons.) He also reveals plans for The Kinks to finally return and tour the US. "In the States, fans have been slow to latch on to The Kinks' style," he says, "but now there is a sudden surge of interest – mostly coming from the West Coast." Jones optimistically claims that the band has emerged as "the leading British underground group" and reckons that final plans for the tour have been completed. Avory continues: "We rehearse a lot these days. Often, of course, it is just to routine numbers for the albums – we spent a lot of time on *Village Green*. But more important is that we're simply getting together and playing – kicking around ideas that come up. We still record at the Pye studios at Marble Arch, with Brian Humphries as the engineer. This suits us best, and of course Ray does most of the producing."

☆ In the US, Reprise Records begin to put the *Four More Respected Gentlemen* album into the early stages of production, after stalling its release following submission of the tapes at the end of June. When the substitute LP promised for September release fails to show, label-copy sheets for *Four More Respected Gentlemen* are prepared (on October 7th) for the pressing of LPs. A small number of white-label test-pressings of the LP are made for technical analysis, and instructions for artwork are roughly sketched out. Details of the LP's planned US release in November are routinely sent to *Schwann's Record Catalog* and for a while a listing is included there among the available Kinks inventory. But further work on the reactivated album's release is halted, mostly likely because of assurances about the quality of the new *Village Green Preservation Society* LP – which will not be logged in to Reprise

until December 20th, and Reprise is apparently willing to substitute this as the next Kinks US album.

Tuesday 9th

In the Denmark Productions vs. Boscobel Productions case a petition for leave to appeal is rejected by the Appeal Committee at the House Of Lords. This ruling finally closes this management dispute and the judgements passed down on June 28th stand, with all obligations between the two parties terminated as of September 14th 1965. However, Kassner Music, separate from Denmark Productions, continues to legally contest its loss of the active Davies catalogue to Carlin Music. The ensuing dispute will not be resolved until October 1970, and Ray's entire ongoing income from publishing since November 1965 remains frozen in escrow until that time.

→ *The Kinks Are The Village Green Preservation Society* original 12-title album released in Norway and Sweden. This version includes two songs – 'Days' and 'Mr Songbird' – dropped from the later version and lacks five songs – 'Sitting By The Riverside', 'All Of My Friends Were There', 'Animal Farm', 'Last Of The Steam Powered Trains' and 'Big Sky' – ultimately added to the final 15-title version (see November 22nd)

Friday 12th

Mayfair Suite, Belfry Hotel *Sutton Coldfield, Warwicks*
The Kinks play probably the first of many regular one-off engagements at this club, which becomes their traditional pre-tour warm-up date for the next few years.

→ ● RECORDING Pye Studios (No.2) *central London*. Even with the 20-song double-LP concept now shot down, The Kinks are evidently recording some new tracks for the rearranged single expanded LP. Probably recorded now are two of the three completely new songs to appear on the restructured album: 'The Last Of The Steam Powered Trains' and 'Big Sky'. 'All Of My Friends Were There' is also newly introduced now, though possibly from an earlier session, maybe in July.

Sunday 20th-Monday 21st

Top Hat Club *Spennymoor, Co. Durham* 7:00pm, with Paul Melva, The John Ray Set
Club Fiesta *Stockton-on-Tees, Co. Durham* 10:00pm & 11:30pm, with Paul Melva, Rosa Roberts
Press reports suggest these cabaret dates and those of the following days were booked as an experiment on the part of The Kinks' management, simply to try something different. But their new booking agent Barry Dickens later admits that British promoters of regular gigs won't touch The Kinks at the time because they think it likely the band won't show up, such is the desperate state of their reputation in Britain. But ultimately The Kinks' volume level live is not conducive to the dinner-dance atmosphere of these northern clubs, and no further dates of this kind are booked. The band certainly does not play the famous Batley Variety Club in Yorkshire, as has been suggested.

Tuesday 22nd

Garden Farm Pub *Chester le Street, Co. Durham* 7:00pm
The performance consists of only a 20-minute show, with the usual early hits plus 'You're Looking Fine'.
Club Fiesta *Stockton-on-Tees, Co. Durham* 10:00pm & 11:30pm, with Paul Melva, Rosa Roberts

Wednesday 23rd – Saturday 26th

Top Hat Club *Spennymoor, Co. Durham* 7:00pm, with Paul

Melva, The John Ray Set
Club Fiesta *Stockton-on-Tees, Co. Durham* 10:00pm &
11:30pm, with Paul Melva, Rosa Roberts
☆ An eight-week Christmas pantomime run in the Midlands,
presumably around Birmingham, and originally scheduled for the
holiday season, intended to present the *Village Green* story as a
pantomime show, is abandoned by this point.

Monday 28th

A press release says Dave Davies as a solo act being is being lined up
for a package tour for December 12th-20th, booked by The Kinks'
former booking agent Arthur Howes.

➔ ● **RECORDING** Pye Studios (No.2) *central London*. Ray remixes
four songs from the July sessions – '**Wicked Annabella**', '**Starstruck**',
'**People Take Pictures Of Each Other**' and '**Do You Remember
Walter**' – presumably because it is now considered that the original
mixes were rushed.

November

➔ Ray submits final tapes to Pye for the rearranged expanded version
of *The Kinks Are The Village Green Preservation Society*. The record
company says that no potential single is present and asks that they
record a suitable song. Ray refuses. He wants Pye to back a stage
presentation of *Village Green Preservation Society* but they have
continued to refuse this. The tensions between Pye and the band and
their management are reportedly coming close to being unworkable.
Manager Collins later admits that he personally retreats from the scene
for a number of months, frustrated that Ray does not want to give Pye
a single and potential hit. Ray stands his ground: if he can't get his stage
production done, he isn't going to tour or play live. This in part explains
the scarcity of live appearances following the recent (and
inappropriate) cabaret bookings.

Pye reportedly does express interest in issuing as a single the song
'Till Death Us Do Part' which The Kinks recorded for the film of the
same name back in September, but Ray resists this idea too. There is
evidence that as a compromise Pye plans an EP using that song as its
title track – it's even assigned a catalogue number, NEP 24303 – but
this too is dropped. There is a stalemate between the two parties.

Friday 22nd

The Kinks Are The Village Green Preservation Society album
released in the UK. The LP is moderately advertised in all the music
weeklies and well represented by reviews. A feature review in *Melody
Maker* declares it easily their best LP. *Disc & Music Echo*: "[Ray]
managed to bypass everything psychedelic and electronic, and has
always concentrated on simple, even rustic melodies with words of
wisdom! ... The Kinks may not be on the crest of the pop wave these
days, but Ray Davies will remain one of our finest composers for many
years." *Top Pop* says: "The themes and styles vary enormously on this
album and a lot of thought has gone into both the lyrics and production
... . Very good value and a set which will command many hours
listening." In what must have been pure music to Ray's ears, Judith
Simons in *The Daily Express* writes: "Ray Davies has written a song
picture of the gentler aspects of British life which could make an idyllic
stage musical." *NME*'s Keith Altham had already chimed in
prematurely back in September, and so the paper has no further review
now. Despite these accolades, the LP does not click with the British
record-buying public and fades into obscurity during the Christmas
rush, eclipsed by the likes of The Beatles' double *White Album* and The
Rolling Stones' career-reviving *Beggars Banquet* LP.

The Kinks Are The Village Green Preservation Society album

A1 '**The Village Green Preservation Society**' (R. DAVIES).
A2 '**Do You Remember Walter**' (R. DAVIES).
A3 '**Picture Book**' (R. DAVIES).
A4 '**Johnny Thunder**' (R. DAVIES).
A5 '**Last Of The Steam Powered Trains**' (R. DAVIES).
A6 '**Big Sky**' (R. DAVIES).
A7 '**Sitting By The Riverside**' (R. DAVIES).
B1 '**Animal Farm**' (R. DAVIES).
B2 '**Village Green**' (R. DAVIES).
B3 '**Starstruck**' (R. DAVIES).
B4 '**Phenomenal Cat**' (R. DAVIES).
B5 '**All Of My Friends Were There**' (R. DAVIES).
B6 '**Wicked Annabella**' (R. DAVIES).
B7 '**Monica**' (R. DAVIES).
B8 '**People Take Pictures Of Each Other**' (R. DAVIES).

UK release November 22nd 1968 (Pye NSPL 18233
stereo/NPL 18233 mono).
US release February 5th 1969 (Reprise RS 6327 stereo).
Musicians Ray Davies lead vocal except as noted, guitar,
keyboard, harmonica (A5). Dave Davies lead vocal (B6), guitar,
backing vocal. Pete Quaife bass guitar, backing vocal. Mick
Avory drums. Nicky Hopkins piano, harpsichord (A7, B1, B2, B8,
possibly other minor parts). David Whitaker string and brass
arrangement (B2).
Recorded Pye Studios (No.2) central London; B2: February
1967; A4, B7: between autumn 1967 and May 1968; B4 March
29th 1968; B1: probably Pye No.1 March 1968; A3: May 1968;
A2, A7, B3 B6, probably B8: July 1968; A1: August 1968; A5, A6,
possibly B5: October 1968; 4-track mixed to mono and stereo.
Producer Raymond Douglas Davies; Shel Talmy & Ray Davies
(B2).
Engineers Brian Humphries; Alan MacKenzie.
Chart high UK none; US none.

Tuesday 26th

⟩⟩⟩ **RADIO** Playhouse Theatre *central London*. BBC Radio 1
Saturday Club studio recordings 'The Village Green Preservation
Society', 'Johnny Thunder', 'Animal Farm' broadcast November 30th.
Only 'Village...' is a new performance; the other two are simply slight
remixes of the issued record versions. The Kinks and other bands will
continue this trend over the next few years at BBC sessions as it
becomes increasingly difficult to quickly replicate more elaborate
studio creations within the constraints of the Beeb's limited session
time. ('The Village Green Preservation Society' will be released in 2001
on *The Kinks BBC Sessions 1964-1977*.)

Thursday 28th

The Kinks Greatest Hits album is certified a gold album today by the
RIAA (Recording Industry Association of America) for list-price sales
of $1,000,000. As in Britain, the band's mid-1960s catalogue of hits is
tending to eclipse sales of their LP work.

➔ On Hampstead Heath, north-west London The Kinks appear in a
promotional film to help promote the European release of 'Starstruck'.

The simple black & white film of the band larking around in the park will at least be broadcast on the Dutch NCRV television programme *Twien* on December 27th, and later is used in band documentaries. It is probably the final surviving footage of the original 1960s line-up.

December

→ A deal with the BBC is finalised early in the month for Ray to write five satirical love songs for the six-show series *Where Was Spring*, to be recorded by The Kinks and aired to accompany special visuals by illustrator and artist Klaus Voorman, who designed The Beatles' *Revolver* sleeve. The shows will star actors John Fortune and Eleanor Bron, produced by Ned Sherrin.

☆ The Kinks begin rehearsing new material, reportedly twice a week, at Ray's new home in Borehamwood, including some early songs for *Arthur*, the next major Kinks project. Also probably worked on is solo material for Dave's upcoming sessions. A US tour is tentatively planned but ultimately The Kinks are unable to go because they still can't get working visas. A proposed appearance by Dave as part of a British package tour December 12th-22nd is also scrapped.

☆ Around the middle of the month, Allan MacDougall's role as Kinks publicist comes to an abrupt end. It follows MacDougall's casual remark to Ray that a chord-change in a Kinks song that came on the radio while they were riding in a car together in Soho reminded him of Donovan's new song 'Atlantis'.

❒ **TV** Southern Television Studios *Southampton*. ITV ***Time For Blackburn (Pop, People & Places)*** lip-synch 'Animal Farm', 'The Village Green Preservation Society' and possibly 'Picture Book' broadcast December 21st.

☆ American band The Turtles make contact with Ray and ask if he is willing to produce their next LP in Los Angeles in the spring. He ultimately agrees.

Reprise Records in America receives master tapes for *The Village Green Preservation Society* album. The album is immediately scheduled for late January 1969 release.

☆ In London the film *Till Death Us Do Part* debuts, going on general release in Britain from January 12th and including The Kinks' recording of the title track buried in the closing credits.

→ ● **RECORDING** Polydor Studios *central London*. Instead of Pye, this less expensive 4-track studio is hired to record four Dave Davies songs in an afternoon. They include what becomes his next solo single, '**Hold My Hand**' and '**Creeping Jean**', as well as '**Do You Wish To Be A Man**' and '**Crying**' planned for inclusion on his solo album. Ray produces, and ex-Pye buddy Alan MacKenzie engineers, but Dave is not pleased with the studio and further recording is halted until the start of next year.

A second daughter, Victoria, is born to Ray and Rasa Davies in Bushey, Herts on Christmas day. The band has time off through the holidays. Quaife and Dave both travel to Copenhagen with their wives and families.

→ ● **RECORDING** Around this time Ray demoes two new compositions, '**Toymaker**' and '**Monday Tuesday Wednesday**', that he gives to former Kinks producer Shel Talmy for use by one of Talmy's acts. Two more Ray compositions – '**Fancy Kitchen Gadgetry**' and '**Could Be Right Could Be Wrong**' – are from this year but no more details are known. Other titles from the initial Carlin contract (November 1965 to November 1970) about which nothing else is known are: 'Give My Fondest Regards To Her', 'I Can't Wait To See You Smile', 'Beginning', and 'Au Nom de la Loi?' (meaning 'In the Name Of The Law').

1969

At the start of the year The Kinks were busy rehearsing and recording behind the scenes, but as they had not issued a single late in '68 they were left even further from the public eye. They rectified this in the spring with 'Plastic Man', but that release forced a major crisis within the band by the final defection of original bassist Pete Quaife, long dissatisfied with the musical direction of the band and his place within it. While they didn't miss a beat, bringing Quaife's former deputy John Dalton back into the fold, Quaife's departure signalled an end to the first incarnation of The Kinks.

The single proved disappointing commercially, but The Kinks' energies were then directed towards an ambitious new album, tied to a made-for-TV programme and a gearing-up for a return to America. Following a visit by Ray to Los Angeles in April to produce an LP by the American top-40 act The Turtles, he and the band's management were finally able to overcome the ban by the American musicians' union that had prevented them from working in the US.

With an album ready by the autumn that they could promote, The Kinks finally returned to American soil in October. But walking cold onto the stage of New York City's Fillmore East on opening night was something of a culture shock – almost a time-travel experience – as The Kinks emerged from the dark ages of the mid 1960s into the modern post-Woodstock rock world of elaborate sound systems and of FM radio devoted to playing album tracks.

In spite of the shock, it was a dream come true of sorts for a band in open rebellion against the top-20 mentality in Britain and their own reputation as "only a singles band". Ray saw a future in America for his ideas for LP-length works. However, once back in the US the band found they were in for a hard slog, in effect having to start from scratch, playing small clubs and colleges in addition to some of the new, hipper venues on the circuit, at first getting work based on their name, if not much else. So many other contemporaries and artists with nowhere near the experience of The Kinks were miles ahead of them because they were able and willing to tour.

But despite the setbacks and disappointments, the band managed to survive the US tour intact and were ready to carry on into a new decade.

January

➜ While on holiday, Quaife informally gives notice of his intention to leave the band, but is talked into staying on at least through the recording and promotion work that will be required surrounding the next single.

Quaife has been writing his own material and has been trying to place some of these songs with other artists.

His disillusion is in part prompted by the recent inactivity of The Kinks, as well as his general feeling that he's not making a creative contribution to the band and that he has no potential or actual outlets outside the band.

Tuesday 7th

❏ **TV** BBC Television Centre *west London*. BBC-1 *Once More With Felix* lip-synch 'The Last Of The Steam Powered Trains', 'Picture Book' broadcast February 1st.

Wednesday 8th

'Starstruck' / 'Picture Book' single issued in the US. (Possibly delayed to the 15th.) Review copies are not sent to any major trade magazines. The only US press comment is a small review in the New York syndicated-radio newspaper *Go!*: "After a period of hibernation The Kinks have reappeared with … a nice, light, happy sound which provides a nice contrast to a lot of the heavy stuff which is being put down today."

➜ The Kinks are rehearsing new material at Ray's new home in Borehamwood roughly twice a week, including songs for the *Where Was Spring* TV show. Ray is now beginning to write songs for *Arthur*. Quaife will recall that 'Victoria' is written around this time, soon after Ray's second daughter, Victoria, was born at Christmas 1968. He also recalls rehearsing 'Australia', possibly 'Some Mother's Son', and 'Shangri-La' during this period. 'Shangri-La' will be specifically mentioned by Ray as one of the earliest songs written for Arthur. Quaife also recalls early rehearsals of two other songs, 'Denmark Street' and

kinks'69

'The Moneygoround', that turn up on the later LP *Part One: Lola Versus Powerman & The Moneygoround*. Both are plausible: the subject matter of both draws on events in the band's early career, and the songs may well have been germinating for some time, far in advance of their final realisation of 1970.

☆ Granada TV producers finalise arrangements for Ray to work with novelist Julian Mitchell. The working title of the experimental TV programme is *The Decline And Fall Of The British Empire*. Ray eventually suggests that it be based on his brother-in-law Arthur, a disillusioned former serviceman who emigrated to Australia in search of a better life than the one he felt he would find in his native England.

● **RECORDING** Pye Studios (No.1) *central London*. Dissatisfied with the pre-Christmas session at what he considered a sub-standard studio, Dave restarts work on his solo LP at the more comfortable and familiar Pye. Not only that, but this next batch of recordings is done using the 8-track recorder that Pye No.1 has had since spring 1968, representing the first recording in that format for The Kinks. It results in a somewhat cleaner and more dynamic sound, and offers more flexibility for overdubs. Believed done at this time are **'Mr Shoemaker's Daughter'**, **'Are You Ready'**, and possibly **'This Man He Weeps Tonight'** (maybe done in March). Engineer is probably Vic Maile or Brian Humphries.

Monday 13th

A press release announces that Ray is to write the title song for the film *The Virgin Soldiers*, and is writing for a special programme for Granada TV with Julian Mitchell, now in preparation. It also notes that The Kinks are to record a song a week for an Eleanor Bron BBC-TV series, that a new Dave Davies single is set for January 17th, and that Dave will go to West Germany and Holland for TV and radio dates at the end of January.

● **RECORDING** Riverside Studios *Hammersmith, west London*. The band convenes to record the first song for the BBC-2 TV series *Where Was Spring*, produced by Ned Sherrin. This week's song is **'We Are Two Of A Kind'**, broadcast on January 27th. Later Ray describes the six *Spring* songs (all mixed in mono) as "critical of love". He says, "I wrote a song each week. They used to phone me up on a Tuesday and I'd have it ready by Thursday. … I really enjoyed it. They wanted a song about some certain subject to fit in the script, so I had to do it as if John [Fortune] were singing to Eleanor [Bron]." (Riverside is an old BBC television studio converted to a recording facility.)

Starstruck single

A 'Starstruck' (R. DAVIES).
B 'Picture Book' (R. DAVIES).

US release January 8th or 15th 1969 (Reprise 0806).
Musicians Ray Davies lead vocal, acoustic guitar (B), piano (A), Mellotron (A, or Nicky Hopkins). Dave Davies acoustic guitar (A), electric guitar (B), backing vocal. Pete Quaife bass guitar, backing vocal. Mick Avory drums. Nicky Hopkins Mellotron (A, or Ray Davies).
Recorded Pye Studios (No.2) central London; A: July 1968; B: May 1968; 4-track mixed to mono and stereo.
Producer Ray Davies.
Engineer Brian Humphries.
Chart high US none.

Hold My Hand single by Dave Davies

A 'Hold My Hand' (D. DAVIES).
B 'Creeping Jean' (D. DAVIES).

UK release January 17th 1969 (Pye 7N 17678).
Musicians Dave Davies electric guitar, lead vocals. Ray Davies piano (A), electric guitar (B). Pete Quaife bass guitar. Mick Avory drums.
Recorded Polydor Studios central London; December 1968; 4-track mixed to mono.
Producer Ray Davies.
Engineer Alan MacKenzie.
Chart high UK none.

Friday 17th

'Hold My Hand' / 'Creeping Jean' single by Dave Davies released in the UK. *NME* says "performance-wise the best he's waxed to date – it's a fiery and impassioned delivery and he really gives it all he's got. … Full marks to brother Ray's production." *Record Mirror* rates it a Chart Certainty and says: "A good song delivered in that drawly powerful way of his, all sliding notes and deliberate brashness on the basic beat."

➜ Dave's promotional dates are cancelled at the last moment, including a TV spot on *Beat-Club* due to be videotaped in Bremen on January 24th, as well as further TV and radio spots in West Germany and Holland in the days following.

➜ ❒ **TV** Granada Television Centre *Manchester*. Granada *Discoteque* lip-synch Dave Davies 'Hold My Hand' broadcast March 26th.
☆ At Ray's house in Borehamwood, Herts, the band rehearses further material for the *Where Was Spring* TV series, as well as a new Kinks single. With the *Arthur* project moving ahead smoothly, Ray seems to end his impasse with Pye and agrees to give them a new recording to be issued as a single. Since 'Days' was issued the previous June he has not been willing to record anything specifically for release as a single.

Tuesday 28th

● **RECORDING** Riverside Studios *Hammersmith, west London*. The second session for BBC-2 TV's *Where Was Spring*, and this time Ray's song is **'Where Did My Spring Go'**, included in the February 3rd broadcast. It will later be issued on the US-only compilation LP *The Great Lost Kinks Album* in January 1973.

Friday 31st

'Toymaker' single by Wild Silk released in the UK, a song by Ray Davies. Produced by Shel Talmy. It registers no attention or response.

February

Monday 3rd

Dave suffers a fractured finger and The Kinks are forced to cancel a scheduled recording session today at the BBC Riverside Studios in west London for *Where Was Spring* and the subsequent days' sessions at Pye Studios intended for the recording of a new single. Any concerts booked for the next four weeks are also cancelled. The scheduled late-February release for his solo LP is delayed as well, pending completion of the remaining tracks.

➜ INDICATES EVENT AROUND THIS TIME BUT WITH NO FIRM DATE

Tuesday 4th

● **RECORDING** Riverside Studios *Hammersmith, west London*. The Kinks return to Riverside, presumably without Dave, to record **'When I Turn Out The Living Room Light'**, broadcast on BBC-2's *Where Was Spring* on February 10th and later released on a promotional various-artists double LP, *The Big Ball*, in April 1970. Further scheduled recording this week at Pye is cancelled and pushed back to early March, pending Dave's recovery.

Wednesday 5th

→ **The Kinks Are The Village Green Preservation Society** album released in the US. (Possibly a week earlier.) This is the first Kinks LP to get extensive if slow-to-appear coverage by the new underground press in the US. But there is no coverage or announcement in any of the major trade magazines, so it is no wonder that nobody knows it has been released. Initially there is virtual press silence, with a small and barely noticeable review in New York City's *The Village Voice* by Johanna Schier. But this is followed in the same paper by critic Robert Christgau writing in his weekly *Rock & Roll* column, where he names it the best album of the year so far.

UCLA student and future Kink kronikler John Mendelssohn writes in his student paper, the *Daily Bruin*, "Ray Davies as you no doubt have little suspected has been writing (and revitalizing) songs of unbelievable charm and wit since the Kinks' descent into obscurity ... The latest Kinks album may, in fact, prove to be one of 1969's two best albums. There are 15 songs on this album and each is a greater delight than the one before ... . I haven't loved an album this much since The *Who Sell Out*, and with each additional listening to *Village Green* ... I grow fonder of it. Don't be without it."

Circus, formerly teen magazine *Hullaballoo*, under the heading "Kinks – Unhip But Original", says: "The Kinks are backdated, cut off from the mainstream of pop progression. Just the same they're originals and now have a fine new album out." Boston's new underground paper *Fusion* says: "The Kinks continue, despite the odds, the bad press and their demonstrated lot, to come across ... Their persistence is dignified, their virtues are stoic. The Kinks are forever, only for now in modern dress." Student paper *California Tech* does not like the record, calling it schmaltz rock, and considers it to be "without imagination, poorly arranged, and a bad copy of The Beatles".

The pièce de résistance will be a lead review in the June 14th issue of the hip and prestigious *Rolling Stone*, written as a guest review by former *Crawdaddy!* editor Paul Williams. He produces a classic piece of "rock writing", heaping accolade upon accolade as he unravels the joys of the album. And he virtually invents the cult of the Kinks freak with his closing remarks: "I'm frustrated now. I was okay trying to make you feel how good The Kinks make me feel, but I can't pass on greatness. I can't sit here and come up with phrases to argue genius, I can only shout, as modestly as possible, about how deeply I am affected. I'm thinking only genius could hit me so directly, destroy me, rebuild so completely ... I've never had much luck turning people on to The Kinks, I can only hope you're on to them already. If you are, brother, I love you. We've got to stick together."

Monday 10th

● **RECORDING** Riverside Studios *Hammersmith, west London*. Possibly again without Dave, The Kinks record the latest song, **'Let's Take Off Our Clothes'**, for the weekly BBC-2 *Where Was Spring* programme, broadcast on February 17th. It is never issued on record.

Friday 14th

Till Death Us Do Part soundtrack album released in the UK. On the title track Ray's lead vocal has been replaced by one Chas Mills, and no mention of The Kinks or their presence on the backing track is made.

Monday 17th

● **RECORDING** Riverside Studios *Hammersmith, west London*. Another *Where Was Spring* BBC-2 song, this time **'Darling I Respect You'**, broadcast on February 24th. The track is never issued on record.

☆ At Ray's house in Borehamwood, Herts the band steps up rehearsal duty to three or four times a week, working on material for the *Arthur* project and a new single.

☆ Meanwhile The Turtles, who have been repeatedly writing to Ray and phoning him to try to persuade him to produce them, get his agreement. This means a paid trip for Ray to Los Angeles – where he can also attempt to talk to the US record company again and sow seeds for The Kinks' return to America later in the year.

'Jessie' / 'Monday Tuesday Wednesday' single by Wild Silk is released in the US, the B-side a song written by Ray Davies. Despite production by Shel Talmy and a *Billboard* ad, the record vanishes without trace. It will become one of the most difficult to find of Ray's recorded compositions.

March

→ ● **RECORDING** Pye Studios (No.1) *central London*. During the first week of the month The Kinks are finally back at Pye where recording again resumes and a new single, **'Plastic Man'**, is done. (They're working in Studio 1 because 2 is being refitted for 8-track.) The new single's B-side, **'King Kong'**, is probably recorded now too.

During this month, work also continues on Dave's solo LP, with two Ray songs probably recorded, **'Groovy Movies'**, and **'Mr Reporter'**, the latter never issued by The Kinks and languishing since their own recording of the song in early 1966. Work on these tracks is not completed until June, when horn parts will be added.

Possibly also dating from now (or January, prior to the recording break) is Dave's **'This Man He Weeps Tonight'**. Although slated for the inevitably aborted solo LP, this will find release in the UK later in the year as the B-side of The Kinks' single 'Shangri-La'.

Furthermore, reports suggest a second song is recorded this month as the intended follow-up single to 'Plastic Man' but that this is scrapped following Quaife's departure; no further details are known. (A stereo mix of 'Plastic Man', with a possibly overdubbed bass part by John Dalton added shortly after his re-joining the band, is released in 1998 as a bonus track added to the CD reissue of the *Arthur Or The Decline And Fall...* album.)

Saturday 8th

Probable concert at unknown venue and location as performing resumes with Dave's finger sufficiently healed.

Monday 10th

A press release reveals the *Arthur* project for the first time. The release notes that it will include material by Dave, will feature The Kinks plus orchestral backing, and is to be filmed in colour for autumn broadcast on Granada TV in Britain.

→ ☆ Rehearsals continue for *Arthur* at Ray's house in Borehamwood.

→ ● **RECORDING** Pye Studios (No.1) *central London*. Quaife is becoming bored by the inactivity of the band and the emphasis on solo projects. He too is increasingly involved in his own side projects, including work with a band without The Kinks' knowledge. Ray, in an effort to involve Quaife more, hires him for this session for a title-theme he's written for a Ned Sherrin-produced movie, *The Virgin Soldiers*. **'The Virgin Soldier March'** is recorded at Pye's larger No.1 studio, produced by the company's head of A&R John Schroeder with string arrangements by Lew Warburton, and will be credited on the resulting record as by The John Schroeder Orchestra.

Quaife will later cherish a lasting memory of taking his place among the seasoned orchestral players, trying to look as comfortable among them as possible, only to have one of the players casually walk by and point out that the music part he is attentively pretending to follow is upside down.

Saturday 15th
Empire Theatre *Sunderland* 5:00 & 8:00pm, *Northeast Folk Song & Dance Festival*
Ray says later that they appear here as part of an attempt to recreate an old-style Music Hall show with traditional Northumbrian folk acts. This is probably The Kinks' last concert performance with Quaife.

➜ With the prospect of a new record, The Kinks finally hire a new publicist to replace Allan MacDougall, the PR man with whom they parted company last December. The new (unnamed) publicist will last less than a year.

☆ Late in the month there is a photo-shoot at a studio in Chelsea, central London, and these last official pictures of Quaife with the band will appear in *Record Mirror*. Ray, Dave and Avory undertake interview duties to support the single's release on the 29th, constituting the first real press campaign since the promotion for 'Days' the previous summer. Ray speaks to Derek Boltwood for *Record Mirror* and expresses his desire to get back in front of audiences again. "I'm looking forward to doing more gigs – I'd like to develop a more professional stage act," he says, "not slick, but a complete act that's entertaining." He confesses that his move to Borehamwood has been less than successful. "I'm so cut off from everyone that I can't manage to get as much done as I'd like to," says Ray. "I just want to be surrounded by people again."

Thursday 27th
❑ **TV** Thames Television Studios *central London*. ITV ***The Eamonn Andrews Show*** lip-synch 'Plastic Man'. Quaife's last public performance with The Kinks. He is interviewed by journalist Mike Ledgerwood for *Disc & Music Echo* regarding his departure, and also gives a statement on the subject to *NME*.

Friday 28th
'**Plastic Man**' / '**King Kong**' single released in the UK. Mostly positive but still mixed reviews greet this long-awaited return to the British singles market. "It is not untimely for The Kinks to indulge in some Cockney & Western, and with great effect, that I am convinced they will be secure in the chart 'ere long. A little spark of brilliance to brighten the pop life," says *Melody Maker*. "This is a sardonic bit of Ray Davies' imagination ... I think it'll make it," writes *Record Mirror* of this "chart certainty". The *Disc & Music Echo* reviewer says: "I'm not as keen on this record as I have been on other Kinks offerings in that it doesn't have quite the charm – but it's a Who type of bitter anti-lyrics." The *NME* is non-committal, acknowledging they've done some nice things, but not much since 'Waterloo Sunset'.

☆ Tomorrow is a day off, with Ray and Dave doubtless keen to see the Arsenal football team play at their home ground, Highbury Stadium, in north London. Both are avid Arsenal supporters and attend many a match into the 1970s.

Monday 31st
A report published later this week in *NME* says that Quaife's notice of resignation from The Kinks is effective from midday today. Ray comments to *Disc & Music Echo* that rumours of The Kinks splitting up are untrue.

Plastic Man single

A '**Plastic Man**' (R. DAVIES).
B '**King Kong**' (R. DAVIES).

UK release March 18th 1969 (Pye 7N 17724).
Musicians Ray Davies lead vocal, electric guitar. Dave Davies electric guitar, backing vocal. Pete Quaife bass guitar, backing vocal. Mick Avory drums, backing vocal (A).
Recorded Pye Studios (No.1) central London; early March 1969 (B-side probably); 8-track mixed to mono.
Producer Ray Davies.
Engineer Vic Maile.
Chart high UK number 28.

April

Tuesday 1st
Manager Robert Wace comments to *NME* that rumours of The Kinks splitting up are untrue.

Wednesday 2nd
))) **RADIO** BBC Aeolian Studios (Studio 1) *central London*. BBC Radio 1 ***Symonds On Sunday*** studio recordings 'Plastic Man', 'Do You Remember Walter', Dave Davies 'Hold My Hand' broadcast April 13th, repeated one-song-per-day on *Sounds Like Tony Brandon* during weeks beginning May 5th and May 19th. At least Ray is present for this radio recording session, and Quaife is almost certainly unavailable. 'Plastic Man' is a remix of the Pye recording with a new lead vocal added by Ray. 'Do You Remember Walter' is simply the same as the commercially issued recording. It's not known what form Dave's 'Hold My Hand' is in.

Thursday 3rd
This is Quaife's "official" date of departure from The Kinks.

Friday 4th
NME out today publishes an exclusive photo of Quaife with his new band (soon named Maple Oak). This prompts The Kinks to read the paper and realise that Quaife is serious this time. Ray reportedly makes a personal plea to Quaife to stay and complete the *Arthur* LP, assuring him that it is going to be something special. Quaife however has made up his mind and declines. This forces The Kinks to contact their former relief bass player John Dalton, who is officially added to the line-up after a phone call from Avory. Dalton has of course been through an almost identical and immediate call to The Kinks' ranks back in June 1966.

☆ It is admitted later that Quaife's departure creates real resentment, with the feeling that he has abandoned the team when it is down but on the verge of a rebound. In some ways the remaining Kinks will never forgive him for bailing out. Years later, Ray reflects: "Pete Quaife was the true amateur. He's not a great music lover, but Pete did it because he enjoyed life. And he was my friend. The saddest thing was that we were very successful, and we toured, and we didn't talk to one another and we weren't friends. The day we stopped communicating offstage was a good time to stop."

Quaife explains later: "The decision to leave The Kinks only came up a while after *Village Green Preservation Society*. I was totally dissatisfied with the conduct of Ray and Dave, the managers … and the

---

New bassman John Dalton, far right, has replaced Pete Quaife and lines up alongside his new bandmates in May 1969.

attitude of the record company. I most certainly felt like a second-rate, hired musician by this point, having nothing to say about my musical abilities, my career or life. I definitely needed a change!"

Asked if his decision to quit had anything to do with their declining popularity, Quaife says: "Leaving the band had nothing to do with 'commercial success'. I have often pointed out that I was not that concerned with the commercial side of the business. I would have been perfectly content to have made my living as a musician – something that I had always wanted to do."

Saturday 5th

❏ **TV** BBC Lime Grove Studios *west London*. BBC-1 *It's Dee Time* lip-synch 'Plastic Man' broadcast April 5th. New bassist John Dalton's first public appearance with The Kinks since 1966.

Monday 7th

A press release confirms that Quaife did indeed leave the band last Thursday and that John Dalton was hired on Friday.

Tuesday 8th

➜ ❏ **TV** Radio Bremen Television Studios *Bremen, West Germany*. German TV **Beat-Club** lip-synch 'Plastic Man' broadcast April 26th.

Wednesday 9th

In a phone interview with the *NME* Ray says that The Kinks are surprised that Quaife has formed a new band after assuring them he would remain with them long enough to fulfil promotional functions for their new single.

Thursday 10th

❏ **TV** BBC Lime Grove Studios *west London*. BBC-1 **Top Of The Pops** lip-synch 'Plastic Man'. The band videotapes an insert for use on an upcoming *TOTP* because Ray will be in the US during the period that the single is likely to chart. (See May 1st.)

☆ With the all-important public image to consider, the revamped line-up of The Kinks is photographed by Dezo Hoffman at his central London studio.

Friday 11th – Thursday 17th

Ray travels to Los Angeles on Friday and stays at the Hollywood Hawaiian Hotel. The following day he begins work producing The Turtles' new album. The Turtles are Mark Volman, Howard Kaylan, Al Nichol, Jim Pons, and John Seiter. The recordings are made at United Recording Studios, with engineer Chuck Britz, plus LA session legend (and *Shindig!* musical director) Ray Pohlman providing string and horn arrangements.

Recorded during this first visit (a second trip will come in June) are: 'You Don't Have To Walk In The Rain', 'House On The Hill', 'Come Over', 'Dance This Dance', 'How You Love Me', and 'Love In The City'. They are mixed to mono for potential release on single.

'House On The Hill' is the first consideration for release, but the US promotional single of it is withdrawn and replaced by the more commercial 'You Don't Have To Walk In The Rain' / 'Come Over' released in the US on White Whale in May and in the UK on London on June 3rd. In the US the record's chart peak is number 51, in July.

☆ Ray takes advantage of his time in Los Angeles to attend to some Kinks business matters, including discussions about the US tour being planned for July. Perhaps most importantly, the problem with the American musicians' union is finally resolved, clearing the way for a working visit by The Kinks.

☆ Meanwhile Dave, Avory and Dalton continue to rehearse additional material for Dave's solo album at Dave's home in Barnet, north London. 'Mindless Child Of Motherhood' is possibly one of the pieces worked into shape now.

Saturday 19th

The Swan *Yardley, Birmingham* 8:00pm-12midnight, with The Spring

Monday 21st +

With Ray back from Los Angeles, the band reassembles at his house in Borehamwood to resume rehearsing *Arthur* material with Dalton on-board. Among the early candidates for recording is a song called 'We All Make Mistakes', but ultimately it does not make it.

☆ A press release announces that Ray is writing a book on the band's career. Maybe this is intended to tie in with a fifth-anniversary retrospective album scheduled for late summer, but this record, the so-called "black album", will not be issued until February 1970, and without a book. It could also refer to the subject of what emerged as the next studio album, *Part One: Lola Versus Powerman & The Moneygoround*, a summary of the band's trials and tribulations in the music business to date.

Friday 25th

The band possibly plays an unknown university show.

Saturday 26th

Mayfair Suite, Belfry Hotel *Wishaw, Warwicks* 8:30pm-2:00am, with Boss White; "admission includes supper"

Monday 28th

● **RECORDING** Pye Studios (No.2) *central London*. Sessions to record a new single take place this week (see following entry).

May

Thursday 1st

● **RECORDING** Pye Studios (No.2) *central London*. Sessions for a new single continue. **'Drivin''** and Dave's **'Mindless Child Of Motherhood'** are worked on early this month. Pye No.2 is now up and running with its new 8-track recorder installed.

☆ While being interviewed for *Record Mirror* the band learn that the BBC will not air the tape made on April 10th of 'Plastic Man' for broadcast on *Top Of The Pops* this evening. The Kinks are annoyed, and claim it's because of the word "bum" in the song's lyrics. The BBC maintains it is simply because the song's chart position does not warrant its inclusion in the programme.

Friday 2nd – Sunday 4th

Planned travel to Beirut, Lebanon for live work is cancelled at the last minute due to local problems. The promoter reschedules the May 3rd and 4th dates for two weeks later. The originally planned venue is the ballroom in the Finosia Hotel but this is changed now to the Cite Sportive, an outdoor arena.

☆ Quaife's new band Maple Oak appears at The Factory, a small club outside Birmingham. The band will work primarily in this area during in its short career.

Monday 5th

A press release suggests a new single will be out at the end of May, and that the new LP will be completed next week.

➜ ● **RECORDING** Pye Studios (No.2) *central London*. The band attempts to record the whole of the *Arthur* album in a set of concentrated sessions over two weeks.

➜ **'You Don't Have To Walk In The Rain' / 'Come Over'** single by The Turtles released in the US, produced by Ray Davies.

Friday 16th

Travel to Beirut. The venue has been changed at the last minute.

Saturday 17th

Pool area, Melkart Hotel *Beirut, Lebanon* 6:00pm

Dalton says later: "It was strange to turn up in a country [soon to be hit by devastating civil wars, that] you weren't used to, and all of a sudden there are soldiers ... and there are tanks going up the road, and soldiers and people with guns, and you're wondering, 'What they hell is going on here?'"

Sunday 18th

Two further shows today at the Melkart Hotel in Beirut are cancelled. The band travels back the following day. Dalton says, "They confiscated our passports for a while [after we refused to play the Sunday shows]. It was about three minutes before the plane was due to take off when they finally gave [them] back, and we just couldn't wait to get out of [there]."

→ ● **RECORDING** Pye Studios (No.2) *central London*. Sessions resume for the *Arthur* LP. The majority of the recording seems to be accomplished during this month. Dave says later he plays his famous Gibson Flying V guitar on 'Australia' and 'Yes Sir No Sir' and then retires it from recording after these sessions.

June

→ ● **RECORDING** Pye Studios (No.2) *central London*. Lew Warburton is the arranger as a number of unidentified studio musicians record string and horn overdubs for *Arthur*. A tour of Sweden, June 3rd-10th, is cancelled to make way for studio time during which the *Arthur* LP is initially completed and mixed.
☆ American photographer Ethan Russell, fresh from his assignment documenting The Beatles' *Get Back* sessions, is hired to shoot a series of promotional shots for the *Arthur* LP and tours.

Thursday 12th

An advertised concert at City Hall, Newcastle Upon Tyne with The Move, The Sect, and Axtree Junction is cancelled the day of show due to poor ticket sales.

Friday 13th

'You Don't Have To Walk In The Rain' / 'Come Over' single by The Turtles released in the UK, produced by Ray Davies. It does not chart.
☆ A concert is possibly done today, venue and location unknown.

Saturday 14th

→ **University of Oxford: Keble College** *Oxford* early evening show, *Roundabout Ball*

Thames Polytechnic *Eltham, south-east London* late evening show

An obscure double university booking (possibly today or the 21st), with a student's bedroom acting as a dressing room.

Monday 16th

● **RECORDING** Pye Studios (No.2) *central London*. Ray and Dave are back at Pye this week putting the finishing touches to Dave's solo LP with engineer Andrew Hendricksen. Horn arrangements by Lew Warburton are probably added now to three tracks recorded during the spring, '**Mr Reporter**', '**Groovy Movies**', and '**Mr Shoemaker's Daughter**'. Final mixing and assembly of the master tape is also finished this week and the completed album will in turn be delivered

to Reprise by Robert Wace on July 3rd when he joins up with Ray in Los Angeles.
☆ Interviewed by *Beat Instrumental*, Ray says *Arthur* is about "a weekend in [Arthur's] life when his son and daughter-in-law stay at his home and the total worthlessness of his life is exposed". He describes Kinks touring as "a couple of gigs here at home most weeks ... and a lot of trips abroad" worked around watching Arsenal football matches with Dave on Saturdays and their own charity games on Sundays. He also discusses problems when foreign promoters renege on payment, leaving the band stranded and unable to pay their bills to get back home, as almost happened recently in Beirut.
☆ Julian Mitchell appears to be getting on well with Ray and so far has enjoyed scriptwriting for the planned TV play of *Arthur*. Mitchell later reveals that the *Arthur* character is a carpet-layer, a concept Ray likes because it means he's spent his life on his knees.
☆ A press release announces that the *Arthur* LP is due for late-July release, and that the plan is to finish off this week the recording and mixing of Dave's solo LP, which had been started last Christmas. The release says a best-of Kinks LP is due for September, accompanied by a book about the band, to commemorate the fifth anniversary of 'You Really Got Me'.

Thursday 19th

❒ **TV** BBC Lime Grove Studios *west London*. BBC-1 *Top Of The Pops* lip-synch 'Drivin'.

Friday 20th

'Drivin'' / 'Mindless Child Of Motherhood' single released in the UK. Reviews are generally strong but to no avail as the record sinks without a trace. *Record Mirror*: "Obviously a big hit and in with chances for the 'smash' category." *Disc & Music Echo*: "Unmistakably Kinks with Ray's rather mournful voice ... it has a pleasant, summery charm. Not an immediately compelling or catchy record but I think it will grow on you."
Melody Maker: "Equally catchy [as 'Plastic Man'] and typically Ray Davies." *NME*: "The Kinks improve with each release but their popularity seems to diminish accordingly. From the quality and production it deserves to be a hit but I can't be too hopeful."

Sunday 22nd – Monday 23rd

Ray travels from London to Los Angeles, staying there at the Hollywood Hawaiian. He will resume work on The Turtles' LP and make further plans for the proposed Kinks US tour, as well as delivering

---

Drivin' single

A '**Drivin'**' (R. DAVIES).
B '**Mindless Child Of Motherhood**' (D. DAVIES).

UK release June 20th 1969 (Pye 7N 17776).
Musicians Ray Davies lead vocal, acoustic guitar, organ (all A), electric guitar, piano (both B). Dave Davies electric guitar, lead vocal (B), backing vocal (A). John Dalton bass guitar. Mick Avory drums. Rasa Davies backing vocal (A).
Recorded Pye Studios (No.2) central London; May 1969; 8-track mixed to mono.
Producer Ray Davies.
Engineer Brian Humphries.
Chart high UK none.

tapes for the band's upcoming US releases. The American tour, originally scheduled for a late-June start and running four weeks, is delayed until late July, and then until October, mostly in order to complete The Turtles project.

Tuesday 24th – Monday 30th

Further recording for The Turtles (Mark Volman, Howard Kaylan, Al Nichol, Jim Pons, John Seiter) at United Recording's 8-track Studio B in Los Angeles, with Ray producing, Chuck Britz engineering, and Ray Pohlman again handling string and horn arrangements. (The earlier sessions were in April.)

Recorded now are: 'John & Julie', 'She Always Leaves Me Laughing', 'Torn Between Temptations', 'Love In The City', 'Bachelor Mother', 'Hot Little Hands', 'How You Love Me', and 'Somewhere Friday Night' (last track unreleased).

Monday 30th

A press release says The Kinks plan to add a brass section on tour, that US and Canadian tours are set for September, and that the *Arthur* LP is complete.

July

Tuesday 1st – Wednesday 2nd

Ray finishes recording and mixing tracks for the Turtles LP at United Recording Studios in Los Angeles.

Wednesday 2nd

Ray and Wace deliver only nine of the 12 eventual songs for *Arthur* to the Reprise Records offices. Tapes include mono as well as stereo mixes so that any song can be chosen as a single. He also delivers the completed Dave Davies solo LP master tape (stereo only), marked "Lincoln County", as well as a reel of 12 recordings, marked "spare tracks".

The Dave Davies album as submitted consists of 12 songs, stereo mixes only: 'This Man He Weeps Tonight', 'Mindless Child Of Motherhood', 'Hold My Hand', 'Do You Wish To Be A Man', 'Are You Ready', 'Creeping Jean', 'Crying', 'Lincoln County', 'Mr Shoemaker's Daughter', 'Mr Reporter', 'Groovy Movies', and 'There Is No Life Without Love'.

The only action taken by Reprise now is to cut a reference acetate disc, adding a stereo mix of 'Susannah's Still Alive' as the opening track for side one. The tapes are not assigned master numbers, implying there are no plans for a release. But even if there were such plans, Dave will not want it released because he considers it a below-par record handed over without his approval. The tapes will languish for over 30 years until Dave agrees to a release by Pye's successor, Sanctuary Records, which results in the tapes being mastered in December 2001 for planned release in 2002. At the time of writing the release is slated for late 2003.

The "spare tracks" reel will eventually form the basis of *The Great Lost Kinks Album*, assembled and released by Reprise in 1973 following the band's defection to RCA in 1971. The reel consists of 12 predominantly mono masters: 'Till Death Us Do Part', 'This Is Where I Belong', 'Lavender Hill', 'Plastic Man', 'King Kong', 'Berkeley Mews', 'Rosemary Rose', 'Easy Come There You Went', 'Pictures In The Sand', 'Mr Songbird', 'When I Turn Out The Living Room Light', and 'Where Did My Spring Go?'.

Like the Dave Davies album, these tracks are not assigned master tape numbers, implying that no release is planned now. Most likely they are simply handed over to top up The Kinks' contractual obligation to deliver a certain number of "sides" as part of a contractually mandated

schedule. Ray says later that he is reluctant to hand over this material, which he doesn't think worthy of release, and says he went so far as to explain that he wanted a note put on the tape box to say "please, we're just fulfilling our contract, just put it in a vault somewhere". The subsequent release of the material in 1973, although a boon to Kinks fans of this era, will be legally challenged by The Kinks.

Thursday 3rd

Ray and manager Wace attend a morning meeting with Reprise executives at the Warner parent-company headquarters in Burbank. They formally launch the *God Save The Kinks* promotional campaign and finalise the US autumn tour. The campaign includes the issuing of an album, *Then Now And Inbetween*, a promotional-only compilation acting as a Kinks career retrospective to reacquaint American media with their work, past and present. Writer and avid Kinks supporter John Mendelsohn is also present in a consultancy role for Reprise. The events are followed by lunch with singer-songwriter Randy Newman.

Friday 4th

Back at United Recording Studios, Ray accomplishes the final mix of The Turtles' *Turtle Soup* LP. His mix is not used for the LP's release in October after the dissatisfied Turtles decide to remix it themselves.

Sunday 6th – Monday 7th

Ray and Wace travel to New York City and then on to London, arriving at 2:00pm Monday.

Tuesday 8th

A press release says the *Arthur* LP and Dave's solo album are scheduled for late August, Ray is to compose incidental music for a new film, *Hushabye*.

Thursday 10th – Friday 11th

Scheduled start of a seven-day jaunt through Scandinavia, though there is no evidence of shows on these two days. If any dates are done now, they are most likely in Sweden.

Saturday 12th

Bruvollen *Blaker, Norway* 10:00pm, with Jim Oddwinds
Grue-tunet *Solør, Norway* 10:00pm, with Giggis Myhrsteens Trio
The Blaker show is possibly relocated to the Ingierstrand in Oslo. Blaker and Solør are small towns just outside Oslo. A concert was originally scheduled for Jylland, Denmark but cancelled in order to do the double Oslo date.

Monday 14th

Tivoli Plaenen, Tivolis Gardens *Copenhagen, Denmark* 9:00pm; with dancing bear act
Revolution Club, Bakken, Klampenborg *Copenhagen, Denmark* 11:00pm, with Sir Henry & His Butlers
For the first show the band performs at the Plaenen (open-air stage) at the centre of the world-renowned amusement park. This is adjacent to the location of the riot at the band's appearance in 1965, but today's return to Copenhagen is considerably quieter than their visits in 1965-66. Besides the usual set of hits and Kinks standards, the band reportedly performs 'She Bought A Hat Like Princess Marina' from their upcoming LP *Arthur*. The late show is at a nightclub inside Copenhagen's second largest amusement park.

Tuesday 15th

Brændegårdshaven *Bornholm, Denmark* 7:30pm-12midnight, with The Vanguards, Black Flowers Liberty
Travel day following to London.

Friday 18th
City Hall *St. Albans, Herts* 9:00pm, with The Pavement, County Jail Blues Band

Saturday 19th
Leas Cliff Hall *Folkestone, Kent* 7:45pm, with Mosaic, Josiah Ben's Fantasy

→ ● **RECORDING** Pye Studios (No.2) *central London*. Around now and over the next few weeks, Ray is back at Pye, remixing in stereo three of the songs for the forthcoming *Arthur* album – 'Mr Churchill Says', 'Young And Innocent Days' and 'Arthur' – which need fine-tuning before they are handed over to Reprise for release on the album. He may also do some mono mixes so that potential singles can be pulled from the album.

Friday 25th
Newton Pavilion *Newton, Ches*
☆ Original planned release date of *Arthur* album, now rescheduled to August.

August

Monday 4th
A press release says a Canadian tour is set with TV, radio and concert appearances and that Dave's LP is due in September.

→ ● **RECORDING** Pye Studios (No.2) *central London*. Around now Ray finishes mixing the *Arthur* tracks.

Wednesday 6th
Warner-Reprise's in-house news publication *Circular* debuts, including an item about plans for a massive promotional campaign to accompany The Kinks' planned autumn tour. A company press release is issued to announce the tour.

Friday 8th
A concert at Bath Pavilion is probably cancelled.
☆ In Los Angeles, Warner-Reprise Records holds the first of four promotional meetings in key markets to preview the label's fall releases, including a scheduled September release of *Arthur*. Sales and promotional staff receive copies of *The 1969 Warner-Reprise Record Show* multiple-artist double-LP promotional set that contains a mono mix of the as-yet-unreleased track 'Nothing To Say'. The LP is then made available to the public through a mail-in offer where anyone paying for shipping and handling will receive a copy. The offer appears in the August 23rd issue of *Billboard* and various other magazines.

Saturday 9th – Sunday 24th
Annual holiday for the band. Ray however flies to California and stays in an apartment on the Sunset strip. He is there to confirm plans for the band's US tour.
☆ On the weekend of 15th-17th in upstate New York the Woodstock Music & Arts Festival unfolds. The Kinks are not part of this landmark event, and are disappointed not to be asked.

Monday 18th
Ray delivers the final three songs, in mono and stereo mixes, for the *Arthur* LP and these are logged into Warner's tape vault. A further almost full set of mono mixes of *Arthur* are logged in on August 26th. The single is chosen from these tapes. Dalton says: "There's a lot of

good tracks on the album and they'd all make good singles. Ray couldn't really make up his mind which track we should use as the single."

Wednesday 20th
Warner-Reprise in-house news publication *Circular* announces the first tentative dates for a Kinks autumn tour.

Saturday 23rd
The band is due to appear at today's *Humberside Pop Festival* at the City Hall, Hull, but cancel, presumably because Ray is still in the States. The Kinks are replaced by Love Sculpture.

Monday 25th
In London the completed *Arthur* LP has presumably by now been presented to Pye Records, prompting the assignment of an initial release date of September 26th, while the 'Shangri-La' single is set for September 12th.

Tuesday 26th
Star Club *Hamburg, West Germany*
In an unusual one-off show The Kinks play the legendary club in Hamburg made famous by The Beatles' early-1960s pre-fame appearances there. Dalton recalls this as a disastrous show. The band use amplifiers supplied by the club (or opening act) with no time for a soundcheck before the show. After having to push their way through the crowd to get on stage, Dalton sees his bass amp fail to work and Ray decides to end their performance after half a song, requiring them to march back through the crowd to the dressing room. The Kinks evidently don't return to the stage after a brawl in the dressing room between Ray and a member of the opening act.

Thursday 28th
Pavilion *Bournemouth* 7:45pm, with The Tension

September

Tuesday 2nd
Ray watches *The Stones In Hyde Park* on Granada TV that features The Rolling Stones' free concert in Hyde Park in the heart of London on July 5th. The programme is co-directed by Jo Durden Smith and Leslie Woodhead. Smith also directed the *Doors Are Open* documentary of The Doors' September '68 concert at London's Roundhouse, aired October 5th that year. Woodhead is the director for the planned Granada version of *Arthur*, in effect to be a TV play with a musical soundtrack by The Kinks. According to the original schedule this should go into production now for broadcast at the end of September, but is delayed.

Thursday 4th
❏ **TV** Killesberg Television Studios *Stuttgart, West Germany*. ZDF *4-3-2-1 Hot 'n' Sweet* lip-synch 'Drivin'' broadcast September 20th.

→ Ray is interviewed by Jonathan Cott for *Rolling Stone* at Kenwood House, Hampstead Heath, north-west London in what turns out to be a revealing and lengthy interview for the new, "serious" rock press, in contrast to the relatively frivolous and ephemeral pop press that the band is beginning to leave behind. He discusses many of his earlier recordings as well as *Arthur* which Cott has heard in advance form. The interview merits Ray a cover story in the British edition of *Rolling Stone*, but in the US it waits until November 1970 for publication, following the success of 'Lola'.
☆ Also around this time Ray is interviewed at BBC Broadcasting

House in central London for the programme *Cool Britannia*, broadcast September 13th.

Monday 8th

A press release says the *Arthur* album is now due October 3rd, because of delays in the associated TV production.

☆ The fifth anniversary of the week that 'You Really Got Me' hit number 1 in the British charts back in 1964 is seized upon in a number of press interviews this week to promote the forthcoming new single, 'Shangri-La'.

Probably today, Ray is interviewed by Ian Middleton for *Record Mirror* and discusses the freshly completed LP of his "pop opera" *Arthur*, which was "finished … about three weeks ago". He says the Granada TV production is underway and it should be screened at the end of October.

Ray defends the release of the lengthy new single that clocks in at five and a half minutes, saying he just couldn't edit it down, aware this will probably kill its chances of radio and TV airplay.

Also discussed is Reprise's promotional plans for The Kinks' fall tour and LP release, including the planting of stories in the press about possession of marijuana and income-tax evasion. Ray dismisses these as "mad" and the campaign is dropped, but the elaborate press kit for the *Arthur* LP will feature a series of six such mocked-up press clippings ("English Pop Group Arrested on Rape Rap" etc), an apparently desperate attempt to give the band anti-establishment and underground credibility. Ultimately this does not help the press discover much about the band's true character.

Tuesday 9th

❑ **TV** BBC Television Centre *west London*. BBC-2 **Peter Sarstedt Show** lip-synch 'Shangri-La' broadcast October 1st.

➜ 'Love In The City' / 'Bachelor Mother' single by The Turtles released in the US this week, produced by Ray Davies.

Friday 12th

'Shangri-La' / 'This Man He Weeps Tonight' single released in the UK. *Record Mirror*: "Must be big, could be very big. Splendid production." *Melody Maker*: "A good pop production as well as a pointed commentary, and should be a hit."

Disc & Music Echo: "A long record – over four minutes – but I hope that deters nobody." Dave will say often that this is one of his favourite Kinks recordings, its utter failure as a single mystifying and disappointing him.

Saturday 13th

Pier Pavilion *Felixstowe, Suffolk* 8:00-11.30pm, with Django's Castle; tickets 10/- (50p).

➜ Dalton is interviewed by Royston Eldridge for *Melody Maker* and confirms the plan to have a brass section on the upcoming US tour to properly present the new material.

☆ Ray is putting final touches to his work with Julian Mitchell on the script for the TV version of *Arthur*.

Saturday 27th

➜ **Top Rank Suite** *Eastbourne, Sussex*

Reportedly only about 100 attend this show, which probably occurs today. While this reveals that the band at a very low point in Britain, it does indicate they are performing at least periodically before their big return trip to America.

Shangri-La single

A 'Shangri-La' (R. DAVIES).
B 'This Man He Weeps Tonight' (D. DAVIES).

UK release September 12th 1969 (Pye 7N 17812).
Musicians Ray Davies lead vocal, acoustic guitar, electric guitar. Dave Davies electric guitar, lead vocal (B), backing vocal (A). John Dalton bass guitar (A). Pete Quaife bass guitar (B). Mick Avory drums.
Recorded Pye Studios (No.2) central London; A: May-June 1969; B: January or March 1969; 8-track mixed to mono.
Producer Ray Davies.
Engineer Andrew Hendricksen (A); Brian Humphries or Vic Maile (B).
Chart high UK none.

October

➜ Ray moves house from Borehamwood back to his now extended home on Fortis Green in East Finchley, north London. Before heading off to the US he does some British press interviews to promote the new album, *Arthur*, release of which is now pushed back one more week, to October 10th.

Saturday 4th

Fishers Melody Rooms *Norwich* with The Black Stump; tickets 7/6 (38p)

"Come early – all your friends will," says the publicity. The Black Stump are from Australia.

➜ *Turtle Soup* album by The Turtles released in the US, produced by Ray Davies. The LP will reach a lowly 117 in the *Billboard* charts.
☆ The tour of Canada booked in July and cancelled sometime in August was originally set for October 1st-15th. Some dates are possibly rescheduled for February 5th-7th 1970 and June 24th-27th 1970.

Friday 10th

Arthur album released in the UK and US. Reviews are generally very favourable in the US as momentum among the new rock press to champion The Kinks gains speed, helped no doubt by the massive publicity campaign by Reprise Records and further fuelled by the presence of the band to promote the album in America.

As with the last LP, the key feature is in *Rolling Stone* which spotlights *Arthur* in its lead spot with two back-to-back reviews. Guest writer Mike Daly gushes about "such an incredible album, the band in their finest form" and concludes it is "a masterpiece on every level; Ray Davies' finest hour, the Kinks' supreme achievement". *Rolling Stone* regular Greil Marcus continues: "Less ambitious than [The Who's] *Tommy*, and far more musical … *Arthur* is by all odds the best British album of 1969. It shows that Pete Townshend still has worlds to conquer and that The Beatles have a lot of catching up to do." Sal Imam in Boston's *Fusion* magazine similarly concludes with the inevitable comparison: "If *Tommy* was the greatest rock opera, then *Arthur* most surely is the greatest rock musical."

In the British music press there is less celebration, and coverage is relatively routine, though everyone sees the rock-opera angle. *Disc & Music Echo*: "*Arthur* works as a complete score because it is basic and simple and pleasing to the ear, and powerfully conjures up pictures in the eye." *Melody Maker*: "Ray Davies' finest hour! ... A pop cavalcade that is beautifully British – to the core." In the *NME* there is something of a backlash against The Kinks' perceived preoccupation with the common man, although the reviewer almost grudgingly admits that the LP is "all cleverly done and performed well. Still The Kinks' recognisable sound, but occasionally with an added toughness that lends more appeal. Should do well".

The LP will do a respectable sales job in the US, buoyed by The Kinks' presence in the country, but in Britain, where the crucial accompanying TV programme will never go into production, the record quickly fades from view.

Wednesday 15th

'Victoria' / 'Brainwashed' single released in the US. Even now *Billboard* manages to miscredit them as The Kings, but says "one of their strongest bids in some time for a top chart inner with this groovy rock item. Should bring them back in a hurry".

➪ **TOUR STARTS** *American Tour '69: North American Tour* (Oct 17th – Dec 8th). **Line-up**: Ray Davies (lead vocal, guitar), Dave Davies (guitar, vocal), Mick Avory (drums), John Dalton (bass). Booking agent Bert Kamerman/Creative Management Associates. Ticket prices range from $1 to $6. This is the only US trip where manager Wace accompanies the band (and he was probably only present in New York

---

Arthur Or The Decline And Fall Of The British Empire album

A1 **'Victoria'** (R. DAVIES).
A2 **'Yes Sir No Sir'** (R. DAVIES).
A3 **'Some Mother's Son'** (R. DAVIES).
A4 **'Drivin''** (R. DAVIES).
A5 **'Brainwashed'** (R. DAVIES).
A6 **'Australia'** (R. DAVIES).
B1 **'Shangri-La'** (R. DAVIES).
B2 **'Mr Churchill Says'** (R. DAVIES).
B3 **'She Bought A Hat Like Princess Marina'** (R. DAVIES).
B4 **'Young And Innocent Days'** (R. DAVIES).
B5 **'Nothing To Say'** (R. DAVIES).
B6 **'Arthur'** (R. DAVIES).

UK release October 10th 1969 (Pye NSPL 18317 stereo/NPL 18317 mono).
US release October 10th 1969 (Reprise RS 6366 stereo).
Musicians Ray Davies lead vocal, electric guitar, acoustic guitar, piano, harpsichord. Dave Davies electric guitar, acoustic guitar, backing vocal. John Dalton bass guitar, backing vocal. Mick Avory drums, percussion. Lew Warburton horn and string arrangements.
Recorded Pye Studios (No.2) central London; A1-A3, A5-A6, B1, B3, B5: May-June 1969; B2, B4, B6: May-August 1969; A4: May 1969; 8-track mixed to stereo and mono.
Producer Ray Davies.
Engineer Andrew Hendriksen; Brian Humphries (A4 only).
Chart high UK none; US number 105.

Victoria single

A **'Victoria'** (R. DAVIES).
B-US **'Brainwashed'** (R. DAVIES).
B-UK **'Mr Churchill Says'** (R. DAVIES).

US release October 15th 1969 (Reprise 0863).
UK release December 12th 1969 (Pye 7N 17865).
Musicians Ray Davies lead vocal, acoustic guitar (A), electric guitar. Dave Davies electric guitar, backing vocal. John Dalton bass guitar, backing vocal. Mick Avory drums, tambourine. Lew Warburton horn arrangement (A, B-US).
Recorded Pye Studios (No.2) central London; May-June 1969 (A, B-US); May-August 1969 (B-UK); 8-track mixed to stereo and mono.
Producer Ray Davies.
Engineer Andrew Hendriksen.
Chart high US number 62, UK none.

---

before returning to London). Collins, the other half of the management team, normally travels with them. Ray says later: "All of a sudden we got our visas to go to the States. We weren't prepared – and [the US audience] hadn't seen us since 'You Really Got Me' – and it was like a complete gap." (Band travels to New York City on the 16th.)

Friday 17th

'Love In The City' / 'Bachelor Mother' single by The Turtles released in the UK, produced by Ray Davies.

Friday 17th – Saturday 18th

The Fillmore East *New York, NY* 8:00 & 11:30pm, with Spirit (headliners), The Bonzo Dog Band
Dave is so rusty and/or nervous that at one point, when called to sing 'Death Of A Clown', he forgets a line and, as at least one audience member recalls, yells off-mike to his bandmates: "I can't remember the fucking lyrics!" A similar thing will happen in Boston next week.

Prestigious showbiz paper *Variety* says: "The Kinks started the weekend somewhat unsure of themselves, but regained their performing composure after a couple of sets. By the last show they were once again delivering the driving rhythms and infectious melodies that racked up a string of disk clicks in the mid-1960s market."

Billboard is less impressed, saying the band's appearance was disappointing. "[As they] wandered through patches of their past hits and an excerpt from their new album, Davies' lyrics were obliterated by the roar of the volume and further plundered by the group's musicianship, which suffered from the drone and sameness of each song."

The *Cash Box* reviewer writes: "Somehow being in the presence of one of rock's newly discovered cult heroes, Ray Davies, wasn't as awe inspiring as it should have been. Here is a man [who] has earned his position as one of Britain's most brilliant songwriters, and he didn't look happy up there performing. As a matter of fact none of The Kinks seemed excited about what they were doing. Consequently their music seemed lukewarm. 'God Save The Kinks?' I think only they can do that."

The two-day gross at the Fillmore, formerly known as the Village Theater, is $35,600 (70 percent capacity).
☆ Various press duties during the day, at magazine offices and the Holiday Inn hotel, including an afternoon press conference.
☆ Dave relates later in *Kink* that he is turned on to 'angel dust' (the hallucinogenic drug phencyclidine) during this weekend. Also, the

band discovers the Haymarket Bar on New York's 8th Avenue, a favourite to many a visiting English rock act and a regular Kinks hangout in the early 1970s.

Sunday 19th

Clarkson College Gymnasium *Potsdam, NY* 3:00pm, with Spirit (headliners), Dan Cooper; sponsored by Potsdam College of the State University of New York as part of annual Homecoming Weekend

The band makes the 300-mile trek north from Manhattan almost to the Canadian border for this afternoon show in remote, rural, upstate New York. Student reviewer Daniel Speer in the *Potsdam College Racquette* is pretty scathing: "I expected more than a bad mix, no-talent singing and playing they gave. I guess it must have been pretty difficult to come to the north country and play in a gym, and that always makes me feel bad for the bands who get conscripted. But it must be a worse drag to have played the same songs over and over for the last six years. 1970 The Kinks are not." A tentative booking for 19th-22nd at Ungano's in New York City is briefly advertised but never finalised. It certainly would have been a more convenient booking.

Monday 20th – Tuesday 21st

Days off, with the band likely back in New York City.

Wednesday 22nd

Leone's *Long Beach, NY*

Thursday 23rd – Saturday 25th

The Boston Tea Party *Boston, MA* two shows, with Lee Michaels, Quill

The Tea Party is a converted warehouse behind Fenway Park, the home of baseball's Red Sox. It's the premier club in this booming college town, a favourite and regular stop on the newly established underground rock circuit. The likes of The Who and the nascent Led Zeppelin passed through the club earlier in the year. Zeppelin's rise has been so fast that on this weekend they are headlining across town at the local indoor sports arena, the Boston Garden, a fact probably not lost on The Kinks who are struggling to regain some momentum in their own career. *Boston After Dark* says: "It was all so quick and so professional and so joyous. Dave radiantly smiled as he flailed away, Ray was more hesitant but just as elated. The Kinks having a good time and hoping everyone else was too." During more press duties, Dave swears live on air at a local radio-station DJ (probably on WBCN) and takes a swing at him. Dave will recall in *Kink* that he has a particular aversion to DJs at this time.

Set-list (Saturday, 1st show): 'Till The End Of The Day', 'You're Looking Fine', 'Waterloo Sunset', medley 'You Really Got Me' / 'All Day And All Of The Night', 'Mr Churchill Says', 'Fancy', 'The Last Of The Steam Powered Trains', 'Louie Louie', 'Mindless Child Of Motherhood', 'Victoria', 'Mr Churchill Says', medley 'A Well Respected Man' / 'Death Of A Clown', 'Dandy', 'Love Me Till The Sun Shines', 'Sunny Afternoon', 'Don't You Fret', medley 'Milk Cow Blues' / 'Rip It Up' / 'See My Friends' / 'Brainwashed', 'The Village Green Preservation Society'.

Sunday 26th – Thursday 30th

Possibly a university booking in the Northeast on Sunday, but the band heads next to Chicago, again biding their time until the weekend booking (though a stray one-off show outside of Chicago is a distinct but unconfirmed possibility). While in town, Ray is squired around the city by Warner/Reprise representative Bob Destocki, no doubt glad-handing and doing some local press. Avory is even figured into the promotional equation and does an interview about drums for national music-trade magazine *Billboard*.

Friday 31st

The Kinetic Playground *Chicago, IL* 7:30pm, with The Who (headliners), Liverpool Scene

A former skating rink converted into a large club of about 2,000 capacity (and just down the street from the scene of the infamous 1920 St. Valentine's Day Massacre) hosts a memorable double billing featuring two of England's finest bands of the era. The Who are soaring to superstar status after two solid years of slogging across the vast American tour circuit and releasing in May this year their career-altering epic double-LP *Tommy*. Despite The Who's very public regard for The Kinks, it must be obvious today what a difference in fortunes they have experienced since the two bands were on the same bill back in London almost exactly five years earlier.

Early in The Who's set Pete Townshend mentions his admiration for The Kinks and that he once dreamed of The Who opening for them. The Kinks had done a single 40-minute opening spot and, despite what is regarded as a strong performance, there is undeniable dissatisfaction within the band. As he relates later in *Kink*, a depressed, drunk and frustrated Dave goes on a rampage after a failed sexual encounter following the show, and eventually cuts his hand after smashing an exit sign back at the Holiday Inn where the band is staying. He later claims frustration with the tour's progress and general homesickness as contributing factors for the outburst. Dave is hospitalised and his hand is stitched up, and he is advised not to use it for a week so that it will heal properly. The Kinks are forced to cancel the following night's show at the Kinetic, as well as the night after that in Cedar Rapids, IA, which is rescheduled for November 12th.

☆ Back in England, Granada Television in Manchester issues the final script for the production of the TV play of *Arthur*, with shooting scheduled to begin on December 1st.

November

Saturday 1st

The Kinks' second scheduled performance at the Kinetic Playground is cancelled the day of show because of Dave's wounded hand. At short notice two bands, Poco and King Crimson, replace The Kinks, with Liverpool Scene still on the bill. The Who aren't booked for this second night, moving instead to Columbus, OH.

Sunday 2nd – Thursday 6th

While the rest of the band stay behind in Chicago, Ray and Dave travel back to London, taking advantage of the unexpected break in the tour. Dave then travels on further to Copenhagen to see wife Lisbet and son Martin who are visiting her family there. Only later in retrospect will it be revealed that morale is at such an all-time low that Ray and Dave seriously consider ending the tour at this point and even breaking up The Kinks. But the idea is reconsidered and dropped after a few days off. While Dave recuperates, Ray sneaks in some press work, including interviews for *Disc & Music Echo* and *Melody Maker*.

☆ In London *The Virgin Soldiers* movie, with its theme song written by Ray, debuts at Rank theatres on Sunday 2nd.

Friday 7th – Saturday 8th

Grande-Riviera Ballroom *Detroit, MI* 8:30pm, with Joe Cocker & The Grease Band (headliners), Grand Funk Railroad, The James Gang

Originally scheduled as two shows: Dr John The Night Tripper here alongside The Kinks and The James Gang (which includes a young Joe Walsh, later of Eagles fame); and a separate concert featuring Joe Cocker, Liverpool Scene and a not-quite-yet-huge Grand Funk Railroad scheduled at Detroit's Eastown Theater. But in the days prior to showtime the two events are combined into this single show at the Grande (briefly renamed the Grande-Riviera). Avory will later recall this booking as particularly disappointing thanks to equipment failures and a poor response to the quieter material they include in their set. (The following few days seem to be time off.)

☆ The Rolling Stones start their own return to US stages tonight after a three-year absence.

Wednesday 12th

Memorial Coliseum *Cedar Rapids, IA* 7:00-11:00pm, with St. John, Brown Sugar, American Legend
The rescheduled date from the November 2nd cancellation, though it's possible this show too may have been cancelled. Travel day following.

Friday 14th – Saturday 16th

The Ludlow Garage *Cincinnati, OH* with Humble Pie, The Glass Harp; presented by Jim Tarbell
Another underground-style venue in the newly burgeoning hip rock club circuit. Tonight the band is co-billed with ex-Small Faces singer Steve Marriott and ex-Herd member Peter Frampton, familiar faces from the British package-tour days. This is reportedly another low point in the tour as the band becomes increasingly demoralised by the long stretches between weekend shows, as they are still unable to command mid-week bookings. Things will change once they hit the West Coast where they are kept busier.

☆ It's possibly here that a determined young fan, Chrissie Hynde (later of The Pretenders), drives from Kent State University in Ohio where she is a student to see The Kinks in concert, which she later recalls as in Ohio on the first tour.

Sunday 16th

Presumably a travel day to Los Angeles, although tonight is originally slated for a show at the Village East, a small club in Mentor, OH, but never finalised. Located in suburban Cleveland, the Village East was formerly the Hullaballoo Scene and has a long tradition of playing host to many British bands passing through this strong rock'n'roll area.

Monday 17th – Wednesday 19th

In Los Angeles the band stays at the Hollywood Hawaiian Hotel, as did Ray earlier this year. Their rooms are in fact separate apartments – reportedly for about $16 a night. This week (probably Wednesday) a press party is held at The Factory, a private discotheque in West Hollywood where many music-biz press functions are held, but The Kinks do not perform as planned. This is reported to be due to Dave's injured hand, but more likely is a result of his fragile, post-drug hangover. As recounted later in *Kink*, Dave goes on a drinking and drug-taking spree, dropping acid (hallucinogenic drug LSD) for the first time and having a very bad experience in the process. During these days off, typically Avory and Dalton will also be off drinking and partying while Ray deals with interviews and other media business. At this time a press release is issued heralding "US tour a success, another being planned".

Thursday 20th – Sunday 23rd

The Whisky A Go Go *Hollywood, CA* two shows nightly, with Gypsy
A four-night stay at this legendary Hollywood rock venue, essentially a dinner club, with a capacity of about 250, and thus the smallest venue on the tour so far. The Kinks are directly up against the triumphant return to LA of The Rolling Stones who have two shows at the massive Inglewood Forum. Dave says later in his book *Kink* that after the first night at the Whisky he is in such a poor state of mind that he wants to cancel the rest of the tour, but is persuaded otherwise.

"So many fans showed up opening night that there wasn't any room,"

writes Pete Senoff in *Music Now!*. "The only major surprise of the evening was that Dave Davies did the majority of the singing. Ray seemed content to play rhythm guitar and contribute occasional verses."

Rock magazine says: "Perhaps their acceptance here and not in other places is because The Kinks are a group's group. That is to say, they are highly respected by others in the recording field. Among those recording luminaries at the show were members of Three Dog Night, The Grassroots, and Kim Fowley. On closing night, Mick Jagger paid a second visit to the club to view his English counterparts."

Set-list (1st show, unspecified night): 'Love Me Till The Sun Shines', 'Mindless Child of Motherhood', 'Last of the Steam Powered Trains', 'Waterloo Sunset', medley 'You Really Got Me' / 'All Day And All Of The Night', 'You're Looking Fine', medley 'Long Tall Shorty' / 'See My Friends' / 'Jailhouse Rock' / 'Tired Of Waiting For You' / 'Fancy', 'Brainwashed'. Second show: 'Till The End Of The Day', 'Victoria', 'Last Of The Steam Powered Trains', 'Big Sky', 'The Village Green Preservation Society', medley 'A Well Respected Man' / 'Death of A Clown' / 'Dandy', 'Milk Cow Blues', 'Australia', 'Louie Louie', 'You Really Got Me'.

☆ Ray optimistically says to *Rolling Stone*: "[The] reception to the band has been enormously gratifying ... I think the audiences are more knowledgeable now. When we came here before ... it was just image then .... We're presently planning our next album and we hope to have it finished by the time we return [in February 1970]. The way things look we may record most of it here. Things are looking brighter now."

Monday 24th

Crawford Hall Gymnasium, University of California *Irvine, CA* 8:30-10:30pm, no opening act; sponsored by Associated Students of UCI; compère (local DJ) Rodney Bigenheimer
The UCLA *Daily Bruin* review reveals an odd venue: "The koncert was held in the gym and for this we had to shed our shoes and shuffle to our seating places on the shellac floor: a veritable Kinks sock-hop! At any rate, amongst the stifling odors of sweaty feet and a poor sound system, The Kinks came alive and so did the audience. Playing for an hour and 20 minutes, they ran through their past hits and a few new ones, zapping the assemblage. How many koncerts have you seen where groups of individuals stormed the stage, leaped onto the same elevated platform as the group, and commenced to frug along with 'You Really Got Me'? The krowd kried in vain for more, and we left to seek our shows." (Following is a travel day to San Francisco.)

☆ Rehearsals are due to begin in Manchester, England today for the filming of the TV version of *Arthur*, without direct Kinks involvement, but this is delayed.

Wednesday 26th

Exhibition Building, Contra Costa Fairgrounds *Antioch, CA* 8:30pm, with It's A Beautiful Day (headliners), Cold Blood, Dry Creek Road; sponsored by the Hedgecock-Piering Family; lights by Deadly Nightshade

Thursday 27th – Sunday 30th

The Fillmore West *San Francisco, CA* two shows nightly, with Taj Mahal, Sha Na Na
The Kinks finally arrive back in San Francisco after more than four years absence and their non-performance at the massive Cow Palace during their troubled first American tour. These nights see an interesting line-up with bluesman Taj Mahal and 1950s doo-wop revivalists Sha Na Na sharing the bill. During the Friday afternoon The Kinks are cajoled to appear in person at an autograph session in the store parking lot of Tower Records, with about 200 people attending. While in the city the band frequents The Edinburgh Castle, an English-style pub on Geary Street.

December

Monday 1st
Sports Center gymnasium, Reed College *Portland, OR*
8:30pm
☆ The scheduled start day (through December 19th) of filming of the Granada TV special *Arthur* on location in London and Southampton, with no direct Kinks involvement but Ray overseeing filming. It is rescheduled for January 5th-23rd 1970, but ultimately abandoned.

Tuesday 2nd
Freeborn Hall, University of California *Davis, CA* 8:30pm, with Bicycle; lights by Deadly Nightshade
"Probably the best and most exciting concert that the Davis community had seen in a while," writes John Kirtland in the *California Aggie*. "A band with seemingly limitless energy, The Kinks seldom stopped playing, even between songs … to a surprisingly small crowd … playing a set that lasted about an hour and 20 minutes." The following day is almost certainly a travel day, and then a day off in New York City. Fellow Brits Fleetwood Mac are in town too, playing at Ungano's, and members of The Kinks at least bump into them. They will see Fleetwood Mac again during the next Kinks tour in the US in February 1970 – when Fleetwood Mac will be continuing on the same US tour. This will underline to The Kinks the level of commitment required to break America, something Fleetwood Mac most certainly do.

Friday 5th
The Spectrum *Philadelphia, PA* 8:00pm, with The Chambers Brothers (headliners), Spirit, American Dream
"The Kinks played a set much different from the one that opened the tour at the Fillmore East," says *Billboard*. "The act was tighter … the music came out clear and sharp. Vocals alternated between composer Ray Davies and lead guitarist Dave Davies. Dave's natural ease and showmanship contrasted his brother's penetrating intensity."

Saturday 6th
The Hawk's Nest *Toronto, ON, Canada* 8:00 & 11:00pm, with Tractor
A small unlicensed club with a capacity of 300-350 owned by Canadian rock'n'roller Ronnie Hawkins. The performance is a pretty loud affair for the size of club, with The Kinks a well-oiled band by this point in the tour. This is their first foray into Canada after cancelling a two-week tour in October this year. "Ray Davies proudly states that he can't compare his opera with The Who's *Tommy* because he'd never heard *Tommy*," reports *Circus*. Ray is also interviewed by Jim Smith for an unpublished piece in NME which breaks down after Ray is asked one too many times about *Tommy*.
☆ The Rolling Stones' US tour ends in disaster as a man is stabbed to death by Hell's Angels at a free concert at the Altamont Speedway in Livermore, CA, today. This is the Stones' own private Woodstock gone awry. In the space of a little over three months the highs and the lows of the 1960s have been played out in a tidily-timed end to the decade.

Sunday 7th
Stamford High School Auditorium *Stamford, CT* 7:30 & 9:30pm, with Roomful Of Blues
An obscure add-on date at this suburban Connecticut highschool, billed as their "last United States show of the year". Opening act Roomful of Blues will go on to be something of an international blues institution; this early version features guitarist Duke Robillard and drummer Fran Christina, who go on to play in The Fabulous Thunderbirds.

Monday 8th
Ungano's *New York, NY*
The tour is stretched to a single show at this small club in New York's upper west side run by Nicky Ungano, no doubt a concession to the tentative but cancelled dates at his club back in October at the start of the tour. The Kinks are reportedly in fine playing form, in marked contrast with the rusty band that opened the tour almost two months earlier at The Fillmore. *Variety* is back to see them again: "Opening with 'Louie Louie' they jumped into a medley that included Elvis Presley's 'Rip It Up' and a number of other oldies." The writer suggests that bands from the mid 1960s are already appealing to nostalgia. Danny Goldberg from *Record World* enthuses: "At the beginning [at The Fillmore] the group had been friendly and good but unspectacular as it adjusted to the country. Then reports spread of great concerts. They came back again for [this] one show before they split. They were great. The Kinks are simply one of the best, most distinctive rock groups in the world. … The evening was an event. The Kinks, as never before, are exciting and relevant rock artists. Bravo!"

Tuesday 9th
Band members travel back to London while Ray stays behind in New York City through Wednesday for business meetings. While the tour has been a rocky one, it has the intended impact, generating record sales and airplay for the band in the US. Reprise is very pleased. With legitimate support from the record company, plans are made to book another tour as soon as possible. The pendulum is now swinging back in The Kinks' favour.

➔ A production meeting is held around now at Granada TV in Manchester with the show's producer who reportedly fails to produce a formal budget, and after some questioning with no satisfactory responses, the show is cancelled on the spot. Co-director Leslie Woodhead and designer Roy Stonehouse have already been appointed and a cast assembled. Ray and co-writer Julian Mitchell are naturally furious that all their hard work has been in vain, and Ray sees his grand artistic visions once again dashed by bureaucracy and internal politics.

Thursday 11th
❏ **TV** BBC Television Centre *west London*. BBC-1 ***Top Of The Pops*** lip-synch 'Victoria'.

Friday 12th
'Victoria' / 'Mr Churchill Says' single released in the UK. Melody Maker thinks "this stands a very good chance [with its] overall sound, which is very commercial." *NME*: "It's a good gutsy pop disc. Not as catchy as many of The Kinks' offerings … not a big hit."

Saturday 13th
Arsenal vs. Burnley at Highbury Stadium, north London – and a good chance that the Davies brothers are in attendance.

Monday 15th
Arthur LP peaks at number 105 in the US *Billboard* charts.

Tuesday 16th
❏ **TV** BBC Television Centre (Studio E) *west London*. British BBC-1 and German ZDF ***Pop Go The 60s*** lip-synch 'Days' simultaneous broadcast December 31st. A New Years Eve retrospective programme about the music of the closing decade.

Thursday 18th
))) **RADIO** Camden Town Theatre *north London*. BBC Radio 1 ***Dave Lee Travis Show*** studio recordings 'Victoria', 'Mr Churchill Says',

'Arthur', 'Days' broadcast December 28th. At least Ray is present as some new vocals and remixes of existing Kinks recordings are prepared for broadcast.

Wednesday 24th – Wednesday 31st

Christmas holidays, and everyone has time off. Ray later recounts that he picks up the records that he'd bought during the recent US tour and had shipped back to London. He later spends some of Christmas Day with his dad in the pub where, he says, Davies senior encourages him to write another worldwide hit, especially given the new possibilities in America. Ray accordingly spends the 26th writing. The reclusive suburban North London band will be irrevocably changed by their acceptance in the US.

☆ On Tuesday 30th a press release proudly announces that the band's "next US tour will start in Philadelphia, then Boston, Chicago, Detroit and New York".

1970

A turning-point year that began with a typical Kinks disaster as their quick return to a US tour was cut short by illness and all the plans were shuffled and delayed. But the time off allowed Ray to craft even more carefully his new composition, 'Lola', and the band spent a good deal of time on it during the spring, before returning to the States. They resumed touring there with an odd combination of tiny club dates and double billings, aiming to renew their exposure in the vast US and Canadian markets.

But everything changed with 'Lola', and the small club dates would be no more. By the time the band returned to the US for their third tour of the year in the late autumn they were triumphantly headlining in theatre-sized venues again.

The Kinks rebounded from a chart lull as 'Lola' became a worldwide hit single. "Underground" FM radio was flourishing in the States and became an important medium, but it had only limited reach, whereas nationwide chart success was still an overpowering experience. The commercial success of 'Lola' was of vast importance to the band. It came towards the end of their US and UK record contracts, at a point where the band seemed an unlikely commercial prospect. Without that hit, finding a new label or renegotiating with the existing companies would have been much more difficult.

The band took full advantage of the desperately needed hit – as they had done with 'Sunny Afternoon' in 1966 – and completely reshuffled all their existing business relationships. The success would spell the beginning of the end of their relationships with their existing US and UK record labels, with their American booking agency, with their publicist, and, by the following year, with their original management team. Things would never be the same again.

January

→ At the turn of the year, Ray accepts a role in an upcoming BBC-produced TV play, *The Long Distance Piano Player*, to be rehearsed and taped during three weeks in March, between scheduled Kinks tours of the US.

Friday 16th

A scheduled appearance at The Fillmore North, Sunderland, Co Durham, with Quintessence, the grand reopening of a venue formerly known as The Locarno Ballroom is probably cancelled. (Day off following likely, with the Davies brothers at Highbury Stadium in north London for an Arsenal football match.)

Saturday 24th
Mayfair Suite, Belfry Hotel *Wishaw, Warwicks*

The Kinks return to one of their favourite venues, a large club within a hotel in the Birmingham area.

The Belfry would become their traditional pre-US-tour warm-up concert. Tonight's booking is billed as "one of their rare appearances in this country" – which is in fact completely accurate.

Wednesday 28th

→ On the eve of their departure back to the States, Avory is interviewed by *Music Now* where he discusses the ups and downs of the last US tour, claiming they had a better response on the West Coast than the East, but thinks some of this may be because at first the band found concerts hard work after such a long period of relative inactivity. He acknowledges that the length of the tour was more than the band could handle, and that upcoming tours will be broken down into East and West Coast legs of one month each. (The band travels to the US the following day.)

⮑ **TOUR STARTS** *Tour Of North America 1970: East Coast leg* (Jan 30th – Feb 14th). **Line-up**: Ray Davies (lead vocal, guitar), Dave Davies (guitar, vocal), Mick Avory (drums), John Dalton (bass). Booking agent is Bert Kamerman of Creative Management Associates.

Friday 30th-Saturday 31st

The Electric Factory *Philadelphia, PA* 8:00 & 11:00pm, with Eric Mercury, The Image; tickets $3

The tours kicks off with a quick return to Philly, now playing this large rock club, an old converted tyre factory and vulcanising plant with a capacity of 2,500.

The Electric Factory is run by local promoter Electric Factory Productions who will continue to book The Kinks/Ray Davies in this area well into the 1990s. The venue will go bust in November this year due to the escalating fees of top rock talent, the same fate that meets many of the large "psychedelic" clubs that sprang up during 1967-68. The Kinks are now catching the tail end of this golden age of the US rock club scene.

February

Sunday 1st

Unknown venue today, possibly a college in New England where the campus Winter Weekend celebrations are taking place. The three days following are likely time off, probably in New York City where the band is happy to bide their time between obligations.

Thursday 5th

F.C. Smith Auditorium, Loyola College *Montreal, PQ, Canada* 7:30 & 9:15pm

Apparently most of the audience are high and Ray, out of frustration with their lethargy, sprays the crowd with beer to get their attention. Although originally meant as something of an insult to the passive crowd, the gesture evolves into a regular audience-participation routine for Ray for much of the 1970s.

Herbert Aronoff, the local student paper's reviewer, is hugely disappointed with The Kinks' performance of a mere 40 minutes, feeling that while they are neglected geniuses in the recording studio, they leave a lot to be desired on stage – a not uncommon charge during this era. Dave says later: "We didn't really want to go [to Canada again] because the Customs in those days were so awful – you couldn't take your own equipment and so you had to just plug into whatever was there. [At the college someone] said, 'Hey man, you want a trip of acid before you go on?' and our bass player turned round and said, 'If you give me any of that stuff I'm gonna knock you out.' But the kids were so out of it, they didn't know what was going on."

Friday 6th

Phys-ed complex, University Of Waterloo *Waterloo, ON, Canada* 8:30pm, with Neil Diamond (headliner), Dion

This appearance was added late, filling in for The Flying Machine who had cancelled. A classic Kinks bill where they are clearly unsuited to play alongside the other performers. The sole reviewer can only say that he thinks The Kinks are too loud – but he's impressed by their professional manner when a guitar string breaks during the performance.

Saturday 7th

Unknown venue and location tonight. Kinks road manager Ken Jones recalls playing at Shea's Theater in Buffalo, NY, around this time but no evidence exists. Possible further (unconfirmed) show tomorrow, with the three days following likely time off.

Thursday 12th-Saturday 14th

The Boston Tea Party *Boston, MA* 7:00 & 10:00pm, with Renaissance

A very quick return booking to Boston where the band found very strong support last October. This interesting double-bill pairs them with a band featuring two ex-Yardbirds (singer Keith Relf and drummer Jim McCarty) and ex-Nashville Teens pianist John Hawken, all former package-tour regulars back in England. Renaissance has just issued its first LP on Elektra, abandoning the guitar-heavy sound of The Yardbirds and that band's successor Led Zeppelin in favour of experimentation with classical and folk flavours.

The Kinks' appearance on opening night is described in the *Boston Globe* as "a far from record-breaking crowd … loud and balanced, the band seems to have tightened its music since its last appearance". The "overly-enthusiastic crowd" succeeds in getting an encore of current hit 'Victoria'. The author attends Saturday's show, noting that Dave's Gibson Flying V guitar is absent for this tour (the instrument will not see regular concert duty again, apart from at a one-off show in Iceland in September).

Ray says he has "an experience" in Boston during this time that is the partial inspiration for the song 'Lola'. Avory struggles through to Saturday's show as he is becoming increasingly ill with hepatitis. In the following days he will be too ill to function and it is finally decided by Wednesday that the band must cancel the remaining tour dates.

Set-list (final night): 'Last Of The Steam Powered Trains', 'You're Looking Fine', 'Big Sky', 'Victoria', medley 'Milk Cow Blues' / 'Naggin' / 'Rip It Up' / 'One Night', 'Louie Louie'.

Thursday 19th

The band minus Ray travels back to London after Avory's illness forces them to cancel the remaining dates of the tour, including an important return to the Fillmore East in New York City. Ray and manager Collins remain in New York to oversee the booking of the next tour. It's set to begin in early April but will ultimately be pushed back until late May.

Cancelled concerts: February 20th-21st The Fillmore East, New York, NY; 22nd Sports Arena, Atlanta, GA; 23rd Music Hall, State Fair Park, Dallas, TX; 25th Music Hall, Houston, TX; 27th The Woodrose Ballroom, Springfield, MA (superseding originally announced booking at The Warehouse, New Orleans, LA which is never finalised); 28th Ritchie Coliseum, University of Maryland, College Park, MD (with second date at The Warehouse, New Orleans originally slated but also never finalised).

Friday 27th

The Kinks (commonly known as ***The Black Album***) double-album released in the UK. It serves as a history of The Kinks on record to date, and was originally planned to include a book by Ray chronicling the band's career. Such a project would have to wait until Ray's 1994 book, *X-Ray*. But Ray's choice of tracks is revealing, both through what is included and what is not included. He puts in some R&B numbers that acknowledge the early influences on the band. He leaves out the cornerstone 'Village Green' song, but includes a standout song from that album, 'Animal Farm'. And he ignores 'Ev'rybody's Gonna Be Happy', perhaps because it was a commercial "failure", as well as 'Set Me Free', maybe to avoid the charges that it "sold out" to gain chart success.

Reviewers generally find the packaging sombre and austere, but the music inside far more cheerful, representing most of the important

kinks'70

The Kinks album (aka *The Black Album*)

A1 'You Really Got Me' (R. DAVIES).
A2 'Long Tall Shorty' (D. COVAY, H. ABRAMSON).
A3 'All Day And All Of The Night' (R. DAVIES).
A4 'Beautiful Delilah' (C. BERRY).
A5 'Tired Of Waiting For You' (R. DAVIES).
A6 'I'm A Lover Not A Fighter' (J. MILLER).
B1 'A Well Respected Man' (R. DAVIES).
B2 'Till The End of The Day' (R. DAVIES).
B3 'See My Friends' (R. DAVIES).
B4 'Don't You Fret' (R. DAVIES).
B5 'Dedicated Follower Of Fashion' (R. DAVIES).
B6 'Sunny Afternoon' (R. DAVIES).
C1 'Dead End Street' (R. DAVIES).
C2 'Death Of A Clown' (D. DAVIES, R. DAVIES).
C3 'Two Sisters' (R. DAVIES).
C4 'Big Black Smoke' (R. DAVIES).
C5 'Susannah's Still Alive' (D. DAVIES).
C6 'Waterloo Sunset' (R. DAVIES).
D1 'Last Of The Steam Powered Trains' (R. DAVIES).
D2 'Wonderboy' (R. DAVIES).
D3 'Do You Remember Walter' (R. DAVIES).
D4 'Dandy' (R. DAVIES).
D5 'Animal Farm' (R. DAVIES).
D6 'Days' (R. DAVIES).

UK release February 28th 1970 (Pye NPL 18326 mono).
Chart high UK none.

recordings from the band's career. The album goes largely unnoticed at home, where the band's fortunes remain at a low point, prior to the resurgence just months later with the release of the 'Lola' single. In the US, a full career history like this cannot be issued because the band's catalogue is now split between two deals with Reprise. The current contract covers *Face To Face* onwards; another, separate arrangement means that recordings before that have to be leased to Reprise from Pye for a limited period, effectively discouraging retrospectives.

March

➜ Recording at Morgan Studios, Willesden, north-west London is originally scheduled for early March but pushed back to late April/early May. US tour plans are shifted too, with the following dates that were planned or announced prior to Avory's illness ultimately cancelled: March 29th *Winters End Festival*, Miami, FL (with Grand Funk Railroad, Joe Cocker, Ten Years After, Sly & the Family Stone, John Mayall, Johnny Winter, Iron Butterfly, Mountain etc), the entire massive event ultimately cancelled on February 19th; April 3rd-4th *Progressive Pop Festival*, Sporthalle, Cologne, West Germany (with T.Rex, Deep Purple, Yes, Procol Harum, Chicken Shack, Barclay James Harvest etc) is a cancellation initially replacing the US tour opening date of April 1st-4th at The Whisky A Go Go, Hollywood, CA, which is then to start April 10th Olympic Auditorium, Los Angeles, CA; 17th-18th The Whisky A Go Go, Hollywood, CA; 23rd-26th Fillmore West, San Francisco, CA; April 30th & May 1st-2nd Fillmore West, San Francisco, CA.

Monday 9th – Friday 20th

Ray presumably spends this two-week period rehearsing for the BBC TV play in which he will appear, *The Long Distance Piano Player*.
✰ Ray's song 'Powerman' is apparently conceived and written one night after dinner with a producer during rehearsals for the play.

Monday 23rd

➜ Location shooting for *The Long Distance Piano Player*, probably during the week, at the Salvation Army Hall, Keighley, Yorks. It stars Ray Davies and Lois Dane, is written by Alan Sharp, directed by Philip Saville (best known for his 1966 movie *Stop The World I Want to Get Off*), and features two musical piano-and-vocal performances by Ray, 'Got To Be Free' and 'Marathon'.

Friday 27th – Sunday 29th

❏ **TV** BBC Television Centre (Studio 3) *west London*. Ray rehearses and videotapes the principal scenes for **The Long Distance Piano Player**, which will eventually be broadcast on BBC TV on October 15th. "It was a good exercise for me," Ray recalls later, "because I don't [act] 12 months a year – I had to do it all in three weeks. I had a lot of pressures, because we had another tour coming up, and I had to think about that at rehearsals: I was getting phone calls from America, phone calls from New Orleans …. That three weeks took six months out of me."
This Is Leon Bibb album by Leon Bibb released in the US, with 'Ballad Of The Virgin Soldier', written by Ray Davies (but with his original lyrics removed and rewritten by outside writers). It's the only US release of this rare Ray composition. The LP fails to chart.

➜ While Ray works on the TV play, Dave may be recording another LP's worth of songs for a new solo album. He tells *Record Mirror*: "It was all my own songs and I recorded it myself, because somehow they didn't fit into the group thing. But they decided not to release the album because of commercial reasons – although one day I think it will be released." The US fan club newsletter will mention a Dave solo album recorded this year and scheduled for July 1970 release, and then considered for issue with the later *Part One: Lola Versus Powerman* Kinks album, but dropped. The newsletter also states that Ray will be working on this same Dave LP in May 1971, hoping for a single during the summer of 1971. This is possibly the source of 'Climb Your Wall', recorded in a makeshift 8-track studio at Dave's home in Cockfosters, north London, only later released on the 1998 career-retrospective 2-CD set *The Dave Davies Anthology – Unfinished Business*.

April

➜ After his acting break and with Avory still recuperating, Ray begins writing new material early in April. "['Lola'] was the first song I wrote after the break," he says later. "The only thing I had to think about was the beginning, getting the thing to sell in the first five seconds. The rest came naturally."
Ray tells *NME* later that the subject-matter of 'Lola' combines two real incidents six months apart: manager Wace in Paris in April 1965, and Ray in Bridlington in January of the same year. "It just happened and it's in the song – but the characters are more extreme. [I] caricature people. Probably I wanted the incident to happen and kind of stage-managed it. I put two people through that incident, and I was one of them."
Later in the month the band begins rehearsals at Ray's house in East Finchley, including work on 'Lola', 'Powerman', 'Got To Be Free' and probably 'Good Good Life'.

● **RECORDING** Morgan Studios *Willesden, north-west London*. In a symbolic move that puts the 1960s behind them, the band moves on to an independent recording studio, Morgan, rather than return to the old Pye standby. At Morgan they jump up a notch in technology, using a state-of-the-art 16-track machine that allows more flexibility for building up recordings. At first it seems a producer is sought for these sessions, but no one is available whom they want to work with, and Ray occupies the role. The sessions are engineered by Morgan staffer Mike Bobak. At least three new songs, possibly a fourth, are recorded at this time: **'Lola'**, **'Powerman'**, **'Got To Be Free'** and possibly **'Good Good Life'**. 'Lola' is recorded in four or five different versions, in various keys and with different feels and beginnings. Dalton recalls that the recording of 'Lola' in particular took a very long time as the sessions stretch into May.

Ray recalls later: "I remember going into a music store on Shaftesbury Avenue in London when we were about to make 'Lola'. I said, 'I want to get a really good guitar sound on this record, I want a Martin.' And in the corner they had this old 1938 Dobro [resonator guitar] that I bought for $150. I put them together on 'Lola' which is what makes that clangy sound; the combination of the Martin and the Dobro with heavy compression."

May

→ ● **RECORDING** Morgan Studios *Willesden, north-west London*. Work continues at the new recording location, Morgan, early this month. The Kinks have decided to look for a keyboard player, and John Gosling is auditioned during overdub sessions. He comes recommended to manager Collins by rock writer Pete Frame, whom Collins phoned for suggestions to avoid having to place ads in Melody Maker and formally audition lots of applicants. Frame is an old acquaintance of Gosling's from school in Luton, Beds. Gosling appears for the audition, and plays a piano part on the final master backing track of **'Lola'**. He is the only person auditioned. At first he is offered the job strictly for the upcoming US tour, to see how it works out, but this evolves into a more permanent position. To accept the job, Gosling gives up his classes at The Royal Academy Of Music where he has been studying since autumn 1966.

By mid May, Ray is working on final mixes of the new tracks. The hard rocking 'Powerman' is briefly considered first choice for the new single, but 'Lola' prevails. With the all-important single nearing completion, it is announced that The Kinks are to resume their tour of US.

Monday 18th

))) **RADIO** BBC Aeolian Studios (Studio 2) *central London*. BBC Radio 1 *Dave Lee Travis Show* studio recordings 'Lola', 'Days', 'Mindless Child Of Motherhood' broadcast May 31st, repeated plus medley 'Dedicated Follower Of Fashion' / 'A Well Respected Man' / 'Death Of A Clown' / 'Sunny Afternoon' *Johnnie Walker Show* week of June 8th-12th. The now typical BBC radio method is adopted of recording some songs from scratch and merely altering existing recordings for others. Here, the issued backing tracks of 'Lola' and 'Days' are given new vocals by Ray, but Dave's 'Mindless Child Of Motherhood' is an entirely new recording. As there is no surviving copy of the medley it's unclear if this is a unique recording or simply a splicing together of studio recordings. ('Mindless Child Of Motherhood' will be released in 2001 on *The Kinks BBC Sessions 1964-1977*.)

Once the recordings are completed, the BBC objects to the use of the word "Coca-Cola" in 'Lola', stating that it violates its policy of no commercial advertising. By the time the band hears of this they will be on tour in America, and Ray will have to fly back to London on May 25th to record a different lyric, replacing "Coca-Cola" with "cherry cola". Later he will also have to dub the new lyric for the videotape of a *Top Of The Pops* BBC TV broadcast, as well as the master studio recording for the single release. No chances are taken that might jeopardise the success of this important single.

☆ It is at this time that John Gosling, following his recent audition as keyboard player, is called to the Boscobel offices in central London where manager Collins asks if he is willing to go on the imminent US tour (and to appear on the taping of *Top Of The Pops* this week). Gosling agrees, and effectively joins The Kinks this week.

Wednesday 20th

❏ **TV** BBC Television Centre *west London*. BBC-1 *Top Of The Pops* lip-synch 'Lola' broadcast June 18th. The new five-man Kinks videotape an insert for *TOTP*, miming to the as yet unreleased 'Lola', ultimately to be aired while the band is in the US. To satisfy the BBC's no-advertising policy the audio portion of the recording is later overdubbed by Ray, probably on the 25th, changing the lyric from "Coca-Cola" to "cherry cola".

☆ The Kinks are photographed backstage in what would be the first photo to feature new member John Gosling, published in the June 6th edition of *NME*. (Band departs for US following day.)

➭ **TOUR STARTS** *Tour Of North America 1970: second leg* (May 22nd – Jul 10th). **Line-up**: Ray Davies (lead vocal, guitar), Dave Davies (guitar, vocal), Mick Avory (drums), John Dalton (bass), John Gosling (keyboard). Gosling plays a modest Hohner Pianet electric piano for this tour. (Ray has played electric piano live on some dates, for example in 1968.) Booked by Bert Kamerman at Creative Management Associates in New York City. No new songs are played, with 'Lola' not yet introduced in public.

Friday 22nd – Saturday 23rd

The Depot *Minneapolis, MN* two shows nightly, with Danny's Reasons

John Gosling's concert debut as The Kinks become a five-piece touring band for the first time.

The age limit and liquor policy of this over-21 nightclub in a newly converted bus terminal restricts many potential under-age Kinks fans from attending. There is also an ongoing attempt by local supporters of musicians in the area to boycott many big-name national touring acts who they characterise as "rip-off artists of the music empire". The cancellation of a Crosby Stills Nash & Young show in nearby Bloomington set for the weekend before, in fact due to the band's internal conflicts rather than the effect of any boycott, has been considered a victory by local organisers. Dalton later proudly tells *Melody Maker* that even though CSN&Y cancelled their appearance, no one tried to stop The Kinks playing.

Opening act Danny's Reasons is led by Danny Rapp, former lead singer of Danny & The Juniors, the Philadelphia-based doo-wop group that scored a big hit with 'At The Hop' in 1957. Ray later says it's "great" playing on the same bill as Rapp.

Local underground paper *Hundred Flowers* reviews the second night's show: "The Kinks opened their seven-week tour [with] some flashes of brilliance that made [them] one of the top rock bands in the 1960s. The group's first set, which lasted only for about a half hour, was very dynamic. The group was really going, even enthusing some of the normally complacent Depot crowd into clapping and dancing. Everything was fast and exciting, not too perfect, yet spontaneously live. The Kinks returned for set number two, everyone anticipating to be swept away by an even better set than the first. It didn't happen, [it] was very loose and uninspired. They finished with a medley of rock'n'roll hits, again playing for only half an hour. The meager audience gave a short, restrained applause."

Sunday 24th

A proposed free concert at the University of Minnesota in Minneapolis is cancelled, probably because Ray has to travel back to London for tomorrow's new-vocal sessions for 'Lola' at BBC studios. The rest of the band travels on to Chicago where they have time off until the next performance on the 29th. Ray reportedly writes three songs over the next few days, probably including 'This Time Tomorrow' and 'A Long Way From Home'.

Monday 25th – Wednesday 27th

))) **RADIO** BBC Aeolian Studios (Studio 2) *central London*.
❏ **TV** BBC Television Centre *west London*.
Ray is back in London to record a new "cherry cola" lyric in place of the forbidden commercial reference to "Coca-Cola" on the existing BBC radio recording of 'Lola' done on the 18th and the video taped on the 20th.
☆ On Tuesday Ray signs The Kinks with the Tony Barrow International Agency as the their new publicists. Barrow's Marion Rainford is assigned as the band's new representative/publicist. With the new agency in place and a potent new single to promote, a new campaign is effectively launched to get the band back into the British charts and the public eye.

Thursday 28th

● **RECORDING** Morgan Studios *Willesden, north-west London*. Ray makes an unsuccessful attempt to overdub to his satisfaction the new "cherry cola" lyric on to the existing master recording of '**Lola**' and is forced to schedule a return visit the following week. He unsuccessfully tries to catch a flight to the island of Jersey to play in a charity football match, but can't make the connecting flight and simply continues on to the US. The new publicist immediately picks up on the missed football game and 6,000-mile round-trip as an interesting angle to pump to the press to herald The Kinks' imminent return to chartdom.

Friday 29th – Saturday 30th

Aragon Ballroom *Chicago, IL* 8:00pm, with Lee Michaels, Frigid Pink, Jesse, Ned; promoted by Triangle Productions
Chicago is becoming a favourite regular haunt of the band. This large line-up at the huge Aragon appears on the popular Memorial Day weekend that traditionally kicks off the American summer season.

Sunday 31st

The band travels to New York City where they have time off until the next scheduled performance on Wednesday, and Ray returns to London to again try to prepare 'Lola' for release and to begin the promotional campaign with a slew of press interviews. As a result, a number of planned activities are cancelled or rescheduled. Originally slated for today was a spot at the *Churubusco Live-In Rock Festival* in Churubusco, NY. The Kinks were a late addition to this ambitious three-day Memorial Weekend festival (May 29th-31st) at the northern tip of New York State near the Canadian border, but ultimately the entire festival was cancelled late in April due to a lack of financial backing.

June

Monday 1st – Tuesday 2nd

● **RECORDING** Morgan Studios *Willesden, north-west London*. This time Ray is successful in seamlessly inserting into the master recording of '**Lola**' the "cherry cola" lyric in place of the original "Coca-Cola" line. With that accomplished, he spends the rest of his short break from the tour handling media duties.
☆ A press release is issued announcing the new single 'Lola' set for

June 12th. It plays up the angle that Ray made two trips to London from the States to change the banned commercial-reference lyric, and notes that John Gosling has been added on piano for the US tour.
☆ In the US, Ray's absence in London forces the shifting to the 22nd of Monday's scheduled TV taping session at the Little Theatre in New York City for *The David Frost Show*.

Wednesday 3rd

Ray travels to New York City but is too late to keep tonight's booking at Ungano's where they are booked for two nights.

Thursday 4th

Ungano's *New York, NY* with Country Funk (headliners), Creedmoor State
Ray is back and The Kinks fulfil this second of a two-night booking at the small, hip club on the Upper West Side where they had played to great response as an after-thought at the end of last year's cross-country tour. The band strolls on stage with Gosling sporting a fright mask he'd taken a liking to. "The Kinks are at their best in a small club where the first row of the audience is sitting on the performers' feet and everybody, for the occasion, loves everybody else," writes Nancy Erlich in *Billboard*. "[The] audience had a guided tour through The Kinks' England as seen through a graceful, raucous, perceptive series of songs …. All went smoothly and with great humor, the kind that can only come in a small hall through a highly personal form of communication."

Friday 5th – Saturday 6th

The Electric Factory *Philadelphia, PA* 8:00pm, with Mott The Hoople; tickets $4
A quick return engagement to Philly, this time with a newly emerging band of fellow Brits who feature an instrumental version of 'You Really Got Me' on their recently issued debut LP.

Sunday 7th – Monday 8th

Basing themselves in New York City and with a few days off, the whole band attends on Sunday afternoon at Madison Square Garden a large-screen simulcast of the England vs Brazil World Cup football match. Unfortunately England loses the game and is eliminated from the final, but The Kinks all buy tickets anyway to the final on June 21st, also broadcast here.
☆ The Who start their 1970 US tour tonight with a special final presentation of their rock opera *Tommy* with two shows at the prestigious Metropolitan Opera House in New York City's Lincoln Center. This further milestone in The Who's career is likely not lost on The Kinks.

Tuesday 9th

Zembo Mosque *Harrisburg, PA* 8:00pm, with East Coast Left, Truth, Justice & The American Way
Off the beaten track tonight, at a small city along the Susquehanna River a few hours west of Philadelphia.

Wednesday 10th – Thursday 11th

The Emergency *Washington, DC* with Stillroven
A record store in the Georgetown section that, remarkably, doubles as an occasional concert venue, with a capacity of about 150 people. This marks The Kinks' debut in the DC area, after a February booking in neighbouring Maryland in was cancelled due to Avory's illness.
☆ Dave's second child, Simon, is born back in London. Dave's absence from the birth is one of the sacrifices made as the band tries to regain lost ground in the US. The birth is not announced to the press.

Friday 12th

A scheduled show tonight at the Allen Theater in Cleveland, OH, with

Traffic (headliners) and Mott The Hoople is called off at the last moment. Traffic are evidently forced to cancel as their equipment truck breaks down.

☆ Reprise Records logs in receipt of their copy of the master tapes for the new Kinks single, 'Lola' and 'Mindless Child Of Motherhood', including short and long-edit versions of 'Lola', implying a concern about the song's length. A new copy of the tape for 'Lola' will be required and evidently the master tape itself is dispatched from London on July 2nd, so perhaps Reprise too want to issue the safer "cherry cola" version as a single. The originally submitted copy still has "Coca Cola".

'Lola' / 'Berkeley Mews' single released in the UK. Along with reasonable advertising in the music press, the single gets promising reviews. The *NME* sums up the overall view: "The Kinks have been out of the public eye for quite a while, but they could well come storming back into the limelight with this catchy piece – always provided that they're able to secure the plugs which are so necessary after a chart absence. This is an engaging and sparkling piece with a gay Latin flavour and a catchy hook chorus that registers right from the outset. The group's driving beat and tingling guitar sound are also well in evidence. I can't recall The Kinks having previously recorded anything like this, but the experiment has certainly paid off, because the net result is an extremely good pop record. It now remains to be seen if the fans will go along with my diagnosis." Ray later credits record plugger Johnny Wise with generating important behind-the-scenes interest in the single, with crucial and virtually career-saving effect.

Saturday 13th
Commodore Ballroom *Lowell, MA* 7:30pm, with The Illusion; tickets $3.50
An old ballroom in a fading mill city 30 miles north of Boston, the venue has been hosting local rock shows for a while, already boasting appearances by such British luminaries as The Yardbirds, Cream, and The Jeff Beck Group. The author attends this show and, while he feels the band's heart isn't entirely in it, notes highlight performances of

Lola single

A 'Lola' (R. DAVIES).
B-UK 'Berkeley Mews' (R. DAVIES).
B-US 'Mindless Child Of Motherhood' (D. DAVIES).

UK release (A/B-UK) June 12th 1970 (Pye 7N 17961).
US release (A/B-US) July 28th 1970 (Reprise 0930).
Musicians Ray Davies lead vocal (A, B-UK), acoustic guitar (A), resonator guitar (A), electric guitar (B-US). Dave Davies lead vocal (B-US), electric guitar, backing vocal (A). John Dalton bass guitar (A, B-US). Pete Quaife bass guitar (B-UK). Mick Avory drums. John Gosling baby grand piano (A). Nicky Hopkins piano (B-UK). Ken Jones maracas (A).
Recorded A: Morgan Studios Willesden, north-west London; April-May 1970; 16-track mixed to mono. B-UK: Pye Studios central London; January-March 1968; 4-track mixed to mono. B-US: Pye Studios central London; May 1969; 8-track mixed to mono.
Producer Ray Davies.
Engineers Mike Bobak (A); probably Alan MacKenzie (B-UK); Andrew Hendriksen (B-US).
Chart high UK number 2; US number 9.

'Some Mother's Son' and Dave's 'Mindless Child Of Motherhood'. Ray wears a straw hat and sometimes plays with it nervously. The presence of John Gosling is something of a mystery to many fans who attended earlier shows at the Boston Tea Party as there is no official word that The Kinks have added a keyboard player. (Following days probably time off.) The opening act pushes a debut LP that features their semi-hit 'Did You See Her Eyes'.
Set-list: 'Till The End Of The Day', 'Last Of The Steam Powered Trains', 'You're Looking Fine', medley 'Sunny Afternoon' / 'A Well Respected Man' / 'Dandy' / 'Death Of A Clown', 'Mr Churchill Says', 'Victoria', 'Some Mother's Son', 'Brainwashed', 'Big Sky', 'Mindless Child Of Motherhood', medley 'Milk Cow Blues' / 'Rip It Up' / 'See My Friends' / 'Mean Woman Blues' / 'Milk Cow Blues' / 'One Night', medley 'You Really Got Me' / 'All Day And All Of The Night'.

Wednesday 17th
Rogers High School Auditorium *Newport, RI* 8:00pm
A typical last-minute fill-in date on The Kinks' ever-shifting itinerary, with local promoter Vic Arman only finalising the venue a matter of days before the show. (Day off following in Newport.)

Friday 19th – Saturday 20th
Capitol Theater *Port Chester, NY* 8:00 & 11:00pm, with Grand Funk Railroad (headliners), Mott The Hoople; tickets $5.50; promoted by Howard Stein
This 1,900-capacity movie house just outside New York City was opened in reaction to Bill Graham's successful Fillmore East venture in the East Village in Manhattan. "Special guest stars" The Kinks fit oddly against the decibel-charged headliners who attract a quite different kind of fan. John Swenson elaborates in *Zygote*: "When The Kinks came on the split in the crowd grew apparent. About half the people stood up and cheered while the other half ho-hummed it. But The Kinks were too much. Shuffling out in straw hats and stripped T-shirts, Lovin' Spoonful-style, Ray Davies pointed his skinny little finger at the audience as the group launched into 'The Last Of The Steam Powered Trains'. The Kinks have been together for a long time and it shows … [they] don't try to make an impression with loudness, they try to leave you with some music playing in your head …. [But] they seemed to have gotten louder and stronger than before. At the first three shows The Kinks had trouble with Grand Funk's part of the audience, but their last set had everybody moving."

Sunday 21st
Ever football-conscious, The Kinks make sure today – Ray's 26th birthday – is set aside as time off so that the whole band can attend a big-screen simulcast of the Brazil vs. Italy World Cup soccer final, even though England had earlier lost to Brazil.

Monday 22nd
❏ **TV** Little Theatre *New York, NY*. Nationally syndicated *The David Frost Show* lip-synch 'Lola' broadcast July 17th. A notable day as The Kinks return to an American TV studio for the first time since July 1965 and the incident then with a union official. Any lingering problems with the AFTRA union have apparently been sorted out so that the band can actively promote a new single to the American television audience (the first since 'Set Me Free' five years earlier). British host Frost plugs the band's last LP, reading out the full title "Arthur or the Decline and Fall of the British Empire," adding, "I hope not!" The show's broadcast on July 17th will unfortunately be a few weeks before 'Lola' is available on vinyl, following a delay in the record company's receipt of the correct master tape.

Tuesday 23rd
Seattle Center Arena *Seattle, WA* *Love Needs Care Concert*,

→ INDICATES EVENT AROUND THIS TIME BUT WITH NO FIRM DATE

with The Sonics, The Bards

The Kinks fly across country for this appearance. Over 6,000 tickets are given away free for a teen health-awareness event sponsored by the Seattle Public Health department and radio station XOL, and a film about preventing venereal diseases, *Love Needs Care*, is shown. But only about 2,000 attend and the event is a partial failure. *The Seattle Times* makes no mention of any of the bands by name, noting instead that the meagre audience "applauded and chuckled during the ten-minute movie, but maybe the response was more intelligent good humor than indifference. Or maybe the teenagers were secure in the thought that no VD germs could have survived the first 150 minutes of well-amplified music".

Wednesday 24th

Centennial Concert Hall *Winnipeg, MB, Canada* 8:00pm, with Justin Tyme

Peter Crossley of the *Winnipeg Free Press* is definitely not happy tonight. "This was The Kinks at their worst," he begins. "After a prolonged intermission due to instrument trouble the audience was mistreated with an avalanche of noise. The Kinks from England are a no-talent group of very poorly groomed not-so-young men whose success seems to lie in their ability to grow lots of long hair and scream unintelligible lyrics into a microphone. The noise was endless and piled layer upon layer until it seemed one's eardrums would break. There are no individual talents in this group. They merely make a pretence at playing music. If this was a sample of the new music coming out of England, perhaps it should stay there."

Thursday 25th

Apollo Theater *Calgary, AB, Canada* 8:00pm

Dave has a revealing comment for a local newspaper: "The Kinks are very much like family now," he says, "more so than we've ever been. We hardly argue at all now. When a group has been together for a time, you realize that arguing is a waste of money and a waste of time."

Friday 26th

Sales Pavilion *Edmonton, AB, Canada* 8:00pm

Saturday 27th

Pacific National Exhibition Gardens Auditorium *Vancouver, BC, Canada* 8:00pm, with Motherhood

Self-confessed middle-aged reviewer Jurgen Hesse enthuses about the show. "It was one of those evenings where you could feel the electricity build up in the audience, where the air became supercharged with anticipation of a great event. [They were] magicians on stage [with] unbelievable togetherness as a group and their beautifully choreographed presentation … It isn't often that a traveling rock group supersedes expectations. The Kinks did." Dave later tells *Music Now*: "We recorded a show in Vancouver and we were amazed when we heard the tapes and compared them to our records." Sadly, no sign of such tapes has emerged since; if they do exist they probably reside with Ray. (Travel day to San Francisco follows.)

Monday 29th

Gosling is fished out of San Francisco Bay after falling in while balancing on the railing on the balcony of Martha's restaurant in Sausalito. Scheduled for June 29th to July 1st are dates at a new rock club, The Earth Station, in Honolulu, HI, but they are cancelled, reportedly due to recent "problems" at local rock shows.

Tuesday 30th

Family Dog on the Great Highway *San Francisco, CA* with Osceola

With the Hawaiian dates cancelled, The Kinks head to San Francisco for dates at Family Dog, a competitor to Bill Graham's Fillmore operation.

July

Wednesday 1st

Family Dog on the Great Highway *San Francisco, CA* with Temporary Optics

Thursday 2nd

Ygnacio Valley High School Auditorium *Concord, CA* 8:00pm with Beggar's Opera; tickets $3.50; presented by the Family Dog in Concord

In addition to the two-night stand at their main SF venue, the Family Dog operation tries its hand at promotion in neighbouring Concord at a high school facility with a capacity of approximately 1,000.

☆ The master copy of the recording of 'Lola' is despatched from London's Heathrow Airport to Los Angeles, to make the July 14th release date, but is lost in transit. It is reported that the group will either have to re-record the song or dub it from the British record. The tape does eventually turn up in New York and is forwarded to Reprise, but this causes a further delay in the US release and will effectively undermine the debut of the song on American TV on the July 17th *David Frost Show*.

Friday 3rd – Sunday 5th

The Whisky A Go Go *Hollywood, CA* two shows, with Toe Fat

A return to the small, prestigious dinner club, where they continue to bang out their standard club-date repertoire of earlier hits and rock'n'roll standards. Annoyed by the lethargy in the set he catches, John Mendelssohn writes in the *Los Angeles Times* about his favourite band: "While it's very likely that The Kinks, who appeared over the weekend at the wonderful Whisky, have as much to offer at their worst as countless lesser British groups have at their best, it's distressingly clear that they could, at the price of a little sweat, do worlds better both by their audience and, more important, by themselves. Endowed in leader Ray Davies with perhaps the idiom's most brilliant living songwriter, the group could conceivably elevate us to heights as yet unexplored by even The Who, were they to perform *Arthur* (Davies' magnificent rock and roll cantata) in something even vaguely resembling its entirety.

"Instead," continues Mendelssohn, " they're content to deal almost exclusively in frazzled vintage standards like 'You're Looking Fine' and 'I Got A Woman', their enthusiasm only infrequently negating their sloppiness. Given to endless improvisations and deafening crescendo finales that often seem to last as long as the songs they close, the group furthermore manages to obscure the charm and wit of the few Davies originals they do perform with heartbreaking regularity. To hear them do it live, for instance, one would scarcely suspect that a song like 'Waterloo Sunset' is at once poignant, beautiful and almost uncomfortably revealing. However wonderful their records may be, it's scarcely fair of them to anyone involved to represent themselves so dismally on stage. Ray's music deserves much better, and so do we."

Monday 6th

With 'Lola' on its way up the British charts, Dave and Dalton return to London for a quick batch of press duties while the rest of the band heads to New York City. The US tour was originally planned to end today but a further weekend of dates is now added to accommodate an unusually lucrative festival booking for Saturday 11th, padded out with a few short-notice shows in and around the New York City area.

Tuesday 7th – Wednesday 8th

Dave is at Boscobel Productions in Mayfair, central London for press duties. Among others he tells *NME* that on the US tour "a lot of people thought we didn't exist", while Dalton talks to *Melody Maker* about the pros and cons of playing in America, the benefits of adding keyboards, and that the recording of a new double-album, of which four songs are already recorded, will begin upon their return. On Thursday the two return to New York City.

Friday 10th
Ritz Theatre *Port Richmond, Staten Island, NY*
It's not certain this is the venue played today. (Regular rock shows began here at the start of the year as a response to the success of Bill Graham and his Fillmore East in the East Village in Manhattan.)

Saturday 11th
An unexpected day off in New York City as the planned *Mountaindale Festival* in the Catskill Mountains area of upstate New York is cancelled one day before the event's scheduled start, thanks to a restraining order issued by Sullivan County. Scheduled to have appeared along with The Kinks in the day-long event were The Band, Blodwyn Pig, The Grateful Dead, Van Morrison, Richie Havens, John Sebastian, Cathy Smith, and The Voices of East Harlem.

The Kinks were added to the bill in late June after a number of already-booked artists dropped out due to conflicts with appearances at the *New York Pop Festival* at Randalls Island, NY, the following weekend (17th-19th).

Sunday 12th
It's possible another gig is played today, details unknown. The Kinks probably depart from New York City this evening and arrive back in London the following morning.

Tuesday 14th
With a day off and the band back in London they are immediately busy dealing with the (possibly unexpected) success of 'Lola' in the British charts.
☆ Reprise Records receives the "lost" replacement master tape of 'Lola' and release in the US is rescheduled for July 28th.

Wednesday 15th
❏ **TV** BBC Television Centre *west London*. BBC-1 **Top Of The Pops** lip-synch 'Lola' broadcast July 30th.

Friday 17th
Student Union, University Of Sheffield *Sheffield*
The first show for some time back on British soil, and no longer as a "former charting band" but with a new hit single to propel them back into demand on the rock circuit.

Monday 20th
Just like the heyday of the 1960s, the press barrage begins, with various newspaper and radio demands on the band's time. It's around this time that Ray is interviewed at Kenwood House on Hampstead Heath, north-west London by Penny Valentine on a typical British summer's day, as it pours down with rain. Ray flatly refuses all questions about his childhood, but utters the classic line: "Dave and I are very close, but we have this feeling toward each other that is almost akin to hatred. It's always been that way."

Speaking of his pet interest in film, Ray says: "I wouldn't make a film unless it was somehow related to the music I write. When I see something in my songs, it looks nice, and I want everybody else to see it the way I do. There may be people around who see life exactly as I see it, and it would be nice to find out if that's true." He talks about his love of classic old films, and of his surprise that *Arthur* did so much better in the States than in Britain. "I realise that England had been through all the *Arthur* thing for real. They'd experienced it first-hand. In America, it's right for now because they're only just having these

things happening to them – like Vietnam. They're only just realising what a big war can do to a family and people."

Tuesday 21st
Pye Records sponsors a Kinks press party in the company's reception room in central London with around 150 attending. Many interviews are done and the band is photographed extensively, resulting in a popular series of shots used repeatedly over the years on sleeves and in the press.
☆ Around this time they are scheduled to appear on Dutch NCRV TV, on *Eddie Steady Go!*, but cancel.

Thursday 23rd
➜ ❏ **TV** Killesberg Television Studios *Stuttgart, West Germany*. ZDF Channel **2 4-3-2-1-Hot 'n' Sweet** lip-synch 'Lola' broadcast August 8th.

Saturday 25th
➜ **Eiderlandhalle** *Pahlhude, West Germany*

Monday 27th +
Ray and family spend time in Cornwall, the county in the extreme south-west of England, where he writes 'Apeman' as well as other songs for the new LP.
☆ A press release announces that Ray will appear in the forthcoming BBC production *The Long Distance Piano Player* but an exact broadcast date has yet to be set.

Tuesday 28th
'Lola' / 'Mindless Child Of Motherhood' single released in the US. *Billboard* says: "Currently a top 10 British chart winner, this infectious rhythm item has all the ingredients to put The Kinks right back up the Hot 100 here with solid impact."

August

Monday 10th
The week is very likely spent considering new material written by Ray over the recent holidays. The weekend brings a pair of one-off British dates that represent the band's return to bankability with British promoters and the public. It begins a pattern where the band, when not on tour in America, will rehearse, record and play occasional dates at home.
☆ A press release announces The Kinks are to record the soundtrack for the upcoming feature film *Percy*.

Friday 14th
Top Rank Suite *Swansea, Wales* 8:00pm-1:00am with Mayfisher, Powerstop

Saturday 15th
Spa Royal Hall *Bridlington, Yorks* 7:45-11:45pm, with Childhood, The Late Arrival

Monday 17th
A press release says the band is currently recording their new LP and that it is expected to be a double set, though issued separately as volume one and volume two, and that the first part of the project is now largely recorded.

The release also states that Ray is currently writing the score for the film Percy, and that the next US tour is slated for six weeks in November and December.

➜ INDICATES EVENT AROUND THIS TIME BUT WITH NO FIRM DATE

→ ● **RECORDING** Morgan Studios *Willesden, north-west London.* Sessions resume for the new LP. Dave, interviewed at the studio by Richard Green for *NME*, speaks of his disappointment when a few of their earlier singles failed to chart. Asked what would have happened if 'Lola' had failed, Dave speculates: "I suppose we'd have gone on making records for another year or so and then drifted apart." Green concludes that The Kinks now need chart success for their albums, not just their singles.

Friday 21st

Outdoor event *Bilzen, Belgium* 11:00am-12midnight, *Jazz Bilzen 70 Festival*, with Arthur Conley (headliner), The Wild Angels, Golden Earring, Black Sabbath
Film of The Kinks playing 'Sunny Afternoon' from this show is later broadcast on the Belgian TV show *The Bilzen Festival* on October 6th.

Saturday 22nd

Outdoor event *Tiel, Netherlands* 8:00pm, *Tiel Pop Festival*, with The Wild Angels, Palace, Arthur Brown, Alan Price, Golden Earring, Sweet Soul Sensation

Sunday 23rd

Fantasio II *Amsterdam, Netherlands*
Travel back to London the next day.

→ ● **RECORDING** Morgan Studios *Willesden, north-west London.* It's likely that more studio work takes place this week.

Saturday 29th

Mayfair Suite, Belfry Hotel *Wishaw, Warwicks*
A thousand fans attend the show, where the band plays 'Till The End Of The Day', 'Last Of The Steam Powered Trains', 'You're Looking Fine', 'Waterloo Sunset', 'Sunny Afternoon', 'Big Sky', 'Lola', medley 'Milk Cow Blues' / 'One Night' / 'You Are My Sunshine', medley 'You Really Got Me' / 'All Day And All Of The Night'.

September

Thursday 3rd

Rebecca's *Birmingham* with Breakdown
About 800 attend this nightclub show. Dave and Gosling join members of the opening act for a post-gig blues jam that includes B.B. King's 'Every Day I Have The Blues'.

Saturday 5th

California Ballroom *Dunstable, Beds*

Sunday 6th

Fehmarn, West Germany Fehmarn Festival, with Procol Harum, Incredible String Band, Cactus, Fat Mattress, Emerson Lake & Palmer
The first of a two-day event on this island off the German coast.

Monday 7th

Laugardalshöllinni *Reykjavik, Iceland* 8:30 pm, *Pop-Hljómleikar*
After the show, The Kinks jam in a club in place of local band Oòmenn.

Tuesday 8th

After a particularly drunken flight and a number of disturbances, members of the band as they arrive in London are escorted off the plane by armed guards and almost arrested. Manager Collins is

becoming increasingly intolerant of such behaviour.

Wednesday 9th

→ ● **RECORDING** Morgan Studios *Willesden, north-west London.* Around now the band is back at Morgan to continue work on the new LP, carrying on throughout the remainder of the month.

Friday 18th

Tonight's show at the Lyceum Ballroom, central London, billed as *Klooks At The Lyceum*, is cancelled at the last moment. A sign posted on the Lyceum door reads, "Show cancelled: Dave Davies ill." The Kinks were scheduled to headline over The Faces, featuring old Grimshaw school-chum Rod Stewart.
☆ Jimi Hendrix dies in London today.

Saturday 19th

Pilton, Somerset 10:00am, *Worthy Farm Pop Folk & Blues Festival*, with Quintessence, Steamhammer, Wayne Fontana, Alan Bown, Duster Bennett, Stackridge, Amazing Blondel

→ ☆ Around this time the start date for the next US tour is pushed back to October, and then November, in order to complete the *Percy* film soundtrack.

October

→ ● **RECORDING** Morgan Studios *Willesden, north-west London.* Ray is mixing completed tracks for the *Part One: Lola Versus Powerman* LP.
→ ● **RECORDING** Morgan Studios *Willesden, north-west London.* The Kinks return to Morgan to begin intensive sessions for the soundtrack for the film *Percy*. Eleven new Ray Davies songs are recorded, six of which are instrumental – **'Completely'**, **'Running Round Town'**, **'Whip Lady'**, **'Helga'**, and **'God's Children (End)'**, plus an instrumental remake of **'Lola'**. The other six feature Ray's lead vocal – **'God's Children'**, **'The Way Love Used To Be'**, **'Moments'**, **'Animals In The Zoo'**, **'Just Friends'**, and **'Dreams'**. The other song, **'Willesden Green'**, is sung under duress by bassist Dalton. A tour of West Germany set for October 13th-25th is scrapped to make time for the work.
☆ Amid the intense recording activity, the long-standing publishing dispute caused by Kassner Music Ltd contesting Ray's signing to Carlin Music Corporation in November 1965 is finally resolved after The Kinks camp tires of threats by Kassner of continued appeals to the House Of Lords and fears a ruling in Kassner's favour. Ray will confirm in his book *X-Ray* that he agrees to an out-of-court settlement, paying Kassner "a small lump sum, and a reduction in royalties due me as a writer on all those early hits". The settlement means that the money that has been held in escrow is finally released to Ray. The five-year Davray Music agreement with Carlin coincidentally terminates at this time, and at first Ray does not re-sign with Carlin. This will cause the British release of the 'Apeman' single to be issued under Copyright Control, the term used when no publisher is assigned. Songs from *Percy* will be published in the interim in a one-off deal with Coronado Music.

Thursday 15th

The Long Distance Piano Player is broadcast in BBC-1 TV's *Play For Today* series. (See March 23rd/29th.) Ray reportedly books studio time this evening so that band members will be unable to see his TV acting debut. Critics are rather unkind, with one headline reading, "Pianist play hits a low note."

Monday 19th

Another member of The Kinks' 1960s camp departs as Robert Ransom, long-serving band accountant, resigns as secretary of Kinks Productions Ltd. Avory takes over the role. It's probably a coincidence that Ransom's exit comes on the heels of the publishing-dispute settlement.

→ ● **RECORDING** Morgan Studios *Willesden, north-west London*. Sessions continue for *Percy* and principal recording is wrapped up at the end of the month, just in time to prepare for the US tour.

November

Tuesday 3rd

→ Probably today, a promotional film for 'Apeman' is shot on Hampstead Heath, north-west London with Gosling willingly donning an elaborate ape costume to play the lead character.

Wednesday 4th

❒ **TV** BBC Television Centre *west London*. BBC-1 **Top Of The Pops** lip-synch 'Apeman' broadcast December 3rd. Following the taping, at which Gosling probably appears in the ape costume again, Ray apparently travels to Los Angeles.

Thursday 5th – Friday 6th

Ray delivers the master tapes of the *Part One: Lola Versus Powerman And The Moneygoround* LP to Reprise Records in the US where they are logged in on the 5th. Tapes have also been handed to Pye before his departure (as this is the first time that a Kinks album has not been recorded at Pye's in-house studios). Other band members travel to Los Angeles on Sunday 8th and Monday 9th.

➭ **TOUR STARTS** *Tour Of North America* (Nov 10th – Dec 12th). **Line-up**: Ray Davies (lead vocal, guitar), Dave Davies (guitar, vocal), Mick Avory (drums), John Dalton (bass), John Gosling (keyboard). New songs include 'Top Of The Pops' and 'Strangers'. This is the first tour where full use is made of acoustic guitars.

Tuesday 10th

Civic Auditorium *Santa Monica, CA* 8:00pm, with Atlee
Los Angeles Times reviewer John Mendelsohn, so critical of the earlier Whisky A Go Go show, finds tonight's appearance proof that The Kinks are a revitalised and unique stage act appealing to a very responsive crowd. Tonight's sell-out show attended by 2,793 fans grosses $15,134.

Wednesday 11th

On their night off in LA the band are back at the Whisky A Go Go to see Black Sabbath opening a four-night stay.

Thursday 12th – Saturday 14th

Fillmore West *San Francisco, CA* with Elton John, Ballin' Jack, Juicy Lucy
The whole band takes advantage of complimentary tickets from Reprise and attends an Elvis Presley concert at the Cow Palace on Friday prior to their own show, partly fuelled by Dalton's love of Presley. Ray is reportedly impressed by Presley's presence as a frontman and his command of the audience.
Set-list (13th): Medley 'Mr Wonderful' / 'Untitled Instrumental', 'Till The End Of The Day', 'Last Of The Steam Powered Trains', 'Big Sky', 'Brainwashed', 'Strangers', 'A Long Way From Home', 'Harry Rag', 'Act Nice And Gentle' (extract), 'Sunny Afternoon', 'Waterloo Sunset', 'Lola', 'Top Of The Pops'.
☆ Reports suggest that The Kinks benefit from a promoter's bidding

war between Bill Graham (Fillmore) and local contender Paul Baratta (Winterland). Baratta intends to book The Kinks for $10,000 but is outbid by Graham's $12,500 for three nights at his Fillmore West.
☆ On Sunday 15th Ray travels back to London. Avory later recalls that he and Dalton extravagantly choose to fly to New York City at their own expense because they prefer the night life there. Dave and Gosling presumably stay in San Francisco.

Monday 16th – Wednesday 18th

● **RECORDING** Morgan Studios *Willesden, north-west London*. Ray mixes the *Percy* soundtrack LP. After an objection from US label Reprise, he also has to redub a new lyric to 'Apeman' for the American single. Reprise takes offence at the line that appears to be "the air pollution is a-fuckin' up my eyes", so Ray redoes it to sound more like "the air pollution is a-foggin' up my eyes".
Ray will say later that he didn't particularly enjoy making *Percy*. "There were a lot of things I wanted to do but it was all working with film people [rather] than playing. … I had no time for music, really. They just wanted The Kinks because we had a record in the charts, and they thought it would help the film. … I learned never to do a film unless you have control." He tells another interviewer: "In a way *Percy* was really good training, having to write with a stopwatch, the same as *Arthur* was good training because I had to work with a script [and] *Piano Player* was good because I worked with theatre." Coming at the peak of a commercial comeback for the band, the *Percy* project ultimately distracts from pressing Kinks activities and causes some resentment from brother Dave.
☆ On the 18th 'Lola' is banned in Australia due to "controversial subject matter".

Thursday 19th

Paramount Theatre *Portland, OR* 8:30pm, with Albert King
For this unusual pairing with Texas blues-guitar legend Albert King, Ray travels to Portland from London while the rest of the band arrives from points south and east.

Friday 20th

Pacific National Exhibition Gardens Auditorium *Vancouver, BC, Canada* 6:30pm, with Stallion, Thumbrock

Saturday 21st

Men's Gymnasium, Pierce College *Woodland Hills, CA* 8:00pm, Young People's Night, with Eyes, The Realm; tickets $2.50
Set-list: 'Last Of The Steam Powered Trains', 'Brainwashed', 'See My Friends', 'You're Looking Fine', 'Strangers', 'Act Nice And Gentle' (extract), 'Waterloo Sunset', 'Big Sky', 'Arthur', 'Top Of The Pops', medley 'Milk Cow Blues' / 'One Night'.

Sunday 22nd

Mesa College field house *Grand Junction, CO* 8:00pm, with The Children
An international chart-topping band playing in Grand Junction is seen as a once-in-a-lifetime event by the local college paper. Playing to a sell-out crowd of almost 1,000, The Kinks appear casually on-stage in T-shirts and play the requisite new hit, 'Lola'. The concert also includes off-the-cuff versions of the English music-hall standard 'Lily Of Laguna' (aka 'She's My Lady Love') and the singalong favourite 'You Are My Sunshine'.

Monday 23rd

Memorial Auditorium, Southern Colorado State College *Pueblo, CO* 8:00pm, with Smith
Continuing into remote Colorado, the band performs with one-hit-wonder Smith, known for their cover of The Shirelles' (via The Beatles'

→ INDICATES EVENT AROUND THIS TIME BUT WITH NO FIRM DATE

Part One: Lola Versus Powerman And The Moneygoround album

A1 'Intro' (R. DAVIES).
A2 'The Contenders' (R. DAVIES).
A3 'Strangers' (D. DAVIES).
A4 'Denmark Street' (R. DAVIES).
A5 'Top Of The Pops' (R. DAVIES).
A6 'Lola' (R. DAVIES).
A7 'The Moneygoround' (R. DAVIES).
B1 'This Time Tomorrow' (R. DAVIES).
B2 'A Long Way From Home' (R. DAVIES).
B3 'Rats' (D. DAVIES).
B4 'Apeman' (R. DAVIES).
B5 'Powerman' (R. DAVIES).
B6 'Got To Be Free' (R. DAVIES).

UK release November 27th 1970 (Pye NSPL 18359).
US release December 2nd 1970 (Reprise RS 6423).
Musicians Ray Davies lead vocal except as noted, acoustic, electric and resonator guitar, harmonica (A2). Dave Davies lead vocal (A3, B3), electric guitar, acoustic guitar, backing vocal. John Dalton bass guitar. Mick Avory drums. John Gosling baby grand piano, electric piano, Hammond organ.
Recorded Morgan Studios Willesden, north-west London; A6, B5, B6: April-May 1970; A1-A5, B1-B4: August-September 1970; 16-track mixed to stereo.
Producer Ray Davies.
Engineer Mike Bobak.
Chart high UK none; US number 35.

'Baby It's You'. The college paper reports that the two bands charge $6,500 in total.

Tuesday 24th – Thursday 26th

With a few more days off, The Kinks head back to Los Angeles for fun. Ray reportedly sees the film *Fellini Satyricon* while the band members again head off to The Whisky A Go Go, this time to see Canned Heat (25th or 26th) as The Kinks hit their peak as rock'n'roll party boys.
☆ This is probably the time of the band's confrontation with Collins, later mentioned in Dave's book *Kink*. The manager is becoming tired of the band's apparently endless party antics. After a particularly debauched evening he assembles them for a lecture, only for Gosling to arrive late still with the Viking outfit on that he'd been wearing all night, and blowing an oversized Viking-type horn to announce his arrival. Everyone finds this very funny … except, of course, for the furious Collins.
☆ Ray, meanwhile, has missed the fun to stay at the hotel and do some interviews. He tells *Melody Maker*: "We've actually started work on another album which I feel may possibly come over as a big change. It will be an extension of the last. It's coming off well at the moment."

Friday 27th

A scheduled show today at the Auditorium Convention Hall in Minneapolis, MN, falls through, perhaps because a reluctant promoter does not want to risk a concert over the Thanksgiving holiday weekend when many college students are out of town.
'Apeman' / 'Rats' single released in the UK. *NME* says: "A very commercial disc with an irresistible hook chorus, which should do well even though The Kinks aren't here to promote it." *Record Mirror*: "As

ever, Ray has something to say. As ever The Kinks do a thoroughly professional, style-changing job." *Disc & Music Echo* can only call the song "controversial" and concludes that it's not a hit. Reviews almost unanimously point out that Ray has altered his moniker on the label to the posh Raymond Douglas Davies.
Part One: Lola Versus Powerman And The Moneygoround album released in the UK. *NME* raves: "Davies has always been one of the finest writers in contemporary rock, relating his personal observations to everyday subjects through the music of The Kinks. … A true original, his subject matter is pure Britannia." *Melody Maker* characterises the LP as Ray "taking a cheeky nibble at capitalism and the hurdy-gurdy pop playground…. The music's pure Kinks simplicity – but it works".

Saturday 28th

Clowes Memorial Hall, Butler University *Indianapolis, IN*
two shows, with Teegarden & Van Winkle; tickets $4.50
Smack dab in the Midwest, and into uncharted Kinks territory. The band hole up at a small motel near the venue and then pile into a station wagon, guitars in hand, to travel to the Hall. Both shows are very sparsely attended, indicating that The Kinks are not quite ready to stray from the stronghold cities they have cultivated in the Northeast, Chicago, and on the West Coast. The opening duo has a recent hit, 'God Love Rock & Roll'.

Sunday 29th

Likely but unconfirmed further Midwest concert date.

Monday 30th

Probable travel day to New York City. It is announced to the British press that the next Kinks LP will be the soundtrack to the film *Percy*.

December

Tuesday 1st – Thursday 3rd

Probably time off in New York City. A concert at Carnegie Hall concert is cancelled as the New York show is instead moved to the Fillmore East.
Part One: Lola Versus Powerman And The Moneygoround album released in the US (Wednesday 2nd). Reviews are generally positive, with *Stereo Review* getting to the core of the album's theme

Apeman single

A 'Apeman' (R. DAVIES).
B 'Rats' (R. DAVIES).

UK release November 27th 1970 (Pye 7N 45016).
US release December 16th 1970 (Reprise 0979).
Musicians Ray Davies lead vocal, guitar. Dave Davies lead vocal (B), electric guitar, acoustic guitar (A), backing vocal (A). John Dalton bass guitar. Mick Avory drums. John Gosling baby grand piano (A), electric piano (A), Hammond organ (B).
Recorded Morgan Studios Willesden, north-west London; August-September 1970; 16-track mixed to mono; US single with "fuckin'" lyric re-recorded to "foggin'" November 16th-18th 1970.
Chart high UK number 6; US number 45.

and tone. "A corrosively bitter tone is common to almost every song in this album, whether it be pop fame ... the shady business dealings of managers, or the mysterious Powerman. So much of the content is devoted to disillusionment with fame, money and success that listening to this album is like reading one of those Hollywood novels."

Thursday 3rd

American Shakespeare Theatre Stratford, CT with Dreams
Unconfirmed but almost certainly this date.

Friday 4th – Saturday 5th

The Fillmore East New York, NY 8:00 & 11:00pm with Love, Quatermass
The Kinks' only New York area appearance of this tour, and the trade magazines report that they sell out all four shows, with a $35,000 total gate. Frank Salvia in the *Polytechnic Reporter* says attendance was not quite this rosy, writing about one of the opening night's show's: "The Kinks carry a kind of atmosphere that tells you that even if there isn't going to be much musicianship or virtuosity on their instruments, it's going to be a fun set. ... You could tell by the style of the first few things that the Kinks were both parodying and taking a serious look at their early days.

"They followed with a series of acoustic numbers from their new album [that] could have been a bring-down after the first songs but some rhythm guitar work was incorporated with the acoustic work. The lyrics also caught and held your attention .... Then the lead electric was picked up again and the group broke into 'Lola' ... The Kinks deserved more than a two-thirds full hall and only an hour and 15 minutes playing time. They also deserve a chance to play a bill with some decent groups. It's very hard to bring a crowd back to life that has been drowned on bad music for over an hour."

Mike Hyland of *Schenectady Gazette* writes: "They opened their set with 'Till The End Of The Day' and the Fillmore audience that heckled Love off the stage was with The Kinks from the first note, right on through the second encore. [Songs included] 'Strangers', 'This Time Tomorrow', 'Apeman', 'Powerman', 'Lola', 'The Moneygoround' and 'The Contender' ... all selections on The Kinks' new album ... Some of their older songs that were fully appreciated by the audience were 'Victoria', 'Big Sky', 'You Really Got Me', 'Last Of The Steam Powered Trains', and 'Sunny Afternoon'."

Reviewers of the second night note that Ray again does an impromptu version of 'Lily Of Laguna' and begins his later-famous Johnny Cash and Merle Haggard routines. Future die-hard supporter Lisa Robinson in *Disc & Music Echo* is surprised at the complete transformation of The Kinks' live act, which she feels was dismal a year earlier at the Fillmore but is now a lot of fun, due she says to Ray's insanity and humour on stage and the able backing of the band.

Sunday 6th

London Arena London, ON, Canada

Monday 7th – Thursday 10th

Back in New York City the band has time off all week, though possibly they are also rehearsing for planned recording sessions back in London. A scheduled concert on the 8th at Patrick Gymnasium, University Of Vermont, Burlington, VT is almost certainly cancelled.

Friday 11th – Saturday 12th

Bowdoin College, Brunswick, ME was offered the Friday or Saturday for $20,000 but declined. Probably the two dates are filled with (unknown) college dates booked at short notice. The originally planned tour-ending show was on the 12th at Carnegie Hall, New York City. Pencilled in back in mid November, this was rescheduled for December 3rd and then cancelled entirely. (Partial day off in New York following, with a night-flight to London, arriving Monday morning.)

Tuesday 15th

❏ **TV** BBC Television Centre *west London*. BBC-1 **Top Of The Pops: Best Of 1970 Part 2** lip-synch 'Lola' broadcast December 26th.

→ ● **RECORDING** Morgan Studios *Willesden, north-west London*. Time is scheduled to work on tracks for the *Part Two...* LP immediately upon return from the US tour. It's unclear if this is done, but it's possible that at least some backing tracks are committed to tape, even if eventually scrapped.

Wednesday 16th

'Apeman' / 'Rats' single released in the US. Because it was necessary to dub in an adjusted lyric, in typical Kinks fashion the 45 hits the airwaves and stores now – just as the band wraps up their US tour. *Billboard* says: "Group made a powerhouse return to the Hot 100 via their Top 10 winner 'Lola'. Follow-up, an easy-beat calypso rocker with a clever lyric, has it to spiral them right back up there again. Currently rushing up the British chart." *Rolling Stone*, not often a singles reviewer, comes in with a slam from Paul Gambaccini: "'Lola' was brilliant and a smash; 'Apeman' is over-ambitious and a dud. The initial reaction to hearing 'Apeman' is outrage that Davies would issue the same single two straight times, but at about 20 seconds in it becomes apparent that at least lyrically something quite different is going on."

Sunday 20th – Tuesday 22nd

Ray travels from London to Los Angeles and back, expressly for the purpose of writing songs that he says he needs to finish by Christmas. He tells *Melody Maker* that The Kinks will then spend January recording the next LP. Around this time, with Ray away and busy writing, Dave, Avory and Dalton take up some of the necessary press duties.

Monday 28th

A press release announces Australian dates for January and UK dates for February and March 1971.

1971

The band continued to ride the good fortune of a revived career, and had a further international chart success with 'Apeman'. But these positive notes were balanced by continued business upheavals and a series of delayed, cancelled or prematurely ended tours during the first part of the year.

Plans from the end of 1970 were delayed to the start of this year because it was decided to devote time to the Percy film soundtrack – which, though containing some genuinely high moments, ultimately proved a commercial and artistic disaster. Percy was dealt a further blow when Reprise deemed it unsuitable for release in the US. During the year, The Kinks would terminate their relationship with both Reprise and their British label, Pye.

In a generally low-key summer, the band negotiated a new record deal and signed a new booking agent. News of The Kinks' defection to RCA came more or less as a surprise to most onlookers when it was announced in November. It coincided with a new album and tour, a new sound, and a revitalised image.

With the RCA deal consummated, the band's original management duo dropped out in quick succession – a momentous event that essentially completed the burial of the 1960s Kinks as the band became a self-managed operation. Other than three of the original four members, little else remained of the first-period Kinks. The house-cleaning completed, Ray pursued his musical visions largely unchallenged, and the year ended optimistically as a promising new LP and record deal held up hope for new directions and fresh successes.

January

Monday 4th
A press release announces The Kinks are to tour the UK in February and that Dave Davies is preparing to record solo tracks.

→ Interviewed by *Melody Maker*, Ray hints at his future working methods. "We went through a period last year of sod-all success," he says. "But I've played Arthur and I like it; I'm glad I did it. And I'm glad I made *Village Green Preservation Society*, because I'm going to … develop them somehow, into things I'm going to do in the future."
☆ Ray is offered an acting part as Aubrey Beardsley, the celebrated British illustrator, for six weeks in March in Edinburgh, Scotland. But he has to turn it down due to touring commitments with The Kinks.

Wednesday 6th
❏ **TV** BBC Television Centre *west London*. BBC-1 ***Top Of The Pops*** lip-synch 'Apeman' broadcast January 7th.

→ ● **RECORDING** Morgan Studios *Willesden, north-west London*. Ray continues mixing tracks for the soundtrack LP, *Percy*. Scheduled recording time for a Kinks project is cancelled.

Saturday 16th
Mayfair Suite, Belfry Hotel *Wishaw, Warwicks*
The band's traditional one-off warm-up show prior to heading off on tour, in this case to Australia. The performance to an audience of

around 1,000 marks the first time the band has used acoustic guitars in concert in the UK, largely ignored previously due to technical and practical difficulties, but worked out on the recent US dates. Ray sings 'Powerman', evidently under consideration as a single for the US.
Set-list: 'Till The End Of The Day', 'Brainwashed', 'You're Looking Fine', 'Waterloo Sunset', 'Big Sky', 'Lola', 'Strangers', 'Apeman', 'Sunny Afternoon', 'Powerman', 'Top Of The Pops', medley 'Milk Cow Blues' / 'You Are My Sunshine' / 'One Night', medley 'You Really Got Me' / 'All Day And All Of The Night'.

Tuesday 19th
The band is due to fly today to Australia for their tour. Reports suggest they arrive at Heathrow Airport to find that no flight tickets are waiting for them, due to the current postal strike. The band plus manager Collins wait until the flight takes off in case the tickets arrive at the last minute. More importantly, contracts and an A\$6,250 advance promised by Australian promoters have not been received, also a casualty of the strike. Two large festival dates, a concert in Perth, a TV date and a show in Hawaii are all scheduled. The tour is effectively cancelled as the band gives up and returns home from the airport. Dave later claims in *Kink* that the tour was delayed because a long flight was too much given his declining mental state. Relations between management and the band are also reportedly tense now, with the Wace/Collins team briefly walking out, only to return a few weeks later.
Dates on the cancelled tour were: January 24th *Odyssey Festival*, Wallacia, New South Wales; undated national TV appearance and concert in Perth, Western Australia; January 31st *Fairlight Festival*, Mittagong, New South Wales; February 1st travel Sydney to Honolulu, HI, where a concert was tentatively scheduled but never confirmed.

Thursday 28th

● **RECORDING** Morgan Studios *Willesden, north-west London*. It's not known what is recorded at this session, presumably booked at short notice after the cancellation of the Australian tour, though Ray is producing and the engineer is Mike Bobak.

Possibly work is done for a Kinks *Part Two* LP, but apparently only backing tracks, if anything, are done, and no masters will be finished. It is also possible that this is additional time for recording a Percy track, or a Dave solo track.

February

Friday 5th

Student Union, Luton College Of Technology *Luton, Beds*
8:00pm, with Junction

Monday 8th

● **RECORDING** Morgan Studios *Willesden, north-west London*. Possibly continuing sessions for planned Kinks *Part Two* album (only backing tracks would be done, with no masters ever completed), the Percy soundtrack LP, or some Dave solo tracks.

Wednesday 10th

❏ **TV** BBC Television Centre *west London*. BBC-1 *Top Of The Pops* live vocal over record backing 'Powerman', 'Got To Be Free' broadcast February 11th.

Thursday 11th

Debut of the *Percy* movie at the ABC Cinema, Shaftesbury Avenue, central London. The Kinks are scheduled to attend, but evidently don't, and the soundtrack LP scheduled for a simultaneous appearance is delayed while Ray completes additional mixing, readying it for vinyl release.

Friday 12th

University of Aberystwyth *Aberystwyth, Cardigans, Wales*
The start of a string of British concerts, something The Kinks have not done on this scale for three full years, since the spring 1968 package tour. The dates are mostly on weekends, providing a relatively easy pace for the band.

Saturday 13th

University of Cardiff *Cardiff, Wales*
No confirmation that this date is played.

Monday 15th

Dave is interviewed in London by Rosalind Russell for a feature in *Disc & Music Echo* and says he wants to perform his own material – not as a solo artist, but as part of a band. Of his writing style, he says: "Probably my songs are more personal than Ray's. Mine are basically folk songs about my impressions of other people and how they see me." He adds: "I'm more of an optimist than Ray is."

Saturday 20th

Gymnasium, Trent Polytechnic *Nottingham* 8:00pm
The Kinks appear on stage two-and-a-half hours late, apparently because they went to the wrong college. (Arsenal are playing Ipswich Town at home, which may be a more likely explanation.) But the crowd of 2,000 doesn't seem to care about this and some terrible sound problems, and the standard show of hits – including 'Till The End Of The Day', 'Sunny Afternoon', 'Waterloo Sunset' and 'Lola' – goes down a storm.

Tuesday 23rd

Bumpers *central London* with Danta
Another unusual booking for the time: a club date in central London. The band hasn't appeared in London proper since August 1967, and are very careful to pick a venue in which they will be comfortable.

Despite this, reportedly only about 150 people show up to this week-night gig. Chris Charlesworth, writing for *Melody Maker*, loves the show, despite the unbalanced sound, and reports snatches of 'You Are My Sunshine', 'A Pub With No Beer' and 'I Left My Heart In San Francisco', as well as the usual hits and a few new album tracks. To cap it off, drummers Avory and The Who's Keith Moon act as judges in a go-go dance contest.

Wednesday 24th

Top Rank Suite *Leicester* 8:00pm-1:00am, with The Octopus; admission £1
Unlike most dates on this tour, this is not at or sponsored by a university, but instead is in one of the old-guard ballrooms from the early touring days.

Friday 26th

Great Hall, University of Lancaster *Lancaster* 8:00pm-3:00am, part of *Rag Ball '71*, with Quintessence, Shaking Stevens & The Sunsets, Brother Love's Travelling Band

Sunday 28th

Colston Hall *Bristol* 7:30pm, with Terry Reid
Another venue from the old days finds The Kinks paired with Terry Reid, the singer originally approached to front Led Zeppelin.

March

Monday 1st

Top Rank Ballroom *Birmingham* with Roger Ruskin Spear's Kinetic Wardrobe; sponsored by the University of Birmingham
Set-list: 'Till The End Of The Day', 'Brainwashed', 'You're Looking Fine', 'Big Sky', 'Sunny Afternoon', 'Powerman', 'Apeman', 'Top Of The Pops', 'A Pub With No Beer', 'Lola', medley 'Milk Cow Blues' / 'One Night' / 'You Are My Sunshine' / 'See My Friends' / 'Powerman', medley 'You Really Got Me' / 'All Day And All Of The Night'.
☆ A press release announces a German tour, and the Percy LP due for release March 26th.

Friday 5th

University of Exeter *Exeter*

Saturday 6th

Loughborough University of Technology *Loughborough, Leics* 8:30pm
Reportedly booked for a 50-minute performance, the band is kept on stage by the audience for close to two hours.

Monday 8th

Student Union, University of Sheffield *Sheffield*
☆ A press release announces US and German tours, *Arthur* for the London West End stage in the autumn, and says Ray has been ordered by his doctor to take a month off, but will continue with commitments as planned.

Tuesday 9th

Reprise receives a rough mix of 'Powerman', likely intended as a new single to promote for the upcoming US tour. But the song is never assigned a catalogue number, nor a B-side, indicating that the idea never gets far. The track will languish in the Warner/Reprise vaults until issued in 1998 as a bonus track on the CD reissue of the *Part One: Lola Versus Powerman* album.

Friday 12th
Chelsea Village *Bournemouth*
☆ Scheduled release of *Percy* LP delayed to April 2nd, probably due to more last-minute mixing.

Saturday 13th
Big Apple/Regent Theatre *Brighton* 7:30pm, part of annual *Rag Ball*, with Patto, Spyrogyra, Randy Grope; sponsored by University of Brighton
Melody Maker singles out Ray's great ability to get an audience response. 'You Are My Sunshine' is again presented as a camp singalong highlight. But a concertgoer writing to *NME* feels The Kinks were hampered by a couldn't-care-less attitude and says the evening was stolen by Patto.

Monday 15th – Sunday 21st
Ray is reported ill in the British pop press. Later in *Kink*, however, Dave says the upcoming West German/Austrian tour is cancelled because of his own continuing and overwhelming depression, especially his paranoia at touring and playing before audiences. Original scheduled dates were: March 17th Stadthalle, Offenbach, West Germany; 18th Konzerhaus, Vienna, Austria; 19th unknown venue, Munich, West Germany, 20th unknown venue, Heilbronn, West Germany; 21st Musikhalle, Hamburg, West Germany. The tour is tentatively rescheduled for early May, but that also fails to happen.

Monday 22nd
A press release says Ray will record a solo LP, and that the new 'God's Children' will appear with 'Lola' on March 26th on a maxi single (EP).

➪ **TOUR STARTS** *Tour Of US* (Mar 25th – Apr 7th). **Line-up**: Ray Davies (lead vocal, guitar), Dave Davies (guitar, vocal), Mick Avory (drums), John Dalton (bass guitar), John Gosling (keyboard). New songs in the repertoire: 'Lola', 'Apeman', 'Get Back In Line', 'Powerman', and (rarely) 'God's Children'. Its their fifth US tour in the last 18 months, ostensibly planned to maintain the momentum of their latest chart-single success, but also with the intention of recording a new single in the States. This short string of dates seems to be littered with more tales of outrageous shows and bizarre onstage antics than almost any other tour by The Kinks.

Thursday 25th
Band members travel to New York City; Ray arrives the following day. A concert scheduled for the Music Hall, Boston, MA, has been cancelled before the tour begins.

Friday 26th
Gymnasium/Allard Field House, State University of New York Agricultural & Technical College at Farmingdale *Farmingdale, NY* 8:00pm, with Trapeze
An obscure, low-key show to start the tour. Support act Trapeze is a heavy rock trio in the style of Grand Funk Railroad, the first signing to The Moody Blues' own Threshold Records.
Percy soundtrack album released in the UK. *NME* gives it a big thumbs up, calling it "forceful and tuneful at the same time .... Altogether a most varied and interesting composing package from Ray, done well by The Kinks." *Sounds* too approves: "This is a far better soundtrack than most, as you would expect from the talented Davies pen." But *Melody Maker*'s reviewer pans it in no uncertain terms. As an LP it "hangs, I'm afraid, limp, rather lank, cold – and lacking in guts"

although "Davies has undoubtedly been successful with the score – if you see the film with it – but it's a shame the album has to be released. It fails to rise to the occasion".
☆ Release of the 'God's Children' maxi-single, due today, is rescheduled to April 2nd.

Percy soundtrack album

A1 'God's Children' (R. DAVIES).
A2 'Lola' (instrumental) (R. DAVIES).
A3 'The Way Love Used To Be' (R. DAVIES).
A4 'Completely' (R. DAVIES).
A5 'Running Round Town' (R. DAVIES).
A6 'Moments' (R. DAVIES).
B1 'Animals In The Zoo' (R. DAVIES).
B2 'Just Friends' (R. DAVIES).
B3 'Whip Lady' (R. DAVIES).
B4 'Dreams' (R. DAVIES).
B5 'Helga' (R. DAVIES).
B6 'Willesden Green' (R. DAVIES).
B7 'God's Children (End)' (R. DAVIES).

UK release March 26th 1971 (Pye NSPL 18365).
Musicians Ray Davies lead vocals (A1, A3, A6, B1, B2, B4), acoustic guitar, electric guitar, harmonica (A4, A5). Dave Davies electric guitar, acoustic guitar, backing vocal (A1, B1, B6). John Dalton lead vocal (B6), bass guitar. Mick Avory drums. John Gosling baby grand piano, Hammond organ, electric piano. Stanley Myers string arrangements. Mike Cotton Sound (possibly) horns (A2).
Recorded Morgan Studios *Willesden, north-west London*; October 1970-January 1971; 16-track mixed to 3-track for film and to stereo for LP.
Producer Ray Davies.
Engineer Mike Bobak.
Chart high UK none.

Saturday 27th
Colden Center Auditorium, Queens College of City University of New York *Flushing, NY* 8:00pm, with Trapeze
Reviewers like Ray's showmanship and his ability to get the audience to sing along, though one finds him almost too spontaneous, to the point that the band can't follow him and verge on the sloppy. The performance is highlighted by the appearance of a Queens College student, one Ben Rosenblatt, who approached Ray before the show and now sits in on piano with the band for unique performances of 'Mister Pleasant' and 'Autumn Almanac', two songs almost certainly never performed before in concert.

Sunday 28th
George C. Marshall High School Gymnasium *Falls Church, VA* 6:30 & 9:30pm, with Rentha; tickets $5.50
Sponsored by local singing group The Marshall Madrigals to help raise money for their own concert tour of Europe. One account suggests the band has a case of beer confiscated, due to a no-alcohol policy in the building. Later, irritated by a poor response from the Falls Church audience, Ray changes the chorus of 'Lola' to: "S-H-I-T spells shit, and that's what this is."

Monday 29th

Ray tells *Crawdaddy!* that the Part Two album has been started, but is being put off for a different LP he really wants to do and which he describes as "a social thing", perhaps referring to an early germination of the idea for *Muswell Hillbillies*.

Tuesday 30th

Philharmonic Hall, Lincoln Center for the Performing Arts
New York, NY 8:00pm, with Trapeze; promoted by Ron Delsner
A legendary Kinks performance. It is among the first rock concerts allowed to be staged at the elegant, prestigious Philharmonic Hall (soon renamed Avery Fisher Hall). Of the host of reviewers attending, several note Ray as somewhat disoriented on stage much of the night, and most feel the performance is very sloppy, even drunken, but entertaining, with Ray into his period of high-camp. Two incidents are highlighted. First, Ray stumbles backwards during 'Apeman' and Dave calmly steps out of his way, allowing Ray to fall into a stack of amps. Ray continues singing, despite the fall. Second, at the end of the set, some of the audience rush the stage for the band's encore of 'Top Of The Pops', after which the band is forced to leave. For the fans it's a show not soon forgotten; for The Kinks it helps strengthen the relationship with their audience.

Ray says later, "I think it all started for me the day we did the Philharmonic Hall … that's when I really started to go for the audience. And I, mmm… let's say had an accident and fell into an amplifier and got knocked out. The audience took over for me. They came up and sang the songs because I couldn't sing. That's when I realised that the audience really likes to get involved; they became a part of the show as much as us. It's worked from then on."

Set-list: 'Give My Love To Rose', 'Till The End Of The Day', 'Brainwashed', 'You're Looking Fine', 'Apeman', 'Waterloo Sunset', 'Sunny Afternoon', 'Get Back In The Line', 'Pub With No Beer', 'Lola', 'Louise', 'Big Sky' 'Milk Cow Blues', 'See My Friends', 'Powerman', 'One Night With You', 'You Are My Sunshine', medley 'You Really Got Me' / 'All Day And All Of The Night', 'Top Of The Pops'.
☆ Ray writes the song 'Life is So Complicated', originally called 'Suicidal', soon after the show.

Wednesday 31st

Community Theatre *North Attleboro, MA* 7:30 & 10:00pm, with Jackie Lomax
A show equally legendary as the night before in New York, despite its relatively obscure location and hardly any reviewers being present. The first show, before a meagre crowd of 300-500 people in a half-full movie theatre, goes without a hitch as the band plays ten songs, including 'Till The End Of The Day', 'You're Looking Fine', 'Apeman', 'Sunny Afternoon', 'Lola', and a medley of 'You Really Got Me' and 'All Day And All Of The Night'.

After finishing the first show and waiting through a further set by Liverpool rocker Jackie Lomax, the band evidently has enough time to slip back to their motel and indulge in more drinking. The second show is apparently a drunken one, equally on a par with the much publicised Philharmonic Hall show yesterday. The band opens the second house as a quartet without Ray, convincing Dalton to sing a tongue-in-cheek blues pastiche he'd written called 'Shoe Without A Lace'. Ray, dressed in lavender suit and hot-pink bow tie, is then mockingly coaxed onto the stage to continue the show. As the set progresses, Dave argues with Ray, who has started to sing a song they have already done. Only when someone from the audience shouts to Ray to "quit fucking around" does the show continue more smoothly.

Ray later mentions from the stage that the band plans on recording a new album in two weeks and that they'll play two songs from it now: Johnny Cash's 'Give My Love To Rose' and another vaguely recalled as something like 'Bozo's Song', more likely an off-the-cuff creation by

Ray. He later explains, "I make up little songs on stage as we go along. The others get around it. I wrote a very good song in Massachusetts. It was the only time I ever performed it, but I've forgotten it."

As happened last night, the show ends with about 50 members of the audience on stage singing along to 'Lola' and 'Louie Louie'. Ray reportedly falls into the drum kit at the end of the show. (Day following is time off or possibly an unknown show.)

April

Friday 2nd – Saturday 3rd

Eastown Theater *Detroit, MI* 8:00pm, with Mylon, Zephyr
A rare performance is included of the new single, 'God's Children', issued today in the UK. Although Dave rocks out on his featured numbers ('Milk Cow Blues' / 'One Night', and 'You're Looking Fine'), a reviewer notes him as subdued, almost angry. Ray returns for an acoustic-guitar encore of 'Days' accompanied only by Gosling on piano.
'God's Children' / **'The Way Love Used to Be'** / **'Moments'** / **'Dreams'** maxi-single (EP) released Friday 2nd as *The Kinks (from the soundtrack of the film Percy)* in the UK. Review copies include a signed note from Ray: "Not everyone can afford LPs and [because so many people] have enjoyed seeing the film *Percy* we have asked Pye to put out four of our favourite tracks from the album in somewhat less expensive form. Indeed I am hoping the next Kinks single as such will be recorded in Los Angeles during our early April tour of America." *NME* calls the title track "a bouncy singalong number with a jangling backing and happy sound", while *Sounds* reckons it's "miles better than the teeth-gritting 'Apeman'".
☆ Ray is interviewed by Gene Davidson and Bill Small for the *Kinks Society Newsletter* and says he is still working on a book about the band's early days. He also talks about putting out a solo LP called the *Ray Davies Songbook*.

Sunday 4th – Tuesday 6th

The band travels to Los Angeles on Sunday and takes three days off, and Ray returns to London. According to his later account in *Kink*, Dave sinks into despair in Los Angeles, downing wine and the hallucinogenic drug mescaline.

Wednesday 7th

Santa Monica Civic Auditorium *Santa Monica, CA* 8:00pm, with Fanny, Jerry Riopelle
Set-list: 'Till The End Of The Day', 'Brainwashed', 'All Right, OK, You

---

The Kinks (from the soundtrack of the film Percy) maxi-single (EP)

A1 'God's Children' (R. DAVIES).
A2 'The Way Love Used To Be' (R. DAVIES).
B1 'Moments' (R. DAVIES).
B2 'Dreams' (R. DAVIES).

UK release April 2nd 1971 (Pye 7NX 8001).
US release (A1/A2 as A/B) July 1971 (Reprise 1017).
Musicians and recording details as Percy LP (see March 26th).
Chart high UK none; US none.

→ INDICATES EVENT AROUND THIS TIME BUT WITH NO FIRM DATE

The early-1970s Kinks look: (L-R) Ray Davies, Dave Davies, John Dalton, John Gosling, Mick Avory.

'Win' (extract), 'Apeman', 'Strangers', 'Arthur', 'Get Back In Line', 'Banana Boat Song', 'Harry Rag' (extract), 'Sunny Afternoon', 'Louise', 'Big Sky', 'Lola', 'Top Of The Pops', 'You Are My Sunshine', medley 'You Really Got Me' / 'All Day And All Of The Night', 'Days', 'Victoria', 'You Are My Sunshine'.

Thursday 8th – Saturday 10th

On Thursday, Dave is hospitalised in Los Angeles for massive depression, a fact only revealed years later in *Kink*. The following day a press release announces cancellation of all remaining dates and planned recording sessions because Dave is "too ill".

Cancelled dates: April 9th Convention Hall, Community Concourse, San Diego, CA; 10th Pauley Pavilion, University Of California, Los Angeles, CA; 16th Capital High School gymnasium, Boise, ID; 17th Omaha Civic Auditorium Music Hall, Omaha, NE; 25th Memorial Coliseum, Dallas, TX.

Cancelled recording sessions: April 11th-15th at Warner Brothers Recording Studios, Burbank, CA, for *Part Two* tracks and new single.

On Saturday 10th, the band travels from Los Angeles to London, though Ray remains in Hollywood in order to write and to take care of Kinks business.

Sunday 11th – Thursday 15th

Ray writes new material. Possibly now, or perhaps later in the summer, he has a meeting with Jay Lasker at ABC Records to discuss the possibility of signing The Kinks to that label. The tour just ended will be the last booked by Bert Kammerman at CMA (Creative Management Agency) in New York City, and probably around now The Kinks sign with the San Francisco-based Millard Agency, co-owned by Herb Spar and Joe Bailey. Millard will last only another year, closing its doors on May 8th 1972, at which time Spar will move to the International Famous Agency and bring a number of his loyal clients, including The Kinks.

Friday 16th

Ray travels back to London from Los Angeles, in time for tomorrow's match at Highbury between Arsenal and Newcastle. The band has time off around now, with Ray probably writing new material.

Wednesday 28th

Percy movie debuts in New York City.

May

Monday 3rd

Reprise Records in the US receives tapes for the 'God's Children' single.

Saturday 8th

Ray and Dave attend Arsenal's defeat of Liverpool at Wembley Stadium marking Arsenal's fourth FA Cup win. A massive victory celebration is held the following day as the team parades from Highbury Stadium to Islington Town Hall, displaying the spoils of their "double": the FA (Football Association) Cup as well as their eighth Football League Championship trophy.

➔ Dave is working on solo material, possibly writing 'You Don't Know My Name', eventually to be included on 1972's *Everyone's In Showbiz* LP. Ray is preparing some of the old songs he wrote for BBC TV's *At The Eleventh Hour* and *Where Was Spring* in 1968 and '69 for a planned solo LP, to be titled either *Songs I Sang For Auntie* or *The Ray Davies Songbook*. But the scheduled recording is never begun.

Friday 21st

Top Rank Suite *Swansea, Wales* 8:00pm-1:00am, with Status Quo, Nine-Thirty Fly

A one-off warm-up date for the upcoming Australian tour.

✫ Ray is interviewed at length by Royston Eldridge for *Sounds*. On the topic of pending recording projects, he mentions the planned collection of old BBC songs and says he would prefer to have an outside producer and arrangements in advance.

Tuesday 25th

Reprise Records logs in tapes for the *Percy* LP, but the US company is evidently not satisfied with them and does not want to release the soundtrack album. Reprise goes so far as to request the multitrack tapes, possibly with the intention of remixing the songs themselves, but this never happens. Perhaps the film's utter failure in America persuades them that strong sales are unlikely. The Kinks' relationship with Reprise further sours now, and will never quite recover.

➪ **TOUR STARTS** *Tour Of Australia* (May 29th – June 6th). **Line-up**: Ray Davies (lead vocal, guitar), Dave Davies (guitar, vocal), Mick Avory (drums), John Dalton (bass guitar), John Gosling (keyboard). Booking agent: John Keefe, David Trew & Paul Dainty (Friendly 3AK). The original plan is to ship the band's own equipment and sound system to Australia, but this is scrapped at the last minute and a different set of rented gear is used for every gig, with the result that the tour is marred by equipment failure. Badfinger are originally to support on all dates but they cancel out of the tour. A date in Auckland, New Zealand is mentioned but never finalised. The entire tour is reportedly sold out. It is notably manager Wace goes with the band this time rather than Collins who normally accompanies them, but who no doubt had enough of the last US debacle. They travel from London on Wednesday 26th, losing a day with the time difference, and arrive in Sydney on Friday 28th.

Saturday 29th

Festival Hall *Brisbane, Queensland, Australia* 8:30pm, with Ted Mulry & Hot Cottage

The Kinks are involved in a disturbance during the flight from Sydney to Brisbane, picked up by Australian tabloid newspaper *The Truth* under the blazing headline "Pop Star Attacks Air Hostess". The piece suggests that the band is quite drunk on the flight, creating a scene which culminates in Gosling hurling an empty beer-can that hits a hostess in the shoulder. No further action is taken, other than airline staff asking the band to cool down. Gosling continues the hi-jinks upon landing, insisting on riding a luggage trolley across the tarmac until he is ordered off by security.

Sunday 30th

Ray and Dave catch a flight to Adelaide to visit their sister Rose and her family, who still reside in Elizabeth, just outside the city. The Kinks will return here five days later for their scheduled performance.

Monday 31st

Broadmeadow Basketball Stadium *Newcastle, New South Wales, Australia*

Three speaker cabinets blow up during the show. Ray leaves the stage in disgust.

June

Tuesday 1st

Canberra Civic Centre Theatre *Canberra, Australian*

➔ INDICATES EVENT AROUND THIS TIME BUT WITH NO FIRM DATE

Capital Territory, Australia 6:30 & 9:00pm, with Ted Mulry & Hot Cottage, Canyon

An amplifier blows up minutes into the show and Ray has to be convinced to continue after a 15-minute break. One reviewer finds the performance very strong and professional, despite no singalong to 'Lola' – which is probably because the song has been banned on Australian radio.

☆ Dave tells a gullible reporter that last year they transferred Dalton from another group for two bottles of Scotch, having shot Pete Quaife, his predecessor.

Thursday 3rd

Festival Hall *West Melbourne, Victoria, Australia* 8:15pm, with The Chain, Ted Mulry & Hot Cottage

Friday 4th

Apollo Stadium *Adelaide, South Australia, Australia* with Spectrum, Daddy Cool

The reviewer for the *Adelaide Advertiser* says that local Australian favourites Daddy Cool clearly upstage the feature attraction before a crowd of 4,700 and that The Kinks' show "folded on a raspy sour note". The Davies brothers again visit sister Rose. Ray Davies recounts in *X-Ray* that this is the last time he sees Rose's husband Arthur, acknowledged inspiration for the main character of The Kinks' album of the same name.

Saturday 5th

Beatty Park Aquatic Centre *Perth, Western Australia, Australia* 8:00pm, with Ted Mulry & Hot Cottage, The Graduate, SSARB

Sunday 6th

Moore Park, Sydney Showgrounds *Sydney, New South Wales, Australia* 2:30-5:30pm, Open Air Festival, with Daddy Cool, Ted Mulry & Hot Cottage, Flake

At the start of Australia's winter season it's a gamble to hold an outdoor event, and this turns out to be a cold, overcast day with icy winds and a constant threat of rain. Nonetheless an estimated 8,000 fans attend. Kinks fans leave disappointed, however, as police insist the show ends at 5:10pm, with The Kinks forced to cut their performance in half from the planned 80 minutes. The *Sydney Morning Herald* notes that, again, Daddy Cool easily wins over the Moore Park crowd with their 50s rock'n'roll act.

Monday 7th

The Kinks decide not to appear for the taping today and tomorrow of a TV special for ABC Television, despite the threat of being sued by the TV company, as Dave returns immediately to London following the frustrating final concert in Sydney. The rest of the band follows soon after, and by Wednesday 9th they're all back in London. They consider the tour a disaster.

➔ Back in London around this time, Ray shoots an experimental film, *The Colossal Shirt*.

☆ Ray spends some time around now at the Archway Tavern pub in north London watching local Irish bands play what he later describes as "bad country & western music".

☆ Work begins in earnest around now on what will become the next Kinks album, and consequently the scheduled recording of the proposed Ray solo LP – *Songs I Sang For Auntie* or *The Ray Davies Songbook* – is never even begun.

☆ A press release at the end of the month notes plans for a UK concert tour in October with a "new concept show", and that a new single is set for mid-summer release.

July

Wednesday 7th

'God's Children' / 'The Way Love Used To Be' single released in the US. *Billboard* writes: "Group follows the Apeman with a potent lyric ballad set to a rock beat featured in the film *Percy*. Strong entry for Top 40, FM and the Hot 100." But the record is released too late for any support from The Kinks and no promotion ensues from Reprise, whose active relationship with The Kinks is rapidly coming to an end.

➔ Early in the month the band may be rehearsing new material for upcoming recording sessions.

☆ Around the middle of the month Ray and manager Wace meet various record company representatives in New York City and Los Angeles. Serious negotiations proceed with Clive Davis at Columbia Records in New York and, notably, with RCA Records in LA where they meet RCA president Rocco Laginestra, A&R head Mike Everett, and legal representative Steve Fisher.

☆ The Kinks record up to 20 demos of songs in London for consideration for their new album, including all the songs eventually on the *Muswell Hillbillies* LP, plus unreleased items including one called 'Rosie Rook'.

August

During the fortnight from Sunday the 1st the band takes its annual holiday. Dave goes to Spain and grows a beard, further distancing himself from the band's 1960s pop image. He decides to keep it upon his return. At some point this month Ray writes the title song 'Nobody's Fool' for the British LWT TV comedy-drama series *Budgie*, starring Adam Faith, which debuts later this year.

Meanwhile, Ray and Wace continue negotiations and finalise an agreement for a new recording contract with RCA. It seems to be a five-year, seven-album deal, and calls for submission of completed masters to RCA who have the rights to release. A strict schedule is written into the contract, plus stipulations that all recordings be of suitable technical quality. There's also a "morals" clause, presumably to prevent the band from serving up any more risqué material.

RCA is a major US company, guaranteeing worldwide distribution of Kinks' product and, hopefully, a tie-in with their important film division – in addition to a healthy dollar advance. After the deal is signed formally on November 12th, the band's British record company, Pye, files a suit against The Kinks for failure to supply the agreed minimum product according to the terms of their contract.

The RCA deal will run to 1976, and the company certainly will offer unparalleled distribution to many countries. But they will not be willing to finance Ray's ambitious plans for Kinks LPs like *Muswell Hillbillies* and *Everybody's In Show-Biz*, both of which Ray will intend as films with accompanying soundtrack LPs. Nor will they underwrite the theatrical productions that accompany the *Preservation (Acts 1&2)*, *Soap Opera*, and *Schoolboys In Disgrace* LPs.

RCA will retain rights to The Kinks catalogue until 1986, when those rights will revert to The Kinks – who can then release the material themselves or lease it to another record company.

On the 20th the band plays at the first day of the *Ruis-Rockfestivaal* in Runsala-parken Turku, Finland. Attendance over the entire three-day event exceeds 100,000, making it the largest festival in Europe this year. This is The Kinks' only summer appearance.

Later in the month the band is back at Morgan Studios in north-west London recording tracks for the forthcoming *Muswell Hillbillies* LP.

Avory has his tonsils removed at Kingston Hospital, south-west London at the end of the month, delaying some work.

September

More work takes place at Morgan Studios with overdub sessions for *Muswell Hillbillies*. A photo session around now at the Archway Tavern pub in Archway, north London provides the cover of that album.

October

→ ● **RECORDING** Morgan Studios *Willesden, north-west London*. Work continues on *Muswell Hillbillies* tracks.
☆ A tentatively scheduled tour of the US is delayed until November

Thursday 7th
● **RECORDING** Audio International Recording Studios *central London*. Ray and Kevin Daly produce 'Girl With Guitar' by Gothic Horizon, a duo of Andy Desmond (who will later record for The Kinks' own label, Konk) and Richard Garrett. Gosling plays keyboards and arranges strings and brass, and sessions will continue with Kevin Daly producing. An entire LP, *Tomorrow's Another Day*, is eventually recorded (with no further involvement from Ray) and released on Argo, a Decca subsidiary.

Saturday 16th
● **RECORDING** Morgan Studios *Willesden, north-west London*. Session for two ultimately unused tracks, '**Mountain Woman**' and '**Kentucky Moon**'. Both are later exhumed and remixed in February 1998 as bonus cuts for that year's CD reissue of *Muswell Hillbillies*.

Monday 18th
A press release says the US tour will start on November 19th and that the new LP is out "soon".

Friday 22nd
● **RECORDING** Morgan Studios *Willesden, north-west London*. Horn overdubs for *Muswell Hillbillies* LP.

November

→ ● **RECORDING** Morgan Studios *Willesden, north-west London*. Ray does final mixing for *Muswell Hillbillies*.
☆ The band rehearses new material: 'Acute Schizophrenia Paranoia Blues', 'Skin And Bones', 'Complicated Life', 'Shangri-La', 'Muswell Hillbilly'.

Friday 12th
Mayfair Suite, Belfry Hotel *Wishaw, Warwicks*
☆ Lawyers for RCA fly to London for the formal signing of the contract between Kinks Productions Ltd and RCA Records. Presumably Ray takes this opportunity to deliver the master tapes of the new album.
   Later, the band appears at this favourite venue just outside Birmingham as a warm-up for the upcoming US tour.

Tuesday 16th
With the RCA deal signed and sealed, the long-serving Grenville Collins resigns as a director of Kinks Productions Ltd and effectively as co-manager of the band, leaving Robert Wace as sole manager – though he too will go in a matter of weeks.

⇨ **TOUR STARTS** *Tour Of Northeast US* (Nov 19th – Dec 5th).
Line-up: Ray Davies (lead vocal, guitar), Dave Davies (guitar, vocal), Mick Avory (drums), John Dalton (bass guitar), John Gosling (keyboard). Booking agent is Herb Spar at Millard Agency. The band minus Ray travels from London to New York City on Wednesday 17th.

Thursday 18th
An elaborate press party is thrown by RCA at exclusive New York City restaurant Etoile to celebrate their signing of The Kinks. The new record company spares no expense, flying in journalists and providing accommodation at the prestigious Plaza Hotel to spotlight the label's most important signing of the year. Celebrity guests include Andy Warhol, The Cockettes theatrical troupe, Keith Moon and John Entwistle of The Who (in town to start their own US tour), and members of Ten Years After, The Guess Who, Lou Reed, Delaney & Bonnie, and Alice Cooper. Ray arrives at the party at the last minute, where a crowd of up to 750 people has gathered. The wild event lasts six hours, with liquor flowing freely. New York radio has been playing an advance copy of the new Kinks LP today, and everyone's hopes are high that this is the start of a mutually beneficial relationship.

Friday 19th
Alumni Field House, Wesleyan University *Middletown, CT*
9:00pm, with Manhattan Transfer, Fancy
The Kinks start their brief tour to promote *Muswell Hillbillies* with today's and tomorrow's warm-up dates at colleges in nearby Connecticut, in preparation for the prestigious debut at New York City's renowned Carnegie Hall on Sunday.

Saturday 20th
Gymnasium, University of Hartford *West Hartford, CT*
8:00pm, with The Glass Harp

Sunday 21st
Carnegie Hall *New York, NY* 7:30pm, with The Glass Harp; promoted by Ron Delsner
A triumphant return to the New York stage following last spring's much publicised concert at the Philharmonic. Around 3,000 fans attend tonight's show. Only one song from the new *Muswell Hillbillies* LP is featured, but Dave does tackle 'Strangers', and 'Shangri-La' reappears in the set. During the pre-encore closer as they play their first two hits, Dave drops to his knees during his solo – just as he used to do during the scream-fest days of the 1960s. The band returns for three encores, all of non-original material, ranging from 'You Are My Sunshine' to 'Louie Louie'. *Record World*'s reviewer writes: "The Kinks proved themselves once again to be the most enduring and entertaining of pop stars. Hits and memories – then, now, and in between – provided high spots in a set marred only by an inadequate sound system." (Time off in New York City follows to the 25th.)
Set-list: 'Top Of The Pops', 'Brainwashed', 'Waterloo Sunset', 'Victoria', 'Till The End Of The Day', 'Lola', 'Strangers', 'Apeman', 'Get Back In The Line', 'A Well Respected Man', 'Acute Schizophrenia Paranoia Blues', 'Big Sky', 'Shangri-La', medley 'You Really Got Me' / 'All Day And All Of The Night', 'Milk Cow Blues', 'One Night With You', 'You Are My Sunshine', 'Louie Louie'.

Wednesday 24th
Muswell Hillbillies album released in the US. American reviewers are

mixed in their reaction, many caught off guard by the change in the band's image and sound and the record's deliberate old-timey production. Mike Saunders, an unabashed Kinks fan, is critical in his *Rolling Stone* review of buried vocals and country-music influences, in the end awarding mixed marks. Michelle Hush in *Rock* is similarly unsure: "Although even when it falters it's still a lot of fun, the Davies brothers can do better than [this], as they illustrate on the best songs on the album. But let's not be too critical, it really is very good."

The always-opinioned Dave Marsh in *Creem* dislikes it. "It's not just poor, it's horrible ... C'mon Ray, how about another 'Lola'?" But Greg Mitchell in *Crawdaddy!* raves, calling it "another instant classic", Jon Tiven in *Phonograph Record Magazine* rates it as "superb", and Robert Palmer in the prestigious *New York Times* dubs it "The Kinks' newest masterpiece".

RCA picks up on the everyman angle and in its publicity campaign uses the slogan "The return of the working class hero" spread across the album's these-are-just-regular-guys-in-a-bar cover shot. Full page ads in *Rolling Stone* and the industry trades reveal a strong commitment to the album, which Boston's *Fusion* magazine goes so far as to vote Album Of The Year, an honour which will be worked into subsequent ads.

Friday 26th
The Spectrum *Philadelphia, PA* 8:00pm, with Edgar Winter's White Trash, Good God
Muswell Hillbillies album released in the UK. British reviewers are more consistent than those in the US, with *NME* saying it's easily worth the year's wait. *Melody Maker* headlines: "Damn Clever These Kinks,"

Muswell Hillbillies album

A1 '20th Century Man' (R. DAVIES).
A2 'Acute Schizophrenia Paranoia Blues' (R. DAVIES).
A3 'Holiday' (R. DAVIES).
A4 'Skin And Bone' (R. DAVIES).
A5 'Alcohol' (R. DAVIES).
A6 'Complicated Life' (R. DAVIES).
B1 'Here Come The People In Grey' (R. DAVIES).
B2 'Have A Cuppa Tea' (R. DAVIES).
B3 'Holloway Jail' (R. DAVIES).
B4 'Oklahoma USA' (R. DAVIES).
B5 'Uncle Son' (R. DAVIES).
B6 'Muswell Hillbilly' (R. DAVIES).

US release November 24th 1971 (RCA Victor LSP-4644).
UK release November 26th 1971 (RCA Victor SF 8243).
Musicians Ray Davies lead vocal, acoustic guitar, 12-string acoustic guitar, electric guitar, resonator guitar. Dave Davies electric guitar, 12-string acoustic guitar, resonator guitar, accompanying lead or backing vocal, bass guitar (B4). John Dalton bass guitar except as noted. Mick Avory drums. John Gosling baby grand piano, Hammond organ, squeeze box, harmonium (pump organ). Mike Cotton trumpet (A2, A5). John Beecham tuba (A2, A5). Alan Holmes clarinet (A2, A5). Ken Jones harmonica (B1). Vicki Brown vocal (A4, B3).
Recorded Morgan Studios *Willesden, north-west London*; August-October 1971; 16-track mixed to stereo.
Producer Raymond Douglas Davies.
Engineers Mike Bobak and Roger Quested.
Chart high US number 100; UK none.

---

and *Sounds* writes, "The album is a joy, worth a good ten of so many of your heavies." But even with RCA's album-oriented marketing force in place, the LP makes no dent in the British charts, especially as no single is released from the album.

Saturday 27th
Ritz Theater *Port Richmond, Staten Island, NY* 8:00 & 11:00pm, with Yes
Annoyed by the length of Yes's extended opening set, Ray allegedly pulls the plug on them in order to keep the show moving.

Sunday 28th
SUNY Gymnasium, State University of New York at Stony Brook *Stony Brook, NY* 8:00 & 11:00pm, with Yes

Monday 29th – Tuesday 30th
Ray has flu, holed up in New York City, and a scheduled appearance on Tuesday at Massey Hall, Toronto, ON, Canada is cancelled.

December

Wednesday 1st
Ray is still in New York City, ill with flu.

Thursday 2nd
Dome Arena, Long Island University, C.W. Post Campus *Brookville, NY* 8:00pm, with Boomerang
The opening act is a new hard-rock outfit fronted by former Vanilla Fudge man Mark Stein. Ray is reportedly still ill, but the show goes on.

Friday 3rd
Unknown location and venue, possibly a college in New Jersey, likely a fill-in date booked at short notice. A tentatively booked concert at the Dario Palce theatre, Providence, RI, falls through.

Saturday 4th
Athletic Center, LeMoyne College *Syracuse, NY* 8:00pm, with Juken Bone
The Kinks only play a little over an hour, including a performance of '20th Century Man' which is announced as their new single, but Ray's flamboyance and the able backing from the band win over the crowd. Juken Bone is a local band recently signed to RCA.

Sunday 5th
Bristol Gymnasium, Hobart College *Geneva, NY* 4:00pm, with Snake Drive; $2 advance / $3 door; co-sponsored by Hobart College and William Smith College
An unusual late-afternoon show, perhaps to allow the band to get back to New York City for one last night of fun before returning to London.

Monday 6th – Thursday 9th
The band minus Ray travels to London on Monday. Ray stays at Loew's Midtown Motor Inn in New York City for another stretch of media functions, and travels home on Thursday.

Friday 10th
Immediately upon his return from New York, Ray signs a form removing Grenville Collins as a director of Kinks Productions Ltd, to formalise Collins's voluntary departure from the management team of The Kinks and sever any further ties to their interests. With only a one percent share as a director, Collins's involvement in the company was only for voting purposes.

Monday 13th

A press release announces a UK tour in 1972. Around this time Ray tells *Melody Maker* that plans for 1972 are virtually all in place, with three US tours set. He mentions that Granada TV has asked him to do another programme for them, despite the failure of their proposed *Arthur* TV project to reach production, and says the recent US tour was generally excellent. He tells *Record Mirror* that six further LPs are due in the RCA deal.

Friday 17th

The Kinks assemble for photographer and friend Barry Wentzell for a rare photoshoot. The session starts at 11:30am at the Archway Tavern pub in north London, site of the recent cover shoot for *Muswell Hillbillies*. After some mid-day imbibing, the entourage moves on to another pub, The Flask in nearby Highgate, as well as posing for

20th Century Man single

A '**20th Century Man**' (R. DAVIES).
B '**Skin And Bone**' (R. DAVIES).

US release late December 1971 (RCA Victor 74-0620).
Musicians and recording details as Muswell Hillbillies LP (see November 24th).
Chart high US number 106.

pictures in various locations in the streets along the way. This shoot supplies some of the most often-used Kinks photos during the RCA period, and they will appear repeatedly in the press photos and on picture sleeves.

Monday 20th

A press release announces upcoming concerts at the Rainbow Theatre in north London, possibly as many as three shows.

☆ With the advance money from the RCA signing, around this time Kinks Productions buys an old warehouse in Tottenham Lane, Hornsey, north London, just down the street from Hornsey Art College, as the site for their future recording studio and offices. Otherwise the band enjoys time off for Christmas and the new year.

➔ '**20th Century Man**' / '**Skin And Bone**' single released in the US.

Thursday 30th

Management by Robert Wace and Boscobel Productions Ltd is completely terminated as Wace resigns in a dispute with Ray over a proposed reduction in the management fee following Collins's recent departure. As with Collins, Wace's relationship with Ray has been in serious decline over the last year and today is simply the breaking point for both sides. But where Collins left because he wanted to, Wace departs in a more acrimonious manner.

Today clearly marks the end of the original Kinks. Besides Ray and Dave and the stalwart Avory, the original associates – management, booking agent, publisher, recording manager, and record company – are all now gone, almost exactly eight years since the original relationships were begun.

1972

For the first time in the band's early history almost every aspect of their career was finally under their control. All ties with previous management had been severed, and they were riding high on a new and lucrative recording contract. Previous publishing problems had also been left behind. They had signed with a new booking agency in Britain, and their first LP under the new RCA Records contract was gathering critical acclaim.

Financed by advance money from the RCA deal, The Kinks took the first step to creating their own recording studio, which would free them from the recently escalating costs of making their records.

Ray's longstanding dream of expanding the line-up to include horn players was finally realised, and the band finally cast off its 1960s pop-group image as Ray reinvented himself as a dynamic frontman backed by his troupe of musicians.

The RCA contract held the band to quite a rigorous schedule of releases, and they found themselves in a hurry to complete the second LP of the term. Steady touring kept them on the road for a large proportion of the year, though never for more than about three weeks at a time. In Britain they returned to the singles chart – and it turned out to be the last time they would do this for over a decade. But the year was certainly one in which The Kinks largely re-established their presence in the contemporary rock music world.

January

Tuesday 4th
❏ **TV** BBC Television Centre *west London*. BBC-2 **The Old Grey Whistle Test** live performance 'Have A Cuppa Tea', 'Acute Schizophrenia Paranoia Blues'. The Kinks videotape two songs, one as a five-man band with Gosling on keyboard, the other adding the Mike Cotton horn section. Both are broadcast later the same day. Also taped are assorted interviews that will be used in an upcoming TV special, *The Kinks At The Rainbow*.

Wednesday 5th
Location footage is shot at the Archway Tavern, north London, interviewing the pub locals for *The Kinks At The Rainbow* BBC TV special.

Tuesday 11th
Location footage shot of The Kinks in rehearsal in London for the TV special.

➜ 'Nobody's Fool' single by Cold Turkey released in the UK, a song written by Ray Davies. It's the theme song from the successful LWT TV series, *Budgie*.

Sunday 23rd
Kinetic Circus *Kenilworth, Warwicks*
Their first live show since returning from the US tour in December, and a warm-up performance for the BBC/Rainbow taping. *Melody Maker* says the band turn a potentially disastrous gig into a total

triumph as, unusually, they use borrowed equipment and have no time for a soundcheck, in a club more familiar with the day's progressive sounds. However, The Kinks' ability to turn their old hits into a singalong and mix in new material wins through, proving they're still a concert draw in England.

➜ On-stage rehearsals with the Mike Cotton horn section for the BBC TV special are held at an unknown "old vaudeville-era theatre" in east London. The band works up horn parts for songs including 'She's Bought A Hat Like Princess Marina', 'Alcohol', 'Acute Schizophrenia Paranoia Blues', a medley of 'Skin And Bone' and 'Dry Bones', 'Holiday', 'Complicated Life', 'Have A Cuppa Tea', and 'Baby Face'.
☆ Also around this time, Ray is interviewed for *Disc & Music Echo* and mentions that ex-manager Wace is suing the band.

Thursday 27th
❏ **TV** BBC Television Studios *Birmingham*. Further interviews for **The Kinks At The Rainbow** are taped.

Sunday 30th
Separate from the live concert, probably today at the Rainbow Theatre in north London a separate staged performance of 'The Moneygoround' with a live vocal sung over the record's backing track is filmed for use in the resulting TV special.

Monday 31st
Rainbow Theatre *Finsbury Park, north London*
Filmed before an invited audience of 2,000, The Kinks appear in concert with The Mike Cotton Sound, produced by Mel Cornish. Songs captured on film include 'Till The End Of The Day', 'Waterloo Sunset',

'Sunny Afternoon', a snatch of 'Mr Wonderful', 'She's Bought A Hat Like Princess Marina', 'Some Mother's Son' (with vocal by opera singer Wendy Ethorne, ultimately not aired), 'Alcohol', 'Acute Schizophrenia Paranoia Blues', 'Lola', and 'You Really Got Me'.

☆ *Muswell Hillbillies* LP peaks in US chart at number 100.

February

Friday 4th
Guildhall *Southampton*

Monday 7th

A press release notes that the band has added brass players to the line-up.

→ ● **RECORDING** Morgan Studios *Willesden, north-west London*. Some time this week, The Kinks return to Morgan to record a single intended to get them back in the charts. (No single was taken from the recent LP for the UK.) The five Kinks successfully put down a backing track for an early version of **'Supersonic Rocket Ship'**.

Friday 11th

● **RECORDING** Morgan Studios *Willesden, north-west London*. A session at 7:00pm to overdub Mike Cotton (trumpet) and John Beecham (trombone) on to **'Supersonic Rocket Ship'**.

Saturday 12th

The traditional pre-US-tour warm-up show at the Mayfair Suite, Belfry Hotel, Wishaw, Warwicks is cancelled and rescheduled for April 15th.

Monday 14th

A press release says The Kinks are to record shows at New York City's Carnegie Hall for a live LP.

Tuesday 15th

Owens Union, University Of Manchester *Manchester* with Patto, Nazareth, Bell & Arc, Brett Marvin & The Thunderbolts, Good Habit
Part of the Rag Ball for Salford and Manchester universities.

Saturday 19th

Central Hall, University Of York *York* 7:30pm, with Plainsong
Tonight's performance includes an off-the-cuff rendition of Bill Haley's 'Rock Around The Clock'.

→ ● **RECORDING** Morgan Studios *Willesden, north-west London*. Further work around this time to complete the recording of **'Supersonic Rocketship'**, although it is apparently not prepared for release until after the forthcoming US tour.

⇨ **TOUR STARTS** *Tour of the US* (Feb 25th – Mar 12th). **Line-up**: Ray Davies (lead vocal, guitar), Dave Davies (guitar, vocal), Mick Avory (drums), John Dalton (bass guitar), John Gosling (keyboard), Mike Cotton (trumpet), John Beecham (trombone), Davy Jones (saxophone, clarinet). The Mike Cotton horn section appears only on the dates between March 1st and 10th. The band departs London on the 23rd, arriving in Tampa, FL, the following day.

Friday 25th

Fort Homer W. Hesterly Armory *Tampa, FL* 8:00pm, with Fairport Convention
The band's first-ever appearance in Florida. Fairport Convention are friends from the Muswell Hill area, later held as prime movers of the British folk revival and folk-rock scene. The Kinks' reception in Florida is strong, and their legendary status and a thoroughly entertaining show will bring rave reviews and full houses throughout the entire tour.

Saturday 26th

Speedway Sportatorium *Hollywood, FL* 8:00pm, with Fairport Convention

Sunday 27th

Berkeley Community Theater *Berkeley, CA* 8:00pm, with Badfinger
All the way to the West Coast for a one-off date before heading straight back east. This is the era of Ray's classic high camp, as he begins to pepper Kinks shows with spontaneous versions of American songbook classics of the 1920s and '30s. Tonight Ray works a snippet of Al Jolson's 'Mammy' into the now routine performance of the Calypso nugget, 'Banana Boat Song'. Ray also satisfies the loyal early-Kinks fans with performances of now rarely played chestnuts from the 1960s catalogue, including 'Dead End Street' and 'Harry Rag'. (Travel day following to New York City and time off. The horn section now flies into New York City from London.)

March

Wednesday 1st

Kleinhans Music Hall *Buffalo, NY* 8:00pm, with Lindisfarne, Fairport Convention; sponsored by State University of NY at Buffalo
The US debut with the horn section, which goes without a hitch. The *Buffalo News* says: "[Ray's] act is a study in exaggerated coyness … like in a striptease [but] no matter how Davies carries on, however, the music emerges unscathed [as] the eight of them fake a joyously full and complex sound." Accompanying The Kinks on most of the dates for the rest of the tour are Lindisfarne, more British folkies, this time from Newcastle, who make their US concert debut tonight promoting the *Fog On The Tyne* LP that includes UK hit 'Meet Me On The Corner'.

Thursday 2nd – Friday 3rd

Carnegie Hall *New York, NY* 8:00pm, with Lindisfarne
Both nights are taped on the RCA Mobile Recording Unit, and some songs from the second night will be used as part of the *Everybody's In Show-Biz* album (see August 25th). (Two further live recordings from Carnegie Hall, 'Till The End Of The Day' and 'She's Bought A Hat Like Princess Marina', will be released as bonus cuts on the 1998 CD reissue of *Show-Biz*, and a third previously unreleased song from these shows, 'You're Looking Fine', is issued on two promotional-only sampler CDs, *The Borders Compilation* and *The Limited Edition Compilation*, alongside that Show-Biz CD reissue.)

The Kinks bring along their photographer friend Barrie Wentzell to take live shots of the show, one of which will be used in the gatefold of the *Show-Biz* LP. Incidental footage of the scene backstage and at their lodgings at the Ramada Inn is filmed by Laurie Lewis on Ray's 16mm camera for possible use in an hour-long TV special shot largely during the stays between New York and Los Angeles. The film is shot with available light for an intentionally grainy look.

Coverage in the New York press is extensive, and The Kinks' good-time carnival atmosphere is by now becoming infectious. *Billboard*: "The Kinks cavorted through burlesque turns reminiscent of a London music hall. … If camp is indeed an art form, The Kinks are its original interpreters."

Set-list (3rd): 'Top Of The Pops', 'You're Looking Fine', 'Mr Wonderful', 'Get Back In Line', 'Muswell Hillbilly', 'Apeman', 'Sunny

Afternoon', '20th Century Man', 'Banana Boat Song', 'Brainwashed', 'Acute Schizophrenia Paranoia Blues', 'Holiday', 'Complicated Life', 'You Are My Sunshine', 'Skin And Bone', 'Mammy', 'Alcohol', 'Have A Cuppa Tea', 'Baby Face', 'Lola', medley 'You Really Got Me' / 'All Day And All Of The Night', 'Victoria'.

Saturday 4th

Scheduled concert at the Palace Theatre, Providence, RI, is cancelled at the last moment on the day of the show because the promoter couldn't get an approved concert license in time. Local promoters are plagued by resistance to rock shows in Providence, with three previous attempts to bring The Kinks to the city also failing.

Sunday 5th

Aquarius/Orpheum Theater *Boston, MA* 7:30pm, with Lindisfarne, Fairport Convention; promoted by New England Productions (Don Law)
Like New York City, Boston has a solid Kinks fan-base and tonight's show sees the band graduating from club to sold-out auditorium, repeating the magic created at Carnegie Hall. The horn section is already seamlessly worked into the show, and tonight includes a rendition of 'Baby Face' tagged onto a reworking of *Arthur*'s 'She Bought A Hat Like Princess Marina'.

Ray also pulls out an off-the-cuff live take of 'Harry Rag'. Both opening acts are impressive and fuel the crowd's enthusiasm for the ensuing show, which rates rave reviews across the board. The show grosses $15,500.

Monday 6th – Tuesday 7th

The band travels to Los Angeles while horn player Davy Jones returns to London for prior commitments. The other two hornmen, Cotton and Beecham, stay on for the LA show, using local session saxophonist Ernie Watts in Jones's place. Staying at the Continental Hyatt House, Watts rehearses with the horn players on Tuesday.

Wednesday 8th

An elaborate RCA press party, *A Night with The Kinks at a Gala Soirée*, is held poolside tonight at 8:30 pm at the Continental Hyatt House Hotel's penthouse in Los Angeles. The ensuing mayhem, with about 500 attending, is also filmed by Laurie Lewis for the proposed Kinks film. Earlier today the band is photographed by Mary Frampton with British consulates at home as part of a publicity stunt.

Thursday 9th

Hollywood Palladium *Los Angeles, CA* 8:00pm, with Jo Jo Gunne, REO Speedwagon, Michael Gately
The party continues onstage with a show similar in content and on a similar high to those in New York and Boston.

Friday 10th

Music Hall *Cincinnati, OH* 8:00pm, with Taj Mahal, Lindisfarne; promoted by Belkins Productions
Cotton and Beecham return to London for prior commitments, and this and the remaining dates are done without the horns. A local report suggests "both temper and light fuses were blown" as power is cut after the band play for too long.

Saturday 11th

Emerson Gymnasium, Case Western Reserve University *Cleveland, OH* 8:30pm, with Taj Mahal, Lindisfarne
Future Pretender Chrissie Hynde is in attendance tonight to take in her second Kinks concert. After dropping out of Kent State University next year, she will move to London to pursue her musical ambitions, eventually crossing paths with Ray Davies again in 1980.

The Kink Kronikles double-album

A1 'Victoria' (R. DAVIES).
A2 'The Village Green Preservation Society' (R. DAVIES).
A3 'Berkeley Mews' (R. DAVIES).
A4 'Holiday In Waikiki' (R. DAVIES).
A5 'Willesden Green' (R. DAVIES).
A6 'This Is Where I Belong' (R. DAVIES).
A7 'Waterloo Sunset' (R. DAVIES).
B1 'David Watts' (R. DAVIES).
B2 'Dead End Street' (R. DAVIES).
B3 'Shangri-La' (R. DAVIES).
B4 'Autumn Almanac' (R. DAVIES).
B5 'Sunny Afternoon' (R. DAVIES).
B6 'Get Back In Line' (R. DAVIES).
B7 'Did You See His Name' (R. DAVIES).
C1 'Fancy' (R. DAVIES).
C2 'Wonder Boy' (R. DAVIES).
C3 'Apeman' (R. DAVIES).
C4 'King Kong' (R. DAVIES).
C5 'Mister Pleasant' (R. DAVIES).
C6 'God's Children' (R. DAVIES).
C7 'Death Of A Clown' (D. DAVIES, R. DAVIES).
D1 'Lola' (R. DAVIES).
D2 'Mindless Child Of Motherhood' (D. DAVIES).
D3 'Polly' (R. DAVIES).
D4 'Big Black Smoke' (R. DAVIES).
D5 'Susannah's Still Alive' (D. DAVIES).
D6 'She's Got Everything' (R. DAVIES).
D7 'Days' (R. DAVIES).

US release March 25th 1972 (Reprise 2XS 6454).
With the exception of 'Did You See His Name' (B7), a casualty from the full-length and aborted Four More Respected Gentlemen LP, all tracks have been previously released on singles and albums, although many are obscure in the US or in a few cases only available in the UK until now.
B7 data Musicians Ray Davies lead vocal, acoustic guitar, organ (or Nicky Hopkins). Dave Davies electric guitar, backing vocal. Pete Quaife bass guitar, backing vocal. Mick Avory drums. Nicky Hopkins organ (or Ray Davies). Recorded Pye Studios (No.2) *central London*; March 1968; 4-track mixed to stereo.
Producer Ray Davies.
Engineer Alan MacKenzie (possibly Brian Humphries).
Chart high US number 94.

Sunday 12th

Auditorium Theater *Chicago, IL* 8:00pm, with Lindisfarne
Without the horns, some older chestnuts are pulled out tonight, including Dave singing his medley of 'Milk Cow Blues' / 'One Night With You', and a final encore of 'Louie Louie'. Reviewer Al Rudis in *Melody Maker* says The Kinks' show has "brought fun back to rock'n'roll". (Following day travel back to London.)

➜ Back in London, Ray begins editing the 16mm colour film shot by Lewis during the US tour, and begins writing songs to accompany it. "I shot the film first and worked on the songs as if I were doing a soundtrack," he says later. Eventually an edit of around 50-60 minutes is produced, plus a 20-minute sampler to be shopped around for possible broadcasters.

Saturday 25th
The Kink Kronikles double-album released in the US. With the band now signed to RCA, the old US label Reprise wastes no time in assembling this double set of its Kinks back-catalogue material – a sort of US equivalent of Pye's British 1970 "*Black Album*".

Compilation is entrusted to company insider and Kinks enthusiast John Mendelssohn, who assembles what will become a classic collection of chestnuts and overlooked remnants of the band's golden period from 1966-70, offering a generous 28 tracks at less than the price of two LPs.

This causes some problems for Ray, who is in effect forced to compete against his own back catalogue. The perennially in-print *Kronikles* will provide reviewers a convenient and classic benchmark against which to measure future Kinks albums coming from a band headed in a completely different direction.

Reviews that appear now of the *Kronikles* set are uniformly strong, with many a writer pointing out that the double-LP provides material that has not been available to fans who may have come along since the time of 'Lola' or the band's return to the US concert circuit in the past two years.

The *New York Times* recommends the new Kronikles collection highly, referring to the double set as "a remarkable cross-cut view through the music of a remarkable group". *Rolling Stone* rates the double-album "an unqualified 100 points". *Phonograph Record Magazine* suggests that "every self-respecting devotee of pop music should possess this new set".

April

→ ● **RECORDING** Morgan Studios *Willesden, north-west London*. Around now an engineer by mistake erases the opening seconds of '**Supersonic Rocketship**' from its master tape, forcing a complete re-recording. Besides one hugely embarrassed engineer, the accident causes delay to the release of the new single. (The partially-erased early version will be inadvertently released on a collection of Kinks tracks, *Backtrackin'*, in 1985.)

☆ Also around this time Ray continues to edit Lewis's film footage and to write new material for it.

Wednesday 12th
❑ **TV** Radio Bremen Television Studios *Bremen, West Germany*. ARD-1 *Beat Club* live performance 'Muswell Hillbilly' broadcast May 27th, repeated in 1981 plus 'Lola', medley 'You Really Got Me' / 'All Day And All Of The Night'.

Thursday 13th
● **RECORDING** Morgan Studios *Willesden, north-west London*. Horn overdub session for re-recorded '**Supersonic Rocket Ship**'. Final mix completed by Ray shortly afterwards; the single is ready for release by the coming weekend.

Friday 14th
Student Union, Lanchester Polytechnic *Coventry* with Steve Peregrine
The band is again supplemented by the Mike Cotton horn section at this sell-out date.

Saturday 15th
Mayfair Suite, Belfry Hotel *Wishaw, Warwicks*
Attendance is around 1,000 at this make-up date following the February postponement. The brass team is not available tonight so this is a regular five-man Kinks show.

→ ● **RECORDING** Morgan Studios *Willesden, north-west London*. With the new single out of the way, The Kinks begin work on their next LP, generally rehearsing and recording during the week alongside occasional duties and sporadic (mostly weekend) gigs.

Saturday 22nd
St. Georges Hall, University Of Bradford *Bradford, Yorks*
With the Mike Cotton horn section.

Friday 28th
University of London: Goldsmiths' College *New Cross, south-east London* with Spyrogyra
Tonight the band tries the classic Muddy Waters blues 'Hoochie Coochie Man' and will feature it occasionally at British gigs over the next few months.

May

→ Laurie Lewis again uses Ray's 16mm camera, this time for a short promotional film for possible broadcast on television to accompany 'Supersonic Rocketship'. Footage is shot at Ray's house on Fortis Green, East Finchley, north London. The highpoint comes when Gosling attempts to fly. The film will be successfully aired in place of an in-person appearance on the Dutch AVRO programme *Top Pop* on May 15th, and is possiblyseen on Australian TV. The film is aired on BBC-1's *Top Of The Pops* on June 1st in place of an in-person appearance, on the Dutch AVRO show *Top Pop* on May 15th, and possibly on Australian TV. But it is never broadcast on American television.

Wednesday 3rd
'**King Kong**' / '**Waterloo Sunset**' single released in the US. Old label Reprise makes a last attempt at singles success with this odd choice of an A-side from the *Kink Kronikles* collection, but it does not chart.

Friday 5th
))) **RADIO** Studio T1, BBC Transcription Service, Kensington House *central London*. BBC Radio-1 *John Peel Show* studio recordings produced by John Walters 'Supersonic Rocketship', 'Acute Schizophrenia Paranoia Blues', 'Skin And Bones', 'Holiday' broadcast May 16th. For this taping session the band has a variant on the Cotton horn section. Cotton himself is unavailable, and the line-up is Michael Rosen (trumpet), John Beecham (trombone), Alan Holmes (saxophone). Cotton's temporary replacement, Canadian trumpeter Rosen, is known to the other horn players from his work with the band Mogul Thrash. ('Skin And Bones' and 'Holiday' will be released in 2001 on *The Kinks BBC Sessions 1964-1977*.)

'**Supersonic Rocketship**' / '**You Don't Know My Name**' single released in the UK. Despite 'God's Children' released in April last year, this is in effect The Kinks' true follow-up to 'Apeman', which came out back in November 1970. *NME*: "A colourful mid-tempo goodie with bits of mandolin, Trinidad steel drums and their recently added brass section. It's great stuff." *Record Mirror* calls it a "chart certainty" because "it's got that Kinks magic touch to it". *Melody Maker* says: "All good clean fun. It could be The Kinks' biggest hit in years."

→ INDICATES EVENT AROUND THIS TIME BUT WITH NO FIRM DATE

Saturday 6th

Bickershaw Festival *Bickershaw, near Wigan, Lancs* with America, Captain Beefheart, Hawkwind, Brinsley Schwarz, Cheech & Chong

An ambitious three-day open-air festival (May 5th-7th) that also features San Francisco's The Grateful Dead. Up to 30,000 attend, but the event is hampered by persistent heavy rain that results in a veritable mud-fest. The Kinks appear on the second day and get a great review from *Melody Maker* that is tinged with mock surprise that the mud-drenched crowd eats up the 1972-style "Americanised" Kinks. "They were great, and the surprising thing was the audience thought so too. The Kinks succeeding in their homeland? Could this be true at last?" Ray says later that he writes the song 'Motorway' for the new LP while travelling up the M1 motorway (freeway) to this performance.

☆ Starting with this date, the horn section – though still separately billed as The Mike Cotton Sound – officially becomes part of The Kinks.

☆ Possible further activity on the tracks recorded on the 5th takes place at BBC Radio's Studio T1 in central London.

Tuesday 9th

Town Hall *Watford* 8:00pm, with Jonathan Kelly; presented by The Friars

→ ● **RECORDING** Morgan Studios *Willesden, north-west London.* Concentrated recording sessions take place around this time for the *Everyone's In Show-Biz* LP.

Saturday 20th

Student Union, North East London Polytechnic *Walthamstow, north-east London* 7:30pm, with Fishbaugh Fishbaugh & Zorn

Monday 22nd

Insel Grun *Fiesenheimer Penninsula, Germersheim, West Germany* *Second British Rock Meeting/Whitsuntide,* with Pink Floyd, The Faces, Humble Pie, Incredible String Band, Atomic Rooster, Buddy Miles Express, The Doors, Family, Osibisa, Curved Air, Linda Lewis, Tom Paxton (40 acts total)

Supersonic Rocketship single

A **'Supersonic Rocketship'** (R. DAVIES).
B **'You Don't Know My Name'** (D. DAVIES).

UK release May 5th 1972 (RCA Victor RCA 2211).
US release September 1972 (RCA Victor 74-0807).
Musicians Ray Davies lead vocals (A), acoustic guitar. Dave Davies acoustic guitar, resonator guitar, backing vocal (A), lead vocal (B). John Dalton bass guitar. Mick Avory drums, maracas (A). John Gosling marimba (A), baby grand piano. Mike Cotton trumpet (A). John Beecham trombone (A). Alan Holmes flute (B).
Recorded Morgan Studios Willesden, north-west London; A: April 1972; B: possibly 1971, or else February 1972; 16-track mixed to stereo.
Producer Raymond Douglas Davies.
Engineer Mike Bobak.
Chart high UK number 16; US none.

This open-air festival runs continuously for three days attracting a crowd estimated at up to 100,000. It takes place on a peninsula along the Rhine river south of Mannheim. The festival was originally set for the motor-racing circuit in Hockenheim but was moved a few weeks prior due to local protests. According to *Variety* The Kinks, who the newspaper suggests have a drunken stage act, are not well received. (Travel back to London following day.)

Friday 26th

Maidstone Art College *Maidstone, Kent* 8:00pm

Saturday 27th – Monday 29th

● **RECORDING** Morgan Studios *Willesden, north-west London.* A single three-hour session and two separate six-hour sessions take place over these three days, working on horn overdubs for the *Show-Biz* LP tracks.

June

Thursday 1st

● **RECORDING** Morgan Studios *Willesden, north-west London.* A further horn-overdub session for the LP, starting at 6:00pm.

Saturday 3rd

City Hall *Newcastle Upon Tyne* 8:00pm, with John Miles Set, Brass Alley

Monday 5th

● **RECORDING** Morgan Studios *Willesden, north-west London.* Sessions continue.

☆ A press release announces negotiations for the film planned to accompany the *Everybody's In Show-Biz* album, to be shown as a TV special in the US.

Friday 9th

Corn Exchange *Cambridge* 9:00pm, with Brinsley Schwarz

While a stage power failure is fixed, Ray plays 'Skin And Bone' on acoustic guitar accompanied by just drums and the horn section.

Saturday 10th – Sunday 11th

● **RECORDING** Morgan Studios *Willesden, north-west London.* The band and horn section are busy with a marathon all-day session on Saturday and an evening session on Sunday in which three tracks are recorded, or re-recorded, including a new song **'Celluloid Heroes'**. For this session The Kinks are augmented by friend and former Mike Cotton Sound keyboard player Dave Rowberry. After this point all the basic backing tracks are apparently complete, and only vocal and minor overdubs plus final mixing remain, occupying Ray over the next four weeks.

Wednesday 14th

❏ **TV** BBC Television Centre *west London.* BBC-1 *Top Of The Pops* backing tracks 'Supersonic Rocket Ship', 'Skin And Bone' broadcast tomorrow.

Thursday 15th

❏ **TV** BBC Television Centre *west London.* BBC-1 *Top Of The Pops* live vocal over backing track 'Supersonic Rocket Ship', 'Skin And Bone'. The band appears with Dave Rowberry on piano while Gosling plays marimba. Remarkably, this will be The Kinks' last appearance on *Top Of The Pops* for 11 years. It ends in controversy as a confrontation develops between Ray and members of Slade in the BBC canteen, resulting in Ray pouring beer over Slade member Jim Lea's head.

→ ● **RECORDING** Morgan Studios *Willesden, north-west London*. Ray is busy with mixing sessions for the LP, and is also reviewing the live tapes from Carnegie Hall recorded in March that require mixing and some overdubbing. Accordingly he sends out Dave and Avory to keep the press interested in the new single. Dave tells *NME* that the band's own new studio in Hornsey, north London is under construction and that they hope it will be ready in "the next few weeks". In fact, it will not open until May 1973.

Thursday 22nd
Kinks' publicist Marion Rainford leaves Barrow International and joins Kinks Productions as a full-time assistant.

Friday 23rd
Civic Hall *Solihull, Warwicks* sponsored by Coventry College of Education, Coventry University
The band faces a tough crowd tonight. They leave the stage once, return shortly after, but soon leave for good, to boos and jeers.

Saturday 24th
Loughborough University of Technology *Loughborough, Leics* with Fishbaugh Fishbaugh & Zorn

Monday 26th
Free Trade Hall *Manchester* with Max Merritt, Steve Goodman
The show is part of the charity War On Want campaign.

→ ● **RECORDING** Morgan Studios *Willesden, north-west London*. Ray probably continues work on the new LP.

Friday 30th
Fantasy Festival *Roskilde, Denmark* with Family, Sha Na Na, others
A local reviewer writes that "The Kinks are a nice mix of old music hall tradition and progressive rock". (Travel day back to London following.)

July

On the 7th they play the Top Rank Suite in Doncaster, Yorks with Edwin Starr, and week later Ray delivers master tapes of the *Everybody's In Show-Biz* LP to RCA Records in New York City, and presumably oversees mastering. Tape copies are also likely delivered to the British RCA offices in Mayfair, central London around the same time. From Saurday the 15th for two weeks comes the band's annual holiday, allowing a rest before the upcoming US tour. During the break, *The Kinks At The Rainbow* TV special airs on BBC-1 on Friday 21st, 6:30-7:15pm.

August

Thursday 3rd
Starkers Royal Ballroom *Bournemouth* 8:00pm with David Blue
Back from holidays, the band warms up for their US tour with this one-off show.
☆ Around now Avory is interviewed by Tony Norman for *NME*. He

reveals the band's current ambitions that, in effect, predict the next phase of their career. "Rather than just going out and [doing] a gig for the sake of it," says the drummer, "we thought a music-hall thing would be much more interesting, both for the audience and us. We'd probably do it in conjunction with other musicians. It could work. This was one idea we had for *Arthur* when we made that album. It had a good strong story and we could have made it into a good musical play."

Wednesday 9th
The Kinks hold a rehearsal today, presumably to work up numbers from the new LP for the tour, including 'Here Comes Yet Another Day'.

➪ **TOUR STARTS** *Tour of US* (Aug 18th – Sep 4th). **Line-up**: Ray Davies (lead vocal, guitar), Dave Davies (guitar, vocal), Mick Avory (drums), John Dalton (bass guitar), John Gosling (keyboard), Mike Cotton (trumpet), John Beecham (trombone), Alan Holmes (saxophone, clarinet). Booking by Chip Rachlin and Herb Spar at International Famous Agency. The tour is originally set to run into late September, but before its start is cut back to three weeks in order to slot in a short British tour. (The band travels to New York City on the 16th and have time off there the following day.)

Friday 18th
Dillon Stadium *Hartford, CT* with The Beach Boys (headliners), The Phlorescent Leech & Eddie, The Doors
The tour to promote *Everybody's In Show-Biz* starts with this interesting bill: Leech & Eddie is the latest guise for the ex-Turtles singers, while a last-gasp post-Jim Morrison version of The Doors promotes their *Full Circle* LP. The Kinks and The Beach Boys now share the same booking agency in the US and are paired together for a short string of dates that expose The Kinks to some stadium-size American crowds.

Saturday 19th
Roosevelt Stadium, New Jersey Fairgrounds *Jersey City, NJ* 7:30pm, with The Beach Boys (headliners), Looking Glass
A paying crowd of 9,318 is reported.

Sunday 20th
Allentown Fairgrounds race track *Allentown, PA* 7:00pm, with The Beach Boys (headliners), Orleans; sponsored by the Allentown Council of Youth; promoted by William Honney; MC (local radio personality) Danny Somach; tickets $3.50
The show attracts more than 10,000, and local officials are upset by The Kinks bringing a case of beer on stage and passing cans out to fans at the front. But the performances by The Beach Boys and The Kinks are very highly rated and the evening is deemed a big success.

Monday 21st
Nassau Veterans Memorial Coliseum *Uniondale, NY* 8:00pm, with The Beach Boys (headliners)
Around 18,000 attend this evening. The band has a day off in New York City tomorrow preceding the show there. Dave says later in *Kink* that it was at some point during the New York stay, while in his hotel room on 8th Avenue, that he reaches a desperate low, a culmination of years of excessive lifestyle and a general neglect of his emotional needs. He resolves to stop his intake of hallucinogens, and eventually will become a vegetarian in a bid to reclaim his mental health. It's ironic, of course, that such personal misery should coincide with a public professional peak.

Wednesday 23rd
Wollman Rink, Central Park *New York, NY* 7:30pm, Schaefer Music Festival, with Orleans
The Kinks headline in Central Park, with 7,000 attending one of their

legendary shows of the period. *Melody Maker* says it's "Kinks mania – there's no doubt about it. There was nearly a riot, ending up with Ray and the lads doing a good half-hour of encores to satisfy an audience that looked like uprooting the stage and eating the cops patrolling the front lines". Lisa Robinson in *Disc* concurs: "They managed to entertain us in a way that no one – and I repeat, no one – has all this season." (Travel day following to Chicago.)

Set-list: 'Top Of The Pops', medley 'You're Looking Fine' / 'Little Queenie' / 'Be Bop A Lula', 'Apeman', 'Dedicated Follower Of Fashion', 'Waterloo Sunset', 'Sunny Afternoon', 'Acute Schizophrenia Paranoia Blues', 'Here Comes Yet Another Day', 'Holiday', 'Alcohol', medley 'Skin And Bone' / 'Dry Bones' / 'The Village Green Preservation Society', 'You Are My Sunshine', 'Victoria', 'Baby Face', 'Lola', medley 'You Really Got Me' / 'All Day And All Of The Night', medley 'Louie Louie' / 'Twist And Shout' / 'Hang On Sloopy', 'Unreal Reality' medley 'Milk Cow Blues' / 'One Night'.

Friday 25th

Aragon Ballroom *Chicago, IL* 8:00pm, with Flash, Doctor Hook & His Medicine Show, Foghat

Perhaps inspired by the home of Chicago blues, The Kinks play a further performance of Muddy Waters's 'Hoochie Coochie Man'.
Everybody's In Show-Biz double-album released in the US. The record has been delayed, evidently due to production problems with the cover. The Kinks are at the top of their game in the States and coverage of album is unprecedented for the band. But reviews are mixed. *Crawdaddy!* observes that this may be "Ray's America album" and calls it good but not great. Lester Bangs in *Phonograph Record Magazine* clearly dislikes the set, dismissing it as "excessive and inconsequential". The *New York Sunday Times* reviewer says he misses Ray's usual ambiguity and emotion in the writing, and that it adds up to "a series of complaints: literate, occasionally charming, at one point obnoxiously cynical, and consistently depressing". *Rolling Stone* is critical too, but says "despite its faults and its unevenness, this is a delightfully varied, endlessly entertaining album". The album's sales will be respectable, with an improved chart peak at number 70, improving on the last album's number 100. Despite consistently strong reviews of the live shows too, this album just can't seem to capitalise on a peak of enthusiasm from an eager new audience.

Saturday 26th

Berkeley Community Theater *Berkeley, CA* 8:00pm, with Doctor Hook & His Medicine Show
Travel to and time off in Los Angeles follows.

Tuesday 29th

Santa Monica Civic Auditorium *Santa Monica, CA* 8:00pm, with Taj Mahal

This show features a number of rock'n'roll oldies, mostly as parts of medleys, including snippets of 'Little Queenie', 'Shakin' All Over' and 'Be Bop A Lula', as well as an encore of 'Louie Louie' / 'Hang On Sloopy'. Portions of the show are recorded from the audience and will form part of an early vinyl bootleg, *Kriminal Kinks*, issued in 1973. (Day off in Los Angeles with travel day to Pittsburgh following.)

September

Friday 1st

Syria Mosque Auditorium *Pittsburgh, PA* 8:00pm, with Argent
A classic double bill providing a fascinating meeting of Kinks-related musicians. Support act Argent includes Jim Rodford – reuniting the ex-Mike Cotton Sound bass player and future Kink with his old pals – as

---

Everybody's In Show-Biz – Everybody's A Star double-album

A1 'Here Comes Yet Another Day' (R. DAVIES).
A2 'Maximum Consumption' (R. DAVIES).
A3 'Unreal Reality' (R. DAVIES).
A4 'Hot Potatoes' (R. DAVIES).
A5 'Sitting In My Hotel' (R. DAVIES).
B1 'Motorway' (R. DAVIES).
B2 'You Don't Know My Name' (D. DAVIES).
B3 'Supersonic Rocketship' (R. DAVIES).
B4 'Look A Little On The Sunny Side' (R. DAVIES).
B5 'Celluloid Heroes' (R. DAVIES).
C1 'Top Of The Pops' live (R. DAVIES).
C2 'Brainwashed' live (R. DAVIES).
C3 'Mr Wonderful' live (J. BOCK, L. HOLLOFCENER, G. WEISS).
C4 'Acute Schizophrenia Paranoia Blues' live (R. DAVIES).
C5 'Holiday' live (R. DAVIES).
D1 'Muswell Hillbilly' live (R. DAVIES).
D2 'Alcohol' live (R. DAVIES).
D3 'Banana Boat Song' live (L. BURGESS, W. ATTAWAY, H. BELAFONTE).
D4 'Skin And Bone' live (R. DAVIES).
D5 'Baby Face' live (B. DAVIS, H, AKST).
D6 'Lola' live (R. DAVIES).

US release August 25th 1972 (RCA Victor VPS 6065).
UK release September 2nd 1972 (RCA Victor DPS-2035).
Musicians Ray Davies acoustic guitar, electric guitar, lead vocal. Dave Davies electric guitar, acoustic guitar, lead vocal (B2), second lead vocal (A4), backing vocal. John Dalton bass guitar. Mick Avory drums. John Gosling baby grand piano, Hammond organ, harmonium (pump organ), backing vocal. Dave Rowberry Hammond organ (B5). Mike Cotton trumpet. John Beecham trombone, tuba. Alan Holmes baritone saxophone, flute, clarinet (A/B sides only). Davy Jones baritone saxophone, clarinet (C/D sides only).
Recorded A/B sides: Morgan Studios *Willesden, north-west London*; May-July 1972 (B3 April 1972, B2 possibly 1971 or else February 1972); 16-track mixed to stereo. C/D sides: RCA Mobile, Carnegie Hall *New York, NY*; March 3rd 1972; post-production Morgan Studios June-July 1972; 16-track mixed to stereo.
Producer Raymond Douglas Davies.
Engineers Mike Bobak (Morgan); unknown (RCA Mobile).
Chart high US number 70; UK none.

---

well as future Kinks drummer Bob Henrit. Both bands play outstanding performances. As one reviewer puts it: "The enthusiasm, the excitement and the sheer power of the Kinks/Argent show … surpassed anything the Stones had to offer [in their recent Pittsburgh appearance]. The Mosque didn't sell out – only about 2,500 were there – but if a repeat performance were to be scheduled word of mouth could sell out the Arena." At the end of the show, Ray brings on Rodford to assist in a singalong, with Henrit too probably there banging a tambourine, making for a memorable finale.

Everybody's In Show-Biz double-album released in the UK. Reviews in general are complimentary about Ray's writing and The Kinks' overall reputation, but don't say much specifically about the album. *NME* does note that the songs seem "more personally experienced than

kinks'72

usual" and isolates the album's studio finale, 'Celluloid Heroes', as "a masterpiece – the best of everything on the album in one track".

Saturday 2nd
Wildwood Convention Hall *Wildwood, NJ*
Part of a series of summer rock concerts held on the Southern Jersey shore near Atlantic City. (Following day off in New York City.)

Monday 4th
Painter's Mill Music Fair *Owings Mill, MD* 8:30pm, with Michael Murphy
A late addition to the tour, and evidently a show the band isn't happy playing. The evening begins with a bomb-scare that temporarily forces the half-capacity crowd outside the venue while a search is made. The show subsequently turns into another legendary shambolic performance. Dave is in such a drunken state that he has to sit on a chair for part of the performance. Later, Ray is knocked unconscious in a fall on-stage and the band is forced to jam on a prolonged blues until Ray finally returns to the stage with his head wrapped in bandages.

Afterwards, the band hurriedly drives all the way back to New York to catch their flight home to London. The venue is not pleased with The Kinks' behaviour, later characterised as "totally unprofessional", and claim the house organ is damaged by quantities of beer being poured inside. There are also stories of members of the band brawling in the dressing room after the show. Some audience members apparently ask for a refund, feeling they are not treated to a full performance due to Ray's prolonged absence from the stage. The Kinks do not make a return booking.

→ Kinks Productions opens an office for their secretary, Marion Rainford, at Highgate House, north London. With the new LP now out in Britain, press duties begin almost immediately the band returns form the US tour, with a newly talkative Dave in an extensive chat with Steve Peacock, running to two parts in *Sounds*. Ray speaks with Connor McKnight for *Zig Zag* and also does phone interviews with Dutch journalists as well as radio spots to highlight their upcoming visit to The Netherlands.
☆ The band is reported to be working on ideas for a new single to follow up 'Supersonic Rocketship', so rehearsals are likely around now.
→ **'Supersonic Rocketship' / 'You Don't Know My Name'** single released in the US. Very little attention is paid to it in the press, but it does manage to briefly get into the bottom of the chart, at number 111.

Friday 22nd
Robert Wace is officially removed as a director of Kinks Productions Ltd, nine months after the band parted company with him as manager.

➪ **TOUR STARTS** *Tour of the UK* (Sep 29th – Oct 21st). **Line-up**: Ray Davies (lead vocal, guitar), Dave Davies (guitar, vocal), Mick Avory (drums), John Dalton (bass guitar), John Gosling (keyboard), Mike Cotton (trumpet), John Beecham (trombone), Alan Holmes (saxophone, clarinet).

Friday 29th
University Of Newcastle *Newcastle Upon Tyne* with Birtha

October

Tuesday 4th
Top Rank Suite *Cardiff, Wales* with Danta, Hookfoot; sponsored by the University of Cardiff

Wednesday 5th
Gymnasium, Trent Polytechnic *Nottingham*
Melody Maker: "Ray Davies and The Kinks give something extra in comparison with other groups: star quality and versatility, which competitors can only acquire through experience."

Saturday 7th
County Cricket Grounds *Northampton* with Birtha

→ ● **RECORDING** Morgan Studios *Willesden, London*. A session is booked around now, details unknown. Also, Ray has been attempting an edit of **'Celluloid Heroes'** to reduce running time for commercial airplay.

Thursday 12th
● **RECORDING** Morgan Studios *Willesden, north-west London*. Horn overdubs for newly-recorded song or songs.

Friday 13th
St. George's Hall, University Of Bradford *Bradford, Yorks*

Saturday 14th
Liverpool Stadium *Liverpool*

Monday 16th
Free Trade Hall *Manchester* 7:30pm, with Blackfoot Sue

Wednesday 18th
Town Hall *Birmingham* 7:30pm, with Blackfoot Sue
● **RECORDING** Morgan Studios *Willesden, north-west London*. Horn overdubs for the newly recorded song or songs are done during the afternoon, between 2:00 and 5:00pm, and then following the Brum gig the band heads back to Morgan for more work from 1:00 to 3:00am.

Thursday 19th
Oxford Polytechnic *Oxford*

Friday 20th
Refectory, University Of Leeds *Leeds* 7:30pm, *Rag Hop*, with Mungo Jerry, Max Merritt, Paintbox, Syncopated Codpiece

Saturday 21st
The Rainbow Theatre *Finsbury Park, north London* 7:30pm, with Suzi Quatro, Birtha
No trouble getting press coverage here, and all of it positive, as the band plays strongly in its own back yard. *Melody Maker*: "There's no Kinks like the Old Kinks." *NME*: "It wasn't an amazing performance by any means, but it was a heck of a lot of fun." *Record Mirror*: "The audience which packed into the Rainbow was wildly enthusiastic. They demanded and got two genuine encores." *Disc*: "A night of beautiful lunacy."

Monday 23rd – Tuesday 24th
● **RECORDING** Morgan Studios *Willesden, north-west London*. More sessions this week, probably Ray mixing just prior to the US tour.

➪ **TOUR STARTS** *US Tour* (Oct 27th – Nov 17th). **Line-up**: Ray Davies (lead vocal, guitar), Dave Davies (guitar, vocal), Mick Avory (drums), John Dalton (bass guitar), John Gosling (keyboard), Mike Cotton (trumpet), John Beecham (trombone), Alan Holmes (saxophone, clarinet). The tour is to prormote the new *Show-Biz* album. Songs added to the repertoire include Dave having a go at Little Richard's 'Good Golly Miss Molly', plus the planned new Kinks single, 'Celluloid Heroes'. During 25th and 26th the band travels to New York City and then on to San Antonio.

→ INDICATES EVENT AROUND THIS TIME BUT WITH NO FIRM DATE

Friday 27th
Laurie Auditorium, Trinity College *San Antonio, TX* 8:00pm, with Pure Prairie League, Steely Dan
The Kinks finally make their debut in Texas with a trio of dates. Steely Dan is an emerging new band, later renowned for an aversion to touring but now out on the road plugging their debut LP, *Can't Buy A Thrill*.

Saturday 28th
Music Hall *Houston, TX* 8:00pm, with Stoneground, Steely Dan
Says the *Houston Daily Cougar*: "The crowd (only half-filling the Music Hall) made up in enthusiasm what it lacked in numbers.... In little over an hour the Kinks wrapped up the eight years of their dynamic music into the most all-inclusive package since The Who performed **Tommy** in its entirety several years ago."

Sunday 29th
Texas Hall, University of Texas at Arlington *Arlington, TX* 8:00pm, with Stoneground, Steely Dan
The following day the band flies to Chicago.

Tuesday 31st
Auditorium Theater *Chicago, IL* 8:00pm, with Steely Dan
A full-scale rehearsal is held in the afternoon in place of the usual soundcheck. Ironically, minor sound problems mar the show tonight, but as the reviewer for the *Sun-Times* points out, "The Kinks seem to thrive on adversity," and for their third Chicago appearance this year they still have the audience and critics in the palms of their hands.

November

Wednesday 1st
Henry & Edsel Ford Auditorium *Detroit, MI* 7:30pm, with Captain Beefheart
Travel to New York the following day.

Friday 3rd
Capitol Theatre *Passaic, NJ* 8:00pm, with Lindisfarne, Revival

Saturday 4th
University Hall, University of Virginia *Charlottesville, VA* 8:00pm, with Lindisfarne

Sunday 5th
Eisenhower Theater, Kennedy Center for The Performing Arts *Washington, DC* 8:30pm, with Lindisfarne

Monday 6th – Tuesday 7th
● **RECORDING** RCA Recording Studios *New York, NY*. Ray edits 'Celluloid Heroes' from its original 6:20 length to 4:39 for single release.
☆ The double *Show-Biz* album peaks in the US charts at number 70.

Wednesday 8th
The Spectrum *Philadelphia, PA* 8:00pm, with Loggins & Messina, Lindisfarne
The Evening Bulletin tips its hat to opening act Loggins & Messina, feeling they upstage The Kinks, acknowledging only that Kinks music "has come right to the edge of music hall-burlesque rock'n'roll".

Thursday 9th
Men's gymnasium, Harpur College, State University of New York *Binghamton, NY* 10:00pm
One reviewer writes: "The Kinks were their normal exuberant selves, being sloppy musically but enthusiastic and campy. Most important, they brought a relatively lethargic audience to a near-frenzied ecstasy at the end."

Friday 10th
Henry Center, Washington & Jefferson College *Washington, PA* 8:30 pm, with Lindisfarne

Saturday 11th – Sunday 12th
The Aquarius/Orpheum Theater *Boston, MA* 7:30pm, with Lindisfarne

Wednesday 15th – Thursday 16th
Felt Forum, Madison Square Garden Center *New York, NY* 8:00pm, with Mom's Apple Pie
The band's appearances in New York are now regular media events, with the shows heavily reviewed. *The Village Voice* is typical in its praise, saying: "The Kinks put on one of the most enjoyable shows seen here in recent memory." Tonight, Dave takes the unusual step of playing his second solo single, 'Susannah's Still Alive'.

Friday 17th
Palace Concert Theater *Providence, RI* 8:00pm, with REO Speedwagon; promoted by Bruce Goldstein/Skip Chernov
Set-list: 'Top Of The Pops', 'Till The End Of The Day', 'Waterloo Sunset', 'A Well Respected Man', 'Sunny Afternoon', 'Muswell Hillbilly', 'Apeman', 'Lola', 'Celluloid Heroes', 'Here Comes Yet Another Day', 'Brainwashed', 'Mr. Wonderful', 'Acute Schizophrenia Paranoia Blues', 'Banana Boat Song', 'Alcohol', medley 'Skin And Bone' / 'Dry Bones', medley 'You Really Got Me' / 'All Day And All Of The Night', 'Good Golly Miss Molly'.

Saturday 18th
The band holds their now customary end-of-tour party at a favourite hangout, the Haymarket Bar in New York City. (Travel day to London following.)

Monday 20th
A press release announces UK tour dates for December.

Wednesday 22nd
Kinks Recording Enterprises Ltd is filed for incorporation as a company by the band's accountants, with the relevant certificate issued December 20th.

→ 'Celluloid Heroes' / 'Hot Potatoes' single released in the US. Ray gets behind promotion of this single, and RCA springs for a full-page ad in the trade magazine *Cash Box*. The press are supportive too, naming the A-side among Ray's finest ever, so expectations for its chart success are high. However, airplay and audience response are poor, and like the previous single on RCA doesn't even make it to the bottom reaches of the charts.

Friday 24th
'Celluloid Heroes' / 'Hot Potatoes' single released in the UK. The British music press too is unanimous in its praise. *Sounds*: "A fine, fine track from The Kinks' fine album." *Melody Maker*: "Curtains up on the greatest rock single ever told." *NME*: "One of the best Ray Davies songs in recent years." But as in the US, the single fails to make any impression on the charts, making one of the more disappointing reactions to a single in the band's career.

kinks'72

Celluloid Heroes single

A '**Celluloid Heroes**' (R. DAVIES).
B '**Sitting In My Hotel**' (R. DAVIES).

UK release November 24th 1972 (RCA Victor RCA 2299).
US release November (around 22nd) 1972 (RCA Victor 74-0852). US A-side is in edited, remixed form.
Musicians Ray Davies acoustic guitar, lead vocal. Dave Davies acoustic guitar (A), electric guitar (B), backing vocal. John Dalton bass guitar. Mick Avory drums. John Gosling baby grand piano (A, B), Hammond organ (B), harmonium (A), backing vocal (A). Mike Cotton trumpet (B). John Beecham tuba (A). Alan Holmes baritone saxophone (A). Dave Rowberry Hammond organ (A).
Recorded Morgan Studios *Willesden, north-west London;* A: June-July 1972; B: May-July 1972; 16-track mixed to stereo.
Producer Raymond Douglas Davies.
Engineer Mike Bobak.
Chart high UK none; US none.

December

Friday 1st
Hatfield Polytechnic *Hatfield, Herts* with Silverhead
First of a short string of UK dates to help bring attention to the release of 'Celluloid Heroes'.

Saturday 2nd
Portsmouth Polytechnic *Portsmouth* with Holy Mackerel

Sunday 3rd – Friday 8th
Ray travels to New York City where he holes up for the week at the Navarro Hotel and does some press for 'Celluloid Heroes', but becomes ill with flu. His scheduled return to London is delayed for two days, causing cancellation of a concert at the Heavy Steam Machine, Stoke-on-Trent on the 7th. Ray makes it back on the 8th in time for the next show.

Saturday 9th
Student Union, University of London: Imperial College of Science and Technology *central London* with Peter Barden's Camel
The opening act is headed by Ray's erstwhile bandmate from the Hamilton King band back in the spring of 1963.

Monday 11th
A press release announces that The Kinks are booked for a concert in mid January as part of the *Fanfare For Europe* celebration. Ray decides to take advantage of this high-profile gig as an opportunity to finally revive his long standing vision of a staged musical version of 1968's *Village Green Preservation Society* LP. But it will be a rush as the concert takes place in four weeks, and Ray turns all his attention to developing the idea and writing new material for it.

Friday 15th
Concertgebouw *Amsterdam, Netherlands* 9:00pm, with Sandy Coast
A lone Continental booking that in effect wraps up promotion of the recent LP. Now all energies are focused on the staged *Village Green* project. (Travel day to London following.)
Set-list: 'Top Of The Pops', medley 'You're Looking Fine' / 'Little Queenie' / 'Shakin' All Over' / 'Be Bop A Lula', 'Dedicated Follower Of Fashion', 'Sunny Afternoon', 'Lola', 'Celluloid Heroes', 'Here Comes Yet Another Day', 'Brainwashed', 'Mr Wonderful', 'Acute Schizophrenia Paranoia Blues', 'Holiday', 'Alcohol', medley 'Skin And Bone' / 'Dry Bones', 'Baby Face', 'Good Golly Miss Molly', 'Victoria', medley 'Louie Louie' / 'Hang On Sloopy'.

Monday 18th
A press release announces the intention to base the special show for *Fanfare For Europe* on the band's 1968 LP *The Village Green Preservation Society*.
☆ While the band is off during the holiday season, Ray is writing intensively for the planned *Village Green* show.

1973

After achieving control of virtually every aspect of their career the previous year, everything came crashing to a halt this spring and summer. Ray began 1973 set on realising the ambitious Preservation project, but that lurched to a standstill as his personal life fell apart, and he made a dramatic on-stage resignation from the business.

But the "retirement" was shortlived. He soon returned to the fold, and with a new determination to recast The Kinks as a means to achieve his theatrical ambitions, at first with the Preservation saga. Ray said, "I used Preservation, because all these things were happening to me. It was like therapy. At the time I was very emotional. It was like I've got to finish the show, and I really put a lot of myself into it."

Little remained of the traditional pop-rock image of The Kinks as an ever-expanding number of musicians and singers were added to the ranks, turning it into a troupe rather than a group. The goal became the production and staging of Ray's rock theatre work. Only a portion of the work was finished on record by year's end, as Ray and Dave were busy forming their own production company and record label with an eye toward developing an in-house miniature music empire. They intended to develop other artists and undertake any personal side projects that came up along the way.

But the result of this year's ambitions was little or no chart success for The Kinks and a prolonged period out of the public eye, all of which would have long-term consequences for the band.

January

➜ Ray continues to work around the clock on new material and new arrangements of some older material from *The Village Green Preservation Society* album for the concert at London's Drury Lane Theatre later this month.

Among new titles are 'I'm Going Home', 'Cricket', 'Where Are They Now?', 'Time Song' and 'Salvation Road'. Some of the "new" material may in fact have been written earlier, as Ray had long envisioned an expanded stage presentation and had probably been working at it over the years.

Older material given new arrangements includes 'Picture Book' and 'People Take Pictures Of Each Other'.

Avory meanwhile is sent off to create some press interest with the media, including an interview with Rob Mackie for *Record Mirror* in which the drummer predicts: "I have the feeling that Drury Lane could be the start of a natural extension of live Kinks concerts that should have started long ago."

Sunday 7th

➜ Full band rehearsal for the new *Village Green Preservation Society* takes place in the function room of the White Hart, a pub in Tottenham, north London.

Wednesday 10th – Thursday 11th

Rehearsals for the new *Village Green* show take place at Konk Studios, Hornsey, north London, which is the band's new but as-yet unfinished recording studio.

Friday 12th

Another full band rehearsal for *Village Green* at the White Hart, Tottenham.

Sunday 14th

Theatre Royal, Drury Lane *central London* 8:00pm, *The Village Green Preservation Society*, with The Pigsty Hill Light Orchestra

Although preparations were rushed, this show marks the first realised incarnation of Ray's long-standing vision of an expanded, multimedia, theatrical presentation based on a single song, 'Village Green', that he wrote back at the end of 1966. The development of the idea is still not complete, however, and Ray will spend the next 18 months pursuing it, in what becomes known simply as *Preservation*.

Tonight's show is presented as part of the *Fanfare For Europe* concert series celebrating Britain's entry into the European Common Market. The standard five-man Kinks plus the three-piece Mike Cotton Sound (Cotton on trumpet, John Beecham on trombone, Alan Holmes on saxophone) is augmented by a chorus of four men (possibly including Lewis Rich) and two women (probably Lee Pavey and Sue Brown). In addition there is a six-piece brass band – two trumpets, trombone, saxophone, sousaphone, plus one other – conducted by Pip Williams, who also acts as the show's musical director.

The opening Pigsty Hill act features 1950s skiffle. Then the main show opens with a brass band overture, with the players in complete bandmaster's gear. The stage is set to resemble London's Vauxhall Gardens, the legendary 18th/19th-century outdoor musical pleasure-grounds, ringed in strings of lights and centred on an ornate gilt gateway through which the stars of the show come on stage. Lighting effects and backdrop projections by Joe's Lights include movie footage and various still photos. Images used during the show including pre-war family photos for 'Picture Book', a red-white-and-blue sunset over Big Ben for 'Waterloo Sunset', and stills of The Rolling Stones, Mary Quant and the Kray Twins for 'Where Are They Now'.

Response in the press is almost universally raving. "One of the best rock concerts it has ever been my pleasure to attend," writes Karl Dallas in *Melody Maker*, and, "The best rock concert I've been to in ages," agrees Mitch Howard in *Record Mirror*, while Michael Wale of *Disc* says, "One of the most enjoyable performances of [Ray's] career." The show only disappoints because, as Jerry Gilbert in *Sounds* relates, "its concept is manifested so blatantly yet so closely to a regular Kinks gig, rather than a full departure from the routine that Ray Davies talks of".

Set-list: 'The Village Green Overture' (brass band only), 'I'm Going Home', 'Victoria', medley 'Dedicated Follower Of Fashion' / 'A Well Respected Man' / 'Sunny Afternoon' / 'Waterloo Sunset', 'Lola', 'Have A Cuppa Tea', 'Acute Schizophrenia Paranoia Blues', 'Cricket', 'Mr Wonderful', 'Alcohol', 'Village Green' (instrumental), 'Where Are They Now?', medley 'You Really Got Me' / 'All Day And All Of The Night', 'Picture Book', 'People Take Pictures Of Each Other', 'Time Song', 'Salvation Road', 'The Village Green Preservation Society', 'Celluloid Heroes', 'Here Comes Yet Another Day', medley 'Louie Louie' / 'Hang On Sloopy'.

Monday 22nd

A press release announces UK tour dates and the re-release of the 'Celluloid Heroes' single.

Tuesday 23rd

The band is at BBC Television Theatre in west London for rehearsals for an appearance on BBC-2's *In Concert*, a TV series that presents rock bands of the day in a live setting. They talk to Danny Holloway for a feature in *NME* in which Ray speaks of his visions for the near future. "At Drury Lane we were doing our regular set with a few new ideas thrown in," he says. "But really that's the last time I want to perform last year's show. We're working on a new repertoire with a few surprises. I think we'd like to present even more of a visual performance. Perhaps we can take a lightshow around with us and present dialogue as well as the usual delivery."

Wednesday 24th

❏ **TV** BBC Television Centre *west London*. BBC-2 *In Concert* live performance 'Victoria', 'Acute Schizophrenia Paranoia Blues', 'Dedicated Follower Of Fashion', 'Lola', 'Holiday', 'Good Golly Miss Molly', medley 'You Really Got Me'/ 'All Day And All Of The Night', 'Waterloo Sunset', 'The Village Green Preservation Society', 'Village Green Overture' broadcast March 15th. Produced by Stanley Dorfman, the show features the five-man Kinks with the three-piece Mike Cotton Sound on all numbers, but for 'Waterloo Sunset' and 'The Village Green Preservation Society' they are augmented by the same six-piece brass band and six-person choir used for the recent Drury Lane show. As an outro, the brass band alone, conducted by Pip Williams, plays the 'Village Green Overture'.

Thursday 25th

The Great Lost Kinks Album released in the US. The record is issued by the band's old US company, Reprise, without Ray's knowledge or approval. It was informally mentioned as a potential release a year earlier, as *Son Of Kink Kronikles*, and has been lying in wait pending the response to the initial post-contract collection, *Kink Kronikles*.

Ray only learns of its existence by reading about it in *Billboard*, and has an American fan send a copy of the LP to his office in London. Particularly upsetting to Ray are the caustic liner notes by the now apparently disgruntled former Kinks-supporter John Mendelssohn,

---

The Great Lost Kinks Album

A1 'Till Death Us Do Part' (R. DAVIES).
A2 'There Is No Life Without Love' (D. DAVIES, R. DAVIES).
A3 'Lavender Hill' (R. DAVIES).
A4 'Groovy Movies' (R. DAVIES).
A5 'Rosemary Rose' (R. DAVIES).
A6 'Misty Water' (R. DAVIES).
A7 'Mr Songbird' (R. DAVIES).
B1 'When I Turn Out The Living Room Light' (R. DAVIES).
B2 'The Way Love Used To Be' (R. DAVIES).
B3 'I'm Not Like Everyody Else' (R. DAVIES).
B4 'Plastic Man' (R. DAVIES).
B5 'This Man He Weeps Tonight' (R. DAVIES).
B6 'Pictures In The Sand' (R. DAVIES).
B7 'Where Did My Spring Go' (R. DAVIES).

US release January 25th 1973 (Reprise MS 2127).
Musicians Ray Davies lead vocal except as noted, acoustic guitar, electric guitar, keyboards except as noted. Dave Davies lead vocal (A2, A4, B3, B5), electric guitar, backing vocal. Pete Quaife bass guitar except as noted. John Dalton bass guitar (B2). Mick Avory drums. Nicky Hopkins piano (A6, A7, B6), Mellotron (A7), harpsichord (A2, A5), organ (possibly A6, or else Ray Davies).
Recorded Pye Studios (No.2) central London; A1: September 1968; A2: probably March 1968; A3: August 1967; A5: probably March 1968; A6 May 5th 1968; A7: probably around November 1967; B3: May 12th 1966; B6 May 27th 1968; 4-track mixed to mono, except A6, A7 mixed to stereo, B3 3-track mixed to mono. Pye Studio (probably No.1) *central London*; A4: probably March 1969; B4: March 1969; B5: January or March 1969; 8-track mixed to stereo, except B4 mixed to mono. BBC Riverside Studios *central London*; B1: February 4th 1969; B7: January 28th 1969; probably 2-track mixed to mono. Morgan Studios *Willesden, north-west London*; B2: October 1970; 16 track-mixed to stereo.
Producer Ray Davies, except (B3) Shel Talmy.
Engineers Alan MacKenzie; Brian Humphries; Vic Maile; Andrew Hendriksen (B5); Mike Bobak (B1); unknown (B1, B7).
Chart high US number 145.

---

who spares nothing in his criticism for the band's current output and bemoans the loss of the reclusive, suburban Ray of the classic 1966-69 stretch. "Instead," he writes, "it's a bitchy, egocentric Davies who dominates [the *Show-Biz* album], one whose primary interest is making clear to his listener the agony he must endure to stay on the road entertaining us." A number of reviewers pick up on Mendelssohn's outburst. Ray is also displeased that a large number of the tracks are rejects that he never intended for public consumption.

The album's title is somewhat misleading as it does not reflect the content of the unreleased *Four More Respected Gentlemen* LP. Instead it's a random collection of leftover tracks, as old as 1966 and as recent as 1970, and this makes for an inconsistent record, both in musical style and in the quality of the recordings. The cornerstone of the album is a batch of songs submitted by The Kinks in July 1969 as "spare tracks", not intended for release and perhaps only provided then as contractual collateral.

Nevertheless, Reprise feels entitled to issue this one last compilation in their interpretation of their contract with The Kinks, although it will result in litigation (and the album is eventually withdrawn around 1975). Despite the controversy, fans of the group's 1960s recordings relish the cache of obscure gems that will help to turn the LP into a collectors' classic.

Crawdaddy! knowingly points out the barrel-scraping inconsistencies in the choice of material. It says the best tracks will make the album a worthwhile purchase for devoted fans, but notes it "lacks both the bountifulness and dramatic highlights of last year's somewhat similarly-intentioned *Kinks Kronikles*". Rock magazine concurs: "All told the album's main value will be to Kink Kultists who don't mind wading through second-rate material to get to the occasional highspots." *Rolling Stone* likewise considers that the record "basically represents dreg-ism" but "contains a surprising number of undeservedly esoteric Kinks classics" and "will sustain those archivists who … remain disappointed with Ray's recent Kinks recordings".

Friday 26th

'Celluloid Heroes'/ 'Hot Potatoes' single re-released in the UK. A rare re-promotion of a failed release from the pre-Christmas season. Ray is confident that the song will be a chart success, but even a second time around it stiffs miserably.

Monday 30th

A press release announces that the band is to record a new LP over the next six weeks and will tour with it as a show. Upcoming UK tour dates also announced.

February

▷ **TOUR STARTS** *UK Tour* (Feb 2nd – Mar 3rd).). **Line-up**: Ray Davies (lead vocal, guitar), Dave Davies (guitar, vocal), Mick Avory (drums), John Dalton (bass guitar), John Gosling (keyboard), Mike Cotton (trumpet), John Beecham (trombone), Alan Holmes (saxophone, clarinet). New songs added to repertoire: 'Picture Book', 'People Take Pictures Of Each Other'.

Friday 2nd

Trentham Gardens Ballroom *Stoke-on-Trent*; sponsored by Madeley College

➔ ● **RECORDING** Morgan Studios *Willesden, north-west London*. Work begins recording backing tracks for the new LP.

Friday 9th

Student Centre, Edinburgh University *Edinburgh, Scotland* with The Alex Harvey Band

Saturday 10th

Union Assembly Hall, University Of Strathclyde *Glasgow, Scotland*

➔ ● **RECORDING** Morgan Studios *Willesden, north-west London*. Continuing to record new LP.

Friday 16th

University College of Wales *Aberystwyth, Cardigans, Wales* with (probably) Babe Ruth

Saturday 17th

Stadium Liverpool with (probably) Babe Ruth

➔ ● **RECORDING** Morgan Studios *Willesden, north-west London*. Continuing to record new LP.

Friday 23rd

● **RECORDING** Morgan Studios *Willesden, north-west London*. Begin horn overdubs for new LP.

Saturday 24th

Sports Centre, University of Kent *Canterbury, Kent* 8:00pm, Kent Rock '73, with Babe Ruth, Mike Maran

Sunday 25th

Guildhall *Southampton* with Nick Pickett; sponsored by University of Southampton

Monday 26th

Top Rank Suite *Reading* 8:00pm-12:30am, *Reading Rag '73*, with Babe Ruth, Glencoe, Betsy Cook; sponsored by University of Reading
Set-list: 'Victoria', medley 'You're Looking Fine' / 'Little Queenie' / Reelin' And Rockin" / 'Shakin' All Over' / 'Be Bop A Lula', 'Till The End of the Day', 'Dedicated Follower of Fashion', 'Sunny Afternoon', 'Waterloo Sunset', 'Lola', medley 'Here Comes Yet Another Day' / 'Acute Schizophrenia Paranoia Blues', 'Mr Wonderful' (extract), 'Alcohol', medley 'Skin And Bone' / 'Dry Bones', medley 'You Really Got Me'/ 'Good Golly Miss Molly'.

➔ ● **RECORDING** Morgan Studios *Willesden, north-west London*. Continuing to record new LP. In addition to the two songs (**'One Of The Survivors'** and **'Scrapheap City'**) ultimately issued in April in the US as a single, songs believed recorded during the sessions in February and March include: a vocal version of **'Morning Song'**, eventually issued on Act 1 with the simpler title 'Morning'; two of the new songs debuted at Drury Lane in January, **'I'm Going Home'** and **'Time Song'**, neither of which are heard from again; and three others from the same show, likely in early versions: **'Cricket'**, **'Where Are They Now'** and **'Salvation Road'**. It is also possible that new recordings are made of **'Picture Book'** and **'People Take Pictures Of Each Other'**, and even **'The Village Green Preservation Society'**, but details are unknown. Two other stray songs about which little else is known are an unreleased song from this year called **'For You'** and another from late 1972/early 1973 called **'Using Me'**.

March

Thursday 1st

● **RECORDING** Morgan Studios *Willesden, north-west London*. Continue horn overdubs for new LP, starting at 8:30pm.

Friday 2nd

University of Exeter *Exeter* 8:00 pm, *Rag Ball '73*, with Jon Hiseman's Tempest

Saturday 3rd

University of Essex *Colchester* 8:00 pm, with Babe Ruth

Monday 5th

● **RECORDING** Konk Studios *Hornsey, north London*. The band's own brand new recording studio isn't officially open or even finished, but recording equipment is in place and running, and from this point sessions for the new LP switch to here from Morgan and work

kinks'73

continues, mostly on overdubs. Dave takes on the additional role of engineer prior to the hiring of a house engineer. These first sessions at Konk probably stretch into the whole of this week.

Friday 9th-Saturday 10th
● **RECORDING** Konk Studios *Hornsey, north London*. More horn overdubs for the new LP, with sessions from 5:00-10:30pm on Friday and 10:30-2:00am on Saturday.
☆ An appearance this weekend at the *Pop Festival* at Sporthall De Vliegermolen in Voorburg, Netherlands is cancelled. The Kinks are announced for the show but say they never booked.

→ ● **RECORDING** Konk Studios *Hornsey, north London*. An album's worth of material is reportedly finished by this time, and Ray completes final mixing on Tuesday 27th. A new single is due to coincide with the upcoming US tour, and two tracks are chosen: 'One Of The Survivors' and 'Scrapheap City'.

⇨ **TOUR STARTS** *Tour Of North America* (Mar 30th – Apr 14th). **Line-up**: Ray Davies (lead vocal, guitar), Dave Davies (guitar, vocal), Mick Avory (drums), John Dalton (bass guitar), John Gosling (keyboard), Mike Cotton (trumpet), John Beecham (trombone), Alan Holmes (saxophone, clarinet). The band leaves for New York City on Tuesday 27th. The two following days are set aside for press functions, primarily with Ray doing interviews from the Hotel Navarro on Central Park South where the band is staying.

Friday 30th
Rose Hill Gymnasium, McGinley Center, Fordham University *Bronx, NY* 8:00pm, with Aerosmith; sponsored by Lehman College & Fordham University
The Kinks opt for two lower-key shows in local colleges in the New York area rather than another of the high-profile venues they have played there of late. Aerosmith is a new young band on Columbia Records pushing their first album.
☆ Earlier in the day, Ray is at Sterling Sound in New York City where he oversees mastering of the 'One Of The Survivors' / 'Scrapheap City' single, which is finally delivered to RCA Records and registered in their tape log the following Monday.

Saturday 31st
Alumni Hall, St. John's University *Jamaica, NY* 8:00pm, with Argent
Reportedly a first rate performance by both bands. Argent includes future Kinks rhythm section Jim Rodford and Bob Henrit. The Kinks' set is characterised by Ray's strong rapport with the crowd. The highpoint for many is the now well-developed routine during 'Alcohol' where Ray sprays the front rows with beer, to which the well-prepared audience responds by spraying beer back on stage. A reviewer from *St. John's Torch* says that during 'Celluloid Heroes' a film is shown of the various characters from the song. Also featured tonight is the new (delayed) single, 'One Of The Survivors', and the revived medley of 'Picture Book' / 'People Tale Pictures Of Each Other', coupled with snatches of old standards 'Maybe It's Because I'm A Londoner' and 'If I Were A Rich Man'.

April

Sunday 1st
Music Hall *Boston, MA* 7:00pm, with Aerosmith
"The very best rock concert of the year," reckons *The Boston Globe*.

"The group was amazingly tight musically and they seemed to be doing their best to erase their shoddy, drunken image of a few years ago."

Monday 2nd
Elting Gymnasium, State University of New York College at New Paltz *New Paltz, NY* 9:00pm, with Aerosmith
Phonograph Record Magazine says the band's stage show has mutated into a mock drunken parody at the expense of their fine musical heritage. Nonetheless, the concert features the never-before-performed-live 'Johnny Thunder' along with the revived coupling of 'Picture Book' and 'People Take Pictures of Each Other'. (Day off following in New York City.)

Wednesday 4th
Palace Concert Theater *Providence, RI* 8:00pm, with Aerosmith

Thursday 5th
Massey Hall *Toronto, ON, Canada* 9:00pm, with Michaeljon

Friday 6th
Century Theater *Buffalo, NY* 8:30pm, with Wet Willie
"The Kinks roared into Buffalo," says the *Buffalo News*, "and were magnificent before a packed house, playing with intensity and exuberance. As a performer [Ray] is a dynamo of energy, campily strutting up and down the stage." The finale includes snatches of 'If I Were A Rich Man', Sinatra's 'My Way', and 'Hava Nagila', and Dave ends with 'Good Golly Miss Molly'.

Saturday 7th
Theater For The Performing Arts, Newark State College *Union, NJ* 8:00pm, with Aerosmith
Tonight is reportedly a poorly attended performance with an estimated crowd of only 300 to 400.

Sunday 8th
Alumni Gymnasium, Rider College *Lawrenceville, NJ* 8:00pm, with Aerosmith
Travel day to Los Angeles and then day off follow.

Wednesday 11th
Hollywood Palladium *Hollywood, CA* 8:00pm, with Rory Gallagher; promoted by KDAY & Pacific Presentations; tickets $5.50 advance / $6 door
After spraying the front row of the audience with beer and doing mock exercises during 'Skin And Bone', Ray slips at the front of the stage and falls or is dragged into the audience, and is passed around by the crowd. Back onstage he emerges from the amps minus his trousers, and does the encore in his underwear. "One of the most fun-filled evenings in LA in a long time," says *Billboard*, "with Ray Davies eligible for one of the best showmen in rock, despite numerous distractions in the form of sound problems [and] guitar tuning problems." (Travel day following.)
Set-list: 'Victoria', 'Brainwashed', 'Acute Schizophrenia Paranoia Blues', 'Holiday', 'Picture Book', 'People Take Pictures Of Each Other', 'Mr Wonderful', 'Till The End Of The Day', 'Celluloid Heroes', 'Muswell Hillbilly', 'Dedicated Follower Of Fashion', 'Here Comes Yet Another Day', 'Harry Rag', 'Alcohol', medley 'Sunny Afternoon' / 'Dead End Street', medley 'Skin And Bone' / 'Dry Bones', 'Good Golly Miss Molly', medley 'You Really Got Me' / 'All Day And All Of The Night'.

Friday 13th-Saturday 14th
Winterland Ballroom *San Francisco, CA* 8:00pm, with Dan Hicks & His Hot Licks, Mason Proffit
"Ray Davies maintains his crown as the king of camp rock, with The

Kinks proving themselves as one of the finest live bands," writes *NME*'s reviewer, "with a range of material and sensibility that is truly peerless." These shows are farewell concerts for Hicks's band. One of their two female singers, Maryann Price, will later be contacted by Ray and hired for a short time as a member of The Kinks, early in 1974. (The band flies home to London the following day.)

Monday 16th

According to his later account in *X-Ray* this is when Ray returns home to an empty house and, slightly later, suffers a concussion in a pub brawl while trying to track down his wife, Rasa. It launches Ray's personal life into turmoil for the coming months, all the while facing a contractual obligation to complete the next Kinks album.

Friday 20th

'One Of The Survivors' / 'Scrapheap City' single released in the US. Typically for The Kinks, this appears just after the tour is completed. Ray is unhappy with the record and there seems to be little support or promotion, but it does manage to creep into the bottom of the chart at number 108, an achievement that even 'Celluloid Heroes' did not match.

→ With pressure to meet a contractually-mandated deadline in about five weeks for completion of the new LP, Ray is supposed to be busy putting finishing touches and doing the mixing of tracks at Konk, while the studio proper is nearing completion. But he is completely out of commission for about three weeks following his return from the States.
→ Cancelled at this time is an April 29th appearance by the band at the *Golden Rose TV Festival* in Montreux, Switzerland.

Monday 30th

A press release publicly announces the formation of Kinks Recording Enterprises Ltd, and says that a resident engineer is being sought for the band's new studio, Konk.

May

A tour of Australia and Japan tentatively scheduled for May is delayed

---

One Of The Survivors single

A **'One Of The Survivors'** (R. DAVIES).
B **'Scrapheap City'** (R. DAVIES).

US release April 20th 1973 (RCA Victor 74-0940).
Musicians Ray Davies electric guitar (A), acoustic guitar (B), lead vocal, harmonica (A). Dave Davies electric guitar, backing vocal (A). John Dalton bass guitar. Mick Avory drums. John Gosling baby grand piano, Hammond organ (B). Alan Holmes baritone saxophone (A), tenor saxophone, flute (B).
Recorded Morgan Studios Willesden, north-west London and Konk Studios Hornsey, north London; March 1973; 16-track mixed to stereo.
Producer Ray Davies.
Engineers Mike Bobak (Morgan); Dave Davies (Konk).
Chart high US none.

---

until November in order to work on the new LP, but a press release announces a concert at London's Festival Hall for June 8th, also saying the new LP is being completed and that the band will return to the US in July.

Around the middle of the month, Ray returns to mixing the new double album, but by the end decides to scrap much of the existing work because he is generally dissatisfied with it.

Trumpet-player Mike Cotton leaves The Kinks around this time to join Acker Bilk's trad-jazz band. Laurie Brown is hired in his place, and the three horn players now officially become an integral part of The Kinks rather than a separately billed augmentation.

On the 31st there's a full band rehearsal for the upcoming shows.

June

Friday 1st

The horn section holds an acoustic rehearsal at the flat of the new trumpet player, Laurie Brown.

Monday 4th – Tuesday 5th

Full band rehearsals for the forthcoming shows.

Wednesday 6th

Town Hall *Birmingham* 7:30pm
A show booked at the last minute as a warm-up for the London show on Friday, and as it goes largely unpublicised only about half the hall's 2,000 seats are filled.
☆ The Kinks send a telegram to Stealer's Wheel, care of their old management company Boscobel Productions, congratulating the group (and in effect The Kinks' former manager) as their single 'Stuck In The Middle With You' moves into the upper reaches of the UK charts.

Friday 8th

Royal Festival Hall *central London* 8:00pm, with Harvey Andrews & Graham Cooper
Kinks admirer Barbara Charone raves about the show in the *NME*. She feels it's a particular challenge because of the inherently cold atmosphere of the venue, by reputation a poor location for a rock show. It was hoped this concert would incorporate more of the recent *Preservation* material, but in fact features a typical range of material for the time.

→ ● **RECORDING** Konk Studios *Hornsey, north London*. Work begins to re-record *Preservation* tracks, starting with **'Sitting In The Midday Sun'**, which will become the next single. It is generally credited as the first recording made at the new Konk Studios.

Wednesday 20th

Rasa Davies leaves the family home in East Finchley with her two daughters.

Saturday 23rd

A promotional film is shot for 'Sitting In The Midday Sun'.

Monday 25th

A press release announces an appearance at London's White City for July 15th. Ray later reveals that he accepts this booking as a means to try to publicly woo back Rasa and family, as he plans to announce his retirement from the stage for their benefit. (It also means the July tour of the US will be slightly delayed, causing the shuffling of a few of the early dates there.)

➔ A week following his wife's departure, an emotionally distraught Ray is admitted to hospital for suspected barbiturate poisoning. He is treated and released.

Friday 29th

'Sitting In The Midday Sun' / 'One Of The Survivors' double-A-side single released in the UK. Reviews are divided. *Melody Maker* loves it: "A lazy summer sound ... another winning tune from Raymond Douglas Davies and the boys." *Disc* offers faint praise, calling it "one of the week's better releases", but *NME* lays into it. "One of those lightweight singles The Kinks put out when they're waiting for Ray Davies to come up with something truly remarkable. It's an adequately pleasant little summer song that will do what it's supposed to do." Owing to Ray's personal crisis and the necessity to finish the next LP, no press work is done to help promote the record. It does not chart – a trend that the band does not seem able to reverse.

July

Monday 2nd

Sitting In The Midday Sun single

A 'Sitting In The Midday Sun' (R. DAVIES).
B-UK 'One Of The Survivors' (R. DAVIES).
B-US 'Sweet Lady Genevieve' (R. DAVIES).

UK release (A/B-UK) June 29th 1973 (RCA Victor RCA 2387).
US release (A/B-US) August 1973 (RCA Victor LPBO 5001).
Musicians Ray Davies acoustic guitar (A, B-US), electric guitar (B-UK), lead vocal, harmonica (B-UK, B-US). Dave Davies electric-acoustic guitar (A, B-UK), electric guitar (B-US), backing vocal. John Dalton bass guitar. Mick Avory drums, bongos (A). John Gosling electric piano, Hammond organ (B-US). Alan Holmes alto flute (A), baritone saxophone (B-UK).
Recorded Konk Studios *Hornsey, north London*; A: June 1973; B-US July 1973; 16-track mixed to stereo. B-UK: Morgan Studios *Willesden, north-west London* and Konk Studios *Hornsey, north London*; March 1973; 16-track mixed to stereo.
Producer Raymond Douglas Davies.
Engineers Roger Beale and Dave Davies (A, B-US); Mike Bobak (Morgan), and Dave Davies (Konk) (B-UK).
Chart high UK none; US none.

Attempting some damage control, a press release announces that Ray did not take an overdose.

➔ ● **RECORDING** Konk Studios *Hornsey, north London*. The Kinks are back in the studio where they record **'Sweet Lady Genevieve'**, a brand new song Ray has written in the course of his personal crisis and another thinly-veiled appeal to his estranged wife. Further recording and/or re-recording is probably done as well for the LP around this time.
☆ A US tour was originally scheduled for July. Once the White City show in London is booked, the earlier American dates are rescheduled. They include: July 11th Pine Knob Music Theater, Independence Township, MI; 15th Kinetic Playground, Chicago, IL; 17th Merriweather Post Pavilion, Washington, DC. Further scheduled dates that are also ultimately scrapped include: July 30th Roseland Ballroom,

New York, NY; 31st Merriweather Post Pavilion, Washington, DC (rescheduled date). The latter is cancelled quite close to the day of the show, indicating that the start of the delayed tour is only cancelled after the events following White City (see 15th).

Friday 13th

RCA receives tapes of the new US single, 'Sitting In The Midday Sun' / 'Sweet Lady Genevieve'. The entire new double album is probably contractually due at this point, but is delayed until the autumn.

Sunday 15th

White City Stadium *west London* 12midday-10:00pm, *Great Western Express Festival*, with Sly & The Family Stone (headliners), Edgar Winter's White Trash, Canned Heat, Lindisfarne, Barclay James Harvest, JSD Band
Guitarist Phil Palmer, The Davies's nephew, joins The Kinks on stage during the finalé, in front of a crowd of 30,000. After the last song Ray announces his "retirement" to the audience, but his message is somewhat masked by pre-recorded music coming through the PA. The band doesn't return for an encore. Ray is later admitted to Whittington Hospital for suspected amphetamine poisoning and then released after having his stomach pumped.
Set-list: 'Victoria', 'Brainwashed', 'Dedicated Follower Of Fashion', 'Lola', 'Waterloo Sunset', 'Celluloid Heroes', 'Acute Schizophrenia Paranoia Blues', 'Holiday', medley 'Skin And Bone' / 'Dry Bones', 'One Of The Survivors', medley 'Alcohol' / 'If I Were a Rich Man' / 'Sunny Afternoon', medley 'You Really Got Me' / 'All Day And All of the Night'.

Monday 16th

Secretary Marion Rainford, based at the Kinks Productions office in Highgate, north London, does phone interviews with the British music press and issues a release in an effort to control the reaction to Ray's announcement. Ray meanwhile takes two weeks off, completely stopping any musical work and staying at Dave's house in Southgate, north London.

Monday 30th

A press release breaks the silence and announces that Ray Davies has returned to the band, and that The Kinks have a tour planned for September.

August

➔ Ray accompanies Dave and family to rural Denmark for a two-week holiday.
☆ **'Sitting In The Midday Sun' / 'Sweet Lady Genevieve'** single released in the US. Alan Betrock in *Rock Marketplace* writes: "The new Kinks record has to bring smiles onto a lot of faces. It seems as if Ray has seen the light and taken to heart the criticism heaped upon him for his trashy work on RCA. Both sides of the new single are vintage Kinks tracks extraordinaire. 'Sitting In The Midday Sun' sounds like it could have come right off of *Village Green* and melodically and lyrically is quite fine. 'Sweet Lady Genevieve' is the most commercial of the sides, and should really be the A-side. This one is so good, it could have come from the *Something Else* LP. Hopefully this is just the start of a new direction for The Kinks. If so, I will retrieve my Kinks Fan Club button from my archives where it has been gathering an enormous amount of dust."
● **RECORDING** Konk Studios *Hornsey, north London*. Ray and the band return in earnest to resume work on the new LP at Konk Studios at this time.

Tuesday 28th

Ray issues a formal statement about his retirement. "Several weeks ago I wrote a letter to the world; it turned out to be a letter to me. But I do feel that I made a decision, whether motivated or not, to change the format of the band. The White City was not a happy place to say goodbye. The sun wasn't shining, my shirt was not clean, and anyway rock festivals have never held many happy memories for me personally, and I want these shows to be happy.

"The Kinks are close enough now to be able to work as a team in whatever they do and anyone who thinks it is only my back-up band is very mistaken. On stage it's like Leeds United – all team work. In the studio there are still things to extract from The Kinks on an artistic level. Whether or not it turns out to be commercial remains to be seen.

"I have just spent a couple of weeks with my brother Dave. At first we didn't talk about music, but then we started singing and playing guitars one day and before we knew it we were like a couple of ordinary 'punk rock punters' trying to play some Chuck Berry riffs."

→ Ray moves into a new house in Surrey, shifting his main operating base south of London.

Thursday 30th

The Kinks with various singers, horn players and a studio engineer are photographed by Chris Hopper outside a pub, The Flask in Highgate, north London. The photo will be used for the cover of the *Preservation Act 1* album.

☆ Ray later told *Making Music*'s Jon Lewin: "I tried to stop being a pop musician in 1973. I wanted genuinely to give up playing in a band, cos I think I'd said everything I wanted to say in that particular form at the time. I'd made *Muswell Hillbillies*, *Everybody's In Show-Biz*, and I felt I wanted to do something else, so I went into making musicals. For about three or four years, all I did was write shows."

September

Monday 3rd

A press release announces a new single and full British tour dates.

Friday 7th

In an effort to re-establish his presence in the public eye, Ray does a quick flurry of media appearances to help smooth over the more sensationalist press coverage he has been afforded since his retirement statement in July.

As a guest DJ he's interviewed today by Stuart Henry at BBC Broadcasting House, central London, for Radio-1 show *Rosko's Roundtable*. And a few days later, on Monday 10th, he's at the Beeb's Television Centre as a guest with writer Charlie Gillett and host Michael Dean in a panel discussion on pop music, which is broadcast on BBC-2's *Opinion* programme.

Saturday 8th

❏ **TV** BBC Television Centre *west London*. BBC-1 **It's Lulu** possibly live performance 'Lola' broadcast September 22nd.

→ ● **RECORDING** Konk Studios *Hornsey, north London*. Ray does final mixes for the *Preservation Act 1* album.

Friday 14th

Rehearsal for upcoming tour at Konk Studios at 3:00pm.

→ ● **RECORDING** Konk Studios *Hornsey, north London*. Ray continues to finish mixing the new LP through the week, having been unable to make the planned trip to RCA in New York City this week before the UK/Netherlands tour begins. The schedule is changed slightly, which requires cancellation of a Birmingham date next week as well as two days of planned filming in London for US television. Although the new record was intended to be a double album from the start, the delay in completion caused by the need to re-record it forces Ray to settle for the release only of what he will term "Act 1" as RCA insists on having an LP to release for the Christmas season. It has already been over a year since the band's last album.

↪ **TOUR STARTS** *Tour Of UK And Netherlands* (Sep 20th – Oct 7th). **Line-up**: Ray Davies (lead vocal, guitar), Dave Davies (guitar, vocal), Mick Avory (drums), John Dalton (bass guitar), John Gosling (keyboard), Laurie Brown (trumpet), John Beecham (trombone, tuba), Alan Holmes (saxophone, clarinet).

Thursday 20th

DeMontfort Hall *Leicester* 7:30pm

There is perhaps some symbolism here, at the start of what *Melody Maker* calls The Kinks' "umpteenth nationwide tour", as DeMontfort Hall was the site of their humiliating demotion to bottom of the rung at the start of their first package tour, way back in March 1964. As a hint that the Davies brothers recall those early roots, a rendition of Lonnie Donegan's skiffle hit, the traditional African-American song 'Long Lost John', is briefly added to the set, with John Beecham on tuba.

Set-list: 'Victoria', 'Brainwashed', medley 'You're Looking Fine' / 'Be Bop A Lula' / 'Shakin' All Over' / 'Little Queenie' / 'Sweet Little Sixteen', 'Dedicated Follower Of Fashion', 'Waterloo Sunset', 'Lola', 'Long Lost John', 'Acute Schizophrenia Paranoia Blues', medley 'Skin And Bones' / 'Dry Bones', 'Holiday', 'Alcohol', 'One Of The Survivors', 'Here Comes Yet Another Day', 'Celluloid Heroes', 'Good Golly Miss Molly', medley 'You Really Got Me'/ 'All Day And All Of The Night'.

Friday 21st

Locarno Ballroom *Sunderland*

'Sweet Lady Genevieve' / 'Sitting In My Hotel' single released in the UK. *Melody Maker* continues to back their efforts: "Opens with a mouth harp and guitar lick from [Beatles track] 'I Should Have Known Better' but troubled troubadour Ray Davies soon stamps Kinks all over the track. … I hope this is the hit it richly deserves to be." *NME* is becoming increasingly tougher in its criticism. "Quite nicely performed with some attractive harmonica and National guitar, and Ray sounds great, but the song ain't much cop (whatever that singularly quaint folk saying actually means)." Again, the single merits not one drop of chart action.

Saturday 22nd

Stadium *Liverpool* with Bloodstone

Sounds: "The Kinks were in great form … as they went through their complete songbook. But what could they finish on, having apparently sung everything? Would you believe that the 2,500-strong audience freaked to a totally Dixieland version of 'Dem Bones, Dem Dry Bones'? After an encore of 'You Really Got Me' The Kinks left the audience chanting for a full 20 minutes."

Sunday 23rd

Concert at Birmingham Hippodrome cancelled as Ray travels to New York.

Monday 24th

Ray oversees mastering of *Preservation Act 1* LP with Robert Ludwig at Sterling Sound in New York City.

Sweet Lady Genevieve single

A 'Sweet Lady Genevieve' (R. DAVIES).
B 'Sitting In My Hotel' (R. DAVIES).

UK release September 21st 1973 (RCA Victor 2418).
Musicians Ray Davies acoustic guitar, lead vocal, harmonica (A). Dave Davies electric guitar, backing vocal. John Dalton bass guitar. Mick Avory drums. John Gosling baby grand piano (A), Hammond organ (A). Mike Cotton trumpet (B).
Recorded A: Konk Studios Hornsey, north London; July 1973; 16-track mixed to stereo. B: Morgan Studios *Willesden, northwest London*; May-July 1972; 16-track mixed to stereo.
Producer Raymond Douglas Davies.
Engineers Roger Beale and Dave Davies (A); Mike Bobak (B).
Chart high UK none.

Tuesday 25th

Ray delivers tapes for *Preservation Act 1* to RCA, logged into their tape vaults on the 26th. He later travels back to London.
☆ Scheduled filming in London for US TV is cancelled, most likely for *Wide World In Concert*, which the band will do in June next year.

Wednesday 26th

The Palais *Manchester* 8:00pm

Friday 28th

De Doelen *Rotterdam, Netherlands* 8:15 pm, with Rob Hoeke Groep

Saturday 29th

Concertgebouw *Amsterdam, Netherlands* 12midnight, with Rob Hoeke Groep
☆ Probably today The Kinks attend a Gala at the Statenzaal, Hotel Hilton in Amsterdam where they are presented with Edison Awards – the Dutch equivalent of Grammys – for their LPs *Muswell Hillbillies* and *Everybody's In Show-Biz*. Presenting the award is Piet Beishuizen of Dutch record-industry association CCGC (Commissie Collectieve Grammofoonplaten Campagne).

October

Monday 1st

A press release says The Kinks will form their own record production company to record other artists, and that Dave Davies plans to issue a solo album in the new year. The production company is named Konkwest Ltd, for which papers are filed for incorporation on November 8th and certified on the 22nd. Artists already lined up for signing include March Hare, which is the Davies nephew Phil Palmer's trio (with bassist Nick South and drummer Neil McBain). Also earmarked for the new operation is singer Claire Hamill, who has already had two albums out on Island. Konkwest will become a focal point for both Ray and Dave's extracurricular activities outside The Kinks as active searching for new talent begins.

Wednesday 3rd

Apollo Theatre/Greens Playhouse *Glasgow, Scotland*

Thursday 4th

City Hall *Newcastle Upon Tyne* 7:30pm, with Raw Spirit

Friday 5th

An announced concert at the Ancienne Belgique in Brussels, Belgium is cancelled, and instead Ray is interviewed at length at The Kinks' office in Highgate, north London by Andrew Tyler for a major two-part feature in the *NME*. Speaking of the recent failure of their singles, Ray says he has on occasion intentionally set out to fail "by releasing certain records I knew were going to be the biggest flops of all time [including 'Shangri-La' and 'Celluloid Heroes']." He also talks about his current state of mind. "I've had number one records. I've done [that]," he says. "I'm trying to get interested in other things now. When you get a number one it really doesn't mean anything."

Sunday 7th

Fairfield Halls *Croydon, south London* with Bloodstone
Andrew Tyler in *NME* writes: "Davies and his Kinks are a thoroughly confusing phenomenon. We have Ray, a man of summer sandwiches and classless frippery, and we have his band of Kinks – now grown to include a three-man horn section – and still as rough-hewn as the junkiest pub band. Ray, except for a few magnificent interludes, can hardly sing, and his band, with the exception of the horns, can hardly play, yet despite everything, Sunday Night at The Fairfield Halls, Croydon, was a magnificently entertaining evening."

➔ In the course of setting up Konk over the past year-plus, Dave has recorded about five or six of his own songs on an 8-track recorder originally installed at the studio. With the formation of the band's separate production company, it is announced around now that Dave intends to finish the recordings and tape additional songs for a solo album in the new year. Gosling recalls writing string arrangements on three or four of eight or nine songs eventually recorded to some level of completion. Only two titles are known for certain, **'Midnight Sun'** and **'How Can I Love You'**.
☆ Soon after the tour ends, Ray unexpectedly takes time off after his brother-in-law Arthur dies in Australia. The scheduled release of the new Kinks album is accordingly delayed for two weeks, to November 16th.

November

➔ A tour of Australia and Japan loosely slated for late in the year is cancelled.
☆ Ray is again approached by Granada Television, this time to write a late-night musical related to his songwriting techniques. This will eventually become the TV special *Starmaker*, subsequently adapted to record and to stage as *A Soap Opera*.
☆ Dave is interviewed at Konk Studios by Rob Mackie for *Sounds* and talks of current progress on his solo album. "There are five songs written, brand new ones. Difficult to say what they're like, really. I think they're quite melodious, sort of folky, but there are a couple of rockers. I've done the back tracks, and I want to add keyboards, probably brass on some tracks. I don't know who, but I'll use people that I know, and I'll probably use the drummer [Neil McBain] and bass player [Nick South] from March Hare who we produce."

Friday 16th

Preservation Act 1 album released in the UK and US. *Melody Maker's* reviewer writes: "The influences of [The Who's] *Tommy* abound and distract from this album. That said, there are some Kinks gems, a pretty good if somewhat hackneyed storyline, and enough good music to swell the ranks of the Kinks Preservation Society." *Sounds*: "The most

Ray at London's White City, about to announce his 'retirement', July 15th 1973.

ambitious and wide-ranging Kinks record yet [is] already a stage nearer sounding like a play than a record. ... As a set it seems strangely disjointed too, in terms of plot, but this may be resolved when *Act 2* reaches us. *Preservation Act 1* contains some lovely songs, the familiar and lovely blend of gentleness and raunch that's kept the Kinks so good, [and] some fine playing, notable in the wide variety of piano styles by John Gosling. As a Kinks album it's fine. I just don't feel that *Preservation* adds up to the sum of its parts, yet." *Rolling Stone*: "Musically it is still too diffuse and inconsistent to rank with past classics, but it is close in spirit to albums like *Village Green Preservation Society* (which inspired the new LP) and indicates that the general pattern for the future is more than promising." *Hit Parader*: "Every

---

Preservation Act 1 album

A1 'Morning Song' (R. DAVIES).
A2 'Daylight' (R. DAVIES).
A3 'Sweet Lady Genevieve' (R. DAVIES).
A4 'There's A Change In The Weather' (R. DAVIES).
A5 'Where Are They Now?' (R. DAVIES).
A6 'One Of The Survivors' (R. DAVIES).
B1 'Cricket' (R. DAVIES).
B2 'Medley: Money & Corruption/I Am Your Man' (R. DAVIES).
B3 'Here Comes Flash' (R. DAVIES).
B4 'Sitting In The Midday Sun' (R. DAVIES).
B5 'Demolition' (R. DAVIES).

US release November 16th 1973 (RCA Victor LPL1-5002).
UK release November 16th 1973 (RCA Victor SF 8392).
Musicians Ray Davies acoustic guitar, electric guitar, lead vocal, harmonica (A6). Dave Davies electric guitar, second lead vocal (B5), backing vocal. John Dalton bass guitar. Mick Avory drums, bongos (B5), tympani (B3). John Gosling baby grand piano, Hammond organ. John Beecham tuba, trombone. Alan Holmes saxophones, clarinet, flute. Laurie Brown trumpet. Lee Pavey, Krysia Kocjan, Sue Brown, Pamela Travis, Lewis Rich backing vocals. Stanley Myers string arrangement (A1).
Recorded Konk Studios Hornsey, north London; June-September 1973 (except A6: Morgan Studios *Willesden, north-west London* and Konk Studios *Hornsey, north London*; March 1973); 16-track mixed to stereo.
Producer Raymond Douglas Davies.
Engineers Roger Beale/Dave Davies; Mike Bobak/Dave Davies (A6).
Chart high UK none; US number 177.

---

song has its own particular charm, ranging from hot blasts of rock to terribly reserved British humor. Thanks Ray."

Tuesday 20th

At the BBC Television Centre, west London Ray is briefly interviewed by *The Old Grey Whistle Test*'s host Bob Harris on videotape for broadcast later the same day on BBC-2. Other than this brief TV appearance, neither The Kinks nor Ray do any major media appearances or press associated with the release of the new LP. The brothers are instead completely immersed in recording and business chores associated with setting up their own record label, Konk Records. As Ray considers *Act 1* to be an incomplete work, it seems he is purposely saving any media push or touring related to the project until the second act is finished and released – which will happen next spring. ☆ In London Ray around this time meets with various record company executives, including Chris Blackwell at Island Records, to find a distributor for Konk Records.

Tuesday 27th

A final settlement is reached between Kinks Productions Ltd and Pye Records, after Pye disputed that the band had delivered the minimum amount of product due according to their contract. Pye seem to have a strong case and in the settlement The Kinks pay a considerable sum of money to account for the shortfall.

Saturday 8th

● **RECORDING** Konk Studios *Hornsey, north London*. Work begins recording 8-track demos for *Preservation Act 2*, including 'Shepherds Of The Nation', 'Money Talks' and three other songs.

December

At the start of the month some work probably begins on Claire Hamill's Konk album, perhaps rehearsals and demos, and on the 14th there's the first of what become annual Konk Christmas parties.

Ray is interviewed on the 17th by George Melly for Melly's Granada TV show in Manchester. Ray is probably also at the company's HQ to negotiate the late-night musical television play that the company wants him to write. "The play was supposed to be how I actually go about writing a song," Ray says later. "They came out and asked me to write anything I wanted to, and explained how I could present that idea as an experimental dream of sorts." Ray would be mulling over ideas for this in the coming months, and it eventually becomes the TV special *Starmaker*, later adapted to LP and stage as *A Soap Opera*.

Around the end of December, Ray and newly-hired Konk Records manager Tony Dimitriades check out a performance by Cafe Society at The Troubadour in Earls Court, west London. Soon afterwards, the group records a demo at Konk Studios as an audition for Konk Records.

➜ INDICATES EVENT AROUND THIS TIME BUT WITH NO FIRM DATE

1974

The focus on bringing Preservation to the world on record and on stage consumed much of this year, although Ray's workaholic ability to juggle multiple projects was demonstrated as he also created, wrote and staged a musical play, Starmaker, for British TV in the middle of a very busy year.

The way in which Ray threw himself into his work was further evidenced by additional recording projects in this, the first full year that Konk Studios was operational, and Ray was busy as producer of one of their first signings, Claire Hamill. Dave and John Gosling also took advantage of the Konk facilities and worked on an album by another Konk signing, Andy Desmond. Konk was a very busy studio this first year, and proved to be a worthwhile investment where the band could apply their creative energies.

In addition to touring East and West Coasts of the US and Scandinavia, and promoting the completed Preservation Act 2 LP, Ray spent the latter part of the year preparing the full-blown stage production of his Preservation epic. It finally went on the road across the US, ending the year with a three-night stand in London – and all accomplished to much critical acclaim. Record sales however continued to falter, even though The Kinks' popularity was still strong in their traditional bases and regular touring haunts.

January

→ ● **RECORDING** Konk Studios *Hornsey, north London*. Around the beginning of the month Ray and Dave continue to record demos for *Preservation Act 2* on the studio's 8-track machine.

On **'Mirror Of Love'** Ray plays acoustic guitar, piano and drums, and sings lead vocal; Dave contributes mandolin, Laurie Brown trumpet, and John Beecham tuba.

The demo – possibly begun in December, and mixed to stereo in February by Ray – will become the first released version of the song, though it will be re-recorded for a second UK release. (See entries for April 5th; July 26th.)

Sunday 6th

The horn section rehearses arrangements for upcoming sessions at Laurie Brown's flat in Brixton, south London.

→ Ray flies to Los Angeles. He negotiates with ABC Records president Jay Lasker for a deal to distribute product from The Kinks' own record label, Konk.

The fact that ABC is a competitor of the band's own label shows how little interest RCA is taking as the relationship between them and The Kinks rapidly erodes.

☆ Ray also meets with California singer Maryann Price whom he'd met when she was in Dan Hicks's band supporting The Kinks in San Francisco last April.

Despite her laryngitis that precludes a proper audition, he hires her. Price and husband John Girton will arrive in London late next month.

Thursday 24th

Papers are filed today for the establishment of a new company, Konkwest Ltd, with directors Ray Davies, Dave Davies, and Tony Dimitriades. Dimitriades is a friend from Muswell Hill, hired as the company's business manager. Konkwest is created to be the parent company that will in effect handle the running of the band's label, Konk Records.

February

Tuesday 12th

● **RECORDING** Konk Studios *Hornsey, north London*. More horn overdubs for *Preservation Act 2*.

Monday 18th – Wednesday 20th

Rehearsals with the horn section for *Act 2* take place at Konk Studios.
☆ A press release announces 'Mirror Of Love' as a new single for March 8th release.

Monday 25th

At a 4:00pm rehearsal at Konk Studios, a few songs that have been slated for recording soon are run through, complete with new singer Maryann Price on board.

New songs rehearsed for the tour on which Price and Pamela Travis will sing are 'Money Talks', 'Mirror Of Love', 'Here Comes Flash', and 'Demolition'.
☆ A press release notes that the 'Mirror Of Love' single is delayed for release until March 22nd.

→ The Kinks are photographed at Konk Studios by Chris Hooper. during the session the band is shot in character for the sleeve of the *Preservation Act 2* album wearing assorted costumes and with professional models, as well as in casual five-man-Kinks poses for use in ads for the new 'Mirror Of Love' single.

⇨ **TOUR STARTS** *Tour Of The UK* (Feb 26th – Mar 23rd). **Line-up**: Ray Davies (lead vocal, guitar), Dave Davies (guitar, vocal), Mick Avory (drums), John Dalton (bass), John Gosling (keyboard), John Beecham (trombone), Alan Holmes (saxophone), Laurie Brown (trumpet), Pamela Travis, Maryann Price (backing vocals). The Kinks are popular now with college crowds who enjoy singalongs of the hits and the inebriated party atmosphere. The band has no trouble maintaining their favour with the British music press, although there is the occasional criticism about augmenting the band so heavily beyond the classic five-man line-up. Unfortunately, the single they should be promoting doesn't reach the shops until well after the tour. Even though this is no great surprise given their chaotic history of such things, in this case it may actually be beyond their control: RCA is between pressing-plant contracts and the single has to be manufactured in France and imported back to Britain for sale.

Tuesday 26th

Town Hall *Birmingham* sponsored by University of Birmingham
NME feels the party atmosphere of the sell-out gig beats "the social satire of that connoisseur of the genre, Ray Davies" and that the horns' presence is merely "to dispel comparisons with Kinks Mark One". However, the *Sounds* writer finds the show "the most effective set I've ever seen from the Kinks".
Set-list: 'Victoria', medley 'You're Looking Fine' / 'Little Queenie' / 'Be-Bop-A-Lula' / 'Shakin' All Over', 'Waterloo Sunset', 'Dedicated Follower Of Fashion', 'Lola', 'Acute Schizophrenia Paranoia Blues', 'Demolition', 'Here Comes Flash', 'Here Comes Yet Another Day', 'Skin And Bone', 'Alcohol', 'Sunny Afternoon', 'Celluloid Heroes', 'Good Golly Miss Molly', medley 'You Really Got Me' / 'All Day And All Of The Night'.

Wednesday 27th – Thursday 28th

● **RECORDING** Konk Studios *Hornsey, north London*. Recording continues for *Act 2*.

March

Friday 1st

Sports Hall, Brunel University *Uxbridge, Middx*
"Crammed with an eager audience," says *Melody Maker*, "[and] highly entertaining."

Saturday 2nd

Refectory, University Of Leeds *Leeds* 8:00pm, with Bill Haley & The Comets
A great double-bill pairing them with rock'n'roll legend Haley, still a draw in his later years for a devoted British audience. This may be the last time that the band plays 'You're Looking Fine', long a concert staple; it effectively disappears from standard set-lists after tonight. (Day off following.)

Monday 4th – Tuesday 5th

● **RECORDING** Konk Studios *Hornsey, north London*. Work continues on *Act 2*. Dave is interviewed by *Record & Radio Mirror* and again refers to his hopes that his solo album will be out this summer.

Wednesday 6th

Central Hall, University of York *York* 8:00pm, with March Hare
"One of the most zany nights of musical entertainment witnessed in a long time," says the University's paper *Nouse*. March Hare includes the Davies' nephew, guitarist Phil Palmer.

Thursday 7th

University Of Leicester *Leicester* 8:00pm, with March Hare

Friday 8th

West Refectory, University Of Hull *Hull* 8:00pm-1:30 am, Union Ball, with March Hare, Snafu

Saturday 9th

Union Assembly Hall, University Of Strathclyde *Glasgow, Scotland* 8:00pm, with Bilbo Baggins; tickets £1
The school concert committee rejects The Kinks' preferred opening acts of March Hare and Claire Hamill, insisting on a band of their own choosing. (Travel day to London follows.)

Monday 11th – Thursday 14th

● **RECORDING** Konk Studios *Hornsey, north London*. Work continues on *Act 2*, including horn overdubs slated for 2:15pm on Tuesday.

Friday 15th

Great Hall, University of Lancaster *Lancaster* 8:00pm, with Snafu; tickets £1

Saturday 16th

University Of Bristol *Bristol*
"The Kinks concert produced an enthusiasm and fervour in the audience to equal the most partisan football choir," says *Sounds*.

Sunday 17th – Friday 22nd

● **RECORDING** Konk Studios *Hornsey, north London*. Ray mixes, and various overdubs are done, including the horns which are booked for a 4:00-8:00pm session on Monday and 2:15-5:00pm on Wednesday.

Friday 22nd

University Of Bath *Bath*
☆ Scheduled release of the 'Mirror Of Love' single again delayed, to April 5th, due to pressing-plant problems.

Saturday 23rd

Hastings Pier Pavilion *Hastings, Sussex*
☆ As the new double-album nears completion, Ray begins his press campaign with a prolonged interview for *Melody Maker* in which he speaks yet again of his desire to make films. "I don't know whether I want to direct, produce or what," he says, "I just want to make films about people." Of the still un-formed project for Granada TV, he reveals: "[It will be a] musical about a writer who becomes so deeply involved in his work that he becomes one of his own characters."

Monday 25th

Band rehearsals at Konk Studios.
☆ Konk Records signs a deal with ABC/Dunhill Records for distribution in the US and Canada, says a press release. This is a master lease deal – meaning Konkwest pays for all recording costs up-front. The deal is initially set for an ambitious five LPs every year.

Sunday 24th – Thursday 28th

● **RECORDING** Konk Studios *Hornsey, north London*. Ray completes the mixing of the *Preservation Act 2* double-LP.

⇨ **TOUR STARTS** *US Tour: 1st Leg* (Apr 3rd – 20th). **Line-up**: Ray Davies (lead vocal, guitar), Dave Davies (guitar, vocal), Mick Avory (drums), John Dalton (bass), John Gosling (keyboard), John Beecham (trombone), Alan Holmes (saxophone), Laurie Brown (trumpet), Pamela Travis, Maryann Price (backing vocals). March Hare guitarist

Phil Palmer tours with band as a roadie and occasional auxiliary guitarist. Henry Gross, ex-1950s revivalists Sha Na Na singer turned rock frontman, opens a number of the shows. This leg of the tour sticks to the main predominantly East Coast cities where The Kinks' reputation is strongest, with only a quick dip into the upper South. Richmond, VA, is a new stop-off in place of the usual booking in the Washington DC area.

Ray takes the tapes of the new LP with him to the US – which, typically, means the record won't reach the public until after this tour. But he does intend to properly stage the complete *Preservation* work later in the year, so he probably considers this tour as more of a stop-gap to get the band back in front of US audiences after a full year's absence.

The tour can be seen as a minor test-run for the more ambitious full staging of *Preservation* later in the year, as the number of band members grows from that of previous US tours.

April

Monday 1st – Tuesday 2nd
Ray heads to New York City, a day ahead of the band. On Tuesday he's at Sterling Sound where he oversees mastering with Robert Ludwig, completing the 'Money Talks' single and getting well into the *Preservation Act 2* album.

Wednesday 3rd
Playhouse, Hofstra University *Hempstead, NY* 8:00pm, probably with Elliott Murphy

Singer Maryann Price is ill and hospitalised upon arrival in the US and misses this and the next two concerts. It seems the other new vocalist Pamela Travis does not appear either, meaning that new numbers from *Preservation* are not done and some impromptu choices are made instead. "A great treat for the noisy Kinks addicts but a decided disappointment to concert-goers accustomed to stage performances, not nightclub acts," says the *Hofstra Chronicle*.

Set-list: 'One Of The Survivors', 'Where Are They Now', 'Dedicated Follower Of Fashion', 'Waterloo Sunset', 'Mirror Of Love', 'Sunny Afternoon', 'Celluloid Heroes', 'Here Comes Yet Another Day', 'Here Comes Flash', 'Demolition', 'Banana Boat Song', 'Lola', 'Money (That's What I Want)', 'Alcohol', medley 'Skin And Bone' / 'Dry Bones', 'Good Golly Miss Molly'.

☆ Masters for the 'Money Talks' single and the *Preservation Act 2* album are logged in at RCA's US office today, but apparently mastering work is not complete and further time will be spent in the studio on the 8th/9th.

Thursday 4th
Providence Civic Center *Providence, RI* 8:00pm, with Poco, Henry Gross

Singer Maryann Price is still ill and does not appear. For this show the normal positioning of the Civic Center stage is moved to allow more intimacy. Hampered by a bad mike, a mediocre sound-monitoring system, and the lack of a prior soundcheck, the band still comes across well. "Ray Davies flounced on stage," says the *Providence Journal*, "and immediately owned the place. From the opening, no doubt was left that The Kinks can transform even a rowdy Civic Center crowd [of 6,000] into the RI chapter of the Village Green Preservation Society."

Friday 5th
Palace Theater *Waterbury, CT* 9:00pm, with Henry Gross
Singer Maryann Price is again ill and does not perform.

'Mirror Of Love' / 'Cricket' single released in the UK. This is the original demo version of 'Mirror'. RCA puts its full weight into advertising and the critics are all raving. *Sounds*: "This is another little gem from the band." *Melody Maker*: "With an alcoholic off-beat and amusing lyrics, zis must be a hit!" But the lateness of the release date following the UK tour doesn't help, and despite the efforts the record is a flop.

NME's review is written by none other than Chrissie Hynd, as she then bills herself, future Pretenders leader and star-to-be. Her reviewing gig is an early job as she hustles to get into the music scene. 'Mirror Of Love' has her gushing: "Yet another Kinks single that positively reeks of white trousers and loafers. Raymond Douglas Davies

---

Mirror Of Love single (first version)

A **'Mirror Of Love'** (R. DAVIES).
B **'Cricket'** (R. DAVIES).

UK release April 5th 1974 (RCA Victor RCA LPBO 5015).
Musicians Ray Davies lead vocals, acoustic guitar, piano, drums. Dave Davies mandolin. John Beecham tuba. Laurie Brown trumpet.
Recorded Konk Studios *Hornsey, north London*; A: December 1973 or January 1974; B: June-September 1973: A: 8-track mixed to stereo; B: 16-track mixed to stereo.
Producer Raymond Douglas Davies.
Engineer Roger Beale (A); Roger Beale/Dave Davies (B).
Chart high UK none.

---

is the only songwriter who can write such personal material (and he is always very personal) and never get embarrassing. One of the true romantics of our time."

Saturday 6th
Felt Forum, Madison Square Garden Center *New York, NY* 7:30 & 11:00pm, with Henry Gross; promoted by Ron Delsner; tickets $6, $7

A second show is added due to popular demand, and both sell out, even after a long 16-month absence by the band from New York City. Reflecting their recent brush with Bill Haley, The Kinks perform an impromptu version of 'Rock Around The Clock' in a medley with 'Shake Rattle And Roll' and 'Blue Suede Shoes'. John Rockwell raves in the *New York Times*: "[Ray] Davies was hopelessly hoarse late Saturday. But his gifts of showmanship go beyond voice alone, and as a showman he was in fine form …. He manages to sing his great songs year after year and still give the illusion that he is enjoying them. And that is what a performing pro is all about." Frank Rose in *Zoo World* calls it "more of a party than a concert". In fact, an RCA Records party is held after the show – and the proceedings are interrupted by a streaker. (Day off in New York City following.)

Monday 8th – Tuesday 9th
Ray oversees final mastering of *Preservation Act 2* LP at Sterling Sound. He also gives press interviews at the Warwick Hotel, also in New York City, and makes a formal announcement of the signing with ABC Records to handle The Kinks' own Konk Records in the US. Tony Dimitriades is named as the Konk business manager. Ray also says that negotiations are underway to record an LP for Konk by actor Vincent Price, though this will never materialise. (The band travels to Boston on the late train Tuesday night to beat an early spring snowstorm.)

Wednesday 10th

Music Hall *Boston, MA* 7:30pm, with Elliott Murphy
'Salvation Road' is performed tonight, not yet a regular song in the repertoire. "It was a rather well ordered Davies," says *The Boston Globe*, "at least compared to certain past performances. Too often [the horns and female singers] sounded hopelessly out of place. The Kinks are one group that should never, ever change. Yet the more than 4,300 people … did not seem to mind."

Thursday 11th

Capitol Theater *Passaic, NJ* 8:00pm, with Elliott Murphy
Laurie Werner in *The Village Voice* chimes in with a sour note on the tour and a reportedly out-of-control Ray. "Once in the spotlight, his flouncing and posing like a marionette run amok brought cheers from the audience but scowls from the band. He either lagged or leaped ahead, breaking into or abandoning numbers at will, leaving the others to fill the void. Singers Maryann and Pamela seemed amused but there was murder in brother Dave's eyes." Werner also feels the new material is disappointing, saying: "I sorely miss Ray's searing or compassionate satire and his controlled recklessness," prompting the writer to close by wondering, "Has he gone too far over the brink to return?".

Friday 12th

The Spectrum *Philadelphia, PA* 8:00pm, with King Crimson, Frampton's Camel

Saturday 13th

Syria Mosque Auditorium *Richmond, VA* 8:00pm

Sunday 14th – Monday 15th

Travel day and then time off in Chicago. Ray is ill, but while he's laid up watching soap operas on TV conceives the *Starmaker/Soap Opera* concept for the TV play that Granada wants him to do. Ray is still ill on Tuesday, but recovers sufficiently to honour Tuesday's show.

Tuesday 16th

Auditorium Theater *Chicago, IL* 8:00pm, with Henry Gross
"The proverbial good time seemed to be had by all," writes Lynn Van Matre in the *Chicago Tribune*, "though I confess The Kinks have lost a lot of their charm for me. After a while the mincing hand-on-hips approach begins to wear a little thin. There was beer on the stage, beer cans tossed into the audience, beer slopped on the audience, and a lot of it slopped into Ray. It was, in short, the usual Kinks concert."
Set-list: 'Victoria', 'One Of The Survivors', 'Celluloid Heroes', 'Money Talks', medley 'You Really Got Me' / 'All Day And All Of The Night', 'Sunny Afternoon', 'Lola', 'Here Comes Yet Another Day', 'Here Comes Flash', 'Mr Wonderful' (extract), 'Alcohol', medley 'Skin And Bone' / 'Dry Bones', 'Good Golly Miss Molly'.

Wednesday 17th

Mershon Auditorium, Ohio State University *Columbus, OH* 8:00pm, with Leo Sayer

Thursday 18th

Albee Theater *Cincinnati, OH* 7:30pm, with Henry Gross

Friday 19th

Gymnasium, John Carroll University *University Heights, OH* 8:00pm, with Henry Gross

Saturday 20th

Century Theater *Buffalo, NY* 8:00pm, with Henry Gross
Buffalo News: "The biggest display of Kinkomania this city has yet seen greeted the British rock band's third annual appearance. And the crowd

sang! Buffalo crowds never sing along. The sold-out crowd [was brought] to a peak from which it refused to descend. [Ray's] voice gave out early but his coy clowning grew bold on the crowd's adoration."

Sunday 21st

As the Kinks travel home to London, singer Maryann Price returns to California for the tour break as there are no recording commitments in London.

Monday 22nd

As a footnote to the other side of public adoration, the music papers report that a girl is forcibly ejected from Ray's house in the middle of the night.

➔ A marathon press reception is held around now at the RCA Records offices in Mayfair, central London at which Ray does a battery of interviews for the international press, including *NME*, *Sounds*, France's *Rock Et Folk* and Andrew Bailey for *Rolling Stone*. He focuses on preparing his audience for the ambitious double album and stage show that will follow, hopefully by summer (though it will be nearer the year's end).

➔ **'Money Talks' / 'Here Comes Flash'** single released in the US. Rather than 'Mirror of Love', which failed to chart in Britain, the US gets this more upbeat A-side as a preview of the new *Act 2* album, but it too fails to chart.

Money Talks single

A **'Money Talks'** (R. DAVIES).
B **'Here Comes Flash'** (R. DAVIES).

US release late April 1974 (RCA Victor APBO 0275).
Musicians (A only; B as Preservation Act 2 album, see November 16th 1973) Ray Davies acoustic guitar, lead vocal. Dave Davies electric guitar, co-lead vocal. John Dalton bass guitar. Mick Avory drums. John Gosling electric piano. Alan Holmes saxophones. Pamela Travis backing vocal. Maryann Price backing vocal.
Recorded (A only; B as Preservation Act 2 album, see November 16th 1973) Konk Studios *Hornsey, north London*; January-March 1974; 16-track mixed to stereo.
Producer Raymond Douglas Davies.
Engineer Roger Beale.
Chart high US none.

● **RECORDING** Konk Studios *Hornsey, north London*. Almost certainly at this time, concentrated sessions for the Claire Hamill album for Konk Records are held, probably the first for the upcoming LP, with Ray producing.

May

➲ **TOUR STARTS** *US Tour: 2nd leg* (May 9th – 16th). **Line-up**: Ray Davies (lead vocal, guitar), Dave Davies (guitar, vocal), Mick Avory (drums), John Dalton (bass), John Gosling (keyboard), John Beecham (trombone), Alan Holmes (saxophone), Laurie Brown (trumpet), Pamela Travis, Maryann Price (backing vocals). For this short and relatively contained set of West Coast dates The Kinks travel predominantly in a group of mobile homes. Unlike the almost unceasing press coverage from the East Coast, press reports from this leg are rare and the few reviewers are not impressed. This stint seems to get off to a bad start amid a wrangle with the musicians' union, and the sudden cancellation of the last weekend of shows is probably related to this. (During Saturday 4th and Sunday 5th the band travels to Los Angeles, with a day off there.)

Monday 6th
Rehearsals take place at NBC Television Studios in Burbank, CA for tomorrow's *Midnight Special* show. Following their history of uneasiness with American unions from the 1965 tour, The Kinks head right back into trouble with the American Federation Of Musicians, which has announced a strike of the three major television networks today. Nevertheless, the band continues with their scheduled taping. In retaliation, the union plans to cause the band further problems when they next try to enter the country, but this will be successfully resolved by lawyers in time for their return in November.

Tuesday 7th
❑ **TV** NBC Television Studios *Burbank, CA*. NBC **The Midnight Special** live performance 'You Really Got Me', 'Money Talks', 'Here Comes Yet Another Day', 'Celluloid Heroes', medley 'Skin And Bone' / 'Dry Bones' broadcast June 7th. Ray also co-hosts the show.

Wednesday 8th
Day off in Los Angeles.
Preservation Act 2 double-album released in the US. There is wild praise in *Rolling Stone*: "Pessimistic as it ultimately is (what Kinks opus could be otherwise?) this is still their most exuberant effort in a long time, even more so than *Everybody's In Show-Biz*. ... Melodies are strong, arrangements careful, and the newly enlarged band combines traditional Kinks restraint with some nice eccentric touches. The new singers are unusual enough to complement Ray perfectly. ... The Kinks have proven here that they don't need to duplicate an earlier sound to match their past triumphs." *Creem* takes an opposing view: "A few good singles on an album with vast pretensions that is merely a mediocre record by an idiosyncratic personality and his studio backing group."

Thursday 9th
Celebrity Theatre *Phoenix, AZ* 8:30pm

Friday 10th
Shrine Civic Auditorium *Los Angeles, CA* 8:00pm, with Maggie Bell, Kansas

Saturday 11th
Warnor Theater *Fresno, CA* 8:00pm, with Lynyrd Skynyrd

Sunday 12th
Robertson Gymnasium, University of California *Santa Barbara, CA* 8:00pm, with Jo Jo Gunne, Kansas
Day off following in Los Angeles.

Tuesday 14th
Celebrity Theatre *Phoenix, AZ* 8:30pm
Oddly, a second show here just five days after the first. (Travel day following to Los Angeles.)

Thursday 16th
Golden Hall, Convention & Performing Arts Center *San Diego, CA* 7:30pm, with Kansas; produced by Jim Pagul
"Not exactly one of those super rock'n'roll occasions," says the *San Diego Union*, "it was just ho-hum dumb. The Kinks ... play for a minuscule gathering of perhaps a thousand persons [and] looked a little like a mini [Joe Cocker's] Mad Dogs & Englishmen group."

Friday 17th
While still in Los Angeles, the band cancels their appearance tonight at the Winterland in San Francisco just hours before showtime, stating that Ray has been hospitalised with a bad back. The following night is also cancelled.

Saturday 18th
The Kinks are still in Los Angeles, and tonight's appearance in San Francisco – which is planned anyway as the last date of the tour – is a forced cancellation.

Preservation Act 2 double-album

A1 'Announcement' *(#1)*
A2 'Introduction To Solution' (R. DAVIES).
A3 'When A Solution Comes' (R. DAVIES).
A4 'Money Talks' (R. DAVIES).
A5 'Announcement' *(#2)*
A6 'Shepherds Of The Nation' (R. DAVIES).
B1 'Scum Of The Earth' (R. DAVIES).
B2 'Second Hand Car Spiv' (R. DAVIES).
B3 'He's Evil'(R. DAVIES).
B4 'Mirror Of Love' (R. DAVIES).
B5 'Announcement' *(#3)*
C1 'Nobody Gives' (R. DAVIES).
C2 'Oh Where Oh Where Is Love' (R. DAVIES).
C3 'Flash's Dream (The Final Elbow)' (R. DAVIES).
C4 'Flash's Confession' (R. DAVIES).
D1 'Nothing Lasts Forever' (R. DAVIES).
D2 'Announcement' *(#4)*
D3 'Artificial Man' (R. DAVIES).
D4 'Scrapheap City' (R. DAVIES).
D5 'Announcement' *(#5)*
D6 'Salvation Road' (R. DAVIES).

US release May 8th 1974 (RCA Victor CPL2-5040).
UK release July 26th 1974 (RCA Victor LPL2-5040).
Musicians Ray Davies acoustic guitar, lead vocal except as noted. Dave Davies electric guitar, acoustic guitar, mandolin (D4), co-lead vocals (A4, D3). John Dalton bass guitar. Mick Avory drums, percussion. John Gosling baby grand piano, electric piano, Hammond organ. John Beecham trombone, tuba. Alan Holmes saxophones, clarinet , flute, piccolo. Laurie Brown trumpet. Pamela Travis backing vocal (A4, A6, B1, B2, B3, D1, D3). Maryann Price lead vocal (D1, D4), backing vocal (A4, B2, B3, D3). Chris Timothy spoken announcements. Chris Musk spoken announcement (as reporter). Stanley Myers string arrangement (C1, D3). Johnny Girton guitar (D4).
Recorded Konk Studios *Hornsey, north London*; January-March 1974 except probably C2, D6: June-September 1973 and B4: December 1973 or January 1974; recorded 16-track mixed to stereo, except B4 recorded 8-track mixed to stereo. Producer Raymond Douglas Davies.
Engineer Roger Beale.
Chart high UK none; US number 114.

Sunday 19th

The band travels to New York City and home to London, while singer Maryann Price remains in California.

Monday 20th

A press release announces a *Preservation* stage show for London's West End in September.

☆ With his concept now taking solid shape, Ray soon starts busily writing music and dialogue for the *Starmaker* Granada TV show.

Monday 27th

A London Palladium concert for June 9th is announced, as well as a new LP, *Preservation Act 2*, for July 5th release.

June

Sunday 2nd

Maryann Price arrives in London around now in time for the next set of band commitments.

Monday 3rd

A likely rehearsal today at the Rainbow Theatre, Finsbury Park, north London for tomorrow's TV taping.

☆ A further press release says the London Palladium gig is delayed until June 16th due to insufficient time for promotion.

Tuesday 4th

❏ **TV** Rainbow Theatre *Finsbury Park, north London.* ABC US **Wide World – In Concert** live performance 'Here Comes Yet Another Day', medley 'Skin And Bone' / 'Dry Bones', 'Here Comes Flash', 'Celluloid Heroes' broadcast August 16th. Produced by Stanley Dorfman, the live show is filmed before an invited audience. *Wide World* is a popular late-night TV concert programme that offers the audio portion simulcast on affiliated FM radio stations in stereo. ('Here Comes Flash' is sung by Maryann Price and Pamela Travis.)

Wednesday 5th

Ray is probably involved in post-production song selection and stereo mixing for the *Wide World – In Concert* programme. Further work is done by the show's producers tomorrow.

Thursday 6th

))) **RADIO** Langham Studios (Studio 1), BBC Broadcasting House *central London.* BBC Radio-1 **John Peel Show** studio recordings produced by Tony Wilson, engineered by Bill Aitken 'Demolition', 'Mirror Of Love', 'Money Talks' broadcast July 11th. In true 1960s tradition, The Kinks record unique BBC versions of three songs from the new double-album. ('Demolition' and 'Money Talks' will be released in 2001 on *The Kinks BBC Sessions 1964-1977*.)

➜ In preparation for the upcoming Palladium show the band rehearses around now, incorporating more material from *Preservation*. It's possible that further work is done on the Claire Hamill LP now, too.

Sunday 16th

The Palladium *central London* 8:00pm, with The Butts Band
"All in all a splendid evening," writes one reviewer, "which is maybe seen as the first step towards the eventual staged show of *Preservation* (you can't hurry The Kinks, you know). Already the show includes two Kinkettes and a variety of props including small lamp-post and a jiving skeleton, in addition to Ray's usual stage additions – cigar, beer, straw

hat and dressing gown. No shortage of ye olde Kinks hits of course … One off the forthcoming [*Act 2* album] called 'Money Talks' was particularly strong and sounded like a future single."
Set-list: 'Victoria', 'Here Comes Yet Another Day', 'Money Talks', medley 'You Really Got Me' / 'All Day And All Of The Night', 'Dedicated Follower Of Fashion', 'Sunny Afternoon', 'Celluloid Heroes', 'Mirror Of Love', 'Daylight', 'A Change In The Weather', 'Cricket', medley 'Money & Corruption' / 'I'm Your Man', 'Here Comes Flash', 'Demolition', 'He's Evil', 'Lola', 'Dead End Street', 'Banana Boat Song', 'Skin And Bone',

Monday 17th – Tuesday 18th

● **RECORDING** Konk Studios *Hornsey, north London*. Ray decides to give **'Mirror Of Love'** a second chance in the charts and re-records a new master, this time using the full band, in contrast to the original demo version released in the UK earlier in the year.

Wednesday 19th

Singer Maryann Price returns to California. She is scheduled to return for the next set of band commitments, beginning July 10th.

➜ ● **RECORDING** Konk Studios *Hornsey, north London*. Ray mixes the new recording of 'Mirror Of Love'. Two separate mixes are prepared, one for the US release and one for the UK. The US mix has more prominent female vocals and is edited to rearrange the song structure.

☆ Also around this time at Konk, Ray continues work on the Claire Hamill LP *Stage Door Johnnies* that will become the first release on the newly formed Konk Records. The 11 songs completed at least by August are roughly split between Hamill's original material and some well-chosen covers.

As producer, Ray uses a number of local musicians forming part of a loose circle of players who will work on Konk projects. Among them is keyboard player Dave Rowberry (who'd guested on The Kinks' 'Celluloid Heroes') and session drummer Clem Cattini (who played on their 1965 LP *The Kinks Kontroversy*). Also present is the Davies' nephew Phil Palmer on guitar, plus bassist Phil South and drummer Neil McBain from his band March Hare.

In some cases members of The Kinks are involved too. Avory plays drums on one song, **'Trying To Work It All Out'**, while Ray contributes minimal guitar as well as keyboard work on at least one, **'All The Cakes She Baked Him'**. Kink horn players Alan Holmes and Laurie Brown will also be credited on the record's sleeve, as is string arranger Lew Warburton.

Friday 28th

Ray delivers tapes of the new version of the 'Mirror Of Love' single to RCA in New York City.

July

➜ Singer Maryann Price decides not to return to London to continue with The Kinks, citing her inability to continue the travel involved in a transatlantic career. With no time to audition a new singer, Ray uses Konk artist Claire Hamill as a temporary stand-in for two upcoming commitments this month.

Thursday 10th – Saturday 13th

Rehearsals for the BBC broadcast, with Claire Hamill now in the band.

Sunday 14th

)))) **RADIO** Hippodrome Theatre *Golders Green, north London.* BBC Radio-1 *In Concert* live performance, produced by Jeff Griffin, engineered by John Edgehill 'Victoria', 'Here Comes Yet Another Day', 'Mr Wonderful' (extract), 'Money Talks', 'Dedicated Follower Of Fashion', 'Mirror Of Love', 'Celluloid Heroes', medley 'You Really Got Me' / 'All Day And All Of The Night', 'Daylight', 'Here Comes Flash', 'Demolition', 'He's Evil', 'Lola', medley 'Skin And Bone' / 'Dry Bones' broadcast July 27th.

For this broadcast to help promote the *Preservation* LPs, the band consists of the five-piece Kinks plus vocalists Pamela Travis and Claire Hamill, and the horn section of John Beecham, Alan Holmes and Laurie Brown. The live in-concert format is now emerging as the standard in rock radio programming, gaining over the formerly predominant practice of the 1960s of strictly live-in-the-studio recordings. The Hippodrome is set up for proper recording of live rock and is able to accommodate a large invited audience, effectively putting the artist in both a concert setting and a studio at the same time. The show is hosted by Alan Black.

Following the main British broadcast, the tapes are passed on to the BBC's Transcription Service where a syndicated version (omitting the medley of 'You Really Got Me' / 'All Day And All Of The Night') is prepared for distribution on disc outside the UK and slotted for broadcast in August. A separate syndicated version (further shortened by the omission of 'Daylight') is prepared in the US by London Wavelength in New York City for airing on subscribing stations around the US on the programme *The BBC Presents...* during the week of January 19th 1975. ('Victoria', 'Here Comes Yet Another Day', 'Money Talks', 'Mirror Of Love', 'Celluloid Heroes', medley 'Skin And Bone' / 'Dry Bones' will be released in 2001 on *The Kinks BBC Sessions 1964-1977*.)

Monday 15th – Saturday 20th

➜ **'Mirror Of Love' / 'He's Evil'** single released in the US. This is the re-recorded version of 'Mirror'.

Monday 22nd

With taping of the Granada TV show imminent, the band's office issues a press release stating that Ray is to take the lead in *Starmaker*.

Tuesday 23rd

The Kinks minus Ray travel to Manchester by train tonight.

Wednesday 24th

Ray travels up to Manchester from London this morning where in the afternoon at Granada Television Centre (Studio 12) there is a run-through of the show during the entire afternoon, mostly to establish lighting and camera set-ups. Much to the band's disappointment, the sound is given just a few hours consideration.

Thursday 25th

❑ **TV** Granada Television Centre (Studio 12) *Manchester.* ITV *Starmaker* 'Starmaker', 'Ordinary People', 'Rush Hour Blues', 'Nine To Five', 'When Work Is Over', 'Have Another Drink', 'You Make It All Worthwhile', 'Ducks On The Wall', 'Face In The Crowd', 'You Can't Stop The Music' broadcast (except 'Ducks On The Wall') September 4th. Back at Granada there is a full rehearsal of the show in the afternoon and then a break for dinner. Formal taping begins at 7:45pm before a small invited audience. The show is directed by Peter Plummer and produced by Dennis Wolfe, with choreography by Dougie Squires.

The main players are Ray Davies as Norman, and June Ritchie as the wife. Musical backing is by The Kinks, plus John Beecham, Alan

---

Mirror Of Love single (second version)

A 'Mirror Of Love' (R. DAVIES).
B 'He's Evil' (R. DAVIES).

US release mid July 1974 (RCA Victor PB 10019).
UK release July 26th 1974 (RCA Victor LPBO 5042).
Different A-side mixes and edits for UK and US versions.
Musicians Ray Davies lead vocals, acoustic guitar (A). Dave Davies mandolin (A), electric guitar (B). John Dalton bass guitar (B). Mick Avory drums. John Gosling baby grand piano, electric piano (B). Laurie Brown trumpet. John Beecham tuba (A), trombone (B). Alan Holmes clarinet. Pamela Travis backing vocal. Maryann Price backing vocal.
Recorded Konk Studios *Hornsey, north London*; A: June 17th-18th 1974; B: January-March 1974; 16-track mixed to stereo.
Producer Raymond Douglas Davies.
Engineer Roger Beale.
Chart high UK none; US none.

Holmes and Laurie Brown (horns), and Claire Hamill and Pamela Travis (vocals). Dancers are Richard Gough, Chris Henner, Ann Chapman, and Linda Lawrence. 'Ordinary People' features June Ritchie duetting with Ray, and Dave takes lead vocal on 'You Can't Stop The Music'.

The original British broadcast is on ITV, Britain's commercial TV network. The programme is later broadcast in the Netherlands by VPRO, Nederland 2 TV, on June 4th 1975. It is never broadcast in the US or anywhere else. A clip of 'A Face In The Crowd' is later excavated and included in the 1986 MGM/UA video documentary *The Story of The Kinks*.

The story presents Ray's character duelling with alter egos: he's a glamorous rock star who decides intentionally to place himself in the role of Norman, a common accountant whose dull routines of everyday married life become fodder for the star's songwriting inspiration. In the ensuing confusion the roles blur in and out of reality.

A little later, Ray reveals that he was too self-conscious to watch *Starmaker* on TV. "I just didn't want to know. I knew it was going to be bad. It wasn't the producer's fault. That guy [Dennis Wolfe, with whom Ray will continue to work] is suffering, trying to use rock bands, trying to break new ground, and his Light Entertainment department don't wanna know. So we got squeezed into some late-night slot, and we got the guy who does the drama sound. ... We always get resentment from those kind of people because we're a rock band trying to do something on a theatrical level. Theatrical people don't like us infringing on their territory."

Dave also talks later, in *Kink*, of his unhappiness with the production, how poorly the band were treated by the crew, and his feeling of being reduced to a sideman in what he sees as a vehicle for Ray alone rather than a Kinks project. Dave further characterises this time as one of great crises about the direction of the band and his role within it. Dave's dissatisfaction will not be far from the surface for the next few years as Ray exorcises his theatrical ambitions within the format of an extended Kinks.

Friday 26th

Preservation Act 2 double-album released in the UK. *Melody Maker* says: "As far as concept albums go, its libretto may be preferable to the ham-fisted stupidity of *Tommy* – what couldn't? – but there's little original music. These extended pieces don't really bring out the best in Davies, because he sacrifices the part to the whole, and there's not one song on this album that bears comparison with the singles he's released. … I hope that if and when Ray Davies stages his musical of the albums, I can offer criticism more favourable to him."

'Mirror Of Love' / 'He's Evil' single released in the UK. For the British market this is the second version of 'Mirror' to be released, now re-recorded in a full band version. But there is no advertising for it, and the pop press more or less fails to review it again, so the single has no chance in the charts.

Monday 29th

A press release announces that Konk Studios is now ready for hire to outside acts. (In fact, Konk does not successfully become available for hire on a regular basis until after it is refitted with 24-track equipment, active on June 24th 1976. Until then it is almost exclusively used by The Kinks and for Konk-related projects.)

August

At Konk Studios around the start of the month, possible last-minute work is done on the first Konk Records release by Claire Hamill. A number of projects are progressing simultaneously, keeping Konk very busy for the entire year.

During August, The Kinks record proper studio masters of the entire *Starmaker* soundtrack at Konk. This will eventually emerge the following year as the album *A Soap Opera*. The track list is identical to the TV broadcast, including 'Ducks On The Wall' which was dropped from the final show. Also at this time Dave does some recording with Konk band March Hare to which Gosling later adds string arrangements. Ray tells *Hit Parader* that Dave has completed four demos recently – details unknown – but that he is pushing Dave to work with an outside producer.

Interspersed among Kinks sessions this month and next, and continuing into next year, Dave and Gosling become joint producers for the recording of another Konk signing, singer-songwriter Andy Desmond. They will use a similar array of musicians as for the Claire Hamill sessions earlier this year. Dave himself plays guitar on one song, **'She Can Move Mountains'**, singing backing vocals on that and two others, **'Can't Bear To Think About You'** and **'Annie'**. Gosling contributes keyboards and does string arrangements on several of the songs, and Alan Holmes provides brass and woodwind arrangements as well as playing on some. Backing vocals are later overdubbed by Pamela Travis and her future Kinks singing partner Shirlie Roden (Roden will be hired in October).

Meanwhile, plans for the staging of *Preservation* early this autumn are again delayed until an appropriate London theatre becomes available.

At the end of the month at Konk, horn overdubs are added to the *Starmaker* tracks (23rd-24th), and on the 26th, with initial recording nearing completion, a press release announces a new LP based on the *Starmaker* TV show – which will turn out to be *A Soap Opera*.

September

Wednesday 4th

The Granada production of *Starmaker* recorded on July 25th is broadcast in the UK on the ITV network. Ray virtually disowned the TV production upon its completion (see July 25th), but the broadcast itself takes some blows.

The *Sounds* reviewer is charitable, but concludes: "There's a lot of truth in what [Ray] says, and his tacky style is, as ever, a delight, but I have an uncomfortable feeling that he's just saying the same few things over and over in slightly different ways without really developing his themes or his arguments." *Melody Maker* is more critical and dismisses the program as "little more than a minor footnote to his 'everyone's in show biz' obsession. … Taken in isolation, the show never really did gel, though to Kinks fans it was no doubt of interest in illustrating their hero's state of mind during his brief retirement … at White City."

A particularly heavy panning comes from the *NME*'s Charles Shaar Murray. He flatly dislikes the show to the point of finding it insulting, and proceeds to pick the entire production to pieces. "*Starmaker* is where two of Ray Davies' most treasured pet fantasies collide. [Here is] his fantasy of the Life Of The Common People meets Everyone's-In-Showbiz-Everybody's-A-Star routine, right in the middle of a stylised set, complete with Dougie Squires choreography." Of the music: "All the songs are indeed glib, shallow and … superficial … . Okay, so it's a first effort – but that shouldn't have to be brought up as an excuse."

→ ● **RECORDING** Konk Studios *Hornsey, north London*. Ray is at Konk early this month to record the backing track for 'Holiday Romance', a new song for release both as the next Kinks single and as part of the studio album from the *Starmaker* show, which will eventually emerge the following year as *A Soap Opera*.

Saturday 7th

Parc de La Courneuve *Paris, France* La Fête De l'Humanité, with Leonard Cohen (headliner) and others
This very large annual festival sponsored by the French Communist Party marks the debut of a slightly altered line-up of the band as vocalist Maryann Price's replacement Lyndsey Moore takes her place. It's The Kinks' first appearance in France in eight years, and the first in Paris proper since April 1966 (at the Locomotive Club). The band will return again to this festival 18 years later, in 1992. Today, The Kinks perform a perfunctory one-hour show to a crowd of what one attendee called "50 percent narrow-minded quinquagenarian communists [who] didn't seem to understand what Ray was singing, and they obviously did not understand rock'n'roll." (Return to London day following.)
Set-list: 'Victoria', 'Here Comes Yet Another Day', medley 'You Really Got Me' / 'All Day And All Of The Night', 'Money Talks', 'Celluloid Heroes', 'Sunny Afternoon', 'Lola', 'One Of The Survivors', 'Here Comes Flash', 'Demolition', 'Alcohol', medley 'Skin And Bone' / 'Dry Bones'.

Monday 9th-Tuesday 10th

● **RECORDING** Konk Studios *Hornsey, north London*. Strings are overdubbed on to the **'Holiday Romance'** backing track, in an arrangement by Stanley Myers.
☆ Ray is interviewed by Allan Jones for *Melody Maker* and some of the problems with *Starmaker* are discussed. He is clearly not deterred by the show's poor execution and reception. "We could have got the whole thing a lot better. I'm thinking of doing it again for America," he says, and then the talk turns to *Preservation*. "The plans are at a standstill at the moment. *Starmaker* held them up, and I'm just getting over that. But I think we'll do it as a pantomime. People have been wanting us to do something like that for a long time. And a pantomime … that's where it's all at, man." Ray acknowledges his bad press. "I'm upsetting a lot of people, and a lot of people think I'm on the wrong track. They think I should be writing two hit singles a year and doing a tour. But that's not what I want to do."
☆ This week marks the tenth anniversary of 'You Really Got Me' hitting the top of the charts, and some of the press picks up on it. Old label Pye Records announces its plans to re-release as a single two

former A-sides, 'Dedicated Follower Of Fashion' and 'Waterloo Sunset', but for reasons unknown this goes no further. The same coupling will finally find a release in 1979.

Wednesday 11th

● **RECORDING** Konk Studios *Hornsey, north London*. A horn overdub session from 3:00-6:00pm is almost certainly for further work on the *Starmaker / Soap Opera* tracks.

→ A proposed booking for The Kinks as part of a September 14th show at Wembley Stadium with Crosby Stills Nash & Young, The Band, Jesse Colin Young, and Joni Mitchell is touted but never realised.

→ *Stage Door Johnnies* album by Claire Hamill is released in the US. This is the first record from the Konk label. Hamill does some limited touring of the US to promote the LP, but it fails to get into the charts.

↪ **TOUR STARTS** *Tour Of Scandinavia* (Sep 16th – 23rd). **Line-up**: Ray Davies (lead vocal, guitar), Dave Davies (guitar, vocal), Mick Avory (drums), John Dalton (bass), John Gosling (keyboard), John Beecham (trombone), Alan Holmes (saxophone), Laurie Brown (trumpet), Pamela Travis, Lyndsey Moore (backing vocals). After a five-year absence the band undertakes this short swing through Sweden and Denmark, with singer Lyndsey Moore now aboard.

Monday 16th

Konserthuset *Stockholm, Sweden* 8:00pm, with Jan Svan, Stefan Liljeholm

"When everything seems to fall apart," writes one reviewer, "the ten-piece group pull themselves together and land on solid ground. … The whole performance seems to be extremely well rehearsed, and yet it still seems like improvisation. [Ray] has enough charisma to make the audience at the Paris Olympia sing 'Rule Brittannia'."

Tuesday 17th

Konserthuset *Gothenburg, Sweden* 8:00pm

Friday 20th

Studenternes Hus, Stakladen *Århus, Denmark* with Side Show Blues

Saturday 21st

Tinghallen *Viborg, Denmark* 8:00pm, with Liza

Evidently a disastrous show as a hostile audience of 1,500 yells, "Kinks out!" The band complies with the request after playing exactly 45 minutes, abruptly leaving the stage and not returning. A reviewer maintains: "The Kinks acted like a bunch of stuck-up supercilious superstars who had come to a musically developing country where the audience weren't smart enough to understand what they were doing."

Monday 23rd

Tivoli Koncertsal *Copenhagen, Denmark* 8:00pm, with Bobby Ball & The Starbox Band

The show is attended by former Kinks bass player Pete Quaife, who now lives in Copenhagen. He is introduced from the stage during the performance but does not perform. Singer Lyndsey Moore leaves The Kinks as this tour is completed.

Set-list: 'Victoria', 'Here Comes Yet Another Day', 'Acute Schizophrenia Paranoia Blues', 'Mr Wonderful', 'Dedicated Follower Of Fashion', 'Sunny Afternoon', 'Get Back In Line', 'Mirror Of Love', 'Money Talks', medley 'You Really Got Me' / 'All Day And All Of The Night', 'Celluloid Heroes', 'Here Comes Flash', medley 'Demolition' / 'Salvation Road', 'He's Evil', 'Lola', 'Alcohol', medley 'Skin And Bone' / 'Dry Bones', 'Good Golly Miss Molly'.

Wednesday 25th – Friday 27th

● **RECORDING** Konk Studios *Hornsey, north London*. Dave and Gosling finish work on the Andy Desmond LP for Konk.

October

Friday 4th

● **RECORDING** Konk Studios *Hornsey, north London*. Keyboard overdubs for *Soap Opera* tracks.

Tuesday 8th

● **RECORDING** Konk Studios *Hornsey, north London*. Horn overdubs 12midday-3:00pm for *Soap Opera* tracks.

→ ● **RECORDING** Konk Studios *Hornsey, north London*. Backing-vocal overdubs for *A Soap Opera* tracks, and Ray probably finishes his initial mix.

☆ Also around now the new US single 'Preservation' is recorded at Konk.

☆ Shirlie Roden is auditioned and hired as a Kinks vocalist. Soon, vocalists Debbie Doss, Anna Peacock, Lewis Rich and Trevor White are auditioned and hired, and tenor saxophone player Nick Newall is hired on the recommendation of John Beecham. A second trombone player, Rob Goodale, is recommended but not hired.

Friday 18th

'Holiday Romance' / **'Shepherds Of The Nation'** single released in the UK. *Melody Maker* says: "Raymond Douglas Davies returns, at last, to the three-minute narrative form of the classic Kinks singles, and confirms that he's far from lost his eccentric, comic vision …. Could this be a hit of impressive proportions? One hopes so."

But over at the *NME* it seems that Kinks stock has now slumped and the record gets an utter panning in the paper. "And still they descend into the quagmire," writes the reveiwer. "Unbearably twee and altogether tiresome in the extreme."

Tuesday 22nd – Wednesday 23rd

→ Rehearsals at Konk Studios for *Preservation*, first with singers only, then just with horns.

Holiday Romance single

A **'Holiday Romance'** (R. DAVIES).
B **'Shepherds Of The Nation'** (R. DAVIES).

UK release October 18th 1974 (RCA Victor RCA 2478).
Musicians A: Ray Davies lead vocals, acoustic guitar, baby grand piano. John Dalton bass guitar. Mick Avory drums. Stanley Myers string arrangement.
Recorded A: Konk Studios Hornsey, north London; September 10th-11th 1974; 16-track mixed to stereo.
Musicians and recording details for B-side as *Preservation Act 2* album (see May 8th).
Producer Raymond Douglas Davies.
Engineer Roger Beale.
Chart high UK none.

Thursday 24th – Wednesday 30th
Full band rehearsals at Konk for the *Preservation* show.

Monday 28th
Ray takes a quick break in rehearsals to deliver the master tape of the 'Preservation' single to RCA in New York City.

November

Monday 4th
→ Negotiations proceed with Anchor Records for a UK distribution deal for Konk.
☆ Around this time, backdrop projection 16mm film segments are shot with Ray as Mr Black for use in the *Preservation* concerts.
☆ The Kinks in *Preservation* costumes are photographed at Konk Studios and outside in Tottenham Lane by Sam Emerson to provide press photos featuring the five-man band plus singers Travis, Roden and Doss.
☆ Amid this busy time, Ray quietly marries school teacher Yvonne Gunner. Unlike his first marriage, which became public, this one is successfully hidden from view. It will only be revealed in 1981 when it ends in divorce following Ray's very public involvement with Chrissie Hynde.

Monday 11th
A press release announces *Preservation* shows for London and the US.

Tuesday 12th
'Preservation' / 'Salvation Road' single released in the US.

Wednesday 13th – Saturday 16th
Full production stage rehearsals for *Preservation* are held at the Royalty Theatre in central London.

↷ **TOUR STARTS** *Preservation: US Tour* (Nov 24th – Dec 14th).
Line-up: Ray Davies (lead vocal, guitar), Dave Davies (guitar, vocal), Mick Avory (drums), John Dalton (bass), John Gosling (keyboard), John Beecham (trombone), Alan Holmes (saxophone), Laurie Brown (trumpet), Nick Newall (saxophone), Anna Peacock, Pamela Travis, Shirley Roden, Debbie Doss, Lewis Rich, Trevor White (vocals).
   Ray performs as Mr Flash (on-stage) and as Mr Black (on film), Dave as Mr Twitch, Avory as Big Ron, Dalton as Mr Lugs, and Gosling as the

---

Preservation single
A 'Preservation' (R. DAVIES).
B 'Salvation Road' (R. DAVIES).

US release November 12th 1974 (RCA Victor PB10121).
Musicians Ray Davies lead vocal. Dave Davies electric guitar. John Dalton bass guitar. Mick Avory drums. John Gosling electric piano. Pamela Travis, Shirlie Roden backing vocals.
Recorded Konk Studios *Hornsey, north London*; October 1974; 16-track mixed to stereo.
Producer Ray Davies.
Engineer Roger Beale.
Chart high US none.

Vicar. Anna Peacock appears as Belle, and Travis, Roden and Doss variously as Villagers, Spivs and Floozies. Belle sings 'Mirror Of Love', 'Nothing Lasts Forever' and 'Scrapheap City'. Rich and White appear variously as Villagers and other minor characters.
   Visual effects used in the show include back-projected stills and film, special lighting, and assorted stage props. Choreography advised by Dougie Squires; producer Dennis Wolf; music director Ray Davies; lighting director Cecily Jaffe; stage director John Kalinowski; stage manager Ken Jones (with roadie Brian Wilcox). All shows start at 8:00pm unless noted, with the opening act of The Kinks as themselves. Ticket prices are generally $4-$6.50.
   While the two *Preservation* albums that preceded the stage presentation received mixed reviews, and their sales reflected a rapidly declining record-buying fan base for the band, Ray's ace in the hole has always been this long-anticipated stage production. It will be a test for his grand vision, over eight years in the making.
   For the most part reviews will reflect the view even of causal fans that the final result is impressive and entertaining – but there a fair number of dissenters.

Wednesday 20th – Friday 22nd
Crew, singers and hornmen travel to New York City and have a day off. The Kinks minus Ray travel on Friday to New York City, then on to Albany with the whole entourage. When the equipment crew arrives at the first venue of the tour, they realise that the stage built by the school (see next entry) is too small, and a new one has to be built to accommodate the set-up.

Saturday 23rd
Huntington Gymnasium, Colgate University *Hamilton, NY*
"Despite the flaws," writes Rob Patterson for *Colgate News*, "[this] was one of the most enjoyable rock concerts I've ever seen. Bits of dry British wit combined with good songs and strong performances made for an evening of just plain fun rock'n'roll, rare in these days of heaviness, mysticism and other assorted trappings in popular music."
Set-list: 'Victoria', 'Here Comes Yet Another Day', medley 'Skin And Bone' / 'Dry Bones', 'Lola', 'Dedicated Follower Of Fashion', medley 'You Really Got Me' / 'All Day And All Of The Night', 'Celluloid Heroes', 'Waterloo Sunset'. Intermission. *Preservation*: 'Morning Song', 'Daylight', 'There's A Change In The Weather', medley 'Money And Corruption' / 'I Am Your Man', 'Here Comes Flash', 'Demolition', 'Money Talks', 'Shepherds Of The Nation', 'He's Evil', 'Scum Of The Earth', 'Slum Kids', 'Mirror Of Love', 'Alcohol', 'Flash's Dream', 'Flash's Confession', 'Nothing Lasts Forever', 'Artificial Man', 'Scrapheap City', 'Salvation Road', 'Finale'.

Sunday 24th
Palace Theater *Albany, NY* possibly sponsored by State University of New York at Albany
A projector breaks down just prior to the show, causing some quick adjustments to the *Preservation* portion of the show.

Monday 25th
Stanley Theater *Pittsburgh, PA*
Travel day follows.

Wednesday 27th – Thursday 28th
Felt Forum, Madison Square Garden Center *New York, NY*
Steve Simels of *Stereo Review* expects the usual chaotic, unprofessional rock show, but "the extravaganza they mounted was easily the most entertaining and impressive rock/theatre venture to date, as well as probably the best-integrated mixed-media show rock or otherwise". But *The Village Voice* pipes in with a negative view: "[It] amounted to a high-school talent show [with] a lame chorus, a tacky split-screen

Ray in character for the Preservation stage show, seen here in Ohio on December 14th 1974.

kinks'74

projection and the whole feeling the show would fall apart the next time Davies left the stage."

Friday 29th
Sanderson Theater *Springfield, MA*

Saturday 30th
Palace Concert Theater *Providence, RI* 7:30pm; sponsored by Rhode Island College

December

Sunday 1st
Music Hall *Boston, MA* 7:00pm
"It was an uncharacteristically calm concert," says *The Boston Globe*. "There was little of the rowdiness that's been known to break out on both sides of the stage lights at a Kinks concert. All things considered, [*Preservation*] was a remarkable achievement." (Travel day to New York City following.)

Tuesday 3rd
Kleinhans Music Hall *Buffalo, NY*
Buffalo News: "[The show] gave Ray and company a juicy chance to solicit boos and hisses for the villains and their cause, which embellished the vaudevillian atmosphere with a crazy, good-time fondness."

Wednesday 4th
Men's gymnasium, State University of New York at Binghamton *Binghamton, NY* 9:00pm
Day off in New York City, following a cancelled show on the 5th at the Casino Arena in Asbury Park, NJ. Travel to Los Angeles on the 6th as planned, with a day off in LA following.

Sunday 8th
Winterland Ballroom *San Francisco, CA* with Climax Blues Band, Aerosmith
Travel day follows.

Tuesday 10th
Santa Monica Civic Auditorium *Santa Monica, CA* 8:00 & 11:30pm
Los Angeles Times: "Who would have thought that the Brooklyn Dodgers of rock'n'roll – sloppy and colorful, eccentric and exciting, eternally lovable – could be the band that would devise and execute one of the most successful of all theatrical-rock productions." (Travel day to St. Louis following.)

Thursday 12th
Ambassador Theater *St. Louis, MO*

Friday 13th
Auditorium Theater *Chicago, IL*
Anna Peacock is unwell and doesn't perform 'Mirror Of Love'. Shirlie Roden sings it instead.

Saturday 14th
Music Hall *Cleveland, OH*
Originally scheduled at the Allen Theater, but moved. (Travel day to London following as the US tour ends.)

Friday 20th – Sunday 22nd
Royalty Theatre *Holborn, central London* 8:00pm nightly
After the throttling they gave Ray and The Kinks for *Starmaker*, the British music press comes rallying back to their defence with unanimous praise for these Preservation shows. *Sounds* says: "The show combines the best elements of a Christmas pantomime – extra evil villains and a degree of hammy pathos, but no dull principal girl and boy – with a story which maintains its interest and (if you want it) is a modern day parable. Better yet, the show has a collection of fine songs and in the dual-role lead character [played by] Ray Davies, The Kinks have maybe the only person capable of combining elements of rock, the music hall tradition and Amateur Dramatics, without ending up with a hybrid beast lacking the charm each form possesses. ... The combination of rock and theatre has rarely been used to such direct effect." *Melody Maker*: "The way it was all pieced together to tell a simplistic morality tale of the struggle against a villain to preserve something sacred was extremely impressive. ... It deserves a long run in a large theatre."

➜ INDICATES EVENT AROUND THIS TIME BUT WITH NO FIRM DATE

1975

The working pattern of 1974 was largely maintained and continued into this year as Ray created, recorded, staged and toured two more rock-theatre works – A Soap Opera and Schoolboys In Disgrace. Even by his own standards, it was a time of almost non-stop creativity for Ray the writer, and he completely threw himself into his work, especially as he was now freed from the confines of management control.

Activity at Konk was high as producers Ray, Dave and John Gosling turned out two more albums by the label's artists – although once the final three LPs were released at the end of the year the label fizzled out quickly. But further evidence of Ray having more than he could handle came when production of a second Claire Hamill LP was passed on to an outside producer, Phil MacDonald.

January

Wednesday 8th
In London today the band assembles for an RCA photo session for a new set of promotional pictures. Some of the images will be used for the cover of the 1976 LP, *The Kinks Greatest/Celluloid Heroes*.

Thursday 9th – Monday 13th
● **RECORDING** Konk Studios *Hornsey, north London*. Dave and Gosling remix some of last year's Andy Desmond recordings for a single. Acetates are made for 'Beware', 'So It Goes', and 'Only Child'.

Friday 10th
Stage Door Johnnies album and **'Geronimo's Cadillac'** single by Claire Hamill released in the UK. The Konk label's debut releases in Britain. *NME*'s review is favourable, calling Ray's production and arrangements imaginative, and sensitive to the broad and esoteric choice of material, although it suggests Hamill's youthful vocals are novice-like compared to Maria Muldaur, offered as the nearest comparison. While naggingly irresistible, the single will not chart, and neither does the LP. Most of the promotional effort for Hamill is made in the US where she has been playing concert dates and doing promotion, mostly from a base in Los Angeles.

→ Around this time Ray's side projects include working on a British TV show called *Billy Boy* about Manchester football (soccer) star George Best, as well as overseeing recording at Konk by potential Konk signing David Sewall, referred to as The Mad Violinist. Some tracks are recorded, but none are ever issued.

☆ ● **RECORDING** Konk Studios *Hornsey, north London*. Late this month Ray does the final mix and the selection and arrangement of tracks for the *Soap Opera* LP.

Thursday 30th
A press release announces the next Kinks LP *A Soap Opera* for April release. It is also revealed that the album will include three new songs ('Holiday Romance,' 'Underneath The Neon Sign,' and 'Ducks On The Wall') not in the original *Starmaker* TV broadcast upon which the record is based.

February

Monday 3rd
● **RECORDING** Konk Studios *Hornsey, north London*. With *A Soap Opera* wrapped up, sessions begin today to record the first LP by another Konk signing, Cafe Society. This is a trio of singer-songwriters – Tom Robinson, Hereward Kaye and Raphael Doyle – and is intended to be another of Ray's personal projects. The initial session produces the first single release, titled 'The Whitby Two Step', which is full of Davies hallmarks.

The sessions continue throughout February and into March. However, Ray becomes less available, and Dave and Gosling (as production duo Dazling Productions) take over his duties along the way. The final session, which produces 'The Family Song', occurs on March 25th. When the album is issued, the production credit will be for Ray Davies "in association with Dave Davies and John Gosling".

Wednesday 5th
The production department at RCA Studios in central London issues the first test pressings of the *Soap Opera* LP.

March

→ Early this month a tentatively planned tour of the US is delayed because no new material is ready, and it is decided instead to stage *A Soap Opera* as a full-blown production.

There is some confusion among promoters and venues as to what is being presented, with omission of *A Soap Opera* in some ads, and many shows initially promoted as *Preservation Acts I & II*.

Ray prepares the *Soap Opera* stage show, and also looks for a possible film deal. "About three or four weeks before we were scheduled to go," he tells *Rolling Stone*, "the band decided that it seemed a bit silly to be going out on the road for a while and not presenting something new."

Ray's touring method returns to that which the band tried with *Preservation*: The Kinks will be their own opening act to draw the audience into the performance – and then they will produce something altogether new.

kinks'75

Thursday 6th

Ray delivers tapes of the 'Starmaker' single to RCA in New York City.

→ ● **RECORDING** Apple Studios *central London*. Probably at this time Dave records two songs at Apple on Savile Row with independent producer Phil MacDonald. They may have been demoed first at Konk. Dave later recalls the songs as **'You've Got It Made'** and **'Long Lonely Road'**, done in the final days of The Beatles' studio that closed in May this year.

Dave plays all the instruments except drums (by Nick Trevisick, currently in Cafe Society). Producer MacDonald will also work with Konk signing Claire Hamill this year on her second album *Abracadabra*, issued in November.

Friday 21st

Ray oversees the mastering of *A Soap Opera* with Robert Ludwig at Sterling Sound in New York, and delivers master tapes to RCA while he is in the city.

→ Stage backing film (16mm) is shot for *A Soap Opera*, used in concert April-June.

Friday 28th

'So It Goes' single by Andy Desmond released in the UK. A further Konk release.

April

Tuesday 1st

'Starmaker' / 'Ordinary People' single released in the US. Despite an upbeat review in *Cash Box*, this preview of the forthcoming LP sinks into oblivion without a trace of chart activity and barely a sentence in the music press.

Tuesday 1st – Thursday 3rd

Music rehearsals are held at Konk Studios where virtually the entire show from the *Soap Opera* LP is routined – a necessity as most of the material was recorded six months ago.

The only omission from the stage production is the late-added album track 'Holiday Romance', which was also absent from the original *Starmaker* TV show.

Friday 4th – Saturday 5th

● **RECORDING** Konk Studios *Hornsey, north London*. Dave and Gosling finish mixing the *Cafe Society* LP, reflecting Ray's virtual disappearance from the project.

Sunday 6th

Today's scheduled departure to the US is cancelled at the last minute. It's claimed this is because of blizzard conditions in the Midwest, and a press release is issued to this effect the following day.

The cancelled dates on the tour are: April 12th RKO Orpheum Theater, Davenport, IA; 13th Memorial Auditorium, Fort Wayne, IN (shuffled to the 17th, then canceled); 14th Veterans War Memorial Auditorium, Columbus, OH.

Monday 7th

A press release announces the start dates for the delayed US tour and reveals that the reshuffled tour will now end with three days in New York City.

Starmaker single

A **'Starmaker'** (R. DAVIES).
B **'Ordinary People'** (R. DAVIES).

US release April 1st 1975 (RCA Victor PB 10251).
Musicians Ray Davies lead vocal, spoken part (B). Dave Davies electric guitar. John Dalton bass guitar. Mick Avory drums. John Gosling Hammond organ (A), baby grand piano (B). John Beecham trombone. Alan Holmes tenor saxophone. Laurie Brown trumpet. Pamela Travis, Shirlie Roden, Lyndsey Moore backing vocals. June Ritchie spoken part (B).
Recorded Konk Studios *Hornsey, north London*; August-October 1974; 16-track mixed to stereo.
Producer Ray Davies.
Engineer Roger Beale.
Chart high US none.

Thursday 10th

A promotional reception attended by representatives of much of the music press is hastily arranged at the RCA Records company offices situated in Mayfair, central London today to make best use of the unexpected free time that the band now have.

Steve Lake's feature in *Melody Maker* reveals that, following the *Soap Opera* tours, the plan is to record a "straightahead no-frills Kinks album of songs around Christmas".

⇨ **TOUR STARTS** *A Soap Opera: US Tour* (Apr 13th – May 9th). **Line-up**: Ray Davies (lead vocal, guitar), Dave Davies (guitar, vocal), Mick Avory (drums), John Dalton (bass), John Gosling (keyboard), John Beecham (trombone), Alan Holmes (saxophone), Laurie Brown (trumpet), Pamela Travis, Shirley Roden, Debbie Doss (backing vocals).

The three singers double in minor acting roles. Theatrical effects include back-projection of slides and film; special lighting; props. In a few cases there is a support act, as noted, but generally The Kinks as themselves open.

Friday 11th

Prior to the band's departure today for New York City, plans are finalised to spend £25,000 for the production of a film featuring The Kinks. This may be the planned filming of *A Soap Opera* in concert in London, or possibly a Kinks-made film of *Preservation*.

There are also plans for The Kinks' company to build a new control room and studio at Konk at an estimated cost of £45,000. These facilities will indeed be opened the following summer. (Following day travelling and time off.)

Sunday 13th

St. Paul Civic Center Theater *St. Paul, MN* 8:00pm.
Set-list: 'Here Comes Flash', 'Here Comes Yet Another Day', medley: 'You Really Got Me' / 'All Day And All Of The Night', 'Demolition', 'Salvation Road', 'Mirror Of Love', 'Money Talks', 'Celluloid Heroes', 'Lola', 'Alcohol', medley: 'Skin And Bone' / 'Dry Bones'. Intermission. *A Soap Opera*.

Monday 14th

Travelling day and time off. Meanwhile back home a press release announces UK tour dates with an as-yet unspecified London date.

→ INDICATES EVENT AROUND THIS TIME BUT WITH NO FIRM DATE

Ducks On The Wall single

A 'Ducks On The Wall' (R. DAVIES).
B 'Rush Hour Blues' (R. DAVIES).

UK release April 18th 1975 (RCA Victor RCA 2546).
Musicians Ray Davies lead vocal. Dave Davies electric guitar. John Dalton bass guitar. Mick Avory drums, duck effects (A). John Gosling baby grand piano. John Beecham trombone. Alan Holmes tenor saxophone. Laurie Brown trumpet. Pamela Travis, Shirlie Roden, Lyndsey Moore backing vocals (B). June Ritchie spoken part (B).
Recorded Konk Studios *Hornsey, north London*; August-October 1974; 16-track mixed to stereo.
Producer Ray Davies.
Engineer Roger Beale.
Chart high UK none.

Tuesday 15th

Akron Civic Theater *Akron, OH* 8:00pm
"Although the production of Soap Opera was a case of reach exceeding grasp at points where it was ragged or even amateurish, the concert otherwise was solidly performed," says the *Akron Beacon Journal*. "The major drawback was a horribly muddy sound which sapped the music of much of its vitality and obscured Davies' lyrics. Even if some preferred to ignore Davies' intellectualizing, the concert was funny, raucous, and entertaining. Not overwhelming, perhaps, but a good evening of rock'n'roll."

Wednesday 16th

Riverside Theater *Milwaukee, WI* 8:00pm.
"The two-and-a-half-hour affair was more English music hall than anything else, a total show," writes Spatz Columbo in *The Bugle*. "Live Kinks is quite a spectacle. Ray Davies center-stage cavorts like a drunken dancer. His voice ran the full gamut of Kinks styles. Growling. Purring. High. Always theatrical. Delightfully tacky at worst. The Kinks seemed quite at ease in the majestically outdated Riverside Theater. At times the whole show seemed like an eerie replay of *The Blue Angel*." (Travel day follows.)

Friday 18th

Barn, Rutgers University *New Brunswick, NJ* 8:00pm
Despite some criticism of the sound system, the concert is described as excellent. *Daily Targum*: "The costuming was both fitting and funny, and the slides projected to the rear of the stage provided an enjoyable visual accompaniment."
'Ducks On The Wall' / 'Rush Hour Blues' single released in the UK. Reaction in the music press is poor. *Melody Maker* pans it – "Kinks come back with a lame duck" – while the *NME* is a little more discreet, noting strong guitar and piano in the backing but complaining of a weak tune and unsubtle satire. Perhaps it is no coincidence that neither paper will ultimately run a review of the *Soap Opera* LP.

Sunday 20th

The Spectrum *Philadelphia, PA* 8:00pm
Tonight's gross takings are $40,000 of a potential $55,000 house.

Monday 21st

Capitol Theatre *Passaic, NJ* 8:00pm

Technically this is *Soap Opera*'s debut in the New York area as Passaic is an easy trip across the river from Manhattan. Despite only about 2,300 attending (80 per cent capacity) this is still deemed a strong turnout in the depressed economic atmosphere. A major blow-by-blow account of this show by US critic John Swenson runs in *Sounds* in Britain, providing a taster for the upcoming UK tour. A local reviewer mentions sound-system shortcomings at the Capitol, and says that the lights "were frequently the wrong color or played on the wrong person. These problems began to bother the band, and everything started to get rushed. Still, it was The Kinks, and despite everything, it was a damned good show".

Tuesday 22nd

With the previews over, today the band meets the New York music press at the Warwick Room in the Warwick Hotel in Manhattan. The cream of the current rock press is in attendance, including many Kinks supporters: Lisa Robinson (*Hit Parader*); Jim Litke (*Rolling Stone*); Stephen Demorest (*Circus*); Danny Fields (*16 Magazine*); and a representative from *Creem*. Even Chris Charlesworth is flown in from London to represent *Melody Maker* and, conveniently, to preview the British tour. Ray reveals to Robinson that he already has "another idea I want to do", likely hinting that *Schoolboys* is a concept in waiting.

Wednesday 23rd

Ritchie Auditorium, University of Maryland *College Park, MD* 8:00pm

Thursday 24th

Charmichael Auditorium, University of North Carolina *Chapel Hill, NC* 8:00pm
The Kinks' very first visit to the South in their long career. The attendance of only a few thousand falls far short of a sell out, and there are complaints of persistent sound problems, but the student paper reports the show an artistic and entertaining triumph.

Friday 25th

William & Mary Hall, College of William & Mary *Williamsburg, VA* 8:00pm
(The Kinks Present) A Soap Opera album released in the US. "It's a tremendous advance in its handling of the traditions of a full-scale musical comedy but it's still not a first rate Kinks album," says *Stereo Review*. "The demands of the storyline intrude upon the songs … Frankly, it sounds just too much like a soundtrack." Vocal critic John Mendelsson in *Rolling Stone* doesn't hide his disappointment, urging Davies to return to his strengths. John Swenson in *Crawdaddy!* takes a more supportive stance, claiming that the album overall manages to stand on its own, but says that parts fail without the help of the visuals of the stage show. Lenny Kaye writes in *Hit Parader* of "a concept album livened by engaging humor, bittersweet romanticism, and a touch of slumming elegance". (Travel day tomorrow.)

Sunday 27th

Charleston Municipal Auditorium *Charleston, SC* 8:00pm

Tuesday 29th

Dixon Meyers/Auditorium Music Hall *Memphis, TN* 8:00pm
Originally scheduled for the larger Ellis Auditorium, but slow ticket sales force a change to this smaller location where 2,200 attend. All these Southern dates are first-time visits for the band, and while the colleges can usually produce a guaranteed audience, it seems to be a tough sell – despite The Kinks' enduring legacy from the 1960s.

Wednesday 30th

Municipal Auditorium *Atlanta, GA* 7:30pm

(The Kinks Present) A Soap Opera album

A1 **'Everybody's A Star (Starmaker)'** (R. DAVIES).
A2 **'Ordinary People'** (R. DAVIES).
A3 **'Rush Hour Blues'** (R. DAVIES).
A4 **'Nine To Five'** (R. DAVIES).
A5 **'When Work Is Over'** (R. DAVIES).
A6 **'Have Another Drink'** (R. DAVIES).
B1 **'Underneath The Neon Sign'** (R. DAVIES).
B2 **'Holiday Romance'** (R. DAVIES).
B3 **'You Make It All Worthwhile'** (R. DAVIES).
B4 **'Ducks On The Wall'** (R. DAVIES).
B5 **'(A) Face In The Crowd'** (R. DAVIES).
B6 **'You Can't Stop The Music'** (R. DAVIES).

US release April 25th 1975 (RCA Victor LPL1-5081).
UK release May 16th 1975 (RCA Victor SF 8411).
Musicians Ray Davies lead vocal, acoustic guitar. Dave Davies electric guitar, backing vocal. John Gosling baby grand piano, Hammond organ. John Dalton bass guitar. Mick Avory drums, duck effects (B4). John Beecham trombone. Alan Holmes saxophones. Laurie Brown trumpet. Pamela Travis, Lyndsey Moore, Shirley Roden backing vocals. June Ritchie spoken female parts (A2, A3, B3). Stanley Meyers string arrangement (B3).
Recorded Konk Studios *Hornsey, north London*; August-October 1974; 16-track mixed to stereo.
Producer Ray Davies.
Engineer Roger Beale.
Chart high UK none; US number 55.

May

Friday 2nd
Scheduled concert at Miami Municipal Auditorium, FL, cancelled on the day of the show due to local (unconnected) rioting.

Saturday 3rd
Jai-Alai Center *West Palm Beach, FL* 8:00pm

Sunday 4th
Bayfront Center *St. Petersburg, FL* 8:00pm
(Following two days off.)

Wednesday 7th – Friday 9th
Beacon Theatre *New York, NY* 8:00pm
Dave Hickey of *The Village Voice* has often been critical of rock posing as theatre, but he raves about the *Soap Opera* show. "Like a lot of great songwriter performers Davies isn't musically sophisticated but he understands rock'n'roll as well as any man alive. He knows it is about a band and an audience, the status gulf between them, and the primitive music that unifies them. ... Every grotesque cliché of rock royalty and the new populism gets a clean funny shot, and it works because Davies doesn't introduce theatrical effects into rock'n'roll, he takes the theatrical effects which are already in rock'n'roll and uses them to his advantage: every variation on the rock rituals ... is used to dramatic effect." Hickey says the effect on the audience "was almost chemical – it was dramatic, funny, touching and so goddamn smart it made you

want to hit a wall". John Rockwell in *The New York Times* acknowledges Davies as a consummate vaudevilian and finds the show an admirable effort in the "study of the links between the reality and fantasy of rock'n'roll". *Rolling Stone* magazine coolly remarks that "from a distance, the show probably seemed heavily overplayed. But the true believers loved it".

Chris Charlesworth, flown in from London to review the show for the British audience, says: "The Kinks have finally become the Ray Davies show ... In terms of a professional theatre concept – à la Bowie or Cooper – the band display the same degree of lackadaisical unprofessionalism that has always been evident in their work. But to criticise The Kinks on that level is unfair. What Ray Davies has done is to write and choreograph an evening of laughter based loosely around the concept of a rock star becoming a normal person, and the result of his labours is a huge success. I laughed a lot and that's what counts ... A clever, amusing show, then, although the English aspects (no one in the US has ever heard of ducks on the wall!) may well baffle US audiences."

One show from the three-night run is videotaped in black and white by RCA Records. This is transferred to 16mm film and will be released theatrically in the US for a very limited time from July. But it is eventually pulled after an objection by the band and because of the film's poor visual quality.

Saturday 10th
Travel to London. Tentatively scheduled shows in two traditional Kinks strongholds were inexplicably never finalised: May 10th Music Hall, Boston, MA; 11th Palace Concert Theater, Providence, RI.

Friday 16th
(The Kinks Present) A Soap Opera album released in the UK. "Despite popular British opinion that The Kinks are only ancient memory-joggers," writes Barbara Charone in *Sounds*, "they continue to be one of Britain's best. *Soap Opera* is proof that Ray Davies is our finest songwriter, touching us deeply, reaching within our own fantasies." The LP garners a four-star rating in the languishing music paper *Disc* where the reviewer asks, "Could this be the album to put The Kinks back in the public eye? I hope so, for it is a work that should not go unnoticed." Sadly, the record-buying public does not share such a view and the album fails to chart. Most telling of all is that neither *NME* nor *Melody Maker* run reviews at all.

Monday 19th
A pre-tour warm-up rehearsal at 2:00pm, presumably at Konk Studios.

⇨ **TOUR STARTS** *A Soap Opera: UK Tour* (May 21st – Jun 14th).
Line-up: Ray Davies (lead vocal, guitar), Dave Davies (guitar, vocal), Mick Avory (drums), John Dalton (bass), John Gosling (keyboard), John Beecham (trombone), Alan Holmes (saxophone), Laurie Brown (trumpet), Pamela Travis, Shirley Roden, Debbie Doss (backing vocals). For some of the shows, generally those closer to London, Konk-label artists Cafe Society are added as special guests. (Entourage travels to Scotland on the 20th.)

Wednesday 21st
Usher Hall *Edinburgh, Scotland*
Set-list: 'Here Comes Flash'; 'Here Comes Yet Another Day'; 'Money Talks'; 'Slum Kids'; 'Mirror Of Love'; 'Celluloid Heroes'; 'Banana Boat Song'; 'Lola'; 'Alcohol'; medley: 'Skin And Bone'/'Dry Bones'; medley: 'You Really Got Me'/'All Day And All Of The Night'. Intermission. *A Soap Opera*.

Thursday 22nd
Apollo Theatre *Glasgow, Scotland*

You Can't Stop The Music single

A 'You Can't Stop The Music' (R. DAVIES).
B 'Have Another Drink' (R. DAVIES).

UK release May 23rd 1975 (RCA Victor RCA 2567).
Musicians and recording details as *Soap Opera* album (see April 25th).
Chart high UK none.

Friday 23rd

Maxwell Hall, University Of Salford *Salford*

'You Can't Stop The Music' / 'Have Another Drink' single released in the UK. This constituted a second attempt to chart a single from the *Soap Opera* LP after the disastrous reaction to 'Ducks On The Wall'. *Melody Maker* likes it much more but still predicts a miss – and is proved correct.

Saturday 24th

Sports Hall, Brunel University *Uxbridge, Middx* 8:30pm, with Cafe Society
Five days off follow.

Friday 30th

Refectory, University Of Leeds *Leeds* 8:00pm

"The Kinks performance demonstrated why they are still one of the best live bands in the country," writes Nick Kehoe in *Leeds Student*. "They grabbed the audience's attention from the start and held it right until the final encore. The music suffered a little from technical problems but the band still managed a credible performance ... A great deal of thought had obviously been put into the stage production of this work ... with full use being made of cine-projectors and lighting to make the 'opera' both visually and musically exciting."

Saturday 31st

Empire Theatre *Liverpool* 8:00pm

June

Sunday 1st

City Hall *Newcastle Upon Tyne* 7:30pm

Monday 2nd

Hippodrome *Birmingham*

A press release announces a special London date added to the UK tour. Rather than tack it on immediately following the end of the tour's normal run on the 3rd, extra time is allowed between to ensure proper technical running and to arrange to record and film the event. *'Everybody's A Star (Starmaker)'* single is remixed (it is slightly speeded up) and re-promoted to radio stations, but the record is never issued commercially.

Tuesday 3rd

Colston Hall *Bristol* 8:00pm

→ Early this month the band have a ten-day break, with preparations underway for the important London show, including plans for filming and recording.

Friday 13th

Pye Records opportunistically re-releases the 1966 hit 'Sunny Afternoon' in Britain, hoping for a summer revival as a result of The Kinks' visibility now. It does not chart.

Saturday 14th

New Victoria Theatre *central London* 8:00pm

"*Soap Opera* was flawless," writes Phil MacNeill in *Let It Rock*. "Costume changes, exits, entrances, back-projected slides and films that changed every ten seconds ... Tears, laughter, love, hate. The band, subdued to the point of seriousness ... was paradoxically active: drunk, brash, sneering, as necessary. Dave, who had hardly put a solo together last year, was playing heavy metal with a swagger whenever he got the chance. Ray may be a poseur rather than an actor, but he times his lines like only a singer can. And his vocal performance and effortless singing was staggering."

☆ During the following days the audio recording of the *Soap Opera* portion of the New Victoria show is mixed by Ray into quadrophonic (four-channel sound). It is broadcast in the US by DIR on their syndicated concert program *A British Biscuit* (August 24th and December 21st) and later partially issued on bootlegs (*Don't Touch That Dial* and *A British Biscuit*). One song from The Kinks' opening set, 'Here Comes Yet Another Day', is later mixed and issued as part of the band's last LP for RCA in 1976, *The Kinks Greatest/Celluloid Heroes*. Three other songs recorded tonight – 'Ordinary People', 'You Make It All Worthwhile' and 'Underneath The Neon Sign' – are later exhumed, remixed and issued as bonus cuts on the 1998 CD reissue of *A Soap Opera*. The entire show is evidently filmed in colour as well, apparently financed by The Kinks themselves for a potential theatrical release, but the project is never mentioned again.

→ Konk engineer Roger Beale leaves and a new house engineer, Roger Wake, is hired.
☆ Ray begins intensive writing sessions for a new album and stage show.
☆ A European leg of the *Soap Opera* tour is pencilled in, initially for October, but this will be abandoned once the next album and show begin to take shape.

July

The band has time off while Ray continues concentrated writing sessions during the first few weeks of the month. The work is interrupted on the 5th by the death of Ray and Dave's father – only publicly revealed years later in Ray's *X-Ray* book. Ray must quickly revert to business matters and will be selling the next conceptual idea to RCA.

The first informal band rehearsals for what will become the *Schoolboys In Disgrace* album begin on Sunday 22nd at Ray's house in Surrey, continuing into Monday. Ray continues to write for the rest of the week. The following Sunday, the 29th, rehearsals resume with the band at the Ray's home for the upcoming *Schoolboys* sessions. Afterwards, Ray again adjourns for two solid weeks of further writing while the band members are officially off for their annual holidays.

August

The week of the 13th to the 18th sees the band reconvene at Konk in London where they set about recording rough demos of some 16 songs of the 30 that Ray is said to have composed for the project by now (indicating he has a double-album in mind). However, it is likely only nine songs will be chosen for re-recording as master versions. Two of the demos made now and not re-recorded as masters are 'History' and 'Drop Out'. Proper sessions for the recording of the masters for *Schoolboys In Disgrace* begin on Tuesday 19th with the recording of at least the backing track for 'I'm In Disgrace'. Sessions are broken again but then resume by Wednesday 27th, when 'Education' is put on tape.

September

Tuesday 2nd
● RECORDING Konk Studios *Hornsey, north London*. Sessions for the *Schoolboys In Disgrace* album continue, recording 'Jack The Idiot Dunce' and 'The First Time We Fall In Love'.

Friday 5th
'Rory' single by Claire Hamill, 'Beware' single by Andy Desmond, '(The) Whitby Two Step' single by Cafe Society all released in the UK. The Konk label unleashes a trio of new singles from its stable of artists. All three preview full-length LPs which follow shortly as Konk makes its biggest push into the marketplace.

Tuesday 9th
With an eye on the new album's strict release deadline, still set for November 10th, photo sessions are held today for the sleeve and accompanying promo shots. At Konk the band is photographed by Chris Hooper in their newly acquired schoolboy costumes. In addition, a separate session is shot with the band in everyday clothes playing billiards in the studio's game room.

Thursday 11th, Saturday 13th, Tuesday 16th
● RECORDING Konk Studios *Hornsey, north London*. *Schoolboys* sessions continue, recording 'Schooldays' (11th), 'The Last Assembly' (13th) and 'No More Looking Back' (16th).

Monday 22nd
Press release announces new LP and a stage show in the works.

Monday 22nd – Wed 24th
● RECORDING Konk Studios *Hornsey, north London*. Sessions for the *Schoolboys In Disgrace* album completed, recording 'The Hard Way' (22nd), 'Headmaster' (23rd) and 'Finale' (24th).

Thursday 25th – Friday Oct 3rd
● RECORDING Konk Studios *Hornsey, north London*. Ray mixes *Schoolboys* tracks.

October

Thursday 2nd
● RECORDING Konk Studios *Hornsey, north London*. John Beecham dubs trombone on to 'The Hard Way' and 'Headmaster'.

Saturday 4th
With the finished mix in hand, Ray travels to New York City.

Sunday 5th
At Sterling Sound in New York City, Ray oversees the mastering of the *Schoolboys In Disgrace* LP by Robert Ludwig.

Monday 6th
Master tapes of *Schoolboys* LP logged in to RCA Records vaults in New York City today.

➜ Early this month at the offices of ABC Records in Los Angeles, Ray personally retrieves tapes of cancelled US Konk releases by Cafe Society, Andy Desmond, Claire Hamill, and Ian Whitcomb, as Konk's distribution deal with ABC is terminated.

Friday 17th
Cafe Society album released in the UK. Another Konk release.

➜ *Living On A Shoestring* album by Andy Desmond released in the UK. A further Konk LP.
☆ Talking to Lisa Robinson for *Hit Parader* magazine at the Savoy Hotel in central London, Ray says of Dave: "My brother is all right, his life is dedicated to getting the [Konk] studio together. He's really into that. He's started recording but I might even have to get a contract with him and say he's got to deliver me [a solo] album. It may be the only way he's going to record is at gunpoint."

Friday 31st
The Kinks begin music rehearsals at Konk Studios for the *Schoolboys* stage show. Also today, Tony Dimitriades resigns as business manager of Konkwest Ltd and in the process sends the Konk label to a relatively early grave.

November

Wednesday 5th
At Konk Studios, interior scenes are shot with Ray's 16mm camera for the stage background film for *Schoolboys In Disgrace*. Also, some location scenes are shot around the Hornsey area.

Thursday 6th
On Hampstead Heath, scene of the famous cover shoot for the 1968 *Village Green Preservation Society* LP, more film footage for the *Schoolboys In Disgrace* stage background film is shot today.
☆ Around this time music rehearsals for the *Schoolboys* stage show continue at Konk Studios.

Wednesday 12th – Saturday 15th
At a 450-seat theatre in Ealing, west London (possibly the Questors Theatre) the band privately rehearses the full stage show for the upcoming *Schoolboys* tour.

Monday 17th
(The Kinks Present) Schoolboys In Disgrace album released in the US. Stephen Demorest reviews the record for *Circus*, saying: "Ray Davies is once again mining his own past … and the characteristic mixture of wistfulness and good humor he brings to it is nothing new. What's special is that those eccentric, charming, slipshod post-adolescents, The Kinks, seem to be entering a new golden age, having served up the most musically mature production of their career."
☆ A press release announces the January 1976 release of the *Schoolboys* LP in Britain and a tour at that time.

➜ Marion Rainford, long-serving Kinks secretary, assistant and gal Friday, retires from the organisation after a frenetic five-and-a-half-year stint.

➜ INDICATES EVENT AROUND THIS TIME BUT WITH NO FIRM DATE

Schoolboys in disgrace: Ray and Dave uniformly snookered, October 1975.

Abracadabra album by Claire Hamill released in the U.K. Says *Melody Maker* of the new Konk album, not this time produced by Ray: "Doesn't perhaps have the impact or immediacy of the excellent [first Konk LP] *Stage Door Johnnies*, and there aren't any tracks with the commercial potential of 'Geronimo's Cadillac' which rightfully should have been a hit single. But this [is] a rewarding showcase of one of Britain's most stylish writers (she's penned seven of the tracks here) and performers."

↪ **TOUR STARTS** *Schoolboys In Disgrace: US Tour: 1st leg* (Nov 21st – Dec 18th). **Line-up**: Ray Davies (lead vocal, guitar), Dave Davies (guitar, vocal), Mick Avory (drums), John Dalton (bass), John Gosling (keyboard), John Beecham (trombone), Alan Holmes (saxophone), Nick Newall (saxophone), Pamela Travis, Shirley Roden, Debbie Doss (backing vocals).

Singers double as schoolgirls, with Travis taking the pregnant role. The horn section and auxiliary singers also have some speaking roles. Theatrical effects include multimedia presentation with rear-projected 16mm films and three slide carousels, and some props. A whipping scene has Avory experiencing the lash in 'The Hard Way'. (Travel London to Philadelphia on the 20th.) International Famous Agency (IFA), which had been booking The Kinks for US tours, has been incorporated into the newly formed International Creative Management (ICM), and all American tours from now through autumn 1985 are booked through this new major New York City-based company.

(The Kinks Present) Schoolboys In Disgrace album

A1 'Schooldays' (R. DAVIES).
A2 'Jack The Idiot Dunce' (R. DAVIES).
A3 'Education' (R. DAVIES).
A4 'The First Time We Fall In Love' (R. DAVIES).
B1 'I'm In Disgrace' (R. DAVIES).
B2 'Headmaster' (R. DAVIES).
B3 'The Hard Way' (R. DAVIES).
B4 'The Last Assembly' (R. DAVIES).
B5 'No More Looking Back' (R. DAVIES).
B6 'Finale' (R. DAVIES).

US release November 17th 1975 (RCA Victor LPL1-5102).
UK release January 23rd 1976 (RCA Victor RS 1028).
Musicians Ray Davies acoustic guitar (A1, B2, B3), baby grand piano (A3, A4, B4, B6), lead vocal, tambourine. Dave Davies electric guitar, backing vocal. John Dalton bass guitar. Mick Avory drums, backing vocal. John Gosling baby grand piano (A1, A2, B1, B2), electric piano (A4, B5), Hammond organ (A1, A3, B3, B4), backing vocal. Nick Newall tenor saxophone (A3, A4, B2, B6). Alan Holmes baritone saxophone (A3, A4, B2, B5, B6), tenor & soprano saxophone (A3, B6). Pamela Travis, Debbie Doss, Shirley Roden backing vocals (A3, B2, B5, B6).
Recorded Konk Studios *Hornsey, north London*; 1975; A1: September 11th; A2, A4: September 2nd; A3: August 27th; B1: August 19th; B2: September 23rd; B3: September 22nd; B4: September 13th; B5: September 16th; B6 September 24th; 16-track mixed to stereo.
Producer Ray Davies.
Engineer Roger Wake.
Chart high UK none; US 45.

Friday 21st
Grace Hall, Lehigh University *Bethlehem, PA* 9:00pm, with Steve Harley & Cockney Rebel
Set-list: Opening set as The Kinks, approximately 45 minutes. Intermission. *Schoolboys In Disgrace*: 'Schooldays', introductory theme, 'Jack The Idiot Dunce', 'Education', 'The First Time We Fall In Love', 'I'm In Disgrace', 'Headmaster', 'The First Time We Fall In Love' (reprise), 'The Hard Way' (narration & whipping), 'The Last Assembly', 'No More Looking Back', 'Education' (reprise).

Saturday 22nd
MacMorland Center, Widener University *Chester, PA* 8:00pm, with Steve Harley & Cockney Rebel

Sunday 23rd
Loew's Buffalo Theater *Buffalo, NY* 8:30pm, with Steve Harley & Cockney Rebel; sponsored by the State University of New York at Buffalo
The crowd is described as the biggest so far this year at the theatre. "It was the ultimate vaudeville low teenage multimedia comic opera, Charles Dickens style," wrote Dale Anderson in the *Buffalo News* after panning opener Steve Harley. "There was no encore (do movies come back after 'The End?') though the student crowd clamored mightily for one. Davies and The Kinks had put on a singularly brilliant show." (Travelling and day off tomorrow.)

Tuesday 25th
War Memorial Auditorium *Trenton, NJ* 8:00pm, with Steve Harley & Cockney Rebel

Wednesday 26th
Capitol Theater *Passaic, NJ* 8:00pm, with Steve Harley & Cockney Rebel
Day off in New York City follows.

Friday 28th
Beacon Theatre *New York, NY* 7:00 & 11:00pm, with Steve Harley & Cockney Rebel
"The great thing about seeing The Kinks live in 1975 is that solid gold oldies serve only as the perfunctory audience/band warm-up," says visiting British music paper *Sounds*. "The burden of having to depend solely on past hits has been lifted from Kinks shoulders, freeing them to give some of their best performances. But the real feeling of discovery and freshness comes the minute they launch into *Schoolboys In Disgrace*. It doesn't take the sold-out crowd long to realise that this new Kinks show is chock full of humour, rock'n'roll and some of the most clever staging in rock."

Saturday 29th – Sunday 30th
The band gets a few days off in New York City including a rare Saturday night to enjoy the nightlife. (Further day off in New York December 1st.)

December

Tuesday 2nd
Palace Theater *Albany, NY* 8:00pm, with Steve Harley & Cockney Rebel

Wednesday 3rd
Physical Education Building, State University of New York College *Brockport, NY* 8:00pm, with Steve Harley & Cockney Rebel

---

➜ INDICATES EVENT AROUND THIS TIME BUT WITH NO FIRM DATE

Thursday 4th – Friday 5th
Orpheum Theater *Boston, MA* 7:00pm, with Steve Harley & Cockney Rebel

"A tight, clever comedy of music and cinema which is as good as anything the well-traveled group has ever displayed," says *The Boston Globe*.

Saturday 6th
Palace Theater *Waterbury, CT* 8:30pm, with Steve Harley & Cockney Rebel

"The concept … is provocative, though the music it uses as a vehicle is often not far from the ordinary," writes Alan Cameron in *The Advocate*. "Davies' lyrics are not as brilliant as they once were; if not understated they are mundane. And the melodies are not as inspired as the bouncy music hall tunes he used to write. Still … The Kinks delight in performing and the music-drama at the Palace, replete with moments of pure camp, nostalgia, poignancy, terror, and loneliness, was fascinating from start to finish." (The following day is time off for the band in New York City.)

Monday 8th
Playhouse, Hofstra University *Hempstead, NY* 8:00pm, with Steve Harley & Cockney Rebel

"Most memorable in performance is Dave Davies for his incredible guitar work and Ray Davies' all around performance," says the *Hofstra Chronicle*. "[Ray] had the audience under his complete control from the moment they opened." (Following days off and travelling.)

Thursday 11th
Music Hall *Cleveland, OH* 8:00pm, with Steve Harley & Cockney Rebel

Friday 12th
Palace Theater *Detroit, MI* 8:00pm, with Steve Harley & Cockney Rebel

Saturday 13th
Aragon Ballroom *Chicago, IL* 8:00pm, with Little Feat, Steve Harley & Cockney Rebel

Tonight's show adds to the bill one of Dave and Gosling's favourite acts, Little Feat, featuring guitarist Lowell George.

Sunday 14th
Oriental Landmark Theater *Milwaukee, WI* 8:00pm, with Steve Harley & Cockney Rebel

Wednesday 17th
Memorial Hall *Kansas City, MO* 8:00pm, with Steve Harley & Cockney Rebel

Thursday 18th
Ambassador Theater *St. Louis, MO* 8:00pm, with Steve Harley & Cockney Rebel

Friday 19th
The entourage returns to London. Original schedule was to end with two West Coast dates (20th Shrine Civic Auditorium, Los Angeles; 21st Winterland, San Francisco) but during the tour it was deemed worthwhile to return in January for a proper West Coast leg of the tour.

Saturday 20th – Saturday 27th
Christmas time off in London.

Sunday 28th
The five-man Kinks with just the three-piece horn section – no female singers – are at the South Bank Television Centre in London where they record backing tracks, used the following day for their TV session.

Monday 29th
❏ **TV** South Bank Television Centre *central London*. ITV *Supersonic* lip-synch 'No More Looking Back', medley 'You Really Got Me' / 'All Day And All Of The Night' broadcast March 6th 1976. The show is under the direction and production of the band's old 1960s ally from Southern TV, Mike Mansfield. They're filmed lip-synching to the backing tracks made the day before for this London Weekend Television production, broadcast in Britain next year to tie in with the release of the 'No More Looking Back' single and their British tour. In the US, the *Supersonic* series will later be picked up by American International Television (AITV) which syndicates the show under the title *Juke Box Featuring Twiggy*. The earliest known broadcast is not until February 1979, rendering The Kinks' segment somewhat redundant as a promotional tool for selling records, but nevertheless a treat for US fans lucky enough to catch it in their area.

1976

The Kinks were out of public gaze for much of this year, but behind the scenes kept as busy as ever. After wrapping up touring commitments for the final stage productions of Schoolboys In Disgrace, Ray handed over a final label-retrospective album to RCA. It had been an unhappy partnership for the band and the record company.

Pressure was building on Ray from The Kinks' camp and accumulating critical opinion to abandon the ambitious stage shows. The rock-theatre productions had generally met with approval from those who attended, but the band's sales of records and tickets were fading in the face of Ray's fondness for the medium.

The Kinks seized the opportunity offered by former Columbia Records head Clive Davis. He had courted them at the time of the RCA deal, and was now heading his own start-up company, Arista Records. Davis had great faith in The Kinks' talents and was now in a better position to make a deal. The band was no longer in a position of commercial strength as they had been when RCA signed them. Davis's deal was designed to curtail what some perceived as the creative dip of the RCA years and return them to commercial success – a goal that both sides seemed to approve.

By mid-year a deal was signed and the remainder of 1976 spent working on the all-important debut album for Arista. It heralded the return of a five-man Kinks as a classic rock group, no longer a theatrical troupe. Perhaps it was no coincidence that this happened at a time when in Britain young new bands, in rebellion against the inflated self-importance of rock stars and their uninspired product, were beginning to emerge in the nascent punk-rock scene.

January

➜ Money is finally allocated by Kinks Productions to move forward with the plans first mooted a year ago to build a new control room at Konk Studios. (The old one will be converted to an isolation booth.) This work occurs simultaneously with the installation of a new 24-track tape recorder that brings Konk's recording capabilities up to date. It will provide The Kinks with a state-of-the-art studio in which to record themselves, but will also attract business from outside acts and bands.

☆ Prompted by working with The Kinks again last month on his regular music series *Supersonic*, LWT producer Mike Mansfield proposes a separate special programme devoted to The Kinks featuring older material as well as excerpts from *Schoolboys In Disgrace*. The idea seems to develop quickly, and filming is set for January 24th. The already planned US tour is consequently pushed back by two weeks, and as tickets for some of the early dates have already gone on sale, the resulting delay and cancellation of a few dates angers some fans who had waited overnight to get their tickets.

Monday 12th
A press release says that a UK tour originally scheduled for January will now take place at the end of February, that a TV special is planned for London Weekend Television, and that a new LP and maxi-single (EP) will be out on the 23rd.

Monday 19th
A press release issued today confirms that The Kinks will play a forthcoming concert at the Drury Lane Theatre, situated in the heart of central London.

Wednesday 21st
➜ 'I'm In Disgrace' / 'The Hard Way' single released in the US.

Friday 23rd
(The Kinks Present) Schoolboys In Disgrace album released in the UK. *Record Mirror & Disc* is upbeat: "Lyrics apart, the album is superb – and a vast improvement on the style they adopted for the

I'm In Disgrace single

A **'I'm In Disgrace'** (R. DAVIES).
B **'The Hard Way'** (R. DAVIES).

US release January (around 21st) 1976 (RCA Victor PB 10551). Musicians and recording details as *Schoolboys* album (see November 17th 1975).
Chart high US none.

Preservation albums. There's more guts, more rock'n'roll and a little less pretension. I think that's more than sufficient to carry the initial idea, which hasn't worked out so convincingly."

But the *NME*'s reviewer is not convinced. "I like The Kinks a lot, but have to say that this album is a pretty uninspired collection of product. The thematic album has become an easy way for The Kinks to get by, but this is no story of the fall of the British Empire or revelation of corruption in the music business, both of which gave rise to some magnificent tracks because Ray Davies believed in what he was writing."

'No More Looking Back' / 'Jack The Idiot Dunce' / 'The Hard Way' maxi-single (EP) released in the UK. *NME* asks: "What's with Raymond Douglas? The man who wrote so many enduring singles seems to be unable to clear his mind of musical clutter. … Bring back Shel Talmy. It's urgent!"

No More Looking Back maxi-single (EP)

A 'No More Looking Back' (R. DAVIES).
B1 'Jack The Idiot Dunce' (R. DAVIES).
B2 'The Hard Way' (R. DAVIES).

UK release January 23rd 1976 (RCA Victor RCM 1). Musicians and recording details as *Schoolboys* album (see November 17th 1975).
Chart high UK none.

Saturday 24th

❏ **TV** South Bank Television Centre *central London*. The Kinks record two songs (titles unknown) with producer Mike Mansfield for a planned TV special. The intention is to use material from *Schoolboys In Disgrace* and some older Kinks songs. However, the taping reaches some sort of impasse and the band plans to resume taping of the show after the US tour in late February, but that ultimately never happens and the show is scrapped.

Wednesday 28th

Just prior to leaving for the States, Ray does some press, including an interview with Rosalind Russell for *Record Mirror & Disc*. He tells her, "I want to go back to the music. In a way I think I have neglected the music and concentrated too much on the lyric form – but I don't think it was overdone. To me the albums were musical plays. I don't think I'm big headed when I say that it worked."

↪ **TOUR STARTS** *Schoolboys In Disgrace: US Tour: 2nd leg* (Jan 30th – Feb 20th). **Line-up**: Ray Davies (lead vocal, guitar), Dave Davies (guitar, vocal), Mick Avory (drums), John Dalton (bass), John Gosling (keyboard), John Beecham (trombone), Alan Holmes (saxophone), Nick Newall (saxophone), Pamela Travis, Shirley Roden, Debbie Doss (backing vocals).

One show nightly, generally at 8:00pm. All dates are with The Pretty Things, unless noted. Like The Kinks, the Pretties have survived relatively intact from the heyday of the mid 1960s, and currently they're signed to a career-reviving deal with Swan Song Records, Led Zeppelin's venture into the record business. (Travel to New York and then on to San Francisco, 28th-29th.)

Friday 30th
San Jose Civic Auditorium *San Jose, CA* 8:00pm

Saturday 31st
Berkeley Community Theater *Berkeley, CA* 8:00pm

February

Sunday 1st
Men's gymnasium, California State University: Sacramento *Sacramento, CA* 7:30pm
Following two days are time off in San Francisco, plus travel day to and day off in Seattle.

Friday 6th
Paramount Northwest Theater *Seattle, WA*

Saturday 7th
Paramount Theatre *Portland, OR*
The Kinks show is plagued by a poor turn-out of only about 800 fans. They are up against both David Bowie and ELO in town this week, competing for the local dollar. (Travel day to Los Angeles on Sunday, which possibly sees an RCA press party for The Kinks there at the Continental Hyatt Hotel.)

Monday 9th – Tuesday 10th
Santa Monica Civic Auditorium *Santa Monica, CA*
Los Angeles Times: "Though not so consistently absorbing as *Preservation*, last year's complex morality play, The Kinks' new production of *Schoolboys In Disgrace* … is another impressive merger of rock'n'roll intensity with high-quality visual aides." *Cash Box* raves: "[The Kinks] are and will continue to be a major force in rock'n'roll…. The show was masterful. Careful attention was paid to theatrics – choreography and gesture – and what emerged was a whole greater than the sum of its parts."

Wednesday 11th
Golden Hall, Convention & Performing Arts Center *San Diego, CA* with Horsefeathers
San Diego Union: "Ambitiously conceived, the show proved flawed in execution. The films, for example, seldom rose above the level of well-made amateur movies. Likewise, Davies' lyrics often seemed to reach for ideas that exceeded their grasp. Still, in its completeness as a show, including pictures, costumes, music and satire, it far surpassed what most rock groups are willing to try."

Thursday 12th
Day off in Los Angeles. At some point, possibly tonight, a press party for the tour's support act The Pretty Things is held at the former mansion of actress Jayne Mansfield in Hollywood, sponsored by Swan Song Records. Ray attends, among a cast of LA's rock elite.

Friday 13th
Crawford Hall, University of California-Irvine *Irvine, CA* 11:00pm

Saturday 14th
Swing Auditorium *San Bernadino, CA*

Sunday 15th
Main gymnasium, California State University *Northridge, CA*
Day off in Los Angeles plus travel day to Texas following.

Wednesday 18th
Austin Municipal Auditorium *Austin, TX*

Thursday 19th
Music Hall *Houston, TX*
Houston Chronicle: "Davies, through skilful manipulation of characters and a delightful vaudevilian zeal, never bogs down in the details of the story. Instead he pulls its decidedly moralistic punch with just enough slapstick humor to make it all go down like a smooth spoonful of honey."

Friday 20th
McAlister Auditorium, Tulane University *New Orleans, LA*
The band returns home the following day.

Monday 23rd
More work at London's South Bank Television Centre on the partially finished TV special is inexplicably cancelled, and nothing more will be heard about the project.

⇨ **TOUR STARTS** *Schoolboys In Disgrace: UK Tour* (Feb 27th – Mar 10th). Kinks personnel and theatrical effects identical to US 1st/2nd legs. Three of the ten dates will in fact be cancelled, making for a very brief tour.

Friday 27th
University of Exeter *Exeter* 8.00pm, with Splinter
Day off in London following, with more press duties to support the album and tour.

Sunday 29th
Drury Lane Royal Theatre *central London* 7:30pm, with Splinter
Reviews are becoming increasingly polarised, with notable dissension from the *NME* which is increasingly embracing the return-to-basics punk movement. Neil Spencer loves the opening set, but doesn't buy the main event. "It was better than I expected, but after dutifully sitting through both album and show I'm still at a loss why an artist of the calibre of Ray Davies should choose to expend so much time and energy on something so evidently empty and directionless as this. … I couldn't help but think that for all the clever and humorous filming, theatre-in-rock artifice, and earnest recitations about 'Education' in Ray's latest grand opus, it didn't say as much in an hour as Chuck Berry's song did in three minutes."

Allan Jones in *Melody Maker* raves: "The Kinks have not been among the most fashionable bands of the 1970s, despite the enormous popular and critical acclaim enjoyed by Ray Davies as one of England's premier rock writers in the last decade. As a commercial force, then, there has been some decline. But the mere fact that The Kinks grace the chart so infrequently these days should be taken as no indictment of their achievements over the last five years. … As ever, The Kinks preceded the evening's set-piece with an adroit selection of old favourites … The Kinks are an individual, eccentric and everlasting joy. Sunday's concert proved that Davies and his band are still ahead of most of their competitors."

Barbara Charone in *Sounds* agrees. "On-stage, *Schoolboys In Disgrace* comes alive with inspiration too often missing from rock'n'roll. The props, costumes, and back-projection are simple but effective, counterpointing the stage antics and fine music perfectly. Really, you should have been there." (Day off following.)
Set-list: 'Starmaker', 'Rush Hour Blues', 'Waterloo Sunset', 'Lola', 'Dedicated Follower Of Fashion', medley 'You Really Got Me' / 'All Day And All Of The Night', 'Alcohol', 'Celluloid Heroes', *Schoolboys In Disgrace*, 'Money Talks'.

March

Tuesday 2nd
Palace Theatre *Manchester* 8.00pm, with Splinter

Friday 5th
City Hall *Newcastle Upon Tyne* 7:30pm, with Splinter
Another two days off follow.

Monday 8th
Colston Hall *Bristol* 8.00pm, with Splinter

Tuesday 9th
Winter Gardens *Bournemouth* 9:15pm, with Splinter

Wednesday 10th
University of Cardiff *Cardiff, Wales* 8.00pm, with Splinter

➔ ● **RECORDING** Konk Studios *Hornsey, north London*. Ray is presumably at Konk during this break to prepare a contract-mandated Best Of The Kinks-style album to close the band's five-year contract with RCA (although one further RCA-assembled collection will appear in 1980). He reviews tracks for selection and does some extensive remixing and editing.

⇨ **TOUR STARTS** *Schoolboys In Disgrace: European Tour* (Mar 26th – 31st). The Kinks wrap up their touring commitments for the album with a quick swing through Scandinavia and a sole date in Germany. These concerts mark the only time that any of the band's three theatrical productions are presented outside the US and UK. (Travel by ferry to Esbjerg, Denmark and then on to Copenhagen for a stopover before heading on to Stockholm, 24th–25th.)

Friday 26th
Konserthuset *Stockholm, Sweden*
Broadcast on *Skivspegeln*, Swedish radio, April 2nd.

Saturday 27th
Olympen *Lund, Sweden*
Local paper *Arbetet* does not care for The Kinks' production, preferring instead their opening set for which the audience was seemingly more prepared than the *Schoolboys* show that followed. Ray later talks with a reporter from the paper who presumably voices his preference. "People must understand that I've been writing for more than ten years," replies Ray. "I just have to try new things." He tells the newspaperman the next LP will be in the old style, and that after that his songs will probably change. "I don't think that I can write more about England. I'd rather go somewhere something's happening, to Portugal or Africa. To write from a stranger's point of view like a visiting Englishman." (This doesn't *quite* predict Ray's eventual move to New York City – and his tackling of American themes by 1979.) He also reveals current projects: a play called *Billy Boy* about British football star George Best for British TV, and a film of *Soap Opera*, possibly with American comedy film maker Mel Brooks directing.

Monday 29th
Tivoli Koncertsal *Copenhagen, Denmark*
Day off in Copenhagen following.

Wednesday 31st
Congress Centrum *Hamburg, West Germany*
Travel day to London following.

➔ INDICATES EVENT AROUND THIS TIME BUT WITH NO FIRM DATE

April

➔ Singer Pamela Travis leaves the band. Dalton later reveals that it is following the European tour that he privately decides that he too no longer wants to travel so extensively. Though he will stay with The Kinks through the recording of the next album, once it is completed he will also leave the band.

☆ A tour of Australia is originally planned at the start of April to follow the European dates, but is cancelled.

☆ ● **RECORDING** Konk Studios *Hornsey, north London.* Ray presumably completes the editing, remixing and sequencing of the so-called "best of" for RCA.

Monday 5th

Ray delivers tapes for *The Kinks' Greatest – Celluloid Heroes* album to RCA in New York City. The album's title is awkwardly constructed to sound like a greatest hits package – but as none of the contents were in fact hits, a compromise is agreed upon.

"At the end of the RCA deal they wanted the usual *Greatest Hits* album," Ray says later. "I pointed out that there was something called the Trades Descriptions Act, and The Kinks hadn't actually had any greatest hits on RCA – 'Supersonic Rocketship' was the only one that even made the charts. But we put together an album with what we thought was our best stuff on it, and they called it *The Kinks' Greatest*. A subtle difference."

☆ Ray remains in NYC, presumably to negotiate a possible new recording deal with Arista Records. He also probably spends time writing new material.

☆ At Konk in London, installation of new recording equipment and construction of a new control booth continue.

Friday 30th

The band assembles to start rehearsing material for the next LP, temporarily relocating to Ray's house in Surrey.

May

➔ The reconstruction and expansion of Konk Studios continues into this month. A further rehearsal to go over new material is held on Friday 7th at Ray's house in Surrey. Possibly Ray is back in New York City to continue negotiations with Clive Davis of Arista Records for a new record contract.

Regular full-band rehearsals of new material for the next LP begin at Konk on Thursday 20th and Friday 21st and continue into the following week on Tuesday and Thursday.

➔ *The Kinks' Greatest – Celluloid Heroes* album released in the US. The final album under the RCA contract.

It's reasonably advertised in the music press, with a campaign reprising the dreaded k-word gimmick of 1964. "Now those kantakerous kurators of komedy and khaos, The Kinks, have kompiled 12 klassik kuts and krammed them into a krowning kommemoration of their kolorful rekording kareer." Kute. The album warrants almost no reviews, but the audiophile rather than rock oriented *Stereo Review* deems it "a rag-tag collection of material [written by Ray Davies, who] seems to be making a lifelong career out of cheeky irreverence".

➔ Around this time Ray rents an apartment in New York City on the upper west side. This will enable him to work more closely with his new record company, and means he will have permanently established bases in England and the US for the remainder of his career.

June

➔ Installation of updated recording equipment and the new control booth nears completion at Konk Studios.

Saturday 5th

An open air festival at Ninian Park Football Grounds in Cardiff, Wales originally for today is rescheduled to the 19th, but The Kinks cancel, and a tentative date at another outdoor festival in Offenbourg, France around this time is never finalised. The band will devote the remainder of the year to recording, with no further concert appearances.

Thursday 17th – Friday 18th

● **RECORDING** Konk Studios *Hornsey, north London*. Rehearsals and demo sessions.

Friday 18th

The Kinks' Greatest – Celluloid Heroes album released in the UK. Barbara Charone in *Sounds* calls it "an honest representation of the last

---

The Kinks' Greatest – Celluloid Heroes album

A1 'Everybody's A Star' (R. DAVIES).
A2 'Sitting In My Hotel' (R. DAVIES).
A3 'Here Comes Yet Another Day' (R. DAVIES).
A4 'Holiday' (R. DAVIES).
A5 'Muswell Hillbilly' (R. DAVIES).
A6 'Celluloid Heroes' (R. DAVIES).
B1 '20th Century Man' (R. DAVIES).
B2 'Sitting In The Midday Sun' (R. DAVIES).
B3 'One Of The Survivors' (R. DAVIES).
B4 'Alcohol' (R. DAVIES).
B5 'Skin And Bone' (R. DAVIES).
B6 '(A) Face In The Crowd' (R. DAVIES).

US release May 1976 (RCA Victor APL1-1743).
UK release June 25th 1976 (RCA Victor RS 1059).
Comprised of previously-issued album tracks, except A3 (detailed below). See original releases for credits: A5, B1 *Muswell Hillbiliies*; A2, A6 *Everybody's In Show-Biz* (studio); A4, B4, B5 *Everybody's In Show-Biz* (live); B2, B3 *Preservation Act 1*; A1, B6 *A Soap Opera*. Tracks A4, B1, B4-B5 all edited from original releases; A1, A2, A5, B2, B3 are remixes. A5 features newly-recorded vocals by Ray and Dave plus acoustic guitar, and is edited.
Musicians (A3 only) Ray Davies lead vocal. Dave Davies electric guitar. John Dalton bass guitar. Mick Avory drums. John Gosling keyboards. John Beecham trombone. Alan Holmes saxophone. Laurie Brown trumpet. Pamela Travis, Shirley Roden, Debbie Doss backing vocals.
Recorded (A3 only) New Victoria Theatre *central London*; June 14th 1975; mobile recording unit; probably 16-track mixed to stereo.
Mixing/editing Ray Davies at Konk Studios *Hornsey, north London*; March-April 1976.
Chart high UK none; US number 144.

kinks'76

five Kinks years" but notes that the much cleaner sound indicates there may have been some remixing. "Nasty marks to RCA for the worst packaging conceivable. The cover is strictly bargain-bin stuff with a tacky New Faces star on the back and an advanced K-Tel collage of The Kinks, Clark Gable and some Hollywood beauty on the front. The RCA years is the end of another Kinks era. Already Davies has promised us that … 'there's no more looking back'. Let's hope he keeps his word. The Kinks could belong to tomorrow."

Bob Edmands in *NME* is sympathetic to The Kinks' continuing curse of having to compete with the firmly-engrained melodies of their own 1960s catalogue. But these songs, he writes, "sound like the work of a man who's moved too fast for his audience and isn't sure if it's his fault or theirs. Uncertainty is the keynote. That said, there's no disguising the abundance of clever, witty ideas. … There's lots on the album to intrigue and amuse you, particularly if you come to these songs fresh, as you're likely to".

Wednesday 23rd

At the Dorchester Hotel in central London, The Kinks formally sign their new record deal with Arista Records. It will be a ten-year contract. Arista is the old Bell Records label, bought in 1975 and subsequently turned into a major operation by industry legend Clive Davis. He was the head of Columbia Records until his ousting in the early 1970s during a big industry scandal. Davis has always been interested in signing The Kinks, dating back to 1966 when the band was renegotiating a separate deal with Warner/Reprise and again in 1971 when they were up for grabs. But he lost out then to RCA, which offered the band more than he was willing to pay.

Unlike the RCA deal, where The Kinks merely submitted completed masters for release, Davis will take a strong interest in influencing the band's recorded output. He will appear to have a considerable say in what is released. Davis begins his relationship with Ray by giving him three songs by outside writers that Davis thinks he ought to try recording.

Thursday 24th

In London a press party is held to announce the grand re-opening of The Kinks' newly outfitted 24-track studio at Konk. Ray tells *Melody Maker* of his plans to start recording the new Kinks album immediately. "Yes, I am looking forward to it, because the situation is right. It's a great studio; I'm proud of it."

Friday 25th

Rehearsal for The Kinks at Konk Studios. Reports suggest up to 30 songs are written for consideration for the new album, 20 of which are eventually recorded. Some rejected titles reportedly include: 'Power Of Gold', 'Stagefright', 'Restless' and 'Elevator Man', all probably only recorded as demos. The only known demo from the May-June period is 'Elevator Man', later exhumed by Ray and included on a 1994 EP release, *Waterloo Sunset 94*.

Monday 28th – Wednesday 30th

● **RECORDING** Konk Studios *Hornsey, north London*. Work begins this week on tracks for the new album. All recording is on the new 24-track machine, with Roger Wake engineering and Ray producing. Only the five-man Kinks are present (Ray, Dave, Dalton, Avory and Gosling) in a conscious return to a traditional, unextended line-up. For the next six months The Kinks effectively vanish from the public eye as the sessions stretch out into January 1977.

July

From the start of the month to the 9th the band is at Konk in London to lay down six initial backing tracks, for **'Hay Fever'** (unreleased version), **'Artifical Light'**, **'Brother'** (see August 13th), **'Jukebox Music'** (unreleased version), **'Life On The Road'** (unreleased version) and **'Lazy Day'** (unreleased song). In addition to Fender Rhodes electric piano and Hammond organ, Gosling is for the first time using a Roland string synthesiser (a keyboard with preset string-section sounds).

Again the following week (12th-16th) sessions for master backing tracks continue, with four more songs committed to tape: **'Back To 64'** / **'Decade'** (unreleased song), **'In A Foreign Land'** (unreleased version), **'Prince Of The Punks'** (unreleased version) and **'The Poseur'** (eventually released as a bonus track on the 1998 reissue of the *Sleepwalker* CD).

And from the 20th to the 23rd there's another session for 'Hay Fever' (unreleased version). It's around now that work is halted at Konk due to a broken air conditioner, which at the height of the summer needs to be repaired before recording can continue.

August

During the break Ray reviews what has been recorded so far. Evidently now, Arista boss Clive Davis, who has been played some of the results, suggests that Ray extends the ending of 'Brother' and adds a string section. Davis believes the song has great potential as a single in the style of Simon & Garfunkel's 'Bridge Over Troubled Water', which he'd helped to produce. At Konk during an overdub and vocal session from 1:00-10:00pm on Friday 13th an end section is added to an edited rearrangement of **'Brother'**. A further session may occur on Tuesday 17th, details unknown. But despite the efforts to accommodate Davis's views, the recording of 'Brother' is never issued as a single.

The remainder of August is probably taken up with holidays for the band, giving Ray time to work up more new material. With The Kinks absent from the studio, producer John Miller probably works there on a second LP with Konk singings Cafe Society.

September

With new material from Ray now to hand, rehearsals are held at Konk from Monday 6th through Wednesday 8th and a recording session is held on Friday 10th, possibly making demos. The following week, Wednesday 15th to Friday 17th, five new backing tracks are put down: **'Child Bride'**, **'Everything Is Alright'**, **'One Woman Man'**, **'On The Outside Of Life'** and **'Full Moon'**. The first three will remain unreleased. 'On The Outside' is dusted off in 1994 for the *Waterloo Sunset 94* EP. Only 'Full Moon' will end up on the new album.

Concentrated recording continues over a nine-day period, from Wednesday 22nd through to the following Thursday, the 30th, breaking only on the Sunday between. At least three new songs emerge: **'Sleepwalker'**, **'Sleepless Night'** and **'Life Goes On'**. The first two of these are apparently of extended length, over seven minutes each, and will only later be edited down for eventual release. All three end up on the new album.

October

Work continues into this month at Konk and re-recordings are made (1st-2nd) of three songs attempted at the initial sessions in July. **'Child Bride'** will remain unreleased, while **'Jukebox Music'** and **'Life On**

New line-up, December 1976: standing (L-R) Dave Davies, Andy Pyle and Mick Avory; seated are Ray Davies and John Gosling trying a new set of keys.

The Road' are released on the album, edited down from their extended original lengths, as is one additional new recording, **'Stormy Sky'**. A further new track recorded between Monday 4th and Wednesday 6th is **'Black Messiah'** (unreleased version).

John Dalton officially leaves the band on the 8th, after finishing all the backing tracks for the new album. He has already made up his mind that he does not want to commit to the intensive level of touring expected in the coming year. (Plans for January through April 1977 have already been made.) A disappointed Ray tries to change Dalton's mind, but he stands firm on his decision – and another classic line-up of The Kinks comes to a close. There is plenty of other work; the task of finding a new bass player is put aside until early December.

Meanwhile, work on the backing tracks continues: Ray, Dave and Gosling record backing vocals for **'Sleepwalker'** (11th) and for **'Stormy Sky'** and **'Full Moon'** (12th). Gosling records synthesiser overdubs for **'Brother'**, **'Full Moon'** and **'Juke Box Music'** (13th), and after some unspecified work on the 14th, probably overdubs, Ray starts mixing tracks. More work, likely overdubs are done on the 27th, Ray and Gosling record keyboard overdubs two days later.

On Friday 22nd the four-man Kinks (Ray, Dave, Avory, Gosling) are photographed at Konk Studios by James Wedge for the sleeve of the new LP.

November

Another month spent largely at Konk on the new *Sleepwalker* album, with some initial press work for the new record. Ray continues to mix tracks for it, and at some point he reportedly begins stripping away "excessive" overdubs. Additional keyboard and vocal overdubs are done (16th-17th, 22nd) with more overdubs and backing vocals added to **'Hay Fever'** (23rd-24th). Towards the end of the month Ray, still mixing, decides to delay the planned Christmas release of the LP and record some new tracks. The US tour originally planned for November/December is delayed.

On Monday 22nd a press release announces the splitting of Konk group Cafe Society. Frontman Tom Robinson is to debut his new outfit, The Tom Robinson Band, on November 28th. After seemingly endless delays, Robinson and co had been working on a second Cafe Society album with producer John Miller since the summer, after Ray became busy with the new Kinks album. But the recording became bogged down in business problems and artistic differences, ultimately prompting Robinson's sudden departure. Cafe Society struggled on without him, subsequently finishing an LP in February 1977, but this would go unreleased, and the remaining members finally called it quits in August of that year. Robinson subsequently went on to fame with The Tom Robinson Band and their autumn 1977 hit '2-4-6-8 Motorway' followed in the spring of 1978 with their *Rising Free* EP track 'Sing If You're Glad To Be Gay' – a song that he wrote, demoed and performed in the latter days of the ill-fated Cafe Society.

December

A demo session is held at Konk 12midday-5:00pm on Monday 6th for new material. Four days later a session there is in effect an audition for potential new Kinks bass players, including Andy Pyle (ex-Blodwyn Pig, Savoy Brown, and Alvin Lee & Co). Later this evening, Ray is at a performance by Tom Robinson at the Nashville Rooms pub in west London. Rehearsals at Konk with Pyle continue on the 13th, 15th and 16th, and he is asked to join the band. From the 17th to the 20th the new five-man Kinks (Ray, Dave, Avory, Pyle, Gosling) record at least one new song, **'Mr Big Man'**. Around the same time, photographer Sam Emerson does a photo session at Konk for future promotional use. These are the first pictures to include Pyle, although none of these pictures will be used on the forthcoming album's sleeve.

The new LP, originally planned for release around now, is rescheduled to February 4th. In the process 'In A Foreign Land' is dropped and the new 'Mr Big Man' added to the final track listing. Ray mixes tracks for what will become *Sleepwalker*.

1977

The Kinks essentially reinvented themselves this year, abandoning Ray's theatre-rock projects (both studio and live) and returning to the public as a timeless rock band. This was helped by Arista head Clive Davis, who saw boundless potential for the band among the record-buying public. What he seemed to be offering The Kinks was a second chance at traditional commercial success in the modern rock era, where platinum-selling albums and stadium-filling tours were still perfectly possible.

If The Kinks could deliver strong albums of rock songs and were willing to tour much more extensively and undertake the necessary promotion to sell tickets and records, then Clive Davis and Arista could provide the mechanism and support to make it all happen. The touring in particular meant a big commitment, especially from Dave who during the early 1970s could only manage being away from home for three weeks at a time. But bassist John Dalton had already made up his mind not to be away from home any more – even on their old schedule.

Albums were expected by Arista on a factory-like timetable. The debut for the company, Sleepwalker, took far longer to complete than planned – and at a relatively leisurely pace with no touring commitments. But the follow-up, Misfits, and most subsequent releases were done largely without the luxury of time off. Almost immediately this caused pressure and friction as the band, back from almost non-stop touring in the first half of the year, were expected to finish an LP by the autumn – with touring resuming straight afterwards.

The abandonment of the theatrical format and the support of a new relationship in Dave's life revived his creative energies and saw him recording solo songs and contributing material to the band again. On the surface, The Kinks were well on the way back to a much more visible and popular success, especially in the US. They were seen on TV, heard on the radio, read about in the rock press, and seen on tour – and well beyond their regular concert round of eight to ten major American cities. But the effort required to reach this new level would almost crippled the band by the end of the year.

January

Saturday 1st – Tuesday 4th
● **RECORDING** Konk Studios *Hornsey, north London*. Ray finishes mixing the *Sleepwalker* album, wrapping up work on the 4th and likely flying out to the US the following day. While he is away, rehearsals are held at the band's Konk Studios in London from the 5th to the 14th to familiarise their new bass guitarist Andy Pyle with the band's complete stage show.

The touring horn section (John Beecham, Nick Newall) and female backing singers (Shirley Roden, Debbie Doss) will also work on the tour. Although they were purposely absent from the new album, it is deemed necessary to include them for the proper presentation of the recent RCA material that they continue to play in concert.

Virtually all of the new LP is worked up, and only 'Sleepless Night' seems not to make it to stage, even once. Otherwise, medleys from *Soap Opera* and *Schoolboys* and of the early hits serve as a convenient way to cover obligatory earlier material.

Saturday 8th
Ray is at Media Sound Studios in New York City to oversee mastering of the new LP. There appears to be some frustration with the track 'Brother' and it is decided to remix it from scratch back in London.

This decision on 'Brother' throws off the already-delayed schedule, and while the planned tour cannot now be shifted, the album will not be ready for release in time to coincide with the opening dates. This is a blow to the master plan – but hardly untypical of The Kinks' working methods.

Sunday 9th
Ray travels on from New York City to Los Angeles for a brief visit to undertake some advance press duties for the tour. Out of curiosity he attends a concert on the following day (the 10th) at the Santa Monica Civic Auditorium given by the latest teen sensations, The Bay City Rollers, before heading back to London.

➔ ● **RECORDING** Konk Studios *Hornsey, north London*. Ray remixes 'Brother'.

kinks'77

Monday 17th – Thursday 20th

Rehearsals continue with the band's new bass player, Andy Pyle, and with the work moved away from Konk to a local Hornsey church, the Moravian Hall.

● **RECORDING** Konk Studios *Hornsey, north London.* On the 18th Ray is busy at the mixing board at Konk, editing out a verse from the new LP's title song 'Sleepwalker'. The verse had the song's character claiming he is gay.

Friday 21st

The band hires the Roxy Theatre in Harlesden, north-west London for a full-blown stage rehearsal to ensure material and stage presentation are in order.

There is increased pressure to get the show right, what with a new band member and the fact that this tour will be heavily reviewed by the press in The Kinks' key cities. Much of the success of the debut Arista LP and the subsequent, more expansive tour rests on the initial response. Over the weekend, Ray once again crosses the Atlantic, returning to New York.

Monday 24th – Tuesday 25th

Ray is back again in New York City, and this time he faces a barrage of press interviews, all of which are designed to help promote the brand new LP. Holed up at the Warwick Hotel in the city, he receives interviewer upon interviewer, and the hard work results in coverage in *Circus, Creem* and *Hit Parader* as well as *The Aquarian* and some of the New York dailies.

➥ **TOUR STARTS** *Sleepwalker: US Tour: 1st leg* (Jan 28th – Feb 20th). **Line-up**: Ray Davies (lead vocal, guitar), Dave Davies (guitar, vocal), Mick Avory (drums), Andy Pyle (bass), John Gosling (keyboard), John Beecham (trombone), Nick Newall (saxophone), Shirley Roden, Debbie Doss (backing vocals). ICM (International Creative Management) continue to book this and all US tours until the end of the Arista period.

Wednesday 26th

Today the rest of the band is gathered together and travels from London to start the tour.

Meanwhile, with customary last-minute flair, Ray is at Masterdisk Studios in New York City to oversee the final mastering of the now finished *Sleepwalker* LP. Even with a rush order to the pressing plant, the album won't get into the stores for at least two weeks. Barring some sneak previews of the material on a few radio stations, fans attending the tour's shows will mostly be hearing the new material for the first time in concert.

Thursday 27th

The Kinks set up a day early at their opening venue in suburban Philadelphia, enabling them not only to feel at ease about the opening might, but also to ensure a full technical as well as musical run-through of the show.

Friday 28th – Saturday 29th

Tower Theater *Upper Darby, PA* 8:00pm, with The Sutherland Brothers & Quiver
A capacity 3,100 audience generates an $18,436 gross. (Following day off in New York City.)

Monday 31st

Albert N. Jorgensen Auditorium, University Of Connecticut *Storrs, CT* 8:00pm, with Jean Luc Ponty
Forever reclaiming their youth, the band are reportedly involved in a massive food fight backstage after the show.

February

Tuesday 1st–Wednesday 2nd

The Palladium *New York, NY* 8:00pm, with The Sutherland Brothers & Quiver
The band opens the show without Ray, as the rest of The Kinks set the scene for his entrance with an instrumental 'You Really Got Me', known officially from now as 'Opening'. Towards its end Ray tosses off a few choruses, quickly ending the song, at which point the band quietly segues into the first full number of the show. John Rockwell writes in *The New York Times*: "What they did at the Palladium was hardly up to their own best efforts. … Mostly this is a conventional rock-song recital, focussed firmly on Mr Davies, and so far he hasn't found the key to making it really interesting to non-cultists." (Day off following in New York City.)
Set-list (Tue): 'Opening', 'One Of The Survivors', 'Sleepwalker', 'Starmaker', 'Rush Hour Blues', 'You Make It All Worthwhile', 'Ordinary People', 'Starmaker' (reprise), 'Celluloid Heroes', 'Death Of A Clown', 'Waterloo Sunset', 'Schooldays', 'Brother', 'Stormy Sky', medley 'A Well Respected Man' / 'Sunny Afternoon', 'Full Moon', 'Lola', 'Alcohol', medley 'You Really Got Me' / 'All Day And All Of The Night', 'Money Talks'.

Friday 4th

Capitol Theater *Passaic, NJ* 8:00pm, with Southside Johnny & The Asbury Jukes (including guest singer Ronnie Spector)

Saturday 5th

Music Hall *Boston, MA* 7:00 & 10:00pm, with The Sutherland Brothers & Quiver, Trent Arterberry (mime act, 7:00pm show only)

Sunday 6th

LeRoy Concert Theater *Pawtucket, RI* 8:00pm, with The Sutherland Brothers & Quiver
Two days off in New York City following. Scheduled release of the new LP on the 7th is now pushed to the 12th.

Wednesday 9th

Shea Auditorum, William Paterson College of New Jersey *Wayne, NJ* 8:00pm, with The Sutherland Brothers & Quiver
"Kinks blow the roof off Shea," writes the student newspaper's reviewer. "Contrary to past performances, The Kinks came out as a tight band." (Time off in New York City and travel to Cleveland following day.)

Friday 11th

Gymnasium, John Carroll University *University Heights, OH* 8:00pm, with The Sutherland Brothers & Quiver
"The concert was a sell-out at showtime, and those who attended saw the finest concert held here in the last few years," says the *Carroll News*. "The Kinks are professionals. The many years of touring haven't seemed to have taken any of the energy from these guys. They played this concert as if it were the first one in a long while."

Saturday 12th

Uptown Theater *Chicago, IL* 8:00pm, with The Sutherland Brothers & Quiver, Cheap Trick
The *Chicago Sunday Times* sums it up: "Though Kinks are sloppy, they're entertaining." (Travel day to LA following, where they again stay at the infamous wild-rock-musicians-on-tour Continental Hyatt Hotel on Sunset Boulevard.)
Sleepwalker album released in the US. The record is available today in certain areas, and nationally by next week. On the whole, critics

welcome the return of a five-man line-up and a collection of songs. A number point to it as their favourite since *Muswell Hillbillies* and in retrospect dismiss most of the band's RCA output. Billy Altman writes in *Rolling Stone*: "The first Kinks album [in a while] that's unencumbered by either a horn section or female vocal chorus is a clear-cut triumph both for Davies and the band. ... The Kinks' playing on *Sleepwalker* is easily their most powerful since 'Lola'. Dave Davies' aggressive guitar work is pushed into the forefront, and the intensity of his lead work seems to rouse the entire group." Advertising and promotion is massive, as is the band's willingness to tour in support and make the big media push required to revive their commercial career. The reward will be that both album and its lead single make the upper

---

Sleepwalker album

A1 'Life On The Road' (R. DAVIES).
A2 'Mr. Big Man' (R. DAVIES).
A3 'Sleepwalker' (R. DAVIES).
A4 'Brother' (R. DAVIES).
B1 'Juke Box Music' (R. DAVIES).
B2 'Sleepless Night' (R. DAVIES).
B3 'Stormy Sky' (R. DAVIES).
B4 'Full Moon' (R. DAVIES).
B5 'Life Goes On' (R. DAVIES).

US release February 12th 1977 (Arista AL 4106).
UK release February 26th 1977 (Arista SPARTY 1002).
Musicians Ray Davies lead vocal except as noted, guitar. Dave Davies lead vocal (B2), co-lead vocal (B1), electric guitar, backing vocal. John Dalton bass guitar except as noted. Andy Pyle bass guitar (A2). Mick Avory drums. John Gosling baby grand piano, Hammond organ, electric piano, string synthesiser, backing vocal.
Recorded Konk Studios *Hornsey, north London*; A1, B1, B3: October 1st-2nd 1976; A2: December 17th-20th 1976; A3, B2, B5: September 23rd-30th 1976; B4: September 15th-17th 1976; A4: July 1st-9th/August 13th 1976; additional overdubs to most tracks October-November 1976; 24-track mixed to stereo.
Producer Ray Davies.
Engineer Roger Wake.
Chart high UK none; US number 21.

reaches of the US charts.

Monday 14th – Wednesday 16th

A week mostly of press duties in New York City. Among the nightlife options this week are two breaking local bands of punk rockers, The Ramones and Blondie, at The Whisky A Go Go all week. Dave reportedly meets a new flame, Nancy Evans, at one of these shows, and the relationship will blossom by summer and continue well into the 1990s.

Thursday 17th – Friday 18th

Santa Monica Civic Auditorium *Santa Monica, CA* 8:00pm (Thu), 7:30 & 11:00pm (Fri), with The Sutherland Brothers & Quiver
Richard Cromelin writes in *The Los Angeles Times*: "For the first time in a long time, the high points of The Kinks' show at Santa Monica Civic on Thursday (the first of three sell-out concerts) came with the group's new material. That this veteran band, seemingly in a holding pattern for so long, can reassert its purpose so freshly and convincingly is one of the

most encouraging signs of the year."

Friday's show is recorded by DIR Broadcasting for airing on their nationally-syndicated rock concert radio show, the *King Biscuit Flower Hour*, broadcast the week of April 24th.

Saturday 19th

Winterland Ballroom *San Francisco, CA* 8:00pm, with The Sutherland Brothers & Quiver, Big Wha-Koo
Tonight's performance is broadcast live on local station KSAN-FM. The complete show consists of 'Opening', 'One Of The Survivors', 'Sleepwalker', 'Rush Hour Blues', 'You Make It All Worthwhile', medley 'Ordinary People' / 'Everybody's A Star (Starmaker)', 'Banana Boat Song', 'A Well Respected Man', 'Sunny Afternoon', 'Waterloo Sunset', 'Celluloid Heroes', 'Schooldays', 'Schooldays (reprise)', 'The Hard Way', 'Education', 'Brother', 'Stormy Sky', 'Life Goes On', 'Full Moon', 'Lola', 'Alcohol', medley 'You Really Got Me' / 'All Day And All Of The Night', 'Victoria'. Many of these tracks subsequently appear on bootlegs.

Sunday 20th

Stockton Civic Memorial Auditorium *Stockton, CA* 8:00pm, with The Sutherland Brothers & Quiver, Ambrosia
Earlier in the day back in LA, Ray goes to a post-Grammy Awards brunch hosted by Arista president Clive Davis in the Crystal Room of the Beverly Hills Hotel. Others in attendance include Brian Wilson, Linda Ronstadt, Paul Simon, and Leonard Cohen.

Monday 21st

The band travels to New York for last-minute TV bookings while the two female singers return to London.

Tuesday 22nd

❐ **TV** KYW Television Studios *Philadelphia, PA*. Group W *The Mike Douglas Show* lip-synch 'Sleepwalker', live performance 'Celluloid Heroes' broadcast March 8th. The band takes advantage of an otherwise free day with a quick drive down to Philadelphia to tape an appearance for this weekday-afternoon variety and entertainment programme. After miming to 'Sleepwalker', Ray is interviewed by Douglas along with the show's other guest singer, Tony Bennett. After this the band does a live-in-the-studio version of 'Celluloid Heroes', with the horn players off-camera but audible. The show is seen later than the March 8th broadcast date in some areas. (Day off following in New York City.)

Thursday 24th

The band finances their own rehearsal at S.I.R. Studios, New York, NY for the upcoming *Saturday Night Live* appearance.

Friday 25th

Official full rehearsals at NBC Television Studios at the RCA Building in New York City for the following day's live broadcast. The programme is broadcast from studio 8H, precisely the studio where The Kinks appeared on *Hullaballoo* in 1965, and the start of their problems with the American TV unions.
Sleepwalker album released in the UK. Allan Jones in *Melody Maker*: "The first album the Kinks have produced for Arista, and it emphatically testifies to the dramatic artistic revival of Raymond Douglas Davies, whose supreme talents as a writer have been so distressingly overlooked during the first half of this decade. [*Sleepwalker*] really is the group's strongest and most organised album in years ... as moving and pertinent [an album] as The Kinks have ever produced. The Kinks, like life, go on." Giovanni Dadomo in *Sounds*: "The absence of a rigid skeleton holding its various parts together ... should bode well ... [but] it's not the great new album one always hopes

for." Julie Burchill in *NME* is cryptic: "*Sleepwalker* seems to be a sign that [Ray] is less of a smart-ass than he once was, though no less perceptive. The j'accuse vignettes are gone and in their place lies a looking glass."

Saturday 26th

❏ **TV** NBC Television Studios (Studio 8H), RCA Building *New York, NY*. NBC *Saturday Night Live* live performance: medley 'You Really Got Me' / 'All Day And All Of The Night' / 'A Well Respected Man' / 'Lola', 'Sleepwalker'.

The Kinks wrap up this first whirlwind tour for Sleepwalker with a prestigious appearance on the hip late-night comedy programme *Saturday Night Live*. It has a massive audience and this single spot helps reintroduce The Kinks to a wide US audience that, unless they were paying close attention to the music scene over the past six or seven years, may well have thought the band had long ago faded away. The Kinks turn in a rapid-fire medley of the early hits, followed quite smartly by the title song from the new LP.

(The band travels back to London the following day for a quick break in the action. Ray stays behind to begin a brief media tour of key US cities this coming week.)

March

Tuesday 1st – Saturday 5th

A week of American press duties for Ray. Back home, the music weeklies carry the announcement that The Kinks are set for a major London appearance at the Rainbow on March 24th. Ray travels to Los Angeles on Saturday.

Sunday 6th

Probably today, Ray serves as a panellist at a symposium about the future of rock music at the NARM convention at the Century Plaza Hotel in Los Angeles.

With him on the panel are Warner Brothers executive vice-president Stan Cornyn, promoter Bill Graham, and singers Linda Rondstadt and Tina Turner. A transcript of the seminar is later published in *The New York Sunday Times* affording The Kinks some very high-profile coverage and revealing Ray's willingness to mix with the record industry, like his time at Cannes in 1968.

"I think the important thing is one person making music and one person listening to it," he tells the panel. "All the rest is just part of the horrible side of capitalism. I'm not saying it's noble to have small audiences, though, because I think that's boring. There's nothing like a big audience getting excited and becoming part of the music. And if you've done something toward that, contributed something, it's a fantastic feeling."

Monday 7th – Thursday 10th

Ray continues with promotional appearances and press interviews. Among radio station appearances is one for 102.1 KTXQ-FM Dallas-Fort Worth where, in addition to an interview, he treats the listening audience to an unusual solo performance of 'Life On The Road', 'A Well Respected Man', 'Here Come The People In Grey', '20th Century Man', 'Acute Schizophrenia Paranoia Blues' and 'Oklahoma USA'.

➜ **'Sleepwalker' / 'Full Moon'** single released in the US. It will be the first Kinks single to enter the American Hot 100 in over six years, since the Reprise 45 of 'Apeman'.

☆ Back at Konk in London the band minus Ray holds rehearsals for the upcoming show. By Thursday Ray is winging his way back to London.

Sleepwalker single

A **'Sleepwalker'** (R. DAVIES).
B **'Full Moon'** (R. DAVIES).

US release March (probably 9th) 1977 (Arista AS 0240).
UK release March 19th 1977 (Arista ARISTA 97).
Musicians and recording details as *Sleepwalker* album (see February 12th). A-side is edited version of album track.
Chart high UK none; US number 48.

Friday 11th – Sunday 13th

On Friday the full band rehearses at Konk Studios for the upcoming Rainbow Theatre shows. During the sessions, Ray is interviewed by Phil McNeill for a major two-part cover feature in *NME*.

McNeill asks probing questions about The Kinks' early history and initially Ray is in a talkative mood. A lot of uncharted ground is covered and Ray appears to reveal a good deal, although the later portion of the published interview is less strong.

McNeill writes: "He was surprisingly forthcoming – yet at the end of it all I was really no nearer to knowing him. Strictly a business association." The interview continues on Saturday on the way to the airport, from where Ray heads back to New York, initially with a day off on Sunday to catch his thoughts.

Monday 14th – Friday 18th

Another week of heavy press duties around the globe for the three principal Kinks, as unusually some of the chat work is farmed out to Dave and Avory.

Friday 18th

'Sleepwalker' / 'Full Moon' single released in the UK. *NME* says: "Set to a backdrop highly reminiscent of the hallowed back-'em-up-shut-'em-down riffing of Phase 1 Kinks … the main squeeze is that The Kinks are making good records again." *Melody Maker*: "Kinks fans/lovers of 'Waterloo Sunset' won't find 'Sleepwalker' very satisfactory. Respect The Right Honorable Davies though one must, this isn't quite the leap back to form which was hoped for. Not for the chart." Correct.

☆ Ray travels back to London, certainly by Saturday 19th, and so presumably do Dave and Avory, from their respective locations. Sunday they resteth.

Monday – Tuesday 21st-22nd

The band is back at Konk for some final rehearsals before their London date at the Rainbow.

Thursday 24th

Rainbow Theatre *Finsbury Park, north London* 7:45pm, with Charlie

The London press is out in force to witness the rebirth of the classic Kinks approach to rock'n'roll. Reviews are wildly mixed.

Melody Maker's Allan Jones finds them uneven but enjoyable, while *NME*'s reviewer, Nick Kent, absolutely thrashes them. This may be expected from a music paper that is now embracing the new punk ethic very enthusiastically and distancing itself from anything considered a 1960s leftover.

Sounds falls somewhere in the middle, commenting that the new material is promising and grows more naturally from their classic catalogue than from the 1970s rock-theatre period.

Ray offers the reborn rock'n'roll Kinks to the Rainbow audience in London, March 24th 1977.

Friday 25th
❏ **TV** South Bank Television Centre *central London*. ITV **Supersonic** live performance 'Sleepwalker' plus jam session with Ray 'Sweet Little Rock'n'Roller', 'Sunny Afternoon' broadcast April 2nd. Of The Kinks only Ray is in the jam with other guests at the end of the programme to celebrate the last show of the series, and including Dave Edmunds, Marc Bolan, Alvin Stardust, Gloria Jones, Nick Lowe, and Bonnie Tyler.

Monday 28th
❏ **TV** BBC Television Centre *west London*. BBC-2 **The Old Grey Whistle Test** live performance 'Sleepwalker', 'Life Goes On', 'Stormy Sky', 'Celluloid Heroes', 'Muswell Hillbilly', 'Full Moon', 'Life On The Road', 'Juke Box Music', medley 'You Really Got Me' / 'All Day And All Of The Night' broadcast April 26th. Filmed before an invited audience, the band adds backing vocalists Shirley Roden and Debbie Doss and hornmen John Beecham and Nick Newall.

Tuesday 29th
Back at the South Bank Television Centre in central London from 2:00-8:00pm the band tapes a promotional film for *Sleepwalker*, lip-synching to the record.

April

➪ **TOUR STARTS** *Sleepwalker: US Tour: 2nd leg* (Apr 5th – May 8th). Details as 1st leg (see the relevant entry in late January). This series of American dates opt for the classic 3,000-seat halls that The Kinks can comfortably fill, assuming they get the proper promotion. Following their relative absence from Texas, the band rediscovers a strong audience in the state, and will return there regularly into the mid 1980s.

Tuesday 5th
Music Hall *Houston, TX* 8:00pm, with Cheap Trick

Wednesday 6th
Will Rogers Memorial Auditorium *Fort Worth, TX* 8:00pm, with Cheap Trick

Thursday 7th
Civic Center Music Hall *Oklahoma City, OK* 8:00pm, with Cheap Trick
Travel day following.

Saturday 9th
Orchestra Hall *Minneapolis, MN* 8:00pm, with Cheap Trick

Sunday 10th
Memorial Hall *Kansas City, MO* 8:00pm, with Cheap Trick

Monday 11th
Hancher Auditorium, University Of Iowa *Iowa City, IA* 8:00pm, with Cheap Trick

Tuesday 12th
Riverside Theater *Milwaukee, WI* 8:00pm, with Cheap Trick
Day off in Chicago plus travel day follow.

Friday 15th
Paramount Theater *Portland, OR* 8:00pm, with The Hollywood Stars

Saturday 16th
Paramount Northwest Theater *Seattle, WA* 8:00pm, with The Hollywood Stars

Sunday 17th
Pacific National Exhibition Gardens Auditorium *Vancouver, BC, Canada* 8:00pm, with The Hollywood Stars
"If it wasn't anyone but The Kinks, I'd say the show was awful," writes a reviewer in *The Province*. "Somehow the generally slipshod, dopey and disreputable show they put together fits the image so well, though, that – while horribly disappointing in itself – it's probably a classic chapter in the eccentric, continuing saga." (Travel day following.)
☆ *Sleepwalker* album peaks in US chart at number 21.

Tuesday 19th
San Jose Center For The Performing Arts *San Jose, CA* 8:00pm, with The Hollywood Stars
Day off in Los Angeles following.

Thursday 21st
Civic Theater, Convention & Performing Arts Center *San Diego, CA* 7:30pm, with The Hollywood Stars

Friday 22nd
Arlington Theater *Santa Barbara, CA* 8:00pm, with The Hollywood Stars

Saturday 23rd
➜ ❏ **TV** NBC Television Studios *Burbank, CA*. NBC **The Midnight Special** live performance 'Sleepwalker', 'Juke Box Music', 'Lola' broadcast May 6th. Probably today, this late-added appearance on NBC's weekly rock concert program is taped in Burbank. The Kinks appear in a concert setting on a sound stage, and of many songs taped or performed for the invited audience, only these three appear when their segment is aired.

Sunday 24th
Field House, Regis College *Denver, CO* 8:00pm, with Stallion
Following this show the tour takes a short break for three days, allowing ever-busy Ray to fly back to New York on Monday where at Masterdisk Studios he helps masters an edit of the next single, 'Juke Box Music'.

Thursday 28th
Cobo Arena *Detroit, MI* 8:00pm, Heart (headliners), Nite City

Friday 29th
Concert Bowl, Maple Leaf Gardens *Toronto, ON, Canada* 8:00pm, with Elliott Murphy
In addition to the basic set they've been playing this tour, the encore today also includes 'Victoria' and an impromptu solo version by Ray of the traditional 'Amazing Grace'.

Saturday 30th
New Century Theater *Buffalo, NY* 8:00pm, probably with Elliott Murphy

May

Sunday 1st
Another indication that The Kinks are more willing now to go along with the type of publicity stunt they have long shunned comes as the entire band appears at a local Buffalo record store, the Record Theatre.

They do an autograph session, and then leave their handprints in cement in the sidewalk in front of the store.

Monday 2nd

Stanley Theater *Pittsburgh, PA* 8:00pm, with Elliott Murphy

Tuesday 3rd

DAR Constitution Hall *Washington, DC* 8:30pm, with Elliott Murphy

Tonight's show will pass into Kinks legend. In the final moments of what one fan describes as a musically sloppy but otherwise fun show, the old animosities between Dave and Avory spill out on stage. Towards the end of the encore of 'Juke Box Music' both abruptly storm off – in opposite directions. Ray is left virtually alone on-stage to apologise for the awkward and sudden end of the programme. It is the climax of an escalating exchange of steel-dagger glares, insults and flying spittle between the two during the latter part of the show. *The Washington Post* reviewer notes this sour end to the evening, but otherwise generally approves, reassured that The Kinks are as strong as ever.

Wednesday 4th

Playhouse, Hofstra University *Hempstead, NY* 8:00pm, with Elliott Murphy

Travel day tomorrow.

Set-list: 'Opening', 'One Of The Survivors', 'Life On The Road', 'Mr Big Man', 'Tired Of Waiting For You', 'Sunny Afternoon', 'Rush Hour Blues', 'You Make It All Worthwhile', 'Ordinary People', 'Stormy Sky', 'Life Goes On', '20th Century Man', 'Schooldays', 'The Hardway', 'Education', 'Full Moon', 'Sleepwalker', 'Lola', 'Alcohol', 'Banana Boat Song', medley 'You Really Got Me' / 'All Day And All Of The Night', 'Juke Box Music', 'Victoria'.

Friday 6th

Fox Theatre *Atlanta, GA* 8:00pm, with Elliott Murphy

Saturday 7th

Miami Jai Alai Fronton *Miami, FL* 8:00pm, with Pablo Cruise

Sunday 8th

Curtis Hixon Hall *Tampa, FL* 8:00pm, with Pablo Cruise

Travel day back to London as the tour ends, followed by a ten-day break. It is at this point that singer Shirlie Roden decides to leave the band, having tired of so much travelling.

Wednesday 18th

'Juke Box Music' / 'Life Goes On' single released in the US.

Juke Box Music single

A 'Juke Box Music' (R. DAVIES).
B-US 'Life Goes On' (R. DAVIES).
B-UK 'Sleepless Night' (R. DAVIES).

US release (A/B-US) May 18th 1977 (Arista AS 0249).
UK release (A/B-UK) June 3rd 1977 (Arista ARISTA 114).
Musicians and recording details as *Sleepwalker* album (see February 12th). A-side is edited version of album track.
Chart high US none; UK none.

Friday 20th; Monday 23rd – Wednesday 25th

With the departure of singer Shirlie Roden, rehearsals are held at Konk Studios with Kim Goody for the next string of concerts, possibly also working up some new material for future recording. This coming weekend The Kinks will hit three key European cities in an effort to re-establish their audience.

Friday 27th

Circus Krone Bau *Munich, West Germany* 8:00pm, with Horslips

Segments of this concert are filmed on home 8mm camera and later broadcast by Dutch Veronica television for *The Story Of The Kinks* on April 24th 1983. (Day off in Munich follows, plus travel day to Cologne and on to Aachen.)

Monday 30th

Voetbalstadion, Burgemeester Damenssportpark *Geleen, Netherlands* 10:30am-8:00pm, *Pinkpop Festival '77*, with Tom Petty & The Heartbreakers, Racing Cars, Golden Earring, Bothy Band, Nils Lofgren, Manfred Mann's Earth Band

A huge crowd of around 50,000 attends this start-of-summer event, where The Kinks are headliners.

On the Continent, the band is still prone to be linked to its 1960s reputation, but here it turns out to be the British press that condemns their performance. *Record Mirror*: "The old hits are jolly enough I suppose … but as far as the new stuff [goes,] it's dull." The event is later broadcast on Dutch KRO radio in June, and while The Kinks do not permit recording of their show, reportedly the radio station subsequently airs a poor audience tape anyway. (Travel day following.)

☆ Back home, a press release announces that *Preservation* is to be staged in London's West End, and that the 'Juke Box Music' single is out on June 3rd.

June

Wednesday 1st

Pavillion *Paris, France* 8:00pm, with Tom Petty & The Heartbreakers, Todd Rundgren

In addition to the band's regular set, as they play 'Life On The Road' Ray leads them through an impromptu medley of oldies, including Bruce Channel's 'Hey Baby' and Buddy Holly's 'Heartbeat', plus their usual revival of 'Louie Louie' / 'Hang On Sloopy'. (Return to London following day.)

Friday 3rd

'Juke Box Music' / 'Sleepless Night' single released in the UK. *NME*: "It's only juke-box music, sings the astute Raymond Douglas Davies with one eye cocked on single sales, but not this one methinks." *Record Mirror*: "From the murky depths of Muswell Hill comes another success. The single reeks of the early 1970s but it's still appealing as Ray Davies hisses through the song. Masterful."

→ It is rumoured that Ray does an impromptu solo performance with acoustic guitar at Pond Square in Highgate, north London as part of a local event connected to the Queen's Silver Jubilee celebrations (5th-7th). With Ray forever a busking troubadour in his own mind, this is just eccentric enough to be possible.

☆ Ray is working on his stage adaptation of *Preservation* planned for London's West End later in the year. Discussions with financial backers are currently underway. The plan grows out of the suggestion that The Kinks' own stage presentation of the show at the Royalty Theatre in

kinks'77

December 1974 was so successful that it merits an extended run – a commitment that The Kinks as a band could not make then, and indeed still cannot.

Monday-Tuesday 13th-14th

Likely owing to an inability or unwillingness to tour, stopgap singer Kim Goody is not available for the upcoming US dates and yet another singer, Linda Kendrick, is quickly hired and the band re-assembled at Konk for rehearsals. It is possible the sessions are also used to begin work on new material for the next album, recording for which is scheduled to begin in the late summer. This last-minute glitch also requires that an opening tour date on June 16th in Chicago is pushed back to the 25th. The band will start the tour instead with a massive open-air show at a 64,573-capacity baseball stadium, home to the California Angels.

➪ **TOUR STARTS** *Sleepwalker: US Tour: 3rd leg* (Jun 19th – Jul 3rd). Details as 1st and 2nd legs (see late January). During Friday 17th and Saturday 18th the band travels to Los Angeles, with a day to catch up with jet lag and a possible soundcheck on Friday.

Sunday 19th

Anaheim Stadium *Anaheim, CA* 1:00-11:00pm, with Alice Cooper (headliners), The Tubes, Nazareth, Flo & Eddie, Sha Na Na
An estimated 45,000 partygoers are present for this day-long extravaganza that marks a return to the LA stage for former freakshow master turned goodtime party man Alice Cooper. Although Los Angeles has been a Kinks stronghold from the start, it is no doubt thought that they should try their hand at a stadium-size rock show, exposing their on-stage charms to as many people in one day here as they might on a typical three-week tour. It is reported that the event is videotaped for a possible network TV special, but nothing transpires.
☆ With a full two days off to unwind in LA following the big event, Avory and Dave hang out with The Who's Keith Moon at the crazy Continental Hyatt House, while Dave reunites with his new female companion, Nancy.
☆ Perhaps The Kinks notice that megastars Led Zeppelin are beginning a six-night stand at the nearby Inglewood Forum on the 21st to wrap up their own US tour.

Thursday 23rd

Pine Knob Music Theatre *Clarkston, MI* 7:30pm

Saturday 25th

Aragon Ballroom *Chicago, IL* 8:00pm, with Widow Maker, Pierce Arrow
Earlier in the day The Kinks again concede to an in-store Record City appearance, at Skokie in suburban Chicago. (Travel day and day off following in Philadelphia.)

Tuesday 28th

Astor Theater *Reading, PA* 8:00pm, with Pierce Arrow

Wednesday 29th

Merriweather Post Pavilion *Columbia, MD* 8:30pm, with Pierce Arrow

July

Friday 1st

Mid-Hudson Civic Center *Poughkeepsie, NY* 8:00pm, with Nils Lofgren, Pierce Arrow

Saturday 2nd

Cape Cod Coliseum South *Yarmouth, MA* with Pierce Arrow
The Kinks perform on a beautiful summer evening to more than 7,000 fans on the unofficial opening weekend of summer in the heart of the Boston area's summer paradise, Cape Cod. The show includes a few more than usual 1960s chestnuts, such as 'Death Of A Clown' and a hit hardly ever performed live, 'Set Me Free'.
☆ Before tonight's show a weary Ray is briefly interviewed by *Boston Globe* reporter Lucinda Smith and tells her how he sees *Preservation* as a film or stage show. "It's kind of a documentary, really, and I want to find unknowns for it. I want to be sure it's sold on its own strength and not because of some star in it. It must be kind of an anonymous thing." He also offers a typically sarcastic view of the new punk rock scene, which he sees as already overly commercialised and marketed, and says to have any effect now the true punk bands will have to try suicide rock.

Sunday 3rd

Convention Hall *Asbury Park, NJ* 8:00pm, with Pierce Arrow
An audience of 3,571 nearly fill this 4,000-capacity venue as the band includes rarely-performed songs 'Who'll Be The Next In Line', 'Set Me Free' and 'Tired Of Waiting For You'.

Monday 4th

The band shoots straight back to London but Ray stays behind in New York City, working on stage and film deals for his *Preservation* saga and continuing to write new material for the next Kinks album, scheduled for the Christmas season.

Tuesday & Thursday 19th & 21st

Rehearsals are held in Hornsey, north London, not at Konk but at the small local Moravian Hall. Ray continues to write and refine new material.

August

Further rehearsals are held at the Moravian Hall, Hornsey (1st-2nd) as more new material is made ready to consider for recording. Shortly afterwards, Ray returns to New York while the band members enjoy a traditional British holiday this month. The Kinks will not resume work on the new album until September. While away, Ray composes a new song, 'A Rock'n'Roll Fantasy', inspired both by the death of Elvis Presley (17th) and a Peter Frampton show he attends at Madison Square Garden (22nd or 23rd).

Meanwhile Dave, inspired by a new romantic relationship, has been writing again and takes advantage of the time before the start of serious recording with The Kinks to record a number of solo tracks. He uses a few outside musicians and produces himself.

Towards the end of the month at Konk band rehearsals take place, and possibly some recording, likely extending into the start of September.

September

At Konk, Dave continues to record solo tracks with Andy Pyle on bass, ex-Konk sessioneer Nick Trevisick on drums, and an unnamed keyboard player.

He records masters of at least four of his new songs, **'Give You All My Love'**, **'Faith'**, **'Violet Dreams'** and **'Trust Your Heart'**. Only 'Heart' will see the light of day when it is ultimately included on the next Kinks album, *Misfits*, edited down from its reported original six nd a half minutes. 'Violet Dreams' will much later be issued on the Dave Davies CD *Fragile*, in 2001.

On the 12th and 13th rehearsals and demo recordings for the new Kinks album begin at Konk, continuing on the 20th-23rd and 26th. Although not specifically dated, demos recorded around this time include **'Permanent Waves'**, **'Out Of The Wardrobe'**, **'Misfits'**, **'A Rock'n'Roll Fantasy'** and **'Get Up'**. All will be re-recorded in master versions and ultimately included on the album.

Another demo made on the 22nd-23rd, **'Still Searchin''**, is passed over for *Misfits* but will be brought back to life for re-recording and inclusion on 1993's *Phobia* album. A further song demoed at these sessions is **'East West'**, which remains unused. On the 28th Ray reaches back to the *Sleepwalker* sessions and records a new version of a leftover track, **'Black Messiah'**, a session that marks the return of trumpeter Mike Cotton. Rehearsals for more new material continue on the 30th.

October

More work at Konk as a full week (3rd-7th) is devoted to the new album, including rehearsals as well as recording. The exact dates of recordings are unknown, but by this month titles on tape are **'Permanent Waves'**, **'Out Of The Wardrobe'**, **'Hay Fever'**, **'Misfits'**, **'A Rock'n'Roll Fantasy'** (unreleased version) and **'Get Up'** (unreleased version). Between scheduled sessions, Ray is busy mixing and/or writing more material. Arista Records reportedly wants a Christmas single from the band to give them something new to promote on the upcoming US tour. Ray evidently writes 'Father Christmas' at this time.

At some point between sessions, bassist Pyle tells Ray that he wants to leave the band, but is persuaded to stay through the coming tour, with assurances of a Christmas bonus.

The band reconvene at Konk for a final series of night-time sessions (24th-28th) for *Misfits*. Finished at least by now is the special one-off Christmas single, **'Father Christmas'**. Its B-side, **'Prince Of The Punks'**, first recorded as part of the early sessions for *Sleepwalker* in July 1976, is entirely re-recorded during these new-LP sessions, with trumpet played by Mike Cotton.

November

Tuesday 1st – Wednesday 2nd
Rehearsals for the upcoming US tour are held at the Moravian Hall in Hornsey. Added to the repertoire is the new single, 'Father Christmas'. The Kinks are photographed probably at this time by James Wedge for future promotional use.

→ ● **RECORDING** Konk Studios *Hornsey, north London*. Ray mixes the new LP, and decides to re-record a few tracks in the new year. A press release on the 14th announces that the LP is now set to be issued early in 1978.
☆ Before leaving for the US tour, and with pressure off from having to deliver the new album, Ray decides to shoot a promotional film for the new Christmas single. This is done at Konk Studios with the band performing the song. But editing is reportedly never completed, and only a working copy finished. However, a copy is later acquired and broadcast by Dutch Veronica television for a 1983 Kinks documentary.
☆ During a further tour rehearsal at Konk, Ray tells *Melody Maker* that he plans to do a solo album next year using musicians other than The Kinks. This could be considered an indication that the current Kinks

recording could potentially be transformed into a Ray Davies album.
☆ Ray is formulating plans for the London Rainbow shows at Christmas to be a veritable history of rock from the 1960s in which the Kinks' own musical history will be presented, including appearances by former Kinks bassists Pete Quaife and John Dalton, but also including other bands to represent various periods in rock such as flower power and heavy metal. None of this materialises beyond the present-day Kinks performing some of their earlier material sporting the original 1960s red hunting jackets.

➪ **TOUR STARTS** *Father Christmas Tour: North America* (Nov 22nd – Dec 11th). **Line-up:** Ray Davies (lead vocal, guitar), Dave Davies (guitar, vocal), Mick Avory (drums), Andy Pyle (bass), John Gosling (keyboard), John Beecham (trombone), Nick Newall (saxophone), Debbie Doss, Linda Kendrick (backing vocals).

Ray performs 'Father Christmas' in Santa costume during the song's regular encore spot. Various backdrop slides are used throughout the show. The Kinks do a handful of shows as opening act for Hall & Oates, which puts them before some very large crowds as Arista intends, but these are balanced by a number of small college shows where The Kinks are far more comfortable and in touch with the audience. (During the 20th the band travels to New York City, with a day off following.)

Tuesday 22nd
Kendall Hall, Trenton State College *Trenton, NJ* 8:00pm, with Artful Dodger
Tonight's show is marred by a number of technical sound problems, including a persistent campus police walkie-talkie bleeding into the sound system.
(The openers, Columbia Records act Artful Dodger, are a heavy power-pop band from the greater Washington DC area.)

Wednesday 23rd
Whitman Auditorium, Brooklyn College of City University of New York *Brooklyn, NY* 8:00pm, with Artful Dodger
Day off in New York City follows.
Set-list: 'Till The End Of The Day' (intro only), 'Sleepwalker', 'Life On The Road', 'Heartbeat', 'Stormy Sky', 'Rush Hour Blues', 'Tired Of Waiting For You', medley 'A Well Respected Man' / 'Dedicated Follower Of Fashion' / 'Sunny Afternoon', 'All Day And All Of The Night', 'Get Back In Line', 'Life Goes On', 'Full Moon', 'Slum Kids', 'The Hard Way', 'Education', 'See My Friends', 'Lola', 'Juke Box Music', 'Father Christmas', 'You Really Got Me'.

Friday 25th
Coliseum *Richfield, OH* 8:00pm, with Hall & Oates (headliners)
'Father Christmas' / **'Prince Of The Punks'** single released in the UK. *NME* says that "successful Xmas songs are more about mood than specifics, but as this is an anti-Christmas song it's fine". Noting sleigh bells out in force, the reviewer concludes: "How the mighty have fallen."

Saturday 26th
Indianapolis Convention Center *Indianapolis, IN* 8:00pm, with Hall & Oates (headliners)

Monday 28th
Concert Bowl, Maple Leaf Garden *Toronto, ON, Canada* 8:00pm, with Eric Carmen, Artful Dodger
Travel day following.

Wednesday 30th
The Forum *Montreal, PQ, Canada* 8:00pm, with Eric Carmen

Father Christmas single

A **'Father Christmas'** (R. DAVIES).
B **'Prince Of The Punks'** (R. DAVIES).

UK release November 25th 1977 (Arista ARISTA 153).
US release December 8th 1977 (Arista AS 0296).
Musicians Ray Davies lead vocal, electric guitar (B). Dave Davies electric guitar, backing vocal. Andy Pyle bass guitar. Mick Avory drums, tambourine, cowbell. John Gosling baby grand piano, synthesiser (A), sleigh-bells (A). Mike Cotton trumpet (B).
Recorded Konk Studios, *Hornsey, north London*; September-October 1977; 24-track mixed to stereo.
Producer Ray Davies.
Engineer Steve Waldman.
Chart high UK none; US none.

December

Friday 2nd-Saturday 3rd
LeRoy Concert Theater *Pawtucket, RI* 8:00pm, with Artful Dodger

Sunday 4th
Lowell Memorial Auditorium *Lowell, MA* 8:00pm, with Artful Dodger; sponsored by the University of Lowell
Travel day to New York City following.

Tuesday 6th
Westchester Premier Theatre *Tarrytown, NY* 8:00pm, with Artful Dodger
Day off/travel day following.

Thursday 8th
Palestra, University Of Rochester: River Campus *Rochester, NY* 8:00pm
'Father Christmas' / 'Prince Of The Punks' single released in the US. Dan Oppenheimer in New York's *Soho News* loves it: "A visionary three-and-a-half-minute Kink song that unites classic Kinks characteristics – observant, forceful and cynically funny lyrics from leader Ray Davies, his droning, magnetic voice and the subtly outraged wall-of-sound that backs him. … It should stand before, during, and after Christmas as one of their finest singles."

Saturday 10th
The Capital Centre *Landover, MD* 8:00pm, with Hall & Oates (headliners)
A disappointing turnout of 10,000 (half the hall's capacity) for the headliners, who are panned by *Washington Post* reviewer Richard Harrington. He also criticises the opening act. "The Kinks," writes Harrington, "were appearing for the first time locally since their brawling finale at Constitution Hall six months ago. The only punches in their opening show were mild cuts at the stage sound system. In fact this once-noble band seems to have thrown in the towel. If rock has a new wave, it also has its old hat. The Kinks are at the head of that category."

Sunday 11th
Gymnasium, Stockton State College *Pomona, NJ* 8:00pm, with Network

Monday 12th
The band returns to London, marking the end of their fourth US tour in a single year. Finalised details of the special Christmas shows and a tie-in to TV and radio are released to the press.

Thursday 22nd
A full soundcheck for Friday and Saturday's concert and broadcast is held at the Rainbow Theatre in north London.

Friday 23rd
Rainbow Theatre *Finsbury Park, north London* 8:00pm,
Christmas Party With The Kinks, with Splinter
The line-up is more or less as the US tour, but Mike Cotton and Alan Holmes briefly return to the horn section, Kim Goody replaces Linda Kendrick as backing singer, and percussionist Ray Cooper is added. The show is held in the same theatre as one of their earliest London shows back in spring 1964, when the venue was known as the Finsbury Park Astoria. Despite the grand plans, the show does at least feature a running history of the band's repertoire, including an opening with three songs they did originally almost 14 years earlier, and with the bonus that they wear their old red 1960s hunting jackets.
"The whole evening was a very odd affair, and at the end of it you weren't sure whether you'd just seen the last – but one – show by The Kinks," writes Tony Stewart in *NME*. "Just before they performed 'Alcohol', for instance, Ray Davies insisted that it'd be the last time they ever played it. And then at the end of the show, as the rest of his gang trooped off, Davies grabbed the mike and sang, "This could be the last time." … Maybe I've been fooled by Davies' sense of humour, but there was also something very final about this Kinks concert. … But really, when you think about it, the show might only have been the end of one era, and as *Sleepwalker* indicates, Davies and The Kinks are going into another. If their Rainbow concert is any guide, they obviously still have both the talent and imagination to last another few years."
Set-list: 'Little Queenie', 'Beautiful Delilah', 'Louie Louie', 'Life On The Road', 'You Really Got Me', 'Tired Of Waiting For You', medley 'A Well Respected Man' / 'Death Of A Clown' / 'Dedicated Follower Of Fashion' / 'Sunny Afternoon', 'Dead End Street', 'Waterloo Sunset', 'All Day And All Of The Night', 'Victoria', 'Rush Hour Blues', 'Slum Kids', 'Celluloid Heroes', 'Get Back In Line', 'The Hard Way', 'Education', 'Alcohol', medley 'Skin And Bone' / 'Dry Bones', 'Sleepwalker', 'Lola', 'Father Christmas', 'You Really Got Me', 'Juke Box Music'.

Saturday 24th
Rainbow Theatre *Finsbury Park, north London* 8:00pm, with Splinter
Before an invited audience, The Kinks round out the year in grand fashion. Tonight's concert is a simulcast, *The Kinks' Christmas Concert*, broadcast on BBC-2 TV and BBC Radio-1. Some feel that the two Rainbow concerts seem like some kind of ending, and the future of this version of the band does indeed seem tenuous. This is indeed the last concert that Pyle and Gosling will play – although both technically continue as members into the new year. Pyle and Gosling will go on to form a new band together, United, though Gosling will do some more recording with The Kinks in January.
Set-list: 'Juke Box Music', 'Sleepwalker', 'Life On The Road', medley 'A Well Respected Man' / 'Death Of A Clown' / 'Sunny Afternoon', 'Waterloo Sunset', 'All Day And All Of The Night', 'Slum Kids', 'Celluloid Heroes', 'Get Back In Line', 'The Hard Way', 'Lola', 'Alcohol', medley 'Skin And Bone' / 'Dry Bones', 'Father Christmas', 'You Really Got Me'.

→ ● **RECORDING** Konk Studios *Hornsey, north London*. Official Kinks holiday time, but Ray mixes tracks for the delayed new LP. Around now he calls in Gosling, who lives near the studio, for some keyboard overdubs.

→ INDICATES EVENT AROUND THIS TIME BUT WITH NO FIRM DATE

1978

Another major transitional year for the band. Dalton had already gone by the time the second classic incarnation of the band had come apart at the end of 1977, with Gosling and Pyle gone by the new year. As well as this, a demoralised Avory let Ray and Dave finish the second Arista album without him. This was as close as the band had ever got to a complete break-up. But the album was finished, and a new version of The Kinks was put together in the spring.

The change in personnel and the paring down of the road band to a five-piece core unit – only augmented live by horns, with no more female singers – completely revitalised The Kinks as a performing unit. They had a renewed commitment to touring, and concert reviews this year almost unanimously reflected this resurgence of live energy, no doubt in part still prompted by the punk and new wave movements of the past few years. Dave said later in his book that he felt they finally had a "cohesive and unified rock band" again.

The first revival of Kinks material by the next generation of rockers came in the spring when upstart LA heavy metal band Van Halen had a success with 'You Really Got Me', followed in England with punk group The Jam covering 'David Watts'. A new manager was appointed too, an American, and he would free Ray from many business burdens.

The new Kinks album, Misfits, was viewed as uneven, but it spawned a successful single in the US, 'Rock'n'Roll Fantasy', which provided momentum for the newly energised live band to tour extensively and make their mark on the established fans. But there was also a new and rapidly growing younger audience who would prove significant in the coming resurgence of The Kinks and their new-found commercial success. One of the challenges for the all-new Mark III Kinks was to prove their worth as a truly contemporary band. While proud of their legacy, they did not want to be shackled by it.

January

Ray begins the year busily mixing tracks at Konk in London, and in the process again decides to re-record some songs. The scheduled US release of the new LP and the start of an accompanying US tour was to have started on February 22nd, but the album is pushed back first to March 29th and then into May. Also rescheduled because of the delay in completion of the album is a short Scandinavian tour, set for February 10th-15th, now pushed into the autumn.

Meanwhile, sessions re-start for the new LP on the 9th in order to record new versions of at least two tracks, with engineer Steve Waldman. Having drummed on the originals, Avory decided to bow out. He agrees to have occasional Konk session drummer Nick Trevisick take a stab at the problematic **'A Rock'n'Roll Fantasy'** and **'Get Up'**, along with bassist Ron Lawrence, Trevisick's partner in the informal Konk rhythm section and in the band Moon. Lawrence also appears on **'Live Life'**, likely overdubbing bass on to the earlier backing track. Gosling is present on the new takes, playing synthesiser on 'A Rock'n'Roll Fantasy' and piano and Hammond on 'Get Up'.

On the 28th, Gosling leaves the studio in a dispute with Ray over the re-recording of 'Get Up' and quits the band. He and Pyle are informed by phone the following day that their services are no longer required, and they are subsequently removed from the payroll.

February

Drummer Nick Trevisick and bassist Ron Lawrence are apparently no longer available for further recording; ironically, they are committed to recording with ex-Konk artist Andy Desmond. Bassist Zaine Griff is brought in now for some unspecified overdubs on to existing recordings originally made with Pyle.

On the 13th, major recording for the LP is completed as veteran session man Clem Cattini (and one-time fill-in Kink) does some drum and percussion overdubs on to tracks existing from earlier sessions, and overdubs a complete drum track on **'Live Life'**, replacing Avory's original. The latter is a particularly difficult feat, demanding an especially good feel for timing, and a tribute to Cattini's abilities.

Initial meetings are held in London this month with Elliot Abbott, an American who is hired as The Kinks' new manager. The band's booking agent Barry Dickens introduced them to his friend Abbott, personally recommending him as someone who can handle the business affairs that Ray has been doing mostly himself. While Ray in effect still makes the decisions, there is now someone to take care of details and advise on business matters. Abbott seems to work well and the band's commercial standing steadily improves from now until his departure in 1985. During the chaos of January and February when the LP is being finished with session players, Ray reportedly considers going out as a solo act to promote the record. No effort is made from February until late April to hire the two missing Kinks, so it seems this is a serious prospect. Later in the month, Ray mixes the completed tracks for the album.

March

Ray continues to mix tracks at Konk for the new LP. On the 6th he does final mixes for **'Misfits'**, **'Hay Fever'**, **'Out Of The Wardrobe'**, **'In A Foreign Land'** and **'Rock'n'Roll Fantasy'**. A press release announces a new Kinks LP, *Permanent Waves*, set for release on April 28th or May 5th, but the US release is pushed to May 17th.

The band's reputation is given a huge boost when a cover version of 'You Really Got Me' by upstart Los Angeles heavy-metal band Van Halen reaches number 36 in the US *Billboard* singles chart. The accompanying debut album, *Van Halen*, including the track, makes number 19. This exposure to a large, young audience gives The Kinks a new credibility that helps strengthen their growing success in the US. Lead guitarist Eddie Van Halen cites Dave Davies as an early influence, and this in turn bolsters Dave's image as an important figure among guitar players.

April

➜ Avory and Dave busy themselves setting up the new Konk Club within the Konk studio complex.

Sunday 9th
● **RECORDING** Konk Studios *Hornsey, north London*. Ray accomplishes the final editing of **'Black Messiah'** and the new LP is deemed complete.

Monday 10th – Tuesday 11th
With the final mixes in hand, Ray travels to New York City, and on Tuesday with Robert Ludwig at Masterdisk masters the new album. Ray also does some press duties while in town.

Monday 17th
A press release announces that John Gosling and Andy Pyle have formed their own band, as news of their departure from The Kinks is made public.

Tuesday 18th
A press release has Ray confirming the departure of Gosling and Pyle from The Kinks, but that new members are not yet chosen. It is briefly considered to ask original bassist Pete Quaife to rejoin. Quaife is living quietly as a commercial artist in Copenhagen, but the offer is apparently never made. Says Avory: "The idea was discussed within the group [but dropped, after reasoning that when Quaife] left in '69 he was fed up with touring and didn't want to make it his career. So I don't think he really has any interest in playing with the Kinks again." Also considered now as a replacement for Gosling is ex-Animals and Mike Cotton Sound keyboardist Dave Rowberry. He is a very good friend of the band, but is politely passed over because of his laidback personal style. (Rowberry died suddenly in June 2003 while an active member of a partially re-formed Animals.)

Thursday 20th
Jim Rodford is phoned by road manager Ken Jones and offered the job

of Kinks bass player. Rodford is well known to the band since they toured together late in 1964 when he had just joined The Mike Cotton Sound. The connection continued as the horn section from that band eventually became part of The Kinks in the early 1970s. Rodford spent 1968-1976 as bassist with Argent, and then an offshoot called Phoenix, and is currently recording with Limey. He accepts the position as The Kinks' new bass player.

Friday 21st
Gordon Edwards is auditioned at Konk and hired as the band's new keyboard player. Edwards was a member in the 1970s of The Pretty Things, who toured with The Kinks in January and February 1976. More recently he's been working with a band called Sunshine which is just splitting up when Avory suggests him as a candidate, recalling his versatility as a keyboard player and a fine backing vocalist. With Rodford and Edwards both very capable singers, it will no longer be necessary to include the long-serving female backing singers on tour, and this too will help contain and tighten the new-look Kinks.

Monday 24th
A press release announces that Jim Rodford and Gordon Edwards have been hired as new members, that UK dates are set for May, and that the new LP, now called *Misfits*, is out on May 5th. Towards the end of the month the new band begins rehearsals at Konk Studios.

May

Monday 1st – Friday 5th
Rehearsals continue at Konk Studios. On the 5th there is an opening party for a private, members-only bar/restaurant/games-room within the Konk studio complex. On Saturday the band's favoured football team, Arsenal, is playing in the FA Cup final, so a day off is essential.

Monday 8th – Friday 12th
➜ Rehearsals continue at Konk this week, but it is announced to the music press that the UK tour is now cancelled due to insufficient time to work in the new members. The cancellations are May 13th Apollo Theatre, Manchester; 14th Empire Theatre, Liverpool; 15th Hippodrome Theatre, Birmingham; 18th New Theatre, Oxford; 19th City Hall, Newcastle Upon Tyne.

Saturday 13th
❏ **TV** Granada Television Centre *Manchester*. ITV **What's On**. Probably already arranged to coincide with the now-cancelled Manchester date, Ray makes a solo appearance on this show, and in addition to the requisite interview with host Tony Wilson he performs a rendition of 'Out Of The Wardrobe', accompanying himself on guitar. Ray also begins to undertake other promotional functions around now to get the ball rolling for the new LP.

Monday 15th
As band rehearsals continue this week, a press release says The Kinks will play the Roundhouse, London as a one-off charity gig.

Wednesday 17th
Misfits album released in the US. "Misfits is nearly a masterpiece," says *Rolling Stone*. "The Kinks aren't getting older, they're getting better." Time: "Fine corrosive fun from one of the perennials of British rock." *Hi-Fidelity*'s reviewer writes: "Bittersweet eloquence is the most striking aspect of the album. ... A tenth of the young upstarts one hears today should be so good as to make a record this enjoyable." *Good Times* says: "Misfits sounds like a hit, feels like a hit, and is receiving the

➜ INDICATES EVENT AROUND THIS TIME BUT WITH NO FIRM DATE

Misfits album

A1 'Misfits' (R. DAVIES).
A2 'Hay Fever' (R. DAVIES).
A3* 'Live Life' (R. DAVIES).
A4 'A Rock'n'Roll Fantasy' (R. DAVIES).
A5 'In A Foreign Land' (R. DAVIES).
B1 'Permanent Waves' (R. DAVIES).
B2* 'Black Messiah' (R. DAVIES).
B3 'Out Of The Wardrobe' (R. DAVIES).
B4 'Trust Your Heart' (D. DAVIES).
B5 'Get Up' (R. DAVIES).
* On the British release, tracks A3 and B2 are transposed, with 'Live Life' an extended edit.

US release May 17th 1978 (Arista AB 4167).
UK release May 19th 1978 (Arista SPARTY 1055).
Musicians Ray Davies lead vocals except as noted, acoustic guitar, electric guitar, backing vocal. Dave Davies lead vocal (B4), electric guitar, backing vocal. Andy Pyle bass guitar except as noted. John Dalton bass guitar (A5). Ron Lawrence bass guitar (A3, A4, B5). Zaine Griff bass guitar overdubs on to some Andy Pyle tracks. Mick Avory drums except as noted. Nick Trevisick drums (A4, B4, B5). Clem Cattini drum overdub (A3) plus possible further minor percussion/drum overdubs. John Gosling baby grand piano, Hammond organ, synthesiser. Mike Cotton trumpet (B2). John Beecham trombone (B2). Nick Newell clarinet (B2).
Recorded Konk Studios *Hornsey, north London*; September-October 1977, January-February 1978; 24-track mixed to stereo.
Producer Raymond Douglas Davies.
Engineer Steve Waldman.
Chart high UK none; US number 40.

humility and sincere superiority about his favourite subjects: losers; little men; dedicated followers; fashion; the crowd; the mundane; fantasy; escape; rock'n'roll; life."

Melody Maker: "For all the glorious exceptions, however, *Misfits* is guilty of a heap of musical and lyrical makeweights. It's compelling listening for Davies' always wonderful lachrymal vocal and for axe histrionics like the Spanish classical guitar intro to 'Misfits' and the acoustic accompaniment on 'Get Up', but genuine freaks like 'Out of The Wardrobe' … are dull dogs indeed."

Sounds gives it an absolute panning. "Had this LP been released under a different group name, it admittedly would not have been quite so offensive, but this is The Kinks!"

'A Rock'n'Roll Fantasy' / 'Artificial Light' single released in the UK. *Melody Maker*'s reviewer comes over all sentimental, writing: "I've always had a tender spot for Raymond Douglas and the boys whatever their shortcomings over the years. … The single isn't great by any means but The Kinks … aaaah."

▷ **TOUR STARTS** *Misfits: US Tour: 1st leg* (May 25th – Jun 25th). **Line-up**: Ray Davies (lead vocal, guitar), Dave Davies (guitar, vocal), Mick Avory (drums), Jim Rodford (bass), Gordon Edwards (keyboards), John Beecham (trombone), Nick Newall (saxophone). This tour sees all material from the theatrical productions dropped. Ticket prices range from $6.50 to $8.50. Venues are generally 2,000-4,000 capacity halls. (Travel day London to New York City on the 24th.)

Thursday 25th
Palace Theater *Waterbury, CT* 8:00pm, with Charlie
Six-piece (two-drummer) British rock band Charlie, signed to Janus Records, support The Kinks on these dates.

Friday 26th
Auditorium Theater *Rochester, NY* with Charlie
"Davies, the guiding light of that venerable rock group, The Kinks, danced, primped, screamed, drank, and generally had a roaring good time," writes Larry King in the *Democrat & Chronicle*. "So did the audience, some of who were born about the same time Ray and his brother Dave Davies first put together The Kinks."

kind of initial radio acceptance essential for a hit. Davies' production technique and brother Dave Davies' guitar playing are at an all-time high."

Friday 19th
The Roundhouse *Chalk Farm, north London* 8:00pm, with Stan Arnold
This 800-capacity club-size gig is a warm-up debut for the new band. *NME* says: "A small triumph and if I say it was too easily won, that's not to knock how good they were. Merely to note that in a few months time and working to a less dedicated audience they'll probably be even better."

Allan Jones is the reviewer for *Melody Maker* and says that after 'A Rock'n'Roll Fantasy', which he considers the evening's most memorable performance, "it was a simple gallop into our hearts, an energetic brace of encores and a 15-minute ovation after the house-lights went up. You don't witness many such receptions, but then The Kinks remain quite unique".
Set-list: 'Opening', 'Life On The Road', 'Lola', 'Waterloo Sunset', 'You Really Got Me', 'Permanent Waves', 'Misfits', 'Hay Fever', 'Celluloid Heroes', 'Sunny Afternoon', 'A Rock'n'Roll Fantasy', medley 'A Well Respected Man' / 'Death Of A Clown' / 'Dedicated Follower Of Fashion', 'Slum Kids', 'Alcohol', 'All Day And All Of The Night', 'Live Life'.
Misfits album released in the UK. *NME* calls it "vintage Kinks with Davies whining, pining, shining, and maligning away in tones of courtly

A Rock'n'Roll Fantasy single

A* 'A Rock'n'Roll Fantasy' (R. DAVIES).
B-UK 'Artificial Light' (R. DAVIES).
B-US 'Live Life' (R. DAVIES).
* US A-side is a shorter edited version.

UK release (A/B-UK) May 19th (Arista ARIST 189).
US release (A/B-US) June (around 21st) 1978 (Arista AS 0342). A, B-US: musicians and recording details as Misfits album (see May 17th).
Musicians B-UK: Ray Davies lead vocal, electric guitar, harmonica, backing vocal. Dave Davies electric guitar. John Dalton bass guitar. Mick Avory drums. John Gosling electric piano, synthesiser.
Recorded B-UK: Konk Studios *Hornsey, north London*; July 1976; 24-track mixed to stereo.
Producer Ray Davies.
Engineer Steve Waldman (A, B-US); Roger Wake (B-UK).
Chart high UK none; US number 30.

Saturday 27th

New Century Theater *Buffalo, NY* 8:00pm, with Charlie
Vinyl Edition says the show "proved the band's long standing excellence. Their newest works provide a heady experience and demonstrate that The Kinks have stayed in touch with the present as well as the future".

Sunday 28th

Syracuse Area Landmark Theater *Syracuse, NY* 8:00pm, with Charlie
Travel day following.

Tuesday 30th

Palace Theater *Cleveland, OH* 8:00pm, with Charlie
A tentative second night here is cancelled. Travel day following, with Ray going to Chicago for press work.

June

Thursday 1st

Stanley Theater *Pittsburgh, PA* 8:00pm, with Charlie

Friday 2nd

The Palladium *New York, NY* 8:00 & 11:30pm, with Charlie
The New York Times: "The Kinks were at their most glorious at the Palladium Friday evening, offering a performance as charged with revitalized energy as it was rich with memories. The set was far from seamless, but technical perfection was very much beside the point; what mattered was the ferocity with which the group attacked the various challenges at hand."
Set-list (11.30 show): 'Opening', 'Life On The Road', 'Sleepwalker', 'Mr Big Man', 'Banana Boat Song', 'Lola', 'Permanent Waves', 'Misfits', 'Waterloo Sunset', medley 'A Well Respected Man' / 'Death Of A Clown' / 'Sunny Afternoon', 'Hay Fever', 'Trust Your Heart', 'You Really Got Me', 'Slum Kids', 'Alcohol', 'A Rock'n'Roll Fantasy', 'All Day And All Of The Night', 'Live Life', 'Juke Box Music'.

Saturday 3rd

Providence Civic Center *Providence, RI* 8:00pm, with Charlie
A significant booking because it represents The Kinks' first headlining date in an arena-size venue since the 1960s. In a way it's a test to see how they do in such a setting and if they can fill the approximately 9,000 concert-seating capacity.

Sunday 4th

Music Hall *Boston, MA* 7:00 & 10:00pm, with Charlie
One of tonight's shows is highlighted by the unusual inclusion in the set of ther song 'Get Up'. (The band has a travel the following day and a day off in Washington DC after a scheduled first night at the Warner Theater there on the 6th is dropped.)

Wednesday 7th

Warner Theater *Washington, DC* 8:00pm, with Charlie
"Seeing The Kinks live in 1978 is like returning to the fold at a Pentacostal revival," says *The Washington Post*, "explosive, wrenching, draining and supremely satisfying."

Thursday 8th – Friday 9th

Tower Theater *Upper Darby, PA* 8:00pm, with Charlie
After the first night Ray travels back to the Warwick Hotel in New York City where the next day he does a number of press interviews, including one with Stan Soocher of *Circus*, saying: "I've returned to the commercial mould now because I want to make direct contact with the audience once again."

Saturday 10th

Veterans Memorial Auditorium *Columbus, OH* 8:00pm, with Charlie

Sunday 11th

Uptown Theater *Chicago, IL* 8:00pm, with Charlie

Monday 12th

Uihlein Hall, Performing Arts Center *Milwaukee, WI* 8:00pm, with Charlie
For tonight's show The Kinks are introduced on stage by television actor Leonard Nimoy, famed for his character Mr Spock in *Star Trek*. Nimoy is in town with a one-man show about artist Vincent Van Gogh.

Tuesday 13th

State Theater *Minneapolis, MN* 7:00 & 11:00pm, with Charlie
First show with 3,200 attending is only three-quarters sold out. *The Minneapolis Tribune* says they "delivered an uplifting 90-minute set that had more rock'n'roll raw edges than the 18-year-old band has bared on stage during previous appearances this decade". (Travel day to and then a day off in San Francisco follow.)

Friday 16th

San Jose Center For The Performing Arts *San Jose, CA* 8:00pm, with Charlie

Saturday 17th

Medford Armory *Medford, OR* 8:00pm, with Charlie

Sunday 18th

Paramount Theatre *Portland, OR* 8:00pm, with Charlie

Monday 19th

Paramount Northwest Theatre *Seattle, WA* 8:00pm, with Charlie

➜ 'A Rock'n'Roll Fantasy' / 'Live Life' single released in the US this week.

Wednesday 21st

Berkeley Community Theater *Berkeley, CA* 8:00pm, with Charlie
"Kinks fans are a loyal lot," writes Larry Kelp in the *Oakland Tribune*. "They guarantee the group sell out shows each year when the London band returns to the Bay Area. It doesn't matter what the group does, for just being on stage is enough to satisfy a Kinks fan. Well, this time it was different. The Kinks weren't just a traditionally grand affair. They also proved that they haven't gone out-of-date. And no longer are they treading water. Now they are pushing forward. The results were breathtaking."

Friday 23rd – Sunday 25th

Universal Amphitheatre *Universal City, CA* 8:00pm, with Charlie
"The Kinks did a delightful three-night-stand engagement," says *Melody Maker*. "Ray Davies has always had a spot in his heart for Los Angeles and Hollywood, echoed in his introduction to 'Celluloid Heroes'. Dave Davies is playing better than ever and really got a chance to open up and play to [a total audience of 15,000] folks." (Travel day to London following as the tour ends slightly ahead of schedule.)

July

➜ Back in London, Ray is approached by the playwright Barrie Keeffe who wants Ray to co-write a musical with him for The National Theatre. *The Poet And The Woman* is to be Keeffe's rewriting of *Thesmophorriazusai* by Greek playwright Aristophanes. Keeffe, who is planning to recast the work in modern form as a story about a strike by actresses at the National Theatre, gets Ray's agreement to write music for the project.

✭ British concert dates for The Kinks that were originally set for July are cancelled.

Tuesday 4th

❐ **TV** Granada Television Centre *Manchester*. ITV **On Site** lip-synch 'Live Life' broadcast July 6th 6.30-7.15 pm. Song(s) performed for this TV programme are unconfirmed, but almost certainly include the forthcoming new single.

Monday 10th

Misfits album peaks in the US *Billboard* chart at number 40.

Friday 14th

'Live Life' / 'In A Foreign Land' single released in the UK. The single gets nowhere in the British charts. An apparently innocent review in *Melody Maker* – "not quite at their best but it's great to hear from them again" – gets a vehement response from one reader, typifying the current punk-inspired backlash against established 1960s and '70s rock artists. "What can you say about patronising prattish ill conceived calculated token gestures of 'understanding the scene maaan' like this?"

Live Life singles

A 'Live Life' (R. DAVIES).
B 'In A Foreign Land' (R. DAVIES).
A is an edited version of UK *Misfits* album edit; same as US album edit (see April 17th).
UK release July 14th 1978 (Arista ARIST 199).
Musicians and recording details as *Misfits* album (see April 17th).
Chart high UK none.

A 'Live Life' (R. DAVIES).
B 'Black Messiah' (R. DAVIES).
A is a significantly remixed and re-edited version. B is new mix, same as later UK single (September 29th).
US release October (around 11th) 1978 (Arista AS 0372).
Musicians and recording details as *Misfits* album (see April 17th). Mixing and editing Konk Studios *Hornsey, north London* September 1978.
Chart high US none.

⇨ **TOUR STARTS** *Misfits: US Tour: 2nd leg* (Jul 16th – Aug 9th). **Line-up**: Ray Davies (lead vocal, guitar), Dave Davies (guitar, vocal), Mick Avory (drums), Jim Rodford (bass), Gordon Edwards (keyboards), John Beecham (trombone), Nick Newall (saxophone). Two oldies are worked into the show: The Isley Brothers' hit 'Twist And Shout' and the Chuck Berry chestnut 'Little Queenie'. Ticket prices are generally $6.50-$8.50. With the exception of the opening date, and as noted, venues are in the 2,000-4,000 capacity range. (Travel day London to New York City to Seattle on the 15th.)

Sunday 16th

Memorial Stadium, Seattle Center *Seattle, WA* 1:00pm, *Summer Sunday '78*, with The Beach Boys (headliners), Randy Hansen, Jr. Cadillac
The tour's opening date marks a quick return to Seattle but gives The Kinks an opportunity to play to an enormous crowd of 22,000 at the city's local baseball stadium. The show is hampered by poor weather and what *Seattle Times* reviewer Patrick MacDonald characterises as soulless performances. "It was a social and economic event, not a musical event," he says, and describes The Kinks' performance as "much like the one they did last month at the Paramount except that it was far less spirited".

Monday 17th

Santa Cruz Civic Auditorium *Santa Cruz, CA* 8:00pm, with Blondie
Tonight is a sell-out at this relatively small 1,967-seat venue. Much of the rest of this tour pairs The Kinks with rapidly emerging New York new-wavers Blondie. It proves to be a happy and mutually beneficial musical pairing. Blondie have just completed their not-yet-released *Parallel Lines* LP, featuring future hit 'Heart Of Glass'. Debbie Harry recalls later, "The Kinks were fun to work with, helpful and friendly rather than competitive, so we appreciated that." The Kinks in turn seem to pick up something from Blondie's refreshing mix of pop and punk, traces of which will be heard on the next Kinks single and album. (Day off following.)

Wednesday 19th

Open Air Theatre, San Diego State University *San Diego, CA* 8:00pm, with Blondie
Two days off in Los Angeles following. A tentative concert in Phoenix, AZ on the 20th is cancelled, probably due to the promoter's fear of stiff competition from The Rolling Stones who are in Tuscon on the 21st.

Saturday 22nd

Uptown Theater *Kansas City, MO* 8:00pm, with Blondie
Originally scheduled at Memorial Hall, the venue is changed to this smaller room due to slow ticket sales. (Day off following plus travel day to St. Louis.)

Tuesday 25th

Kiel Opera House *St. Louis, MO* 8:00pm, with Blondie
"Always experimenting, always cultivating a warped sense of humor, The Kinks never have been has-beens," says the *St. Louis Post-Dispatch*. "But for those in the crowd who were fans of the band more than a decade ago, the Tuesday night performance must have been especially gratifying. But for anyone else who saw the show … it was simply an evening of good unadulterated rock'n'roll." (Travel day following.)

Thursday 27th

Red Rocks Amphitheatre *Morrison, CO* 7:30pm, with Cheap Trick
The Kinks are ambitiously booked at this 9,000-capacity outdoor venue; 4,000 attend.

Friday 28th

Armadillo World Headquarters *Austin, TX* 8:00pm, with Blondie

Saturday 29th

McFarlin Memorial Auditorium, Southern Methodist University *Dallas, TX* 8:00pm, with Blondie

kinks'78

Set-list: 'Opening', 'Sleepwalker', 'Life On The Road', 'Permanent Wave', 'Hay Fever', 'Lola', 'Misfits', 'Celluloid Heroes', medley 'A Well Respected Man' / 'Sunny Afternoon', 'Trust Your Heart', 'You Really Got Me', 'Alcohol', 'Slum Kids', 'A Rock'n'Roll Fantasy', 'All Day And All Of The Night', 'Live Life', 'Juke Box Music', 'Twist And Shout'.

Sunday 30th

Music Hall *Houston, TX* 8:00pm, with Blondie
Houston Post: "Through it all, Ray had never seemed happier or more involved with his singing, and brother Dave has never played more ferocious guitar. And new members Gordon Edwards and Jim Rodford teamed with the veteran Mick Avory to push forward the tightest band sound the Kinks have ever had in a Houston show. It was all simply unbeatable … and living proof of just why The Kinks inspire more true affection from their fans than any other rock group in the world." (Travel day following.)

August

Tuesday 1st

Civic Center Music Hall *Oklahoma City, OK* 8:00pm, with Tom Petty & The Heartbreakers
Petty's band is promoting their second album, *You're Gonna Get It*, and although Petty is some way from his eventual stardom, his classic 1960s-based sound is a fine complement to The Kinks. (Travel day following.)

Thursday 3rd

The Warehouse *New Orleans, LA* 8:00pm, with Tom Petty & The Heartbreakers
"The Kinks and Tom Petty & The Heartbreakers delivered an impressive, high-powered concert to a below capacity crowd," says *Figaro*. "Both groups, some of the very oldest and the very newest rockers, played hot sets for the already sweating audience. … The newest Kinks style is straightahead rock'n'roll, tight and powerful. Ray literally bounces through the set like an energetic youngster. Indeed they seem to be accepting the challenge of the 'new wave' by appearing with the likes of Tom Petty." (Travel day following.)

Saturday 5th – Sunday 6th

Fox Theatre *Atlanta, GA* 8:00pm, with Tom Petty & The Heartbreakers, Blondie
Travel day following.

Tuesday 8th

Springfield Civic Center Arena *Springfield, MA* 7:30pm, with The Cars
The opening act is a rapidly emerging band from Boston whose debut LP spawns the hit singles 'My Best Friend's Girl' and 'Just What I Needed', providing yet another great pairing of acts on this tour.
☆ The Kinks travel with and are interviewed by Fred Schruers for a possible cover story in *Rolling Stone*, though it ultimately emerges as just a regular feature.

Wednesday 9th

Wollman Rink, Central Park *New York, NY* 7:00pm, *Dr. Pepper Music Festival*, with Eddie Money
The site of a memorable Kinks appearance six years earlier. (Day off in New York City follows, then travel day to Belgium as US tour finishes.)

Saturday 12th

Outdoor event *Bilzen, Belgium* 8:00pm, *Bilzen Rock/Jazz*

Festival, with Blondie, Radio Stars, Little Bob Story, Tyla Gang, Japan, Lindisfarne
Travel day following to London by ferry.

➔ The band takes a well-deserved break for the remainder of the month. Dave heads off to Portugal and Avory is more than occupied with the birth of a daughter on the 24th – making him the last member of The Kinks to enter the world of the family man. Ray busies himself on his new side project, writing *The Poet And The Woman* with Barrie Keeffe.
☆ While The Kinks have been away on tour, the latest revival of their back catalogue has hit the charts in the form of The Jam's latest single, a faithful cover version of 'David Watts'. This was the lead track from their 1967 LP, *Something Else By The Kinks*. The chart success of the song helps boost awareness of The Kinks among a new generation of young listeners and record buyers in Britain – and in a shrewd move the band adds the old song to their new live set (see, for example, October 1st).

September

➔ ● **RECORDING** Konk Studios *Hornsey, north London*. With a scheduled month-off from Kink duties, Dave takes advantage by beginning work on songs he has been writing, possibly recording some demos for a proposed solo album.
☆ Ray continues work on his play with Barrie Keeffe.
☆ On the 8th drummer Keith Moon dies in London, marking the end of an era for The Kinks' old London rivals The Who.

Monday 11th

A press release today says a London concert is scheduled and that a new single, 'Black Messiah', is due September 29th. A further release on the 18th announces that Dave is planning a solo LP.
☆ 'A Rock'n'Roll Fantasy' single peaks in the US charts at number 30.

Monday 18th

● **RECORDING** Konk Studios *Hornsey, north London*. Ray remixes and re-edits 'Live Life' and 'Black Messiah' for American single releases.

Friday 29th

Ray is probably in New York City as remixes of 'Black Messiah' and 'Live Life' are mastered at Masterdisk Studios with Bob Ludwig today, set for release soon in the US by Arista Records.
'Black Messiah' / 'Misfits' single released in the UK. *Melody Maker*'s reviewer almost reluctantly pans it. "Why this week? Why me? Thirteen years ago I loved The Kinks and went on liking more of their singles

---

Black Messiah single

A* **'Black Messiah'** (R. DAVIES).
B **'Misfits'** (R. DAVIES).
* A is a remixed version with sections of the song edited into a different order.

UK release September 29th 1978 (Arista ARIST 210).
Musicians and recording details as *Misfits* album (see April 17th).
Chart high UK none.

---

than I didn't for a good few years after, but now like Slade and The Moody Blues, they sound old and irrelevant. 'Black Messiah' is reggae, but it's Ray Davies, and the rhythm and the Linguaphone Rasta accent feel uncomfortable without the wit and invention of 10cc's 'Dreadlock Holiday' which it unavoidably calls to mind."

October

Sunday 1st

Odeon *Hammersmith, west London* 8:00pm
Whatever it is The Kinks have discovered that reconnects them to their American audience, it seems no longer to be in favour with the ever-fickle British press.

Graham Lock in *NME* is scathing, calling them "a second-rate Heavy Metal band living on past glories. If this sounds extreme, well, I've rarely felt so angry at, and insulted by, a concert performance as I was by [this one … but] the fans loved it, of course. I should say that Dave Davies tossed in some pretty good HM guitar every now and again, but the rest of the night was a travesty of rock'n'roll".

In *Melody Maker*, long-time supporter Penny Valentine writes: "The Kinks are set in aspic, a minor British institution, and that's where they will remain." Chris White in *Music Week* is far more charitable. "Maybe it was an evening of semi-nostalgia for many of the rather old 'teenagers' in the audience. … Maybe Ray Davies has lost some of his bite and satire … but he proved that old pop stars don't always just fade away – they can go on writing good stuff and appealing to kids who were barely out of rompers during their first wave of success. … The Kinks are still entertainment originals in the pop world and Ray Davies has few songwriting peers. He'll still be doing what he's doing in another 13 years time."
Set-list: 'Opening', 'Sleepwalker', 'Life On The Road', 'Mr Big Man', 'Misfits', 'Hay Fever', 'Dedicated Follower Of Fashion', 'Lola', 'Waterloo Sunset', 'Tired Of Waiting For You', 'Alcohol', 'Sunny Afternoon', 'A Well Respected Man', 'Death Of A Clown', 'Slum Kids', 'Trust Your Heart', 'You Really Got Me', 'A Rock'n'Roll Fantasy', 'Celluloid Heroes', 'Permanent Waves', 'All Day And All Of The Night', 'Live Life', 'David Watts', 'Twist And Shout', 'Juke Box Music'.

Wednesday 11th

➔ **'Live Life' / 'Black Messiah'** single released in the US.

➔ **TOUR STARTS** *European Tour* (Oct 10th – 30th). **Line-up**: Ray Davies (lead vocal, guitar), Dave Davies (guitar, vocal), Mick Avory (drums), Jim Rodford (bass), Gordon Edwards (keyboards), John Beecham (trombone), Nick Newall (saxophone). The first full-length tour of Europe since the mid 1960s. Reception is strong and will prompt the band to routinely schedule similar tours during the three commercially successful years that follow. The tours are attractive as travelling distances aren't as unnerving as for US tours, and the band can often travel by train rather than fly. Venues are generally in the vicinity of 1,500-2,000-seat halls. Show-time is usually 8:00 or 8:30pm unless noted.

Tuesday 10th

Falconer Theatre *Copenhagen, Denmark* with Cafe Jacques
Arbetet raves: "It was sheer music hall, and Ray Davies is a great singalong leader."
Set-list: 'Opening', 'Sleepwalker', 'Life On The Road', 'Mr Big Man', 'Lola', 'Dedicated Follower Of Fashion', 'Misfits', 'Tired Of Waiting For You', 'Hay Fever', medley 'A Well Respected Man' / 'Death Of A Clown' / 'Sunny Afternoon', 'Celluloid Heroes', 'Banana Boat Song', 'Trust Your Heart', 'You Really Got Me', 'Slum Kids', 'Alcohol', 'A

Rock'n'Roll Fantasy', 'All Day And All Of The Night', 'Live Life', 'Little Queenie', 'Twist And Shout'.

Wednesday 11th

Olympen *Lund, Sweden* with Cafe Jacques, The Buddyboys
A disappointing turnout with only a half-full auditorium and reportedly much resistance to the non-1960s material. "It's hardly the music of 1978, but The Kinks are all right for a pleasant evening," says *Expressen*.

Thursday 12th

Chateau Neuf *Oslo, Norway* with Cafe Jacques
Travel day following to Stockholm.

Saturday 14th

Konserthuset *Stockholm, Sweden* 9:30pm, with Cafe Jacques
Travel day following.

Monday 16th

Deutschlandhalle *Berlin, West Germany* with Cafe Jacques

Tuesday 17th

Musikhalle *Hamburg, West Germany* with Cafe Jacques

Wednesday 18th

Volkhaus *Zürich, Switzerland* with Cafe Jacques
"The concert … was sold out," says *Tagesanzeiger*. "No wonder, as everybody from the scene back in the 1960s wanted to see this legendary band. It proved how important The Kinks were and still are [but] it was a little sad that more younger people didn't attend; really, the band's current work is only known to insiders." (Travel day following to Vienna.)

Friday 20th

Sporthalle *Linz, Austria* with Cafe Jacques

Saturday 21st

Kammersaal *Graz, Austria* with Cafe Jacques

Sunday 22nd

Sophiensaal *Vienna, Austria* with Cafe Jacques
Along with band interviews, segments of 'Lola', 'Slum Kids', 'Alcohol' and 'All Day And All Of The Night' from this show are filmed and later broadcast on the Austrian TV show *Ohne Malukorb* in November.

Monday 23rd

Stadthalle *Offenbach, West Germany* with Cafe Jacques

Tuesday 24th

Stadthalle *Erlangen, West Germany* with Cafe Jacques

Wednesday 25th

Circus Krone Bau *Munich, West Germany* with Cafe Jacques

Thursday 26th

Travel day to Frankfurt and on to The Hague. The Kinks are slated to be at the BBC Television Centre in London to tape an appearance on *The Leo Sayer Show* but this is cancelled.

Friday 27th

Congresgebouw *The Hague, Netherlands* with Cafe Jacques

Saturday 28th

Arenahal Deurne *Antwerp, Belgium* with Cafe Jacques

kinks'78

Stadsschouwburg *Sittard, Netherlands* with Cafe Jacques

Théâtre Mogador *Paris, France* with Cafe Jacques
Travel day to London following as the European tour ends.

November

Immediately following the European tour, The Kinks are set to head on to Australia and New Zealand and possibly Japan. But it is decided at short notice to cancel their part of the Australasian tour in order to devote time to the current projects of Dave (a solo album) and Ray (a play). The press reports that the cancellation is made so that the band can work on a new Kinks album. The Australian promoters are not pleased and scramble to find a replacement for their spot. The Kinks were set to leave for Australia on the 6th for a string of dates in arena and stadium-sized venues and would open for guitarist and currently platinum-selling superstar Peter Frampton, with local band Sherbert in support. Frampton was a former member of The Herd, a band with whom The Kinks had appeared on the less-than-successful British package tour in spring 1968.

The Australasian tour continues on without The Kinks, with the following shows: November 9th Perth Entertainment Centre, Perth; 13th The Oval, Adelaide; 15th Myer Music Bowl, Melbourne; 18th Sports Ground, Sydney; 22nd Western Springs, Auckland, NZ; 25th Queen Elizabeth II Park, Christchurch, NZ. Tentative dates for Japan were to have followed into early December.

At Westdeutscher Rundfunk studios in Cologne, West Germany around this time the band lip-synch to 'Father Christmas' for the ARD TV show *Plattenküche*, broadcast November 18th. Precise date of the taping session is unknown, but it's probably done independently of the recent European tour. No horn players are present.

Ray continues to work with playwright Barrie Keeffe, and a press release later this month says their play/musical *The Poet And The Woman* is scheduled to open at the Olivier Auditorium, London, in March 1979.

Dave spends time at Konk with new engineer John Rollo. Dave is working with the same rhythm section – Ron Lawrence on bass and Nick Trevisick on drums – that he used for his solo recordings last year, which resulted in 'Trust Your Heart' from *Misfits*. Reportedly Ray planned to play rhythm guitar and piano but due to his unavailability Andy Desmond assumes that role. Tracks are reportedly cut live in the studio.

Songs probably recorded now include three new titles, all Dave originals: **'Heartbreaker'**, **'Same Old Blues'** and **'Long Lonely Road'** (the latter evidently a re-recording of the same song put on tape at Apple studios in spring 1975). They will form the first hints of what will eventually turn into Dave's first solo album, released on RCA in 1980, though ultimately none of the songs from these initial sessions are used.

Only 'Long Lonely Road' is eventually released – but only on *Fragile*, a limited-release CD in January 2001 of some of Dave's demos.

'Father Christmas' / **'Prince Of The Punks'** single is re-released in the UK on Friday 24th. The Kinks' Christmas single on Arista is given another full release, but again meets with resistance from the press. *Melody Maker*: "They tried it last year and it didn't work. The intervening year hasn't improved its quality or upped its chances." Bob Edmands in the *NME* is no fan, cleverly damning the record: "A wrister, indeed." The film clip shot for the song back in November 1977 is unearthed and partially aired on a weekend children's TV programme, *The Saturday Banana*, but fails to generate any interest.

December

On the 4th a press release announces pre-Christmas concert dates which The Kinks characterise as "back to the roots" where they'll return to the sort of venue they played in their early days. These are evidently trial dates of sorts to test the waters for the British college market, perhaps to see if the band can reconnect directly to a young audience away from the glare of London reviewers – who have lately described the band as out of date.

Friday 8th
Student Union, Manchester Polytechnic *Manchester*

Saturday 9th
Student Union, University Of Reading *Reading*

Monday 11th
University of Exeter *Exeter*

Wednesday 13th
Student Union, University of Keele *Keele, Staffs*

➔ Dave presumably continues work on his planned solo album while Ray works on the musical, with time off for the Christmas/New Year holidays.

Reportedly just after Christmas, Ray goes to see the new feature film *Superman – The Movie* based on the classic American comic strip superhero. He is immediately inspired to write a new song that emerges quickly as '(Wish I Could Fly Like) Superman'. Following the four college dates plans are put into place for The Kinks to do a full tour of colleges in January. When they ask Arista for tour support, the label wants a new single out in exchange. Once he has his inspiration, Ray moves quickly to get the new song down on tape. Initial sessions take place as early as the last few days of this year, but almost certainly immediately following New Year's Day.

1979

This was the year The Kinks delivered, the year they got everything right, and it marked the start of the band's second golden era. With new bassist Jim Rodford in place to lock them together musically, the band was tighter than it had ever been.

They had already found a new credibility through heavy metal band Van Halen and punksters The Jam, but in the spring their back-catalogue was given a further fashionable boost when another upstart band, The Pretenders, covered 'Stop Your Sobbing'. They unearthed this Ray Davies gem from The Kinks' very first album and transformed it with a classic modern sound, propelling it up the British charts.

None of this hurt The Kinks' reputation at all, and if anything the band seemed to feed off the energy of this new recognition. They were handed an opportunity to prove themselves to a totally new audience, and they did not hold back. They appeared to be bursting with creative energy and an unprecedented willingness to tour and work hard.

The Kinks had learned from the long, demoralising sessions of the last two albums and knew the importance of a strong single and fresh product. In a wise move that broke them from a stale routine, the band recorded in mid-town New York City, stripped down to a quartet and focused on making an energised, vibrant album of songs. Whether intentional or not, the record targeted and resonated with the young disaffected American stadium-rock audience. Warm-up tours of British and then American colleges also helped to connect the band to a young, eager audience.

Following the highly successful US college dates, Ray went on a writing spree. It was so productive that an intended half-live/half-studio album was rejected in favour of a full studio outing, with leftovers to spare that would form the basis of their subsequent studio album. The momentum generated by the release and immediate US chart success of Low Budget would carry them to year's end and a new peak of commercial success.

January

→ ● **RECORDING** Konk Studios *Hornsey, north London*. Sessions are held in the first few days of the new year in a rush to get a new single/EP ready.

Arista have insisted on new product if they are to even consider subsidising The Kinks' planned tour of British colleges, and Ray works under pressure to produce something quickly. He often manages to be inspired when under pressure.

Three new songs are recorded around now, all newly written and inspired by recent events, including the crippling series of strikes that are hitting Britain: **'(Wish I Could Fly Like) Superman'**, **'Low Budget'** and **'Pressure'**.

It's possible that the track 'Superman' was started during the last days of December 1978, and it is apparently written and recorded during the course of four days.

☆ Plans for Ray's musical collaboration with Barrie Keeffe seemingly end around this time.

Ray and Keeffe are of course disappointed, but they enjoy working together and attempt to find another home for their play – and almost two years later the Theatre Royal in Stratford will become seriously interested in the project.

Monday 8th

A press release announces a 16-date UK tour for January, and that The Kinks will start recording a new album following the tour.

→ Possible rehearsals around now at Konk Studios to work up new material for concerts, including '(Wish I Could Fly Like) Superman' and 'Low Budget'.

Although the single coupling these two songs will – in typical Kinks fashion – not be issued until late in the tour, the song is included in their upcoming shows.

↪ **TOUR STARTS** *Low Budget: UK Tour* (Jan 18th – Feb 2nd). **Line-up**: Ray Davies (lead vocal, guitar), Dave Davies (guitar, vocal), Mick Avory (drums), Jim Rodford (bass), Gordon Edwards (keyboards), John Beecham (trombone), Nick Newall (saxophone).

The tour is intentionally booked with continuous shows for 16 out of 17 nights in a row, in an effort to recreate the conditions under which hungry young bands play. There is a musical benefit too: it allows the band to be on top form.

Thursday 18th

Oxford Polytechnic *Oxford* 7:30pm, with Stadium Dogs
NME writer Mark Ellen is kind: "After 15 years and various

kinks'79

'experimental' phases, the Muswell Hillbillies have finally found a near perfect format. This time round it's a smoothly accessible product, conservative in the extreme yet undeniably enjoyable. Revamped for added impact in heavy metal guise, we have The Kinks as medium slick vaudeville, as hack social commentary, as ageing sentimentality, as showband rock-a-boogie."

Friday 19th

University Of Sheffield *Sheffield* 7:30pm, with Stadium Dogs
'Stop Your Sobbing' single by The Pretenders released in the UK, a cover version of The Kinks song.

The Pretenders effectively demonstrate how Ray's early songs can be recast as contemporary hits, and for a brief period in the early 1980s a personal relationship will develop between Ray and the band's leader, Chrissie Hynde.

Saturday 20th

Leicester Polytechnic *Leicester* 7:30pm, with Stadium Dogs

Sunday 21st

Empire Theatre *Liverpool* 7:30pm, with Stadium Dogs

Monday 22nd

City Hall *Newcastle Upon Tyne* 7:30pm, with Stadium Dogs

Tuesday 23rd

Odeon Cinema *Edinburgh, Scotland* 7:30pm, with Stadium Dogs
Record Mirror's reviewer chastises Ray for a disappointing show. "Nostalgia was last year's thing. If Davies could come up with some new material with the venom and conviction of his past work but relating more to the present day, there may yet be hope. If not, I'll be sorry to see so much talent going to waste."
Set-list: 'Opening', 'Sleepwalker', 'Hay Fever', 'Sunny Afternoon', 'Misfits', 'Low Budget', 'Muswell Hillbillies', 'David Watts', 'The Hard Way', 'Celluloid Heroes', 'A Gallon Of Gas', 'Trust Your Heart', 'Full Moon', 'Juke Box Music', 'Slum Kids', 'Lola', 'Life On The Road', 'Skin

(Wish I Could Fly Like) Superman single

A '(Wish I Could Fly Like) Superman' (R. DAVIES).
B 'Low Budget' (R. DAVIES).

UK release January 26th 1979 (Arista ARIST 240).
US release March 12th 1979 (Arista AS 0409).
A-side UK is without synthesiser; A-side US is with synthesiser, remixed and edited. B-side US is an edited version.
Musicians Ray Davies lead vocal, synthesiser (A remix only, B). Dave Davies electric guitar, backing vocal. Jim Rodford bass guitar, backing vocal. Mick Avory drums. Gordon Edwards piano (B).
Recorded Konk Studios *Hornsey, north London*; early January 1979; 24-track mixed to stereo.
Producer Ray Davies.
Engineer John Rollo.
Chart high UK none; US number 41.

(Wish I Could Fly Like) Superman 12-inch single

A '(Wish I Could Fly Like) Superman' (R. DAVIES).
B 'Low Budget' (R. DAVIES).

UK release January 26th 1979 (Arista ARIST 12240).
US release March 12th 1979 (Arista CP 700).
A-side is extended six-minute edit; US is synthesiser mix; UK initially without synthesiser but replaced in later pressings with synthesiser mix. Musicians and recording details, see above.

And Bone', 'Till The End Of The Day', 'All Day And All Of The Night', '(Wish I Could Fly Like) Superman'.

Wednesday 24th

Apollo Theatre *Glasgow, Scotland* 7:30pm, with Stadium Dogs

Thursday 25th

St. George's Hall *Bradford, Yorks* 7:30pm, with Stadium Dogs

Friday 26th

Apollo Theatre *Manchester* 7:30pm, with Stadium Dogs
'(Wish I Could Fly Like) Superman' / 'Low Budget' single released in the UK. The *NME* has nothing good to say about the record, and *Melody Maker* calls it "erratic".

Saturday 27th

Odeon Cinema *Birmingham*
Day off following.

Monday 29th

Student Union Dance Hall, University Of Essex *Colchester*

Tuesday 30th

Colston Hall *Bristol*

Wednesday 31st

Kingdom Room, Brunel University *Uxbridge, Middx*

February

Thursday 1st

The Dome *Brighton*

Friday 2nd – Saturday 3rd

City Hall *St Albans, Herts*
In honour of Dave's 32nd birthday on Saturday, The Kinks reportedly perform a one-off version of the Buddy Holly classic 'Peggy Sue'. Dave is a big fan of the influential singer from Lubbock, Texas, who died in a plane crash exactly 20 years ago to the day – on February 3rd 1959, "the day the music died". (St. Albans is bassist Rodford's homeground and likely a special occasion for him too, his first time in town with his new band.)

➔ INDICATES EVENT AROUND THIS TIME BUT WITH NO FIRM DATE

→ ● **RECORDING** Konk Studios *Hornsey, north London.* Dave does some sessions, almost certainly demos for his planned solo album, with just Dave, drummer Nick Trevisick and bassist Ron Lawrence.

☆ Ray too is at Konk for further work on the existing recording of **'(Wish I Could Fly Like) Superman'**, on to which he overdubs synthesiser, and then remixes the track.

☆ Recording sessions for a new Kinks LP originally scheduled for now have been delayed until mid May and moved to New York City.

☆ Ray is interviewed by Colin Larkin and Nick Ralph for independent magazine *Dark Star*, and is surprisingly candid. When asked if it angers him that the music press have been scathing of late, he replies: "No, it's happened two or three times over the years. They give you a good run and give you a hard time, then they give you a good run again." Referring to a specific weekly: "[For a while] the *NME* has been a difficult newspaper. I call it the Enemy. ... I think I'm more upset if I'm knocked in the *Melody Maker* than I am in the *NME* because I don't really ... count the *NME*." But surely *Melody Maker* panned the October 1978 Hammersmith show? "Yeah, well, that's unfortunate. I think I said that I couldn't go on after that. I said that for about ten seconds ... it's nothing really." He's then asked about the 'Father Christmas' single being ignored two years running. "Of course I get upset; it's a great record, you see. If it was a stiff I'd know it was a stiff, and if it's bad show, I know it's a bad show. I don't need a reviewer to tell me I've done a bad show. I know it." And the recent UK tour? "We should have done about 50 dates [because] when you actually confront people ... that's what it's all about, because audiences don't lie."

↻ **TOUR STARTS** *Northeast US Tour* (Feb 16th – Mar 11th). **Line-up**: Ray Davies (lead vocal, guitar), Dave Davies (guitar, vocal), Mick Avory (drums), Jim Rodford (bass), Gordon Edwards (keyboards), John Beecham (trombone), Nick Newall (saxophone). Venues are around 1,500-2,500 capacity, and many are sell-outs. Ticket prices range from $5-$7.50, usually cheaper for students. A number of new songs are in the show, probably with a live album in mind. Songs introduced on the coming US tour include: 'Sleepless Night', 'The Hard Way', 'Victoria', 'Where Have All The Good Times Gone', and '20th Century Man'. (Band travels to New York City on the 15th, with Ray at Konk Studios up to the last minute preparing the final mix of the overdubbed version of the new US single.)

Friday 16th
Haas Auditorium, Bloomsburg University of Pennsylvania *Bloomsburg, PA* 8:00pm, with TKO

Saturday 17th
Einsenhower Auditorium, Pennsylvania State University *University Park, PA* 8:00pm, with TKO
Set-list: 'Opening', 'Sleepwalker', 'Life On The Road', 'Permanent Waves', 'Where Have All The Good Times Gone', 'Lola', 'Sleepless Night', 'Misfits', 'Live Life', 'Low Budget', '(Wish I Could Fly Like) Superman', medley 'A Well Respected Man' / 'Death Of A Clown' / 'Sunny Afternoon', 'Trust Your Heart', 'You Really Got Me', 'Slum Kids', 'Alcohol', 'A Rock'n'Roll Fantasy', 'All Day And All Of The Night', medley 'Little Queenie' / 'New Orleans'.

Sunday 18th
Men's gymnasium, State University of New York at Binghamton *Binghamton, NY* 8:00pm, with TKO
Special treats tonight are impromptu versions of 'Get Back In Line' and 'David Watts'. "The band was happy and responsive, and the audience was wild," says *Pipe Dream*. "A new song 'Low Budget' became an audience effort when Davies ceded his microphone to members of the front row during the chorus. The guy knows how to work with crowds." (Two days off follow in New York City. On the 20th Ray is at Masterdisk

Studios overseeing the mastering of the new US single with Robert Ludwig.)

Wednesday 21st
Fine Arts Center Concert Hall, University of Massachusetts *Amherst, MA* 8:00pm, with TKO

Thursday 22nd
Palace Theater *Albany, NY* 8:00pm, with TKO; sponsored by State University of New York at Albany

Friday 23rd
Bailey Hall, Cornell University *Ithaca, NY* 8:00pm, with TKO
Echoing a number of other reviewers' sentiments on this tour, Dennis Conway writes in the *Cornell Sun*: "Perhaps the most poignant moment of the evening was Ray's rendition of 'A Rock'n'Roll Fantasy'. Here's a man singing to his audience about how unreal, and maybe even cowardly, it seems to be a stage performer at his age."

Saturday 24th
Laker Hall, State University of New York College at Oswego *Oswego, NY* 8:00pm, with TKO

Sunday 25th
SUCO Gymnasium, State University of New York College at Oneonta *Oneonta, NY* 7:00pm
Support band TKO is scheduled tonight but don't perform, and The Kinks end up starting very late, at 10:45pm, due to their equipment truck breaking down en route. (Day off in Syracuse following.)

Tuesday 27th
Syracuse Area Landmark Theater *Syracuse, NY* 8:00pm, with TKO; sponsored by Syracuse University

Wednesday 28th
Alumni Gymnasium, Hamilton College *Clinton, NY* 8:00pm, with TKO
"The Alumni Gym which is usually awful acoustically was rendered listenable by the thoroughly professional Showco sound system," says *The Spectator*. "Only one third of The Kinks' sound and lights were set up for the small hall. The sound was good and the band was hot."

March

Thursday 1st
Wilkins Theater For The Performing Arts, Kean College of New Jersey *Union, NJ* 8:00pm, with TKO
☆ Promotional copies of '(Wish I Could Fly Like) Superman' are issued to US radio stations.

Friday 2nd
Harrington Auditorium, Worcester Polytechnic Institute *Worcester, MA* 8:00pm, *Winter Weekend '79*, with TKO

Saturday 3rd
Barn, Rutgers University *New Brunswick, NJ* 8:00pm, with TKO
Tonight's is the first of at least two shows that are recorded by sound company Showco Inc's 16 or 24-track mobile recording unit, with engineer Brooks Taylor at the board. Probably tonight's performances of '20th Century Man', 'All Day And All Of The Night' and 'The Hard Way' will be included on next year's live album, *One For The Road*. It's

probably at this show backstage that The Kinks are photographed by Ebet Roberts, the results of which will be used for both the *Low Budget* album sleeve and the promotional campaign that accompanies it.

Sunday 4th
Gymnasium, Fairleigh Dickinson University: Florham-Madison Campus *Madison, NJ* 8:00pm, with TKO
Day off in New York City following.

Tuesday 6th
Lowell Memorial Auditorium *Lowell, MA* 8:00pm, with TKO; sponsored by University of Lowell
This show is also recorded by Showco Inc. Probably used on next year's *One For The Road* are tonight's performances of 'Where Have All The Good Times Gone' and 'You Really Got Me'. Reportedly, Dave and Avory almost come to blows during this show.

Wednesday 7th
Philips Memorial Auditorium, West Chester State College *West Chester, PA* 8:00pm, with TKO
Travel day following.

Friday 9th
King Concert Hall, Rockefeller Art Center, State University of New York College at Fredonia *Fredonia, NY* 8:00pm, with TKO

Saturday 10th
Kuhl Gymnasium, State University of New York College at Geneseo *Geneseo, NY* 8:00pm, with TKO
"Beyond a shadow of a doubt, The Kinks conquered our campus … with one of the most stunning shows I've seen them produce," writes Russ Donahue in *Lamron*. "In place of the old swaggering (and more often than not, drunken) Ray Davies, who sang wishfully about being a star, was Ray Davies: Star and Survivor."
Set-list: 'Opening', 'Sleepwalker', 'Life On The Road', 'Where Have All The Good Times Gone', 'Geneseo Way' (improvisation), 'Hay Fever', 'Lola', 'Celluloid Heroes', 'Low Budget', '(Wish I Could Fly Like) Superman', 'Trust Your Heart', 'You Really Got Me', 'Batman Theme', 'Slum Kids', 'A Rock'n' Roll Fantasy', 'All Day And All Of The Night', 'The Hard Way', 'Ducks On The Wall', 'Victoria', 'Twist And Shout'.

Sunday 11th
Gymnasium, Bergen Community College *Paramus, NJ* 8:00pm, with TKO

Monday 12th
The band returns to London. This tour marks trombonist John Beecham's last performances with The Kinks, who decide in July to have only Nick Newall as their live horn player. Thus comes to an end Beecham's seven years of continuous work with the band.
'(Wish I Could Fly Like) Superman' / **'Low Budget'** single released in the US. With classic Kinks timing, it hits the shops the day the band goes home. *Trouser Press* says: "Leave it to The Kinks. Misfits they may be, but here they tackle disco and come away with more than a shred of dignity. And 'Low Budget' isn't nothin' to sneeze at – raunchier still. … Ray's vocal is so raw and hoarse it sounds like Tom Robinson imitating him. Ray's rarely been funnier nor Dave's guitar tougher-sounding."

→ ● **RECORDING** Blue Rock Studios *New York, NY*. In the city, possibly at this studio, Ray is reviewing live tapes from the recent concert recordings. Reportedly a total of four shows have been recorded for potential use on the upcoming LP, which until recently has

been seen as half live, half new studio recordings. But Ray apparently now assembles a full album's worth of recordings from the four shows for future consideration.
☆ Dave is likely working on solo recordings, probably in demo form.

April

Dave is reportedly visiting both Los Angeles and New York City at this time, shopping solo tapes for a record deal. Ray stays in New York, writing material for a new LP. In a contemporary interview he refers to three songs written at the time, cited as 'Television', 'Radio' and 'Oil' – which seem more like subjects than titles. Only one will end up on the forthcoming album: 'Oil' is probably 'A Gallon Of Gas' on *Low Budget*. 'Television' is almost certainly 'Give The People What They Want', recorded in an early version for *Low Budget* but later re-recorded and used as the title track for a subsequent studio album. Ray says later that it is about TV programmers intentionally aiming at the lowest common denominator in audiences – an irony that many will misunderstand when he names a Kinks album with the song's title. 'Radio' is possibly an early reference to the later song 'Around The Dial'.

May

Ray makes a conscious effort to remove himself and the band from the comfortable confines of their own London studio. Aiming to conjure up the experience of NY living, the band stays at a shabby hotel in New York City (possibly the Wellington). Ray organises a week-long rehearsal schedule to learn the new batch of songs he's written in the city over the past few months.

Edwards has grown unhappy with the lack of musical contribution he's made to the band, and he simply fails to show up for the trip. The Kinks likewise have been unhappy of late with Edwards; the no-show prompts his firing and removal from the payroll. (Edwards dies at age 56 in London in March 2003.) Rather than immediately seeking a replacement, Dave reportedly coaxes Ray into handling the keyboard chores for the rehearsals and sessions, which forces the band to become an even tighter unit. The hiring of a new keyboard player will be dealt with after the recording sessions.

During the week of the 14th to the 19th The Kinks are rehearsing at Daily Planet Studios, New York City. Ray has evidently had a burst of creative productivity and comes ready with up to 16 new songs, all of which are worked into shape for recording.

From the 20th for ten days they move to The Power Station (Studio 2) in the city, and it seems at least 15 new songs are attempted. Completed recordings are made of **'Attitude'**, **'National Health'**, **'In A Space'**, **'A Little Bit Of Emotion'**, **'Misery'**, **'Moving Pictures'**, **'Catch Me Now I'm Falling'** and **'A Gallon Of Gas'**, all of which will end up on the resulting *Low Budget* album.

Also recorded at this time are **'Destroyer'** and **'Give The People What They Want'**, both of which will be held back, and the latter re-arranged for concert play in 1980 and re-recorded in 1981 at Konk. Two further songs – **'Hidden Qualities'** and **'Laugh At The World'** – are completed but never issued. Another song, **'Massive Reductions'**, will be issued as a B-side to the 1981 'Better Things' single, only to be re-recorded in 1984 for the *Word Of Mouth* LP. **'The Optimist'** is reportedly attempted but not finished. Ray says later that an early version of 1981's **'Better Things'** is first attempted at this time. It is also reported that an early unfinished version of **'Yo-Yo'**, later redone for 1981's *Give The People What They Want* LP, is first attempted but scrapped now.

→ INDICATES EVENT AROUND THIS TIME BUT WITH NO FIRM DATE

The 78/79 band, backstage in New Jersey, March 11th 1979: (L-R) Dave Davies, Jim Rodford, Ray Davies, Mick Avory, Gordon Edwards.

kinks'79

June

Early in the month work is evidently shifted to Blue Rock Studios in New York City as vocals are recorded for the new LP, while mixing of the tracks is likely done back at the Power Station.

On the 15th Ray is at Masterdisk Studios to master an early version of the new album with a trial running order: at this point it includes both 'Destroyer' (or 'Massive Reductions') and 'Give The People What They Want' in place of 'Attitude' and 'National Health'. The scheduled release date is June 27th (with the US tour starting on July 6th) but this will be pushed into early July. 'Destroyer' is dropped because it's not possible to achieve a satisfactory mix (it will be revived for the next studio LP).

Ray evidently returns to Konk in London around the middle of the month where work is done on two songs, **'National Health'** and **'Attitude'**, both of which appear in the album's next proposed running order. Ray then goes back to Masterdisk to finalise tapes for the album. On the 22nd at the Power Station final mixes are done for **'Catch Me Now I'm Falling'** and **'In A Space'**, and three days later Ray is again at Masterdisk with Robert Ludwig to master the new and final running order for the album as it will be released. But this is not before he decides to remix 'Attitude' and slightly re-edit 'Catch Me Now' and 'A Gallon Of Gas'. Shortly afterwards Ray returns to London and the search for a new keyboard player.

On the 30th, at Konk in London, Ian Gibbons auditions at a session where Avory is dubbing congas and Dave playing acoustic guitar. Gibbons has been on tour with The Records for all of June, finishing up with two dates at the Marquee club in central London on June 28th and 29th. He does some background singing and keyboard playing at this session; afterwards he is given a tape to learn a couple of songs and asked to come back the next day.

July

Sunday 1st – Wednesday 4th

It is probably on Sunday that Ian Gibbons returns to Konk and begins rehearsing with The Kinks over the next few days. Ray is still tweaking the mixes and edits on **'Attitude'**, **'Catch Me Now I'm Falling'** and **'A Gallon Of Gas'**.

➭ **TOUR STARTS** *Low Budget: US Tour: 1st leg* (Jul 11th – Aug 19th). **Line-up:** Ray Davies (lead vocal, guitar), Dave Davies (guitar, vocal), Mick Avory (drums), Jim Rodford (bass), Ian Gibbons (keyboards), Nick Newall (saxophone, second keyboard, congas). Some shows towards the end of the tour are taped for a double live album planned for release early next year. Ticket prices range from $6-$10. Venue sizes are generally 2,000-5,000 capacity, but in the band's stronger areas 9,000-12,000. Arista launches a major advertising and promotional campaign behind the new album, with multiple full-page ads in the industry trade magazines and a heavy push to radio stations, which pick up on the album quickly. Sales are strong from the outset. As the band is for once perfectly timed to "be in your town" to back it up, the album will reach the edge of the US top ten, a first for The Kinks with an album of original new material.

Thursday 5th

Travel to New York City, staying at the Warwick Hotel. Ray finally has all the pieces together for the new LP, and a final version is mastered and sent off for pressing. It is pressed literally over the weekend, ready to ship the following week – which, almost unheard of, will be in time for the tour. The campaign is so well co-ordinated that an advance copy of the album arrives at *Billboard* in time for a review to appear in the issue on sale Monday 9th. Album covers have been readied, initially without song title information printed on the back to allow for inevitable last-minute changes.

Friday 6th – Saturday 7th

Rehearsals for the tour take place at Daily Planet Studios in New York City. New keyboard player Ian Gibbons has a lot of material to learn quickly. Besides a standard set he must also know some other songs so he is ready for off-the-cuff and back-catalogue numbers that pop up over the course of a typical evening. (Travel day to Dallas following.)

Monday 9th – Tuesday 10th

The band continues to rehearse, now in Dallas, Texas.

Tuesday 10th

Low Budget album released in the US. The press largely applauds The Kinks' return to an energetic sounding album. David Fricke in *Rolling Stone* writes: "There is no energy crisis on *Low Budget*, the hardest rocking Kinks record in recent memory. ... The Kinks haven't mounted this kind of rock'n'roll attack since 'Lola'. *Low Budget* may not be the best of their 20-odd albums released in America, but it's not bad either." Philip Bashe in *Good Times* says: "Strangely, *Low Budget* is an encouraging album. 'Times are tough, but we'll all survive,' [Ray] tells us right away. His own band is living proof of that statement, and with the addition of Jim Rodford they should remain a vital unit for years to come. Their playing on this record is heartier than ever, and Ray himself is no longer coy in his delivery; most of the LP's 11 tunes have him shouting and barking but never sermonizing." And Mark Fleischmann in *Trouser Press*: "Flaws aside, it's still a great album,

Low Budget album

A1 'Attitude' (R. DAVIES).
A2 'Catch Me Now I'm Falling' (R. DAVIES).
A3 'Pressure' (R. DAVIES).
A4 'National Health' (R. DAVIES).
A5 '(Wish I Could Fly Like) Superman' (R. DAVIES).
B1 'Low Budget' (R. DAVIES).
B2 'In A Space' (R. DAVIES).
B3 'Little Bit Of Emotion' (R. DAVIES).
B4 'A Gallon Of Gas' (R. DAVIES).
B5 'Moving Pictures' (R. DAVIES).

US release July 10th 1979 (Arista AB 4240).
UK release September 7th 1979 (Arista SPART 1099).
Musicians Ray Davies lead vocal, acoustic guitar, electric guitar, piano, synthesiser, harmonica (B2). Dave Davies electric guitar, harmony lead vocal (B2), backing vocal. Jim Rodford bass guitar, backing vocal. Mick Avory drums. Nick Newall saxophone (A3, B4).
Recorded The Power Station *New York, NY*, May 20th-30th 1979; Blue Rock Studios *New York, NY*, June 1979; Konk Studios *Hornsey, north London*, June 1979; 24-track mixed to stereo.
Producer Ray Davies.
Engineer John Rollo.
Chart high UK none; US number 11.

certainly one of the year's best so far. … By my own (suspect) count this is Kinks album number 20, not counting compilations. I can't wait for the next 20."

Wednesday 11th – Thursday 12th
The Palladium *Dallas, TX* 8:00 & 11:00pm, with Herman Brood & His Wild Romance
The scheduled 11:00pm show on the 12th is cancelled earlier in the day for fear of over-taxing Ray's voice and rescheduled for September 11th at McFarlin Auditorium. Ticket holders are refunded and given free tickets for the rescheduled show. "Two years ago I saw The Kinks at Will Rogers Auditorium and during that performance they seemed moribund," writes Pete Oppel of the *Dallas Morning News*. "At the end of the Palladium show, I realized what had transformed the performance. At that concert two years ago Davies was more interested in displaying and acting out all the characters he had created through the years on the various concept albums. Not so Thursday night. His only intention for this particular evening was to sing and play straightahead rock'n'roll. And when the band roared through something like 'You Really Got Me', I realized that The Kinks may, in fact, have been the world's first punk rock band. … There was nothing low budget about this show."

Friday 13th
Manor Downs *Manor, TX* 8:00pm, with Herman Brood & His Wild Romance

Saturday 14th
Music Hall *Houston, TX* 8:00pm, with Herman Brood & His Wild Romance
Set-list: 'Sleepwalker', 'Life On The Road', 'Permanent Waves', 'Misfits', 'Low Budget', '(Wish I Could Fly Like) Superman', 'National Health', 'Lola', 'A Gallon Of Gas', 'Muswell Hillbilly', medley 'A Well Respected Man' / 'Death Of A Clown' / 'Sunny Afternoon', 'You Really Got Me', 'The Hard Way', 'Alcohol', 'Celluloid Heroes', 'All Day And All Of The Night', 'Pressure', 'Twist And Shout'.

Sunday 15th
Municipal Auditorium *New Orleans, LA* 8:00pm, with Herman Brood & His Wild Romance
Travel day following.

Tuesday 17th
Birmingham-Jefferson County Civic Center Concert Hall *Birmingham, AL* 8:00pm, with Herman Brood & His Wild Romance

Wednesday 18th
War Memorial Auditorium *Nashville, TN* 8:00pm, with Herman Brood & His Wild Romance
Travel day following.

Friday 20th – Saturday 21st
Fox Theatre *Atlanta, GA* 8:00pm, with Herman Brood & His Wild Romance
Sell outs both nights, each with 4,000 attending. "Like fine wine," says the *Atlanta Constitution*, "The Kinks seem to get better and better the longer they go on." (Travel day to New York City follows, and then a day off.)

Tuesday 24th – Wednesday 25th
Convention Hall *Asbury Park, NJ* 8:00pm, with Herman Brood & His Wild Romance
Dave is interviewed by Elliot Cohen for *Good Times* and talks about a

solo album that he says he has now finished, with drummer Nick Trevisick and bassist Ron Lawrence, and that it's currently being considered by three different record labels. He also mentions the planned live album.
"The Kinks always have a live album in the works," says Dave. "I don't know yet if we're going to release it. Some of it's very good, some of it's bloody horrible. … A lot of people who make live albums now, they never turn out [to have been recorded] live anyway. Nowadays you can keep all the shouting and screaming in, and do everything else again in the studio." (Day off in New York City following.)

Friday 27th
Nassau Veterans Memorial Coliseum *Uniondale, NY* 8:00pm, with The Ian Hunter Band
Nearly 9,500 attend in this 12,000-capacity hall. "There aren't many times when attending a rock concert can be considered a privilege," says *Record World*, "but The Kinks' show at the Nassau Coliseum was one of those rare events. The Kinks are once again able to communicate the wild, electric spirit of rock'n'roll that they first generated in 1963. The enthusiasm that The Kinks put into these songs and the whole evening made one forget the countless years of disappointment and frustration when the group did not live up to expectation."

Saturday 28th
The Spectrum *Philadelphia, PA* 8:00pm, with The Ian Hunter Band
Attended by 16,000-plus. Ray is interviewed by Ed Sciaky, broadcast on Philadelphia radio WIOQ-FM and later released on the promotional LP *The Low Budget Interview*.

Sunday 29th
New Haven Veterans Memorial Coliseum *New Haven, CT* 7:30pm, with The Ian Hunter Band
This show is recorded for the planned live LP, but no material from it will be used. (Day off in New York City following.)

Tuesday 31st
Poughkeepsie Civic Center *Poughkeepsie, NY* 8:00pm, with Herman Brood & His Wild Romance
Day off following.

August

Thursday 2nd
Glens Falls Civic Center *Glens Falls, NY* 8:00pm, with The Ian Hunter Band
Attended by 3,000 at this 5,600-capacity hall.

Friday 3rd
Cumberland County Civic Center *Portland, ME* 8:00pm, with The Ian Hunter Band

Saturday 4th
Cape Cod Coliseum *South Yarmouth, MA* 8:00pm, with Herman Brood & His Wild Romance
A 7,200-capacity sell-out.

Sunday 5th
Music Inn *Lenox, MA* 4:30pm, with The Ian Hunter Band
The Kinks are photographed in concert by Lauren Recht and some of the shots are later used for the *One For The Road* album sleeve. (Travel day following.)

kinks'79

Tuesday 7th
Kleinhans Music Hall *Buffalo, NY* 8:00pm, with The Ian Hunter Band
Sell out. (Travel day following.)
'A Gallon Of Gas' / 'Low Budget' single released in the US this week. It doesn't click on the charts.

Thursday 9th
Music Hall *Cleveland, OH* 8:00pm, with Herman Brood & His Wild Romance
"Much of the sold-out crowd probably came on a nostalgia trip," says the *Cleveland Scene*. "But more than 3,000 fans returned to their

A Gallon Of Gas single

A **'A Gallon Of Gas'** (R. DAVIES).
B **'Low Budget'** (R. DAVIES).
A is atypically in extended form from album version

US release August 7th 1979 (Arista AS 0448).
Musicians and recording details as *Low Budget* album (see July 10th).
Chart high US none.

homes as devout Kinks fans …. Songs from the past spurred happy memories; songs from the group's new album *Low Budget* spurred respect. Gauging the reaction of the fans at this show I'd have to say The Kinks have never been stronger."

Friday 10th
Cobo Arena *Detroit, MI* 8:00pm, with The Ian Hunter Band
Tonight 10,655 attend at this 12,359-capacity venue.

Saturday 11th
Uptown Theater *Chicago, IL* 8:00pm, with Herman Brood & His Wild Romance

Sunday 12th
MECCA-Milwaukee Auditorium *Milwaukee, WI* 8:00pm, with Herman Brood & His Wild Romance
Travel day following with two days off in Los Angeles.

Thursday 16th – Sunday 19th
Universal Amphitheatre *Universal City, CA* 8:00pm, with Herman Brood & His Wild Romance
Set-list (16th): 'Sleepwalker', 'Where Have All The Good Times Gone', 'Life On The Road', 'Permanent Waves', medley 'A Well Respected Man' / 'Death Of A Clown' / 'Sunny Afternoon', 'Misfits', 'I'm On An Island' (extract), 'Lola', 'Low Budget', '(Wish I Could Fly Like) Superman', 'Catch Me Now I'm Falling', 'You Really Got Me', 'A Gallon Of Gas', 'Alcohol', 'Celluloid Heroes', 'All Day And All Of The Night', 'Pressure', 'Twist And Shout', 'The Hard Way', 'Victoria', 'Live Life', medley 'Little Queenie' / 'New Orleans'.
All these LA shows are recorded for the planned live album, but no material is ultimately used for the finally released version, *One For The Road*. Some material from these shows is planned for an early version briefly known as *Double Life*, but this is dropped when more live songs are recorded the following spring. (The band now travels back to London as the first leg of the tour is finished, with a seven-day break in London.)

Monday 27th
Low Budget album peaks at number 11 in the US charts.

☛ **TOUR STARTS** *Low Budget: US Tour: 2nd leg* (Aug 29th – Sep 23rd). **Line-up**: Ray Davies (lead vocal, guitar), Dave Davies (guitar, vocal), Mick Avory (drums), Jim Rodford (bass), Ian Gibbons (keyboards), Nick Newall (saxophone, second keyboard, congas). Band travels to Seattle on the 28th, while Ray is in New York City at Sterling Sound Studios where the next single, 'Catch Me Now I'm Falling', is edited and mastered for release.

Wednesday 29th
Paramount Northwest Theatre *Seattle, WA* 8:00pm, with The Heaters
"A classic performance (and then some) from one of the remaining threesome of 1960s British rock giants," says the *Seattle Post-Intelligencer*. "They made the evening matter and appeared to have a wonderful time doing it. The show was in turn, and sometimes simultaneously, funny, moving, exciting, silly, important, surprising, traditional, personal, and powerful. The performance made the audience forget how limited rock'n'roll is supposed to be and remember how great it can make you feel."

Thursday 30th
Paramount Theater *Portland, OR* 8:00pm, with Herman Brood & His Wild Romance
This show and yesterday's are sell-outs. (Travel day following.)

September

Saturday 1st
San Francisco Civic Auditorium *San Francisco, CA* 8:00pm, with Herman Brood & His Wild Romance
A sell-out with 6,837 attending. The following two shows are also sell-outs.

Sunday 2nd
Santa Barbara County Bowl *Santa Barbara, CA* 8:00pm, with Herman Brood & His Wild Romance

Monday 3rd
Open Air Theater San Diego State University *San Diego, CA* 8:00pm, with Herman Brood & His Wild Romance
Three days off in Los Angeles follow.

Wednesday 5th
'Catch Me Now I'm Falling' / 'Low Budget' single released in the US, probably today. Released quickly after 'A Gallon Of Gas', this too fails to follow the success of '(Wish I Could Fly Like) Superman'.

Friday 7th
Tucson Community Center Theater *Tucson, AZ* 8:00pm, with Herman Brood & His Wild Romance
Tonight's show and tomorrow's are first-time performances for The Kinks in these Southwest cities as the band continues to expand its fan base. *The Arizona Daily Star* welcomes them: "They put on an act so classy it made performances from legions of better-paid rock bands pale."
Low Budget album released in the UK. The *NME* this time rebounds with praise, as Charles Shaar Murray writes: "Ray Davies is writing great songs again. We must repeat: the first great Kinks album in eight years. To go even further: *Low Budget* is actually worth spending money on, even in these El Skinto times. A miracle yet." *Melody*

Catch Me Now I'm Falling single

A 'Catch Me Now I'm Falling' (R. DAVIES).
B 'Low Budget' (R. DAVIES).
A-side is an edit of the album version.

US release September (probably 5th) 1979 (Arista AS 0458).
Musicians and recording details as *Low Budget* album (see July 10th).
Chart high US none.

Maker: "The barely subliminal message may be about the lowering of one's standards, but my impression is that The Kinks have perceptibly raised theirs."

Saturday 8th
Johnson Gymnasium, University Of New Mexico *Albuquerque, NM* 8:00pm, with Herman Brood & His Wild Romance

Sunday 9th
Red Rocks Amphitheatre *Morrison, CO* 8:00pm, with Moon Martin
Travel day following.

Tuesday 11th
McFarlin Memorial Auditorium, Southern Methodist University *Dallas, TX* 8:00pm, with The Bugs Henderson Group featuring Marc Benno
Dallas Morning News: "A perfect setting for rock'n'roll: a smoke-filled auditorium, rather small by today's standards; an audience that spent most of the evening on its feet; and a band that was hot."

Wednesday 12th
Old Lady Of Brady Auditorium *Tulsa, OK* 8:00pm, with The Bugs Henderson Group featuring Marc Benno
Travel day following, and at the Sterling Sound studio in New York City the promotional 12-inch record titled *The Low Budget Interview* is mastered.

Friday 14th
Memorial Hall *Kansas City, MO* 8:00pm, with John Cougar & The Zone

Saturday 15th
Northrup Memorial Auditorium, University of Minnesota *Minneapolis, MN* 8:00pm, with John Cougar & The Zone
This 5,000-capacity hall and last night's show are both sell-outs.

Sunday 16th
Dane County Memorial Coliseum *Madison, WI* 8:00pm, with John Cougar & The Zone

Monday 17th
Western Hall, Western Illinois University *Macomb, IL* 8:00pm, with John Cougar & The Zone
Western Courier: "This band does more than any other I've seen to get the audience involved in the show. … They just came on stage and played their music with an enthusiasm that ran through the crowd like a hot current." (Travel day following.)

Wednesday 19th
Music Hall *Cincinnati, OH* 8:00pm, with John Cougar & The Zone

Friday 21st
McDonough Arena, Georgetown University *Washington, DC* 8:00pm, with John Cougar & The Zone

Saturday 22nd
Esby Gymnasium, Glassboro State College *Glassboro, NJ* 8:00pm, with John Cougar & The Zone
☆ Perhaps owing to his favourable review of the *Low Budget* album in the formerly hostile *NME*, journalist Charles Shaar Murray is invited to accompany The Kinks on the final two dates on their wildly successful American tour. This might allow the British press to better understand the nature of The Kinks' huge popularity there.
Ray speaks again of the transition from the RCA to the Arista period. "When we were doing *Soap Opera* and *Preservation*, judged on the level of a Yes or Genesis spectacular or an Elton John spectacular those shows were amateurish and bad, but I made those statements in the simplest and most direct way I could. Now I feel liberated, and that's why the new album sounds more positive," Ray continues. "I was liberated from … everything I had done before. I just shed the burden. I shed my 'Waterloo Sunset' and 'Sunny Afternoon's and realised that I was a writer … and that writers can only keep going on new ideas. It's going back to what we were when we started. … We know you can hit a riff and you can play an offbeat and I can sing in a limited sort of way and write something around that and use the materials that are there. That's what we're doing, and that's why I think the album's worked."

Sunday 23rd
Providence Civic Center *Providence, RI* 8:00pm, with John Cougar & The Zone
Tonight's show is recorded and videotaped. Recorded are 'Lola', 'Misfits', 'Low Budget', 'Pressure', 'Catch Me Now I'm Falling', and these are possibly the versions that will be released on the double live album *One For The Road*. The show is videotaped tonight using three cameras, with probably a rough cut done live. The resulting commercial video, also called *One For The Road*, will be released next year by Time/Life Video, directed by Ken O'Neill for John Roseman Productions. Songs edited out of the video are 'Sleepwalker', 'Life On The Road', 'Misfits', 'A Gallon Of Gas', 'Twist And Shout' and 'Live Life'. (Travel day following: band members to London; Ray to New York City.)
Set-list: 'Opening', 'Sleepwalker', 'Life On The Road', 'Where Have All The Good Times Gone', 'Lola', 'Misfits', 'Low Budget', '(Wish I Could Fly Like) Superman', 'Attitude', 'You Really Got Me', 'A Gallon Of Gas', 'The Hard Way', 'Celluloid Heroes', 'All Day And All Of The Night', 'Pressure', 'Twist And Shout', 'Catch Me Now I'm Falling', 'Live Life', 'Victoria'.

Monday 24th
In New York City, Ray and director/editor Ken O'Neill finalise the multiple-camera footage for the Time/Life video. This condenses the show down from the three camera shots into a single continuous tape that can also be edited for length and song arrangement at a later time. Ray says later the work was completed in one day-long session. A short edit is assembled for use as a promotional aid to find broadcasters in Europe.

➔ At Konk Studios, Dave is rehearsing solo tracks for recording.

Friday 28th
'Moving Pictures' / 'In A Space' single released in the UK. *Melody Maker*: "An amiable, proficient shuffle, but the lyrics … hardly approach the timeless elliptical acuity of 1960s material like 'Fancy' or 'Wonder Boy'."

October

→ ● **RECORDING** Konk Studios *Hornsey, north London.* Reportedly Dave records an entire album's worth of material during sessions across ten days at the start of the month, including some songs that will be re-recorded early in 1980. He is again backed by the rhythm section of Nick Trevisick (drums) and Ron Lawrence (bass guitar). Probably recorded at this time are '**Where Do You Come From**', '**Move Over**'

Moving Pictures single

A '**Moving Pictures**' (R. DAVIES).
B '**In A Space**' (R. DAVIES).

UK release September 28th 1979 (Arista ARIST 300).
Musicians and recording details as *Low Budget* album (see July 10th).
Chart high UK none.

---

and '**See The Beast Run**' (which will be released next year on Dave's solo album). Two further songs, '**Heartbreaker**' and '**Within Each Day**', will remain unreleased.

Sunday 14th
● **RECORDING** Regent Sound Studios *central London.* Ray is probably mixing live tapes from the recent concerts.

Monday 15th
Ray is in Stockholm for the day where he does advance press for the upcoming concert.

Tuesday 16th
● **RECORDING** Regent Sound Studios *central London.* Ray is again probably mixing live tapes, with Peter Frank, including takes of 'All Day And All Of The Night', 'Low Budget', 'Lola', 'Superman', 'Attitude', 'A Gallon Of Gas', 'You Really Got Me', 'Catch Me Now I'm Falling', 'Pressure'. Concert sources unknown; possibly from Providence, RI.

Friday 19th
Ray flies ahead to Copenhagen to do advance press and media duties to promote the upcoming show there.

➡ **TOUR STARTS** *Low Budget: European Tour* (Oct 20th – Nov 19th). **Line-up**: Ray Davies (lead vocal, guitar), Dave Davies (guitar, vocal), Mick Avory (drums), Jim Rodford (bass), Ian Gibbons (keyboards), Nick Newall (saxophone, second keyboard, congas). Following the pattern set this time last year, The Kinks begin what will for the next few years be a regular tour of Europe. Prompted by criticism that the band was pigeonholed as a nostalgia act by some reviewers on last year's European tour, the standard set-list now cuts down the 1960s hits and concentrates on new material, with a large dose from the *Low Budget* album. Venues are largely in the 1,000-2,000 capacity with some larger exceptions, such as a 6,000-capacity hall in Paris.

Saturday 20th
Tivoli Koncertsal, Tivoli Gardens *Copenhagen, Denmark*
Set-list: 'Sleepwalker', 'Life On The Road', 'Where Have All The Good Times Gone', 'Lola', 'Misfits', 'Low Budget', '(Wish I Could Fly Like) Superman', 'A Gallon Of Gas', 'You Really Got Me', 'Celluloid Heroes', 'Catch Me Now I'm Falling', 'All Day And All Of The Night', 'Pressure', 'Twist And Shout', 'New Orleans', 'Attitude', 'Live Life'.

Sunday 21st
Chateau Neuf *Oslo, Norway* 8:00pm, with magician Jan Krosby

Monday 22nd
Konserthuset *Gothenburg, Sweden* 8:00pm, with local troubadour
In an interview with Jan-Olov Andersson for *Aftonbladet*, Ray reiterates the philosophy for this tour. "We have toured a lot in the States lately," he says. "The audience there wants to hear the new songs. Therefore we will also, during our European tour, only play songs from our last three LPs to try to convince the audience that we still make good music. Right now it feels as if I could play rock for at least another 15 years." He is also candid about some of the RCA records. "I'm not too pleased with our concept albums. Sometimes I tried to describe English society, sometimes English society the way I wanted it to be. Very often it ended up somewhere in between."

Tuesday 23rd
Konserthuset *Stockholm, Sweden*
Travel day following.

Thursday 25th
Audimax *Hamburg, West Germany* with Kanyon

Friday 26th
Westfallenhalle *Dortmund, West Germany* 8:00pm, with Kanyon

Saturday 27th
Neue Welt *Berlin, West Germany* with Kanyon
Day off in Berlin following.

Monday 29th
Stadthalle *Bremen, West Germany* with Kanyon

Tuesday 30th
Niedersachsenhalle *Hanover, West Germany* with Kanyon

Wednesday 31st
Jahrhunderthalle *Frankfurt, West Germany* with Kanyon
"Two-thousand fans were left electrified by The Kinks' performance after this concert," says the *Frankfurter Nachtausgabe.* "The Kinks had total control over the audience. What a show, with all these Kinks classics as well as new songs from *Low Budget.* The encore of 30 minutes was definitely not enough for the fans, who kept shouting for more." (Travel day following.)

November

Friday 2nd
Circus Krone Bau *Munich, West Germany* with Kanyon

Saturday 3rd
Sporthalle *Crailsheim, West Germany* with Kanyon

Sunday 4th
Philipshalle *Düsseldorf, West Germany* 8:00pm, with Kanyon

Monday 5th
Rosengarten *Mannheim, West Germany* with Kanyon
Travel day following.
☆ Back home, a press release says the planned UK tour is cancelled.

Wednesday 7th
Konzerthaus *Vienna, Austria*

Thursday 8th
Unknown venue *Klagenfurt, Austria*

Friday 9th
Kammersaal *Graz, Austria* 8:00pm
Travel day following.

Sunday 11th
Volkhaus *Zürich, Switzerland* 8:30pm, with Chicken Fisher &
John Brack
Probably at least three or even four songs are recorded tonight that end
up on *One For The Road*: 'Celluloid Heroes', '(Wish I Could Fly Like)
Superman', 'Attitude', and possibly 'Victoria'. Recording is by Mobile I
Recording Unit, engineered by Barry Ainsworth. The opening act fills in
at the last moment after the scheduled band Kanyon is held at the Swiss
border. "No comparison to last year's concert at the same place," says
Tagesanzeiger. "The band played with an incredible power that nobody
in the sold-out venue was expecting, with a clever mix of Kinks classics
and the best songs from their new album *Low Budget*. Even the punks
in the front row couldn't believe their eyes." (Travel day following.)

Tuesday 13th
Stadthalle *Offenbach, West Germany* with Kanyon
Travel day following.

Thursday 15th
Concertgebouw *Amsterdam, Netherlands* 8:15pm, with
Michael Robinson

Friday 16th
Muziekcentrum Vredenburg *Utrecht, Netherlands* 8:15pm,
with Michael Robinson

Saturday 17th
Vorst Nationaal *Brussels, Belgium*
Travel day following.

Monday 19th
Pavilion *Paris, France* 8:00pm, with Edith Nylon
This concert is also recorded by Mobile I Recording Unit with engineer
Barry Ainsworth, potentially for the proposed live LP. Ultimately no
material from this show is used, though tracks from here will briefly be
intended for use on the planned but unreleased *Double Life* version (see
August 16th-19th). (Travel day home to London follows as tour ends.)
Set-list: 'Sleepwalker', 'Till The End Of The Day', 'Where Have All
The Good Times Gone', 'Lola', 'Misfits', 'Low Budget', '(Wish I Could
Fly Like) Superman', 'You Really Got Me', 'A Gallon Of Gas',
'Celluloid Heroes', medley 'A Well Respected Man' / 'Death Of A
Clown' / 'Sunny Afternoon', 'All Day And All Of The Night', 'Pressure',
'Twist And Shout', 'Get Back In Line', 'A Rock'n'Roll Fantasy',
'Victoria', 'Attitude'.
● **RECORDING** Konk Studios *Hornsey, north London*. Probably
around now Ray reviews live tapes for potential release. As there will be
evidence of significant re-recording on the final product, overdubs by
the band are done around this time.
☆ As a sign of the extent of The Kinks' resurgence, some of the early

Pye albums are reissued by PRT, the company that recently bought the
Pye catalogue. For now the first four LPs are reissued in their original
form, allowing a new generation of British fans to discover the band's
formative recordings.
☆ The UK leg of the *Low Budget* tour, originally planned to run from
November 22nd to December 5th, has been cancelled.

Friday 30th
'Pressure' / 'National Health' single released in the UK. *Melody
Maker*: "Pressure has been whipped off the album, and it works well as
a single. Rowdy, rousing and instantly accessible, it sounds as if Ray
Davies might have jotted it down after heavy exposure to The Clash and
Ramones. Go on – give 'em a hit." They do not.

Pressure single

A **'Pressure'** (R. DAVIES).
B **'National Health'** (R. DAVIES).

UK release November 30th 1979 (Arista ARIST 321).
Musicians and recording details as *Low Budget* album (see July
10th).
Chart high UK none.

December

Dave narrows down the three interested parties and signs a solo
recording contract with RCA in New York City this month.
At Konk in London, Ray does the final mixing of the live-album
tracks, scheduled for February release. Six of the "final" choices will not
eventually make it: 'Sleepwalker', medley 'A Well Respected Man' /
'Death Of A Clown' / 'Sunny Afternoon', 'A Rock'n'Roll Fantasy', 'Slum
Kids', 'A Gallon Of Gas', 'Live Life', 'Till The End Of The Day' (non-
reggae arrangement), from shows recorded March 3rd-6th, August
16th-19th, and November 11th.

kinks'80

1980

The Kinks were on a roll. Buoyed by the momentum of commercial success that at last came their way in the US, much of the year was focused on the band. But while Ray was consumed with the preparation of an ambitious double live album and accompanying video, Dave surprised everyone and methodically chipped away at recording his first commercially available solo album. It was a personal, professional and commercial success for him, and the year turned into a win-win combination for both The Kinks and Dave Davies.

The long-delayed double live album was eventually issued mid-year and raced up the US charts in a similar fashion to last year's Low Budget. A major cross-country tour of the States even included some larger arena-sized venues, helping the band secure a solid new fan-base.

While much emphasis was still focused on the US, the now standard European trek in the autumn was also successful. There was however no major tour of the homeland, instead just a few key shows and a handful of dates at year's end that were well attended and positively received by fans. But the UK critics were largely suspicious of the band's arena success in the US, and British airplay and chart success were non-existent.

January

At the start of the month Ray is making the final song selection of live tracks and mixing them for the proposed *Double Life* album. He decides to record more songs, delaying and rearranging upcoming work. The album, scheduled for February 6th, is delayed until April and then June, and the accompanying tour due to start at the same time is pushed back two weeks. Rather than promoting the album, it will offer the means for further live recording.

On the 7th the *Low Budget* album is certified gold. Four days later, a change of name is filed turning Kinks Productions Ltd, the original company formed in April 1965 to handle the band's financial transactions, into Kinks Properties Ltd. This new company will handle income and ownership of all past interests and holdings, based since the departure of Pete Quaife on a three-way split between the Davies brothers and Avory. A dummy company which was set up in autumn 1973 now becomes Kinks Productions, reflecting an adjustment to the number of shares held among the three principals, and this company will handle all current and forthcoming group interests.

Dave begins another set of sessions at Konk in London to record more songs for his new solo LP. With house engineer John Rollo at the controls, he is producing and also now handling all guitars, vocals, bass and drums. Effectively re-recorded now are **'Visionary Dreamer'**, **'Nothing More To Lose'**, **'Imagination's Real'** and **'In You I Believe'**, all of which will appear on his LP.

Taking a break from work on the live album until more new recordings are available, Ray continues his worldwide travels, heading down-under to Australia and New Zealand to arrange a planned tour of those countries in March and April. He negotiates directly with the Australian and New Zealand promoters and checks out possible venues because the previous trip, in 1971, had been so badly planned and he wants to avoid similar mistakes. The band's label in Australasia, Festival

Records, convinces Ray to do some press dates in conjunction with the visit. He brings along a promotional cut of the live *One For The Road* video to show as necessary.

February

→ Ray wraps up his trip down-under, departing for London on the 2nd. Meanwhile Dave is presumably still at Konk, continuing work on his solo recordings begun last month. Probably around now he records **'Wild Man'**, relegated to a later B-side.

▷ **TOUR STARTS** *Northeast US College Tour* (Feb 21st – Mar 9th). **Line-up**: Ray Davies (lead vocal, guitar), Dave Davies (guitar, vocal), Mick Avory (drums), Jim Rodford (bass), Ian Gibbons (keyboards), Nick Newall (saxophone, second keyboard, congas). The band travels to New York City on Monday 18th. Venues are mainly in the 2,000-6,000-capacity range. Tour shirts sold at the shows are promoting the original name of the live album, *Double Life*. The main reason for delaying release of a live LP is to record some new material that will give the band added currency in light of the revival of some of their older songs by new wave and punk bands. Before the tour starts, The Kinks book time at Daily Planet Studios in New York City where they start to work up and rehearse four songs, 'Stop Your Sobbing', 'David Watts', 'Prince Of The Punks' and 'National Health', all of which it is hoped can be captured on tape later in the tour for the LP.

Thursday 21st

Monroe County Dome Arena, Rochester Institute Of Technology *Rochester, NY* 8:00pm, with Steve Forbert
Set-list: 'Opening', 'The Hard Way', 'Catch Me Now I'm Falling', 'Where Have All The Good Times Gone', 'Lola', 'Low Budget', '(Wish

Could Fly Like) Superman', 'Attitude', 'You Really Got Me', 'A Gallon Of Gas', 'Celluloid Heroes', medley 'A Well Respected Man' / 'Death Of A Clown' / 'Sunny Afternoon', 'All Day And All Of The Night', 'A Rock'n'Roll Fantasy', 'Pressure', 'Twist And Shout', 'Prince Of The Punks', 'Live Life', 'David Watts', 'Money (That's What I Want)'.

Friday 22nd

Heiges Field House, Shippensburg University of Pennsylvania Shippensburg, PA 8:00pm

Saturday 23rd

Alumni Hall, St John's University Jamaica, NY 8:00pm, with Falcon Eddy

The only New York City-area show is treated to an unusual encore of 'Money (That's What I Want)' performed as 'Beer (That's What I Want)'. "The Kinks provided 6,250 fans with a tremendous night of almost two hours of solid music which will be difficult to forget," says *The Torch*. "It was great to see a band that enjoyed what they were doing and that was not just going through the motions."

Sunday 24th

Ray is ill and tonight's show at Seton Hall University, South Orange, NJ is cancelled early today. (Day off following in New York City.)

Tuesday 26th

Memorial Hall, Muhlenberg College Allentown, PA 8:00pm, with The Brains

Atlanta, Georgia-based punk band The Brains join the tour – and garner almost universal scorn from reviewers. According to one fan's account The Kinks play an off-the-cuff version of their first single, 'Long Tall Sally'.

Wednesday 27th

College Avenue Gymnasium, Rutgers University New Brunswick, NJ 8:00pm, with The Brains

(Day off following.)

Friday 29th

Westchester Premier Theatre Tarrytown, NY with The Brains

March

Saturday 1st

Gymnasium, County College Of Morris Randolph, NJ 8:00pm, with The Brains

Sunday 2nd

Bailey Hall, Cornell University Ithaca, NY 8:00pm, with The Brains

RCA's mobile recording unit (probably 16-track) is hired for this and the remaining shows on the tour, with Mike Moran engineering. A total of six shows are captured on tape from which to choose additional recordings for the live album. (Following day off.)

Tuesday 4th

Syracuse Area Landmark Theater Syracuse, NY 8:00pm, with The Brains; sponsored by Syracuse University.

Following day off.

Thursday 6th

Fine Arts Center Concert Hall, University of Massachusetts Amherst, MA 8:00pm, with The Brains

"The Kinks gave a supercharged show for an equally revved up audience," writes Norma J. Coates in *The Collegian*. "The sell-out crowd was on their feet most of the concert and rightly so, for Ray Davies and company gave one of the best musical performances seen in the Valley for some time. … Ray and his brother Dave were able to feed off the crowd's energy throughout the show, with Ray jumping into the ecstatic audience at one point. … Dave was incredible all night, tearing off solos which kept the audience on their feet while putting himself on his knees."

Friday 7th

Gymnasium, Southeastern Massachusetts University North Dartmouth, MA 8:00pm, with The Brains

Saturday 8th

Eisenhower Hall Theater, United States Military Academy West Point, NY 8:00pm, with The Brains

Sunday 9th

Palace Theater Albany, NY 8:00pm, with The Brains; sponsored by the University of New York at Albany

Monday 10th

The tour is finished and the band presumably heads back to London.

➜ Ray has homes in both New York City and Surrey, England now, so it's not always clear where work on the live LP takes place. Later album credits include Blue Rock Studios in New York City, with engineer Michael Ewaskow, so it seems this may be where much of the reviewing of tapes and then mixing is done now. Ray is certainly there with Ewaskow on the 22nd and 23rd working on some of the newly recorded choices for the live LP, including 'National Health', 'Catch Me Now I'm Falling' and 'Prince Of The Punks'. Any necessary re-recording of Ray's vocals on these tracks is likely done now. At least 'Prince Of The Punks' and 'David Watts' have backing vocals overdubbed, also probably done now.

☆ The tentatively planned tour of Australia, New Zealand and Japan fails because of the delay in preparation of the live album. In fact, no dates have been announced or tickets sold. A tentatively rescheduled start date of May 21st is touted, but this is pushed back to November and eventually fails too. Plans to tour Australia will have to wait until after the next studio album.

April

Ray continues mixing and making any necessary minor overdubs for the live LP, presumably accomplished in New York City. Mixing is finalised by the end of the month.

Meanwhile, Dave is at Konk in London where final sessions are held for his first RCA LP. He is again producing and playing all instruments – a more laborious and time-consuming task than working with a rhythm section. The Konk engineer is the latest to fill the spot, Ben Fenner. Recorded at this time are **'The World Is Changing Hands'** and **'Doing The Best For You'**.

May

Ray oversees the mastering of the live album at Masterdisk Studios in New York City on the Thursday 1st, and 4th-6th. After the 6th the

kinks'80

album is ready for production, with release scheduled for June 4th. He returns to Masterdisk on the 8th to oversee the mastering of a four-song 12-inch promotional EP that will be used by Arista Records in its intensive campaign among radio stations and general press. Ray begins to do some advance media duties around now.

With the live record finally wrapped up, the focus now switches to the live video scheduled for commercial release at the same time. A final one-hour edit needs to be done, and Ray works on it this month with film editor Wayne Hyde in New York.

It is probably during this process that Ray is introduced to singer Chrissie Hynde of The Pretenders. After turning down two previous offers of a meeting, Ray recalls later, "I didn't really want to meet her. I'd rather people just liked my songs from a distance than try to meet me. I finally gave in because the meeting place was just around the block from my flat in New York and I thought I'd take a stroll." A relationship develops quickly between the two over the course of the next month, with Hynde quietly accompanying Ray on a trip to Paris early in July.

By now, Dave has wrapped up all recording and mixing for his first RCA album. By the middle of the month, he flies in to New York City from London to take care of some business associated with the record's release. He oversees the mastering with Robert Ludwig at Masterdisk Studios, and a photo session with Nick Sangiamo is completed both for the cover shot and promotional photos.

Dave also spends time at the RCA Records offices where he begins the promotional campaign for the release of his new solo album, which is scheduled to be issued on July 9th. He's back in London later in the month and begins press work at RCA's central London offices, promoting the solo album as well as some upcoming Kinks festival dates on the Continent.

It's possible Ray is back in England towards the end of the month for a band rehearsal at his home in Surrey. Among the songs possibly worked up is a new arrangement of a song recorded for *Low Budget* but left off the LP, 'Give The People What They Want'.

Also around this time Ray is back at Konk in London where he gets a co-writing credit on the song 'Long Island' recorded by guitarist Trevor Rabin for his album *Wolf*, which is being recorded with engineer Ben Fenner. The LP will be released in January 1981 on Chrysalis, and while it's produced by Rabin, the sleeve will carry an "executive production" credit for Ray.

June

Wednesday 4th

One For The Road double-album released in the US. Accompanying the records is an insert offering the Time/Life video release. It was hoped they would be simultaneously issued, but the video is now set for June 25th and later delayed to early July. Unlike most Kinks albums to date, which have been rushed out as a tour is in progress, the tactic with this one seems to be to let the record company do the initial push, as the band is not scheduled to begin touring in support until August – about ten weeks after the LP's release.

"The [instruments] this time around sound more tight and controlled than they usually do in a real concert," writes John Rockwell in *The New York Times*, "which means that the music is more accessible but also more conventional. Yet fans of Mr Davies will find plenty to keep them happy." Tom Smucker in *The Village Voice* says: "[The LP] has some nice moments, because The Kinks have written some great songs. But does anyone really need a third live album from them? … We get your average live rock album mix and, worst of all, an audience that sounds as mindless and pre-trained as the ones on [TV's] *Rock Concert.*"

Saturday 20th

Ray is probably back in New York City at Masterdisk to edit a version of 'Lola' from the new live LP and master it for release as a single.

July

Friday 4th

The Kinks are in France to play at the huge *Pulsar 80 Festival* in

---

One For The Road double-album

A1 'Opening' (R. DAVIES).
A2 'The Hard Way' (R. DAVIES).
A3 'Catch Me Now I'm Falling' (R. DAVIES).
A4 'Where Have All The Good Times Gone' (R. DAVIES).
A5 'Introduction To Lola' [LARGELY SPEECH].
A6 'Lola' (R. DAVIES).
A7 'Pressure' (R. DAVIES).
B1 'All Day And All Of The Night' (R. DAVIES).
B2 '20th Century Man' (R. DAVIES).
B3 'Misfits' (R. DAVIES).
B4 'Prince Of The Punks' (R. DAVIES).
B5 'Stop Your Sobbing' (R. DAVIES).
C1 'Low Budget' (R. DAVIES).
C2 'Attitude' (R. DAVIES).
C3 '(Wish I Could Fly Like) Superman' (R. DAVIES).
C4 'National Health' (R. DAVIES).
D1 'Till The End Of The Day' (R. DAVIES).
D2 'Celluloid Heroes' (R. DAVIES).
D3 'You Really Got Me' (R. DAVIES).
D4 'Victoria' (R. DAVIES).
D5 'David Watts' (R. DAVIES).

US release June 4th 1980 (Arista A2L 8401).
UK release August 1st 1980 (Arista DARTY 6).
Musicians Ray Davies lead vocal, acoustic guitar, electric guitar. Dave Davies electric guitar, backing vocal. Jim Rodford bass guitar, backing vocal. Mick Avory drums. Ian Gibbons keyboards, backing vocal. Nick Newall saxophone (A3), additional keyboards, percussion. (The original keyboard parts played by Gordon Edwards on B1, B2, D3 were erased and new parts overdubbed in the studio by Gibbons in late 1979.)
Recorded A2, B1, B2: The Barn, Rutgers University *New Brunswick, NJ* March 3rd 1979; A4, D3: Lowell Memorial Auditorium *Lowell, MA* March 6th 1979; A3, A5-A7, B3, C1: Providence Civic Center *Providence, RI* September 23, 1979; C2, C3, D2 (possibly D4): The Volkhaus *Zürich, Switzerland* November 11th 1979; A1, B4, B5, C4, D1, D5: Syracuse Landmark Theatre *Syracuse, NY* March 4th 1980 or Fine Arts Center, University of Massachusetts *Amherst, MA* March 6th 1980 or Gymnasium, Southeastern Massachusetts University *North Dartmouth, MA* March 7th 1980; overdubs Konk Studios *Hornsey, north London* and Blue Rock Studios *New York, NY* November-December 1979 and March 1980; probably 16-track mixed to stereo.
Engineers Mike Moran, Arnie Rosenberg, Brooks Taylor, Michael Ewaskow. **Producer** Ray Davies.
Chart high US number 14; UK none.

→ INDICATES EVENT AROUND THIS TIME BUT WITH NO FIRM DATE

Vierzon but it is cancelled at the last minute due to local rioting. Ray nevertheless does the scheduled media appearances.

Saturday 5th

Outdoor event *Torhout, Belgium* 11:00am-10:15pm, *Woodland Festival*, with Jo Lemaire & Flouze, Kevin Ayers & Band, Steel Pulse, Mink DeVille, Fischer Z, The Specials

Sunday 6th

Outdoor event *Werchter, Belgium* 12midday-12midnight, *Woodland Festival*, with Jo Lemaire & Flouze, Kevin Ayers & Band, The Blues Band, Mink DeVille, Fischer Z, The Specials
The Kinks return to London the following day. Further European festival dates tentatively scheduled in West Germany and Yugoslavia this month are never finalised.

➜ *One For The Road* video released in the US. Initially it is available mail-order only. It probably arrives in the stores by mid August. Press screenings occur at the Bottom Line club, New York City, and the Roxy, Los Angeles, to mark the release of the *One For The Road* video. Jay Cocks in *Time* calls it "a tidy audiovisual chronicle of fierce, reckless endurance, a gone-to-hell charm that is distinctly, and triumphantly, Kinky". Michael Shore in *Soho News Weekly* is less sure. "This concert just isn't that good … it's simply boring. That's a shame. In fact it makes me mad because I know they're a better band than this. Not until the last song, 'Victoria' … do The Kinks work up to a really meaningful froth."

Wednesday 9th

AFL1-3603 album by Dave Davies released in the US. Reviews are strong. "Lyrically and vocally it lacks Ray Davies' distinctiveness," says *The New York Times*. "But in its slightly cluttered, slickly produced way, the disk conforms more to contemporary musical tastes than the determined traditionalism of The Kinks." *Rolling Stone*: "Though [it] boasts the trebly echo and buzz-bomb dynamics of heavy metal, it's

One For The Road videocassette

1 **'Opening'** (R. DAVIES).
2 **'All Day And All Of The Night'** (R. DAVIES).
3 **'Lola'** (R. DAVIES).
4 **'Low Budget'** (R. DAVIES).
5 **'Superman'** (R. DAVIES).
6 **'Attitude'** (R. DAVIES).
7 **'Celluloid Heroes'** (R. DAVIES).
8 **'The Hard Way'** (R. DAVIES).
9 **'Where Have All The Good Times Gone'** (R. DAVIES).
10 **'You Really Got Me'** (R. DAVIES).
11 **'Pressure'** (R. DAVIES).
12 **'Catch Me Now I'm Falling'** (R. DAVIES).
13 **'Victoria'** (R. DAVIES).

US release July 1980 (Time Life Video TLV 4000 [VHS] TLB 4000 [Beta]).
UK release November 17th 1983 (VTC/Vestron MUS 1136 [VHS] BUS 1136 [Beta]).
Videotaped/recorded Providence Civic Center *Providence, RI*; September 23rd 1979.

AFL1-3603 / Dave Davies album by Dave Davies

A1 **'Where Do You Come From'** (D. DAVIES).
A2 **'Doing The Best For You'** (D. DAVIES).
A3 **'Visionary Dreamer'** (D. DAVIES).
A4 **'Nothin' More To Lose'** (D. DAVIES).
A5 **'The World Is Changing Hands'** (D. DAVIES).
B1 **'Move Over'** (D. DAVIES).
B2 **'See The Beast'** (D. DAVIES).
B3 **'Imagination's Real'** (D. DAVIES).
B4 **'In You I Believe'** (D. DAVIES).
B5 **'Run'** (D. DAVIES).

US release July 9th 1980 (RCA Victor AFL1-3603).
UK release re-titled *Dave Davies* and with different cover, Sept 26th 1980 (RCA Victor PL 13603).
Musicians Dave Davies lead vocal, guitars, keyboards, bas guitar, drums except as noted. Ron Lawrence bass guitar (A1, B1, B2, B5). Nick Trevisick drums (A1, B1, B2, B5).
Recorded Konk Studios *Hornsey, north London*; A1, B1, B2, B5: October 1979; A3, A4, B3, B4: January-February 1980; A2, A5: April 1980; 24-track mixed to stereo.
Producer Dave Davies.
Engineers John Rollo, except A2, A5 Ben Fenner.
Chart high US number 50; UK none.

really the cat-in-heat, rockabilly hiccupping that Dave displays in songs like 'Move Over' that makes *AFL1-3603* so distinctive in its honest frenzy." *Good Times*: "Although overall a fine effort, the album is sometimes flawed by too many multi-layered guitar tracks, sometimes as many as 20, which not only clutter the sound but distract from Davies' interesting lyrics."

Friday 11th

The Kinks Live EP released in the UK.

➜ Both Ray and Dave busy themselves with concentrated press duties for their respective albums.
At Konk, Ray does a major interview – a rarity now – with Colin Irwin for the generally loyal-to-Kinks music paper *Melody Maker*. Irwin reports Ray's forecast of the dominance of all-powerful radio monopolies and their pre-programmed effects on the music industry, and his dark hints that if there isn't a good reaction to *One For The Road* he'll wash his hands of Britain. Ray tells him, "I'm not bitter … but I'm confused."
Ray is also in a concerned frame of mind – about British indifference to his newer work. "The audience is there, no doubt about that," Ray says to the *Melody Maker* interviewer. "What's wrong is the middle ground. Radio in particular. The only things the radio stations play are the old stuff. … If there were more competition in radio we'd get more airplay. Capital [Radio, a London commercial station] should have more competition. It's the only one in town and that's … dangerous. I get competition from new bands coming up and that's healthy, it drives you on."
Speaking of the now failed Konk Records label, Ray reveals further disappointment with the effects of big business in the music industry. "I couldn't get across what I wanted to do. People always wanted to drag it into the big money scene. It would always get into a situation

where [the distributors would] be really excited about a new band, and then the album didn't come up to expectations and they'd shelve it. I had the idea of bringing along one or two groups slowly, but you'd always get dragged into this thing of product commitment and five albums a year, or something."

Ray tells Irwin he thinks *One For The Road* is "technically imperfect, but it captures the atmosphere of fun and chaos, and that's The Kinks on stage, isn't it?"

He further muses: "Everything I say is a cliché. Everything is predictable. That's the thing about the world now, it's so predictable. The predictability of something like television is a joke. I'm sure that's why people like to watch the Olympics because it's unreliable – like us. We're so unpredictable that we're predictable."

Friday 18th

Scheduled release of the *One For The Road* live LP in the UK is delayed to August 1st.

The Kinks Live EP

A1 'David Watts' (R. DAVIES).
A2 'Where Have All The Good Times Gone' (R. DAVIES).
B1 'Attitude' (R. DAVIES).
B2 'Victoria' (R. DAVIES).

UK release July 11th 1980 (Arista ARIST 360).
Musicians and recording details as *One For The Road* album (see June 4th).
Chart high UK none.

Sunday 20th – Friday August 1st

Dave travels from London to New York City on Sunday to begin a two-week promotional tour of the US. He and companion Nancy are accompanied throughout by RCA publicist Barbara Pepe, and they visit radio stations and meet members of the press in key cities right across the country, from New York to Los Angeles. Response to Dave's album has been positive, and he later recalls this as a very happy point in his career.

Wednesday 23rd

→ 'Lola' / 'Celluloid Heroes' single released in the US.

August

Friday 1st

Dave winds up his promo tour and stays behind in LA for the weekend before heading back to London to resume Kinks duties. A string of tentatively scheduled French dates for The Kinks are scrapped.
One For The Road double-album released in the UK. Sandy Robertson writes in *Sounds*: "With lots of hip young pop stars plundering The Kinks' past, the band themselves have chosen to challenge the challengers by tarting up the very same tunes that the newcomers have been raking in the bucks with." Nick Kent in *NME*:

Lola live single

A 'Lola' (R. DAVIES).
B 'Celluloid Heroes' (R. DAVIES).

US release July 23rd 1980 (Arista AS 0541).
Musicians and recording details as *One For The Road* album (see June 4th).
Chart high US number 81.

"Will probably succeed admirably in its chosen intention – ie to plant The Kinks firmly in the rich soil of US Top Ten success."

Allan Jones in *Melody Maker*: "The Kinks now sound like a rock band. Unfortunately they no longer sound very much like The Kinks. [This] seeks to remind us of former glories while attempting to stress some kind of continuity [but] the performances are mostly characterised by the kind of drab, impersonal competence the Americans think passes for rock'n'roll."

→ Around now a rehearsal probably occurs at Konk where four of Dave's songs are worked up: 'Imagination's Real', 'Nothing More To Lose', 'Doing The Best For You' and 'The World Is Changing Hands', though the latter two are not played in concert. Also worked up is a cover of The Everly Brothers' 'Bird Dog' and a revised 'Give The People What They Want', reworked since first recorded during the *Low Budget* sessions.

Wednesday 6th

Maxwell Hall, Friars *Aylesbury, Bucks* 8:00pm, with The Step
Sell-out show with 1,000 attending.
Set-list: 'Opening', 'The Hard Way', 'Where Have All The Good Times Gone', 'Catch Me Now I'm Falling', 'Bird Dog', 'Lola', 'Low Budget', '(Wish I Could Fly Like) Superman', 'Nothing More To Lose', 'Dedicated Follower Of Fashion' (rock'n'roll version), 'A Well Respected Man', 'Sunny Afternoon', 'Death Of A Clown', 'Dead End Street', 'Tired Of Waiting For You', 'See My Friends', 'You Really Got Me', 'A Gallon Of Gas', 'Celluloid Heroes', 'All Day And All Of The Night', 'Pressure', 'David Watts', 'Waterloo Sunset', 'Give The People What They Want', 'Louie Louie'.

Thursday 7th

Strand Lyceum Ballroom *central London* 8:00pm, with The Step
It's London and so the music press is out in force at this concert, with reviews dividing in a way that now seems set.

Patrick Humphries in *Melody Maker* says, "I couldn't believe how much I enjoyed the following 100 or so minutes. Where Have All The Good Times Gone? queried Ray early on in the set. Right here, mate. Lyceum Ballroom, Thursday night! … A band honed down to basics, filled with a fervour and enthusiasm which would have put bands half their age to shame."

Meanwhile the *NME* turns in its usual criticism, even if it is this time laced with a dose of respect. "Songs from the *Low Budget* era come across as drab and plain," writes Paul Du Noyer, "while the catalogue of the 60s hits gets only the most perfunctory treatment from the stage. … As a one-off event, and a rare one at that, any Kinks show is worth taking a look at – in Ray Davies we're dealing with rock's most accomplished showman. But don't expect excellence or too much in the way of contemporary relevance. The Kinks survive because they're an institution with a preservation order held in all our hearts."

→ PRT Records, which now owns the Pye catalogue, is gradually reissuing the old Kinks albums, and around now releases *Kelvin Hall* and *Village Green Preservation Society*. As a typical spoiler, budget label Hallmark issues a two-LP set of 1960s hits around now. Although the reissue programme is motivated by the band's current prominence, it nonetheless makes available the classic back-catalogue to a new generation of fans who now have easier access to the band's rich heritage.

↪ **TOUR STARTS** *One For The Road: US Tour* (Aug 22nd – Oct 27th). **Line-up**: Ray Davies (lead vocal, guitar), Dave Davies (guitar, vocal), Mick Avory (drums), Jim Rodford (bass), Ian Gibbons (keyboards). Size of hall ranges from 2,000-capacity (Nashville) to the uncharted territory of an 18,000 one in LA, averaging somewhere in the middle. Not all shows are sell-outs but attendance is healthy and the tour a success. Ticket prices range from $6.50-$11.

Friday 22nd-Saturday 23rd
Sunrise Musical Theatre *Fort Lauderdale, FL* 8:00pm, with LeRoux
Set-list (23rd): 'Opening', 'The Hard Way', 'Where Have All The Good Times Gone', 'Catch Me Now I'm Falling', 'Bird Dog', 'Lola', 'Low Budget', 'Superman', 'Attitude', medley 'A Well Respected Man' / 'Death Of A Clown' / 'Sunny Afternoon', 'Nothing More To Lose', 'You Really Got Me', 'A Gallon Of Gas', 'Celluloid Heroes', 'All Day And All Of The Night', 'Pressure', 'Twist And Shout', 'Louie Louie', 'Hang On Sloopy', 'David Watts'.
Second Time Around album released in the US (Friday). This compilation amounts to a disappointing collection of RCA Records-period Kinks tracks.

Sunday 24th
Curtis-Hixon Convention Hall *Tampa, FL* 8:00pm, with LeRoux
Travel day follows.

Tuesday 26th
Jacksonville Civic Auditorium *Jacksonville, FL* 8:00pm, with LeRoux

Wednesday 27th
Boutwell Municipal Auditorium *Birmingham, AL* 8:00pm, with LeRoux
Travel day following.

Friday 29th
Tennessee Theater *Nashville, TN* 8:00pm, with Piggys

Saturday 30th
Orpheum Theatre *Memphis, TN* 8:00pm, with The Suspicions
The band spends the following few days travelling and with a day off in Chicago.

September

Tuesday 2nd
MECCA-Milwaukee Auditorium *Milwaukee, WI* 8:00pm, with John Cougar & The Zone
Day off in Chicago follows.

Thursday 4th
Assembly Hall, University Of Illinois *Champaign, IL* 8:00pm, with John Cougar & The Zone

Friday 5th
Elliot Hall Of Music, Purdue University *West Lafayette, IN* 8:00pm, with The Fabulous Poodles
'Imagination's Real' / 'Wild Man' single by Dave Davies released in the US. Probably released today or August 29th.

Imagination's Real single by Dave Davies

A 'Imagination's Real' (D. DAVIES).
B 'Wild Man' (D. DAVIES).
A-side is shorter edited version than album.

US release September (probably 5th) 1980 (RCA Victor PB 12089).
Musicians A: as AFL1-3603 album (see July 9th). B: Dave Davies lead vocals, electric guitars, electric bass, drums.
Recorded A: as AFL1-3603 album (see July 9th). B: Konk Studios *Hornsey, north London*; likely January-February 1980; 24-track mixed to stereo.
Engineer B: John Rollo.
Chart high US none.

Saturday 6th
Cobo Arena *Detroit, MI* 8:00pm, with John Cougar & the Zone
"A young frenzied crowd met them head on, cheering the first licks of 'You Really Got Me' and 'All Day And All Of The Night' as if they were far more recent memories (or as if they could remember when they first hit the charts)," writes Ben Brown in the *Detroit News*. "And lead-singer-songwriter Ray Davies sang them as if they were written yesterday. Now in his third decade of stardom, Ray Davies seems to have lost none of his enthusiasm for performance, for prancing and vamping along the stage apron just out of reach of the stage-front loonies. And although the familiar games are there – the 'Lola' tease, the Harry Belafonte 'De-oh, de-eh-eh-oh...' business – Davies so enthusiastically invites everyone into the act that the old tricks are welcome … . That the Kinks have been this good for this long is nothing short of an inspiration for the aging doubters among us."

Sunday 7th
Veterans War Memorial Auditorium *Columbus, OH* 8:00pm, with John Cougar & The Zone
Travel day following.

Tuesday 9th
Armory Fieldhouse, University of Cincinnati *Cincinnati, OH* 8:00pm, with John Cougar & The Zone
The Kinks' equipment truck is stolen before the show but recovered in time to do the concert.

Wednesday 10th
Louisville Gardens *Louisville, KY* 8:00pm, with John Cougar & The Zone
Travel day following.

Friday 12th
Stanley Theater *Pittsburgh, PA* 8:00pm, with John Cougar & The Zone

Saturday 13th
The Coliseum *Richfield, OH* 8:00pm, with John Cougar & The Zone

Sunday 14th
Indianapolis Convention Center *Indianapolis, IN* 8:00pm, with John Cougar & The Zone
Travel day following.

Tuesday 16th
Minneapolis Auditorium *Minneapolis, MN* **8:00pm, with Robert Palmer**

Wednesday 17th – Thursday 18th
Uptown Theater *Chicago, IL* 8:00pm, with Angel City

Friday 19th
Memorial Hall *Kansas City, MO* 8:00pm, with John Cougar & The Zone

Saturday 20th
Kiel Opera House *St. Louis, MO* 8:00pm, with John Cougar & The Zone
The band spends the following day travelling, and then has some days off in New Orleans.

Wednesday 24th
Riverside Centroplex Performing Arts Theatre *Baton Rouge, LA* 8:00pm, with LeRoux, The Shieks
Original venue was the smaller Assembly Center at Louisiana State University.

Thursday 25th
Sam Houston Coliseum *Houston, TX* 8:00pm, with LeRoux
Set-list: 'Opening', 'The Hard Way', medley 'Where Have All The Good Times Gone' / 'Tired Of Waiting For You', 'Catch Me Now I'm Falling', 'Bird Dog', 'Lola', 'Low Budget', '(Wish I Could Fly Like) Superman', 'Imagination's Real', 'Nothing More To Lose', 'You Really Got Me', 'A Gallon Of Gas', 'Celluloid Heroes', 'All Day And All Of The Night', 'Attitude', 'Pressure', 'Twist And Shout', 'Give The People What They Want', 'David Watts'.

Friday 26th
Austin Municipal Auditorium *Austin, TX* 8:00pm, with LeRoux
American Statesman: "For a band that spearheaded the British Invasion, nearly destroyed itself, influenced the punk movement, and came back as strong as ever, rocking into their sixties shouldn't be a problem."
Dave Davies album by Dave Davies released in the UK. Otherwise identical to US album *AFL1-3603* (see July 9th). Fred Dellar in *NME* gives "an approving nod".

Saturday 27th
Dallas Convention Center Arena *Dallas, TX* 8:00pm, with LeRoux
Two days off in Dallas follow.

Tuesday 30th
Events Center, University of Colorado *Boulder, CO* 8:00pm, with Angel City

→ INDICATES EVENT AROUND THIS TIME BUT WITH NO FIRM DATE

October

Wednesday 1st-Thursday 2nd
Day off in Denver, then travel day to Seattle.

Friday 3rd
Seattle Center Arena *Seattle, WA* 8:00pm, with Angel City
This sell-out concert is disrupted towards the finish when a gatecrasher falls 80 feet from a catwalk above the crowd … and while walking away without apparent effect seriously injures two crowd members. The Kinks' performance is stopped before any encores to help clear the way so that emergency personnel can move in.

Saturday 4th
Pacific Coliseum *Vancouver, BC, Canada* 8:00pm, with Angel City
"The Kinks don't lose fans, they just keep gaining them," suggests the *Vancouver Sun*. "There were people old enough to have bought The Kinks first singles when they first started coming out, and there were children who could only be familiar with The Kinks from their latest album … . Few rock bands have a wide enough appeal to attract so many family groups."

Sunday 5th
Memorial Coliseum *Portland, OR* 8:00pm, with Angel City
While returning into the US from Canada, Ray is arrested upon arrival at Portland airport by Oregon State Troopers. There is a warrant out for the arrest of a person who has been impersonating Ray and running up unpaid bills in his name. The misunderstanding is sorted out in time for the evening's show. (Travel day following.)

Tuesday 7th – Wednesday 8th
Oakland Auditorium Arena *Oakland, CA* 8:00pm, with Angel City
Travel day follows.

Friday 10th
The Forum *Inglewood, CA* 7:30pm, with Angel City
Despite a comment by Ray at this show that they will return to a smaller, more intimate venue next time in LA, the band continues to play here during tours in 1981 and '83. "Count on The Kinks to comment on the prevailing atmospheric conditions by sporting smog masks during their opening number of their two-hour set," says the *Los Angeles Times*. "It was typical of the playfulness of the veteran British quintet, which is enjoying a renewed surge of popularity among younger rock fans drawn by its *One For The Road* live album."

Saturday 11th
San Diego Sports Arena *San Diego, CA* 8:00pm, with Angel City

Sunday 12th
Late added date in Los Angeles area, details unknown.

Monday 13th – Thursday 16th
Tour break, and the band takes time off in Los Angeles. However, Ray returns to New York City and at Masterdisk oversees mastering of 'You Really Got Me' from the live LP for single release. Dave does more media work for his LP.

Friday 17th
War Memorial Auditorium *Buffalo, NY* 8:00pm, with Dear Daddy

Ray and guitar communing with the Spectrum audience in Philadelphia, October 24th 1980.

kinks'80

"The Kinks cast themselves as heavy rockers," writes Dale Anderson in the *Buffalo News*, "and slammed their hits home to a wildly enthusiastic throng of newly coined Kinks fanatics. It was nothing short of a triumph for this long-lived British band. A year ago in Kleinhans Music Hall, they played the part of seasoned concert-hall troupers, a venue they'd trodden for years.

"This time in front of 8,000 fans, many introduced to the group by its successful double live album this year, they shed the subtleties and cranked everything up full tilt. Guitarist Dave Davies, one of the most underrated journeymen in rock, rammed home riff after riff on one side of the stage while on the opposite side, brother Ray Davies sang and pranced like a born-again screamer."

Saturday 18th

Providence Civic Center *Providence, RI* 8:00pm, with Robin Lane & The Chartbusters
Travel day following.

Monday 20th – Tuesday 21st

Fox Theatre *Atlanta, GA* 8:00pm, with John Cougar & The Zone
A third night was planned but cancelled, so Wednesday is a day off, with a travel day following.

Friday 24th

The Spectrum *Philadelphia, PA* 8:00pm, with The John Cougar Band

Saturday 25th

Cape Cod Coliseum *South Yarmouth, MA* 8:00pm, with The John Cougar Band

Sunday 26th

Nassau Veterans Memorial Coliseum *Uniondale, NY* 8:00pm, with The John Cougar Band

Monday 27th

The Spectrum *Philadelphia, PA* 8:00pm, with The A's
Extra show in addition to that of the 24th, due to local demand.
Set-list: 'Opening', 'The Hard Way', medley 'Where Have All The Good Times Gone' / 'Tired Of Waiting For You', 'Catch Me Now I'm Falling', 'Bird Dog', 'Lola', 'Misfits', 'Low Budget', 'Imagination's Real', 'Nothing More To Lose', 'See My Friends', 'You Really Got Me', 'A Gallon Of Gas', 'Celluloid Heroes', 'All Day And All Of The Night', 'Pressure', 'Twist And Shout', 'Attitude', 'Stop Your Sobbing', 'David Watts', 'A Rock'n'Roll Fantasy', medley 'A Well Respected Man' / 'Death Of A Clown' / 'Sunny Afternoon', 'Give The People What They Want'.

You Really Got Me live single

A **'You Really Got Me'** (R. DAVIES).
B **'Attitude'** (R. DAVIES).
A-side is edited from album version.

US release October 29th 1980 (Arista AS 0577).
Musicians and recording details A: as *One For The Road* album (see June 4th), B: as *Low Budget* album (see July 10th 1979).
Chart high US none.

Tuesday 28th

The tour ends slightly sooner than planned with dates cancelled on the 28th at Capitol Theater, Passaic, NJ and 30th at New Haven Veterans Memorial Coliseum, New Haven, CT. The band goes home to London.

Wednesday 29th

'You Really Got Me' / 'Attitude' single released in the US. A complete non-click and doesn't even chart.

Doing The Best For You single by Dave Davies

A **'Doing The Best For You'** (D. DAVIES).
B-US **'Nothing More To Lose'** (D. DAVIES).
B-UK **'Wild Man'** (D. DAVIES).
A and B-US are shorter edited versions than album

US release (A/B-US) November 14th 1980 (RCA Victor PB 12147).
UK release (A/B-UK) December 5th 1980 (RCA Victor PB 9620).
Musicians and recording details A, B-US as *AFL1-3603/Dave Davies* album (see July 9th), B-UK as US 'Imagination's Real' single (see September 5th).
Chart high US none; UK none.

November

→ The endlessly rescheduled tour of Australia and New Zealand pencilled in for this time is again cancelled, and instead the band gets a brief holiday from touring. Dave is off to north Devon in England for rest and relaxation, but not without squeezing in a quick visit to the RCA Records offices in central London for a series of press interviews to help support the release of his solo LP and a single from it.

Friday 14th

'Doing The Best For You'/ 'Nothing More To Lose' single by Dave Davies released in the US.

⇨ **TOUR STARTS** *One For The Road: European Tour* (Nov 18th – Dec 19th). **Line-up**: Ray Davies (lead vocal, guitar), Dave Davies (guitar, vocal), Mick Avory (drums), Jim Rodford (bass), Ian Gibbons (keyboards). Added to the repertoire is 'Dead End Street'. All German dates promoted by Mike Scheller Concerts.

Tuesday 18th

DeVereeniging *Nijmegen, Netherlands* 8:30pm, with Nine Below Zero
Dave is ill with food poisoning, but performs anyway.

Wednesday 19th

Muziekcentrum Vredenburg *Utrecht, Netherlands* 8:30pm, with Nine Below Zero

Thursday 20th

De Doelen *Rotterdam, Netherlands* 8:30pm, with Nine Below Zero
Travel day following.

→ INDICATES EVENT AROUND THIS TIME BUT WITH NO FIRM DATE

Saturday 22nd
Friedrich-Eberthalle *Ludwigshafen, West Germany* 8:00pm, with Nine Below Zero
Travel day following, then day off in Munich.

Monday 24th
Deutsches Museum *Munich, West Germany* 8:00pm, with Nine Below Zero
"The best Kinks concert I have ever seen – and I've seen many," writes the *Musik Express* reviewer. "Ray was outstanding: a rock poseur par excellence. It's hard to believe, but they really got us again."

Tuesday 25th
Hemmerleinhalle *Neunkirchen, West Germany* 8:00pm, with Nine Below Zero

Wednesday 26th
Audimax *Hamburg, West Germany* 8:00pm, with Nine Below Zero
Originally at the Stadthalle, Kassel but cancelled.

Thursday 27th
Neue Welt *Berlin, West Germany* 8:00pm, with Nine Below Zero

Friday 28th
Stadthalle *Hanover, West Germany* 8:00pm, with Nine Below Zero
Travel day follows.

Sunday 30th
Philipshalle *Düsseldorf, West Germany* 7:30 pm, with Nine Below Zero
Set-list: 'Opening', 'The Hard Way', medley 'Where Have All The Good Times Gone' / 'Tired Of Waiting For You', 'Bird Dog', 'Catch Me Now I'm Falling', 'Düsseldorf Blues' (improvisation), 'Lola', 'Dead End Street', 'Low Budget', 'Imagination's Real', 'Nothing More To Lose', '20th Century Man', 'All Day And All Of The Night', 'Attitude', 'Pressure', 'Twist And Shout', 'Give The People What They Want', 'David Watts', 'A Land Of 1,000 Dances'.

December

Monday 1st
Vorst Nationaal *Brussels, Belgium* 8:30pm, with Nine Below Zero

Tuesday 2nd
Stadthalle *Offenbach, West Germany* 8:00pm, with Nine Below Zero
"A perfect, energetic show," says *Die Welt*. "Ray Davies is a first class performer. After all the boring monotony in rock music, he celebrates the almost forgotten quality of entertainment."

Wednesday 3rd
Kongresshau *Zürich, Switzerland* 8:30pm, with Nine Below Zero
Travel day following.

Friday 5th
Unexpected day off in Nice, France as a scheduled show in Aix-en-Provence, probably at the Théàtre Municipal, is cancelled.

'Doing The Best For You' / 'Wild Man' single by Dave Davies released in the UK.

Saturday 6th
Théâtre de Verdure *Nice, France* 8:00pm, with Nine Below Zero
Set-list: 'Opening', 'The Hard Way', medley 'Where Have All The Good Times Gone' / 'Tired Of Waiting For You', 'Bird Dog', 'Catch Me Now I'm Falling', 'Nice Blues' (improvisation), 'Lola', 'Dead End Street', 'Low Budget', 'Imagination's Real', 'Nothing More To Lose', 'You Really Got Me', 'A Gallon Of Gas', 'Till The End Of The Day', 'Celluloid Heroes', 'All Day And All Of The Night', 'Attitude', 'Pressure', 'Twist And Shout', 'Stop Your Sobbing', 'David Watts', 'A Well Respected Man', '20th Century Man'.

Sunday 7th
Palais d'Hiver *Lyon, France* 8:00pm, with Nine Below Zero

Monday 8th
Pavillion Baltard *Nogent Sur Marne, Paris, France* 8:00pm, with Nine Below Zero
In the US, the *One For The Road* double-album is certified gold by the RIAA for sales of 500,000 or more copies. This is The Kinks' second consecutive gold album, following hot on the heels of the previous year's *Low Budget*, and their third to date (*The Kinks Greatest Hits* was the first to go gold, on November 25th 1968).

Tuesday 9th – Thursday 11th
Travel day, then two days off in London, England and Paris, France. British portion of the European leg commences.

Friday 12th
Gaumont Cinema *Southampton* 8:00pm, with Gas

Saturday 13th
The Dome *Brighton* 8:00pm, with Gas

Sunday 14th
Victoria Apollo Theatre *central London* 8:00pm, with Gas

Monday 15th
Queensway Hall *Dunstable, Beds* 8:00pm, with Gas
Day off following.

Wednesday 17th
Apollo Theatre *Manchester* 8:00pm, with Gas

Thursday 18th
Odeon Cinema *Birmingham* 8:00pm, with Gas

Friday 19th
Rock City *Nottingham* 8:00pm, with Gas
Week off for Christmas holidays follows.

Sunday 28th
Travel to Washington DC. Notable additions to the repertoire now are 'I'm Not Like Everybody Else' and 'Come On Now'.

Monday 29th
Capital Centre *Landover, MD* 8:00pm, with Alvin Lee

Wednesday 31st
The Palladium *New York, NY* 9:00pm, *New Year's Eve With The Kinks*
This concert at New York's Palladium is recorded by the Starfleet

Mobile Unit 16-track, guided to tape by engineers Robert L. DeMeuth and Michael Ponczek.

The entire show is broadcast live in Britain on the BBC's Radio-1 station, and in the United States on the NBC syndicated programme *The Source – The Kinks Concert*, February 19th-21st 1982 (omitting 'Bird Dog', 'New York City Blues', 'I'm Not Like Everybody Else' and 'Come On Now').

The complete set-list is as follows: 'Opening', 'The Hard Way', medley 'Where Have All The Good Times Gone' / 'Tired Of Waiting For You', 'Catch Me Now I'm Falling', 'Bird Dog', 'New York City Blues' (improvisation), 'Lola', 'Dead End Street', 'Till The End Of The Day', 'Low Budget', 'Imagination's Real', 'Nothing More To Lose', 'I'm Not Like Everybody Else', 'Come On Now'. New Year's Eve countdown. 'You Really Got Me', 'Give The People What They Want', 'A Gallon Of Gas', 'Celluloid Heroes', 'All Day And All Of The Night', 'Stop Your Sobbing', 'Pressure'.

1981

On the surface this was a year of strong professional and commercial achievements. Following 1980's intense devotion to all things Kinks, this one started with brief diversions to separate projects for the brothers: Ray to the Chorus Girls show, Dave to his second solo LP, Glamour. In fairly quick order The Kinks then put together another winning album, Give The People What They Want, a record that sustained their new arena-based sound and was well received in press and charts.

In the US they sustained touring of arena-size venues, culminating in a triumphant and symbolic sold-out show at New York City's Madison Square Garden, a personal goal for Ray after a promoter told him years ago that The Kinks would never be big enough to play there. But the successes paled, at least temporarily, when Dave pulled out of the European leg of the world tour, partly because of the disappointing reception to his solo album.

Once Ray had done the Madison Square Garden gig, he shifted his energies to a pet project – just as he'd done in 1967 after the achievement of getting 'Waterloo Sunset' to number 2. Back in '67 the new challenges he took on included writing for TV and film and planning a concept album. This time the pet project was another film, and in the final weeks of the year the idea that would become Return To Waterloo took shape. It would affect the band's activities and fortunes for the next three years.

January

Presumably after taking a short break from the recent touring, the band begins rehearsing new material for the next LP and starts to record demos at Konk Studios in north London.

Principal recording is originally scheduled to take place during January and February, and a tour is set for March, but the schedule is changed at short notice when an offer comes up to stage the musical that Ray has collaborated on with Barrie Keeffe since 1978, now to be called *Chorus Girls*.

The offer is to do this in April, and it's decided that the work needs serious rewriting as well as a month of rehearsals if that' target is going to be achieved.

Accordingly, The Kinks' schedule is shifted. Recording for a new album is still set to happen during February, although the band won't return to the project until late April, and the scheduled March UK tour is pushed to May.

All this has the benefit of allowing Dave to devote time to his next solo LP, which presumably he has been working on and continues to write for.

February

Rehearsals and recording of demos continue at Konk.

An initial set of proper recording sessions for the new LP takes place in the week of the 16th to the 20th, and reportedly five tracks are recorded (two are described as "ballads", while three are characterised as "rockers").

Ray later implies that nothing that is recorded at Konk at this time is ultimately used. "I've had a lot of trouble writing this year," he tells an interviewer in September.

Sessions also begin at Konk Studios in north London late this month for tracks aimed at Dave's next solo album, and this recording work continues into March.

Dave again handles all the instruments himself, although this time he calls in ex-Argent drummer Bob Henrit to cut the backing tracks, with Dave playing bass.

March

For the entire month, beginning on Monday 2nd, rehearsals tale place at the Theatre Royal in Stratford, north-east London for the production of Ray and Barrie Keeffe's *Chorus Girls*. Ray is often present, and occasionally acts as pianist while overseeing the fine tuning of his music. A March tour by The Kinks had been pencilled in but once this show is in place with such lengthy rehearsals, all Kinks plans are pushed back eight weeks, to the very end of April.

Probably early this month Ray undertakes a brief side project at Konk Studios, producing a session for pop-influenced punk band The Moondogs from Londonderry, Northern Ireland. The band has so far issued a few independent singles and gained some industry attention. They've supported The Pretenders and no doubt caught the attention of Chrissie Hynde, who took Ray along to see them in London late in February. At Konk, with Ben Fenner engineering, a single is recorded (released April 17th on Real Records) coupling two original songs, 'The Imposter' and 'Body Snatcher', both written by guitarist/singer Gerry McCandles.

Meanwhile Dave is free to devote the entire month to continuing sessions at Konk for his next solo album. All nine of the eventually used tracks are completed: **'Reveal Yourself'**, **'Body'**, **'World Of Our Own'**, **'7th Channel'**, **'Glamour'**, **'Telepathy'**, **'Too Serious'**, **'Is This The Only Way'** and **'Eastern Eyes'**. Overdubs and final mixing continue into the middle of April.

April

Thurday 2nd – Sunday 5th

Press previews are staged for *Chorus Girls* at the Theatre Royal, Stratford, north-east London. The production is directed by Adrian Shergold, choreographed by Charles Augins. Playwright is Barrie Keeffe, with music by Ray Davies, and the musical director is Peter Brewis. (Jim Rodford plays bass in the pit band for the first two weeks, then returns to playing with The GB Blues Co, his extra-curricular band that also includes ex-Argent drummer Bob Henrit and ex-Kinks horn players John Beecham and Mike Cotton.)

Patrick Humphries writes in *Melody Maker*: "Prince Charles falling through a trapdoor at an East London theatre and held hostage by a group of feminist dancers? This unlikely premise is expanded into a gloriously entertaining play by Barrie (*Long Good Friday*) Keeffe, with songs by Ray Davies. Davies' songs topically touch on unemployment, patriotism and royalty, and one uncharacteristic number at the beginning of the second act concerning the function of dildos! His songs are of interest because virtually all of them come from a feminist standpoint, the most militant of which is the anthemic 'All Men Are Fools'.

"There's a lovely song about a tower block palace sung by Lesley Manville, and [Marc] Sinden contributes an in-character reggae song to wrap the proceedings up, 'Celebrate England', which is vintage Davies. The acting is unanimously excellent ... Davies' songs integrate well into the narrative. ... Whether Mary Whitehouse, the Conservative Party and *The Daily Express* will be offended by the anti-monarchist irreverence is entirely a matter for them. With any luck they will, and the ensuing notoriety will bring *Chorus Girls* the success it deserves."

Monday 6th

Opening of *Chorus Girls* at the Theatre Royal, Stratford, running through to May 9th. Capacity at the hall is 467. Ray's songs performed in the production are: 'Newham At Work' and 'A Woman In Love Will Do Anything' (sung by Charlotte Cornwell), 'Privilege' and 'Payback'

(both sung by Charlotte Cornwell and Sandy Ratcliff), 'Reputation' (sung by Michael Elphick, Peter Halliday and Howard Lew Lewis), 'Up On A High Rise Block' (Lesley Manville and Marc Sinden), 'Glorious Sight' (Henrietta Baynes, Anita Dobson, Helen Gemmell, Lesley Manville, Sandy Ratcliff, Mary Sheen and Kate Williams), 'Let's Have A Dance' (Anita Dobson), 'Newham At Work' (sung by Charlotte Cornwell).

'Men Are Fools' (sung by Kate Williams and Howard Lew Lewis), 'The Man Of Destiny' (Michael Elphick), 'England' (Marc Sinden), and 'Everybody's Got A Body' (Charlotte Cornwell, Kate Williams, Marc Sinden and Michael Elphick).

During the run, Channel 4 TV's commissioning editor Walter Donahue approaches Ray to write an experimental filmed play for the channel's *Film On 4* series. Ray later submits a one-page proposal to the company's drama-department head.

➜ In the middle of the month, Dave travels to New York City. First he oversees mastering of his new LP with Robert Ludwig at Masterdisk Studios. He also meets RCA marketing and promotion people to map out the visual presentation for the record. Dave ultimately agrees to present himself as a 1920s-style Hollywood movie star, and is subsequently photographed in character by Nick Sangiamo for the LP's cover and promotional materials.

➜ ● **RECORDING** Konk Studios *Hornsey, north London*. Late in April and beginning on the 20th, **'Better Things'** and **'Predictable'** are recorded and **'Give The People What They Want'** re-recorded. Ray says later that 'Better Things' was written in New York about the impending split with his second wife, Yvonne. And the style of the recording is, he says, "a total send up".

☆ Reportedly, a full set of demos of Ray's final songs for *Chorus Girls* are recorded by The Kinks at Konk; this is the most likely time for the session(s).

⤳ **TOUR STARTS** *UK & Ireland Tour* (Apr 29th – May 15th). **Line-up**: Ray Davies (lead vocal, guitar), Dave Davies (guitar, vocal), Mick Avory (drums), Jim Rodford (bass), Ian Gibbons (keyboards). Billed as a "rare series of UK concerts". Venue sizes range from 1,500-3,000 seaters. The Kinks are still booked by Barry Dickens, their same British agent since 1968, now with ITB (International Talent Bureau.

Wednesday 29th

Ulster Hall *Belfast, Northern Ireland* 7:30pm, with The AK Band

The Kinks play their first Irish date since autumn 1967. Ray says later the band was advised not to go to the troubled city, but that "the audience was wonderful. They were really wonderful. They were rocking out. We had all the Mods jumping. It was brilliant. And yet we finished the gig, went to the car and were going back to the hotel, and there we were, tanks on every corner, nobody in the streets. But somehow rock'n'roll has got this power to make people really want to enjoy themselves, because it goes beyond economics somehow".

Thursday 30th

National Stadium, Royal Dublin Society *Dublin, Ireland* 7:30pm, with The AK Band

Ray meets novelist Christy Brown tonight, whose book *Down All The Days* will later inspire at least in title Ray's 1989 composition of the same name. Neil Stokes in *Hot Press* reviews the gig: "It was way over the top, but what the hell? Everyone enjoyed themselves. ... The Kinks are a powerful rock'n'roll band, still possessed of the primordial surge that gives the music its most potent thrust. But Ray Davies holds all the aces in their pack – if he's in form then the band can't fail. At this moment, he's got the raison d'etre of live rock'n'roll back in focus and he's revelling in the fun."

May

Friday 1st
National Stadium, Royal Dublin Society *Dublin, Ireland*
7:30pm, with The AK Band

Saturday 2nd
● RECORDING Konk Studios *Hornsey, north London*. Final mixes
are done for **'Better Things'**, **'Massive Reductions'**, 'Destroyer'
and **'Predictable'**.

Sunday 3rd
Wessex Hall, Poole Arts Centre *Poole, Dorset* 7:30pm, with
The AK Band

Monday 4th
Cornwall Coliseum *St Austell, Cornwall* 7:30pm, with The AK
Band

Tuesday 5th
New Theatre *Oxford* 7:30pm, with The AK Band

Wednesday 6th
DeMontfort Hall *Leicester* 7:30pm, with The AK Band
Day off following.
Set-list: 'Opening', 'The Hard Way', medley 'Where Have All The
Good Times Gone' / 'Tired Of Waiting For You', 'Come On Now',
'Bird Dog', 'Till The End Of The Day', 'Lola', 'Dead End Street',
'Better Things', 'Low Budget', 'Nothing More To Lose', 'You Really
Got Me', 'A Gallon Of Gas', 'Celluloid Heroes', '20th Century Man',
'All Day And All Of The Night', 'David Watts', 'Pressure', 'Twist And
Shout'.

Friday 8th
Victoria Hall *Hanley, Stoke-on-Trent* 7:30pm, with The AK
Band

Saturday 9th
City Hall *Newcastle Upon Tyne* 7:30pm, with The AK Band

Sunday 10th
Apollo Theatre *Manchester* 7:30pm, with The AK Band
Day off following.

Tuesday 12th
Empire Theatre *Liverpool* 7:30pm, with The AK Band
Travel day follows to Edinburgh, the day on which an assassination
attempt is made on Pope John Paul II. This will become the inspiration
for Ray's new song 'Killer's Eyes' which he says later was written on the
coach ride to Glasgow. He says the song is also inspired by Peter
Sutcliffe, the "Yorkshire Ripper" serial rapist and murderer.

Thursday 14th
Apollo Theatre *Glasgow, Scotland* 7:30pm, with The AK Band

Friday 15th
St. George's Hall, University of Bradford *Bradford, Yorks*
7:30pm, with The AK Band
The tour ends today and the band heads straight back into the studio
for more recording.

→ ● RECORDING Konk Studios *Hornsey, north London*. Recording
sessions continue for the new LP, details unknown.

Thursday 28th
Dauwtrappers Festival *Lochem, Netherlands* 9:00am, with
The Stray Cats, Slade, Joe Ely, Mother's Finest, SST
The festival is broadcast by Dutch Television, but typically The Kinks'
performance is excluded. (Travel day following.)

June

→ ● RECORDING Konk Studios Hornsey, north London. Sessions
continue for the new LP throughout the month, details unknown.

Friday 19th
'Better Things' / 'Massive Reductions' single released in the UK.
NME dismisses it outright, but *Melody Maker* hits the mark:
"Everyone is rooting for The Kinks to break their duck in the 1980s.
This has all the vital ingredients – it's throwaway, simple and summery,
with Ray's vocals wavering unsteadily through the higher reaches. Yet
you just know the [populist radio DJs] will prefer to wheel out 'Sunny
Afternoon' and 'Lola' one more time, for this so determinedly
recreates the characteristic Kinks sound of the 1960s that they begin
to sound like a parody of themselves. I can't wait for The Pretenders'
version."

Better Things double-single

A **'Better Things'** (R. DAVIES).
B **'Massive Reductions'** (R. DAVIES).
C **'Lola' live** (R. DAVIES).
D **'David Watts' live** (R. DAVIES).

UK release June 19th 1981 (Arista ARIST 415).
Musicians A/B: Ray Davies lead vocal, electric guitar. Dave
Davies electric guitar, backing vocal. Jim Rodford bass guitar,
backing vocal. Mick Avory drums. Ian Gibbons keyboards.
Recorded A: Konk Studios *Hornsey, north London*; April-May
1981; possibly 8-track mixed to stereo. B: The Power Station
New York, NY; May-June 1979; 24-track mixed to stereo.
Producer Ray Davies.
Engineers Ben Fenner (A); John Rollo (B).
Sides C/D, musicians and recording details as *One For The
Road* double-album (see June 4th 1980).

⇨ **TOUR STARTS** *Mini UK Tour* (Jun 25th – 28th). **Line-up:** Ray
Davies (lead vocal, guitar), Dave Davies (guitar, vocal), Mick Avory
(drums), Jim Rodford (bass), Ian Gibbons (keyboards). All venues are
1,800-3,200 capacity; all well-attended if not sell outs.

Thursday 25th
Gaumont Cinema *Ipswich* 7:30pm, with Jody Street

Friday 26th
Rainbow Theatre *Finsbury Park, north London* 7:30pm, with
Jody Street
NME: "A soirée of nostalgia dedicated to the spectre of rock'n'roll. At
the centre of it all is ringmaster Ray Davies, resplendent in red coat; he
is the man of a hundred jackets and faces to match. While his songs now

lack the classic 20th century imagery of Springsteen or the social poignancy and wit of Costello, they have a solid, unpretentious charm enhanced no end by Davies' personality. Say what you like, but you cannot fault his genuine commitment and energy, shown by his sheer enthusiasm for the event and his personable and overt contact with the audience." *Melody Maker* is ruthless this time: "Nostalgia's something we all indulge in from time to time, but if it means giving blind worship to a grotesque heavy-metal cabaret act, then count me out."

Colston Hall *Bristol* 7:30pm, with Jody Street

Sunday 28th
Coventry Theatre *Coventry* 7:30pm, with Jody Street
Set-list: 'The Hard Way', medley 'Where Have All The Good Times Gone' / 'Tired Of Waiting For You', 'Come On Now', 'Bird Dog', 'Back To Front', 'Yo Yo', 'Lola', 'Till The End Of The Day', 'Better Things', 'Low Budget', 'Nothing More To Lose', 'Give The People What They Want', 'You Really Got Me', 'A Gallon Of Gas', '20th Century Man', 'Celluloid Heroes', 'All Day And All Of The Night', 'David Watts', 'Stop Your Sobbing', 'Pressure', 'Twist And Shout'.

July

Wednesday 1st
Glamour album by Dave Davies released in the US. The most prominent review, by Nicholas Schaffner in *Rolling Stone*, is positive. "It's a solo tour de force, with Davies playing every instrument except drums. The guitar riffs remain ferocious, while the voice … continues to sound as if its owner were in the throes of death by strangulation. Dave still lacks Ray's lyrical touch. ... But the new LP is much more disciplined and melodic than the noisy and unfocused *AFL1-3603*. … For Kinks fans … *Glamour* should come as a welcome surprise." But there is little other coverage, disappointing given the healthy sales of Dave's first solo album and the continued high visibility of The Kinks in the charts and

Glamour album by Dave Davies

A1 **'Reveal Yourself'** (D. DAVIES).
A2 **'Body'** (D. DAVIES).
A3 **'World Of Our Own'** (D. DAVIES).
A4 **'7th Channel'** (D. DAVIES).
B1 **'Glamour'** (D. DAVIES).
B2 **'Telepathy'** (D. DAVIES).
B3 **'Too Serious'** (D. DAVIES).
B4 **'Is This The Only Way'** (D. DAVIES).
B5 **'Eastern Eyes'** (D. DAVIES).

US release July 1st 1981 (RCA Victor AFL1-4036).
UK release October 16th 1981 (RCA Victor RCALP 6005).
Musicians Dave Davies vocal, electric guitar, bass guitar, keyboards, extra percussion. Bob Henrit drums.
Recorded Konk Studios *Hornsey, north London*; mid-February to mid-April 1981; 24-track mixed to stereo.
Producer Dave Davies.
Engineer Ben Fenner.
Chart high US number 152.

in concert. Dave later attributes this partly to the loss of his right-hand man at RCA and less rapport with the company. He says RCA feels it's just too "serious" to sell, and no single is issued in an evident disagreement over which track to issue. The LP enters the lower reaches of the US charts but peaks at a disappointing number 152.

➔ Early in the month, photographer Robert Ellis takes an album cover shot of The Kinks in front of Konk Studios. The LP's title *Give The People What They Want* has been stylishly spray-painted across the front window of the studio, boarded up in response to a local police warning to businesses to prepare for the rioting that has been breaking out in various parts of Britain.
● **RECORDING** Konk Studios *Hornsey, north London*. Ray is involved in intense mixing sessions for the new LP. Unlike the last studio record, *Low Budget*, new material is not bountiful, with only one likely outtake, a song mentioned in interviews by Ray as 'Blasé Blasé'. He also says that the songs on this album have generally been less demoed in advance, which is his normal recording method. Recordings are completed by this time of **'Around The Dial'**, **'Killer's Eyes'**, **'Add It Up'**, **'Yo-Yo'**, **'Back To Front'**, **'Art Lover'** and **'A Little Bit Of Abuse'**.
✰ The album's planned release date passes and the proposed start of the US tour is delayed, with early dates rescheduled to the end of the tour in October.

Monday 26th
Ray with Robert Ludwig masters the new LP today, but some further editing of tracks is necessary. At this stage the album includes a song from the recent sessions, 'Entertainment', in place of 'Better Things'. The former is held back for release, possibly as the title cut for the planned 1982 album, but is then relegated to the Konk vaults until 1989 when, in slightly altered form, it will be included on *UK Jive*. Another unused song, 'Bernadette', is also present on the acetates cut today, but it's quickly dropped (and will appear on 1983's *State Of Confusion*).
✰ Around this time in New York City, Ray meets acclaimed movie director Martin Scorsese who advises Ray on his as-yet-untitled upcoming film project, which becomes *Return To Waterloo*.

August

Saturday 1st
With Ray overseeing, Robert Ludwig accomplishes the final mastering of the new LP and the finished item is ready for production. Some time during this final mastering, Ray previews a few songs from the LP on a local New York radio station. Ironically on this same day a new cable TV channel debuts devoted entirely to music. MTV (Music Television) opens with the prophetically titled video for The Buggles' 'Video Killed The Radio Star'. Ray no doubt notices this event, a fusion of the two mediums that he has long considered, and that will finally provide an outlet for the visual presentation of his music.
✰ With a relationship blossoming between Ray and Chrissie Hynde, their respective US tours are timed approximately in parallel this month: The Pretenders dates are the 8th-24th, The Kinks 5th-22nd.

⤳ **TOUR STARTS** *Give The People What They Want: North American Tour: 1st leg* (Aug 5th – 22nd). **Line-up**: Ray Davies (lead vocal, guitar), Dave Davies (guitar, vocal), Mick Avory (drums), Jim Rodford (bass), Ian Gibbons (keyboards). The first tour for new roadie Big Bob Suzinski. Ticket prices range from $7.50-$13. Venue sizes differ dramatically depending on how popular The Kinks are locally; at the low end just under 3,000 capacity, up to about 15,000 (such as The Forum in Inglewood, CA).

Tuesday 4th

Today is likely set aside for rehearsals at the tour's opening venue, the Saenger Performing Arts Center in New Orleans. A number of new songs are worked up for the tour, including 'Around The Dial', 'Yo Yo', 'Destroyer', 'Art Lover', 'Back To Front', 'Add It Up', 'Killer's Eyes' and Dave's solo feature 'Too Serious'.

Wednesday 5th

Saenger Performing Arts Center *New Orleans, LA* 8:00pm, with Bill Wray
A sell-out at this 2,847-capacity venue.

Thursday 6th

Frank C. Erwin Jr. Special Events Center, University of Texas *Austin, TX* 8:00pm, with Bill Wray
Tonight 5,034 attend at this 6,151-capacity room.

Friday 7th

Summit Arena *Houston, TX* 8:00pm, with The Joe Perry Project
Attendance is 8,963.

Saturday 8th

Dallas Convention Center Arena *Dallas, TX* 8:00pm, with Lightning
Capacity is 9,810, with 6,001 showing up tonight. Were you that one? (Two days off in Dallas follow.)

Tuesday 11th

Albuquerque Civic Auditorium *Albuquerque, NM* 8:00pm, with The Kamakazi Klones
Sell-out with 5,000 attendance.

Wednesday 12th

Veterans Memorial Coliseum, State Fairgrounds *Phoenix, AZ* 8:00pm, with The Ramones
Travel day following.

Friday 14th

The Forum *Inglewood, CA* 7:30pm, with Joe Ely
"Lead singer Ray Davies was as animated as ever and the band was tight but, like the current TV season, it all seemed to be a rerun," says *Billboard*. "The 23-song, one-hour-50-minute show did feature many new songs which have many of the biting textures of some of Davies' early compositions. This is a hopeful sign of things to come in the future."
Set-list: 'Around The Dial', 'The Hard Way', 'Bird Dog', 'Catch Me Now I'm Falling', 'Yo-Yo', 'Tired Of Waiting For You', 'Killer's Eyes', 'Lola', 'Back To Front', 'Too Serious', 'You Really Got Me', 'Misfits', 'A Gallon Of Gas', 'Celluloid Heroes', '20th Century Man', 'All Day And All Of The Night', 'Give The People What They Want', 'Twist And Shout', 'Low Budget', 'David Watts', '(Wish I Could Fly Like) Superman'.

Saturday 15th

San Diego Sports Arena *San Diego, CA* 8:00pm, with Joe Ely

Sunday 16th

Santa Barbara County Bowl *Santa Barbara, CA* 7:00pm, with Joe Ely
Travel day following.

Tuesday 18th – Wednesday 19th

Hollywood Palladium *Los Angeles, CA* 8:00pm, with Joe Ely
Sell-out show with 4,400 in the audience. (Travel day following.)

Friday 21st – Saturday 22nd

Greek Theatre, University of California *Berkeley, CA* 7:30pm, with Joe Ely
British journalist Paul Du Noyer has been following The Kinks around this string of California dates for a feature piece in *NME*. Ray complains to him: "Oh God, you always see us at the worst gigs, you *NME* people. Like tonight, or that poxy open-air place in San Whatsit. The best gigs are when we're all pissed off and when there's no one there. You should have seen us in Dunstable." Du Noyer does get an interview with Ray … in December, back in London.

Sunday 23rd

Travel day from Los Angeles back home to London.

Wednesday 26th

Give The People What They Want album released in the US. Some of the LP, says *Rolling Stone*, "may seem pedestrian back to back with *Face To Face* et al, and the lyrics probably won't qualify as timeless literature and all that. But compared with most of the other yo-yo's heard around my dial lately, tunes like 'Around The Dial' and 'Yo-Yo' certainly provide an exhilarating noise delivered with a lightness of touch that hardly suggests the stamp of a dinosaur. They're funny and they're fun, and that, I'll venture, should be enough until Ray Davies gets around to *Preservation Act III*." Meanwhile *Creem* thinks it will be the band's biggest seller yet. "[It] gives the people – whoever we are – accessible, entertaining rock'n'roll, [and] it is also the best Kinks album … since *Muswell Hillbillies*." Ray tells Jeff Tamarkin of *Aquarian* about some of the songs. He says 'Art Lover' was written about his lack of visitation rights to his two daughters from his first marriage, and 'A

Give The People What They Want album

A1 'Around The Dial' (R. DAVIES).
A2 'Give The People What They Want' (R. DAVIES).
A3 'Killer's Eyes' (R. DAVIES).
A4 'Predictable' (R. DAVIES).
A5 'Add It Up' (R. DAVIES).
B1 'Destroyer' (R. DAVIES).
B2 'Yo-Yo' (R. DAVIES).
B3 'Back To Front' (R. DAVIES).
B4 'Art Lover' (R. DAVIES).
B5 'A Little Bit Of Abuse' (R. DAVIES).
B6 'Better Things' (R. DAVIES).

US release August 26th 1981 (Arista AL 9567).
UK release January 15th 1982 (Arista SPART 1171).
Musicians Ray Davies lead vocal, acoustic guitar, electric guitar, backing vocal. Dave Davies electric guitar, backing vocal. Jim Rodford bass guitar, backing vocal. Mick Avory drums. Ian Gibbons keyboards, backing vocal. Chrissie Hynde backing vocal (A5). Sarah Murray backing vocal (B2).
Recorded Konk Studios *Hornsey, north London*; April-July 1981 (except B1: The Power Station *New York, NY*; May-June 1979, backing track); 24-track mixed to stereo.
Producer Ray Davies.
Engineers Ben Fenner; John Rollo (B1).
Chart high US number 15; UK none.

Ray and Dave in six-string harmony, Veterans Memorial Auditorium, Columbus, Ohio, September 21st 1981.

kinks'81

Little Bit Of Abuse' was inspired when women from *Chorus Girls* indirectly challenged him to write about a serious women's issue, such as domestic violence. 'Better Things' was written in New York City at a depressing time, he says.

→ Business affairs tidied up around now include the liquidation of Konkwest Ltd, the production company that was in effect the now defunct Konk Records. Oddly, the Konk Records logo will be briefly revived with the next Kinks single, 'Predictable', issued on October 31st. While released on Arista, it will also carry a credit for Konk Records And Tapes.

Sunday 30th
21st National Jazz Blues & Rock Festival *Reading* with Wishbone Ash, Nine Below Zero, Midnight Oil, .38 Special, The Enid, The Thompson Twins, Greg Lake

The Kinks are headliners on the third of this three-day annual event. High marks from Paul Colbert in *Melody Maker*: "It's possible to forget how good a rock band The Kinks are. When at last they hit ['Lola', 'You Really Got Me' and 'All Day And All Of The Night'] they could have been written yesterday. I don't know how they managed it, but after taking the boards as one of the oldest and longest-established bands to play Reading that day, they left sounding the freshest. All that and suntan too."

Monday 31st
Ray takes the 11-hour flight from London to Los Angeles where, along with guitarist Nils Lofgren and an impromptu four-piece horn section, he joins Chrissie Hynde and The Pretenders on-stage at the Santa Monica Civic Auditorium for the encore of the band's own 'Mystery Achievement' and the Jackie Wilson hit 'Higher And Higher'. Ray's appearance in public with Hynde is tantamount to a coming out for the previously "secret romance". Hynde is named as the corespondent in divorce papers filed earlier in the year by Ray's second wife Yvonne and finalised by the London High Court at around this time, bringing further publicity for the relationship between Ray and Hynde. There is some public benefit, in that each seems to be boosted in the eyes of fans of the other, often across different generational lines.

September

➲ **TOUR STARTS** *Give The People What They Want: North American Tour: 2nd leg* (Sep 3rd – Oct 16th). **Line-up**: Ray Davies (lead vocal, guitar), Dave Davies (guitar, vocal), Mick Avory (drums), Jim Rodford (bass), Ian Gibbons (keyboards). On the 2nd the band flies in from London to Portland, OR, and Ray arrives from Los Angeles. (The Pretenders are also on a US tour this month, promoting their second album, with the two bands overlapping on the 9th.)

Thursday 3rd
Memorial Coliseum *Portland, OR* 8:00pm, with Red Rider

Friday 4th
Seattle Center Coliseum *Seattle, WA* 8:00pm, with Red Rider

Saturday 5th
Pacific Coliseum *Vancouver, BC, Canada* 8:00pm, with Red Rider

Tom Harrison writes in *Province*: "[Tonight] confirmed the renaissance that has taken place in The Kinks' Kamp: playing for 12,000 fans now instead of a few hundred, this 17-year-old band is more popular than it's

ever been … a case of a band really playing for its audience and the audience actually participating in the excitement of the show." (Travel day follows.)

Monday 7th
Northlands Coliseum *Edmonton, BC, Canada* 8:00pm, with Red Rider
Travel day following.

Wednesday 9th
McNichols Sports Arena *Denver, CO* 8:00pm, with The Pretenders
"The concert proved to be the finest double billing in recent memory," says the *Denver Post*. "The Pretenders were simply outstanding. … Any band other than The Kinks would have worried about following The Pretenders' set, but Ray Davies & Co were working crowds before 50 percent of the Denver audience was even born." (Day off following.)

Friday 11th
Municipal Auditorium *Kansas City, MO* 8:00pm, with Red Rider
An attendance of 4,921 at this 5,500-capacity room.

Saturday 12th
C.Y. Stephens Auditorium, Iowa State University *Ames, IA* 8:00pm, with Red Rider
Sell-out show for 2,639 fans.

Sunday 13th
Metropolitan Sports Center *Bloomington, MN* 8:00pm, with Red Rider
Day off in Minneapolis follows.

Tuesday 15th
The Rosemont Horizon *Rosemont, IL* 8:00pm, with Red Rider
The Kinks normally play the 4,000-seat Uptown Theatre, but now bump up to this 20,000-capacity stadium, making many loyal local fans wince. It's an ambitious experiment that slightly backfires, with some large empty sections in the place, but the band makes it feel intimate. "As it turned out The Kinks managed matters better than might have been expected," reports the *Chicago Tribune*. "The quintet's joyous, melodic, and often witty rock'n'roll – even the songs from the 1960s – came across as fresh and powerful."
✪ At Masterdisk in New York City the 'Destroyer' / 'Back To Front' single is mastered.

Wednesday 16th
Pine Knob Music Theatre *Clarkston, MI* 7:30pm with Red Rider

Thursday 17th
Wings Stadium *Kalamazoo, MI* 8:00pm, with Red Rider
Day off in Detroit follows.

Saturday 19th
Millet Hall, Miami University *Oxford, OH* 8:00pm, with Red Rider
An attendance of 9,100 at this 11,000-capacity hall. Soundcheck consists of a rock'n'roll medley of songs by Buddy Holly, Elvis Presley and Chuck Berry.

Sunday 20th
Public Hall *Cleveland, OH* 8:00pm, with Red Rider

Monday 21st

Veterans Memorial Auditorium *Columbus, OH* 8:00pm, with Red Rider

"Packed to the rafters," says the *Columbus Monthly Planet*, "as yet another sell-out crowd was treated to the cynical, tongue-in-cheek rock of the legendary Kinks." And the *Columbus Dispatch*: "Even after 17 years as the backbone of The Kinks, Ray and Dave Davies are still locked in struggle. Dave wants to play rock'n'roll; Ray wants to tell stories and make wry social comments." (Travel day follows plus day off in Buffalo.)

Thursday 24th

War Memorial Auditorium *Buffalo, NY* 8:00pm, with Red Rider

Friday 25th

Maple Leaf Gardens *Toronto, ON, Canada* 8:00pm, with Red Rider

Original Kinks bass player Pete Quaife, now resident in Toronto, joins the band on-stage for the last encore, playing on Chuck Berry's 'Little Queenie'. It marks the only reunion of the original four Kinks in public since Quaife left the band in March 1969. "For some time The Kinks had been the grand old also-rans of the first British invasion," says the *Toronto Sun*. "Now they are heroes to a generation that never saw The Beatles and never cared about the Stones. But while they catered [tonight] primarily to the newest members of their fan clubs, they managed to do so without alienating their peers."

Saturday 26th

Concert Bowl *Montreal, PQ, Canada* 8:00pm, with Nine Below Zero

Sunday 27th & Tuesday 29th

Boston Garden *Boston, MA* 7:30pm, with Red Rider

Demand is so strong in Boston, traditionally a big market for The Kinks, that a date is added by moving tonight's originally scheduled show in Montreal up a night and cancelling a show in Ottawa to accommodate the switch. (Day off in Boston between shows.) **'Destroyer'** / **'Back To Front'** single released in the US.

Wednesday 30th

Providence Civic Center *Providence, RI* 8:00pm, with Red Rider

An audience of 11,186 make this a sell-out.

Destroyer single

A **'Destroyer'** (R. DAVIES).
B **'Back To Front'** (R. DAVIES).

US release September 28th 1981 (Arista AS 0619).
Musicians and recording details as *Give The People What They Want* album (see August 26th).
Chart high US number 85.

October

Thursday 1st

Nassau Veterans Memorial Coliseum *Uniondale, NY*

8:00pm, with Red Rider
The last song of the evening is interrupted by an on-stage verbal spat between Dave and Avory, and Avory leaves the stage. Ray says to the audience: "I think our drummer's had a phone call..."

Saturday 3rd

Madison Square Garden *New York, NY* 8:00pm, with Red Rider

A milestone for The Kinks who have made it a goal to play this prestigious 15,000-capacity venue. Ray partly attributes this to a promoter's offhand remark in the 1970s that The Kinks would never be popular enough to play the Garden.

"Lead singer/showman Ray Davies was in fine form, bantering with the audience like a camp counselor stuck with an unruly bunch of kids," writes Ed Naha in the *New York Post*. "Dave Davies turned in some stellar performances on guitar. The rhythms concocted by Mick Avory, Jim Rodford and Ian Gibbons on drums, bass and keyboard were solid without being overpowering. If there was any fault to be found it was because of the size of the Garden. These musicians' zany presence works better in smaller, more intimate halls where there's more of an exchange between Ray and his ardent fans. Nonetheless the audience got an expertly crafted avalanche of Kinky epics."

Set-list: 'Around The Dial', 'The Hard Way', 'Destroyer', 'Yo-Yo', 'Catch Me Now I'm Falling', 'Better Things', 'Blues' (improvisation), 'Lola', 'Too Serious', 'Art Lover', 'Waterloo Sunset', 'You Really Got Me', 'Back To Front' / 'Get Back', 'A Gallon Of Gas', 'Till The End Of The Day', 'Celluloid Heroes', '20th Century Man', 'Killer's Eyes', 'All Day And All Of The Night', 'Give The People What They Want', 'Misfits', 'Low Budget', 'Add It Up', medley '(Wish I Could Fly Like) Superman' / 'Shakin' All Over', 'Pressure', 'The Village Green Preservation Society', 'Twist And Shout'.

Sunday 4th & Tuesday 6th

The Spectrum *Philadelphia, PA* 8:00pm, with Red Rider

Exactly 24,013 fans attend over the two nights. (Day between is time off in New York City; the 7th is a travel day.)

Thursday 8th

Atlanta Civic Center *Atlanta, GA* 8:00pm, with Blackfoot

Friday 9th

NBC Television Studios (8H), RCA Building *New York, NY*. Rehearsals for tomorrow's appearance. (A second concert at the Atlanta Civic Center originally scheduled for today is cancelled.)

Saturday 10th

☐ **TV** NBC Television (Studio 8H), RCA Building *New York, NY*. NBC *Saturday Night Live* live performance 'Destroyer', 'Art Lover' 11:30pm-1:00am. The Kinks return to this hugely popular late-night live comedy/variety show playing two songs from the new LP, and as the show fades to a commercial the band start into a third, 'Give The People What They Want'.

Sunday 11th

Tallahassee-Leon County Civic Center *Tallahassee, FL* 8:00pm

Tonight sees 3,716 fans at the 5,000-capacity room. Following the show, $8,000 cash and $14,000-worth of airline tickets are stolen from road manager Ken Jones's hotel room while he is out for a late-night meal with the band. (Travel day following.)

Monday 12th

As the band travels from Tallahassee to Fort Lauderdale, the *Give The People What They Want* LP peaks in the *Billboard* chart at number 15.

Tuesday 13th – Wednesday 14th

Sunrise Musical Theatre *Fort Lauderdale, FL* 8:00pm
Travel day following.

Friday 16th

Lakeland Civic Center *Lakeland, FL* 8:00pm, with Molly Hatchet
Band members remain in Florida for rest and relaxation and then return home. Ray stays in the US.
Glamour album by Dave Davies released in the UK. *Melody Maker's* Patrick Humphries mercilessly trashes the record, calling it nothing less than a "truly depressing experience" and ends by saying, "The only worrying thing about this regressive outing is that it'll probably be number one before Christmas." It isn't.

Jack Lynch in Irish rock paper *Hot Press* is a little more polite in his criticism. "There was never any doubt that Dave Davies has his act together as a guitarist. Added to this he has an alarming vocal range (in The Kinks' vocal signature he sings lines an octave above Ray). But on the evidence of *Glamour* I'll continue to prefer to know and love him as a Kink."

Tuesday 20th

Ray is probably at Masterdisk in New York City as Robert Ludwig masters the new US single, 'Better Things' and 'Yo-Yo'.
☆ Around this time Ray and Dave are interviewed by Chris Welch for *International Musician* at Konk. Ray tells Welch, a veteran rock reporter, "Well, I was never happy in the 1960s. You met me. I was never happy. The Kinks feel much better in the 1980s. This is the happiest band we've had, certainly the most exciting, and, I hope, the most successful. It's got a few years left in it." Ray flies straight back to NYC to work on the financing for a full-length video of *Give The People What They Want*.
➔ In New York City Ray is writing the script for a *Give The People What They Want* video and negotiating a deal with RCA Video Productions, eventually sealing a long-term development deal that underwrites the making of future Kinks videos.

He tells *Creem* how the script is going. "I'm using the thing of the DJ – the guy who's missing – as a very important part of the story, because he's pissed off at the way the media is run, the way people tell him how to play records.

"He's being hyped up and he's had enough and can't take it any more. He disappears. It's all going to be a show. I'm not saying that this album is a concept album. It's still a load of songs put together, but I think the videodisc [version] will be a good concept, and I'd like to try it." While a working script for the project is completed, the full *Give The People* video is never made.

Friday 30th

'Predictable' / 'Back To Front' single released in the UK.

Predictable single

A **'Predictable'** (R. DAVIES).
B **'Back To Front'** (R. DAVIES).

UK release October 30th 1981 (Konk [Arista] ARIST 426).
Musicians and recording details as *Give The People What They Want* album (see August 26th).
Chart high UK none.

'I Go To Sleep' single by The Pretenders released in the UK, a song by Ray Davies. The song was demoed by The Kinks back in the 1960s – see May 24th 1965 – and never released by them, but recorded that year by Peggy Lee. The Pretenders' version peaks in the British *Music Week* singles chart at number 7.

November

➔ At the start of the month Ray is back in London, continuing the press duties that have taken up much time over the last few months.

Monday 2nd

➔ 'Better Things' / 'Yo-Yo' single released in the US probably this week.
➔ The Kinks cancel their entire European tour except two Irish dates, with the usual vague "Dave Davies ill" excuse. Dave reveals later in *Kink* that he is suffering from depression and feels he can't cope with another tour now. Instead he gets away to north Devon for some time alone.
☆ While commuting between his home in Surrey and Konk in London, Ray comes up with the idea for an experimental film project, *Return To Waterloo*, that will tell the story through song of a suburban estate agent (real-estate agent) suspected of rape. Channel 4 Television is already hoping that Ray will develop a TV play for broadcast, and the two ideas merge for the next proposed Kinks project (though in 1982 Dave will drop out and it becomes a venture for a Dave-less Kinks).

Better Things single

A **'Better Things'** (R. DAVIES).
B **'Yo-Yo'** (R. DAVIES).

US release November (probably 2nd) 1981 (Arista AS 0649).
Musicians and recording details as *Give The People What They Want* album (see August 26th).
Chart high US number 92.

Thursday 19th

Ulster Hall *Belfast, Northern Ireland*

Friday 20th – Saturday 21st

National Stadium, Royal Dublin Society *Dublin, Ireland*
"It was the early 1960s again minus the screams," says *Hot Press*, "and it's warming to witness the band come full-circle in terms of recognition [to a] crowd close on 5,000."

➔ The planned filming of a videodisc for the entire *Give The People What They Want* LP is cancelled due to a lack of finance. But Ray does get backing for a video for one of the songs, 'Predictable', produced in London around now. It is essentially a Ray solo performance as he plays himself evolving from the 1950s into the 1980s. The video is produced by Michael Hamlyn and directed for Midnight Films by Julien Temple, who is just beginning to make his mark as a music-video maker (and last year directed The Sex Pistols' film *The Great Rock'n'Roll Swindle*). There is an early broadcast for the video in the US on MTV in December 1981, and on French TV programme *Jacques Martin* on December 13th.

December

Friday 4th

❏ **TV** Westdeutscher Rundfunk Studios *Cologne, West Germany.* ARD-channel 1 *Bananas* lip-synch 'Give The People What They Want' broadcast January 26th 1982 8:15-9:00pm. (Kinks without Dave.)
☆ Ray does a good deal of press work in place of the cancelled German Kinks concerts.

Tuesday 8th

❏ **TV** Bayerischer Rundfunk Studios *Munich, West Germany.* ARD-channel 1 *Bayern III* lip-synch 'Predictable', 'Destroyer' broadcast December 31st. Again, the band performs on this German TV show without Dave.

Friday 18th

Ray is in Paris, France for a series of interviews to take the place of live appearances by the band, and then returns to London shortly after completing this work.

Ray continues to do press work for the LP, including phone interviews with Australian journalists in preparation for upcoming Australian and Japanese tours. Dave has been talked into honouring these dates, despite his fragile emotional state.

1982

The final two legs of the lengthy worldwide tour to promote Give The People What They Want wrapped up as spring began and, just as in the previous year, the brothers again veered off to pursue individual interests. Dave recorded a third solo LP (Chosen People) while Ray largely continued to develop his film project, Return To Waterloo. Ray saw this as the next Kinks project, but Dave withdrew his support from the ambitious venture early on. Return To Waterloo dominated much of the following two years, contributing to a tense atmosphere in the band.

The summer began and ended with two very brief visits to the US, each centred on a big festival appearance, allowing the band major exposure without the necessity to commit to extensive touring. Work on the next Kinks LP began in earnest in the autumn, but the sessions stretched well into 1983.

Having achieved album and arena-tour success in the States, Ray shifted his focus a little, paying attention to the British market and having a stab at a hit pop single again, a strategy that hadn't quite worked with last year's return to a 1960s sound, 'Better Things'.

Two new recordings, each with a dancing theme, became the focal point late in the year, and a full British tour rounded off 1982 to promote the first one, 'Come Dancing'. At first the effort didn't pay off in the British charts, but it showed The Kinks were making an attempt to connect once more to a home audience, and the plan would work very well in the end.

January

▷ **TOUR STARTS** *Give The People What They Want: North American Tour: 3rd leg* (Jan 8th – 24th). **Line-up**: Ray Davies (lead vocal, guitar), Dave Davies (guitar, vocal), Mick Avory (drums), Jim Rodford (bass), Ian Gibbons (keyboards). This relatively quick jaunt is booked to finance the trip to Australia. 'Bernadette', an as-yet unreleased song, is added to the repertoire. (The band travels from London to New York City on the 6th and 7th.)

Friday 8th

War Memorial Auditorium *Syracuse, NY* 8:00pm, with Bryan Adams

Saturday 9th

Westchester Premier Theater *Tarrytown, NY* 8:00pm, with Bryan Adams

Sunday 10th

Brendan Byrne Arena, Meadowlands *East Rutherford, NJ* 8:00pm, with Bryan Adams
"It was by all accounts a perfect rock concert with good sound, professional performances [and] exciting solos," reports *The Aquarian* of this sell-out show. "It just wasn't The Kinks! They were too good, if that's possible." (Day off in New York City follows.)
Set-list: 'Around The Dial', 'The Hard Way', medley 'Where Have All The Good Times Gone' / 'Tired Of Waiting For You', 'Catch Me Now I'm Falling', 'Bird Dog', 'Destroyer', 'Yo-Yo', 'Lola', 'A Gallon Of Gas',

'Low Budget', 'Back To Front', 'Art Lover', 'Celluloid Heroes', 'Till The End Of The Day', 'Bernadette', 'All Day And All Of The Night', 'Give The People What They Want', 'Pressure', 'Twist And Shout', 'You Really Got Me', 'Stop Your Sobbing'.

Tuesday 12th
Stabler Arena, Lehigh University *Bethlehem, PA* 8:00pm, with Bryan Adams
A sell-out, attracting 5,800 fans.

Wednesday 13th
Hampton Coliseum *Hampton, VA* 8:00pm, with Bryan Adams
Dave recounts later in full detail in his book *Kink* that this afternoon he has his first experience of what he describes as a visitation – a telepathic revelation that is a life-altering experience for him. It has a profound influence on both his next album if not all of his future work as an artist and as a person. More mundanely, Ray is busy doing long-distance phone-interviews with Australian journalists as part of his massive advance operation to prepare for the dates there.

Thursday 14th
Capital Centre *Landover, MD* 8:00pm, with Bryan Adams

Friday 15th – Saturday 16th
The band's equipment truck is snowed in en route and, with Ray ill anyway, Friday's show in Charlotte is delayed to Sunday. This also forces the delay of Sunday's originally scheduled show in Memphis, which gets pushed back until June. As the 12th was a night off anyway, Ray and Dave return to New York City for two days, while the remaining band members enjoy time off in Washington DC.
Give The People What They Want album released in the UK. Plans to remix the album for the British public have been scuttled, as has Ray's dream for the financing of an accompanying full-length video. So the LP is simply offered up for British release, in the middle of a Kinks tour of the US, with virtually no promotion from Arista or the band – tantamount to an admission of defeat with the home crowd. The Kinks' problem persists: they have a profoundly etched reputation with the British public and press … based almost entirely on their 1960s classics.

The main review of the latest LP is eloquent in recognising and describing this problem in their home country. While riding high on a Stateside reputation, writes Patrick Humphries in *Melody Maker*, "they triumphed in America with an unfortunate brand of [heavy metal] riffing over their old classics. Yet they played a great gig at the [London] Lyceum last year, before a new generation of Kinks fans. It was like The Kinks were out to prove they could still cut it. That seems to be the message behind *Give The People What They Want*, but behind the unambiguous title are 11 songs that at least show Ray Davies trying to recapture some of his former glory. … The album shows that Davies hasn't wholly lost that ability, and for that we should be grateful, even it is only in small doses."

Sunday 17th
Charlotte Coliseum *Charlotte, NC* 8:00pm, with The George Hatcher Band

Monday 18th
Further disaster strikes and tonight's concert at the Palace Theatre, Louisville, KY, is cancelled one hour before showtime due to a strike by stage hands. Accordingly this show has to be rescheduled too, ultimately for June 15th as part of a brief make-up tour.

Tuesday 19th
Stanley Theater *Pittsburgh, PA* 8:00pm, with Bryan Adams
Day off follows in Pittsburgh.

Thursday 21st
New Haven Veterans Memorial Coliseum *New Haven, CT* 8:00pm, with Bryan Adams

Friday 22nd
State University of New York College fieldhouse *Plattsburgh, NY* 8:00pm, with Bryan Adams

Saturday 23rd
Proctor Theater *Schenectady, NY* 8:00pm, with Bryan Adams; sponsored by Union College
Tonight's performance prompts a *Sunday Gazette* headline: "Kinks-Mania Explodes In Schenectady – Finest Rock Show Ever At Proctor's."

Sunday 24th
Springfield Civic Center Arena *Springfield, MA* 7:30pm, with Bryan Adams

Monday 25th
Tonight is scheduled as an added second show at the Brendan Byrne Arena, Meadowlands at East Rutherford, NJ, but appears not to take place. (The band has two days off in New York City and departs for Los Angeles and on to Sydney on the 27th.)
☆ *Give The People What They Want* is certified a gold album by the RIAA in the US for sales of 500,000 or more copies.

February

➡ **TOUR STARTS** *Give The People What They Want: Australia/Japan Tour* (Feb 2nd – 27th). **Line-up**: Ray Davies (lead vocal, guitar), Dave Davies (guitar, vocal), Mick Avory (drums), Jim Rodford (bass), Ian Gibbons (keyboards). The Kinks finally return to Australia after an 11-year absence, following their disastrous foray there in 1971. Tours had been planned again in 1973 and then seriously in '78 when they pulled out at the last minute. Plans were again put into place in 1980 as part of the *Low Budget* tours but again fell through. Now finally they get there as they ride a crest of popularity in the US, and battle for acceptance of new material in an attempt not to be tied down to their 1960s reputation.

Very careful advance planning has been done to ensure control over production, especially bearing in mind that the main problems before came when they travelled without their own equipment. In addition to the five-man Kinks, the entourage includes American manager Elliot Abbott, tour manager Ken Jones, plus a stage manager, bodyguard, and six-man road crew. Venues are in the 2,000-3,000 capacity range. Promoter is Gary Van Egmond Promotions Ltd of Melbourne. (The band departs New York on January 27th heading for Sydney via Los Angeles, and arrives in Sydney on Friday 29th – losing a day in the process by crossing the international dateline. The weekend of 30th/31st is off to recover from the long trip, though Ray is available for some press duties.)

Monday 1st
Tonight the band sets up at the Capitol Theatre in Sydney for rehearsals, in particular to make sure their stage equipment and PA are in perfect working order.

Tuesday 2nd – Wednesday 3rd
Capitol Theatre *Sydney, New South Wales, Australia* 8:00pm, with The Boys
"It seemed as if The Kinks were not only determined to Give The People What They Want," writes Elly MacDonald in *The Australian*,

"but to give them rather more than they'd anticipated. Anyone who bought tickets expecting to see this durable band, now approaching its third decade of existence, work their way through a string of old hits can only have been pleasantly surprised. As the handful of classic favourites were concentrated at the very end, the show relied on the strength of material with which the audience were not necessarily familiar." Support band The Boys are from Perth. (Travel day following, with a press conference in Brisbane.)

Friday 5th
Festival Hall *Brisbane, Queensland, Australia* 8:00pm, with The Boys
Travel day follows.

Sunday 7th
Festival Hall *Melbourne, Victoria, Australia* 8:00pm, with The Boys
Travel day following.

Tuesday 9th – Wednesday 10th
Thebarton Concert Hall *Adelaide, South Australia, Australia* 8:00pm, with The Boys
The opening night's show gets off to a bad start but soon bounces back. The *Adelaide Advertiser* reports Ray shouting, "I didn't travel 12,000 miles for the amusement of you morons," to the crowd and then storming off stage "muttering profanities". The reporter notes the bandleader's return soon after. "One had to wonder whether he was still annoyed about the lukewarm reception in Adelaide [in 1971. In the end] this band delivered all that had been promised, and showed [Ray] in particular to be rejuvenated. Grinning frequently and bending to kiss some girls and shake hands, he leapt about the stage and gave the fans what they came for – a bit of fun, a few oldies and evidence that he can still cut the mustard."

Thursday 11th
A day off in Adelaide before heading on to Perth. Ray writes the song 'Long Distance' around now (recorded later for the *State Of Confusion* sessions) after his frustration at trying to make long-distance calls to Chrissie Hynde in the US where she is on tour with The Pretenders. It's also a tribute to Ray's band and their road crew, many of whom are named in the song. (A travel day follows, and then a day off in Perth.)

Sunday 14th
Perth Entertainment Centre *Perth, Western Australia, Australia* 8:00pm, with The Boys
Travel day to Melbourne follows.

Tuesday 16th
❏ **TV** Channel 9 Studios *Melbourne, Victoria, Australia.* Channel 9 *The Don Lane Show* live performance 'You Really Got Me', 'Destroyer'. An appearance on this popular variety programme sees some energetic live takes, and Ray briefly interviewed by host Lane.

Wednesday 17th
Festival Hall West *Melbourne, Victoria, Australia* 8:00pm, with The Sherbs
Support band The Sherbs are from Sydney. (Travel day follows.)

Friday 19th
Hordern Pavilion, Paddington Showground *Sydney, New South Wales, Australia* 8:00pm, with The Sherbs

Saturday 20th – Tuesday 23rd
The band travels to Tokyo, followed by two days off before travelling on to Osaka. Ray arrives in Tokyo on the 22nd. There is no opening act for the four Japanese dates.

Wednesday 24th
Mainichi Hall *Osaka, Japan* 6:30pm
The band's first ever concert in Japan.

Thursday 25th – Saturday 27th
Nihon Seinenkan *Tokyo, Japan* 6:30pm
The final night's show is recorded and later broadcast on Radio NHK-FM in September. "How cool a guy is Ray Davies?" asks *Weekly FM*'s reviewer. "He shouts into the microphone, plays guitar, appeals to the audience, throws a guitar pick. I've never seen a guy change his clothes on the stage three times!" Ray does quite a bit of press, and when asked by Youichi Hirose of *Rock'n On* about how Japanese audiences are receiving the band, he replies, "I was so surprised! They know all about us. I never thought they'd know the lyrics – and not only the old songs, but the new songs too. I'm so happy about coming to Japan now, and I intend to return within 18 months."
Set-list: 'Around The Dial', 'The Hard Way', 'Where Have All The Good Times Gone', 'Tired Of Waiting For You', 'Come On Now', 'Destroyer', 'Yo-Yo', 'Oh Oh Tokyo' (improvisation), 'Lola', 'Low Budget', '(Wish I Could Fly Like) Superman', 'Back To Front', 'Celluloid Heroes', 'Till The End Of The Day', 'Bernadette', 'All Day And All Of The Night', 'Give The People What They Want', 'Pressure', 'Stop Your Sobbing', 'David Watts', 'You Really Got Me'.

Sunday 28th
The tour officially ends and the entourage heads back to London, except for Ray who remains behind for an extended break in Japan. While there he does at least two interviews on Japanese TV, one of which is broadcast today. The Pretenders start a Japanese tour in Tokyo today, adding to the appeal for Ray. The Pretenders are here through the first week of March. Ray later recalls buying a Casio keyboard in Tokyo on which he starts to write 'Come Dancing' during the plane trip back from Japan.

March

The band takes the entire month off, with a German date early in April wrapping up an intense period of touring. They're well aware that finally making it back to Australia and to Japan was a real feat. Having returned from his extended stay in Tokyo, Ray then travels all the way back to Australia with Chrissie Hynde as The Pretenders tour continues with Australian dates from March 16th-30th. Ray is there until he has to resume Kinks obligations. The Pretenders finally end up in Bangkok early in April before taking a break from touring themselves. Ray takes advantage of his time off to write, including material for an early version of *Return To Waterloo*, at present a play based on a song of the same name. He also works on various other projects, as well as new material for the next Kinks LP. (The band flies to Germany for a full-scale soundcheck at the Grugahalle in Essen on the 31st in preparation for a Europe-wide telecast.)

April

Band members enjoy some time off in Essen, West Germany on the 1st and 2nd while Ray dashes back to London. The concert takes place on the 3rd (and into the early hours of the 4th) at the Grugahalle, Essen with Rick James and Van Morrison. It is widely broadcast live around

Europe, allowing The Kinks to reach a vast audience in a single appearance – in part perhaps as a make-up for their own cancelled German concert tour set for the previous autumn.

Broadcasters taking the concert live include West German WDR/Channel 3 TV (*Rockpalast*), Swedish television's *Maraton Rock*, Danish television's *Rockpalast*, and in delayed transmission on April 15th on French Antenne 2 (*Rockpalast* again). (Travel day back to London follows.) **Set-list**: 'Opening', 'Around The Dial', 'The Hard Way', 'Where Have All The Good Times Gone', 'Catch Me Now I'm Falling', 'Come On Now', 'Destroyer', 'Yo-Yo', 'Lola', 'Dead End Street', 'Add It Up', 'Low Budget', 'Art Lover', 'Back To Front', 'Till The End Of The Day', 'Bernadette', 'All Day And All Of The Night', 'Give The People What They Want', 'Pressure', 'Stop Your Sobbing', 'David Watts'.

Some Scandinavian dates have been announced for this time including a show in Oslo, Norway but these are never finalised.

Dave leaves for a holiday in Portugal, writing songs for his new LP while there. He also writes in Los Angeles around now. Ray is in London writing and developing an early version of his TV play *Return To Waterloo* and working on an ultimately unfulfilled project called *See My Friends (A History of Britain 1900-)*. Ray and Chrissie Hynde have time off from touring schedules, and are both present at the Guildford Registrar's Office to be married on the 21st, but decide against it and continue their relationship on its present basis.

May

Dave starts rehearsals for a new solo LP. Ray continues writing and developing songs and script for *Return To Waterloo* – but Dave is entirely against the idea as a Kinks project. It is unclear at which point he decides to opt out of it, forcing Ray to continue with it as a solo venture (with the Dave-less Kinks on board), but it is at this time that the first serious work seems to begin, with early demos likely made at Konk.

June

→ ● **RECORDING** Konk Studios *Hornsey, north London*. At the start of the month Dave is at Konk for the first set of sessions for his third solo LP. This time he assembles a full studio band rather than playing most of the parts himself. Returning is Dave's preferred drummer, Bob Henrit, plus bassist Dave Wintour and keyboards player Chris Parrin. The sessions are engineered and co-produced by Steve Churchyard.

⤵ **TOUR STARTS** *US Mini Tour* (Jun 14th – 19th). **Line-up**: Ray Davies (lead vocal, guitar), Dave Davies (guitar, vocal), Mick Avory (drums), Jim Rodford (bass), Ian Gibbons (keyboards). Originally scheduled as three weeks of East Coast dates through the July 4th weekend, the trip is now reduced to only a few required make-up dates and one major festival. (Band travels to US on Saturday 12th, with a day off following in Memphis.)

Monday 14th
Dixon-Meyers/Auditorium Music Hall *Memphis, TN* 8:00pm, with Debra DeJean

Tuesday 15th
Palace Theatre *Louisville, KY* 8:00pm, with The Producers
The Kinks return with a vengeance to an eager audience who are keen to see the band. This follows the January 18th cancellation due to a dispute between the theatre and union stage hands.

Tensions are high between Ray and Dave tonight, with several publicly visible exchanges reported in the *Louisville Times*. When Ray makes to leave the stage at the end of the set he gestures to the crew that his brother is nuts, and Dave retaliates by kicking into 'All Day And All Of The Night' so that Ray has to return to the stage – grinning – and the band does two encores for an out-of-control crowd of 3,000. "Sibling rivalry settled peacefully once again," suggests the *Times*. Meanwhile, Dave's inspired playing is described by John Herzfeld in the *Courier-Journal* as "rabid guitar runs … his solos took off like jets, soared, and then crashed violently".

Wednesday 16th
Knoxville Civic Coliseum *Knoxville, TN* 8:00pm, with The Producers
In London today Pretenders guitarist James Honeyman-Scott dies of drug-related causes, just a day after bassist Pete Farndon was fired because of continuing problems with his own drug abuse. Farndon too will die a drug-related death, on April 14th 1983.

Friday 18th
Pre-concert soundcheck at John F. Kennedy Stadium in Philadelphia. Chrissie Hynde flies in from London today to join Ray following the death of her bandmate.

Saturday 19th
John F. Kennedy Stadium *Philadelphia, PA* 10:00am, with Foreigner (co-headliners), Joan Jett & The Blackhearts, Huey Lewis & The News, Loverboy
"Leading the crowd in calling them back for a final encore was none other than The Pretenders' Chrissie Hynde," says *The Aquarian*, "who, although looking understandably dishevelled as a result of the sudden death three days earlier of Pretenders guitarist James Honeyman-Scott, apparently got caught up in The Kinks' performance."

Dave is angered by Ray bringing Hynde on-stage with The Kinks, even if she does appear in a momentary non-performing capacity, and later in his book *Kink* admits to "taking a swipe at her" at the time. Although Dave admits to later becoming friends with Hynde, his actions at the time make it obvious that tensions are at a peak between the brothers concerning personal as well as artistic matters. (A travel day follows the Philadelphia concert as the band heads back home to London.)

→ ● **RECORDING** Konk Studios *Hornsey, north London*. At the end of the month Dave is back at Konk in order to resume sessions for his new LP.

July

Sessions continue at Konk for Dave's new solo LP. During June and July tracks recorded include **'Tapas'**, **'Charity'**, **'Mean Disposition'**, **'Love Gets You'**, **'Danger Zone'**, **'True Story'**, **'Matter Of Decision'**, **'Take One More Chance'**, **'Freedom Lies'**, **'Is It Any Wonder'**, **'Fire Burning'**, **'Chosen People'**, **'Cold Winter'** and **'One Night'**.

Ray works on various projects, including the writing of new material for the next Kinks LP.

Exact timing is unknown, but possibly around this time Ray appears in a film that is directed by Julien Temple and titled *Scenes From A Video Marriage*. The film will be broadcast on British Channel 4 TV in May 1983.

Thousands watch The Kinks on-stage at the John F. Kennedy Stadium, Philadelphia, June 19th 1982.

August

→ Rehearsals take place at Konk and presumably demos of new material are made, with the intention of recording masters at US studios during September.

A US Mini Tour starts on the 30th, lasting only until September 4th. The opening date is at Saenger Performing Arts Center, New Orleans, LA, at 8:00pm, with The Sheiks, and the following night they're at the City Coliseum Austin, TX, at 8:00pm, with Lords Of The New Church. There's a rare performance in Austin of the as-yet unreleased song 'Entertainment', which will not be released until 1989. "Three encores finished this two-hour offering," says the *Daily Texan*, "not a bad show for a group of 35-year-old men." The opening act includes punk rockers Stiv Bators and Brian James, formerly of The Dead Boys and The Damned respectively. (Travel day follows.)

September

Thursday 2nd

Ahead of Saturday's show, today sees a soundcheck at the Glen Helen Regional Park in San Bernadino, CA, and then a day off in Los Angeles as the three-day *US Festival* begins. Among other acts: (3rd) The Police, Talking Heads, and The B-52s; (5th) Fleetwood Mac, Jackson Browne, and Jimmy Buffet. The festival is the brainchild of Apple Computer's Steve Wozniak.

Saturday 4th

Glen Helen Regional Park *San Bernadino, CA* 10:00am-12midnight, *The US Festival*, with Tom Petty & The Heartbreakers, Pat Benetar, The Cars, Santana, Eddie Money, Dave Edmunds, The Ramones, Joe Sharino

The Kinks perform on the second of the three-day event, with 205,000 attending and the temperature peaking at over 100 degrees. Ray is involved in a battle of wills with "talent organizer" Bill Graham, who is used to running things with precision timing. It's reported that The Kinks are slated to go on at 6:20pm before sets by Petty and Benetar, a schedule they evidently want changed so they will appear at dusk for better dramatic effect, but which Graham won't accommodate. As their scheduled showtime approaches there are no Kinks to be found, and reportedly it is only after Graham threatens to up-end manager Elliot Abbott's Mercedes that the manager retrieves his band, who successfully stall by 40 minutes, long enough for darkness to be almost descending.

→ Dave negotiates and secures a recording contract around now with Warner Brothers Records at the company's offices in Burbank, CA.
☆ On the quiet, The Kinks are booked into the 24-track Grand Slam Studios in East Orange, NJ, with former Konk engineer John Rollo. The sessions are intended to provide backing tracks for the next LP, similar to the way in which they made *Low Budget* in New York City three years earlier.

One of the seven or eight titles put on tape is probably the backing for **'Don't Forget To Dance'**, which turns out to be the only track apparently salvaged and subsequently used. **'Regret It'** is another song probably recorded now, although it is never heard of again (other than some soundcheck work-outs in December). Otherwise the tracks are eventually scrapped: any songs from this time that eventually end up on the new Kinks LP will be re-recorded in February and March 1983.
☆ Back at Konk Studios in London the band works with engineer Damian Korner to add vocals and overdubs to 'Don't Forget To Dance'.

October

In London Ray finishes writing a new song, **'Come Dancing'**, which he'd reportedly begun on the flight home from Tokyo in March with a newly purchased Casio keyboard. At Konk a demo is made first, and later a master backing track with bass, drums and acoustic guitar, followed by overdubs. Dave later says that the recording is done the day after a particularly heated argument with Ray. The track is completed and final mixing done 20th-21st, as is a completed recording of **'Don't Forget To Dance'**, which becomes first choice of Arista's British arm as a potential single release.

November

→ Dave spends a good deal of time at Ray's house in Surrey, England during this month, working up arrangements for new material. A mix and edit session for 'Bernadette' takes place on the 8th and 9th.
☆ Ray pushes for 'Come Dancing' rather than 'Don't Forget To Dance' as the new single; UK Arista agrees, and it's released in 7-inch and 12-inch forms on the 19th. Clive Davis of US Arista decides against releasing 'Come Dancing' as a single for now.

The Kinks are at the Ilford Palais in Essex, England on the 30th where footage is shot from 6:00pm for ballroom scenes for a video of the new single, 'Come Dancing'. Some local fans are invited to help make up an audience. The video is produced by Michael Hamlyn and directed by Julien Temple, with choreography by Jim Cameron. It recreates the storyline of the song, recalling Ray's youth and his sister's night out on a date with a slick, pencil-moustached suitor at the local Palais where a big-band orchestra is playing. The Kinks as themselves are seen later in the video performing in the same ballroom.

The video will be aired in Britain on Channel 4 TV's *The Tube* in December, and debuts on American television on the MTV channel on March 25th 1983.

Come Dancing single

A **'Come Dancing'** (R. DAVIES).
B **'Noise'** (R. DAVIES).

UK release November 19th 1982 (Arista ARIST 502 7-inch; ARIST 12502 12-inch with extended versions); re-released July 1983.
US release April 21st 1983 (Arista AS 1054).
Edits of A and B differ slightly between US and UK releases.
Musicians Ray Davies lead vocal, acoustic guitar. Dave Davies electric guitar, backing vocal. Jim Rodford bass guitar, backing vocal. Mick Avory drums. Ian Gibbons keyboards. John Beecham trombone. Noel Morris trumpet. Andy Hamilton tenor saxophone. Alan Holmes baritone saxophone. Kate Williams spoken voice.
Recorded A: Konk Studios *Hornsey, north London*; October 1982; 24-track mixed to stereo. B: probably same, but details unknown.
Producer Ray Davies.
Engineer Damien Korner.
Chart high UK number 12; US number 6.

December

▷ **TOUR STARTS** *Come Dancing: UK Tour* (Dec 2nd – 22nd). **Line-up**: Ray Davies (lead vocal, guitar), Dave Davies (guitar, vocal), Mick Avory (drums), Jim Rodford (bass), Ian Gibbons (keyboards). A classic 1960s-style tour of England and Scotland. (The band travels from London to Edinburgh on the 1st.)

Thursday 2nd
Playhouse Theatre *Edinburgh, Scotland* 7:30pm, with Idle Flowers

Friday 3rd
Apollo Theatre *Manchester* 7:30pm, with Idle Flowers
Ray talks to *Time Out* about the new album. "It's about half finished. It's proving incredibly slow. I'm not too worried though. To be honest, I know the world isn't holding its breath waiting for the new Kinks album, and Arista must know that." (Day off follows, with Ray returning to London to work on an edit at Konk for the proposed US single, 'Don't Forget To Dance'.)

Sunday 5th
Royal Court Theatre *Liverpool* 7:30pm, with Idle Flowers

Monday 6th
Town Hall *Middlesbrough, Yorks* 7:30pm, with Idle Flowers

Tuesday 7th
Odeon *Birmingham* 7:30pm, with Idle Flowers

Wednesday 9th
❏ **TV** BBC Pebble Mill Studios *Birmingham*. BBC-1 *Pebble Mill At One* live performance Ray solo (not Kinks) 'A Well Respected Man', 'Celluloid Heroes' broadcast December 16th, 'Come Dancing', 'You Really Got Me' not broadcast.

Thursday 10th
Friars, Maxwell House *Aylesbury, Bucks* 7:30pm, with The Truth

Friday 11th
Gaumont Cinema *Ipswich, Suffolk* 7:30pm, with The Truth

Saturday 12th
Lower Common Room, University Of East Anglia *Norwich* 7:30pm, with The Truth
Day off follows.

Monday 14th
Royal Court Centre *Nottingham* 7:30pm, with The Truth

Tuesday 15th
Victoria Hall *Hanley, Stoke-on-Trent, Staffs* 7:30pm, with The Truth

Wednesday 16th
Caesar's *Bradford, Yorks* 7:30pm, with The Truth

Thursday 17th
Lyceum Ballroom *Sheffield* 7:30pm, with The Truth
● **RECORDING** Konk Studios *Hornsey, north London*. Today sees an edit session for the US single 'Don't Forget To Dance' / 'Noise'. (Day off follows.)

Saturday 19th
Winter Gardens *Bournemouth* 7:30pm, with The Truth

Sunday 20th
Civic Hall *Guildford, Surrey* 7:30pm, with The Truth

Monday 21st
Dome Arena *Brighton* 7:30pm, with The Truth

Tuesday 22nd
Strand Lyceum Ballroom *central London* 7:30pm, with Idle Flowers
Some rare good words from the British music press for a London show come in a review by Paul Roland published in *Sounds*. He says that Ray seems to be the epitome of boundless energy. Roland says Ray's band "stormed through a whole barrage of hits without a single mistake and jacked all the usual effects in favour of a stunning light show. ... As a tribute to The Jam, they steamed through 'David Watts'. ... I hate to say it, but The Jam were made to look like a schoolkids' garage band next to the real thing."
Set-list: 'Around The Dial', 'The Hard Way', medley 'Where Have All The Good Times Gone' / 'Tired Of Waiting For You', 'Come On Now', 'Destroyer', 'Yo-Yo', 'London Blues' (improvisation), 'Lola', 'Come Dancing', 'Low Budget', 'David Watts', 'Dead End Street', 'A Gallon Of Gas', 'Back To Front', 'Celluloid Heroes', 'Till The End Of The Day', 'Bernadette', 'All Day And All Of The Night', 'Pressure', 'Twist And Shout', medley 'A Well Respected Man' / 'Death Of A Clown', 'Waterloo Sunset', 'You Really Got Me', 'Victoria', 'Louie Louie'.

➜ Towards the end of the month Ray secures a financing deal with Britain's new Channel 4 TV for his *Return To Waterloo* project. Starting life as an intended TV play, it's now to be a TV special based on music. Meanwhile, at Konk, sessions continue for the new Kinks album.

kinks'83

1983

At first, efforts to get back into the British singles chart failed, and throughout the winter and into the spring the band shifted its focus to completing the next album, typically behind schedule.

The band had State Of Confusion under their belt and headed off across the US to pick up the momentum started with the success of Give The People What They Want. 'Come Dancing' started selling well as an import single and, almost against the wishes of the US record label, turned into a runaway hit there. It was then re-promoted in Britain and likewise headed up the charts.

The success of 'Come Dancing' came at a tricky point. Ray was committed to recording and filming his Return To Waterloo project and Dave to promoting his Chosen People solo album. The commercial failure of Dave's record put him into a momentary tailspin, and a crucial US tour in the autumn was postponed as the band faced one of the larger internal crises of its career.

The Kinks rebounded at the close of the year with a series of shows at New York City's Roseland Ballroom, but the inner conflict continued. 'Come Dancing' – which turned out to be the band's last major charting single – was just like their first, 'You Really Got Me', in that it came at a time of conflict within the band and was released after differences of opinion between Ray and the record company about its suitability.

January

→ Work at Konk on the new LP seems to be nearing completion, with a February release date scheduled. The working title is probably *Entertainment*, the track left off the *Give The People What They Want* album and saved for this one.

On the 11th Ray does another edit and dubs some additional vocals to **'Don't Forget To Dance'**. Two new tracks recorded around the middle of the month are **'Young Conservatives'** and **'Heart Of Gold'**. Ray says later that 'Heart Of Gold' is partly about the birth of a daughter to him and Chrissie Hynde on the 22nd.

Mixes are likely completed by the time Ray leaves for New York City, where on the 27th he oversees mastering of 'Don't Forget To Dance' with Robert Ludwig at Masterdisk for the intended US single release. Arista head Clive Davis has refused to release 'Come Dancing' for the US market.

Ray returns to London and announces that he will re-record a number of the LP tracks, causing tour dates set for February and March to be shifted forward by six weeks. The album is also delayed.

While in London, Ray tells *Music World*: "I want our albums to sound the way we want to play, to have the excitement of playing the Lyceum or the Royal Court in Liverpool together with the bigness of Madison Square Garden … combined with the tightness and excitement of the smaller gigs. That's what I am trying to capture on our album. And that influences the sort of songs I use. You've got to reflect what the group is. It is not just my songs, it's a point the group has reached, which is a big sound. I'm trying to make a great band record."

He goes on in the interview to mention the film and album of *Return To Waterloo*, the attempt to work together again with playwright Barrie

Keeffe for the Stratford Theatre Royal, and advance plans for a Kinks 20th anniversary, including an authorised biography and an accompanying film.

"The sort of film I'd want to make, people would never take us seriously again!" Ray tells *Music World*. "But it's the only way you could tell our particular story, because we're such complete idiots. You just have to look at me and Mick, we're a complete mess. There's a certain way you can tell our story, because people still haven't got it. There's not really anything to tell, other than how we got together or what I was doing the day we recorded 'You Really Got Me'. They can't pin us down. We're inconsistent."

February

→ Sessions for the new album begin again at Konk and many of the tracks are re-recorded.

Probably done now and into March are the issued versions of **'Definite Maybe'**, **'Labour Of Love'**, **'Clichés Of The World'**, **'Once A Thief'**, **'Property'** and **'Long Distance'**.

Ray says later that he commutes daily from his home in Surrey to Konk in London during the next two months, and that he spends the time creatively, devises much of the final form of *Return To Waterloo* during his travelling.

On the 20th Ray further remixes 'Don't Forget To Dance' for an American single, also slated for British release. But in the US import copies of the British single 'Come Dancing' are selling well, and Arista head Clive Davies finally concedes to Ray's wish and agrees to issue it as the next US single.

March

On the 1st, Ray does a final mix of 'Come Dancing' for the US single release. Also at Konk early in the month The Kinks continue recording for the new album, including an entirely new song, **'State Of Confusion'**, which at the eleventh hour becomes the new title track, with the old contender, 'Entertainment', dropped altogether from the proposed running order.

On the 14th, 15th and 18th Ray does edits and final mixes on a number of completed recordings, including 'Definite Maybe' and 'State of Confusion' and on the 26th final edits of 'Definite Maybe' and 'Young Conservatives'. The tentative March release date of the album is pushed to April by now.

In the midst of finishing the new album, the sudden interest in 'Come Dancing' in America prompts Ray to videotape a few interviews at Konk, including one for the important American cable channel MTV, aired on the 25th, marking the premiere of the 'Come Dancing' video on US TV. Ray is also interviewed on camera for an ambitious television special on the history of The Kinks being assembled by Veronica TV in Holland, included in the resulting programme *The Story Of The Kinks* that is broadcast April 24th.

Business moves are made to incorporate a company that becomes Waterloo Films, indicating that interest is gathering in the *Return To Waterloo* film project.

April

➜ The Kinks are again photographed by Robert Ellis in front of Konk Studios for the new album's cover. The band are possibly rehearsing at Konk around now to work up new songs for the tour, including 'Don't Forget To Dance', 'State Of Confusion', 'Labour Of Love' and the intro only of 'Definite Maybe', used to lead into 'State Of Confusion'.

Tuesday 5th

At Konk Studios in north London Ray assembles a proposed album master, but after travelling to the US he decides that some songs still need remixing. This further delays the album's release – but the tour must begin. The following day at Konk he produces a new concert-opening tape.

⇨ **TOUR STARTS** *State Of Confusion: US Tour: 1st leg* (Apr 8th – Jun 11th). **Line-up**: Ray Davies (lead vocal, guitar), Dave Davies (guitar, vocal), Mick Avory (drums), Jim Rodford (bass), Ian Gibbons (keyboards). Tickets $8.50-$13.50, venue sizes are in the range of 6,000-18,000 capacity.

Friday 8th

Cincinnati Gardens *Cincinnati, OH* 8:00pm, with The Rockets

Saturday 9th

UIC Pavilion, University of Illinois-Chicago *Chicago, IL* 8:00pm, with The Shoes

"A number of tunes from the band's forthcoming album *State Of Confusion* sounded as tough and tight as anything the band has recorded in recent years," writes Don McLeese in the *Chicago Sun Times* of this sell-out attended by 10,638 fans. "'Don't Forget To Dance' is gracefully melodic in the 'Waterloo Sunset' tradition [and] 'Come Dancing' which has received considerable airplay as an import single is already being greeted as a hit."

Sunday 10th

Evans Field House, Northern Illinois University *DeKalb, IL* 8:00pm

Day off in Chicago follows.

Tuesday 12th

Dane County Memorial Coliseum *Madison, WI* 8:00pm, with The Rockets

Wednesday 13th

MECCA-Milwaukee Auditorium *Milwaukee, WI* 7:30pm, with The Rockets

A sell-out with 6,120 attending. *Milwaukee Sentinel*: "The band was tight, vibrant and polished – a matchless musical import."

Thursday 14th

Cobo Arena *Detroit, MI* 8:00pm, with Jon Butcher Axis

Friday 15th

● **RECORDING** Grand Slam Studios *East Orange, NJ*. The band has the day off in Detroit but Ray is off to New York City and then East Orange where he remixes 'Bernadette'. The forthcoming 'Come Dancing' / 'Noise' single is issued to US radio stations.

Saturday 16th

The Met Center *Bloomington, MN* 8:00pm, with The Rockets

Attendance is 8,825 at this 12,731-capacity room.

Sunday 17th

Pershing Municipal Auditorium *Lincoln, NB* 7:30pm, with The Rockets

Monday 18th

Events Center, University of Colorado *Boulder, CO* 8:30pm, with Looker

"The British musicians are still the masters of chunky three-chord rock'n'roll, thanks in no small part to … Dave Davies," says the *Denver Post*. Travel day following: the band to Vancouver, where they have time off for the two following days; Ray heads to New York City where he works on mixing and editing tracks for the new LP.

Tuesday 19th+

● **RECORDING** The Hit Factory *New York, NY*. Ray edits **'Young Conservatives'**, with further work without him on the 23rd and 26th. On the 20th-21st he remixes and re-edits **'Property'**, now finished. A concert at Memorial Coliseum, Portland, OR scheduled for the 21st is cancelled to accommodate the studio work in NYC.

Friday 22nd

Pacific National Exhibition Coliseum *Vancouver, BC, Canada* 8:00pm, with The Ray Roper Band

A sell-out with an audience of 13,113.

Saturday 23rd

Seattle Center Coliseum *Seattle, WA* 8:00pm, with The Original Kingsmen

Sunday 24th – Monday 25th

Travel day to San Francisco and a day off following for the band. Ray switches gears and is writing intensely to complete the final script of his TV/video special *Return To Waterloo* that he needs to submit for financing from RCA Video Productions. A concert scheduled for the 25th at The Forum, Inglewood, CA, is delayed to May 6th to accommodate Ray's work schedule.

Tuesday 26th

Cow Palace *San Francisco, CA* 8:00pm, with Scandal
An crowd of 10,244 nearly fill this famous 13,752-capacity venue.
Set-list: 'Around The Dial', 'State Of Confusion', 'The Hard Way', 'Catch Me Now I'm Falling', 'Destroyer', 'Yo-Yo', 'Come Dancing', 'Don't Forget To Dance', 'Lola', 'Back To Front', 'Where Have All The Good Times Gone', 'A Gallon Of Gas', '(Wish I Could Fly Like) Superman', 'Art Lover', 'Till The End Of The Day', 'Bernadette', 'All Day And All Of The Night', 'Pressure', 'David Watts', 'Low Budget', 'Celluloid Heroes', '20th Century Man', 'You Really Got Me'
☆ Ray evidently phones in one last edit instruction to New York for the song 'Young Conservatives' and gives Arista the final OK for the new LP's release.

The release date for the album is now set to May 24th. A travel day follows as the band returns to London for a break from touring. Ray heads to New York City for final work on the *Return To Waterloo* script and for business related to the project. Scheduled California concerts on the 29th in San Diego and the 30th at Laguna Hills are pushed back a week.

May

➔ At the RCA Video Productions offices in New York City, Ray submits the recently finished script for *Return To Waterloo* which subsequently is approved for the necessary financing for release as a videodisc in the US. The band travels to Las Vegas from London and Ray from New York City on Tuesday 3rd.

Wednesday 4th

Las Vegas Convention Center Rotunda *Las Vegas, NV* 8:00pm, with Scandal

Thursday 5th

San Diego Sports Arena *San Diego, CA* 8:00pm, with Scandal
Attended by 6,484 in an 8,500-capacity arena.

Friday 6th

The Forum *Inglewood, CA* 7:30pm, with Scandal
Almost full: 11,135 fans crowd this 13,705-capacity venue.

Ray has all the necessary work for the new LP completed and the submission deadline for the *Return To Waterloo* script behind him, and so while in Los Angeles he and Dave begin to involve themselves in the press work for the record, doing an array of interviews and photo shoots over the weekend.

Saturday 7th

Irvine Meadow Amphitheatre *Laguna Hills, CA* 8:00pm, with Scandal
The Kinks are briefly filmed in concert tonight and Ray is interviewed for a featured segment on the syndicated TV show *Entertainment Tonight* which airs nationally in two parts on May 27th-28th. (Travel day follows.)

Monday 9th

Veterans' Memorial Coliseum, State Fairgrounds *Phoenix, AZ* 8:00pm, with Scandal

Tuesday 10th

Tingley Coliseum, State Fairgrounds *Albuquerque, NM* 8:00pm, with Scandal
Ray receives a test pressing of the new Kinks LP today and stage

manager Colin Boyd gets a local fan to rent a stereo so he can listen to it in his hotel room. (Travel day following.)

Thursday 12th

Frank C. Erwin Jr. Special Events Center, University of Texas at Austin *Austin, TX* 8:00pm, with Scandal
Tonight 4,988 attend in this 6,243-capacity room.

Friday 13th

The Summit *Houston, TX* 8:00pm, with Scandal

Saturday 14th

Reunion Arena *Dallas, TX* 8:00pm, with Scandal
Almost a sell-out, with 6,351 in a 7,000-capacity venue.

Sunday 15th

Starlight Theatre *Kansas City, MO* 8:00pm, with Scandal
(Travel day follows.)

Tuesday 17th

Grand Ole Opry House *Nashville, TN* 8:00pm, with White Animals
Originally booked at the 9,654-capacity Nashville Municipal Auditorium but the venue is changed one week prior due to slow sales; 2,987 attend in this famous 4,424-capacity room.

Wednesday 18th

Rupp Arena, Lexington Center *Lexington, KY* 8:00pm
Travel day to New York City follows.

Friday 20th

Stabler Arena, Lehigh University *Bethlehem, PA* 8:00pm, with INXS

Saturday 21st

The Spectrum *Philadelphia, PA* 8:00pm, with Kix

Sunday 22nd

Community War Memorial *Rochester, NY* 8:00pm, with Backseat Sally
Tonight there are 6,848 fans in this 10,200-capacity venue. (Travel day to New York follows.)

Tuesday 24th

Montreal Forum *Montreal, PQ, Canada* 8:00pm, with Sherriff
"Last night [Ray] was a masterful, relaxed showman, and his audience, though less than capacity, was clearly keyed into the band's every note," writes John Griffin in the *Montreal Gazette* as more than 5,000 attend in this 13,000-capacity room. "What's especially surprising about this is that about one-third of the evening was given over to new material released on The Kinks' latest album, *State Of Confusion*. The immediate impression is that the band hasn't rocked this hard nor written so well since at least *Low Budget* and the result was one of the most purely entertaining rock shows since the band's last visit."
Set-list: 'Around The Dial', medley 'Definite Maybe' (intro) / 'State Of Confusion', 'The Hard Way', 'Destroyer', 'Yo-Yo', 'Come Dancing', 'Don't Forget To Dance', 'Untitled' (improvisation), 'Lola', '(Wish I Could Fly Like) Superman', 'A Gallon Of Gas', 'Art Lover', 'Till The End Of The Day', 'Bernadette', 'All Day And All Of The Night', 'Pressure', 'Low Budget', 'Celluloid Heroes', 'You Really Got Me'.
State Of Confusion album released in the US. "The album is not quite perfect," says *Rolling Stone*, "but in the breadth of its songwriting, the zip and assurance of the playing, the comeliness of the melodies and the gritty determination of Ray Davies himself, [it] cuts the competition

State Of Confusion album

1/A1 'State Of Confusion' (R. DAVIES).
2/A2 'Definite Maybe' (R. DAVIES).
3/A3 'Labour Of Love' (R. DAVIES).
4/A4 'Come Dancing' (R. DAVIES).
5/A5 'Property' (R. DAVIES).
6 'Noise' (R. DAVIES).
7/B1 'Don't Forget To Dance' (R. DAVIES).
8/B2 'Young Conservatives' (R. DAVIES).
9/B3 'Heart Of Gold' (R. DAVIES).
10/B4 'Clichés Of The World' (R. DAVIES).
11/B5 'Bernadette' (R. DAVIES).
12 'Long Distance' (R. DAVIES).

US release May 24th 1983 (LP A1-5/B1-5 Arista AL8-8018; cassette 1-12 Arista AC8-8018).
UK release June 10th 1983 (Arista 205 275).
Musicians Ray Davies lead vocal (except B5), electric guitar, acoustic guitar, backing vocal. Dave Davies lead vocal (B5), electric guitar, backing vocal. Jim Rodford bass guitar, backing vocal. Mick Avory drums. Ian Gibbons keyboards, backing vocal.
Recorded Konk Studios *Hornsey, north London*; 1: March 1983; 2, 3, 5, 10, 12: February-March 1983; 4, probably 6: October 1982; 8, 9: January 1983; 11: May-July 1981; 24-track mixed to stereo. 7: possibly Grand Slam Studios *East Orange, NJ*; September 1982; with overdubs at Konk October 1982; 24-track mixed to stereo.
Producer Ray Davies.
Engineers John Rollo, Damian Korner, Ben Fenner (B5).
Chart high US number 12; UK none.

to shreds. Nobody but The Kinks could have made such a record in 1983, and no band deserves more to be at the very top – which is where this LP ought to place them."

Good Times goes further when they take their turn to review the new *State Of Confusion* album: "Far from being a muddled mess, a failed experiment, or even an exercise in now-that-we've-made-it-we'll-just-give-the-people-what-they-want, [this] is close to being as perfect a record as The Kinks have yet made."

Wednesday 25th

Maple Leaf Gardens *Toronto, ON, Canada* 8:00pm, with INXS
Attended by 9,005 at this 10,000-capacity venue. (Travel day to New York follows.)

Friday 27th

Brendan Byrne Arena, Meadowlands *East Rutherford, NJ* 7:30pm, with Sherriff
"Musically The Kinks are tighter than they've ever been," says *The Aquarian* of this sell-out at the Brendan Byrne Arena that is attended by 18,007 fans.
"Dave Davies," continues the reviewer, "is one of rock's most underrated guitarists, and a consummate rocker. Charter member Mick Avory can still drum with the best of them. Jim Rodford is the best bass player The Kinks ever had. Ian Gibbons is a flexible supportive keyboardist. Together their playing is the most spontaneous I've seen in any Kinks line-up."
☆ Scheduled release in UK of 'Don't Forget To Dance' single is delayed to June 24th.

Saturday 28th

Glens Falls Civic Center *Glens Falls, NY* 8:00pm, with Red Rockers
"Davies is one of the few rock performers who uses the concert as theatre," writes Steve Webb in *Knickerbocker News*, "not with loads of lights and props, but by communicating the roles of his songs to the audience in a way that records don't."

Sunday 29th

Providence Civic Center *Providence, RI* 7:30pm, with Robert Ellis Orall
Almost a sell-out as 8,891 of a 9,826 capacity attend. An originally proposed concert at Madison Square Garden in New York City in two days' time (May 31st) is never announced. (Following two days are time off in New York City.)

June

Wednesday 1st

The Capital Centre *Landover, MD* 8:00pm, with The Greg Kihn Band
Travel day follows.

Friday 3rd

War Memorial Auditorium *Buffalo, NY* 8:00pm, with Sheriff
John Curran tells readers of *Buffalo News* that the audience of 6,300 gets a furious one-hour-45-minute performance. His piece is headlined: "Crowd Gets a Kick as Kinks Show Mastery of Old and New", underlining that the band still has to please both the teenagers and the old-time original fans.

Saturday 4th

The Coliseum *Richfield, OH* 8:00pm, with Sheriff
A sell-out audience attends the concert tonight at this big 14,125-capacity venue.

Sunday 5th

War Memorial Auditorium *Syracuse, NY* 8:00pm, with Sheriff

Monday 6th

New Haven Veterans Memorial Coliseum *New Haven, CT* 8:00pm, with Sherriff
Day off in New York City follows.

Wednesday 8th

Nassau Veterans Memorial Coliseum *Uniondale, NY* 8:00pm, with Sheriff

Thursday 9th

Cumberland County Civic Center *Portland, ME* 8:00pm, with Robert Ellis Orall
A sell-out audience of 9,500.

Friday 10th – Saturday 11th

The Centrum *Worcester, MA* 8:00pm, with Robert Ellis Orall
Sell-outs both nights, with a combined attendance of 19,080. "It only takes one Kinks concert to turn the worst skeptic into a true Kinks fan," reckons Joe Pinder in the *Worcester Daily Telegram*. "And last night's performance … was one of the better examples of what Ray, his brother Dave and the rest of the band can do. … Every song from [*State Of Confusion*] sounded as though it should be a single, and a hit at that. The night had so many high points it's hard to single out special

moments, but Dave Davies' torrid 'Bernadette' – and Ray's 'Property', a song about divorce – were simply stunning."

State Of Confusion album released in the UK. "They struggle manfully, but vainly, to hold on to that famous wit and somehow wrap it up in a supposedly fashionable thrash. The result is disjointed and ultimately unsatisfying," complains Colin Irwin in *Melody Maker*.

Sunday 12th

The band returns to London, but Dave heads to Los Angeles to deliver his new LP and to do some preliminary preparation for its release, and Ray stays behind in New York City for some further promotional work for the new Kinks album.

Monday 13th

Dave delivers master tapes of his third solo LP to Warner Brothers Records. An initial test pressing indicates the title as *Mean Disposition* but it's subsequently changed to *Chosen People*. While in LA, Dave hires publicist Shelly Heber of Image Consultants to assist with an independent publicity campaign. A photo shoot is done with a white-faced Dave decked out in a clown suit, and one of the shots is used for a promotional poster to accompany the LP's release. Dave will return to the US in September shortly after the album comes out to help promotion, similar to the efforts for his 1980 LP but lacking for 1981's *Glamour*.

Friday 24th

In Britain the scheduled release as a single of 'Don't Forget To Dance' is again delayed, to September 30th, as it's decided to re-promote 'Come Dancing' because of its chart success in the US.

→ Towards the end of the month Ray is back in London for pre-production for upcoming shoots for two Kinks videos. During the summer he will also be involved with many aspects of his film project, *Return To Waterloo*, including the assembly of cast and crew.

July

Early in the month staged concert footage is shot at The Venue Theatre in central London before an invited audience, including local fans, and used for part of the later 'State Of Confusion' video. Footage for the video is also shot inside Konk Studios and on Muswell Hill Broadway. It is produced by Michael Hamlyn and directed by Julien Temple for Midnight Films, and receives its world premiere on MTV on July 24th. It's first shown in the UK on BBC-1 television's *Breakfast Time* on March 28th 1984.

'Come Dancing' / 'Noise' single re-released in the UK (originally released November last year). The re-issue is based on its success in the US, where on the 11th it peaks at number 6.

The Kinks shoot a video for the song 'Don't Forget To Dance' at a ballroom in London, exact location and date unknown. In part it reprises the scenes in the popular 'Come Dancing' video, with The Kinks playing themselves on a ballroom stage, and Ray's spiv character pursues a girl.

The video is highlighted by a sophisticated dream sequence based on early Kinks history, showing the early band in their red hunting jackets, and recreating one of The Ravens' society bashes with an elaborate costume ball at an impressive mansion. The video is again produced by Michael Hamlyn and directed by Julien Temple for Midnight Films and is first aired in Germany on August 1st on ARD-TV's *Tommy's Popshow*, in the US on MTV (September 3rd), and in November in the UK on Channel 4's *The Tube*.

Probably later this month and into August at Konk in London the

bulk of the soundtrack for the *Return To Waterloo* film is recorded.

With engineer Damian Korner helping out for this recording work at Konk Studios in London – and minus Dave Davies – the rest of The Kinks record **'Intro'**, **'Return To Waterloo'**, **'Missing Persons'**, **'Sold Me Out'**, **'Going Solo'**, **'Lonely Hearts'**, **'Not Far Away'**, **'Expectations'**, **'Ladder Of Success'** and **'Good Times Are Gone'**.

Ray recalls later: "Dave refused to play and so it had to be 'Ray Davies and members of The Kinks'. If he had worked with me on it, it would have been a *great* record, but he let me down."

On the 25th a change of name is filed, turning Step Ahead Productions into Waterloo Films Ltd, and the change is officially accepted on August 17th, naming Ray Davies and Dennis Woolf as directors and equal partners. Davies and Woolf had first worked together on *Starmaker* back in 1974 when Woolf was a producer for Granada TV.

August

Monday 1st

'Don't Forget To Dance' / 'Bernadette' single released in the US.
Chosen People album by Dave Davies released in the US. "In spite of all its metallic proclivities," says *Rock Magazine*, "*Chosen People* is an intelligently conceived and executed album which should move Dave

---

Don't Forget To Dance single

A 'Don't Forget To Dance' (R. DAVIES).
B 'Bernadette' (R. DAVIES).
UK 12-inch A-side is a slightly extended mix

US release August 1st 1983 (Arista AS1-9075).
UK release September 30th 1983 (7-inch Arista ARIST 524, 12-inch ARIST 12524).
Musicians and recording details as *State Of Confusion* album (see May 24th).
Chart high US number 29; UK none.

---

from the penumbra of his brother, Ray. This is the work of a concerned individual." *Long Island Ear*: "An odd album, running a full spectrum between pleasant lyricism ('Is It Any Wonder') and relative cacophony ('Matter Of Decision') but somehow it all seems to fit together nicely. As you might expect, it's a quirky album with some quirky things to say; let the quirkiness of the album grow on you, and it can also be a rewarding one."

Atlantic City Press: "Sounding more contemporary than The Kinks, Davies has created a record that has some strong arrangements and memorable tunes. He even connects on a couple of his more quiet songs. Davies' guitar solos also impress!"

→ Ray seems to be mostly working at Konk to complete the soundtrack for *Return To Waterloo*.

☆ With the success of the 'Come Dancing' single in the UK, Ray's time is also taken up with a number of media duties this month.

Friday 19th

'Love Gets You' / 'One Night With You' single by Dave Davies released in the US.

Chosen People album by Dave Davies

A1 'Tapas' (D. DAVIES).
A2 'Charity' (D. DAVIES).
A3 'Mean Disposition' (D. DAVIES).
A4 'Love Gets You' (D. DAVIES).
A5 'Danger Zone' (D. DAVIES).
A6 'True Story' (D. DAVIES).
A7 'Take One More Chance' (D. DAVIES).
B1 'Freedom Lies' (D. DAVIES).
B2 'Matter Of Decision' (D. DAVIES).
B3 'Is It Any Wonder' (D. DAVIES).
B4 'Fire Burning' (D. DAVIES).
B5 'Chosen People' (D. DAVIES).
B6 'Cold Winter' (D. DAVIES).

US release August 1st 1983 (Warner Brothers 23917-1).
UK release October 7th 1983 (Warner Brothers 92-3917-1).
Musicians Dave Davies lead vocal, guitars, bass guitar (A6), keyboards (some parts). Dave Wintour bass guitar (except A6). Chris Parrin keyboards. Bob Henrit drums. Kim Goody second vocal (B3). Martin Ford string arrangements (A7, B6).
Recorded Konk Studios *Hornsey, north London*; June-August 1982; 24-track mixed to stereo.
Producers Dave Davies, Steve Churchyard.
Engineer Steve Churchyard.
Chart high US none; UK none.

Wednesday 24th

❏ **TV** BBC Television Centre *west London*. BBC-1 **Top Of The Pops** lip-synch 'Come Dancing'. The Kinks plus three-piece horn section are on tonight's Top Of The Pops, the band's first appearance since June 1972 on this important hits show.

☆ Dave's video for 'Mean Disposition' from the recent album is shot now. Warners refuse to finance it and so Dave pays for it himself on the cheap. It will be first broadcast in the US on MTV in October just before it's released as a single.

Love Gets You single by Dave Davies

A 'Love Gets You' (D. DAVIES).
B 'One Night With You' (D. BARTHOLOMEW, P. KING).

US release August 19th 1983 (Warner Brothers 7-29509).
Musicians Dave Davies lead vocal, guitars. Dave Wintour bass guitar. Chris Parrin keyboards. Bob Henrit drums.
Recorded Konk Studios *Hornsey, north London*; June-August 1982; 24-track mixed to stereo.
Producer Dave Davies.
Engineer Steve Churchyard.
Chart high US none.

September

→ Ray is given a script for a proposed film adaptation of the Colin MacInnes novel *Absolute Beginners* and asked to consider contributing music and taking an acting role. Presumably the book's setting in the coffee bar scene of late-1950s London appeals to him.

☆ Probably starting on the 5th, Ray begins three weeks of formal pre-production for the filming of *Return To Waterloo*, working with art director Terry Pritchard, the first technician hired for the project. Pritchard has worked on Kinks stage shows in the past.

Wednesday 7th

❏ **TV** ABC Television Center *Hollywood, CA*. ABC **American Bandstand** Dave Davies lip-synch 'Love Gets You' broadcast scheduled October 22nd but delayed to December 3rd. Dave is in Los Angeles for a week (5th-12th) of media work to promote his new LP. In addition to meetings with Warner Brothers, he works with publicist Shelly Heber who sets up a full schedule including interviews and syndicated radio shows. This videotaped TV appearance on the perennial music show *American Bandstand* also sees Dave briefly interviewed by host Dick Clark.

Tuesday 13th – Thursday 15th

Dave is probably in Chicago (13th) and certainly in New York City (14th-15th) for more press work, largely at the Warner Brothers Records offices in NYC.

Friday 16th

As Dave later recounts in *Kink*, he feels the interviews go badly and that the press are resistant to open discussion of his personal beliefs about metaphysics and spirituality that inspired the album. Particularly upsetting is what he feels is Warner Brothers' lack of support for the LP. It is a dejected and depressed Dave who returns to London, having put every effort into promoting the new record. Meanwhile, its British release is set in three weeks time and Dave does some minor British promo work too. Despite a second single from the album in November in the US, the album fails to chart or to get much support in the press.

Friday 23rd

An agreement signed between Waterloo Films Ltd and RCA Video Productions in effect allows filming of *Return To Waterloo* to proceed, with work starting probably on Monday 26th.

Friday 30th

'Don't Forget To Dance' / 'Bernadette' single released in the UK. Also issued today in Britain is a re-release on PRT of 'You Really Got Me' in three formats: a regular single; a 12-inch single; and a special-edition picture disc.

October

Monday 3rd – Friday 7th, Monday 10th – Friday 14th

→ Work continues on *Return To Waterloo* film, with the second and third weeks of principal 35mm filming with Ray as director. Included is location shooting in Wimbledon, south-west London and Guildford, Surrey, as well as at Waterloo Station in central London.

Finance is received from the Channel 4 television company on the last day of shooting. The producer is Dennis Wolf, the choreographer is Jim Cameron, and the director of photography for *Return To Waterloo* is Roger Deakins. Editing is done in London in November and from late January to March 1984.

Friday 7th

Chosen People album by Dave Davies released in the UK. The British music paper *NME* (*New Musical Express*) is once again unmerciful and dismisses Dave's record outright. "When old Kinks start droning on about the inner self shining through the mere hush, which is the Outer Self, it's time to get worried," says the reviewer. "They are not being beautiful, they are leaking." Such a generally poor reception in the press to this and his previous LP makes a further solo deal for Dave unlikely for a time.

Monday 10th

At some point this week, with The Kinks upcoming tour of the US finalised and tickets beginning to go on sale, Dave decides to pull out. It will prove to be a costly decision financially and strategically, and generates negative publicity.

Thursday 13th

➔ The decision is made around now to cancel the US tour. Dave will take six weeks off, and is ordered to rest. A rumour spreads that Ray momentarily considers doing the tour without Dave, using in his place guitarist Chris Spedding. If this is considered then it is also quickly dismissed, and the tour is partially cancelled or delayed pending Dave's return.

Friday 14th

The Kinks Greatest – Dead End Street album with bonus 10-inch record released in the UK. The Kinks immediately instigate legal proceedings to have this PRT album withdrawn because it includes unreleased material not covered in their contract-settlement agreement with Pye Records (now owned by PRT). The album is later altered and retitled to correct this.

The Kinks Greatest – Dead End Street bonus 10-inch LP

C1 **'Misty Water'** (R. DAVIES).
C2 **'Pictures In The Sand'** (R. DAVIES).
C3 **'Spotty Grotty Anna'** (NO CREDIT).
D1 **'Groovy Movies'** (R. DAVIES).
D2 **'Time Will Tell'** (R. DAVIES).
D3 **'Rosemary Rose'** (R. DAVIES).
A/B sides contain a routine selection of greatest hits

UK release October 14th 1983 (PRT KINK1).
C1, C2, D1, D3: see *The Great Lost Kinks Album* January 25th 1973, but with the following variations: C1, D1: different stereo mixes; C2: stereo backing track only with no vocals.
Musicians Ray Davies lead vocal (D2), electric guitar. Dave Davies electric guitar. Pete Quaife bass guitar. Mick Avory drums.
Recorded D2: Pye Studios *central London* probably October 1965; C3: Pye Studios *central London* around 1968.
Producers Shel Talmy (D2); Raymond Davies (C3).
Engineers Alan MacKenzie (D2); probably Brian Humphries (C3).
Chart high UK none.

Mean Disposition single by Dave Davies

A **'Mean Disposition'** (D. DAVIES).
B **'Cold Winter'** (D. DAVIES).

US release November 18th 1983 (Warner Brothers 7-29425). Musicians and recording details as *Chosen People* album (see August 1st).
Chart high US none.

Monday 17th

A press release announces the cancellation of the US tour and that Dave is to take six weeks off.

➔ At a film studio in London, Ray begins the task of editing *Return To Waterloo* with film editor David Mingay.

November

➔ Ray continues editing *Return To Waterloo* with film editor David Mingay at a London studio.
☆ Music critic Jon Savage is commissioned by The Kinks to write the band's official biography, and begins his research.
☆ The band has time off in London around now.

Friday 18th

'Mean Disposition' / 'Cold Winter' single by Dave Davies released in the US.

Tuesday 29th

New York City radio station WAPP announces that tickets for three special local shows in December by The Kinks will go on sale on the 30th. This ends six weeks of silence since the sudden cancellation of The Kinks' autumn tour in mid October and speculation that the band has split.

December

Sunday 4th – Friday 9th

Rehearsals for the upcoming shows are held at Konk Studios in north London during the entire week, including the working up of a few new songs such as 'Definite Maybe', 'Clichés Of The World', 'Heart Of Gold' and 'Property'.

➔ Ray agrees to appear in an undetermined role in Julien Temple's full-length feature film *Absolute Beginners*. Keith Richards is to play comedian Max Miller and will sing a Ray Davies song. Shooting is initially set for summer 1984 but delayed due to the loss of the film's original financial backing.

➪ **TOUR STARTS** *Mini US Tour: make-up dates* (Dec 28th – 31st). **Line-up**: Ray Davies (lead vocal, guitar), Dave Davies (guitar, vocal), Mick Avory (drums), Jim Rodford (bass), Ian Gibbons (keyboards). The

---

➔ INDICATES EVENT AROUND THIS TIME BUT WITH NO FIRM DATE

Kinks travel to New York City on the 27th and the following day drive up to Massachusetts for a warm-up date before their high-profile shows in the Big Apple.

Wednesday 28th
Springfield Civic Center Arena *Springfield, MA* 7:30pm, with Cyndi Lauper
Some rarely-performed songs are included during the evening, including 'Two Sisters' and 'Harry Rag' mid-show, and, perhaps revealing a reflective mood, a complete version of 'Days' during the encore. Lauper is just breaking nationally now with her album *She's So Unusual*, and its big hit 'Girls Just Want To Have Fun' is just taking off in the charts.

Thursday 29th – Saturday 31st
Roseland Ballroom *New York, NY* 9:00pm (Thu-Fri), 10:00pm (Sat), Sat billed as *Come Dancing with The Kinks – New Year's Eve Ball*, with Cyndi Lauper (Thu-Fri), The Catholic Girls (Sat); tickets $15 (Thu-Fri), $35 & $50 (Sat)
Saturday's big event in effect marks the 20th anniversary concert for the band, to the day, although no mention is made of the fact. The New Year's Eve ball at Hornsey Town Hall in 1963 is commonly regarded by Ray as the real beginning of The Kinks, even though technically it was

prior to Avory joining the band. Among reviewers of the new year's eve date, Harold DeMuir in *The Aquarian* bemoans the loss of the shabby but loveable Kinks, saying the show was overly similar "to the one they delivered last May at the Byrne Arena" and "weighted heavily toward the band's newer, inferior material".

But still, writes DeMuir, the band plays tighter and stronger than ever and give it their all, "which is often more than the material deserved".

Barry Millman in Long Island's *Good Times* publication is not impressed. "A nonchalant Ray Davies had little to say or do, while brother Dave and company did their best to cover the warts of a largely lackluster set. ... Sticking slavishly to stuff from their recent *State Of Confusion*, Ray's ever-present nice-guy delivery seemed hollow and forced. ... Celluloid Heroes may certainly never really die but vinyl ones most certainly do."

Set-list (31st): 'Around The Dial', 'Definite Maybe', 'Catch Me Now I'm Falling', 'Where Have All The Good Times Gone', 'State Of Confusion', 'Don't Forget To Dance', 'The Hard Way', 'Come On Now', '20th Century Man', 'Come Dancing', 'Destroyer', 'Yo-Yo', medley 'Batman Theme' / '(Wish I Could Fly Like) Superman' / 'Shakin' All Over', 'Till The End Of The Day', 'All Day And All Of The Night', 'Lola', 'David Watts', 'Celluloid Heroes', 'You Really Got Me', 'Days', 'Low Budget'.

1984

The internal band problems of 1983 carried straight into this year, and The Kinks seemed to come close to calling it quits. Ray finally finished his Return To Waterloo film, and his relationship with Chrissie Hynde ended abruptly, followed quickly by key member Mick Avory leaving the band. After this came a twist only possible for The Kinks: Larry Page, who was ousted as their manager in 1965, was re-hired to take over the management reins in the UK.

But still the band forged ahead, despite these potentially catastrophic upheavals – and with Ray's do-or-die film behind him, The Kinks were able to survive intact, even if in altered form. Ray said later: "It was a hellish year and it cost me dearly in my personal life. But the point is, I did what I wanted to do. 1983-84 was the most unhappy yet the most fulfilling time for me." Bassist Jim Rodford characterised the time since the autumn of '83 as "tense, tenuous and traumatic".

Yet despite the traumas, The Kinks delivered a new Arista album at the end of the year. It generated a respectably successful single to boot and some of Dave's best contributions to the band's catalogue in years.

January

▷ **TOUR STARTS** *Winter Of Confusion: US Tour* (Jan 6th – 20th).
Line-up: Ray Davies (lead vocal, guitar), Dave Davies (guitar, vocal), Mick Avory (drums), Jim Rodford (bass), Ian Gibbons (keyboards).
This two-week outing for the band is in effect a reduced version of the cancelled November-December '83 tour.

Friday 6th
Charlotte Coliseum *Charlotte, NC* 8:00pm, with The SpongeTones

Saturday 7th
Hampton Coliseum *Hampton, VA* 8:00pm, with The Romantics
Ray falls on stage and seriously injures his knee. Reportedly his kneecap is broken and several ligaments are torn. After the following day's

concert the band unexpectedly stays in Richmond, VA, where his injuries are treated. The remainder of the tour is completed as scheduled with Ray performing in a flexible knee brace. (Detroit-based support act The Romantics are promoting their hit single 'Talking In Your Sleep'.)

The *Virginian-Pilot* reviewer notes that the British are saying The Kinks have sold out to American commercialism. "But for almost 6,000 souls at the Coliseum Saturday night all that was irrelevant [as] the group tore through a frenetic 90-minute rendition of their songbook along with two encores. ... With Ray's keen lyrics, Dave's powerhouse deliveries and the band's form of inspired lunacy, it's no wonder fans and critics alike have come to say God Save The Kinks!"

Setlist: 'All Day And All Of The Night', 'Around The Dial', 'Catch Me Now I'm Falling', 'Come Dancing', 'Come On Now', 'David Watts', 'Dead End Street', 'Definite Maybe', 'Destroyer', 'Don't Forget To Dance', 'A Gallon Of Gas', 'The Hard Way', 'Heart Of Gold', medley 'Muswell Hillbilly' / 'Lola', 'State Of Confusion', 'Till The End Of The Day', '20th Century Man', medley 'Where Have All The Good Times Gone' / 'Tired Of Waiting For You', medley '(Wish I Could Fly Like) Superman' / 'Shakin' All Over', 'Yo-Yo'.

Monday 9th
Knoxville Civic Coliseum *Knoxville, TN* 8:00pm, with The Romantics

Tuesday 10th
Charleston Municipal Auditorium *Charleston, WV* 8:00pm, with The Romantics
Following day off.

Friday 13th
Indiana University Auditorium, Indiana University *Bloomington, IN* 8:00pm, with The Romantics
IU Press: "Toying with an enthusiastic capacity crowd ... the mercurial leader of The Kinks played familiar snatches of hits like 'Lola' only to launch into something else, often grabbed his acoustic guitar and then decided he'd rather play his electric, and disappeared off-stage briefly for at least five jacket changes. ... With a satisfying 105-minute set that relied heavily on its last few albums, the band performed with a vigor that belied its members ages."

Saturday 14th
Louisville Gardens *Louisville, KY* 8:00pm, with The Romantics

Sunday 15th
Hara Arena *Dayton, OH* 8:00pm, with The Romantics

Tuesday 17th
Ohio Center *Columbus, OH* 8:00pm, with The Romantics

Wednesday 18th
Elliot Hall Of Music, Purdue University *West Lafayette, IN* 8:00pm, with The Romantics

Thursday 19th
Assembly Hall, University of Illinois at Urbana-Champaign *Champaign, IL* 8:00pm, with The Romantics

Friday 20th
Five Seasons Center *Cedar Rapids, IA* 8:00pm, with The Romantics
Dave says later in *Kink* that he and Avory almost come to blows on the tour, but that they at least manage to complete the dates. (Travel day back home to London follows.) Ray is present at the Apollo Theatre,

Manchester on the 22nd where The Pretenders are performing the last night of a string of British dates before the they are off for a quick tour of Australia.

➜ Ray resumes work in a London editing studio on his *Return To Waterloo* film, its scheduled debut on British TV now delayed until summer. He is also recuperating from his knee injury, and after prematurely jogging and working out at a gym ends up at a physical therapy clinic in London this spring – providing inspiration for a new song, 'Too Hot'.

February

Ray continues to edit *Return To Waterloo* in London. Kinks members are interviewed by writer Jon Savage presses on with work for *The Kinks: The Official Biography*. The Pretenders finished their Australian dates on January 31st and return to London until an extensive US tour starts in Honolulu on the 14th, ending in New York City on May 3rd. Once Hynde leaves for the US tour, her relationship with Ray is again a long-distance one, and this perhaps adds to the overall tension within The Kinks now.

March

➜ Jon Savage continues interviews with The Kinks into the start of the month for his band biography, the initial manuscript for which is completed on the 5th. Ray continues editing *Return To Waterloo*.

State Of Confusion EP

A1 'State Of Confusion' (R. DAVIES).
A2 'Heart Of Gold' (R. DAVIES).
B1 'Lola' (R. DAVIES).
B2 '20th Century Man' (R. DAVIES).
B1/B2 are edits of the album versions

UK release March 23rd 1984 (7-inch EP Arista 560, 12-inch ARIST 12560).
A1/A2 musicians and recording details as *State Of Confusion* album (see May 24th 1983). B1/B2 musicians and recording details as *One For The Road* album (see June 4th 1980).
Chart high UK none.

Friday 23rd
State Of Confusion EP released in the UK.

➜ **TOUR STARTS** UK Tour (Mar 23rd – Apr 9th). **Line-up**: Ray Davies (lead vocal, guitar), Dave Davies (guitar, vocal), Mick Avory (drums), Jim Rodford (bass), Ian Gibbons (keyboards).

Friday 23rd
Odeon Cinema *Birmingham* 7:30pm, with The Truth

Saturday 24th
St David's Hall *Cardiff, Wales* 7:30pm, with The Truth

Sunday 25th
Victoria Hall *Hanley, Stoke-on-Trent, Staffs* 7:30pm, with The Truth

"I've never managed to connect with The Kinks," admits Simon Scott in *Melody Maker*.

Scott continues: "The fundamental reason why they command the attention of thousands of Americans remains a complete mystery to me. ... Last time The Kinks played here [December 15th 1982] they were bright, clever, breezy, fun to watch. This time they were clichéd, loud, one-dimensional and turgid."

Thursday 29th
Guildford Civic Hall *Guildford, Surrey* 7:30pm, with The Truth

Friday 30th
Royal Court Centre *Nottingham* 7:30pm, with The Truth

April

Monday 2nd – Tuesday 3rd
Hammersmith Palais *Hammersmith, west London* 8:00pm, with The Truth

Robin Denselow writes in *The Guardian*: "A master of melody, sentiment, nostalgia and crowd-control, with his throwaway music-hall showmanship, [Ray] Davies still has to match these skills against the heavy metal wailing guitar style of brother Dave. This has long been one of The Kinks' many contradictions, and one that has actually helped them in America, but in the cheerful dancehall atmosphere of the Palais it seemed particularly wrong." (Two days off in London follow.)

Setlist (2nd): 'All Day And All Of The Night', 'Around The Dial', 'Come Dancing', 'David Watts', 'Dead End Street', 'Destroyer', 'Don't Forget To Dance', 'The Hard Way', Heart Of Gold', 'I Gotta Move', 'Improvised Blues', 'Lola', 'Oklahoma USA', 'Pressure', 'Property', 'State Of Confusion', '20th Century Man', 'Waterloo Sunset', medley 'Where Have All The Good Times Gone' / 'Tired Of Waiting For You', 'You Really Got Me'.

Friday 6th
Apollo Theatre *Manchester* 7:30pm, with The Truth

Saturday 7th
Royal Court Theatre *Liverpool* 7:30pm, with The Truth

Sunday 8th
Town Hall *Middlesbrough, Yorks* 7:30pm, with The Truth

Monday 9th
DeMontfort Hall *Leicester* 7:30pm, with The Truth

This show marks the end of the band's current set of British dates – and while no one within the band or among their many fans knows it yet, this will turn out to be drummer Mick Avory's last ever live appearance with The Kinks.

→ In order for Ray to complete the final edit of *Return To Waterloo*, a number of tentatively scheduled European tour dates this month are cancelled.

☆ Towards the end of this month the master copy of Ray's film project, *Return To Waterloo*, is finalised, and on the 27th Ray flies into New York City where he delivers the finished work to the RCA Video offices.

May

Without warning, Ray, like the rest of the world, learns through press reports of Chrissie Hynde's sudden marriage to Simple Minds singer Jim Kerr in New York City on the 5th.

With Ray's film project behind him, the focus shifts back to The Kinks and, inspired by the abrupt termination of his relationship with Hynde, he writes his first song of 1984, 'Good Day', followed in close succession by 'Too Hot'.

Late this month or early in June Ray's new songs are worked up and demoed at Konk in London.

June/July

Sessions are held at Konk Studios with Ray producing and Damian Korner engineering.

At least two new songs are recorded. Tensions are high in the studio and relations between Avory and Dave have evidently reached a point where it is decided to use a programmable drum machine for '**Good Day**' (which otherwise features the regular Kinks line-up). For '**Too Hot**', which ends up as the B-side of 'Good Day', Dave brings in session drummer Bob Henrit – who worked with Dave on the guitarist's 1982 solo album.

Ray's daughter Louisa sings on 'Good Day' and performs the spoken parts on 'Too Hot'. A four-man horn section comes in for 'Hot': John Beecham (trombone), Noel Morris (trumpet), Nick Payne (tenor saxophone) and Alan Holmes (baritone saxophone). Mixing is finished in July. A new vocal will later be added to 'Too Hot' for its inclusion on the *Word Of Mouth* album in the autumn.

In the midst of these sessions, around the second week of July, there is a sequence of major shake-ups in the Kinks organisation. Most significantly, Ray decides that the tension between Dave and Avory is no longer workable, and in a quiet moment with Avory agrees that the drummer should now part company from the band, just over 20 years after he joined.

Avory is subsequently hired as manager at Konk Studios; former manager Pete Smith leaves. Bob Henrit, ex-Argent bandmate of Jim Rodford's, is hired as Avory's replacement.

Ray approaches ex-manager Larry Page who, on a handshake agreement, returns as The Kinks' business manager in the UK. To top off the house-cleaning, Konk engineer Damian Korner is replaced by David Baker.

As part of a continuing effort to upgrade Konk, an SSL 6000E mixer for computerised 46-track recording is purchased for eventual installation, and planning of a second Konk studio begins.

A tentative booking at the Swansea Marina, Swansea, Wales on June 29th, which was to be videotaped, is cancelled in light of the recent personnel changes. Avory's departure is announced on Friday July 13th. Without missing a beat, the band starts work on a new Kinks album, rehearsing and working up demos and master recordings.

August/September

The '**Good Day**' single is out on August 10th in the UK, where at the end of the month (29th) a book by Johnny Rogan, *The Kinks: The Sound And The Fury*, is published.

During August and September six songs are recorded at Konk in north London – '**Do It Again**', '**Massive Reductions**' (second version), '**Summer's Gone**', '**Living On A Thin Line**', '**Guilty**', and kinks '84

'**Word Of Mouth**' – with Ray producing, Dave as associate producer, and engineers David Baker and Dave Powell. Bob Henrit is on drums for all these tracks.

Dave wrote 'Living On A Thin Line' around June/July and, he will recall later in *Kink*, it is inspired in part by the precarious roller-coaster ride of The Kinks' long career, as well as his general distaste for politicians and his view of their attitudes towards the world. The recording work is wound up in September, probably including overdubs and mixing of finished tracks.

Good Day single

A '**Good Day**' (R. DAVIES).
B/B2 '**Too Hot**' (R. DAVIES).
B1 '**Don't Forget To Dance**' (R. DAVIES).

UK release August 10th 1984 (7-inch A/B Arista ARIST 577; 12-inch A/B1/B2 ARIST 12577).
B1 musicians and recording details as *State Of Confusion* album (see May 24th 1983).
Musicians Ray Davies lead vocal, acoustic guitar, electric guitar. Dave Davies electric guitar, backing vocal. Jim Rodford bass guitar, backing vocal. Bob Henrit drums (B). Ian Gibbons keyboards. Louisa Davies backing/spoken vocal. John O'Donnel drum machine, percussion (A). John Beecham trombone (B). Noel Morris trumpet (B). Nick Payne tenor saxophone (B). Alan Holmes baritone saxophone (B).
Recorded Konk Studios *Hornsey, north London*; July 1984; 24-track mixed to stereo.
Producer Ray Davies.
Engineer Damian Korner.
<u>*Chart high*</u> UK none.

October

Three days of work at Konk (9th-11th) result in mixes of 'Do It Again', 'Guilty', 'Sold Me Out', 'Missing Persons', 'Too Hot', 'Living On A Thin Line', 'Massive Reductions' (second version), 'Good Day', 'Summers Gone', and two versions of 'Word Of Mouth'.

On the 15th Ray oversees disc mastering of 'Do It Again' at Masterdisk Studios in New York City with Robert Ludwig for a 12-inch promotional release. The following day he's back at Konk in London to assemble the tape master for the *Word Of Mouth* album. Final edits are made at Konk of 'Word Of Mouth', 'Sold Me Out', 'Too Hot' and 'Going Solo' on the 20th, and two days later Ray is back at Masterdisk to supervise disc mastering of Word Of Mouth.

Late in the month Ray attempts to halt publication of Jon Savage's *The Kinks: The Official Biography*, as *The Observer* reports: "He has made three attempts to get the book stopped, even though he collaborated with the author and his manager set up the original deal with [publisher] Faber. The first was an objection to the text, even though the singer had approved it earlier. Then there came a threatened injunction against the book because of objections to some of the photographs. Then there was a curious demand that Fabers should pay £50,000 permission fee for quoting some lyrics. All these threats have failed and Fabers [say] the book will be published... ."

On the 27th Ray is given a One Of The Most Played Songs Of 1983 award for 'Come Dancing' by the US performing-rights organisation ASCAP at a ceremony at Claridges Hotel in central London.

November

The 'Do It Again' promotional 12-inch single is sent out to radio stations on the 1st as a taster for the new LP *Word Of Mouth*. Airplay begins immediately and the song quickly features on rock-radio programming charts.

Around this time The Kinks shoot a video for 'Do It Again' produced by Julien Temple for Nitrate Films at various UK locations, including the London Underground and Brighton Pier. The video is soon ready and debuts in the US on MTV on the 19th, and the following day in the UK on BBC-2's *The Old Grey Whistle Test*.

Ray's film **Return To Waterloo** is broadcast 9:00-10.05pm on Channel 4 TV in the UK on Sunday 4th. Response is mixed. "It could have been a load of pretentious rubbish," says Miles Kington in *The Listener*. "Instead it was like a long and very good poem. Ray Davies wrote, directed, composed, sang and even played the part of a busker. I hope he is feeling extremely pleased with himself and is planning something else."

Nigel Fountain writes in the same publication a few weeks later: "If one blends fantasy and what passes for reality, it is often useful if some illumination ensues. Well it certainly passed me by, whatever it was. The soundtrack [says] the empire is dying ... oh no it isn't, it's dead. Stone dead. But in this decade of nostalgia, warming over the corpse still passes muster for social criticism. *Return To Waterloo* is well shot and performed. A faint echo of one of the tunes still lingers in my post-imperial skull, but it won't do. It made me yearn for something really old-fashioned, like an interest in the future."

Around the middle of the month a press release says that the film *Absolute Beginners*, in which Ray has agreed to play a cameo role, is back on track pending signing soon with Orion Pictures in the US, and that production will start in spring 1985.

Also around this time the band rehearses at Konk Studios in north London for the upcoming tour, with Bob Henrit on drums. They travel to New York City on the 14th and, after a few days rehearsals, on the 17th appear at NBC Television Studios for an NBC Network TV simulcast of *Saturday Night Live* where they perform 'Do It Again' and 'Word Of Mouth'.

The **Word Of Mouth** album is released in the UK and US on the 19th. "A ringing open-chord sound that harkens to earlier Kinks albums and their mid-1960s peers rings through *Word Of Mouth*," says *Billboard*. "Full of the quirks, turns and sleight-of-hand that have endeared them to diehard fans, this Kinks set is, alas, devoid of a single to rival 'Come Dancing' or 'Superman'."

Three books on the band are published the same week as *Word Of Mouth* is released: Jon Savage's *The Kinks: The Official Biography* is out simultaneously in the US and UK; in the US *The Kinks Kronikles* by John Mendelssohn appears; and *The Kinks: A Mental Institution* by Johnny Rogan is published in the US (it's already out in the UK as *The Kinks: The Sound & The Fury*).

On the 20th at Masterdisk Studios in New York City, Ray oversees the mastering of the commercial 7-inch single of 'Do It Again' / 'Guilty'. Two days later the band is deep in rehearsal at the Festhalle, Frankfurt, West Germany.

Not only is the band preparing themselves in Frankfurt for the live debut of their new line-up, but there is also a need to prepare technically as the Festhalle concert (at 7:00pm on Friday 23rd) will be simultaneously recorded for radio broadcast by West German HR3 radio (*The Kinks In Concert*, December 29th 1985) and videotaped by West German ZDF & SWF television (*Rock Und Ballads*, December 2nd 1984).

In the UK, on the 30th, three compilation albums are individually released – *Greatest Hits*, *Kollectables*, and *Kovers* – as well as together for the 20th Anniversary three-LP box set.

➜ INDICATES EVENT AROUND THIS TIME BUT WITH NO FIRM DATE

kinks'84

Word Of Mouth album

A1 'Do It Again' (R. DAVIES).
A2 'Word Of Mouth' (R. DAVIES).
A3 'Good Day' (R. DAVIES).
A4 'Living On A Thin Line' (D. DAVIES).
A5 'Sold Me Out' (R. DAVIES).
B1 'Massive Reductions' [second version] (R. DAVIES).
B2 'Guilty' (D. DAVIES).
B3 'Too Hot' (R. DAVIES).
B4 'Missing Persons' (R. DAVIES).
B5 'Summer's Gone' (R. DAVIES).
B6 'Going Solo' (R. DAVIES).
B3 is remixed and includes a new lead vocal, differing from the August 10th single B-side

UK release November 19th 1984 (Arista 206 685).
US release November 19th 1984 (Arista AL8-8264).
Musicians Ray Davies lead vocal except as noted, acoustic guitar, electric guitar, keyboards, harmonica. Dave Davies electric guitar (except A5, B4, B6), lead vocal (A4, B2). Jim Rodford bass guitar, backing vocal. Mick Avory drums (A5, B4, B6). Bob Henrit drums (A1, A2, A4, B1-B3, B5). Ian Gibbons keyboards, synthesisers. Louisa Davies backing/spoken vocal (A3, B3). John O'Connel drum machine (A3).
Recorded Konk Studios *Hornsey, north London*; A1, A2, A4, B1, B2, B5: August-September 1984; A3, B3: June 1984; A5, B4, B6: June-July 1983.
Producer Ray Davies; associate producer Dave Davies.
Engineers David Baker, except Damian Korner (A3, A5, B3, B4, B6); second engineer Dave Powell.
Chart high UK none; US number 57.

⇨ **TOUR STARTS** *Word Of Mouth: North American Tour: 1st leg* (Nov 27th – Dec 21st). **Line-up**: Ray Davies (lead vocal, guitar), Dave Davies (guitar, vocal), Bob Henrit (drums), Jim Rodford (bass), Ian Gibbons (keyboards). A rehearsal on Monday 26th at the Lakefront Arena is necessary for both musical and technical run-throughs.

Tuesday 27th
Kiefer UNO Lakefront Arena, University Of New Orleans *New Orleans, LA* 8:00pm, with Tommy Shaw

Wednesday 28th
Atlanta Civic Center *Atlanta, GA* 8:00pm, with Tommy Shaw

Friday 30th
Rupp Arena *Lexington, KY* 8:00pm, with Tommy Shaw

December

Saturday 1st
Cincinnati Gardens *Cincinatti, OH* 8:00pm, with Tommy Shaw

Sunday 2nd
UIC Pavilion, University of Illinois-Chicago *Chicago, IL* 8:00pm, with Tommy Shaw
Chicago Tribune: "Something for every kind of fan: an obscure early

song ('I Gotta Move') for old-timers; a handful of 1960s favorites ('Victoria', 'Where Have All The Good Times Gone') for die-hards; the most recent hits ('Destroyer', 'Come Dancing') for newcomers; and a roaring finale of 'You Really Got Me' for everybody."

Tuesday 4th
Mecca-Milwaukee Auditorium *Milwaukee, WI* 8:00pm, with Tommy Shaw
'Do It Again' / 'Guilty' single released in the US.

Wednesday 5th
Rose Arena, Central Michigan University *Mount Pleasant, MI* 8:00pm, with Tommy Shaw

Friday 7th
Cobo Arena *Detroit, MI* 8:00pm, with Tommy Shaw

Saturday 8th
The Metro Center *Rockford, IL* 8:00pm, with Tommy Shaw

Monday 10th
Pittsburgh Civic Arena *Pittsburgh, PA* 8:00pm, with Tommy Shaw

Tuesday 11th
Broome County Veterans Memorial Arena *Binghamton, NY* 8:00pm, with Tommy Shaw

Wednesday 12th
War Memorial Auditorium *Syracuse, NY* with Tommy Shaw

Thursday 13th
Ray attends a press screening of *Return To Waterloo* at the RCA Video offices in New York City.

Friday 14th
The Spectrum *Philadelphia, PA* 8:00pm, with Tommy Shaw

Saturday 15th
Providence Civic Center *Providence, RI* 8:00pm, with Tommy Shaw

Sunday 16th
Boston Garden *Boston, MA* 7:30pm, with Tommy Shaw
The Boston Globe: "The combination of Ray's songs and singing, Dave's note-wrenching guitar, and the wildly careening harmonies of the brothers Davies remains one of the most exhilarating sounds in all of rock."

Do It Again single

A 'Do It Again' (R. DAVIES).
B1 'Guilty' (D. DAVIES).
B2 'Summer's Gone' (R. DAVIES).

US release (A/B1) December 4th 1984 (Arista ASI 9309).
UK release April 19th 1985 (7-inch A/B1 Arista ARIST 617; 12-inch A/B1/B2 Arista ARIST 12617).
Musicians and recording details as *Word Of Mouth* album (see November 19th).
Chart high UK none; US number 41.

Tuesday 18th
Community War Memorial *Rochester, NY* 8:00pm, with Tommy Shaw

Thursday 20th
Veterans Memorial Arena, Hartford Civic Center *Hartford, CT* 7:30pm, with Tommy Shaw

Friday 21st
Madison Square Garden *New York, NY* 8:00pm, *WNEW-FM Christmas Party*, with Tommy Shaw

With the Madison Square Garden show the first leg of the tour ends and the band returns to London the following day. They now have a little time off for the Christmas and New Year holidays.
Setlist: 'All Day And All Of The Night', 'Around The Dial', 'Art Lover', 'Celluloid Heroes', 'Come Dancing', 'David Watts', 'Dead End Street', 'Definite Maybe' (intro), 'Destroyer', 'Do It Again', 'Don't Forget To Dance', 'A Gallon Of Gas', 'Good Day' 'The Hard Way', 'I Gotta Move', 'Living On A Thin Line', 'Lola', 'Low Budget', 'Missing Persons', 'State Of Confusion', '20th Century Man', 'Victoria', 'Where Have All The Good Times Gone', 'Waterloo Sunset', 'We Wish You A Merry Christmas', '(Wish I Could Fly Like) Superman', 'Word Of Mouth'.

1985

The new-look Kinks with drummer Bob Henrit continued to tour in support of the latest album. It was their last for Arista, ending what was arguably the most successful commercial and professional relationship of their career. At the same time their association with long-serving US manager Elliot Abbott – an equally beneficial relationship – was wrapped up by the end of the year. Although sales of that last Arista album and its lead single paled compared to the golden period from Low Budget to State Of Confusion, both charted respectably, and the feeling was that there was no reason the momentum couldn't be revived in the new year – even on a new record label. But The Kinks disappeared from public view for the last quarter of the year as they re-examined themselves and their future.

January

The second leg of the *Word Of Mouth* North American tour was set to begin sometime early to mid January, but is delayed to allow Ray time to record and film a song for the film *Absolute Beginners*. January dates are pushed back and rescheduled to March at the tail end of the tour that is now planned to begin at the start of February. Keith Altham, an old ally from the 1960s, is hired this month as The Kinks' press agent, but his tenure does not last the year.

Early in the month at Konk in London a session is held to record Ray's song **'Quiet Life'** intended for *Absolute Beginners*. Overdubs for the version as heard in the film will be done later, arranged by Gil Evans. Producer for the Konk session is Clive Langer, engineer probably David Baker. Ray does the lead vocal, with Jim Rodford on bass guitar and Bob Henrit playing drums. Ray says later, "I was kind of conned into making the film. Julien Temple, who was a good friend, was obsessed about making it. … Nobody else had a song ready. I said I'd do it, but I want the option [for it] to be cut out later on. … I was just rehearsing the scene I was doing and I just set a tempo and wrote the chords down. … In the middle of rehearsals, I popped down and did a vocal. When we did the film, I just had the backing track with a click and the vocal. Then when they did the film [soundtrack] they added all these overdubs – and I've actually never heard it."

Later in the month, at Twickenham Film Studios in west London, Ray films one portion of his Father role in Absolute Beginners as a sample for the producers to help secure US financing from Goldcrest.

The remainder of the Virgin/Palace movie is indeed filmed, beginning in June.

The band's British manager Larry Page announces that The Kinks will begin accepting offers for a new record deal as their obligations to Arista are complete.

February

Radio stations in the US were sent 12-inch promotional copies of 'Living On A Thin Line' at the very end of January. Automatically, the song is getting airplay on AOR stations and enters *Billboard's* Rock Action (top 50) charts in early February, rising to number 24 in an eight-week run. Prompt release of the song as a single could well have given The Kinks a much needed hit, but for unclear reasons no release is forthcoming, and instead 'Summer's Gone' is issued. It's less strong as a single, and will not be released until the end of the forthcoming North American tour. The stalled tour probably doesn't help album sales either, and *Word Of Mouth* peaks at number 57 in the US charts just as the concerts start.

▷ **TOUR STARTS** *Word Of Mouth: North American Tour: 2nd leg* (Feb 3rd – Mar 28th). **Line-up**: Ray Davies (lead vocal, guitar), Dave Davies (guitar, vocal), Bob Henrit (drums), Jim Rodford (bass), Ian Gibbons (keyboards). Ticket prices range from $10-$16 and venue size varies considerably, from 2,500-12,000 capacity, with most in the

4,000-6,000 range. Support acts are generally local bands. Attendance on this tour shows signs of weakness, with many of the bookings apparently over-ambitious as sales of the single and album slump. (Band travels to Fort Lauderdale, FL, on the 2nd, with Dave possibly in town a few days in advance to begin press work.)

Sunday 3rd – Monday 4th
Sunrise Musical Theatre *Fort Lauderdale, FL* 8:00pm, with The David Shelley Band
There's a 38th birthday party for Dave after the first show. (Travel day follows.)

Wednesday 6th
Lakeland Civic Center *Lakeland, FL* 8:00pm, with Lefty
Attendance is 2,438 at this 5,000-capacity room.

Thursday 7th
Stephen C. O'Connell Center, University Of Florida *Gainesville, FL* 8:00pm, with Twigs
Travel day following.

Saturday 9th
Dixon Meyers Hall/Auditorium-Music Hall *Memphis, TN* 8:00pm, with Larry Raspberry
Travel day follows.

Monday 11th
Music Hall *Houston, TX* 8:00pm, with Hershel Berry & The Natives
Perhaps disappointed that they have to switch to this far smaller venue from the much bigger Summit where they have played before in Houston, the band gets a scathing review.

"The Kinks, England's legendary rouges of sloppy rock'n'roll, overstepped artistic license … and came up with their worst set I've ever witnessed," writes Marty Racine in the *Houston Chronicle*. "Instead of compensating for the shortened acoustics, the sound crew blasted the building as if they were in an arena. … The show was too loud. Too short. Too dispassionate. Too *big* for the room.

"Well maybe it was a bad night," Racine reflects, "and that only. The Kinks never were a perfect band. But when a band overblows their speakers you wonder what they're covering up. Monday night it seemed like indifference."

Tuesday 12th
City Coliseum *Austin, TX* 8:00pm, with The True Believers
Travel day following.

Thursday 14th
Reunion Arena *Dallas, TX* 8:00pm, with Honeymoon Suite

Friday 15th
Majestic Theater/Performing Arts Center *San Antonio, TX* 8:00pm, with Emerald
A sell-out at this 2,539-capacity venue.

Saturday 16th
Lloyd Noble Center, University Of Oklahoma *Norman, OK* 8:00pm
There follows a travel day for the band, and after this comes a day off for them in Phoenix.

Tuesday 19th
Activity Center, Arizona State University *Tempe, AZ* 8:00pm, with The Out Crowd

Wednesday 20th
Golden Hall, Convention & Performing Arts Center *San Diego, CA* 8:00pm, with Army Of Love
A sell-out audience of 3,644.

Thursday 21st
Los Angeles Memorial Sports Arena *Los Angeles, CA* 8:00pm, with The Blasters

Friday 22nd
Arlington Theatre *Santa Barbara, CA* 8:00pm, with Giant Eden

Sunday 24th
Henry J. Kaiser Convention Center *Oakland, CA* 7:30pm, with Wire Train
Attendance is 6,147 at this 7,100-capacity hall. (Day off in LA follows.)

Tuesday 26th
At the 27th Annual Grammy Awards Ceremony at the Shrine Civic Auditorium in Los Angeles, Ray makes an award presentation, included in the CBS TV *Grammy Awards Show*.

Wednesday 27th
Arlene Schnitzer Concert Hall, Portland Center For The Performing Arts *Portland, OR* 8:00pm, with The Blasters

Thursday 28th
Paramount Northwest Theater *Seattle, WA* 8:00pm, with The Blasters

March

Friday 1st
Paramount Northwest Theater *Seattle, WA* 8:00pm, with The Blasters

Saturday 2nd
Pacific Coliseum *Vancouver, BC, Canada* 8:00pm, with The Blasters

Sunday 3rd – Friday 8th
Band members return to London for a week-long break from the tour. Ray possibly does some additional work on *Absolute Beginners*. They fly back to the US on the 8th.

Saturday 9th
Roy Wilkins Auditorium/Civic Center Theatre *St Paul, MN* 8:00pm, with Ipso Facto
A sell-out show.

Sunday 10th
Dane County Memorial Coliseum *Madison, WI* 8:00pm, with Flash Kahan
Attended by 3,949 fans at this 4,300-capacity room. (Travel day following.)

Tuesday 12th
Franklin County Veterans War Memorial Auditorium *Columbus, OH* 8:00pm, with Donny Iris & The Cruisers

Wednesday 13th
Hara Arena *Dayton, OH* 8:00pm, with Donny Iris & The Cruisers

Thursday 14th
The Coliseum *Richfield, OH* 8:00pm, with Donny Iris & The Cruisers
Travel day follows.

Saturday 16th
Minges Coliseum, East Carolina University *Greenville, NC* 8:00pm, with Glass Moon

Sunday 17th
Halsey Field House, United States Naval Academy *Annapolis, MD* 5:00pm
A free private concert for Academy midshipmen. Some tickets are available for faculty, staff and immediate families at $12.

Monday 18th
DAR Constitution Hall *Washington, DC* 8:30pm, with The Slickee Boys
Day off following.
'Summer's Gone' / 'Going Solo' single released in the US. Rather than issue the promo'd 'Living On A Thin Line', Arista instead pulls this weaker track from the album.

Summer's Gone single

A **'Summer's Gone'** (R. DAVIES).
B **'Going Solo'** (R. DAVIES).

US release March 18th 1985 (Arista AS1-9334).
Musicians and recording details as *Word Of Mouth* album (see November 19th 1984).
Chart high US none.

Wednesday 20th
Maple Leaf Gardens *Toronto, ON, Canada* 8:00pm, with Gowan
Set-list: 'Around The Dial', medley 'Definite Maybe' (intro) / 'State Of Confusion', 'The Hard Way', 'Don't Forget To Dance', 'Come Dancing', 'Do It Again', 'Living On A Thin Line', 'Guilty', 'Word Of Mouth', 'Missing Persons', 'Lola', 'All Day And All Of The Night', 'I Gotta Move', 'Till The End Of The Day', 'Celluloid Heroes', 'You Really Got Me', '(Wish I Could Fly Like) Superman'.

Thursday 21st
Ottawa Civic Centre Arena *Ottawa, ON, Canada* 8:00pm, with Honeymoon Suite
Travel day following.

Saturday 23rd
Carr Center, Saint Anselm College *Manchester, NH* 8:00pm, with The Del Fuegos

Sunday 24th
Brendan Byrne Arena, Meadowlands *East Rutherford, NJ* 8:00pm, with LaBamba & The Hubcaps; sponsored by the St. Pauli Girl Concert Series and WNEW-FM
Gary S. Lewis, among the audience of 12,768 who almost fill this 14,509-capacity venue, writes in *The Aquarian*: "The concert had a nice off-hand feel to it, as if the stop were a spur-of-the-moment decision.

At the same time, I think it regrettable that The Kinks' status prevents them from appearing in smaller halls. Some of their subtlety, humor, and wistfulness are lost when they are compelled to play to the gallery." The encore tonight includes an impromptu version of the 1965 US-only hit 'Who'll Be The Next In Line'.

Monday 25th
Cassell Coliseum, Virginia Polytechnic Institute and State University *Blacksburg, VA* 8:00 pm, with The Dads
Day off in Roanoke follows.

Wednesday 27th
Convocation Center, James Madison University *Harrisonburg, VA* 8:00 pm, with The Sparkplugs

Thursday 28th
Robins Center, University of Richmond *Richmond, VA* 8:00pm, with Skip Castro
Tour ends, and the band travels back to London the following day. Ray returns to New York City to do press work for the *Return To Waterloo* film.

April

➔ While the band has time off and Dave is on holiday, Ray does a barrage of press interviews in New York City for *Return To Waterloo*. Part of a European tour is cancelled and a mini-tour of a few cities is rescheduled in its place.
➔ ● **RECORDING** Konk Studios *Hornsey, north London*. Ray finishes **'Return To Waterloo'** (second version) and **'Voices In The Dark'** for a *Return To Waterloo* LP, with engineers David Baker and Dave Powell.
On these sessions, Ray sings lead vocals and plays guitars and synthesiser, with Jim Rodford on bass and backing vocal, Bob Henrit on drums, Ian Gibbons on keyboards, backing vocal and synth percussion programming, and John O'Donnel on extra percussion.

⮑ **TOUR STARTS** *Mini European Tour* (Apr 18th – 24th). **Line-up**: Ray Davies (lead vocal, guitar), Dave Davies (guitar, vocal), Bob Henrit (drums), Jim Rodford (bass), Ian Gibbons (keyboards). The band travels to Utrecht on the 17th.

Thursday 18th
Muziekcentrum Vredenburg *Utrecht, Netherlands* 9:00pm

Friday 19th
Pavillion Baltard Nogent Sur Marne, Paris, France
Filmed by MTV but not broadcast, except for a small clip shown in conjunction with winners of an MTV contest.
'Do It Again' / 'Guilty' single released in the UK. Issued as 7-inch and 12-inch, the latter with extra track 'Summer's Gone'.

Saturday 20th
Cirque Royal *Brussels, Belgium* 8:30pm, with The Kreuners
Set-list: 'Around The Dial', medley 'Definite Maybe' (intro) / 'State Of Confusion', 'Dead End Street', 'The Hard Way', 'Do It Again', 'Don't Forget To Dance', 'Living On A Thin Line', 'Guilty', 'Massive Reductions', 'Come Dancing', 'Lola', 'Missing Persons', 'David Watts', 'All Day And All Of The Night', 'I Gotta Move', 'Till The End Of The Day', 'Celluloid Heroes', 'Waterloo Sunset', medley 'Hang On Sloopy' / 'Louie Louie' / 'You Really Got Me' (accompanied by the show's promoter on piano). (Travel day follows.)

kinks'85

Monday 22nd
Apollo Theatre *Oxford* 7:30pm, with Catch

Tuesday 23rd
Odeon Cinema *Birmingham* 7:30pm, with Terry & Gerry

Wednesday 24th
Apollo Theatre *Manchester* 7:30pm
➜ Partially on location at Waterloo Station, central London, Ray shoots a video for the song 'Return To Waterloo' for use in the US, directed by Ray for Waterloo Films. It will first be shown on MTV, on May 23rd.

Sunday 28th
● **RECORDING** Konk Studios *Hornsey, north London*. Dave records solo tracks **'Earache'**, **'Please Stay'**, both unissued.

May/June

Ray is at Konk in London in early May finishing work on the *Return To Waterloo* album, and on the 16th there is a press preview of the film at the Waverly Theater in Greenwich Village, New York City. Although originally intended solely for the small screen, in the US the film is enlarged for full theatrical release around the country, opening at the Waverly on the 17th and playing in smaller art and independent theaters through the coming summer.

"What is invigorating about the entire affair," says Ira Mayer in the *New York Post*, "is that Davies has never lost sight of the sense of rebellion and confusion that are the essence of rock'n'roll. He has always given voice to the emotional conflicts of adolescence; here he illustrates them. … Like a French-made *Twilight Zone* in which a man about to be hanged fantasizes his escape, *Return To Waterloo* is emotionally charged. The charge may not warrant a $5 ticket but if it ever hits TV, it's worth an hour's time."

Proposed dates at Sun City, Bophuthatswana, South Africa are cancelled. A tour of Australia is pencilled in for June, but dates are never announced.

At Twickenham Film Studios in west London Ray does further filming for his role as the Father in the *Absolute Beginners* movie. Filming continues through the summer without further involvement from Ray. Ray recalls later that he writes a song called 'She's So Contrary' for the film's Max Miller character to sing, to be played by Keith Richards, but this is never filmed.

July

Monday 1st
Return To Waterloo soundtrack album by Ray Davies released in the US. "Ray Davies is again writing vignettes about recognizable people," says Parke Puterbaugh in *Rolling Stone*. "They don't have the scope of The Kinks' crowd-pleasing anthems, but as those who fell in love with *Arthur*, *Something Else*, or the *Village Green Preservation Society* years ago already know, they mean more. … The songs are crafted with an exceptional sensitivity to nuance. … Whatever its limitations as a film, *Return To Waterloo* advances Ray Davies' desire to bridge music and drama far better than the string of Kinks concept LPs in the mid-1970s. And while Davies' preoccupations on *Return To Waterloo* are unrelentingly gloomy, they are powerfully haunting as well."

➜ At the end of the month at Konk, Ray and Ian Gibbons play synthesisers for a recording to be used as a concert introduction tape in August.

***

Return To Waterloo soundtrack album by Ray Davies

A1 'Intro' (R. DAVIES).
A2 'Return To Waterloo' (R. DAVIES).
A3 'Going Solo' (R. DAVIES).
A4 'Missing Persons' (R. DAVIES).
A5 'Sold Me Out' (R. DAVIES).
B1 'Lonely Hearts' (R. DAVIES).
B2 'Not Far Away' (R. DAVIES).
B3 'Expectations' (R. DAVIES).
B4 'Voices In The Dark (End Title)' (R. DAVIES).
Album omits 'Ladder Of Success' and 'Good Times Are Gone' from original film

US release July 1st 1985 (Arista AL6-8386).
Musicians Ray Davies lead vocal, electric guitar, acoustic guitar, synthesiser. Jim Rodford bass guitar, backing vocal. Mick Avory drums. Bob Henrit drums and percussion (A2, B4), and some overdubs to existing tracks. Ian Gibbons keyboards, synth percussion programming. Louisa Davies backing vocal (A1, B4). John O'Donnel percussion (B4).
Recorded Konk Studios *Hornsey, north London*; probably July-August 1983; B4 and overdubs A1, A2: April 1985; possibly some early work May 1982; 24-track mixed to stereo.
Producer Ray Davies.
Engineers Damian Korner, David Baker; possible early work John Rollo.
Chart high US none.

August

➜ Early in the month the band rehearses new material at Konk for the upcoming concerts and tour, including 'Brother', 'Better Things' and 'Return To Waterloo'.

Thursday 15th
Ostend Airport *Ostend, Belgium* 12midday, *Belga Festival*, with ZZ Top (headliners), The Blasters, Screaming Blue Messiahs, T.C. Matic
Travel day back to London follows for the band, plus a day's rest before they're off again.

Sunday 18th
Royal Dublin Society National Stadium *Dublin, Ireland* with ZZ Top [headliners], Light A Big Fire
Travel day to London following, and then a travel day to Los Angeles.

➦ **TOUR STARTS** *Under The Skies: US Tour* (Aug 22nd – Sep 22nd). **Line-up**: Ray Davies (lead vocal, guitar), Dave Davies (guitar, vocal), Bob Henrit (drums), Jim Rodford (bass), Ian Gibbons (keyboards). The tour features new screen-projected backdrops and a taped introduction, plus a taped musical segue mid-show that feeds into a Dave Davies section. It's the last tour booked by long-time US booking agency ICM and co-ordinated by American manager Elliot Abbot's company Renaissance Management. Representatives of various record companies are invited to see the shows as part of the build-up to signing a new post-Arista record deal.

Much of the first two-thirds of the tour is booked into popular outdoor amphitheatres that typically range from 9,000 up to as many as 20,000 with lawn seating, though often a reduced number of tickets are offered for sale.

Ticket sales are not strong for The Kinks in many of these larger venues now, suggesting in some cases that there has been some over-ambitious booking. On the 21st the band rehearses at the Open Air Theater at San Diego State University prior to the start of the tour there the following day.

Thursday 22nd
Open Air Theater, San Diego State University *San Diego, CA* 8:00pm, with Cock Robin

Friday 23rd
Concord Pavilion *Concord, CA* 8:00pm, with Cock Robin

Saturday 24th
Irvine Meadow Amphitheatre *Laguna Hills, CA* 8:00pm, with Cock Robin
A day off for the band in California follows, and then there's a travel day on to Kansas City.

Tuesday 27th
Starlight Theatre *Kansas City, MI* 8:00pm, with Translator

Wednesday 28th
Omaha Civic Auditorium Music Hall *Omaha, NE* 8:00pm, with Translator
Travel day follows, then a day off in St Louis.

Friday 30th
Fox Theatre *St Louis, MI* 8:00pm, with Translator

Saturday 31st
Poplar Creek Music Theatre *Hoffman Estates, IL* 8:00pm, with Translator

September

Monday 1st
Pine Knob Music Theatre *Clarkston, MI* 8:00pm, with Translator

Monday 2nd
Alpine Valley Music Theatre *East Troy, WI* 8:00pm, with Translator
Tonight's concert in East Troy is attended by 4,000 out of 15,000 tickets offered for sale.

Translator are scheduled to complete the tour but are dropped now and replaced at short notice by Donnie [Miller] & The Rock who play the support spot for the rest of the tour. (Two days off in Chicago follow for the band.)

Thursday 5th
Blossom Music Center *Cuyahoga Falls, OH* 8:00pm, with Donnie & The Rock
Attendance is 8,000 in this 18,723-capacity room.

Friday 6th
Mann Music Center *Philadelphia, PA* 8:00pm, with Donnie & The Rock

Saturday 7th
Jones Beach Theatre *Wantagh, NY* 8:00pm, with Donnie & The Rock
Encore at tonight's show includes the rarely performed 'Sold Me Out'.

Sunday 8th
Manning Bowl *Lynn, MA* 3:00 pm, with Donnie & The Rock, Jon Butcher Axis
There are 7,000 fans here tonight, out of 15,000 tickets offered for sale. (Travel day follows.)

Tuesday 10th
Garden State Arts Center *Holmdel, NJ* 8:00pm, with Donnie & The Rock
Day off in New York City following.

Thursday 12th – Friday 13th
Pier 84 *New York, NY* 8:00pm, *Miller Music on the Pier*, with Donnie & The Rock
Set-list: 'Do It Again', medley 'Definite Maybe' (introduction) / 'State Of Confusion', 'The Hard Way', 'Better Things', 'Don't Forget To Dance', 'Come Dancing', 'A Well Respected Man', 'Return To Waterloo', 'Destroyer', 'Missing Persons', medley 'Batman Theme' / '(Wish I Could Fly Like) Superman', 'Brother', 'Guilty', 'A Gallon Of Gas', 'Lola', 'You Really Got Me', 'Living On A Thin Line', '20th Century Man', 'Celluloid Heroes', 'Low Budget', 'All Day And All Of The Night'.

☆ Director Des McAnuff telegrams Ray suggesting he might write songs for a proposed Broadway musical based on Jules Verne's *Around The World In 80 Days*. McAnuff is developing the show with Ray's former associate, playwright Barrie Keeffe. After contacting Ray, McAnuff attends a Kinks concert at the Pier, and Ray in turn attends McAnuff's successful Broadway show *Big River*. Eventually they agree to work together on the project, though Ray says later that at first he is resistant to the concept, thinking Verne's novel too much of a travelogue, and the two steer it into a show about Verne and creativity.

Saturday 14th
Merriweather Post Pavilion *Columbia, MD* 8:00pm, with Donnie & The Rock
In the audience is Howard Thompson, head of A&R for Elektra Records, which is interested in signing The Kinks. (Thompson had attended Grimshaw Secondary Modern School along with the Davies brothers in the late 1950s.) This is the last of the large outdoor amphitheatres on this tour; the coming final week of dates reverts to smaller 3,000 to 4,000-seat venues.

Sunday 15th
Recreation Hall, Pennsylvania State University *University Park, PA* 8:00pm, with Donnie & The Rock
Travel day follows.

Tuesday 17th
Monroe County Dome Arena, Rochester Institute Of Technology *Rochester, NY* 8:00pm, with Donnie & The Rock

Wednesday 18th
Fieldhouse, State University of New York College *Plattsburgh, NY* 8:00pm, with Donnie & The Rock
Travel day following.

Friday 20th
West Gymnasium, State University of New York *Binghamton, NY* 8:00pm, with Donnie & The Rock

Still life with Telecaster: Dave Davies on-stage at the Pavilion in Concord, California, August 23rd 1985.

Saturday 21st
Einsenhower Hall Theater, United States Military Academy
West Point, NY 8:00pm, with Donnie & The Rock
Tensions are flaring between the Davies brothers by this point on the Under The Skies tour.

Ray says later about this show: "I was trying to do the song 'Celluloid Heroes' and … Dave got his guitar to make a farting sound so everybody laughed." He tells another interviewer: "He was pissing me off all night, you know. And I had enough. … I got so frustrated … I'd run out of words and insults so I just dropped my trousers on stage and mooned the audience. … I don't think they'll ask us back there!"

Sunday 22nd
Gymnasium, State University of New York at Stony Brook
Stony Brook, NY 8:00pm, with Donnie & The Rock
There's an end-of-tour party tonight at the English Pub, New York City. Band members travel home to London the day after, while Ray stays behind in NYC for business. In the following days he undertakes negotiations for a new record deal, with EMI, CBS and MCA among the candidates.

Friday 27th
Hurricane Gloria strikes New York City. Ray later writes 'Lost And Found' based partially on this event.

October/November/December

Early in October, Ray is in New York City for negotiations with MCA for a new Kinks record deal. On his return he runs into ex-Kinks manager Grenville Collins on the street – possibly the inspiration for the song 'How Are You'.

On October 23rd, in London, Ray and Dave form a new limited company in preparation for signing the new record contract. Papers are signed to create Kinks 85 Ltd, with ownership split solely between Ray and Dave, and through which monies from all current and future Kinks touring and record contracts will flow. It essentially replaces Kinks Productions, the previous operating company of which Mick Avory too was a partner. Dave says later in *Kink* that at this same time Ray and Dave also sign a written agreement between the two of them stating that the name "The Kinks" is a jointly-owned entity and that the name can only ever be used by one with the consent of the other.

On November 8th it is announced on MTV News that The Kinks are scheduled to sign a recording contract with MCA Records, a report later described as "premature". Later in *Kink*, Dave writes that it is MCA that jumps the gun, squashing any chance of a re-signing with Arista, which he says is still a possibility at this time.

1986

As far as the public was concerned, The Kinks vanished from view for much of this year – the first year they did not tour the US since 1968. The band signed new record contracts (MCA Records for North America and London Records for Europe) which gave them a fresh outlook.

Yet as the first sessions began on a new album and quickly ground to a halt, it seemed as if the whole thing might come apart amid a crisis of panic and self-doubt.

A period of reflection and a morale-building tour away from the limelight provided the motivation to continue with what would be the final version of The Kinks. New drummer Bob Henrit ably filled Avory's shoes and completed an album and tours. With a new label and fresh personnel The Kinks were again ready to re-invent themselves and optimistically head into the future. They were focused on making as strong an album as possible and committing themselves to touring in support of the record during the coming year.

January

→ Early in the month The Kinks formally sign with MCA Records for the US and Canada. The contracts with Elliot Abbott and his Renaissance Management and with US booking agency International Creative Management expire around now.

With engineer David Baker still at the board at Konk in London, The Kinks begin recording demos of new material, one of which is **'How Are You'**. Ray says later that he likes his vocal performance so much that he bounces the vocal track from the demo on to the studio's 24-track machine and builds up a new instrumental performance around the existing vocal. This is a novel way to record a master – but indicates how sophisticated modern recording has become and how so many new creative and technical possibilities are at hand compared to the band's early days.

Another new master recorded at this time is **'The Video Shop'**. Ray says: "That song was going to form the concept of the LP. I took the spiv character I played in the 'Come Dancing' video and threw him into the environment of a video shop. I thought it might be interesting to see how he functioned in the cruel, modern world where factories are closing and everybody's redundant. It is very much the central theme of the record." Together with 'How Are You' it is probably earmarked as a potential first single for MCA's newest signing.

On the 25th Ray quietly marries Irish dancer Pat Crosbie in Surrey, England, his third marriage. Ray had met her almost two years before at a physical therapy clinic in London where both were recovering from job-related injuries. A small reception follows at Ray's house with immediate family and friends. Music is reportedly provided by the band of Ray's daughter Victoria, with Dave's son Simon joining in on drums. Many of the British dailies pick up on the story and a news feature in *Rolling Stone* magazine eliminates any semblance of secrecy.

February

Still at Konk, The Kinks record a special new version of their 1970 hit 'Apeman' exclusively for inclusion in the soundtrack of feature comedy film *Club Paradise*, directed by Harold Ramis of National Lampoon's *Animal House* fame, starring comedian Robin Williams, and released theatrically in the US by Warner Brothers on July 11th. As has happened before, The Kinks' performance is not included in the accompanying soundtrack LP also issued this summer, nor is it ever issued on vinyl or CD.

The scheduled US release of the soundtrack LP for *Absolute Beginners* is rescheduled to March 20th.

Mastering of The Kinks' final Arista offering – a double-album "best of" called *Come Dancing With The Kinks* – is done at Masterdisk in New York City between the 11th and the 18th.

In London, Dave's first daughter, Lana, is born. He spends some of the advance money from the new record contract on a small cottage in Devon, which he will use often in the coming years to get away from it all.

March

The band probably has the month off. Installation of equipment for Konk's new second studio continues which will provide the facility with state-of-the-art digital recording and mixing.

Absolute Beginners has its UK premier at the Leicester Square Theatre cinema in central London. The film includes Ray's on-camera performance of 'The Quiet Life'. The soundtrack album is released in the US on the 20th and in the UK four days later. "[Ray's] 'Quiet Life' is glorious," says *Sounds*, "and, when choreographed, is Ray Davies with a cherry on top."

Probably towards the end of the month Ray provides a copy of 'The Video Shop' for MCA and it is reportedly played at a company sales meeting as a sample of upcoming product. Release of the Arista label-retrospective *Come Dancing With The Kinks* is delayed to June 2nd due to a pressing backlog.

On the 31st The Kinks attempt to restart rehearsals for the new LP at Konk, but Ray reportedly has no new material and it is later reported that rehearsals come to a standstill, almost to the point of the band calling it quits because morale is so low. "We were coming apart during [that time]," Ray says later.

April

The band is reportedly at an impasse, almost at the point of splitting up. It is agreed however to book a short string of concerts off the beaten path – in Spain and Portugal – as a means of re-examining their feelings about playing as a group in front of an audience, and before deciding

---

Absolute Beginners soundtrack album

A4 'Quiet Life' (R. DAVIES).
The record also includes performances by David Bowie, Sade, Gil Evans, and Style Council

US release March 20th 1986 (EMI-America SV 17182).
UK release March 24th 1986 (Virgin V 2386), April 1st 1986 (2-LP set Virgin VD 2514).
Musicians Ray Davies lead vocal. Jim Rodford bass guitar. Bob Henrit drums. Further (non-Kinks) instrumentation overdubbed later, arranged by Gil Evans.
Recorded Konk Studios *Hornsey, north London*; January 1985; 24-track mixed to stereo.
Producers Clive Langer; Alan Winstanley.
Engineer probably David Baker.
Chart high US none; UK none.

---

whether to try to continue the recording.

On the 18th *Absolute Beginners* has its US premier at the Ziegfield Theater in New York City. The movie receives mixed notices, with many reviewers openly critical, and it does not fare well at the box office. Caryn James, writing in *The New York Times*, makes an astute observation of Ray's cameo as the put-upon Father. "[He] sings about the 'Quiet Life' in the family's chaotic boarding house, seen in cross-section like a doll's house. Mr Davies's music-hall-influenced song not only matches his character, but also suits the slapstick scrambling all around him. It's one of the film's euphoric moments, but stylistically it belongs in another movie."

May

⇨ **TOUR STARTS** *Spain/Portugal Tour* (May 8th – 17th). **Line-up**: Ray Davies (lead vocal, guitar), Dave Davies (guitar, vocal), Bob Henrit (drums), Jim Rodford (bass), Ian Gibbons (keyboards). Ray travels from New York City on the 5th, and the band members from London to Lisbon on the 6th. This will be the first visit to Spain by The Kinks since two brief visits 20 years earlier.

Thursday 8th
Pavillion do Dramatico *Cascais, Portugal*
The band plays to a receptive crowd of about 3,000 and performs among others 'Good Golly Miss Molly' and 'Waterloo Sunset'. (Travel day follows.)

Saturday 10th
Amphitheatre, Casa de Campo *Madrid, Spain* *San Isidro Festival*
The Kinks play to a massive crowd of many tens of thousands on this steamy day. (Travel day following.)

Monday 12th
La Maestranza *Seville, Spain* with Yos Yacentes
Although reportedly 4,000 attend, the turn-out is disappointing and blamed largely on poor promotion locally. (Travel day follows.)
'Quiet Life' / 'Voices In The Dark' single by Ray Davies released in

Quiet Life single by Ray Davies

A 'Quiet Life' (R. DAVIES).
B 'Voices In The Dark' (R. DAVIES).

UK release May 12th 1986 (Virgin VS 865; 12-inch VS 865 12).
A: musicians and recording details as *Absolute Beginners* album (see March); B musicians and recording details as *Return To Waterloo* soundtrack album (see July 1st 1985).
Chart high UK none.

the UK. "A sprightly but old fashioned tiddly-bum sort of song," says *Smash Hits*, "which extols the virtues of avoiding trouble by heading in the opposite direction, to an accompaniment of tubas a-parping, lightly jazzy drums a-scritching and fake birds a-tweeting. All of which is fairly unnecessary when it comes down to it , but it's a nice character study all the same."

The more established British music paper *Record Mirror* is more down to earth: "The song, from one of the stand out sequences of *Absolute Beginners*, has one foot in the boozer, the other planted firmly at the end of a two-piece tartan suit. This is English pop straight from the music hall tradition and not bad at it."

Wednesday 14th

Placio Municipale de Deportes *Barcelona, Spain*
Travel day following.

Friday 16th

Plaza de Toros (bullring) *Gijon, Spain*

Saturday 17th

Polideportiro Anoeta *San Sebastian, Spain* 7:30pm, with Los Santos
Evidently in a good mood today, The Kinks play a Troggs song and The Who's 'My Generation' during their soundcheck. (Travel day back to London follows.)
Set-list: 'Around The Dial', 'State Of Confusion', 'The Hard Way', 'Where Have All The Good Times Gone', 'Don't Forget To Dance', 'Come Dancing', 'Lola', 'David Watts', 'Dead End Street', 'Living On A Thin Line', 'Guilty', 'Low Budget', 'A Gallon Of Gas', 'Celluloid Heroes', '(Wish I Could Fly Like) Superman', 'All Day And All Of The Night', 'I Gotta Move', 'Pressure', '20th Century Man', 'You Really Got Me', 'Till The End Of The Day'.

➔ Ray later admits that since the break in touring last September he is still concerned about the loss of Mick Avory and unsure if this new incarnation of The Kinks is right. After the Spanish dates and seeing how well the band plays on-stage, however, the inspiration returns. Ray sets out to prove that the current band is, after all, The Kinks and that they have something to offer both in the studio and on stage. Preliminary work on the new LP is begun now and the band is busy preparing new material and recording demos. Sometime around now Konk engineer David Baker leaves and Ben Fenner returns.

June

On the 1st, sessions for the album begin at Konk's new No.2 studio and continue throughout the month. "It was a very planned-out album,"

Ray recalls later, adding: "It's the first album The Kinks have ever made where we knew the songs and made demos for them before we started to record.

Ray continues, "We didn't actually spend that much time in the studio. … [Dave] put a lot into the album – he was always there, and his attitude was pretty good throughout."

On the 2nd, Arista release the label retrospective double-album *Come Dancing With The Kinks* in the US.

July

Saturday 5th

Midtfyns Festival *Ringe, Denmark* four-day festival (3rd-6th) with Jethro Tull, John Mayall, The Fall, Roger Chapman & The Short List, Pentangle, Kate & Anna McGarrigle, The Dubliners and more
A tremendous success that provides the band with a pleasant mid-way break in their summer recording schedule. "The Kinks were the biggest name at Midfyns Festival and they were also the biggest event," writes Jakob Lambertsen in *Jyllandsposten*. "With almost insane energy and uncontrolled enthusiasm they underlined the fact that The Kinks are here and now – just like they were 22 years ago when their first appearance in Denmark ended in chaos." Ray speaks to the reviewer and says that the new album will be accompanied by a film-musical, and that its theme concerns "the fears caused by big monopolies".

☆ Meanwhile this month the band continues to record the new album at Konk No.2 back in London as the finishing touches are made to the studio upgrade.

Come Dancing With The Kinks double-album

A1 'You Really Got Me' live (R. DAVIES).
A2 'Destroyer' (R. DAVIES).
A3 '(Wish I Could Fly Like) Superman' (R. DAVIES).
A4 'Juke Box Music' (R. DAVIES).
A5 'A Rock'n'Roll Fantasy' (R. DAVIES).
B1 'Come Dancing' (R. DAVIES).
B2 'Sleepwalker' (R. DAVIES).
B3 'Catch Me Now I'm Falling' (R. DAVIES).
B4 'Do It Again' (R. DAVIES).
B5 'Better Things' (R. DAVIES).
C1 'Lola' live (R. DAVIES).
C2 'Low Budget' (R. DAVIES).
C3 'Long Distance' (R. DAVIES).
C4 'Heart Of Gold' (R. DAVIES).
C5 'Don't Forget To Dance' (R. DAVIES).
D1 'Misfits' (R. DAVIES).
D2 'Living On A Thin Line' (D. DAVIES).
D3 'Father Christmas' (R. DAVIES).
D4 'Celluloid Heroes' live (R. DAVIES).

US release June 2nd 1986 (Arista AL11-8428).
UK release October (probably 6th) 1986 (Arista 302 778).
All released previously on various Arista albums and singles, except (C3) 'Long Distance', only available before on tape.
Chart high US number 159; UK none.

August

By now nine new songs of Ray's are completed on tape at Konk: **'Killing Time'**, **'Working At The Factory'**, **'Repetition'**, **'Welcome To Sleazy Town'**, **'Think Visual'**, **'Natural Gift'**, **'Lost And Found'**, **'Possession'** and **'The Informer'**. Ray mixes them this month.

Also early this month, Dave as producer has completed two of his songs, **'When You Were A Child'**, made at Konk No.2, and **'Rock'n'Roll Cities'**, done as a demo presumably in the old No.1 room, with Mick Avory on drums rather than Bob Henrit. Dave decides that he will use the demo as the final master version for inclusion on the album.

By mid-month, Ray has completed all mixing and assembling of the tracks for the LP, and flies to New York City where mastering is done at Masterdisk on the 16th and again on the 25th and 28th.

At this point two tracks, 'The Informer' and 'Possession', are dropped. 'Possession' is never issued on record and nor is the track heard of again, while 'The Informer' will reappear a full seven years later, likely in re-recorded form, on 1993's *Phobia* CD. While in New York, Ray begins initial collaborations with Des McAnuff for the musical *80 Days*.

September

On the 10th at Konk Ray does a new mix of 'How Are You', without strings. Release of the new album is delayed into November because some minor remixing needs to be done and in order that videos can be prepared in advance for simultaneous release with singles in the US and UK.

In London The Kinks sign European record deals with London Records and the LP is prepared for release. A photograph of Ray used for the back cover of the LP is shot during a one-day stop-over in London on his way to Ireland.

Sequestered away in Cork, Ireland, Ray shifts his attention to working on the music for the musical *80 Days*, as well as making preparations for filming videos for The Kinks, and planning a book he wants to write about the recording of the new LP based on a diary he kept during the process.

Ray reportedly directs a few minor remixes by phone from Cork, and work on the new album's cover art with graphic designer Richard Evans is also done long-distance.

October

At the start of the month Ray has done the very final mix for the new album at Konk. He then flies to New York City and oversees the final mastering at Masterdisk with Robert Ludwig, on the 2nd. Then, back in London, the 'Rock'n'Roll Cities' video is shot on location around town and at Konk Studios.

'Rock'n'Roll Cities' is the humorous story of a house-bound Dave tending to a gaggle of young children, forced to help audition candidates for a replacement for a gone-missing Ray Davies on the eve of a pending Kinks tour – for which Ray sheepishly appears at the last moment. Following his experience with *Return To Waterloo*, this is Ray's debut directing a Kinks video (earlier videos were directed by Julien Temple).

Later in the month, possibly after more time back in Cork, Ray begins shooting a video for 'How Are You' with The Kinks on location in London. It's again directed by Ray, for his Waterloo Films.

November

➔ Work is completed on the video for 'How Are You'. It's aired in the UK in December and in the US on MTV on June 3rd 1987.
☆ In London the 'Rock'n'Roll Cities' video is assembled and finished by mid-month.

Wednesday 12th
'Rock'n'Roll Cities' promotional single released to US radio stations.

Monday 17th
Today Ray starts the press launch at BBC Broadcasting House, London appearing on BBC-1 TV. Portions of the interview are later issued as *The Official Ray Davies Interview* on a London Records 12-inch single and on video. On the 18th or 19th he makes a quick trip to Paris for the European press where for a day he does up to 15 interviews, including one which is taped and later broadcast on French Antene 2 television's *Les Enfants Du Rock* on February 28th 1987.
Think Visual album is released in the UK. *Sounds*: "This old dog may not know any new tricks but he can still perform his old ones to perfection." But the *NME* continues its hard line on The Kinks and unmercifully trashes it. "It's simple: the music on this album is very, very poor. … There aren't many ways of being substandard that aren't explored here."
'Rock'n'Roll Cities' / 'Welcome To Sleazy Town' single released in the US. "A loud jangly bit of life-in-the-fast-lane stadium rock," says *Billboard*, "featuring the usually second-billed younger Davies; label

Think Visual album

A1 'Working At The Factory' (R. DAVIES).
A2 'Lost And Found' (R. DAVIES).
A3 'Repetition' (R. DAVIES).
A4 'Welcome To Sleazy Town' (R. DAVIES).
A5 'The Video Shop' (R. DAVIES).
B1 'Rock'n'Roll Cities' (D. DAVIES).
B2 'How Are You' (R. DAVIES).
B3 'Think Visual' (R. DAVIES).
B4 'Natural Gift' (R. DAVIES).
B5 'Killing Time' (R. DAVIES).
B6 'When You Were A Child' (R. DAVIES).

UK release November 17th 1986 (London LONLP-27).
US release November 24th 1986 (MCA Records MCA-5822).
Musicians Ray Davies lead vocal except as noted, electric guitar, acoustic guitar, incidental keyboards. Dave Davies lead vocal (B1), electric guitar, backing vocal. Jim Rodford bass guitar, backing vocal. Bob Henrit drums, percussion except as noted. Mick Avory drums (B1). Ian Gibbons keyboards. Kim Goody backing vocal (B3).
Recorded Konk Studios (No. 2) *Hornsey, north London*; June-August 1986, except A5, B2: January 1986; B1: August 1986; 46-track mixed to stereo, except B1: probably 8-track mixed to stereo.
Producer Ray Davies, except B1, B6: Dave Davies.
Engineers Ben Fenner; Dave Powell (assistant), except A5, B2: David Baker; Damian Korner (unconfirmed track).
Chart high UK none; US number 81.

debut for the long-lived band." Despite the initial push from their new label, MCA, the song just doesn't connect to the audience. Although no one knows this now, The Kinks will never get another single in the charts.

Rock'n'Roll Cities single

A **'Rock'n'Roll Cities'** (D. DAVIES).
B **'Welcome To Sleazy Town'** (R. DAVIES).

US release November 17th 1986 (MCA MCA-52960).
Musicians and recording details as *Think Visual album* (see above).
Chart high US none.

Thursday 20th

Ray flies in to New York City today to begin a week of media blitzing to tie in with the new LP's release in the US. At Masterdisk, he helps to master the 'Lost And Found' 12-inch single.

Sunday 23rd

))) RADIO Ray is interviewed by the irreverent DJ Howard Stern at WXRK-FM studios. During the show Ray joins in with Stern for off-the-cuff versions of 'Lola', 'You Really Got Me' and 'Come Dancing' with Stern's informal house band Pig Vomit, which tonight consists of the show's writer Fred Norris on guitar and an intern known as Danny on a minimal drum kit. *The Howard Stern Show* is broadcast live on K-Rock (WXRK-FM) and in syndication the following week on DIR's *The National Howard Stern Show*.

Monday 24th

Think Visual album is released in the US. Reviews are generally positive, with many critics noting the return to a slightly calmer band sound. "Although there's plenty of rock'n'roll on The Kinks' first album for MCA," says the *Boston Herald*, "the veteran English outfit has toned down the hard-rock stance of its last couple of albums for a sound closer to The Kinks' best work." *The Los Angeles Times* agrees: "[Ray] has been one of the most consistently interesting and entertaining auteurs of rock for the past two decades. This album does nothing to alter that perception."

☆ During the week Ray continues with media duties and does a series of interviews at the MCA Records offices. On Thanksgiving Day (27th) he departs for Munich for a TV commitment.

Friday 28th

Rehearsal at Bavarian Rundfunk, Munich, for tomorrow's show.

Saturday 29th

❏ **TV** Bavarian Rundfunk Studios *Munich, West Germany*. ZDF Channel 2 *Na Sowas* lip-synch 'How Are You'.

December

Dave travels from London to Los Angeles where separately he begins his own media duties for the new single and album. An interview conducted at MCA's LA office is later issued as part of a promotional 12-inch in February 1987, *A Look At Think Visual*. Partly due to Dave's removal to Los Angeles, a number of planned German TV shows are not done.

On the 9th The Kinks minus Dave appear at Veronica Television Studios in Amsterdam, Netherlands where they lip-synch to 'How Are You' and Ray is interviewed. This is broadcast live on *Countdown* on VOO/Nederland 1 and later on the European Satellite Channel programme *Music Box*.

Ray is back in New York City by the 16th for more media work over the next few weeks. Among the more novel efforts is a feature taped at a video store called *Video Haven* where Ray appears as guest VJ, broadcast on MTV January 6th 1987. The **'How Are You' / 'Killing Time'** single is released in the UK on Monday 22nd.

On the 23rd Ray masters the US 7-inch 'Lost And Found' single. Around this time playwright Barry Keeffe leaves the *80 Days* project. The eventual replacement is British humorist Snoo Wilson, but the show's scheduled start is delayed from summer 1987 to summer 1988.

How Are You single

A **'How Are You'** (R. DAVIES).
B1 **'Killing Time'** (R. DAVIES).
B2 **'Welcome To Sleazy Town'** (R. DAVIES).
A-side is an edit of the album version

UK release December 22nd 1986 (7-inch A/B1 London LON 119; 12-inch A/B1/B2 LONX 119).
Musicians and recording details as *Think Visual* album (see November 17th).
Chart high UK none.

1987

Following their virtual invisibility in 1986, The Kinks were now committed to a very full year of activities which in effect began in the final months of '86 and continued throughout the new year. Now there was the promise and excitement of a re-energised band, new labels – MCA and London – and the unified, focused Think Visual album that was recorded over a short period of time and could be reproduced perfectly in concert.

A strategy for the year was mapped out, underlining MCA's commitment to the album and The Kinks' resolve to tour in reasonable bursts. The record company was seemingly committed to breaking a single from the LP, and while Dave's 'Rock'n'Roll Cities' did not perform well, two further tracks were pulled during the year, with tours and videos to help. Everything pointed to a relatively cohesive and co-operative organisation at work and, unlike the debacles that plagued their later Arista years, The Kinks made no false moves. But none of the songs and videos captured the public's attention: the singles sank without trace, and the album stalled at number 81 in the US.

Perhaps with an air of resignation at this failure, Ray wrote 'The Road', a tribute to The Kinks' halcyon touring days and a song that would help launch them into 1988. But MCA evidently were not behind a new live album and video, and the relationship between band and label began to falter this summer.

All the while, Ray pursued his main side project this year, the musical 80 Days. He was moving it forward between band commitments, and the work provided him with the always necessary outlet for his non-Kinks interests.

January

Ray undertakes a brief tour of key European cities to speak to the press about the new *Think Visual* LP and to pave the way for some European concert dates later in the spring.

On the 16th Ray is at Channel 4 Television studios in London where he is interviewed by Jonathan Ross for *The Last Resort*, broadcast the same day. He agrees to perform with the studio band and delivers two chestnuts: 'Lola' and 'Come Dancing'. He does not attempt songs from the new album – which no doubt it is felt would require all The Kinks.

Probably later in the month, Ray begins work on a music video for the next single from *Think Visual*, 'Lost And Found'. The Kinks play themselves as they record a soundtrack to an otherwise silent black-and-white movie that features Ray in the role of an 18th century soldier pining for his lost love. At the song's climax he finds her, a cellist from the soundtrack session set in the present day who crosses over into the film.

February

Friday 6th

Shooting and editing of the new video apparently take more time than anticipated and an appearance on British TV's *The Tube*, set to be taped at Tyne Tees Television Studios in Newcastle Upon Tyne today, is one of the casualties.

Monday 9th

Ray appears at the British Phonograph Institute Awards at the Grosvenor House Hotel in central London where he makes an award presentation to Kate Bush. The event is broadcast in the UK on BBC-1 television and via satellite to the US, France, Sweden and other countries.

'Lost And Found' / **'Killing Time'** single released in the US.

Lost And Found single

A **'Lost And Found'** (R. DAVIES).
B1 **'Killing Time'** (R. DAVIES).
B2 **'The Ray Davies Interview'**.
US A-side is an edit of the album version

US release (A/B1) February 9th 1987 (MCA Records MCA-53015).
UK release April 3rd 1987 (7-inch A/B1 London LON 132; 12-inch A/B1/B2 LONX 132).
Musicians and recording details as *Think Visual* album (see November 17th 1986).
Chart high US none; UK none.

→ Ray is at the offices of MCA in New York around mid-month as he delivers the finished video of the new single, slightly behind the record's release on the 9th but still in time for the start of the short upcoming tour.

☆ The Kinks finally reconvene at Konk in London where proper rehearsals are held to prepare for the upcoming tour. Unlike many tours before, The Kinks rehearse every song on the album for possible inclusion in their set-list. Before, many songs were deemed inappropriate for live presentation or weren't considered reproducible in concert.

Sunday 22nd

Ray flies into New York City, ahead of the rest of the band, for press and broadcast work. The band arrives in Philadelphia on the 24th, and the following day set up at the first venue, the Tower Theater in Philadelphia, where they fine-tune their repertoire and stage show for the tour.

↪ **TOUR STARTS** *Think Visual: North American Tour: 1st leg* (Feb 26th – Mar 16th). **Line-up**: Ray Davies (lead vocal, guitar), Dave Davies (guitar, vocal), Bob Henrit (drums), Jim Rodford (bass), Ian Gibbons (keyboards). Meant as a lightning promotional tour of the key Kink cities – Philly, Boston, Providence, Cleveland, Passaic (NJ), Chicago, LA, Detroit, and New York City, missing only San Francisco and DC – it will reacquaint major groups of fans with the band and prepare for the more extensive summer tour when they'll aim at the larger-capacity "sheds".

Reviews on the tour are almost universally positive and generally welcome the band's return to relatively intimate venues (mostly 2,500-4,000-capacity). It's the first tour booked by a new outfit, the LA-based Creative Artists Agency, through Rob Light. All shows are sell-outs or close, with tickets selling in the $15-$20 range. An important event is a live broadcast in Chicago mid-tour that will be syndicated nationally.

Thursday 26th – Friday 27th

Tower Theater *Upper Darby, PA* 8.00pm, with John Eddie
These opening dates are in suburban Philadelphia; Eddie is a New Jersey roots rocker. In perfect modern rock-biz synchronicity, MTV broadcasts a world debut of the 'Lost And Found' video to tie in with the opening night of the tour.

Saturday 28th

Wang Center for the Performing Arts *Boston, MA* 7.30pm, with John Eddie
Day off in Boston follows.

March

Monday 2nd

Providence Performing Arts Center *Providence, RI* 8:00pm, with John Eddie
Tonight is only a near sell-out, considered disappointing by the band but a reasonable feat for a Monday night.

Tuesday 3rd – Wednesday 4th

Capitol Theatre *Passaic, NJ* 8:00pm, with John Eddie
Special 15th anniversary shows celebrating the opening of the Capitol Theatre as a rock venue. Ray is suffering from an extremely bad throat and the show is nearly cancelled. (Day following is time off in New York City, and then a travel day to Chicago.)

Saturday 7th – Sunday 8th

Riviera Nightclub *Chicago, IL* 8:00pm, with The Insiders (7th), The Verandas (8th)
Sunday's show is broadcast live on Chicago WXRT-FM radio's *Budweiser Sunday Night Concert Special*, and edited and remixed for re-broadcast in national syndication on *The King Biscuit Flower Hour*, May 10th and 17th. The work is done by Fanta Sound Recording Services with engineer Bruce Rains and assistant engineer John Hanson.
Set-list (8th): 'Do It Again', 'The Hard Way', 'Low Budget', 'Come Dancing', 'Working At The Factory', 'Lost And Found', 'Welcome To Sleazy Town', 'Think Visual', 'The Video Shop', 'Living On A Thin Line', 'Guilty', 'Misfits', 'Lola', 'State Of Confusion', 'A Gallon Of Gas', 'All Day And All Of The Night', 'I Gotta Move', 'Celluloid Heroes', '20th Century Man', 'You Really Got Me', 'Till The End Of The Day'.

Monday 9th

Orpheum Theater *Minneapolis, MN* 8:00pm, with Royal Court Of China
Travel day follows.

Wednesday 11th

Music Hall *Cleveland, OH* 8:00pm, with Royal Court Of China

Thursday 12th

Fox Theatre *Detroit, MI* 8:00pm, with Royal Court Of China
Travel day following.

Saturday 14th

Hollywood Palladium *Los Angeles, CA* 8:00pm, with Legal Weapon
Travel day follows. "The veteran British quintet charmed the capacity crowd with selections from its 20-plus years of sporadic hits, but most of the show was devoted to beery renditions of head Kink Ray Davies' versions of radio fodder," writes Don Waller in the *Los Angeles Times*. "The best of which sounded as off-handedly raunchy and funny as the bust-up-the-dance-hall band The Kinks have always prided themselves on being. The rest of which was as forgettable as it was tightly performed.

"For years," Waller continues in the *Times*, "The Kinks have been the great outsiders, the true poets of small lives, small pleasures, simultaneously savage 'n' sentimental. Despite their intellect and their considerable artistic accomplishments, their audience remains – somewhat ironically – almost exclusively working-class yobs, not unlike the Kinks themselves."

Monday 16th

Beacon Theatre *New York, NY* 8:00pm, with Peter Himmelman
The grand reopening of this recently renovated venue on Broadway on the Upper West Side where the Kinks played in the 1970s.
→ A post-tour party for The Kinks is thrown by MCA Records at the Hard Rock Café. Guests include Mark Harmon and guitarist Jeff Beck. (Travel day to London following.)

→ ● **RECORDING** Calliope Studios *New York, NY*. Possibly at this studio, Ray and Gibbons record demo versions of songs for the *80 Days* musical, following the end of the tour. Pieces recorded include **'Let It Be Written'**, **'Our World'** (aka 'Empire Song'), **'Well-Bred Englishman'**, **'Against The Tide'**, **'Ladies Of The Night'**, **'On The Map'**, **'It Could Have Been Him'**, **'Mongolia Song'**, **'No Surprises'**, **'Welcome To India'**, **'Passing Through'**, **'Who Do You Think You Are'**, **'80 Days'**, **'Members Of The Club'**, **'Conspiracy'**, **'Tell Him Tell Her'**, and **'Be Rational'**.

→ INDICATES EVENT AROUND THIS TIME BUT WITH NO FIRM DATE

April

On the 3rd The Kinks appear on Channel 4's hip TV show *The Tube*. Their performances are videotaped at the Tyne Tees Television Centre (Studio 5) in Newcastle Upon Tyne. Broadcast the same day are 'Lost And Found' and 'Think Visual'. 'Come Dancing' is taped but not broadcast; 'I Gotta Move' is played for the studio audience and not broadcast. The same day sees the UK release of the **'Lost And Found' / 'Killing Time'** single.

More TV follows in Germany on the 7th, when at the Bayerischen Rundfunk studios in Nürnberg, West Germany they lip-synch to 'Lost And Found', broadcast on ARD/channel 1's *Vier Gegen Willi* on the 18th. Back at Konk they rehearse a new song inspired while they were in Germany, 'It (I Want It)'.

Some time this spring, Dave records demos of two of his new songs, **'Emergency'** and **'No More Mysteries'**, at his home studio in Maida Vale, north-west London. They are submitted to EMI Publishing as part of a deal for which he will record more demos over the course of this year. 'No More Mysteries' will be released in demo form on a Dave solo CD in January 2001, *Fragile*, part of a series of demos he issues at that time.

Towards the end of the month the scheduled US tour is delayed, with dates in May either cancelled or moved to June. The cancelled May dates: 7th Sam Houston Coliseum, Houston, TX; 8th Starplex Amphitheatre, Dallas, TX; 10th Tingley Coliseum, Albuquerque, NM; 11th Mesa Amphitheatre, Mesa, AZ; 13th Golden Hall, San Diego, CA; 15th Pacific Amphitheatre, Orange County Fairgrounds, Costa Mesa, CA; 16th ARCO Arena, Sacramento, CA; 17th Concord Pavilion, Concord, CA.

May

➪ **TOUR STARTS** *Think Visual: German Mini Tour* (May 23rd – 28th). **Line-up**: Ray Davies (lead vocal, guitar), Dave Davies (guitar, vocal), Bob Henrit (drums), Jim Rodford (bass), Ian Gibbons (keyboards). Though brief, this is the band's first proper tour of Germany since autumn 1980. It's promoted by Z-Concerts and Music GMBH. (Band travels to Zurich on the 22nd.)

Saturday 23rd
Bodenseestadion Konstanz, West Germany 2:00pm, *Rock Am See Festival*, with Santana (headliners), Gary Moore, FM, Phil Carmen, Whats Up

Sunday 24th
Freilichtbühne Loreley, St Goarshausen, West Germany 2:00pm, *Loreley '87 Open Air Festival*, with Santana (headliners), Gary Moore, Flatsch, FM, Anno Domini

Monday 25th
Stadthalle Heidelberg, West Germany with The Jocco Abendroth Band
Travel day follows.

Wednesday 27th
Musikhalle Hamburg, West Germany with The Jocco Abendroth Band

Thursday 28th
Westfallenhalle 2 Dortmund, West Germany with The Jocco Abendroth Band

Set-list: 'Do It Again', 'Where Have All The Good Times Gone', 'Tired Of Waiting For You', 'The Hard Way', 'Low Budget', 'Come Dancing', 'Waterloo Sunset', 'Working At The Factory', 'Lost And Found', 'Think Visual', 'Welcome To Sleazy Town', 'Guilty', 'Living On A Thin Line', 'Lola', 'Dead End Street', 'David Watts', 'All Day And All Of The Night', 'I Gotta Move', 'Celluloid Heroes', 'Pressure', 'How Are You', 'You Really Got Me', 'Victoria', 'Twist And Shout'.

Saturday 30th
❏ **TV** television studio *Basel, Switzerland*. ZDF/Channel 2 *Na Sowas Extra* lip-synch 'Lost And Found'.
Travel day to Los Angeles follows.

June

Monday 1st
'How Are You' / 'Working At The Factory' single released in the US.

How Are You single

A **'How Are You'** (R. DAVIES).
B **'Working At The Factory'** (R. DAVIES).
A-side is an edit of the album version

US release June 1st 1987 (MCA Records MCA-53093). Musicians and recording details as *Think Visual* album (see November 17th 1986).
Chart high US none.

➪ **TOUR STARTS** *Think Visual: North American Tour: 2nd leg* (Jun 2nd – Jul 5th). **Line-up**: Ray Davies (lead vocal, guitar), Dave Davies (guitar, vocal), Bob Henrit (drums), Jim Rodford (bass), Ian Gibbons (keyboards), Pat Crosbie, Annie Cox (dancers, from June 8th). Tickets prices are generally $10.50 to $18.50.

Tuesday 2nd
Civic Theatre Convention And Performing Arts Center San Diego, CA 7:30pm, with The Knack

Wednesday 3rd
Pacific Amphitheatre, Orange County Fairgrounds Costa Mesa, CA 7:30pm, with Joan Jett & The Blackhearts
Day off following in LA; Ray has media duties including radio interviews to promote shows on the tour.

Friday 5th
Greek Theatre Los Angeles, CA 8:00pm, with Joan Jett & The Blackhearts

Saturday 6th
Santa Barbara County Bowl Santa Barbara, CA 8:00pm, with Joan Jett & The Blackhearts

Sunday 7th
Concord Pavilion Concord, CA 8:00pm, with Joan Jett & The Blackhearts
Travel day following.

kinks'87

Tuesday 9th

An unexpected day off in Santa Fe, NM, due to the evening's show at the Paolo Soleri Amphitheater being rained out. The show is instead moved to tomorrow in Albuquerque. The Kinks take advantage of the time and hold rehearsals for a new song called 'It (I Want It)'.

Wednesday 10th

Exhibit Area, New Mexico State Fairgrounds *Albuquerque, NM*

New song 'It (I Want It)' debuts tonight. It's also the first show to feature Ray's wife Pat along with Annie Cox performing a ballet-influenced piece that is integrated into the song's story line. It becomes a staple of the live act for the next four years.

Thursday 11th

Red Rocks Amphitheatre *Morrison, CO* 7:30pm, with Joan Jett & The Blackhearts
Travel day follows.

Saturday 13th

Riverside Theatre *Milwaukee, WI* 8:00pm, with Pat McCurdy & The Confidentials

Sunday 14th

Poplar Creek Music Theatre *Hoffman Estates, IL* 8:00pm, with Joan Jett & the Blackhearts

Monday 15th

Blossom Music Center *Cuyahoga Falls, OH* 8:00pm, with Joan Jett & The Blackhearts

Tuesday 16th

Riverbend Music Center *Cincinnati, OH* 7:30pm, with Joan Jett & The Blackhearts
Travel day following.

Thursday 18th

DeVos Hall Grand Center *Grand Rapids, MI* 8:00pm

This late added date at a small theatre impressed Marie Havenga of *Grand Rapids Press* who seems unused to such talent in town. "No questions. No ifs, ands, or buts. Name a current rock group better than The Kinks. Not just one aspect. We're talking totality – style, longevity, material, vocals, lyrics, sincerity. Forget musical taste, personal favorites and current chart toppers. Forget The Rolling Stones. The Kinks' Ray Davies can out-sing Mick Jagger with his tongue tied behind his back. He proved it Thursday night at DeVos Hall before a crowd of 1,650."

Friday 19th

Kingswood Music Theatre, Canada's Wonderland theme park *Maple, ON, Canada* 8:00pm, with The Jitters
Former bassist Pete Quaife is in the audience at tonight's show and hangs out with the band back at the hotel following the show. (Travel day follows.)

Sunday 21st

Stanley Theater *Utica, NY* 8:00pm, with Steve Jones
The ex-Sex Pistol and new band open tonight's show and are slated to do the rest of the dates, but for unknown reasons are dropped from the tour after the Maryland show on the 29th.

Monday 22nd

Saratoga Performing Arts Center *Saratoga Springs, NY* 8:15pm, with Steve Jones

The two dancers are featured tonight performing during 'Clichés Of The World' which also becomes a regular part of the show. The following day sees unexpected time off in Saratoga following the cancellation of a gig at the Finger Lakes Performing Arts Center, Canandaigua, NY. With Wednesday also open, Ray takes advantage of the free time and two additional dance routines are worked up for 'Welcome To Sleazy Town' and 'Think Visual'.

Thursday 25th

Lakeside Amphitheatre – Darien Lake *Darien Center, NY* 8:00pm, with Steve Jones

Friday 26th

Mid-Hudson Civic Center *Poughkeepsie, NY* 8:00pm, with Todd Hobin & The Heat

Saturday 27th

Pier 84 *New York, NY* 7:30pm, with Steve Jones
Earlier in the day Ray (and possibly Dave) meet MCA executives, including president Irving Azoff, who say they want The Kinks to present more saleable product in future. Ray has plans for the next album to be a double-live package with an accompanying video, but MCA are resistant and relations between the two parties begin to strain hereafter. On-stage tonight Ray is clearly in a bad mood and can barely conceal his anger at the day's earlier meeting, bellowing to the crowd at one point his frustration at the corporate attitude and its financially-driven products: "C'mon MCA … *Beverly Hills Cop, Starlight Express* … Suck it! Fuck you!"

On a more artistic note, the dancers are by now also incorporated into 'Think Visual' and 'Welcome To Sleazy Town' as well as 'Clichés Of The World' and 'It (I Want It)'. Ray is videotaping incidental footage for possible inclusion in his planned video to accompany the recording of a live album. Despite the earlier on-stage rancour, MCA holds an after-show party for The Kinks at the Tunnel Club on 12th Avenue and 27th Street. (Following day is time off in New York City).

Monday 29th

Merriweather Post Pavilion *Columbia, MD* 8:00pm, with Steve Jones
Tonight's show is recorded by the Fanta Sound 32-track mobile recording unit with engineer Johnie Rosen. 'Lost And Found' from tonight's performance ends up on the forthcoming live album. The concert is also filmed for a possible video to accompany the live album, but is never used. (Day off follows.)
Set-list: 'Destroyer', 'Low Budget', 'Apeman', 'Come Dancing', 'Clichés Of The World', 'Working At The Factory', 'Think Visual', 'Welcome To Sleazy Town', 'Muswell Hillbilly', 'A Well Respected Man', 'Art Lover', 'Living On A Thin Line', medley 'Batman Theme' / '(Wish I Could Fly Like) Superman', 'It (I Want It)', 'Guilty', 'Lola', 'All Day And All Of The Night', 'Give The People What They Want', 'I Gotta Move', 'Celluloid Heroes', 'Around The Dial', 'You Really Got Me'.

July

Wednesday 1st

Mann Music Center *Philadelphia, PA* 8:00pm, with Todd Hobin & The Heat
This show too is recorded by the Fanta Sound mobile and filmed for the proposed video. 'Destroyer', 'Apeman', 'Art Lover', 'Clichés Of The World', 'Think Visual', 'Lost And Found', 'Come Dancing', 'Living On A Thin Line', 'It (I Want It)', 'Give The People What They Want' and 'Around The Dial' from tonight's performance end up on the resulting

→ INDICATES EVENT AROUND THIS TIME BUT WITH NO FIRM DATE

Ray Davies live at London's Town & Country Club, December 20th 1987; just out of shot is bassist Jim Rodford, in front of Bob Henrit's drums.

live album, *The Road*. 'You Really Got Me' will be issued as the B-side of 1989's 'Down All The Days' single, and 'I Gotta Move' on 1991's *Did Ya* CD maxi-single. (Day off following in New York City as the scheduled show at Jones Beach Theater is rained out.)

Friday 3rd
Great Woods Center For The Performing Arts *Mansfield, MA* 7:30pm, with Todd Hobin & The Heat
Day off in New York City follows.

Sunday 5th
Jones Beach Theatre *Wantagh, NY* 7:30pm, with Todd Hobin & The Heat
For old times' sake Ray performs the 1970s concert staple 'Alcohol' tonight. The band hold a traditional end-of-tour party back in New York City, this time at a low-key Irish bar, Mulligan's Bar & Grille on 7th Avenue. (Band travels home to London the following day, except Ray who stays in New York.)

→ Ray spends much of the remainder of the summer in New York City, collaborating with director Des McAnuff and writer Snoo Wilson on the *80 Days* musical project.
☆ Probably around this time, following the tour, and with Ray consumed by his project, Dave records two more demos of his new songs at his home studio in Maida Vale, north-west London – **'Wait'** and **'Bright Lights'** – and both are submitted to EMI Publishing. They will be released in this demo form as part of Dave's solo CD *Fragile* of January 2001. A master version of 'Bright Lights' is recorded probably shortly after, and will be included as a bonus cut on the 1989 Kinks CD *UK Jive*.

August

Ray is reported to be at Calliope Studios in New York City working with producer Chris Julian on *80 Days* demos.
Dave is reportedly in New York mid-month, possibly to meet Ray and discuss the upcoming live album.
Ray later recalls writing the verses for a new song 'The Road' that will accompany the live album he is pushing MCA to put out as the next Kinks release.
He needs to complete this song so he can play it for MCA executives, probably to convince them of the worthiness of the project, and also to demonstrate that the album will have a new studio recording that can be released as an accompanying single.

September

Saturday 5th
Steinberggasse *Winterthur, Switzerland* 8:15pm, *Winterthurer Musikfestwochen*, with Toy Dolls, Triffids
This appearance is a one-off festival date that takes place outside Zurich and is dampened by rain – hence Ray's impromptu Gene Kelly tribute with a rendition of 'Singing In The Rain'. During the encore Ray is hit on the head by a record thrown from the crowd, and stitches are required afterwards.
☆ Back in London on the 13th, the band has worked up Ray's new song **'The Road'** and they head into Konk Studios (No.2) with engineer Dave Powell and assistant George Holt to put a master version on tape. It is probably now and through to the end of the month that any post-production overdubs required for the live recordings from the two

shows recorded this summer are done.
☆ Two lots of old Pye material are released on the 28th by owners PRT: a double-album, *The Kinks Are Well Respected Men*; and the single LP *Hit Singles*.

October

Ray books Friday 2nd to Monday 12th at PUK Recording Studios in Gjerlev in rural Denmark, bringing with him noted British mix engineer Jeremy Allom, known for his work at Air Studios in London on albums by The Pretenders and The Clash among others. Ray and Allom work on tapes for the new live Kinks album and spend this intense 11-day stretch mixing tracks. Time is also spent remixing tracks at Konk on 17th-18th, 21st, 22nd, and 27th.
Probably around this time, with Ray deep into his projects, Dave records three more demos of new songs at his home studio in London, **'Every Little Once In A While'**, **'Give Something Back'** and **'Hope'**, which are submitted to EMI Publishing. The latter two are released in this demo form on Dave's January 2001 *Fragile* CD. 'Every Little Once In A While' remains unissued.
In Ray's absence, Dave also seems to record around this time at least a master version of **'Bright Lights'** at Konk with Rodford, Henrit and Gibbons. Other recent Dave songs may be recorded too, details unknown.

November

Ray travels to New York City, spending the 2nd, 4th-5th and 9th overseeing the mastering of the new live LP, *The Road*, at Masterdisk Studios with Robert Ludwig. He also has meetings with MCA, negotiating for an accompanying video. Otherwise Ray is working intensively at the Alcott Hotel with Des McAnuff & Snoo Wilson on *80 Days*. On the 23rd he receives news of his mother's death in London and flies back the following day for her funeral.

December

➪ **TOUR STARTS** *The Road: European Tour* (Dec 7th – 20th).
Line-up: Ray Davies (lead vocal, guitar), Dave Davies (guitar, vocal), Bob Henrit (drums), Jim Rodford (bass), Ian Gibbons (keyboards), Pat Crosbie, Annie Cox (dancers). The band begins the tour by travelling to Berlin on Sunday 6th.

Monday 7th
Eissporthalle *Berlin, West Germany* 8:00pm, with Marquee Moon

Tuesday 8th
Capitol Veranstaltungszentrum *Hanover, West Germany* 8:00pm, with Marquee Moon
Ray is not well and is too exhausted for the encore, instead handing vocal duties to Dave on 'You Really Got Me'.

Wednesday 9th
Jahrhunderthalle *Frankfurt, West Germany* 8:00pm, with Marquee Moon
Dave again takes over vocals on 'You Really Got Me' tonight.
The Road album released in West Germany.

The Road album

A1 'The Road' (R. DAVIES).
A2 'Destroyer' (R. DAVIES).
A3 'Apeman' (R. DAVIES).
A4 'Come Dancing' (R. DAVIES).
A5 'Art Lover' (R. DAVIES).
A6 'Clichés Of The World' (R. DAVIES).
B1 'Think Visual' (R. DAVIES).
B2 'Living On A Thin Line' (D. DAVIES).
B3 'Lost And Found' (R. DAVIES).
B4 'It (I Want It)' (R. DAVIES).
B5 'Around The Dial' (R. DAVIES).
B6 'Give The People What They Want' (R. DAVIES).

US release January 11th 1988 (MCA Records MCA-42107).
UK release May 23rd 1988 (London LONLP 49).
Musicians Ray Davies lead vocal except as noted, guitars.
Dave Davies lead guitar, lead vocal (B2), backing vocal. Jim
Rodford bass guitar, backing vocal. Bob Henrit drums. Ian
Gibbons keyboards, backing vocal.
Recorded A1: Konk Studios No.2 *Hornsey, north London*;
September 1987; 46-track mixed to stereo. A2-A6, B1, B2, B4-
B6: Mann Music Center *Philadelphia, PA*; July 1st 1987. B3:
Merriweather Post Pavilion *Columbia, MD*; June 29th 1987; live
tracks recorded by Fanta Sound Mobile Unit. Post-production
for live recordings at Konk Studios *Hornsey, north London*,
probably September 1987; mixed October 1987 at PUK Studios
Gjerlev, Denmark; 32-track mixed to stereo.
Producer Ray Davies.
Engineers Johnie Rosen, assistants Mervin and Billy (Fanta
Sound); Dave Powell, assistant George Holt (Konk); mix Jeremy
Allom, assistant Peter Everson (PUK).
Chart high US number 110; UK none.

Thursday 10th
Sporthalle *Böblingen, West Germany* 8:00pm, with Marquee
Moon
Travel day following.

Saturday 12th
Sporthalle *Linz, Austria* 8:00pm

Sunday 13th
Rolling Stone Club *Milan, Italy* 9:30pm
The Kinks make their only appearance ever in Italy. (Travel day
follows.)

Tuesday 15th
Oberlaa Kurhalle *Vienna, Austria* 8:00pm

Wednesday 16th
Kongressaal Deutsches Museum *Munich, West Germany*
8:00pm, with Marquee Moon

Thursday 17th
Schwarzwaldhalle *Karlsruhe, West Germany* 8:00pm, with
Marquee Moon

Friday 18th
Philipshalle *Düsseldorf, West Germany* 8:00pm, with
Marquee Moon
Travel day to London follows.

Sunday 20th
Town & Country Club *Kentish Town, north-west London*
7:30pm, with Voice Of The Beehive
Despite an adoring crowd and numerous encores, including a guest
spot with Mick Avory on drums for 'A Well Respected Man', the British
music press largely writes off the band, essentially for what they
perceive as Americanisation and the embracing of heavy metal.
  NME is ruthless, apparently sensing a betrayal of the band's former
ideals. "Terry and Julie wave goodbye to Ray with water in their eyes.
The man who helped fill the pages of their scrapbook now deals in
scrap metal." *Melody Maker*: "How did they bore me? Let me count
the ways."
  The other British weekly music paper, *Record Mirror*, is only slightly
more charitable: "[Ray] will be back, because … he's still worth it, even
just for those few moments." The concert is videotaped by MTV for an
intended concert special, but this remains unaired. Footage from this
concert of the title song 'The Road' is used in *The Road* video, with
audio from the record overdubbed. (Time off for Christmas holidays
follow; Ray's health deteriorates.)
Set-list: 'Do It Again', 'Destroyer', 'Low Budget', 'Apeman', 'Come
Dancing', 'Clichés Of The World', 'Lost And Found', 'Think Visual',
'Living On A Thin Line', 'Dead End Street', 'Sunny Afternoon', 'It (I
Want It)', 'Guilty', 'Lola', 'All Day And All Of The Night', 'The Road',
'You Really Got Me', 'A Well Respected Man', 'David Watts', 'Till The
End Of The Day', 'Waterloo Sunset', 'Give The People What They
Want'.

Monday 21st
A single of 'The Road' / 'Apeman' is mastered today in 7-inch and 12-
inch forms but ultimately will not be issued commercially in the US.

Wednesday 23rd
US radio stations are sent copies of the album's title song, the studio-
recorded 'The Road', in various programming samplers. However,
release of the album scheduled for the 28th is delayed until January
11th 1988.

kinks'88

1988

Chaos seemed to dominate this year, as Ray's ill health and his commitment to a major theatrical production cut into The Kinks' schedule. It was certainly an anti-climactic year for the band, but resulted in a major accomplishment for Ray with the 80 Days musical. Disappointment with MCA continued to fester after the false start and let-down of the Think Visual studio LP and the company's apparent resistance to what the band felt was a strong live album, The Road. Dave would later write off the entire year with a single paragraph in his book, Kink.

January

In London early in the new year it is initially reported in the media that Ray Davies is ill with bronchitis and exhaustion (or alternatively that he has had a heart attack). There follows a delay to the upcoming US tour by one month.

Doctors decide that Ray should enter hospital to correct what is later described as a blood clot and a build-up of fluid in his lungs. He is treated in Dublin, Ireland and is reportedly discharged over the weekend of the 15th-16th when he removes to his in-laws near Cork to convalesce.

As he recuperates in Cork, Ray busies himself writing two film scripts. It's at this time a publisher approaches him to write his autobiography. Ray writes about 100 pages at this point but doesn't get back to it seriously until 1993/94 when his Canadian editor pushes the project again. Ray says later that at some point towards the end of this month The Kinks come to Cork to rehearse in a local hotel ballroom.

The Road album is released in the US. "It's so charmingly like The Kinks to release a live album *after* Christmas, thus minimizing whatever revenues such an obvious stocking stuffer would normally produce," writes George Kalogerakis in *Rolling Stone*. "[The album] is representative of the band's latest concerts; it's less predictable and more textured than the tiresome arena-rock performances of the early-1980s Kinks. … Davies still has much to offer, and judging from this album, so may The Kinks."

The Kinks pick up some additional credibility as a cover version of 'All Day And All Of The Night' by The Stranglers hits the British Top Ten this month.

February

Ray travels to New York City where he edits *The Road* video, a compilation of various film and video footage. There are excerpts from TV footage of *Beat Room* (October 1964) and *Shindig!* (filmed in London, December 1964), promotional film for 'Starstruck' shot in north London (November 1968), live concert film from K.B. Hallen, Copenhagen, Denmark (February 1966), arrival at Reykjavik, Iceland (September 1965), the 'Everybody's In Showbiz' film (shot March 1972), concert footage from *A Soap Opera* (probably New Victoria Theatre, London, June 1975), unknown concert footage from 1980 and May 1983, and film from the Town And Country Club, London

(December 1987). The finished video debuts on US television on MTV on March 3rd.

Following The Stranglers into the British charts with a Kinks cover are The Fall who revive 'Victoria' in an energetic reading. While its peak of number 35 is not quite the hit that The Stranglers enjoyed, its reworking by this fashionable band only helps to highlight Ray's writing and bring The Kinks' early catalogue back to life.

In New York City, once the video is completed, Ray sprinkles media appearances around his work on the *80 Days* musical. On Friday 19th he's at NBC Television Studios in the Rockefeller Center where he performs 'The Road' on the popular *Late Night With David Letterman* show. Backing Ray is The Paul Shaffer Band (Paul Shaffer keyboards, Will Lee bass, Anton Fig drums, Sid McGinnis guitar). Three days later he's at WXRK-FM Studios (aka K-Rock), a return visit to the nationally syndicated radio phone-in programme *Rockline*, on which he sings brief off-the-cuff extracts from 'The Quiet Life' and 'The Road'.

March

➜ Ray continues to work on a number of projects in New York City. On Tuesday 1st he rather uncharacteristically attends a pre-Grammy Awards party at the Helmsley Palace. The following week on the 8th he again appears on the popular but controversial *Howard Stern Show* at WXRX Studios where he is interviewed by Stern and co-host Robin Quivers. Meanwhile he works diligently with Des McAnuff and Snoo Wilson and by late in the month they have a final working version of *80 Days* ready. Casting for the show begins this spring, with rehearsals set for August.

✰ Back in London, with Ray unavailable, the band convenes at Konk to work up a couple of new songs for the pending US tour that Dave will sing, likely in an effort to allow Ray to rest his voice a little in concert. Dave chooses to revive two favoured old chestnuts, 'Too Much On My Mind' (from 1966) and 'Sleepwalker' (from '77).

➪ **TOUR STARTS** *The Road Tour 88: US Tour* (Mar 26th – Apr 23rd). **Line-up**: Ray Davies (lead vocal, guitar), Dave Davies (guitar, vocal), Bob Henrit (drums), Jim Rodford (bass), Ian Gibbons (keyboards), Pat Crosbie, Annie Cox (dancers). As worked out on last summer's tour, the dancers are included on 'Clichés Of The World', 'Welcome To Sleazy Town' (which often gets a bit of 'A Gallon Of Gas' worked into the beginning), 'Think Visual' and of course the feature piece 'It (I Want It)'. Ray gives off a definite air of finality on this tour, implying or making outright statements to the press and audience alike that this could be the last time. At the Beacon in New York the *Daily News* quotes Ray as saying: "This is the last time you'll see the greatest band in the world," uttered after the first of three encores that night. The astute Lisa Robinson writing in the *New York Post* knows Ray well enough not to take it seriously, and she proves to be correct. Reviews throughout The Road tour are still strong as the band stays in its strong cities, playing comfortable-sized venues and hitting a good balance of material.

Saturday 26th – Sunday 27th

Tower Theatre *Upper Darby, PA* 8:00pm, with Original Sin
Ray is interviewed by Pierre Robert at the soundcheck for tonight's Tower Theatre appearance, where Ray in a humorous reference to his recent illness performs an impromptu segment of the Broadway standard 'Heart', and this is broadcast on local radio WMMR-FM. (Day off in New York follows.)

Tuesday 29th

Beacon Theatre *New York, NY* 8:00pm, with Tonio K

Wednesday 30th

Orpheum Theatre *Boston, MA* 7:30pm, with Tonio K

April

Friday 1st

Springfield Symphony Hall *Springfield, MA* 8:00pm, with Tonio K

Saturday 2nd

Mid-Hudson Civic Center *Poughkeepsie, NY* 8:00pm, with Tonio K
Day off in New York follows.

Monday 4th

Massey Hall *Toronto, ON, Canada* 8:00pm, with Tonio K

Tuesday 5th

Music Hall *Cleveland, OH* 8:00pm, with Tonio K
Travel day follows, then day off in Chicago.

Friday 8th

Riverside Theatre *Milwaukee, WI* 8:00pm, with Tonio K
Tonight's Milwaukee concert is recorded by Westwood One Concert Master One mobile recording unit with engineer Fred Lindgren. Most of the recording will later be broadcast on the syndicated radio programme *Superstar Concert* which airs on August 22nd-23rd. The individual recording of 'You Really Got Me' is later heard as part of the syndicated special titled *Isle Of Dreams Festival 1988* and broadcast September 2nd-5th.

Saturday 9th

Auditorium Theater *Chicago, IL* 8:00pm, with Tonio K

Sunday 10th

Holiday Star Theatre *Merrillville, IN* 8:00pm, with Tonio K
The Westwood One Concert Master One mobile recording unit is present again but any recording from tonight is unused. (Two days off in Chicago follow, and then a travel day and a preparation day for recording.)

Thursday 14th

Fox Theatre *St Louis, MO* 8:00pm, with Tonio K
A further recording is made tonight by the Westwood One Concert Master One mobile recording unit with engineer Bob "Sparky" DeMuthe, and most of the concert is broadcast by satellite US Westwood One syndicated radio on *The Kinks – Live From The Fox Theatre, St. Louis*.
Set-list: 'Do It Again', 'Destroyer', 'Low Budget', 'Apeman', 'Sleepwalker', 'Art Lover', 'Come Dancing', 'Clichés Of The World', 'Lost And Found', 'Welcome To Sleazy Town', 'Think Visual', 'Too Much On My Mind', 'Living On A Thin Line', 'A Well Respected Man', 'It (I Want It)', 'Guilty', 'All Day And All Of The Night', 'The Road', 'You Really Got Me', 'Celluloid Heroes', 'Lola'.

Friday 15th

Memorial Hall *Kansas City, MO* 8:00pm, with Tonio K
Travel day following.

Sunday 17th

Denver Auditorium Theater *Denver, CO* 8:00pm, with Tonio K
Travel day follows.

Tuesday 19th

Berkeley Community Theatre *Berkeley, CA* 8:00pm, with Tonio K

Wednesday 20th

Arlington Theater *Santa Barbara, CA* 8:00pm, with Tonio K
Day off following in Los Angeles.

Friday 22nd

Open Air Theater San Diego State University *San Diego, CA* 8:00pm, with Tonio K

Saturday 23rd

Universal Amphitheater *Universal City, CA* 8:00pm, with Tonio K
End of tour, with the band returning to London and Ray and Dave staying behind for further press functions.

May

Plans for work in Britain due to start during this month are repeatedly delayed. On the 23rd *The Road* album is eventually released there. *Sounds* in its review says: "A fair few atrocities have been committed to vinyl in recent years in the name of Kinkdom and regrettably this is the worst yet. … [It's the] kind of riff-heavy Americana that only serves to besmirch the reputation of this once brilliant band. Buy *Face To Face* instead."

June

⇨ **TOUR STARTS** *The Road: UK / Denmark Tour* (Apr 8th – 19th).
Line-up: Ray Davies (lead vocal, guitar), Dave Davies (guitar, vocal), Bob Henrit (drums), Jim Rodford (bass), Ian Gibbons (keyboards), Pat Crosbie, Annie Cox (dancers).

Wednesday 8th

Apollo Theatre *Manchester* 7:30pm, with Brian Spence & The Storm

Thursday 9th

Town & Country Club *Kentish Town, north-west London*
7:30pm, with Brian Spence & The Storm

From a fan's perspective this two-hour marathon sold-out show at the popular Town & Country venue finds the band in top form: energetic, and eager to please the crowd, but the British music press apparently no longer bothers to cover their concerts. (Day off in London follows.)

Set-list: 'Do It Again', 'Destroyer', 'Low Budget', 'Apeman', 'A Well Respected Man', 'Sleepwalker', 'Clichés Of The World', 'Art Lover', 'Lost And Found', 'Think Visual', 'Too Much On My Mind', 'Living On A Thin Line', 'Welcome To Sleazy Town', 'Sunny Afternoon', 'Dead End Street', 'It (I Want It)', 'Guilty', medley 'Till The End Of The Day' (intro) / 'All Day And All Of The Night' / 'Got Love If You Want It', 'I Gotta Move', 'The Road', 'Celluloid Heroes', 'You Really Got Me', 'Days', 'Lola'.

Saturday 11th

Guildhall *Portsmouth* 7:30pm, with Brian Spence & The Storm

Sunday 12th

Hippodrome *Bristol* 7:30pm, with Brian Spence & The Storm

Monday 13th

Wessex Hall, Poole Arts Centre *Poole, Dorset* 7:30pm, with Brian Spence & The Storm
Day off in London following.

Wednesday 15th

Royal Court Theatre *Liverpool* 7:30pm, with Brian Spence & The Storm

Thursday 16th

Royal Court Centre *Nottingham* 7:30pm, with Brian Spence & The Storm
Travel day follows.

Saturday 18th

Mølleparken *Ålborg, Denmark* 7:30pm, *Open Air '88 Festival*, with Anne Linnet & Band, Dissidenten, Lilholt Band, Anne Dorte, Monrad & Rislund

Sunday 19th

Lisbjerg Fællespark *Århus, Denmark* 8:30pm, *Århus Festival*, with Anne Linnet & Band, Lars Muhl, Kasper Winding, Intellectuals, Axidenz, others

"Despite their 20 years of existence, or perhaps because of it, Ray Davies and The Kinks played a muscular kind of rock that shook the audience," writes *BT*'s reviewer.

➡ Late in the month, Ray travels to New York City where he prepares for *80 Days* rehearsals.

Ray is also spending some time working on three different film treatments (proposals), all at different stages of completion. *Medication Abuse In America* is a comedy about drug misuse in American society; *Man Of Aran* is the story of an ex-hitman attempting to flee his home in southern Ireland; and *Playing The Crowd* is about the music business.

☆ Ray tells an interviewer that The Kinks have "sort of half-made another album. Depending how [*80 Days*] goes, and how the band feels about it, there might be some songs on the next album from the show".

July

From Tuesday 5th Ray is at the La Jolla Playhouse, La Jolla, San Diego, CA, where rehearsals begin for *80 Days* and he oversees music direction.

Ray returns to London, reportedly to begin some recording at Konk Studios of a few new Kinks or related tracks (these are possibly demos) before the more intensive work on his new musical project, *80 Days*, begins.

August

Early in the month, Ray travels from London to San Diego, CA, where he attends the last three weeks of the seven-week rehearsals for *80 Days* at La Jolla Playhouse.

Towards the middle of the month, while rehearsals continue, he begins to talk to the local press to promote the opening of the show. Press preview performances run from Tuesday 23rd to Saturday 27th, with opening night on Sunday 28th. Capacity at the La Jolla Playhouse is 492, with a $28 top ticket.

"There are 40 set changes, 40 costume changes, 24 actors playing 200 parts, and a stage built atop another stage that contains two mechanical treadmills and a raised slip-stage with a revolving platform," describes *The Tribune*. "And it's not cheap: $700,000 for the entire production, making it the most expensive show ever done at the La Jolla Playhouse."

Sandra Kreiswirth in the *Daily Breeze* says that, instead of simply following Jules Verne's novel *Around The World In 80 Days*, the show looks at the creative process and what made Jules Verne tick. "What was he thinking when he sat down to write his novel, and what were the problems along the way? It's also a British look at the foibles and prejudices of the Empire of the day, Britain, and the empire of tomorrow, America."

The Register emphasises that *80 Days* is certainly not a rock musical. "Notwithstanding its musical author's pedigree or a few mildly electric riffs, Davies' pop songs have always ordered from a much broader musical menu than straight rock; here, the main courses are bouncy little two-steps from the Gilbert & Sullivan cookbook and from traditional music hall."

Variety refers to Ray's score in particular. "[He] demonstrates a definite flair for this type of work. He uses an appropriate variety of styles and rhythms to capture moods and locales. And the renowned Kinkian satire helps the general attitude of spoofery in such numbers as the mock anthem 'Members Of The Club' and the biting 'Well Bred Englishman' which sounds like a Gilbert & Sullivan spin-off of The Kinks' hit 'A Well Respected Man'. Davies' penchant for clever hooks makes the title tune catchy enough to be remembered beyond the parking lot."

September

There is no Kinks activity during September.

80 Days plays throughout the month at the LaJolla Playhouse. Reviews in the press have generally been enthusiastic, but a number of the critics have pointed to the necessity of some serious editing and re-writing if the show is to have a chance to make it to Broadway – the immediate goal.

Ray is probably involved now with helping to determine the show's future presentation.

Kink Ray Davies with Gibson Les Paul, Beacon Theater, New York City, March 29th 1988.

kinks'88

80 Days – A New Musical

Act 1
'Let It Be Written' (sung by Verne, Family, Publishers)
[originally called 'It Must Be Written, I've Got A Deadline To Meet']
'The Empire Song' (sung by Preacher, Mrs Fix, Gladstone, Archbishop, Astronomer, Fix, Company)
'Well-Bred Englishman' (sung by Fogg, Club Members)
'Against The Tide' (sung by Fogg, Verne, Company)
'Ladies Of The Night' (sung by Ladies, Fogg, Madam)
'On The Map' (sung by Club Members)
'It Could Have Been Him' (sung by Mrs Fix)
'Mongolia Song' / 'No Surprises' (sung by Verne, Fogg, Fix, Mrs Fix, Cumberland)
'It Could Have Been Him' (reprise) (sung by Queen Victoria)
'Welcome To India' (sung by Governor, Soldiers)
'Just Passing Through' (sung by Fogg, Verne, Company)
'On The Map' (reprise) (sung by Club Members, Queen Victoria)
'Members Of The Club' (sung by Gladstone, Club Members)
'80 Days' (sung by Verne, Fogg, Fix, Aouda, Mrs Fix, Company)

Act 2
'Tell Him Tell Her' (sung by Fogg, Aouda, Verne, Mrs Fix, Company)
'Let It Be Written' (reprise) (sung by Verne, Family, Publishers)
'Who Is This Man' (sung by Aouda)
'Here!' (sung by Bly, Company)
'On The Map' (reprise) (sung by Club Members)
'A Place In Your Heart' (sung by Mudge, Mrs Mudge, Aouda, Fogg, Fix, Mrs Fix)
'Be Rational' (sung by Fogg, Verne)
'80 Days' (reprise) (sung by Aouda, Bly, Mrs Fix, Fogg, Nemo, Verne)
'Finale' (sung by Company)

Director Des McAnuff.
Writer Snoo Wilson.
Music & lyrics Ray Davies.

October / November

The extended run of *80 Days* at La Jolla Playhouse in San Diego ends on October 9th.

The Kinks meet up and begin rehearsals of new material at a small studio in Holloway, north London but the scheduled start of recording at Konk later in the month is delayed until November.

Ray says later that the next album for MCA is strictly a contractually mandated one that the band have to do, in spite of the generally low morale.

Talking about *80 Days* later, Ray says: "I've got to do these things, otherwise I won't be happy playing with the band. … I've always been at my best when I've come off something else and then made a record. This has been tough for me because I *had* to make [*UK Jive*], but I was sick for a while [in 1988] and there was a chance that we'd never tour again anyway. I had a circulatory problem. I had stomach pains and pains in my arms."

The rescheduled recording with The Kinks at Konk is further delayed during November while Ray continues work on new material for The Kinks, plus other projects including the rejigging of *80 Days* and a film, *Breakfast In Berlin* (also known as *Million Pound Semi*).

December

In London, Ray is working on solo projects, including the revisions for *80 Days*. It's announced that runs of the show are being considered for San Francisco, CA, and Portland, OR, with the hope of bringing it to Broadway in New York City in March 1989. The target date for New York is later pushed to summer that year, then spring 1991. Eventually, hope for a Broadway staging will fade.

Sometime this month The Kinks finally return to Konk Studios with engineers Joe Gibb and their old colleague "Irish" from the 1960s, aka Alan O'Duffy, and some initial tracks for the next Kinks LP are recorded. These may include Dave's **'Dear Margaret'** plus two new Ray songs, **'What Are We Doing'** and **'War Is Over'**, with work on the latter at least continuing into the new year.

1989

This year seemed to be a trying one for the band. They had a contractual obligation to complete a new album, but morale was low following all the hard work of 1987 and the let-down of 1988. Relations between Ray and Dave also appeared to be strained at this time, and the pressure of the recording sessions over the first three months of the year saw a kind of replay of the house-cleaning of 1984.

First to go was long-serving keyboardist Ian Gibbons, followed by the departure of manager Larry Page after his second term with the band. A new keyboard player was immediately sought, and Mark Haley got the job. Page almost made it to his fifth anniversary, but the relationship ended with a simple parting of the ways and there were no legal complications.

Work on the new album stretched from its first "completion" at the end of April through to July. It proved troublesome in finding a release, and although The Kinks finally got out on the road in the US in the autumn, the album faltered and did not do well, leaving the band virtually in limbo.

A new manager was hired but he could not salvage a workable relationship with either MCA or London Records. If it hadn't been for the encouraging news that The Kinks had been inducted into the Rock & Roll Hall of Fame in their first year of eligibility, then this troubled year would have ended entirely on a series of disappointing notes.

January / February / March

Early into new-album sessions at Konk, Ray submits what he feels should be the title track, 'The Million Pound Semi-Detached', to London Records – possibly for consideration for release as a single. This idea is rejected, and the LP takes a different shape. *The Million Pound Semi-Detached* is instead saved as the title for a proposed but never realised television film by Ray (alternatively called *Breakfast In Berlin*).

A reworking of the original demo of 'The Million Poud Semi-Detached' will later be issued on the bonus CD *The Songs Of Ray Davies: Waterloo Sunset* that is issued with 1997's *The Kinks Singles Collection* on Essential Records in the UK.

Songs recorded over this three-month period include 'Aggravation', 'How Do I Get Close' (recorded early in the sessions with full live band on the backing track, with only the guitar solo dubbed later), 'Now And Then' (reportedly begun with Ray and Dave on acoustic guitars, with vocal track and band built around it later and the acoustics dropped), 'Down All The Days (Till 1992)', and 'Scattered' (early version).

Probably also done at this time is 'New World' which is pieced together in sections.

Although timing isn't confirmed, Dave with the other Kinks records a new song, 'Perfect Strangers' which he has written for the new album, with Dave as producer and Dave Powell engineering. It will feature in the first proposed running order for the LP, but is later dropped, ending up as a bonus track on CD and cassette versions only (as opposed to vinyl).

Dave later tells the *Providence Sunday Journal* that he and Ray "had quite a few fights" during these sessions. "When there are other people around it's not too bad. But when we're alone .... We're so different, and yet we're forced together, practically living out of each other's pockets."

Late in March, at the end of the main sessions for the new LP, Ian Gibbons gives notice that he is leaving the band due to continuing dissent between Ray and Dave. Generally, Gibbons feels he can no longer comfortably remain uncommitted during these disputes. Reportedly, Dave is particularly unhappy with the progress of the LP. Ray subsequently writes Gibbons a letter asking him to stay, but the keyboard player decides to accept more reliable touring work instead. He is first seen post-Kinks in West Germany, touring with singer Roger Chapman, in May.

April

On Saturday 1st – within days of Gibbons's defection – manager Larry Page announces his resignation, in a dispute with Ray over his commission on the deal that Page has secured with Penguin Books for Ray's autobiography.

Page in fact never signed a contract with The Kinks when he accepted the management position in July 1984, and so just walks away, with little business to care of.

This again leaves The Kinks with no manager – and at a crucial moment, too, just as the band is about to launch a new album.

Ray does further overdubs and mixing at Konk. In the meantime the search begins for a new keyboard player, with a German tour pending. Road manager Ken Jones speaks with keyboard player Mark Haley as he appears with The Monkees at a concert in London on Thursday 20th. On the following Monday, Kinks bassist Jim Rodford attends the final date of The Monkees' European tour at the Rivermead Centre in Reading to see the proposed candidate in action. Following the show, Rodford talks to Haley about The Kinks' opening, and Haley agrees to audition.

On the 27th, Ray oversees mastering with Robert Ludwig of an early version of the new LP for MCA, but this is ultimately rejected for release and Ray returns to London to re-work the album.

May

An audition is held either at Konk Studios or at a rehearsal studio in Ripley, Surrey.

Prospective new keyboard player Mark Haley has quickly learned some of the songs from *The Road* LP, and after successfully playing through these, along with some jamming on rock'n'roll classics, he is hired for the band.

'Loony Balloon', an older song written in 1987, is probably recorded now, the one new track added since it was decided to rework the LP. 'Scattered' is dropped because Ray is dissatisfied with the lyric. It will get a revised lyric in 1990, though isn't released until late 1993 when it becomes a last-minute addition to the *Phobia* CD.

Rehearsals are held with new keyboard player Haley while Ray is busy re-working the new LP, but the June tour of West Germany is cancelled late this month.

June

In London, PRT (current owner of the old Pye material) is sold for £3million to Castle Communications Ltd, an established British record label specialising in reissues. Castle wastes no time and quickly assembles a Kinks hits package in time for the 25th anniversary of 'You Really Got Me' topping the charts in September.

Rehearsals continue at Konk with Mark Haley. Footage of the band in action is shot for use in Ray's proposed film *Breakfast In Berlin*. On Tuesday 6th, Haley is invited to do one piece of recording for the new LP, dubbing the fanfare keyboard part on to **'Down All The Days'**. This is probably one of the final recordings; Ray has final mixing and track selection completed by the last weekend of the month.

Over the weekend of the 24th/25th, at a meeting between Ray and Dave in a London hotel, the two come to blows in a disagreement over the final track selection for the new LP.

Dave later says in his book *Kink* that the argument is about Ray not including Dave's songs 'Perfect Strangers' and 'Bright Lights' on the final track selection.

Larry Page later confirms the incident, saying that Dave is so upset that he quits on the spot and phones Page for guidance – even though Page is no longer representing the band. Page's advice is to do nothing until the situation settles down. When this eventually happens a compromise is worked out where Dave's two songs are included on the CD and cassette versions as bonus tracks but not on the vinyl LP, still the main format at the time.

Ray is in New York City on the 27th overseeing the mastering of the single 'How Do I Get Close' with Robert Ludwig at Masterdisk Studios, and subsequently delivers the results to MCA.

July

WNEW-FM in New York City obtains an advance cassette copy of the first single from the new album, 'How Do I Get Close', which DJs Scott Muni and Dennis Elsis play as a world exclusive over the weekend of July 4th. However, further broadcast is halted by MCA, who say the song is not yet cleared for airplay.

On the 11th Ray does final mixes for the new 10-title LP and 12-title CD. Three days later he's at Masterdisk in NYC to re-master the 'How Do I Get Close'/ 'Entertainment' single. Back at Konk, Ray continues with minor final mixing, editing and assembly of the new LP and CD. He oversees mastering of the new album: on the 25th at PRT Studios in central London for London Records, and a day later at Masterdisk in NYC for MCA. Ray then starts promotional work for the new records in New York.

August

On the 1st Konk issues a press release signalling that The Kinks are still among the living, announcing a London date for the 15th, a US tour for September, the arrival of new keyboard player Mark Haley, a UK single for this month, and a new album in September. Two days later Ray is again at Masterdisk in New York City to master a new B-side 'War Is Over' to replace 'Entertainment' for the planned US single 'How Do I Get Close'.

Ray continues his re-emergence to public view with more press work. In one of the interviews, with Charles Shaar Murray for *Q* magazine, he says his current side projects include the rewrite of *80 Days*, a film called *Breakfast In Berlin*, and a documentary about jazz bassist/composer Charles Mingus tentatively titled *Goodbye Pork Pie Hat* for which he is currently in negotiations with Mingus's widow Sue. Ray is also said to be writing a play about 'You Really Got Me' for the BBC, and a reference is made about him preparing to write his memoirs, a project that has been in the works since he became ill in January 1988 but that will not see fruition for another five years.

Murray writes in *Q* that the *Breakfast In Berlin* project is a semi-autobiographical sequel to Ray's TV film, *Return To Waterloo*, based on events leading up to the recent death of his mother and featuring some of the songs from the new album. The film, also known as *Million Pound Semi*, is described in an early publicity flyer as seeking "to put Ray's current activities with The Kinks into historical perspective. Ray Davies has been developing the ideas for the last 18 months. It will reflect on his childhood and youth, probe into some of his past and present fears and touch on some of his roles and responsibilities. The film will include all the music from [forthcoming album] *UK Jive* plus three songs specially written for the film, live concert performance, rehearsals and studio footage".

At band rehearsals at Konk in London, Robin James is hired as a dancer. New material being worked on from the album includes 'How Do I Get Close', 'Aggravation', 'UK Jive', 'Down All The Days', 'Now And Then', 'War Is Over', 'Dear Margaret' and 'Loony Balloon'.

Tuesday 15th

Town & Country Club *Kentish Town, north-west London*
7:30pm, with River City People
Singer Kirsty MacColl, who has a remake of 'Days' in the British Top 20, is brought on stage to perform with the band. The concert is filmed for possible use by Ray for his *Breakfast In Berlin* project.

Meanwhile, delays are made to the forthcoming US tour and to album release dates. Late in the month Dave returns to London from LA, where he has been doing press work, to film the video for 'Down All

The Days', but in the end doesn't appear in it. It's filmed at Ray's old house on Fortis Green in East Finchley, north London. It has stayed in the family, the last residents being his sister Gwen and her husband Brian and, prior to her death, Ray and Dave's mother.

In the video, Ray again revives the pencil-moustached spiv character from 'Come Dancing', but it also includes a young Ray revisiting early family parties from his youth while observing the carryings-on of the household's post-War adults. It opens with Ray in the present day, absorbing the brilliant summer sunshine of a beautiful afternoon, recalling no doubt the look and feel of the place back when he was inspired to write 'Sunny Afternoon'.

September

Monday 4th

The Ultimate Collection double-LP released in the UK. This compilation from the new owners of the Pye material, Castle, is a classic bit of record company "spoiling", diverting public attention from The Kinks' new product and making the band compete against their own back-catalogue. There is heavy promotion for the collection that in effect forces the band to postpone release of their new LP to distance themselves from this competition. The release of the UK single, 'Down All The Days', is delayed to the 25th, and the album to October 2nd.

➪ **TOUR STARTS** *UK Jive: US Tour* (Sep 9th – Oct 16th). **Line-up:** Ray Davies (lead vocal, guitar), Dave Davies (guitar, vocal), Bob Henrit (drums), Jim Rodford (bass), Mark Haley (keyboards), Pat Crosbie, Robin James (dancers). The band travels from London on the Thursday 7th, and on Friday hold a rehearsal at the Mann Music Center.

Saturday 9th
Mann Music Center *Philadelphia, PA* 8:00pm, with John Eddie

Sunday 10th
Laker Hall, State University of New York College at Oswego *Oswego, NY* 8:00pm, with John Eddie

Monday 11th – Wednesday 13th
Ray is ill in Syracuse and the Poughkeepsie concert scheduled for the 12th is postponed to October 8th. (Two days off in New York City follow.)
☆ It's possibly around this time that a meeting is arranged with an American managerial candidate, Eugene Harvey, whose principal client is Whitney Houston. Harvey is now the main contender for the manager's job along with ex-Tommy James & The Shondells keyboardist/singer Kenny Laguna.

Thursday 14th
Garden State Arts Center *Holmdel, NJ* 8:00pm, with John Eddie

Friday 15th
Jones Beach Theatre *Wantagh, NY* 8:00pm, with John Eddie

Saturday 16th
Merriweather Post Pavilion *Columbia, MD* 8:00pm, with John Eddie

Sunday 17th
Great Woods Center For The Performing Arts *Mansfield, MA* 7:30pm, with John Eddie
Day off in Boston following, and then a travel day.

Wednesday 20th
West Gymnasium, State University Of New York at Binghamton *Binghamton, NY* 8:00pm, with John Eddie
Tonight's concert at the State University of New York is interrupted midway through the proceedings due to an electrical fire in the gymnasium where the performance is taking place. (A travel day for the band follows, and MCA Records issues 'How Do I Get Close' on a promo CD single.)

Friday 22nd
Pine Knob Music Theatre *Clarkston, MI* 8:00pm, with John Eddie
"One of the worst-attended [shows] in [the Center's] 17-year history," says the *Detroit Free Press*, "with another poor turnout for a terrific show. Just 2,100 fans turned out … despite a half-price ticket promotion."

Saturday 23rd
Poplar Creek Music Theatre *Hoffman Estates, IL* 8:00pm, with John Eddie

Sunday 24th
Music Hall *Cleveland, OH* 8:00pm, with John Eddie
Travel day follows.

Down All The Days (Till 1992) single

A 'Down All The Days (Till 1992)' (R. DAVIES).
B1 'You Really Got Me' live (R. DAVIES).
B2 'Entertainment' (R. DAVIES).

UK release September 25th 1989 (7-inch A/B1 London LON 239; 12-inch A/B1/B2 LONX 239; CD-single A/B1/B2 LONCD 239).
Recorded Konk Studios (No.2) *Hornsey, north London*; A: January-April 1989, May-June 1989; 32-(or 48-)track mixed to stereo. B1: Mann Music Center *Philadelphia, PA*; July 1st 1987; 24-track mixed to stereo. B2: Konk Studios *Hornsey, north London*; May-June 1981; 24-track mixed to stereo.
Producer Ray Davies; assistant producer Alan O'Duffy.
Engineers Joe Gibb/Alan O'Duffy (A) & Ben Fenner original recording (B2); Johnie Rosen and assistants Mervin & Billy (Fanta Sound), Dave Powell and assistant George (Boy) Holt (Konk) (B1).
Chart high UK none.

Monday 25th
'**Down All The Days (Till 1992)**' / '**You Really Got Me**' single (various formats) released in the UK.

Tuesday 26th
Syria Mosque Auditorium *Pittsburgh, PA* 8:00pm, with John Eddie

Wednesday 27th
The Boathouse *Norfolk, VA* 8:00pm, with John Eddie
Travel day follows.

Friday 29th
Chastain Park Amphitheatre *Atlanta, GA* 8:00pm, with John Eddie

Saturday 30th
Ocean Center *Daytona Beach, FL* 8:00pm, with John Eddie

October

Sunday 1st
Sunrise Musical Theatre *Fort Lauderdale, FL* 8:00pm, with John Eddie

Monday 2nd
UK Jive album released in the UK. Never at a loss for an inspired slagging-off, the *NME* does not miss the opportunity here. "You want to love it for what The Kinks once were," writes Ian McCann, "except that's not what they are now. Dry, irritable nostalgia went out when Ian Dury's career evaporated; this is a high-gloss, all tacky island full of rampant Australians living in an eternal high octane leaded present. The door is still open to The Kinks in America; heritage sells there –

UK Jive album

1/A1 **'Aggravation'** (R. DAVIES).
2/A2 **'How Do I Get Close'** (R. DAVIES).
3/A3 **'UK Jive'** (R. DAVIES).
4/A4 **'Now And Then'** (R. DAVIES).
5/A5 **'What Are We Doing'** (R. DAVIES).
6/B1 **'Entertainment'** (R. DAVIES).
7/B2 **'War Is Over'** (R. DAVIES).
8/B3 **'Down All The Days (Till 1992)'** (R. DAVIES).
9/B4 **'Loony Balloon'** (R. DAVIES).
10/B5 **'Dear Margaret'** (D. DAVIES).
11 (CD bonus) **'Bright Lights'** (D. DAVIES).
12 (CD bonus) **'Perfect Strangers'** (D. DAVIES).
1, 3 and 9 are extended versions on CD

UK release October 2nd 1989 (London 828.165-1/LON 54). US release October 31st 1989 (MCA Records MCA-6337). Musicians Ray Davies lead vocal except as noted, guitar, keyboards. Dave Davies lead vocal (10, 11, 12), lead guitar, backing vocal. Jim Rodford bass guitar, backing vocal. Bob Henrit drums. Mick Avory original drum track (6). Ian Gibbons keyboards except as noted. Mark Haley keyboard (8).
Recorded Konk Studios (No.1 & 2) *Hornsey, north London*; 1-4, 8, 9, 12: January-April 1989, possible further recording May-June 1989; 5, 10: December 1988; 6: May-July 1981, overdubs probably January-March 1989; 7: December 1988-April 1989; 11: probably October 1987; 32-track and/or two 24-track (46 tracks) mixed to stereo.
Producer Ray Davies except as noted; Dave Davies (11, 12); assistant producer Alan O'Duffy (except 5, 6, 10).
Engineer Joe Gibb/Alan O'Duffy except as noted; Jeremy Allom (11); Dave Powell (12); Ben Fenner (6 original backing track).
Chart high US number 122; UK none.

---

just look at The Stones and The Who." Otherwise the British press is inattentive, and the LP barely warrants mention.

Tuesday 3rd – Wednesday 4th
In Miami, FL, film is shot on the beach and at an old hotel for the 'How Do I Get Close' video. Ray's guitar technician Larry Rowell fills in for Rodford on bass, who flies home following a death in the family.
☆ The release in the US of the *UK Jive* album, scheduled for today, is inexplicably pushed back each week this month, to the 10th, 17th, 24th, and 31st.

Thursday 5th
Florida Theatre *Jacksonville, FL* 8:00pm, with The Motion
Travel day follows.

Saturday 7th
Syria Mosque Auditorium *Richmond, VA* 8:00pm, with John Eddie

Sunday 8th
Mid-Hudson Civic Center *Poughkeepsie, NY* 8:00pm, with John Eddie
Day off in New York City follows.

Tuesday 10th
F. M. Kirby Center *Wilkes-Barre, PA* 8:00pm, with John Eddie
Day off in New York City following, when the surprise addition of the show at the Beacon Theatre in NYC on the 16th is announced.

Thursday 12th
Livingston College Gymnasium, Rutgers University *Piscataway, NJ* 8:00pm, with John Eddie
Potential new manager Kenny Laguna meets the whole band tonight.

Friday 13th
Rose Hill Gymnasium, McGinley Center, Fordham University *Bronx, NY* 8:00pm, with John Eddie
Tonight's show is for Fordham students only. (Two days off in New York City follow, after failing to secure a venue for the 14th and settling for the Beacon on Monday.)

Monday 16th
Beacon Theatre *New York, NY* 8:00pm, with The Peregrins
"The Kinks aren't playing at stadiums like their contemporaries, The Who and The Rolling Stones – just middle-sized theaters like the Beacon," writes Jon Parales in the *New York Times*. "And their shows aren't elaborate spectacles, but amiable, scrappy, slightly disheveled concerts that reaffirm the band's perseverance and moxie. Twenty-five years after The Kinks had their first hit single 'You Really Got Me' The Kinks still take rock'n'roll seriously enough to knock it around. Ray … seemed to intersperse the planned set with Kinks oldies chosen on the spot, dipping into the band's 1960s catalog for fondly remembered songs … . With his lop-sided grin, his deceptively diffident-sounding (but unmistakable) voice, and his cheerfully unassuming attitude on stage, Mr Davies shows that modesty – backed by a no-nonsense rhythm section – can carry a band through the decades." (Band members return to London, with the exception of Ray and Dave who remain in New York City on business.)
Set-list: 'Around The Dial', 'The Hard Way', 'Low Budget', 'Apeman', 'The Village Green Preservation Society', 'A Well Respected Man', 'How Do I Get Close', 'UK Jive', 'Stop Your Sobbing' (extract), 'Come Dancing', 'It (I Want It)', 'Guilty', 'Living On A Thin Line', 'Waterloo Sunset', medley 'A Gallon Of Gas' / 'Welcome To Sleazy Town', 'Lola', 'All Day And All Of The Night', 'Aggravation', 'David Watts', 'Days', 'You Really Got Me', 'Twist And Shout'.

➜ INDICATES EVENT AROUND THIS TIME BUT WITH NO FIRM DATE

Tuesday 17th – Wednesday 18th

Ray is editing the 'How Do I Get Close' video in a rush to get it on the air to coincide with the release of the single. MCA sends promo CD copies of 'How Do I Get Close' to radio stations for advance airplay.

Thursday 19th – Sunday 22nd

Over these four days, Kenny Laguna is at the Hit Factory in New York City producing the next LP by his prime charge, Joan Jett. The record consists of Jett's interpretation of some of her favourite songs. Ray is present for at least one session, during which he plays acoustic guitar on her recording of his song 'Celluloid Heroes'. The album will be released in the US as *Hit List* on January 16th 1990.

Tuesday 24th

Ray hears the news that The Kinks have been inducted into the Rock & Roll Hall Of Fame in their first year of eligibility (25 years since their first issued recording).

Monday 30th

In New York, Kenny Laguna signs as The Kinks' new US business manager.

UK Jive album released in the US. *Metropolis*: "Ray Davies is the auteur of hackneyed rock riffs, directing cinematic foils for his political irony. *UK Jive* rocks harder because brother Dave's metal tendencies aren't kept in check, but Ray still manages a few aces, especially 'Loony Balloon'."

Billboard: "Soon-to-be Rock and Roll Hall of Famers, The Kinksters let loose with a spotty effort that showcases their brilliance and mediocrity at the same time. Worthy tracks such as 'How Do I Get Close' and the musically jaunty 'War Is Over' are juxtaposed against such cheerleading anthemic fillers as 'UK Jive' and 'Down All The Days (To 1992)'. The good far outweighs the bad, however, for even at their worst, the Brothers Davies are much better than most."

Tuesday 31st

MCA issues the promotional video for 'How Do I Get Close' for industry previewing. It appears that MTV soon objects to some of the more suggestive or revealing shots of women and a further edit will be required before it will broadcast the video. Consequently the scheduled November 14th release date for the single is delayed to the 28th.

November

Dave and the band members have time off this month in London while Ray busies himself in New York City, working on his Charles Mingus project. He also evidently does a few edits to the promotional video for 'How Do I Get Close'.

Dave makes an unusual guest appearance on stage playing guitar as part of a Jerry Lee Lewis All-Star concert at the Hammersmith Odeon, west London on the 21st. (The concert is filmed and subsequently issued on videocassette by MCA in February 1991.)

On the 27th the 'How Do I Get Close' video finally debuts on MTV and VH-1. The following day the single, **'How Do I Get Close' / 'War**

Is Over', is released in US. *Billboard* says: "Highlight from the venerable band's current *UK Jive* album is a crunchy chorded rocker that could mark a welcome return to the Top 40."

December

Wednesday 13th

Ray is at NBC Television Studios, Rockefeller Center, New York City to tape an appearance on the popular talk and variety show *Late Night With David Letterman*. Dave is scheduled to fly in and appear too but cancels, and Ray performs alone backed by the house musicians, Paul Shaffer & The World's Most Dangerous Band. 'How Do I Get Close' is performed live during the show's 5:00-6:00pm taping session and broadcast 11:30-12:30pm EST the same night. Later, Ray catches a flight to Munich, Germany to start the Kinks tour, with the band arriving on the 14th.

➡ **TOUR STARTS** *UK Jive 89: German Tour* (Dec 15th – 22nd). **Line-up**: Ray Davies (lead vocal, guitar), Dave Davies (guitar, vocal), Bob Henrit (drums), Jim Rodford (bass), Mark Haley (keyboards), Pat Crosbie, Robin James (dancers).

Friday 15th

Deutsches Museum *Munich, West Germany* 8:00pm, with The Case
Travel day following.

Sunday 17th

Biskuithalle *Bonn, West Germany* 8:00pm, with The Case

Monday 18th

Jovel Music Hall *Münster, West Germany* 8:00pm, with The Case
"The legendary 1960s/70s group let their fans wait for some time," says the *Westfälische Nachrichten*, "but they stormed the stage and set hearts beating fast with songs like 'Apeman'. There's no question about it: The Kinks don't rely on their famous name to make easy money – they were really good!" (Travel day following.)

Wednesday 20th

Stadthalle *Offenbach, West Germany* 8:00pm, with The Case

Thursday 21st

Stadthalle *Neumarkt, West Germany* 8:00pm, with The Case

Friday 22nd

Musikhalle *Hamburg, West Germany* 8:00pm, with The Case
Travel day following as the tour ends tonight. While the band members return to London for the coming holiday break, Ray stays behind in Hamburg for a short while for additional press work. He says later: "There was a time at the end of 1989 and the beginning of 1990 when I thought there might not [be a Kinks any more]. That … was a really difficult time. Actually we didn't begin to record the [next] album proper until the beginning of 1991."

1990

Another transitional year, and this one began with what might be considered a pinnacle in many a band's career: induction into the record industry's Rock And Roll Hall Of Fame. But while their past and their legacy was being heralded, The Kinks were in crisis. Relations with their record label had deteriorated to the point where late in the year the connection was ended prematurely. Turmoil continued behind the scenes as the new manager, hired to replace the departing Larry Page, himself left after less than a year of working with The Kinks, and again the band was in search of new management.

There was almost no recording activity this year as the band rode out their MCA contract. Ray predominantly occupied himself with a Charles Mingus documentary, for which principal filming was completed, and did some re-working of the Preservation albums, slated for reissue next year.

January

Ray arrives in New York a few days ahead of the band's induction into the Rock And Roll Hall Of Fame for some independent media appearances that include TV and press interviews. On Tuesday 16th Dave, original drummer Mick Avory, and current bassist Jim Rodford fly in from London, and original bassist Pete Quaife flies in from Toronto. The four meet up at the Waldorf Astoria hotel to attend a music industry party at the Hard Rock Café thrown by legendary producer Don Kirschner. (Also on the 16th, Joan Jett's album *The Hit List* is released, to which Ray contributes guitar on Jett's recording of his song 'Celluloid Heroes'.)

The following day is the **Rock And Roll Hall Of Fame 1990 Fifth Annual Induction Dinner**, starting at 7:00pm and continuing to 1:20am, held at the Grand Ballroom of the Waldorf-Astoria Hotel in New York City. Pre-event duties for The Kinks include a rehearsal at 3:00pm followed by a press conference three hours later where inductees are available for interviews and photographs. The dinner and ceremony begin at 7:00pm, and in addition to The Kinks, fellow British invaders The Who are also inducted, along with The Four Seasons, The Four Tops and Simon & Garfunkel among others. All inductions begin with a short film reviewing the artist's career, highlighted by early TV footage and talkovers, leading up to a formal introduction by Atlantic founder Ahmet Ertegun.

The four original Kinks – Ray Davies, Dave Davies, Mick Avory, and Pete Quaife – are introduced by ex-Hollie and early Kinks supporter Graham Nash. He recalls the two bands on a package tour in the spring of 1964, before The Kinks hit the charts with 'You Really Got Me'. All four Kinks are then allotted a brief moment to make a short statement or speech following the presentation of statuettes. After The Kinks' induction comes that of The Who.

A very loosely structured post-awards jam session follows, with individual artists and band members backed by musical director Paul Shaffer with The World's Most Dangerous Band. The four original Kinks briefly appear with singers Sting and Rickie Lee Jones for a medley of 'You Really Got Me' / 'Mack The Knife' / 'Set Me Free'. Immediately afterwards is The Who's segment, with Dave and Quaife (on guitar) assisting in backing them on 'Substitute', 'Pinball Wizard'

and 'Won't Get Fooled Again'. Further free-for-all jamming ensues, with Dave and Quaife backing Bruce Springsteen and John Fogerty for a version of 'Long Tall Sally' and then Simon & Garkunkel on 'The Boxer', after which Dave and Quaife leave the stage. Ray and Dave head their separate ways following the dinner, while Avory, Quaife and Rodford convene for drinks in Quaife's room and some stories of the old days. Quaife and Rodford fly home the following day, Avory a few days later.

Meanwhile, back in London, the 'How Do I Get Close' single is delayed for UK release until February 19th. On the 23rd the *Muswell Hillbillies*, *Soap Opera* and *Schoolboys In Disgrace* albums are reissued by Rhino Records. A promotional CD single for a proposed new release of 'Entertainment' is issued in the US by MCA, but commercial release of the song is stalled and then cancelled, for unknown reasons.

February

In New York City, Ray is developing ideas for proposed shows there in May, while in London Dave possibly does some recording.

Ray makes an award presentation in London on the 19th to U2 for Best International Group at the British Phonograph Record Institute Awards ceremony, broadcast by BBC Radio-1. The day also sees UK

How Do I Get Close single

A '**How Do I Get Close**' (R. DAVIES).
B '**Down All The Days (Till 1992)**' (R. DAVIES).

UK release Feb 19th 1990 (London LON 250; 12-inch LONX 250). Musicians and recording details as *UK Jive* album (see October 2nd 1989).
Chart high UK none.

➜ INDICATES EVENT AROUND THIS TIME BUT WITH NO FIRM DATE

release for the new Kinks single, **'How Do I Get Close' / 'Down All The Days (Till 1992)'**, and Ray devotes time to intense press duties over the coming weeks to help promote it.

Around this time Ray seemingly abandons hope of developing his video/film production of *Million Pound Semi*, aka *Breakfast In Berlin*, which is being described by now as "delayed indefinitely".

March

Between about the 12th and the 23rd the band rehearses at Konk Studios in north London for *The Kinks On Broadway*. This is intended as an eight-day residency in a theatre on Broadway in New York City, in the style of a recently successful similarly-styled show there. It's viewed by Kinks management as a good opportunity for the band to take advantage of the recent avalanche of publicity associated with their Hall Of Fame induction. The show is initially pencilled-in for mid May, on the tail end of a quick tour of East Coast US colleges being set up as promotion for the next MCA single. The 45's original release date of March 28th is pushed to April and then May.

Songs worked on at the rehearsal include 'Victoria', 'The Hard Way', 'I'm Not Like Everybody Else', 'Come Dancing', 'Till The End Of The Day' and 'Top Of The Pops'. All of these will later appear on an interesting tape circulated privately and derived from a partial run-through of the show. It's often called the *Club Vegas Tape* thanks to an off-the-cuff reference by Ray about the potential lounge-like atmosphere of the show. Other songs rehearsed include 'Australia' and 'Animal Farm'.

Ray is back in New York City during the last week of the month, partially in preparation for initial filming of recording sessions for his Charles Mingus documentary project, but also for a brief interview videotaped at United Video-Studio 55 for MTV's promotion of the upcoming Kinks tour. The interview will be aired on MTV on April 7th.

April

Monday 2nd

The Kinks receive their second gong of the year, this time an Ivor Novello Award for Outstanding Service To British Music. The ceremony is held at the Grosvenor House Hotel in central London. Key members past and present receive awards, including the full current line-up. Former bassist Pete Quaife receives his award by mail.

Tuesday 3rd

→ Around this time Ray and a film crew are present at the Mastersound Astoria in Queens, New York City to shoot an initial recording session for record producer Hal Willner's multi-artist tribute to jazz bassist and composer Charles Mingus.

The recording of the CD and Ray's documentary film of the recording sessions are two separate projects, but they must be co-ordinated around the participants' busy schedules. (Mastersound is in the renovated complex where the legendary Marx Brothers films were made in the 1930s, a fact probably not lost on the film-history-conscious Ray.)

Probably done at this time are Elvis Costello's contribution, 'Weird Nightmare' – which ultimately becomes the title song for both the CD release and the accompanying documentary – as well as recordings of 'Meditation', 'Work Song' and 'Freedom', the latter including one of Ray's more unusual recording credits – for "humming".

Filming also includes interview footage with Costello and Willner at the Court Square Diner in Queens, as well as location filming around the local area and in Times Square, Manhattan. Willner's CD will finally be released in September 1992, while Ray's documentary only airs on British TV in June 1993 and is commercially issued in Japan in October of the same year. Ray is mentioned in the *New York Daily News* on the 15th concerning his involvement with Ray Gaspard, the black owner of a commercial theatre with whom he is developing a musical.

Monday 16th

'Down All The Days' promotional CD is released to US radio stations.

➪ **TOUR STARTS** *Down All The Days: Northeast US College Tour* (Apr 19th – May 13th). **Line-up**: Ray Davies (lead vocal, guitar), Dave Davies (guitar, vocal), Bob Henrit (drums), Jim Rodford (bass), Mark Haley (keyboards), Pat Crosbie, Robin James (dancers). The band travels to New York City on the 17th.

Thursday 19th

McLane Center Gymnasium, Alfred University *Alfred, NY*
8:00pm, with Janata

Friday 20th

McDonough Arena, Georgetown University *Washington, DC* 8:00pm, with Janata

Saturday 21st

Delaware Fieldhouse, University of Delaware *Newark, DE*
8:00pm, with Janata
Concert for students only.

Sunday 22nd

Kline Center, Dickinson College *Carlisle, PA* 8:00pm, with Janata

Monday 23rd

Will Orr Auditorium, Westminster College *New Wilmington, PA* 8:00pm, with Janata
Day off in Pittsburgh following.

Wednesday 25th

Fisher Auditorium, Indiana University of Pennsylvania *Indiana, PA* 8:00pm, with Janata
"In the tradition of *Give The People What They Want*, The Kinks delivered the rock'n'roll goods to a near capacity audience," writes Tim Thompson in *The Penn*. "After 25 years, the Kinks are obviously experienced in working up an audience, and this was evident in their performance. Perhaps the only complaint that anyone could have given about [their] performance was that it lasted only about 90 minutes. From the satisfied look of the crowd, however, no one appeared to be disappointed."

Thursday 26th

Dillon Gymnasium, Princeton University *Princeton, NJ*
10:00pm, with Janata
Concert for students only, closed to the public. (Day off in Rochester follows.)

Saturday 28th

Louis A. Alexander Palestra, University Of Rochester *Rochester, NY* 8:00pm, with Janata

Sunday 29th

Alumni Ice Arena, State University Of New York College at Cortland *Cortland, NY* 8:00pm, with Janata

Monday 30th

Physical Fitness Center, Hofstra University *Hempstead, NY*
8:00pm, with Janata
Concert free for students only, closed to the public. (Day off in New York City follows.)
☆ MCA release 'Down All The Days' as a promotional cassette single in the US.

May

Wednesday 2nd

David Mead Field House, Allegheny College *Meadville, PA*
8:00pm, with Janata
Attendance at this performance in Meadville is around 800-900. (Travel day following.)

Friday 4th

Palace Theatre *Albany, NY* 8:00pm, with Janata; sponsored by Rensselaer Polytechnic Institute, Troy, NY

Saturday 5th

Paolino Recreation Center, Roger Williams College *Bristol, RI* 8:00pm, with Janata
This concert was staged for students only and is attended by around 700 fans.

Sunday 6th

Morrell Gymnasium, Bowdoin College *Brunswick, ME*
8:00pm, with The 39 Steps
Two days off in Portland follow.

Tuesday 8th

'**Down All The Days**' cassette single released in the US. Strangely, this is issued only on cassette. Vinyl 45s are on their way out now, but

---

Down All The Days (Till 1992) cassette single

A '**Down All The Days (Till 1992)**' (R. DAVIES).
B blank

US release (cassette only) May 6th 1990 (MCA MCAC-53840). Musicians and recording details as *UK Jive* album (see October 2nd 1989).
Chart high US none.

---

it's not released on CD, which is becoming the industry standard for singles.

Wednesday 9th

UMB Baseball Field, University Of Massachusetts at Boston/Harbor Campus *Dorchester, MA* 4:00pm, with The 39 Steps
Concert free for students only, attended by about 1,000. (Day off in Boston follows.)
Set-list: 'Around The Dial', 'The Hard Way', 'UK Jive', 'I'm Not Like

Everybody Else', 'Too Much On My Mind', medley 'State Of Confusion' / '(Wish I Could Fly Like) Superman' / 'Destroyer', 'Days', 'It (I Want It)', 'Come Dancing', 'Living On A Thin Line', medley 'A Gallon Of Gas' / 'Welcome To Sleazy Town', 'Down All The Days', 'Low Budget', 'Loony Balloon', 'Till The End Of The Day', 'Lola', 'All Day And All Of The Night', 'Now And Then', 'You Really Got Me'.

Friday 11th

Leede Arena, Berry Center, Dartmouth College *Hanover, NH* 8:00pm, with The 39 Steps

Saturday 12th

Ives Center For The Performing Arts, Western Connecticut State University *Danbury, CT* 8:00pm, with The 39 Steps
An outdoor event that finds the band housed inside a gazebo. The sound is apparently so appalling that the performance is cut after 14 songs.

Sunday 13th

UNH Fieldhouse/Lundholm Gymnasium, University Of New Hampshire *Durham, NH* 8:00pm, with The 39 Steps
The band travels to New York City following the show and the next day returns to London, while Ray, Dave and road manager Ken Jones remain in NYC. If the tour continued as originally planned, rehearsals would begin today at a venue in New Jersey for three days, with *The Kinks On Broadway* starting an eight-show run in New York City from the 17th. But these dates, initially pushed to September, do not happen.
☆ It seems that at this time the future of the management contract with Kenny Laguna is being seriously considered as the band has apparently become unhappy with the relationship.

June / July

Early in June, Ray heads out to Los Angeles where he meets writers on the Jules Verne musical *80 Days*. It is being rewritten for consideration for Broadway presentation, and is tentatively scheduled for a workshop in New York in the autumn. Ray probably goes back to New York City for a stretch, possibly working on the *Weird Nightmare* Charles Mingus film, for which filming began in April. Later in the month he is back in London in time for the *Midtfyns Festival-Ringe '90* in Ringe, Denmark on Thursday June 28th, the first of a four-day festival. The band travels back to London the following day.

It is almost certainly at this time that Ray and a local film crew shoot a one-off recording session in London for Hal Willner's Charles Mingus CD project. Taking part are Rolling Stones Keith Richards and Charlie Watts during a break from the English leg of their *Urban Jungle* European Tour. They're joined by musicians from the tour, including keyboardist Chuck Leavell, tenor saxophonist Bobby Keyes and the Uptown Horns – Crispin Cioe, Bob Frank, Arno Hecht and Hollywood Paul – and record the song 'Oh Lord, Don't Let Them Drop That Atomic Bomb On Me'.

In July, Ray returns to New York City to continue work on the Mingus project. He begins moves to extract The Kinks from their management deal with Kenny Laguna, to make one last album in their commitment to MCA, and to shop for a new record deal. Ray says later of MCA: "They changed their personnel continually, so I had no consistent [person] I could work with. I could not really strike a relationship there."

Kinks new and old at an Ivor Novello bash in London, April 2nd 1990: (L-R) Dave Davies, Ray Davies, Jim Rodford, Mick Avory, Bob Henrit.

kinks'90

August

➔ Early this month Ray makes a short trip from New York to Los Angeles where he is meeting with a potential new manager as well as scouting around for a new record label. Relations with manager Kenny Laguna have been severed by this point. Reportedly among potential replacements is Shep Gordon, one-time manager of Alice Cooper and Debbie Harry among others. Ray then returns to London for some press duties and a rehearsal at Konk Studios for upcoming shows.

Sunday 12th

Alexandra Palace *Wood Green, north London* 3:30-11:00pm, with Squeeze, Voice Of The Beehive, The 4 Of Us, 29 Palms
The final day of the Town & Country Club's three-day Fifth Birthday Celebration Party, with a sell-out crowd of 5,000. Portions are filmed for possible transmission via satellite television, but not of The Kinks' performance.
Set-list: 'Around The Dial', 'The Hard Way', 'Apeman', 'Muswell Hillbilly', 'UK Jive', 'I'm Not Like Everybody Else', 'Come Dancing', 'Dead End Street', medley 'State Of Confusion' / 'Destroyer', 'It (I Want It)', 'Low Budget', 'Living On A Thin Line', 'Where Have All The Good Times Gone', 'Tired Of Waiting For You', 'Welcome To Sleazy Town', 'Dedicated Follower Of Fashion', 'A Well Respected Man', 'Sunny Afternoon', 'Catch Me Now I'm Falling', 'I'm Not Like Everybody Else', 'Days', 'Lola', 'All Day And All Of The Night', 'Aggravation', 'Now And Then', 'You Really Got Me'.

Wednesday 15th

Outdoor event *Leuven, Belgium* 2:30pm-12midnight, *Marktrock*, with Noordkapp, The Paranoiacs, Candy Dulfer, Dan Reed Network, Nils Lofgren
The final day of a four-day open-air festival held in the centre of the city. Admission is free and attendance for the band's performance is about 15,000. "It was packed to capacity and pouring down with rain," says Ray. "We got drenched and the crowd got drenched, but they wouldn't go home. For an encore we went out and did 'Twist And Shout' which we haven't done for years and years. It was a wonderful moment. It had nothing to do with pride, but it summed up the whole idea about being in a rock band. The crowd were uncomfortable and soaked but they forgot about it. The energy on stage was incredible. Basically, it was what we got into this silly lifestyle for all those years ago. I was amazed that I still got the same thrill out of it."

➔ A proposed tour of the US West Coast is tentatively in place for this time, but is delayed indefinitely. The opening date of August 16th was slated for New Orleans with gigs following in Georgia, Texas, California, Oregon, and Washington, ending with a concert in Honolulu, HI, on September 10th. This was to be followed by two dates in Tokyo, Japan on September 18th and 19th. This tour is temporarily pushed to October, with Japan pencilled in for November 1st, but by the end of this month these plans are scrapped. Instead, Ray returns to New York City where he probably does more filming for *Weird Nightmare* at the Mastersound Astoria in Queens, completed by month's end.

September

Back at Konk Studios, Ray is prompted by the need to provide Rhino Records with a useable master of *Preservation Acts 1 & 2* to begin work on the tapes. At first he cleans them up and adds the songs 'Preservation' and 'Slum Kids', but then decides that to improve the mixes he needs to re-record the bass and drum parts.

Ray is reportedly inspired by the idea of reviving *Preservation* in its best possible form after watching the September 1st worldwide broadcast of Roger Waters' ambitious presentation of Pink Floyd's *The Wall* to a crowd of 300,000 and more at Potsdamer Platz in Berlin on July 21st.

By mid month Ray is dubbing new drum tracks by Bob Henrit into fresh mixes of the original recordings. But the re-recording is speculative, and not agreed by Rhino. Ray also hopes to revive a production of *Preservation*, last visited as an idea back in 1977. This would not be a Kinks project, and would mean finding a theatrical producer willing to take on the project.

Ray says of *Preservation*: "It's kind of my lost lifelong project, the thing that I constantly find myself going back to, just like Rembrandt kept painting his self-portrait. It's about lost innocence and lost friendship, and things that can never be recaptured, which are things that have always interested me."

The band is still not completely out of the MCA contract, and there is a need for new material to be prepared. However, the separate European deal with London Records was fulfilled with the last album. At some point, probably around now, Ray and Dave meet a British manager, Nigel Thomas, and both the Davies brothers take a liking to him.

While the bulk of the filming for Ray's Mingus project is now complete, there is still the need to shoot narration segments, but this is now delayed. As a reflection of Ray's constant interest in film, late in the month he attends the British Film Institute's launch party for their Connoisseur Video Collection series in London.

October

At the start of the month Ray continues mixing the revamped *Preservation* records and prepares material for a new Kinks album, still intended for MCA.

It's hoped the work can be done quickly, and possibly somewhere other than Konk, as a means of fulfilling the contract with MCA and being free to find another record deal.

MCA meanwhile issues a statement that The Kinks intend to have a new album out at the start of 1991, with an East Coast tour planned, but this does not happen. It is probably during this time that the band reassembles at Konk Studios in north London to begin early sessions for the next album. Although impossible to date exactly, three songs (**'Scattered'**, **'Still Searching'** and **'Somebody Stole My Car'**) that end up on 1993's *Phobia* CD are possibly recorded, or recording is begun, now and into the following month. 'Still Searching' dates back to 1977 when at least a demo of it was recorded for possible inclusion on the *Misfits* album.

'Scattered' too has a previous life. Ray says later that it took him ten years to write. "I originally wrote the song because I ended a relationship and my trousers were in New York and my shoes were in London," he says. "But it took until 1990 when I lost a dear friend for the song to take on a cosmic thread. Until the person died – she died of cancer – I couldn't finish the song." As a completed master of 'Scattered' was finished early in 1989, it's possible that only part of the lyrics are changed now to Ray's satisfaction, or that it is entirely re-recorded.

Remarkably, all five members of The Kinks attend a Kinks fan-club event, *Kinks Konvention 1990*, on Saturday 27th at Muswell Hill Civic Centre in north London. Ray even agrees to do a bit of local press in advance of the event by speaking to the hometown newspaper, *The Hornsey Journal*.

➔ INDICATES EVENT AROUND THIS TIME BUT WITH NO FIRM DATE

November

➜ Early in the month at Konk there is probably some more work done on songs for the next album.

⇨ **TOUR STARTS** *Stimmen Für Oskar / UK Jive Across Germany: Mini German Tour* (Nov 9th – 13th). **Line-up:** Ray Davies (lead vocal, guitar), Dave Davies (guitar, vocal), Bob Henrit (drums), Jim Rodford (bass), Mark Haley (keyboards), Pat Crosbie, Robin James (dancers). The first visit by The Kinks since reunification of the two Germanys, with two appearances in cities formerly in East Germany (Erfurt and Schwerin). The tour is part of a package show that continues for a further five dates without The Kinks, promoting candidate Oskar Lafontein for Chancellor.

Friday 9th

Thüringenhalle *Erfurt, Germany* 8:00pm, with Laid Back, Klaus Lage, Angelo Branduardi, Dissidenten, Thomas Freitag, Knobi-Bonbon
"This was an outstanding concert," says the *Erfurter Tagespost*, "with the famous British band on stage in the former DDR [German Democratic Republic] for the first time."
Set-list: 'Around The Dial', 'UK Jive', 'Come Dancing', 'Low Budget', 'Loony Balloon', 'State Of Confusion' / 'Destroyer', 'It (I Want It)', 'Living On A Thin Line', medley 'Where Have All The Good Times Gone' / 'Tired Of Waiting For You', medley 'A Gallon Of Gas' / 'Welcome To Sleazy Town', 'Lola', 'All Day And All Of The Night', 'You Really Got Me', 'Louie Louie'.

Saturday 10th

Eilenrieder Halle *Hannover, Germany* 8:00pm, with Laid Back, Angelo Branduardi, Dissidenten, Chinchilla Green, Thomas Freitag, Eisi Gulp
Ray also appears on the local FFN Radio programme *Oldies* aired on the 18th, where in addition to being interviewed he plays an impromptu version of 'Celluloid Heroes'.

Sunday 11th

Kongresshalle *Schwerin, Germany* 6:00pm, with Laid Back, Konstantin Wecker, Anne Haigis, Lutz Gorner, Salto Vitale

Monday 12th

Schwabenhalle *Augsburg, Germany* 8:00pm, with Angelo Branduardi, Klaus Lage, Runrig, Chinchilla Green, Eisi Gulp, Andreas Giebel

Tuesday 13th

Friedrich-Ebert-Halle *Ludwigshafen, Germany* 8:00pm, with Gipsy Kings, Runrig, Frankfurter Kurorchester, Thomas Frietag, Marx, Rootschilt Tillerman, Ley Gaga Show
The band finishes the mini German tour with this performance and travels back to London the following day.

➜ After this tour of Germany, Ray reportedly gets the initial inspiration for an apocalyptic theme that will underlie the next Kinks album (*Phobia*), and many of the songs for the record are begun now. While writing songs for the new album Ray is also working on the *80 Days* rewrite.

☆ Despite MCA's recent promise of new Kinks product, at some point around now the band is able successfully to end their contract with MCA. Both parties are unhappy working with each other. Exact timing of the release from the label is unknown, but The Kinks now continue the process of looking for a new record deal, as well as searching for a new manager.

☆ Late in the month Ray flies from London to Los Angeles where he continues work on the *80 Days* rewrite. He also negotiates with Rhino Records to help him finance his incomplete production work on the *Preservation* reissue, and pursues leads on a new label deal for the band, including the possibility of a return to Warner Brothers (which owns Reprise).

December

After Ray's return from the US, The Kinks are reportedly rehearsing some new material. As Ray handles all the keyboards work, and with no prospect for any major upcoming tours in the new year, keyboardist Mark Haley is taken off retainer around this time. He will only be summoned for future live work if he's available. Towards the end of the month, the band is officially on Christmas holidays through to the first week of January.

kinks'91

1991

Early this year The Kinks were still in a holding pattern, but a new manager was hired in the spring and the band signed to the prestigious Columbia Records. Virtually all the remainder of the year was then spent recording for the grand debut for their new label. By the end of 1991 a five-song preview CD at least made fans aware of the affiliation to Columbia, if nothing else.

January

Work probably continues on re-recording parts of *Preservation* at Konk for the Rhino reissue, but otherwise time is taken with attempts to net a new manager. Late in the month, Ray is back in New York City for further label shopping. One of the possibilities is Columbia Records (owned by Sony Music), now headed by Don Ienner, formerly head of promotion at Arista Records during The Kinks' tenure there.

February

Early in the month, Ray flies to Los Angeles and in Santa Monica works on the rewrite of the *80 Days* musical with an unidentified collaborator. This is probably when he delivers copies of the original master tapes of the revised *Preservation Acts 1 & 2* to Rhino Records. Rhino has wanted up to four bonus cuts, including possibly a live recording of 'Slum Kids', but the plan is dropped, and only the studio recording of the song 'Preservation' is used as a bonus track. It is also decided to issue the two "acts" together as a double CD set rather than separately as originally issued on vinyl. Later, Ray returns to New York City.

March

Ray meets Nigel Thomas in New York City at the start of the month to discuss the possibility of Thomas becoming The Kinks' manager. Thomas has managed numerous British acts since the 1960s, including Alexis Korner, Steampacket, Joe Cocker, Kiki Dee, and Morrissey.

Planned recording at Konk is delayed pending Ray's return. The possibility of some British colleges dates has now been dropped. By the third week of the month some rehearsals are done and sessions finally begin. The engineer at Konk is now Richard Edwards. Believed done at this time at Konk is one of Dave's songs, **'Open Up Your Heart'**, already demoed recently at his cottage in Devon (and issued in that form in 2001 on Dave's *Fragile* CD). When transformed into a Kinks track it emerges as **'Look Through Any Doorway'**.

April

Nigel Thomas formally signs up as The Kinks' new manager. Serious negotiations with interested record labels begin. Dave will recall in his book *Kink* that he and Ray are both in New York City now, shopping around the various offers. Tour plans for Japan and Europe proposed at the end of 1990 are long abandoned by now. A more recently proposed US tour of colleges for April/May to oil the band's rusty musical wheels is also scrapped.

May

Early in the month, The Kinks sign a preliminary agreement with Columbia Records. The formal contract will not be signed until July, and no announcement is made yet. But the initial plan is for a new album for autumn release. At almost the same time, Ray decides to pull *Preservation* from release by Rhino Records, pending the possibility of issuing it through the new company. Columbia is interested in getting the entire back catalogue in order to issue a Kinks box-set of some kind. Meanwhile, new material is being readied and the band is preparing to begin serious record sessions at Konk now that the new record deal is in place.

June

The band is at Konk Studios in north London for the initial recording sessions for the new record label, with Ray producing and Richard Edwards engineering. Among the first songs recorded is 'Did Ya', which clearly harks back to The Kinks of the 1960s. "I wanted to recapture the sound we had on 'Sunny Afternoon'," Ray says later. "It was interesting trying to get the new technology to sound like the 1960s. I don't mind doing that when there's a purpose behind it, because I was trying to recreate the time for that particular song. I think it's wrong to do it just for the sake of it, to make people feel nostalgic."

On the issued recording of **'Did Ya'** the band sounds fresh and revitalised, no doubt aided by the promising new outlook. They are released from their unhappy management and record label commitments, and have in place new relationships that seem comfortable and encouraging for band, manager and label alike. Ray is playing all the keyboard parts during the sessions, as Mark Haley is now only employed for concert appearances. The plan is to work through this month and next, with a break for some concerts and a holiday in August, and then to resume recording in September with the aim of finishing the album by the end of the year.

On Wednesday 12th Ray presents the Songwriter Of The Year award to Don Henley during the *3rd Annual International Rock Awards* at the Docklands Arena in east London. Other rock celebrities attending the event include Chrissie Hynde and Pete Townshend. The event is broadcast on the British Sky Channel and in the US by the ABC Network.

Ray settles on a final deal with Rhino Records where the original mixes of *Preservation* will be issued as originally planned, with no re-recordings or additional material other than the inclusion of the original studio recording of the title song.

In a typical bit of Kinks eccentricity, Ray agrees at short notice to do a favour for a promoter friend from the old days, and as a result the band plays the *Commemoration Ball* at Magdalen College, Oxford University on the 21st.

The Kinks dress in ball attire for the occasion. Far from the critical London music press, the band allows some nostalgic leanings, giving the crowd a healthy dose of their 1960s classics, highlighted by a three-song encore that starts with back-to-back faithful recreations of two of the band's most reflective songs, 'Days' and 'Waterloo Sunset', and ends with a rip-roaring reading of their first hit, 'You Really Got Me'. It's also Ray's 47th birthday and the crowd sings 'Happy Birthday' to him.

Fresh from that happy booking, The Kinks head back into Konk Studios apparently "within days", and lay down a new version of the 1960s classic **'Days'**, inspired by their performance at Oxford. Ray has never been satisfied with the original recording and wants to give it a new airing.

July

The band works hard, with continued concentrated recording for the album at Konk, with the aim to finish by the autumn. Early in the month plans are made to first issue a five-song CD single in Britain, scheduled for release during the following month.

Formal signing of the contract with Columbia Records takes place on Friday 19th. At the end of the month, Ray and manager Nigel Thomas fly to New York City for a meeting with Columbia to discuss progress on the album. The decision is made now to push release of the new record until after the Christmas season and instead release the five-song CD as a preview, to keep the band's name in the public eye and to announce their new label affiliation. In Ray's absence the rest of the band rehearses for the upcoming dates, working up a version of Dave's 'Susannah's Still Alive'.

On the 30th, Rhino Records finally issues the long-delayed two-CD set of **Preservation: A Play In Two Acts**. Besides re-mastering from the original tapes and inclusion of the title song 'Preservation', the only musical difference to the original *Act 1* and *Act 2* albums is a slightly elongated edit of the medley 'Money & Corruption' / 'I Am Your Man'.

August

➪ **TOUR STARTS** *Mini European Tour: 1st leg* (Aug 7th – 13th).
Line-up: Ray Davies (lead vocal, guitar), Dave Davies (guitar, vocal), Bob Henrit (drums), Jim Rodford (bass), Mark Haley (keyboards), Pat Crosbie and (probably) Robin James (dancers). The band travels to Brussels on the 6th.

Wednesday 7th

Bellekouter Halle *Affligem, Belgium* 8:00pm, *Rock Affligem Indoors*, with William Souffreau
Travel day follows.
Set-list: 'Around The Dial' (intro), 'The Hard Way', 'UK Jive', 'A Well Respected Man', 'Apeman', 'Sunny Afternoon', 'Low Budget',

'Susannah's Still Alive', 'Come Dancing', 'Till The End Of The Day', medley 'Where Have All The Good Times Gone' / 'Tired Of Waiting For You', It (I Want It)', 'Living On A Thin Line', 'Days', 'Welcome To Sleazy Town', 'Lola', 'All Day And All Of The Night', 'Aggravation', 'You Really Got Me'.

Friday 9th

Dyrehaven *Skanderborg, Denmark* 1:00-11:00pm, *Danmarks Smukkeste Festival 1991*, with Malurt, Ray Dee Ooh, Poormouth, Fielfraz, Allan Olsen, Big Fat Snake, Poul Krebs & The Bookhouse Boys

Saturday 10th

Cyklebane *Odense, Denmark* 12midday-10:00pm, *Open Air Festival*, with Malurt, Shu Bi Dua, Moonjam, Ian Gillan
Ray plays a passage of 'Sweet Lady Genevieve' solo during the course of the show at this bicycling stadium.

Sunday 11th

Amager Strandpark *Copenhagen, Denmark* 2:00-10:00pm, *5-Øren Musikforeningen*, with Malurt, Big Fat Snake, The Scampi, Fritti Family
Ray pulls out an impromptu 'Singing In The Rain' for this free concert on a rainy day. (Travel day follows).

Tuesday 13th

Stadtpark *Hamburg, Germany* 7:00pm, with Edo Zanki & Band
Ray plays piano and sings for fans at the hotel after the show. The band travels back to London the following day. British dates and a London show have been considered to follow the Danish dates, but these do not materialise. Recording is scheduled to resume now but is pushed back to early September while Ray is off writing and the band takes a break.

Tuesday 27th

Lost And Found (1986-89) album released in the US. This label retrospective is the last album issued by MCA Records.

Lost And Found (1986-89) album

1 **'The Road'** (R. DAVIES).
2 **'UK Jive'** (R. DAVIES).
3 **'Lost And Found'** (R. DAVIES).
4 **'Working At The Factory'** (R. DAVIES).
5 **'Think Visual'** (R. DAVIES).
6 **'Welcome To Sleazy Town'** (R. DAVIES).
7 **'How Do I Get Close'** (R. DAVIES).
8 **'The Video Shop'** (R. DAVIES).
9 **'Now And Then'** (R. DAVIES).
10 **'Apeman' live** (R. DAVIES).
11 **'Living On A Thin Line' live** (D. DAVIES).
12 **'Give The People What They Want' live** (R. DAVIES).

US release August 27th 1991 (MCA Records MCAD-10338). All material previously issued on the three Kinks MCA albums. Compilation assembled by Andy McKaie of MCA Records. Digital preparation by Kevin Hatunga at MCA Studios, *North Hollywood, CA*. This is the first official Kinks album to be issued in CD format rather than vinyl LP as the principal format.
Chart high US none.

kinks'91

September

Following the break from recording, Dave and long-time companion Nancy decide to move the family to Los Angeles. Nancy is from Los Angeles and her family still live there. They make the move at the start of the month, selling their flat in Maida Vale in London and leasing a house in Hollywood.

With the band midway through the recording of a new album, Dave's move will no doubt slow down progress as the operating base of the two principal Kinks, Ray and Dave, is now spread between Los Angeles and London, some 3,000 miles apart.

Ray delivers the master tapes for the 'Did Ya' five-song CD single to CBS UK, the British arm of Columbia, for preparation for release. The scheduled mid-month resumption of sessions for the new album is pushed back, pending Dave's return to London. Slightly later in the month, Ray travels to New York City where he delivers masters of the CD single to Columbia Records there, and remains in NYC until early next month.

October

Advance promotional copies of the *Did Ya* CD single are issued on cassette the week of the 7th to radio stations in the US. By mid month, with Dave back in London, the band reconvenes at Konk Studios to resume work on the new album, including some re-recording. Meanwhile, it is decided to cancel UK release of the new CD single. On Thursday 24th the **Did Ya** five-song CD single is released in the US. It warrants virtually no press coverage, nor does it register any noticeable airplay, and is perhaps the victim of its experimental five-song format – not quite a single, and not quite an album.

Steve Simuels manages to evaluate it for *Stereo Review*, however, and calls it "the most interesting thing they've released in what seems

---

Did Ya CD maxi-single

1 '**Did Ya**' (R. DAVIES).
2 '**I Gotta Move**' live (R. DAVIES).
3 '**Days**' 2nd version (R. DAVIES).
4 '**New World**' (R. DAVIES).
5 '**Look Through Any Doorway**' (D. DAVIES).

US release October 24th 1991 (Columbia 44K-74050).
Musicians Ray Davies lead vocal, guitar, keyboards except as noted. Dave Davies lead vocal (5), guitar, backing vocal. Jim Rodford bass guitar, backing vocal. Ian Gibbons keyboards (2, probably 4).
Recorded Konk Studios (No.1 & 2) *Hornsey, north London*; 1, 3: June 1991; 4: January-June 1989; 5: March-June 1991; 32-track and/or two 24-track (46 tracks) mixed to stereo. 2: Mann Music Center, *Philadelphia, PA*; July 1st 1987; Fanta Sound Mobile Unit; 24-track mixed to stereo.
Producer Ray Davies.
Engineers Richard Edwards (1, 3, 5); Johnie Rosen with Mervin & Billy (mobile unit), Dave Powell with George Holt (post-production at Konk) (2); Joe Gibb and "Irish" Alan O'Duffy (4).
Chart high US none.

---

like ages". Simuels nominates Dave's 'Look Through Any Doorway' as the standout track, "an ingratiating bit of melancholia in a style splitting the difference between The Kinks' original crunch-guitar and folk-rock modes". He concludes: "A very pleasant surprise. If the band's next full length album displays the level of energy and inspiration on display here, then 1992 could be a better year than anybody around my house anticipated."

November

➜ Ray continues at Konk in London to work on overdubs, mixing and editing of existing recordings for the new album. Dave is back in Los Angeles at some point.

A brief media campaign to help promote the new CD single and to publicise the band's signing to Columbia is arranged, and on the 19th and 20th Ray and Dave fly in from their respective bases to meet up in Philadelphia. Long-serving road manager Ken Jones is scheduled to come as well, but at the last moment doesn't go. His relationship with the band deteriorates quickly thereafter.

Almost certainly on the 21st, photographer Kate Garner captures a shot of the brothers exiting their limo in New York City which will eventually be used on the cover of the 1993 CD *Phobia*.

On Friday 22nd Ray and Dave appear at the Boston Garden in Boston, MA, for the *WBCN Rock Of Boston* event. Also on are The Raindogs, RTZ, The Smithereens, and Foreigner, with a pre-concert set by The Stools. Originally billed as Kinks Unplugged (and supposedly with a third member), the brothers' appearance is changed to an acoustic set by "Ray & Dave Davies of The Kinks". They dedicate their performance to former roadie/bodyguard "Big" Bob Suszynski, who died in Chicago earlier this week of a heart attack at age 36.

Ray and Dave's set is largely spontaneous, and consists of 'Low Budget', 'Alcohol', 'Dedicated Follower Of Fashion', 'Celluloid Heroes', 'Days', 'A Well Respected Man', 'Apeman', 'Lola' and 'You Really Got Me'.

On the spot they arrange for the New Jersey-based Smithereens to back them for the last song and a half. This provides the audience with a pleasant surprise as the closed curtain that is behind the duo for most of the set is raised in the middle of 'Lola' to reveal The Smithereens joining in. A rousing set-closer of 'You Really Got Me' follows, and Ray and Dave bring the crowd to their feet.

"The Kinks and The Smithereens played as if they'd almost rehearsed," writes Ted Drozdowski in *Musician*, "bashing along with ragged abandon while Ray pogo'd behind his microphone." Dave will later consider using The Smithereens as his first backing band in 1997, but ultimately the partnership never materialises. Dave subsequently heads back to LA, while Ray remains in New York City for the next week before heading back to London.

December

Early in the month Dave is in Los Angeles. Ray resumes work on tracks at Konk Studios, but the album is now behind schedule and the January target release date is delayed.

There is more rehearsing mid month for some new material at Konk. Probably completed by now among the sessions from June-July and October-December are '**Surviving**', '**It's Alright (Don't Think About It)**', '**Close To The Wire**', '**The Informer**', '**Hatred (A Duet)**', '**Don't**', '**Over The Edge**', '**Babies**', '**Drift Away**' and '**Phobia**'. The band takes a break for the Christmas/New Year holidays, with Dave back in LA.

1992

Another year where the band was almost completely absent from the public eye, barring a handful of European dates. While an album was essentially ready by January, even by Kinks standards 1992 turned into a year of utter chaos, with endless delays and setbacks for the release of their long-awaited new album. It was unclear if the problems arose mainly from the record company's dissatisfaction with the proposed product or from Ray's inclination to tweak and remix and rethink his work. In any event, the year was a non-stop roller-coaster ride of delays and reshuffled plans, and no doubt a frustrating and trying period for musicians, record company executives, and the band's ever-patient fans.

January / February

Ray is completing the mixing and assembly of the new album, with a reported 14 or 15 songs, including three by Dave. Release was tentatively slated by Columbia for February, but by now it's set to March. Also around this time, road manager Ken Jones parts company with the band after a 24-year stint.

Ray flies in to New York City from London on January 16th with a nearly completed version of the new album for a progress review and the hope of bringing the release date forward. While in town he takes in a concert by John Cougar Mellencamp and Billy Squire at the Meadowlands in East Rutherford, NJ.

Probably on the 17th Ray arrives at the offices of Columbia Records in midtown Manhattan for a meeting with company representatives that evidently does not go well. Release plans are tied to a scheduled US and then world tour to follow, so these plans shift as the release date changes, along with proposed video shoots and advance press requirements. Ray later describes the meeting as almost deal breaking. But a chance encounter with a stranger in the record company's lift (elevator) at least inspires a last song for the record that Ray writes on his plane trip back to London. Upon his return, Ray takes The Kinks back into Konk Studios to record the song, **'Only A Dream'**. It will end up as one of the featured singles from the new CD when it ultimately appears next year.

In the rush to record the last track for the CD, tentative plans to shoot a video for 'Did Ya' and another song in Los Angeles at the end of January are scrapped. Also dropped are plans for two weeks of US college dates early in March with a finale at the Paramount Theater in New York City – all of which have been contingent on a March release of the CD, but this is again pushed back, to June.

Ray does final mixes for the finished album with engineer John Rollo at Konk. At some point mid February, Ray takes a break to attend part of the Olympics in Albertville, France, which run from the 8th to the 23rd.

March

A Columbia Records press release slips out announcing a new Kinks album titled *Don't* for release later this month, and the news runs in the March 9th issue of *New York* magazine. The slant of the piece is that Columbia Records' newest signing, The Kinks, has been contacting

fashion magazines with an eye for Ray Davies to have a column as a fashion critic once he finishes the group's next album, *Don't*. Any further talk of this scheme is immediately halted.

Meanwhile, the band is said to be rehearsing at Konk Studios, are announced as playing an upcoming Boston gig and possibly a few other big dates, and planning a major tour for the second half of June. Reportedly, the new album undergoes more revision at Konk now.

A Yorkshire-produced TV police series called *Heartbeat* debuts this month that was originally intended to air with a theme song composed by Ray. In the chaos of the previous month, however, no such song is forthcoming, and at the eleventh hour the show instead opts for the old Buddy Holly song of the same name.

April

➔ Early in the month, Columbia shifts the release date of the new Kinks album from June to August.

Wednesday 15th

Ray is at the Grosvenor Hotel in central London for the Ivor Novello Awards ceremony where he presents an award to singer Seal.

Friday 24th

Ray and Dave with manager Nigel Thomas travel from London to Boston for a concert appearance by the duo tomorrow. They hole up at the Hilton Hotel in Dedham just outside the city. The brothers pick up some local musicians: pianist Dan Lewis, bassist Brad (unknown surname) and drummer Steve (unknown surname)

Saturday 25th

Sullivan Stadium *Foxboro, MA* 12midday-7:30pm, *National Earth Day '92 Sound Action Concert*, with The Steve Miller Band, Midnight Oil, Indigo Girls With Mary Chapin-Carpenter & Joan Baez, Robin Hitchcock, Bruce Cockburn, Youssou N'Dour, The Violent Femmes, Fishbone, The Disposable Heroes of Hiphopcracy, John Trudell & Graffitti Man, Sofie B. Hawkins, Young Nation; promoted by Concerts For The Environment

Part of a series of concerts around the country to help promote and celebrate Earth Day. It is a bitterly raw New England spring day, and attendance is relatively disappointing at about 20,000, despite ticket

kinks'92

sales of 28,000 from 40,000 offered for sale in this football stadium outside Greater Boston. The weather is so poor that a planned finale of all artists appearing en masse is scrapped, and the show ends earlier than the scheduled 10:00pm finish due to rain.

Ray and Dave initially appear as an acoustic duo for the first five songs, and are joined by pianist Dan Lewis for 'Now And Then' and then Lewis's bassist and drummer for the remainder of the brief set. "The stadium-savvy Kinks blistered through 'Lola', 'Low Budget' and 'You Really Got Me'," says *The Boston Globe*, presumably without noticing it wasn't the whole Kinks. Sony Music tapes the entire event with plans to issue a CD, with proceeds going to worthy causes, but this is later abandoned. (Ray heads straight back to London to finish mixing the new album, which he wants completed by May 5th so that release can be set for the end of June. Dave heads back to LA.)

Set-list: 'Apeman', 'Days', 'A Well Respected Man', 'Celluloid Heroes', 'Dedicated Follower Of Fashion', 'Now And Then', 'Lola', 'All Day And All Of The Night', 'Low Budget', 'You Really Got Me'.

May

At Konk, Ray is busy mixing the new album. Six of the songs deemed as potential singles – 'Wall Of Fire', 'Still Searching', 'Phobia', 'Drift Away', 'Only A Dream', 'Hatred (A Duet)' – are remixed with Bob Clearmountain at this time. As the May submission deadline for the new album passes, all temporary plans for June release and a tour then are pushed to the autumn.

Papers are filed in London for the creation by Ray of a new film company, Weird Films Ltd, to handle his Charles Mingus documentary, although its incorporation doesn't occur until February 9th 1993.

June

Friday 12th
Rockefeller's Music Hall *Oslo, Norway* 9:00pm
Tonight sees a sell-out crowd of 1,000 at this large rock club, with no opening act. Local paper *Verdens Gang* notes the crowd as largely in their 40s, of the same generation who went to see The Kinks when they first played Oslo in 1966. The reaction is wildly enthusiastic, with two encores totalling almost 30 minutes. During the set the band plays the rarely-performed 'Get Back In Line' and, as a finale, 'Louie Louie'. Dancers Pat Crosbie and probably Brenda Edwards perform during 'Aggravation'.

Saturday 13th
Slottsskogen *Gothenburg, Sweden* *Gothenburg Park Festival*, with Sonia, Katrina & The Waves
An open-air festival attended by around 4,000 fans. Those lucky enough to catch the soundcheck heard off-the-cuff run-throughs of 'Misfits', 'Who'll Be The Next In Line' and even The Yardbirds' hit 'Still I'm Sad'. Like last night, the dancers are present only on 'Aggravation'. (Band travels back to London the following day, where Dave remains to take care of Kinks business before returning to LA.)

Set-list: 'Around The Dial', 'The Hard Way', 'Low Budget', 'European Cup Blues' (improvisation sung to Marty Robbins US/Guy Mitchell UK hit 'Singing The Blues'), 'Come Dancing', 'Apeman', 'Celluloid Heroes', 'I'm Not Like Everybody Else', 'UK Jive', 'Did Ya', 'Sunny Afternoon', 'Till The End Of The Day', 'Welcome To Sleazy Town', 'Living On A Thin Line', 'Lola', 'All Day And All Of The Night', medley 'Aggravation' / 'New World', 'You Really Got Me', 'Days', 'David Watts', 'Louie Louie'.

July

Presumably Ray is at Konk throughout the month busy refining the final mixes for the new album, with Dave also in London at some point. By month's end Ray travels from London to New York City yet again, to deliver a finished version of the album to Columbia Records, including the six new mixes for possible singles done by remix engineer Bob Clearmountain, and to make arrangements for a promotion and tour schedule. At this point the CD is announced for release on September 18th.

August

Ray presumably is in New York City briefly to co-ordinate the CD's artwork, for which he has commissioned New York City-based artist Sue Coe, known for her bleak, cartoon-like depictions of tormented souls and political and moral corruption – which presumably appeal to Ray's own dark views of the world. Towards the middle of the month, Columbia Records announces that release of The Kinks CD is again pushed back, now to October 19th, due to delays in its artwork. Columbia further reveals that the album will now be titled *Phobia*, rather than *Don't*.

Dave flies from LA to London late in the month for a few weeks of rehearsals prior to the September German and French dates as it is intended to play material from the new album. These concerts were booked on the basis of a of European release of the CD in September, but that will shortly be pushed to December.

At this point 'Wall Of Fire' is being pushed to Columbia as the single. Dave says later in his book *Kink* it's his favoured choice – and also that of Ray and manager Thomas – but Columbia doesn't agree, preferring 'Hatred'.

September

Friday 4th
The Boston Globe runs a news item indicating that the October 27th release date of *Phobia* is now indefinitely delayed, reflecting Ray's desire to avoid the Christmas rush and release it in the new year. Columbia, meanwhile, is holding to its schedule, with the first single due the second week of October, and the CD in the third week of that month. The record company is also setting up plans for a mini-tour to follow in November, and the promotions department is developing an advance release campaign.

➪ **TOUR STARTS** *Germany/France Mini Tour* (Sep 6th – 12th).
Line-up: Ray Davies (lead vocal, guitar), Dave Davies (guitar, vocal), Bob Henrit (drums), Jim Rodford (bass), Mark Haley (keyboards), Pat Crosbie, Brenda Edwards (dancers). Following rehearsals, the band travels to Germany on the 5th.

Sunday 6th
Outdoor event *Trochtelfingen, Germany* 6:00pm, *Trochtelfinger Festival Am See*, with Steppin' Out, Lizard
The last of a three-day festival that also featured Johnny Winter, Miriam Makeba, and King Sunny Ade. In a European festival setting, Ray tilts the set-list heavily towards Kinks classics, while still presenting the cornerstone piece from *UK Jive*. One new song from the forthcoming CD is played on this tour, a revived 1977 composition 'Still Searching'. For this show only among these dates, they play a final

encore of The Kingsmen's classic 'Louie Louie', recorded by The Kinks in 1964.

Set-list: 'Concert Prelude #2', 'Around The Dial' (extract), 'The Hard Way', 'Low Budget', 'UK Jive', 'Celluloid Heroes', 'Come Dancing', 'I'm Not Like Everybody Else', 'Till The End Of The Day', 'Where Have All The Good Times Gone', 'Dead End Street', 'Welcome To Sleazy Town', 'Still Searching', 'Living On A Thin Line', 'Too Much On My Mind', 'Lola', 'All Day And All Of The Night', 'Death Of A Clown', medley 'Aggravation' / 'New World' (tape), 'Days', 'You Really Got Me', 'Louie Louie'.

Monday 7th

Open-air event *Miltenberg, Germany* Festival Michaelismesse, with The Little River Band

Another festival date maintains a healthy dose of oldies, but The Kinks also try out 'Wall Of Fire' from the forthcoming *Phobia* CD as well as 'Still Searching'.

Tuesday 8th

Serenadenhof *Nürnberg, Germany* 7:30pm

Wednesday 9th

E-Werk *Cologne, Germany*

Ray begins losing his voice after the third song tonight and accordingly the show is trimmed a little. He sees a doctor directly after the concert.

Thursday 10th – Friday 11th

Ray is ill with laryngitis, and rests in bed in Cologne. Concerts at Huxley's Neue Welt, Berlin, Germany on the 10th and a tentatively scheduled gig in Saabrücken, Germany the following day are cancelled.

Saturday 12th

La Corneuve *Paris, France* Fête de l'Humanité 1992; sponsored by French Socialist Party

The Kinks make a grand return to the same festival they played in 1974. The band has not performed in Paris since 1985.

Sunday 13th

The band travels back to London. In New York City the *Sunday News* reports that the new CD will still be out in the third week of October.

Tuesday 15th

In New York City, Columbia Records now announces that the new single and CD, *Phobia*, are delayed again, until January 1993. As there have been firm plans in place for release of the CD in the US on October 27th, some general multi-artist promotional products have already been manufactured and are sent out this week. Advance promotional copies of *Phobia* album on cassette featuring the 15-song version of the CD have also been manufactured for distribution to reviewers, and a few copies leak out. Discussions between record company and The Kinks mostly seem to relate to a choice of song for the single.

Sunday 20th – Thursday 24th

Ray tutors a five-day songwriting workshop held at Fen Farm, a writer's retreat near Blo' Norton on the Norfolk/Suffolk border. He takes on this twice-yearly commitment as a way of sharing his songwriting talents and experience with young hopefuls.

➔ Towards the end of the month at Konk, Ray probably prepares the track 'Scattered' for inclusion on the new CD. The lyric at least was likely re-recorded back at the end of 1990 (on to a backing-track probably the same as the 1989 recording submitted to MCA as part of the initial version of *UK Jive*). Like all the other contenders for single release, the track is mixed by Bob Clearmountain. Ray also does a remix of 'Still Searching', either now or slightly later in the autumn.

October

Ray travels to New York City at the start of the month where he again meets with Columbia Records executives to discuss the latest revised plans. 'Scattered' is added to the track listing, making the new album now officially a 16-title CD, with release announced for January 1993.

Ray is also in town to arrange production of videos. Under consideration are the Quay Brothers, avant-garde animated filmmakers whose Kafkaesque style evoking nightmarish scenes appeals to Ray for this project, and German film-maker Wim Wenders, a long-standing admirer of Ray's work.

The promotional campaign will call for a trend-setting, so-called electronic press kit, offered also on video rather than paper alone. Current concert plans call for a US tour for the spring and through the summer, and there is a plan to start with club dates – something that will occur the following spring. Ray travels back to London later in the month, and Dave is probably there too.

November

Early in the month the Konk office issues a memo to the Kinks fan club outlining existing plans, including a proposed UK release of the *Did Ya* EP (minus 'I Gotta Move'), two weeks of concerts in Europe at the end November into December, and then five UK dates. The memo also says that Ray and Dave will do some US promotional work prior to Christmas for a US album release in mid January. All these plans will be dropped almost as quickly as they are announced.

December

Ray is back in New York City by mid month, working on his *Weird Nightmare* Charles Mingus documentary, and reportedly meeting New York artist Sue Coe about the final artwork for the *Phobia* CD. It's possible that Ray assists in the mastering of the now absolutely finalised version of the new CD with long-time mastering colleague Robert Ludwig. Any tentative plans to shoot videos this month are pushed into January. Ray is seen around town, and at the China Club he suggests a late-February release date for the apparently endlessly delayed CD. Late in the month, Columbia names a new release date – March – as they now have a finalised CD and all their promotional and tour plans in place.

1993

An unparalleled year of touring and promotion for The Kinks, unlike almost any other in their long career. Despite the seemingly endless false starts, once the juggernaut got rolling it rarely came to a halt, barring a few typical Kinks instances of utter disaster. This would in effect turn out to be The Kinks' last shot to catapult themselves back into the big time. In fact, much of the previous two years had been taken up by preparations for such a re-launch. But however sincere and energy-filled that effort was, the Phobia album failed to click with record buyers, whether due to the music itself or the record company's ability to market it. Once again The Kinks were almost completely at odds with their record label, and this very busy year ended in a disappointing atmosphere.

January

On Monday the 4th Columbia announces the latest confirmed release date for The Kinks' new album, *Phobia*, as March 9th. Later in the month it's shifted to the 16th. Ray is sorting out plans to shoot two separate videos for pending singles.

On the 9th, in London, manager Nigel Thomas dies of a massive stroke at age 45. The Kinks' business plans and arrangements for an upcoming media tour to start on the 18th in Europe are thrown into disarray. Dave flies in to attend the manager's funeral and to sort out a new schedule for Kinks activities that have been laid out for the year.

Late in the month advance cassette copies of *Phobia* begin to circulate to selected members of the US press.

February

Wednesday 3rd
Sony Music cafeteria *Santa Monica, CA*
Ray and Dave play a special private performance, about a 40-minute set that includes 'Apeman', 'Harry Rag', 'A Well Respected Man', 'Celluloid Heroes', 'Scattered', 'Hatred (A Duet)', 'Still Searching' and 'Lola'. It's said that Columbia head Don Ienner particularly likes 'Still Searching' and 'Scattered'. 'Scattered' is set as the first single for release on February 15th, instead of 'Hatred (A Duet)'. But it is learned that MCA has filed an injunction against Columbia to prevent them issuing 'Scattered'. MCA claims they have rights to this song under their contract with The Kinks, as at least a version of it was submitted to them during that period. So 'Scattered', already pressed up for distribution, is now in jeopardy as the first single from the new album. It's ultimately abandoned, with Columbia seemingly dumping the pressed-up copies in late June, but these will still make their way into the collectors' market. (It's Dave's 46th birthday, and a cake in the shape of a guitar is presented to him at the Sony/Columbia event.)

Thursday 4th
Among other press activities, Ray and Dave appear at 9:00pm on the *Mark & Brian KLOS Morning Show* on 95.5 FM in Los Angeles, and in addition to being interviewed they perform in the studio 'Hatred (A Duet)', 'Sweet Lady Genevieve' (the latter with fans Greg Romayo and

Scott Gilbertson singing and playing guitars), 'Still Searching' and 'A Well Respected Man' (with the show's DJs Mark Thompson and Brian Phelps joining in on the chorus). As an example of the chaos already occurring, Ray mentions on air that 'Hatred (A Duet)' is the next single, but the Sony rep present in the studio later corrects him, indicating that 'Scattered' has been announced for release on March 15th. (Ray then travels to New York for media duties, and after the weekend heads back to London and thence to Europe.)

Wednesday 10th – Thursday 11th
Ray and Dave are in Paris where in addition to numerous interviews they film a video for the planned European-only single, 'Only A Dream'. Ray and Dave are shown strolling the sites of Paris with acoustic guitars in hand as they sing along to the recording. Interview footage is also shot for a French TV documentary on *The Kinks, Saga Du Rock*, which is broadcast on French M6 on April 1st.

Thursday 11th
La Péniche BOER 2, Port Henri IV *Paris, France* 9:00pm
Ray and Dave perform with local backing musicians Vincent Palmer (guitar), Hugues Urvoy de Portzampac (bass) and Gérard Coullondre (drums) at a Columbia Records invitation-only press party held on this barge at the water's edge. They play 'Louie Louie', 'You Really Got Me', 'Lola', 'Still Searching', 'Long Tall Shorty' and 'Only A Dream', and Ray performs 'Waterloo Sunset' solo.

Friday 12th
Ray and Dave are in Amsterdam, Netherlands for a day of interviews.

Saturday 13th
Ray and Dave possibly in Copenhagen, Denmark for more press.

Sunday 14th – Monday 15th
Ray and Dave move on to the Strand Hotel, Stockholm with a full schedule of interviews with the Swedish press plus appearances on Swedish radio and TV. At Berns, a restaurant in Stockholm, Ray and Dave perform 'Sunny Afternoon' and 'Scattered', broadcast on Swedish TV4 March 15th and 20th.

Monday 15th – Tuesday 16th
Ray and Dave are available for interviews at the Sony Records offices in Frankfurt, Germany.

➡ Possibly a few other European cities are visited on this promo tour. Ray and Dave are certainly in Brussels, Belgium at some point, but by the weekend of 20th-21st are back in London.

✰ Once back in England, Ray and Dave finalise business and tour arrangements. A planned tour of Europe that was scheduled mid January is cancelled now. Decisions about which singles are to be released where must be made soon as videos have to be shot well in advance of issue dates. At this time, Columbia in New York announces *Phobia* for release March 23rd, with 'Hatred (A Duet)' now the first single, set for March 8th.

March

➡ Plans are on hold pending the hiring of a new manager, following the death of Nigel Thomas, and no tour dates can be finalised until that decision is made.

Monday 8th

Scattered CD single is released in Switzerland and Germany. It has been set for release today in the UK and Europe but is only issued in these two countries, with UK release delayed. It was intended that Europe should get 'Only A Dream' as a single now, and this seems to be briefly issued in Holland but likely withdrawn. Release of 'Hatred (A Duet)' as a single in the US is delayed to the 29th.

➡ By mid-month, new manager Eugene Harvey is hired. Harvey was formerly Whitney Houston's manager and had been considered as a potential Kinks manager in autumn 1989. With a new manager in place, plans begin to move forward more smoothly.

Monday 15th

After a week's delay 'Scattered' is released to radio stations in the UK and gets some initial airplay, but regular release is delayed first to April 5th and then to July 12th. During this week a video for 'Scattered' is filmed, including scenes with Ray and Dave driving through expansive country fields, intermingled with footage of The Kinks performing the song at Konk. The young Ray Davies character as introduced in 1982's 'Come Dancing' video is also worked into the song's basic storyline. Shooting for the video is completed by the 20th and submitted to Columbia Records on March 25th (with Ray likely popping over to New York City briefly on the 21st-22nd).

Thursday 18th

Phobia album released in Switzerland, Germany and Sweden.

Scattered CD single

1 'Scattered' (R. DAVIES).
2 'Hatred (A Duet)' (R. DAVIES).
3 'Days' 2nd version (R. DAVIES).

European release March 8th 1993 (Columbia 658992 2).
UK release July 12th 1993 (Columbia 658992 2).
Musicians and recording details: 1, 2: as *Phobia* album (see 18th); 3: as *Did Ya* CD maxi-single (see October 24th 1991).
Chart high UK none.

Phobia album

1 'Opening' (R. DAVIES).
2 'Wall Of Fire' (R. DAVIES).
3 'Drift Away' (R. DAVIES).
4 'Still Searching' (R. DAVIES).
5 'Phobia' (R. DAVIES).
6 'Only A Dream' (R. DAVIES).
7 'Don't' (R. DAVIES).
8 'Babies' (R. DAVIES).
9 'Over The Edge' (R. DAVIES).
10 'Surviving' (R. DAVIES).
11 'It's Alright (Don't Think About It)' (D. DAVIES).
12 'The Informer' (R. DAVIES).
13 'Hatred (A Duet)' (R. DAVIES).
14 'Somebody Stole My Car' (R. DAVIES).
15 'Close To The Wire' (D. DAVIES).
16 'Scattered' (R. DAVIES).
17 'Did Ya' (R. DAVIES).
Track 17 is on UK/European release but not on US release

European release March 18th 1993 (Columbia 472489 2).
UK release March 29th 1993 (Columbia 472489 2).
US release April 13th 1993 (Columbia CK 48724).
Musicians Ray Davies lead vocal except as noted, electric guitar, acoustic guitar, keyboards, harmonica (13), backing vocal. Dave Davies lead vocal (11, 15), electric guitar, acoustic guitar, backing vocal. Jim Rodford bass guitar, backing vocal. Bob Henrit drums.
Recorded Konk Studios (No.1 & 2) *Hornsey, north London*; 1-3, 5, 7-11, 13, 15: 1991; 6: February 1992; 4, 14: probably late 1990; 12: 1991 (or possibly June-August 1986); 16: January-April 1989 and/or late 1990; 17: May-June 1991; 32-track and two 24-track (46 tracks) mixed to stereo.
Producer Ray Davies (credited as R. Douglas Davies).
Engineers Richard Edwards; assistant engineers Stan Loubieres, Kevin Paul. Mixed by John Rollo.
Chart high UK none; US number 166.

Tuesday 23rd

The Kinks are in Paris to help celebrate and promote the release of the *Phobia* CD, issued in France today. There's an in-store appearance at the Virgin Megastore and at a local TV studio where they tape an appearance on popular French music show **Taratata** performing live in the studio 'Only A Dream' and 'Sunny Afternoon' plus an unexpected spontaneous version of 'You Really Got Me'. The show is broadcast on French TV 2 on June 5th.

Thursday 25th

❏ **TV** BBC Television Centre *west London*. BBC-2 **The Late Show** live performance 'Scattered', 'Days' broadcast 11:15-11:55pm.
✰ Columbia Records receives the 'Scattered' video today, and the promotional CD single 'Hatred (A Duet)' is issued to US radio stations.

Saturday 27th

Barrowlands *Glasgow, Scotland*
The regular live line-up – the four-man Kinks plus Mark Haley on keyboards and two dancers (Pat Crosbie and probably Suzie Thomas) – plays to 1,800 fans in this 2,000-capacity ballroom.

kinks'93

Sunday 28th

Royal Concert Hall *Nottingham* with unknown folk singer
A sell-out audience of 2,200.

Monday 29th

The Grand *Clapham, south London*
Opening night of this newly renovated theatre, with a sell-out audience of 1,600, and no opening act. It's filmed by MTV for broadcast April 5th but not aired.
Set-list: medley 'Around The Dial'/ 'The Hard Way', 'Low Budget', 'Come Dancing', 'Apeman', 'Scattered', 'Only A Dream', 'I'm Not Like Everybody Else', 'Hatred (A Duet)', 'Sunny Afternoon', 'Celluloid Heroes', 'Harry Rag', 'Welcome To Sleazy Town', 'Still Searching', 'Death Of A Clown', 'Wall Of Fire', 'Till The End Of The Day', medley 'Where Have All The Good Times Gone' / 'Tired Of Waiting For You', 'Living On A Thin Line', 'Dead End Street', 'Phobia', 'Lola', 'All Day And All Of The Night', medley 'Aggravation' / 'New World' (tape), 'Days', 'You Really Got Me', 'Great Balls Of Fire', 'Twist And Shout'.
Phobia album released in the UK. Although sales are typically slow in the UK, the CD does pick up some positive reviews. The stranglehold by the old-guard music papers like *NME* and *Melody Maker* that dominated Britain for years has finally expanded with a healthy assortment of new music-magazine titles. "Ray Davies is shown here at his best," writes Andy Bradshaw in *Rock World*, "his voice alternating between uncertain fragility to hard edged meanness. ... This is by no means an out-and-out hard rock record, by any stretch of the imagination. But it is a well balanced and, yes, classy album by a bunch of old guard rockers who have been written off so many times their existence has been completely overlooked."

Rock Compact Disc Magazine says: "*Phobia* is some kind of return to form and serves as a long-overdue reminder of [Ray's] knack for conveying precise emotions in concise three-minute explosions of sound. His lightness of touch seemingly deserted him years ago, but on this album that debit is more than compensated for by the sheer tenacity of approach."

Meanwhile Ray summarises *Phobia*'s governing image for *The Observer* newspaper. "It's of a man on top of a skyscraper, and the skyscraper is on fire. He's scared of heights and the only way to escape is across a tightrope to another building. A dilemma, you might say."

Tuesday 30th

● **RECORDING** Konk Studios *Hornsey, north London*. Ray works on an electronic press kit (EPK) of around 25 minutes duration to boost the new CD's promotion. Done entirely on videotape, it consists of performance and interview footage. Ray is also at Broadcasting House in London for BBC Radio-1's *Nicky Campbell Show* at 10:00pm on which he sings excerpts of 'Days', 'Still Searching' and 'Two Sisters' and plays the records of 'Scattered' and 'Hatred (A Duet)'.

April

→ All original plans set for early this month are pushed back or cancelled. A tour of US clubs originally set to start on the 2nd is pushed to the 13th.
☆ Early in the month, filming is finished for the EPK (Electronic Press Kit). Some shots of the band playing at Konk will likely be used for the planned video for 'Hatred (A Duet)' to be completed after the US mini tour.

Monday 12th

Ray and Dave are in New York City this week, and today a press conference is held to announce the release of *Phobia* on Tuesday and to begin a barrage of press and radio interviews. Ray also finishes editing the electronic press kit. Although 'Hatred (A Duet)' has now been sent to radio stations, Ray reportedly still wants to produce a proper video for it, but Columbia says it is too late. An already delayed string of club dates around the US is delayed a further ten days.

Tuesday 13th

Phobia album released in the US. While there are many positive reviews, the public doesn't notice. The record has an initial surge of sales, no doubt thanks to the loyal followers; it enters the US charts at 166 but immediately drops out. This is surely viewed by the band as a massive disappointment. "*Phobia* is prime late-model Kinks," writes Paul Evans in *Rolling Stone*. "Dave Davies drives home customarily tough, wry guitar work, and the rhythm section of Bob Henrit and Jim Rodford provides resolutely unflashy accompaniment. But the spotlight, as always, is less on playing than on the songs themselves. Mining Ray's trademark obsessions – anxiety, nostalgia and longing – these sturdy melodies support decidedly disturbing themes: eco-apocalypse, suicide, urban threat and multiform angst. But while Lou Reed or Nick Cave might employ such subject matter for something darkly baroque, Davies's thin, affecting singing and caustic, romantic vision render these phobias as disconcertingly comical, bitterly Chaplinesque."

Carl Cafarelli in *Goldmine* says: "Their prototypical British stiff upper lip has long been augmented by an American-bred combativeness that's willing to dig in for a long drawn out fight. Now, as ever, The Kinks are one of pop music's greatest treasures." Ray describes the basic theme of *Phobia* for *Billboard*. "It's a bittersweet record," he says. "A lot of it is about society driving people right to the edge. ... People are on the brink of comedy and tragedy every day, between despair and elation. It's the way the world swings."

Wednesday 21st

Palais des Congrès *Bourges, France* *Printempes de Bourges Festival*
This ongoing festival also includes Sade, Suzanne Vega and others. (The Kinks travel on to Miami, FL, the following day.)

⇨ **TOUR STARTS** *Phobia Spring Tour Of US* (Apr 23rd – May 13th, Jun 2nd – 5th). **Line-up**: Ray Davies (lead vocal, guitar), Dave Davies (guitar, vocal), Bob Henrit (drums), Jim Rodford (bass), Mark Haley (keyboards). Ticket prices $15-$20. Venue capacities 500-1,500 except as noted. The two dancers are absent from this club tour, mainly because the venues are too small to accommodate their performance, but probably also because the band wants to appear back-to-basics. Virtually all shows are sell-outs. At almost every stop both Ray and Dave do local radio spots to help promote the evening shows and advertise the new CD. Booked by Rob Light at CAA (Creative Artists Agency).

Friday 23rd

Button South *Hallandale, FL* 8:00pm, with The Rockafellas

Saturday 24th

Vinoy Park *St Petersburg, FL* 4:00pm, *95-YNF Birthday Concert*, with Paul Rodgers & Company, Gene Loves Jezebel, U-ROK
Free outdoor concert attended by 35,000 on the occasion of radio station 95-YNF's fifth birthday. The Kinks go on stage one hour late, at 8:30pm. (Day off in Tampa follows.)

Monday 26th

The Roxy (Theatre) *Atlanta, GA* 8:00pm, with The Ottoman Empire

---

→ INDICATES EVENT AROUND THIS TIME BUT WITH NO FIRM DATE

Tuesday 27th
Rocky's *Charlotte, NC* with Flat Earth
The Kinks play late, 12:05am-1:25am. (Travel day follows.)

Thursday 29th
The Boathouse *Norfolk, VA* with Boy-O-Boy
Attended by 750 out of 1,500 tickets on sale.

Friday 30th
The Bayou *Washington, DC*
Green Berry Woods were scheduled to open but cancelled or simply didn't show up. A sell-out audience of 500 attend, but the band plays only a 75-minute set.

May

Saturday 1st
Theatre Of Living Arts *Philadelphia, PA* with Ken Kwedder
The opening act is booed off stage after three songs. (Travel day follows.)

Monday 3rd
Toad's Place *New Haven, CT* 7:30pm, with Velvet & Becker

Tuesday 4th
Avalon Ballroom *Boston, MA* 8:00pm, with Charlie Feron
Tonight's venue is the site of the former Boston Tea Party where The Kinks played in 1969 and 1970. (Day off follows in Boston.)
Set-list: 'Around The Dial' (intro), 'Destroyer', 'Low Budget', 'Misfits', 'Apeman', 'Phobia', 'Drift Away', 'Wall Of Fire', 'Only A Dream', 'Harry Rag', 'I'm Not Like Everybody Else', 'Hatred (A Duet)', 'Celluloid Heroes', 'Welcome To Sleazy Town' (intro only), 'Still Searching', 'Till The End Of The Day', 'Come Dancing', 'All Day And All Of The Night', 'Scattered', 'Lola', 'Days', 'Muswell Hillbilly', medley 'You Really Got Me'/ 'Boston Massachusetts USA' (improvisation).

Thursday 6th
The Chance *Poughkeepsie, NY* 8:00pm, with Joe Durso
Marathon two-hour show at this 600-capacity club.

Friday 7th
J.R.'s Fastlane *Providence, RI* 7:30pm, with The Gift
Although not announced to the audience, the show is terminated prematurely due to a bomb scare phoned in toward the end of the show.

Saturday 8th
Einsenhower Hall Theatre, United States Military Academy *West Point, NY* 8:00pm, with Golden & Carillo
Day off in New York City follows.

Monday 10th
Hammerjacks *Baltimore, MD*

Tuesday 11th
The Stone Pony *Asbury Park, NJ* 7:00pm, with Jeffrey Gaines
Tension between Ray and Dave is noticeably high on-stage tonight, especially during 'Hatred (A Duet)' when there are a number of exchanges of hand gestures and glares.

Wednesday 12th
))) **RADIO** Electric Lady Studios *New York, NY.* WNEW-FM *Richard Neer Show* live performance 'Around The Dial' (intro), 'Destroyer', 'Phobia', 'Drift Away', 'Only A Dream', 'Apeman', 'Harry Rag', 'Hatred (A Duet)', 'Come Dancing', 'Somebody Stole My Car', 'Low Budget', 'Death Of A Clown' 8:50-9:30pm. Live radio broadcast hosted by Richard Neer in front of an invited audience of about 25 people. 'Death Of A Clown' is an encore for the audience, not broadcast. Ray is unhappy with the performance and leaves with the tapes. Earlier in the day Ray has been editing video all day at National Video Studios.

Thursday 13th
The Academy *New York, NY* 8:00pm, with Brenda Kahn
"The Kinks are expert at the informal," writes Peter Watrous in *The New York Times*, "and for over an hour they turned the show into a private concert for friends. Where most bands from the 1960s have long ago succumbed to the necessities of the pop process – canned comments, a spectacular show – and can barely disguise contempt for the audience or self-disgust, The Kinks are shockingly spontaneous, and completely willing to sell themselves for the thrill of a singalong. It's as if they actually believe that a rock concert can be an improvisational event, featuring both the band and the audience, and that anything can happen in the admixture." (Travel day to London follows.)
☆ At Christie's auction house in London, Dave's green hunting jacket and shirt are sold for £1,870 (about $2,900).

Tuesday 25th
❏ **TV** NBC Television Studios *Burbank, CA.* NBC *The Tonight Show With Jay Leno* Ray & Dave Davies live performance 'Hatred (A Duet)', 'Celluloid Heroes' 11:30pm-12:30am EDT. First anniversary show, broadcast in stereo. 'Hatred' is backed by members of The Branford Marsalis Band. (Ray flies back to London directly after the show, while Dave remains in LA.)

Thursday 27th – Sunday 30th
Ray is again teaching at a British songwriting seminar, now a regular event that he began last October.

Monday 31st
Ray does press duties to promote the upcoming TV broadcast of his *Weird Nightmare* Charles Mingus documentary. Travel day back to US follows, in order to honour three Midwest dates remaining from the longer tour originally planned.

June

Wednesday 2nd
Star Plaza Theatre *Merrillville, IN* 8:00pm, with comedian Ken Sevara

Thursday 3rd
Union Station *St Louis, MO* 7:00pm, with Suave Octopus; sponsored by KSHE-FM/Budweiser
Free concert, part of a summer series. (Travel day follows.)

Saturday 5th
Central Park *Kaukauna, WI* 1:00-10:45pm, *River Jam Festival 93*, with Bad Haji, Roller, Tambora, The Ozark Mountain Daredevils, Nuff Z' Nuff
During the show The Kinks play an impromptu version of 'It's Only Make Believe' as a tribute to Conway Twitty who died today. A scheduled taping in Chicago for MTV's popular *Unplugged* show, possibly at the Club Park West, was scheduled at this time but cancelled. (Travel day follows to London.)

Monday 7th+

Ray is in London doing more press to help promote the British debut of his Mingus documentary, to be shown on TV this week.

Sunday 13th

Channel 4 TV in the UK broadcasts Ray's Charles Mingus documentary *Weird Nightmare* at 7:00pm in the *Sound Stuff* series.

Monday 14th

❏ **TV** BBC Television Centre (Studio 4) *west London*. BBC-2 *Later With Jools* live performance 'Over The Edge', 'The Informer', 'Till The End Of The Day' broadcast June 18th 11:45pm. Also on are Aimee Mann, Belly, and others. (Day off follows, then travel day to Stockholm.)

➪ **TOUR STARTS** *Phobia: European Tour* (Jun 17th – Jul 11th). **Line-up**: Ray Davies (lead vocal, guitar), Dave Davies (guitar, vocal), Bob Henrit (drums), Jim Rodford (bass), Mark Haley (keyboards), Pat Crosbie, Suzie Thomas (dancers).

Thursday 17th

Moderna Museets Trädgård *Stockholm, Sweden* 8:00pm, with Blur

Emerging young UK act Blur is personally chosen by Ray to appear as openers at the Museum Of Modern Art garden area tonight, with about 900 in attendance.

Set-list: 'Around The Dial' (intro), 'The Hard Way', 'Low Budget', 'Drift Away', 'Over The Edge', 'Scattered', 'Wall Of Fire', 'Dead End Street', 'Only A Dream', 'Come Dancing', 'I'm Not Like Everybody Else', 'Phobia', 'Welcome To Sleazy Town', 'Hatred (A Duet)', 'Till The End Of The Day', 'All Day And All Of The Night', 'Apeman', 'Sunny Afternoon', medley 'Aggravation' / 'New World' (tape), 'David Watts', 'Days', 'Lola', 'You Really Got Me'.

Friday 18th

Hellerudsletta *Oslo, Norway* 7:30pm, *Sommerfestivalen 1993*, with Uriah Heep, Glenn Hughes & Friends, Ace Of Base, Bee Flat

Saturday 19th

Mølleparken *Ålborg, Denmark* 11:00am-10:00pm, *Open Air 93 Festival*, with Shu-bi-dua, Lisa Nilsson, Bachman-Turner Overdrive, Ancient Tribe

Attended by around 12,000 fans. (Travel day follows.)

Monday 21st

Huxley's Neue Welt *Berlin, Germany*

Tuesday 22nd

Batschschkapp *Frankfurt, Germany*

Early into tonight's show Ray does an impromptu rendition of the rock standard 'Hey Joe', but sings it as 'Hey Donnie' with bitterly sarcastic lyrics, aimed at Columbia Records' chief Don Ienner who according to the previous day's *New York Post* "plans to ditch dinosaur rock on the label" and "now wants to drop the Kinks". The comment reaches Ray in Germany, who clearly takes offence at the public reference, and it likely weakens the relationship between The Kinks and Columbia. (The dancers do not appear with The Kinks tonight because the stage is too small.) Shows at the Lycabettus, Athens, Greece originally set for 23rd-24th are cancelled. (Travel day to London follows and then two days off.)

Saturday 26th

Pyramid Stage *Glastonbury, Somerset* *Glastonbury Festival Of Contemporary Performing Arts*, with Hothouse Flowers, Christy Moore, Lenny Kravitz; sponsored by *NME*

Three-day festival running June 25th-27th. The Kinks' spot is added after Crosby Stills & Nash cancel, originally as headliners on Sunday. The Kinks are then moved to Saturday with Lenny Kravitz as headliner, but he defers to them at the last moment and lets them close the show. (Two days off in London follow.)

Tuesday 29th

Forum am Schlosspark *Ludwigsburg, Germany* 7:30pm
Travel day follows.

July

Thursday 1st

Beurs van Berlage *Amsterdam, Netherlands* 93 *Drum Rhythm Festival*, with Pat Mears

First of a three-day festival held at various locations around Amsterdam, this one with up to 1,500 capacity.

☆ Tonight and the next a full-scale production of Ray's *Preservation Act 2* is staged by the Boston Rock Opera at the Middle East, a club in Cambridge, MA. The theatrical organisation consists of area musicians and actors and actresses. Their show is reprised December 11th-12th this year at the same venue, and will be revived in 1998 on an even larger scale in Boston.

Friday 2nd

E-Werk *Cologne, Germany*

Saturday 3rd

Stadtpark Open Air *Hamburg, Germany*
Travel day follows.

Monday 5th

Circus-Krone Bau *Munich, Germany*

Tuesday 6th

Sommer Arena *Vienna, Austria* 8:00pm

Wednesday 7th

Schlossberg-Kasemattenbüne *Graz, Austria* 7:00pm
Travel day follows.

Friday 9th

Arena de Riazor *La Coruña, Spain* *Concierto de los Mil Años*, with Bob Dylan, Chuck Berry, Wilson Pickett
Attended by a crowd of 30,000.

☆ 'Still Searching' US promo single released around this time.

Saturday 10th

Outdoor event *Frauenfeld, Switzerland* *Out In The Green Festival*, with Bryan Adams (headliner), The Beach Boys (special guests), Mr Big, Heroes Del Silencios, Inner Circle, The Jeff Healey Band, Saga

Part of a three-day festival, also featuring Faith No More, Lenny Kravitz, Midnight Oil, and Sting. There is a confrontation between Dave and keyboardist Mark Haley backstage during the 'New World' segment. Haley will play tomorrow's London show but quits The Kinks thereafter.

Sunday 11th

Royal Albert Hall *Kensington, central London* 7:30pm, with David Gray

Ray is quoted as ranting on stage at one point during this sell-out show: "If there are any journalists here, don't review the show. I'm tired of

Ray belts it out in Amsterdam, July 1st 1993, with keyboardist Mark Haley in the shadows.

kinks'93

reading that The Kinks are a 1960s band. We're not a 1960s band. Our songs are part of Britain's heritage, and that heritage is being thrown away." Tony Patrick is certainly there, for *The Times*. "The Kinks (est. 1964) may be prehistoric," he writes, "but dinosaurs, as *Jurassic Park* is reminding the world, were often fast-moving and quick-witted creatures, and can be reborn; the saurian smiles of the Davies brothers confirmed that they are entering their fourth decade in blockbusting form."

Set-list: 'Opening' (tape), 'Till The End Of The Day', 'Where Have All The Good Times Gone', 'Low Budget', 'Apeman', 'Phobia', 'Only A Dream', 'Scattered', 'Celluloid Heroes', medley 'Loony Balloon' / 'Drift Away', 'I'm Not Like Everybody Else', 'Dedicated Follower Of Fashion', 'Harry Rag', 'The Informer', 'Dead End Street', 'Still Searching', 'Come Dancing', 'Aggravation', 'Death Of A Clown', 'Sunny Afternoon', 'Welcome To Sleazy Town', 'All Day And All Of The Night', 'Lola', 'Days', 'You Really Got Me', 'Waterloo Sunset', 'Twist And Shout'.

Monday 12th

Mark Haley faxes his resignation to Kinks road manager Dave Bowen at Konk.

✰ During this week at Konk Ray edits the song 'Phobia' as a possible new single.

Scattered CD single released in the UK.

Wednesday 21st – Friday 23rd

Following Haley's resignation, Rodford and Henrit rehearse with their old keyboard-playing colleague Ian Gibbons at Konk Studios in north London during these three days, with Ray joining them on the Friday. Gibbons will play with The Kinks on the upcoming US dates. (Day off on the 24th and travel to the US on 25th.)

➪ **TOUR STARTS** *Phobia: US Tour Summer '93* (Jul 26th – Aug 22nd). **Line-up**: Ray Davies (lead vocal, guitar), Dave Davies (guitar, vocal), Bob Henrit (drums), Jim Rodford (bass), Ian Gibbons (keyboards), Pat Crosbie, Suzie Thomas (dancers). Tickets $12.50-$35.50. Venues are generally the large "sheds" or amphitheatres with quite large capacities, able to accommodate additional thousands on the large lawns typically found to the rear of the roofed seating. Capacity of these is around 9,000 up to about 20,000, but attendance on the tour is not strong and the bookings seem over-ambitious, especially considering the relatively poor sales of the *Phobia* CD.

Monday 26th

Saratoga Performing Arts Center *Saratoga Springs, NY* 8:15pm, with Aimee Mann

Tuesday 27th

Great Woods Center For The Performing Arts *Mansfield, MA* 7:30pm, with Aimee Mann

As a spur-of-the-moment gesture Ray comes on stage solo prior to The Kinks' performance and does a song and a half before the taped introduction, 'Opening', that regularly begins the band's show. Inspired by the wild reception it receives, Ray from this point on will start concerts in this manner. The solo spot will expand from the song and a half here to often three or four and a half songs, at first adding 'A Well Respected Man' and then 'Dedicated Follower Of Fashion' as the tour progresses.

The *Providence Journal* says: "In concert the band has a rough-hewn unpredictability that is part of its charm. ... A high-spirited Ray Davies led the band through an engaging 90-minute set, and if he dropped a microphone at one point, it wasn't about to bother anyone. Sadly only 3,500 were on hand, a disappointing turnout for a rock legend." (Three days off in New York follow.)

Set-list: 'Sweet Lady Genevieve' (Ray solo); 'Do It Again' (Ray solo, extract), 'Opening' (tape), 'Till The End Of The Day', 'Where Have All The Good Times Gone', 'Phobia', 'Low Budget', medley 'Loony Balloon' / 'Drift Away', 'Only A Dream', 'Apeman' (full version with spoken section), 'The Informer', 'Come Dancing', medley 'Aggravation' / 'New World' (tape, with dancers), 'Still Searching', medley 'A Gallon Of Gas' (intro) / 'Welcome To Sleazy Town' (with dancers), 'All Day And All Of The Night', 'David Watts', 'You Really Got Me', 'Victoria', 'Lola'.

Friday 30th

Jones Beach Theatre *Wantagh, NY* 8:00pm, with Aimee Mann

Saturday 31st

Big Birch ski lodge *Patterson, NY* 8:00pm, with Aimee Mann

August

Sunday 1st

Riverside Park Stadium *Agawam, MA* 7:00pm, with Joan Jett & The Blackhearts

Day off in New York City follows, originally booked for the Roseland Ballroom there.

Tuesday 3rd

Garden State Arts Center *Holmdel, NJ* 8:30pm, with Aimee Mann

Ray announces on-stage during tonight's show that 'Phobia' may soon be a new single.

Wednesday 4th

State Theatre *Easton, PA* 7:30pm, with Aimee Mann

Thursday 5th

Merriweather Post Pavilion *Columbia, MD* 8:00pm, with Aimee Mann

Around 1,000 to 2,000 attend at this 15,000 capacity venue. (Travel day follows.)

Saturday 7th

Iron City Light Amphitheatre *Pittsburgh, PA* with Aimee Mann

Pittsburgh Regatta Festival is happening the same night and its fireworks distract the audience. Ray is irritated by this and sings an impromptu song, 'Regatta My Ass'.

Evidently he has broken a couple of toes while kicking something in a fit of anger before coming on . Despite all this, tonight's performance is later voted top concert of 1993 by reviewer Ed Masley of the *Pittsburgh Post Gazette*. (A travel day for the band follows and then a day off in Toronto.)

Tuesday 10th

Kingswood Music Theatre, Canada's Wonderland *Maple, ON, Canada* 8:00pm

Thursday 12th

Mann Music Center *Philadelphia, PA* 8:00pm, with Aimee Mann

Tonight's show is recorded, and 'You Really Got Me' later included on *To The Bone*, first issued in 1994. (Travel day follows.)

Saturday 14th

While the band has time off in Columbus, OH, Ray sees an insurance doctor who authorises cancellation of the remaining tour dates because

➜ INDICATES EVENT AROUND THIS TIME BUT WITH NO FIRM DATE

of the condition of the broken toes, pending examination over the weekend by a second doctor. The decision to cancel will be made on Monday. It is believed that the relationship with Columbia goes completely dead after the decision to cancel tour dates.

Sunday 15th
Newport Music Hall *Columbus, OH* 8:00pm, with Aimee Mann

Monday 16th
Club Eastbrook *Grand Rapids, MI* 8:00pm
Aimee Mann cancels at short notice, including the tour's remaining dates, and with no replacement found The Kinks are without an opening act. In Los Angeles The Kinks' booking agency, CAA, announces that all "western dates of the tour are cancelled" due to the aggravated condition of Ray's broken toes, and that they are now rescheduling dates for October, including Mexico.

Tuesday 17th
New Pine Knob Music Theatre *Clarkston, MI* 7:30pm, with Vudu Hippies
Reportedly only 547 turn up to this venue, which potentially has a capacity of 7,253 (reduced from its maximum 15,253). A travel day and then a day off in Cleveland follows, where Ray visits the Rock & Roll Hall Of Fame site and meets museum officials there. He discusses loaning items for a proposed Kinks exhibit there.

Thursday 19th
Nautica Stage *Cleveland, OH* 7:30pm, with Oroboros
A sell-out at this 4,000 capacity amphitheatre. During their soundcheck the band plays 'The Last Of The Steam Powered Trains' and 'Johnny Thunder'. (Day off follows in Chicago.)

Saturday 21st
Poplar Creek Music Theatre *Hoffman Estates, IL* 8:00pm, with Rattlin' Bones

Sunday 22nd
River's Edge Water Park *Somerset, WI* *Jurassic Jam*, with Kansas, Lamont Cranston
The second of a two-day festival located in Greater St Paul, MN. Pat Travers and The Jeff Healey Band headlined the previous day. (Travel day to London follows for the band minus Ray and Dave; Ray stays in the US a few days.)
☆ The postponed tour dates are generally pushed to October. Some of these shows are not cancelled locally until as late as the 26th. The cancelled concerts are: August 24th Grizzily Rose, Denver, CO; 25th Salt Air Amphitheater, Ogden, UT; 27th Hearst Greek Theatre, University of California-Berkeley, Berkeley, CA; 28th Sacramento Community Theatre, Sacramento, CA; 30th Copley Symphony Hall, San Diego, CA; 31st Celebrity Theatre, Anaheim, CA; September 1st Wiltern Theatre, Los Angeles, CA; 2nd *MTV Music Awards*, Los Angeles, CA; 5th *23rd Annual Bumbershoot Festival*, Seattle Center Coliseum, Seattle, WA; 6th Portland, OR.
There was also a tentative booking for Mexico City on September 11th. A pencilled-in visit to Australia is cancelled, but the Japanese jaunt following that remains in place.

September

Ray is in London for the entire month working on projects. The tentative deal for the Mingus documentary *Weird Nightmare* to be

aired in the US on the Arts & Entertainment Channel falls through around this time. Dave remains in Los Angeles, where on the 2nd he and Nancy have a third child, a son named Eddie. Late in the month, Columbia issues 'Drift Away' as a promotional CD single in the US.

October

☞ **TOUR STARTS** *Tour Of Japan* (Oct 3rd – 14th). **Line-up**: Ray Davies (lead vocal, guitar), Dave Davies (guitar, vocal), Bob Henrit (drums), Jim Rodford (bass), Ian Gibbons (keyboards) Pat Crosbie plus Dana (surname unknown) or Suzie Thomas (dancers). Promoted by Smash/Hot Stuff Promotions. The band travels to Japan on the 1st and has time off in Osaka on the 2nd. No opening acts at any shows, as is the tradition in Japan. Venue sizes are typically 2,000-2,400 except as noted.

Sunday 3rd – Monday 4th
Kosei-Nenkin Hall *Osaka, Japan*
Set-list (3rd): 'Sweet Lady Genevieve' (Ray solo), 'A Well Respected Man' (Ray solo), 'Do It Again' (Ray solo, extract), 'Opening' (tape), 'Till The End Of The Day', 'Destroyer', 'Low Budget', 'Phobia', medley 'Loony Balloon' / 'Drift Away', 'Did Ya', 'Apeman', 'Celluloid Heroes', 'Over The Edge', 'Only A Dream', 'Come Dancing', medley 'Aggravation' / 'New World' (tape), 'I'm Not Like Everybody Else', medley 'A Gallon Of Gas' (intro) / 'Welcome To Sleazy Town', 'All Day And All Of The Night', 'Lola', 'You Really Got Me'.

Tuesday 5th – Wednesday 6th
Kani Hoken Hall *Tokyo, Japan*
Travel day follows.

Friday 8th
Shimin Hall *Fukuoka, Japan*
Travel day follows.

Sunday 10th
Kani Hoken Hall *Tokyo, Japan*

Monday 11th
Diamond Hall *Nagoya, Japan*
At this smaller venue there are 390 attending. The Kinks include 'Village Green Preservation Society' and Buddy Holly's 'Peggy Sue' in the set tonight. (Travel day follows.)

Wednesday 13th
Factory Hall *Saporo, Japan*

Thursday 14th
Public Hall *Shibuya, Japan*
Day off following, with travel to London. Time off follows.
☆ The US make-up dates were cancelled late on the 12th, still citing Ray's toe injuries as the reason. Cancelled dates: October 16th Wiltern Theatre, Los Angeles, CA; 17th Celebrity Theatre, Anaheim, CA; 18th Copley Symphony Hall, San Diego, CA; 20th Grizzily Rose, Denver, CO; 22nd Portland, OR; 23rd Hearst Greek Theatre, University of California-Berkeley, Berkeley, CA; 24th Ziegfield Ballroom, Reno Hilton, Reno, NV (replacing the original Sacramento date which was not available).

→ ● **RECORDING** Konk Studios *Hornsey, north London*. Later in the month Ray is doing demos with his daughter Victoria Davies. Ray also produces some recordings with Shut Up Frank, a band including ex-Kinks drummer Mick Avory, but nothing is ever issued.

kinks'93

November

▷ **TOUR STARTS** *Phobia: British Tour* (Nov 1st – 25th). **Line-up**: Ray Davies (lead vocal, guitar), Dave Davies (guitar, vocal), Bob Henrit (drums), Jim Rodford (bass), Ian Gibbons (keyboards), Dana (surname unknown) and Pat Crosbie (dancers). An old-style full scale tour of Britain that harks back to The Kinks' tour circuit in their package-show days of the 1960s. Venue size is in the range of 1,000-2,000 capacity and most are sell-outs or close, though a few poor turnouts are noted. The tour is initially set to start in Lincoln on October 29th but the first weekend of dates are moved later into the tour.

Monday 1st
Empire Theatre *Sunderland* 8:00pm, with Strangeways

Tuesday 2nd
Victoria Theatre *Halifax, Yorks* 8:00pm, with Strangeways

Wednesday 3rd
DeMontfort Hall *Leicester 8:00pm, with Strangeways*
Only 900 in this 2,000 capacity hall. (Day off follows.)

Friday 5th
Mansfield Leisure Centre *Mansfield, Notts* 8:00pm, with Strangeways

Saturday 6th
Brentwood Centre *Brentwood, Essex* 8:00pm, with Strangeways

Sunday 7th
Mayflower Theatre *Southampton* 8:00pm, with Strangeways
Day off follows.

Tuesday 9th
English Riviera *Torquay* 8:00pm, with Strangeways
Day off follows.

Thursday 11th
Barbican Centre *York* 8:00pm, with Strangeways

Friday 12th
Apollo Theatre *Manchester* 8:00pm, with Strangeways

Saturday 13th
Floral Pavilion Theatre *New Brighton, Wallasey, Ches* 8:00pm, with Strangeways
Day off follows.

Monday 15th
The Hexagon *Reading* 8:00pm, with Strangeways
Only A Dream CD maxi-single/vinyl single released in the UK.

Tuesday 16th
A day off from the tour, but Ray and Dave keep busy with media duties, including an interview at BBC Broadcasting House broadcast on BBC Greater London Radio after midnight where the two perform an acoustic version of 'Days'.

It is probably at this time that the two Davies appear at Virgin 1215 Radio studios in London for the *Big Red Mug Show* (broadcast on Saturday 20th 10:00am-1:00pm and further on December 28th) during which they perform 'Somebody Stole My Car'.

Only A Dream single

1/A **'Only A Dream'** (R. DAVIES).
2/B **'Somebody Stole My Car'** (R. DAVIES).
3 **'Babies'** (R. DAVIES).

UK release November 15th 1993 (vinyl 7-inch A/B Columbia 659922 7; CD maxi-single 1/2/3 Columbia 659922 2). Musicians and recording details as *Phobia* album (see March 18th). **Chart high** UK none.

Wednesday 17th
Lower Common Room, University of East Anglia *Norwich* 8:00pm, with Strangeways
The *UEA News* reviewer writes: "[We're here] to sing along to the old ones. And the chances are we sing them more faithfully than Ray, whose relationship with most of the tunes resembles playful flirtation more than obsessive commitment. ... A particularly jaunty 'All Day And All Of The Night' has the elderlies trembling for an encore."

Thursday 18th
Corn Exchange *Cambridge* 8:00pm, with Strangeways

Friday 19th
St David's Hall *Cardiff, Wales* 8:00pm, with Strangeways
Day off follows.

Sunday 21st
Ritz Theatre *Lincoln* 8:00pm, with Strangeways
A bit of Dave's 'Lincoln County' is played tonight in honour of the locale. Also played is 'Oklahoma USA', which is some miles away.

Monday 22nd
Civic Hall *Wolverhampton* 8:00pm, with Strangeways

Tuesday 23rd
The Dome *Doncaster, Yorks* 8:00pm, with Strangeways
Day off follows.

Thursday 25th
Royal Concert Hall *Glasgow, Scotland* 8:00pm, with Strangeways
This sell-out show attended by 2,400 fans is recorded and filmed, and material from it will be used for the next project, a career-retrospective CD *To The Bone*. (Travel back to London follows the next day as the British portion of the tour ends. Tentative dates in the Channel Islands on the 28th-29th are never finalised.)
Set-list: 'Sweet Lady Genevieve' (Ray solo, extract), A Well Respected Man (Ray solo), 'Autumn Almanac' (Ray solo), 'Stop Your Sobbing' (Ray solo), 'Do It Again' (Ray solo, extract), 'Opening' (tape), 'Till The End Of The Day', 'Scattered', 'Low Budget', 'Apeman', 'Phobia', 'Too Much On My Mind', 'Harry Rag', 'It's Alright (Don't Think About It)', 'Death Of A Clown', medley 'Dead End Street' / 'Sunny Afternoon', 'Only A Dream', 'I'm Not Like Everybody Else', 'Wall Of Fire', 'Dead End Street', 'Oklahoma USA', 'Over The Edge', 'Come Dancing', medley 'Aggravation' / 'New World' (tape), 'All Day And All Of The Night', 'Lola', 'Welcome To Sleazy Town', 'Days', 'You Really Got Me'.

December

▷ **TOUR STARTS** *Phobia: Germany/Switzerland Tour* (Dec 2nd – 17th). **Line-up**: Ray Davies (lead vocal, guitar), Dave Davies (guitar, vocal), Bob Henrit (drums), Jim Rodford (bass), Ian Gibbons (keyboards). Dana (surname unknown) and Pat Crosbie (dancers). The band travels from London on the 1st. Gibbons is involved in a car crash on the way to the airport in which he is slightly injured. He continues on with his flight, is examined at a hospital in Germany, and is able to complete the tour. The dancers are primarily featured on 'Aggravation' / 'New World' and 'Welcome To Sleazy Town'. This tour has been completely re-booked and many dates shuffled and changed before being finalised.

Thursday 2nd
Jurahalle *Neumarkt, Germany* with Katrina & The Waves

Friday 3rd
Music-Zirkus *Dresden, Germany* with Katrina & The Waves

Saturday 4th
Terminal 1 *Munich, Germany* 3:00pm, *Rock 'N' Bayern 93*, with Katrina & The Waves
Five local bands are also on the bill. (Day off in Munich follows.)

Monday 6th
Capitol *Hannover, Germany* with Katrina & The Waves
Hans-Christian Jacobi writes in the *Hannoversche Allgemeine Zeitung*: "Katrina & The Waves had already brought a fresh breeze into the concert hall that grew to a hurricane when Ray, Dave and the band played. They blew away any questions about age, up-to-date-ness, or the past. I never knew how productive it can be when brothers hate each other."

Tuesday 7th
Neufang-Kulturhalle *Saarbrücken, Germany* with Katrina & The Waves
Travel day and then a day off follow.

Friday 10th
Halle Gartlage *Osnabrück, Germany* with Katrina & The Waves

Saturday 11th
Westfallenhalle 2 *Dortmund, Germany* with Katrina & The Waves

Sunday 12th
Kulturzentrum *Erfurt, Germany* with Katrina & The Waves
Travel day follows.

Tuesday 14th
Roxy-Hallen *Ulm, Germany* with Katrina & The Waves
Set-list: 'Sweet Lady Genevieve' (Ray solo, extract), 'Stop Your Sobbing' (Ray solo), 'Sunny Afternoon' (Ray solo), 'Do It Again' (Ray solo, extract), 'Opening' (tape), 'Till The End Of The Day', 'Low Budget', 'Phobia', 'Scattered', 'A Well Respected Man', 'Death Of A Clown', 'It's Alright (Don't Think About It)', '20th Century Man', 'Dead End Street', 'Celluloid Heroes', 'Only A Dream', 'Apeman', 'Over The Edge', 'Come Dancing', medley 'Aggravation' / 'New World' (tape), 'All Day And All Of The Night', 'Waterloo Sunset', 'Welcome To Sleazy Town', 'Days' (extract), 'Hatred (A Duet)', 'Lola', 'You Really Got Me'.

Wednesday 15th
Schützenhaus Albisgüetli *Zürich, Switzerland* with Katrina & The Waves
Travel day follows.

Friday 17th
Wikinghalle *Flensburg-Handewitt, Germany* with Katrina & The Waves
Late-added final date for the tour. (Travel day back to London follows.)

Tuesday 21st
Ray is at BBC Broadcasting House where he is interviewed by Donna Luke, broadcast on BBC Greater London Radio 94.9 FM at 4:00pm. Ray is scheduled to perform solo but doesn't. He says that The Kinks have recorded a couple of new songs since *Phobia* with the plan to release a new single in March, and that he hopes to stage a musical based on *Phobia* by the end of next year.

The radio spot is probably tied in to the appearance The Kinks were due to make this same evening at a special year-end show, *The Kinks At Kristmas*, at Wembley Arena in north-west London (with guests Nine Below Zero).

The ambitious booking at the 12,000-capacity venue was cancelled only five days before showtime and rescheduled for March 16th. Slow ticket sales were reportedly part of the problem. Barring an upcoming radio and TV booking early in January – for which Dave is not present – the next five weeks are scheduled as time off, and the year ends as an ultimately disappointing if busy one for the band.

1994

The Kinks had given everything they had to offer in 1993, and the process of winding up the show began this year. Finally they were about to celebrate their past rather than fight it. This year marked the 30th anniversary of the band's initial success, and there seemed to be an unspoken recognition of that fact.

Once the band were freed from their contract with Columbia – and while still primed from a year of touring – they began the process of revisiting their entire catalogue and, perhaps with an eye towards issuing some sort of career retrospective, the never-say-die Kinks assembled at Konk to re-record a number of their early chestnuts. Ray had the foresight to film the proceedings and in effect created his own Kinks unplugged-style presentation in the process.

In September, 30 years since the band's jump to fame, Ray's unique "unofficial autobiography" was published, followed in short order by the release of a one-off Kinks album featuring some of the re-recordings done earlier in the year plus live material from the finale of their extensive 1993 touring. Although never announced as such, everything they did at this time seemed to speak silently of wrapping up their career. Short of the appearance of a full-career boxed set – which at the time was still a contractual nightmare – no better series of convenient bookending activities could have taken place.

January

On the 7th at the BBC's Maida Vale Studios in central London the band performs material for a radio broadcast 3:30-4:30pm on Radio-1's *Johnny Walker Show*. The Kinks are without Dave – who is "ill" – and so at short notice they substitute Level 42's guitarist, Jakko Jakszyk. They play 'Phobia', 'Over The Edge', 'Wall Of Fire' and 'Till The End Of The Day'. Cancelled, however, is an appearance today on BBC TV's *Danny Baker Show*.

It's a quiet month otherwise, as Ray and Dave pursue solo interests. Ray speaks of plans to do a solo album next, but there seems little progress with that idea.

Talk of a new Kinks single in March is dropped pending their official separation from Columbia Records.

Who singer Roger Daltrey is reportedly in contact with Ray to convince him to take part in a *Daltrey Sings Townshend* concert at Carnegie Hall in New York City on February 23rd-24th.

Daltrey is trying to get Ray to sing 'Pictures Of Lily' for the show as the vocalist always thought it was more of a Kinks song than a Who song. Ray declines.

February

As far as the public are concerned, The Kinks continue to be quiet. Ray and Dave continue to pursue separate interests.

Discussions of potential slots in February and March for make-up dates for the recently cancelled appearances on the US West Coast are never finalised.

March

→ On or about the 1st, The Kinks are officially released from their contract with Columbia Records. They are free to sign elsewhere. Dave is busy in Los Angeles on an unspecified film project. Ray's autobiography is being completed and is set for publication in September. Ray is also working on a proposed Kinks box-set and is shopping around various record companies.

Thursday 10th
❏ **TV** Channel 4 TV Studios *central London*. Channel 4 **Don't Forget Your Toothbrush** Ray with Jools Holland & His Big Band live performance 'You Really Got Me', 'Dead End Street', 'Bring Me Sunshine' broadcast March 12th. Ray also participates in a Kinks trivia competition on the show with American fan Tracy Noonan.

➪ **TOUR STARTS** *UK/Ireland Mini Tour* (Mar 19th – 26th). **Line-up**: Ray Davies (lead vocal, guitar), Dave Davies (guitar, vocal), Bob Henrit (drums), Jim Rodford (bass), Ian Gibbons (keyboards), Pat Crosbie, Louise Wodwell (dancers).

Saturday 19th
National Stadium, Royal Dublin Society *Dublin, Ireland*
8:00pm

Sunday 20th
Ulster Hall *Belfast, Northern Ireland*
Travel day follows.

→ INDICATES EVENT AROUND THIS TIME BUT WITH NO FIRM DATE

Tuesday 22nd

The Town & Country Club *Leeds* 7:00pm, with Nine Below Zero
Set-list: 'A Well Respected Man' (Ray solo), 'Autumn Almanac' (Ray solo), 'Stop Your Sobbing' (Ray solo), 'Sunny Afternoon' (Ray solo), 'Dedicated Follower Of Fashion' (Ray solo), 'Do It Again' (Ray solo, extract), 'Opening' (tape), 'Till The End Of The Day', 'The Hard Way', 'Low Budget', 'Scattered', 'Death Of A Clown', 'Phobia', 'Wall Of Fire', 'Living On A Thin Line', 'The Informer', 'Come Dancing', medley 'Aggravation' / 'New World' (tape), 'Dead End Street', 'Welcome To Sleazy Town', 'All Day And All Of The Night', 'Lola', 'Days', 'You Really Got Me', 'Twist And Shout'.

Thursday 24th

Aston Villa Sports & Leisure Centre *Birmingham* with Nine Below Zero

Friday 25th

Guildhall *Portsmouth* with Nine Below Zero
This show is filmed by the BBC for an upcoming documentary for which two songs will be used, 'Dead End Street' and 'I'm Not Like Everybody Else'. The BBC has also been conducting interviews with band members for the documentary. Tonight's show is also recorded: 'Sunny Afternoon' and 'Dedicated Follower' will appear on the 1994 single-CD and 1996 two-CD versions of *To The Bone*; 'Lola', 'Come Dancing', 'Till The End Of The Day', 'Give The People What They Want' and 'State Of Confusion' will be on the two-CD version only.

Saturday 26th

Wembley Arena *Wembley, north-west London* 7:30pm, with The Stranglers, Nine Below Zero

April

➔ Early in the month there are rehearsals for the four-man Kinks plus keyboard-player Ian Gibbons at Konk Studios in Hornsey, north London for their upcoming "unplugged" sessions.

On Sunday 10th the band probably records a backing track for a re-recording of **'The Village Green Preservation Society'** and **'Two Sisters'**. Both are recorded for possible use the following night, but remain unused.

'Village Green' will later be completed in the studio and issued on the *To The Bone* CD.

During a session from 10:30pm-2:30am on Monday 11th/Tuesday 12th at Konk, a session is filmed for the BBC documentary, scheduled for September broadcast. The format is an unplugged-style studio performance in front of 16 invited guests.

Performed on camera and recorded are **'Do You Remember Walter'** (two takes), **'Death Of A Clown'** (four takes, one with Ray rather than Dave on vocals), **'Too Much On My Mind'**, **'Sweet Lady Genevieve'**, **'Uncle Son'** (three takes), **'Muswell Hillbillies'** (three takes), **'Set Me Free'**, **'See My Friends'** (with a drum backing-track), **'Tired Of Waiting For You'**, **'Apeman'** (done Cajun-style), and **'A Gallon Of Gas'** (long version).

Performed off-camera and informally for the audience are versions of oldies including: 'Singing The Blues', 'Sea Of Love', 'Untitled' (improvisation), medley 'You're Going To Get Trashed Tomorrow' (based on the traditional Latin American folk song 'Guantanamera') / 'Twist And Shout', 'When You Were A Child' (Dave acoustic instrumental), and 'So You Want To Be A Rock'n'Roll Star' (Dave acoustic instrumental).

Not everything planned is completed because the film crew has to leave at 2:30am.

The BBC has been filming interview footage during March. Further unplugged recording is done on the 12th at Konk, without an audience, including **'Waterloo Sunset'** and **'Picture Book'**; also probably recorded for the project around this time are **'Better Things'** and **'Don't Forget To Dance'**.

Dave returns to Los Angeles some time after the Konk sessions to continue work on a film project, details unknown.

May

Dave is still in Los Angeles working on his film project.

Ray is shopping for a new record label, including Island Records, but nothing comes to fruition at this time. He continues work on a possible Kinks box-set.

On the 26th Christie's auction house in London sells Mick Avory's hunting-jacket stage suit for £1,100 (about $1,700).

BBC-2 television broadcasts on the 30th Ray's 'Sitting In The Stands', a football song based on 'Autumn Almanac', on the programme *Dear Football: Goalmouthing*.

June

⤷ **TOUR STARTS** *Scandinavian Mini Tour* (Jun 9th – 11th). Line-up: Ray Davies (lead vocal, guitar), Dave Davies (guitar, vocal), Bob Henrit (drums), Jim Rodford (bass), Ian Gibbons (keyboards), Pat Crosbie and (probably) Louise Wodwell (dancers).

Thursday 9th

Rockefeller's Music Hall *Oslo, Norway* 9:00pm

Friday 10th

Excersisheden *Heden, Gothenburg, Sweden* *Göteborg All Star Festival*, with No Limits, Scam, Electric Boys, Pride & Glory (replacing ELO who cancelled)
A three-day festival, beset with bad weather during The Kinks' show. Following their performance Ray agrees at the last minute to appear as a substitute for Van Morrison at a competing Swedish festival, *Brunnsparkenfestivalen*, at Brunnsparken in Gothenburg, but the crowd has already left when he arrives at 1:00am.
Set-list: 'A Well Respected Man' (Ray solo), 'Sunny Afternoon' (Ray solo), 'Autumn Almanac' (Ray solo), 'Dedicated Follower Of Fashion' (Ray solo), '20th Century Man', 'Till The End Of The Day', 'Give The People What They Want', 'State Of Confusion', 'Low Budget', 'Gothenburg Blues' (improvisation), 'Scattered', 'Phobia', 'Wall Of Fire', 'Apeman', 'Alcohol', 'Come Dancing', medley 'Aggravation' / 'New World' (tape), 'All Day And All Of The Night', 'Welcome To Sleazy Town', 'Lola', 'Days', 'You Really Got Me'.

Saturday 11th

Outdoor event *Middelfart, Denmark* 11:00am, *Rock Under Broen Festival*, with Status Quo (headliners), Gnags, Smokie, Shakin' Stevens, Bamses Venner, Dizzy Miss Lizzy, Bachman-Turner Overdrive
Attendance at this festival is 20,000. (Travel day back to London follows.)

➔ Dave remains behind in London for a short while. One of his plans is to re-record some of his 1960s performances with The Kinks for use in his film project, but this doesn't appear to happen.
☆ *Publishers Weekly* announces that Dave Davies is writing a new

book called *Getting All The Kinks Out* with New York freelance writers Roger Friedman and Marianne Naples. Both will eventually be dropped from the project.

☆ By mid month Dave is back in Los Angeles and is a guest at a Smithereens concert on Sunday 19th. He joins the New Jersey-based band on-stage at The House Of Blues in LA during their encore and performs 'Creeping Jean' and two other songs. The performance will later lead Dave to consider using The Smithereens for solo shows in 1997.

☆ Dave's film project is now dropped from contention as he concentrates on his book.

July / August

Dave is in Los Angeles in the early part of July working on his book, but flies to London mid month for at least a few weeks work at Konk – presumably further post-production on the *To The Bone* CD that Ray is assembling.

During August, Ray is probably working on the finalising of mixes for *To The Bone* and also preparing for the upcoming promotional work for his book.

September

Dave is in London shopping for a UK deal for his book. He later recounts that he now learns that Ray has written his own book, which is out shortly. He feels he's been beaten to it, and that publishers might be less interested in his work because the market for Kinks books is saturated.

Nicky Hopkins, who played on many classic Kinks recordings of the 1960s, dies on the 6th at age 50 in Nashville, TN.

On the 12th *X-Ray: The Unauthorised Biography* by Ray Davies is published in the UK by Penguin/Viking, and Ray begins a press tour.

Tom Hibbert reviews the book for *The Mail On Sunday*, identifying it as beyond the regular rock tome. "Davies employs a peculiar and crafty device: he assumes the identity of an unnamed biographer being commissioned by a mysterious firm, the 'Corporation', to interview and write about this Kinks person – and to expose him as a charlatan. … The process allows the author to declare himself both a nincompoop (he does not flinch at describing his many human shortcomings) and a genius (his biographer begins to find his subject's words and music quite remarkable), and to write a novel and a true story, all at the same time. Pretentious? Perhaps. But clever with it."

Robert Sandall in *The Sunday Times* is less sure. "*X-Ray* makes a decently readable tale of pop life in the 1960s," he writes. "There is a good crop of anecdotes about The Beatles, The Rolling Stones and the rest. It is a bit of a surprise to discover that the north-London boy who tiptoed around love and sex in his songs was such an avid off-duty womaniser. Indeed, the book would be more interesting if we heard less of the laddish capers and more about how the music was made. … What seems to have gone missing here, aside from a convincing sense of humour, is Davies's skill as an editor. His best songs were masterpieces of concise observation: *X-Ray* would be twice as entertaining at half the length."

Ray is at BBC Broadcasting House on the 13th for a guest appearance with host Simon Mayo, broadcast on Radio-1 9:00pm-12midnight. Besides being interviewed, Ray performs with acoustic guitar and sings three songs, 'Waterloo Sunset', 'Days' and a brand new composition based on a character from his new book, 'The Ballad Of Julie Finkle'. In the course of the interview, which naturally centres

on the new book, he announces the new Kinks album, *To The Bone*, which he describes as in unplugged style, with live and studio recordings.

The same evening, Ray appears at the formal reception party for the launch of his book, thrown by his publishers at the legendary jazz club, Ronnie Scott's, in central London. The highlight is a short performance by Ray accompanied by guitarist Pete Mathison, a guitarist from Hornsey whom Ray will use subsequently as his accompanist for "solo" shows. The party also sees a guest appearance by his daughter, Victoria (known as Tor). Songs performed are: 'Dedicated Follower Of Fashion', 'Waterloo Sunset', 'The Ballad Of Julie Finkle', 'Sunny Afternoon', 'Tired Of Waiting For You' (with Tor Davies), 'No Guarantees' (with Tor), 'Lola', 'Days', 'You Really Got Me'.

In the following weeks Ray keeps up a steady schedule of in-store appearances. He usually does a traditional reading of excerpts from his book with a signing session at the end. Initial dates: September 17th Waterstones, central London; 20th Dillons, central London; 21st Dillons, Manchester; 23rd Dillons, Birmingham. The dates continue into October as his schedule allows.

On the 29th at BBC Television Centre in west London The Kinks appear on the perennial chart TV programme *Top Of The Pops*. This is the first time they've been on *TOTP* since August 1983. They play a live version of 'You Really Got Me', and it's broadcast today on BBC-1, virtually a 30th anniversary performance in the show's own 30th year. For dramatic effect the slot starts out in black & white and gradually builds into colour.

To The Bone album (single-CD version)

1/A1 'All Day And All Of The Night' live (R. DAVIES).
2/A2 'Apeman' live (R. DAVIES).
3/A3 'Tired Of Waiting For You' live (R. DAVIES).
4/A4 'See My Friends' live (R. DAVIES).
5/A5 'Death Of A Clown' live (D. DAVIES, R. DAVIES).
6/A6 'Waterloo Sunset' (R. DAVIES).
7/B1 'Muswell Hillbillies' (R. DAVIES).
8/B2 'Better Things' (R. DAVIES).
9/B3 'Don't Forget To Dance' (R. DAVIES).
10/B4 Ray Davies 'Autumn Almanac' (R. DAVIES).
11/B5 Ray Davies 'Sunny Afternoon' (R. DAVIES).
12/B6 Ray Davies 'Dedicated Follower Of Fashion' (R. DAVIES).
13/B7 'You Really Got Me' live (R. DAVIES).

UK release October 3rd 1994 (Konk/Grapevine KNKLP 1).
Musicians Ray Davies lead vocal except as noted, electric guitar, acoustic guitar. Dave Davies electric guitar, acoustic guitar, lead vocal (A5), backing vocal. Jim Rodford bass guitar, backing vocal. Bob Henrit drums. Ian Gibbons keyboards.
Recorded 1, 10: Royal Concert Hall *Glasgow, Scotland*, November 25th 1993; 2-5, 7: live Konk Studios (No.2) *Hornsey, north London*, April 11th, 1994; 6, 8, 9: Konk Studios (No.2) *Hornsey, north London*, April 1994. 11, 12: Guildhall *Portsmouth*, March 25th 1994. 13: Mann Music Center *Philadelphia, PA*, August 12th 1993.
Producer Ray Davies.
Engineers Stan Loubieres, assistant Will Titt.
Chart high UK none.

October

Monday 3rd

Ray begins a five-day stretch this week for his now twice-yearly British songwriting workshop. He is still able to take in some in-store appearances at this time too.

To The Bone album (single-CD version) released in the UK.

Friday 7th

))) **RADIO** BBC Maida Vale Studios *central London*. BBC Radio-1 *Emma Freud Show* studio recordings 'All Day And All Of The Night', 'Waterloo Sunset', 'I'm Not Like Everybody Else', 'Till The End of The Day', 'You Really Got Me' broadcast October 8th. The Kinks make a return to BBC radio and record a traditional five-song session of some of their 1960s classics.

Sunday 9th

At the Civic Hall, Broxbourne, Herts approximately 400 fans show up for *The Kinks 30th Anniversary Konvention*, the annual gathering sponsored by the Official Kinks Fan Club. There's a performance by The Kast-Off Kinks, including former band members Mick Avory, John Dalton and John Gosling. The current rhythm section of Jim Rodford and Bob Henrit attend the event. While Ray and Dave are both in London at the time, neither makes an appearance this year, although Ray sends a special videotaped message.

Wednesday 12th

Ray does a noteworthy in-store reading and book-signing tonight in his old back yard – at The Muswell Hill Book Shop in north London. Among the audience is at least one friend from the old days, erstwhile Bonzos frontman Vivian Stanshall.

Friday 14th

❑ **TV** RTE TV Studios *Donnybrook, Dublin, Ireland*. RTE-1 *The Late Late Show* live performance 'You Really Got Me' (Ray and Dave, acoustic), 'Waterloo Sunset' (The Kinks with an unidentified stand-in for an absent Ian Gibbons). Also, Ray is interviewed by host Gay Byrne. The show's edited highlights are broadcast in the UK on Channel 4 on Monday October 17th 5:00-6:00 pm, including only 'You Really Got Me'.

Saturday 15th

❑ **TV** BBC Television Centre *west London*. BBC-1 *Steve Wright People Show* live performance 'You Really Got Me' broadcast 5:30-6:10pm.

➪ **TOUR STARTS** *To The Bone: UK / Ireland Tour* (Oct 16th – Nov 23rd). **Line-up**: Ray Davies (lead vocal, guitar), Dave Davies (guitar, vocal), Bob Henrit (drums), Jim Rodford (bass), Ian Gibbons (keyboards), Pat Crosbie and (probably) Louise Wodwell (dancers). Venues are generally 1,000-2,000 capacity. Ticket sales are far less consistent than last year's tour.

Sunday 16th

Rothes Halls *Glenrothes, Scotland* with David Gardiner
Set-list: 'A Well Respected Man' (Ray solo), 'See My Friends' (Ray solo), 'Come Dancing' (Ray solo), 'Autumn Almanac' (Ray solo), 'I Go To Sleep' (Ray solo), 'Dedicated Follower Of Fashion' (Ray solo), 'Do It Again' (Ray solo), 'Opening' (tape), 'Till The End Of The Day', 'State Of Confusion', 'Set Me Free', 'I'm Not Like Everybody Else', 'Muswell Hillbillies', 'Scattered', 'Alcohol', 'Phobia', 'Apeman', 'Too Much On My Mind', medley 'Aggravation' / 'New World' (tape), 'All Day And All Of The Night', 'Welcome To Sleazy Town', 'Lola', 'Waterloo Sunset', 'Days', 'You Really Got Me'.

Waterloo Sunset 94 EP

1 'Waterloo Sunset' version 2 (R. DAVIES).
2 'You Really Got Me' live (R. DAVIES).
3 'Elevator Man' (R. DAVIES).
4 'On The Outside' (R. DAVIES).
Track 1 is a slight edit of the album version (no audience at start)

UK release October 17th 1994 (Konk/Grapevine KNKCD 2).
1, 2: Musicians and recording details as *To The Bone* album (see October 3rd) except 1 in slightly edited form.
Musicians 3, 4: Ray Davies lead vocal, electric guitar, acoustic guitar. Dave Davies electric guitar, backing vocal. John Dalton bass guitar. Mick Avory drums. John Gosling keyboards.
Recorded 3: Konk Studios, *Hornsey, north London*; May-June 1976; probably 8-track mixed to stereo. 4: Konk Studios *Hornsey, north London*; September 15th-17th 1976; 24-track mixed to stereo.
Producer Ray Davies.
Engineer 3, 4: Roger Wake.
Chart high UK none.

Monday 17th

Capitol Theatre *Aberdeen, Scotland* with David Gardiner
Waterloo Sunset 94 EP released in the UK.

Tuesday 18th

Barrowlands *Glasgow, Scotland* with David Gardiner
Dave writes the last chapter of his forthcoming book. (Travel day follows.)

Thursday 20th

Queen Elizabeth Hall *Oldham* with Strangeways
Day off follows.

Friday 21st

❑ **TV** UTV Studio 1 *Belfast, Northern Ireland*. UTV *The Kelly Show* live performance medley 'You Really Got Me' (instrumental) / 'All Day And All Of The Night' (with organ player in addition to Ian Gibbons).

Saturday 22nd

Brentwood Leisure Centre *Brentwood, Essex* 8:00pm, with Strangeways
Ray regularly includes his new song, 'The Ballad Of Julie Finkle', among his opening solo set from about this time.

Sunday 23rd

Town Hall *Cheltenham, Glos* 8:00pm, with Strangeways

Monday 24th

Congress Hall *Eastbourne, Sussex* with Strangeways
Day off follows.

Wednesday 26th

Victoria Hall *Halifax, Yorks* 7:30 pm, with unnamed local band
"Ray Davies, the wrong side of 50, still looks the part," writes Stephen Firth in the *Evening Courier*. "He's still got a fine band, steered through by brother Dave and that driving lead guitar. Most important of all, he's got the songs. Songs that launched one of the most original talents British rock has produced ... There's humour, there's pathos in

this mould-breaker of a character," wrote the *Evening Courier* reviewer of the Halifax show. "Above all there's a deep-seated and genuine love for his craft that will ensure he remains one of rock's great survivors."

Thursday 27th
Assembly Rooms *Worthing, Sussex*

Friday 28th
Fairfield Hall *Croydon, south London* with John Fiddler
Day off follows.

Sunday 29th
Wessex Hall, Poole Arts Centre *Poole, Dorset* with Pout
Pout, the support act, is the band of Ray's daughter Tor (Victoria). They are added to the tour for most dates from this point on. Tor's set usually consists of six songs, including two Kinks oldies, 'I Need You' and 'Heart Of Gold'.

Monday 31st
King George's Hall *Blackburn, Lancs* with Pout
Day off follows.

November

Wednesday 2nd
New Pavilion *Rhyl, Flints, Wales* with Pout

Thursday 3rd
Civic Theatre *Barnsley, Yorks* 7:30pm, with unnamed local band
Ray storms off stage after the first 15 minutes of the show after being heckled at what is described as a large workingmen's-club. Dave takes over until Ray eventually returns, but rather than continue with the show predominantly plays the old hits for the demanding crowd.

Friday 5th
Barbican Centre *York* 8:00pm, with Marc Atkinson & Company
Day off follows.

Sunday 6th
Lower Common Room, University of East Anglia *Norwich* 7:30pm, with Pout

Monday 7th
Dacorum Pavilion *Hemel Hempstead, Herts* with Pout

Tuesday 8th
Empire *Shepherd's Bush, west London* with Pout
Day off follows.
Set-list: 'A Well Respected Man' (Ray solo), 'Autumn Almanac' (Ray solo), 'The Ballad Of Julie Finkle' (Ray solo), 'Dedicated Follower Of Fashion' (Ray solo), 'Do It Again' (Ray solo), 'Opening' (tape), 'Till The End Of The Day', 'Give The People What They Want', 'Low Budget', 'Scattered', 'Apeman', 'Too Much On My Mind', 'Death Of A Clown', 'Missing Persons', 'Phobia', 'Come Dancing', medley 'Aggravation' / 'New World' (tape), 'All Day And All Of The Night' (with extract from 'Green Onions'), 'Welcome To Sleazy Town', 'Waterloo Sunset', 'Lola' (short version), 'Days', 'You Really Got Me', 'Twist And Shout'.

Thursday 10th
Royal Concert Hall *Nottingham* with Pout

Friday 11th
Civic Hall *Wolverhapmton* with Pout

Sunday 13th
Prince's Theatre *Clacton, Essex* with Pout

Monday 14th
Leas Cliff Hall *Folkestone, Kent* with Pout

Tuesday 15th
Assembly Rooms *Tunbridge Wells, Kent* with Pout
Days off follow.

Thursday 17th
The Empire *Sunderland* 7:30pm, with Pout

Friday 18th
The Bowl *Redcar, Yorks* with Pout
There's a packed house tonight in this old ballroom, and the band in elated mood includes 'Not Fade Away', 'Susannah's Still Alive', 'See My Friends', 'Victoria' and '20th Century Man'.

Saturday 19th
Alexandra Theatre *Birmingham* 7:30pm, with Pout
Day off follows.

Monday 21st
Ulster Hall *Belfast, Northern Ireland*

Tuesday 22nd
Opera House *Cork, Ireland*

Wednesday 23rd
The Point *Dublin, Ireland* 8:00pm
Travel day follows; end of tour.

Friday 25th
❐ **TV** BBC Television Centre *west London*. BBC-1 *Children In Need* live performance 'All Day And All Of The Night' 7:00-9:00pm, 9:30pm-2:00am.

➔ Current plans are to release a full-length video to accompany *To The Bone* consisting of highlights of the Konk unplugged session and concert highlights. Tour dates for Australia and Japan and the US are set for the coming year.

December

Tuesday 6th
Docklands Arena *east London* *BT Birthday Concert In Aid Of The Prince's Trust*, with Bjorn Again, Brand New Heavies, Belinda Carlisle, Sophie B. Hawkins, East 17, Eternal, Kylie Minogue, Pulp, Roachford, Dave Stewart, Paul Young, Squeeze, plus on-screen Phil Collins & Meatloaf, Joe Cocker, Cliff Richard, M-People
Ray and Dave with members of Pink Floyd perform 'You Really Got Me', 'All Day And All Of The Night' and 'Lola'. The 'Lola' performance is broadcast as part of *The Prince's Trust Gala Concert* on BBC-1 TV and BBC Radio-1 December 26th 11:05pm.

➔ It is around this time that Granada Television in Britain begins working on a 30-minute documentary that will cover The Kinks' 1960s career and is planned to be broadcast during March 1995. Ray has been

➔ INDICATES EVENT AROUND THIS TIME BUT WITH NO FIRM DATE

"I can't hear you!" Ray encourages the crowd at the Civic Hall, Wolverhampton, England, November 11th 1994.

interviewed and the TV company is scheduled to interview Dave as well.

Hans Martin Schleierhalle *Stuttgart, Germany* 7:30pm, *The Heroes Of Rock*, with Kansas, Electric Light Orchestra II
The Kinks play a 60-minute set including 'All Day And All Of The Night', 'Dead End Street', 'Come Dancing', 'You Really Got Me', 'Lola', 'Days'. Excerpts are televised by SWR3 TV on *Rocknacht* and simulcast in stereo on SDR3 radio on December 27th at 7:00pm. (Travel day follows.)

❏ **TV** London Weekend Television Studios *South Bank, central London*. LWT *Richard Littlejohn's Christmas Offensive* Ray Davies & Pete Mathison live performance 'You Really Got Me'.

→ Back in Los Angeles for the Christmas and new year holidays, Dave at the end of this year or early in January does a guitar solo overdub on a piece called 'In The Mouth Of Madness' at either Westlake or Capitol Studio B in Los Angeles. It's for a John Carpenter movie to which Dave is contributing.

1995

Although not quite the end of the road for The Kinks, this was the year when they played their last proper tours, and throughout there seemed to be an air of finality about the band and its limited undertakings. There was no record contract to speak of and no plans for recording. Relations with manager Eugene Harvey seemed to have come to an end as well, and an unknown replacement considered this spring didn't work out, so the band continued manager-less for the remainder of this year. The two tours appeared to be energetic, heartfelt displays of playing for enjoyment, celebrating the band's legacy and almost revelling in the glory.

The Kinks agreed to participate in two separate British documentaries that again underscored an unusual willingness to look back at their career and recognise their achievements rather than busy themselves with current preoccupations and ignore nostalgia. Ray's continuing focus was the promotion of his book and, ultimately, the development of a show that celebrated his most fertile creative period. Ray's so-called one-man show came to life this year, and it spawned a new songs-and-anecdotes genre.

January / February

Over the weekend of January 21st-22nd at Guernsey's Auction in New York City, Dave's legendary Gibson Flying V guitar is sold for $24,000 (about £15,000).

Also in the US, the movie *In The Mouth Of Madness* opens on February 3rd. The film's title song is co-composed by Dave, along with director John Carpenter and Jim Lang.

On the 17th, Dave appears as a special guest performer at the Morgan-Wixson Theatre in Santa Monica, CA, for *A Kinks Preservation Revue*, a charity performance in aid of Habitat For Humanity. He plays a six-song set – 'Susannah's Still Alive', 'Death Of A Clown', 'Too Much On My Mind', 'Dead End Street', 'I'm Not Like Everybody Else' and 'You Really Got Me' – backed by Andrew, a band of local LA musicians fronted by Andrew Sandoval (guitar, backing vocal) with Dave Jenkins (bass, backing vocal), Jim Laspesa (drums, backing vocal), Matt Lederman (guitar), Danny McGough (keyboards), Brian Kehew (Mellotron, certain songs only) and Probyn Gregory (french horn on 'You Really Got Me' only).

Dave is in LA working with film director John Carpenter on music for a forthcoming movie. By now writer Roger Friedman has been dropped from Dave's book project, which he is completing on his own.

At the Brit Awards '95 at Alexandra Palace in north London on February 20th Ray presents an award to Oasis, broadcast on ITV the following day.

March

Ray continues his schedule of in-store appearances where he has been reading from his book *X-Ray* and signing copies. He decides at some point that he should sing some of the songs he is talking about in his readings, and arranges to have a few small theatres booked to present a show where he can continue his readings from *X-Ray* but also work in some performances. For the project, Ray writes a number of new songs based on incidents in the book – including 'Americana', 'London Song', 'Animal', 'X-Ray' and 'Art School Babes' – in the same way that he wrote some last year with the book in mind ('The Ballad Of Julie Finkle' and 'To The Bone'). He rehearses with guitarist Pete Mathison for a first test show later in the month.

Ray and Pete Mathison appear at Channel 4 TV Studios in central London on the 13th and perform 'You Really Got Me' (in blues style),

'To The Bone', 'Waterloo Sunset' (with Damon Albarn from Blur) and 'Parklife' (a Blur song, also with Albarn). The set is broadcast on Channel 4's TV music show **The White Room** on March 18th at 10:05pm. (This performance of 'Waterloo Sunset' will be released on a cassette-only various-artists sampler, *The White Room Album*, given away with the February 1996 Q magazine.)

Ray's very first official solo performance occurs on Tuesday 28th at the small 200-capacity Hazlitt Theatre in Maidstone, Kent, with little commotion. The same day, a 30-minute documentary on The Kinks is broadcast on the Channel 4 TV programme *Without Walls*, a Granada Arts Production and part of a three-show mini-series called *My Generation* that focuses on 1960s British bands (the other two are The Animals and The Troggs). It features numerous 1960s TV clips of the band, plus recent interview footage of Ray, Dave and Mick Avory, as well as contributions from Blur's Damon Albarn, Q magazine editor Danny Kelly, former Kinks manager Larry Page, music journalist Charles Shaar Murray, biographer Johnny Rogan, and former Kinks publicist Keith Altham. The programme covers the 1960s only, finishing in 1970 with 'Lola'.

April

Monday 3rd
Grosvenor House Hotel *central London* *Advertising World Annual Awards Ceremony*
The Kinks play a private one-off date at this corporate party. Two further dates are due to be booked in the Channel Islands, on the 4th in Jersey and the 5th in Guernsey, but these never materialise. A Kinks tour of the United States had been pencilled in for this month, but it is delayed.

↳ **TOUR STARTS** *An Evening With Ray Davies* (Apr 9th – 13th). Ray Davies (lead vocal, guitar), Pete Mathison (guitar). Venues on this short tour away from the press have capacities in the 440-700 range. Tickets £9-12.

Sunday 9th
Prince Of Wales Centre *Cannock, Staffs* 8:00pm, with Lisa Rhodes & Roger Crombie

Monday 10th
Coronation Hall *Ulverston, Lancs* 8:00pm, with Lisa Rhodes & Roger Crombie
Set-list: 'Autumn Almanac', 'Dedicated Follower Of Fashion', 'Victoria', '20th Century Man', 'London Song', 'Sunny Afternoon', 'That Old Black Magic', 'Tired Of Waiting For You', 'Set Me Free', 'X-Ray', 'See My Friends', 'Art School Babes', 'You Really Got Me' (two versions), 'Apeman', 'Animal', 'A Well Respected Man', 'Americana', 'Scattered', 'Lola', 'I Go To Sleep', 'The Moneygoround', 'Dead End Street', 'The Ballad Of Julie Finkle', 'Still Searching', 'To The Bone', 'Days', 'Waterloo Sunset', 'The Village Green Preservation Society', 'You Really Got Me'.

Tuesday 11th
The Venue *Borehamwood, Herts* 8:00pm, with Lisa Rhodes & Roger Crombie

Wednesday 12th
Castle Theatre *Wellingborough, Northants* 8:00pm, with Lisa Rhodes & Roger Crombie
Ray performs 'Village Green' tonight, probably the song's first live airing since it was written in November 1966.

Thursday 13th
Music Hall *Shrewsbury, Shrops* 8:00pm, with Lisa Rhodes & Roger Crombie
The concert is filmed by the BBC, and portions will be broadcast on the BBC documentary *I'm Not Like Everybody Else*.

→ ● **RECORDING** Cherokee Recording Studio *Los Angeles, CA*. By mid month Dave is finishing up guitar overdubs for the soundtrack of the John Carpenter movie *Village Of The Damned*.

Friday 28th
In the US, John Carpenter's film *Village Of The Damned* opens. It has music by Carpenter and Dave Davies.

May

Friday 5th
A Kinks show at the House Of Blues in Los Angeles is announced today for May 25th and some tickets go on sale the following day. By the 8th sales are halted temporarily, and by the 12th the date is officially cancelled and set to be rescheduled for June.

Tuesday 9th
Village Of The Damned soundtrack album is released in the US, with music by John Carpenter and Dave Davies. Copies are exported to the UK and Europe for release on May 26th.

↳ **TOUR STARTS** *Tour Of Japan* (May 10th – 19th). **Line-up**: Ray Davies (lead vocal, guitar), Dave Davies (guitar, vocal), Bob Henrit (drums), Jim Rodford (bass), Ian Gibbons (keyboards). The band leaves on Monday 8th, arriving the following day, which is time off in Tokyo. All appearances are one show nightly with no opening acts, which is traditional in Japan.

Wednesday 10th – Thursday 12th
Shibuya Kokaido (Public Hall) *Tokyo, Japan*

Friday 13th
Nakano Sun Plaza *Tokyo, Japan*
Day off follows.

Sunday 14th – Monday 15th
Sankei Hall (Kokusai Kouryu Center) *Osaka, Japan*

Tuesday 16th
Club Diamond Hall *Nagoya, Japan*
Day off follows.

Thursday 18th – Friday 19th
Cine Chitta (aka Club Chitta) *Kawasaki, Japan*
Day off follows. Band members travel back to London, Dave to Los Angeles, and Ray to New York City.
Set-list: 'Stop Your Sobbing' (Ray solo), 'Sunny Afternoon' (Ray solo), 'Dedicated Follower Of Fashion (Ray solo), 'Do It Again' (Ray solo), concert prelude (tape), 'Do It Again', 'The Hard Way', 'Till The End Of The Day', 'It's Alright', 'Low Budget', 'Sleepwalker', 'Apeman', 'I'm Not Like Everybody Else', 'Alcohol', 'Days', 'Come Dancing', 'It's Alright (If You Don't Think)', 'Living On A Thin Line', 'Set Me Free', 'Lola', 'David Watts', 'Welcome To Sleazy Town', 'All Day And All Of The Night', 'Good Golly Miss Molly', 'Victoria'.

✗ The Kinks were booked to continue to Australia but the tour has been cancelled since mid April, with a promise of rescheduling at the end of the year. Scheduled dates were May 24th Concert Hall, Perth; 26th Thebarton Theatre, Adelaide; 27th-28th The Palais, Melbourne; 30th-31st State Theatre, Sydney; June 1st Brisbane Concert Hall (briefly moved to the 3rd before cancelling).

→ Ray is in New York City where he signs a deal for US publication of his book *X-Ray* with Overlook Press, based in Woodstock, NY. The book was originally said to be coming out with EP Dutton. The deal is announced on the 24th, with publication set for September.

☆ Dave is back in LA where he reportedly takes in a show by The Smithereens at the House Of Blues on the 24th. The Kinks have been scheduled to play there the following night but this is being rescheduled. In London on the 25th two more of Dave's guitars hit the auction block as his gold-top Gibson Les Paul and a white 1956 Fender Telecaster are sold.

June

Early in the month Ray returns to London where he cancels a scheduled appearance on July 1st at *Meltdown Festival '95* at the Royal Festival Hall in London. Ray was due to sing with The Moon Dog Bog Band that also includes Elvis Costello and June Tabor on vocals.

July

Saturday 8th
Ray presents an award at the British Music Awards ceremony in London.

➭ **TOUR STARTS** *US Tour* (Jul 11th – Aug 1st). **Line-up**: Ray Davies (lead vocal, guitar), Dave Davies (guitar, vocal), Bob Henrit (drums), Jim Rodford (bass), Ian Gibbons (keyboards). The band travels to LA on Sunday 9th with a day off following. Ticket prices are generally $25. Ray says that this brief tour is "to see if I can face playing here again. … Last time I was here [1993] I had two really bad injuries on the tour. It's like a football player. Something telling you something." He tells another interviewer: "We have nothing to promote, we just wanted to go out and tour." Following the three-night stand in LA, the band flies to New England where all shows are concentrated within relatively easy driving distances, making for a comfortable clutch of dates on the summer "tent" circuit (primarily outdoor musical theatres).

Tuesday 11th – Thursday 13th
House Of Blues *Los Angeles, CA* with The Wild Colonials
"Ray Davies is often portrayed as one of rock's prime neurotics, but at the House Of Blues on Tuesday the leader of The Kinks was all smiles," writes Richard Cromelin in the *Los Angeles Times*. "'This is a very emotional return for us,' he said at one point, referring to the British Invasion veterans' long absence from shows here. Davies' spirits were bubbling in something of a void for the band: a Hall Of Fame member without a record deal and with no recent or new material worth playing. But they sold out their three nights at the 1,000-capacity club, matching the numbers they used to draw in their annual visits to the Santa Monica Civic. … Fronting the music, Ray Davies was less campy, teasing and sarcastic than in his 1970s incarnation. He was irreverent enough, but also more genuine as he appeared sincerely energized by performing and touched by the response." (Travel day to New York City follows, and then a day off.)

Set-list (11th): 'A Well Respected Man' (Ray solo), 'Dedicated Follower Of Fashion' (Ray solo), 'Sunny Afternoon' (Ray solo), 'I Go To Sleep' (Ray solo), 'Do It Again' (Ray solo), 'Till The End Of The Day', medley 'The Hard Way' / 'Give The People What They Want', 'Low Budget', 'It's Alright', 'Sleepwalker', '20th Century Man', 'Apeman', 'Set Me Free', 'Dead End Street', 'Living On A Thin Line', 'Muswell Hillbillies', 'Celluloid Heroes', 'Welcome To Sleazy Town', 'David Watts', 'Lola', 'All Day And All of The Night', 'Days', 'You Really Got Me'.

Sunday 16th
Valley Forge Music Fair *Devon, PA* with Stacy Wilde

Monday 17th
The Bayou *Washington, DC* with Stacy Wilde
Travel day follows.

Wednesday 19th
Melody Fair North *Tonawanda, NY* with Stacy Wilde

Thursday 20th
Starlight Musical Theatre *Lantham, NY* with Stacy Wilde
The air conditioning is broken and the show is short. (Day off follows.)

Saturday 22nd
Oakdale Music Theatre *Wallingford, CT* with Stacy Wilde

Sunday 23rd
Warwick Musical Theatre *Warwick, RI* with Stacy Wilde

Monday 24th
North Shore Musical Theatre *Beverly, MA* with Stacy Wilde
"What's bad for rock bands can be good for their fans," says Dean Johnson in the *Boston Herald*. "For example, British rock legends The Kinks are touring the US this summer without a new album to promote. That's bad for them. But it was good for the 1,250 fans who showed up for the group's 90-minute concert. No album means no unfamiliar songs inserted into the set. It gave The Kinks the delicious freedom to do anything they wanted, and the band responded with a wonderfully eclectic and upbeat performance, among its best here in recent years." (Day off follows.)

Wednesday 26th
Hampton Beach Casino Ballroom *Hampton, NH* with Stacy Wilde

Thursday 27th
Cape Cod Melody Tent *Hyannis, MA* with Stacy Wilde
Another venue with no air conditioning on a hot sweaty night, so the show is again cut short.

Friday 28th
South Shore Music Circus *Cohasset, MA* with Stacy Wilde
Ray unusually includes 'A Rock'n'Roll Fantasy' among his solo set, and in the course of The Kinks' set they play 'Dead End Street', 'The Village Green Preservation Society' and 'Skin And Bone'.

Saturday 29th
Ski area *Stratton Mountain, VT* with Stacy Wilde
Travel day follows with time off in New York City.

Monday 31st
Westbury Music Fair *Westbury, NY* with Stacy Wilde
Ray again pulls out 'A Rock'n'Roll Fantasy' in his solo preamble, and The Kinks' set includes 'Waterloo Sunset' and 'Dead End Street'.

→ INDICATES EVENT AROUND THIS TIME BUT WITH NO FIRM DATE

August

Tuesday 1st
Westbury Music Fair *Westbury, NY* with Stacy Wilde
A post-tour party is held at the Irish Pub at 7th Avenue & 53rd St, New York City, with all five Kinks attending, and the fun lasts until 5:00am. Though no one knows it, this will be the last proper tour by The Kinks, apart from three isolated appearances over the next 11 months. It is fitting that Dave ends the show with the Little Richard song 'Good Golly Miss Molly' that he recalls as the first he ever sang with the very earliest incarnation of The Kinks back around the autumn of 1961. (Travel day to London follows.)
☆ New record deals are being considered around now; in the running are EMI, SBK, and Virgin.

↪ **TOUR STARTS** *Ray Davies solo tour UK* (Aug 5th – 27th). Ray Davies (lead vocal, guitar), Pete Mathison (guitar). Ray books another small group of small off-the-beaten-track gigs as warm-ups for his proper high-profile debut at the prestigious Edinburgh Fringe Festival. Venue capacities are in the range 500-1,275.

Saturday 5th
Theatre Royal *Norwich* with Lisa Rhodes & Roger Crombie

Sunday 6th
North Wales Theatre *Llandudno, Caernarfs, Wales* with Lisa Rhodes & Roger Crombie
Day off follows.

Tuesday 8th
Princess Theatre *Clacton-on-Sea, Essex* with Lisa Rhodes & Roger Crombie

Wednesday 9th
Wulfrun Hall *Wolverhampton* with Lisa Rhodes & Roger Crombie
Day off follows.
Set-list: 'Autumn Almanac', 'Sweet Lady Genevieve', 'Sunny Afternoon', 'Dedicated Follower Of Fashion', 'Victoria', '20th Century Man', 'London Song', 'Tired Of Waiting For You', 'That Old Black Magic', 'You Really Got Me' (blues version), 'Set Me Free', 'See My Friends', 'Art School Babes', 'I Go To Sleep', 'X-Ray', 'A Well Respected Man', 'Americana', 'The Moneygoround', 'Dead End Street', 'Two Sisters', 'The Ballad Of Julie Finkle', 'Lola', 'Animal', 'Village Green', 'To The Bone', 'Waterloo Sunset', 'You Really Got Me' (electric guitar).
☆ Sometime this week, Pete Quaife is interviewed on film at the El Macombo Club, Toronto, Canada for the upcoming BBC Kinks documentary.

Friday 11th
Leas Cliff Hall *Folkestone, Kent* with Lisa Rhodes & Roger Crombie
Very poor attendance, and the concert is marred by a persistent heckler.

Saturday 12th
Assembly Hall *Tunbridge Wells, Kent* with Lisa Rhodes & Roger Crombie
Week off follows.

Friday 18th – Sunday 27th
Assembly Theatre Hall *Edinburgh, Scotland* Edinburgh Fringe Festival
Ray performs his standard show, with no opening act. "Among the true highlights of this year's Edinburgh Festival were Ray Davies' Unplugged-style appearances at the Assembly Rooms," says *Time Out*. "Davies' set is far from being a one-man affair; he has backing from an awesomely talented guitarist, Pete Mathison, who moved effortlessly from Spanish fingerpicking to Hendrix wah-wah, just as Davies progressed from song to song, beginning perkily with 'Autumn Almanac', including some old faves like 'You Really Got Me', 'Victoria' and 'Lola', and climaxing musically with two of the finest English pop songs ever written, 'Days' and 'Waterloo Sunset'."

September

Saturday 2nd
Memorial Stadium *Cleveland, OH* Benefit For The Rock & Roll Hall Of Fame
At the time of writing this marks The Kinks' last appearance in America. From Friday 1st and throughout the weekend there is the official opening of the long awaited Rock & Roll Hall Of Fame And Museum in downtown Cleveland, OH. There are a number of dinners and events to celebrate the opening.
Pete Quaife is in town at the invitation of the Hall Of Fame. Quaife, who has always been an artist and specialises in cartoons and airbrush work, participates in a celebrity art show. He also donates some of his work to the Hall Of Fame. The Kinks are represented in the Museum with an exhibit devoted to them, largely based on their 1966 hit 'Dedicated Follower Of Fashion' and featuring various artefacts related to the song as well as Ray's Ivor Novello Award for the song, which he has loaned for the exhibit.
On Saturday The Kinks perform at the Hall Of Fame's *Benefit* concert. Initially it seemed that only Ray and Dave might appear, but ultimately the whole band is there for the brief spot. They take the stage at about 10:30pm for a crowd that is estimated at around 63,000 of a 77,000 capacity.
The Kinks are among the best-received acts of the show, even though they play just two songs, 'All Day And All Of The Night' and 'Lola' (included in the live broadcast on HBO cable channel 7:30pm-2:30am EDT, re-broadcast on *Hilights* September 26th). At the band's soundcheck earlier in the day they played 'Apeman' in addition to 'All Day And All Of The Night'. (Travel day back to London follows.)

Monday 25th
Ray is scheduled to start a tour to promote his X-Ray book in the US, which is published today by Overlook Press, but the dates are pushed back to October. "X-Ray stands as an indispensable eyewitness account of the golden age of British pop," says Ken Schlager in *Billboard*. "Unfortunately, what is missing is the probing eye of an independent observer. Thus, there is no corroboration for Davies' tales. And we never really get to the root of the sadness, alienation, and paranoia that he contends dogged him throughout his life. One thing is clear: Davies' prose is as clever as his poetry. Thankfully, the book's final twist suggests a sequel." The mainstream literary press is a little more critical. "Throughout, Mr Davies seems to be saying that he is the most misunderstood artist in rock'n'roll," writes Lauren Thierry in the *New York Times Book Review*. "His book seems intended to keep it that way."
☆ Ray is in New York City for a week doing press work for *X-Ray*. Before returning to London on the 29th he also meets record company executives, including some from Guardian Records, the popular-music subsidiary of classical music label Angel Records. Dave meanwhile has been in Los Angeles completing all work on the manuscript for his book, which his agent will be delivering to the London publisher on October 1st.

October

→ The Kinks are reportedly recording a track at Konk around this time, details unknown. Ray teaches another of his songwriting classes, at Fen Farm near Blo' Norton on the Norfolk/Suffolk border, a writer's retreat where various classes are held.

❑ **TOUR STARTS** *Ray Davies: X-Ray: World Tour* (Oct 9th – Dec 21st). Ray Davies (lead vocal, guitar), Pete Mathison (guitar). Bob Adcock is tour manager. Tickets are $25-45. Ray does various TV interviews and in-store appearances around the shows. (The entourage travels to Los Angeles on the 7th, with a day off on the 8th.)

Monday 9th
Galaxy Concert Theatre *Santa Ana, CA* with Kevin Fisher
"No other rocker presents as potent a combination of comic wit and timing, an actor's hamminess, joy and ferocity in rocking out, and invention, warmth, insight and grace in song composition as Davies, the driving force of The Kinks since 1964," says Mike Boehm in the *Los Angeles Times*. "Backed by guitarist Pete Mathison, Davies offered much more than another fashionably 'unplugged' evening.

"The two-hour performance was a fully realized one-man theatrical show, coherently structured and beautifully paced as Davies astutely balanced songs old and new with reminiscences and readings from [*X-Ray*] which focuses on the early days of The Kinks. This music was so humane and so fully and fervently felt in Davies' performance, that to hear it was to be granted a privileged moment. In a warm, elegiacally satisfying climax, Davies lovingly etched two of his greatest achievements, 'Days' and 'Waterloo Sunset', with a special mixture of pathos and dignity."
Set-list: 'Dedicated Follower Of Fashion', 'Autumn Almanac', 'Sunny Afternoon', 'Victoria', '20th Century Man', 'London Song', 'That Old Black Magic', 'Tired of Waiting For You', 'Set Me Free', 'See My Friends', 'X-Ray', 'Art School Babes', 'You Really Got Me', 'Animal', 'You Really Got Me', 'A Well Respected Man', 'Americana', 'I Go To Sleep', 'Two Sisters', 'The Moneygoround', 'Dead End Street', 'Lola', 'The Ballad Of Julie Finkle', 'To The Bone', 'Village Green', 'Days', 'Waterloo Sunset', 'You Really Got Me'.

Tuesday 10th
Henry Fonda Theatre *Hollywood, CA* with unconfirmed support artist

Wednesday 11th
Galaxy Concert Theatre *Santa Ana, CA* with Daughter V

Thursday 12th
Fillmore Auditorium *San Francisco, CA* with John Wesley Harding

Sunday 15th
Park West *Chicago, IL* with Ralph Covert

Monday 16th
The Paradise *Boston, MA* 9:00pm

Tuesday 17th
Theatre Of The Living Arts *Philadelphia, PA* with Ken Kweder
Day off follows in New York City, working on the new record deal.

Thursday 19th
The Academy *New York, NY* with Hamell On Trial
Day off follows.

Sunday 22nd
Toad's Place *New Haven, CT* 8:00pm

Monday 23rd
❑ **TV** NBC Studios, Rockefeller Center *New York, NY*. NBC *Late Night With Conan O'Brien* broadcast 12:30am EDT (Tuesday). Taped in the late afternoon, Ray in addition to being interviewed performs with Pete Mathison on guitar backed by The Max Weinberg Band, playing 'Victoria' and 'You Really Got Me'. Ray travels to Cork, Ireland later today where he has a day off before his appearance with Mathison in Dublin.

Wednesday 25th
Olympia Theatre *Dublin, Ireland* 8:00pm
Two days off in London follow.

Saturday 28th – Monday 30th
Bloomsbury Theatre *central London* 8:00pm (plus 4:00pm matinee 29th), with Lisa Rhodes & Roger Crombie
Day off follows.

November

Wednesday 1st
Custom House Theatre *South Shields, Co Durham*
Ray and Pete Mathison continue the "one-man" shows in the UK.

Thursday 2nd
Rothes Hall *Glenrothes, Fife, Scotland*

Friday 3rd
The Pavilion *Glasgow, Scotland*
Day off follows.

Sunday 5th
Gaiety Theatre *Ayr, Scotland*

Monday 6th
King George's Hall *Blackburn, Lancs*

Tuesday 7th
Town Hall *Cheltenham, Gloucs*

Wednesday 8th
Day off in London. Guardian Records executives fly to London to discuss with Ray the final details for a deal.

Thursday 9th
Pavilion *Rhyl, Flints, Wales*
Day off follows.

Saturday 11th
Darlington Arts Centre *Darlington, Co Durham*

Sunday 12th
Floral Pavilion *New Brighton, Wallasey, Ches*

Monday 13th
Civic Centre *Aylesbury, Bucks*

Tuesday 14th
Playhouse Theatre *Weston-Super-Mare, Somerset*

→ INDICATES EVENT AROUND THIS TIME BUT WITH NO FIRM DATE

At the time of writing this counts as the last US Kinks concert, at the Memorial Stadium, Cleveland, Ohio, September 2nd 1995.

kinks'95

Wednesday 15th
Orchard Theatre *Dartford, Kent*

Thursday 16th
Guildhall, Civic Centre *Southampton*
Three days off follow. Shows at the Empire, Willesden, north-west London on the 18th and the Barbican Centre, York on the 19th are cancelled due to Ray's ill health.

Monday 20th
Queen Elizabeth Hall *Oldham*
Day off follows.

Tuesday 21st
Attack Of The Smithereens album by The Smithereens released in the US. It includes a unique version of 'You Really Got Me' performed by Ray and Dave with The Smithereens, recorded live at Boston Garden, Boston, MA, on November 22nd 1991.

Wednesday 22nd
South Holland Centre *Spalding, Lincs*

Thursday 23rd
Lewisham Theatre *Catford, south-east London*

Friday 24th
Grand Pavilion *Porthcawl, Glam, Wales*
End of the UK portion of the tour. Travel on to Australia for more Ray solo dates, via New York City, which is possibly when the new recording contract with Guardian Records is formally signed. The Kinks were scheduled to tour Australia back in June following the Japanese dates, but this was cancelled and rescheduled for later in the year – which becomes this Ray solo tour.

Tuesday 28th
Regal Theatre *Perth, Western Australia, Australia*

Wednesday 29th
Her Majesty's Theatre *Adelaide, South Australia, Australia*
Travel day follows.

December

→ Dave is busy in Los Angeles finishing work on his book.

Friday 1st
❏ **TV** unknown location. Network Nine *Hey Hey It's Saturday* Ray Davies and Pete Mathison live performance 'You Really Got Me' broadcast December 2nd 6:30-8:30pm. The duo are backed by the house band on this national variety programme.

Ray is ill and at short notice cancels tonight's show at the Mission Theatre, Newcastle, New South Wales, which is rescheduled for the 6th. (Travel day follows.)

Sunday 3rd
Labour Club *Canberra, Australian Capital Territory, Australia*

Monday 4th – Tuesday 5th
Everest Theatre, Seymour Centre *Sydney, New South Wales, Australia*
"Davies is a charming storyteller with a finely honed sense of theatre,"

writes Bruce Elder in the *Sydney Morning Herald*. "A slight gesture, a raised eyebrow, a gentle song, a few bars of a long forgotten tune, a warm recollection – these are the elements which make this night special. In the end there is a feeling that a 'true Londoner' who was once a star … has let you enter his world and has shared the special moments of his life. When at the end Davies launches into the marvellous and evocative 'Waterloo Sunset', and then offers a reprise of his first hit, 'You Really Got Me', you feel as though you have been on a journey full of good times and the joys of youth."

Wednesday 6th
Mission Theatre *Newcastle, New South Wales, Australia*
Travel day follows.

Friday 8th – Saturday 9th
Athenaeum Theatre *Melbourne, Victoria, Australia*
Travel day following, plus day off in Auckland.

Tuesday 12th
Town Hall *Auckland, New Zealand*
Travel day follows to Japan for more Ray solo dates, with two days off in Tokyo.

Friday 15th – Saturday 16th
Shibuya Parco *Tokyo, Japan*
To aid the non-English-speaking audience, a Japanese-language guide to the spoken portions of the show is handed. All Japanese shows are at small, approximately 500-seat venues, without an opening act. (Day off follows.)

Monday 18th – Tuesday 19th, Thursday 21st
Yomiuri Hall *Tokyo, Japan*
After a day off, the third night is added. (Travel day back to London follows.)

Thursday 21st
In Britain, BBC-2 television airs its Kinks career-retrospective documentary, *I'm Not Like Everybody Else: The World Of Ray Davies And The Kinks*. The show is largely interview-based and includes contributions by Ray and Dave, as well as Pete Quaife, Mick Avory, Robert Wace, Larry Page, Shel Talmy, and Ned Sherrin, and includes only minor clips of vintage film.

Friday 22nd
Dave appears on a Compuserve internet forum during which he says he has been in the UK a lot lately and may be moving back there.
☆ The band has time off for the Christmas and New Year holidays.

Sunday 31st
The Kinks are scheduled to appear at the Princess Street Theatre, Edinburgh, Scotland, headlining Edinburgh's *New Year's Eve Concert* with Edwyn Collins, Big Country, and The Scottish Fiddle Orchestra. But as of December 14th the band cancels out, claiming that as Ray suffered a perforated eardrum while in Australia they will not be able to appear.

→ INDICATES EVENT AROUND THIS TIME BUT WITH NO FIRM DATE

1996

By this year, The Kinks were reduced to a couple of recording sessions and two festival dates. There was no indication that anything was amiss or not going according to plan; on the contrary, it was implied that the lull would soon be rectified by band action, especially as a new manager had been hired.

The Kinks had also signed a new record deal, already manifesting itself in the form of a two-CD set (albeit live versions and re-recordings of earlier material). But the CDs did include two new studio recordings of a typically strong and vibrant quality, suggesting that the beast still had life but that it would just have to wait for the second contracted Kinks CD, to follow the planned Ray Davies solo effort.

The significant event, however, was the publication of Dave's own memoirs, hot on the heels of Ray's. Unlike his brother, Dave offered a rather complex telling of The Kinks' history, and pulled no punches in the process. Dave spoke candidly of his love and admiration for his brother and his talent, but didn't mince words when giving a brutally honest assessment of his side of their relationship. Meanwhile, Ray devoted the year to fine-tuning and touring his so-called one-man show.

The Kinks assembled for what would turn out to be one last time – ironically at a 50th birthday party celebration for Dave, organised by Ray. The symbolism of the event was impossible to overlook. The party was held at the site of the brothers' very first musical endeavour, the Clissold Arms pub, across the street from their childhood home on Fortis Green in north London.

It almost seemed too picture-book-perfect, but it was from this point that The Kinks as a band ground to a halt – though this was never officially stated. Despite a record contract stipulating one more CD to be recorded by The Kinks, following the party Dave began seriously to work up his own band back in Los Angeles. From then until the time of writing, The Kinks – meaning at the very least Ray Davies and Dave Davies – have never worked together again.

January

The Kinks are scheduled to record two new tracks for an expanded US version of *To The Bone*. The US release has been planned for now, but is delayed, as is a US tour.

This month, Deke Arlon is hired as The Kinks' manager. His duties also include management of any solo affairs of Ray and Dave. Arlon has long been on the British music scene, predating The Kinks. As early as 1959 he was in a band billed as Deke Arlon & The Tremors, and in 1964 issued a few UK singles with Deke Arlon & The Offbeats. He later moved into music publishing with his own company, and into management in the 1980s, his most famous client being singer Sheena Easton.

February

➔ Dave travels from London to Los Angeles early in the month. The new two-CD version of To The Bone is tentatively set for May release.

Monday 12th, Wednesday 14th – Sunday 18th
Westbeth Theatre Center Music Hall *New York, NY* 7:30pm, except Saturday 6:30 & 10:30pm, *20th Century Man: An Evening With Ray Davies In Concert*

Ray Davies (lead vocal, guitar) plus Pete Mathison (guitar). Theatre producer James Nederlander "presents" the show, so there is an acknowledged theatrical element to the performance.

The dates at this 300-capacity venue are first announced as a one-week booking, with a second and then third week added as demand continues. Tickets are $35, and $40 on Friday and Saturday.

Neil Strauss reviews Wednesday's show in the *New York Times*, describing the venue as decorated to look like an English pub.

"Mr Davies of The Kinks chronicled his life in song and spoken word," writes Strauss. "His account, based on [*X-Ray*], took him from normal child to misfit teenager to upstart musician to exploited songwriter to wistful old-timer.

"For a songwriter of Mr. Davies's stature, Wednesday's show … was surprisingly intimate, honest and well-staged. … At other times, Mr. Davies offered new ways of listening to his songs. … When an old song didn't fit into Mr Davies's narration, he played new ones. … These songs written in his late-1960s style showed that Mr Davies's powers as a lyricist have hardly waned and that his voice was still capable of hitting the sweet high notes that can turn detailed observations into perfect pop."

Following the show on the 14th, Ray is honoured guest at a party thrown by Guardian Records at the Harley-Davidson Cafe, and his friend Elvis Costello is present. The following day, Ray and new manager Deke Arlon are in meetings with Guardian Records.

Tuesday 20th

❒ **TV** NBC Studios *New York, NY*. NBC *Live With Regis & Kathy Lee* Ray Davies and Pete Mathison live performance 'You Really Got Me'. Ray is also interviewed by hosts Regis Philbin and Kathy Lee Gifford on this popular morning talk/variety programme.

Wednesday 21st – Sunday 25th

Westbeth Theatre Center Music Hall *New York, NY* 7:30pm, except Saturday 6:30 & 10:30pm, *20th Century Man: An Evening With Ray Davies In Concert*
More solo shows with Ray accompanied by Mathison.
❒ **TV** Westbeth Theatre *New York, NY*. VH-1 **The Storyteller** live performance 'Lola', 'Sunny Afternoon', 'Come Dancing', 'London Song', 'Dead End Street', 'Celluloid Heroes', medley 'A Well Respected Man' / 'Harry Rag', 'To The Bone', 'You Really Got Me', 'Days', 'Waterloo Sunset' broadcast June 2nd and multiple times in days following that debut. Shot before Wednesday's show, for a VH-1 cable TV Special based on *20th Century Man*. 'The Ballad Of Julie Finkle' is evidently also taped for the show but not included in the broadcast.

➜ Dave travels to London around this time for a month of press work, and possibly some recording.

Tuesday 27th – Thursday 29th

Westbeth Theatre Center Music Hall *New York, NY* 7:30pm, *20th Century Man: An Evening With Ray Davies In Concert*
On the 28th Ray is scheduled on the TV show *Late Night With David Letterman* but doesn't appear because of a dispute over song selection.

Wednesday 28th

Kink: An Autobiography by Dave Davies is published in the UK. "On one level," writes D.J. Taylor in *The Mail On Sunday*, "the history of The Kinks is simply the history of a personal grievance: a furious argument about whose band it was, whose songs were going to get played, and in what style. ... All of this has been told before, discreetly (in Jon Savage's official biography of the group), indiscreetly (in numerous press stories), as well as being gestured at in Ray's rather good autobiography *X-Ray*. What startling condiments can Dave Davies add to this stew? It has to be said that in a genre characterised by a hankering for the archetypal, this is a highly archetypal book. ... A work of considerable cultural significance: another exemplary account of what happens if you take an impressionable teenager, give him lots of money and then let him make his own unguided way through a fraught and exploitive world. The comforting thing, perhaps, is how old-fashioned Dave Davies' version turns out to be, and his ability to emerge from the six-in-a-bed pill orgies as a halfway likeable character."

March

Friday 1st & Sunday 3rd

Westbeth Theatre Center Music Hall *New York, NY* 7:30pm, *20th Century Man: An Evening With Ray Davies In Concert*
A party with fans follows at local Mexican restaurant Tortilla Flats.

➜ While Ray is busy in New York, Dave does a string of media dates in Britain to promote his book.
☆ Some time this month, Dave writes the song 'Unfinished Business' with Dr Richard Lawrence – author, friend and psychic lecturer – after what Dave describes as a visitation by John Lennon at a cafe in Fulham.
☆ At Konk in London, The Kinks work on new tracks **'Animal'** and **'To The Bone'** for the expanded version of To The Bone.

April

➜ At Konk Studios, Ray completes all work on the two-CD version of *To The Bone*. While two new studio recordings will be included, probably four were recorded between the January and March sessions. Release is ready for June, but Guardian Records may delay until August.

▷ **TOUR STARTS** *20th Century Man: Ray Davies in Concert: US mini tour* (Apr 10th – May 18th). Ray Davies (lead vocal, guitar), Pete Mathison (guitar).

Wednesday 10th – Saturday 13th

Ohio Theatre *Cleveland, OH* 7:30pm
An extra show at this 1,035 capacity venue is planned for the 13th but that and an originally scheduled show on the 14th are cancelled due to poor ticket sales.
☆ Ray appears as a featured speaker in the *Lecture* series at the Rock & Roll Hall Of Fame in Cleveland, reading from *X-Ray* and answering questions from the audience. (Day off plus travel day follow.)

Tuesday 16th – Sunday 21st; Wednesday 24th – Saturday 27th

Apollo Theatre *Chicago, IL* 7:30pm (plus 10:00pm 20th)
Travel day plus two days off in San Francisco follow.

May

Wednesday 1st – Sunday 5th; Wednesday 8th – Saturday 11th

Alcazar Theatre *San Francisco, CA* 8:00pm
"The smartest thing the 50-ish singer-songwriter could have done," says Barry Walters in the *San Francisco Examiner* of Ray's songs-and-stories format. (Travel day following to Los Angeles.)
☆ The Kinks are advertised among the line-up for *Die Mega Party* on the 11th at the Elan Fitnesspark, Hildesheim, Germany (with Pygmalion, Hot Chocolate, Suzi Quatro, The Troggs, and Moulin Rouge) but the booking is never finalised.

Wednesday 15th – Saturday 18th

Henry Fonda Theatre *Los Angeles, CA* 8:00pm (7:30 & 10:30pm 18th)
A second show added for the 18th and a show on the 19th are cancelled due to slow ticket sales. Ray stays behind briefly in Los Angeles before heading back to London.

Thursday 30th

Ray makes an Ivor Novello Award presentation to The Small Faces at the annual ceremony at the Grosvenor House in central London.

Friday 31st

The Kinks reportedly hold an impromptu rehearsal at a rented building near tomorrow's festival site in Sweden to shake off the cobwebs prior to their performance and for the benefit of temporary keyboard player Dave Dulake. Dulake is filling in for Ian Gibbons who evidently has prior commitments, and is primarily known as the drummer in a band called The Phrogs from Southend (Gibbons's hometown).

June

Saturday 1st
Idrottsplats *Kristinebergs, Sweden* *12 Timmar 70-Tal På Festival ("12 Hours Of Seventies Music"),* with Van Morrison, Gary Glitter, Gilbert O'Sullivan, Boney M, Nationalteatern, Harpo, Sister Sledge, Cheap Trick, Gloria Gaynor, Pugh Pogefeldt
Much of the approximately 8,000 crowd has thinned out and gone home because of bad weather by the time The Kinks come on as the final act at 10:30pm, in what is almost universally described as an uninspired performance. "Ray destroyed one Kinks classic after another," says *Expressen*, while *Dagens Nyheter* describes them as "a clumsy rock band that played for a handful of fans at a deserted football arena".

Saturday 15th
Frognerbadet *Oslo, Norway* *Norwegian Wood Music Festival,* with Iggy Pop, Bel Canto, Ocean Colour Scene and others
At the time of writing, this is the final concert appearance by The Kinks. A further festival date in Munich in July will be considered, but is never booked. The band is headlining on the first of this two-day festival, and in contrast to the off-night two weeks earlier is back in fine form, winning over the crowd. "To say that The Kinks are good-looking would be an exaggeration," writes reviewer Haakon Moslet in *Dagbladet*, naturally unaware of the significance of the event. "Still, the audience, numbering about 5,000, sang along when the 33-year-old London band finished with 'You Really Got Me'. While Iggy Pop impressed with physical vitality, The Kinks appeared as very old men. Say what you like about Ray Davies, but elegant he is not. Nevertheless, it was a lot of fun. Grown-ups went down on their knees and cried when Ray and Dave played their hits. Some of the songs sounded a bit half-hearted, but when The Kinks played 'Lola', the audience became very enthusiastic. For the first time that day, most of the otherwise very relaxed crowd were up on their feet. When The Kinks played 'You Really Got Me' as the last encore, the middle-aged members of the audience were overjoyed at hearing one of rock'n'roll's greatest classics played live."

Friday 21st
❑ **TV** London Weekend Television Studio *central London*. ITV *Richard Littlejohn's Live & Uncut UK* Ray and Pete Mathison live performance 'Sunny Afternoon', 'London Song'.

July

Sunday 7th
Royal Albert Hall *central London* *Poetry Olympics*, Ray Davies, with Damon Albarn, John Cooper Clarke, Kylie Minogue, Patti Smith, Moondog, others
Lucy O'Brien is there for *Q* magazine, reporting that the crowd sings along as Ray plays a medley of 'Sunny Afternoon' / 'Lola' / 'Dedicated Follower Of Fashion'. "Albarn joins him for a chorus of 'Waterloo Sunset', and Davies does an irreverent version of 'Parklife'. A strange mix of method and mood, the day hadn't always gelled. But finally, at 11 at night, there is at last a real sense of easy intimacy. No mean feat."

☆ At Right Track Studios, Woodstock, NY, remix specialists Bob Clearmountain and Jason Goldstein mix 'To The Bone' and 'Animal' for the expanded version of The Kinks' *To The Bone*.

Thursday 18th
Ray oversees mastering by Ted Jenson of the two-CD *To The Bone* at Sterling Sound in New York City. Release date is now set for October 15th. Ray is also in NYC to being recording a solo album, but it's unclear if work is started.

Sunday 28th
Cherry Hinton Hall Grounds *Cambridge* *32nd Cambridge Folk Festival*, Ray Davies, with The Rankin Family, Luka Bloom, Townes Van Zandt, Chris Smither, Penguin Cafe Orchestra, Oysterband, Eileen Ivers, others

August

Ray is in New York City and scheduled to record a solo album, but evidently this does not happen. On the 26th, Guardian Records issues a CD5 (more than a CD single, less than an album) that includes the two new studio recordings, 'To The Bone' and 'Animal', plus the live version of 'Celluloid Heroes' as a preview of the new two-CD album. Reportedly only 500 copies are manufactured and distributed to radio stations, with no plans to issue it as commercial single. 'To The Bone' debuts the following day on Los Angeles radio and other stations.

September

Tuesday 17th
A two-CD set, *The Concert For The Rock'n'Roll Hall Of Fame*, is issued, but does not contain either performance by The Kinks from September 2nd 1995.
☆ Around this time, Ray's projects include a musical, *Come Dancing*, based on The Kinks' song of the same name, and a follow-up book to *X-Ray*.

➪ **TOUR STARTS** *Ray Davies: Storyteller US Tour* (Sep 25th – Nov 22nd). Ray Davies (lead vocal, guitar), Pete Mathison (guitar). Travel to New York City 23rd; press and technical rehearsals 24th in Stockbridge, MA. Heavy media schedule during the tour, including in-store, radio and TV appearances. Venue size 300-900. Tickets $25-35.

Wednesday 25th – Sunday 29th
Berkshire Theater Festival *Stockbridge, MA* 7:30pm (Sunday 6:00pm)
Travel day following. (Dave travels to Los Angeles at about this time.)

Thursday 26th
Am I The Kinda Girl album by Cathy Dennis released in Japan, with a new song by Ray Davies co-written with Dennis, 'The Date'. Issued in the UK March 17th 1997.

October

Tuesday 1st
Rhode Island Convention Center *Providence, RI* 8:00pm
Ray does a private performance 11:25am-12:25pm for a local record-store event, the *Strawberries/Maxie Waxie Convention*.

kinks'96

Tuesday 1st-Thursday 3rd
Lansdowne Street Playhouse *Boston, MA* 7:30pm
Further shows scheduled to take place from the 4th to the 6th are cancelled following tonight's performance due to excessive noise. The three remaining shows will be combined into a single show on the 6th at the Orpheum Theatre.

Ray instead devotes much of the 4th to media and press duties, and for part of the 4th and much of the 5th books time at a local recording studio, Sound Techniques, to remix and edit 'To The Bone' for commercial single release.

Sunday 6th
Orpheum Theatre *Boston, MA* 7:30pm

Monday 7th
❏ **TV** Ed Sullivan Theatre *New York, NY*. CBS **David Letterman Show** Ray Davies, Pete Mathison and Paul Schaffer live performance 'To The Bone', 'You Really Got Me' (extract), 'Victoria' (extract). The TV taping session begins at 8:00pm.

Tuesday 8th – Saturday 12th
Music Hall *Toronto, ON, Canada* 8:00pm
☆ On the 9th, during this season of appearances at the Music Hall, Dave conducts an online chat session on Prodigy, from the Continental Hyatt House in Los Angeles.
☆ Former Kinks road manager Ken Jones dies of cancer in Florida on the 12th.

Tuesday 15th
To The Bone album (two-CD version) released in the US.

Wednesday 16th – Thursday 17th
The Barns of Wolf Trap *Vienna, VA* 8:00pm
"Hilarious one moment and poignant the next," writes Geoffrey Hines in the *Washington Post* of tonight's show by Ray and Mathison. Hines goes on to pronounce the show he sees in Vienna as "unlike any other rock theater ever attempted".

Friday 18th
❏ **TV** ABC TV Studios *New York, NY*. ABC **Good Morning America** Ray and Pete Mathison live performance 'A Well Respected Man' (extract), 'Come Dancing', 'To The Bone' broadcast 7:00-9:00am EDT.

Saturday 19th
Music Hall *Portsmouth, NH* 8:00pm

Sunday 20th
Rich Forum, Stamford Center For The Arts *Stamford, CT* **2:00 & 8:00pm**
Day off in New York City follows.

Tuesday 22nd – Saturday 26th
Theatre Of The Living Arts *Philadelphia, PA* 8:00pm
Travel day follows to Seattle, and then a day off.

Thursday 24th
))) **RADIO** Tongue & Groove Studios *Philadelphia, PA*. WXPN-FM **World Cafe** Ray and Pete Mathison live performance '20th Century Man' (extract), 'To The Bone', 'Waterloo Sunset', 'Days' broadcast November 28th.

Tuesday 29th – Thursday 31st
Moore Theatre *Seattle, WA* 8:00pm

→ INDICATES EVENT AROUND THIS TIME BUT WITH NO FIRM DATE

To The Bone album (two-CD version)

1/1 'All Day And All Of The Night' live (R. DAVIES).
1/2 'Apeman' live (R. DAVIES).
1/3 'Tired Of Waiting For You' live (R. DAVIES).
1/4 'See My Friends' live (R. DAVIES).
1/5 'Death Of A Clown' live (D. DAVIES, R. DAVIES).
1/6 'Muswell Hillbiliies' live (R. DAVIES).
1/7 'Better Things' (R. DAVIES).
1/8 'Don't Forget To Dance' (R. DAVIES).
1/9 Ray Davies 'Sunny Afternoon' live (R. DAVIES).
1/10 Ray Davies 'Dedicated Follower Of Fashion' live (R. DAVIES).
1/11 Ray Davies 'Do It Again' live (R. DAVIES).
1/12 'Do It Again' live (R. DAVIES).
2/1 'Celluloid Heroes' live (R. DAVIES).
2/2 'Picture Book' 2nd version (R. DAVIES).
2/3 'The Village Green Preservation Society' 2nd version (R. DAVIES).
2/4 'Do You Remember Walter' live (R. DAVIES).
2/5 'Set Me Free' live (R. DAVIES).
2/6 'Lola' live (R. DAVIES).
2/7 'Come Dancing' live (R. DAVIES).
2/8 'I'm Not Like Everybody Else' live (R. DAVIES).
2/9 'Till The End Of The Day' live (R. DAVIES).
2/10 'Give The People What They Want' live (R. DAVIES).
2/11 'State Of Confusion' live (R. DAVIES).
2/12 'Dead End Street' live (R. DAVIES).
2/13 'A Gallon Of Gas' live (R. DAVIES).
2/14 'Days' live (R. DAVIES).
2/15 'You Really Got Me' live (R. DAVIES).
2/16 'Animal' (R. DAVIES).
2/17 'To The Bone' (R. DAVIES).

US release October 15th 1996 (Guardian 7243 8 37303 22).
UK release March 3rd 1997 (Guardian 7243 8 37303 21).
Disc 1 contents same as UK single-CD release (see October 3rd 1994) except omits that disc's tracks 6 and 10 and adds this disc's tracks 1/11 and 1/12.
Musicians Ray Davies lead vocal, acoustic guitar, electric guitar. Dave Davies acoustic guitar, electric guitar, backing vocal. Jim Rodford bass guitar, backing vocal. Bob Henrit drums. Ian Gibbons keyboards.
Recorded 1/11, 1/12, 2/8, 2/14: Royal Concert Hall *Glasgow, Scotland*; November 25th 1993. 2/1, 2/12: live concert recording, unknown location and date. 2/2, 2/3: Konk Studios *Hornsey, north London*; April 1994. 2/4, 2/5, 2/13: live Konk Studios *Hornsey, north London*; April 11th 1994. 2/6, 2/7, 2/9-11: Guildhall *Portsmouth*; March 25th 1994. 2/15: Mann Music Center *Philadelphia, PA*; August 12th 1993. 2/16, 2/17: Konk Studios (No.2) *Hornsey, north London*; March-April 1996.
Producer Ray Davies.
Engineers except as noted: Stan Loubieres; assistant engineers Graham Hogg, Mark Aubrey, Will Pitt; studio assistant Phillip Crosbie. 2/16, 2/17: Richard Edwards; assistant engineer Mark Aubrey. Mixed at Right Track Studios New York, NY by Bob Clearmountain assisted by Jason Goldstein.
Chart high US none; UK none.

November

Friday 1st – Saturday 2nd

Moore Theatre *Seattle, WA* 8:00pm
Travel day to New York City follows.

Monday 3rd

→))) **RADIO** United Stations Network Studios *New York, NY*. United Stations Radio Network *The Difference* Ray live performance 'To The Bone', 'Waterloo Sunset' syndicated broadcasts November 16th-22nd.

Tuesday 5th – Sunday 10th

Westbeth Theatre *New York, NY* 8:00pm
Songs added to the regular set at various points during this run as special treats for the fans include 'Animal Farm', 'Come Dancing', 'Shangri-La' (extract), 'Celluloid Heroes', 'Get Back In Line', 'Ducks On The Wall' (extract), 'The Ballad Of Julie Finkle', 'I'm Not Like Everybody Else', 'Dead End Street', 'Powerman' and 'The Village Green Preservation Society'. An extended run from the 13th-17th was pencilled in but is dropped. (Travel day back to London on the 11th, and then a return to the States on the 15th for more dates.)
☆ Around now, Ray is interviewed by long-time Kinks supporter and friend Lisa Robinson for *The New York Post*. "I'm not doing anything with The Kinks at the moment," he tells her. "It's a coincidence that we have this double-CD *To The Bone* out, but that was ready last year. I've only been in the studio with [The Kinks] to do two tracks for that." When asked how he gets along with his brother these days, he responds: "Not great. We're trying to make it so that we don't have any business dealings together any more, which will hopefully make it easier for us to work as musicians."

Saturday 16th

))) **RADIO** Buddy Guy's Legend *Chicago, IL*. WXRT-FM *Brunch With Ray* Davies Ray and Pete Mathison live performance 'Apeman', 'Animal', 'A Well Respected Man', 'To The Bone' broadcast 3:00-6:00pm. Hosted by DJs Lin Brehmar and Kathy Voltmar. Ray also good-naturedly participates in a comedy skit called Dueling Insanities.

Sunday 17th

Vic Theatre *Chicago, IL* 8:00pm
Ray's "solo" shows with Mathison continue. Tonight's at this 1,200-capacity venue is reportedly recorded for possible future use. (Travel day follows, plus day off in Atlanta.)
☆ Edward Kassner, Ray's first music publisher, dies today at age 76.

Wednesday 20th – Thursday 21st

Variety Playhouse *Atlanta, GA* 8:00pm
These shows are reportedly filmed.

Friday 22nd

Carefree Theatre *West Palm Beach, FL* 8:00pm
End of this *Storyteller* US tour.

December

→ At the start of the month, Dave is shopping a recently finished script for a film or play around London. He also makes arrangements with Castle Communications for the upcoming release of a Dave Davies anthology record.
    Ray is scheduled to begin recording solo tracks, apparently with Cliff Richard's rhythm section, details unknown.

Monday 2nd

Guardian Records issues a promo CD of 'To The Bone' in full-length and edited form, along with a demo version by Ray. This is intended to re-activate the song over Christmas; the possibility of a quick tie-in Kinks tour is also mentioned.

Sunday 8th

The Kast Off Kinks – with Mick Avory, John Dalton and John Gosling – perform at the Archway Tavern in north London, with Jim Rodford and Bob Henrit sitting in.

Tuesday 10th

❏ **TV** BBC Television Centre *west London*. BBC-2 *Later With Jools Holland* Ray and Pete Mathison live performance 'To The Bone', 'Sunny Afternoon' (latter with guest Dominic Greensmith from Reef on spoons), 'Lola' broadcast December 14th.

→ During the autumn a TV advertising campaign begins in the UK that is planned to celebrate the 30th anniversary of British Telecom's *Yellow Pages* phone directory, and the campaign prominently uses The Kinks' recording of 'Days'.
    Originally, a re-release of the song in Britain to capitalise on the ads is planned on a CD EP for December 9th, delayed to January 6th. It's difficult to ignore the symbolism of the release of a song that in part is clearly about the ending of relationships, at a time when the band itself seems to be imploding.
☆ Back in early November a BBC studio or a London club was tentatively reserved for December 12th-15th to tape a Kinks special for US radio syndicator Westwood One.
    Ray's intention was to have the original four Kinks reunite to record a one-off radio show, but the idea is pushed to January and then dropped entirely.
☆ Dave is back in Los Angeles for the Christmas/New Year holidays. He is considering using some of the local LA musicians from his February 1995 charity appearance for future dates.

After 1996...

Dave Davies returned to London on January 12th 1997 to plan with Ray Davies and manager Deke Arlon any potential Kinks activities and to shoot his inserts for the Kinks video of 'To The Bone'. The completed video was full of symbolism at a precarious time for the band and for the relationship between Ray and Dave.

It largely reprised Ray's 1970s hippy character from the 1981 video for 'Predictable', looking back on his life and career as a series of flashback scenes and TV images, with the inevitable ending of relationships along the way. The final scene cuts to Dave alone snapping a photo of one of Ray's irate lovers from the song's story as she storms off in anger, seemingly mirroring the brothers' own crumbling relationship. The video, made available in time to coincide with the UK release on March 3rd of the two-CD version of *To The Bone*, went virtually unaired, and the CD set too was similarly overlooked.

During the evening of Monday February 3rd Ray threw a surprise 50th birthday party for Dave at the Clissold Arms pub on Fortis Green in north London. Kinks members Rodford, Henrit and Gibbons and many of the remaining Davies family were present. It marked a turning point after which Ray and Dave's professional relationship seemed to fall apart.

Dave returned to the US shortly afterwards to promote the US publication of his book, **Kink**, and pursued his own solo career in earnest, finally assembling his own band from LA musicians he'd befriended. He would make his true solo debut on April 21st at Luna Park, west Hollywood, CA, and toured sporadically thereafter.

Ray continued his solo activities, including the popular "one-man" shows. His solo career had developed in parallel with The Kinks over the course of 1995-96 once he happened upon the concept for his **Storyteller** stage show. It was a perfect vehicle for him and an ideal way to move on from The Kinks. It provided freedom from the shackles of the huge entourage that any modern touring band requires, it relieved him of the stress – but also the benefits – of working with his brother, and it distanced him from the sheer on-stage volume of the rock'n'roll experience.

No formal break-up of The Kinks was evident, and plans for future band activities were floated well into 1998. The Rodford/Henrit band was evidently long off retainer by 1996 and no longer an active outfit by 1997. During the autumn of 1997, Ray and Mick Avory were both in contact with Pete Quaife, and all three were willing to undertake a strictly recording-only Kinks project, designed to fulfil an outstanding obligation to Guardian Records for that label's second Kinks album. Dave, however, was not in favour, and despite public airing of the plan it never happened.

Quaife came down from his home in Canada to New York City in May 1998 to catch back-to-back solo shows by the Davies brothers. On the 23rd he attended a performance by Dave at the Bottom Line and sat in on bass for 'You Really Got Me'. The following night, Quaife saw

Ray in performance at the Trump Arena's Shell Theatre in Atlantic City, NJ, but didn't even get to speak to Ray. Any further thoughts of reforming the original band were essentially put to rest, and The Kinks just seemed to fade away.

All this was taking place amid the largest ever reorganisation and promotion of most of the band's back catalogue, including the exhumation of some bonus material. The business was spearheaded by manager Arlon, who worked hand in hand with Ray to win back some control over the old Pye catalogue, and because of a worldwide licensing deal for the RCA and Arista catalogues that went to an upstart US label, Velvel Records. Dave's career got a similar backwards look and reassessment with two CD sets issued on both sides of the Atlantic, **Unfinished Business** and **The Dave Davies Anthology**.

In 1998 Ray issued his first and, to date, only solo effort. *The Storyteller* was a combination of live and new studio recordings that captured his now long-running "one-man" show for posterity. It was issued through EMI Records, parent company of the now defunct Guardian Records. Ray wrote a second book, **Waterloo Sunset – Stories**, this one a collection of essays based on the titles of some of his songs, and it was published in 1999. At the same time, a Kinks hits CD (*The Singles Collection*) was released with a bonus disc, **The Songs Of Ray Davies: Waterloo Sunset**, which was intended to accompany the book, including some previously unreleased and newly-exhumed performances by Ray and by The Kinks.

The limited company Kinks 85, the last business partnership that Ray and Dave formed to handle ongoing Kinks business, was formally terminated at the very end of 1998. This certainly closed down the late-1980s/1990s version of The Kinks. But it doesn't prevent Ray and Dave entering into a new venture of their own choosing at any time.

Both Ray and Dave continued to tour their respective solo projects. Dave, based in Los Angeles, maintained a relatively high public profile through the establishment of a well-maintained official website, DaveDavies.com, and released new CDs through conventional channels as well as private releases through his website.

Early in May 2000 Dave reportedly had dinner with Ray in London and discussed future Kinks plans. But they realised their ideas about what The Kinks could be were too far apart. Any further mention of the final Kinks album that was still owed had faded by this time, and it seems the matter was eventually somehow settled with EMI. Another piece of the band's recorded history was filled in with the release in 2001 of some of their long-lost recordings made at the BBC during the 1960s and '70s, on the two-CD set **The Kinks BBC Sessions 1964-77**.

At the time of writing, in May 2003, Ray and Dave and The Kinks are all still managed by Deke Arlon, currently affiliated with Sanctuary Music Management. In spring 2003, Dave began to speak favourably of the chances that he and Ray would team up again in the foreseeable future. With the 40th anniversary of the band's rise to fame approaching in 2004, there is still at least a hope that the two can work together and make some more musical magic.

RADIO SESSIONS

Key to Entries
Broadcast date / Recording date (one date only = broadcast date) / Show name / Radio station / Station channel / Time of broadcast / Location / Songs (syndication if any)
Notes
Mono recordings to circa 1970; stereo thereafter.
TOTP = *Top Of The Pops* (syndicated radio show)
record = same as commercial recording
record+ = commercial recording with minor element added at the BBC

1964

Sep 19 / Sep 7 / Saturday Club / BBC / Light / 10am-12 noon / Playhouse Theatre, London / Got Love If You Want It, Little Queenie (*TOTP 1 Dec 4*), Cadillac (*TOTP 1 Dec 4*), You Really Got Me (*TOTP 1 Dec 4*).

Nov 13 / Nov 6 / Joe Loss Pop Show / BBC / Light / 12:30-1:30 pm / Playhouse Theatre, London / All Day and All of the Night, It's Alright, You Really Got Me, I'm a Lover Not a Fighter. (Before invited audience. BBC files list You Really Got A Hold On Me but believed to be clerical error and actual song performed is You Really Got Me.)

Nov 19 / Oct 30 / Top Gear / BBC / Light / 10-11.55pm / Playhouse Theatre, London / I'm a Lover Not a Fighter (*TOTP 6 Jan 8*), Long Tall Shorty, You Really Got Me (*TOTP 6 Jan 8*), Too Much Monkey Business, All Day and All Of The Night (*TOTP 6 Jan 8*), Bye Bye Johnny.

Dec 12 / Dec 9 / Saturday Club / BBC / Light / 10am-12 noon / Piccadilly Studio 1, London / I'm a Lover Not a Fighter (*TOTP 9 Jan 29*), I've Got That Feeling (*TOTP 9 Jan 29*), All Day and All of the Night (*TOTP 9 Jan 29*), Stop Your Sobbing, Louie Louie

1965

Feb 26 / live / Joe Loss Pop Show / BBC / Light / 12:30-1:30 pm / Playhouse Theatre, London / Naggin', Come On Now, Tired of Waiting For You, All Day and All of the Night. (Before invited audience.)

Feb 28 / Feb 23 / Musicorama / French Europe 1 Radio / Olympia Theatre, Paris / Bye Bye Johnny, You Really Got Me, Long Tall Shorty, All Day And All Of The Night, Tired Of Waiting For You, (unconfirmed additional song).

Apr 24 / Apr 20 / Saturday Club / BBC / Light / 10am-12noon / Maida Vale Studios, London / Dancing In The Street, Naggin', Nothin' In This World, Ev'rybody's Gonna Be Happy (*TOTP 26 May 28*), You Shouldn't Be Sad (*TOTP 26 May 28*), Tired of Waiting For You [not aired] (*TOTP 26 May 28*).

Aug 30 / Aug 6 / You Really Got (Holiday Pop) / BBC / Light / 10:45am-12noon / Aeolian Hall, Studio 1, London / Hide And Seek (*TOTP 43 Sep 24*), This Strange Effect (*TOTP 43 Sep 24*), See My Friends (*TOTP 43 Sep 24*), Never Met a Girl Like You Before, Milk Cow Blues, You Really Got Me [intro & outro] (*TOTP 56 Dec 24*).

Sep 4 / Aug 10 / Saturday Club / BBC / Light / 10am-12 / Playhouse Theatre, London / Never Met A Girl Like You Before (*TOTP 47 Oct 22*), Milk Cow Blues (*TOTP 47 Oct 22*), Wonder Where My Baby Is Tonight (*TOTP 47 Oct 22*) / Got My Feet On The Ground, See My Friends.

Nov 19 / live / Joe Loss Pop Show / BBC / Light / 12:30-1:30pm / Camden Theatre, London / A Well Respected Man, Milk Cow Blues, Never Met A Girl Like You Before, You Really Got Me. (Before invited audience.)

Dec 18 / Dec 13 / Saturday Club / BBC / Light / 10am-12noon / Playhouse Theatre, London / A Well Respected Man (*TOTP 60 Jan 21*), Till the End of the Day (*TOTP 60 Jan 21*), Where Have All The Good Times Gone (*TOTP 60 Jan 21*), I Am Free.

1967

Aug 5 / Aug 4 / Saturday Club / BBC / Light / 10am-12noon / Playhouse Theatre, London / Death Of A Clown (*TOTP 146 Sep 15*), Good Luck Charm [not aired] (*TOTP 146 Sep 15*), Love Me Till The Sun Shines

[not aired] (*TOTP 146 Sep 15*). 'Clown' also aired Saturday Club Aug 26.

Oct 29 / Oct 25 / Top Gear / BBC / Radio-1 / 2-4pm / Maida Vale Studio 4, London / David Watts (*TOTP 161 Dec 29*), Mister Pleasant (*TOTP 161 Dec 29*), Sunny Afternoon (*TOTP 158 Dec 8*), Harry Rag (*TOTP 158 Dec 8*), Suzannah's Still Alive (*TOTP 161 Dec 29*), Autumn Almanac [record + vocals] (*TOTP 158 Dec 8*). Tracks also aired on Radio-1 shows: Happening Sunday (Nov 11), Saturday Club (Nov 11), Jimmy Young Show (Nov 20-24), Dec 11-15), Top Gear (Nov 26), Saturday Club (Dec 2).

1968

July 7 / July 1 / Top Gear / BBC / Radio-1 / 2-4pm / BBC Piccadilly Studio 1, London / Days (*TOTP 193 Aug 9*), Monica, Love Me Till the Sun Shines, (*TOTP 193 Aug 9*), Waterloo Sunset (*TOTP 193 Aug 9*). Tracks also aired on Top Gear (Aug 4).

July 13 / July 9 / Saturday Club / BBC / Radio-1 / 10am-12noon / Playhouse Theater, London / Days (*TOTP 196 Aug 30*), Monica (*TOTP 196 Aug 30*), Love Me Till the Sun Shines (*TOTP 196 Aug 30*), Suzannah's Still Alive. Tracks also aired on Radio-1 shows: Afternoon Pop Show (July 20, 21-26), Stuart Henry Show (July 21), Dave Cash Show (Aug 15).

Nov 30 / Nov 26 / Saturday Club / BBC / Radio-1 / 10am-

12noon / Playhouse Theatre, London / The Village Green Preservation Society (*TOTP 215 Jan 10*), Animal Farm [record+] (*TOTP 215 Jan 10*), Johnny Thunder [record] (*TOTP 215 Jan 10*), Last Of The Steam Powered Trains [record] (*TOTP 222 Feb 28*). Tracks also aired on Radio-1 shows: Afternoon Pop Show (Dec 7, 9-13), Dave Cash Show (Dec 9-13; Dec 30-Jan 3), David Symmonds Show (Dec 23-25).

1969

Apr 13 / Apr 2 / Symonds On Sunday / BBC / Radio-1 / 10am-12noon / Aeolian Hall, Studio 1, London / Plastic Man [record+] (*TOTP 234 May 23*), Do You Remember Walter [record+] (*TOTP 235 May 30*), King Kong [record remix] (*TOTP 234 May 23*), Hold My Hand [record?]. Tracks also aired on Radio-1 show Sounds Like Tony Brandon (May 5-9; 19-23).

Dec 28 / Dec 18 / Dave Lee Travis / BBC / Radio-1 / 10am-12noon / Camden Theatre, London / Victoria [record+] (*TOTP 270 Jan 30*), Mr. Churchill Says [record+] (*TOTP 270 Jan 30*), Arthur [record remix/edit] (*TOTP 270 Jan 30*), Days. Unconfirmed if Days is unique or reused version from earlier session. Tracks also aired on Radio-1 show Dave Cash Show (Jan 12-16; 26-30).

1970

May 31 / May 18 / Dave Lee Travis / BBC / Radio-1 / 10am-12noon / Aeolian Hall, Studio 2, London / Lola [record+] (*TOTP 295 Jul 24*), Days [record +] (*TOTP 298 Aug 14*), Mindless Child Of Motherhood (*TOTP 295 Jul 24*), medley Dedicated Follower Of Fashion / A Well Respected Man / Death Of A Clown / Sunny Afternoon. Medley is likely a unique BBC recording. Tracks also aired on Radio-1 shows: Johnnie Walker Show (June 8-12), Jimmy Young Show (June 29-July 3).

Dec 13 / Nov / Dave Lee Travis / BBC / Radio-1 / 10am-12noon / "own studio" not BBC / Apeman [record+] (*TOTP 318? Jan 1*), This Time Tomorrow [record] (*TOTP 323 Feb 5*), Top Of The Pops [record] (*TOTP 323 Feb 5*), Lola [record?]. Tracks also aired on Radio-1 shows: Sounds Like Tony Brandon (Jan 12-15), Terry Wogan Show (Feb 1-5), Radio 1 Club/Dave Cash (Feb 8-12).

1972

May 16 / May 5 / John Peel Top Gear / BBC / Radio-1 / Studio T1, Transcription Service, Kensington House, London / Supersonic Rocketship (*TOTP 394 Jun 16*), Holiday (*TOTP 394 Jun 16*), Acute Schizophrenia Paranoia Blues (*TOTP 394 Jun 16*), Skin and Bone (*TOTP 394 Jun 16*). Tracks also aired on Radio-1 shows: Afternoon Pop Show (May 27), Alan Freeman (May 29; June 2), Johnnie Walker Show (June 5-9; July 10-14), Dave Lee Travis (July 3-7).

1974

July 11 / Jun 6 / John Peel / BBC / Radio-1 / 10-12pm / Langham Studio 1, London / Demolition (*TOTP 503 Jul 19*), Mirror of Love (*TOTP 503 Jul 19*), Money Talks (*TOTP 503 Jul 19*).

Jul 27 / Jul 14 / In Concert / BBC / Radio-1 / 6-7pm / Hippodrome Theatre, Golders Green, London / Victoria, Here Comes Yet Another Day, Mr. Wonderful, Money Talks, Dedicated Follower Of Fashion, Mirror of Love, Celluloid Heroes, medley You Really Got Me / All Day & All of the Night, Daylight, Here Comes Flash, Demolition, He's Evil, Lola, medley Skin & Bone / Dry Bones. All tracks except first medley syndicated on Pop Special 76 Aug. Before an invited audience.

1975

Jun 14 / syndication only / DIR / New Victoria Theatre, London / Everybody's A Star (Starmaker)*, Ordinary People*, Rush Hour Blues*, Nine To Five*, When Work Is Over*, Have Another Drink*, Underneath the Neon Sign*, You Make It All Worthwhile*, medley: A Well Respected Man / Dedicated Follower of Fashion / Sunny Afternoon**, Ducks On The Wall* **, Face In The Crowd* **, You Can't Stop The Music* **. (Tracks syndicated to British Biscuit Aug 24*, Dec 21 **.) Recorded live in concert.

1977

Feb 18 / syndication only / DIR / Santa Monica Civic Auditorium, Santa Monica, CA / One Of The Survivors Sleepwalker, Waterloo Sunset, A Well Respected Man, Sunny Afternoon, Celluloid Heroes, Schooldays, Education, Life Goes On, Lola, Alcohol, medley You Really Got Me / All Day And All Of The Night. (All tracks syndicated to King Biscuit Flower Hour Apr 23.) Recorded live in concert and as back up for live broadcast from Winterland, San Francisco, CA Feb 19; ultimately 12 songs from recording this night chosen for syndication, presumably due to better performance and/or recording results. Full concert details unconfirmed. Eight recordings subsequently re-syndicated on LP as *Supergroups In Concert* Aug 7 '82.

Feb 19 / The Kinks Live From Winterland / KSAN-FM / 107.7 / Winterland Ballroom, San Francisco, CA / Opening, One Of The Survivors, Sleepwalker, Rush Hour Blues, You Make It All Worthwhile, medley Ordinary People / Everybody's A Star (Starmaker), Banana Boat Song, A Well Respected Man, Sunny Afternoon, Waterloo Sunset, Celluloid Heroes, Schooldays (reprise), The Hard Way, Education, Brother, Stormy Sky, Life Goes On, Full Moon, Lola, Alcohol, medley You Really Got Me / All Day And All Of The Night, Victoria. Recorded live in concert.

Mar 7 / KTXQ-FM / 102.1 / KTXQ Studios, Dallas, TX / Life On The Road (Ray), A Well Respected Man (Ray), Here Come The People In Grey (Ray), 20th Century Man (Ray), Acute Schizophrenia Paranoia Blues (Ray), Oklahoma USA (Ray). Impromptu performanc; Ray accompanies himself on acoustic guitar.

Dec 24 / Old Grey Whistle Test: The Kinks Christmas Concert / BBC / Radio-1 / 10-10:45pm / Rainbow Theatre, Finsbury Park, London / Juke Box Music * ** (probably back-up recording from Dec 23 show), Sleepwalker* **, Life On The Road* **, medley A Well Respected Man / Death Of A Clown / Sunny Afternoon, Waterloo Sunset* **, All Day And All Of The Night* **, Slum Kids* **, Celluloid Heroes* **, Get Back In Line* **, The Hard Way* **, Lola* **, Alcohol* **, medley Skin And Bones / Dry Bones*, Father Christmas, You Really Got Me*. Syndicated to In Concert (UK) Apr 23 *, BBC Rock Hour (US) Apr 23 **. Recorded live in concert; simulcast with BBC-1 TV broadcast.

1980

Dec 31 / New Year's Eve With The Kinks / Starfleet Stereo Network / worldwide via satellite / 11pm / Palladium, New York City / Opening*, The Hard Way*, medley Where Have All The Good Times Gone / Tired Of Waiting For You*, Catch Me Now, I'm Falling*, Bird Dog, New York City Blues (improvisation), Lola*, Dead End Street*, Till The End Of The Day*, Low Budget*, Imagination's Real*, Nothing More To Lose*, I'm Not Like Everybody Else, Come On Now, New Year's Eve countdown, You Really Got Me*, Give The People What They Want*, A Gallon Of Gas*, Celluloid Heroes*, All Day And All Of The Night*, Stop Your Sobbing*, Pressure*. Syndicated to Source: The Kinks Concert Feb 19 *. Recorded live in concert. Broadcast worldwide via satellite.

1982

Sep / Feb 27 / NHK Radio / Seinen-Kan, Tokyo / Around The Dial, The Hard Way, Where Have All The Good Times Gone, Tired Of Waiting For You, Come On Now, Destroyer, Yo-Yo, Oh Oh Tokyo (improvisation), Lola, Low Budget, (Wish I Could Fly Like) Superman, Back To Front, Celluloid Heroes, Till The End Of The Day, Bernadette, All Day And All Of The Night, Give The People What They Want, Pressure, Stop Your Sobbing, David Watts, You Really Got Me. Recorded live in concert.

1984

Dec 29, 1985 / Nov 23 / The Kinks In Concert / HR-3 / Festhalle, Frankfurt, West Germany / Around The Dial, (Definite Maybe intro) / State Of Confusion, Where Have All The Good Times Gone, The Hard Way, Don't Forget To Dance, Come Dancing, Low Budget, Do It Again, Word Of Mouth, Lola, David Watts, Dead End Street, Living On A Thin Line, Good Day, All Day And All Of The NIght, Till The End Of The Day, Celluloid Heroes, You Really Got Me, I Gotta Move. Recorded live in concert. Full broadcast of audio portion of West German ZDF & SWF TV show *Rock Und Ballads,* originally broadcast Dec 2 '84.

1986

Nov 23 / The Howard Stern Show / WXRK-FM / 92.3 / WXRK Studios, New York City / Lola, You Really Got Me, Come Dancing. Ray Davies with Pig Vomit; off-the-cuff versions with Howard Stern also singing. All tracks syndicated to National Howard Stern Show, Nov 29-Dec 5.

1987

Mar 8 / Budweiser Sunday Night Concert Special: The Kinks / WXRT-FM / 93.1 / 9-10pm CST / The Riviera Nightclub, Chicago, IL / Do It Again*, The Hard Way, Low Budget*, Come Dancing*, Working At The Factory*, Lost And Found*, Welcome To Sleazy Town*, Think Visual*, The Video Shop, Living On A Thin Line*, Guilty*, Misfits, Lola*, State Of Confusion*, A Gallon Of Gas, All Day And All Of The Night*, I Gotta Move*, Celluloid Heroes*, 20th Century Man*, You Really Got Me*, Till The End Of The Day*. Syndicated to King Biscuit Flower Hour May 10 & 17 *. Recorded live in concert. Edited and remixed for syndication.

1988

Apr 8 / syndication only / Westwood One Radio Networks / Riverside Theatre, Milwaukee, WI / Do It Again*, Destroyer*, Low Budget*, Apeman, Sleepwalker*, Come Dancing*, Art Lover*, Cliches Of The World*, Lost And Found*, A Gallon Of Gas (intro) / Welcome To Sleazy Town*, Think Visual*, Too Much On My Mind*, Living On A Thin Line*, A Well Respected Man*, It (I Want It), Guilty*, All Day And All Of The Night*, The Road, You Really Got Me**, Celluloid Heroes*, Lola*. Syndicated to Superstar Concert July 29-31 *; Isle Of Dreams Festival 1988 **. This recording was back-up show for *Live From The Fox Theatre* broadcast and was used in syndication.

Apr 14 / The Kinks: Live From The Fox Theatre, St. Louis / Fox Theatre, St. Louis, MO / Do It Again, Destroyer, Low Budget, Apeman, Sleepwalker, Art Lover, Come Dancing, Cliches Of The World, Lost And Found, Welcome To Sleazy Town, Think Visual, Too Much On My Mind, Living On A Thin Line, A Well Respected Man, It (I Want It), Guilty, All Day And All Of The Night, The Road, You Really Got Me, Celluloid Heroes, Lola. Live broadcast by satellite US Westwood One syndicated radio. Do It Again, Cliches Of The World, Too Much On My Mind omitted from broadcast for station breaks.

1993

Feb 4 / Mark & Brian KLOS Morning Show / KLOS-FM / 95.5 / 9am / KLOS Studios, LA / Hatred (A Duet), Sweet Lady Genevieve, Still Searching, A Well Respected Man. Ray & Dave Davies; 'Genevieve' with fans Greg Romayo and Scott Gilbertson singing; 'Well Respected' with hosts Mark Thompson and Brian Phelps singing.

May 12 / The Kinks Live At Electric Ladyland / WNEW-FM / 102.7 / 8:50-9:30pm / Electric Ladyland Studios, New York / Around The Dial (extract), Destroyer, Phobia, Drift Away, Only A Dream, Apeman, Harry Rag, Hatred (A Duet), Come Dancing, Somebody Stole My Car, Low Budget. Death Of A Clown is unbroadcast encore for invited audience of about 25 people.

Nov 16/17 / BBC / Greater London Radio / 12midnight / BBC Broadcasting House, London / Days. Ray & Dave Davies.

Nov 20 / Nov 16? / Big Red Mug Show / Virgin / 1215 / 10am-1pm / Virgin Radio Studios, London / Somebody Stole My Car. Ray & Dave Davies.

1994

Jan 7 / Johnny Walker Show / BBC / Radio-1 / 3:30-4:30pm / Maida Vale Studios, London / Phobia, Over The Edge, Wall Of Fire, Till End Of The Day. The Kinks minus Dave Davies and with guitarist Jakko Jakszyk.

Sep 13 / Simon Mayo / BBC / Radio-1 / 9-12 pm / BBC Broadcasting House, London / The Ballad Of Julie Finkle, Waterloo Sunset, Days. Ray Davies accompanying himself on acoustic guitar.

Oct 8 / Oct 7 / Emma Freud Show / BBC / Radio-1 / Maida Vale Studios, London / All Day And All Of The Night, Waterloo Sunset, I'm Not Like Everybody Else, Till The End of The Day, You Really Got Me. Kinks' final appearance at BBC studios, almost 30 years since first appearance.

Dec 27 / Dec 21 / Rocknacht / SDR / SDR-3 / 7 pm / Hans Martin Schleierhalle, Stuttgart / All Day And All Of The Night, Dead End Street, Come Dancing, You Really Got Me, Lola, Days. Simulcast on German SWR-3 TV of *The Heroes Of Rock* concert, also with Kansas and Electric Light Orchestra II.

1996

Oct 23 / Oct 23 / WMMR-FM / 93.3 / WMMR Studios, Philadelphia / Animal, To The Bone, X-Ray. Ray Davies & Pete Mathison. Not all complete versions.

Nov 28 / Oct 24 / World Cafe / WXPN-FM / 88.5 / 2:30-4pm / Tongue & Groove Studios, Philadelphia / 20th Century Man, To The Bone, Waterloo Sunset, Days. Ray Davies (& Pete Mathison). Broadcast nationally.

Nov 3 / syndicated only / United Stations / United Nations Studios, New York / To The Bone, Waterloo Sunset. Ray Davies & Pete Mathison; syndicated to The Difference Nov 16-22.

Nov 16 / Brunch with Ray Davies / WXRT-FM / 93.1 / 3-6pm / Buddy Guy's Legend, Chicago / Apeman, Animal, A Well Respected Man, To The Bone. Ray Davies & Pete Mathison. Before an invited audience. Ray Davies also participates in comedy skit 'Duelling Insanities' with show hosts.

TV SESSIONS

Key to Entries

Broadcast date / Recording date (one date only = broadcast date) / Show name / TV company / Channel / Time of broadcast / Location / Songs

Abbreviations

RSG = *Ready Steady Go!*

TOTP = *Top Of The Pops*

TC = BBC Television Centre

1964

Feb 7 / RSG / Rediffusion / ITV / Kingsway / Long Tall Sally.

Jul 31 / RSG /Rediffusion / ITV / Kingsway / You Really Got Me, Got Love ... (live).

Aug 14 / RSG / Rediffusion / ITV / Kingsway / You Really Got Me.

Aug 17 / Aug 12 / Discs A Go Go / TWW / ITV / Bristol / You Really Got Me.

Aug 19 / TOTP / BBC / BBC-1 / Manchester / You Really Got Me.

Aug 20 / For Teenagers Only / ATV / ITV / Borehamwood / You Really Got Me.

Aug 26 / TOTP / BBC / BBC-1 / Manchester / You Really Got Me.

Sep 2 / TOTP / BBC / BBC-1 / Manchester / You Really Got Me.

Sep 9 / Sep 2 / TOTP / BBC / BBC-1 / Manchester / You Really Got Me.

Sep 16 / Sep 15 / TOTP / BBC / BBC-1 / Manchester / You Really Got Me.

Oct 5 / Oct 1 / Beat Room / BBC / BBC-2 / 7-7.30pm / You Really Got Me (live) / TC / Got Love .. (live).

Oct 22 / Dig This! / Scottish TV / Glasgow / You Really Got Me(?), All Day And All Of The Night.

Oct 30 / / RSG / Rediffusion / ITV / All Day And All Of The Night / Kingsway / Just Can't Go To Sleep(?), Long Tall Shorty(?).

Nov 5 / Nov 4 / TOTP / BBC / BBC-1 / 7-7.30pm / Manchester / All Day And All Of The Night.

Nov 11 / Nov 9 / Top Beat / BBC / BBC-2 / Royal Albert Hall / All Day And All Of The Night(?) (live).

Nov 12 / Nov 4 / TOTP / BBC / BBC-1 / 7-7.30pm / Manchester / All Day And All Of The Night.

Nov 19 / Nov 18 / TOTP / BBC / BBC-1 / 7-7.30pm / Manchester / All Day And All Of The Night.

Nov 26 / Nov 4 / TOTP / BBC / BBC-1 / 7-7.30pm / Manchester / All Day And All Of The Night. Rebroadcast of insert taped Nov 4 broadcast Nov 12.

Dec 24 / Dec 15 / TOTP '64 / BBC / BBC-1 / Manchester / You Really Got Me.

Dec 31 / Beat In The New... / BBC-2 / 7-7.30pm / You Really Got Me (live) / TC / It's Alright ... (live).

Dec 31 / Dec 31 / RSG / Rediffusion / ITV / Kingsway / All Day And All Of The Night(?).

1965

Jan 7 / TOTP / BBC / BBC-1 / 7-7.30pm / Manchester / Tired Of Waiting.

Jan 9 / Jan 3 / ABC / ITV / Thank Your Lucky Stars / Birmingham / Tired Of Waiting.

Jan 15 / RSG / Rediffusion / ITV / Kingsway / Tired Of Waiting.

Jan 20 / Dec 17 / Shindig! / ABC / Shepperton Film / You Really Got Me, All Day And All Of The Night.

Jan 21 / Jan 6 / TOTP / BBC / BBC-1 / 7-7.30pm / Manchester / Tired Of Waiting.

Jan 28 / Jan 6 / TOTP / BBC / BBC-1 / 7-7.30pm / Manchester / Tired Of Waiting.

Feb 4 / Jan 6 / TOTP / BBC / BBC-1 / 7-7.30pm / Manchester / Tired Of Waiting.

Feb 11 / Jan 6 / TOTP / BBC / BBC-1 / 7-7.30pm / Manchester / Tired Of Waiting.

Feb 16 / Feb 12 / Hullaballoo / New York / You Really Got Me, All Day And All Of The Night.

Feb 18 / TOTP / BBC / BBC-1 / 7-7.30pm / Manchester / Tired Of Waiting.

Feb 20 / Feb 19 / ABC / ITV / Thank Your Lucky Stars / Birmingham / Tired Of Waiting.

Feb 26? / Feb 24 / Discorama(?) / ORTF / Ch. 1 / Paris.

Mar 7? / Jan 12 / Dim-Dam-Dom / ORTF / Ch. 2 / Marseilles / You Really Got Me(?).

Mar 18 / Three Go Round / Southern / ITV / Southampton / cancelled.

Mar 30 / Nov 24 / Red Skelton / CBS / London / Got Love If You Want It.

Apr 5 / Scene At 6.30 / Granada / ITV / Manchester / Everybody's Gonna Be Happy.

Apr 10 / Apr 4 / Thank Your Lucky Stars / ABC / ITV / Birmingham / Everybody's Gonna Be Happy.

Apr 15 / TOTP / BBC / BBC-1 / 7-7.30pm / Manchester / Everybody's Gonna Be Happy.

Apr 16 / Ready Steady Goes Live! / Rediffusion / ITV / 6.08-7.00pm / Wembley / Everybody's Gonna Be Happy, Hide And Seek. Also end-of-show jam with whole cast including John Lennon, George Harrison for off-the-cuff rendition of I Need Your Loving.

Apr 18 / Apr 11 / NME Poll Winners / ABC / ITV / Wembley / Tired Of Waiting, You Really Got Me.

May 14 / RSG / Rediffusion / ITV / Wembley / Set Me Free, Wonder Where... .

May/June/Apr? / Hollywood A Go Go / KHJ / London.

Jun 3 / TOTP / BBC / BBC-1 / 7-7.30pm / Manchester / Set Me Free.

Jun 4 / RSG / Rediffusion / ITV / Wembley / Set Me Free.

Jun 8 / Jun 2 / Discs A Go Go / TWW / ITV / Bristol / Set Me Free.

Jun 10 / Jun 3 / TOTP / BBC / BBC-1 / 7-7.30pm / Manchester / Set Me Free.

Jun 12 / Jun 6 / Thank Your Lucky Stars / ABC / ITV / Birmingham / Set Me Free.

Jun 20 / Jun 17 / Clay Cole Show / WPIX / WPIX / New York / Set Me Free.

Jul 30? / Jun 29? / Lloyd Thaxton / KCOP / Los Angeles / Set Me Free, I Need You

Jul 3? / Jun 28 / Shivaree / KABC / syndicated / Los Angeles / Set Me Free, All Day And All Of The Night.

Jul 7 / Jul 1 / Shindig! / ABC / ABC / Los Angeles / Tired of Waiting, Set Me Free, It's Alright, I'm A Lover Not..., Long Tall Shorty.

Jul 23 / Jul 2 / Where The Action Is / Los Angeles / You Really Got Me, Set Me Free, Ev'rybody's Gonna Be Happy.

Jul 25 / Apr 24 / Discorama / ORTF / Ch 1 / Paris / Louie Louie (+ others).

Jul 30 / RSG / Rediffusion / ITV / Wembley / See My Friends.

Aug 3 / Jul 28 / Discs A Go Go / TWW / ITV / Bristol / See My Friends.

Aug 5 / TOTP / BBC / BBC-1 / 7-7.30pm / TC / See My Friends.

Aug 12 / Aug 10 / TOTP / BBC / BBC-1 / 7-7.30pm / TC / See My Friends.

Aug 14 / Aug 8 / Thank Your Lucky Stars / ABC / ITV / Birmingham / See My Friends.

Aug 18 / Jul 2 / Where The Action Is / Los Angeles / Who'll Be The Next In Line, Tired Of Waiting, All Day And All Of The Night.
Aug 19 / TOTP / BBC / BBC-1 / 7-7.30pm / TC / See My Friends.
Aug / Discotech / ITV / unaired pilot / UK / See My Friends.
Sep 1 / Dec 17 / Shindig! / ABC / London / I'm A Lover..., Beautiful Delilah.
Sep 24 / RSG / Rediffusion / ITV / Wembley / A Well Respected Man, Don't You Fret.
Oct 4 / Drehscheibe(?) / unconfirmed / W Germany
Oct 7 / Aug 4 / Shindig! / ABC / London / See My Friends.
Dec 4 / Nov 28 / Thank Your Lucky Stars / ABC / ITV / Birmingham / Till The End Of The Day.
Dec 9 / TOTP / BBC / BBC-1 / 7.30-8pm / Till The End Of The Day.
Dec 10 / Five O'Clock Club / Rediffusion / ITV / Wembley / Till The End Of The Day, Milk Cow Blues.
Dec 16 / TOTP / BBC / BBC-1 / 7.30-8pm / Till The End Of The Day.
Dec 24 / Dec 21 / RSG / Rediffusion / ITV / Wembley / Till The End Of The Day, All I Want For Xmas.
Dec 25 / Dec 21 / TOTP / BBC / BBC-1 / 7-8pm / TC / Tired Of Waiting
Dec 30 / Sep 2 / Drop In / Stockholm / Set Me Free, See My Friends, Wonder Where My... .
Dec 29 / Dec 22(?) / Now! / TWW / ITV / Bristol / Till The End Of The Day.
Dec 30 / Aug 4 / Shindig! / Twickenham / Milk Cow Blues.
Dec 31 / RSG / Rediffusion / ITV / Wembley / A Well Respected Man.

1966

Jan 6 / TOTP / BBC / BBC-1 / 7.30-8pm / TC / Till The End Of The Day.
Jan 6 / Aug 4 / Shindig! / Twickenham / I Gotta Move.
Jan 7 / Nov 23 / Beat Beat Beat / Offenbach / Till The End Of The Day, I'm A Lover Not A Fighter, A Well Respected Man, Milk Cow Blues, You Really Got Me.
Jan 13 / Jan 13 / TOTP / BBC / BBC-1 / 7.30-8pm / TC / Till The End Of The Day.
Jan 14 / RSG / Rediffusion / ITV / Wembley / Till The End Of The Day.
Jan 13 / Jan 13 / TOTP / BBC / BBC-1 / 7.30-8pm / TC / Till The End Of The Day.
Jan 19 / A Whole Scene... / 6.30-7pm / TC / A Well Respected Man, All Day And All Of The Night.
Feb 12 / Feb 6 / Thank Your Lucky Stars / ABC / ITV / Birmingham / A Well Respected Man(?).
Feb 14 / Sep 14-18 / Hvadmorer-I Island / Reykjavik / You Really Got Me.
Mar 5 / Feb 25 / Thank Your Lucky Stars / ABC / ITV / 5.15-5.55pm / Birmingham / Dedicated Follower...
Mar 10 / Feb 24 / TOTP / BBC / BBC-1 / 7.30-8pm / TC / Dedicated Follower... .
Mar 23 / A Whole Scene... / 6.30-7pm / Barry Fantoni: Little Man In A Little Box.
Mar 31 / TOTP / BBC / BBC-1 / 7.30-8pm / TC / Dedicated Follower... .
Jun 8 / A Whole Scene... / 6.30-7pm / TC / Sunny Afternoon.
Jun 11 / Jun 5 / Thank Your Lucky Stars / ABC / ITV / 5.15-5.55pm / Birmingham / Sunny Afternoon.
Jun 16 / June 9 / TOTP / BBC / BBC-1 / 7.30-8pm / TC / Sunny Afternoon.
Jun 22 / Jun 20 / Scene At 6.30 / Granada / 6.30pm / Manchester / Sunny Afternoon.
Jun 23 / TOTP / BBC / BBC-1 / 7.30-8pm / Lime Grove / Sunny Afternoon.
Jun 24 / RSG / Rediffusion / ITV / Wembley / Sunny Afternoon, Dandy.
Jun 30 / Jun 9 / TOTP repeat / BBC / BBC-1 / 7.30-8pm / Lime Grove / Sunny Afternoon.
Jul 7 / TOTP / BBC / BBC-1 / 7.30-8pm / Lime Grove / Sunny Afternoon.
Jul 14 / Jul 7 / TOTP repeat / BBC / BBC-1 / 7.30-8pm / Lime Grove / Sunny Afternoon.
Jul ? / Apr 16 / Discorama (La Mutualité) / ORTF / Paris.
Sep 19? / Sep 19 / Zwischen Beat Und Bach / HRS / ZDF-1 / Frankfurt / Party Line, Sunny Afternoon.
Dec 8 / TOTP / BBC / BBC-1 / 7.30-8pm / Lime Grove / Dead End Street.
Dec 22 / Dec 8 / TOTP repeat / BBC / BBC-1 / 7.30-8pm / Lime Grove / Dead End Street.

1967

Jan 5 / TOTP / BBC / BBC-1 / 7.30-8pm / Lime Grove / Dead End Street.
Feb 21 / Feb 20? / Vibrato / Belgian TV / Astridplein, Antwerp / Sunny Afternoon.
May 4 / TOTP / BBC / BBC-1 / 7.30-8pm / Lime Grove / Waterloo Sunset.
May 5 / Apr 28 / Fan Club / VARA / NOS-1 / Zaandam / Mister Pleasant, This Is Where I Belong.
May 18 / May 10 / It's Dee Time / BBC / BBC-1 / 6.25-7.05pm / Manchester / Waterloo Sunset.
May 18 / May 17 / TOTP / BBC / BBC-1 / 7.30-8pm / Lime Grove / Waterloo Sunset.
May 20 / May / Beat-Club / ARD / Radio Bremen / Mister Pleasant.
May 23 / May / As You Like It / Southern / ITV / Southampton / Waterloo Sunset.
Jun 1 / TOTP / BBC / BBC-1 / 7.30-8pm / Lime Grove / Waterloo Sunset.
Jun 5 / Apr 29 / Adele Bloementhal / VPRO / VPRO, Hilverum / Dead End Street, Sunny Afternoon, Mister Pleasant.
Jun 24 / May / Beat-Club / Radio Bremen / Waterloo Sunset.
Jul 13 / TOTP / BBC / BBC-1 / 7.30-8pm / Lime Grove / Death Of A Clown.
Jul 22 / Jul / Beat-Club / ARD / Radio Bremen / Death Of A Clown.
Jul 27 / TOTP / BBC / BBC-1 / 7.30-8pm / Lime Grove / Death Of A Clown.
Aug 3 / TOTP / BBC / BBC-1 / 7.30-8pm / Lime Grove / Death Of A Clown.
Oct 12 / TOTP / BBC / BBC-1 / 7.30-8pm / Lime Grove / Autumn Almanac.
Oct 16 / Oct / Beat Beat Beat / HR / Stadthalle, Offenbach / Death Of A Clown.
Oct 21 / It's Dee Time / BBC / BBC-1 / 6.25-7.05pm / Manchester / Autumn Almanac.
Oct 24 / Oct / Vibrato / Belgian TV / Antwerp / Death Of A Clown.
Oct 26 / Oct 25 / TOTP / BBC / BBC-1 / 7.30-8pm / Lime Grove / Autumn Almanac.
Nov 9 / TOTP / BBC / BBC-1 / 7.30-8pm / Lime Grove / Autumn Almanac.
Dec 7 / TOTP / BBC / BBC-1 / 7.30-8pm / Lime Grove / Susannah's Still Alive.

1968

Apr 13 / Apr / Time For Blackburn / Southern / ITV / 5:50pm / Southampton / Wonder Boy.
Apr 18 / Apr 3 / TOTP / BBC / BBC-1 / 7.30-8pm / Lime Grove / Wonder Boy.
June 28 / Jun 26 / Basil Brush / BBC / BBC-1 / 4:55-5:25pm / Golders Green / Days.
Jul 6 / Jul / Time For Blackburn / Southern / ITV / Southampton / Days.
Jul 11 / TOTP / BBC / BBC-1 / 7.30-8pm / Lime Grove / Days.
Jul 26 / Jul 22 / BBC / BBC-2 / Late Night Line-Up, Colour Me Pop / 10:50pm / TC / Lincoln County, Picture Book, Days, medley Dedicated/Well Respected/Death Of A Clown, Sunny Afternoon, Two Sisters, Sitting By The Riverside.
Aug 1 / Jun 26 / TOTP / BBC / BBC-1 / 7.30-8pm / Lime Grove / Days.
Aug 15 / TOTP / BBC / BBC-1 / 7.30-8pm / Lime Grove / Days.
Aug 24 / It's Dee Time / BBC / BBC-1 / 6:15-6.55pm / Lime Grove / Lincoln County.
Dec 21 / Dec / Time For Blackburn / Southern / ITV / Southampton / Animal Farm, Village Green Preservation, Picture Book.

1969

Feb 1 / Jan 7 / BBC / Once More With Felix / BBC / BBC-1 / 9:45pm / TC / Last of Steam Powered Trains / Picture Book.
Mar 26 / Jan? / Discoteque / Granada / ITV / Manchester / Hold My Hand.
Mar 27 / Mar / Eamonn Andrews / Thames / ITV / London / Plastic Man.
Apr 5 / It's Dee Time / BBC / BBC-1 / 6:15pm / Lime Grove / Plastic Man.
unaired / Apr 10 / TOTP / BBC / BBC-1 / Lime Grove / Plastic Man.
Jun 19 / TOTP / BBC / BBC-1 / 7.30-8pm / Lime Grove / Drivin'.
Sep 20 / Sep 4 / 4-3-2-1 Hot n Sweet / ZDF / Ch. 2 / 5.10-6pm / Killesberg, Stuttgart / Drivin'.
Oct 1 / Sep 9 / Peter Sarstedt / BBC / BBC-2 / TC / Shangri-La.
Dec 11 / TOTP / BBC / BBC-1 / 7.30-8pm / Lime Grove / Victoria.
Dec 31 / Dec 19 / Pop Go The 60s / BBC / BBC-1 / TC / Days.

1970

Jun 18 / May 21 / TOTP / BBC / BBC-1 / 7:15-8pm / TC /Lola.
Jul 17 / Jun 22 / David Frost / Group W syndicated / 4:30-5:30pm EDT / Little Theater, NYC / Lola.
Jul 30 / Jul 15 / TOTP / BBC / BBC-1 / 7:15-8pm / TC / Lola.
Aug 8 / 4-3-2-1 Hot n Sweet / ZDF / Channel 2 / 4-4:45pm / Killesberg, Stuttgart / Lola.
Oct 15 / Mar 29 / Play For Today / BBC / BBC-1 / 9:20-10:35pm / Long Distance Piano Player, Got To Be Free, Marathon.
Dec 3 / Nov 4 / TOTP / BBC / BBC-1 / 7:15-8pm / TC / Apeman.
Dec 26 / Dec 15 / TOTP Best of 1970 pt.2 / BBC / BBC-1 / 7:15-8pm / TC / Lola.

1971

Jan 7 / Jan 6 / TOTP / BBC / BBC-1 / 7:05-7:45pm / TC / Apeman.
Feb 11 / Feb 10 / TOTP / BBC / BBC-1 / 7:05-7:45pm / TC / Powerman, Got To Be Free.

1972

Jan 4 / Jan 4 / Old Grey Whistle Test / BBC / BBC-2 / 11pm / TC / Cuppa Tea, Acute Schizophrenia Paranoia Blues.
May 27 / Apr 12 / Beat-Club / 3:15-4pm / Muswell Hillbillies. Taped but unaired until 1981: medley You Really Got Me / All Day And All Of The Night, Lola.
Jun 15 / TOTP / BBC / BBC-1 / 7:30-8pm / TC / Supersonic Rocket Ship, Skin & Bone.
Jul 21 / Jan 31 / The Kinks At the Rainbow / BBC / BBC-1 / 6:30-7:15pm / Rainbow Theatre / Till The End Of The Day, Waterloo Sunset, Sunny Afternoon, Mr.Wonderful (excerpt), She's Bought A Hat Like Princess Marina(?), Alcohol, Acute Schizophrenia Paranoia Blues, You Really Got Me. Also included is a conceptual film for the song 'Top Of The Pops'.

1973

Mar 15 / Jan 24 / In Concert / BBC / BBC- 2 / 10:45-11:15pm / Shepherds Bush / Victoria, Acute Schizophrenia Paranoia Blues, Dedicated Follower Of Fashion, Lola, Holiday, Good Golly Miss Molly, medley You Really Got Me / All Day And / All Of The Night, Waterloo Sunset, The Village Green Preservation Society, Village Green Overture.
Sep 22 / Sep 8 / It's Lulu / BBC/ BBC-1 / 10:30pm / TC / Lola.

1974

June 7 / May 7 / The Midnight Special / NBC / Burbank / You Really Got Me, Money Talks, Here Comes Yet Another Day, Celluloid Heroes, medley Skin And Bone / Dry Bones.
Aug 16 / June 4 / Wide World In Concert / ABC / Rainbow, London / Here Comes Yet Another Day, medley Skin & Bone / Dry Bones, Here Comes Flash, Celluloid Heroes.

1975

Sept 4 / Jul 25 / Starmaker.

1976

Mar 6 / Dec 28 / Supersonic / LWT / ITV / No More Looking Back, You Really Got Me, All Day And All Of The Night.

1977

Mar / Feb / Mike Douglas Show / Sleepwalker, Celluloid Heroes.
Feb 26 / Saturday Night Live / NBC / New York City / medley You Really Got Me/All Day And All Of The Night/A Well Respected Man/Lola, Sleepwalker.
Apr 2 / Mar 25 / Supersonic / LWT / ITV / London / Sleepwalker, Ray Davies in jam Sweet Little Rock'n'Roller.
Apr 26 / Mar 20 / Old Grey Whistle Test / BBC / BBC-2 / London / Sleepwalker, Life Goes On, Stormy Sky, Celluloid Heroes, Muswell Hillbilly, Full Moon, Life On The Road, Juke Box Music.
May 7 / Apr 23 / Midnight Special / NBC / Burbank / Sleepwalker, Juke Box Music, Lola.
Dec 24 / Old Grey Whistle Test: Kinks Christmas Concert / BBC / BBC-2 / Rainbow, London / Juke Box Music, Sleepwalker, Life On The Road, medley A Well Respected Man / Death Of A Clown / Sunny Afternoon, Waterloo Sunset, All Day And All Of The Night, Slum Kids, Celluloid Heroes, Get Back In Line, The Hard Way, Lola, Alcohol, medley Skin And Bone / Dry Bones, Father Christmas, You Really Got Me.

1978

May 13 / May / What's On / Granada / ITV / Manchester / Out Of The Wardrobe. Ray Davies.
July 6 / July 4 / On Site / Granada / ITV / Manchester / Live Life.
Nov 17 / Nov / Plettenkueche / ARD / Ch. 1 / Cologne / Father Christmas.
Nov / Oct 22 / Ohne Maulkorb / Vienna.

1981

Oct 10 / Saturday Night Live / NBC / Destroyer / New York City / Art Lover.
Dec 31 / Dec 8 / Bayern III / ARD / Ch 1 / Munich / Predictable, Destroyer.

1982

Jan 26 / Dec 4 / Bananas / ARD / Ch 1 / Cologne / Give The People... .
Feb 16 / Don Lane Show / Ch.9 / You Really Got Me / Melbourne / Destroyer.
Apr 3/4 / Rockpalast / Essen/ Opening, Around The Dial, The Hard Way, Where Have All The Good Times Gone, Catch Me Now I'm Falling, Come On Now, Destroyer, Yo-Yo, Lola, Dead End Street, Add It Up, Low Budget, Art Lover, Back To Front, Till The End Of The Day, Bernadette, All Day And All Of The Night, Give The People What They Want, Pressure, Stop Your Sobbing, David Watts.
Dec 16 / Dec 9 / Pebble Mill At One / BBC / BBC-1 / Birmingham / A Well Respected Man, Celluloid Heroes / Ray Davies.

1983

Aug 24 / Top Of The Pops / BBC / BBC-1 / TC / Come Dancing
Dec 3 / Sept 7 / American Bandstand / Hollywood / Love Gets You. Dave Davies

1984

Nov 2 / 1983-84 / Return To Waterloo / Channel 4 / feature film.
Nov 17 / Saturday Night Live / NBC / NYC / Do It Again, Word Of Mouth.
Dec 2 / Nov 23 / Rock Und Ballads / ARD & SWF / Frankfurt / Don't Forget To Dance, Do It Again, Lola, David Watts, Dead End Street, Good Day, All Day And All Of The Night, You Really Got Me.

1986

Nov 29 / Na Sowas / ZDF Ch 2 / Munich / How Are You.
Dec 9 / Countdown / VOO Ch1 / Amsterdam / How Are You.

1987

Jan 16 / The Last Resort / Channel 4 / London / Lola, Come Dancing. Ray Davies.
Apr 3 / The Tube / Channel 4 / Newcastle / Lost And Found, Think Visual.
Apr 18 / Apr 7 / Vier Gegen Willi / ARD Ch 1 / Nurnberg / Lost And Found.
May 30 / Na Sowas Extra / ZDF / Basel / Lost And Found.

1988

Feb 19 / Late Night With David Letterman / NBC / NYC / The Road. Ray Davies.

1989

Dec 14 / Dec 13 / Late Night With David Letterman / NBC / NYC / How Do I Get Close. Ray Davies.

1990

Jan 17 / My Generation – The Kinks / VH-1 / UK Jive documentary.

1993

Mar 15 / Feb 14 / Berns / TV-4 / Stockholm / Sunny Afternoon, Scattered. Ray & Dave Davies.
Mar 25 / The Late Show / BBC / BBC-2 / TC / Scattered, Days.
June 5 / Mar 23 / Taratata / TV2 / Paris / Only A Dream, Sunny Afternoon, You Really Got Me.
May 25 / Tonight Show / NBC / LA / Hatred (A Duet), Celluloid Heroes. Ray & Dave Davies.
June 18 / June 14 / Later With Jools Holland / BBC / BBC-2 / TC / Over The Edge, The Informer, Till The End Of The Day.

1994

Mar 12 / Mar 10 / Don't Forget Your Toothbrush / Channel 4 / Channerl 4 / You Really Got Me, Dead End Street, Bring Me Sunshine. Ray Davies.
Sep 29 / Top Of The Pops / BBC / BBC-1 / TC / You Really Got Me.
Oct 14 / Late Late Show (Gay Byrne) / RTE / Dublin / Waterloo Sunset, You Really Got Me. Ray & Dave Davies. Also YRGM shown Channel 4 UK Oct 17.
Oct 15 / Steve Wright People Show / BBC / BBC-1 / TC / You Really Got Me.
Oct 21 / The Kelly Show / UTV / Belfast / You Really Got Me, All Day And All Of The Night, Waterloo Sunset. Ray & Dave Davies.
Nov 25 / Children In Need / BBC / BBC-1 / All Day And All Of The Night.
Dec 23 / Richard Littlejohn's Christmas Offensive / LWT / ITV / You Really Got Me. Ray Davies.
Dec 26 / Dec 6 / Prince's Trust Gala / BBC / BBC-1 / Lola.
Dec 27 / Dec 21 / Rocknacht-Heroes of Rock / SWR / All Day And All Of the Night, Dead End Street, Come Dancing, You Really Got Me, Lola, Days.

1995

Mar 18 / Mar 14? / White Room / Channel 4 / Channel 4 / You Really Got Me, To The Bone. Ray Davies. Waterloo Sunset, Parklife. Ray Davies & Damon Albarn.
Mar 28 / Dec 94-Mar / Without Walls: My Generation: The Kinks / Channel 4 / Channel 4 / Documentary on The Kinks.
Sept 2 / Benefit for the R & R Hall of Fame / HBO / All Day And All Of The Night, Lola.
Oct 24 / Oct 23 / Late Night With Conan O'Brien / NBC / Victoria, You Really Got Me. Ray Davies.
Dec 2 / Dec 1 / Hey Hey It's Saturday / Ch. 9 (Australia) / You Really Got Me. Ray Davies.
Dec 21 / Mar-May / BBC / BBC-2 / The World of Ray Davies and The Kinks / I'm Not Like Everybody Else. Documentary on The Kinks.

1996

Feb 20 / Live With Regis & Cathy Lee / NBC / You Really Got Me. Ray Davies.
June 2 / Feb 21 / Storytellers / VH-1 / London / Lola, Sunny Afternoon, Come Dancing, Celluloid Heroes, Dead End Street, medley A Well Respected Man / Harry Rag, To The Bone, You Really Got Me, Days, Waterloo Sunset. Ray Davies' Storytellers Show.
June 21 / Richard Littlejohn's Live & Uncut / LWT / ITV / Ray Davies: Sunny Afternoon / LWT / London Song. Ray Davies.
Oct 7 / Late Night With David Letterman / CBS / To The Bone, You Really Got Me (excerpt), Victoria (excerpt). Ray Davies.
Oct 18 / Good Morning America / ABC / Come Dancing, To The Bone. Ray Davies.
Dec 14 / Dec 10 / Later With Jools Holland / BBC / BBC-2 / To The Bone, Sunny Afternoon. Ray Davies.

LIVE SHOW LOCATIONS

/can = cancelled show (many not included in main year-by-year listings).
/re = rescheduled show.
u/v = unconfirmed venue.

AUSTRALIA. Adelaide (South Australia) Centennial Hall, Wayville Jan 21 '65; Apollo Stadium, Richmond June 4 '71; Adelaide Oval, North Adelaide Nov 13 '78/can; Apollo Stadium, Richmond Mar 19 '80/can; Thebarton Concert Hall, Torrensville Feb 9, 10 '82; Her Majesty's Theatre (Ray Davies) Nov 29 '95. **Albury-Wodonga** (Victoria) Regent Theatre Mar 24, 25 '80/can. **Brisbane** (Queensland) Festival Hall Jan 26 '65; Festival Hall May 29 '71; Festival Hall Mar 29 '80/can; Festival Hall Feb 5 '82. **Canberra** (Australian Capital Territory) Canberra Theatre Jun 1 '71; Canberra Theatre Mar 22, 23 '80/can; Labour Club (Ray Davies) Dec 3 '95. **Hobart** (Tasmania) u/v Jun 2 '71/can. **Melbourne** (Victoria) Festival Hall, West Melbourne Jan 22, 23 '65; Festival Hall, West Melbourne Jun 3 '71; Myers Music Bowl Nov 15 '78/can; Palais Theatre, St. Kilde Mar 20, 21 '80/can; Festival Hall Feb 7 '82; Festival Hall Feb 17 '82; Victoria Athenaeum Theatre (Ray Davies) Dec 8-9 '95. **Mittagong** (New South Wales) Mittagong Festival Jan 31 '71/can. **Newcastle** (New South Wales) Century Theatre, Broadmeadow Jan 27 '65; Basketball Stadium, Broadmeadow May 31 '71; Civic Theatre Mar 27 '80/can; Mission Theatre (Ray Davies) Dec 6 '95. **Perth** (Western Australia) Capitol Theatre Jan 20 '65; u/v Jan '71/can; Beatty Park Aquatic Centre Jun 5 '71; Perth Entertainment Centre Nov 9 '78/can; Perth Entertainment Centre Mar 17 '80/can; Perth Entertainment Centre Feb 14 '82; Regal Theatre (Ray Davies) Nov 28 '95. **Sydney** (New South Wales) Sydney Stadium Jan 29, 30 '65; Odyssey Festival, Wallacia Jan 24 '71/can; Moore Park, Sydney Showground, Paddington Jun 6 '71; Sportsground, Paddington Nov 18 '78/can; Capitol Theatre Mar 26 '80/can; Capitol Theatre Feb 2, 3 '82; Hordern Pavilion, Sportsground, Paddington Feb 19 '82; Everest Theatre, Seymour Centre (Ray Davies) Dec 4-5 '95.

AUSTRIA. Dornbirn Messehalle Mar 6 '66/re from Mar 5; u/v Oct 21 '78/can. **Graz** Arbeiter Kannersaal Nov 9 '79; Schlossberg Jul 7 '93. **Klagenfurt** u/v Nov 8 '79. **Salzburg** u/v Nov 8 '79/can. **Linz** Sporthalle Nov 9 '79/can; Sporthalle, Dec 12 '89. **Vienna (Wien)** Stadthalle Sep 20 '66; Konzerthaus Mar 20 '71/can (re from Mar 18); Sophiensaal Oct 22 '78; Konzerthaus Nov 7 '79; Oberlaa Kurhalle Dec 15 '87; Arena Jul 6 '93.

BELGIUM. Affligem Rock Afffligem Indoors, Bellekouter Halle Aug 7 '91. **Antwerp (Antwerpen, Anvers)** Koningen Elizabethzaal Mar 15 '66; Zaal Roma Nov 17 '67; Arenahall, Deurne Oct 28 '78. **Bilzen** Bilzen Festival 70, Aug 21 '70; Bilzen Festival 73, Aug 19 '73/can; Bilzen Festival 78, Aug 12 '78. **Brussels (Brussel, Bruxelles)** Palace Regina Mar 19 '66; Théâtre 140, Feb 16-18 '68; Ancienne Belgique Oct 5 '73/can; Vorst Nationaal (Forest National) Nov 17 '79; Vorst Nationaal (Forest National) Dec 1 '80; Vorst Nationaal (Forest National) Dec 12 '81/can; Cirque Royal Apr 20 '85; **Châtelet** Teenagers Festival, Gemeentepark Sep 8 '68. **Deurne** *see* **Antwerp**. **Ertvelde** Club 67, Nov 19 '67; **Kieldrecht** Festival Nov 19 '67; **Lebbeke** Corso Club, Zaal Casino Nov 18 '67. **Leige** Leige Palace Mar 18 '66. **Leuven** Marktrock Aug 15 '90. **Mechelen** Margriet Youth Club Nov 18 '67. **Mouscron** Place Gerard Kaiser Mar 12 '66. **Oostende** Belga Festival, Oostende Airport Aug 15 '85. **Putte** De Toekomst Sep 8 '68. **Torhout** Torhout Festival Jul 5 '80. **Verviers** Coliseum Mar 17 '66. **Werchter** Festival Jul 6 '80.

CANADA. Placenames in Canada in the main text of this book include standard two-letter state abbreviations. The list here includes those abbreviations alongside the state name. **Calgary** (Alberta; AB) Apollo Rock Club Jun 25 '70. **Edmonton** (Alberta; AB) Sales Pavilion Jun 26 '70; Northlands Coliseum Sep 7 '81. **London** (Ontario; ON) London Arena Dec 6 '70. **Maple** (Ontario; ON) Kingswood Music Theater, Canada's Wonderland Jun 19 '87; Kingswood Music Theater, Canada's Wonderland Aug 10 '93. **Montreal** (Quebec; PQ) FC Smith Auditorium, Loyola College (later Concordia College) Feb 5 '70; Montreal Forum Nov 30 '77; Concert Bowl Sep 26 '81/re from Sep 27; Montreal Forum May 24 '83/re from Apr 3. **Ottawa** (Ontario; ON) Ottawa Civic Center Nov 29 '77/can; Ottawa Civic Center Sep 26 '81/can; Ottawa Civic Center, Mar 21 '85. **Toronto** (Ontario; ON) (*see also* Maple) Hawk's Nest Dec 6 '69; Massey Hall Nov 30 '71/can; Massey Hall Apr 5 '73; Concert Bowl, Maple Leaf Gardens Apr 30 '77; Concert Bowl, Maple Leaf Gardens Nov 28 '77; Maple Leaf Gardens Sep 25 '81; Maple Leaf Gardens May 25 '83/re from Apr 4; Maple Leaf Gardens Mar 20 '85; Massey Hall Apr 4 '88; Massey Hall Sep 3 '89/can; Music Hall (Ray Davies) Oct 8-12 '96. **Vancouver** (British Columbia; BC) Pacific National Exhibition Gardens Auditorium (PNEGA) Jun 27 '70; PNEGA Nov 20 '70; PNEGA Feb 8 '76/can; PNEGA Apr 17 '77; Pacific Coliseum Oct 4 '80; Pacific Coliseum Sep 5 '81; Pacific Coliseum Apr 22 '83; Pacific Coliseum Mar 2 '85. **Waterloo** (Ontario; ON) Phys-Ed Complex, University of Waterloo Feb 6 '70. **Winnipeg** (Manitoba; MB) Centennial Concert Hall Jun 24 '70. **NOTE:** Tour of Canada scheduled for Oct 1-15 '69, all dates /can.

DENMARK. Ålborg Hit Club Sep 27 '66; Open Air 88 Festival Mølleparken Jun 18 '88; Open Air 91 Festival, Mølleparken Aug 11 '91/can; Open Air 93 Festival, Mølleparken Jun 19 '93. **Århus** Stakladen, Studenternes Hus Sep 20 '74; Århus Festival, Lisberg Fællespark Jun 19 '88. **Bornholm** Brændegardshaven Jul 15 '69. **Copenhagen** Tivoli Koncertsal Apr 9 '65; Tivoli Koncertsal Apr 10 '65/can; KB Hallen Sep 11 '65; KB Hallen Feb 12 '66; Hit House Sep 28 '66/can; Tivoli Plænen Jul 14 '69; Revolution Club, Balken Jul 14 '69; Tivoli Koncertsal Sep 23 '74; Tivoli Koncertsal Mar 29 '76; Falconerteatret Oct 10 '78; Tivoli Koncertsal Oct 20 '79; Tivoli Koncertsal Nov 29 '81/can; Tivoli Koncertsal Apr '84/can; Tivoli Koncertsal Apr 12 '85/can; Open-air festival, Amager Strandpark Aug 11 '91. **Helsingør** Industriforeningen (rumoured '69, unconfirmed). **Middelfart** Rock Under Broen Festival (Ray Davies) Jun 11 '94. **Nyköbing** Industrihotellet Apr 8 '65. **Odense** Fyens Forum Sep 10 '65; Fyens Forum Feb 12 '66; Fyens Forum Sep 27 '66; Open-air festival, Syklebanen Aug 10 '91. **Ringe** Midtfyns Festival Jul 5 '86; Midtfyns Festival-Ringe '90 Jun 28 '90. **Roskilde** Fantasy Festival Jun 30 '72. **Skanderberg** Danmarks Smukkeste Festival 1991, Aug 9 '91. **Viborg** Tinghallen Sep 21 '74.

ENGLAND *see* United Kingdom

FRANCE. Aix-En-Provence Théâtre Municipal? Dec 5 '80/can. **Amiens** u/v Mar 13 '66. **Bourges** Palais des Congres Apr 21 '93. **Bruay** u/v Mar 20 '66. **Cambrai** Palais des Grottes Nov 18 '79/can. **Clermont-Ferrand** Casino de Royat Feb 25 '67. **Dunkirk** u/v Mar 20 '66. **Fleurs Les Lille** Peau de Vache Cabaret Mar 11 '66. **La Courneuve** (Greater Paris) La Fête d'Humanité Sep 7 '74; La Fête d'Humanité Sep 12 '92. **Lens** Bal du Boxing, Eden Ranch Mar 12 '66. **Lille** Salle Roger Salengro Mar 14 '66; Théâtre Sebastopol? Nov 18 '79/can. **Lyon** Palais d'Hiver Dec 7 '80. **Mulhouse** Palais Des Fêtes Oct 10 '65. **Menton** Viking Club, rumoured '65, unconfirmed. **Nice** Théâtre de Verdure Dec 6 '80. **Nogent Sur Marne** (Greater Paris) Pavillion Baltard Dec 8 '80; Pavillion Baltard Apr 29 '85. **Normandy** (town unconfirmed) Casino Tharon Aug 11-13 '67/can. **Offenbourg** open air festival Jun '76/can. **Paris** (*see also* Nogent Sur Marne, La Courneuve) Olympia Théâtre Feb 23 '65; Grand Bretagne Hotel Apr 26 '65; Locomotive Club May 30 '65/can; Locomotive Club Apr 16 '66; Alhambra Théâtre Feb 23, 24 '67; Olympia Théâtre Apr 23 '67/can; Golden Trophy Party, Le Plessis-Robinson Jun 11 '67 possibly /can; Pavillion Jun 1 '77; Pavillion Nov 19 '79; Mogador Théâtre Oct 30 '78; Pulsar 80, Vierzon Jul 4 '80/can; u/v Dec 16 '81/can. **St. Quentin** u/v Mar 13 '66.

GERMANY. Augsburg Sporthalle Jan 18 '67; Schwabenhalle Nov 12 '90. **Berlin (West Berlin)** Waldbühne Aug 14 '65; u/v Jun '66/can; Berliner Sportsplast Sep 21 '66; Deutschlandhalle Oct 16 '78; Neue Welt Oct 27 '79; Neue Welt Nov 27 '80; Neue Welt Dec 2 '81/can; Eissporthalle Dec 7 '87; Huxley's Neue Welt June 21 '93. **Böblingen** Sporthalle Dec 10 '87. **Bonn** Bürgerverein Jan 21 '67; Biskuithalle Dec 17 '89. **Bremen** Stadthalle Aug 15 '65; Stadthalle Oct 29 '79/re from Oct 31. **Celle** u/v Oct 14 '65/can. **Cologne** Sporthalle Jan 21 '67/re from Dec 4 '66; Sporthalle Apr 3 '70/can; Sporthalle Dec 3 '81/can; E-Werk Sep 9 '92; E-Werk Jul 2 '93. **Crailsheim** Sporthalle Nov 3 '79. **Darmstadt** Stadthalle Oct 13 '65. **Delmenhorst** Delmenhalle Oct 17 '65. **Dortmund** Westfallenhalle 2, Oct 26 '79; Westfallenhalle 2, May 28 '87; Westfallenhalle 2, Dec 11 '93. **Dresden** Music-Zirkus Dec 3 '93. **Dusseldorf** Rheinhalle Jan 17 '67/re from Nov 27 '66; Philipshalle Nov 4 '79; Philipshalle Nov 30 '80; Philipshalle Dec 5 '81/can; Philipshalle Dec 18 '87; Philipshalle Jun 22 '89/can; Westfallenhalle 2, Dec 11 '93. **Erlangen** Stadthalle Oct 24 '78. **Erfurt** Thüringen Halle Nov 9 '90; Kulturzentrum Dec 12 '93. **Essen** Grugahalle Apr 3 '82. **Fehmarn** Festival Sep 6 '70. **Flensburg-Handewitt** Wikinghalle Dec 17 '93. **Frankfurt** Kongresshalle Jan 16 '67; Jahrhunderthalle Oct 31 '79; Jahrhunderthalle Dec 10 '81/can; Festhalle Nov 23 '84; Jahrhunderthalle Dec 9 '87; Jahrhunderthalle Jun 25 '89/can; Batschschkapp Jun 22 '93. **Gelsenkirchen** Hans-Sach Haus Oct 5 '65. **Germersheim** Whitsuntide Festival May 23 '72. **Göttingen** Rock Im Stadtpark Festival Jul 1 '89/can. **Hamburg** Star Club Aug 26 '69; Musikhalle Mar 21 '71/can; Congress Centrum Mar 31 '76; Musikhalle May 27 '77/can; Musikhalle Oct 17 '78; Audimax Oct 25 '79; Audimax Nov 26 '80; Congress Centrum Dec 1 '81/can; Musikhalle May 27 '87; Musikhalle Dec 22 '89; Stadtpark Aug 13 '91; Stadtpark Jul 3 '93. **Hanover** Niedersachsenhalle Oct 14 '65; Niedersachsenhalle Oct 30 '79; Stadthalle Nov 28 '80; Capitol Veranstaltungszentrum Dec 8 '87; Eilenrieder Halle Nov 10 '90; Capitol Dec 6 '93. **Heidelberg** Stadthalle May 25 '87. **Heilbronn** u/v Mar 20 '71/can. **Ingolstadt** ESV-Halle Jan 18 '67. **Iserlohn** Parkhalle Oct 6 '65. **Kaiser Lautern** Fruchthalle Oct 11 '65. **Karlsruhe** Schwarzwaldhalle Dec 17 '87. **Kassel** Stadthalle Nov 26 '80/can. **Kiel** Ostseehalle Oct 16 '65. **Koblenz** Stadthalle Oct 7 '65. **Konstanz** Bodenseestadion May 23 '87. **Krefeld** Niederrheinhalle Jan 17 '67. **Ludenscheid** Neue Schutzenhalle Oct 6 '65. **Ludwigsburg** open-air festival Jun '75/can; Forum am Schlosspark Jun 29 '93; **Ludwigshafen** Friedrich-Ebert Halle Oct 8 '65; Friedrich-Ebert Halle Nov 22 '80; Friedrich-Ebert-Halle Nov 13 '90. **Mainz** Kurfurstal Schloss Oct 13 '65. **Mannheim** Rosegarten Nov 5 '79; Musensaal Dec 9 '81/can; u/v Jun 24 '89/can. **Miltenberg** Festival Michaelismesse Sep 7 '92. **Munich** PN Hit House Oct 1-3 '65; Circus Krone-Bau Jan 22 '67; u/v Mar 19 '71?; Circus Krone-Bau May 27 '77; Circus Krone-Bau Oct 25 '78; Circus Krone-Bau Nov 2 '79; Deutsches Museum Nov 24 '80; Deutsches Museum Dec 7 '81/can; Kongressaal Deutsches Museum Dec 16 '87; Kongressaal Deutsches Museum Jun 29 '89/can; Kongressaal Deutsches Museum Dec 15 '89; Circus Krone-Bau Jul 5 '93; Terminal 1, Dec 4 '93. **Munster** Münsterlandhalle Oct 15 '65; Jovel-Music Hall Dec 18 '89. **Neumarkt** Jurahalle Dec 21 '89; Jurahalle Dec 2 '93. **Neunkirchen** TuS-Sporthalle Oct 11 '65; Hemmerleinhalle Nov 25 '80. **Neu-Isenburg** Hugenottenhalle Jun 22 '93/can. **Nurnberg** Messehalle Jan 22 '67/re from Nov 30 '66; Serenadenhof, Sep 8 '92. **Offenbach** Stadthalle Nov 23 '65; Stadthalle Jan 16 '67; Stadthalle Mar 17 '71/can; Stadthalle Oct 23 '78; Stadthalle Nov 13 '79; Stadthalle Dec 2 '80; Stadthalle Dec 20 '89; Stadthalle Jun 22 '93/can. **Oldenberg** Weser-Ems-Halle Oct 17 '65. **Osnabrück** Halle GartlageDec 10 '93. **Pahlhude** Eiderlandehalle Jul 25? '70. **Pforzheim** Universum Kino Jan 20 '67. **Reckinghausen** Vestlandhalle Oct 12 '65. **Rendsburg** Nordmarkhalle Oct 16 '65. **Saarbrücken** Neufang-Kulturhalle Dec 7 '93. **St. Goarshausen** Freilchtbuhne May 24 '87. **Stuttgart** (*see also* Böblingen) Sporthalle Jan 20 '67; Liederhalle Dec 6 '81/can; Liederhalle, Jun 28 '89/can; Hans Martin Schleierhalle (Heroes Of Rock) Dec 21 '94. **Schwerin** Kongresshalle Nov 11 '90. **Trochtelfinger** Trochtelfinger Festival Am See Sep 6 '92. **Ulm** Roxy-Hallen Dec 14 '93. **Wolfsburg** Stadthalle Oct 26 '79/can.

FINLAND. Åbo *see* Turku. **Helsinki** Peacock Theatre, Linnanmäki Sep 7 '65; u/v Sep. 30 '66/can. **Lahti** Field House Sep 8 '65. **Turku (Åbo)** Turun Konserttisal Sep 6 '65. Ruis-Rockfestival, Runsala-parken Aug 20 '71.

GREECE. Salonika u/v Sep 23 '67/can. **Athens** u/v Sep 24 '67/can; Lycabettus, Jun 23, 24 '93/can.

HOLLAND *see* The Netherlands

HONG KONG. Football Club Stadium Feb 6 '65.

ICELAND. Reykjavik Austurbæjarboi Sep 14-18 '65; Austurbæjarboi Sep 13, 14 '66/can; Laugardalshöllinni Sep 7 '70.

IRELAND. For Northern Ireland *see* United Kingdom. **Bray** (Wicklow) New Arcadia Ballroom Sep 30 '67; New Arcadia Ballroom Jun 1 '68. **Bundoran** (Donegal) Astoria Ballroom Jul 11 '66. **Cork** Arcadia Ballroom Oct 1 '67; u/v Nov 21 '81/can; Opera House Nov 22 '94. **Dublin** Royal Dublin Society National Stadium (RDSNS) Apr 30, May 1 '81; RDSNS Nov 20, 21 '81; RDSNS Aug 18 '85; RDSNS Mar 19 '94; The Point Nov 23 '94; Olympia Theatre (Ray Davies) Oct 29 '95. **Dundalk** (Louth) Adelphi Theatre Nov 7 '65. **Drogheda** (Louth) unconfirmed ballroom Jul 10 '66. **Galway** u/v Nov 22 '81/can. **(South of Ireland)** u/v Oct 2, 3 '67.

ITALY. Rome u/v Sep 5, 6 '66/can; Piper's Club Jun 1 '68/can. **Milan** Piper's Club May 29 '68/can; Rolling Stone Club Dec 13 '87.

JAPAN. Fukuoka Shimin Hall Oct 8 '93. **Kawasaki** Cine Chitta (aka Club Chitta) May 18-19 '95. **Nagoya** Diamond Hall Oct 11 '93; Club Diamond Hall May 16 '95. **Osaka** Mainchi Hall Feb 24 '82; Kosei-Nenkin Hall Oct 3-4 '93; Sankei Hall (Kokusai Kouryu Center) May 14-15 '95. **Saporo** Factory Hall Oct 13 '93. **Shibuya** Public Hall Oct 14 '93. **Tokyo** u/v Nov '78/can; u/v Apr 11, 12 '80/can; Seinen-Kan Hall Feb 25-27 '82; u/v Nov 1 '90/can; Kani Hoken Hall Oct 5-6, 10 '93; Shibuya Kokaido (Public Hall) May 10-12 '95; Nakano Sun Plaza May 13 '95; Shibuya Parco (Ray Davies) Dec 15-16 '95; Yomiuri Hall (Ray Davies) Dec 18-19, 21 '95.

LEBANON. Beirut Melkart Hotel May 17, 18 '69/re from Cite Sportive May 3, 4.

NETHERLANDS. Amsterdam Concertgebouw Sep 9 '67; Fantasio II (orig Open Lucht Theatre) Aug 23 '70; Concertgebouw Dec 15 '72; Concertgebouw Sep 29 '73; Concertgebouw Nov 15 '79; 93 Drum Rhythm Festival, Beurs van Berlage Jul 1 '93. **Apeldoorn** De Eurobeurs May 19 '68. **Beverwijk** Veilinghal Oct 24 '65/can; VEB-Garage Nov 21 '65; Garage Wijkermereweg May 8 '66. **The Hague** Houtrusthal Oct 23 '65/can; Houtrusthal Nov 20 '65/can; Houtrusthal Sep 3 '66; Congressgebouw Oct 27 '78. **Den Helder** Sporthal May 9 '66. **Dordrecht** Session Club 66, Sep 18 '66. **Eindhoven** Philips Schouwburg Nov 21 '65/can. **Geleen** Pink Pop Festival, Voetbalstadion May 30 '77. **Hoorn** Bierfeesten Sep 18 '66. **Lochem** Dauwtrappers Festival May 28 '81. **Marum** De Kruisweg Hotel May 7 '66; De Kruisweg Hotel Sep 17 '66. **Nijmegen** DeVereeniging Nov 18 '80. **Roermond** u/v Sep 18 '66/can. **Rotterdam** DeDoelen Sep 28 '73; DeDoelen Nov 20 '80; Ahoy Dec 11 '81/can. **Scheveningen** Casino May 8 '66. **Sittard** Stadsschouwburg May 18 '68; Stadsschouwburg Oct 29 '78. **Soesterberg** Circus Toni Boltini Sep 17 '66. **Tiel** Veiling Septer Nov 20 '65/can/re from Oct 23; Tiel Pop Festival Aug 22 '70. **Utrecht** Meifest, Irenhal May 7 '66; Muziekcentrum Vredenburg Nov 16 '79; Muziekcentrum Vredenburg Nov 19 '80; Muziekcentrum Vredenburg Apr 18 '85. **Vlagtwedde** Zaal Beyering May 19 '68. **Voorburg** Pop Festival, Vliegermolen Mar 9, 10 '73/can. **Winterswijk** Feestgebouw Nov 21 '65.

NEW ZEALAND. Auckland Town Hall Feb 1 '65; Western Springs Nov 22 '78/can; Town Hall Apr 2, 3 '80/can; Town Hall (Ray Davies) Dec 12 '95. **Christchurch** Majestic Theatre Feb 4 '65; Queen Elizabeth II Park Nov 25 '78/can; Town Hall Apr 7 '80/can. **Hamilton** Founder's Theatre Feb 2 '65. **Wellington** Town Hall Feb 3 '65; Town Hall Mar 31, Apr 1 '80/can.

NORTHERN IRELAND *see* United Kingdom

NORWAY. Bergen Landåshallen Jun 17 '66; National Youth Festival (Dave Davies) Sep 3 '67/can. **Hedmark** Grue-tunet Jul 12 '69. **Oslo** Nordstrandshallen Jun 16 '66; Ingierstrand Jul 11 '69; Chateau Neuf Oct 12 '78; Chateau Neuf Oct 21 '79; Chateau Neuf Nov 26 '81/can; u/v Apr '84/can; Skedsmohallen Apr 11 '85/can; Rockefeller's Music Hall Jun 12 '92; Sommerfestivalen, Hellerudsletta Jun 18 '93; Rockefeller's Music Hall Jun 9 '94; Norwegian Wood Music Festival, Frognerbadet Jun 15 '96.

PORTUGAL. Cacais Pavillion do Dramatico May 8 '86/re from May 7.

SCOTLAND *see* United Kingdom

SINGAPORE. Badmington Stadium Feb 7, 8 '65.

SOUTH AFRICA. Bopthuthatswana Super Bowl, Sun City May 25, 26, 30, 31, Jun 1-3 '85/can.

SPAIN. Madrid Yulia Club, Sale de Fiesta Yulia Jun 13 '66; Yulia Club, Sale de Fiesta Yulia Jun 14, 15 '66/can; Ampitheatre May 10 '86/re from May 9. **Barcelona** u/v Jul 16 '66/can; Palacio Municipale de Deporte, May 14 '86. **Gijon** Plaza de Toros May 16 '86. **La Coruna** festival Jul 9 '93. **Palma, Mallorca** Plaza De Toros Jul 17 '66. **San Sebastian** Polideportiro de Anoeta May 17 '86. **Seville** La Maestranza May 12 '86.

SWEDEN. Åhus Folkets Park, Jun 15 '68. **Alingsås** Alingsåsparken Jun 12 '68. **Ängelholm** Torslund, Sep 29 '66. **Boden** Ishallen May 14 '67/can. **Borlänge** Folkets Park Jun 22 '68. **Bollnäs** Folkets Park Jun 23 '68. **Eskiltuna** Sporthallen Sep 24 '66. **Finspång** Folkets Park Jun 19 '68. **Fagersta** Folkets Park Jun 22 '68. **Gamleby** Folkpark Jun 18 '68. **Gävle** Folkparken Jun 23 '68. **Gothenburg** Liseberg Konserthallen Sep 3 '65; Liseberg Konserthallen Sep 23 '66; Liseberg Konserthallen May 11 '67/can; Liseberg Konserthallen Jun 11 '68; Konserthuset Sep 17 '74; Konserthuset Oct 22 '79; Göteberg Park Festival, Slottsskogen Jun 13 '92; Göteborg All Star Festival Jun 10 '94. **Hultsfred** Folkets Park Jun 18 '68. **Hunnesbostrand** Folkets Park Jun 13 '68. **Jönköping** Rigoletto May 12 '67/can. **Karlstad** Mariebergsskogen Jun 9 '68. **Karlshamn** Bellevueparken Jun 15 '68. **Kalmar** Folkets Park Jun 16 '68. **Knivsta** Folkets Park Sep 2 '65. **Kristinebergs** 12 Timmar 70-Tal På Festival, Idrottsplats Jun 1 '96. **Kristinehamn** Folkets Park Tallunden Jun 8 '68. **Lund** Olympen Sep 18 '74/can; Olympen Mar 27 '76; Olympen Oct 11 '78; Olympen Nov 28 '81/can; Olympen Apr 12 '84/can; Olympen Apr 10 '85/can. **Malmö** MFF Station Sep 29 '66; Folkets Park Jun 14 '68. **Örebro** Club 700, Sep 24 '66; Brunnsparken Jun 8 '68. **Oskarshamn** Parken Jun 16 '68. **Pitea** Norrmalmia, May 14 '67/can. **Sandviken** u/v May 13 '67/can. **Södertalje** u/v Sep 25 '66. **Stockholm** Nalen Sep 25 '66; Gröna Lund May 15 '67/can; Stora Scenen, Gröna Lund Jun 20 '68; Jump-In Discotheque, Gröna Lund Jun 20 '68; Konserthuset Sep 16 '74; Konserthuset Mar 26 '76; Konserthuset Oct 14 '78; Konserthuset Oct 23 '79; Konserthuset Nov 25 '81/can; Konserthuset Apr 14 '84/can; Konserthuset Apr 9 '85/can; Moderna Museets Trädgård Jun 17 '93. **Vara**; Kommunalhusets (orig Friluftsscenen) Sep 4 '65. **Note:** Concerts scheduled for following dates venue or city not known: Sep 20-22 '67/can; Nov '67/can; Jun 1-8 '69/can. Concerts scheduled for following dates may or may not have been booked or performed, venue or city unknown: Jun 11, 19, 21 '68.

SWITZERLAND. Basel Gundeldinger Casino Oct 10 '65; Kino Union Mar 5 '66. **Bern** Casino Oct 10 '65/can; Kursaal Mar 4 '66. **Biel** Casino Oct 10 '65/can. **Chur** u/v Mar 5 '66/can. **Frauenfeld** Out In The Green Festival Jul 10 '93. **Kreuzlingen** Hotel Löwen Mar 6 '66/can. **Lausanne** Palais de Beaulieu Dec 14 '81/can. **Luzern** Hotel Union Mar 1 '66. **Montreaux** Golden Rose TV Festival Apr 29 '73/can. **Neuchâtel** Maison de Syndicates Mar 4 '66. **Olten** Hammer Restaurant Oct 9 '65. **Schaffhausen** Hotel Schaffhauserhof Mar 2 '66. **St. Gallen** Tonhalle Feb 28 '66/can. **Winterthur** Winterthurer Musikfestwochen, Steinberggasse Sep 5 '87. **Zurich** Allmend Brunau Oct 9 '65; Hotel Spirgarten

Mar 3 '66; Volkhaus Oct 18 '78; Volkhaus Nov 11 '79; Kongresshaus Dec 3 '80; Kongresshaus Dec 15 '81/can; Schützenhaus Albisgüetli Dec 15 '93.

UNITED KINGDOM. Sub-headings follow for England, Isle Of Man, Northern Ireland, Scotland, Wales. Well-known large cities named in the main text of this book (for example Edinburgh, Sheffield, Liverpool etc) stand alone without a county name. Other cities, towns etc are named in this book followed by the abbreviated traditional county name (which in some cases will differ from the current local-government name). The list here includes the full traditional county name for each town or city.

ENGLAND. Accrington (Lancashire) Majestic Ballroom Jan 21 '66. **Aldershot** (Hampshire) ABC Cinema May 5 '65. **Altrincham** (Cheshire) Stamford Hall May 30 '64; Stamford Hall Jun 27 '64. **Ardwick** *see* Manchester. **Atherton** (Lancashire) Formby Hall Sep 19 '64. **Aylesbury** (Buckinghamshire) Friars, Maxwell Hall Aug 6 '80; Friars, Maxwell Hall Dec 10 '82; Bucks Civic Centre (Ray Davies) Nov 13 '95. **Barnsley** (Yorkshire) Civic Theatre Nov 3 '94. **Barnstaple** (Devon) Queen's Hall Sep 1 '66/can (re from Aug 17). **Barnsley** (Gloucestershire) Civic Hall Jul 2 '66/can. **Barrow-In-Furness** (Lancashire) Public Hall Jul 28 '66. **Basildon** (Essex) Mecca Ballroom Sep 4 '64. **Bath** (Somerset) Forum Cinema Jun 7 '64; Pavilion Jan 4 '65; Pavilion Sep 27 '65; Pavilion Ballroom Jul 4 '66/can; Pavilion Aug 8 '69 probably /can; University Of Bath Mar 22 '74. **Bedford** (Bedfordshire) Granada Cinema (GC) Apr 10 '64; GC Oct 13 '64; GC Nov 17 '64; GC May 13 '65; GC Feb 5 '67; GC Apr 8 '68. **Bickershaw** (Lancashire) Bickershaw Festival May 6 '72. **Birmingham** (Warwickshire) Carlton Club, Erdington Sep 24 '64; Hippodrome Nov 15 '64; Smethwick Baths Feb 27 '65; Town Hall Mar 22 '65; Silverblades Ice Rink Nov 15 '65; Smethwick Baths Dec 4 '65; Hippodrome May 15 '66/can; Plaza Ballroom, King's Heath Jun 11 '66; Plaza Ballroom, Oldhill Jun 17 '67; Kyrle Oct 6 '67; Town Hall Apr 15 '68; Rebecca's Sep 3 '70; Top Rank Ballroom Mar 1 '71; Town Hall Oct 18 '72; Town Hall Jun 6 '73; Hippodrome Sep 23 '73/can; Town Hall Feb 26 '74; Hippodrome Jun 2 '75; Hippodrome May 15 '78/can; Odeon Cinema Jan 27 '79; Odeon Cinema Dec 18 '80; Odeon Cinema Dec 7 '82; Odeon Cinema Mar 23 '84; Odeon Cinema Apr 23 '85; Aston Villa Sports & Leisure Centre Mar 24 '94; Alexandra Theatre Nov 19 '94. **Blackburn** (Lancashire) King George's Hall Jun 14 '64; King George's Hall Oct 31 '94; King George's Hall (Ray Davies) Nov 6 '95. **Blackheath** *see* Colchester. **Blackpool** (Lancashire) Opera House Aug 16 '64; Queen's Theatre Aug 30 '64; Queen's Theatre Sep 13 '64; Queen's Theatre Sep 27 '64; Casino Ballroom Apr 11 '66/can; Opera House Jul 3 '66/can; Opera House Aug 14 '66. **Bolton** (Lancashire) Odeon Cinema Oct 8 '64; Boneyard Apr 20 '65/can; Odeon Cinema May 21 '65/can. **Borehamwood** (Hertfordshire) The Venue (Ray Davies) Apr 11 '95. **Boston** (Lincolnshire) Starlite Room Mar 20 '65; Starlite Room Gliderdrome Oct 30 '65; Starlite Room Gliderdrome Aug 13 '66/can. **Bournemouth** (Hampshire) Winter Gardens Apr 25 '64; Gaumont Cinema Aug 2 '64; Winter Gardens Nov 28 '64; Winter Gardens May 15 '65; Winter Gardens Apr 27 '68; Bournemouth Pavilion Aug 28 '69; Chelsea Village Mar 12 '71; Starkers Royal Ballroom Aug 3 '72; Winter Gardens Mar 9 '76; Winter Gardens Dec 19 '82. **Bradford** (Yorkshire) Gaumont Cinema Apr 5 '64; Odeon Cinema c. Sep '64; St. George's Hall, Univ of Bradford (SHUB) Apr 22 '72; SHUB Oct 13 '72; SHUB Jan 25 '79; SHUB May 15 '81; Caeser's Dec 16 '82. **Brentwood** (Essex) Brentwood Centre Nov 6 '93; Brentwood Leisure Centre Oct 22 '94. **Bridlington** (Yorkshire) Spa Royal Hall Aug 27 '66; Spa Royal Hall Dec 17 '66 Spa Royal Hall Aug 15 '70. **Brighton** (Sussex) Hippodrome Theatre Apr 26 '64; u/v Jun '64; Locarno Ballroom Sep 5 '64; Regent Ballroom Mar 9 '65/can; Mecca Ballroom Jun 1 '66; Big Apple (formerly Regent Ballroom) Mar 13 '71; Dome Arena Feb 1 '79; Dome Arena Dec 13 '80; Dome Arena Dec 21 '82. **Bristol** (Gloucestershire) Colston Hall May 12 '64; Corn Exchange May 27 '64; Broadway Cinema Jul 2 '64; Colston Hall Nov 29 '64; Colston Hall Mar 21 '65/can; Corn Exchange Aug 18 '65; Colston Hall Nov 27 '65; Top Rank Suite Jan 12 '66; Corn Exchange Jun 3 '67; Colston Hall Feb 28 '71; Bristol University Mar 16 '74; Colston Hall Jun 3 '75; Colston Hall Mar 8 '76; Colston Hall Jan 30 '79; Colston Hall Jun 27 '81; Hippodrome Theatre Jun 12 '88/re from May 27. **Brixton** *see* London. **Bromley** (Kent) Bromley Court Hotel May 1 '66/re from Mar 26. **Broughton** (Cheshire) u/v Jul 6 '64/can. **Burnley** (Lancashire) Casino Club Sep 25 '64; Locarno Ballroom Aug 25 '66. **Burton-on-Trent** (Staffordshire) Jubilee Hall Sep 28 '64. **Bury** (Lancashire) Palais de Danse Sep 19 '64; Palais de Danse Apr 9 '66/can. **Buxton** (Derbyshire) Pavilion Gardens Ballroom Apr 17 '65; Pavilion Gardens Ballroom Feb 5 '66; Pavilion Gardens Ballroom May 21 '66. **Cambridge** (Cambridgeshire) Corn Exchange Jun 9 '72; ABC Cinema Apr 9 '64; ABC Cinema Nov 25 '64; ABC Cinema Apr 24 '68; Marcam Ballroom Apr 4 '65/can; Corn Exchange Nov 18 '93. **Cannock** (Staffs) Prince Of Wales Centre (Ray Davies) Apr 9 '95. **Canterbury** (Kent) University of Kent May 13 '66; Sports Centre, University of Kent Feb 24 '73. **Carlisle** (Cumberland) ABC Cinema Apr 2 '64; ABC Cinema Oct 7 '64; Market Hall Jul 23 '66. **Carlyon Bay** (Cornwall) New Cornish Riviera Lido Sep 2 '67; New Cornish Riviera Lido Jun 24 '67. **Chalk Farm** *see* London. **Chatham** (Kent) Central Hall Apr 26 '68. **Chelmsford** (Essex) Odeon Cinema Apr 16 '64. **Cheltenham** (Gloucestershire) Town Hall Oct 23 '94; Town Hall (Ray Davies) Nov 7 '95. **Chesterfield** (Derbyshire) ABC Cinema Apr 18 '68. **Chester le Street** (Co. Durham) Garden Farm Oct 22 '68. **Cheshunt** (Hertfordshire) Wolsey Hall Feb 9 '66. **Chester** (Cheshire) ABC Cinema Nov 18 '64; ABC Cinema Apr 19 '68. **Chesterfield** (Derbyshire) Victoria Ballroom Jan 13 '66. **Chippenham** (Wiltshire) Neald Hall Sep 3 '64. **Clacton-On-Sea** (Essex) Town Hall Jul 11 '64; Essex Prince's Theatre Nov 13 '94; Princess Theatre (Ray Davies) Aug 8 '95. **Cleethorpes** (Lincolnshire) ABC Cinema Apr 1 '64. **Cleveleys** (Lancashire) Fabulous Queens Ballroom Jul 21 '64; Fabulous Queens Ballroom Sep 15 '64. **Coalville** (Leicestershire) Grand Ballroom May 26 '67. **Colchester** (Essex) South East R&B Festival, Blackheath Jul 1 '67; University of Essex Mar 3 '73; Colchester University Jan 29 '79. **Coventry** (Warwickshire) Coventry Theatre Mar 29 '64; Coventry Theatre Nov 22 '64; Coventry Theatre May 9 '65; Matrix Hall Aug 21 '65; Union, Lanchester Technical College Jan 27 '68; Coventry Theatre Apr 28 '68; Lanchester Polytechnic Apr 14 '72; College Of Education Jun 23 '72; Coventry Theatre Jun 28 '81. **Cranford** (Northamptonshire) Town Hall May 26 '66. **Croydon** *see* London. **Darlington** (Co. Durham) Darlington Arts Centre (Ray Davies) Nov 11 '95. **Dartford** (Kent) Orchard Theatre (Ray Davies) Nov 15 '95. **Derby** (Derbyshire) Gaumont Cinema May 9 '64; Gaumont Cinema Nov 21 '64; Gaumont Cinema May 23 '65/can. **Doncaster** (Yorkshire) Gaumont Cinema Apr 21 '64; Top Rank Suite Mar 8 '65/can; Top Rank Suite Jan 24 '66; Top Rank Suite Jul 7 '72; The Dome Nov 23 '93. **Dover** (Kent) ABC Cinema Apr 14 '64; ABC Cinema Nov 24 '64. **Droylsden** *see* Manchester. **Dudley** (Worcestershire) Hippodrome Theatre Feb 16 '66. **Dunstable** (Bedfordshire) California Pool Ballroom (CPB) Jan 1 '65; CPB Nov 12 '65/can?; CPB Jun 25 '66/can; CPB Sep 5 '70; Queensway Hall Dec 15 '80. **Eastbourne** (Sussex) Winter Gardens May 11 '66/re from Apr 27; Sussex Congress Hall Oct 24 '94. **East Grinstead** (Sussex) White Hall Dec 27 '64. **East Ham** *see* London. **Eccles** (Lancashire) Broadway Theatre Nov 19 '64. **Edgware** *see* London. **Eltham** *see* London. **Erdington** *see* Birmingham. **Exeter** (Devon) University of Exeter Jun 23 '67; ABC Cinema Apr 9 '68; University of Exeter (UE) Mar 5 '71; UE Mar 2 '73; UE Feb 27 '76; UE Dec 11 '78. **Farnborough** (Hampshire) Carousel Club May 16 '66/re from Mar 28. **Felixstowe** (Suffolk) Pier Pavilion Sep 13 '69; **Finsbury Park** *see* London. **Folkestone** (Kent) Leas Cliff Hall Jul 19 '69; Leas Cliff Hall Nov 14 '94; Leas Cliff Hall (Ray Davies) Aug 11 '95. **Forest Gate** *see* London. **Forest Hill** *see* London. **Frodsham** (Cheshire) Merseyview Ballroom Feb 21 '64; Merseyview Ballroom Aug 29 '64. **Glastonbury** (Somerset) Glastonbury Festival Jun 26 '93/re from Jun 27. **Gloucester** (Gloucestershire) ABC Cinema Apr 7 '64; ABC Cinema Oct 17 '64; ABC Cinema Apr 10 '68. **Golders Green** *see* London. **Grantham** (Lincolnshire) Granada Cinema Oct 9 '64; Drill Hall Feb 19 '66. **Gravesend** (Kent) Co-op Oct 29 '65. **Great Malvern** (Worcestershire) Winter Gardens Nov 2 '65; Winter Gardens Aug 23 '66/can/re from Jul 12/re from Jun 7; Winter Gardens Jul 18 '67. **Great Yarmouth** (Norfolk) ABC Cinema Jul 12 '64; ABC Cinema Aug 21 '66. **Greenford** (Middlesex) Starlite Ballroom Oct 31 '65/re from Sep 24. **Greenwich** *see* London. **Grimsby** (Lincolnshire) Mecca Gaiety Ballroom Mar 25 '66/can; Mecca Gaiety Ballroom Aug 19 '66. **Guildford** (Surrey) Odeon Cinema Apr 19 '64; Odeon Cinema Oct 15 '64; Civic Hall Dec 20 '82; Civic Hall Mar 29 '84. **Halifax** (Yorkshire) Princess Ballroom Sep 11 '64; Victoria Theatre Nov 2 '93; Victoria Hall Oct 26 '94; **Handsworth** (Warwickshire) Plaza Ballroom Mar 21 '64; Plaza Ballroom Jun 11 '66; Plaza Ballroom Jun 17 '67. **Hammersmith** *see* London. **Hanley** *see* Stoke-On-Trent. **Harleston** (Norfolk) 32 Club, Oct 22 '65. **Harrow** *see* London. **Harrogate** (Yorkshire) Royal Hall Jan 7 '65; **Hastings** (Sussex) Pier Ballroom May 23 '64; Pier Ballroom Jul 3 '64; Pier Ballroom Aug 6 '67; Hastings Stadium Aug 28 '67; Pier Pavilion Mar 23 '74. **Hatfield** (Hertfordshire) Hatfield Polytechnic Institute Dec 1 '72. **Hemel Hempstead** (Hertfordshire) Pavilion Ballroom Jan 10 '68/can; Dacorum Pavilion Nov 7 '94. **Hereford** (Herefordshire) Hillside Ballroom Feb 19 '65. **Hertford** (Hertfordshire) Corn Exchange Jun 25 '66. **High Wycombe** (Buckinghamshire) Town Hall Sep 1 '64; Town Hall May 3 '66. **Hinckley** (Leicestershire) St George's Ballroom Aug 15 '64; Football Grounds Jul 15 '67; St George's Ballroom Nov 4 '67. **Holborn** *see* London. **Hornsey** *see* London. **Huddersfield** (Yorkshire) ABC Cinema May 6 '64; Teen Plaza Club Jun 18 '67. **Hull** (Yorkshire) ABC Cinema May 5 '64. ABC Cinema Oct 10 '64; ABC Cinema Dec 2 '64; Locarno Ballroom Jun 15 '67; Skyline Ballroom Oct 18 '67; City Hall Aug 23 '69; West Refectory, University of Hull Mar 8 '74. **Ipswich** (Suffolk) Gaumont Cinema Sep 23 '64/can; Gaumont Cinema May 16 '65; Gaumont Cinema Jun 25 '81. **Keele** (Staffordshire) University of Keele Dec 13 '78. **Kenilworth** (Warwickshire) Kinetic Cinema Jan 23 '72. **Kentish Town** *see* London. **Kidderminster** (Worcestershire) Town Hall Sep 23 '65/can; Town Hall Oct 21 '65; Town Hall Feb 17 '66. **King's Lynn** (Norfolk) Theatre Royal Sep 29 '64. **King's Heath** *see* Birmingham. **Kingston-Upon-Thames** *see* London. **Kingston upon Hull** *see* Hull. **Krumlin** (Yorkshire) Yorkshire Festival Aug 16 '70/can (never booked). **Lancaster** (Lancashire) University of Lancaster (UL) Feb 26 '71; UL Feb 18 '72/can; UL Mar 15 '74; UL Mar 6 '76/can. **Langley Mill** (Derbyshire) Working Men's Club Oct 5 '67. **Leeds** (Yorkshire) Odeon Cinema May 22 '65/can; Refectory, University of Leeds (RUL) Oct 26 '67; RUL Oct 20 '72; RUL Mar 2 '74; RUL May 30 '75; Town And Country Club Mar 22 '94. **Leicester** (Leicestershire) Drill Hall Dec 16 '64; DeMontfort Hall (DMH) Apr 18 '65; DMH May 6 '66; Granby Halls Feb 23 '68; DMH Apr 14 '68; Top Rank Suite Feb 24 '71; DMH Sep 20 '73; University of Leicester Mar 7 '74; Leicester Poly Jan 20 '79; DMH May 6 '81; DMH Apr 9 '84; DMH Nov 3 '93. **Lewisham** *see* London. **Leyton** *see* London. **Lincoln** (Lincolnshire) ABC Cinema Apr 17 '64; ABC Cinema Nov 13 '64; City Football Club May 30 '66; Ritz Theatre Nov 21 '93. **Liverpool** (Lancashire) Cavern Feb 21 '64; Cavern Mar 31 '65/can; Union, University of Liverpool Oct 21 '67; Empire Theatre Apr 21 '68; Stadium Oct 14 '72; Stadium Feb 17 '73; Stadium Sep 22 '73; Empire Theatre May 31 '75; Empire Theatre May 14 '78/can; Empire Theatre Jan 21 '79; Empire Theatre May 12 '81; Royal Court Theatre Dec 5 '82; Royal Court Theatre Apr 7 '84; Royal Court Theatre Jun 15 '88/re from Jun 1. **London** *As **The Kelley Brothers***: Clissold Arms, Muswell Hill c. Dec '60. *As **Ray Davies Quartet***: William Grimshaw Secondary Modern School, Muswell Hill, Oct '61; Athaeneum, Muswell Hill, Nov? '61; Clissold Arms, Muswell Hill '62; El Toro Coffee Bar, Muswell Hill '62; Crouch End School, Crouch End '62; Coldfall Youth Club, Muswell Hill spring '62; Muswell Hill Youth Club spring '62; Hendon Police Academy spring '62; u/v Crouch End spring '62; u/v Edmonton spring '62; Railway Tavern, Crouch End, c. autumn '62; Lyceum Dec 31 '62. *Ray Davies as part of **Dave Hunt's R&B Band***: Piccadilly Club (Soho) Jan 4 '63; Station Hotel, Richmond Jan 6 '63; Six Bells Club, Chelsea Jan 9 '63; Elm Park Hotel, Hornchurch Jan 10 '63; Piccadilly Club, Soho Jan 11 '63; Station Hotel, Richmond Jan 13 '63; Six Bells Club, Chelsea Jan 16 '63; Piccadilly Club, Soho Jan 18 '63; Station Hotel, Richmond Jan 20 '63; Six Bells Club, Chelsea Jan 23 '63; Piccadilly Club, Soho Jan 25 '63; Station Hotel, Richmond Jan 27 '63; Station Hotel, Richmond Feb 3 '63; Station Hotel, Richmond Feb 10 '63. *As **Ray Davies Quartet/Ramrods***: Town Hall, Hornsey Apr 13 '63; Dance Institute Of London c. '63 ***Ramrods:*** Toc H, Muswell Hill crica '63. ***Rick Wayne & The Muscle Men:*** various US Air Force bases Aug '63. *Ray Davies as part of **Hamilton King's Blues Messengers***: Kaleidoscope, Soho spring '63; Flamingo Club, Soho spring '63; Count Suckles, Edgware tube (possible) spring '63; Roaring Twenties, spring '63. *As **Robert Wace & The Boll-Weevils***: Dorchester Hotel? Sep 28 '63; Grocer's Hall Oct 3 '63; Brady's Oct 30 '63. *As **The Ravens***: Camden Head, Islington Oct '63; private party, Belgravia Nov '63; private party, Chelsea Nov '63; Daily Mail offices Nov '63; Methodist Youth Hostel, Muswell Hill Nov 23 '63; Twycross Country club Dec '63; Town Hall, Hornsey Dec 17 '63; Archway Tavern, Holloway Dec 18 '63; Town Hall, Hornsey Dec 31 '63; Lotus House Restaurant Dec 31 '63. *As **The Kinks***: Goldhawk Beat Club, Shepherds Bush Feb 7 '64; Moravian Hall, Hornsey Feb 15 '64; Glenlyn Ballroom, Forest Hill Feb 28 '64; Astoria Theatre, Finsbury Park May 2 '64; Odeon Cinema, Lewisham May 3 '64; Granada Cinema, Walthamstow May 10 '64; Granada Cinema, Harrow May 13 '64; Granada Cinema, Kingston-Upon-Thames May 14 '64; Goldhawk Beat Club, Shepherds Bush May 15 '64; Easybeat Club, Tottenham Jun 9 '64; Club Noreik, Tottenham Jul 4 '64; Goldhawk Beat Club, Shepherds Bush Jul 24 '64; Goldhawk Beat Club, Shepherd Bush Aug 28 '64; Silverblades Ice Rink, Streatham Sep 7 '64; 100 Club Sep 9 '64; Lotus Ballroom, Forest Gate Sep 22 '64/can; Granada Cinema, East Ham Oct 11 '64; Granada Cinema, Brixton Oct 14 '64; Granada Cinema, Tooting Oct 18 '64; Lotus Ballroom, Forest Gate Oct 27 '64; Granada Cinema, Walthamstow Nov 7 '64; Royal Albert Hall Nov 9 '64; ABC Cinema, Harrow Nov 11 '64; ABC Cinema, Kingston-Upon-Thames Nov 27 '64; Polar Baths Dec 18 '64; Celebrity Club Dec 20 '64; Baths, Eltham Dec 28 '64; Baths, Eltham Feb 22 '65; Baths, Leyton Mar 5 '65; Palais, Wimbledon Mar 6 '65; Fairfield Hall, Croydon Mar 19 '65; Empire Pool, Wembley Apr 11 '65; Granada Cinema, Walthamstow May 1 '65; Odeon Cinema, Lewisham May 2 '65; Granada Cinema, Kingston-Upon-Thames May 6 '65; Granada Cinema, East Ham May 7 '65; Granada Cinema, Tooting May 14 '65; Empire Pool, Wembley Nov 19 '65; Palais, Wimbledon Dec 3 '65; Town Hall, Greenwich Dec 10 '65; Silverblades Ice Rink, Streatham Jan 17 '66; Notre Dame Hall Feb 4 '66; Locarno Ballroom, Streatham May 12 '66/re from Apr 7; Goldsmiths' College May 20 '66; Town Football Club, Edgware May 22 '66; Fairfield Hall, Croydon May 27 '66; Ram Jam, Brixton Jun 9 '66/can; Palais, Wimbledon Nov 26 '66; Royal Albert Hall Feb 4 '67; Empire Pool, Wembley Apr 16 '67; Upper Cut Club, Forest Gate May 20 '67/can; Fanny Boutique, Croydon (Dave Davies) Feb 9 '68/can; Granada Cinema, Walthamstow Apr 7 '68; Thames Polytechnic, Eltham Jun 14 or 21 '69; Bumper's Feb 23 '71; Rainbow Theatre, Finsbury Park Jan 31 '72; Goldsmiths' College Apr 28 '72; North East London Polytechnic, Walthamstow May 20 '72; Rainbow Theatre, Finsbury Park Oct 21 '72; Imperial College Dec 9 '72; Drury Lane Theatre Royal Jan 14 '73; Royal Festival Hall Jun 8 '73; White City Stadium Jul 15 '73; Fairfield Hall, Croydon Oct 7 '73; Palladium Jun 16 '74; Hippodrome, Golders Green Jul 14 '74; Wembley Stadium Sep 14 '74/can; Royalty Theatre Dec 20-22 '74 New Victoria Theatre,Jun 14 '75; Drury Lane Theatre Royal Feb 29 '76; Rainbow Theatre, Finsbury Park Mar 24 '77; Rainbow Theatre, Finsbury Park Dec 23 '77; Rainbow Theatre, Finsbury Park Dec 24 '77; Roundhouse, Chalk Farm May 19 '78; Odeon Cinema, Hammersmith Oct 1 '78; Dominion Theatre Nov-Dec '79/can; Strand Lyceum Ballroom Aug 7 '80; Victoria Apollo Theatre Dec 14 '80; Rainbow Theatre, Finsbury Park Jun 26 '81; Strand Lyceum Ballroom Dec 22 '82; Palais, Hammersmith Apr 2, 3 '84; Town & Country Club, Kentish Town (T&C) Dec 20 '87; T&C Jun 9 '88; T&C Aug 15 '89; T&C Apr 17 '90/can; Alexandra Palace Aug 12 '90; The Grand, Clapham Mar 29 '93; Royal Albert Hall Jul 11 '93; Wembley Arena Mar 26 '94; Fairfield Hall, Croydon Oct 28 '94; Empire, Shepherd's Bush Nov 8 '94; BT Birthday Concert, Docklands Arena Dec 6 '94; Advertising World Annual Awards, Grosvenor House Hotel Apr 3 '95; Bloomsbury Theatre (Ray Davies) Oct 28-30 '95; Poetry Olympics, Royal Albert Hall (Ray Davies) Jul 7 '96; Empire, Willesden (Ray Davies) Nov 18 '95/can; Lewisham Theatre, Catford (Ray Davies) Nov 23 '95. **Lowestoft** (Suffolk) Nautilus Club, South Pier Pavilion Aug 5 '67. **Loughborough** (Leicestershire) Loughborough University Of Technology (LUT) Mar 6 '71; LUT Jun 24 '72. **Luton** (Bedfordshire) Majestic Ballroom Jul 9 '64; Ritz Cinema Nov 26 '64; Majestic Ballroom Mar 11 '65/can; Luton College of Technology Feb 5 '71. **Lydney** (Gloucestershire) Town Hall, Feb 26 '65. **Maidenhead** (Berkshire) Ready Steady Club, Pearce Hall Nov 25 '67. **Maidstone** (Kent) Maidstone Art College May 26 '72; Hazlitt Theatre (Ray Davies) Mar 28 '95. **Malvern** *see* Great Malvern. **Manchester** (Lancashire) Bodega Club Mar 13 '64; Palace Theatre Mar 22 '64; Apollo Theatre, Ardwick Green Apr 18 '64; Co-op Hall, Droylsden Mar 15 '64; Jung Frau Jun 12 '64; Oasis Jun 29 '64; Mr. Smith's Jul 5 '64; Domino Jul 26 '64; Princess Jul 26 '64; Cavern Aug 7 '64; Jung Frau Aug 21 '64; Twisted Wheel Oct 28 '64; New Century Hall Dec 24 '64; Plaza Ballroom Feb 18 '65; Student Union, University of Manchester Mar 1 '65; Top Twenty Nov 13 '65; Oasis Dec 5 '65; Princess Ballroom Dec 11 '65; Oasis Apr 9 '66/can; Top Ten Jun 19 '66; Belle Vue Aug 26 '66; Belle Vue Apr 6 '67; Odeon Cinema Apr 22 '68; Owens Union, University Of Manchester Feb 15 '72; Free Trade Hall Jun 26 '72; Free Trade Hall Oct 16 '72; Palais Sep 26 '73; Palace Theatre Mar 2 '76; Student Union, Manchester Polytechnic Dec 8 '78; Apollo Theatre, Ardwick Green (Apollo) May 13 '78/can; Apollo Jan 26 '79; Apollo Dec 17 '80; Apollo May 10 '81; Apollo Dec 3 '82; Apollo Apr 6 '84; Apollo Apr 24 '85; Apollo Jun 8 '88/re from Jun 7; Apollo Nov 12 '93. **Mansfield** (Nottinghamshire) Granada Cinema Apr 22 '64; Granada Cinema Apr 6 '68; Mansfield Leisure Centre Nov 5 '93. **March** (Cambridgeshire) Marcam Hall Aug 7 '65. **Margate** (Kent) Dreamland Ballroom Jul 14 '66; Dreamland Ballroom Aug 29 '66. **Middlesborough** (Yorkshire) Town Hall Dec 6 '82; Town Hall Apr 8 '84. **Morecambe** (Lancashire) Floral Hall Ballroom Oct 2 '64; Central Pier Marine Ballroom Jun 3 '66. **Nelson** (Lancashire) Imperial Ballroom Aug 8 '64; Imperial Ballroom Sep 2 '64; Imperial Ballroom Oct 23 '65/can; Imperial Ballroom Feb 26 '66; Imperial Ballroom Jun 4 '66/can; Imperial Ballroom Jan 28 '67; Imperial Ballroom Jan 6 '68/can. **New Brighton** *see* Wallasey (Cheshire). **Newcastle-under-Lyme** (Staffordshire) PMC Clayton Lodge Mar 8 '64; PMC Clayton Lodge Mar 15 '64. **Newcastle Upon Tyne** (Northumberland) City Hall Apr 3 '64; Majestic Ballroom Sep 14 '64; City Hall Dec 5 '64; City Hall Mar 14 '65; Majestic Ballroom Dec 15 '65; Majestic Ballroom Jan 25 '66; City Hall Apr 29 '66; City Hall Apr 13 '68; City Hall Jun 12 '69/can; City Hall Jun 3 '72; University Sep 29 '72; City Hall, Oct 4 '73; City Hall Jun 1 '75; City Hall Mar 5 '76; City Hall May 19 '78/can; City Hall Jan 22 '79; City Hall May 9 '81; City Hall Jun 5 '88/can. **New Cross** *see* London, **Newton** (Cheshire) Pavilion Jul 25 '69. **Northampton** (Northamptonshire) ABC Cinema Apr 28 '64; ABC Cinema Nov 12 '64; ABC Cinema Apr 16 '68; County Cricket Grounds Oct 7 '72. **Northwich** (Cheshire) Memorial Hall Jun 6 '64; Memorial Hall Sep 12 '64. **Norwich** (Norfolk) Theatre Royal Apr 11 '64; Gala Ballroom Sep 17 '64; Earlham Park Jun 18 '66; Earlham Park May 6 '67; Fishers Melody Rooms Oct 4 '69; University of East Anglia Feb 27 '74/can; University of East Anglia Dec 12 '82; University of East Anglia Nov 17 '93; University of East Anglia Nov 6 '94; Theatre Royal (Ray Davies) Aug 5 '95. **Nottingham** (Nottinghamshire) Dungeon Jul 18 '64; Dungeon Aug 9 '64; Elizabethan Rooms Mar? '65; Sherwood Rooms Apr 28 '66; Trent Polytechnic Feb 20 '71; Trent Polytechnic Oct 5 '72; Rock City Dec 19 '80; Royal Court Centre Dec 14 '82; Royal Court Centre Mar 30 '84; Royal Court Centre Jun 16 '88/re from Jun 2; Royal Concert Hall Mar 28 '93; Royal Concert Hall Nov 10 '94. **Nuneaton** (Warwickshire) Co-op Ballroom Mar 12 '65. **Oakham** (Rutland) Rutland County Showgrounds Aug 20 '66. **Oldham** (Lancashire) Astoria Ballroom May 28 '64; Human Jungle Oct 25 '64; Queen Elizabeth Hall Oct 20 '94; Queen Elizabeth Hall (Ray Davies) Nov 20 '95. **Oldhill** *see* Birmingham. **Oxford** (Oxfordshire) Town Hall Feb 8 '64; New Theatre Dec 7-11 '64; University of Oxford: Balliol College Jun 21 '66; University of Oxford: Keble College Jun 14 or 21 '69; Oxford Poly Oct 19 '72; New Theatre May 18 '78/can; Oxford Poly Jan 18 '79; New Theatre May 5 '81; Apollo Theatre Apr 22 '85; Apollo Theatre May 29 '88/can; University of Oxford: Magdalen College Jun 21 '91. **Peterborough** (Northamptonshire) Embassy Theatre Apr 12 '64; Palais Jan 10 '65/ re to Mar 13; Palais Mar 13 '65; Palais Dec 18 '65; ABC Cinema Apr 17 '68. **Pilton** (Somerset) Worthy Farm Sep 19 '70. **Pinhoe** (Devon) Beat Barbeque Festival Jul 30 '66. **Poole** (Dorset) Wessex Hall, Poole Arts Centre (WHPAC) May 3 '81; WHPAC Apr 1 '84/can; WHPAC Jun 13 '88; WHPAC Nov '94; WHPAC Oct 29 '94. **Portsmouth** (Hampshire) Guildhall May 4 '65; Guildhall Apr 3 '66/can; Portsmouth Polytechnic Dec 2 '72; Guildhall Jun 11 '88/re from May 28; Guildhall Mar 25 '94. **Ramsgate** (Kent) West Cliff Tavern Mar 28 '64; Supreme Ballroom May 28 '66. **Rawtenstall** (Lancashire) Astoria Ballroom Jun 20 '64; Astoria Ballroom Oct 3 '64; Astoria Ballroom Jun 5 '65. **Reading** (Berkshire) Majestic Ballroom Jun 22 '64; Olympia Theatre Feb 25 '65; Top Rank Suite Feb 26 '73; University of Reading Dec 9 '78; Reading Festival Aug 30 '81; The Hexagon Nov 15 '93. **Redcar** (Yorkshire) The Scene May 17 '64; The Bowl Nov 18 '94. **Redhill** (Surrey) Market Hall Aug 22 '64. **Redruth** (Cornwall) Flamingo

Ballroom Aug 17 '66; Flamingo Ballroom Aug 9 '67. **Richmond** *see* London. **Rochdale** (Lancashire) Cubicklub Sep 18 '64; New Pyramid Beat Club Oct 4 '64. **Rochester** (Kent) Casino Ballroom Jun 23 '66. **Romford** (Essex) ABC Cinema Apr 15 '64; ABC Cinema Nov 10 '64. **Ross-on-Wye** (Herefordshire) Top Spot Ballroom Jul 29 '66/re from Jun 10/re from Apr 1. **Rugby** (Warwickshire) Ben Memorial Ballroom Jun 16 '67. **St. Albans** (Hertfordshire) City Hall Jul 18 '69; City Hall Feb 2, 3 '79; City Hall Dec 15 '80/can. **St. Austell** (Cornwall) Cornwall Coliseum May 4 '81. **Salford** (Lancashire) Whiskey A-Go-Go Jul 6 '64; University Of Salford May 23 '75. **Salisbury** (Wiltshire) City Hall May 21 '64; City Hall Apr 21 '65/re from Mar 17; City Hall Feb 10 '66. **Scarborough** (Yorkshire) Futurist Theatre (FT) Mar 30 '64; FT Dec 6 '64; FT Apr 19 '65; FT Aug 1 '65; FT Aug 29 '65. **Sheffield** (Yorkshire) City Hall Apr 4 '64; Esquire May 19 '64; Mojo Sep 20 '64; City Hall Nov 14 '64; University of Sheffield Jul 17 '70; University of Sheffield Mar 8 '71; University of Sheffield Jan 19 '79; Lyceum Ballroom Dec 17 '82. **Shrewsbury** (Shropshire) Granada Cinema Apr 23 '64; Granada Cinema Nov 20 '64; Music Hall (Ray Davies) Apr 13 '95. **Skegness** (Lincolnshire) Derbyshire Miner's Holiday Camp May 27 '67. **Slough** (Buckinghamshire) Adelphi Cinema Apr 30 '65; Adelphi Cinema Apr 25 '68. **Smethwick** *see* Birmingham. **Southampton** (Hampshire) Gaumont Cinema May 1 '64; Gaumont Cinema Dec 12 '80; Gaumont Cinema Apr 4 '84/can; ABC Cinema Oct 16 '64; Top Rank Ballroom Feb 20 '66; Guildhall Feb 25 '73; Mayflower Theatre Nov 7 '93; Guildhall, Civic Centre (Ray Davies) Nov 16 '95. **South Shields** (Co. Durham) Marine & Technical College Dec 19 '67/can?; Custom House Theatre (Ray Davies) Nov 1 '95. **Southend-On-Sea** (Essex) Odeon Cinema May 11 '64; Odeon Cinema May 12 '65. **Southport** (Lancashire) Floral Hall Jan 15 '66; Floral Ballroom May 21 '66/can; Floral Ballroom Jun 10 '67; Southport Theatre Mar 3 '76/can. **Southsea** (Hampshire) Savoy Ballroom May 16 '64; Birdcage Aug 15 '66. **Spalding** (Lincolnshire) South Holland Centre (Ray Davies) Nov 22 '95. **Spennymoor** (Co. Durham) Top Hat Oct 20, 21, 23-26 '68. **Stevenage** (Hertfordshire) Locarno Ballroom Oct 27 '65/can; Locarno Ballroom Apr 6 '66/can; Locarno Ballroom,Aug 31 '66. **Stockport** (Cheshire) Manor Lounge Nov 14 '65. **Stockton-On-Tees** (Co. Durham) ABC Cinema Dec 4 '64; Globe Cinema May 7 '64; Fiesta Club Oct 20-26 '68. **Stoke-On-Trent** (Staffordshire) Gaumont Cinema, Hanley May 8 '64; Gaumont Cinema, Hanley May 8 '65; Top Rank Ballroom, Hanley Mar 10 '65/can; King's Hall May 14 '66/can; Golden Torch Ballroom May 14 '66/can?; King's Hall Feb 4 '67; Trentham Gardens Feb 2 '73; Victoria Hall, Hanley May 8 '81; Victoria Hall, Hanley Dec 15 '82; Victoria Hall, Hanley Mar 25 '84. **Stourbridge** (Worcestershire) Town Hall Dec 30 '64. **Streatham** *see* London. **Stroud** (Gloucestershire) Subscription Rooms Feb 20 '65. **Sunderland** (Co. Durham) Locarno Ballroom Jun 2 '66; Empire Theatre Mar 15 '69; Fillmore North (Locarno Ballroom) Jan 19 '70/can; Locarno Ballroom Sep 21 '73; Empire Theatre Nov 1 '93; Empire Theatre Nov 17 '94. **Sutton Coldfield** (Warwickshire) Belfry's Hotel (BH) Oct 12 '68; BH Apr 26 '69; BH Jan 24 '70; BH Aug 28 '70; BH Jan 16 '71; BH Nov 12 '71; BH Feb 12 '72/can; BH Apr 15 '72. **Sutton-In-Ashfield** (Nottinghamshire) Golden Diamond Social Club Sep 21 '64/can. **Swindon** (Wiltshire) Locarno Ballroom Mar 18 '65; Odeon Cinema May 11 '65; Locarno Ballroom Nov 26 '65. **Taunton** (Somerset) Gaumont Cinema Apr 30 '64; Gaumont Cinmea May 18 '65. **Tooting** *see* London. **Tottenham** *see* London. **Torquay** (Devon) Princess Theatre Jul 19 '64; Princess Theatre Sep 6 '64/ re from Aug 23; Princess Theatre Jul 31 '66; Town Hall Aug 16 '66; Town Hall Aug 8 '67; English Riviera Nov 9 '93. **Tunbridge Wells** (Kent) Assembly Rooms Nov 15 '94; Assembly Hall (Ray Davies) Aug 12 '95. **Ulverston** (Lancs) Coronation Hall (Ray Davies) Apr 10 '95. **Tunbridge Wells** (Kent) Assembly Hall Mar 16 '65/can. **Uxbridge** (Middlesex) Brunel University (BU) Mar 1 '74; BU May 24 '75; BU Jan 31 '79. **Wallasey** (Cheshire) Tower Ballroom, New Brighton Jan 9 '65; Floral Pavilion Theatre, New Brighton Nov 13 '93; Floral Pavilion, New Brighton (Ray Davies) Nov 12 '95. **Wallington** (Surrey) Public Hall, Wallington Jun 5 '64. **Walthamstow** *see* London. **Warrington** (Lancashire) Paar Hall Jun 2 '64; Paar Hall Apr 5 '65. **Watford** (Hertfordshire) Town Hall May 9 '72. **Wellingborough** (Northamptonshire) Castle Theatre (Ray Davies) Apr 12 '95. **Wembley** *see* London. **West Bromwich** (Staffordshire) Adelphi Ballroom Feb 27 '65/re from Jan 2?; Adelphi Ballroom Dec 4 '65. **Weston-Super-Mare** (Somerset) Somerset Playhouse Theatre (Ray Davies) Nov 14 '95. **Wigan** (Lancashire) ABC Cinema Mar 6 '64; ABC Cinema Dec 1 '64. **Wimbledon** *see* London. **Windsor** (Berkshire) Festival Aug 11 '67/can. **Winchester** (Hampshire) Lide Ballroom Jun 26 '64. **Wolverhampton** (Staffordshire) Gaumont Cinema Apr 29 '64; Gaumont Cinema May 20 '65; Civic Hall Nov 22 '93; Civic Hall Nov 11 '94; Wulfrun Hall (Ray Davies) Aug 9 '95. **Worthing** (Sussex) Assembly Hall Jul 16 '64; Assembly Hall Jul 20 '64; Pier Pavilion Jan 27 '66; Pier Ballroom Jun 30 '66; Sussex Assembly Rooms Oct 27 '94. **Woolwich** *see* London. **York** (Yorkshire) University Of York Feb 19 '72; University Of York Mar 6 '74; Barbican Centre Nov 11 '93; Barbican Centre Nov 5 '94; Barbican Centre (Ray Davies) Nov 19 '95/can.

ISLE OF MAN. Douglas Palace Theater (PT) Aug 12 '65; PT Aug 11 '66.

NORTHERN IRELAND. Banbridge (Down) Castle Ballroom Nov 5 '65. **Bangor** (Down) Milano's Ballroom Nov 6 '65; Milano's Ballroom Jul 9 '66. **Belfast** Romano's Ballroom Nov 5 '65; Romano's Ballroom Jul 8 '66; Starlite Ballroom Jun 2 '67; Starlite Ballroom Sep 29 '67; Ulster Hall Apr 29 '81; Ulster Hall Nov 19 '81; Ulster Hall Mar 20 '94; Ulster Hall Nov 21 '94. **Lisburn** (Antrim) Top Hat Jun 2 '67. **Newtownards** (Down) Queen's Ballroom Nov 6 '65. **Portstewart** (Londonderry) Strand Ballroom Jul 8 '66.

SCOTLAND. Aberdeen (Aberdeenshire) Beach Ballroom Oct 21 '64; Beach Ballroom Aug 26 '65; Capitol Theatre Mar 30 '65/can; Capitol Theatre Oct 17 '94. **Ayr** (Ayrshire) Ice Rink Aug 28 '65; Ice Rink Jul 20 '66; Gaiety Theatre (Ray Davies) Nov 5 '95. **Dumfries** (Dumfriesshire) Drill Hall Jul 23 '66. **Dunfermline** (Fife) Kinema Ballroom Mar 24 '65; Kinema Ballroom Apr 20 '66/can. **Dundee** (Angus) Caird Hall Mar 28 '65/can; Caird Hall Aug 24 '65/can. **Edinburgh** (Midlothian) Eldorado Ballroom, Leith Oct 24 '64; ABC Cinema Dec 3 '64; Fountainbridge Palais Aug 25 '65; McGoo's Apr 24 '66; McGoo's Jul 24 '66; McGoo's Aug 28 '66/can; University May 3 '67; University Feb 9 '73; Usher Hall May 21 '75; Odeon Cinema Jan 23 '79; Playhouse Theatre Dec 2 '82; Playhouse Theatre Jun 4 '88/can; Fringe Festival, Assembly Theatre Hall (Ray Davies) Aug 18-27 '95; New Year's Eve Concert, Princes Street Theatre Dec 31 '95/can. **Elgin** (Morayshire) Town Hall Oct 20 '64; Town Hall Aug 24 '65. **Glasgow** (Lanarkshire) Odeon Cinema Sep 30 '64; Barrowland Oct 19 '64; Barrowland Aug 23 '65/re from May 26-29?/re from Mar 29; Barrowland (possible venue) Jan 9 '66; Odeon Cinema Jun 5 '66/can; Kelvin Hall Apr 1 '67; University of Glasgow May 5 '67; University of Strathclyde Feb 10 '73; Apollo Oct 3 '73; University of Strathclyde Mar 9 '74; Apollo May 22 '75; Apollo Jan 24 '79; Apollo May 14 '81; Barrowlands Mar 27 '93; Royal Concert Hall Nov 25 '93; Barrowlands Oct 18 '94; Pavilion (Ray Davies) Nov 3 '95. **Glenrothes** (Fife) Rothes Halls Oct 16 '94; Rothes Hall (Ray Davies) Nov 2 '95. **Greenock** (Renfrewshire) Palladium Mar 27 '65/can; Palladium Aug 25 '65/can. **Kirkcaldy** (Fife) Raith Ballroom Jan 7 '66; Raith Ballroom Jul 22 '66. **Lamlash** (Isle Of Arran) Lamlash Hall Jul 21 '66. **Leith** *see* Edinburgh. **Perth** (Perthshire) City Hall (CH) Oct 23 '64; CH May 26-29? '65/can/re from Mar 26; CH Aug 27 '65; CH Apr 23 '66. **Stirling** (Stirlingshire) Albert Hall Mar 25 '65. **Stranraer** (Wigtownshire) Kinema Dance Hall Jul 19 '68/can; Marquee, Agnew Park Jul 20 '68/can. **Unconfirmed venues** Jan 8 '66; Apr 25 '66.

WALES. Aberystwyth (Cardiganshire) Aberystwyth University (AU) Feb 12 '71; AU Feb 16 '73; AU Mar 1 '76/can. **Cardiff** (Glamorgan) Capitol Theatre Apr 24 '64; Capitol Theatre May 19 '65; Sophia Gardens Nov 27 '65; Top Rank Suite Apr 24 '67; Capitol Theatre Apr 11 '68; University Feb 13 '71; University Oct 4 '72; University Mar 10 '76; Ninian Park Festival Jun 15 '77/can/re from Jun 5; University Jan 29 '79/can; St. David's Hall Mar 24 '84; St David's Hall Nov 19 '93. **Llandudno** (Caernarfonshire) North Wales Theatre (Ray Davies) Aug 6 '95. **Llanelli** (Carmarthenshire) Llanelli Glen Oct 28 '65. **Neath** (Glamorgan) Empire Ent/Social Club Nov 18 '65. **Pontypridd** (Glamorgan) Municipal Hall Jul 1 '66/can. **Porthcawl** (Glamorgan) Grand Pavillion Nov 18 '65; Glam Grand Pavilion (Ray Davies) Nov 24 '95. **Prestatyn** (Flintshire) Royal Lido Ballroom Oct 31 '64/re from Sep 26. **Rhyl** (Flintshire) New Pavilion Nov 2 '94; Pavilion (Ray Davies) Nov 9 '95. **Shotton** (Flintshire) Vaughn Hall, Sep 26 '64. **Swansea** (Glamorgan) Top Rank Suite (TRS) Jun 14 '67; TRS Aug 14 '70; TRS May 21 '71; TRS Feb 28 '73/can; Marina, Jul 29 '84/can.

UNITED STATES OF AMERICA. Placenames in the main text include standard two-letter state abbreviations. The list here includes those abbreviations alongside the state name.

ALABAMA (AL): **Birmingham** Birmingham-Jefferson County Civic Center Concert Hall Jul 17 '79; Boutwell Municipal Auditorium Aug 27 '80. **ARIZONA** (AZ): **Chandler** Compton Terrace Sep 6 '79/can. **Mesa** Amphitheatre May 11 '87/can. **Phoenix** (*see also* Mesa, Chandler, Tempe) Celebrity Theatre May 9 '74; Celebrity Theatre May 14 '74; u/v Jan 20 '76/can; Veterans Memorial Coliseum Aug 12 '81; Veterans Memorial Coliseum May 9 '83; u/v Apr 21 '88/can. **Tempe** Arizona State University Feb 19 '85. **Tucson** Community Center Theatre Sep 7 '79; University of Arizona Jan 21 '76/can. **CALIFORNIA** (CA): **Anaheim** Stadium Jun 19 '77. **Antioch** Contra Costa Fairgrounds Nov 26 '69. **Berkeley** Community Theate (CT) Feb 27 '72; CT Aug 26 '72; CT Jan 31 '76/re from Jan 30; CT, Feb 17 '77/can; CT Jun 21 '78; Greek Theatre Aug 21, 22 '81; CT Apr 19 '88. **Concord** Ygnacio Pavilion Jul 2 '70; Pavilion, Aug 23 '85; Pavilion, Jun 7 '87/re from May 17. **Costa Mesa** Pacific Amphitheatre Jun 3 '87/re from May 15. **Davis** University of California-Davis Dec 2 '69. **Fresno** Warnor Theater May 11 '74. **Hollywood** *see* Los Angeles. **Inglewood** Forum Oct 10 '80; Forum Aug 14 '81; Forum May 6 '83/re from Apr 25. **Irvine** University of CA-Irvine Nov 24 '69; University of CA-Irvine Feb 13 '76/re from Jan 22, 23. **Laguna Hills** Irvine Meadow Amphitheatre May 7 '83/re from Apr 30; Irvine Meadow Amphitheatre Aug 24 '85. **Los Angeles** (*see also* Santa Monica; Inglewood; Irvine; Laguna Hills; Northridge) Hollywood Bowl Jul 3 '65; Whisky A Go Go Nov 20-23 '69; Whisky A Go Go Apr '70/can; Whisky A Go Go Jul 3-5 '70; Pauley Pavilion Apr 10 '71/can; Hollywood Palladium Mar 9 '72; Hollywood Palladium Apr 11 '73; Shrine Civic Auditorium May 10 '74; Shrine Civic Auditorium Dec 20 '75/can; Hollywood Palladium Aug 18 ' '81; Memorial Sports Arena Feb 21 '85; Hollywood Palladium Mar 14 '87; Greek Theatre Jun 5 '87; Hollywood Henry Fonda Theatre (Ray Davies) Oct 10 '95; House of the Blues Jul 11-13 '95; Hollywood Henry Fonda Theatre (Ray Davies) May 15-18 '96. **Northridge** California State University Feb 15 '76/re from Jan 25. **Oakland** Auditorium Arena Oct 7, 8 '80; Henry J. Kaiser Convention Center Feb 24 '85. **Sacramento** Memorial Auditorium (MA) Jun 26 '65; MA May 19 '74/can; California State University Feb 1 '76; MA Apr 20 '77/can; MA Aug 23 '81/can; ARCO Arena May 16 '87/can. **San Bernadino** Glen Helen Regional Park Sep 4 '82; Swing Auditorium Feb 22 '85/can. **San Diego** Convention Hall Apr 9 '71/can; Golden Hall May 16 '74; Golden Hall Feb 11 '76/re from Jan 24; Civic Theater Apr 21 '77; Open Air Theatre, University Jul 19 '78; Open Air Theatre, University Sep 3 '79; Sports Arena Oct 11 '80; Sports Arena Aug 15 '81; Sports Arena May 5 '83/re from April 29; Golden Hall Feb 20 '85; Open Air Theatre, University Aug 22 '85; Golden Hall May 13 '87/can; Civic Theatre Jun 2 '87; Open Air Theatre, University Apr 22 '88. **San Francisco** (*see also* Berkeley; Concord; Oakland; Antioch) Cow Palace (Kinks present but don't perform) Jul 4 '65; Fillmore West Nov 27-30 '69; Family Dog Great Highway Jun 30, Jul 1 '70; Fillmore Nov 12-14 '70; Winterland Apr 13, 14 '73; Winterland May 17, 18 '74/can; Winterland Dec 8 '74; Winterland Dec 21 '75/can; Winterland Feb 19 '77; Civic Auditorium, Sep 1 '79; Cow Palace Apr 26 '83; Fillmore (Ray Davies) Oct 12 '95; Alcazar Theatre (Ray Davies) May 1-5, 8-11 '96. **San Jose** Civic Auditorium Jan 30 '76; Center For Performing Arts Apr 19 '77; Center For Performing Arts Jun 16 '78. **Santa Ana** Galaxy Concert Theatre (Ray Davies) Oct 9, 11 '95. **Santa Barbara** University of California-Santa Barbara May 12 '74; University of California-Santa Barbara Jan 29 '76/can; Arlington Theater Apr 22 '77/re from Feb 16; County Bowl Sep 2 '79; County Bowl Aug 16 '81; Arlington Theater Feb 22 '85; County Bowl Jun 5 '87; Arlington Theater Apr 20 '88. **Santa Cruz** Civic Auditorium Jul 17 '78. **Santa Monica** Civic Auditorium (CA) Nov 10 '70; CA Apr 7 '71; CA Aug 29 '72; CA Dec 10 '74; CA Feb 9, 10 '76/re from Jan 27, 28; CA Feb 17,18 '77; Morgan-Wixson Theatre (Dave Davies) Feb 17 '95. **Stockton** Civic Memorial Auditorium (CMA) Jun 27 '65/can; CMA Feb 20 '77. **Universal City** Amphitheatre Jun 23-25 '78; Amphitheatre Aug 16-19 '79; Amphitheatre Apr 23 '88; Amphitheatre Oct 2 '89/can. **Woodland Hills** Pierce College, Nov 21 '70. **COLORADO** (CO): **Boulder** University of Colorado Sep 30 '80; University of Colorado Apr 18 '83. **Denver** (*see also* Morrison) City Auditorium Theatre Jun 24 '65; Mammoth Gardens Nov 22 '70/can; Regis College Apr 24 '77; McNichols Sports Arena Sep 9 '81; u/v Mar 5 '85/can; Auditorium Theatre Apr 17 '88; Grizzly Rose Aug 24 '93/can. **Grand Junction** Mesa College, Nov 22 '70. **Morrison** Red Rocks Amphitheatre (RRA) Jul 27 '78; RRA Sep 9 '79; RRA Jun 11 '87. **Pueblo** Memorial Auditorium Nov 23 '70. **CONNECTICUT** (CT): **Danbury** Ives Center For Performing Arts May 12 '90. **Hartford** Dillon Stadium Aug 18 '72; Veterans Memorial Arena Mar 24 '83/can; Veterans Memorial Arena Dec 20 '84. **Middletown** Wesleyan University Nov 19 '71; Wesleyan University Feb 14 '79/can. **New Haven** Veterans Memorial Coliseum (VMC) Jul 29 '79; VMC Oct 30 '80/can; VMC Jan 21 '82; VMC Jun 6 '83; Toad's Place, May 2 '93; Toad's Place (Ray Davies) Oct 22 '95. **Stamford** High School Auditorium Dec 7 '69; Rich Forum (Ray Davies) Oct 20 '96. **Stratford** American Shakespeare Festival Theatre Dec 3 '70. **Storrs** Albert N. Jorgensen Auditorium Jan 31 '77; University of Connecticut May 8? '90/can. **Wallingford** Oakdale Music Theatre Jul 22 '95. **Waterbury** Palace Theater (PT) Apr 5 '74; PT Dec 6 '75; PT May 25 '78. **West Hartford** University of Hartford Nov 20 '71. **DELAWARE** (DE): **Newark** University Of Delaware, Apr 21 '90. **DISTRICT OF COLUMBIA** (DC): **Washington** (*see also* Falls Church, Virginia; Landover, Maryland) Emergency Jun 10, 11 '70; Eisenhower Theater Nov 5 '72; DAR Constitution Hall May 3 '77; Warner Theater Jun 7 '78; McDonough Arena Sep 21 '79; DAR Constitution Hall Mar 18 '85; DAR Constitution Hall Feb 3 '88/can; McDonough Arena Apr 20 '90; Bayou Apr 30 '93; Bayou Jul 17 '95. **FLORIDA** (FL): **Daytona Beach** Ocean Center Sep 30 '89/re from Sep 22. **Gainesville** O'Connell Center Oct 10 '81/can; O' Connell Center Feb 7 '85. **Hallandale** Button South Apr 23 '93. **Jacksonville** Civic Auditorium Aug 26 '80; Coliseum Dec 9 '83/can; Florida Theatre Oct 5 '89. **Lakeland** (*see also* Tampa) Civic Center Oct 16 '81/re from Oct 11/re from Jul; Civic Center, Dec 10 '83/can; Civic Center, Feb 6 '85. **Fort Lauderdale** Sunrise Musical Theater (SMT) Aug 22, 23 '80; SMT Oct 13,14 '81/re from Jul; SMT Feb 3, 4 '85; SMT Oct 1 '89/re from Sep 19. **Hollywood** Speedway Sportatorium Feb 26 '72. **Miami** (*see also* Hollywood; West Palm Beach; Fort Lauderdale) Pop Festival Mar 29 '70/can; Jai-Alai Fronton May 25 '74/can; Municipal Auditorium May 2 '75/can; Jai-Alai Fronton May 7 '77/re from Apr 1?; James L. Knight International Center Dec 6, 7 '83/can. **St. Petersburg** Bayfront Center Theatre May 4 '75; Vinoy Park Apr 24 '93. **Tallahassee** County Civic Center Oct 11 '81. **Tampa** (*see also* St. Petersburg, Lakeland) Fort Homer Hesterly Armory Feb 25 '72; State Fairground Speedway Nov 29 '74/can; Curtis Hixon Convention Hall May 8 '77; Curtis Hixon Convention Hall Aug 24 '80; Tampa Fair Oct 4 '89/can/re from Sep 21. **West Palm Beach** Jai-Alai Center May 3 '75; Carefree Theatre (Ray Davies) Nov 22 '96. **GEORGIA** (GA): **Atlanta** Sports Arena Feb 22 '70/can; Municipal Auditorium Apr 30 '75; Fox Theatre (FT) May 6 '77; FT Aug 5, 6 '78; FT Jul 20, 21 '79; FT Oct 20, 21 '80; FT Oct 22 '80/can; Civic Center Oct 8 '81/re from Jul; Civic Center Oct 9 '81/can; Civic Center Nov 28 '84; Chastain Park Amphitheatre Sep 29 '89/re from Sep 23; Roxy Apr 26 '93; Variety Playhouse (Ray Davies) Nov 20-21 '96. **HAWAII** (HI): **Honolulu** International Center Arena Jul 6 '65; Conroy Bowl Jul 6 '65; Earth Station Jun 29-Jul 1 '70/can; u/v Feb 10 '77. **IDAHO** (ID): **Boise** Capital High School Apr 16 '71/can. **ILLINOIS** (IL): **Carbondale** SIU Arena Nov 5 '83/can. **Champaign** University of Illinois-Champaign Jan 19 '84/re from Nov 4 '83. **Chicago** (*see also* Rosemont; Hoffman Estates) Arie Crown Theater Jun 21 '65; Kinetic Playground Oct 31 '69; Kinetic Playground Oct 30, Nov 1 '69/can; Kinetic Playground? Feb '70/can; Aragon May 29, 30 '70; Auditorium Theater Mar 12 '72; Aragon Aug 25 '72; Auditorium Theater (AT) Oct 31 '72; AT Apr 16 '74; AT Dec 13 '74; Aragon Dec 13 '75; Uptown Theater Feb 12 '77; Aragon Jun 25 '77/re from Jun 16; Uptown Theater Jun 11 '78; Uptown Theater Aug 11 '79; Uptown Theater Sep 17,18 '80; UIC Pavilion Apr 9 '83; UIC Pavilion Dec 2 '84; Riviera Mar 7, 8 '87; Auditorium Theatre Apr 9 '88/can; Park West (Ray Davies) Oct 15 '95; Apollo Theatre (Ray Davies) Apr 16-21, 24-27 '96; Vic Theatre (Ray Davies) Nov 17 '96. **DeKalb** Northern Illinois University Apr 10 '83. **Hoffman Estates** Poplar Creek Music Theatre (PCMT) Aug 31 '85; PCMT Jun 14 '87; PCMT Sep 23 '89/re from Sep 1; PCMT Aug 21 '93. **Macomb** Western Illinois University Sep 17 '79. **Peoria** Exposition Gardens Jun 20 '65. **Rockford** Metro Center Nov 8 '83/can; Metro Center Dec 8 '84. **Rosemont** Horizon Sep 15 '81. **Springfield** State Armory Jun 23 '65; u/v Dec 1 '84/can. **INDIANA** (IN): **Bloomington** Auditorium Jan 13 '84/re from Nov 12 '83. **Fort Wayne** Memorial Auditorium Apr 13 '75/can. **Indianapolis** Clowes Memorial Auditorium Nov 26 '77; Convention Center Sep 14 '80. **Merillville** Holiday Star Theatre Apr 10 '88; Star Plaza Theatre Jun 2 '93. **Noblesville** Deer Creek Music Center Aug 19 '93/can. **West Lafayette** Purdue University Sep 5 '80; Purdue University Jan 18 '84/re from Nov 9 '83. **IOWA** (IA): **Ames** C.Y. Stephens Auditorium Sep 12 '81; C.Y. Stephens Auditorium Apr 12 '88/can. **Cedar Rapids** Veterans Memorial Coliseum Nov 12 '69/can/re from Nov 2; Veterans Memorial Auditorium Apr 10 '75/can; Five Seasons Center Jan 20 '84/re from Nov 11 '83. **Davenport** u/v Nov '69 or '70; RKO Orpheum Theatre Apr 12 '75/can. **Iowa City** Hancher Auditorium Apr 11 '77. **KENTUCKY** (KY): **Louisville** Gardens Sep 10 '80; Gardens Jan14 '84/re from Nov 6 '83; Palace Theatre Jun 15 '82/re from Jan 18. **Lexington** Rupp Arena May 19 '83; Rupp Arena Nov 30 '84. **LOUISIANA** (LA): **Baton Rouge** Riverside Centroplex Performing Arts Theater Sep 24 '80/re from Assembly Center, Louisiana State University Sep 24. **New Orleans** Warehouse Feb 27, 28 '70/can; McAlister Auditorium Feb 20 '76; Warehouse Aug 3 '78; Municipal Auditorium Jul 15 '79; Saenger Performing Arts Center (SPAC) Aug 5 '81; SPAC Aug 30 '82; Kiefer UNO Lakefront Arena Nov 27 '84. **MAINE** (ME): **Brunswick** Bowdoin College May 6 '90. **Portland** Cumberland County Civic Center (C4) Dec 2 '77/can; C4 Aug 3 '79; C4 Jun 9 '83/re from Mar 25. **MARYLAND** (MD): **Annapolis** Halsey Field House Mar 17 '85. **Baltimore** (*see also* Owings Mill; Columbia) Hammerjacks May 10 '93. **College Park** Ritchie Auditorium Apr 23 '75; University Of Maryland Nov 28 '83/can. **Columbia** Merriweather Post Pavilion (MPP) Jun 29 '77; MPP Sep 14 '85; MPP Jun 29 '87 MPP Sep 16 '89; MPP Aug 5 '93. **Landover** Capital Centre (CC) Dec 10 '77; CC Dec 29 '80; CC Jan 14 '82; CC Jun 1 '83/re from Mar 17. **Owings Mill** Painter's Mill Music Fair Sep 4 '72. **MASSACHUSETTS** (MA): **Agawam** Riverside Park Stadium Aug 1 '93. **Amherst** Fine Arts Center Feb 21 '79; Fine Arts Center Mar 6 '80. **Beverly** North Shore Musical Theatre Jul 24 '95. **Boston** (*see also* Dorchester; Lynn) Tea Party Oct 23-25 '69; Tea Party Feb 12-14 '70; Music Hall Mar 25 '71/can; Aquarius Theatre Mar 5 '72; Aquarius Theatre Nov 11,12 '72; Music Hall (MH) Apr 1 '73; MH Apr 10 '74; MH Dec 1 '74; MH May 10 '75/can; Orpheum Theater Dec 4, 5 '75; MH Feb 5 '77/re from Feb 4, 5; MH Jun 4 '78; Orpheum Theater Oct 26 '80/can; Garden Sep 27, 29 '81; Garden Dec 16 '84; Wang Center For Performing Arts Feb 28 '87; Orpheum Theater Mar 30 '88; Garden (Ray & Dave Davies) Nov 22 '91; Avalon May 4 '93; Paradise (Ray Davies) Oct 16 '95; Lansdowne Street Playhouse (Ray Davies) Oct 1-3 '96; Orpheum Theatre (Ray Davies) Oct 6 '96. **Cape Cod** *see* South Yarmouth). **Cohasset** South Shore Music Circus Jul 28 '95. **Dorchester** UMB Baseball Field May 9 '90. **Foxboro** Sullivan Stadium Apr 25 '92. **Hyannis** Cape Cod Melody Tent Jul 27 '95. **Lenox** Music Inn Aug 5 '79. **Lowell** Commodore Ballroom Jun 13 '70; Memorial Auditorium Dec 4 '77; Memorial Auditorium Mar 6 '79. **Lynn** Manning Bowl Sep 8 '85. **Mansfield** Great Woods Center For Performing Arts (GWPA) Jul 3 '87; GWPA Sep 17 '89; GWPA Jul 27 '93. **North Attleboro** Community Theater Mar 29 '71. **North Dartmouth** South Eastern Massachusetts University Mar 7 '80. **South Yarmouth** Cape Cod Coliseum (C3) Jul 2 '77; C3 Aug 4 '79; C3 Oct 25 '80. **Springfield** (*see also* Agawam) Civic Center Arena (CCA) Aug 8 '78; CCA Jan 24 '82; CCA Dec 28 '83/re from Nov 22; Symphony Hall Apr 1 '88/re from Feb 1. **Stockbridge** Berkshire Theater Festival (Ray Davies) Sep 25-29 '96. **Worcester** Harrington Auditorium Mar 2 '79; Centrum Jun 10,11 '83/re from Mar 30, 31. **MICHIGAN** (MI): **Clarkston** Pine Knob Music Theatre (PKMT) Jun 23 '77; PKMT Sep 16 '81; PKMT Sep 1 '85; PKMT Sep 22 '89/re from Aug 30/re from Aug 31; PKMT Aug 17 '93. **Detroit** (*see also* Clarkston) Grande Ballroom Nov 7, 8 '69; u/v Feb '70/can; Eastown Theater Apr 2, 3 '71/re from Dec 11, 12 '70; u/v Dec 1 '71/can; Ford Auditorium Nov 1 '72; Palace Theater Dec 12 '75; Cobo Arena (CA) Apr 12 '78; CA Aug 10 '79; CA Sep 6 '80; CA Apr 14 '83/re from Apr 7; CA Dec 7 '84; Fox Theatre Mar 12 '87. **Grand Rapids** DeVos Hall Jun 18 '87; Club Eastbrook Aug 16 '93. **Kalamazoo** Wings Stadium Sep 17 '81. **Lansing** Civic Center Arena Apr 6

'83/can. **Mount Pleasant** Rose Arena Dec 5 '84. **MINNESOTA** (MN): **Bloomington** Metropolitan Sports Center (MSC) Sep 13 '81; MSC Apr 16 '83. **Minneapolis** Depot May 22, 23 '70; Auditorium Convention Hall Nov 27 '70/can; u/v Dec 2 '71/can; Orchestra Hall Apr 9 '77; State Theater Jun 13 '78; Northrup Memorial Auditorium Sep 15 '79; Auditorium Sep 16 '80; Orpheum Theater Mar 9 '87. **St. Paul** Civic Center Theatre Apr 13 '75/re from Apr 11; Roy Wilkins Auditorium Mar 9 '85. **MISSOURI** (MO): **Kansas City** Memorial Hall (MH) Dec 17 '75; MH Apr 10 '77; MH Jul 22 '78; Uptown Theater Jul 22 '78; MH Sep 14 '79; MH Sep 19 '80; Municipal Auditorium Sep 11 '81; Starlight Theater May 15 '83; Starlight Theater Aug 27 '85; Memorial Hall, Apr 15 '88. **St. Louis** Ambassador Theater (AT) May 23 '74/can; AT Dec 12 '74; AT May 7 '75/can; AT Dec 18 '75; Kiel Opera House (KOH) Jul 25 '78; KOH Sep 13 '79/can; KOH Sep 20 '80; Fox Theater Aug 30 '85; Fox Theater Apr 14 '88; Union Station Jun 3 '93. **NEBRASKA** (NE): **Lincoln** Pershing Municipal Auditorium Apr 17 '83. **Omaha** Civic Auditorium Music Hall or University of Omaha Apr 17 '71/can; Civic Auditorium Dec 16 '75/can; Civic Auditorium Aug 28 '85. **NEVADA** (NV): **Las Vegas** u/v Feb 2 '76/can; Convention Center Rotunda May 4 '83. **Reno** Centennial Coliseum Jun 25 '65. **NEW HAMPSHIRE** (NH): **Durham** University Of New Hampshire May 13 '90. **Hampton** Beach Casino Ballroom Jul 26 '95. **Hanover** Leede Arena May 11 '90. **Manchester** JFK Coliseum Jun 11 '65/can; Saint Anselm College Mar 23 '85. **Portsmouth** Music Hall (Ray Davies) Oct 19 '96. **NEW JERSEY** (NJ): **Asbury Park** Casino Arena Dec 5 '74/can; Convention Hall Jul 3 '77; Convention Hall Jul 24, 25 '79; Stone Pony May 11 '93. **East Rutherford** Brendan Byrne Arena (BBA) Jan 10 '82; BBA Jan 25 '82/can; BBA May 27 '83/re from Mar 28, 29; BBA Mar 24 '85. **Glassboro** State College Sep 22 '79. **Holmdel** Garden State Arts Center (GSAC) Sep 10 '85; GSAC Sep 14 '89; GSAC Aug 3 '93. **Jersey City** Roosevelt Stadium Aug 19 '72. **Lawrenceville** Rider College, Apr 8 '73. **Madison** Farleigh Dickinson University Mar 4 '79. **New Brunswick** Rutgers University (RU) Apr 18 '75; RU Mar 3 '79; RU Feb 27 '80. **Paramus** Bergen Community College Mar 11 '79. **Passaic** Capitol Theater (CT) Nov 3 '72; CT Apr 11 '74; CT Apr 21 '75; CT Nov 26 '75; CT Feb 4 '77/re from Jan 30; CT Oct 28 '80/can; CT Mar 3, 4 '87. **Piscataway** Rutgers University Oct 12 '89. **Pomona** Stockton State College, Dec 11 '77. **Princeton** University Apr 26 '90. **Randolph** County College Of Morris Mar 1 '80. **South Orange** Seton Hall University Feb 24 '80/can. **Trenton** War Memorial Auditorium Nov 25 '75; State College Nov 22 '77. **Union** Newark State College Apr 7 '73; Kean College of NJ Mar 1 '79. **Wayne** Shea Auditorium Feb 9 '77. **Wildwood** Convention Hall Sep 2 '72. **NEW MEXICO** (NM): **Albuquerque** Civic Auditorium?, Nov 25 '70/can; University Of New Mexico, Sep 8 '79; Civic Auditorium, Aug 11 '81; Tingley Coliseum May 10 '83; Tingley Coliseum May 10 '87/can; State Fairgrounds Jun 10 '87/re from Paolo Soleri Amphitheater Jun 9. **Santa Fe** Paolo Soleri Amphitheater Jun 9 '87/re to Tingley Coliseum, Albuquerque, Jun 10. **NEW YORK** (NY): **Alfred** University Apr 19 '90. **Albany** Palace Theater (PT) Nov 24 '74; PT Dec 2 '75; PT Feb 22 '79; PT Mar 9 '80; PT May 4 '90. **Binghamton** State University (SU) Nov 9 '72; SU Dec 4 '74; SU Feb 18 '79; Broome County Veterans Memorial Arena (BCVM) Nov 20 '83/can; BCVM Dec 11 '84; SU Sep 20 '85; SU Sep 20 '89. **Brockport** State University Dec 3 '75. **Bronx** *see* New York City. **Brooklyn** *see* New York City. **Brookville** Dome Arena Dec 2 '71. **Buffalo** (*see also* Darien Center) Shea's Theater Feb 7? '70; Kleinhans Music Hall Mar 1 '72; Century Theater Apr 6 '73; Century Theater Apr 20 '74; Kleinhans Music Hall Dec 3 '74; Loew's Buffalo Theater Nov 23 '75; New Century Theater Apr 30 '77/re from Feb 10; New Century Theater May 27 '78; Kleinhans Music Hall Aug 7 '79; War Memorial Auditorium (WMA) Oct 17 '80; WMA Sep 24 '81; WMA Jun 3 '83/re from Mar 19. **Canandaiqua** Finger Lakes Performing Arts Center Jun 23 '87/can. **Clinton** Hamilton College Feb 28 '79. **Cortland** Alumni Ice Arena Apr 29 '90. **Darien Center** Lakeside Amphitheatre Jun 25 '87; Lakeside Amphitheatre Aug 8 '93/can. **Farmingdale** College of Technology Mar 26 '71. **Flushing** *see* New York City. **Fredonia** King Concert Hall Mar 9 '79. **Geneseo** State University Mar 10 '79. **Geneva** Hobart College Dec 5 '71. **Glens Falls** Civic Center Aug 2 '79; Civic Center May 28 '83. **Hamilton** Colgate University Nov 23 '74. **Hempstead** Hofstra University (HU) Apr 3 '74; HU Dec 8 '75; HU May 4 '77; HU Apr 30 '90. **Island Park** Action House Dec 4, 5 '70/can. **Ithaca** Cornell University Feb 23 '79; Cornell University Mar 2 '80. **Jamaica** *see* New York City. **Lantham** Starlight Musical Theatre Jul 20 '95. **Long Beach** Leone's Oct 22 '69. **Long Island** *see* Long Beach; Island Park; Hempstead; Watagh; Stony Brook. **Mountaindale** Festival Jul 11 '70/can. **New Paltz** State University Apr 2 '73. **New York City** Academy Of Music Jun 18 '65/re from Jun 19/re from Jun 12; Fillmore Oct 17, 18 '69; Ungano's Dec 8 '69; Fillmore Feb 20, 21 '70/can; Ungano's Jun 3 '70/can; Ungano's Jun 4 '70; Fillmore Jun 12, 13 '70/can; Ritz Theater, Port Richmond Jul 10? '70; Carnegie Hall Dec 3 '70/can/re from Dec 12; Fillmore Dec 4, 5 '70; Colden Auditorium Mar 27 '71; Philharmonic Hall Mar 30 '71; Carnegie Hall Nov 21 '71; Ritz Theater, Port Richmond Nov 27 '71; Carnegie Hall Mar 2, 3 '72; Wollman Rink Aug 23 '72; Felt Forum, Madison Square Garden Center Nov 15, 16 '72; Fordham University, Bronx Mar 30 '73; St. John's University, Jamaica Mar 31 '73; Felt Forum, Madison Square Garden Center Apr 6 '74; Felt Forum, Madison Square Garden Center Nov 27, 28 '74; Beacon Theatre May 7-9 '75; Beacon Theatre Nov 28 '75; Palladium Feb 1, 2 '77; Whitman Auditorium, Brooklyn Nov 23 '77; Palladium Jun 2 '78; Wollman Rink Aug 9 '78; St. John's University, Jamaica Feb 23 '80; Palladium Dec 31 '80; Madison Square Garden Oct 3 '81; Madison Square Garden Nov 25 '83/can; Roseland Ballroom Dec 29-31 '83; Madison Square Garden Dec 21 '84; Pier 84, Sep 12, 13 '85; Beacon Theatre Mar 16 '87; Pier 84, Jun 27 '87; Beacon Theatre Mar 29 '88; Palladium Sep 12 '89/can; Fordham University, Bronx Oct 13 '89; Beacon Theatre Oct 16 '89; Academy May 13 '93; Roseland Aug 1 '93/can; Academy (Ray Davies) Oct 19 '95; Westbeth Theatre (Ray Davies) Feb 12, 14-18, 21-25, 27-29, Mar 1, 3 '96; Westbeth Theatre (Ray Davies) Nov 5-10 '96. **North Tonawanda** Melody Fair Jul 19 '95. **Oneonta** State University Feb 25 '79. **Oswego** State University Feb 24 '79; State University Sep 10 '89. **Patterson** Big Birch Jul 31 '93/re from Jul 28. **Plattsburgh** State University Jan 22 '82; State UniversitySep 18 '85. **Port Chester** Capitol Theater Jun 19, 20 '70. **Potsdam** Clarkson College Oct 19 '69. **Poughkeepsie** Mid-Hudson Civic Center (MHCC) Jul 1 '77; MHCC Jul 31 '79; MHCC Jun 26 '87; MHCC Apr 2 '88; MHCC Oct 8 '89/re from Sep 10, 12; The Chance, May 6 '93. **Queens** *see* New York City. **Rochester** Palestra, University Dec 8 '77; Auditorium Theater May 26 '78; Monroe County Dome Arena Feb 21 '80; Community War Memorial May 22 '83/re from Apr 1/re from Mar 21; Community War Memorial Dec 18 '84; Monroe County Dome Arena Sep 17 '85; Palestra, University Apr 28 '90. **Saratoga Springs** Performing Arts Center Jun 22 '87; Performing Arts Center, Jul 26 '93. **Schenectady** Aerodome Dec 6 '69/can; Proctor Theater Jan 23 '82; Proctor Theater Feb 2 '88/can. **Staten Island** *see* New York City. **Stony Brook** State University Nov 28 '71; State University Sep 22 '85. **Syracuse** LeMoyne College Dec 4 '71; Landmark Theater (LT) May 28 '78; LT Feb 27 '79; LT Mar 4 '80; War Memorial Auditorium (WMA) Jan 8 '82; WMA Jun 5 '83/re from Apr 2; WMA Nov 19 '83/can; WMA Dec 12 '84. **Tarrytown** Westchester Premier Theater (WPT) Dec 6 '77; WPT Feb 29 '80; WPT Jan 9 '82. **Uniondale** Nassau Veterans Memorial Coliseum (NVMC) Aug 21 '72; NVMC Jul 27 '79; NVMC Oct 26 '80; NVMC Oct 1 '81; NVMC Jun 8 '83/re from Mar 23. **Utica** Stanley Theater Jun 21 '87; Raceway Jul 28 '93/can. **Wantagh** Jones Beach Theatre (JBT) Sep 7 '85; JBT Jul 5 '87 (rained out from Jul 2); JBT Sep 15 '89; JBT Jul 30 '93. **West Point** Eisenhower Hall Theater (EHT) Mar 8 '80; EHT Sep 21 '85; EHT May 8 '93. **Westbury** Music Fair Jul 31-Aug 1 '95. **Westchester** *see* Tarrytown; Port Chester. **NORTH CAROLINA** (NC): **Chapel Hill** Charmichael Auditorium Apr 24 '75. **Charlotte** Coliseum Jan 17 '82/re from Jan 15; Coliseum Jan 6 '84/re from Dec 4 '83; Rocky's Apr 27 '93. **Durham** Duke University Nov 30 '83/can. **Fayetteville** State University Apr 26 '75/can. **Greenville** Minges Coliseum Mar 16 '85. **OHIO** (OH): **Akron** (*see also* Cuyahoga Falls) Civic Theatre Apr 15 '75. **Cincinnati** Ludlow Garage Nov 14, 15 '69; Music Hall Mar 10 '72; Albee Theater Apr 18 '74; Music Hall Feb 9 '77; Music Hall Sep 19 '79; University of Cincinnati Sep 9 '80; Gardens Apr 8 '83; Gardens Dec 1 '84; Riverbend Music Center Jun 16 '87; Zoo Aug 17 '93/can. **Cleveland** (*see also* Akron; University Heights; Richfield; Mentor) Allen Theater Jun 12 '70/can; Case Western Reserve University Mar 11 '72; Music Hall, Dec 14 '74; Music Hall Dec 11 '75; Palace Theater May 30 '78 (May 31 '78/can); Music Hall Aug 9 '79; Public Hall Sep 20 '81; Music Hall Mar 11 '87; Music Hall Apr 5 '88; Music Hall Sep 24 '89; Nautica Stage Aug 19 '93; Rock & Roll Hall Of Fame Sep 4 '95; Ohio Theatre (Ray Davies) Apr 10-13 '96. **Columbus** Ohio State University Apr 17 '74; Veterans War Memorial Auditorium Apr 14 '75/can; Ohio Center Jan 17 '84/re from Nov 15 '83; Veterans War Memorial Auditorium (VWMA) Jun 10 '78; VWMA Sep 7 '80; VWMA Sep 21 '81; VWMA Mar 12 '85; Newport Music Hall, Aug 15 '93. **Cuyahoga Falls** (*see also* Akron) Blossom Music Center Sep 5 '85; Blossom Music Center Jun 15 '87. **Dayton** u/v Apr 15 '75/can; Hara Arena Jan 15 '84/re from Nov 16 '83; Hara Arena Mar 13 '85. **Mentor** Village East Nov 16 '69/can. **Oxford** Miami University Sep 19 '81. **Richfield** Coliseum Nov 25 '77; Coliseum Sep 13 '80; Coliseum Jun 4 '83/re from Apr 5; Coliseum Mar 14 '85. **Toledo** Sports Arena Apr 26 '75/can/re from Apr 17; Sports Arena Sep 22 '81/can; Sports Arena Jan 11 '84/can/re from Centennial Hall Nov 17 '83. **University Heights** John Carroll University Apr 19 '74; John Carroll University Feb 11 '77. **OKLAHOMA** (OK): **Norman** University Of Oklahoma Feb 16 '85. **Oklahoma City** (*see also* Norman) Civic Center Music Hall Apr 7 '77. **Tulsa** Old Lady Of Brady Auditorium Sep 12 '79. **OREGON** (OR): **Eugene** University of Oregon Feb 5 '76/can. **Medford** Armory Jun 17 '78. **Portland** Reed College Dec 1 '69; Paramount Theater (PT) Nov 19 '70; PT Feb 6 '76; PT Apr 15 '77; PT Jun 18 '78; PT Aug 30 '79; Memorial Coliseum (MC) Oct 5 '80; MC Sep 3 '81; MC Apr 21 '83/can; Center For Performing Arts Feb 27 '85. **PENNSYLVANIA** (PA): **Allentown** Fairgrounds Aug 20 '72; Muhlenberg College Feb 26 '80; Fairgrounds Aug 6 '93. **Bethlehem** Lehigh University (LU) Nov 21 '75; LU Jan 12 '82; LU May 20 '83; LU Sep 15 '87/can. **Bloomsburg** University of Pennsylvania Feb 16 '79. **Carlisle** Dickinson College Apr 22 '90. **Chester** Widener University Nov 22 '75. **Devon** Valley Forge Music Fair Jul 16 '95. **Easton** State Theatre Aug 4 '93. **Erie** Civic Center Sep 6 '89/can. **Harrisburg** Zembo Mosque Jun 9 '70. **Indiana** University of Pennsylvania Apr 25 '90. **Meadville** Allegheny College May 2 '90. **New Wilmington** Westminster College Apr 23 '90. **Philadelphia** (*see also* Upper Darby; Chester; West Chester; Trenton, New Jersey) Convention Hall Jun 19 '65; Spectrum Arena Dec 5 '69; Electric Factory Jan 30, 31 '70; Electric Factory Jun 5, 6 '70; Spectrum (SM) Nov 26 '71; SM Nov 8 '72; SM Apr 12 '74; SM Apr 20 '75; SM Jul 28 '79; SM Oct 24, 27 '80; SM Oct 4, 6 '81; JFK Stadium Jun 19 '82; Spectrum, May 21 '83/re from Mar 18; Spectrum Dec 14 '84; Mann Music Center (MMC) Sep 6 '85; MMC Jul 1 '87; MMC Sep 9 '89/re from Tower Theater, Upper Darby, Sep 8, 9 '89; Theatre of Living Arts May 1 '93; Mann Music Center Aug 12 '93; Theatre Of The Living Arts (TLA) (Ray Davies) Oct 17 '95; TLA (Ray Davies) Oct 22-26 '96. **Pittsburgh** Syria Mosque Auditorium Sep 1 '72; Stanley Theater (ST) Nov 25 '74; ST May 2 '77; ST Jun 1 '78; ST Sep 12 '80; ST Jan 19 '82; Civic Arena Nov 27 '83/can; Civic Arena Dec 10 '84; Syria Mosque Auditorium, Sep 26 '89; IC Light Amphitheatre, Aug 7 '93. **Reading** Astor Theater Jun 28 '77. **Scranton** University Feb 6 '88/can. **Shippensburg** Shippensburg University Feb 22 '80. **University Park** Pennsylvania State University (PSU) Feb 17 '79; PSU Sep 15 '85; PSU Feb 7 '88/can. **Upper Darby** Tower Theater (TT) Jan 28, 29 '77; TT Jun 8, 9 '78; TT Feb 26, 27 '87; TT Mar 26, 27 '88; TT Sep 8, 9 '89/re to Mann Music Center, Philadelphia, Sep 9. **Villanova** University Feb 17 '79/can. **Washington** Washington & Jefferson College Nov 10 '72. **West Chester** State College Mar 7 '79. **Wilkes-Barre** King's College Sep 14 '87/can; F. M. Kirby Center Oct 10 '89/re from Sep 5/re from Sep 8. **RHODE ISLAND** (RI): **Bristol** Roger Williams College May 5 '90. **Cranston** Rhodes-On-The-Pawtuxet Ballroom Mar 4 '72/re to Palace Concert Theater, Providence. **Providence** (*see also* Pawtucket; Cranston; North Attleboro; Mansfield; Massachusetts) Dario Palace Theater (DPT) Dec 3 '71/can; DPT Mar 4 '72/can; Palace Concert Theater (PCT) Nov 17 '72; PCT Apr 4 '73; Civic Center, Apr 4 '74; PCT Nov 30 '74; PCT May 11 '75/can; Civic Center (CC) Jun 3 '78; CC Sep 23 '79; CC Oct 18 '80; CC Sep 30 '81; CC May 29 '83/re from Mar 26; CC Dec 15 '84; Performing Arts Center Mar 2 '87; JR's Fastlane May 7 '93; Convention Center (Ray Davies) Oct 1 '96. **Newport** Rogers High School Jun 17 '70. **Pawtucket** LeRoy Concert Theater Feb 6 '77; LeRoy Concert Theater Dec 2, 3 '77. **Warwick** Musical Theatre Jul 23 '95. **SOUTH CAROLINA** (SC): **Charleston** Municipal Auditorium, Apr 27 '75. **TENNESSEE** (TN): **Nashville** War Memorial Auditorium Jul 19 '79; Tennessee Theater Aug 29 '80; Municipal Auditorium (venue changed to Grand Ole Opry House) May 17 '83; Grand Ole Opry House May 17 '83. **Knoxville** Civic Coliseum Jun 16 '82; Civic Coliseum Jan 9 '84/re from Jan 8/re from Dec 2 '83. **Memphis** Dixon-Meyers Auditorium (DMA) Apr 29 '75; Orpheum Theatre Aug 30 '80; DMA Jun 14 '82/re from Jan 17/re from Jul '81; DMA Nov 13 '83/can; Ellis Auditorium Nov 30 '84/can; DMA Feb 9 '85. **TEXAS** (TX): **Arlington** University Of Texas Oct 29 '72; University Of Texas Jan 16 '76/can (possibly re to Feb 17). **Austin** (*see also* Manor) Municipal Auditorium Feb 18 '76/re from Jan 17,18; Armadillo World Headquarters Apr 4? '77/can; Armadillo World Headquarters Jul 28 '78; Municipal Auditorium Sep 26 '80; University Of Texas Aug 6 '81; City Coliseum Aug 31 '82; University Of Texas May 12 '83; City Coliseum Feb 12 '85; u/v May '87/can. **Dallas** (*see also* Arlington; Fort Worth) Music Hall, Fair Park Feb 23 '70/can; Memorial Coliseum Apr 25 '71/can; Southern Methodist University Jul 29 '78; Palladium Jul 11, 12 '79/re from Jul 7-10; Southern Methodist University Sep 11 '79; Convention Center Arena Sep 27 '80; Convention Center Arena Aug 8 '81; Reunion Arena May 14 '83; Reunion Arena Feb 14 '85; u/v May 8 '87/can. **Fort Worth** Will Rogers Memorial Center, Apr 6 '77. **Houston** Music Hall (MH) Feb 25 '70/can; MH Oct 28 '72; MH Feb 19 '76/re from Jan 15; MH Apr 5 '77; MH Jul 30 '78; MH Jul 14 '79; Sam Houston Coliseum Sep 25 '80; Summit Arena Aug 7 '81; Summit Arena May 13 '83/re from Mar 4; Music Hall Feb 11 '85; Sam Houston Coliseum May 7 '87/can. **Manor** Manor Downs Jul 13 '79/re from Jul 12. **San Antonio** Trinity College Oct 27 '72; Majestic Theatre Feb 15 '85. **VERMONT** (VT): **Burlington** University of Vermont Dec 8 '70/can. **Stratton Mountain** Ski Area Jul 29 '95. **VIRGINIA** (VA): **Blacksburg** Virginia Polytechnic Institute & State University Mar 25 '85. **Charlottesville** University Of Virginia Nov 4 '72. **Falls Church** George C. Marshall High School Mar 28 '71. **Hampton** Coliseum Jan 13 '82; Hampton Coliseum Jan 7 '84/re from Nov 29 '83. **Harrisonburg** James Madison University Mar 27 '85. **Norfolk** Scope Convention Center Arena May 31 '83/can; Boathouse Sep 27 '89; Boathouse Apr 29 '93. **Richmond** (*see also* Hampton) Syria Mosque Auditorium Apr 13 '74; University Mar 28 '85; Syria Mosque Auditorium, Oct 7 '89; u/v Aug 13 '93/can. **Vienna** Barns of the Wolf Trap (Ray Davies) Oct 16-17 '96. **Williamsburg** College Of William & Mary (CWM) Apr 25 '75; CWM Mar 16 '85/can. **WASHINGTON** (WA): **Seattle** Center Coliseum Jul 10 '65; Center Arena Jun 23 '70; Paramount Northwest Theatre (PNT) Feb 7 '76; PNT Apr 16 '77; PNT Jun 19 '78; Memorial Stadium Jul 16 '78; PNT Aug 29 '79; Center Arena Oct 3 '80; Center Coliseum Sep 4 '81; Center Coliseum Apr 23 '83; PNT Feb 28, Mar 1 '85; Moore Theatre (Ray Davies) Nov 1-2 '96. **Spokane** Coliseum Jul 8 '65. **WASHINGTON DC** *see* District Of Columbia. **WEST VIRGINIA** (WV): **Charleston** Charleston Municipal Auditorium, Jan 10 '84/re from Civic Center Coliseum. **WISCONSIN** (WI): **East Troy** Alpine Valley Music Theater Sep 2 '85. **Kaukauna** Central Park Jun 5 '93. **Madison** Dane County Memorial Coliseum (DCMC) Sep 16 '79; DCMC Apr 12 '83; DCMC Mar 10 '85. **Milwaukee** Riverside Theater Apr 16 '75/re from Apr 8; Oriental Landmark Theater Dec 15 '75; Riverside Theater Apr 26 '77/re from Apr 12; Performing Arts Center Jun 12 '78; MECCA-Milwaukee Auditorium (MMA) Aug 12 '79; MMA Sep 2 '80; MMA Apr 13 '83; MMA Dec 4 '84; Riverside Theatre (RT) Jun 13 '87; RT Apr 8 '88; RT Aug 28 '89/can. **Somerset** River's Edge Water Park Aug 22 '93.

WALES *see* United Kingdom

WEST GERMANY *see* Germany

SONGS INDEX

Kinks and Kinks-related songs: brackets refer to feature block in text (page number, A/album, E/EP, M/musical, S/single); general references are dated.

***Absolute Beginners* soundtrack album** (281A), Feb '86, Mar '86. **Acute Schizophrenic Paranoia Blues** (157A, 165A), Nov '71, Nov 21 '71, Jan 4 '72, Jan '72, Jan 31 '72, Mar 2-3 '72, May 5 '72, Aug 23 '72, Nov 17 '72, Dec 15 '72, Jan 14 '73, Jan 24 '73, Feb 26 '73, Apr 11 '73, Jul 15 '73, Sep 20 '73, Feb 26 '74, Sep 23 '74, Mar 7-10 '77. **Act Nice And Gentle** (99S), Mar '67, May 5 '67, Nov 12-14 '70, Nov 21 '70. **Add It Up** (250A), Jul '81, Aug 4 '81, Oct 3 '81, Apr '82. ***AFL1-3603* album** (239A), Jul 9 '80. **Afternoon Tea** (104A), Nov 24-25 '66, Mar '67, Oct 12 '67, Oct 23 '67. **Against The Tide** (296M), Mar '87. **Aggravation** (300A), Jan/Feb/Mar '89, Aug '89, Oct 16 '89, Aug 12 '90, Aug 7 '91, Jun 12 '92, Jun 12 '92, Sep 6 '92, Mar 29 '93, Jun 17 '93, Jul 11 '93, Jul 27 '93, Oct 3 '93, Nov 25 '93, Dec '93, Dec 14 '93, Mar 22 '94, Jun 10 '94, Oct 16 '94, Nov 8 '94. **Alcohol** (157A, 165A, 203A), Jan '72, Jan 31 '72, Mar 2-3 '72, Aug 23 '72, Nov 17 '72, Dec 15 '72, Jan 14 '73, Feb 26 '73, Mar 31 '73, Apr 11 '73, Jul 15 '73, Sep 20 '73, Feb 26 '74, Apr 3 '74, Apr 16 '74, Sep 7 '74, Sep 23 '74, Nov 23 '74, Apr 13 '75, May 21 '75, Feb 29 '76, Feb 1-2 '77, Feb 19 '77, May 4 '77, Dec 23 '77, May 19 '78, Jun 2 '78, Jul 29 '78, Oct 1 '78, Oct 10 '78, Oct 22 '78, Feb 17 '79, Jul 14 '79, Aug 16 '79, Nov '91, Jun 10 '94, Oct 16 '94, May 18-19 '95. **All Day And All Of The Night** (38S, 88A, 89A, 139A, 238A, 239V, 326A, 340A), Sep 19 '64, Sep 20 '64, Sep '64, Sep 26 '64, Sep 28 '64, Oct 7 '64, Oct 11 '64, Oct 22 '64, Oct 23 '64, Oct 30 '64, Nov 4 '64, Nov 6 '64, Nov 9 '64, Nov 18 '64, Nov 26 '64, Dec 9 '64, Dec 16-17 '64, Dec 31 '64, Jan 13-14 '65, Feb 4 '65, Feb 12 '65, Feb 23 '65, Feb 26 '65, Mar 13 '65, Apr 19 '65, Apr 30 '65, Jun 28 '65, Jul 2 '65, Oct 1-3 '65, Oct 5 '65, Jan 14 '66, Jun 13 '66, Sep 24 '66, Sep 29 '66, Apr 19 '68, Oct 23-25 '69, Nov 20-23 '69, Jun 13 '70, Aug 29 '70, Jan 16 '71, Mar 1 '71, Mar 30 '71, Apr 7 '71, Nov 21 '71, Mar 2-3 '72, Apr 12 '72, Aug 23 '72, Nov 17 '72, Jan 14 '73, Jan 24 '73, Apr 11 '73, Jul 15 '73, Sep 20 '73, Feb 26 '74, Apr 16 '74, Jul 16 '74, Jul 14 '74, Sep 7 '74, Sep 23 '74, Nov 23 '74, Apr 13 '75, May 21 '75, Dec 29 '75, Feb 29 '76, Feb 1-2 '77, Feb 19 '77, Feb 26 '77, Mar 28 '77, May 4 '77, Nov 23 '77, Dec 23 '77, Dec 24 '77, May 19 '78, Jun 2 '78, Jul 29 '78, Oct 1 '78, Oct 10 '78, Oct 22 '78, Jan 23 '79, Feb 17 '79, Mar 3 '79, Mar 10 '79, Jul 14 '79, Aug 16 '79, Sep 23 '79, Oct 16 '79, Oct 20 '79, Nov 19 '79, Feb 21 '80, Aug 6 '80, Aug 23 '80, Sep 25 '80, Oct 27 '80, Nov 30 '80, Dec 5 '80, Dec 31 '80, May 6 '81, Jun 28 '81, Aug 14 '81, Oct 3 '81, Jan 10 '82, Feb 25-27 '82, Apr '82, Dec 22 '82, Apr 26 '83, May 24 '83, Dec 31 '83, Jan 7 '84, Apr 2 '84, Dec 21 '84, Mar 20 '85, Apr 20 '85, Sep 12-13 '85, May 17 '86, Mar 8 '87, May 28 '87, Jun 29 '87, Dec 20 '87, Jan '88, Apr 14 '88, Jun 9 '88, Oct 16 '89, May 9 '90, Aug 12 '90, Nov 9 '90, Aug 7 '91, Apr 25 '92, Jun 12 '92, Sep 6 '92, Mar 29 '93, May 4 '93, Jun 17 '93, Jul 11 '93, Jul 27 '93, Oct 3 '93, Nov 25 '93, Dec 14 '93, Mar 22 '94, Jun 10 '94, Oct 7 '94, Oct 16 '94, Oct 21 '94, Nov 8 '94, Nov 25 '94, Dec 6 '94, Dec 21 '94, May 18-19 '95, Jul 11-13 '95, Sep 2 '95. **All I Have To Do Is Dream** Oct '61. **All I Want For Christmas…** Dec 21 '65. **All Night Stand** Dec '65, Dec 13 '65, Sep 30 '66, Oct 18 '66. **All Of My Friends Were There** (121A), Jul 1 '67, Oct '68. **All Right OK You Win** Apr 7 '71. **All The Cakes She Baked Him** Jun '74. **Amazing Grace** Apr 29 '77. **Americana** Jul 2 '65, Mar '95, Apr 10 '95, Aug 9 '95, Oct 9 '95. **And I Will Love You** Dec 29/30 '65, Mar 6 '67. **Animal** (340A), Mar '95, Apr 10 '95, Aug 9 '95, Oct 9 '95, Mar '96, Jul 7 '96, Aug '96, Nov 16 '96. **Animal Farm** (121A, 139A), Mar '68, Jun 20 '68, Nov 22 '68, Dec '68, Mar '90, Nov 5-10 '96. **Animals In The Zoo** (151A), Oct '70. **Annie** Aug '74. **Apache** Oct '61. **Apeman** (147A, 147S, 161A, 291A, 309A, 326A, 340A), Oct '70, Nov 3 '70, Nov 4 '70, Nov 16-18 '70, Nov 27 '70, Dec 16 '70, Jan 6 '71, Jan 16 '71, Mar 1 '71, Mar 30 '71, Apr 7 '71, Nov 21 '71, Mar 2-3 '72, Aug 23 '72, Nov 17 '72, Feb '86, Jun 29 '87, Jul 1 '87, Dec 20 '87, Dec 21 '87, Apr 14 '88,

Jun 9 '88, Oct 16 '89, Aug 12 '90, Aug 7 '91, Nov '91, Apr 25 '92, Jun 12 '92, Feb 3 '93, Mar 29 '93, May 4 '93, May 12 '93, Jun 17 '93, Jul 11 '93, Jul 27 '93, Oct 3 '93, Nov 25 '93, Dec 14 '93, Apr '94, Jun 10 '94, Oct 16 '94, Nov 8 '94, Apr 10 '95, May 18-19 '95, Jul 11-13 '95, Sep 2 '95, Nov 16 '96. **Are You Ready** Jan '69, Jul 2 '69. **Around The Dial** (250A, 291A), Apr '79, Jul '81, Aug 14 '81, Oct 3 '81, Jan 10 '82, Feb 25-27 '82, Apr '82, Dec 22 '82, Apr 26 '83, May 24 '83, Dec 31 '83, Jan 7 '84, Apr 2 '84, Dec 21 '84, Mar 20 '85, Apr 20 '85, May 17 '86, Jun 29 '87, Jul 1 '87, Oct 16 '89, May 9 '90, Aug 12 '90, Nov 9 '90, Aug 7 '91, Jun 12 '92, Sep 6 '92, Mar 29 '93, May 4 '93, May 12 '93, Jun 17 '93. **Art Lover** (250A, 291A), Jul '81, Aug 4 '81, Aug 26 '81, Oct 3 '81, Oct 10 '81, Jan 10 '82, Apr '82, Apr 26 '83, May 24 '83, Dec 21 '84, Jun 29 '87, Jul 1 '87, Apr 14 '88, Jun 9 '88. **Art School Babes** Mar '95, Apr 10 '95, Aug 9 '95, Oct 9 '95. **Arthur** (song) (133A), Jul '69, Dec 18 '69, Nov 21 '70, Apr 7 '71. ***Arthur Or The Decline And Fall Of The British Empire*** **album** (133A), Jan 21 '65, Aug 19 '68, Dec '68, Jan '69, Feb 17 '69, Mar 10 '69, Apr 21 '69, May '69, Jun '69, Jun 16 '69, Jun 30 '69, Jul 2 '69, Jul 8 '69, Jul 25 '69, Aug '69, Aug 8 '69, Aug 18 '69, Aug 25 '69, Sep 2 '69, Sep 8 '69, Oct 10 '69, Oct 31 '69, Nov 24 '69, Dec 1 '69, Dec 15 '69, Jun 22 '70, Jul 20 '70, Jun 4 '71, Dec 13 '71. **Artificial Light** (219S), Jul '76, May 19 '78. **Artificial Man** (183A), Nov 23 '74. **Attitude** (230A, 238A, 239V, 240E, 244S), May '79, Jun '79, Jul 1-4 '79, Sep 23 '79, Oct 16 '79, Oct 20 '79, Nov 11 '79, Nov 19 '79, Dec '79, Feb 21 '80, Aug 23 '80, Sep 25 '80, Oct 27 '80, Oct 29 '80, Nov 30 '80, Dec 5 '80. **Au Nom De La Loi** Dec '68. **Australia** (133A), Jan '69, May '69, Nov 20-23 '69, Mar '90. **Autumn Almanac** (105S, 161A, 326A), Apr 13 '67, Sep '67, Oct 12 '67, Oct 15 '67, Oct 21 '67, Oct 25 '67, Nov 9 '67, Nov 14 '67, Nov 29 '67, Jun '68, Jun 20 '68, Mar 27 '71, Nov 25 '93, Mar 22 '94, May '94, Jun 10 '94, Oct 16 '94, Nov 8 '94, Apr 10 '95, Aug 9 '95, Oct 9 '95.

Babies (315A, 322S), Dec '91. **Baby Face** (165A), Jan '72, Mar 2-3 '72, Aug 23 '72, Dec 15 '72. **Bachelor Mother** Jun 24-30 '69, Sep 9 '69, Oct 17 '69. **Back To Front** (250A, 253S, 254S), Jun 28 '81, Jul '81, Aug 4 '81, Aug 14 '81, Sep 15 '81, Sep 28 '81, Oct 3 '81, Oct 30 '81, Jan 10 '82, Feb 25-27 '82, Apr '82, Dec 22 '82, Apr 26 '83. **Back To '64** Jul '76. **Bad To Me** Sep 28 '63. **Bald Headed Woman** (37A, 41A), Aug 25 '64, Sep 26 '64. **Ballad Of Julie Finkle, The** Sep '94, Oct 22 '94, Nov 8 '94, Mar '95, Apr 10 '95, Aug 9 '95, Oct 9 '95, Feb 21-25 '96, Nov 5-10 '96. **Banana Boat Song** (165A), Apr 7 '71, Feb 27 '72, Mar 2-3 '72, Nov 17 '72, Apr 3 '74, Jun 16 '74, May 21 '75, Feb 19 '77, May 4 '77, Jun 2 '78, Oct 10 '78. **Batman Theme** (103A), Apr 19 '68, Mar 10 '79, Dec 31 '83, Sep 12-13 '85, Jun 29 '87. **Be Bop A Lula** Aug 23 '72, Aug 29 '72, Dec 15 '72, Feb 26 '73, Sep 20 '73, Feb 26 '74. **Be Rational** (296M), Mar '87. **Beautiful Delilah** (37A, 41A, 139A), Jan 28-31 '64, Mar 29 '64, Aug 18 '64, Dec 16-17 '64, Apr 30 '65, May 19 '65, Sep 1 '65, Oct 1-3 '65, Dec 23 '77. **Beginning** Dec '68. **Berkeley Mews** (142S, 161A), Mar '68, Jun 20 '68, Jul 2 '69, Jun 12 '70. **Bernadette** (265A, 266S), Jul 26 '81, Jan '82, Jan 10 '82, Feb 25-27 '82, Apr '82, Nov '82, Dec 22 '82, Feb 15 '83, Apr 26 '83, May 24 '83, Aug 1 '83, Sep 30 '83. **Better Things** (248S, 250A, 254S, 282A, 326A, 340A), May '79, Apr '81, May 2 '81, May 6 '81, Jun 19 '81, Jun 28 '81, Jul 26 '81, Aug 26 '81, Oct 3 '81, Oct 20 '81, Nov 2 '81, Aug '85, Sep 12-13 '85, Apr '94. **Beware** Jan 9-13 '75, Sep 5 '75. **Big Black Smoke** (93S, 106A, 139A, 161A), Apr 11/12 '66, May 23-25 '66, Oct 15 '66, Oct 21-22 '66, Nov 15 '66, Nov 30 '66. **Big Noise From Winetka** Oct '61. **Big Sky** (121A), Jan 24 '68, Oct '68, Nov 20-23 '69, Feb 12-14 '70, Jun 13 '70, Aug 29 '70, Nov 12-14 '70, Nov 21 '70, Jan 16 '71, Mar 1 '71, Mar 30 '71, Apr 7 '71, Apr 21 '71. **Bird Dog** Aug '80, Aug 6 '80, Aug 23 '80, Sep 25 '80, Oct 27 '80, Nov 30 '80, Dec 5 '80, Dec 31 '80, May 6 '81, Jun 28 '81, Aug 14 '81, Jan 10 '82. ***Black Album, The,*** **album** see *Kinks, The* album (1970). **Black Messiah** (219A, 221S, 222S), Oct '76, Sep 27 '77, May 4 '77, Jun 2 '78, Sep 18 '78, Sep 29 '78, Oct 11 '78. **Blasé Blasé** Jul '81. **Blue Suede Shoes** Apr 6 '74. **Bo Diddley** Oct '63, Jan 28-31 '64, Mar 29 '64. **Body** (249A), Mar '81. **Body Snatcher** Mar '81. **Boll-Weevil Blues** Sep '63. **Boll Weevil Song** Sep '63. **Boston Massachusetts USA** May 4 '93. **Bring Me Sunshine** Mar 10 '94. **Bye Bye Johnny** Jan 28-31 '64, Mar 29 '64, Oct 30 '64, Feb 23 '65. **Brainwashed** (133A, 133S, 165A), Oct 15 '69, Oct 23-25 '69, Nov 20-23 '69, Jun 13 '70, Nov 12-14 '70, Nov 21 '70, Jan 16 '71, Mar 1 '71, Mar 30 '71, Apr 7 '71, Nov 21 '71, Mar 2-3 '72, Nov 17 '72, Dec 15 '72, Apr 11 '73, Jul 15 '73, Sep 20 '73. **Bright Lights** (300A), Jul '87, Oct '87, Jun '89. **Brother** (209A), Jul '76, Aug '76, Oct '76, Jan 8 '77, Jan '77, Feb 1-2 '77, Feb 19 '77, Aug '85, Sep 12-13 '85.

Cadillac (37A, 41A), Jan 28-31 '64, Aug 18 '64, Sep 7 '64, Sep 26 '64, Nov 23 '65. **Can't Bear To Think About You** Aug '74. **Catch Me Now I'm Falling** (230A, 233S, 238A, 239V, 282A), May '79, Jun '79, Jul 1-4 '79, Aug 16 '79, Aug '79, Sep 5 '79, Sep 23 '79, Oct 16 '79, Oct 20 '79, Feb 21 '80, Mar '80, Aug 6 '80, Aug 23 '80, Sep 25 '80, Oct 27 '80, Nov 30 '80, Dec 5 '80, Dec 31 '80, Aug 14 '81, Oct 3 '81, Jan 10 '82, Apr '82, Apr 26 '83, Dec 31 '83, Jan 7 '84, Aug 12 '90. **Celluloid Heroes** (165A, 168S, 203A, 238A, 239V, 240S, 282A, 340A), Jun 10-11 '72, Oct '72, Nov 6-7 '72, Nov 17 '72, Nov '72, Nov 24 '72, Dec 15 '72, Jan 14 '73, Jan 22 '73, Jan 26 '73, Mar 31 '73, Apr 11 '73, Jul 15 '73, Sep 20 '73, Feb 26 '74, Apr 3 '74, Apr 16 '74, May 7 '74, Jun 4 '74, Jun 16 '74, Jul 14 '74, Sep 7 '74, Sep 23 '74, Nov 23 '74, Apr 13 '75, May 21 '75, Feb 29 '76, Feb 1-2 '77, Feb 19 '77, Feb 22 '77, Mar 28 '77, Dec 23 '77, Dec 24 '77, May 19 '78, Jun 23-25 '78, Jul 29 '78, Oct 1 '78, Oct 10 '78, Jan 23 '79, Mar 10 '79, Jul 14 '79, Aug 16 '79, Sep 23 '79, Oct 20 '79, Nov 11 '79, Nov 19 '79, Feb 21 '80, Jul 23 '80, Aug 6 '80, Aug 23 '80, Sep 25 '80, Oct 27 '80, Dec 5 '80, Dec 31 '80, May 6 '81, Jun 28 '81, Aug 14 '81, Oct 3 '81, Jan 10 '82, Feb 25-27 '82, Dec 9 '82, Dec 22 '82, Apr 26 '83, May 24 '83, Dec 31 '83, Dec 21 '84, Mar 20 '85, Apr 20 '85, Sep 12-13 '85, May 17 '86, Mar 8 '87, May 28 '87, Jun 29 '87, Apr 14 '88, Jun 9 '88, Oct 19-22 '89, Jan '90, Nov 10 '90, Nov '91, Apr 25 '92, Jun 12 '92, Sep 6 '92, Feb 3 '93, Mar 29 '93, May 4 '93, May 25 '93, Jul 11 '93, Oct 3 '93, Dec 14 '93, Jul 11-13 '95, Feb 21-25 '96, Aug '96, Nov 5-10 '96. ***Celluloid Heroes*** **album** see *Kinks Greatest....* **Charity** (267A), Jul '82. **Child Bride** Sep '76, Oct '76. **Chosen People** (song), (267A), Jul '82. ***Chosen People*** **album** (267A), Jun 13 '83, Aug 1 '83, Oct 7 '83. **Clichés Of The World** (265A, 291A), Feb '83, Dec 4-9 '83, Jun 22 '87, Jun 29 '87, Jul 1 '87, Dec 20 '87, Mar '88, Apr 14 '88, Jun 9 '88. **Climb Your Wall** Mar '70. **Close To The Wire** (315A), Dec '91. ***Club Vegas Tape*** **bootleg** Mar '90. **Cold Winter** (267A, 268S), Jul '82, Nov 18 '83. **Come Dancing** (260S, 265A, 282A, 291A, 340A), Dec 31 '63, Feb 25-27 '82, Oct '82, Nov '82, Dec 9 '82, Dec 22 '82, Jan '83, Feb '83, Mar '83, Apr 9 '83, Apr 15 '83, Apr 26 '83, May 24 '83, Jun 24 '83, Jul '83, Aug '83, Aug 24 '83, Dec 31 '83, Jan 7 '84, Apr 2 '84, Oct '84, Dec 2 '84, Dec 21 '84, Mar 20 '85, Apr 20 '85, Sep 12-13 '85, Jan '86, May 17 '86, Nov 23 '86, Jan '87, Mar 8 '87, Apr '87, May 28 '87, Jun 29 '87, Jul 1 '87, Dec 20 '87, Apr 14 '88, Jun 9 '88, Oct 16 '89, Mar '90, May 9 '90, Aug 12 '90, Nov 9 '90, Aug 7 '91, Jun 12 '92, Sep 6 '92, Mar 29 '93, May 4 '93, May 12 '93, Jun 17 '93, Jul 11 '93, Jul 27 '93, Oct 3 '93, Nov 25 '93, Dec 14 '93, Mar 22 '94, Mar 25 '94, Jun 10 '94, Oct 16 '94, Nov 8 '94, Dec 21 '94, May 18-19 '95, Feb 21-25 '96, Oct 18 '96, Nov 5-10 '96. ***Come Dancing With The Kinks*** **album** (282A), Feb '86, Mar '86, Jun '86. **(Come On Baby) Got My Rabbit's Foot Working** Apr 10 '64. **Come On Now** (46S, 50A, 103A), Dec 22-23 '64, Feb 26 '65, Oct 1-3 '65, Oct 5 '65, Dec 28 '80, Dec 31 '80, May 6 '81, Jun 28 '81, Feb 25-27 '82, Apr '82, Dec 22 '82, Dec 31 '83, Jan 7 '84. **Come Over** Apr 11-17 '69, May '69, Jun 13 '69. **Completely** (151A), Oct '70. **Complicated Life** (157A), Mar 30 '71, Nov '71, Jan '72, Mar 2-3 '72. **Conspiracy** Mar '87. **Contenders, The** (147A),. **Could Be Right Could Be Wrong** Dec '68. **Could Be You're Getting Old** Jan 22 '68. **Creeping Jean** (124S), Dec '68, Jan 17 '69, Jul 2 '69, Jun '94. **Cricket** (178A, 181S), Jan '73, Jan 14 '73, Feb '73, Apr 5 '74, Jun 16 '74. **Crying** Dec '68, Jul 2 '69.

Dance This Dance Apr 11-17 '69. **Dancin' In The Street** (50A), Nov 9 '64, Feb 15-17 '65, Apr 20 '65. Dandy, (92A, 103A, 139A), Jun 9 '66, Jun 24 '66, Aug 11 '66, Sep 12 '66, Oct 30 '66, Dec 27 '66, Mar 28 '67, Apr 16 '67, Apr 28 '68, Oct 23-25 '69, Nov 20-23 '69, Jun 13 '70. **Danger Zone** (267A), Jul '82. **Darling I Respect You** Feb 17 '69. **Date, The** Sep 26 '96. ***Dave Davies*** **alb. um** (239A), Sep 26 '80. ***Dave Davies Hits*** **EP** Apr 19 '68. **David Watts** (104A, 105S, 161A, 238A, 240E, 248S), Aug 20 '66, Jan '67, Jan 23 '67, Feb 6 '67, Oct 12 '67, Oct 23 '67, Oct 25 '67, Nov 29 '67, Aug 12 '78, Oct 1 '78, Jan 23 '79, Feb 18 '79, Feb '80, Feb 21 '80, Mar '80, Aug 6 '80, Sep 25 '80, Oct 27 '80, Nov 30 '80, Dec 5 '80, May 6 '81, Jun 19 '81, Jun 28 '81, Aug 14 '81, Feb 25-27 '82, Apr '82, Dec 22 '82, Apr 26 '83, Dec 31 '83, Jan 7 '84, Apr 2 '84, Dec 21 '84, Apr 20 '85, May 17 '86, May 28 '87, Dec 20 '87, Oct 16 '89, Jun 12 '92, Jun 17 '93, Jul 27 '93, May 18-19 '95, Jul 11-13 '95. **Daylight** (178A), Jun 16 '74, Jul 14 '74, Nov 23 '74. **Days** (117S, 139A, 161A, 310S, 315A, 340A), May '68, May 27 '68, Jun '68, Jun 20 '68, Jun 24 '68, Jun 26 '68, Jun 27 '68, Jun 28 '68, Jul 1 '68, Jul 9 '68, Jul 11 '68, Jul 22 '68, Jul 24 '68, Aug 15 '68, Aug 19 '68, Sep 4-6 '68, Oct '68, Dec 16 '69, Dec 18 '69, May 18 '70, Apr 7 '71, Dec 28 '83, Dec 31 '83, Jun 9 '88, Aug 15 '89, Oct 16 '89, May 9 '90, Aug 12 '90, Jun '91, Aug 7 '91, Nov '91, Apr 25 '92, Jun 12 '92, Sep 6 '92, Mar 29 '93, Mar 30 '93, May 4 '93, Jun 17 '93, Jul 11 '93, Nov 16 '93, Nov 25 '93, Dec 14 '93, Mar 22 '94, Jun 10 '94, Sep '94, Oct 16 '94, Nov 8 '94, Dec 21 '94, Apr 10 '95, May 18-19 '95, Jul 11-13 '95, Oct 9 '95, Feb 21-25 '96, Oct 24 '96, Dec '96. **Dead End Street** (93S, 106A, 139A, 161A, 340A), May 23-25 '66, Oct 21-22 '66, Nov '66, Nov 14 '66, Nov 15 '66, Nov 18 '66, Nov 21 '66, Nov 30 '66, Dec 8 '66, Dec 29 '66, Jan 5 '67, Jan '67, Apr 29 '67, Feb 27 '72, Apr 11 '73, Jun 16 '74, Dec 23 '77, Aug 6 '80, Nov '80, Nov 30 '80, Dec 5 '80, Dec 31 '80, May 6 '81, Apr '82, Dec 22 '82, Jan 7 '84, Apr 2 '84, Dec 21 '84, Apr 20 '85, May 17 '86, May 28 '87, Dec 20 '87, Jun 9 '88, Aug 12 '90, Sep 6 '92, Mar 29 '93, Jun 17 '93, Jul 11 '93, Nov 25 '93, Dec 14 '93, Mar 10 '94, Mar 22 '94, Mar 25 '94, Dec 21 '94, Jan/Feb '95, Apr 10 '95, Jul 11-13 '95, Jul 28 '95, Jul 31 '95, Aug 9 '95, Oct 9 '95, Feb 21-25 '96, Nov 5-10 '96. ***Dead End Street*** **album** see *Kinks Greatest – Dead End Street*. Dear Margaret, (300A), Dec '88, Aug '89. **Death Of A Clown** (101S, 104A, 139A, 161A, 326A, 340A), Jun '67, Jun 26 '67, Jul 7 '67, Jul 13 '67, Jul 25 '67, Jul 27 '67, Aug 2 '67, Aug 3 '67, Aug 4 '67, Aug 10 '67, Oct 16-17 '67, Apr 15 '68, Apr 19 '68, Apr 28 '68, Jun 11 '68, Jul 22 '68, Oct 17-18 '69, Oct 23-25 '69, Nov 20-23 '69, May 18 '70, Jun 13 '70, Feb 1-2 '77, Jul 2 '77, Dec 23 '77, Dec 24 '77, May 19 '78, Jun 2 '78, Oct 1 '78, Oct 10 '78, Feb 17 '79, Jul 14 '79, Aug 16 '79, Nov 19 '79, Dec '79, Feb 21 '80, Aug 6 '80, Aug 23 '80, Oct 27 '80, Dec 22 '82, Sep 6 '92, Mar 29 '93, May 12 '93, Jul 11 '93, Nov 25 '93, Dec 14 '93, Mar 22 '94, Apr '94, Nov 8 '94, Jan/Feb '95. **Decade** Jul '76. **Dedicated Follower Of Fashion** (77S, 88A, 106A, 139A, 326A, 340A), Dec '65, Dec 23 '65, Dec 29/30 '65, Feb 2 '66, Feb 7 '66, Feb 10 '66, Feb 14 '66, Feb 24 '66, Feb 27 '66, Mar 8 '66, Mar 9 '66, Mar 10 '66, Mar 31 '66, Apr 25-27 '66, May 8 '66, Dec 27 '66, Apr 28 '68, Jun 11 '68, Jul 22 '68, May 18 '70, Aug 23 '72, Dec 15 '72, Jan 14 '73, Jan 24 '73, Feb 26 '73, Apr 11 '73, Jul 15 '73, Sep 20 '73, Feb 26 '74, Apr 3 '74, Jun 16 '74, Jul 14 '74, Sep 9-10 '74, Sep 23 '74, Nov 23 '74, Feb 29 '76, Nov 23 '77, Dec 23 '77, May 19 '78, Oct 1 '78, Oct 10 '78, Aug 6 '80, Aug 12 '90, Nov '91, Apr 25 '92, Jul 11 '93, Mar 22 '94, Mar 25 '94, Jun 10 '94, Sep '94, Oct 16 '94, Nov 8 '94, Apr 10 '95, May 18-19 '95, Jul 11-13 '95, Aug 9 '95, Sep 2 '95, Oct 9 '95, Jul 7 '96. **Definite Maybe** (265A), Feb '83, Mar '83, Apr '83, May 24 '83, Dec 4-9 '83, Dec 31 '83, Jan 7 '84, Dec 21 '84, Mar 20 '85, Apr 20 '85, Sep 12-13 '85. **Demolition** (178A), Feb 25 '74, Feb 26 '74, Apr 3 '74, Jun 6 '74, Jun 16 '74, Jul 14 '74, Sep 7 '74, Sep 23 '74, Nov 23 '74, Apr 13 '75. **Denmark Street** (147A), Jan '69. **Destroyer** (250A, 253S, 282A, 291A), May '79, Jun '79, May 2 '81, Aug 4 '81, Sep 15 '81, Sep 28 '81, Oct 3 '81, Oct 10 '81, Dec 8 '81, Jan 10 '82, Feb 16 '82, Feb 25-27 '82, Apr '82, Dec 22 '82, Apr 26 '83, May 24 '83, Dec 31 '83, Jan 7 '84, Apr 2 '84, Dec 2 '84, Dec 21 '84, Sep 12-13 '85, Jun 29 '87, Jul 1 '87, Dec 20 '87, Apr 14 '88, Jun 9 '88, May 9 '90, Aug 12 '90, Nov 9 '90, May 4 '93, May 12 '93, Oct 3 '93. **Did Ya** (310S, 315A), Jun '91, Sep '91, Oct '91, Jan/Feb '92, Jun 12 '92, Nov '92, Oct 3 '93. **Did You See his Name** (161A), Feb 19-21 '68, Mar '68, Jun 20 '68. **Do It Again** (273A, 273S, 282A, 340A), Aug/Sep '84, Oct '84, Nov '84, Dec 4 '84, Dec 21 '84, Mar 20 '85, Apr 19 '85, Apr 20 '85, Sep 12-13 '85, Mar 8 '87, May 28 '87, Dec 20 '87, Apr 14 '88, Jun 9 '88, Jul 27 '93, Oct 3 '93, Nov 25 '93, Dec 14 '93, Mar 22 '94, Oct 16 '94, Nov 8 '94, May 18-19 '95, Jul 11-13 '95. **Do You Remember Walter** (121A, 139A, 340A), Jul '68, Oct '68, Apr 2 '69, Apr '94. **Do You Want To Dance** Oct '61. **Do You Wish To Be A Man** Dec '68, Jul 2 '69. **Doing The Best For You** (239A, 244S), Apr '80, Aug '80, Nov '80, Dec 5 '80. **Don't** (315A), Dec '91, Aug '92. ***Don't*** **proposed album title** Jan/Feb '92. **Don't Ever Change** (50A), Dec 29 '64. **Don't Ever Let Me Go** Sep 4 '64, Sep 8 '64. **Don't Forget To Dance** (265A, 266S, 272S, 282A, 326A, 340A), Dec 31 '63, Jun 9 '64, Sep '82, Oct '82, Dec 3 '82, Dec 17 '82, Jan '83, Feb '83, Apr '83, Apr 9 '83, Apr 26 '83, May 24 '83, May 27 '83, Jun 24 '83, Aug 1 '83, Sep 30 '83, Dec 31 '83, Jan 7 '84, Apr 2 '84, Dec 21 '84, Mar 20 '85, Apr 20 '85, Sep 12-13 '85, May 17 '86, Apr '94. **Don't You Fret** (66E, 72A, 89A, 139A), Aug '65, Aug 6 '65, Sep 24 '65, Oct 23-25 '69. ***Double Life*** **proposed album** Aug 16-19 '79, Nov 19 '79, Jan '80, Feb '80. **Down All The Days (Till 1992)** (299S, 300A, 302S, 304S), Apr 30 '81, Jan/Feb/Mar '89, Jun '89, Aug '89, Sep 4 '89, Sep 25 '89, Feb '90, Apr 16 '90, Apr 30 '90, May 8 '90, May 9 '90. **Dreams** (151A, 152S), Oct '70, Apr 2 '71. **Drift Away** (315A), Dec '91, May '92, May 4 '93, May 12 '93, Jun 17 '93, Jul 11 '93, Jul 27 '93, Sep '93, Oct 3 '93. **Drivin'** (129S, 133A), May 1 '69, Jun 19 '69, Jun 20 '69, Sep 4 '69. **Drop Out** Aug '75. **Dry Bones** Jan '72, Aug 23 '72, Nov 17 '72, Dec 15 '72, Feb 26 '73, Apr 11 '73, Jul 15 '73, Sep 20 '73, Sep 22 '73, Apr 3 '74, Apr 16 '74, May 7 '74, Jun 4 '74, Jul 14 '74, Sep 7 '74, Sep 23 '74, Nov 23 '74, Apr 13 '75, May 21 '75, Dec 23 '77, Dec 24 '77. **Ducks On The Wall** (193S, 194A), Jul 25 '74, Jan 30 '75, Feb 18 '75, Mar 10 '79, Nov 5-10 '96. **Düsseldorf Blues** Nov 30 '80.

Earache Apr 28 '85. **East West** Sep '77. **Eastern Eyes** (249A), Mar '81. **Easy Come There You Went** Mar 29 '68, Jul 2 '69. **Education** (198A), Aug '75, Nov 21 '75, Feb 19 '77, May 4 '77, Nov 23 '77, Dec 23 '77. **80 Days** (296M), Mar '87. **Elevator Man** Jun 25 '76. **Emergency** Apr '87. **Empire Song** (296M), Mar '87. **Emptiness** May 10 '65, Dec 17 '65. **End Of The Season** (104A), Apr '66, Jun 9 '66, Sep 30 '66. **England** Apr 6 '81. **Entertainment** (song), (299S, 300A), Jul 26 '81, Mar '83, Jul '89, Aug '89, Sep 25 '89, Jan '90. ***Entertainment*** **proposed album title** Jan '83, Mar '83. **Et Moi Et Moi Et Moi** Aug '67. **European Cup Blues** Jun 12 '92. **Every Little Once In A While** Oct '87. **Everybody Wants To Be A Personality** Apr 11/12 '66. **Everybody's A Star (Starmaker)** (194A, 203A), Jun 2 '75, Feb 19 '77. **Ev'rybody's Gonna Be Happy** (51S, 88A), Nov 7 '64, Dec '64, Dec 22-23 '64, Mar 19 '65, Mar 30 '65, Apr 4 '65, Apr 5 '65, Apr 8 '65, Apr 15 '65, Apr 16 '65, Apr 19 '65, Apr 20 '65, Apr 30 '65, Jul 2 '65, Jul 21 '65, Feb 27 '70. **Everybody's Got A Body** Apr 6 '81. ***Everybody's In Show-Biz – Everybody's A Star*** **album** (165A), Mar 2-3 '72, May '72, May 27-29 '72, Jun 1 '72, Jun 5 '72, Jun 10-11 '72, Jun '72, Jul '72, Aug 25 '72, Sep 1 '72, Nov 6-7 '72, Sep 29 '73. **Everyday** Oct '61. **Everything Is Alright** Sep '76. **Expectations** (277A), Jul '83.

Face In The Crowd, A (194A, 203A), Jul 25 '74, . ***Face To Face*** **album** (92A), Jun 27-28 '66, Jul 6 '66, Jul 13-14 '66, Jul 28 '66, Aug 12 '66, Sep 2 '66, Oct 21 '66, Oct 28 '66, Dec 7 '66, Dec 8 '66. **Faith** Sep '77. **Fallen Idol** Dec 14 '65, Apr 11/12 '66, Apr '66, Jun 6 '66, Jun 9 '66. **Family Song** The, Feb 3 '75. **Fancy** (92A, 161A), May 12-13 '66, Oct 23-25 '69, Nov 20-23 '69. **Fancy Kitchen Gadgetry** Dec '68. **Father Christmas** (216S, 282A), Oct '77, Nov 1-2 '77, Nov 23 '77, Nov 25 '77, Dec 8 '77, Dec 23 '77, Dec 24 '77, Nov '78, Feb '79. **Finale** *(80 Days)*, (296M). **Finale** *(Preservation)*, Nov 23 '74, . **Finale** *(Schoolboys)*, (198A), Sep 24 '75. **Fire Burning** (267A), Jul '82. **First Time We Fall In Love, The** (198A), Sep 2 '75, Nov 21 '75. **Flash's Confession** (183A), Nov 23 '74. **Flash's Dream (The Final Elbow)** (183A), Nov 23 '74. **For You** Feb '73. ***Four More Respected Men*** **proposed album** Jun '68, Jun 20 '68, Jun 26 '68, Oct '68. **Freedom** Apr 3 '90. **Freedom Lies** (267A), Jul '82. **Full Moon** (209A, 210S), Sep '76, Oct '76, Feb 1-2 '77, Feb 19 '77, Mar 7-10 '77, Mar 18 '77, Mar 28 '77, May 4 '77, Nov 23 '77, Nov 23 '77, Jan 23 '79. **Funny Face** (104A, 107S), May 15 '67, Jun '67, Nov 24 '67, Jan 31 '68.

Gallon Of Gas, A (230A, 232S, 340A), Jan 23 '79, Apr '79, May '79, Jun '79, Jul 1-4 '79, Jul 14 '79, Aug 7 '79, Aug 16 '79, Sep 23 '79, Oct 16 '79, Oct 20 '79, Nov 19 '79, Dec '79, Feb 21 '80, Aug 6 '80, Aug 23 '80, Sep 25 '80, Oct 27 '80, Dec 5 '80, Dec 31 '80, May 6 '81, Jun 28 '81, Aug 14 '81, Oct 3 '81, Jan 10 '82, Dec 22 '82, Apr 26 '83, May 24 '83, Jan 7 '84, Dec 21 '84, Sep 12-13 '85, May 17 '86, Mar 8 '87, Mar '88, Oct 16 '89, May 9 '90, Nov 9 '90, Jul 27 '93, Oct 3 '93, Apr '94. **Geneseo Way** Mar 10 '79. **Geronimo's Cadillac** Jan 10 '75. **Get Back** Oct 3 '81. **Get Back In Line** (161A), Mar '71, Mar 30 '71, Apr 7 '71, Nov 21 '71, Mar 2-3 '72, Sep 23 '74, Nov 23 '77, Dec 23 '77, Dec 24 '77, Feb 18 '79, Nov 19 '79, Jun 12 '92, Nov 5-10 '96. **Get Up** (219A), Sep '77, Oct '77, Jan '78, Jun 2 '78. **Girl Who Goes To Discotheques, A** Apr 11/12 '66. **Girl With Guitar** Oct 7 '71. **Give My Fondest Regards To Her** Dec '68. **Give My Love To Rose** Mar 30 '71, Mar 31 '71. **Give Something Back** Oct '87. **Give The People What They Want** (song), (250A, 291A, 309A, 340A), Apr '79, May '79, Jun '79, May '80, Aug '80, Aug 6 '80, Sep 25 '80, Oct 27 '80, Nov 30 '80, Dec 31 '80, Apr '81, Jun 28 '81, Aug 14 '81, Oct 3 '81, Oct 10 '81, Dec 4 '81, Jan 10 '82, Feb 25-27 '82, Apr '82, Jun 29 '87, Jul 1 '87, Dec 20 '87, Mar 25 '94, Jun 10 '94, Nov 8 '94, Jul 11-13 '95. ***Give The People What They Want*** **album** (250A), Jul '81, Aug 26 '81, Oct 12 '81, Jan 15-16 '82, Jan 25 '82. **Give You All My Love** Sep '77. **Glamour** (song), (249A), Mar '81. ***Glamour*** **album** (249A), Jul 1 '81, Oct 16 '81. **Glorious Sight** Apr 6 '81. **God's Children** (151A, 152S, 161A), Oct '70, Mar 22 '71, Mar '71, Mar 26 '71, Apr 2 '71, May 3 '71, Jul 7 '71. **Going Solo** (273A, 276S, 277A), Jul '83, Oct '84, Mar 18 '85. **Good Day** (272S, 273A), May '84, Jun/Jul '84, Aug/Sep '84, Oct '84, Dec 21 '84. **Good Golly Miss Molly** Oct '61, Jan 28-31 '64, Oct '72, Nov 17 '72, Dec 15 '72, Jan 24 '73, Feb 26 '73, Apr 11 '73, Sep 20 '73, Feb 26 '74, Apr 3 '74, Apr 16 '74, Sep 23 '74, May 8 '74, May 18-19 '95, Aug 1 '95. **Good Good Life** Apr '70. **Good Luck Charm** *see* Good Luck Child. **Good Luck Child** Jan '66, Aug 4 '67, Aug '67. **Good Times Are Gone** Jul '83. **Got Love If You Want It** (37A, 41A), Oct '63, Jan 28-31 '64, Mar 29 '64, Jul 31 '64, Aug 18 '64, Sep 7 '64, Oct 1 '64, Nov 24 '64, Oct 1-3 '65, Jun 9 '88. **Got My Feet On The Ground** (50A), Feb 15-17 '65, Aug 10 '65. **Got To Be Free** (147A), Mar 23 '70, Apr '70, Feb 10 '71. **Gothenburg Blues** Jun 10 '94. **Gotta Get The First Plane Home** (72A). **Great Balls Of Fire** Mar 29 '93. ***Great Lost Kinks Album, The*** **album** (170A), Jul 2 '69, Jan 25 '73. ***Greatest Hits*** **album** Nov '84. **Green Onions** Nov 8 '94. **Greenback Dollar** Oct '61. **Groovy Movies** (170A, 268A), Mar '69, Jun 16 '69, Jul 2 '69. **Guantanamera** Apr '94. **Guilty** (273A, 273S), Aug/Sep '84, Oct '84, Nov '84, Dec 4 '84, Mar 20 '85, Apr 19 '85, Apr 20 '85, Sep 12-13 '85, May 17 '86, Mar 8 '87, May 28 '87, Jun 29 '87, Dec 20 '87, Apr 14 '88, Jun 9 '88. **Guitar Boogie** Oct '61.

Hang On Sloopy Aug 23 '72, Aug 29 '72, Dec 15 '72, Jan 14 '73, Jun 1 '77, Aug 23 '80, Apr 20 '85. **Hard Way, The** (198A, 200S, 201S, 238A, 239V), Sep 22 '75, Oct 2 '75, Nov '75, Nov 21 '75, Jan 21 '76, Jan 23 '76, Feb 19 '77, May 4 '77, Dec 23 '77, Dec 24 '77, Jan 23 '79, Feb '79, Mar 3 '79, Mar 10 '79, Jul 14 '79, Aug 16 '79, Sep 23 '79, Feb 21 '80, Aug 6 '80, Aug 23 '80, Sep 25 '80, Oct 27 '80, Nov 30 '80, Dec 5 '80, Dec 31 '80, May 6 '81, Jun 28 '81, Aug 14 '81, Oct 3 '81, Jan 10 '82, Feb 25-27 '82, Apr '82, Dec 22 '82, Apr 26 '83, May 24 '83, Dec 31 '83, Jan 7 '84, Apr 2 '84, Dec 21 '84, Mar 20 '85, Apr 20 '85, Sep 12-13 '85, May 17 '86, Mar 8 '87, May 28 '87, Oct 16 '89, Mar '90, May 9 '90, Aug 12 '90, Aug 7 '91, Jun 12 '92, Sep 6 '92, Mar 29 '93, Jun 17 '93, Mar 22 '94, May 18-19 '95, Jul 11-13 '95. **Harry Rag** (98S, 104A), Jan '67, Feb 6 '67, May 4 '67, May 17 '67, May 24 '67, Oct 25 '67, Nov 12-14 '70, Apr 7 '71, Feb 27 '72, Mar 5 '72, Apr 11 '73, Nov 23 '77, Dec 28 '83, Feb 3 '93, Mar 29 '93, May 4 '93, May 12 '93, Jul 11 '93, Nov 25 '93, Feb 21-25 '96. **Hatred (A Duet)** (315S, 315A), Dec '91, May '92, Aug '92, Feb 3 '93, Feb 4 '93, Feb '93, Mar 8 '93, Mar 25 '93, Mar 29 '93, Apr 12 '93, May 4 '93, May 11 '93, May 12 '93, May 25 '93, Jun 17 '93, Dec 14 '93. **Hava Nagila** Apr 6 '73. **Have A Cuppa Tea** (157A), Jan 4 '72, Jan '72, Mar 2-3 '72, Jan 14 '73. **Have Another Drink** (194A, 195S), Jul 25 '74, May 23 '75. **Having A Good Time** Aug '65, Aug 6 '65. **Hay Fever** (219A), Jul '76, Nov '76, Oct '77, Mar '78, May 19 '78, Jun 2 '78, Jul 29 '78, Oct 1 '78, Oct 10 '78, Jan 23 '79, Mar

10 '79. **He Spent More Than He Had** *see* You Can't Give More…. **He's Evil** (183A, 185S), Jun 16 '74, Jul 14 '74, Jul 15-20 '74, Jul 26 '74, Sep 23 '74, Nov 23 '74. **Headmaster** (198A), Sep 23 '75, Oct 2 '75, Nov 21 '75. **Heart** Mar 26-27 '88. **Heart Of Gold** (265A, 270E, 282A), Jan '83, Dec 4-9 '83, Jan 7 '84, Mar 23 '84, Apr 2 '84, Oct 29 '94. **Heartbeat** Jun 1 '77, Nov 23 '77. **Heartbreaker** Nov '78, Oct '79. **Helga** (151A), Oct '70. **Here!** (296M). **Here Come The People In Grey** (157A), Mar 7-10 '77. **Here Comes Flash** (178A, 182S), Feb 25 '74, Feb 26 '74, Apr 3 '74, Apr 16 '74, Apr '74, Jun 4 '74, Jun 16 '74, Jul 14 '74, Sep 7 '74, Sep 23 '74, Nov 23 '74, Apr 13 '75, May 21 '75. **Here Comes Yet Another Day** (165A, 203A), Aug 9 '72, Aug 23 '72, Nov 17 '72, Dec 15 '72, Jan 14 '73, Feb 26 '73, Apr 11 '73, Sep 20 '73, Feb 26 '74, Apr 3 '74, Apr 16 '74, May 7 '74, Jun 4 '74, Jun 16 '74, Jul 14 '74, Sep 7 '74, Sep 23 '74, Nov 23 '74, Apr 13 '75, May 21 '75, Jun 14 '75. **Hey Baby** Jun 1 '77. **Hey Joe** Jun 22 '93. **Hidden Qualities** May '79. **Hide And Seek** Apr 16 '65, Apr 30 '65, Aug 6 '65. **Higher And Higher** Aug 31 '81. **History** Aug '75. ***Hit Singles* album** Sep 5 '87. **Hold My Hand** (124S), Dec '68, Jan 17 '69, Apr 2 '69, Jul 2 '69. **Holiday** (157A, 165A, 203A), Jan '72, Mar 2-3 '72, May 5 '72, Aug 23 '72, Dec 15 '72, Jan 24 '73, Apr 11 '73, Jul 15 '73, Sep 20 '73. **Holiday In Waikiki** (92A, 161A), Jul 7 '65, Apr '66. **Holiday Romance** (187S, 194A), Sep '74, Sep 9-10 '74, Oct 18 '74, Jan 30 '75, Apr 1-3 '75. **Holloway Jail** (157A). **Hoochie Coochie Man** Apr 28 '72, Aug 25 '72. **Hope** Oct '87. **Hot Little Hands** Jun 24-30 '69. **Hot Potatoes** (165A), Nov '72, Nov 24 '72, Jan 26 '73. **House In The Country, A** (92A), Mar 18 '66, Apr '66, May 12-13 '66, Jul 1-3 '66. **House On The Hill** Apr 11-17 '69. **How Are You** (283A, 284S, 287S), Oct/Nov/Dec '85, Jan '86, Sep '86, Nov '86, Nov 29 '86, Dec '86, May 28 '87, Jun 1 '87. **How Can I Love You** Oct '73. **How Can We Hang On To A Dream** Jun '67. **How Do I Get Close** (300A, 302S, 309A), Jan/Feb/Mar '89, Jun '89, Jul '89, Aug '89, Sep 20 '89, Oct 16 '89, Oct 17-18 '89, Oct 31 '89, Nov '89, Dec 13 '89, Jan '90, Feb '90. **How You Love Me** Apr 11-17 '69, Jun 24-30 '69.

I Am Free (72A), Dec 13 '65. **I Am Your Man** (178A), Jun 16 '74, Nov 23 '74, Jul '91. **I Believe In You Girl** Jan 15 '67. **I Believed You** Oct 19 '63, Dec 5 '63, Jan 14 '64, Jan 20 '64. **I Bet You Won't Stay** May 24 '65, Jun '65, Aug 17 '65, Sep 17 '65 . **I Can't Wait To See You Smile** Dec '68. **I Don't Need You Anymore** Jan '64, Jan 13 '64, Jan 14 '64, Jan 20 '64. **I Go To Sleep** May 23 '65, May 24 '65, Jun '65, Jun 30 '65, Aug 27 '65, Apr 22 '66, Oct 30 '81, Oct 16 '94, Apr 10 '95, Jul 11-13 '95, Aug 9 '95, Oct 9 '95. **I Gotta Go Now** (41E), Sep '64 . **I Gotta Move** (38S, 89A, 310S), Aug 31 '64, Sep 3 '64, Aug 4 '65, Apr 2 '84, Dec 2 '84, Dec 21 '84, Mar 20 '85, Apr 20 '85, May 17 '86, Mar 8 '87, Apr '87, May 28 '87, Jun 29 '87, Jul 1 '87, Jun 9 '88. **I Just Wanna Walk With You** Sep 2 '64, Sep 4 '64, Sep 8 '64 . **I Left My Heart In San Francisco** Feb 23 '71. **I Like It** Sep 28 '63. **I Need You** (56S, 72A, 106A), Aug 17 '64, Mar 31 '65, Apr 13-14 '65, May 21 '65, May 26 '65, Jun 6 '65, Jun 29 '65, Oct 29 '94. **I Need Your Loving** Apr 16 '65. **I Took My Baby Home** (21S, 37A), Nov 16 '63, Dec 5 '63, Jan 14 '64, Jan 20 '64, Feb 7 '64. **If Christmas Could Last Forever** Jan 1-3 '68. **If I Had A Hammer** Sep 28 '63. **If I Were A Rich Man** Mar 31 '73, Apr 6 '73, Jul 15 '73. **I'll Remember** (92A), Oct 25-26 '65. **I'll Tell Her Tomorrow** Apr 10 '64 . **I'm A Hog For You** Oct 19 '63, Jan 28-31 '64. **I'm A Lover Not A Fighter** (37A, 139A), Jan 28-31 '64, Aug 25 '64, Sep 26 '64, Oct 30 '64, Nov 6 '64, Dec 9 '64, Dec 16-17 '64, Jul 1 '65, Sep 1 '65, Sep 14-18 '65, Nov 23 '65. **I'm Going Home** Jan '73, Jan 14 '73, Feb '73. **I'm In Disgrace** (198A, 200S), Aug '75, Nov 21 '75, Jan 21 '76. **I'm Not Like Everybody Else** (106A, 170A, 340A), Jan 3 '66, Feb '66, Mar 31 '66, May 12-13 '66, Jun 3 '66, Jul 20 '66, Dec 28 '80, Dec 31 '80, Mar '90, May 9 '90, Aug 12 '90, Jun 12 '92, Sep 6 '92, Mar 29 '93, May 4 '93, Jun 17 '93, Jul 11 '93, Oct 3 '93, Nov 25 '93, Mar 25 '94, Oct 7 '94, Oct 16 '94, Jan/Feb '95, May 18-19 '95, Nov 5-10 '96. **I'm On An Island** (72A, 103A), Aug 16 '79. **I'm Telling You Now** Sep 28 '63. **I'm Your Hoochie Coochie Man** Jan 28-31 '64, Sep 26 '64. **Imagination's Real** (239A, 241S), Jan '80, Aug '80, Sep 5 '80, Sep 25 '80, Oct 27 '80, Nov 30 '80, Dec 5 '80, Dec 31 '80. **Imposter, The** Mar '81. **In A Foreign Land** (219A, 221S), Jul '76, Dec '76, Mar '78, Jul 14 '78. **In A Space** (230A), May '79, Jun '79, Sep 28 '79. **In The Mouth Of Madness** Dec '94, Jan/Feb '95. **In You I Believe** (239A), Jan '80. **Informer, The** (315A), Aug '86, Dec '91, Jun 14 '93, Jul 11 '93, Jul 27 '93, Mar 22 '94. **Interview, The** Sep '67. **Intro** (*Powerman*), (147A). **Intro** (*Waterloo*), (277A), Jul '83. **Introduction To Solution** (183A). **Is It Any Wonder** (267A), Jul '82. **Is This The Only Way** (249A), Mar '81. **It Could Have Been Him** (296M), Mar '87. **It (I Want It)** (291A), Apr '87, Jun 9 '87, Jun 10 '87, Jul 1 '87, Dec 20 '87, Mar '88, Apr 14 '88, Jun 9 '88, Oct 16 '89, May 9 '90, Aug 12 '90, Nov 9 '90, Aug 7 '91. **It's All Over** Apr 30 '65. **It's Alright** (31S, 72A), Mar 18 '64, Mar 19 '64, Apr 27 '64, Jun 14 '64, Aug 4 '64, Oct 11 '64, Nov 6 '64, Dec 31 '64, Apr 30 '65, Jul 1 '65, Oct 5 '65. **It's Alright (Don't Think About It)** (315A), Dec '91, Nov 25 '93, Dec 14 '93, May 18-19 '95, May 18-19 '95, Jul 11-13 '95. **It's Only Make Believe** Jun 5 '93. **It's So Easy** Sep 28 '63. **It's Too Late** (72A). **It's You** Mar 18 '64, Mar 19 '64, Apr 27 '64. **I've Been Driving On Bald Mountain** (37A, 41A), Aug 25 '64. **I've Got That Feeling** (41E), Feb 11 '64, Feb 18 '64, Mar 13 '64, Oct '64, Dec 9 '64.

Jack The Idiot Dunce (198A, 201S), Sep 2 '75, Nov 21 '75, Jan 23 '76. **Jailhouse Rock** Nov 20-23 '69. **John & Julie** Jun 24-30 '69. **Johnny B Goode** Oct '61, Oct '63. **Johnny Thunder** (121A), Mar 29 '68, Jun 20 '68, Nov 22 '68, Apr 2 '73, Aug 19 '93. **Juke Box Music** (209A, 213S, 282A), Jul '76, Oct '76, Mar 28 '77, Apr 23 '77, Apr 24 '77, May 4 '77, May 18 '77, Jun 3 '77, Nov 23 '77, Dec 23 '77, Dec 24 '77, Jun 2 '78, Jul 29 '78, Oct 1 '78, Jan 23 '79. **Just A Poor Country Girl** Feb 5-7 '68. **Just Can't Go To Sleep** (37A, 41A), Sep 3 '64, Feb 26 '65. **Just Friends** (151A), Oct '70. **Just Passing Through** (296M), Mar '87.

Kentucky Moon Oct 16 '71. **Killer's Eyes** (250A), May 12 '81, Jul '81, Aug 4 '81, Aug 14 '81, Oct 3 '81. **Killing Time** (283A, 284S, 285S), Aug '86, Dec '86, Feb 9 '87, Apr '87. ***Kinda Kinks* album** (50A), Apr 4 '62, Mar 5 '65, Aug 11 '65. **King Kong** (126S, 161A), Mar '69, Mar 28 '69, Jul 2 '69, May 3 '72. **King Of The Whole Wide World** Feb '66, Mar 18 '66. ***Kink Kronikles, The* album** (161A), Mar 25 '72. ***Kinkdom* album** (72A), Nov '65. ***Kinks, The* album** (1964), (37A), Sep 7 '64, Sep 14 '64, Oct 2 '64. ***Kinks, The* album** (1970), (139A), Feb 27 '70. ***Kinks, The* EP** Apr 19 '68. ***Kinks Are Well Respected Men, The* album** Sep 5 '87. ***Kinks Are The Village Green Preservation Society, The* album** see *Village Green Preservation….* ***Kinks Greatest Hits* album** (88A), Aug 10 '66, Nov 14 '66, Nov 28 '68. ***Kinks Greatest/Celluloid Heroes, The* album** (203A), Jan 8 '75, Apr 5 '76, May '76, Jun 18 '76. ***Kinks Greatest – Dead End Street, The* album** (268A), Oct 14 '83. ***Kinks Kontroversy, The* album** (72A), Nov 26 '65, Mar 30 '66. ***Kinks Live, The* EP** (240E), Jul 11 '80. ***(Kinks Present) A Soap Opera* album** see *Soap Opera….* ***Kinks-Size* album** (52A), Mar 24 '65. ***Kinksize Session* EP** (41E), Nov 27 '64 . ***Kinky Folky* EP** Jun 14 '65. ***Kinky Music* album** Jun 15 '65, Jun 18 '65, Aug 8 '65. ***Kollectables* album** Nov '84. ***Kovers* album** Nov '84. ***Kriminal Kinks* bootleg** Aug 29 '72. ***Kwyet Kinks* EP** (66E), Sep 17 '65.

Labour Of Love (265A), Feb '83, Apr '83. **Ladies Of The Night** (296M), Mar '87. **Ladder Of Success** Jul '83. **Land Of 1,000 Dances** A, Nov 30 '80. **Last Assembly, The** (198A), Sep 13 '75, Nov 21 '75. **Last Of The Steam Powered Trains, The** (121A, 139A), Oct '68, Jan 7 '69, Oct 23-25 '69, Nov 20-23 '69, Feb 12-14 '70, Jun 13 '70, Aug 29 '70, Nov 12-14 '70, Nov 21 '70, Aug 19 '93. **Laugh At The World** May '79. **Lavender Hill** (170A), Aug '67, Jul 2 '69. **Lazy Day** Jul '76. **Lazy Old Sun** (104A), Jun '67. **Let It Be Written** (296M), Mar '87. **Let's Have A Dance** Apr 6 '81. **Let's Take Off Our Clothes** Feb 10 '69. **Life Goes On** (209A, 213S), Sep '76, Feb 19 '77, Mar 28 '77, May 4 '77, May 18 '77, Nov 23 '77. **Life On The Road** (209A), Jul '76, Oct '76, Mar 7-10 '77, Mar 28 '77, May 4 '77, Nov 23 '77, Dec 23 '77, Dec 24 '77, May 19 '78, Jun 2 '78, Jul 29 '78, Oct 1 '78, Oct 10 '78, Jan 23 '79, Feb 17 '79, Mar 10 '79, Jul 14 '79, Aug 16 '79, Oct 20 '79. **Lilacs And Daffodils** (*see also* Sir Jasper) May 12-13 '66, Jun 27-28 '66. **Lily Of Laguna** Nov 22 '70. **Lincoln County** (119S), Mar '68, Apr 1 '68, May '68, Jun 20 '68, Jul 15 '68, Jul 19 '68, Jul 22 '68, Aug 24 '68, Aug 30 '68, Jul 2 '69, Nov 21 '93. **Listen To Me** Oct 25-26 '65. **Little Bit Of Abuse, A** (250A), Jul '81, Aug 26 '81. **Little Bit Of Emotion, A** (230A), May '79. **Little Bit Of Sunlight, A** Jan 6 '64, May 24 '65. **Little Man In A Little Box** Feb 18 '66, Mar 8 '66, May 20 '66. **Little Miss Queen Of Darkness** (92A), Apr 11/12 '66, Jun 21 '66. **Little Queenie** Oct '63, Jan 28-31 '64, Sep 7 '64, Aug 23 '72, Aug 29 '72, Dec 15 '72, Feb 26 '73, Sep 20 '73, Feb 26 '74, Dec 23 '77, Jul '78, Oct 10 '78, Feb 17 '79, Aug 16 '79, Sep 23 '79, Sep 25 '81. **Little Women** Jun '67. ***Live At Kelvin Hall* album** see *Live Kinks*. ***Live Kinks, The* album** (103A), Apr 1 '67, Apr 3 '67, Apr 24 '67, Aug 16 '67, Jan 12 '68, Aug '80. **Live Life** (219A, 219S, 221S), Jan '78, Feb '78, May 19 '78, Jun 2 '78, Jun '78, Jul 4 '78, Jul 14 '78, Jul 29 '78, Sep 18 '78, Sep 29 '78, Oct 1 '78, Oct 11 '78, Oct 10 '78, Feb 17 '79, Aug 16 '79, Sep 23 '79, Oct 20 '79, Dec '79, Feb 21 '80. **Living Doll** Oct '61, Apr '62. **Living On A Thin Line** (273A, 282A, 291A, 309A), Aug/Sep '84, Oct '84, Dec 21 '84, Feb '85, Mar 20 '85, Apr 20 '85, Sep 12-13 '85, May 17 '86, Mar 8 '87, May 28 '87, Jun 29 '87, Jul 1 '87, Dec 20 '87, Apr 14 '88, Jun 9 '88, Oct 16 '89, May 9 '90, Aug 12 '90, Nov 9 '90, Aug 7 '91, Jun 12 '92, Sep 6 '92, Mar 29 '93, Mar 22 '94, May 18-19 '95, Jul 11-13 '95. **Lola** (142S, 147A, 151A, 161A, 165A, 238A, 239V, 240S, 248S, 270E, 282A, 340A), Jan 8 '65, Apr 23 '65, Feb 12-14 '70, Apr '70, May '70, May 18 '70, May 20 '70, May 24 '70, May 25-27 '70, May 28 '70, May 31 '70, Jun 1-2 '70, Jun 12 '70, Jun 22 '70, Jul 2 '70, Jul 6 '70, Jul 14 '70, Jul 15 '70, Jul 23 '70, Jul 28 '70, Aug 29 '70, Oct '70, Nov 12-14 '70, Nov 16-18 '70, Dec 15 '70, Jan 16 '71, Mar 1 '71, Mar 22 '71, Mar '71, Mar 30 '71, Apr 7 '71, Nov 21 '71, Jan 31 '72, Mar 2-3 '72, Apr 12 '72, Aug 23 '72, Nov 17 '72, Dec 15 '72, Jan 14 '73, Jan 24 '73, Feb 26 '73, Jul 15 '73, Sep 8 '73, Sep 20 '73, Feb 26 '74, Apr 3 '74, Apr 16 '74, Jun 16 '74, Jul 14 '74, Sep 7 '74, Sep 23 '74, Nov 23 '74, Apr 13 '75, May 21 '75, Feb 29 '76, Feb 1-2 '77, Feb 19 '77, Feb 26 '77, Apr 23 '77, May 4 '77, Nov 23 '77, Dec 23 '77, Dec 24 '77, May 19 '78, Jun 2 '78, Jul 29 '78, Oct 1 '78, Oct 10 '78, Oct 22 '78, Jan 23 '79, Feb 17 '79, Mar 10 '79, Jul 14 '79, Aug 16 '79, Sep 23 '79, Oct 16 '79, Oct 20 '79, Nov 19 '79, Feb 21 '80, Jun 20 '80, Jul 23 '80, Aug 6 '80, Aug 23 '80, Sep 25 '80, Oct 27 '80, Nov 30 '80, Dec 5 '80, Dec 31 '80, May 6 '81, Jun 19 '81, Jun 28 '81, Aug 14 '81, Oct 3 '81, Jan 10 '82, Feb 25-27 '82, Apr '82, Dec 22 '82, Apr 26 '83, May 24 '83, Dec 31 '83, Jan 7 '84, Mar 23 '84, Apr 2 '84, Dec 21 '84, Mar 20 '85, Apr 20 '85, Sep 12-13 '85, May 17 '86, Nov 23 '86, Jan '87, Mar 8 '87, May 28 '87, Jun 29 '87, Dec 20 '87, Apr 14 '88, Jun 9 '88, Oct 16 '89, May 9 '90, Aug 12 '90, Nov 9 '90, Aug 7 '91, Nov '91, Apr 25 '92, Jun 12 '92, Sep 6 '92, Feb 3 '93, Feb 11 '93, Mar 29 '93, May 4 '93, Jun 17 '93, Jul 11 '93, Jul 27 '93, Oct 3 '93, Nov 25 '93, Dec 14 '93, Mar 22 '94, Mar 25 '94, Jun 10 '94, Sep '94, Nov 8 '94, Dec 6 '94, Dec 21 '94, Apr 10 '95, May 18-19 '95, Jul 11-13 '95, Aug 9 '95, Sep 2 '95, Oct 9 '95, Feb 21-25 '96, Jul 7 '96, Dec 2 '96. ***Lola Versus Powerman & The Moneygoround* album** see *Part One: Lola Versus….* **London Blues** Dec 22 '82. **London Song** Mar '95, Apr 10 '95, Aug 9 '95, Oct 9 '95, Feb 21-25 '96, Jun 21 '96. **Lonely Hearts** (277A), Jul '83. **Long Distance** (265A, 282A), Feb 11 '82, Feb '83. **Long Island** May '80. **Long Lonely Road** Mar '75, Nov '78. **Long Lost John** Sep 20 '73. **Long Tall Sally** (21S, 139A), Jan 17 '64, Jan 20 '64, Jan 21 '64, Jan 28-31 '64, Feb 7 '64, Feb 13 '64, Feb 21 '64, Mar '64, Mar 29 '64, Jun 19 '64, Feb 26 '80, Jan '90. **Long Tall Shorty** (37A, 41A), Aug 25 '64, Oct 30 '64, Feb 4 '65, Mar 13 '65, Jun 30 '65, Jul 1 '65, Nov 20-23 '69, Feb 11 '93. **Long Way From Home, A** (147A), May 24 '70, Nov 12-14 '70. **Look A Little On The Sunny Side** (165A). **Look For Me Baby** (50A), Feb 15-17 '65, Feb 23 '65. **Look Through Any Doorway** (310S), Mar '91. **Loony Balloon** (300A), May '89, Aug '89, May 9 '90, Nov 9 '90, Jul 11 '93, Jul 27 '93, Oct 3 '93. **Lost And Found** (song), (283A, 285S, 291A, 309A), Sep 27 '85, Aug '86, Nov 20 '86, Dec '86, Jan '87, Feb 9 '87, Mar 8 '87, Apr '87, May 28 '87, May 30 '87, Jul 1 '87, Dec 20 '87, Apr 14 '88, Jun 9 '88. ***Lost And Found* album**, (309A), Aug 27 '91. **Louie Louie** (41E, 72A, 106A), Jan 30 '64, Jan 28-31 '64, Mar 29 '64, Oct '64, Dec 9 '64, Mar 13 '65, Apr 19 '65, Apr 24 '65, Aug 18 '65, Nov 21 '65, May 8 '66, Jun 13 '66, Oct 23-25 '69, Nov 20-23 '69, Dec 8 '69, Feb 12-14 '70, Nov 21 '71, Aug 23 '72, Aug 29 '72, Dec 15 '72, Jan 14 '73, Jun 1 '77, Dec 23 '77, Aug 6 '80, Aug 23 '80, Dec 22 '82, Apr 20 '85, Nov 9 '90, Jun 12 '92, Jun 12 '92, Sep 6 '92, Feb 11 '93. **Louise** Mar 30 '71, Apr 7 '71. **Love Gets You** (267S, 267A), Jul '82, Aug 19 '83, Sep 7 '83. **Love In The City** Apr 11-17 '69, Jun 24-30 '69, Sep 9 '69, Oct 17 '69. **Love Me Till The Sun Shines** (101S, 104A), Mar '67, Jul 3 '67, Jul 7 '67, Aug 2 '67, Aug 4 '67, Apr 28 '68, Jul 1 '68, Jul 9 '68, Oct 23-25 '69, Nov 20-23 '69. **Low Budget** (song), (226S, 230A, 232S, 233S, 238A, 239V, 282A), Jan '79, Jan 23 '79, Jan 26 '79, Feb 17 '79, Feb 18 '79, Mar 3 '79, Mar 10 '79, Mar 12 '79, Jul 14 '79, Aug 7 '79, Aug 16 '79, Sep 5 '79, Sep 23 '79, Oct 16 '79, Oct 20 '79, Nov 19 '79, Feb 21 '80, Aug 6 '80, Aug 23 '80, Sep 25 '80, Oct 27 '80, Nov 30 '80, Dec 5 '80, Dec 31 '80, May 6 '81, Jun 28 '81, Aug 14 '81, Oct 3 '81, Jan 10 '82, Feb 25-27 '82, Apr '82, Dec 22 '82, Apr 26 '83, May 24 '83, Dec 31 '83, Dec 21 '84, Sep 12-13 '85, May 17 '86, Mar 8 '87, May 28 '87, Jun 29 '87, Dec 20 '87, Apr 14 '88, Jun 9 '88, Oct 16 '89, May 9 '90, Aug 12 '90, Nov 9 '90, Aug 7 '91, Nov '91, Apr 25 '92, Jun 12 '92, Sep 6 '92, Mar 29 '93, May 4 '93, May 12 '93, Jun 17 '93, Jul 11 '93, Jul 27 '93, Oct 3 '93, Nov 25 '93, Dec 14 '93, Mar 22 '94, Jun 10 '94, Nov 8 '94, May 18-19 '95, Jul 11-13 '95. ***Low Budget* album** (230A), May '79, Jun '79, Jul 10 '79, Aug 27 '79, Sep 7 '79, Jan '80.

Mack The Knife Jan '90. **Malaguena** Oct '61, '62, Dec 8 '66. **Mammy** Feb 27 '72, Mar 2-3 '72. **Man Of Destiny** The, Apr 6 '81. **Man Who Conned Dinner From The Ritz, The** Feb 12-14 '68. **Marathon** Mar 23 '70. **Massive Reductions** (248S, 273A), May '79, Jun '79, May 2 '81, Jun 19 '81, Aug/Sep '84, Oct '84, Apr 20 '85. **Matter Of Decision** (267A), Jul '82. **Maximum Consumption** (165A). **Maybe It's Because I'm A Londoner** Mar 31 '73. **Mean Disposition** (song) (267A, 268S), Jul '82, Nov 18 '83. ***Mean Disposition* proposed album title** Jun 13 '83. **Mean Woman Blues** Jun 13 '70. **Meditation** Apr 3 '90. **Members Of The Club** (296M), Mar '87, Aug '88. **Memphis** Oct '61. **Men Are Fools** Apr 6 '81. **Mick Avory's Underpants** Mar 29 '68. **Midnight Sun** Oct '73. **Milk Cow Blues** (72A, 103A), Jun 30 '65, Aug 4 '65, Aug 6 '65, Aug 10 '65, Nov 19 '65, Nov 23 '65, Dec 13 '65, Jun 13 '66, Sep 17 '66, Sep 24 '66, Sep 29 '66, Apr 19 '68, Apr 28 '68, Jun 9 '68, Oct 23-25 '69, Nov 20-23 '69, Feb 12-14 '70, Jun 13 '70, Aug 29 '70, Nov 21 '70, Jan 16 '71, Mar 1 '71, Mar 30 '71, Nov 21 '71, Aug 23 '72. **Million Pound Semi-Detached, The** Jan/Feb/Mar '89. **Mindless Child Of Motherhood** (129S, 142S, 161A), Aug 19 '68, Apr 11-17 '69, May 1 '69, Jun 20 '69, Jul 2 '69, Oct 23-25 '69, Nov 20-23 '69, May 18 '70, Jun 12 '70, Jun 13 '70, Jul 28 '70. **Mirror Of Love** (181S, 183A, 185S), Jan '74, Feb 18-20 '74, Feb 25 '74, Mar 22 '74, Apr 3 '74, Apr 5 '74, Jun 6 '74, Jun 16 '74, Jun 17-18 '74, Jun '74, Jun 28 '74, Jul 14 '74, Jul 15-20 '74, Jul 26 '74, Sep 23 '74, Nov 23 '74, Apr 13 '75, May 21 '75. **Misery** May '79. **Misfits** (song), (219A, 222S, 238A, 282A), Sep '77, Oct '77, Mar '78, May 19 '78, Jun 2 '78, Jul 29 '78, Sep 29 '78, Oct 1 '78, Oct 10 '78, Jan 23 '79, Feb 17 '79, Jul 14 '79, Aug 16 '79, Sep 23 '79, Oct 20 '79, Nov 19 '79, Oct 27 '80, Aug 14 '81, Oct 3 '81, Mar 8 '87, Jun 12 '92, May 4 '93. ***Misfits* album** (219A), Oct '77, Mar '78, Apr 10-11 '78, Apr 24 '78, May 17 '78, May 19 '78, Jul 10 '78. **Missing Persons** (273A, 277A), Jul '83, Oct '84, Dec 21 '84, Mar 20 '85, Apr 20 '85, Sep 12-13 '85, Nov 8 '94. **Mr. Big Man** (209A), Dec '76, May 4 '77, Jun 2 '78, Oct 1 '78, Oct 10 '78. **Mr. Churchill Says** (133A, 133S), Jul '69, Oct 23-25 '69, Dec 12 '69, Dec 18 '69, Jun 13 '70. **Mister Pleasant** (98S, 105S, 161A), Jan '67, Feb 6 '67, Mar 6 '67, Apr 3 '67, Apr 21 '67, Apr 28 '67, Apr 29 '67, May 4 '67, May 17 '67, May '67, May 24 '67, Aug '67, Aug 28 '67, Oct 13 '67, Oct 25 '67, Mar 27 '71. **Mr. Reporter** Dec '65, Feb 2 '66, Apr 11/12 '66, Apr 30 '66, Jul '66, Mar 6 '67, Mar '69, Jun 16 '69, Jul 2 '69. **Mr. Shoemaker's Daughter** Jan '69, Jun 16 '69, Jul 2 '69. **Mr. Songbird** (170A), Nov '67, Jun 20 '68, Oct '68, Jul 2 '69. **Mr. Wonderful** (165A), Nov 12-14 '70, Jan 31 '72, Mar 2-3 '72, Nov 17 '72, Dec 15 '72, Jan 14 '73, Feb 26 '73, Apr 11 '73, Apr 16 '74, Jul 14 '74, Sep 23 '74. **Misty Water** (170A, 268A), May '68, Jun 20 '68. **Moments** (151A, 152S), Oct '70, Apr 2 '71. **Monday Tuesday Wednesday** Dec '68, Feb 17 '69. **Money & Corruption** (178A), Jun 16 '74, Nov 23 '74, Jul '91. **Money Talks** (182S, 183A), Dec 8 '73, Feb 25 '74, Apr 1-2 '74, Apr 3 '74, Apr 16 '74, Apr '74, May 7 '74, Jun 6 '74, Jun 16 '74, Jul 14 '74, Sep 7 '74, Sep 23 '74, Nov 23 '74, Apr 13 '75, May 21 '75, Feb 29 '76, Feb 1-2 '77. **Money (That's What I Want)** Oct '61, Oct '63, Jan 28-31 '64, Apr 3 '74, Feb 21 '80, Feb 23 '80. **Moneygoround, The** (147A), Jan '69, Apr 10 '95, Aug 9 '95, Oct 9 '95. **Mongolia Song** (296M), Mar '87. **Monica** (121A), Jan 22 '68, Jun 20 '68, Jul 1 '68, Jul 9 '68, Jul 16 '68. **Morning Song** (178A), Feb '73, Nov 23 '74. **Most Exclusive Residence For Sale** (92A), Apr '66, Jun 9 '66. **Motorway** (165A), May 6 '72. **Mountain Woman** Oct 16 '71. **Move It** Oct '61. **Move Over** (239A), Oct '79. **Moving Pictures** (230A), May '79, Sep 28 '79. **Music Music Music** Jan 23 '67. ***Muswell Hillbillies* album** (157A), Mar 29 '71, Jul '71, Aug '71, Sep '71, Oct '71, Oct 22 '71, Nov '71, Nov 24 '71, Nov 26 '71, Jan 31 '72, Sep 29 '73, Jan '90. **Muswell Hillbilly** (157A, 165A, 203A, 326A, 340A), Nov '71, Mar 2-3 '72, Apr 12 '72, Nov 17 '72, Apr 11 '73, Mar 28 '77, Jan 23 '79, Jul 14 '79, Jan 7 '84, Jun 29 '87, Aug 12 '90, May 4 '93, Apr '94, Oct 16 '94, Jul 11-13 '95. **My Way** Apr 6 '73. **My Street** Sep '67. **Mystery Achievement** Aug 31 '81.

Naggin' (50A, 72A), Feb 15-17 '65, Feb 26 '65, Apr 20 '65, Feb 12-14 '70. **National Health** (230A, 235S, 238A), May '79, Jun '79, Jul 14 '79, Nov 30 '79, Feb '80, Mar '80. **Natural Gift** (283A), Aug '86. **Never Met A Girl Like You Before** (62S, 72A), Mar 31 '65, Apr 13-14 '65, Jul 30 '65, Aug 6 '65, Aug 10 '65, Nov 19 '65. **Never Say Yes** Dec '65. **New Orleans** Feb 17 '79, Aug 16 '79, Oct 20 '79. **New World** (310S), Jan/Feb/Mar '89, Jun 12 '92, Sep 6 '92, Mar 29 '93, Jun 17 '93, Jul 27 '93, Oct 3 '93, Nov 25 '93, Dec '93, Dec 14 '93, Mar 22 '94, Jun 10 '94, Oct 16 '94, Nov 8 '94. **New York City Blues** Dec 31 '80. **Newham At Work** Apr 6 '81. **Nice Blues** Dec 5 '80. **Night Time Is The Right Time** Apr '63 . **Night Train** Apr '63. **Nine To Five** (194A), Jul 25 '74. **No Guarantees** Sep '94. **No More Looking Back** (198A, 201S), Sep 16 '75, Nov 21 '75, Dec 29 '75, Jan 23 '76. **No More Mysteries** Apr '87. **No Return** (104A), Jan '67, Jul 3 '67. **No Surprises** (296M), Mar '87. **Nobody Gives** (183A). **Nobody's Fool** Aug '71, Jan '72. **Noise** (260S, 265A), Dec 17 '82, Apr 15 '83, Jul '83. **Not Fade Away** Nov 18 '94. **Not Far Away** (277A), Jul '83. **Nothin' In This World (Can Stop Me Worryin' 'Bout That Girl)** (50A), Feb 15-17 '65, Mar 5 '65, Apr 20 '65. **Nothing Lasts Forever** (183A), Nov 23 '74. **Nothing More To Lose** (239A, 244S), Jan '80, Aug '80, Aug 6 '80, Aug 23 '80, Sep 25 '80, Oct 27 '80, Nov 14 '80, Nov 30 '80, Dec 5 '80,
Dec 31 '80, May 6 '81, Jun 28 '81. **Nothing To Say** (133A), Aug 8 '69. **Now And Then** (300A, 309A), Dec 14 '65, Jan/Feb/Mar '89, Aug '89, May 9 '90, Aug 12 '90, Apr 25 '92.

Oh Boy Oct '61. **Oh Lord Don't Let Them Drop That Atom Bomb On Me** Jun/Jul '90. **Oh Oh Tokyo** Feb 25-27 '82. **Oh What A Day It's Gonna Be** Sep 30 '66. **Oh Where Oh Where Is Love** (183A). **Oh! Yeah** Mar '63 . **Oklahoma USA** (157A), Mar 7-10 '77, Apr 2 '84, Nov 21 '93, Nov 25 '93. **On The Map** (296M), Mar '87. **On The Outside Of Life** Sep '76. **Once A Thief** Feb '83. **One Fine Day** Oct 19 '63, Nov 16 '63, Jan 20 '64, Feb '64, Mar 6 '64. ***One For The Road* album** (238A), Aug 5 '79, Aug 16-19 '79, Sep 23 '79, Nov 11 '79, Nov 19 '79, Dec '79, Mar 2 '80, Mar '80, Apr '80, May '80, Jun 4 '80, Jul '80, Jul 18 '80, Aug 1 '80, Dec 8 '80. ***One For The Road* videocassette** (239V), Jul '80. **One Night With You** (266S), Oct '61, Feb 12-14 '70, Jun 13 '70, Aug 29 '70, Nov 21 '70, Jan 16 '71, Mar 1 '71, Mar 30 '71, Nov 21 '71, Aug 23 '72, Jul '82, Aug 19 '83. **One Of The Survivors** (173S, 174S, 178A, 203A), Feb '73, Mar '73, Mar 30 '73, Apr 20 '73, Jun 29 '73, Jul 15 '73, Sep 20 '73, Apr 3 '74, Apr 16 '74, Sep 7 '74, Feb 1-2 '77, Feb 19 '77, May 4 '77. **One Woman Man** Sep '76. **Only A Dream** (315A, 322S), Jan/Feb '92, May '92, Feb 10-11 '93, Feb 11 '93, Mar 8 '93, Mar 23 '93, Mar 29 '93, May 4 '93, May 12 '93, Jun 17 '93, Jul 11 '93, Jul 27 '93, Oct 3 '93, Nov 15 '93, Nov 25 '93, Dec 14 '93. **Only Child** Jan 9-13 '75. **Ooladiooba** Dec 16 '63 . **Open Up Your Heart** Mar '91. **Optimist, The** May '79. **Ordinary People** (192S, 194A), Jul 25 '74, Apr 1 '75, Jun 14 '75, Feb 1-2 '77, Feb 19 '77, May 4 '77. **Our World** Mar '87. **Out Of The Wardrobe** (219A), Sep '77, Oct '77, Mar '78, May 13 '78. **Over The Edge** (315A), Dec '91, Jun 14 '93, Jun 17 '93, Oct 3 '93, Nov 25 '93, Dec 14 '93, Jan '94.

Parklife Mar '95, Jul 7 '96. ***Part One: Lola Versus Powerman & The Moneygoround* album** (147A), Apr 21

all day and all of the night 351

'69, Oct '70, Nov 5-6 '70, Nov 27 '70, Dec 2 '70. ***Part Two* proposed album** Dec '70, Jan 28 '71, Feb 8 '71, Mar 29 '71, Apr 8-10 '71. **Party Line** (92A), Apr 11/12 '66, Sep 19 '66. **Payback** Apr 6 '81. **Peggy Sue** Sep 28 '63, Feb 2-3 '79. **People Take Pictures Of Each Other** (121A), Jul '68, Oct '68, Jan '73, Jan 14 '73, Feb '73, Apr 11 '73. ***Percy* soundtrack album** (151A), Aug 10 '70, Aug 17 '70, Oct '70, Nov 16-18 '70, Nov 30 '70, Jan '71, Jan 28 '71, Feb 8 '71, Feb 11 '71, Mar 1 '71, Mar 8 '71, Mar 12 '71, Mar 26 '71, Apr 28 '71, May 25 '71. **Perfect Strangers** (300A), Jan/Feb/Mar '89, Jun '89. **Perfidia** Oct '61. **Permanent Waves** (219A), Sep '77, Oct '77, May 19 '78, Jun 2 '78, Jul 29 '78, Oct 1 '78, Feb 17 '79, Jul 14 '79, Aug 16 '79. ***Permanent Waves* proposed album title** Mar '78. **Peter Gunn** Oct '61. **Phenomenal Cat** (121A), Jan 22 '68, Jun 20 '68, Sep 4-6 '68. **Phobia** (song), (315A), Dec '91, May '92, Mar 29 '93, May 4 '93, May 12 '93, Jun 17 '93, Jul 11 '93, Jul 12 '93, Jul 27 '93, Oct 3 '93, Nov 25 '93, Dec 14 '93, Jan '94, Mar 22 '94, Jun 10 '94, Oct 16 '94, Nov 8 '94. ***Phobia* album** (315A), Nov '90, Nov '91, Aug '92, Sep 4 '92, Sep 15 '92, Dec '92, Jan '93, Feb '93, Mar 18 '93, Mar 29 '93, Apr 12 '93, Apr 13 '93, Dec 21 '93. **Picture Book** (121A, 124S, 340A), May '68, Jun 20 '68, Jul 22 '68, Dec '68, Jan 7 '69, Jan 8 '69, Jan '73, Jan 14 '73, Feb '73, Apr 11 '73, Apr '94. **Pictures In The Sand** (170A, 268A), May 27 '68, Jul 2 '69. **Place In Your Heart, A** (296M). **Plastic Man** (126S, 170A), May 12-13 '66, Mar '69, Mar 27 '69, Mar 28 '69, Apr 2 '69, Apr 5 '69, Apr 8 '69, Apr 10 '69, May 1 '69, Jul 2 '69. **Please Stay** Apr 28 '85. **Poison Ivy** Oct '63, Jan 28-31 '64. **Polly** (112S, 161A), Mar '68, Apr 5 '68, Apr 22 '68, May 15 '68, Jun 20 '68. **Poor Old Intellectual Sadie** Jan 15-17 '68. **Poseur, The** Jul '76. **Possession** Aug '86. **Power Of Gold** Jun 25 '76. **Powerman** (147A), Mar 9-20 '70, Apr '70, May '70, Jan 16 '71, Feb 10 '71, Mar 1 '71, Mar 9 '71, Mar '71, Mar 30 '71, Nov 5-10 '96. **Predictable** (250A, 254S), Apr '81, May 2 '81, Aug '81, Oct 30 '81, Nov '81, Dec 8 '81. **Preservation** (song), (188S), Oct '74, Oct 28 '74, Nov 12 '74, Sep '90, Feb '91, Jul '91. ***Preservation: A Play In Two Acts* reissued albums** Sep '90, Oct '90, Nov '90, Jan '91, Feb '91, May '91, Jun '91, Jul '91. ***Preservation Act I* album** (178A), Nov 25-25 '66, Jun 8 '73, Jun '73, Aug 30 '73, Sep '73, Sep 25 '73, Nov 16 '73 (see also *Preservation: A Play In Two Acts*). ***Preservation Act 2* album** (183A), Dec 8 '73, Jan '74, Feb 12 '74, Feb 18-20 '74, Feb '74, Feb 27-28 '74, Mar 4-5 '74, Mar 11-14 '74, Mar 24-28 '74, Apr 1-2 '74, Apr 3 '74, Apr 8-9 '74, May 8 '74, May 27 '74, Jul 26 '74, Jul 1 '93 (see also *Preservation: A Play In Two Acts*). **Pressure** (230A, 235S, 238A, 239V), Jan '79, Jul 14 '79, Aug 16 '79, Sep 23 '79, Oct 16 '79, Oct 20 '79, Nov 19 '79, Nov 30 '79, Feb 21 '80, Aug 6 '80, Aug 23 '80, Sep 25 '80, Oct 27 '80, Nov 30 '80, Dec 5 '80, Dec 31 '80, May 6 '81, Jun 28 '81, Oct 3 '81, Jan 10 '82, Feb 25-27 '82, Apr '82, Dec 22 '82, Apr 26 '83, May 24 '83, Apr 2 '84, May 17 '86, May 28 '87. **Pretty Polly** *see* Polly. **Prince Of The Punks** (216S, 238A), Jul '76, Oct '77, Nov 25 '77, Dec 8 '77, Nov '78, Feb '80, Feb 21 '80, Mar '80. **Priscilla & Sybilla** Nov 24-25 '66, Dec 27 '66 (*see also* Two Sisters),. **Privilege** Apr 6 '81. **Property** (265A), Feb '83, Mar 19 '83, Dec 4-9 '83, Apr 2 '84. **Pub With No Beer, A** Feb 23 '71, Mar 1 '71, Mar 30 '71.

Quiet Life (281A, 282S), Jan '85, Mar '86, Apr '86, May 12 '86, Feb '88.

Rainy Day In June (92A), Jun 6 '66. **Ramrod** Oct '61, Apr '63 . **Rats** (147A, 147S), Nov 27 '70, Dec 16 '70. **Rave On** Oct '61, Sep 28 '63. ***Ray Davies Songbook* proposed album** Apr 2 '71, May '71, Jun '71. **Reelin' And Rockin'** Feb 26 '73. **Regatta My Ass** Aug 7 '93. **Regret It** Sep '82. **Repetition** (283A), Aug '86. **Reporter, The** Apr '66 *see also* Mr Reporter. **Reputation** Apr 6 '81. **Restless** Jun 25 '76. **Return To Waterloo** (song), (277A), Jul '83, Apr '85, Aug '85, Sep 12-13 '85. ***Return To Waterloo* soundtrack album** (277A), Apr '85, May/Jun '85, Jul 1 '85. **Reveal Yourself** (249A), Mar '81. **Revenge** (37A), Dec 16 '63, Jan 28-31 '64, Sep 26 '64, Oct 27 '64, Feb 19 '65. **Riders In The Sky** Oct '61. **Ring The Bells** (72A), Jun 30 '65, Jul 7 '65, Aug '65, Aug 6 '65. **Rip It Up** Jun 11 '68, Oct 23-25 '69, Dec 8 '69, Feb 12-14 '70, Jun 13 '70. **Road, The** (song), (291A, 309A), Mar 6 '64, Mar 21 '64, Aug '87, Sep 5 '87, Dec 20 '87, Dec 21 '87, Dec 23 '87, Feb '88, Apr 14 '88, Jun 9 '88. ***Road, The,* album** (291A), Jul 1 '87, Nov '87, Dec 9 '87, Jan '88, May '88. **Rock Around The Clock** Feb 19 '72, Apr 6 '74. **Rock'n'Roll Cities** (283A, 284S), Aug '86, Oct '86, Nov 12 '86, Nov 17 '86. **Rock'n'Roll Fantasy, A** (219A, 219S, 282A), Aug '77, Sep '77, Oct '77, Jan '78, Mar '78, May 19 '78, May 19 '78, Jun 2 '78, Jun '78, Jul 29 '78, Sep 11 '78, Oct 1 '78, Oct 10 '78, Feb 17 '79, Feb 23 '79, Mar 10 '79, Nov 19 '79, Dec '79, Feb 21 '80, Oct 27 '80, Jul 28 '95, Jul 31 '95. **Rory** Sep 5 '75. **Rosemary Rose** (170A, 268A), Mar '68, Jul 2 '69. **Rosie Rook** Jul '71. **Rosy Won't You Please Come Home** (92A), Jun 6 '66. **Route 66** Oct '63, Jan 28-31 '64. **Run** (239A). **Running Round Town** (151A), Oct '70. **Rush Hour Blues** (193S, 194A), Jul 25 '74, Apr 18 '75, Feb 29 '76, Feb 1-2 '77, Feb 19 '77, May 4 '77, Nov 23 '77, Dec 23 '77.

St Louis Blues Oct '61. **Salvation Road** (183A, 188S), Jan '73, Jan 14 '73, Feb '73, Sep 23 '74, Nov 12 '74, Nov 23 '74, Apr 13 '75. **Same Old Blues** Nov '78. **Sand In My Shoes** Nov 24-25 '66, Feb 6 '67. **Sausages And Eggs** Jan 15 '67. **Save The Last Dance For Me** Oct 11 '64. **Scattered** (315S, 315A), Jan/Feb/Mar '89, May '89, Oct '90, Sep '92, Oct '92, Feb 3 '93, Feb 14-15 '93, Mar 8 '93, Mar 15 '93, Mar 25 '93, Mar 29 '93, May 4 '93, Jun 17 '93, Jul 11 '93, Jul 12 '93, Nov 25 '93, Dec 14 '93, Mar 22 '94, Jun 10 '94, Oct 16 '94, Nov 8 '94, Apr 10 '95. ***Schoolboys In Disgrace* album** (198A), Apr 22 '75, Jul '75, Aug '75, Sep 2 '75, Sep 11/13/16 '75, Sep 22-24 '75, Sep 25-Oct 3 '75, Oct 5 '75, Oct 6 '75, Nov 17 '75, Jan 23 '76, Jan '90. **Schooldays** (198A), Sep 11 '75, Nov 21 '75, Feb 1-2 '77, Feb 19 '77, May 4 '77. **Scrapheap City** (173S, 183A), Feb '73, Mar '73, Mar 30 '73, Apr 20 '73, Nov 23 '74. **Scum Of The Earth** (183A), Nov 23 '74. **Sea Of Love** Apr '94. **Second Hand Car Spiv** (183A). ***Second Time Around* album** Aug 22 '80. **See My Friends** (62S, 72A, 106A, 139A, 326A, 340A), Aug 17 '64, Jan 18 '65, Jan 24 '65, Mar 31 '65, Apr 8 '65, Apr 9 '65, Apr 13-14 '65, May 3 '65, Jul 7 '65, Jul 12 '65, Jul 28 '65, Jul 30 '65, Aug 4 '65, Aug 5 '65, Aug 6 '65, Aug 8 '65, Aug 10 '65, Aug 19 '65, Aug 20 '65, Sep 1 '65, Sep 29 '65, Oct 5 '65, Jun 24 '66, Jun 9 '68, Jun 11 '68, Oct 23-25 '69, Nov 20-23 '69, Jun 13 '70, Nov 21 '70, Mar 1 '71, Mar 30 '71, Nov 23 '77, Aug 6 '80, Oct 27 '80, Apr '94, Oct 16 '94, Nov 18 '94, Apr 10 '95, Aug 9 '95, Oct 9 '95. **See The Beast** (239A), Oct '79. **Session Man** (92A), Jun 6 '66. **Set Me Free** (56S, 88A, 89A, 340A), Mar 31 '65, Apr 13-14 '65, May 14 '65, May 21 '65, May 26 '65, Jun 2 '65, Jun 3 '65, Jun 4 '65, Jun 6 '65, Jun 14 '65, Jun 28 '65, Jun 29 '65, Jul 1 '65, Jul 2 '65, Aug 3 '65, Aug 8 '65, Sep 1 '65, Oct 5 '65, Jun 9 '68, Feb 27 '70, Jul 2 '77, Jul 3 '77, Jan '90, Apr '94, Oct 16 '94, Apr 10 '95, May 18-19 '95, Jul 11-13 '95, Aug 9 '95, Oct 9 '95. **7th Channel** (249A), Mar '81. **Shake Rattle And Roll** Apr 6 '74. **Shakin' All Over** Aug 29 '72, Dec 15 '72, Feb 26 '73, Sep 20 '73, Feb 26 '74, Oct 3 '81, Dec 31 '83, Jan 7 '84. **Shangri-La** (132S, 133A, 161A), Jan 21 '65, Jan '69, Aug 25 '69, Sep 8 '69, Sep 9 '69, Sep 12 '69, Nov '71, Nov 21 '71, Nov 5-10 '96. **She Always Leaves Me Laughing** Jun 24-30 '69. **She Bought A Hat Like Princess Marina** (133A), Jul 14 '69, Jan '72, Jan 31 '72, Mar 2-3 '72. **She Can Move Mountains** Aug '74. **She's Got Everything** (117S, 161A), Feb 7 '66, Jun '68, Jun 20 '68, Jun 28 '68, Jul 22 '68, Jul 24 '68. **She's Got It** Jun 13 '66. **She's My Girl** Jun 27-28 '66. **She's So Contrary** May/Jun '85. **Shepherds Of The Nation** (183A, 187S), Dec 8 '73, Nov 23 '74. **Shoe Without A Lace** Mar 31 '71. **Singing In The Rain** Sep 5 '87, Aug 11 '91. **Singing The Blues** Jun 12 '92, Apr '94. **Sir Jasper** Apr 11/12 '66, May 12-13 '66 (*see also* Lilacs And Daffodils). **Sitting By The Riverside** (121A), Jul '68, Jul 22 '68. **Sitting In My Hotel** (165A, 168S, 176S, 203A), Sep 21 '73. **Sitting In The Midday Sun** (174S, 178A, 203A), Jun '73, Jun 23 '73, Jun 29 '73, Jul 13 '73, Aug '73. **Sitting In The Stands** May '94. **Sittin' On My Sofa** (77S, 106A), Dec 29/30 '65, Jan '66, Feb 24 '66, Apr 25-27 '66. **Situation Vacant** (104A), Mar '67. **Skin And Bone** (157A, 158S, 165A, 203A), Nov '71, Dec '71, Jan '72, Mar 2-3 '72, May 5 '72, Jun 9 '72, Jun 14 '72, Jun 15 '72, Aug 23 '72, Nov 17 '72, Dec 15 '72, Feb 26 '73, Apr 11 '73, Apr 11 '73, Jul 15 '73, Sep 20 '73, Feb 26 '74, Apr 3 '74, Apr 16 '74, May 7 '74, Jun 4 '74, Jun 16 '74, Jul 14 '74, Sep 7 '74, Sep 23 '74, Nov 23 '74, Apr 13 '75, May 21 '75, Dec 23 '77, Dec 24 '77, Jan 23 '79, Jul 28 '95. **Sleepless Night**, (209A, 213S), Sep '76, Jan 1-4 '77, Jun 3 '77, Sep '78, Feb 17 '79. **Sleepwalker** (song), (209A, 210S, 282A), Sep '76, Oct '76, Jan 17-20 '77, Jan 26 '77, Feb 1-2 '77, Feb 19 '77, Feb 22 '77, Feb 26 '77, Mar 7-10 '77, Mar 18 '77, Mar 25 '77, Mar 28 '77, Apr 23 '77, May 4 '77, Nov 23 '77, Dec 23 '77, Dec 24 '77, Jun 2 '78, Jul 29 '78, Oct 1 '78, Oct 10 '78, Jan 23 '79, Feb 17 '79, Mar 10 '79, Jul 14 '79, Aug 16 '79, Sep 23 '79, Oct 20 '79, Nov 19 '79, Dec '79, Mar '88, Apr 14 '88, May 18-19 '95, Jul 11-13 '95. ***Sleepwalker* album** (209A), Nov '76, Dec '76, Jan 1-4 '77, Feb 12 '77, Feb 25 '77, Apr 17 '77. **Slum Kids** Nov 23 '74, May 21 '75, Nov 23 '77, Dec 23 '77, Dec 24 '77, May 19 '78, Jun 2 '78, Jul 29 '78, Oct 1 '78, Oct 10 '78, Oct 22 '78, Jan 23 '79, Feb 17 '79, Mar 10 '79, Dec '79, Sep '90, Feb '91. **Smokestack Lightning** Oct '63, Jan 28-31 '64, Mar 29 '64, Aug 18 '64. **So It Goes** Jan 9-13 '75, Mar 28 '75. **So Long** (50A), Feb 15-17 '65, Mar 5 '65. **So Mystifying** (37A, 41A), Sep 3 '64, Sep 26 '64. **So You Want To Be A Rock'n'Roll Star** Apr '94. ***Soap Opera, A* album** (194A), Aug '74, Sep '74, Sep 11 '74, Oct 4 '74, Oct 8 '74, Oct '74, Jan '75, Jan 30 '75, Feb 5 '75, Mar 21 '75, Apr 25 '75, May 16 '75, Jan '90. **Sold Me Out** (273A, 277A), Jul '83, Oct '84, Sep 7 '85. **Some Mother's Son** (133A), Aug 19 '68, Jan '69, Jun 13 '70, Jan 31 '72. **Somebody Stole My Car** (315A, 322S), Oct '90, May 12 '93, Nov 16 '93. **Something Better Beginning** (50A, 88A), Dec '64, Dec 22-23 '64, Mar 23 '65. ***Something Else By The Kinks* album** (104A), Nov 24-25 '66, Apr 24 '67, Jul 24 '67, Sep 15 '67, Nov 14 '67, Jan 2-6 '68, Jan 24 '68. **Somewhere Friday Night** Jun 24-30 '69. ***Songs I Sang For Auntie* proposed album** May '71, Jun '71. **Spotty Grotty Anna** (268A). **Stagefright** Jun 25 '76. **Starmaker** (192S), Jul 25 '74, Mar 6 '75, Apr 1 '75, Feb 29 '76, Feb 1-2 '77. **Starstruck** (121A, 124S), Jul '68, Oct '68, Nov '68, Jan 8 '69, Feb '88. **State Of Confusion** (song), (265A, 270E, 340A), Mar '83, Apr '83, Apr 26 '83, May 24 '83, Dec 31 '83, Jan 7 '84, Mar 23 '84, Apr 2 '84, Dec 21 '84, Mar 20 '85, Apr 20 '85, Sep 12-13 '85, May 17 '86, Mar 8 '87, May 9 '90, Aug 12 '90, Nov 9 '90, Mar 25 '94, Jun 10 '94, Oct 16 '94. ***State Of Confusion* album** (265A), Mar '83, Apr 9 '83, May 10 '83, May 24 '83, Jun 10-11 '83. **Still I'm Sad**, Jun 12 '92. **Still Searching** (315A), Sep '77, Oct '90, May '92, Sep 6 '92, Sep 7 '92, Sep '92, Feb 3 '93, Feb 4 '93, Feb 11 '93, Mar 29 '93, Mar 30 '93, May 4 '93, Jul 9 '93, Jul 11 '93, Jul 27 '93, Apr 10 '95. **Stop Your Sobbing** (37A, 41A, 238A), Jul 27-30 '64, Sep 3 '64, Dec 9 '64, Jan 19 '79, Feb '80, Oct 27 '80, Dec 5 '80, Dec 31 '80, Jun 28 '81, Jan 10 '82, Feb 25-27 '82, Apr '82, Oct 16 '89, Nov 25 '93, Dec 14 '93, Mar 22 '94, May 18-19 '95. **Stormy Sky** (209A), Oct '76, Feb 1-2 '77, Feb 19 '77, Mar 28 '77, May 4 '77, Nov 23 '77. **Strangers** (147A), Nov 12-14 '70, Nov 21 '70, Jan 16 '71, Apr 7 '71, Nov 21 '71. **Such A Shame** (66E, 72A, 106A), Mar 31 '65, Apr 13-14 '65, Aug '65, Nov 3-4 '65. **Suicidal** Mar 30 '71. **Summer's Gone** (273A, 273S, 276S), Aug/Sep '84, Oct '84, Feb '85, Mar 18 '85, Apr 19 '85. **Sunny Afternoon** (92A, 103A, 106A, 139A, 161A, 326A, 340A), May 12-13 '66, May 16 '66, May 23 '66, May 23-25 '66, Jun 3 '66, Jun 4 '66, Jun 8 '66, Jun 9 '66, Jun 11 '66, Jun 20 '66, Jun 23 '66, Jun 24 '66, Jun 30 '66, Jul 4 '66, Jul 7 '66, Jul 20 '66, Sep 17 '66, Sep 19 '66, Sep 24 '66, Sep 29 '66, Dec 27 '66, Feb 20 '67, Apr 29 '67, Oct 25 '67, Apr 28 '68, Jun 9 '68, Jun 11 '68, Jul 22 '68, Oct 23-25 '69, May 18 '70, Jun 13 '70, Aug 21 '70, Aug 29 '70, Nov 12-14 '70, Jan 16 '71, Mar 1 '71, Mar 30 '71, Apr 7 '71, Jan 31 '72, Mar 2-3 '72, Aug 23 '72, Nov 17 '72, Dec 15 '72, Jan 14 '73, Feb 26 '73, Apr 11 '73, Jul 15 '73, Feb 26 '74, Apr 3 '74, Apr 16 '74, Jun 16 '74, Sep 7 '74, Sep 23 '74, Jun 13 '75, Feb 1-2 '77, Feb 19 '77, Mar 25 '77, May 4 '77, Nov 23 '77, Dec 23 '77, Dec 24 '77, May 19 '78, Jun 2 '78, Jul 29 '78, Oct 1 '78, Oct 10 '78, Jan 23 '79, Feb 17 '79, Jul 14 '79, Aug 16 '79, Sep 23 '79, Nov 19 '79, Dec '79, Feb 21 '80, Aug 6 '80, Aug 23 '80, Oct 27 '80, Dec 20 '87, Jun 9 '88, Aug 12 '90, Jun '91, Aug 7 '91, Jun 12 '92, Feb 14-15 '93, Mar 23 '93, Mar 29 '93, Jun 17 '93, Jul 11 '93, Nov 25 '93, Dec 14 '93, Mar 22 '94, Mar 25 '94, Jun 10 '94, Sep '94, Apr 10 '95, May 18-19 '95, Jul 11-13 '95, Aug 9 '95, Oct 9 '95, Feb 21-25 '96, Jun 21 '96, Jul 7 '96, Dec 2 '96. ***Sunny Afternoon* album** (106A), Oct 21 '66, Apr 24 '67, Nov 17 '67. **Supersonic Rocketship** (163S, 165A), Feb '72, Feb 11 '72, Apr '72, Apr 13 '72, May '72, May 5 '72, Jun 14 '72, Jun 15 '72, Jun 22 '72. **Surviving** (315A), Dec '91. **Susannah's Still Alive** (107S, 139A, 161A), Aug 12-13 '67, Oct '67, Oct 25 '67, Nov 14 '67, Nov 24 '67, Dec 7 '67, Dec 13 '67, Jan 12 '68, Jan 31 '68, Jun 20 '68, Jul 9 '68, Jul 2 '69, Aug 7 '91, Nov 18 '94, Jan/Feb '95. **Suspicion**, Jul '62 . **Sweet Lady Genevieve** (174S, 176S, 178A), Jul '73, Jul 13 '73, Aug '73, Sep 21 '73, Aug 10 '91, Feb 4 '93, Jul 27 '93, Oct 3 '93, Nov 25 '93, Dec 14 '93, Apr '94, Aug 9 '95. **Sweet Little Rock'n'Roller** Mar 25 '77. **Sweet Little Sixteen** Jan 28-31 '64, Sep 20 '73.

Take One More Chance (267A), Jul '82. **Talkin' Bout You** Jan 28-31 '64, Mar 29 '64. **Tapas** (267A), Jul '82. **Taxi** Jan 15 '67. **Telepathy** (249A), Mar '81. **Tell Him Tell Her** (296M), Mar '87. **Tell Me Now So I'll Know** May 24 '65. **That Is What The World Is All About** Feb 26-28 '68. **That Old Black Magic** Apr 10 '95, Aug 9 '95, Oct 9 '95. **That's All I Want** Jan 6 '64. ***Then Now And Inbetween* promo album** Jul 3 '69. **There Is No Life Without Love** (119S, 170A), Mar '68, Apr 1 '68, Jun 20 '68, Aug 30 '68, Jul 2 '69. **There's A Change In The Weather** (178A), Jun 16 '74, Nov 23 '74. **There's A New World (That's Opening For Me)** May 24 '65, Jun '65 . **Things Are Getting Better** (41E), Oct '64, Nov 16 '64 . **Think It Over** Sep 28 '63. **Think Visual** (song), (283A, 291A, 309A), Aug '86, Mar 8 '87, Apr '87, May 28 '87, Jun 22 '87, Jun 29 '87, Jul 1 '87, Dec 20 '87, Mar '88, Apr 14 '88, Jun 9 '88. ***Think Visual* album** (283A), Jun '86, Jul '86, Aug '86, Oct '86, Nov 17 '86, Nov 24 '86, Jan '87. **This I Know** May '65, Jun '65. **This Is Where I Belong** (98S, 161A), Mar 31 '66, May 12-13 '66, Mar 6 '67, Apr 16 '67, Apr 28 '67, Jul 2 '69. **This Man He Weeps Tonight** (132S, 170A), Jan '69, Mar '69, Jul 2 '69, Sep 12 '69. **This Strange Effect** Jan 24 '65, May 24 '65, Jul 2 '65, Aug 6 '65, Aug 8 '65. **This Time Tomorrow** (147A), May 24 '70. **Till Death Us Do Part** (170A), Sep '68, Nov '68, Dec 20 '68, Feb 14 '69, Jul 2 '69. **Till The End Of The Day** (70S, 72A, 88A, 89A, 103A, 139A, 238A, 340A), Jun 30 '65, Nov 3-4 '65, Nov 10 '65, Nov 17 '65, Nov 19 '65, Nov 23 '65, Nov 28 '65, Dec 9 '65, Dec 10 '65, Dec 13 '65, Dec 16 '65, Dec 21 '65, Dec 22 '65, Jan 6 '66, Jan 13 '66, Jan 14 '66, Mar 2 '66, May 8 '66, Sep 17 '66, Sep 24 '66, Sep 29 '66, Apr 3 '67, Apr 16 '67, Jun 8 '68, Jun 9 '68, Oct 23-25 '69, Jun 13 '70, Aug 29 '70, Nov 12-14 '70, Jan 16 '71, Mar 1 '71, Mar 30 '71, Apr 7 '71, Nov 21 '71, Jan 31 '72, Mar 2-3 '72, Nov 17 '72, Feb 26 '73, Apr 11 '73, Nov 23 '77, Jan 23 '79, Nov 19 '79, Dec '79, Dec 5 '80, Dec 31 '80, May 6 '81, Jun 28 '81, Oct 3 '81, Jan 10 '82, Feb 25-27 '82, Apr '82, Dec 22 '82, Apr 26 '83, May 24 '83, Dec 31 '83, Jan 7 '84, Mar 20 '85, Apr 20 '85, May 17 '86, Mar 8 '87, Dec 20 '87, Jun 9 '88, Mar '90, May 9 '90, Aug 7 '91, Jun 12 '92, Sep 6 '92, Mar 29 '93, May 4 '93, Jun 14 '93, Jun 17 '93, Jul 11 '93, Jul 27 '93, Oct 3 '93, Nov 25 '93, Dec 14 '93, Jan '94, Mar 22 '94, Mar 25 '94, Jun 10 '94, Oct 7 '94, Oct 16 '94, Nov 8 '94, May 18-19 '95, Jul 11-13 '95. **Time Song** Jan '73, Jan 14 '73, Feb '73. **Time Will Tell** (268A), Oct 25-26 '65. **Tin Soldier Man** (104A), Nov 24-25 '66, Feb 6 '67, Jul 3 '67. **Tired Of Waiting For You** (46S, 50A, 88A, 89A, 103A, 139A, 326A, 340A), Aug 24 '64, Aug 28 '64, Sep 2 '64, Sep 3 '64, Dec 29 '64, Jan 3 '65, Jan 6 '65, Jan 7 '65, Jan 15 '65, Feb 5 '65, Feb 7-8 '65, Feb 18 '65, Feb 19 '65, Feb 23 '65, Feb 24 '65, Feb 26 '65, Mar 13 '65, Apr 11 '65, Apr 19 '65, Apr 30 '65, Jul 1 '65, Jul 2 '65, Oct 1-3 '65, Oct 5 '65, Dec 21 '65, Nov 20-23 '69, May 4 '77, Jul 3 '77, Nov 23 '77, Dec 23 '77, Oct 1 '78, Oct 10 '78, Aug 6 '80, Sep 25 '80, Oct 27 '80, Nov 30 '80, Dec 5 '80, Dec 31 '80, May 6 '81, Jun 28 '81, Aug 14 '81, Jan 10 '82, Feb 25-27 '82, Dec 22 '82, Jan 7 '84, Apr 2 '84, May 28 '87, Aug 12 '90, Nov 9 '90, Aug 7 '91, Mar 29 '93, Apr '94, Sep '94, Apr 10 '95, Aug 9 '95, Oct 9 '95. **To The Bone** (song), (340A), Mar '95, Apr 10 '95, Aug 9 '95, Oct 9 '95, Feb 21-25 '96, Mar '96, Jul 7 '96, Aug '96, Oct 4-5 '96, Oct 7 '96, Oct 18 '96, Oct 24 '96, Nov 3 '96, Nov 16 '96, Dec 2 '96, Dec 10 '96. ***To The Bone* album** (326A, 340A), Nov 25 '93, Apr '94, Jul/Aug '94, Sep '94, Oct 3 '94, Jan '96, Feb '96, Mar '96, Apr '96, Jul 18 '96, Oct 15 '96. **Too Hot** (272S, 273A), Feb 20 '84, May '84, Jun/Jul '84, Oct '84. **Too Much Monkey Business** (37A, 41A), Jan 28-31 '64, Mar 29 '64, Aug 18 '64, Oct 30 '64. **Too Much On My Mind** (92A), Jun 6 '66, Mar '88, Apr 14 '88, Jun 9 '88, May 9 '90, Sep 6 '92, Nov 25 '93, Apr '94, Oct 16 '94, Nov 8 '94, Jan/Feb '95. **Too Serious** (249A), Mar '81, Aug 4 '81, Aug 14 '81, Oct 3 '81. **Top Of The Pops** (147A, 165A), Nov 12-14 '70, Nov 21 '70, Jan 16 '71, Mar 1 '71, Mar 30 '71, Apr 7 '71, Nov 21 '71, Mar 2-3 '72, Aug 23 '72, Nov 17 '72, Dec 15 '72, Mar '90. **Torn Between Temptations** Jun 24-30 '69. **Toymaker** Dec '68, Jan 31 '69. **Train And The River, The** '62 . **True Story** (267A), Jul '82. **Trust Your Heart** (219A), Sep '77, Jun 2 '78, Jul 29 '78, Oct 1 '78, Oct 10 '78, Jan 23 '79, Feb 17 '79, Mar 10 '79. **Trying To Work It All Out** Jun '74. **Tutti Frutti** Jan 28-31 '64, Mar 29 '64. **20th Century Man** (157A, 158S, 203A, 238A, 270E), Dec 4 '71, Dec '71, Mar 2-3 '72, Mar 7-10 '77, May 4 '77, Feb '79, Mar 3 '79, Nov 30 '80, Dec 5 '80, May 6 '81, Jun 28 '81, Aug 14 '81, Oct 3 '81, Apr 26 '83, Dec 31 '83, Jan 7 '84, Mar 23 '84, Apr 2 '84, Dec 21 '84, Sep 12-13 '85, May 17 '86, Mar 8 '87, Dec 14 '93, Jun 10 '94, Nov 18 '94, Apr 10 '95, Jul 11-13 '95, Aug 9 '95, Oct 9 '95, Oct 24 '96. **Twist And Shout** Sep 28 '63, Aug 23 '72, Jul '78, Jul 29 '78, Oct 1 '78, Oct 10 '78, Jul 14 '79, Aug 16 '79, Sep 23 '79, Oct 20 '79, Nov 19 '79, Feb 21 '80, Aug 23 '80, Sep 25 '80, Oct 27 '80, Nov 30 '80, Dec 5 '80, May 6 '81, Jun 28 '81, Aug 14 '81, Oct 3 '81, Jan 10 '82, Dec 22 '82, May 28 '87, Oct 16 '89, Aug 15 '90, Mar 29 '93, Jul 11 '93, Mar 22 '94, Apr '94, Nov 8 '94. **Two Sisters** (99S, 104A, 139A), Nov 24-25 '66, Feb 6 '67, Mar 6 '67, Apr 21 '67, May 4 '67, Jul 26 '67, Jul 22 '68, Dec 28 '83, Mar 29 '93, Apr '94, Aug 9 '95, Oct 9 '95.

UK Jive (song), (300A, 309A), Aug '89, Oct 16 '89, May 9 '90, Aug 12 '90, Nov 9 '90, Aug 7 '91, Jun 12 '92, Sep 6 '92. ***UK Jive* album** (300A), Oct/Nov '88, Aug '89, Sep 4 '89, Oct 2 '89, Oct 3-4 '89, Oct 30 '89. ***Ultimate Collection, The* album** Sep 4 '89. **Uncle Son** (157A), Apr '94. **Underneath The Neon Sign** (194A), Jan 30 '75, Jun 14 '75. **Unfinished Business** Mar '96 . **Unreal Reality** (165A), Aug 23 '72. **Up On A High Rise Block** Apr 6 '81. **Using Me** Feb '73. .

Victoria (133A, 133S, 161A, 238A, 239V, 240E), Jan '69, Oct 15 '69, Oct 23-25 '69, Nov 20-23 '69, Dec 11 '69, Dec 12 '69, Dec 18 '69, Feb 12-14 '70, Jun 13 '70, Apr 7 '71, Nov 21 '71, Mar 2-3 '72, Aug 23 '72, Dec 15 '72, Jan 14 '73, Jan 24 '73, Feb 26 '73, Apr 11 '73, Jul 15 '73, Sep 20 '73, Feb 26 '74, Apr 16 '74, Jun 16 '74, Jul 14 '74, Sep 7 '74, Sep 23 '74, Nov 23 '74, Feb 19 '77, Apr 29 '77, May 4 '77, Dec 23 '77, Feb '79, Mar 10 '79, Aug 16 '79, Sep 23 '79, Nov 11 '79, Nov 19 '79, Dec 22 '82, Dec 2 '84, Dec 21 '84, May 28 '87, Feb '88, Mar '90, Jul 27 '93, Nov 18 '94, Apr 10 '95, May 18-19 '95, Aug 9 '95, Oct 9 '95, Oct 23 '95, Oct 7 '96. **Video Shop, The** (283A, 309A), Jan '86, Mar '86, Mar 8 '87. **Village Green** (121A), Aug 16 '66, Aug 20 '66, Nov 24-25 '66, Feb 6 '67, Mar 6 '67, Apr 16 '67, Apr 21 '67, Jun '68, Jan 14 '73, Jan 14 '73, Apr 12 '95, Aug 9 '95, Oct 9 '95. **Village Green Overture, The** Jan 14 '73, Jan 24 '73. **Village Green Preservation Society, The** (song), (121A, 161A, 340A), Aug 12 '68, Nov 26 '68, Dec '68, Oct 23-25 '69, Nov 20-23 '69, Aug 23 '72, Jan 14 '73, Jan 24 '73, Feb '73, Oct 3 '81, Oct 16 '89, Oct 11 '93, Apr '94, Apr 10 '95, Jul 28 '95, Nov 5-10 '96. ***Village Green Preservation Society, The Kinks Are* album** (121A), Nov 24-25 '66, Apr 24 '67, Nov '67, Jun '68, Jul 1 '68, Jul 15 '68, Aug 12 '68, Aug 16 '68, Sep '68, Sep 23 '68, Sep 27 '68, Oct '68, Oct 23-26 '68, Nov '68, Nov 22 '68, Dec 20 '68, Feb 5 '69, Dec 11 '72, Dec 18 '72, Jan '73, Jan 7 '73, Jan 10-11 '73, Jan 12 '73, Jan 14 '73, Aug '80. **Violet Dreams** Sep '77. **Virgin Soldiers (March; Ballad Of The)** Jan 13 '69, Mar '69, Nov 2 '69, Mar 27-29 '70. **Visionary Dreamer** (239A), Jan '80. **Voices In The Dark** (277A, 282S), Apr '85, May 12 '86. .

Wait Jul '87. **Wait Till The Summer Comes Along** (66E, 72A, 89A), May 3 '65. **Walk Don't Run** Oct '61. **Wall Of Fire** (315A), May '92, Aug '92, Sep 7 '92, Mar 29 '93, May 4 '93, Jun 17 '93, Nov 25 '93, Jan '94, Mar 22 '94, Jun 10 '94. **War Is Over** (300A), Dec '88, Aug '89, Nov '89. **Waterloo Sunset** (99S, 104A, 139A, 161A, 326A), Mar '67, Mar 27 '67, Apr 3 '67, Apr 10 '67, Apr 13 '67, Apr 16 '67, Apr 21 '67, May 4 '67, May 5 '67, May 10 '67, May 17 '67, May '67, May 25 '67, Jun 1 '67, Jul 26 '67, Apr 19 '68, Jun 9 '68, Jun 11 '68, Jul 1 '68, Oct 23-25 '69, Nov 20-23 '69, Aug 29 '70, Nov 12-14 '70, Nov 21 '70, Jan 16 '71, Mar 30 '71, Nov 21 '71, Jan 31 '72, May 3 '72, Aug 23 '72, Nov 17 '72, Jan 14 '73, Jan 24 '73, Feb 26 '73, Jul 15 '73, Sep 20 '73, Feb 26 '74, Apr 3 '74, Sep 9-10 '74, Nov 23 '74, Feb 29 '76, Feb 1-2 '77, Feb 19 '77, Dec 23 '77,

ACKNOWLEDGEMENTS

AUTHOR'S THANKS

My profuse thanks to various Kinks people for their time and cooperation: Pete Quaife, Mick Avory, John Gosling, John Dalton, Jim Rodford, Bob Henrit, John Beecham, Ian Gibbons, Maryann Price, Grenville Collins, Robert Wace, Larry Page, Marion Rainford, Clem Cattini, Shel Talmy, Giorgio Gomelsky, and the late Ken Jones, and of course to Ray Davies and Dave Davies for most everything this book is about.

Special thanks to kindred spirits who shared my interest over so many years: Marianne Spellman, Jim Napoli, Urs Steiger, Gordon Peel, Russell Smith, Peter Seeger, Henrik Jönsson, Bill Small, Hiroshi Uchida, Jason Brabazon, David Queenan, Johnny Rogan, Freaky Frank Reda; and to my 1990s-era research buddies Joe McMichael, Greg E. Shaw, Andy Neill, Keith Badman, Christopher Hjort and Stu Rosenberg for making this kind of work fun and rewarding.

In no particular order whatsoever, my thanks to Bill Orton, Gary Forsyth, Ian McLeod, Mike Fearn, Mike Henry, Michel Triton, Helge Buttkereit, Reinhard Schmidt, Erich Cohrs, Frank Mootz, Alfred Hebing, Eddy Smit, Jean Pierre De Saedeleer, Eddie Paes, Gert Eggens, Richard Groothuizen, Rob Kopp, Ruud Kerstiens, Henny Stahli, Cees Hoogstrate, Jurrien Schadron, Klaus Göran Björnarwe. Thomas Gjurup, Dag Balsvik, Willy Bakken, Pertti Mälkki, Anne Koivunen, Hrafnkell Gislason, Miguel M. Sanz, Bill Tikellis, Stuart Penny, John Horne, Phil Richards, John Wray, Piers Hemmingsen, Jimmy Beaudry, Paul Bazylinski, Dave Emlen, Kevin Walsh, Norm Meder, Bill Crowley, James Amodio, Bobby Poe, Bernie Greene, Clark Besch, Joel Davis, Ed Mertz, Jeff Heiser, John Becker, Mike Markov, John Ellis, Mark Ritucci, George Brouthers, Paul Bazylinski, Steve Emming, Rick Acosta, James Boyden, David Terralavoro, Armando Luna, Danny Osterweil, Gregg Landis, Paul Hippensteel, Bill Malloy, Bill Wheelhouse, Paul Dregseth, Gregg Landis, Mike Meshew, Gary Gasper, Erick Schlosser, Joseph Hedio, Miriam Moore, Ed Radzwich, Mark Scholz, Steve Kent, Jeffrey Heiser, George Kalogerakis, Rebecca Bailey, Andy Mitchell, Billy Blackmon, Larry Brown, Rebecca Reed, Mark Seiler, Neil Skok, Julian Bailey, the late Alan Betrock, Ray Rivers, Alec Palao, Joey Dryfka, Linda and the much missed Mike Kraus, Tom Kitts, Olga Ruocco, Dave Collins, Jerry Helmfrid, Kieron Tyler, Richard Arfin, Wes Gottlock, Jerry Birenz, George Coelho, Jeff James, Bob Gill, Dennis Hecht, the Mighty Frank Lima, Garret Hashimoto, Bruce Kawakami, Jerry Fuentes, Mary Cozzaglio, Sharon Knerr/Weaver, Alan Lakey, Andy Miller, Klaus Schmalenbach, John Villanova, Steve Kolanjian, Ron Furmanek, Johan Bowkes, Paul Jacobs, Michael Holt, Michael Powell, Kevin Laffey, Steve Lang, Marlyn Yager, Ernie Cannadeo; Madeleine Hawkyard; Harold Bronson, Andrew Sandoval, Bill Inglot, Mick Carpenter, Steve Hammonds Jayne Grodd, Hanne Kinnes, Zena & Rachel Brabazon and Alan Stanton. Jon Savage, Fred Schruers, John Mendelssohn, John Koenig (Discoveries); Jeff Tamarkin (late of Goldmine), Greg Shaw (Bomp), Gary Massucco, "The Dawg", Sean Egan. Anyone I overlooked, please forgive me … this project took 18 years to complete and I've lost track of everyone by this point. In general, thanks to all the great new friends and acquaintances I've made since publishing *You Really Got Me* in 1994 and to the very supportive Kinks community on the internet.

Thanks to the following libraries for on-site use of their facilities: British Museum Colindale Newspaper Library Branch, London; New York Public Library at Lincoln Center, New York, NY; Lamont Library, Harvard University, Cambridge, MA; Library of Congress, Washington, DC; Boston Public Library, Boston, RI; Providence Public Library, Providence, RI. A huge collective thank you to the literally hundred of librarians and the libraries around the world I have been in

contact with by mail, email, phone and in person, which contributed so much to adding pieces of this huge puzzle and for inspiring me to become a librarian myself as a result of the experience. A special hello and thanks to all my friends and colleagues on the fifth floor at PPL.

The following music papers have been consulted extensively and much information checked against their contents: *Melody Maker*; *New Musical Express*; *Record Mirror*; *Disc*; *Sounds*; *Mersey Beat*; *Music Echo*; *Music Week*; *Record Collector*, *Goldmine*; *Discoveries*; *Billboard*; *Cashbox*; *Record World*; *Amusement Business*; *Variety*; *Mojo*; *Q*; *Circus*; *Hit Parader*; *Trouser Press*; *Crawdaddy*; *Creem*; *Rolling Stone*; *Strange Fruit*; and many more.

The following books have all been invaluable each in their own way: *The Kinks: The Sound And The Fury* by Johnny Rogan (Elm Tree, London, 1984) (in the US as *The Kinks: A Mental Institution* (Proteus, NY 1984); *The Kinks: The Official Biography* by Jon Savage (Faber & Faber, London 1984); *The Kinks Kronikles* by John Mendelssohn (Quill, NY 1984); *The Kinks* by Mikel Barsa (Los Juclares, Madrid, 1987; Spanish text); *You Really Got Me: An Illustrated World Discography Of The Kinks 1964-1993* by Doug Hinman with Jason Brabazon (D. Hinman, Rumford, RI, 1994) [*Supplement 1994-1996/97* (D. Hinman, Rumford, RI, 1997)]; *X-Ray* by Ray Davies (Viking, London, 1994); *The Kinks: Well Respected Men* by Neville Marten & Jeffrey Hudson (Castle Communication, Chesssington 1996); *Kink: An Autobiography* by Dave Davies (BoxTree, London, 1996); *The Kinks* by Neville Marten & Jeffrey Hudson (Sanctuary Books London, 2001); *Living On A Thin Line: Crossing Aesthetic Borders With The Kinks* edited by Thomas M. Kitts and Michael J. Kraus (Rock 'n' Roll Research Press, Rumford, RI, 2002).

The following books have been consulted for discographical information: *Blues & Gospel Records 1902-1942* by John Godrich & Robert M. W. Dixon (Storyville Pub. & Co. London 1969); *Popular Music: 1920-1979 A Revised Cumulation* by Nat Shapiro, Bruce Pollock (Gale Research Co); *Detroit Blues Records: 1943-1966* by Mike Leadbitter, Neil Slaven (Oak Publications, New York, NY, 1968); *The Complete Book Of The British Charts, Singles And Albums* by Tony Brown, Jon Kutner & Neil Warwick (Omnibus Press, London, 2000).

Thanks to all the various fan clubs from over the years: Gene Davidson and Bill Small (Kinks Society-US) and Ben Derksen (Dedicated Kinks Followers Association-Holland) were both pioneers in the pre-internet era of the dissemination of Kinks information during the early 1970s. Also, in no particular order, thanks to the following people who over the years have helped contribute to the body of Kinks information: Hiroshi Uchida (Japan Kinks Preservation Society); Bernard de Gioanni & Ann-Marie Savy (French Kinks Konnektion-France); Rob & Vicky Davies (Kinky Kapers-UK); Carole & Phil Higham (Out Of The Wardrobe-UK); Rafael Phillipi (Kinks Kontroversy-US); Hans de Roodt (Kinks Promo Centre-Holland); Kevin Ford and Dena Ford Tarlin (Autumn Almanac-US); Carolyn Mitchell (Kinks Preservation Society-UK); Barbara Crossley (Kinks Appreciation Society-UK); Earle Law, Tony DeWitt and Gloria Taylor (Official Kinks Fan Club); and Peter Seeger (Kinks Info). *Kinks Info* is occasionally still published as an insert to Peter's excellent German-text 60s-80s magazine, *GoodTimes* (Postfach 111321, D-64228 Darmstadt, Germany; www.goodtimes-magazin.de). Still active is The Dave Davies Official Fan Club, PO Box 564198, College Point, NY 11356-4198 USA. And last but certainly not least is the essential Official Kinks Fan Club, PO Box 30, Atherstone, Warwickshire CV9 2ZX, UK and which needs your support.

Much of this book was researched and completed in the pre-internet era

but the following key websites are all excellent sources of current and recent information. Many more excellent sites can be found from these main sources: Dave Emlen's Unofficial Kinks Web Site http://kinks.it.rit.edu; the Official Kinks Fan Club http://kinks.it.rit.edu/okfc; the Dave Davies Website http://www.davedavies.com; official Ray Davies website http://www.raydavies.net; subscribe to Neil Ottenstein's Kinks Digest by sending an email to kps-admin@kinks.org.

Special thanks to Tony Bacon for support, encouragement, enthusiasm, patience and "good phone."

PICTURE CREDITS

The photographs reproduced came from the following sources, listed here by location or page number. Jacket: main picture Pictorial Press; rear Castle/Retna. 2/3 Pictorial Press. 7 Mick Gold/Redfern's . 23 Pictorial Press. 33 Castle/Retna. 62 Val Wilmer/Redfern's. 71 Gary Forsyth Collection. 81 SKR Photos/London Features International. 97 Pictorial Press. 127 Ivan Keeman/Redfern's. 153 Harry Goodwin/Redfern's. 176 Retna. 188 Janet Macoska/London Features International. 197 Michael Putland/Retna. 205 London Features International. 211 Ian Dickson/Redfern's. 229 Ebet Roberts/Redfern's. 243 Ebet Roberts/Redfern's. 250 Marianne Spellman. 259 Doug Hinman Collection. 279 Norm Meder. 289 Gordon Peel. 295 Ebet Roberts/Redfern's. 305 Phil Loftus/Retna. 319 Ruud Ketstiens. 329 Julie Orton. 335 Jay Blakesberg/Retna.

LATE GIG ADDITIONS

All UK: Dec 7 '65 Town Hall, High Wycombe; Feb 25 '66 Royal Hall, Harrogate with The Kokomos, The Vikings; Aug 29 '65 Cosmopolitan Club, Carlisle; Jan 5 '66 Locarno Ballroom, Stevenage; Apr 2 '66 Drill Hall, Bedford; Apr 17 '66 Buxton Pavilion, Buxton, Derbyshire, with The Detours; Oct 5 '66 Dreamland Ballroom, Margate, with The Writ, make-up date for Jul 14 cancellation, likely Dalton's last performance in his first go-round as bass player; Nov 10 '67 Union Ball, University College of Wales, Aberystwyth, Wales.

UPDATES

In a work documenting a career of such enormous range and magnitude there will inevitably be additions and corrections to the research set forth in this book. The author would be pleased to be informed of any such details and may be contacted c/o Rock'n'Roll Research Press, PO Box 4759, Rumford, RI 02916 USA, or by email info1@rocknrollresearchpress.com. For further updates and extra information you may visit the publisher's site, www.backbeatuk.com.

CHART HIGH positions are drawn from *Melody Maker* (albums and singles) and *Record Retailer* (EPs) for the UK, and from *Billboard* for the US.

THE PUBLISHER wishes to thank Keith Badman, Julie Bowie, Paul Cooper, Kim Devlin, Joyce Mason, Andy Neill, Bill Orton, Heinz Rebellius, Ebet Roberts, Klaus Schmalenbach, Marianne Spellman.

"One of our aims is to stay amateurs. As soon as we become professionals, we'll be ruined." RAY DAVIES, 1965